The Definitive Resource in Preparation for the CPA Exam:

WILEY CPA EXAMINATION REVIEW

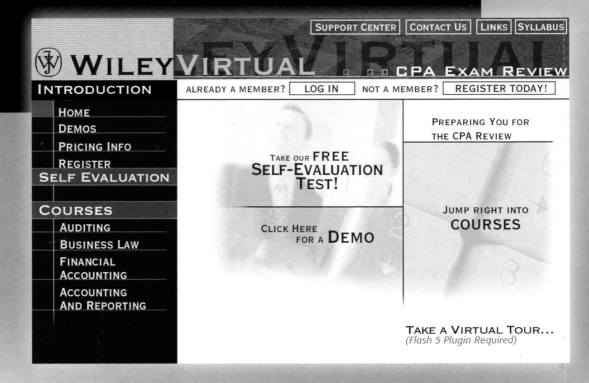

CONTENTS

[1] *As explained in Chapter 1, this book is organized into 11 modules (manageable study units). The numbering of the modules commences with number 34 to correspond with the numbering system used in our two-volume set.*

PREFACE

Passing the CPA exam upon your first attempt is possible! The *Wiley CPA Examination Review* preparation materials provide you with the necessary materials (visit our website at www.wiley.com/cpa for more information). It's up to you to add the hard work and commitment. Together we can beat the first-time pass rate of less than 20%. All Wiley CPA products are continuously updated to provide you with the most comprehensive and complete knowledge base. Choose your products from the Wiley preparation materials and you can proceed confidently. You can select support materials that are exam-based and user-friendly. You can select products that will help you pass!

Remaining current is one of the keys to examination success. Here is a list of what's new in this edition of the *Wiley CPA Examination Review Accounting and Reporting* **text.**

- The latest AICPA Content Specification Outline for Accounting and Reporting
- Discussion of the newly designed Objective Answer Sheet with complete instructions on how to complete
- Tax law changes for 2002 (tested on 2003 examination)
- Updated information and questions on the Financial Governmental Reporting Model covered in

  - GASB 39, *Determining Whether Certain Organizations Are Component Units—an amendment of GASB Statement No. 14*
  - GASB 38, *Certain Financial Statement Note Disclosures*
  - GASB 37, *Basic Financial Statements—and Management's Discussion and Analysis—for State and Local Governments: Omnibus—an amendment of GASB Statements No. 21 and No. 34*

The objective of this work is to provide you with the knowledge to pass the Accounting and Reporting portion of the Uniform Certified Public Accounting (CPA) Exam. The text is divided up into fifteen areas of study called modules. Each module contains written text with discussion, examples, and demonstrations of the key exam concepts. Following each text area, actual American Institute of Certified Public Accountants (AICPA) unofficial questions and answers are presented to test your knowledge. We are indebted to the AICPA for permission to reproduce and adapt examination materials from past examinations. Author constructed questions are provided for new areas or areas that require updating. All author constructed questions are modeled after AICPA question formats. The multiple-choice questions are grouped into topical areas, giving candidates a chance to assess their areas of strength and weakness. Selection and inclusion of topical content is based upon current AICPA Content Specification Outlines. Only testable topics are presented. If the CPA exam does not test it, this text does not present it.

The CPA exam is one of the toughest exams you will ever take. It will not be easy. But if you follow our guidelines and focus on your goal, you will be thrilled with what you can accomplish.

Ray Whittington
November 2002

**Don't forget to visit our website at www.wiley.com/cpa
for supplements and updates.**

ABOUT THE AUTHORS

Patrick R. Delaney was the Arthur Andersen LLP Alumni Professor of Accountancy and Department Chair at Northern Illinois University. He received his PhD in Accountancy from the University of Illinois. He had public accounting experience with Arthur Andersen LLP and was coauthor of *GAAP: Interpretation and Application*, also published by John Wiley & Sons, Inc. He served as Vice President and a member of the Illinois CPA Society's Board of Directors, and was Chairman of its Accounting Principles Committee; was a past president of the Rockford Chapter, Institute of Management Accountants; and had served on numerous other professional committees. He was a member of the American Accounting Association, American Institute of Certified Public Accountants, and Institute of Management Accountants. Professor Delaney was published in *The Accounting Review* and was a recipient of the Illinois CPA Society's Outstanding Educator Award, NIU's Excellence in Teaching Award, and Lewis University's Distinguished Alumnus Award. He was involved in NIU's CPA Review Course as director and instructor.

Ray Whittington, PhD, CPA, CMA, CIA, is the Ledger & Quill Director of the School of Accountancy at DePaul University. Prior to joining the faculty at DePaul, Professor Whittington was the Director of Accountancy at San Diego State University. From 1989 through 1991, he was the Director of Auditing Research for the American Institute of Certified Public Accountants (AICPA), and he previously was on the audit staff of KPMG. He previously served as a member of the Auditing Standards Board of the AICPA and as a member of the Accounting and Review Services Committee and the Board of Regents of the Institute of Internal Auditors. Professor Whittington has published numerous textbooks, articles, monographs, and continuing education courses.

ABOUT THE CONTRIBUTORS

John C. Borke, MAS, CPA, is an Associate Professor of Accounting at the University of Wisconsin-Platteville. He has been a recipient of the UW-Platteville Excellence in Teaching Award, and has worked as a staff auditor with KPMG Peat Marwick. Professor Borke prepared the revision of Chapter 6, Managerial Accounting.

John H. Engstrom, DBA, CPA, is the KMPG Peat Marwick Professor of Accountancy at Northern Illinois University. He is the coauthor of *Essentials of Accounting for Governmental and Not-for-Profit Organizations*, Richard D. Irwin, Inc. He revised Chapter 7, Governmental and Not-for-Profit Accounting.

Edward C. Foth, PhD, CPA, is an Associate Professor and Administrator of the Master of Science in Taxation Program at DePaul University. He has public accounting experience with Arthur Andersen LLP and teaches in their Basic and Intermediate U.S. Tax School. Professor Foth is the author of Commerce Clearing House's *Study Guide For Federal Tax Course*, *Study Guide for CCH Federal Taxation: Basic Principles*, and coauthor of their *S Corporations Guide*. He prepared Chapter 8, Federal Taxation.

John R. Simon, PhD, CPA, is the Coopers & Lybrand Professor of Accountancy and a Presidential Teaching Professor at Northern Illinois University. He has taught in NIU's CPA Review Course for the past 24 years and was the director of the course for 11 years. He is a recipient of NIU's Excellence in Teaching Award. Professor Simon prepared multiple-choice and other objective type questions for Modules 38 and 39.

1 BEGINNING YOUR CPA REVIEW PROGRAM

To maximize the efficiency of your review program, begin by studying (not merely reading) this chapter and the next three chapters of this volume. They have been carefully organized and written to provide you with important information to assist you in successfully completing the Accounting and Reporting section of the CPA exam. Beyond providing a comprehensive outline to help you organize the material tested on the Accounting and Reporting section of the exam, Chapter 1 will assist you in organizing a study program to prepare for the Accounting and Reporting section. Self-discipline throughout your preparation is essential.

GENERAL COMMENTS ON THE EXAMINATION

Successful completion of the Accounting and Reporting section of the Uniform CPA Examination is an attainable goal. Keep this point foremost in your mind as you study the first four chapters in this volume and develop your study plan.

Purpose of the Examination[1]

The CPA examination is designed to measure the wide range of knowledge and skills that entry-level CPAs are expected to possess. The examination assesses candidates' knowledge and skills at three different levels of increasing difficulty:

1. Understanding—The ability to recognize or recall learned materials and grasp the meaning.
2. Application—The ability to use learned materials in new situations.
3. Evaluation—The ability to draw conclusions, make decisions, and communicate judgments.

Presently, at least 60% of each examination section assesses candidates' knowledge and skills at the application and evaluation levels. As the majority of the exam is testing at these higher levels of comprehension, **it is crucial that candidates know the material rather than merely being familiar with the material**.

The CPA examination is one of many screening devices to assure the competence of those licensed to perform the attest function and to render professional accounting services. Other screening devices include educational requirements, ethics examinations, and work experience.

The examination appears to test the material covered in accounting programs of the better business schools. It also appears to be based upon the body of knowledge essential for the practice of public accounting

---

[1] *The following general comments are largely adapted from Information for Uniform CPA Examination Candidates, published by the American Institute of Certified Public Accountants. Information for Uniform CPA Examination Candidates is usually sent to CPA candidates by their State Board of Accountancy as they apply to sit for the CPA examination. If you will not be immediately applying to your State Board of Accountancy to sit for the exam, you may purchase the latest edition by contacting the AICPA order department at 888-777-7077. You can find some of the information on the web at www.aicpa.org/edu/index.htm.*

and the audit of a medium-sized client. Since the examination is primarily a textbook or academic examination, you should plan on taking it as soon as possible after completing your undergraduate accounting education.

Examination Content

Guidance concerning topical content of the Accounting and Reporting part of the CPA exam can be found in a document prepared by the Board of Examiners of the AICPA entitled *Content Specification Outlines for the Uniform Certified Public Accountant Examination*. We have included the content outlines for Accounting and Reporting in Chapter 5. Although the exam is now nondisclosed, these outlines should be used as an indication of the topics' relative importance on past exams.

The Board's objective in preparing this detailed listing of topics tested on the exam is to help "in assuring the continuing validity and reliability of the Uniform CPA Examination." These outlines are an excellent source of guidance concerning the areas and the emphasis to be given each area on future exams.

The AICPA Board of Examiners issued revised Content Specification Outlines in May 2000. These are provided to each candidate in *Information for Uniform CPA Examination Candidates,* along with the examination application or may be purchased by contacting the AICPA order department at 888-777-7077.

New accounting and auditing pronouncements, including those in the governmental and not-for-profit areas, are tested six months after the pronouncement's *effective* date. If early application is permitted, a pronouncement is tested six months after the *issuance* date; candidates are also responsible for the old pronouncement until it is superseded. The exam covers the Internal Revenue Code and federal tax regulations in effect six months before the date of the exam. For the Business Law and Professional Responsibilities section, federal laws are tested six months following their *effective* date and of uniform acts one year after their adoption by a simple majority of jurisdictions. The AICPA posts content changes regularly on its Internet site. The address is www.aicpa.org.

Nondisclosure of Examination Questions and Answers

Beginning May 1996, the Uniform CPA Examination became nondisclosed. For each exam section, candidates are required to sign a *Statement of Confidentiality,* which states that they will not divulge the nature and content of any exam question. Candidates no longer retain or receive their question booklets after the exam. Complete examination questions and answers are no longer published. The AICPA does, however, periodically release selected questions and answers. The released questions are no longer used on actual exams, but they are representative of questions appearing on future exams.

Schedule of Examinations

The two-day Uniform Certified Public Accountant Examination is given twice a year, usually on the first consecutive Wednesday-Thursday in May and November. The subject and time schedules are

CPA EXAM SCHEDULE AND FORMAT

SECTION	TIME PERIOD	MC	FORMAT OOAF	FRE/P
Business Law and Professional Responsibilities	Wed. 9:00 - Noon	50-60%	20-30%	20-30%
Auditing	Wed. 1:30 - 6:00	50-60%	20-30%	20-30%
Accounting and Reporting (Taxation; Managerial; and Governmental and Not-for-Profit Organizations)	Thurs. 8:30 - Noon	50-60%	40-50%	--
Financial Accounting and Reporting (Business Enterprises)	Thurs. 1:30 - 6:00	50-60%	20-30%	20-30%
TOTAL	15.5 Hours			

MC = Multiple-Choice; OOAF = Other Objective Answer Formats; FRE/P = Free Response Essay/Problem

The above schedule presents three basic questions formats.

1.   Multiple-Choice
2.   Other Objective Answer Formats
3.   Free Response Essay/Problem (not used for Accounting and Reporting)

See the beginning of Chapter 5 for a table of contents of question formats by module and topic. The exact number of multiple-choice, other objective answer format, and essay questions that appear on the exam is unknown. Approximately 10 to 15% of the multiple-choice questions are considered to be "pretest" questions. Pretesting means that some questions are not counted in the tabulation of the candidate's final grade. The pretest questions are used to help the AICPA develop future examination test question databases.

The AICPA no longer lists suggested time limits. In order to avoid the possibility of running out of time, it is imperative that today's candidate utilize some form of time management. See Chapter 4, Allocation of Time, for suggested time management techniques.

The following chart lists upcoming examination administrations and the corresponding uniform mailing dates (dates grades will be mailed by the state boards).

Examination Administration	*Uniform Mailing Date*
May 7 and 8, 2003	August 4, 2003
November 5 and 6, 2003	February 2, 2004

In 2004, the AICPA plans to begin using a computerized Uniform CPA Examination. As of the publication date of this text, very little information has been released. We will post more detailed information as it becomes available, on the CPA Examination Review Wiley website at www.wiley.com/cpa.

State Boards of Accountancy

The right to practice public accounting as a CPA is governed by individual state statutes. While some rules regarding the practice of public accounting vary from state to state, all State Boards of Accountancy use the Uniform CPA Examination and AICPA advisory grading service as one of the requirements to practice public accounting. Every candidate should contact the applicable State Board of Accountancy to determine the requirements to sit for the exam (e.g., education, filing dates, references, and fees). A frequent problem candidates encounter is failure to apply by the deadline. **Apply to sit for the examination early. Also, you should use extreme care in filling out the application and mailing required materials to your State Board of Accountancy.** If possible, have a friend review your completed application before mailing with check, photo, etc. Candidates can be turned down for a particular CPA examination simply because of minor technical details that were overlooked (check not signed, photo not enclosed, question not answered on application, etc.). **Because of the very high volume of applications received in the more populous states, the administrative staff does not have time to call or write to correct minor details and will simply reject your application.** This can be extremely disappointing, particularly after spending many hours preparing to sit for a particular exam.

The various state boards, their addresses, and telephone numbers are listed on the following page. Be sure to inquire to your state board for specific and current requirements.

It is possible for candidates to sit for the examination in another state as an out-of-state candidate. Candidates desiring to do so should contact the State Board of Accountancy in their home state.

ATTRIBUTES OF EXAMINATION SUCCESS

Your primary objective in preparing for the Accounting and Reporting section of the CPA exam is to pass. Other objectives such as learning new and reviewing old material should be considered secondary. The six attributes of examination success discussed below are **essential**. You should study the attributes and work toward achieving/developing each of them **before** taking the examination.

1. **Knowledge of Material**

    Two points are relevant to "knowledge of material" as an attribute of examination success. **First,** there is a distinct difference between being familiar with material and knowing the material. Frequently candidates confuse familiarity with knowledge. Can you remember when you just could not answer an examination question or did poorly on an examination, but maintained to yourself or your instructor that you knew the material? You probably were only familiar with the material. On the CPA examination, familiarity is insufficient; you must know the material. For example, you may be familiar with the tax concepts in accounting for like-kind exchanges, but can you compute the basis of like-kind property received if boot is also received? Once again, a major concern must be to know the material rather than just being familiar with it. Knowledgeable discussion of the material is required on the CPA examination. **Second,** the Accounting and Reporting exam tests a literally overwhelming amount of material at a rigorous level. From an undergraduate point of view, the CPA examination in Accounting and Reporting includes material from the following courses:

    Cost/Managerial
    Governmental/Not-For-Profit
    Tax

	STATE BOARD ADDRESS	TELEPHONE #
AK	Dept. of Comm. and Econ. Dev. Div. of Occ. Licensing • P.O. Box 110806 • Juneau, AK • 99811-0806	(907) 465-3811
AL	P.O. Box 300375 • Montgomery, AL • 36130-0375	(334) 242-5700
AR	101 E. Capitol • STE 430 • Little Rock, AR • 72201	(501) 682-1520
AZ	3877 N. 7th St. • STE 106 • Phoenix, AZ • 85014	(602) 255-3648
CA	2000 Evergreen St.• STE 250 • Sacramento, CA • 95815-3832	(916) 263-3680
CO	1560 Broadway • STE 1340 • Denver, CO • 80202	(303) 894-7800
CT	Secretary of State • 30 Trinity Street • PO Box 150470 • Hartford, CT • 06115	(860) 509-6179
DC	941 North Capital St., NE • Rm. 7200 • Washington, DC • 20002	(202) 442-4461
DE	Cannon Bldg. • STE 203 • 861 Silver Lake Blvd.• Dover, DE • 19904	(302) 744-4500
FL	240 NW 76 Dr. • STE A • Gainesville, FL • 32607	(352) 333-2500
GA	237 Coliseum Drive • Macon, GA • 31217-3858	(478) 207-1400
GU	GCIC Bldg 414 W. Soledad Ave., STE 508 • Hagatua, Guam • 96910-5014	(671) 477-1050
HI	Dept. of Commerce & Consumer Affairs • P.O. Box 3469 • Honolulu, HI • 96801-3469	(808) 586-2696
IA	1918 S.E. Hulsizer Ave. • Ankeny, IA • 50021-3941	(515) 281-4126
ID	P.O. Box 83720 • Boise, ID • 83720-0002	(208) 334-2490
IL	505 E. Green St. • Room 216 • Champaign, IL • 61820-5723	(217) 333-1565
IN	302 W. Washington St. • Rm E034 • Indianapolis, IN • 46204-2246	(317) 232-5987
KS	900 S.W. Jackson Street • STE 556 • Topeka, KS • 66612-1239	(785) 296-2162
KY	332 W. Broadway • STE 310 • Louisville, KY • 40202-2115	(502) 595-3037
LA	Pan-American Life Center • 601 Poydras St. • STE 1770 • New Orleans, LA • 70139	(504) 566-1244
MA	239 Causeway St. • STE 450 • Boston, MA • 02114	(617) 727-1806
MD	500 N. Calvert St. • 3rd Floor • Baltimore, MD • 21202-3651	(410) 333-6322
ME	Dept. of Prof. & Fin. Reg. • #35 State House Station • Augusta, ME • 04333	(207) 624-8603
MI	Dept. of Consumer & Industry Services • P.O. Box 30018 • Lansing, MI • 48909-7518	(517) 241-9249
MN	85 E. 7th Pl. • STE 125 • St. Paul, MN • 55101	(651) 296-7938
MO	P.O. Box 613 • Jefferson City, MO • 65102	(573) 751-0012
MS	653 N. State St. • Jackson, MS • 39202-3304	(601) 354-7320
MT	301 S. Park • P.O. Box 200513 • Helena, MT • 59620-0513	(406) 841-2389
NC	1101 Oberlin Rd. • STE 104 • P.O. Box 12827 • Raleigh, NC • 27605-2827	(919) 733-4222
ND	2701 S. Columbia Rd. • Grand Forks, ND • 58201-6029	(701) 775-7100
NE	P.O. Box 94725 • Lincoln, NE • 68509-4725	(402) 471-3595
NH	6 Chenell Dr. • STE 220 • Concord, NH • 03301	(603) 271-3286
NJ	P.O. Box 45000 • Newark, NJ • 07101	(973) 504-6380
NM	1650 University N.E. • STE 400A • Albuquerque, NM • 87102	(505) 841-9108
NV	200 S. Virginia St. • STE 670 • Reno, NV • 89501-2408	(775) 786-0231
NY	Div. of Pro. Lic. Ser. • 89 Washington Ave. • 2nd Fl. E. Mezz. • Albany, NY • 12230	(518) 474-3817
OH	77 S. High St. • 18th Floor • Columbus, OH • 43266	(614) 466-4135
OK	4545 Lincoln Blvd. • STE 165 • Oklahoma City, OK • 73105-3413	(405) 521-2397
OR	3218 Pringle Rd SE #110 • Salem, OR • 97302-6307	(503) 378-4181
PA	124 Pine St. • 1st Floor • Harrisburg, PA • 17101-2649	(717) 783-1404
PR	Box 9023271 • Old San Juan Station • San Juan, PR • 00902-3271	(787) 722-4816
RI	Dept. of Bus. Reg. • 233 Richmond St. • STE 236 • Providence, RI • 02903-4236	(401) 222-3185
SC	P.O. Box 11329 • Columbia, SC • 29211	(803) 896-4492
SD	301 E. 14th St. • STE 200 • Sioux Falls, SD • 57104	(605) 367-5770
TN	500 James Robertson Prkwy. • 2nd Floor • Nashville, TN • 37243-1141	(615) 741-2550
TX	333 Guadalupe Tower 3 • STE 900 • Austin, TX • 78701-3900	(512) 305-7800
UT	P.O. Box 146741 • Salt Lake City, UT • 84114-6741	(801) 530-6720
VA	3600 West Broad Street • STE 696 • Richmond, VA • 23230-4917	(804) 367-8505
VI	Office of Boards & Comm. • Golden Rock Shopping Center • Christiansted • St. Croix, VI • 00822	(340) 773-4305
VT	26 Terrace St. • Drawer 09 • Montpelier, VT • 05609-1106	(802) 828-2191
WA	Box 9131 • Olympia, WA • 98507-9131	(360) 753-2585
WI	1400 E. Washington Ave. • P.O. Box 8935 • Madison, WI • 53708-8935	(608) 266-5511
WV	122 Capitol St. • Charleston, WV • 25301	(304) 558-3557
WY	2020 Carey Ave. • Cheyenne, WY • 82002-0610	(307) 777-7551

NOTE: The publisher does not assume responsibility for errors in the above information. You should request information concerning requirements in your state at least six months in advance of the exam dates.

Furthermore, as noted earlier, the CPA exam will test new material in all of these areas, sometimes as early as six months after issuance. In other words, you are not only responsible for material in the above courses, but also for all new developments in each of these areas.

This text contains outlines of accounting topics from GASB pronouncements, governmental accounting, cost accounting courses, etc. Return to the original material (e.g., GASB, your accounting textbooks, etc.) only if the outlines do not reinforce the material you already know.

2. **Commitment to Exam Preparation**

Your preparation for the CPA exam should begin at least three months prior to your scheduled exam date. Over the course of your preparation, you will experience many peaks and valleys. There will be days when you feel completely prepared and there will also be days when you feel totally overwhelmed. This is not unusual and, in fact, should be expected.

The CPA exam is a very difficult and challenging exam. How many times in your college career did you study months for an exam? Probably not too many. Therefore, candidates need to remain focused on the objective—succeeding on the CPA exam.

Develop a personal study plan so that you are reviewing material daily. Of course, you should schedule an occasional study break to help you relax, but don't schedule too many breaks. Candidates who dedicate themselves to studying for the exam have a much greater chance of only going through this process one time. On the other hand, a lack of focus and piecemeal preparation will only extend the process over several exams.

3. **Solutions Approach**

The solutions approach is a systematic approach to solving the problems found on the CPA examination. Many candidates know the material fairly well when they sit for the CPA exam, but they do not know how to take the examination. Candidates generally neither work nor answer questions efficiently in terms of time or grades. The solutions approach permits you to avoid drawing "blanks" on CPA exam questions; using the solutions approach coupled with grader orientation (see below) allows you to pick up a sizable number of points on questions testing material with which you are not familiar. Chapter 3 outlines the solutions approach for multiple-choice questions and other objective questions. Example questions are worked as well as explained.

4. **Grader Orientation**

Your score on each section of the exam is determined by the sum of points assigned to individual questions. Thus, you must attempt to maximize your points on each individual question.

This text helps you develop grader orientation by analyzing AICPA grading procedures. The author believes that the solutions approach and grading orientation, properly developed, are worth at least ten to fifteen points on each section to most candidates.

5. **Examination Strategy**

Prior to sitting for the examination, it is important to develop an examination strategy (i.e., a preliminary inventory of the questions, the order in which to work questions, etc.). Your ability to cope successfully with the 3 ½ hours of examination in Accounting and Reporting can be improved by

a. Recognizing the importance and usefulness of an examination strategy
b. Using Chapter 4 "Taking the Examination" and previous examination experience to develop a "personal strategy" for the exam
c. Testing your "personal strategy" on CPA questions under examination conditions (using no reference material and with a time limit)

6. **Examination Confidence**

You need confidence to endure the physical and mental demands of 3½ hours of problem solving under tremendous pressure. Examination confidence results from proper preparation for the exam, which includes mastering the first five attributes of examination success. Examination confidence is also necessary to enable you to overcome the initial frustration with problems for which you may not be specifically prepared.

This study manual, when properly used, contributes to your examination confidence. Build confidence by completing the questions contained herein.

Common Candidate Mistakes

The CPA Exam is a formidable hurdle in your accounting career. With a first-time pass rate of less than 20%, the level of difficulty is obvious. The good news, though, is that about 20% of all candidates (first-time and re-exam) sitting for each examination eventually pass. The authors believe that the first-time pass rate could be higher if candidates would be more careful. Six common mistakes that many candidates make are

1. Failure to understand the exam question requirements
2. Misunderstanding the supporting text of the problem
3. Lack of knowledge of material tested, especially recently issued pronouncements
4. Inability to apply the solutions approach
5. Lack of an exam strategy (e.g., allocation of time)
6. Sloppiness and computational errors

These mistakes are not mutually exclusive. Candidates may commit one or more of the above items. Remind yourself that when you decrease the number of common mistakes, you increase your chances of successfully becoming a CPA. Take the time to read carefully the exam question requirements. Don't jump into a quick start, only to later find out that you didn't understand what information the examiners were asking for. Read slowly and carefully. Take time to recall your knowledge. Respond to the question asked. Apply an exam strategy such as allocating your time among all question formats. Don't spend too much time on the multiple-choice questions, leaving no time to spend on preparing your other objective responses. Answer questions quickly but precisely, avoiding common mistakes, and increase your score.

PURPOSE AND ORGANIZATION OF THIS REVIEW TEXTBOOK

This book is designed to help you prepare adequately for the Accounting and Reporting examination. There is no easy way to prepare for the successful completion of the CPA Examination; however, through the use of this manual, your approach will be systematic and logical.

The objective of this book is to provide study materials supportive to CPA candidates. While no guarantees are made concerning the success of those using this text, this book promotes efficient preparation by

1. Explaining how to **"satisfy the grader"** through analysis of examination grading and illustration of the solutions approach.
2. **Defining areas tested** through the use of the content specification outlines. Note that predictions of future exams are not made. You should prepare yourself for all possible topics rather than gambling on the appearance of certain questions.
3. **Organizing your study program** by comprehensively outlining all of the subject matter tested on the examination in eleven easy-to-use study modules. Each study module is a manageable task which facilitates your exam preparation. Turn to the Table of Contents and peruse it to get a feel for the organization of this book.
4. **Providing CPA candidates with previous examination problems** organized by topic (e.g., standard cost, voluntary health and welfare organizations, etc.) Questions have also been developed for new areas.
5. **Explaining the AICPA unofficial answers** to the examination questions included in this text. The AICPA publishes unofficial answers for all questions from exams administered prior to 1996 and for any released questions from exams administered on or after May 1996. However, no explanation is made of the approach that should have been applied to the examination questions to obtain these unofficial answers. Relatedly, the AICPA unofficial answers to multiple-choice and other objective questions provide no justification and/or explanation.

As you read the next few paragraphs which describe the contents of this book, flip through the chapters to gain a general familiarity with the book's organization and contents. Chapters 2, 3, and 4 are to help you "satisfy the grader."

Chapter 2   Examination Grading and Grader Orientation
Chapter 3   The Solutions Approach
Chapter 4   Taking the Examination

Chapters 2, 3, and 4 contain material that should be kept in mind throughout your study program. Refer back to them frequently. Reread them for a final time just before you sit for the exam.

Chapter 5, Accounting and Reporting Exam Content, outlines and discusses the coverage of the Accounting and Reporting section of the CPA examination. It also contains the AICPA Content Specification Outlines for all the Accounting and Reporting topics tested in this part of the exam. Chapters 6, 7, and 8 contain

1. Multiple-choice questions
2. Other objective questions
3. AICPA unofficial answers with the author's explanations for the multiple-choice questions
4. AICPA unofficial answers with the author's explanations for the other objective questions

Also included at the end of this text is a complete sample Accounting and Reporting CPA Examination. The sample exam is included to enable candidates to gain experience in taking a "realistic" exam. While studying the modules, the candidate can become accustomed to concentrating on fairly narrow topics. By working through the sample examination near the end of their study programs, candidates will be better prepared for taking the actual examination. The selection of multiple-choice and other objective questions was based on a statistical analysis of recent exams.

Other Textbooks

This text is a comprehensive compilation of study guides and outlines; it should not be necessary to supplement them with accounting textbooks and other materials for most topics. You probably already have some of these texts or earlier editions of them. In such a case, you must make the decision whether to replace them and trade familiarity (including notes therein, etc.), with the cost and inconvenience of obtaining the newer texts containing a more updated presentation.

Before spending time and money acquiring new texts, begin your study program with *CPA EXAMINATION REVIEW: ACCOUNTING AND REPORTING* to determine your need for supplemental texts.

Ordering Other Textual Materials

You probably already have cost accounting, governmental, and taxation texts for accounting and reporting. Governmental accounting is generally covered sufficiently in one or two chapters of an advanced accounting text. If you cannot order desired texts through a local bookstore, write the publisher directly.

If you want to order AICPA materials, locate an AICPA educator member to order your materials, since educator members are entitled to a 30% discount and may place telephone orders. The backlog at the order department is substantial; telephone orders decrease delivery time.

Telephone: 888-777-7077   Address: Order Department
American Institute of Certified
Public Accountants
P.O. Box 2209
Jersey City, NJ 07303-2209

A variety of supplemental CPA products are available from John Wiley & Sons, Inc. By using a variety of learning techniques, such as software, computer-based learning, and audio CDs, the candidate is more likely to remain focused during the study process and to retain information for a longer period of time. Visit our website at **www.wiley.com/cpa** for other products, supplements, and updates.

Working CPA Problems

The AICPA content outlines, study outlines, etc., will be used to acquire and assimilate the knowledge tested on the examination. This, however, should be only **one-half** of your preparation program. The other half should be spent practicing how to work questions. Some candidates probably spend over 90% of their time reviewing material tested on the CPA exam. Much more time should be allocated to working previous examination questions **under exam conditions**. Working previous examination questions serves two functions. First, it helps you develop a solutions approach. Second, it provides the best test of your knowledge of the material. Candidates should be sure to work one of the more complex and difficult questions (e.g., standard cost) in each area or module.

The multiple-choice questions and answers can be used in many ways. First, they may be used as a diagnostic evaluation of your knowledge. For example, before beginning to review estate taxes you may wish to answer 10 to 15 multiple-choice questions to determine your ability to answer CPA examination questions on estate taxes. The apparent difficulty of the questions and the correctness of your answers will allow you to determine the necessary breadth and depth of your review. Additionally, exposure to examination questions prior to review and study of the material should provide motivation. You will develop a feel for your level of proficiency and an understanding of the scope and difficulty of past examination questions. Moreover, your review materials will explain concepts encountered in the diagnostic multiple-choice questions.

Second, the multiple-choice questions can be used as a poststudy or postreview evaluation. You should attempt to understand all concepts mentioned (even in incorrect answers) as you answer the questions. Refer to the explanation of the answer for discussion of the alternatives even though you selected the correct response. Thus, you should read the explanation of the unofficial answer unless you completely understand the question and all of the alternative answers.

Third, you may wish to use the multiple-choice questions as a primary study vehicle. This is probably the quickest but least thorough approach in preparing for the exam. Make a sincere effort to understand the question and to select the correct response before referring to the unofficial answer and explanation. In many cases, the explanations will appear inadequate because of your unfamiliarity with the topic. Always refer back to an appropriate study source, such as the outlines and text in this volume, your accounting textbooks, etc.

One problem with multiple-choice questions is that you may overemphasize them. Candidates generally prefer to work multiple-choice questions because they are

1. Shorter and less time-consuming
2. Solvable with less effort
3. Less frustrating than other objective questions

Another problem with the large number of multiple-choice questions is that you may tend to become overly familiar with the questions. The result may be that you begin reading the facts and assumptions of previously studied questions into the questions on your examination. Guard against this potential problem by reading each multiple-choice question with **extra** care.

Beginning with the May 1992 examination, the AICPA began testing with other objective formats. The other objective format questions that were given on previous exams and others prepared by the author are incorporated in the modules to which they pertain (see the listing of question and problem material at the beginning of Chapter 6). Working other objective questions from start to finish is just as important as working multiple-choice questions. The other objective questions and unofficial answers may also be used for study purposes without preparation of answers. Before turning to the unofficial answers, study the question and outline the solution (either mentally or in the margin of the book). Next, read the unofficial answer, underlining keywords and phrases, and compare it to your own. The underlining should reinforce your study of the answer's content.

Note that the Accounting and Reporting section includes no essay questions or problems. However, some of the other objective type questions involve calculating numbers that are part of a more comprehensive question.

The questions and solutions in this volume provide you with an opportunity to diagnose and correct any exam-taking weaknesses prior to sitting for the examination. Continually analyze your incorrect solutions to determine the cause of the error(s) during your preparation for the exam. Treat each incorrect solution as a mistake that will not be repeated (especially on the examination). Also attempt to generalize your weaknesses so that you may change, reinforce, or develop new approaches to exam preparation and exam taking.

After you have finished reviewing for the Accounting and Reporting exam, work the complete sample exam provided in Appendix A.

SELF-STUDY PROGRAM

CPA candidates generally find it difficult to organize and to complete their own self-study programs. A major problem is determining **what** and **how** to study. Another major problem is developing the self-discipline to stick to a study program. Relatedly, it is often difficult for CPA candidates to determine how much to study (i.e., determining when they are sufficiently prepared).

The following suggestions will assist you in developing a **systematic, comprehensive,** and **successful** self-study program to help you complete the Accounting and Reporting exam. Remember that these are only suggestions. You should modify them to suit your personality, available study time, and other constraints. Some of the suggestions may appear trivial, but CPA candidates generally need all the assistance they can get to systemize their study programs.

Study Facilities and Available Time

Locate study facilities that will be conducive to concentrated study. Factors that you should consider include

1. Noise distraction
2. Interruptions
3. Lighting
4. Availability (e.g., a local library is not available at 5:00 a.m.)
5. Accessibility (e.g., your kitchen table vs. your local library)
6. Desk or table space

You will probably find different study facilities optimal for different times (e.g., your kitchen table during early morning hours and local libraries during early evening hours).

Next review your personal and professional commitments from now until the exam to determine regularly available study time. Formalize a schedule to which you can reasonably commit yourself. At the end of this chapter, you will find a detailed approach to managing your time available for the exam preparation program.

Self-Evaluation

The *CPA EXAMINATION REVIEW: ACCOUNTING AND REPORTING* self-study program is partitioned into eleven topics or modules. Since each module is clearly defined and should be studied separately, you have the task of preparing for the Accounting and Reporting section of the CPA exam by tackling 11 manageable tasks. Partitioning the overall project into 11 modules makes preparation psychologically easier, since you sense yourself completing one small step at a time rather than seemingly never completing one or a few large steps.

By completing the following "Preliminary Estimate of Your Knowledge of Subject" inventory, organized by the 11 modules in this program, you will tabulate your strong and weak areas at the beginning of your study program. This will help you budget your limited study time. Note that you should begin studying the material in each module by answering up to 1/4 of the total multiple-choice questions covering that module's topics (see instruction 4.A. in the next section). This "mini-exam" should constitute a diagnostic evaluation as to the amount of review and study you need.

PRELIMINARY ESTIMATE OF YOUR PRESENT KNOWLEDGE OF SUBJECT*

No.	Module	Proficient	Fairly Proficient	Generally Familiar	Not Familiar
34	Costing Systems				
35	Planning, Control, and Analysis				
36	Standards and Variances				
37	Nonroutine Decisions				
38	Governmental Accounting				
39	Not-for-Profit Accounting				
40	Taxes: Individual				
41	Taxes: Transactions in Property				
42	Taxes: Partnership				
43	Taxes: Corporate				
44	Taxes: Gift and Estate				

* *The number of modules in this text commences with number 34 to correspond with the numbering system used in our two-volume set.*

Time Allocation

The study program below entails an average of 65 hours (Step 5. below) of study time. The breakdown of total hours is indicated in the left margin.

[2 1/2 hrs.]   1. Study Chapters 2-4 in this volume. These chapters are essential to your efficient preparation program. (Time estimate includes candidate's review of the examples of the solutions approach in Chapters 2 and 3.)

[1/2 hr.]   2. Begin ACCOUNTING AND REPORTING by studying Chapter 5.

          3. Study one module at a time. The modules are listed above in the self-evaluation section.

          4. For each module

[10 hrs.]   A. Work 1/4 of the multiple-choice questions (e.g., if there are 40 multiple-choice questions in a module, you should work every 4th question). Score yourself. This diagnostic routine will provide you with an index of your proficiency and familiarity with the type and difficulty of questions. Time estimate: 3 minutes each, not to exceed 1 hour total.

[20 hrs.]   B.   Study the outlines and illustrations. Also refer to your accounting textbooks (this will occur more frequently for topics in which you have a weak background).
Time estimate: 1 hour minimum per module, with more time devoted to topics less familiar to you.

[20 hrs.]   C.   Work the remaining multiple-choice questions. Study the explanations of the multiple-choice questions you missed or had trouble answering.
Time estimate: 3 minutes to answer each question and 2 minutes to study the answer explanation of each question missed.

[6 hrs.]   D.   Work the other objective format questions.
Time estimate: 20 minutes for each other objective question and 10 minutes to study the answer explanations for each item missed.

[6 hrs.]   E.   Work through the sample Accounting and Reporting section presented at the end of this text. The exam should be taken in one sitting.
Take the examination under simulated exam conditions (i.e., in a strange place with other people present [e.g., your local municipal library]). Apply your solutions approach to each problem and your exam strategy to the overall exam.
You should limit yourself to the time that you will have when taking the actual CPA exam section (3.5 hours for the Accounting and Reporting section). Spend time afterwards grading your work and reviewing your effort. It might be helpful to do this with other CPA candidates. Another person looking over your exam might be more objective and notice things such as logic of calculations, etc.
Time estimate: 5-6 hours to take the exam and review it later.

5.   The total suggested time of 65 hours is only an average. Allocation of time will vary candidate by candidate. Time requirements vary due to the diverse backgrounds and abilities of CPA candidates.

Allocate your time so you gain the most proficiency in the least time. Remember that while 65 hours will be required, you should break the overall project down into 11 more manageable tasks. Do not study more than one module during each study session.

Using Notecards

Below are one candidate's notecards on accounting and reporting topics which illustrate how key definitions, formulas, lists, etc., can be summarized on index cards for quick review. Since candidates can take these anywhere they go, they are a very efficient review tool.

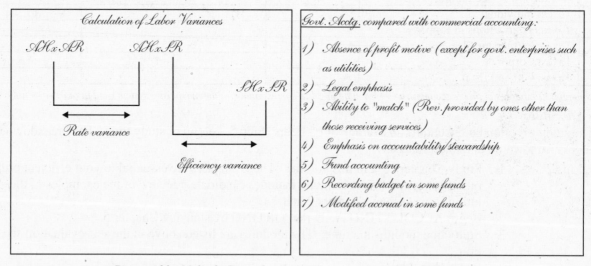

Prepared by Melinda Stees, former student, Northern Illinois University

Levels of Proficiency Required

What level of proficiency must you develop with respect to each of the topics to pass the exam? You should work toward a minimum correct rate on the multiple-choice questions of 80%. Working towards these correct rates or higher ones for Accounting and Reporting will allow for a margin.

Multiple-Choice Feedback

One of the benefits of working through previous exam questions is that it helps you to identify your weak areas. Once you have graded your answers, your strong areas and weak areas should be clearly evident. Yet, the important point here is that you should not stop at a simple percentage evaluation. The percentage only provides general feedback about your knowledge of the material contained within that particular module. The percentage **does not** give you any specific feedback regarding the concepts which were tested. In order to get this feedback, you should look at the questions missed on an individual basis because this will help you gain a better understanding of **why** you missed the question.

This feedback process has been facilitated by the fact that within each module where the multiple-choice answer key appears, two blank lines have been inserted next to the multiple-choice answers. As you grade the multiple-choice questions, mark those questions which you have missed. However, instead of just marking the questions right and wrong, you should now focus on marking the questions in a manner which identifies **why** you missed the question. As an example, a candidate could mark the questions in the following manner: ✓ for math mistakes, x for conceptual mistakes, and ? for areas which the candidate was unfamiliar with. The candidate should then correct these mistakes by reworking through the marked questions.

The objective of this marking technique is to help you identify your weak areas and thus, the concepts which you should be focusing on. While it is still important for you to get 80% correct when working multiple-choice questions, it is more important for you to understand the concepts. This understanding applies to both the questions answered correctly and those answered incorrectly. Remember, questions on the CPA exam will be different from the questions in the book; however, the concepts will be the same. Therefore, your preparation should focus on understanding concepts, not just getting the correct answer.

Conditional Candidates

If you have received conditional status on the examination, you must concentrate on the remaining part(s). Unfortunately, many candidates do not study after conditioning the exam, relying on luck to get them through the remaining part(s). Conditional candidates will find that material contained in Chapters 1-4 and the information contained in the appropriate modules will benefit them in preparing for the remaining part(s) of the examination.

PLANNING FOR THE EXAMINATION

Overall Strategy

An overriding concern should be an orderly systematic approach toward both your preparation program and your examination strategy. A major objective should be to avoid any surprises or anything else that would rattle you during the examination. In other words, you want to be in complete control as much as possible. Control is of paramount importance from both positive and negative viewpoints. The presence of control on your part will add to your confidence and your ability to prepare for and take the exam. Moreover, the presence of control will make your preparation program more enjoyable (or at least less distasteful). On the other hand, a lack of organization will result in inefficiency in preparing and taking the examination, with a highly predictable outcome. Likewise, distractions during the examination (e.g., inadequate lodging, long drive) are generally disastrous.

In summary, establishing a systematic, orderly approach to taking the examination is of paramount importance. Follow these six steps.

1. Develop an overall strategy at the beginning of your preparation program (see below)
2. Supplement your overall strategy with outlines of material tested on the Accounting and Reporting section (see Chapters 5 through 9)
3. Supplement your overall strategy with an explicitly stated set of problem-solving procedures—the solutions approach
4. Supplement your overall strategy with an explicitly stated approach to each examination session (see Chapter 4)
5. Evaluate your preparation progress on a regular basis and prepare lists of things "to do" (see Weekly Review of Preparation Program Progress on following page)
6. RELAX: You can pass the exam. About 10,000 candidates successfully complete the exam each sitting. You will be one of them if you complete an efficient preparation program and execute well (i.e., use your solutions approach and exam strategy) while writing the exam.

The following outline is designed to provide you with a general framework of the tasks before you. You should tailor the outline to your needs by adding specific items and comments.

A. Preparation Program (refer to Self-Study Program discussed previously)

1. Obtain and organize study materials
2. Locate facilities conducive for studying and block out study time
3. Develop your solutions approach
4. Prepare an examination strategy
5. Study the material tested recently and prepare answers to actual exam questions on these topics under examination conditions
6. Periodically evaluate your progress

B. Physical Arrangements

1. Apply to and obtain acceptance from your state board
2. Reserve lodging for examination nights

C. Taking the Examination (covered in detail in Chapter 4)

1. Become familiar with exam facilities and procedures
2. Implement examination strategies and the solutions approach

Weekly Review of Preparation Program Progress

The following pages contain a hypothetical weekly review of program progress. You should prepare a similar progress chart. This procedure, which takes only about five minutes per week, will help you proceed through a more efficient, complete preparation program.

Make notes of materials and topics

1. That you have studied
2. That you have completed
3. That need additional study

Weeks to go		Comments on progress, "to do" items, etc.
12	1)	Mods read: Costing Systems and Planning, Control, and Analysis
	2)	Made notecards
	3)	Worked MC and Other Objective questions
	4)	Need to use solutions approach
11	1)	Mods read: Standards and Variances and Nonroutine decisions
	2)	Made notecards
	3)	Worked the MC and Other Objective questions
	4)	Need to work more variance analysis problems
10	1)	Read Governmental Module
	2)	Made notecards
	3)	Worked some MC and Other Objective questions
	4)	Need to review financial statements for governmental units
9	1)	Read Nonprofit Module
	2)	Made notecards
	3)	Worked some MC and Other Objective questions
	4)	Need to finish governmental and nonprofit MC

8	1)	*Review Nonprofit Standards*
	2)	*Completed governmental and nonprofit MC*
	3)	*Read Individual Tax Module Sections I. and II.*
	4)	*Made notecards*
	5)	*Worked some MC and Other Objective questions*
7	1)	*Read Individual Tax Module Sections III. through VIII.*
	2)	*Made notecards*
	3)	*Worked the MC and Other Objective questions*
	4)	*Need to memorize most of individual tax rules*
6	1)	*Read Transactions in Property and Gift and Estate Tax Modules*
	2)	*Made notecards*
	3)	*Worked the MC and Other Objective questions*
	4)	*Need to review income tax return preparer's responsibilities section*
5	1)	*Read Partnership Module*
	2)	*Made notecards*
	3)	*Worked the MC and Other Objective questions*
	4)	*Need to review pro rata distributions and partnership basis*
4	1)	*Read Corporate Tax Module*
	2)	*Made notecards*
	3)	*Worked the MC and Other Objective questions*
	4)	*Took one night off to "get away from it all" in order to devote full-time in last 3 weeks*
3	1)	*Took Accounting and Reporting Sample Exam*
	2)	*Wrote down topics I still do not feel confident in*
	3)	*Worked variance analysis, governmental, and passive activity loss questions—Am now finally confident in these areas*
2	1)	*Reviewed all prior topics, working out a few MC for each*
	2)	*Worked extra process cost and variance analysis questions*
	3)	*Worked some Other Objective questions*
1	1)	*Reviewed the Tax Modules and worked the MC again*
	2)	*Reviewed all notecards*
0	1)	*Tried to relax and review topics*

Time Management of Your Preparation

As you begin your CPA exam preparation, you obviously realize that there is a large amount of material to cover over the course of the next three to four months. Therefore, it is very important for you to organize your calendar, and maybe even your daily routine, so that you can allocate sufficient time to studying. An organized approach to your preparation is much more effective than a last week cram session. An organized approach also builds up the confidence necessary to succeed on the CPA exam.

An approach which we have already suggested, is to develop weekly "to do" lists. This technique helps you to establish intermediate objectives and goals as you progress through your study plan. You can then focus your efforts on small tasks and not feel overwhelmed by the entire process. And as you accomplish these tasks you will see yourself moving one step closer to realizing the overall goal, succeeding on the CPA exam.

Note, however, that the underlying assumption of this approach is that you have found the time during the week to study and thus accomplish the different tasks. Although this is an obvious step, it is still a very important step. Your exam preparation should be of a continuous nature and not one that jumps around the calendar. Therefore, you should strive to find available study time within your daily schedule, which can be utilized on a consistent basis. For example, everyone has certain hours of the day which are already committed for activities such as jobs, classes, and, of course, sleep. There is also going to be the time you spend relaxing because CPA candidates should try to maintain some balance in their lives. Sometimes too much studying can be counterproductive. But there will be some time available to you for studying and working through the questions. Block off this available time and use it only for exam prep. Use the time to accomplish your weekly tasks and to keep yourself committed to the process. After awhile your preparation will develop into a habit and the preparation will not seem as overwhelming as it once did.

**NOW IS THE TIME
TO MAKE YOUR COMMITMENT**

2 EXAMINATION GRADING AND GRADER ORIENTATION

All State Boards of Accountancy use the AICPA advisory grading service. As your grade is to be determined by this process, it is very important that you understand the AICPA grading process and its **implications for your preparation program and for the solution techniques you will use during the examination.**

The AICPA has a full-time staff of CPA examination personnel whose responsibilities include

1. Preparing questions for the examination
2. Working with outside consultants who prepare questions
3. Preparing grading guides and unofficial answers
4. Supervising and reviewing the work of examination graders

The AICPA examination staff is under the supervision of the AICPA Board of Examiners, which has the responsibility for the CPA examination.

This chapter contains a description of the AICPA grading process including a determination of the passing standard and a description of AICPA grading in *Information for Uniform CPA ExaminationCandidates*.

Setting the Passing Standard of the Uniform CPA Examination

Until May 1997, the passing standard for the CPA examination was based on the policy that all candidates who achieved a raw score of 75 on each section would pass; however, if nationally fewer than 30% of the candidates achieved this standard, candidates' raw scores were bumped up to 75 or higher; this policy passed the top 30% on each section for every examination administration. Consequently, if a group of candidates were particularly well prepared or not, the top 30% would pass, regardless.

Today, the 30% criterion no longer exists, since neither the Board of Examiners (BOE) nor the state boards were comfortable with it. The passing standard for each section of the Uniform CPA Examination is currently based on the Angoff passing standard studies which were held during 1996. The procedure, known as a modified Angoff standard-setting method, generally involves convening a panel of judges familiar with the work of entry-level professionals who evaluate each question of each section of an examination. Each panelist's task is to estimate the probability that a "borderline" or "minimally qualified" professional would answer each question correctly. For the May 1996 exam, the panelists were given the questions and official answers for the specific section they were assigned. They were instructed to read each question and assign a minimum pass level (MPL). The individual MPLs were tallied and the panelists were provided with a summary of the range of MPLs they has assigned. Then the panelists were given the statistics on actual candidate performance. They were then instructed to rate each question again. The second set of MPLs for all questions were tallied to arrive at the "initial passing score" that, in the judgment of the panelists, was needed for the minimally qualified candidate to pass that section of the examination.

The BOE uses a method called "equating" to determine if one examination is more or less difficult than another examination and to test for evidence that the candidate pools are significantly different. Examinations are "equated" by imbedding questions from earlier examinations into later ones. If the candidate pools are equal in ability, they should perform equally well on the equating questions. If the candidates perform significantly better or worse on the equating questions, it is assumed the candidate pools were different.

Grading the Examination

The AICPA exercises very tight control over all of the examination papers during the grading process and prior to their return to individual State Boards of Accountancy.

Only multiple-choice and other objective type questions appear on the Accounting and Reporting section. Multiple-choice and other objective questions are graded electronically and, therefore, only the candidates' responses are graded. No consideration is given to any comments or explanations. **The AICPA has begun to pretest multiple-choice questions on the exam; approximately 10-15% of the questions in each section of the exam are pretest questions that are not included in the candidate's grade.** Different versions of each exam section contain different pretest questions. Objective questions are analyzed to determine whether a significant number of candidates selected an answer other than the one identified as the best answer by the AICPA. If an alternative answer is determined to be valid, the Grading Subcommittee may accept both answers. Because this section of the exam is all objective, the grading review process for essays followed by the AICPA is not described in this volume. However, the AICPA has announced in *Information for Uniform CPA Examination Candidates* that the Advisory Grading Service will manually verify the accuracy of the objective answer score for candidates with adjusted scores of 72, 73, or 74 on the Accounting and Reporting section of the exam, assuming that a passing grade on the section would at least allow the candidate to attain conditioning status.

The examination grades are returned to the individual state boards several weeks prior to the official grade release date. The grade release date is usually at the beginning of February for the November exam and at the beginning of August for the May exam.

Multiple-Choice Grading

Your answers to the multiple-choice questions are graded by an optical scanner. The candidate's grade is based on an overall curve using a combined difficulty adjustment for all types of questions for the Accounting and Reporting section. Thus, candidates should do their best regardless of the difficulty of the questions. Perfect and use the "multiple-choice question solutions approach" discussed in Chapter 3. If you are unsure about a question, you should make an educated guess (i.e., pick the "best" answer). Your grade will be based on your total correct answers since no penalty exists for incorrect answers. The grading procedure for multiple-choice questions is explained in the instructions at the beginning of each section of the exam. As mentioned earlier, 10-15% of the multiple-choice questions are pretest items that are not included in the candidate's grade. The importance of carefully reading and following these and all other instructions cannot be overemphasized.

Other Objective Question Grading

These questions are also graded electronically. The weight for each item will depend on the number of points assigned to the question. For example, if a question that has been assigned 10 points contains 13 items, each correct response would be worth .77 (10/13) of a point. Again, do not be discouraged by your performance; the Accounting and Reporting section, like the other sections, is curved on an overall basis.

Overall Grade

A hypothetical example appears below to indicate how a candidate's grade is determined for the Accounting and Reporting Exam. The example presents one possibility for the format and point assignment on this section of the exam. Candidates should remember that the point distribution of the exam consists of 50 - 60% multiple-choice and 40-50% other objective question format.

Type question	*Question number*	*Points allocated*	*Earned points*
Multiple-Choice	1	60	42.6*
Other Objective Answer Format	2	10	9.0
	3	20	18.0
	4	10	8.5
Raw points earned		100	78.1
Rounding adjustment**			(.1)
			78.0
Angoff adjustment			6.0
Grade reported to candidate			84.0

    * *Excluding pretested questions.*
  ** *If equal to or greater than .5, score is rounded up.*

Allocation of Points to Questions

Candidates should be concerned with point allocations for the purpose of allocating their time on the exam. When answering each question, candidates should allocate the total examination time in proportion to the question's point value. See "Allocation of Time" in Chapter 4.

Grading Implications for CPA Candidates

Analysis of the grading process helps you understand what graders are looking for and how you can present solutions to "satisfy the grader." Before turning to Chapter 3 for a discussion of how to prepare solutions, consider the following conclusions derived from the foregoing grading analysis.

1. Allocate your time based on point value
2. Do your best on every question, no matter how difficult
   a. Remember that the exam grade is adjusted for its difficulty
   b. If a question is difficult for you, it probably is difficult for others also
   c. Develop a "solutions approach" to assist you
3. No supporting notes or computations are required for the multiple-choice or other objective questions. The multiple-choice and other objective answers are machine-graded, and any related work on space provided next to the questions is ignored.

Candidate Diagnostic Report

State boards may include a "Candidate Diagnostic Report" along with the candidates' scores. A sample Auditing report appears below. The report provides useful information to candidates who must repeat a section. In those areas where the percentage of points is low (10% or less), be cautious as the results are based on very few questions.

JURISDICTION ILLINOIS		CANDIDATE NUMBER 1-09-000426			EXAMINATION DATE MAY 2000					
SECTION	GRADE	CONTENT AREAS AND PERCENT COVERAGE			PERCENTAGE OF AREA EARNED					
					≤50	51-60	61-70	71-80	81-90	>90
ARE	83	I	Federal Taxation – Individuals	20%				*		
		II	Federal Taxation – Corporations	20%					*	
		III	Federal Taxation – Partnerships	10%					*	
		IV	Federal Taxation – Other	10%						*
		V	Governmental and Not-For-Profit Organizations	30%			*			
		VI	Managerial Accounting	10%					*	
				100%						

**NOW IS THE TIME
TO MAKE YOUR COMMITMENT**

3 THE SOLUTIONS APPROACH

The solutions approach is a systematic problem-solving methodology. The purpose is to assure efficient, complete solutions to CPA exam problems, some of which are complex and confusing relative to most undergraduate accounting problems. Unfortunately, there appears to be a widespread lack of emphasis on problem-solving techniques in accounting courses. Most accounting books and courses merely provide solutions to specific types of problems. Memorization of these solutions for examinations and preparation of homework problems from examples is "cookbooking." "Cookbooking" is perhaps a necessary step in the learning process, but it is certainly not sufficient training for the complexities of the business world. Professional accountants need to be adaptive to a rapidly changing, complex environment. For example, CPAs have been called on to interpret and issue reports on new concepts such as price controls, energy allocations, and new taxes. These CPAs rely on their problem-solving expertise to understand these problems and to formulate solutions to them.

The steps outlined below represent only one of many possible series of solution steps. Admittedly, the procedures suggested are **very** structured; thus, you should adapt the suggestions to your needs. You may find that some steps are occasionally unnecessary, or that certain additional procedures increase your own question-solving efficiency. Whatever the case, substantial time should be allocated to developing an efficient solutions approach before taking the examination. You should develop your solutions approach by working questions.

Note that the steps below relate to any specific questions; overall examination and section strategies are discussed in Chapter 4.

Multiple-Choice Questions Solutions Approach Algorithm

1. **Work individual questions in order.**

    a. If a question appears lengthy or difficult, skip it until you can determine that extra time is available. Put a big question mark in the margin to remind you to return to questions you have skipped or need to review.

2. **Cover the choices before reading each question.**

    a. The answers are sometimes misleading and may cause you to misread or misinterpret the question.

3. **Read each question *carefully* to determine the topical area.**

    a. Study the requirements **first** so you know which data are important.
    b. Underline keywords and important data.
    c. Identify pertinent information with notations in the margin of the exam.
    d. Be especially careful to note when the requirement is an **exception** (e.g., "Which of the following is **not** included in gross income?")
    e. If a set of data is the basis for two or more questions, read the requirements of each of the questions before beginning to work the first question (sometimes it is more efficient to work the questions out of order or simultaneously).
    f. Be alert to read questions as they are, not as you would like them to be. You may encounter a familiar looking item; don't jump to the conclusion that you know what the answer is without reading the question completely.
    g. For comprehensive questions, prepare intermediary solutions as you read the question.

4. **Anticipate the answer before looking at the alternative answers.**

    a. Recall the applicable principle (e.g., job order costing), the applicable model (e.g., net present value), or the applicable code section (e.g., 1245).
    b. If a question deals with a complex area like standard costing, set up full-blown diagrams in the margins of the Examination Question Booklet, if necessary, using abbreviations that enable you to follow your work (remember that these multiple-choice questions are machine-graded).

5. **Read the answers and select the *best* alternative.**

    a. If the answer you have computed is not among the choices, quickly check your math and the logic of your solution. If you don't arrive at one of the given answers in the time you have allotted for that particular problem, make an educated guess.

6. **Mark the correct answer (or your educated guess) on the examination booklet itself.**
7. **After completing all of the individual questions in an overall question, transfer the answers to the machine gradable answer sheet with extreme care.**

    a. Be very careful not to fall out of sequence with the answer sheet. A mistake would cause most of your answers to be wrong. **Since the AICPA uses answer sheets with varying formats, it would be very easy to go across the sheet instead of down or vice versa.** Note the format of your answer sheet carefully!
    b. Review to check that you have transferred the answers correctly.
    c. Do not leave this step until the end of the exam as you may find yourself with too little time to transfer your answers to the answer sheet. **The exam proctors are not permitted to give you extra time to transfer your answers.**

    EXAMPLE: The following is an example of the manner in which the answer sheet should be marked for a Multiple-Choice question. A No. 2 pencil should be used to blacken the appropriate oval(s) on the Objective Answer Sheet to indicate the answer.

Item	Select One
19	Ⓐ ● Ⓒ Ⓓ
20	Ⓐ Ⓑ Ⓒ ●

Multiple-Choice Question Solutions Approach Example

A good example of the multiple-choice solutions approach is provided, using an actual multiple-choice question from a previous examination in Accounting and Reporting.

Step 3:
Topical area? Job order costing

Step 4a:
Production costs include direct materials used, direct labor, and manufacturing overhead applied. Since there is no ending WIP inventory, all production costs are for jobs completed.

Under Pick Co.'s job order costing system manufacturing overhead is applied to work in process using a predetermined annual overhead rate. During January 2000, Pick's transactions included the following:

Direct materials issued to production	$90,000
Indirect materials issued to production	8,000
Manufacturing overhead incurred	125,000
Manufacturing overhead applied	113,000
Direct labor costs	107,000

Pick had <u>neither beginning nor ending work-in-process inventory</u>. What was the cost of jobs completed in January 2000?

a. $302,000
b. $310,000
c. $322,000
d. $330,000

WIP
90
107 | 310
113
0

Currently, all multiple-choice questions are scored based on the number correct (i.e., there is no penalty for guessing). The rationale is that a "good guess" indicates knowledge. Thus, you should answer all multiple-choice questions.

Other Objective Questions Solutions Approach Algorithm

The following types of other objective questions have been tested previously on the Accounting and Reporting section:

a)	Matching	c)	Fill-in-the-number (No longer used)
b)	Yes/No	d)	Graphs

The AICPA no longer uses the free response essay/problem format to test taxation, managerial or, governmental and not-for-profit accounting. Instead, the AICPA has increased its use of the other objective answer format question. The OOAF questions now account for between 40-50% of the Accounting and Reporting section. Consequently, on the Accounting and Reporting exam candidates will not have to worry about constructing a well-written essay or a properly formatted schedule. But candidates will still need to apply the ideas of developing intermediate solutions or keyword outlines in order to fully understand the key concepts of the question. Note that while fill-in-the-number questions are no longer used, candidates should continue to be prepared for computational questions where the answers will be presented in a list of numeric choices. Therefore, it is still very important for candidates to have an organized solutions approach.

The following solutions approach is suggested for answering other objective questions:

1. **Glance over the entire problem.** Scan the problem in order to get a feel for the topical area and related concepts that are being tested. Even though the format of the question may vary, the exam continues to test your understanding of applicable principles or concepts. Relax, take a deep breath, and determine your strategy for conquering the problem.
2. **Identify the requirements of the problem.** This step will help you focus in more quickly on the solution(s) without wasting time reading irrelevant material.
3. **Study the items to be answered.** As you do this and become familiar with the topical area being tested, you should review the concepts of that area. This will help you organize your thoughts so that you can relate logically the requirements of the question with the applicable concepts.
4. **Answer each item one at a time.** The type of OOAF question determines how the candidate should accomplish this step. For instance, when the answer choices are presented in a matching question, the candidate must first understand how the answer choices apply to the question items. The candidate will then be able to differentiate among the answer choices in order to select the appropriate answer for each question.

    You may want to work backwards from the answers to the questions. Don't be afraid to answer questions out of order. Just be careful to place your selected answer next to the appropriate item number in your question booklet.
5. **Use journal entries, T-accounts, time lines, schedules, etc. as appropriate.** The use of these items helps to lay out the information in a logical manner to avoid silly mistakes.
6. **Mark your selected answer on the examination booklet itself.** Once the candidate has selected an answer it should be clearly marked on the examination booklet before moving on to the next question.
7. **After completing all of the items, carefully transfer the answers to the answer sheet.** Be careful to follow the instructions given for the correct placement of zeros. It is very important that all items be recorded on the objective answer sheet, as they cannot be graded if they are not.

Other Objective Question Solutions Approach Example

Problem 5 (20 to 30 minutes)[1]

Required:

Classify the gains and losses resulting from the following independent transactions. For each transaction (**Items 101 through 112**), select the appropriate tax treatment. A tax treatment may be selected once, more than once, or not at all.

---

[1] *Estimated time is no longer provided on the Uniform CPA Examination. See "Allocation of Time" in Chapter 4.*

Transaction

<table>
<tr><td>

101. Gain from sale of business inventory held thirteen months.

102. Gain from sale of personal residence held three years.

103. Gain from sale of unimproved land used as business parking lot and held seventeen months.

104. Loss from sale of eight-year-old boat held for personal use.

105. Gain from sale of lot held as investment for eleven months.

106. Casualty gain on personal residence held ten years (this was taxpayer's only casualty during year).

107. Casualty loss on truck used in business and held seven months.

108. Loss from nonbusiness bad debt that was outstanding two years.

109. Loss from sale of factory building held twenty-two months.

110. Loss from sale of business warehouse held four months.

111. Collection of cash method taxpayer's accounts receivable.

112. Gain from sale of unimproved land used as parking lot for business and held nine months.

</td><td>

Tax treatment

A. Long-term capital gain
B. Long-term capital loss
C. Short-term capital gain
D. Short-term capital loss
E. Sec. 1231 gain
F. Sec. 1231 loss
G. Ordinary income
H. Ordinary loss
I. Not deductible

</td></tr>
</table>

Step 1

Understand the requirements: The candidate must match **items 101 - 112** with the appropriate tax treatment. Note that a tax treatment may be selected once, more than once, or not at all.

Step 2

Analyze the answers: Spend time analyzing the answers. Can the answers be sorted into groups? Yes. There are basically five groups.

1. Capital Gains and Losses—Long-term
2. Capital Gains and Losses—Short-term
3. Section 1231 Gains and Losses
4. Ordinary Income or Loss
5. Not Deductible

Step 3

List what you know about the answers: Think about the knowledge base for types of gains and losses. Spend time listing what you know. For example, the knowledge base for the above information might be listed as follows:

What are capital gains and losses? They result from the sale or exchange of capital assets
    Capital assets **include**
        Investment property
        Property held for personal use (if sold at gain). No deduction is allowed if personal-use property is sold for loss
    Capital assets **exclude**
        Property used in a trade or business
        Inventory, accounts and notes receivable

What differentiates long-term gains and losses from short-term?
    Long-term is the property was held more than one year

What are Sec. 1231 gains and losses? They result from the sale or exchange of Sec. 1231 assets.
    Sec. 1231 assets **include**
        Property used in a trade or business if hold for **more than one year**
    Sec. 1231 assets **exclude**
        Property used in a trade or business if held one year or less
        Inventory, accounts and notes receivable

What are ordinary gains and losses? (Think of the default setting on a computer) If a gain or loss is neither capital nor
  Sec. 1231, then by default it is simply treated as an ordinary gain or loss

Step 4

Answer each question applying your knowledge base.

ANSWER 5

101.   **(G)**   Gain from sale of business inventory. Inventory is neither a capital nor Sec. 1231 asset—so it results in ordinary income. Here the holding period of thirteen months is just a distracter.

102.   **(A)**   Gain from a personal residence. Capital gain rules apply as property is held for personal use. Now apply the holding rule—more than one year so gain is long-term.

103.   **(E)**   Since the land was used for business, it does not fit the definition of a capital asset. Now apply the holding period rules. Recall, Sec. 1231 property is business property held for more than one year. Yes, this is a Sec. 1231 gains since the land was business property and held for seventeen months.

104.   **(I)**   The boat was held for personal use and sold at a loss so the loss is not deductible. The holding period is not relevant.

105.   **(C)**   The key word is investment. Since the land was held as an investment, it is a capital asset. The holding period of eleven months results in a short-term gain (one year or less).

106.   **(A)**   This was personal-use property. which is a capital asset—not a Sec. 1231 asset. Since the gain resulted from the taxpayer's only casualty during the year, it is a capital gain. The holding period of ten years results in a long-term capital gain.

107.   **(H)**   Truck was used in business so it is not a capital asset. Also, Sec. 1231 does not apply since the truck was held less than one year. By default, this is an ordinary loss.

108.   **(D)**   The key word is nonbusiness. A nonbusiness bad debt can only be deducted s a short-term capital loss. The period of time that the debt was outstanding is just a distracter.

109.   **(F)**   A factory building is a business asset. Therefore, it does not fit the definition of a capital asset. The loss is a Sec. 1231 loss because the building was business property held for more than one year.

110.   **(H)**   Capital loss treatment does not apply since the warehouse was used for business. Sec. 1231 also does not apply because the warehouse was held less than one year. By default, the loss on the warehouse held four months is an ordinary loss.

111.   **(G)**   Accounts receivable are excluded from both the capital and Sec. 1231 categories. Since the taxpayer is using the cash method, the income on the receivables had not previously been recognized. So the collection of the accounts receivable results in ordinary income.

112.   **(G)**   The land was used for business so it is not a capital asset. Sec. 1231 also does not apply since the land was held less than one year. By default, the gain from the sale of land held nine months is treated as ordinary income.

Other objective questions can be easy if you understand that the form of the question is not what is important. What's important, is to maintain a working knowledge of the topic. Also, candidates must realize that the first step is to understand the requirements. Next analyze the answers and list what you know about the topics. As you can see from the above example, it was crucial that the candidate spend time listing the applicable knowledge base and terms that are relevant to the question requirements.

Time Requirements for the Solutions Approach

Many candidates bypass the solutions approach because they feel it is too time-consuming. Actually, the solutions approach is a time-saver, and more importantly, it helps you prepare better solutions to all problems.

Without committing yourself to using the solutions approach, try it step-by-step on several multiple-choice questions and other objective questions. After you conscientiously go through the step-by-step routine a few times, you will begin to adopt and modify aspects of the technique which will benefit you. Subsequent usage will become subconscious and painless. The important point is that you have to try the solutions approach several times to accrue any benefits.

Efficiency of the Solutions Approach

The mark of an inefficient solution is one wherein the candidate immediately begins to write a solution. Remember, the final solution is one of the last steps in the solutions approach. You should have the solution under complete control before you begin your final solution.

While the large amount of intermediary work in the solutions approach may appear burdensome and time-consuming, this technique results in more complete solutions in less time than do haphazard approaches. Moreover, the solutions approach really allows you to work out problems that you feel unfamiliar with at first reading. The solutions approach, however, must be mastered prior to sitting for the CPA examination. In other words, the candidate must be willing to invest a reasonable amount of time into perfecting the solutions approach.

In summary, the solutions approach may appear foreign and somewhat cumbersome. At the same time, if you have worked through the material in this chapter, you should have some appreciation for it. Develop the solutions approach by writing down the seven steps in the solutions approach algorithm at the beginning of this chapter, and keep them before you as you work previous CPA exam questions. Remember that even though the suggested procedures appear **very structured** and **time-consuming**, integration of these procedures into your own style of problem solving will help improve **your** solutions approach. The next chapter discusses strategies for the overall examination.

**NOW IS THE TIME
TO MAKE YOUR COMMITMENT**

---

4 TAKING THE EXAMINATION

This chapter is concerned with developing an examination strategy (e.g., how to cope with the environment at the examination site, the order in which to work problems, etc.).

EXAMINATION STRATEGIES

Your performance during the two-day examination is final and not subject to revision. While you may sit for the examination again if you are unsuccessful, the majority of your preparation will have to be repeated, requiring substantial, additional amounts of time. Thus, examination strategies (discussed in this chapter) which maximize your exam-taking efficiency are very important.

Getting "Psyched Up"

The CPA exam is quite challenging and worthy of your best effort. Explicitly develop your own psychological strategy to get yourself "up" for the exam. Pace your study program such that you will be able to operate at peak performance when you are actually taking the exam. Many candidates give up because they have a bad day or encounter a rough problem. Do the best you can; the other candidates are probably no better prepared than you.

Examination Supplies

The AICPA recommends that candidates prepare their solutions in pencil. As you practice your solutions approach, experiment with pencils, lead types, erasers, etc., that are comfortable to use and that also result in good copy for the grader.

In addition to an adequate supply of pencils and erasers, it is very important to take a watch to the examination. Also, take refreshments (as permitted) which are conducive to your exam efficiency. Finally, dress to assure your comfort during the exam. Layered clothing is recommended for possible variations in temperature at the examination site.

Do **not** take study materials to the examination room. You will not be able to use them. They will only muddle your mind and get you "uptight." Finally, **do not** carry notes or crib sheets upon your person—this can only result in the gravest of problems. Do not risk being expelled from the exam.

Lodging, Meals, Exercise

Make advance reservations for comfortable lodging convenient to the examination facilities. Do not stay with friends, relatives, etc. Both uninterrupted sleep and total concentration on the exam are a must. Consider the following in making your lodging plans:

1. Proximity to exam facilities
2. Lodging and exam parking facilities
3. Availability of meals and snacks
4. Recreational facilities

Plan your meal schedule to provide maximum energy and alertness during the day and maximum rest at night. Do not experiment with new foods, drinks, etc., during the examination time period. Within reasonable limits, observe your normal eating and drinking habits. Recognize that overconsumption of coffee during the exam could lead to a hyperactive state and disaster. Likewise, overindulgence in alcohol to overcome nervousness and to induce sleep the night before might contribute to other difficulties the following morning.

Tenseness should be expected before and during the examination. Rely on a regular exercise program to unwind at the end of the day. As you select your lodging for the examination, try to accommodate your exercise pleasure (e.g., running, swimming, etc.). Continue to indulge in your exercise program on the days of the examination.

To relieve tension or stress while studying, try breathing or stretching exercises. Use these exercises before and during the examination to start and to keep your adrenaline flowing. Do not hesitate to attract attention by doing pushups, jumping jacks, etc., in a lobby outside of the examination room if it will improve your exam efficiency. Remain determined not to go through another examination to obtain your certificate.

A problem you will probably experience during the exam related to general fatigue and tenseness is writer's cramp. Experiment with alternate methods of holding your pencil, rubbing your hand, etc., during your preparation program.

In summary, the examination is likely to be both rigorous and fatiguing. Expect it and prepare for it by getting in shape, planning methods of relaxation during the exam and exam evenings, and finally building the confidence and competence to complete the exam (successfully).

Examination Facilities and Procedures

Visit the examination facilities at least the evening before the examination to assure knowledge of the location. Remember: no surprises. Having a general familiarity with the facilities will lessen anxiety prior to the examination. Talking to a recent veteran of the examination will give you background for the general examination procedures, such as

1. Procedure for distributing exam booklets, papers, etc.
2. Accessibility of restrooms
3. Availability of beverages and snacks at exam location
4. Admissibility of beverages and snacks in the exam room
5. Peculiar problems of exam facilities (e.g., noise, lighting, temperature, etc.)
6. Permissibility of early departure from exam
7. His/her experience in taking the exam
8. Other important information

As you might see, it is important to talk with someone who recently sat for the examination at the same location where you intend to sit. The objective is to reduce your anxiety just prior to the examination and to minimize any possible distractions. Finally, if you have any remaining questions regarding examination procedure, call or write your state board.

On a related point, do not be distracted by other candidates who show up at the examination completely relaxed and greet others with confidence. These are most likely candidates who have been there before. Probably the only thing they are confident of is a few days' vacation from work. Also, do not become distracted when candidates leave early. A candidate's early departure may mean s/he is giving up.

Arrive at the Examination Early

On the day of the exam, be sure to get to the examination site at least 30 minutes early to reduce tension and to get yourself situated. Most states have assigned seating. If this is the case, you will be seated by your candidate ID number. However, if you have a choice, it is probably wise to sit away from the door and the administration table to avoid being distracted by candidates who arrive late, leave early, ask questions, etc., and by proctors who occasionally converse. **Avoid all possible distractions. Stay away from friends.** Find a seat that will be comfortable; consider sunlight, interior lighting, heating/air conditioning, pedestrian traffic, etc.

Usually the proctors open the sealed boxes of exams and distribute the Examination Question and Answer Booklets to candidates 10 minutes before the scheduled beginning of the examination. Shown below is the cover sheet and the back page of the Examination Question and Answer Booklet from the November 1995 Accounting and Reporting Exam, the last disclosed exam. Now candidates receive only one booklet that contains both the questions and the answer sheets. Record your 7-digit candidate number in the boxes provided at the upper right-hand corner of the front cover of the Examination Booklet. You are not permitted to open the booklet until the starting signal is given, but you should study the instructions printed on the front cover. The instructions generally explain

1. How to turn in examination papers
2. Handling of the Examination Question and Answer Booklet

CANDIDATE NUMBER

Record your 7-digit candidate number in the boxes.

Print your **STATE** name here.

UNIFORM CERTIFIED PUBLIC ACCOUNTANT EXAMINATION

Accounting & Reporting—Taxation, Managerial, and Governmental and Not-for-Profit Organizations

ARE

November 2, 1995; 8:30 A.M. to 12:00 NOON

The point values for each question, and estimated time allotments based primarily on point value, are as follows:

	Point Value	Estimated Minutes Minimum	Maximum
No. 1	60	120	130
No. 2	5	5	10
No. 3	20	25	40
No. 4	5	5	10
No. 5	10	15	20
Totals	**100**	**170**	**210**

INSTRUCTIONS TO CANDIDATES

Failure to follow these instructions may have an adverse effect on your Examination grade.

1. Do not break the seal around the *Examination Questions* (pages 3 through 26) until you are told to do so.

2. All questions should be answered on the *Objective Answer Sheet*, which is pages 27 and 28. You should attempt to answer all objective items. There is no penalty for incorrect responses. Work space to solve the objective questions is provided in the *Examination Questions* on pages 5 through 19. Since the objective items are computer graded, your comments and calculations associated with them are not considered. Be certain that you have entered your answers on the *Objective Answer Sheet* before the examination time is up. Your examination will not be graded if you fail to record your answers on the *Objective Answer Sheet*. You will not be given additional time to record your answers.

3. You are required to turn in by the end of each session:

   a. Attendance Record and Calculator Sign-off Record Form, page 1;
   b. *Examination Questions*, pages 3 through 26;
   c. *Objective Answer Sheet*, pages 27 and 28;
   d. Calculator; and
   e. All unused examination materials.

   Your examination will not be graded unless the above listed items are handed in before leaving the examination room.

4. Unless otherwise instructed, if you want your *Examination Questions* mailed to you, write your name and address in both places indicated on page 26 and place 55 cents postage in the space provided. *Examination Questions* will be distributed no sooner than the day following the administration of this examination.

Prepared by the Board of Examiners of the American Institute of Certified Public Accountants and adopted by the examining boards of all states, the District of Columbia, Guam, Puerto Rico, and the Virgin Islands of the United States.

Copyright © 1995 by the American Institute of Certified Public Accountants, Inc.

Examination Questions Booklet No.

4 07178 Q

ATTENDANCE RECORD
(To Be Retained by State Board)

CANDIDATE NUMBER

Record your 7-digit candidate number in the boxes.

Print your **STATE** name here.

Name (please print)

Home Address

City _____ State _____ Zip Code

CALCULATOR SIGN-OFF RECORD
Test Calculations

Keystroke			Display
CA	53000	+	100600
CA	125000	=	47600
CA	98300	=	26700
CA	5000	×	1.667	8335
CA	39000	÷	1300	30

I hereby certify that the calculator I received was tested by me and performed all test functions accurately.

Signature _____ Date _____

ARE
VERSION 2

407178 S

Attendance Record Booklet No.

UNIFORM CERTIFIED PUBLIC ACCOUNTANT EXAMINATION

Accounting & Reporting—Taxation, Managerial, and Governmental and Not-for-Profit Organizations
November 2, 1995; 8:30 A.M. to 12:00 NOON

INSTRUCTIONS TO CANDIDATES

(This *Examination Question and Answer Booklet* contains an *Attendance Record and Calculator Sign-Off Record, Examination Questions, Essay Ruled Paper,* and *Objective Answer Sheet*)

1. Do not begin writing on this *Booklet* until you are told to do so.

2. Complete the *Attendance Record and Calculator Sign-off Record,* and your 7-digit candidate number above. Detach the page at the perforation so it can be collected and retained by the State Board.

3. Test your calculator and sign the *Calculator Sign-off Record.* Press CA once to turn the calculator on. The display will read "0." Perform the *test calculations.* The calculator automatically turns itself off approximately 8 minutes after the last entry. Instructions on

how to use the calculator are on pages 2 and 4.

4. Turn the *Booklet* over and record your 7-digit candidate number and state on the *Objective Answer Sheet.*

5. The *Objective Answer Sheet* is on pages 27 and 28. Your examination will not be graded if you fail to record your answers on the *Objective Answer Sheet.*

6. In order to grade your *Objective Answer Sheet,* the Booklet No. above must be identical to the Booklet Nos. on pages 3 and 28.

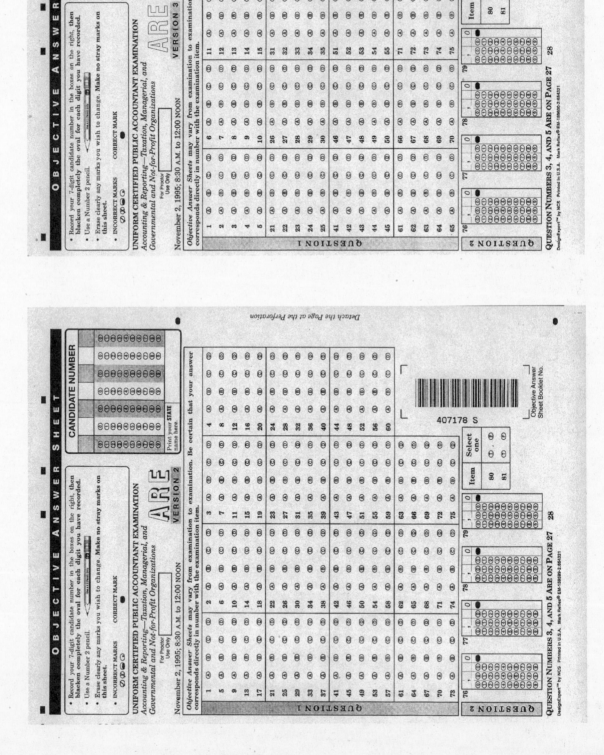

101	(A)(B)	(C)(D)	(E)(F)	(G)(H)	(I)(J)	(K)(L)	(M)(N)	(O)(P)	(Q)(R)	(S)(T)	(U)(V)	(W)(X)	(Y)(Z)
102	(A)(B)	(C)(D)	(E)(F)	(G)(H)	(I)(J)	(K)(L)	(M)(N)	(O)(P)	(Q)(R)	(S)(T)	(U)(V)	(W)(X)	(Y)(Z)
103	(A)(B)	(C)(D)	(E)(F)	(G)(H)	(I)(J)	(K)(L)	(M)(N)	(O)(P)	(Q)(R)	(S)(T)	(U)(V)	(W)(X)	(Y)(Z)
104	(A)(B)	(C)(D)	(E)(F)	(G)(H)	(I)(J)	(K)(L)	(M)(N)	(O)(P)	(Q)(R)	(S)(T)	(U)(V)	(W)(X)	(Y)(Z)
105	(A)(B)	(C)(D)	(E)(F)	(G)(H)	(I)(J)	(K)(L)	(M)(N)	(O)(P)	(Q)(R)	(S)(T)	(U)(V)	(W)(X)	(Y)(Z)
106	(A)(B)	(C)(D)	(E)(F)	(G)(H)	(I)(J)	(K)(L)	(M)(N)	(O)(P)	(Q)(R)	(S)(T)	(U)(V)	(W)(X)	(Y)(Z)
107	(A)(B)	(C)(D)	(E)(F)	(G)(H)	(I)(J)	(K)(L)	(M)(N)	(O)(P)	(Q)(R)	(S)(T)	(U)(V)	(W)(X)	(Y)(Z)
108	(A)(B)	(C)(D)	(E)(F)	(G)(H)	(I)(J)	(K)(L)	(M)(N)	(O)(P)	(Q)(R)	(S)(T)	(U)(V)	(W)(X)	(Y)(Z)
109	(A)(B)	(C)(D)	(E)(F)	(G)(H)	(I)(J)	(K)(L)	(M)(N)	(O)(P)	(Q)(R)	(S)(T)	(U)(V)	(W)(X)	(Y)(Z)
110	(A)(B)	(C)(D)	(E)(F)	(G)(H)	(I)(J)	(K)(L)	(M)(N)	(O)(P)	(Q)(R)	(S)(T)	(U)(V)	(W)(X)	(Y)(Z)
111	(A)(B)	(C)(D)	(E)(F)	(G)(H)	(I)(J)	(K)(L)	(M)(N)	(O)(P)	(Q)(R)	(S)(T)	(U)(V)	(W)(X)	(Y)(Z)
112	(A)(B)	(C)(D)	(E)(F)	(G)(H)	(I)(J)	(K)(L)	(M)(N)	(O)(P)	(Q)(R)	(S)(T)	(U)(V)	(W)(X)	(Y)(Z)
113	(A)(B)	(C)(D)	(E)(F)	(G)(H)	(I)(J)	(K)(L)	(M)(N)	(O)(P)	(Q)(R)	(S)(T)	(U)(V)	(W)(X)	(Y)(Z)
114	(A)(B)	(C)(D)	(E)(F)	(G)(H)	(I)(J)	(K)(L)	(M)(N)	(O)(P)	(Q)(R)	(S)(T)	(U)(V)	(W)(X)	(Y)(Z)
115	(A)(B)	(C)(D)	(E)(F)	(G)(H)	(I)(J)	(K)(L)	(M)(N)	(O)(P)	(Q)(R)	(S)(T)	(U)(V)	(W)(X)	(Y)(Z)
116	(A)(B)	(C)(D)	(E)(F)	(G)(H)	(I)(J)	(K)(L)	(M)(N)	(O)(P)	(Q)(R)	(S)(T)	(U)(V)	(W)(X)	(Y)(Z)
117	(A)(B)	(C)(D)	(E)(F)	(G)(H)	(I)(J)	(K)(L)	(M)(N)	(O)(P)	(Q)(R)	(S)(T)	(U)(V)	(W)(X)	(Y)(Z)
118	(A)(B)	(C)(D)	(E)(F)	(G)(H)	(I)(J)	(K)(L)	(M)(N)	(O)(P)	(Q)(R)	(S)(T)	(U)(V)	(W)(X)	(Y)(Z)
119	(A)(B)	(C)(D)	(E)(F)	(G)(H)	(I)(J)	(K)(L)	(M)(N)	(O)(P)	(Q)(R)	(S)(T)	(U)(V)	(W)(X)	(Y)(Z)
120	(A)(B)	(C)(D)	(E)(F)	(G)(H)	(I)(J)	(K)(L)	(M)(N)	(O)(P)	(Q)(R)	(S)(T)	(U)(V)	(W)(X)	(Y)(Z)
121	(A)(B)	(C)(D)	(E)(F)	(G)(H)	(I)(J)	(K)(L)	(M)(N)	(O)(P)	(Q)(R)	(S)(T)	(U)(V)	(W)(X)	(Y)(Z)
122	(A)(B)	(C)(D)	(E)(F)	(G)(H)	(I)(J)	(K)(L)	(M)(N)	(O)(P)	(Q)(R)	(S)(T)	(U)(V)	(W)(X)	(Y)(Z)
123	(A)(B)	(C)(D)	(E)(F)	(G)(H)	(I)(J)	(K)(L)	(M)(N)	(O)(P)	(Q)(R)	(S)(T)	(U)(V)	(W)(X)	(Y)(Z)
124	(A)(B)	(C)(D)	(E)(F)	(G)(H)	(I)(J)	(K)(L)	(M)(N)	(O)(P)	(Q)(R)	(S)(T)	(U)(V)	(W)(X)	(Y)(Z)
125	(A)(B)	(C)(D)	(E)(F)	(G)(H)	(I)(J)	(K)(L)	(M)(N)	(O)(P)	(Q)(R)	(S)(T)	(U)(V)	(W)(X)	(Y)(Z)
126	(A)(B)	(C)(D)	(E)(F)	(G)(H)	(I)(J)	(K)(L)	(M)(N)	(O)(P)	(Q)(R)	(S)(T)	(U)(V)	(W)(X)	(Y)(Z)
127	(A)(B)	(C)(D)	(E)(F)	(G)(H)	(I)(J)	(K)(L)	(M)(N)	(O)(P)	(Q)(R)	(S)(T)	(U)(V)	(W)(X)	(Y)(Z)
128	(A)(B)	(C)(D)	(E)(F)	(G)(H)	(I)(J)	(K)(L)	(M)(N)	(O)(P)	(Q)(R)	(S)(T)	(U)(V)	(W)(X)	(Y)(Z)
129	(A)(B)	(C)(D)	(E)(F)	(G)(H)	(I)(J)	(K)(L)	(M)(N)	(O)(P)	(Q)(R)	(S)(T)	(U)(V)	(W)(X)	(Y)(Z)
130	(A)(B)	(C)(D)	(E)(F)	(G)(H)	(I)(J)	(K)(L)	(M)(N)	(O)(P)	(Q)(R)	(S)(T)	(U)(V)	(W)(X)	(Y)(Z)
131	(A)(B)	(C)(D)	(E)(F)	(G)(H)	(I)(J)	(K)(L)	(M)(N)	(O)(P)	(Q)(R)	(S)(T)	(U)(V)	(W)(X)	(Y)(Z)
132	(A)(B)	(C)(D)	(E)(F)	(G)(H)	(I)(J)	(K)(L)	(M)(N)	(O)(P)	(Q)(R)	(S)(T)	(U)(V)	(W)(X)	(Y)(Z)
133	(A)(B)	(C)(D)	(E)(F)	(G)(H)	(I)(J)	(K)(L)	(M)(N)	(O)(P)	(Q)(R)	(S)(T)	(U)(V)	(W)(X)	(Y)(Z)
134	(A)(B)	(C)(D)	(E)(F)	(G)(H)	(I)(J)	(K)(L)	(M)(N)	(O)(P)	(Q)(R)	(S)(T)	(U)(V)	(W)(X)	(Y)(Z)
135	(A)(B)	(C)(D)	(E)(F)	(G)(H)	(I)(J)	(K)(L)	(M)(N)	(O)(P)	(Q)(R)	(S)(T)	(U)(V)	(W)(X)	(Y)(Z)
136	(A)(B)	(C)(D)	(E)(F)	(G)(H)	(I)(J)	(K)(L)	(M)(N)	(O)(P)	(Q)(R)	(S)(T)	(U)(V)	(W)(X)	(Y)(Z)
137	(A)(B)	(C)(D)	(E)(F)	(G)(H)	(I)(J)	(K)(L)	(M)(N)	(O)(P)	(Q)(R)	(S)(T)	(U)(V)	(W)(X)	(Y)(Z)
138	(A)(B)	(C)(D)	(E)(F)	(G)(H)	(I)(J)	(K)(L)	(M)(N)	(O)(P)	(Q)(R)	(S)(T)	(U)(V)	(W)(X)	(Y)(Z)
139	(A)(B)	(C)(D)	(E)(F)	(G)(H)	(I)(J)	(K)(L)	(M)(N)	(O)(P)	(Q)(R)	(S)(T)	(U)(V)	(W)(X)	(Y)(Z)
140	(A)(B)	(C)(D)	(E)(F)	(G)(H)	(I)(J)	(K)(L)	(M)(N)	(O)(P)	(Q)(R)	(S)(T)	(U)(V)	(W)(X)	(Y)(Z)
141	(A)(B)	(C)(D)	(E)(F)	(G)(H)	(I)(J)	(K)(L)	(M)(N)	(O)(P)	(Q)(R)	(S)(T)	(U)(V)	(W)(X)	(Y)(Z)
142	(A)(B)	(C)(D)	(E)(F)	(G)(H)	(I)(J)	(K)(L)	(M)(N)	(O)(P)	(Q)(R)	(S)(T)	(U)(V)	(W)(X)	(Y)(Z)
143	(A)(B)	(C)(D)	(E)(F)	(G)(H)	(I)(J)	(K)(L)	(M)(N)	(O)(P)	(Q)(R)	(S)(T)	(U)(V)	(W)(X)	(Y)(Z)
144	(A)(B)	(C)(D)	(E)(F)	(G)(H)	(I)(J)	(K)(L)	(M)(N)	(O)(P)	(Q)(R)	(S)(T)	(U)(V)	(W)(X)	(Y)(Z)
145	(A)(B)	(C)(D)	(E)(F)	(G)(H)	(I)(J)	(K)(L)	(M)(N)	(O)(P)	(Q)(R)	(S)(T)	(U)(V)	(W)(X)	(Y)(Z)
146	(A)(B)	(C)(D)	(E)(F)	(G)(H)	(I)(J)	(K)(L)	(M)(N)	(O)(P)	(Q)(R)	(S)(T)	(U)(V)	(W)(X)	(Y)(Z)
147	(A)(B)	(C)(D)	(E)(F)	(G)(H)	(I)(J)	(K)(L)	(M)(N)	(O)(P)	(Q)(R)	(S)(T)	(U)(V)	(W)(X)	(Y)(Z)
148	(A)(B)	(C)(D)	(E)(F)	(G)(H)	(I)(J)	(K)(L)	(M)(N)	(O)(P)	(Q)(R)	(S)(T)	(U)(V)	(W)(X)	(Y)(Z)
149	(A)(B)	(C)(D)	(E)(F)	(G)(H)	(I)(J)	(K)(L)	(M)(N)	(O)(P)	(Q)(R)	(S)(T)	(U)(V)	(W)(X)	(Y)(Z)
150	(A)(B)	(C)(D)	(E)(F)	(G)(H)	(I)(J)	(K)(L)	(M)(N)	(O)(P)	(Q)(R)	(S)(T)	(U)(V)	(W)(X)	(Y)(Z)
151	(A)(B)	(C)(D)	(E)(F)	(G)(H)	(I)(J)	(K)(L)	(M)(N)	(O)(P)	(Q)(R)	(S)(T)	(U)(V)	(W)(X)	(Y)(Z)
152	(A)(B)	(C)(D)	(E)(F)	(G)(H)	(I)(J)	(K)(L)	(M)(N)	(O)(P)	(Q)(R)	(S)(T)	(U)(V)	(W)(X)	(Y)(Z)
153	(A)(B)	(C)(D)	(E)(F)	(G)(H)	(I)(J)	(K)(L)	(M)(N)	(O)(P)	(Q)(R)	(S)(T)	(U)(V)	(W)(X)	(Y)(Z)
154	(A)(B)	(C)(D)	(E)(F)	(G)(H)	(I)(J)	(K)(L)	(M)(N)	(O)(P)	(Q)(R)	(S)(T)	(U)(V)	(W)(X)	(Y)(Z)
155	(A)(B)	(C)(D)	(E)(F)	(G)(H)	(I)(J)	(K)(L)	(M)(N)	(O)(P)	(Q)(R)	(S)(T)	(U)(V)	(W)(X)	(Y)(Z)
156	(A)(B)	(C)(D)	(E)(F)	(G)(H)	(I)(J)	(K)(L)	(M)(N)	(O)(P)	(Q)(R)	(S)(T)	(U)(V)	(W)(X)	(Y)(Z)
157	(A)(B)	(C)(D)	(E)(F)	(G)(H)	(I)(J)	(K)(L)	(M)(N)	(O)(P)	(Q)(R)	(S)(T)	(U)(V)	(W)(X)	(Y)(Z)
158	(A)(B)	(C)(D)	(E)(F)	(G)(H)	(I)(J)	(K)(L)	(M)(N)	(O)(P)	(Q)(R)	(S)(T)	(U)(V)	(W)(X)	(Y)(Z)
159	(A)(B)	(C)(D)	(E)(F)	(G)(H)	(I)(J)	(K)(L)	(M)(N)	(O)(P)	(Q)(R)	(S)(T)	(U)(V)	(W)(X)	(Y)(Z)
160	(A)(B)	(C)(D)	(E)(F)	(G)(H)	(I)(J)	(K)(L)	(M)(N)	(O)(P)	(Q)(R)	(S)(T)	(U)(V)	(W)(X)	(Y)(Z)
161	(A)(B)	(C)(D)	(E)(F)	(G)(H)	(I)(J)	(K)(L)	(M)(N)	(O)(P)	(Q)(R)	(S)(T)	(U)(V)	(W)(X)	(Y)(Z)
162	(A)(B)	(C)(D)	(E)(F)	(G)(H)	(I)(J)	(K)(L)	(M)(N)	(O)(P)	(Q)(R)	(S)(T)	(U)(V)	(W)(X)	(Y)(Z)
163	(A)(B)	(C)(D)	(E)(F)	(G)(H)	(I)(J)	(K)(L)	(M)(N)	(O)(P)	(Q)(R)	(S)(T)	(U)(V)	(W)(X)	(Y)(Z)
164	(A)(B)	(C)(D)	(E)(F)	(G)(H)	(I)(J)	(K)(L)	(M)(N)	(O)(P)	(Q)(R)	(S)(T)	(U)(V)	(W)(X)	(Y)(Z)
165	(A)(B)	(C)(D)	(E)(F)	(G)(H)	(I)(J)	(K)(L)	(M)(N)	(O)(P)	(Q)(R)	(S)(T)	(U)(V)	(W)(X)	(Y)(Z)

Prior to the start of the exam, you will be instructed to complete and detach the Attendance Record, which will be retained by the State Boards of Accountancy. You should record your 7-digit candidate number on this record and on all other papers you submit. You will also be permitted to record your 7-digit candidate number in the upper right-hand corner and blacken the corresponding oval below each box on the front and back covers of your booklet.

The Objective Answer Sheet contained in the booklet will be used to record answers to both the multiple-choice section of the exam and other objective format questions. In some states, you will be asked to detach the Objective Answer Sheet and turn it in separately; however, in other states the Objective Answer Sheet is to remain attached to the booklet. Follow the instructions of your state board. Also, record your candidate number where indicated.

The AICPA is now using a "generic" two-sided objective answer sheet (shown below). The multiple-choice answers should be entered on side 1, and the other objective answers should be entered on side 2. The information and numbering for each side is as follows:

- **Side 1: Multiple-choice** answers contain spaces to answer question numbers **1 to 100,** with letter **choices "a" through "d."** Use only what you need. For example, the Law exam usually contains 60 multiple-choice questions (excluding pretest). In this case, the remaining numbers up to 100 will be left blank. The Auditing exam might contain 90 multiple-choice questions (excluding pretest). Again, use only what you need. **Then, turn over the answer sheet to side 2 to use for the other objective questions.**
- **Side 2: Other objective** answers contain spaces to answer questions numbers **101 to 165,** with letter **choices "a" through "z."** Again, use only what you need. For example, if the other objective questions end at number 150, leave numbers 151 through 165 blank.

It is very important to turn the answer sheet over and always begin the other objective answers with question number 101. Take your time, darkening an oval for each answer, one question at a time.

Two different versions of the Objective Answer Sheet from the November 1995 Accounting and Reporting Exam are shown below. **Candidates should be aware that different versions of the answer sheet have different arrangements for the multiple-choice questions. The answer sheet may be organized vertically, horizontally, or a combination of the two. The candidate, therefore, must be sure to correctly transfer all answers to the answer sheet.**

Inventory of the Examination Content

When you receive your booklet, carefully read the instructions. The objective is to review the standard instructions, to note any new or special items, and to comply with the examination procedures. After reviewing the instructions on the front of your booklet, make note of the number of questions and the point value of each. Immediately after receiving permission to open the question booklet, glance over each of the questions sufficiently and jot down the topics on the front of the question booklet. This will give you an overview of the ensuing 3½ hours of work. You may find it to your advantage to write down keywords, acronyms, etc. on the front of the question booklet **before** you forget them, but only **after** you have been told to begin the examination.

Allocation of Time

Budget your time. Time should be carefully allocated in an attempt to maximize points per minute. While you must develop your own strategy with respect to time allocation, some suggestions may be useful. First, consider the Accounting and Reporting Examination, which is 210 minutes long. Allocate 5 minutes to reading the instructions and to taking an inventory, jotting the topics tested by question on the front cover. Budget your time based on the points allocated to each question. The ARE exam is a three and one-half hour (210 minutes) exam which would have points allocated as follows:

Hypothetical Time Budget
(3 1/2 hour exam)

Question	*Type*	*Point value*	*Calculated maximum time*
No. 1	Multiple-Choice	60	60/100 x 210 min = 126 min
No. 2	OOAF	10	10/100 x 210 min = 21 min
No. 3	OOAF	10	10/100 x 210 min = 21 min
No. 4	OOAF	10	10/100 x 210 min = 21 min
No. 5	OOAF	10	10/100 x 210 min = 21 min
Total		100	210 min

It is your responsibility to be ready at the start of the session and to stop writing when told to do so. Therefore, take control of the exam from the very start. Assuming seventy-five individual multiple-choice (excluding test questions) and four other objective questions, you should plan on spending about two minutes working each of the individual multiple-choice questions. Next, work the other objective answer format questions. Finally, complete the objective question answer sheet by **carefully** transferring your answers from the exam booklet to the machine gradable form. This should take about five minutes. The answers must be transferred before the exam session ends. **The proctors are not allowed to give you extra time to do this.**

It is important to keep track of the time spent on each question during the examination. Write the time you start each problem near the top of the question to preclude your spending more than the suggested time on any one question.

Techniques for Time Management

The Accounting and Reporting exam has historically had about 75 multiple-choice questions (not including pretest questions). Referring to the above hypothetical time budget, note that the maximum time you should take to complete a group of 25 questions is about 40 minutes per group. Remember that you alone control watching your progress towards successfully completing this exam.

One possible way of monitoring your progress is to write check times throughout the exam. For example, if you begin the multiple-choice at 8:30 a.m. go to question number 15 and write 9:00. By question number 30, write 9:30, and by question number 45, write 10:00. By question number 60, write 10:30 a.m. Now you have benchmarks to check your time against as you proceed through the exam. If you complete the multiple-choice questions by 10:10 a.m., you have successfully banked 20 minutes to use when answering the other objective and essay questions.

Order of Working Questions

Select the question that you are going to work first from the notes you made on the front of your examination. Some will select the question that appears easiest to get started and build confidence. Others will begin with the question they feel is most difficult to get it out of the way. Once you select a question you should apply the solutions approach. You should, however, leave a question if you get stuck, rather than just "spinning your wheels." Later, when you come back and retool the question, you may be able to think of a new approach to "unlock" the solution.

Never, but never, leave a question blank, as this almost certainly precludes a passing grade on that section. Some candidates talk about "giving certain types of questions to the AICPA," (i.e., no answer). The only thing being given to the AICPA is grading time since the grader will not have to read a solution. Expect a couple of "far out" or seemingly insurmountable questions. Apply the solutions approach—imagine yourself having to make a similar decision, computation, explanation, etc., in an actual situation—and come up with as much as possible to answer the question.

Calculator Use

Candidates are provided with calculators at the examination sites for use on the Accounting and Reporting—Taxation, Managerial, and Governmental and Not-for-Profit Organizations, and the Financial Accounting and Reporting sections.

Candidates should only need to use the calculators' four primary functions—add, subtract, multiply, and divide. However, the calculators also have function keys for square root, percentage, and memory. Candidates are given an opportunity to test the calculators to ensure that the calculators are functioning properly. **It is the candidate's responsibility to notify one of the proctors immediately in the event of a malfunction.** Replacement calculators are available. Test calculations are printed in the examination booklets.

To turn the calculator on press $\textcircled{C\cdot CE}$. The display will read "0." The calculator automatically turns itself off approximately eight minutes after the last entry. All data in the calculator will be lost once the calculator is off. When you complete a calculation, we recommend that after you press $\textcircled{=}$, you press $\textcircled{C\cdot CE}$ before beginning a new calculation. The basic key descriptions are as follows:

On and Clear—Turns the calculator on and clears the display. To clear the calculator of all entries, press ⊂=⊃ , then press ⊂C·CE⊃

Numericals—Inputs that number.

Decimal—Indicates that all numbers to follow are decimals.

Change sign—Changes plus (minus) to minus (plus).

Add & Subtract—Adds the next number entered to, or subtracts the next number entered from, the displayed number.

Multiply & Divide—Multiplies or divides the displayed number by the next number entered.

Equal—Displays the results of all previously entered operations.

Square Root—Calculates the square root of the displayed number. It is unlikely that you will need to use this key during the exam.

Percentage—When performing a calculation, converts the displayed number to a percentage and completes the calculation. It is unlikely that you will need to use this key during the exam.

Memory Add—Adds the displayed number to the balance in memory.

Memory Subtract—Subtracts the displayed number from the balance in memory.

Recall Clear Memory—Pressed once, displays the balance in memory. Pressed twice in a row, eliminates the balance in memory but not the displayed number.

Since each AICPA calculator provided has these basic functions, the only difference between calculators is in the placement of the keys. While it may be helpful to have the exact calculator that you are familiar with, this is not essential to your examination success.

Test Calculations

Keystroke						Display
C·CE	53000	+	47600	=		100600
C·CE	125000	−	98300	=		26700
C·CE	5000	x	1.667	=		8335
C·CE	39000	÷	1300	=		30

Pitfalls of Calculator Use

The use of calculators is designed to save candidates time on performing and verifying manual calculations. However, there are some pitfalls that the candidate must remain aware of throughout the entire exam. For instance, how many times have you simply hit the wrong key (e.g., a six instead of a nine?) Or, how many times have you forgotten to clear the calculator before beginning a new calculation? Both of these mistakes are simple errors that everyone makes at one time or another. Yet, these simple mistakes could be the difference between a candidate receiving a passing grade or a failing grade. In order to guard against these errors, candidates should avoid rushing through the questions. Accuracy is just as important, if not more so, as speed. Candidates should work each section of the exam with a time budget in mind to avoid any last-minute panic attacks. There are no points given for finishing first, and so, candidates should concentrate on working accurately, by using the calculator carefully to ensure such accuracy.

The candidate should also guard against using the calculator as a crutch. For example, there should be no need to multiply an amount by 10%. This calculation simply distracts the candidate from the real issue of solving the problem.

In addition, candidates should avoid the urge to overcalculate. While the calculator may give you some extra time, there is no benefit to number crunching all the different possibilities. The focus of the exam remains understanding and applying the basic concepts of accounting. A candidate will not be able to successfully pass the exam simply by using the calculator to back into the answer.

Postmortem of Your Performance

Don't do it and especially don't do it until Thursday evening. Do not speak to other candidates about the exam after completing sections on Wednesday noon, Wednesday evening, and Thursday noon. Exam postmortem will only upset, confuse, and frustrate you. Besides, the other candidates probably will not be as well prepared as you, and they certainly cannot influence your grade. Often, those candidates who seem very confident have overlooked an important requirement(s) or fact(s). As you leave the exam room after each session, think only ahead to achieve the best possible performance on each of the remaining sections. In addition, past candidates felt they had failed all four parts; yet they had actually passed the exam.

AICPA GENERAL RULES
GOVERNING EXAMINATION*

Rules for Examination Day

The examination is a closed-book examination and no reference materials are permitted to be taken to an examination site. Candidates are not permitted to bring calculators, computers, other electronic data storage, or communication devices into the examination room.

At the examination site, candidates are provided with an Examination Question and Answer Booklet for each section they are taking. In addition, for the Accounting & Reporting-Taxation, Managerial, Governmental and Not-For-Profit Organizations, and Financial Accounting & Reporting sections, candidates are provided with official AICPA calculators. Candidates should bring adequate supplies of Number 2 pencils and erasers. Rulers are not allowed.

The general candidate instructions are as follows:

1. Prior to the start of the examination, you will be required to sign a *Statement of Confidentiality* which states:

   I hereby attest that I will not divulge the nature or content of any question or answer to any individual or entity, and I will report to the board of accountancy any solicitations and disclosures of which I become aware. I will not remove, or attempt to remove, any Uniform CPA Examination materials, notes, or other unauthorized materials from the examination room. I understand that failure to comply with this attestation may result in invalidation of my grades, disqualification from future examinations, and possible civil and criminal penalties.

2. The only aids you are allowed to take to the examination tables are pens, No. 2 pencils, and erasers.

3. You will receive a prenumbered identification card (or admission notice) with your 7-digit candidate number on it. The prenumbered identification card must be available for inspection by the proctors throughout the examination.

4. Any reference during the examination to books or other materials or the exchange of information with other persons shall be considered misconduct sufficient to bar you from further participation in the examination.

   Penalties will be imposed on any candidate who is caught cheating before, during, or after the examination. These penalties may include expulsion from the examination, denial of applications for future examinations, and civil or criminal penalties.

5. You must observe the fixed time for each session. It is your responsibility to be ready at the start of the session and to stop writing when told to do so.

6. The following is an example of point values for each question as they might appear in the *Examination*

Questions portion of the *Examination Question and Answer Booklet* (*Booklet*).

	Point value
No. 1	60
No. 2	10
No. 3	10
No. 4	10
No. 5	10
Total	100

When answering each question, you should allocate the total examination time in proportion to the question's point value.

7. The *Booklet* will be distributed shortly before each session begins. Do not break the seal around the *Examination Questions* portion of the *Booklet* until you are told to do so.

   Prior to the start of the examination, you are permitted to complete page 1 of the *Booklet* by recording your 7-digit candidate number in the boxes provided in the upper right-hand corner of the page and by filling out and signing the *Attendance Record*. You are also permitted to turn the *Booklet* over and record your 7-digit candidate number and State on the *Objective Answer Sheet* portion of the *Booklet*.

   You must also check the booklet numbers on the *Attendance Record*, *Examination Questions*, *Objective Answer Sheet*, and *Essay Paper*. Notify the proctor if any of these numbers do not match.

   You must also review the *Examination Questions* (after you are told to break the seal), *Objective Answer Sheet*, and *Essay Paper* for any possible defects, such as missing pages, blurred printing, or stray marks (*Objective Answer Sheet* only). If any defects are found, request an entirely new *Booklet* from a proctor before you answer any questions.

8. For the Business Law and Professional Responsibilities (LPR), Auditing (AUDIT), and Financial Ac-

---

* *Information for Uniform CPA Examinaiton Candidates*, Sixteenth Edition, AICPA, 2000, p.44.

counting and Reporting (FARE) sections, your answers to the essay questions or problems must be written on the paper provided in the *Essay Paper* portion of the *Booklet*. After the start of the examination, you should record your 7-digit candidate number, state, and question number on the first page of the *Essay Paper* portion of the *Booklet* and on the other pages where indicated.

9. For the ARE and FARE examination sections, you will be given a calculator. You should test the calculator in accordance with the instructions on the cover page of the *Booklet*. Inform your proctor if your calculator is defective. Calculators will not be provided for the LPR and AUDIT examination sections because the number of questions requiring calculations is minimal and the calculations are simple.

10. All amounts are to be considered material unless otherwise stated.

11. Answer all objective items on the *Objective Answer Sheet* provided. Use a No. 2 pencil only. You should attempt to answer all objective items, as there is no penalty for incorrect responses. Since the objective items are scanned optically, your comments and calculations associated with them are not considered. You should blacken the ovals as darkly as possible and erase clearly any marks you wish to change. You should make no stray marks.

Approximately 10-15% of the multiple-choice items are included for pretesting only and are not included in your final grade.

12. It is important to pay strict attention to the manner in which your *Objective Answer Sheet* is structured. As you proceed with the examination, be certain that you blacken the oval that corresponds exactly with the item number in the *Examination Questions* portion of your *Booklet*. If you mark your answers in the *Examination Questions* portion of your *Booklet*, be certain that you transfer them to the *Objective Answer Sheet* before the session ends. Your examination paper will not be graded if you fail to record your answers on the *Objective Answer Sheet*. You will not be given additional time to record your answers.

13. Answer all essay questions and problems on the *Essay Paper* provided. Always begin your answer to a question on the top of a new page (which may be the reverse side of a sheet of paper). Cross out anything that you do not want graded.

14. Selected essay responses will be graded for writing skills.

15. Include all computations to the problems in the FARE section. This may assist the graders in understanding your answers.

16. You may not leave the examination room with any examination materials, nor may you take notes about the examination with you from the examination room. You are required to turn in by the end of each session:

   a. *Attendance Record* and *Statement of Confidentiality*
   b. *Examination Questions*
   c. *Essay Paper* (for LPR, AUDIT, and FARE). Do not remove unused pages.
   d. *Objective Answer Sheet*
   e. Calculator (for ARE and FARE)
   f. All unused examination materials
   g. Prenumbered Identification Card (or Admission Notice) at the last examination section for which you sit (if required by your examining jurisdiction)

   Your examination will not be graded unless you hand in these items before you leave the examination room.

17. If you believe one or more questions contain errors and want your concerns evaluated, you must fax your comments to the AICPA (201-938-3443). The fax should include the precise nature of any error; your rationale; and, if possible, references. The fax should include your 7-digit candidate identification number and must be received by the AICPA within 4 days of the completion of the examination administration. This will ensure that all comments are reviewed before the grading bases for the Uniform CPA Examination are confirmed. Although the AICPA cannot respond directly to each fax, it will investigate all comments received within the 4-day period.

18. Contact your board of accountancy for information regarding any other applicable rules.

In addition to the above general rules, oral instructions will be given by the examination supervisor shortly before the start of each session. They should include the location and/or rules concerning

   a. Storage of briefcases, handbags, books, personal belongings, etc.
   b. Food and beverages
   c. Smoking (usually not permitted)
   d. Rest rooms
   e. Telephone calls and messages
   f. Requirements (if any) that candidates must take all parts not previously passed each time they sit for the examination. Minimum grades (if any) needed on parts failed to get credit on parts passed.
   g. Official clock, if any
   h. Additional supplies
   i. Assembly, turn-in, inspection, and stapling of solutions

The next section provides a detailed listing (mind-jogger) of things to do for your last-minute preparation. It also contains a list of strategies for the exam.

CPA EXAM CHECKLIST

One week before exam

___ 1. Look over major topical areas, concentrating on schedule formats and the information flow of the formats.
For example:
FIFO and Wtd.-Avg. Process Costing Flow
Capital Budgeting Models
Cost of Goods Manufactured Schedule
Governmental Fund Accounting
Individual and Corporate Tax Formats

___ 2. If time permits, work through a few questions in your weakest areas so that techniques/concepts are fresh in your mind.

___ 3. Assemble notecards and key outlines of major topical areas into a manageable "last review" notebook to be taken with you to the exam.

What to bring

___ 1. *Registration material*—for the CPA exam. You will save time at the examination site by filling out ahead of time the survey that you received with your registration materials.

___ 2. *Hotel confirmation.*

___ 3. *Cash*—payment for anything by personal check is rarely accepted.

___ 4. *Major credit card*—American Express, Master Card, Visa, etc.

___ 5. *Alarm clock*—this is too important an event to trust to a hotel wake-up call that might be overlooked.

___ 6. *Food*—candidates should carefully review the instructions provided by their State Board Examiners regarding policies about food at the exam.

___ 7. *Clothing*—should be comfortable and layered to suit the temperature range over the two-day period and the examination room conditions.

___ 8. *Watch*—it is imperative that you be aware of the time remaining for each session.

___ 9. *Earplugs*—even though an examination is being given, there is constant activity in the examination room (e.g., proctors walking around, rustling of paper, people coughing, etc.). The use of earplugs may block out some of this distraction and help you concentrate better.

___ 10. *Other*—"last review" materials, pencils, erasers, leads, sharpeners, pens, etc.

While waiting for the exam to begin

1. Put your ID card on the table for ready reference to your number. The front page of your Examination Booklet contains an Attendance Record and Statement of Confidentiality. When told to do so, complete this information so that the proctor can collect it prior to the start of the exam.

2. Realize that proctors will be constantly circulating throughout each exam session. You need only raise your hand to receive more paper at any time or paper will be available at nearby tables.

3. Take a few deep breaths and compose yourself. Resolve to do your very best and to go after every point you can get!

Before leaving for exam each day

1. Put your ID card in your wallet, purse, or on your person for entry to take the exam. This is your official entrance permit that allows you to participate in all sections of the exam.

2. Remember your hotel room key.

3. Pack snack items and lunch (optional).

4. Limit consumption of liquids.

5. Realize that on Thursday morning you must check out and arrange for storage of your luggage (most hotels have such a service) **prior to** departing for the exam to prevent late charges on your hotel bill.

Evenings before exams

1. Reviewing the evenings before the exams could earn you the extra points needed to pass a section. Just keep this last-minute effort in perspective and do NOT panic yourself into staying up all night trying to cover every possible point. This could lead to disaster by sapping your body of the endurance needed to attack questions creatively during the next 7-8 hour day.

2. Before the Accounting and Reporting session, scan the general schedule formats to imprint the *flow* of information on your mind (e.g., individual and corporate tax formats, etc.).

3. Scan tax notes, imprinting required percentages used for figuring charitable contributions, tax credit for the elderly, etc., on your mind.

4. Read over **key** notecards or the most important outlines on topics in which you feel deficient.

5. Go over mnemonics and acronyms you have developed as study aids. Test yourself by writing out the letters on paper while verbally giving a brief explanation of what the letters stand for.

6. Scan outlines and any other notes pertinent to answering accounting and reporting questions, to imprint keywords.

7. Avoid postmortems during the examination period. Nothing you can do will affect your grade on sec-

tions of the exam you have already completed. Concentrate only on the work ahead in remaining sections.

8. **Set your alarm and get a good night's rest!** Being well rested will permit you to meet each day's challenge with a fresh burst of creative energy.

Exam-taking strategy

1. Open the exam booklet, noting the number of objective questions and the areas they cover (individual tax, managerial, etc.).

2. Reconcile the question numbers for each set of multiple-choice or other objective answer format questions with the numbers listed on the front of the exam booklet and check consecutive page numbers in your booklet to reassure yourself that it is complete, that no pages are stuck together, etc.

3. Begin working the objective questions, noting the time begun at the start of each set. Realize that you have approximately 1 1/2 to 2 minutes per question. Use blank space provided in the Examination Booklet for computations so that you have ample room to develop minischedules, time lines, etc. Do not waste time labeling computations because the grader will not use objective question computation sheets. It is wise to number your computations for your own use if you come back to a question, however.

4. Read each question **carefully!** Dates are extremely important! (For example, a tax question may give information for medical expenses incurred in 20**X0** but paid in 20**X1**.)

5. If you are struggling with problems beyond your time limit, use the strategy of dividing objective questions into two categories

   a. Questions for which you **know** you lack knowledge to answer: Drawing from any resources you have, narrow answers down to as few as possible; then make an **educated guess**.

   b. Questions for which you feel you should be getting correct answer: Put "?" by the objective question number on your Booklet and label your computations so you can return to them later. Your mental block may clear, or you may spot a simple math error that now can be corrected, thus giving you extra points.

6. Remember: **Never** change a first impulse objective question answer later unless you are **absolutely certain** you are right. It is a proven fact that your subconscious often guides you to the correct answer.

7. Work questions that you consider easiest first, noting time begun and time allotted. Your goal is to pick up extra time to allocate to problems you are weaker on.

8. Read the "required" section, underlining and noting **every** requirement that you are asked for.

9. Read the information given, underlining key facts, circling percentages and tax rates that you plan to use, and crossing out extraneous information, etc.

10. Draw graphs, visualize schedule formats, etc., that will help you respond to requirements.

11. Constantly compare your progress with the time remaining. **Never** spend more than the maximum allotted time on any problem until **all** problems are answered and time remains. Fight the urge to **complete** one problem at the expense of another problem.

12. Each test will include a question for which you may feel unprepared. Accept the challenge and go after the points! Draw from all your resources. Ask yourself how tax rules, etc. would be applied to similar situations, scan the objective questions for clues, look for relationships in **all** the available information given in the problem, try "backing into" the problem from another angle, etc.

13. The cardinal rule is **never,** but **never,** leave an answer blank.

14. If time permits, go back to any question that you "guessed" on.

15. Double check to make certain you have answered **all** questions to the best of your ability.

16. Transfer objective question answers to the form provided in your Examination Booklet. Be especially careful to follow the numbers exactly, because number patterns differ on each answer form! Don't wait until it's too late. The proctors are not authorized to give you extra time for this.

17. Take your Examination Booklet to the front of the exam room.

HAVE YOU MADE YOUR COMMITMENT?

---

5 ACCOUNTING AND REPORTING EXAM CONTENT

Preparing for the Accounting and Reporting Exam

Beginning with the May 1994 examination, the last disclosed exam, the AICPA began testing the areas of taxation, managerial accounting, and governmental and not-for-profit accounting on the Accounting and Reporting section of the exam. These areas are covered as shown below.

Taxation	60%
Managerial	10%
Governmental and Not-For-Profit Organizations	30%
	100%

As previously mentioned, the Accounting and Reporting section of the exam only tests using multiple-choice (50-60%) and other objective format questions (40-50%). **No essays or problems appear on this section of the exam.**

Despite this change in the format of the exam, the basic concepts tested remain the same. Thus, the candidate still needs to have the skills and knowledge necessary to solve both **how** (number crunching) and **why** (conceptual) type questions.

First, become acquainted with the nature of the Accounting and Reporting exam itself. In addition to the format changes, the AICPA has made some modifications to the content specifications. These content specification outlines are printed on the following page.

Relatedly, you should evaluate your competence by working 10 to 20 multiple-choice questions from each of the modules (34-44) in this volume. This diagnostic routine will acquaint you with the specific nature of the questions tested on each topic as well as indicate the amount of study required per topic. You should work toward a 75% correct response rate as a minimum on each topic. However, do not get discouraged. Remember that a difficulty adjustment is made in arriving at the overall exam grade. See discussion of self-study programs (Chapter 1) and examination grading (Chapter 2).

Second, study the content of modules 34-44, emphasizing the mechanics of each topic such as fund accounting, equivalent units of productions, etc. Use simple examples, journal entries, and diagrams to get a handle on the basic concepts underlying each topic. You may have to refer to your textbooks, etc., for topics to which you have had no previous exposure.

Third, work the other objective format type questions under examination conditions. Refer back to Chapter 3 and review the solutions approach for other objective questions.

Candidates should note that beginning with the May 2001 exam, the new Governmental Reporting model according to GASB 34 is the only reporting model tested. Be sure to allocate additional study to Module 38, Governmental Accounting, as this material has changed substantially.

AICPA Content Specification Outlines

The AICPA Content Specification Outline of the coverage of Accounting and Reporting appears on the following page. This outline was issued by the AICPA, effective as of November 2000.

AICPA CONTENT SPECIFICATION OUTLINE: ACCOUNTING AND REPORTING

I. Federal Taxation—Individuals **(20%)**

  A. Inclusions in Gross Income
  B. Exclusions and Adjustments to Arrive at Adjusted Gross Income
  C. Deductions from Adjusted Gross Income
  D. Filing Status and Exemptions
  E. Tax Accounting Methods
  F. Tax Computations, Credits, and Penalties
  G. Alternative Minimum Tax
  H. Tax Procedures

II. Federal Taxation—Corporations **(20%)**

  A. Determination of Taxable Income or Loss
  B. Tax Accounting Methods
  C. S Corporations
  D. Personal Holding Companies
  E. Consolidated Returns
  F. Tax Computations, Credits, and Penalties
  G. Alternative Minimum Tax
  H. Other

    1. Distributions
    2. Incorporation, Reorganization, Liquidation, and Dissolution
    3. Tax Procedures

III. Federal Taxation—Partnerships **(10%)**

  A. Basis of Partner's Interest and Bases of Assets Contributed to the Partnership
  B. Determination of Partner's Share of Income, Credits, and Deductions
  C. Partnership and Partner Elections
  D. Partner Dealing with Own Partnership
  E. Treatment of Partnership Liabilities
  F. Distribution of Partnership Assets
  G. Termination of Partnership

IV. Federal Taxation—Estates and Trusts, Exempt Organizations, and Preparers' Responsibilities **(10%)**

  A. Estate and Trusts

    1. Income Taxation
    2. Determination of Beneficiary's Share of Taxable Income
    3. Estate and Gift Taxation

  B. Exempt Organizations

    1. Types of Organizations
    2. Requirements for Exemption
    3. Unrelated Business Income Tax

  C. Preparers' Responsibilities

V. Accounting for Governmental and Not-for-Profit Organizations **(30%)**

  A. Governmental Entities

    1. Measurement Focus and Basis of Accounting
    2. Objectives of Financial Reporting
    3. Uses of Fund Accounting
    4. Budgetary Process
    5. Financial Reporting Entity
    6. Elements of Financial Statements
    7. Conceptual Reporting Issues
    8. Accounting and Financial Reporting for State and Local Governments

      a. Governmental-type Funds and Account Groups
      b. Proprietary-type Funds
      c. Fiduciary-type Funds

    9. Accounting and Financial Reporting for Governmental Not-for-Profit Organizations (Including Hospitals, Colleges and Universities, Voluntary Health and Welfare Organizations, and Other Governmental Not-for-Profit Organizations)

  B. Nongovernmental Not-for-Profit Organizations

    1. Objectives of Financial Reporting
    2. Elements of Financial Statements
    3. Formats of Financial Statements
    4. Accounting and Financial Reporting for Nongovernmental Not-for-Profit Organizations

      a. Revenues and Contributions
      b. Restrictions on Resources
      c. Expenses, Including Depreciation

VI. Managerial Accounting **(10%)**

  A. Cost Estimation, Cost Determination, and Cost Drivers
  B. Job Costing, Process Costing, and Activity-Based Costing
  C. Standard Costing and Flexible Budgeting
  D. Inventory Planning, Inventory Control, and Just-in-Time Purchasing
  E. Budgeting and Responsibility Accounting
  F. Variable and Absorption Costing
  G. Cost-Volume-Profit Analysis
  H. Cost Allocation and Transfer Pricing
  I. Joint and By-Product Costing
  J. Capital Budgeting
  K. Special Analyses for Decision Making
  L. Product and Service Pricing

6 MANAGERIAL ACCOUNTING

Cost and managerial accounting, as contrasted with financial accounting, produce data primarily for management decision making. Management needs data for

1. Planning and controlling day-to-day operations (e.g., use of standard costs to evaluate production efficiency)
2. Long-range planning and decision making (e.g., use of capital budgeting techniques in making decisions concerning investment projects)

Another function is to determine inventory costs for financial reporting purposes. Determining inventory costs is the more traditional role of cost accounting.

The AICPA Content Specification Outline of the coverage of managerial accounting on the Accounting and Reporting Exam (Taxation; Managerial; and Governmental and Not-for-Profit Organizations) appeared in the previous chapter. As shown in the outline, managerial accounting will be weighted 10% of this exam.

BASIC COST ACCOUNTING TERMINOLOGY

Overview

1. **Managerial accounting** emphasizes data for managerial decisions, planning, performance evaluation, and control in contrast to **cost accounting,** which provides cost information for both management accounting and for external reporting.
2. **Planning** is selecting goals and choosing methods to attain those goals. **Control** is the implementation of the plans and evaluation of their effectiveness in attaining goals.
3. **Management by exception** focuses attention on material deviations from plans (e.g., variances in a performance report) while allowing areas operating as expected to continue to operate without interference.
4. **Strategic cost analysis** is a broad-based analysis of a firm's products or services that supports management's development of the strategic plan.
5. **Computer-integrated manufacturing (CIM)** is a highly automated and integrated production process that is controlled by computers.
6. A **flexible manufacturing system (FMS)** is a series of computer controlled manufacturing processes that can be easily changed to make a variety of products.

Cost of Goods Manufactured and Cost Flows

7. **Product costs** are costs that can be associated with the production of specific goods. Product costs attach to a physical unit and become an expense in the period in which the unit to which they attach is sold. Product costs normally include direct manufacturing labor, direct materials, and factory overhead. **Period costs** cannot be associated (or matched) with manufactured goods (e.g., advertising expenditures). Period costs become expenses when incurred.
8. **Prime costs** are easily traceable to specific units of production and include direct manufacturing labor and direct materials. **Direct costs** are those easily traced to a specific business segment (e.g., product, division, department). **Indirect costs** are not easily traceable to specific segments and include factory overhead.
9. **Direct materials** is the cost of materials directly and conveniently traceable to a product. Minor material items (nails, glue) are not deemed conveniently traceable. These items are treated as **indirect materials** along with production supplies.
10. **Direct manufacturing labor** is the cost of labor directly transforming a product. This theoretically should include fringe benefits, but frequently does not. This is contrasted with **indirect manufacturing labor,** which is the cost of supporting labor (e.g., material handling labor, factory supervisors).
11. **Factory (manufacturing) overhead** normally includes indirect manufacturing labor costs, supplies cost, and other production facility costs such as plant depreciation, taxes, etc. It is comprised of all manufacturing costs that are not direct materials or direct manufacturing labor.
12. **Conversion costs** include direct manufacturing labor and manufacturing overhead. They're the costs of converting direct materials into finished products.
13. **Cost assignment** encompasses both **cost tracing** (assignment of direct costs to a cost object) and **cost allocation** (assignment of indirect costs to the cost object). A **cost object** is the item (product, department, process, etc.) for which cost is being determined.

14. **Direct materials inventory** includes the cost of materials awaiting entry into the production system. **Work in process inventory** includes the cost of units being produced but not yet completed. **Finished goods inventory** includes the cost of units completed but unsold.

15. **Cycle time** (or **throughput time**) is the time required to complete a good from the start of the production process until the product is finished.

16. **Product life-cycle costing** tracks the accumulation of costs that occur starting with the research and development for a product and ending with the time at which sales and customer support are withdrawn.

17. **Cost of quality (COQ)** is the cost necessary to prevent or correct product quality problems and equals the sum of four categories of quality related costs.

   a. **Prevention costs,** such as employee training and vendor certification, designed to prevent quality problems.

   b. **Appraisal costs** such as inspectors' salaries incurred to identify quality problems.

   c. **Internal failure costs,** such as rework costs, incurred to correct identified quality problems that are discovered before goods leave the company.

   d. **External failure costs,** such as warranty costs and the opportunity cost of lost customers, incurred because a quality problem has escaped internal detection and has been identified by the customer. The objective is to reduce COQ by shifting resources to prevention. It is much less costly to prevent a quality problem than to correct it either internally or externally.

Costing Systems

18. **Job-order costing** is a system for allocating costs to groups of unique products made to customer specifications. **Process costing** is a system for allocating costs to homogeneous units of a mass-produced product.

19. **Activity-based costing (ABC)** is a cost system that focuses on activities, determines their costs, and then uses appropriate cost drivers to trace costs to the products based on the activities. The following terminology is encountered in ABC:

   a. A **cost driver** is a factor that causes a cost to be incurred. Cost drivers may be volume-related (e.g., repair costs may depend on the volume of machine hours) and transaction-related (purchasing costs may depend on the number of purchase transactions).

   b. **Non-value-added costs** are the cost of activities that can be eliminated without the customer perceiving a decline in product quality or performance.

   c. A **value-added cost** is the cost of activities that **cannot** be eliminated without the customer perceiving a decline in product quality or performance.

   d. A **value chain** is the sequence of business functions in which value is added to a firm's products or services. This sequence includes research and development, product design, manufacturing, marketing, distribution, and customer service.

   e. **Engineered costs** are determined from industrial engineering studies that examine how activities are performed and if/how performance can be improved.

20. **Activity-based management (ABM)** integrates ABC with other concepts such as Total Quality Management (TQM) and target costing to produce a management system that strives for excellence through cost reduction, continuous process improvement, and productivity gains.

21. A **cost management system (CMS)** is a planning and control system that measures the cost of significant activities, identifies non-value-added costs, and identifies activities that will improve organizational performance.

Joint and By-Products

22. **Joint costs** are costs common to multiple products that emerge at a split-off point. **Joint costing** is a system of assigning joint costs to **joint products** whose overall sales values are relatively significant. When a product has insignificant sales value relative to the other products, it is called a **by-product**.

Cost Behavior

23. **Fixed costs** do not vary with the level of activity within the relevant range for a given period of time (usually one year), for example, plant depreciation.

24. **Variable costs** vary proportionately **in total** with the activity level throughout the relevant range (e.g., direct materials).
25. **Stepped costs (or semifixed costs)** are fixed over relatively short ranges of production levels (e.g., supervisors' salaries). Fixed, variable, and semifixed costs are diagrammed below.

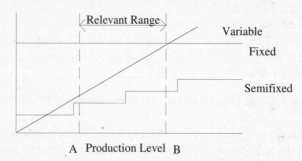

26. **Mixed costs (semivariable)** are costs that have a fixed component and a variable component. These components are separated by using the scattergraph, high-low, or linear regression methods.
27. **Relevant range** is the operating range of activity in which cost behavior patterns are valid (A to B in the preceding illustration). Thus, it is the production range for which fixed costs remain constant (e.g., if production doubles, an additional shift of salaried foremen would be added and fixed costs would increase).

Cost-Volume-Profit Analysis

28. **Cost-volume-profit (CVP) analysis** is a planning tool used to analyze the effects of changes in volume, sales mix, selling price, variable expense, fixed expense, and profit.

Variable (Direct) vs. Absorption Costing

29. **Variable (direct) costing** considers all fixed manufacturing overhead as a period cost rather than as a product cost. Conversely, **absorption (full) costing** considers fixed manufacturing overhead to be product cost. The treatment of fixed manufacturing cost as a period cost rather than as a product cost is the only difference between variable costing and absorption costing. All other costs (i.e., variable manufacturing, fixed selling, and variable selling) are treated the same under both systems. Variable costing is not acceptable for external reporting per GAAP.

Budgeting, Responsibility Accounting, and Performance Measurement

30. A **budget** is a quantification of the plan for operations. A **flexible budget** is a budget that is adjusted for changes in volume. **Performance reports** compare budgeted and actual performance.
31. **Responsibility accounting** measures subunit performance based on the costs and/or revenues assigned to responsibility centers.
32. **Controllable costs** can be affected by a manager during the current period (e.g., amount of direct manufacturing labor per unit of production is usually under the control of a production supervisor). Uncontrollable costs are those that cannot be affected by the individual in question (e.g., depreciation is not usually controllable by the production supervisor).
33. **Contribution margin** equals revenue less **all** variable costs.
34. **Nonfinancial performance measures** are performance measures in the form of production, marketing, or industry data, and not accounting data.

Product and Service Pricing and Transfer Pricing

35. **Target costing** identifies the estimated cost of a new product that must be achieved for that product to be priced competitively and still produce an acceptable profit. Often the product is redesigned and the production process simplified several times before the target cost can be met.
36. **Transfer pricing** is the determination of the price at which goods and services will be "sold" to profit or investment centers via internal company transfers.

Inventory Models

37. The **just-in-time (JIT)** concept may be applied to purchasing so that raw material arrives just as it is needed for production. JIT may also be applied to production so that each component of the manufactured good is produced only when needed by the next production step.

38. The **economic order quantity (EOQ)** is the optimal quantity of inventory purchased (or manufactured) per order that minimizes the sum of ordering and carrying costs.

Standards and Variances

39. **Standard costs** are predetermined target costs. **Variances** are differences between standards and actual results.

40. **Benchmarking** requires that products, services, and activities be continually measured against the best levels of performance either inside or outside the organization.

Nonroutine Decisions

41. The following terminology is encountered in nonroutine decisions:

  a. **Sunk, past, or unavoidable costs** are committed costs which are not avoidable and are therefore irrelevant to the decision process.

  b. **Avoidable costs** are costs that will **not** continue to be incurred if a department or product is terminated.

  c. **Committed costs** arise from a company's basic commitment to open its doors and engage in business (depreciation, property taxes, management salaries).

  d. **Discretionary costs** are fixed costs whose level is set by current management decisions (e.g., advertising, research and development).

  e. **Relevant costs** are future costs that will change as a result of a specific decision.

  f. **Differential (incremental) cost** is the difference in cost between two alternatives.

  g. **Opportunity cost** is the maximum income or savings (benefit) foregone by rejecting an alternative.

  h. **Outlay (out-of-pocket) cost** is the cash disbursement associated with a specific project.

42. **Capital budgeting** is the planning for and control of long-term capital outlays.

COSTING SYSTEMS

The basic purpose of any costing system is to allocate the costs of production (direct materials, direct manufacturing labor, and manufacturing overhead) to the units produced. This basic purpose of costing systems (job-order, process, activity-based) is discussed in this module.

A. Cost of Goods Manufactured

Regardless of which costing system is used, a cost of goods manufactured (CGM) statement is prepared to summarize the manufacturing activity of the period. CGM for a manufacturing firm is equivalent to purchases for a merchandising firm. Although it may take different forms, essentially the CGM statement is a summary of the direct materials and work in process (WIP) accounts.

$$BWIP + DM + DML + MOH - EWIP = CGM$$

A typical CGM statement is presented below.

Uddin Company
COST OF GOODS MANUFACTURED
Year Ended December 31, 2002

Direct materials		
Inventory, Jan. 1	$ 23,000	
Purchases	98,000	
Materials available for use	121,000	
Inventory, Dec. 31	16,000	
Direct materials used		$105,000
Direct manufacturing labor		72,000
Factory overhead		
Indirect labor	$ 14,000	
Supplies	4,000	
Utilities	8,000	
Depreciation	13,000	
Other	3,000	42,000
Manufacturing costs incurred, 2002		219,000
Add work in process inventory, Jan. 1		25,000
Manufacturing costs to account for		244,000
Deduct work in process inventory, Dec. 31		30,000
Cost of goods manufactured (completed)		$214,000

The result of the CGM statement is used in the cost of goods sold (CGS) statement or cost of goods sold section of the income statement, as indicated below.

Uddin Company
COST OF GOODS SOLD
Year Ended December 31, 2002

Finished goods, Jan. 1		$ 40,000
Add cost of goods manufactured (completed) per statement above		214,000
Cost of goods available for sale		254,000
Deduct finished goods, Dec. 31		53,000
Cost of goods sold		$201,000

B. Cost Flows

Before discussing any particular costing system, it is important to understand the flow of costs through the accounts, as summarized in the diagram below.

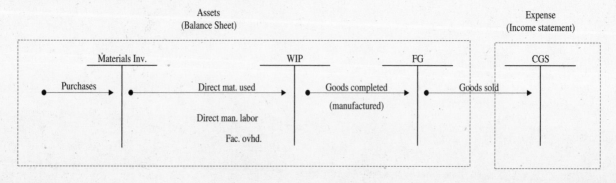

Analyze the diagram carefully before proceeding. The details will be explained further in the next few pages.

C. Job-Order Costing

Job-order costing is a system for allocating costs to groups of unique products. It is applicable to the production of customer-specified products such as the manufacture of special machines and even to cost a particular service (e.g., providing legal services for the client of a law firm). Each job becomes a cost center for which costs are accumulated. A subsidiary record (job-order cost sheet) is needed to keep track of all unfinished jobs (work in process) and finished jobs (finished goods). Note that the total of unfinished job cost sheets will equal the work in process balance.

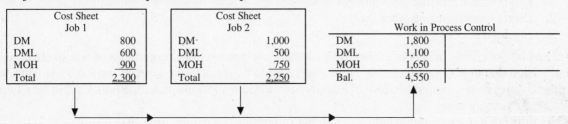

Note that whenever work in process is debited or credited in the above entries, the amount of the entry is the sum of the postings on the job-order cost sheets. The balances on the job-order cost sheets are also the basis for the entries transferring completed goods to finished goods inventory and transferring the cost of goods shipped to customers to cost of goods sold. The work in process account is analyzed below.

Work in Process Control		
1. Beginning balance		
2. Direct materials used		
3. Direct labor used		
4. Overhead applied	5.	Cost of goods manufactured (CGM)
6. Ending balance		

A similar analysis can be performed on the finished goods account.

Finished Goods Control		
1. Beginning balance		
2. Cost of goods manufactured	3.	Cost of goods sold (CGS)
4. Ending balance		

D. Accounting for Overhead

Accounting for manufacturing overhead is an important part of job-order costing and any other costing system. Overhead consists of all manufacturing costs other than direct materials and direct manufacturing labor. The distinguishing feature of manufacturing overhead is that while it must be incurred in order to produce goods, **it cannot be directly traced to the final product** as can direct materials and direct manufacturing labor. Therefore, overhead must be **applied**, rather than directly charged, to goods produced. The overhead application process is described below.

1. Overhead items are grouped by cost behavior, such as fixed and variable.
2. The fixed and variable overhead costs are estimated for the forthcoming year (e.g., $500,000).
3. A denominator (activity) base is chosen (see discussion below). A common choice is direct labor hours or machine hours.
4. The activity level is estimated for the forthcoming year (e.g., 80,000 hours).
5. A predetermined overhead rate is computed.

$$\frac{\text{Estimated overhead costs}}{\text{Estimated activity level}} = \frac{\$500,000}{80,000 \text{ hours}} = \$6.25/\text{hour}$$

6. As actual overhead costs are incurred, they are debited to the factory overhead account (e.g., $400).

Factory overhead (actual)	400	
Various accounts		400

7. As jobs are completed, the predetermined overhead rate is used to apply overhead to these jobs. For example, if job 17 used 52 direct labor hours, $325 of overhead (52 x $6.25) would be charged to work in process and entered on the job cost sheet.

Work in process control   325
    Factory overhead (applied)   325

To allocate the costs of overhead to units produced, an **activity base** must be chosen for use in the computation of a predetermined overhead rate. This activity base should bear a causal relationship to the incurrence of overhead costs. Examples of activity bases are

1. Direct manufacturing labor hours
2. Direct manufacturing labor cost
3. Machine hours

For example, overhead may result from (be a function of) hours worked regardless of who works, which would mean that direct manufacturing labor hours should be the activity base. If, on the other hand, more overhead costs were incurred because of heavily automated operations, machine hours might be a more appropriate activity base.

As illustrated in the diagram below, a number of approaches can be used to determine the activity level, (step D.4. above).

Approach	*Definition*
Theoretical capacity	Output is produced efficiently 100% of the time.
	↓
Practical capacity	ADJUSTED FOR: factors such as days off, down-time, etc. Output is produced maximum percentage of time practical (75-85%).
	↓
Normal volume	ADJUSTED FOR: long-run product demand. Average annual output necessary to meet sales and inventory fluctuations over 4-5 year period.
	↓
Expected annual capacity	ADJUSTED FOR: current year fluctuations. Expected output for current year.

Note that theoretical capacity is larger than practical capacity, which is larger than normal volume. Expected annual capacity fluctuates above and below normal volume. Most firms use expected annual capacity.

At year-end overhead may be

1. **Overapplied**—More is applied than incurred because

    a. Overhead costs were overestimated,
    b. More than expected activity took place, and/or
    c. Actual overhead costs were less than expected

2. **Underapplied**—Less overhead is applied than incurred because

    a. Overhead costs were underestimated,
    b. Less than expected activity took place, and/or
    c. Actual overhead costs were more than expected

E. Disposition of Under- and Overapplied Overhead

1. If the under- or overapplied overhead is immaterial, it is frequently written off to cost of goods sold on grounds of expediency.

Cost of goods sold (debit or credit)   xx
    Factory overhead   xx

2. If the balance is significant, then an adjustment must be made to all goods which were costed at the erroneous application rate during the current period. The goods with the incorrect costs will be in three accounts: Work in Process Control, Finished Goods Control, and Cost of Goods Sold.

Proration may be made based upon total ending balance (before proration) of the three accounts or on some other equitable basis. The exam will normally give specific directions on what allocation base should be used.

F. Service Department Cost Allocation

A large firm will have several production departments, each of which may compute a separate predetermined overhead rate. A problem arises when a **service** department (maintenance, receiving, etc.) incurs costs and benefits multiple production departments.

Costs of these service departments must be allocated to production departments because all manufacturing costs must ultimately be traced to products. For example, the costs of the materials-handling cost center may need to be allocated to the production departments (and possibly other service departments). Apportionment of service department costs should be based on meaningful criteria such as

1. Services provided
2. Services available
3. Benefits received
4. Equity

Examples of apportionment bases are

1. Square feet for building costs
2. Usage for electricity
3. Employees for cafeteria, personnel, and first aid
4. Usage for materials handling, maintenance, etc.

Service department costs can be allocated by

1. Direct method
2. Step method

1. Direct Method

The direct method simply allocates the costs of each service department to each of the producing departments based on a relative level of the apportionment base. For example, if a service department had costs of $140,000, and producing departments X and Y used 80% and 20% of the apportionment base, X and Y would be assigned $112,000 and $28,000 respectively. Note that the direct method ignores use of services by other service departments. For example, the direct method would ignore the fact that service department A uses the services of service department B. The essence of the direct method is shown in the following diagram.

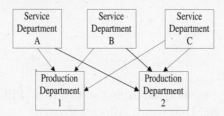

2. Step Method

The step method allocates service department costs to other service departments as well as production departments. The allocation process is

a. Select the service department serving the most other service departments

  1) When more than one service department services an equal number of service departments, select the department with the highest costs

b. Allocate the costs of the service department selected in step a. to the production departments and other service departments based on a relative level of the apportionment base as in the direct method.

c. Costs of service departments are never allocated back to departments whose costs have already been allocated.

Note that the step method ignores the fact that reciprocal services are used between some service departments.

EXAMPLE:

DEPARTMENTS

	Service		Production		
	A	*B*	*1*	*2*	*Totals*
Costs	$4,000	$6,000	$38,000	$42,000	$90,000
Use of A		10%	40%	50%	100%
Use of B	30%		40%	30%	100%

Direct Method—Allocate A's and B's costs directly to production departments 1 and 2.

	A	*B*	*1*	*2*
Costs prior to allocation	4,000	6,000	38,000	42,000
Allocation of A's costs*	(4,000)		1,778	2,222
Allocation of B's costs**		(6,000)	3,429	2,571
	0	0	43,207	46,793

* *4/9 and 5/9*

** *4/7 and 3/7* $90,000

Step Method—Allocate B's costs (B has more costs than A) to departments A, 1 and 2. Next allocate A's costs to departments 1 and 2; you cannot allocate A's costs back to B, as B's costs have already been allocated.

	A	*B*	*1*	*2*
Costs prior to allocation	4,000	6,000	38,000	42,000
Allocation of B's costs*	1,800	(6,000)	2,400	1,800
Allocation of A's costs				
($4,000 + $1,800)**	(5,800)		2,578	3,222
	0	0	42,978	47,022

* *3/10, 4/10, and 3/10*

** *4/9 and 5/9* $90,000

G. Process Costing

Process costing, in contrast to job-order costing, is applicable to a continuous process of production of the same or similar goods, for example, oil refining and chemical production. Since the product is uniform, there is no need to determine the costs of different groups of products and each processing department becomes a cost center.

Process costing computations can be broken down into the 5 steps listed below.

1. Visualize the **physical flow of units**
2. Compute the **equivalent units of production**
3. Determine **costs to allocate**
4. Compute **unit costs**
5. **Allocate total costs** to

   a. Goods completed
   b. Ending work in process

Note that the five steps above can be memorized using the acronym: PECUA (**P**hysical Flow, **E**quivalent Units of Production, **C**osts to Allocate, **U**nit Costs, **A**llocate Costs).

1. Flow of Units

The cost flow diagram shown under Section B in this module is the same for process costing except there will typically be several WIP accounts (i.e., one for every department). When solving a process costing problem, it is helpful to visualize the physical flow of units, as illustrated in the diagram below.

The units in BWIP are either completed or become spoiled. Units started during the period but not completed become EWIP.

2. Equivalent Units of Production (EUP)

An EUP is the amount of work equivalent to completing one unit from start to finish. In a process costing system, products are assigned costs periodically (usually monthly). At any one moment some units are incomplete which makes the EUP calculations necessary to allocate manufacturing costs between

1. Goods finished during the period (cost of goods manufactured)
2. Ending work in process

The two primary EUP methods used for process costing are first-in, first-out (FIFO) and weighted-average (WA). Past questions on the exam have emphasized the weighted-average method. Under the weighted-average approach, current costs are combined with prior period costs, and all units are carried at an average cost of production. Importantly, the method assumes that all units completed during a period are started and completed during that period. As a result, the **percentage** of work done last period on the beginning work in process inventory is ignored.

3. **Simple Process Costing Example**

The BW Toy Company uses a weighted-average process cost system to collect costs. Data relevant to 2000 production is given below. Assume we begin with 800 units 25% complete for labor and overhead (conversion costs), and 100% complete for materials because they are introduced at the start of the process. We start 4,200 units. 4,000 units are completed, while 1,000 remain in EWIP (20% complete for labor and overhead and 100% complete for materials). No spoilage exists. The costs are summarized in the following T-account:

Work in Process Control

BWIP				
materials	900			
labor + OH	532	1,432	???	Goods finished
Current				
materials	4,200			
labor + OH	14,000	18,200		
EWIP		???		

Step 1: The physical flow of units is accounted for.

BWIP	800
Started	4,200
To account for	5,000
Units completed	4,000
EWIP	1,000
Accounted for	5,000

Step 2: The units completed and ending work in process are converted to equivalent units.

		Equivalent units	
Description	Total	Direct mtls.	Conv.
Physical units to account for			
Beginning inventory	800		
Units started	4,200		
Units to be accounted for	5,000		
Equivalent units of production			
Good units completed and transferred out	4,000	4,000*	4,000**
Ending WIP	1,000	1,000*	200
Units accounted for	5,000	5,000	4,200

* These units are 100% complete with respect to materials because materials are introduced at the start of the process.

** These units are 100% complete with respect to conversion because all units completed are **assumed** to be started and completed during the period.

Step 3 and 4: Determine costs to allocate and equivalent unit costs.

Manufacturing costs			
Beginning inventory	$ 1,432	$ 900	$ 532
Current costs	18,200	4,200	14,000
Total costs to account for	$19,632	$ 5,100	$14,532
Cost per equivalent unit		$ 1.02*	$ 3.46**

* Notice the resulting costs are averages: $5,100 ÷ 5,000 equivalent units = $1.02.

** $14,532 ÷ 4,200 equivalent units = $3.46.

Step 5: Allocate total costs to goods completed and ending work in process.

Units completed [4,000 x ($1.02 + $3.46)]		$17,920
Ending WIP:		
Mat. (1,000 x $1.02)	$1,020	
Conv. (200 x $3.46)	692	1,712
Total costs accounted for		$19,632

The allocation is accomplished by multiplying the individual equivalent unit figures by the unit costs.

4. **EUP for Material**

In the above example, material was assumed to be added at the beginning of the production process. Material can also be added at different points in the process (e.g., 10%, 70%) or gradually during the process.

5. **FIFO Work in Process Assumption**

The FIFO approach is not as popular as the weighted-average approach on the exam. Thus, we will focus solely on the calculation of equivalent units. With FIFO, the first batch into production (i.e., the beginning work in process inventory) is assumed to be the first batch completed. This batch is treated as a separate, distinct layer—separate from goods that are started and completed during the period.

The weighted-average assumption (all goods are assumed to be started and completed during the period) no longer holds for FIFO. Thus, any work done last period on the beginning work in process inventory must be taken into consideration. After all is said and done, the equivalent unit figures reflect the work done during the current accounting period. Also, the only difference between the two methods is the treatment of the beginning work in process inventory.

The equivalent-unit calculations for BW Toy follow.

Description	*Total*	*Direct mtls.*	*Conv.*
Physical units to account for			
Beginning inventory	800		
Units started	4,200		
Units to be accounted for	5,000		
Equivalent units of production			
Good units completed and transferred out:			
From beg. WIP	800	-0-*	600**
Started and completed	3,200	3,200***	3,200***
Ending WIP	1,000	1,000	200
Units accounted for	5,000	4,200	4,000

     * All material was introduced last period.
     ** 75% of the work was necessary this period to complete the units.
     *** 100% of the materials and conversions were introduced this period.

6. **Spoilage in Process Costing**

The following terms are commonly used:

1. **Spoilage**—Inferior goods either discarded or sold for disposal value
2. **Defective units**—Inferior goods reworked and sold as normal product

A major distinction is made between normal and abnormal spoilage.

a. Normal spoilage is the cost of spoiled units caused by the nature of the manufacturing process (i.e., which occur under efficient operating conditions).

     (1) Normal spoilage is a necessary cost in the production process and is, therefore, a **product cost**.

b. Abnormal spoilage is the cost of spoiled units which were spoiled through some unnecessary act, event, or condition.

     (1) Abnormal spoilage is a **period cost** (e.g., "loss on abnormal spoilage").
     (2) Abnormal spoilage costs should not be included in cost of goods sold.

Spoilage must be considered in EUP calculations. For example, if spoilage is discovered at the 60% point in processing and 100 units of abnormal spoilage are discovered, 60 EUP have occurred. The amount of abnormal loss would be the cost of 60 EUP (processing) plus the materials added to 100 units of production up to the 60% point. In contrast, if the spoilage was considered normal in nature, the spoilage cost would be treated as a product cost and simply added to the cost of the good units completed.

7. **Spoilage in Job Costing**

In a job-order costing system, the costs of normal spoilage and defective units can be handled in two different ways. When spoilage is attributable to general factory conditions, net spoilage costs are allocated to all jobs through overhead application (i.e., estimated spoilage costs are included with other overhead in the computation of the overhead application rate). Alternatively, when spoilage is attributable to exacting job specifications, net spoilage costs are charged to specific jobs. With this approach, spoilage is **not** reflected in the predetermined overhead rate. Under both methods, the proceeds from the sale of spoiled goods should be offset against the cost of spoiled goods produced. Net spoilage cost would be charged to factory overhead in the first case and left in work in process in the second case.

Costs of abnormal spoilage should **not** be charged to jobs but should be written off as a loss of the period.

H. Activity-Based Costing

Activity-based costing (ABC) is based upon two principles. First, activities consume resources. Second, these resources are consumed by products, services, or other cost objectives (output). ABC allocates overhead costs to products on the basis of the resources consumed by each activity involved in the design, production, and distribution of a particular good. This is accomplished through the assignment of costs to homogeneous cost pools that represent specific activities and then the allocation of these costs, using appropriate cost drivers, to the product.

Central to ABC are the activities performed to fulfill organizational objectives (producing products or services for customers). Activities may be value-added or non-value-added. **Value-added activities** are those which customers perceive as increasing the worth of a product or service and for which customers are willing to pay. They include only production activities. **Non-value-added activities** increase the cost of a product but do not increase its value to customers. Examples include materials handling and rework. Packaging is required for some products such as milk or potting soil, but it may be non-value-added for other products such as books (it is also costly and takes up huge amounts of landfill space). Thus, these activities may be eliminated and/or restructured without customers perceiving a decline in the value of the product/service. An activity (process) map is a flowchart which indicates all activities involved in the production process and identifies both value-added and non-value-added activities.

Cost drivers are those activities which have a direct cause and effect relationship to the incurrence of a particular cost. Traditional costing uses only variable and fixed or total overhead cost pools and views cost drivers at the output unit level, wherein costs are allocated based on labor hours, machine hours, etc. Some costs though, such as setup costs, vary at the batch level (batch-level costs) and should be spread over the units in the batch to which they relate (**not** machine hours). Product-sustaining (process-level) costs such as engineering change orders should be assigned to the products for which the orders were issued. Facility-sustaining costs incurred at the organizational level support operations and can only be arbitrarily assigned to products. As shown by the following table, ABC uses both transaction-related (e.g., purchase orders) and volume-related (e.g., machine hours) cost drivers. Traditional product costing tends to use only volume-related cost drivers.

Activity	*Cost driver*
Purchase of materials	Number of purchase transactions
Receiving	Number of shipments received
Disbursing	Number of checks issued
Setup costs	Number of setups or setup hours
Machining	Number of machine hours
Repair costs	Number of machine hours
Engineering changes to products	Number of engineering change notices

The activities listed above are all examples of direct activities which can be traced to an output or service. In contrast, indirect activities such as human resources are not directly attributable to output. The cost of indirect activities may be allocated or simply labeled as nontraceable.

To illustrate, ABC traces the costs of setup activities to the production batch that caused the setup costs to be incurred. The cost of each setup is then spread over the units in that batch. On the other hand, a traditional costing system would typically allocate setup costs as overhead on the basis of a volume-related cost driver such as direct manufacturing labor hours. Assume that product A and product B incur setup costs as follows:

		A	B	Total
Production volume		7,500	10,000	
Batch size		250	1,000	
Number of setups		30	10	
Total setup costs incurred		$60,000	$20,000	$80,000
Total cost per setup		$2,000	$2,000	
Direct manuf. labor hours/unit		3	3	
Total direct manuf. labor hours		22,500	30,000	52,500
Setup cost per DMLH ($80,000 ÷ 52,500)				$1.52
Traditional setup cost/unit				
A	($1.52 x 3 DMLH required)	$ 4.56		
B	($1.52 x 3 DMLH required)		$ 4.56	
ABC setup cost/unit				
A	($2,000/setup ÷ 250 units/batch)	$ 8.00		
B	($2,000/setup ÷ 1,000 units/batch)		$ 2.00	

In this case, products A and B are assigned different total setup costs. However, because they require the same number of direct manufacturing labor hours per unit, traditional costing allocates equal setup costs per unit to both products. In effect, one product picks up cost that was caused by another product (cross-subsidization), which distorts product costing information. ABC assigns different setup costs per unit to each product because **each unit** of product A demands more resources for setup activity than does **each unit** of product B. Note that the **total** setup cost remains the same under either method.

Activity-based management (ABM) integrates ABC with other concepts such as Total Quality Management (TQM) and target costing to produce a management system that strives for excellence through cost reduction, continuous process improvement, and productivity gains.

I. Joint Products

Joint products are two or more products produced together up to a split-off point where they become separately identifiable. They cannot be produced by themselves. For example, a steak cannot be produced without also producing roasts, ribs, liver, hamburger, etc. Other industries which produce joint products include

1. Chemicals	3. Mining
2. Lumber	4. Petroleum

Joint products incur common, or joint costs, before the split-off point. The split-off point is the point of production at which the joint products can be individually identified and removed from the joint, or common, process. The joint products can then be sold or processed further. Costs incurred after the split-off point for any one of the joint products are called separable costs.

Common costs are allocated to the joint products at the split-off point, usually on the basis of sales value at the split-off point, estimated net realizable value (NRV) at split-off point, or some physical measure. The estimated net realizable value method allocates joint costs using the estimated sales values of the joint products after further processing less the separable processing costs. Of the first two methods listed, the sales value at split-off method **must** be used if a sales value at split-off point exists. The following example illustrates the sales value at split-off and estimated net realizable value methods.

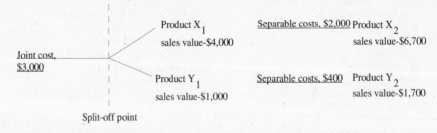

SALES VALUE AT SPLIT-OFF

Product	Sales value @ split-off	Ratio	x	Joint costs	=	Allocated joint costs
X_1	$4,000	$\frac{\$4,000}{\$5,000}$	x	$3,000	=	$2,400
Y_1	$1,000	$\frac{\$1,000}{\$5,000}$	x	$3,000	=	$ 600
Total	$5,000					$3,000

If the sales value at split-off were not available or one did not exist, we would use the estimated net realizable value method (NRV).

ESTIMATED NET REALIZABLE VALUE METHOD (NRV)

Product	Final sales value	–	Separable costs	=	Estimated net realizable value	Ratio	x	Joint costs	=	Allocated joint costs
X_2	$6,700	–	$2,000	=	$4,700	$\frac{\$4,700}{\$6,000}$	x	$3,000	=	$2,350
Y_2	$1,700	–	$ 400	=	$1,300	$\frac{\$1,300}{\$6,000}$	x	$3,000	=	$ 650
Total					$6,000					$3,000

Physical measures (units, pounds, etc.) generally are not used because of the misleading income statement effect. With an allocation based on pounds, steak would show a big profit while ground beef would be a consistent loser; each pound would carry the same cost although steak sells for more per pound.

Joint cost allocation is performed for the purpose of inventory valuation and income determination. However, joint costs should be **ignored** for any internal decisions including the decision on whether to process a joint product beyond the split-off point. Such costs are not relevant to the sell or process further decision. The **sell or process further** decision should be based on incremental revenues and costs beyond the split-off point. If incremental revenue from further processing exceeds incremental costs, then process further. If incremental costs exceed incremental revenues, then sell at the split-off point. In the previous example in which we assumed a sales value at the split-off point, both X_1 and Y_1 should be further processed.

	Incremental revenue		Incremental cost		Advantage of further processing
X_1:	$6,700 – $4,000 = $2,700	–	$2,000	=	$700
Y_1:	$1,700 – $1,000 = $ 700	–	$ 400	=	$300

If X_1 could have sold for only $5,500 after further processing, the incremental revenue ($1,500) would not cover the incremental cost ($2,000), and X_1 should not be further processed.

J. By-Products

By-products, in contrast to joint products, have little market value relative to the overall value of the product(s) being produced. Joint (common) costs are usually not allocated to a by-product. Instead, by-products are frequently valued at market or net realizable value (NRV) and accounted for as a contra production cost, that is, a reduction in the joint costs that will be allocated to the joint products.

Rather than recognizing by-product market value as a reduction of production cost, it is sometimes recognized when sold and disclosed as

1. Ordinary sales
2. Other income
3. Contra to cost of sales

Given the variety of approaches, the exam will normally specify the method that is to be followed.

MULTIPLE-CHOICE QUESTIONS (1-42)

1. The following information was taken from Kay Company's accounting records for the year ended December 31, 2002:

Increase in raw materials inventory	$ 15,000
Decrease in finished goods inventory	35,000
Raw materials purchased	430,000
Direct manufacturing labor payroll	200,000
Factory overhead	300,000
Freight-out	45,000

There was no work in process inventory at the beginning or end of the year. Kay's 2002 cost of goods sold is

   a. $950,000
   b. $965,000
   c. $975,000
   d. $995,000

Items 2 through 4 are based on the following information pertaining to Arp Co.'s manufacturing operations:

Inventories	3/1/02	3/31/02
Direct materials	$36,000	$30,000
Work in process	18,000	12,000
Finished goods	54,000	72,000

Additional information for the month of March 2002:

Direct materials purchased	$84,000
Direct manufacturing labor payroll	60,000
Direct manufacturing labor rate per hour	7.50
Factory overhead rate per direct labor hour	10.00

2. For the month of March 2002, prime cost was

   a. $ 90,000
   b. $120,000
   c. $144,000
   d. $150,000

3. For the month of March 2002, conversion cost was

   a. $ 90,000
   b. $140,000
   c. $144,000
   d. $170,000

4. For the month of March 2002, cost of goods manufactured was

   a. $218,000
   b. $224,000
   c. $230,000
   d. $236,000

5. During the month of March 2002, Nale Co. used $300,000 of direct material. At March 31, 2002, Nale's direct materials inventory was $50,000 more than it was at March 1, 2002. Direct material purchases during the month of March 2002 amounted to

   a. $0
   b. $250,000
   c. $300,000
   d. $350,000

6. Fab Co. manufactures textiles. Among Fab's 2002 manufacturing costs were the following salaries and wages:

Loom operators	$120,000
Factory foreman	45,000
Machine mechanics	30,000

What was the amount of Fab's 2002 direct manufacturing labor?

   a. $195,000
   b. $165,000
   c. $150,000
   d. $120,000

7. The fixed portion of the semivariable cost of electricity for a manufacturing plant is a

	Period cost	Product cost
a.	Yes	No
b.	Yes	Yes
c.	No	Yes
d.	No	No

8. Gram Co. develops computer programs to meet customers' special requirements. How should Gram categorize payments to employees who develop these programs?

	Direct costs	Value-added costs
a.	Yes	Yes
b.	Yes	No
c.	No	No
d.	No	Yes

9. Rework costs should be regarded as a cost of quality in a manufacturing company's quality control program when they are

   I. Caused by the customer.
  II. Caused by internal failure.

   a. I only.
   b. II only.
   c. Both I and II.
   d. Neither I nor II.

10. Costs are accumulated by responsibility center for control purposes when using

	Job order costing	Process costing
a.	Yes	Yes
b.	Yes	No
c.	No	No
d.	No	Yes

11. Birk Co. uses a job order cost system. The following debits (credit) appeared in Birk's work in process account for the month of April 2002:

April	Description	Amount
1	Balance	$ 4,000
30	Direct materials	24,000
30	Direct manufacturing labor	16,000
30	Factory overhead	12,800
30	To finished goods	(48,000)

Birk applies overhead to production at a predetermined rate of 80% of direct manufacturing labor costs. Job No. 5, the only job still in process on April 30, 2002, has been charged with direct manufacturing labor of $2,000. What was the amount of direct materials charged to Job No. 5?

   a. $ 3,000
   b. $ 5,200
   c. $ 8,800
   d. $24,000

12. In a job cost system, manufacturing overhead is

	An indirect cost of jobs	A necessary element in production
a.	No	Yes
b.	No	No
c.	Yes	Yes
d.	Yes	No

13. Under Pick Co.'s job order costing system manufacturing overhead is applied to work in process using a predetermined annual overhead rate. During January 2002, Pick's transactions included the following:

Direct materials issued to production	$ 90,000
Indirect materials issued to production	8,000
Manufacturing overhead incurred	125,000
Manufacturing overhead applied	113,000
Direct labor costs	107,000

Pick had neither beginning nor ending work in process inventory. What was the cost of jobs completed in January 2002?

a. $302,000
b. $310,000
c. $322,000
d. $330,000

14. A direct manufacturing labor overtime premium should be charged to a specific job when the overtime is caused by the

a. Increased overall level of activity.
b. Customer's requirement for early completion of job.
c. Management's failure to include the job in the production schedule.
d. Management's requirement that the job be completed before the annual factory vacation closure.

15. In developing a predetermined factory overhead application rate for use in a process costing system, which of the following could be used in the numerator and denominator?

	Numerator	Denominator
a.	Actual factory overhead	Actual machine hours
b.	Actual factory overhead	Estimated machine hours
c.	Estimated factory overhead	Actual machine hours
d.	Estimated factory overhead	Estimated machine hours

16. A job order cost system uses a predetermined factory overhead rate based on expected volume and expected fixed cost. At the end of the year, underapplied overhead might be explained by which of the following situations?

	Actual volume	Actual fixed costs
a.	Greater than expected	Greater than expected
b.	Greater than expected	Less than expected
c.	Less than expected	Greater than expected
d.	Less than expected	Less than expected

17. Worley Company has underapplied overhead of $45,000 for the year ended December 31, 2002. Before disposition of the underapplied overhead, selected December 31, 2002 balances from Worley's accounting records are as follows:

Sales	$1,200,000
Cost of goods sold	720,000
Inventories:	
Direct materials	36,000
Work in process	54,000
Finished goods	90,000

Under Worley's cost accounting system, over- or underapplied overhead is allocated to appropriate inventories and cost of goods sold based on year-end balances. In its 2002 income statement, Worley should report cost of goods sold of

a. $682,500
b. $684,000
c. $756,000
d. $757,500

18. Parat College allocates support department costs to its individual schools using the step method. Information for May 2002 is as follows:

	Support departments	
	Maintenance	Power
Costs incurred	$99,000	$54,000
Service percentages provided to:		
Maintenance	--	10%
Power	20%	--
School of Education	30%	20%
School of Technology	50%	70%
	100%	100%

What is the amount of May 2002 support department costs allocated to the School of Education?

a. $40,500
b. $42,120
c. $46,100
d. $49,125

19. Kerner Manufacturing uses a process cost system to manufacture laptop computers. The following information summarizes operations relating to laptop computer model #KJK20 during the quarter ending March 31:

	Units	Direct Materials
Work in process inventory, January 1	100	$70,000
Started during the quarter	500	
Completed during the quarter	400	
Work-in-process inventory, March 31	200	
Costs added during the quarter		$750,000

Beginning work in process inventory was 50% complete for direct materials. Ending work-in-process inventory was 75% complete for direct materials. What were the equivalent units of production with regard to materials for March?

a. 450
b. 500
c. 550
d. 600

20. Kerner Manufacturing uses a process cost system to manufacture laptop computers. The following information summarizes operations relating to laptop computer model #KJK20 during the quarter ending March 31:

	Units	Direct Materials
Work in process inventory, January 1	100	$50,000
Started during the quarter	500	
Completed during the quarter	400	
Work in process inventory, March 31	200	
Costs added during the quarter		$720,000

Beginning work in process inventory was 50% complete for direct materials. Ending work-in-process inventory was 75% complete for direct materials. What is the total value of material costs in ending work-in-process inventory using the FIFO unit cost, inventory valuation method?

   a. $183,000
   b. $194,000
   c. $210,000
   d. $216,000

21. In a process cost system, the application of factory overhead usually would be recorded as an increase in

   a. Finished goods inventory control.
   b. Factory overhead control.
   c. Cost of goods sold.
   d. Work in process inventory control.

22. The following information pertains to Lap Co.'s Palo Division for the month of April:

	Number of units	Cost of materials
Beginning work in process	15,000	$ 5,500
Started in April	40,000	18,000
Units completed	42,500	
Ending work in process	12,500	

All materials are added at the beginning of the process. Using the weighted-average method, the cost per equivalent unit for materials is

   a. $0.59
   b. $0.55
   c. $0.45
   d. $0.43

23. The Forming Department is the first of a two-stage production process. Spoilage is identified when the units have completed the Forming process. Costs of spoiled units are assigned to units completed and transferred to the second department in the period spoilage is identified. The following information concerns Forming's conversion costs in May 2002:

	Units	Conversion costs
Beginning work in process (50% complete)	2,000	$10,000
Units started during May	8,000	75,500
Spoilage—normal	500	
Units completed and transferred	7,000	
Ending work in process (80% complete)	2,500	

Using the weighted-average method, what was Forming's conversion cost transferred to the second production department?

   a. $59,850
   b. $64,125
   c. $67,500
   d. $71,250

24. In computing the current period's manufacturing cost per equivalent unit, the FIFO method of process costing considers current period costs

   a. Only.
   b. Plus cost of beginning work in process inventory.
   c. Less cost of beginning work in process inventory.
   d. Plus cost of ending work in process inventory.

25. In process 2, material G is added when a batch is 60% complete. Ending work in process units, which are 50% complete, would be included in the computation of equivalent units for

	Conversion costs	Material G
a.	Yes	No
b.	No	Yes
c.	No	No
d.	Yes	Yes

26. A process costing system was used for a department that began operations in January 2002. Approximately the same number of physical units, at the same degree of completion, were in work in process at the end of both January and February. Monthly conversion costs are allocated between ending work in process and units completed. Compared to the FIFO method, would the weighted-average method use the same or a greater number of equivalent units to calculate the monthly allocations?

	Equivalent units for weighted-average compared to FIFO	
	January	February
a.	Same	Same
b.	Greater number	Greater number
c.	Greater number	Same
d.	Same	Greater number

27. A department adds material at the beginning of a process and identifies defective units when the process is 40% complete. At the beginning of the period, there was no work in process. At the end of the period, the number of work in process units equaled the number of units transferred to finished goods. If all units in ending work in process were 66 2/3% complete, then ending work in process should be allocated

   a. 50% of all normal defective unit costs.
   b. 40% of all normal defective unit costs.
   c. 50% of the material costs and 40% of the conversion costs of all normal defective unit costs.
   d. None of the normal defective unit costs.

28. In its April 2002 production, Hern Corp., which does not use a standard cost system, incurred total production costs of $900,000, of which Hern attributed $60,000 to normal spoilage and $30,000 to abnormal spoilage. Hern should account for this spoilage as

   a. Period cost of $90,000.
   b. Inventoriable cost of $90,000.
   c. Period cost of $60,000 and inventoriable cost of $30,000.
   d. Inventoriable cost of $60,000 and period cost of $30,000.

29. In a quality control program, which of the following is (are) categorized as internal failure costs?

  I. Rework.
  II. Responding to customer complaints.
  III. Statistical quality control procedures.

   a. I only.
   b. II only.
   c. III only.
   d. I, II, and III.

30. What is the normal effect on the numbers of cost pools and allocation bases when an activity-based cost (ABC) system replaces a traditional cost system?

	Cost pools	Allocation bases
a.	No effect	No effect
b.	Increase	No effect
c.	No effect	Increase
d.	Increase	Increase

31. Which of the following is true about activity-based costing?

a. It should not be used with process or job costing.
b. It can be used only with process costing.
c. It can be used only with job costing.
d. It can be used with either process or job costing.

32. In an activity-based costing system, what should be used to assign a department's manufacturing overhead costs to products produced in varying lot sizes?

a. A single cause and effect relationship.
b. Multiple cause and effect relationships.
c. Relative net sales values of the products.
d. A product's ability to bear cost allocations.

33. In an activity-based costing system, cost reduction is accomplished by identifying and eliminating

	All cost drivers	Non-value-adding activities
a.	No	No
b.	Yes	Yes
c.	No	Yes
d.	Yes	No

34. Nile Co.'s cost allocation and product costing procedures follow activity-based costing principles. Activities have been identified and classified as being either value-adding or non-value-adding as to each product. Which of the following activities, used in Nile production process, is non-value-adding?

a. Design engineering activity.
b. Heat treatment activity.
c. Drill press activity.
d. Raw materials storage activity.

35. Hoger Corporation accumulated the following cost information for its two products, A and B:

	A	B	Total
Production volume	2,000	1,000	
Total direct man. labor hrs.	5,000	20,000	25,000
Setup cost per batch	$ 1,000	$2,000	
Batch size	100	50	
Total setup costs incurred	$20,000	$40,000	$60,000
DMLH per unit	2	1	

A traditional costing system would allocate setup costs on the basis of DMLH. An ABC system would trace costs by spreading the costs per batch over the units in a batch. What is the setup cost per unit of product A under each costing system?

	Traditional	ABC
a.	$4.80	$10.00
b.	$2.40	$10.00
c.	$40.00	$200.00
d.	$4.80	$20.00

36. Lane Co. produces main products Kul and Wu. The process also yields by-product Zef. Net realizable value of by-product Zef is subtracted from joint production cost of Kul and Wu. The following information pertains to production in July 2002 at a joint cost of $54,000:

Product	Units produced	Market value	Additional cost after split-off
Kul	1,000	$40,000	$ 0
Wu	1,500	35,000	0
Zef	500	7,000	3,000

If Lane uses the net realizable value method for allocating joint cost, how much of the joint cost should be allocated to product Kul?

a. $18,800
b. $20,000
c. $26,667
d. $27,342

37. The diagram below represents the production and sales relationships of joint products P and Q. Joint costs are incurred until split-off, then separable costs are incurred in refining each product. Market values of P and Q at split-off are used to allocate joint costs.

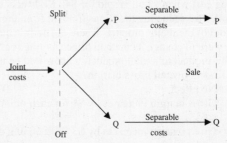

If the market value of P at split-off increases and all other costs and selling prices remain unchanged, then the gross margin of

	P	Q
a.	Increases	Decreases
b.	Increases	Increases
c.	Decreases	Decreases
d.	Decreases	Increases

38. For purposes of allocating joint costs to joint products, the sales price at point of sale, reduced by cost to complete after split-off, is assumed to be equal to the

a. Joint costs.
b. Total costs.
c. Net sales value at split-off.
d. Sales price less a normal profit margin at point of sale.

39. Mig Co., which began operations in 2002, produces gasoline and a gasoline by-product. The following information is available pertaining to 2002 sales and production:

Total production costs to split-off point	$120,000
Gasoline sales	270,000
By-product sales	30,000
Gasoline inventory, 12/31/02	15,000
Additional by-product costs:	
Marketing	10,000
Production	15,000

Mig accounts for the by-product at the time of production. What are Mig's 2002 cost of sales for gasoline and the by-product?

	Gasoline	By-product
a.	$105,000	$25,000
b.	$115,000	$0
c.	$108,000	$37,000
d.	$100,000	$0

40. The following information pertains to a by-product called Moy:

Sales in 2002	5,000 units
Selling price per unit	$6
Selling costs per unit	2
Processing costs	0

Inventory of Moy was recorded at net realizable value when produced in 2001. No units of Moy were produced in 2002. What amount should be recognized as profit on Moy's 2002 sales?

    a. $0
    b. $10,000
    c. $20,000
    d. $30,000

41. Kode Co. manufactures a major product that gives rise to a by-product called May. May's only separable cost is a $1 selling cost when a unit is sold for $4. Kode accounts for May's sales by deducting the $3 net amount from the cost of goods sold of the major product. There are no inventories. If Kode were to change its method of accounting for May from a by-product to a joint product, what would be the effect on Kode's overall gross margin?

    a. No effect.
    b. Gross margin increases by $1 for each unit of May sold.
    c. Gross margin increases by $3 for each unit of May sold.
    d. Gross margin increases by $4 for each unit of May sold.

42. In accounting for by-products, the value of the by-product may be recognized at the time of

	Production	*Sale*
a.	Yes	Yes
b.	Yes	No
c.	No	No
d.	No	Yes

OTHER OBJECTIVE QUESTIONS

Problem 1   (45 to 55 minutes)

Webb & Company is engaged in the preparation of income tax returns for individuals. Webb uses the weighted-average method and actual costs for financial reporting purposes. However, for internal reporting, Webb uses a standard cost system. The standards, based on equivalent performance, have been established as follows:

Labor per return	5 hrs. @ $20 per hr.
Overhead per return	5 hrs. @ $10 per hr.

For March 2002 performance, budgeted overhead is $49,000 for the standard labor hours allowed. The following additional information pertains to the month of March 2002:

Inventory data

Returns in process, March 1	
(20% complete)	200
Returns started in March	825
Returns in process, March 31	
(80% complete)	125

Actual cost data

Returns in process, March 1:	
Labor	$ 3,000
Overhead	3,000
Labor, March 1 to 31, 4,000 hours	89,000
Overhead, March 1 to 31	45,000

Required:

For items 1 through 5, using the inventory data, the actual cost data, and the standard cost data given, compute the amount asked for in each item. Since a numerical answer is required, the candidate would be given a list of numbers to choose from.

1. Equivalent units of performance for labor (weighted-average method).

2. Equivalent units of performance for overhead (weighted-average method).

3. Labor costs used in the computation of cost per equivalent unit for labor (weighted-average method).

4. Overhead costs used in the computation of cost per equivalent unit for overhead (weighted-average method).

5. Actual cost of returns in process at March 31.

For items 6 through 11, compute the amount of each variance to be reported in an analysis of March performance, and state whether each variance is favorable (F) or unfavorable (U).

*NOTE: **Items 6-11** should be completed after studying Module 36, Standards and Variances. A cross-reference from the problem material for Module 36 will refer you back to this requirement later if you don't want to review standard costs and variance analysis at this time.*

Items to be answered

6. Labor efficiency.

7. Labor rate.

8. Total labor.

9. Overhead budget.

10. Overhead volume.

11. Total overhead.

1. a __ __	10. a __ __	19. b __ __	28. d __ __	37. d __ __
2. d __ __	11. b __ __	20. d __ __	29. a __ __	38. c __ __
3. b __ __	12. c __ __	21. d __ __	30. d __ __	39. d __ __
4. d __ __	13. b __ __	22. d __ __	31. b __ __	40. a __ __
5. d __ __	14. b __ __	23. c __ __	32. d __ __	41. b __ __
6. d __ __	15. d __ __	24. a __ __	33. c __ __	42. a __ __
7. c __ __	16. c __ __	25. a __ __	34. d __ __	
8. a __ __	17. d __ __	26. d __ __	35. a __ __	1st: __/42 = __%
9. b __ __	18. c __ __	27. a __ __	36. c __ __	2nd: __/42 = __%

MULTIPLE-CHOICE ANSWER EXPLANATIONS

A. Cost of Goods Manufactured

1.   (a)   Three computations must be performed: raw materials used, cost of goods manufactured, and cost of goods sold.

(1)	Raw materials purchased	$430,000
	Less: Increase in raw materials inventory	15,000
	Raw materials used	$415,000
(2)	Beginning WIP	--
	Raw materials used (from above)	415,000
	Direct manufacturing labor	200,000
	Factory overhead	300,000
	Cost to account for	$915,000
	Less: Ending WIP	--
	Cost of goods manufactured	$915,000
(3)	Cost of goods manufactured	$915,000
	Add: Decrease in finished goods inventory	35,000
	Cost of goods sold	$950,000

The increase in raw materials inventory represents the amount of inventory that was purchased but was not used. Therefore, this increase must be subtracted from raw materials purchased to determine the amount of raw materials used. Work in process inventory is an adjustment in arriving at cost of goods manufactured (as shown above). For this question no adjustment is necessary because Kay has no work in process inventory. The decrease in finished goods inventory represents the amount of inventory that was sold in excess of the inventory manufactured during the current period. Therefore, this amount must be added to cost of goods manufactured to determine cost of goods sold. The freight-out of $45,000 is irrelevant for this question because freight-out is a selling expense and thus, would not be used in computing cost of goods sold.

2.   (d)   Prime cost is the sum of direct materials and direct manufacturing labor. Direct manufacturing labor is $60,000. Direct materials used must be computed. The solutions approach is to enter the information given into the materials T-account and solve for the unknown:

Direct Materials Control			
3/1/02 bal.	36,000		
Purchases	84,000	?	Materials used
3/30/02	30,000		

Using the T-account above, direct materials used are easily computed as $90,000. Thus, prime cost incurred was $150,000 ($90,000 + $60,000).

3.   (b)   Conversion cost is the sum of direct manufacturing labor ($60,000, as given) and applied factory overhead. The factory overhead rate per direct manufacturing labor

hour is $10.00. To compute the number of direct manufacturing labor hours worked, the direct manufacturing labor payroll ($60,000) is divided by the direct manufacturing labor rate per hour ($7.50), resulting in 8,000 direct manufacturing labor hours. Factory overhead applied is 8,000 hours at $10 per hour, or $80,000. Thus, conversion cost incurred was $140,000 ($60,000 of direct manufacturing labor plus $80,000 of applied factory overhead).

4.   (d)   Cost of goods manufactured (CGM) is the cost of goods completed **and** transferred to finished goods. It is the sum of direct materials used, direct manufacturing labor used, applied factory overhead, and any adjustment for work in process inventories. Direct manufacturing labor used ($60,000) is given. Direct materials used ($90,000) and applied factory overhead ($80,000) were computed in the answers to the two previous questions. Beginning work in process ($18,000) and ending work in process ($12,000) are given. Using this data, CGM can be computed as follows:

BWIP	$ 18,000
DM used	90,000
DML	60,000
OH applied	80,000
Costs to account for	$248,000
EWIP	(12,000)
CGM	$236,000

5.   (d)   To determine Nale's direct materials purchases for the month of March, trace the flow of costs through the direct materials account.

Direct materials			
Beg. bal.	x		
Purchased		$300,000	Used
End. bal.	x + $50,000		

The beginning balance was not given, but the problem states that the ending balance was $50,000 greater. Thus, we can label the beginning balance X and the ending balance X + $50,000. Purchases may be determined as follows:

$$(x + \$50,000) + \$300,000 - x = \$350,000$$

6.   (d)   Direct manufacturing labor costs include all labor costs which can be directly traced to the product in an economically feasible way. All other factory labor is considered indirect manufacturing labor. For Fab Co., the wages of loom operators can be directly traced to the textiles produced. However, the labor cost of factory foremen and machine mechanics are **not** direct manufacturing labor since these workers do not work directly on the product. Thus, answer (d) is correct because the amount of Fab's direct manufacturing labor is the loom operator cost of $120,000.

7. **(c)** Product costs are costs that can be associated with the production of specific revenues. These costs attach to a physical unit and become expenses in the period in which the unit to which they attach is sold. Product costs include direct labor, direct material, and factory overhead. Period costs, on the other hand, cannot be associated with specific revenues and, therefore, become expenses as time passes. Answer (c) is correct because the cost of electricity for a manufacturing plant, whether fixed or variable, is included in factory overhead and, therefore, is a product cost.

8. **(a)** The labor cost incurred to develop computer programs for sale to customers represents both a direct cost and a value-adding cost. The software is the cost object, and direct costs include any costs that are both related to it and which are easily traceable to specific units of production. Value-adding costs are those that cannot be eliminated without the customer perceiving a decline in product quality or performance. Obviously, the computer programmers cannot be eliminated from the software development process, so these payroll costs add value to the product.

9. **(b)** In calculating the cost of quality, rework costs related to internal failure are considered but rework costs caused by the customer are not. Answer (a) is incorrect because rework costs caused by the customer are not considered. Answer (c) is incorrect because rework costs caused by the customer are not considered. Answer (d) is incorrect because rework costs caused by internal failure are considered.

B.   Cost Flows

10. **(a)** A responsibility center is any point within an organization where control exists over cost incurrence, revenue generation, and/or the use of investment funds. A responsibility center can be an operation, a department, a division, or even an individual. The key point to note for this question is that no matter what product costing method is used, the responsibility center is always used for control purposes. In job order costing, costs are accumulated by responsibility center and then assigned to specific jobs or orders through the use of a job cost sheet. Even though the job cost sheet will usually reflect the efforts of a number of responsibility centers, it will not be used for control purposes. Any needed cost control will be handled on the responsibility center level. In process costing, costs are accumulated by the responsibility center and recorded on a production cost report that will be used to develop a product's cost. Since the production cost report shows the efforts of only one responsibility center, it is used for both product costing and control purposes. Thus, for control purposes, costs are accumulated by responsibility center for both job-order and process costing.

C.   Job-Order Costing

11. **(b)** The requirement is to determine the amount of direct materials charged to Job No. 5. The problem states that Job 5 is the only job still in process on April 30, so the total costs charged to this job must equal the ending balance in work in process.

Work in Process Control			
Beg. bal.	4,000		
DM	24,000		
DML	16,000		
O/H	12,800	48,000	To FG
End. bal.	8,800		

The total costs charged to Job 5 are $8,800. Direct manufacturing labor accounts for $2,000 of this figure and overhead accounts for $1,600 ($2,000 DL x 80% O/H rate).

Direct manufacturing labor	$2,000
Factory overhead	1,600
Direct materials	--
Total cost of Job 5	$8,800

The remaining cost of $5,200 [$8,800 – ($2,000 + $1,600)] must be the amount of direct materials.

12. **(c)** Manufacturing overhead is considered an indirect cost because it is not directly traceable to specific jobs, although overhead is a necessary (inevitable) cost of production.

13. **(b)** The requirement is to determine the cost of jobs completed in January 2002. In a job order costing system, manufacturing overhead cannot be traced to specific jobs. Instead, overhead is accumulated in an overhead control account and applied to work performed based on some predetermined overhead rate. The difference between actual and applied overhead is normally either allocated to work in process, finished goods, and cost of goods sold or written off to cost of goods sold. In this case the cost of jobs completed is being determined for January only. Under- or overapplied overhead is not usually considered on a monthly basis. Therefore, the cost of jobs completed should include allocated overhead only. The amount of indirect materials issued to production has already been included in overhead applied. These costs do not need to be considered again in determining the cost of jobs completed. The cost of jobs completed can be computed as follows:

Direct materials issued to production	$ 90,000
Manufacturing overhead applied	113,000
Direct labor costs	107,000
Cost of jobs completed	$310,000

14. **(b)** The requirement is to determine which situation would cause a direct manufacturing labor overtime premium to be charged directly to a specific job. Answer (b) is correct because overtime resulting from a customer's requirement of early completion of a job would result in overtime directly traceable to that job. Answer (a) is incorrect because overtime incurred because of an overall high level of activity should be prorated over all jobs. Since production scheduling is generally at random, a specific job should not be penalized simply because it happened to be scheduled during overtime hours. Answers (c) and (d) are incorrect because the overtime is a result of management inefficiency.

D.   Accounting for Overhead

15. **(d)** An overhead application rate is commonly called a predetermined overhead rate and is computed as follows:

$$\frac{\text{Estimated overhead costs}}{\text{Estimated activity level}} = \text{Predetermined rate}$$

Estimated figures are used because actual figures are not known at the beginning of a period. Estimated factory overhead (the numerator) is estimated overhead costs, and estimated machine hours (the denominator) is an estimated activity level. Actual figures (either overhead costs or activity levels) are not known until the end of the period.

16. **(c)** A predetermined factory overhead rate is developed by dividing estimated fixed overhead costs by an estimated volume of a selected cost driver (DML cost, machine hours, etc.). Overhead costs are then applied by multiplying the predetermined rate by the actual volume of the cost driver during the period. Overhead costs will be underapplied if (1) overhead costs are underestimated, making the application rate too small (actual costs are larger than expected), or (2) expected activity is overestimated, making the application rate too small (actual volume is less than expected).

E. Disposition of Under- and Overapplied Overhead

17. (d) The requirement is to determine the amount of costs of goods sold to be reported on the 2002 income statement. The balance in the cost of goods sold account is $720,000. This amount must be increased by the portion of underapplied overhead allocated to cost of goods sold. The underapplied overhead is appropriately allocated to work in process, finished goods, and cost of goods sold. No overhead is allocated to direct materials inventory, since this account contains only the cost of unused materials. The other three accounts contain the cost of materials, labor, and overhead. The amounts to be allocated to work in process, finished goods, and cost of goods sold are determined by each account's relative balance as compared to the total balance in the accounts. The total balance of the three accounts is $864,000 ($720,000 + $54,000 + $90,000). Therefore, the amount allocable to cost of goods sold is [$720,000/$864,000 x ($45,000)] or $37,500. Since overhead was underapplied, not enough costs were applied to production during the year. Thus, cost of goods sold is increased to $757,500 ($720,000 + $37,500).

F. Service Department Cost Allocation

18. (c) The step method of allocating support department costs uses a sequence of allocations which result in partial recognition of services rendered by one support department to another. Total costs of the support department that provides the greatest proportion of its services to other support departments are allocated first, followed by the department with the next highest proportion, and so forth. As each "step" is allocated, each succeeding step involves one less department. Parat College's support department cost allocation is

| | Support Departments | | Operating Departments | |
	Maintenance	Power	School of Education	School of Technology
Costs before allocation	$99,000	$54,000		
Allocation of maintenance $(\frac{2}{10}, \frac{3}{10}, \frac{5}{10})$	(99,000)	19,800	$29,700	$49,500
	$____0			
Allocation of power $(\frac{2}{9}, \frac{7}{9})$		(73,800)	16,400	57,400
		$____0	$46,100	$106,900

Therefore, $46,100 of May 2002 support department costs are allocated to the School of Education.

G. Process Costing

19. (b) Equivalent units of production are calculated as follows:

Completed units	400
Plus: Equivalent units in ending inventory (200 x 75%)	150
Less: Equivalent units in beginning inventory (100 x 50%)	(50)
Equivalent units of production	500

20. (d) Material costs in ending work in process inventory is calculated as $216,000 = 150 (equivalent units in ending inventory) x $144 ($720,000/500) per equivalent unit. Equivalent units of production are calculated as: 500 = 400 completed units + 150 (200 x 75%) equivalent units in ending inventory – 50 (100 x 50%) equivalent units in beginning inventory.

21. (d) The application of factory overhead would increase the work in process inventory control account. In addition, the work in process account would be increased for other product costs (direct manufacturing labor and direct material). Only costs of completed products increase finished goods inventory control. Factory overhead control is increased by actual factory overhead costs incurred. Cost of goods sold is increased by the product costs of the finished units sold.

22. (d) The requirement is to determine the cost per equivalent unit for materials using the weighted-average method. Under the weighted-average method, equivalent units of production and cost per unit are based on **all** work (this period's and last period's) done on units completed plus all work done to date on the units in ending work in process. Since materials are added at the beginning of the production process, both the units completed and the ending work in process are 100% complete with respect to materials. The cost per equivalent unit can be computed as follows:

Units completed	42,500
Ending WIP	12,500
Total equivalent units	55,000
Cost of materials:	
Beginning WIP	$ 5,500
Units started	18,000
Total costs incurred	$23,500
Divide by EUP	÷ 55,000
Cost per equivalent unit	$ .43

23. (c) The requirement is to calculate the amount of conversion cost transferred by Forming to the next production department. First, the physical flow of units must be determined.

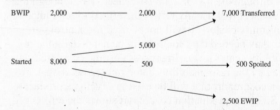

Next, equivalent units of production (EUP) must be calculated, in this case using the weighted-average (WA) method. The WA computations of EUP and cost per equivalent unit include both work done **last** period on the current period's BWIP and all work done in the current period on units completed and on EWIP. Forming's EWIP is 80% complete.

Spoiled units must be accounted for separately because Forming adds their cost only to the cost of units transferred. To ignore spoiled units would result in the same total cost being allocated to 500 fewer units, thus spreading spoilage costs over all work done during the period, including EWIP.

	Total units	Equivalent units
Started and completed	7,000	7,000
Spoilage—normal	500	500
EWIP (80% complete)	2,500	2,000*
	10,000	9,500

*2,500 units x 80% completion

Since conversion costs total $85,500 for the period ($10,000 for BWIP + $75,500 for units started), Forming's conversion cost per equivalent unit is $9.00 ($85,000 ÷ 9,500 EUP). These costs are assigned as follows:

Good units completed (7,000 x $9)	$63,000
Spoiled units (500 x $9)	4,500
Conversion cost transferred	$67,500
EWIP (2,000 x $9)	18,000
Total costs accounted for	$85,500

Therefore, $67,500 was transferred to the second department.

24. (a) The FIFO method determines equivalent units of production (EUP) based on the work done in the current period only. The work done in the current period can be dichotomized as: (1) the work necessary to complete beginning work in process (BWIP), and (2) the work performed on the units started in the current period.

25. (a) Conversion costs consist of direct manufacturing labor and factory overhead. Because the EWIP units are 50% in process 2, some conversion costs have been incurred. These units would be included in the computation of equivalent units for conversion costs. However, because material G is added only when a batch is 60% complete, this material has not yet been added to this batch. These units would not be included in the computation of equivalent units for material G.

26. (d) The requirement is to compare the number of equivalent units of production (EUP) computed using the weighted-average method to the EUP computed using the FIFO method for two months. The weighted-average method determines EUP based on the work done on the units in all periods, while the FIFO method uses only the work done in the current period. Because the system began in January, there was no beginning inventory for the first month of the comparison. Both methods would compute the same number of EUP for January because the only work done on these units was done in the period under consideration. Because there was ending inventory in January, however, February would have a beginning inventory. The weighted-average method would therefore compute a greater number of EUP than FIFO for February because it would include the work done in January while FIFO would not.

27. (a) The requirement is to determine the proper allocation of **normal** defective unit costs to the ending work in process. **Normal** defective unit costs are spread over the units of **good** output because the attaining of good units necessitates the appearance of normal spoiled units. The cost of the normal defective units is included in the total costs of the **good** equivalent units of output. Ending inventory comprised one-half of the total units of good output produced during the year; therefore, it will bear 50% of the normal defective unit costs incurred during the year.

28. (d) Normal spoilage is the cost of spoiled units which results due to the nature of the manufacturing process. Normal spoilage may be unavoidable under efficient operating conditions and is thus a necessary cost in the production process. Since it is treated as a product cost, the $60,000 normal spoilage should be inventoried. Conversely, units become abnormally spoiled as a result of some unnecessary act, event, or condition. Therefore, the $30,000 abnormal spoilage is treated as a period cost.

29. (a) Internal failure costs are defined as costs incurred when a nonconforming product is detected **before** its shipment to customers. Reworked units are defined as unacceptable units of production that are reworked and sold as finished goods. Responding to customer complaints is an external failure cost and statistical quality control procedures are appraisal costs.

H. Activity-Based Costing

30. (d) An activity-based costing system allocates costs to products by determining which activities being performed by the entity are driving the costs. An activity-based costing approach differs from traditional costing methods that accumulate costs by department or function. Activity-based costing accumulates and allocates costs by the specific activities being performed. Since most entities perform a variety of activities, the number of cost pools and allocation bases greatly increases under activity-based costing.

31. (d) Activity-based costing can be used in conjunction with either process or job costing. Answer (a) is incorrect because activity-based costing can be used in conjunction with either process or job costing. Answer (b) is incorrect because activity-based costing can be used in conjunction with job costing. Answer (c) is incorrect because activity-based costing can be used in conjunction with process costing.

32. (b) In an activity-based costing (ABC) system, the activities which drive the manufacturing department's overhead costs would be analyzed. Overhead would then be allocated to products based on the resources consumed in their production. The effect of producing different products in different lot sizes is that some products incur more setup costs than others; products produced in small batches must be produced more often, and thus require more setups to achieve a given level of output. Therefore, setup costs bear a cause and effect relationship with and should be assigned to each production **batch** (and then spread over the units in the batch). However, setups are not the only activities driving overhead costs. Other overhead cost drivers identifiable in production systems may include materials handling, engineering changes to products, and rework costs. Therefore, manufacturing overhead should be assigned to products based on **multiple** cause and effect relationships [answer (b) is correct and answer (a) is incorrect]. Answers (c) and (d) are incorrect because allocation via these methods would wholly defeat the purpose of ABC, which is founded upon cause and effect allocation of costs to products.

33. (c) Activity-based costing (ABC) involves the allocation of overhead costs to products based on the cost driver that actually **caused** those costs to be incurred. In contrast to traditional costing methods which accumulate costs by department or function, ABC accumulates costs by the specific activity being performed. For example, costs related to the purchase of materials may be allocated according to the number of purchase transactions which occurred. Therefore, cost drivers comprise a necessary part of any ABC system. On the other hand, non-value-added activities represent expenditures for which no value is added to the product. Hence, costs can be reduced by eliminating non-value-added activities without affecting the salability of the product.

34. **(d)** Activity-based costing focuses on incorporating into product costs only those activities that provide value to the product. Design engineering is a fundamental activity needed to design a good product. Heat treatment activities would strengthen and protect the product being produced. A drill press activity alters the physical product as it moves on toward becoming a finished good. Raw materials storage activity does nothing to alter or improve the value of a product. It is a non-value-adding activity.

35. **(a)** Under a traditional costing system, setup costs are allocated using a cost driver, in this case, direct manufacturing labor hours. The first step is to calculate the setup costs per direct manufacturing labor hour ($60,000 incurred ÷ 25,000 total DMLH) of $2.40. Since two DMLH are needed to produce one unit of product A, the total setup cost per unit of A is ($2.40 x 2 DMLH) $4.80. Under ABC, one **batch** of product A creates the demand for setup activities that produce value. The setup cost per unit of A under ABC is calculated as the setup cost **per batch** of A ($1,000) divided by the number of units per batch (100), or, $10.00.

I. Joint Products

36. **(c)** The requirement is to determine how to allocate joint cost using the net realizable value (NRV) method when a by-product is involved. NRV is the predicted selling price in the ordinary course of business less reasonably predictable costs of completion and disposal. The joint cost of $54,000 is reduced by the NRV of the by-product ($4,000) to get the allocable joint cost ($50,000). The computation is

	Sales value at split-off	Weighting	Joint costs allocated
Kul	$40,000	40,000/75,000 x 50,000	$26,667
Wu	35,000	35,000/75,000 x 50,000	23,333
	$75,000		$50,000

Therefore, $26,667 of the joint cost should be allocated to product Kul.

37. **(d)** When using the relative sales value at split-off method for joint products, joint costs are allocated based on the ratio of each product's sales value at split-off to total sales value at split-off for all joint products. If the market value at split-off (sales value) of joint product P increases, then a larger proportion of the total joint costs will be allocated to that product. Because all other costs and selling prices remain unchanged, the gross margin of product P will, therefore, decrease. Product Q's gross margin will, however, increase because a smaller proportion of the total joint costs will be allocated to it.

38. **(c)** Joint costs may be allocated to joint products based on either sales price or some physical measure. Methods which use estimated sales price include relative sales value at split-off, estimated net realizable value (NRV), and constant gross margin percentage NRV. Under the sales value at split-off method, joint costs are allocated based on the ratio of each product's sales value at split-off to total sales value at split-off for all joint products. The estimated NRV method allocates joint costs at the split-off point based on net sales value (Estimated sales value of the joint products – Separable processing costs). Under the constant gross margin percentage NRV method, the overall gross margin (GM) percentage for all joint products combined (after deducting both joint and separable costs) is used to determine the GM for each joint product. This GM is deducted from the sales price of each joint product to determine total costs, and separable costs are then deducted from total costs to determine the joint cost allocation. However, this is not the same as answer (d), which uses a predetermined profit margin and ignores actual costs. The constant GM percentage NRV method does not use a preset GM, it uses the actual overall GM and spreads it uniformly among products so that all joint products yield the same GM percentage. The sales price cannot be based solely on costs. Conversely, costs must be based on sales price (or some physical measure) because joint costs can only be allocated arbitrarily.

J. By-Products

39. **(d)** The requirement is to find the cost of sales for both gasoline and the gasoline by-product. The value of the by-products may be recognized at two points in time: (1) at the time of production, or (2) at the time of sale. Under the production method (as given in the problem), the net realizable value of the by-products **produced** is deducted from the cost of the major products **produced**. The net realizable value of the by-product is as follows:

Sales value of by-product	$30,000	
Less: separable costs	25,000	(10,000 + 15,000)
	$ 5,000	

Therefore, cost of sales for gasoline is calculated as follows:

Total production (joint) costs	$120,000
Less: net realizable value of by-product	5,000
Net Production Cost	115,000
Less: costs in 12/31/02 inventory	15,000
	$100,000

Therefore, total cost of gasoline sales is $100,000, and no cost of sales is reported for the by-product.

40. **(a)** Because the inventory of by-product Moy was recorded at its net realizable value of $20,000 [($6 – $2) x 5,000] when produced in 2001, no profit will be recognized in 2002. When the units of Moy were sold in 2002, the proceeds equaled the inventory cost plus disposal costs, resulting in $0 profit for 2002. The following journal entries help to illustrate the situation:

2001	Main product(s) inventory	xxxx	
	By-product inventory	20,000	
	Work in process control		xxxx
2002	Cash or accounts receivable	30,000	
	Inventory		20,000
	Selling expenses		10,000

41. **(b)** The difference between treating the product named "May" as a joint product versus a by-product would be that under by-product treatment, the selling cost is netted against May's selling price thus reducing gross margin whereas under joint-product accounting, the selling cost would be deducting below the gross margin line as a selling expense. Thus, if the change to joint-product accounting were made, gross margin would increase.

42. **(a)** The value of the by-products may be recognized at two points in time: (1) at the time of production, or (2) at the time of sale. Under the production method, the net realizable value of the by-products **produced** is deducted from the cost of the major products **produced**. Under the sale method, net revenue from by-products **sold** (gross revenue from by-product sales minus separable costs incurred) is deducted from the cost of the major products **sold**.

OTHER OBJECTIVE ANSWERS AND ANSWER EXPLANATIONS

Problem 1

1.   (1,000) In order to compute equivalent units of performance (EUP) you need to first visualize the physical flow of units:

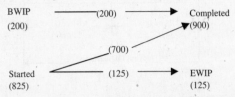

Under the WA method, EUP are computed as the sum of all units completed plus the work to date on EWIP. The diagram above indicates that 900 units were completed. The additional information in the problem indicates that 125 units were in EWIP and that 80% of the work on these units was complete. Thus, for labor, the EUP are 1,000 [900 + 80% (125)].

2.   (1,000) Since labor hours are used as the overhead base, the EUP for overhead are identical to those for labor. Thus, for overhead, the EUP are 1,000 [900 + 80% (125)].

3.   ($92,000) Under the WA method, cost per EUP utilizes the sum of the previous cost in BWIP plus current cost. The previous cost in BWIP is included because the WA calculation of EUP included all work done on BWIP (i.e., no distinction was made between work done last period and work done this period). Thus, the actual costs to be used in the computation of cost per EUP for labor are $92,000 ($3,000 + $89,000).

4.   ($48,000) Under the WA method, cost per EUP utilizes the sum of the previous cost in BWIP plus current cost. The previous cost in BWIP is included because the WA calculation of EUP included all work done on BWIP (i.e., no distinction was made between work done last period and work done this period). Thus, the actual costs to be used in the computation of cost per EUP for overhead are $48,000 ($3,000 in process March 1 + $45,000 March 1 to 31).

5.   ($14,000) Since 80% of the work was done on EWIP, 100 EUP (80% x 125) are contained in EWIP. The actual cost per EUP can be computed as $92.00 and $48.00 for labor and for overhead, respectively [($92,000 ÷ 1,000) and ($48,000 ÷ 1000)]. Thus, the actual cost of returns in process at 3/31 is $9,200 (100 x $92.00) for labor and $4,800 (100 x $48.00) for overhead that is a total cost in EWIP of $14,000.

6.   ($16,000, F) The labor efficiency variance is computed by taking the actual hours (AH) times the standard rate (SR) less the standard hours (SH) times the standard rate (SR) [(AH x SR) – (SH x SR)]. The actual hours of 4,000 and the standard rate of $20 per hr. are given in the problem. The standard hours are computed by taking the standard five hrs. labor per return times the 960 Equivalent Units of Production (EUP) (5 x 960 = 4,800). The EUP for March is computed by adding up the EUP needed to complete BWIP during March, units started and completed, and the EUP done on EWIP during March. This calculation is as follows:

EUP for BWIP (80% of 200)	160
Units started and completed (825 – 125)	700
EUP for EWIP (80% of 125)	100
Total EUP	960

The labor efficiency variance is computed as follows:

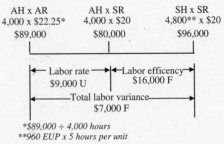

AH x AR	AH x SR	SH x SR
4,000 x $22.25*	4,000 x $20	4,800** x $20
$89,000	$80,000	$96,000

Labor rate
$9,000 U

Labor efficiency
$16,000 F

Total labor variance
$7,000 F

*$89,000 ÷ 4,000 hours
**960 EUP x 5 hours per unit

7.   ($9,000, U) The labor rate variance is computed by taking the actual hours (AH) times the actual rate (AR) less the actual hours times the standard rate (SR). The AH is given as 4,000 and the SR is given as $20. The actual rate can be computed as $22.25 by taking the total labor cost of $89,000 divided by 4,000 hours. The labor rate variance is computed as shown in item 6. above.

8.   ($7,000, F) The total labor variance is computed by taking the labor rate variance computed in item 7 ($9,000, U), plus the labor efficiency variance computed in item 6 ($16,000, F) ($16,000 F – $9,000 U = $7,000 F). See chart in item 6. above.

9.   ($4,000, F) The overhead budget variance is computed by subtracting the actual overhead, given as $45,000, from the budgeted overhead, given as $49,000, ($49,000 – $45,000 = $4000). The variance is favorable because the actual overhead ($45,000) is less than the budgeted overhead ($49,000).

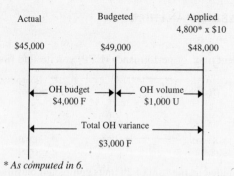

* As computed in 6.

10.   ($1,000, U) The overhead volume budget variance is computed by taking the budgeted overhead ($49,000) less the applied overhead. The applied overhead of $48,000 is computed by taking the $10 overhead rate per hour, which is given, times the standard hours of 4,800 that were computed in number 6. The variance is unfavorable because the anticipated volume was not achieved. See chart in item 9. above.

11.   ($3,000, F) The total overhead variance is the sum of the overhead budget ($4,000, F) and the overhead volume variance ($1,000, U). [$4000 (F) – $1000 (U) = $3000 (F)]. See chart in item 9. above.

PLANNING, CONTROL, AND ANALYSIS

This module discusses a number of tools used internally for financial planning, control, and analysis.

A. Analyzing Cost Behavior

Many of the tools discussed later require the separation of costs into their fixed and variable components (refer to the definitions of fixed, variable, and mixed costs under "Basic Cost Accounting Terminology" beginning on the third page of this chapter).

1. High-Low Method

The high-low method computes the slope for the variable rate based on the highest and lowest observations.

$$\text{Slope} \quad = \quad \frac{\text{Change in cost between high and low points}}{\text{Change in activity between high and low points}}$$

This method is illustrated using the following observations for factory maintenance costs (DMLH = Direct manufacturing labor hours).

Month	DMLH	Factory maintenance cost
1	45,000 (low)	$110,000
2	50,000	115,000
3	70,000	158,000
4	60,000	135,000
5	75,000 (high)	170,000
6	65,000	145,000

The difference in cost is divided by the difference in activity to obtain the variable cost. The fixed cost can then be computed by using either the high observation or the low observation. The same result will be obtained with either one. The computation for separating factory maintenance cost is detailed below.

Variable rate computation

$$\frac{\$170,000 - \$110,000}{75,000 - 45,000} = \$2/\text{DMLH}$$

Fixed rate computation

$\$170,000 - (75,000 \times \$2) = \$20,000$

or

$\$110,000 - (45,000 \times \$2) = \$20,000$

The high-low method is a rather crude technique compared to regression analysis. For example, this method may be inaccurate if the high and low points are not representative (i.e., are outliers) as illustrated in the following chart by the solid line.

2. **Scattergraph Method.** The scattergraph method is a graphical approach to computing the relationship between two variables. The dependent variable is plotted on the vertical axis and the independent variable on the horizontal axis. A straight line is then drawn through the observation points which best describes the relationship between the two variables. In the graph above, the broken line illustrates the relationship. This method lacks precision, because by freely drawing the line through the points, it is possible to obtain a line that does not minimize the deviations of the points from the line.

3. **Regression Analysis.** Regression (least squares) analysis determines the functional relationship between variables with a measure of probable error. It is important to determine that a cause-and-effect relationship actually exists between the cost driver and the resulting costs. For example, you may wish to determine the relationship of electricity cost to level of activity. Based on activity levels and electricity charges of past months, the following chart (scattergraph) might be prepared.

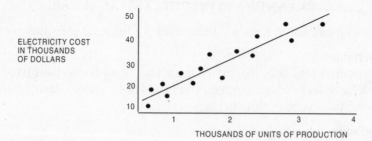

ELECTRICITY COST IN THOUSANDS OF DOLLARS

THOUSANDS OF UNITS OF PRODUCTION

As production increases, electric costs increase. The relationship appears linear. Linearity is an assumption underlying regression. If the power costs begin to fall after 3,000 units of production, the relationship between electricity and production would not be linear, and linear regression would not be appropriate.

The method of least squares fits a regression line between the observation points such that the sum of the squared vertical differences between the regression line and the individual observations is minimized.

The goodness of the least squares fit (i.e., how well the regression line fits the observed data) is measured by the coefficient of determination (R^2). The better the line fits the observed data points (i.e., the closer the observed data points are to the line), the closer R^2 will be to 1.00 — R^2s of 90-99% are considered very good.

If only one independent variable exists, the analysis is known as simple regression (as in the above example). **Multiple regression** consists of a functional relationship with multiple independent variables (e.g., cost may be a function of several variables).

4. **Correlation Analysis.** Correlation is the relationship between variables. If the variables move with each other, they have a direct relationship (positive correlation) as in A. If the variables move in opposite directions, they have an inverse relationship (negative correlation) as in B.

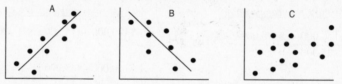

The degree and direction of correlation is measured from -1 to 1. The sign (negative or positive) describes whether the relationship is inverse or direct. The coefficient of correlation is measured by

$$\sqrt{\frac{\text{Amount of variation explained}}{\text{Total variation}}}$$

If all of the observations were in a straight line, all of the variation would be explained and the coefficient of correlation would be 1 or -1 depending upon whether the relationship is positive or negative. If there is no correlation, as in C above, the coefficient of correlation is 0.

Note that the coefficient of correlation is similar in concept to the coefficient of determination discussed above in "method of least squares." The coefficient of determination cannot have a negative value, as can the coefficient of correlation, because the coefficient of determination is based on squared deviations (i.e., if you square a negative number, the result is positive).

B. Cost-Volume-Profit (CVP) Analysis

1. **Overview**

   Cost-volume-profit (CVP) analysis provides management with profitability estimates at all levels of production in the relevant range (the normal operating range). CVP (or breakeven) analysis is based on the firm's profit function. Profit is a function of sales, variable costs, and fixed costs.

   Profit (NI) = Sales (S) –   Fixed Costs (FC) – Variable Costs (VC)
   When profit is zero   0 = S – FC – VC
                               S = FC + VC

   Fixed costs are constant in the relevant range, but both sales and variable costs are a function of the level of activity, and vary with respect to a single, output-related driver (e.g., units manufactured or sold). For example, if widgets are sold at $2.00/unit, variable costs are $.40/unit, and fixed costs are $20,000, breakeven is 12,500 units.

$$
\begin{aligned}
X &= \text{Units of production and sales to breakeven} \\
\$2.00X &= \$.40X + \$20,000 \\
\$1.60X &= \$20,000 \\
X &= 12,500 \text{ units (breakeven point)}
\end{aligned}
$$

The cost-volume-profit relationship is diagrammed below.

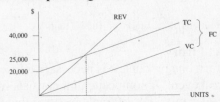

The breakeven point can be thought of as the amount of contribution margin (sales minus variable costs) required to cover the fixed costs, or the point of zero profit. In the previous example, the unit contribution margin (CM) is $1.60 ($2.00 – $.40). Thus, sales of 12,500 units are required to cover the $20,000 of fixed costs. This illustrates the possibility of two shortcut approaches.

Shortcut 1

$$
\text{Units to breakeven} = \frac{\text{Fixed costs}}{\text{Unit CM}} = \frac{\$20,000}{\$1.60} = 12,500 \text{ units}
$$

Shortcut 2

$$
\begin{aligned}
\text{Dollars to breakeven} &= \frac{\text{Fixed costs}}{\text{CM percentage (ratio)}} = \frac{\text{Fixed costs}}{\dfrac{\text{CM per unit}}{\text{Selling price per unit}}} = \frac{\$20,000}{\dfrac{\$1.60}{\$2.00}} = \frac{\$20,000}{80\%} = \$25,000 \text{ sales dollars}
\end{aligned}
$$

A number of variations on the basic CVP calculation are found on the CPA exam. These are illustrated in the following paragraphs:

a. **Target net income.** Selling price is $2, variable cost per unit is $.40, fixed costs are $20,000, and desired net income is $5,000. What is the level of sales in units?

Equation ⟶ Sales = VC + FC + NI
                $2X = $.4X + $20,000 + $5,000

Shortcut ⟶ $\dfrac{FC + NI}{CM} = \dfrac{\$20,000 + \$5,000}{\$1.60}$

Solution ⟶ 15,625 units

b. **Target net income-percentage of sales.** Same facts, except desired net income is 30% of sales. What is the level of sales in units?

Equation ⟶ Sales = VC + FC + NI
                $2X = $.4X + $20,000 + .30($2X)

Solution ⟶ 20,000 units

c. **No per-unit information given.** Fixed costs are $20,000, and variable expenses are 20% of sales. What is the breakeven level of sales in dollars?

Equation ⟶ Sales = VC + FC
                S = .2(S) + $20,000

Shortcut ⟶ $\dfrac{FC}{CM\%} = \dfrac{20,000}{.8}$

Solution ⟶ $25,000 sales dollars

d. **Decision making.** Selling price is $2, variable cost per unit is $.40, and fixed costs are $20,000. Purchasing a new machine will increase fixed costs by $5,000, but variable costs will be cut by 20%. If the selling price is cut by 10%, what is the breakeven point in units?

Equation $\longrightarrow$ Sales = VC + FC

$$\$1.8X = \$.32X + \$25,000$$

Shortcut $\longrightarrow$ $\dfrac{FC}{CM} = \dfrac{\$25,000}{\$1.48}$

Solution $\longrightarrow$ 16,892 units

2. **Breakeven: Multiproduct Firm**

   If a firm makes more than one product, it is necessary to use composite units to find the number of units of each product to breakeven. A composite unit consists of the proportionate number of units which make up the firm's sales mix. For example, assume that a firm has two products with the following selling prices and variable costs.

Product	*Selling price*	*Variable costs*	*Contribution margin*
A	$.60	$.20	$.40
B	$.40	$.15	$.25

   Also assume that the sales mix consists of 3 units of A for every 2 units of B (3:2) and fixed costs are $34,000.

   The **first** step is to find the composite contribution margin.

   Composite contribution margin = 3($.40) + 2($.25) = $1.70

   Next compute the number of composite units to breakeven.

   $$\frac{\$34,000 \text{ fixed costs}}{\$1.70 \text{ composite contribution margin}} = 20,000 \text{ composite units}$$

   Finally, determine the number of units of A and B at the breakeven point by multiplying the composite units by the number of units of A (i.e., 3) and the number of units of B (i.e., 2) in the mix.

   A: 20,000 x 3 = 60,000 units
   B: 20,000 x 2 = 40,000 units

3. **Assumptions of CVP Analysis**

   When applying CVP to a specific case and in interpreting the results therefrom, it is important to keep in mind the assumptions underlying CVP which are listed below.

   a. Selling price does not change with the activity level
   b. The sales mix remains constant
   c. Costs can be separated into fixed and variable elements
   d. Variable costs per unit are constant
   e. Total fixed costs are constant over the relevant range
   f. Productivity and efficiency are constant
   g. Units produced = Units sold

C. Variable (Direct) and Absorption (Full) Costing

Variable (direct) costing is a form of inventory costing. Variable costing considers fixed manufacturing costs as period rather than product costs. It is advocated because, for internal reporting, it presents a clear picture of performance when there is a significant change in inventory. However, remember that variable costing is not acceptable as GAAP for external reporting.

Variable and absorption costing methods of accounting for fixed manufacturing overhead differ: under variable costing, fixed manufacturing overhead is expensed whereas under absorption costing, such amounts are treated as a product cost and inventoried. The treatment of fixed manufacturing overhead often results in different levels of net income between the absorption and variable costing methods. The differences are timing differences, which result from recognizing the fixed manufacturing overhead as an expense.

1. In the period incurred—variable costing

2. In the period in which the units to which fixed overhead has been applied are sold—absorption costing

The relationship between variable costing (VC) income and absorption costing (AC) income follows:

Sales = Production (no change in inventory)	No difference in income
Sales > Production (inventory decreases)	VC income greater than AC income
Sales < Production (inventory increases)	VC income less than AC income

EXAMPLE: Production begins in period A with 5,000 units. Fixed manufacturing costs equal $5,000 and variable manufacturing costs are $1/unit. Sales were 4,000 units at $3/unit. In period B, units produced and production costs were the same as in period A. Sales were 6,000 units at $3/unit.

	Variable costing		Absorption costing	
	Period A	*Period B*	*Period A*	*Period B*
Sales	$12,000	$18,000	$12,000	$18,000
Less costs	9,000	11,000	8,000	12,000
Profit	$ 3,000	$ 7,000	$ 4,000	$ 6,000

*With absorption costing, $1 of fixed manufacturing overhead is attached to each unit produced ($5,000 ÷ 5,000 units). Notice that both variable and absorption costing recognized $10,000 profit in periods A + B. Variable costing income in period A was less than absorption income, because production exceeded sales which resulted in $1,000 of fixed costs being **inventoried** under AC that were **expensed** under VC.*

	Fixed costs expensed		Variable costs expensed		Total costs expensed	
	Period A	*Period B*	*Period A*	*Period B*	*Period A*	*Period B*
Variable	$5,000*	$5,000*	$4,000	$6,000	$9,000	$11,000
Absorption	4,000**	6,000**	4,000	6,000	8,000	12,000

* *The same every period.*
** *$1 per unit x number of units sold.*

The yearly income difference between the two methods can normally be reconciled as follows:

Change in inventory units x Fixed overhead per unit (e.g., 1,000 units x $1)

If the example above included either variable or fixed selling costs, they would be handled the same under either method—deducted in total on the income statement in the period in which they were incurred.

Note that the format of the income statement changes under variable costing to reflect the alternate treatment given to the fixed manufacturing costs and to emphasize the contribution margin. The recommended format under variable costing follows:

Sales
−   Variable manufacturing costs
=   Manufacturing contribution margin
−   Variable selling and administrative expenses
=   Contribution margin
−   Fixed manufacturing, selling, and administrative expenses
=   Net income

D. Budgeting

Budgeting is a plan of action for future operations. The most important functions of a budget are to coordinate the various functional activities of the firm and to provide a basis for control of the activities. Budgets may be prepared for all elements of the value chain, which includes R&D, design, production, marketing, distribution, customer service, and administration. The budget process begins with an estimate of sales and then proceeds systematically as outlined below.

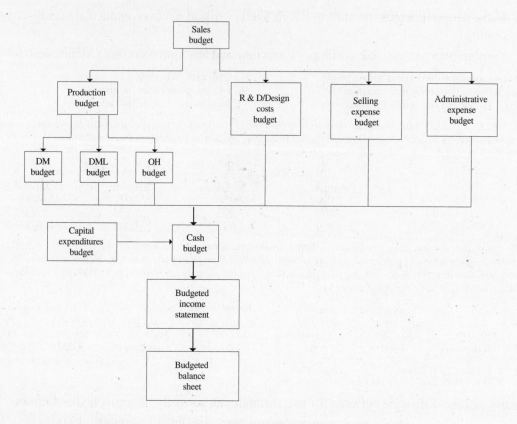

The basic formats of some of the key budgets are presented below.

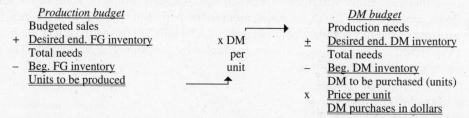

Note that before proceeding to the cash budget, DM purchases would have to be converted to **payments** for DM purchases, based on some payment schedule (e.g., 70% in month of purchase, 30% in month following).

Cash budget
    Beginning cash balance
\+   <u>Receipts</u> (collections from customers, etc.)
    Cash available
–   <u>Payments</u> (materials, expenses, payroll, etc.)
    Estimated cash balance before financing
\+/– <u>Financing</u> (planned borrowing or short-term investing to bring cash to desired balance)
=   <u>Ending cash balance</u>

To illustrate, Adams Company prepared the following cash budget for 2001.

Adams Company
CASH BUDGET
For Year Ending December 31, 2001

Cash balance, beginning		$ 15,000
Add receipts		
Collections from customers		723,000
Total cash available		$738,000
Less payments		
Direct materials	$184,000	
Other costs and expenses	126,000	
Payroll	395,000	
Income taxes	13,000	
Total cash needed		718,000
Estimated cash balance before financing		$ 20,000
Financing		
Borrowings	$25,000	
Repayments	(17,000)	
Interest payments	(1,600)	
Total effects of financing		6,400
Cash balance, ending		$ 26,400

Kaizan budgeting projects costs on the basis of improvements yet to be implemented rather than upon current conditions. The budget will not be achieved unless the improvements are actually made.

Activity-based budgeting (ABB) complements activity-based costing (ABC) by focusing on the costs of activities necessary for production and sales. In this approach, costs are segregated into homogeneous cost pools based upon cause-and-effect cost drivers. An ABB budget determines the costs of performing certain activities, in contrast to traditional budgeting which budgets costs for functional or spending categories.

E. Flexible Budgets

A flexible budget is a budget adjusted for changes in volume. In the planning phase, a flexible budget is used to compare the effects of various activity levels on costs and revenues. In the controlling phase, the flexible budget is used to help analyze actual results by comparing actual results with a flexible budget for the level of activity achieved in the period (see Module 36, Standards and Variances). Standard costing naturally complements flexible budgeting. However, even without standard costing, flexible budgeting can be used based upon actual costs and quantities of outputs (although lack of input data precludes computation of price and efficiency variances).

Presented below is a sample flexible budget for overhead costs.

FACTORY OVERHEAD
FLEXIBLE BUDGET

	18,000	20,000	22,000
Direct manufacturing labor hours			
Variable factory overhead			
Supplies	$ 18,000	$ 20,000	$ 22,000
Power	99,000	110,000	121,000
Idle time	3,600	4,000	4,400
Overtime premium	1,800	2,000	2,200
Total ($6.80 per DMLH)	$122,400	$136,000	$149,600
Fixed factory overhead			
Supervision	$ 15,000	$ 15,000	$ 15,000
Depreciation	32,000	32,000	32,000
Power	8,000	8,000	8,000
Property taxes	5,000	5,000	5,000
Insurance	1,500	1,500	1,500
Total	$ 61,500	$ 61,500	$ 61,500
Total overhead	$183,900	$197,500	$211,100

F. Responsibility Accounting

Responsibility accounting allocates those revenues and/or assets which a manager can control to that manager's responsibility center and holds the manager accountable for operating results. If a manager is only responsible for costs, his/her area of responsibility is called a **cost center**. Cost centers represent the most basic activities or responsibilities. Nonrevenue generating departments (purchasing and billing, for example) are usually organized as cost centers.

If the manager is responsible for both revenues and costs, his/her area of responsibility is called a **profit center**. A contribution income statement similar to the one shown below would be prepared for each profit center. Finally, if the manager is responsible for revenues, costs, and asset investment, his/her area of responsibility is called an **investment center**.

G. Segmented Reporting and Controllability

The variable costing income statement shown in Section C. Variable (Direct) and Absorption (Full) Costing can be broken into further detail to emphasize controllability.

1. Variable manufacturing costs are deducted from sales to obtain **manufacturing contribution margin**.
2. Variable selling and administrative expenses are deducted from manufacturing contribution margin to obtain **contribution margin**.
3. Fixed costs controllable by segment managers at various levels (e.g., division, department) are deducted from contribution margin to obtain the **controllable contribution** at that level.
4. Fixed costs controllable by others at various levels are deducted from controllable contribution to obtain the **segment contribution** at that level.
5. Costs common to all operations are finally deducted to obtain **income before taxes**.

EXAMPLE CONTRIBUTION APPROACH INCOME STATEMENT

	Total	*Segment 1*	*Segment 2*
Sales	*$600*	*$350*	*$250*
− *Variable manufacturing costs*	*220*	*115*	*105*
Manufacturing contribution margin	*380*	*235*	*145*
− *Variable selling and admin. exp.*	*100*	*70*	*30*
Contribution margin	*280*	*165*	*115*
− *Controllable, traceable fixed costs*	*80*	*35*	*45*
Controllable contribution	*200*	*130*	*70*
− *Uncontrollable, traceable fixed costs*	*90*	*60*	*30*
Segment contribution	*110*	*$ 70*	*$ 40*
− *Unallocable common costs*	*60**		
Income before taxes	*$ 50*		

* *Not allocated to any segment of the firm. Examples include corporate office salaries and advertising for firm name.*

Costs not controllable by a subdivision (cost or profit center) of a firm should not be allocated to the subdivision for evaluation or decision making purposes (see Section F. Responsibility Accounting).

Contribution margin data can be used in a variety of situations, including planning (CVP analysis) and decision making (which products to emphasize, which products should be retained and which should be eliminated, and so forth).

H. Performance Analysis

As entities become more decentralized, it becomes necessary to evaluate each department or division in terms of profitability. The most popular measure for analyzing the profitability of a division is **return on investment** (ROI). ROI measures the relationship between a division's profit and the capital invested in the division.

$$\text{ROI} = \text{Profit margin} \quad \times \quad \text{Capital turnover}$$

$$\text{ROI} = \frac{\text{Net income of division}}{\text{Sales of division}} \quad \times \quad \frac{\text{Sales of division}}{\text{Invested capital of division}}$$

$$\text{ROI} = \frac{\text{Net income of division}}{\text{Invested capital of division}}$$

A division may improve ROI by lowering its asset base while keeping income and sales constant, lowering expenses while keeping sales and assets constant, or increasing sales while keeping assets and net profit as a proportion of sales constant. Although ROI is quite popular as a performance evaluation measure, it can, at times, motivate a manager to reject a project which is profitable from the entire company's point of view, because it may lower the division's ROI and thus adversely affect the manager's performance evaluation.

EXAMPLE: Borke Company's cost of capital is 10%. One of Borke Company's division managers has the opportunity of investing in a project that will generate $45,000 of net income per year for eight years on an initial investment of $300,000. The division's current income is $250,000 from a total divisional asset base of $1,000,000. The manager should accept the *project since it offers a 15% return and the company's cost of capital is 10%. Chances are the manager will reject the project since it will lower the division current ROI from*

$$\frac{250,000}{1,000,000} \quad = \quad 25\% \quad to \quad \frac{250,000 + 45,000}{1,000,000 + 300,000} = 22.7\%$$

In this case the use of ROI has led to an incorrect decision.

An alternative method for evaluating divisional performance is the **residual income method**. Residual income is the net income of a division less the cost of capital on the division's assets. The division's residual income before the project would be [$250,000 – (.10 x $1,000,000)] = $150,000. Under the residual income approach a manager would be evaluated as to how well s/he maximizes dollars of residual income instead of maximizing a profit percentage. Using the example above, the manager would have accepted the project under consideration since it would raise his/her residual income by [$45,000 – (.10 x $300,000)] = $15,000 per year.

In addition to financial measures, a company may also use **nonfinancial performance measures** to monitor the organization's performance. These performance measures include production, marketing, or industry data which may be gathered at the customer/market level, the total organizational level, the individual facility level, or the individual activity level. Nonfinancial performance measures such as throughput time for products and machine set-up times are used heavily by operations managers in the day-to-day control of operations. Measures such as returns and allowances, customer complaints, on-time deliveries, and competitive rank may be used by engineering and operations managers in assessing product quality. Other nonfinancial performance measures include number of new product introductions, number of new patents filed, and product market share.

I.   Product and Service Pricing

Product pricing requires the use of judgment by the cost accountant and management to maximize the entity's profits and to increase shareholder wealth. To find the combination of sales price and volume yielding the greatest profits, management must make many assumptions regarding customer preferences, competitors' reactions, economic conditions, cost structures, etc. In maximizing shareholders' wealth, management must consider not only product costs but must also react to external changes, for example, a competitor's price on a relatively undifferentiated product. Additionally, management must consider the company's cost of capital in determining a desired **rate of return**. This rate of return represents the desired minimum markup on the cost of goods.

Costs are usually the starting point in determining prices. In the long run, all costs, including fixed costs, must be considered. However, decisions involving short-range pricing, such as a special order, may be evaluated on the basis of contribution margin. The **contribution margin approach** considers all relevant variable costs plus any additional fixed costs needed to sustain the new production level. Which costs are relevant is determined by analyzing how total costs of each component of the value chain will change if the order is accepted.

Cost-plus pricing is one model for the pricing decision; prices are set at variable costs plus a percentage markup, at full manufacturing or service cost plus a percentage markup, or at target ROI per unit. The percentage markup must cover fixed costs and profit (variable approach), operating expenses and a profit (full cost approach), or invested capital (target ROI approach). Consider the following example:

Annual sales—10,000 units		Invested capital—$100,000		Target ROI—15%
Manufacturing costs:			Operating costs:	
Fixed	$20,000		Fixed	$10,000
Variable	$3/unit		Variable	$2.50/unit

If price is set at total variable cost plus 60% ($5.50 x 160%), or full manufacturing cost plus 76% ($5.00 x 176%), the selling price would be $8.80. The selling price under the target ROI approach is calculated as follows:

Invested capital	$100,000
x Target ROI	x 15%
Total target ROI	$ 15,000
÷ Annual sales	÷ 10,000
Target oper. inc. per unit	$ 1.50
+ Cost base (total cost)	+ 8.50
Selling price	10.00

Note that the rate of markup ($1.50/$8.50 = 17.65%) has nothing to do with target ROI (15%), which expresses operating income as a percentage of **investment**.

Another alternative is **target pricing**, which sets prices at the amount that consumers are willing to pay based on their perceived value of the product or service. Based on targeted prices and income, a target cost is determined; the targeted cost is the estimated cost of the product or service that yields the targeted income at the target price. To meet target costs, a company must often improve its products or increase efficiency. **Value engineering** examines all components of the value chain to find opportunities for improvements and cost reduction. Activity-based costing helps to identify opportunities for cost reduction by improving specific activities.

Finally, the use of **standard costs** that are attainable eliminates the effect of unusual efficiency/inefficiency on price. Refer to Module 36 for a discussion of standard costs.

J. Transfer Pricing

Decentralization of profit or investment centers requires pricing policies for optional internal transfers of intermediate goods or services between those centers. The transfer price represents revenue to the selling subunit and cost to the purchasing subunit, which are included in the operating income of the divisions. The goal of transfer pricing is to provide autonomous segment managers with incentive to maximize profits of the company as a whole, not just the performance of their own divisions.

In theory, outlay cost plus opportunity cost should determine the transfer price. However, opportunity cost may be difficult or impossible to measure. Therefore, three transfer pricing alternatives exist: cost-based price, market price, and negotiated price. Transfer prices based on cost may consider variable manufacturing costs, total manufacturing (absorption) costs, or full product costs. Actual costs are unstable (vary seasonally, etc.) and allow the producing division to pass its inefficiencies to the buyer; thus, standard costs should be used. Any variances from standard affect the operating income of the selling division (cannot be passed on).

A transfer price based on **full cost** includes the transferring division's fixed costs (absorption costing). A problem with full cost transfer pricing is that special orders at below full cost but above variable cost may be rejected because they result in losses for the selling division even though the contribution to fixed costs benefits the company as a whole (suboptimization). Thus, the use of full cost for transfer pricing could lead to poor motivation and dysfunctional decision making.

A **full product cost** transfer price includes absorption manufacturing cost plus a share of other costs of the value chain, such as R&D or other administrative, selling, or general expenses.

A transfer price based on the **market price** of similar products or services is justified if a competitive market exists for the product/service. A market transfer price may also be based on the transferring division's price to outside customers. However, if any costs can be avoided by selling internally rather than externally (e.g., commissions, advertising) then the market price should be reduced by these cost savings. Market transfer prices are useful because they are objective, they avoid the need to define cost, and because they show each division's contribution to company profit.

Alternatively, two divisions may establish a **negotiated transfer price**. Cost and market price information may be useful in the bargaining process, but it is not required that the transfer price be specifically related to either. However the resulting transfer price should fall within a range limited by a ceiling and a floor. The ceiling, which is the lowest external market price, helps the purchasing subunit keep costs down. The floor equals the transferring division's outlay plus opportunity costs, so the seller can cover costs. The transfer price serves to divide this amount between the divisions involved, which affects divisional operating income and thus performance measurement and responsibility accounting.

To enhance cooperation between divisions, prevent suboptimization by managers, encourage the transferring division to maximize income, and provide the purchasing division with cost information relevant for short-term decision making, a **dual transfer pricing** system may be established. Here, transfers are recorded by the selling subunit at one price while the purchaser records the transfer at a different transfer price.

K. Inventory Models

1. Just-in-Time (JIT)

Just-in-time (JIT) is a demand-pull inventory system which may be applied to purchasing so that raw material arrives just as it is needed for production. JIT may also be applied to production so that each component of the completed good is produced only when needed by the next production step. And, finished goods are produced only when sales orders are received. The major features of JIT are described below.

Reduction of inventories, ideally to zero. Because of its non-value-added nature, inventory is regarded as undesirable. In a JIT system, vendors inspect their own goods and make frequent deliveries of materials, which are placed into production immediately upon receipt. This process eliminates the need for incoming inspection and the storeroom. In addition, since each component of the completed good is produced only as needed, work in process inventories are minimized.

Emphasis on solving production problems immediately. If it is discovered that parts are absent or defective, production is stopped until the problem is corrected. This practice contrasts with traditional systems, in which the production of defective products often continues because defective goods are sitting in inventory—awaiting sale and thus ultimate feedback from the customer. In a JIT system, each worker is responsible for the quality of his own work. Thus, JIT results in reductions in scrap and rework.

Emphasis on reducing production cycle time. Cycle time (throughput time) is the time required to complete a product from the start of its production until it is finished. Cycle time is reduced—keep in mind that everything is happening "just in time."

Focus on simplifying production activities. The goal of JIT is to identify and eliminate non-value-added activities. Less factory space is used for inventory storage and production activities, and materials handling between workstations is streamlined.

JIT may offer many advantages over traditional systems, including the following:

a. Lower investments in inventories and in space to store inventory.
b. Lower inventory carrying and handling costs.
c. Reduced risk of inventory obsolescence.
d. Reduced manufacturing costs.
e. The luxury of dealing with a reduced number (when compared with traditional systems) of reliable, quality-oriented suppliers.

2. **Economic Order Quantity**

How much to order? The amount to be ordered is known as the **economic order quantity** (EOQ). The EOQ minimizes the sum of the ordering and carrying costs. The total inventory cost function includes **carrying costs** (which increase with order size) and **ordering costs** (which decrease with order size). The EOQ formula is derived by setting the annual carrying costs equal to annual ordering cost or by differentiating the cost function with respect to order size.

$$EOQ = \sqrt{\frac{2aD}{k}}$$

A	=	cost of placing one order
D	=	annual demand in units
K	=	cost of carrying one unit of inventory for one year.

When to reorder? The objective is to order at a point in time so as to avoid **stockouts** but not so early that an excessive **safety stock** is maintained. Safety stocks may be used to guard against stockouts; they are maintained by increasing the lead time (the time that elapses from order placement until order arrival). Thus, safety stocks decrease stockout costs but increase carrying costs. Examples of these costs include

Carrying costs of safety stock (and inventory in general)		*Stockout costs*
1. Storage	1.	Profit on lost sales
2. Interest	2.	Customer ill will
3. Spoilage	3.	Idle equipment
4. Insurance	4.	Work stoppages
5. Property taxes		

The amount of safety stock held should minimize total stockout and carrying costs, as shown below.

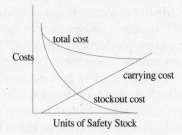

The most common approach to setting the optimum safety-stock level is to examine previous lead-time periods to determine the probabilities of running out of stock (a stockout) for different assessed levels of safety stock.

MULTIPLE-CHOICE QUESTIONS (1-57)

1. Day Mail Order Co. applied the high-low method of cost estimation to customer order data for the first four months of 2002. What is the estimated variable order filling cost component per order?

Month	Orders	Cost
January	1,200	$ 3,120
February	1,300	3,185
March	1,800	4,320
April	1,700	3,895
	6,000	$14,520

   a. $2.00
   b. $2.42
   c. $2.48
   d. $2.50

2. Sender, Inc. estimates parcel mailing costs using data shown on the chart below.

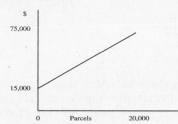

What is Sender's estimated cost for mailing 12,000 parcels?
   a. $36,000
   b. $45,000
   c. $51,000
   d. $60,000

3. Which of the following may be used to estimate how inventory warehouse costs are affected by both the number of shipments and the weight of materials handled?
   a. Economic order quantity analysis.
   b. Probability analysis.
   c. Correlation analysis.
   d. Multiple regression analysis.

4. Sago Co. uses regression analysis to develop a model for predicting overhead costs. Two different cost drivers (machine hours and direct materials weight) are under consideration as the independent variable. Relevant data were run on a computer using one of the standard regression programs, with the following results:

	Coefficient
Machine hours	
Y Intercept	2,500
B	5.0
$R^2 = .70$	
Direct materials weight	
Y Intercept	4,600
B	2.6
$R^2 = .50$	

What regression equation should be used?
   a. Y=2,500 + 5.0X
   b. Y=2,500 + 3.5X
   c. Y=4,600 + 2.6X
   d. Y=4,600 + 1.3X

5. Using regression analysis, Fairfield Co. graphed the following relationship of its cheapest product line's sales with its customers' income levels:

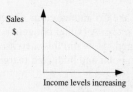

If there is a strong statistical relationship between the sales and customers' income levels, which of the following numbers best represents the correlation coefficient for this relationship?
   a. -9.00
   b. -0.93
   c. +0.93
   d. +9.00

6. At the breakeven point, the contribution margin equals total
   a. Variable costs.
   b. Sales revenues.
   c. Selling and administrative costs.
   d. Fixed costs.

7. The most likely strategy to reduce the breakeven point, would be to
   a. Increase both the fixed costs and the contribution margin.
   b. Decrease both the fixed costs and the contribution margin.
   c. Decrease the fixed costs and increase the contribution margin.
   d. Increase the fixed costs and decrease the contribution margin.

8. Del Co. has fixed costs of $100,000 and breakeven sales of $800,000. What is its projected profit at $1,200,000 sales?
   a. $ 50,000
   b. $150,000
   c. $200,000
   d. $400,000

9. During 2001, Thor Lab supplied hospitals with a comprehensive diagnostic kit for $120. At a volume of 80,000 kits, Thor had fixed costs of $1,000,000 and a profit before income taxes of $200,000. Due to an adverse legal decision, Thor's 2002 liability insurance increased by $1,200,000 over 2001. Assuming the volume and other costs are unchanged, what should the 2002 price be if Thor is to make the same $200,000 profit before income taxes?
   a. $120.00
   b. $135.00
   c. $150.00
   d. $240.00

10. Breakeven analysis assumes that over the relevant range
   a. Unit revenues are nonlinear.
   b. Unit variable costs are unchanged.
   c. Total costs are unchanged.
   d. Total fixed costs are nonlinear.

11. Product Cott has sales of $200,000, a contribution margin of 20%, and a margin of safety of $80,000. What is Cott's fixed cost?
   a. $16,000
   b. $24,000
   c. $80,000
   d. $96,000

12. On January 1, 2002, Lake Co. increased its direct manufacturing labor wage rates. All other budgeted costs and revenues were unchanged. How did this increase affect Lake's budgeted breakeven point and budgeted margin of safety?

	Budgeted Breakeven point	*Budgeted margin of safety*
a.	Increase	Increase
b.	Increase	Decrease
c.	Decrease	Decrease
d.	Decrease	Increase

Items 13 and 14 are based on the following:

The diagram below is a cost-volume-profit chart.

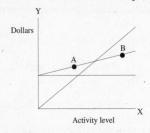

13. At point A compared to point B, as a percentage of sales revenues

	Variable costs are	*Fixed costs are*
a.	Greater	Greater
b.	Greater	The same
c.	The same	The same
d.	The same	Greater

14. If sales dollars are used to measure activity levels, total costs and total revenues may be read from the X and Y axis as follows:

	Total costs	*Total revenues*
a.	X or Y	X or Y
b.	X or Y	X only
c.	Y only	X or Y
d.	Y only	X only

15. In the profit-volume chart below, EF and GH represent the profit-volume graphs of a single-product company for 2001 and 2002, respectively.

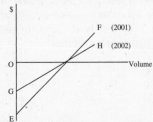

If 2001 and 2002 unit sales prices are identical, how did total fixed costs and unit variable costs of 2002 change compared to 2001?

	2002 total fixed costs	*2002 unit variable costs*
a.	Decreased	Increased
b.	Decreased	Decreased
c.	Increased	Increased
d.	Increased	Decreased

16. Thomas Company sells products X, Y, and Z. Thomas sells three units of X for each unit of Z, and two units of Y for each unit of X. The contribution margins are $1.00 per unit of X, $1.50 per unit of Y, and $3.00 per unit of Z. Fixed costs are $600,000. How many units of X would Thomas sell at the breakeven point?

  a.   40,000
  b.   120,000
  c.   360,000
  d.   400,000

17. In calculating the breakeven point for a multi-product company, which of the following assumptions are commonly made when variable costing is used?

  I.   Sales volume equals production volume.
  II.   Variable costs are constant per unit.
  III.   A given sales mix is maintained for all volume changes.

  a.   I and II.
  b.   I and III.
  c.   II and III.
  d.   I, II, and III.

18. In the budgeted profit/volume chart below, EG represents a two-product company's profit path. EH and HG represent the profit paths of products #1 and #2, respectively.

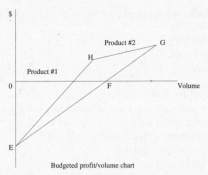

Budgeted profit/volume chart

Sales prices and cost behavior were as budgeted, actual total sales equaled budgeted sales, and there were no inventories. Actual profit was greater than budgeted profit. Which product had actual sales in excess of budget, and what margin does OE divided by OF represent?

	Product with excess sales	*OE/OF*
a.	#1	Contribution margin
b.	#1	Gross margin
c.	#2	Contribution margin
d.	#2	Gross margin

19. In its first year of operations, Magna Manufacturers had the following costs when it produced 100,000 and sold 80,000 units of its only product:

Manufacturing costs	Fixed	$180,000
	Variable	160,000
Selling and admin. costs	Fixed	90,000
	Variable	40,000

How much lower would Magna's net income be if it used variable costing instead of full absorption costing?

  a. $36,000
  b. $54,000
  c. $68,000
  d. $94,000

20. Using the variable costing method, which of the following costs are assigned to inventory?

	Variable selling and administrative costs	Variable factory overhead costs
a.	Yes	Yes
b.	Yes	No
c.	No	No
d.	No	Yes

21. At the end of Killo Co.'s first year of operations, 1,000 units of inventory remained on hand. Variable and fixed manufacturing costs per unit were $90 and $20, respectively. If Killo uses absorption costing rather than variable (direct) costing, the result would be a higher pretax income of
- a. $0
- b. $20,000
- c. $70,000
- d. $90,000

22. A manufacturing company prepares income statements using both absorption and variable costing methods. At the end of a period actual sales revenues, total gross profit, and total contribution margin approximated budgeted figures, whereas net income was substantially greater than the budgeted amount. There were no beginning or ending inventories. The most likely explanation of the net income increase is that, compared to budget, actual
- a. Manufacturing fixed costs had increased.
- b. Selling and administrative fixed expenses had decreased.
- c. Sales prices and variable costs had increased proportionately.
- d. Sales prices had declined proportionately less than variable costs.

23. A single-product company prepares income statements using both absorption and variable costing methods. Manufacturing overhead cost applied per unit produced in 2002 was the same as in 2001. The 2002 variable costing statement reported a profit whereas the 2002 absorption costing statement reported a loss. The difference in reported income could be explained by units produced in 2002 being
- a. Less than units sold in 2002.
- b. Less than the activity level used for allocating overhead to the product.
- c. In excess of the activity level used for allocating overhead to the product.
- d. In excess of units sold in 2002.

24. Mien Co. is budgeting sales of 53,000 units of product Nous for October 2002. The manufacture of one unit of Nous requires four kilos of chemical Loire. During October 2002, Mien plans to reduce the inventory of Loire by 50,000 kilos and increase the finished goods inventory of Nous by 6,000 units. There is no Nous work in process inventory. How many kilos of Loire is Mien budgeting to purchase in October 2002?
- a. 138,000
- b. 162,000
- c. 186,000
- d. 238,000

25. Rolling Wheels purchases bicycle components in the month prior to assembling them into bicycles. Assembly is scheduled one month prior to budgeted sales. Rolling pays 75% of component costs in the month of purchase and 25%

of the costs in the following month. Component cost included in budgeted cost of sales are

April	May	June	July	August
$5,000	$6,000	$7,000	$8,000	$8,000

What is Rolling's budgeted cash payment for components in May?
- a. $5,750
- b. $6,750
- c. $7,750
- d. $8,000

26. A 2002 cash budget is being prepared for the purchase of Toyi, a merchandise item. Budgeted data are

Cost of goods sold for 2002	$300,000
Accounts payable 1/1/02	20,000
Inventory—1/1/02	30,000
12/31/02	42,000

Purchases will be made in twelve equal monthly amounts and paid for in the following month. What is the 2002 budgeted cash payment for purchases of Toyi?
- a. $295,000
- b. $300,000
- c. $306,000
- d. $312,000

27. Cook Co.'s total costs of operating five sales offices last year were $500,000, of which $70,000 represented fixed costs. Cook has determined that total costs are significantly influenced by the number of sales offices operated. Last year's costs and number of sales offices can be used as the bases for predicting annual costs. What would be the budgeted costs for the coming year if Cook were to operate seven sales offices?
- a. $700,000
- b. $672,000
- c. $614,000
- d. $586,000

28. The basic difference between a master budget and a flexible budget is that a master budget is
- a. Only used before and during the budget period and a flexible budget is only used after the budget period.
- b. For an entire production facility and a flexible budget is applicable to single departments only.
- c. Based on one specific level of production and a flexible budget can be prepared for any production level within a relevant range.
- d. Based on a fixed standard and a flexible budget allows management latitude in meeting goals.

29. A flexible budget is appropriate for a

	Marketing budget	Direct material usage budget
a.	No	No
b.	No	Yes
c.	Yes	Yes
d.	Yes	No

30. When production levels are expected to increase within a relevant range, and a flexible budget is used, what effect would be anticipated with respect to each of the following costs?

	Fixed costs per unit	Variable costs per unit
a.	Decrease	Decrease
b.	No change	No change
c.	No change	Decrease
d.	Decrease	No change

31. Controllable revenue would be included in a performance report for a

	Profit center	Cost center
a.	No	No
b.	No	Yes
c.	Yes	No
d.	Yes	Yes

32. The following is a summarized income statement of Carr Co.'s profit center No. 43 for March 2002:

Contribution margin		$70,000
Period expenses:		
Manager's salary	$20,000	
Facility depreciation	8,000	
Corporate expense allocation	5,000	33,000
Profit center income		$37,000

Which of the following amounts would most likely be subject to the control of the profit center's manager?
- a. $70,000
- b. $50,000
- c. $37,000
- d. $33,000

33. Wages earned by machine operators in producing the firm's product should be categorized as

	Direct labor	Controllable by the machine operators' foreman
a.	Yes	Yes
b.	Yes	No
c.	No	Yes
d.	No	No

34. The following information pertains to Bala Co. for the year ended December 31, 2002:

Sales	$600,000
Net income	100,000
Capital investment	400,000

Which of the following equations should be used to compute Bala's return on investment?
- a. $(4/6) \times (6/1) = ROI$
- b. $(6/4) \times (1/6) = ROI$
- c. $(4/6) \times (1/6) = ROI$
- d. $(6/4) \times (6/1) = ROI$

35. Select Co. had the following 2002 financial statement relationships:

Asset turnover	5
Profit margin on sales	0.02

What was Select's 2002 percentage return on assets?
- a. 0.1%
- b. 0.4%
- c. 2.5%
- d. 10.0%

36. The following selected data pertain to the Darwin Division of Beagle Co. for 2002:

Sales	$400,000
Operating income	40,000
Capital turnover	4
Imputed interest rate	10%

What was Darwin's 2001 residual income?
- a. $0
- b. $ 4,000
- c. $10,000
- d. $30,000

37. Division A is considering a project that will earn a rate of return which is greater than the imputed interest charge for invested capital, but less than the division's historical return on invested capital. Division B is considering a project that will earn a rate of return that is greater than the division's historical return on invested capital, but less than the imputed interest charge for invested capital. If the objective is to maximize residual income, should these divisions accept or reject their projects?

	A	B
a.	Accept	Accept
b.	Reject	Accept
c.	Reject	Reject
d.	Accept	Reject

38. Which combination of changes in asset turnover and income as a percentage of sales will maximize the return on investment?

	Asset turnover	Income as a percentage of sales
a.	Increase	Decrease
b.	Increase	Increase
c.	Decrease	Increase
d.	Decrease	Decrease

39. Which measures would be useful in evaluating the performance of a manufacturing system?

  I. Throughput time.
 II. Total setup time for machines/Total production time.
III. Number of rework units/Total number of units completed.

- a. I and II only.
- b. II and III only.
- c. I and III only.
- d. I, II, and III.

40. Cuff Caterers quotes a price of $60 per person for a dinner party. This price includes the 6% sales tax and the 15% service charge. Sales tax is computed on the food plus the service charge. The service charge is computed on the food only. At what amount does Cuff price the food?
- a. $56.40
- b. $51.00
- c. $49.22
- d. $47.40

41. Based on potential sales of 500 units per year, a new product has estimated traceable costs of $990,000. What is the target price to obtain a 15% profit margin on sales?
- a. $2,329
- b. $2,277
- c. $1,980
- d. $1,935

42. Briar Co. signed a government construction contract providing for a formula price of actual cost plus 10%. In addition, Briar was to receive one-half of any savings resulting from the formula price being less than the target price of $2,200,000. Briar's actual costs incurred were $1,920,000. How much should Briar receive from the contract?

    a. $2,060,000
    b. $2,112,000
    c. $2,156,000
    d. $2,200,000

43. Vince, Inc. has developed and patented a new laser disc reading device that will be marketed internationally. Which of the following factors should Vince consider in pricing the device?

  I. Quality of the new device.
  II. Life of the new device.
  III. Customers' relative preference for quality compared to price.

    a. I and II only.
    b. I and III only.
    c. II and III only.
    d. I, II, and III.

44. The budget for Klunker Auto Repair Shop for the year is as follows:

Direct labor per hour	$ 30
Total labor hours	10,000
Overhead costs:	
Materials handling and storage	$ 10,000
Other (rent, utilities, depreciation, insurance)	$120,000
Direct materials cost	$500,000

Klunker allocates materials handling and storage costs per dollar of direct materials cost. Other overhead is allocated based on total labor hours. In addition, Klunker adds a charge of $8 per labor hour to cover profit margin. Tardy Trucking Co. has brought one of its trucks to Klunker for an engine overhaul. If the overhaul requires twelve labor hours and $800 parts, what price should Klunker charge Tardy for these repair services?

    a. $1,160
    b. $1,256
    c. $1,416
    d. $1,472

45. Ajax Division of Carlyle Corporation produces electric motors, 20% of which are sold to Bradley Division of Carlyle and the remainder to outside customers. Carlyle treats its divisions as profit centers and allows division managers to choose their sources of sale and supply. Corporate policy requires that all interdivisional sales and purchases be recorded at variable cost as a transfer price. Ajax Division's estimated sales and standard cost data for the year ending December 31, 2002, based on the full capacity of 100,000 units, are as follows:

	Bradley	Outsiders
Sales	$ 900,000	$ 8,000,000
Variable costs	(900,000)	(3,600,000)
Fixed costs	(300,000)	(1,200,000)
Gross margin	$(300,000)	$ 3,200,000
Unit sales	20,000	80,000

Ajax has an opportunity to sell the above 20,000 units to an outside customer at a price of $75 per unit during 2001 on a continuing basis. Bradley can purchase its requirements from an outside supplier at a price of $85 per unit.

Assuming that Ajax Division desires to maximize its gross margin, should Ajax take on the new customer and drop its sales to Bradley for 2001, and why?

    a. No, because the gross margin of the corporation as a whole would decrease by $200,000.
    b. Yes, because Ajax Division's gross margin would increase by $300,000.
    c. Yes, because Ajax Division's gross margin would increase by $600,000.
    d. No, because Bradley Division's gross margin would decrease by $800,000.

46. The management of James Corporation has decided to implement a transfer pricing system. James' MIS department is currently negotiating a transfer price for its services with the four producing divisions of the company as well as the marketing department. Charges will be assessed based on number of reports (assume that all reports require the same amount of time and resources to produce). The cost to operate the MIS department at its full capacity of 1,000 reports per year is budgeted at $45,000. The user subunits expect to request 250 reports each this year. The cost of temporary labor and additional facilities used to produce reports beyond capacity is budgeted at $48.00 per report. James could purchase the same services from an external Information Services firm for $70,000. What amounts should be used as the ceiling and the floor in determining the negotiated transfer price?

    a. Floor, $36.00; Ceiling $56.00.
    b. Floor, $45.60; Ceiling $56.00.
    c. Floor, $48.00; Ceiling $70.00.
    d. Floor, $57.00; Ceiling $82.00.

47. Which of the following statements regarding transfer pricing is false?

    a. When idle capacity exists, there is no opportunity cost to producing intermediate products for another division.
    b. Market-based transfer prices should be reduced by any costs avoided by selling internally rather than externally.
    c. No contribution margin is generated by the transferring division when variable cost-based transfer prices are used.
    d. The goal of transfer pricing is to provide segment managers with incentive to maximize the profits of their divisions.

48. Which changes in costs are most conducive to switching from a traditional inventory ordering system to a just-in-time ordering system?

	Cost per purchase order	Inventory unit carrying costs
a.	Increasing	Increasing
b.	Decreasing	Increasing
c.	Decreasing	Decreasing
d.	Increasing	Decreasing

49. To determine the inventory reorder point, calculations normally include the

    a. Ordering cost.
    b. Carrying cost.
    c. Average daily usage.
    d. Economic order quantity.

50. In Belk Co.'s just-in-time production system, costs per set-up were reduced from $28 to $2. In the process of reducing inventory levels, Belk found that there were fixed facility and administrative costs that previously had not been included in the carrying cost calculation. The result was an increase from $8 to $32 per unit per year. What were the effects of these changes on Belk's economic lot size and relevant costs?

	Lot size	*Relevant costs*
a.	Decrease	Increase
b.	Increase	Decrease
c.	Increase	Increase
d.	Decrease	Decrease

51. The benefits of a just-in-time system for raw materials usually include
- a. Elimination of non-value-added operations.
- b. Increase in the number of suppliers, thereby ensuring competitive bidding.
- c. Maximization of the standard delivery quantity, thereby lessening the paperwork for each delivery.
- d. Decrease in the number of deliveries required to maintain production.

52. Bell Co. changed from a traditional manufacturing philosophy to a just-in-time philosophy. What are the expected effects of this change on Bell's inventory turnover and inventory as a percentage of total assets reported on Bell's balance sheet?

	Inventory turnover	*Inventory percentage*
a.	Decrease	Decrease
b.	Decrease	Increase
c.	Increase	Decrease
d.	Increase	Increase

53. Which of the following is **not** a typical characteristic of a just-in-time (JIT) production environment?
- a. Lot sizes equal to one.
- b. Insignificant setup times and costs.
- c. Push-through system.
- d. Balanced and level workloads.

54. As a consequence of finding a more dependable supplier, Dee Co. reduced its safety stock of raw materials by 80%. What is the effect of this safety stock reduction on Dee's economic order quantity?
- a. 80% decrease.
- b. 64% decrease.
- c. 20% increase.
- d. No effect.

55. The economic order quantity formula assumes that
- a. Periodic demand for the good is known.
- b. Carrying costs per unit vary with quantity ordered.
- c. Costs of placing an order vary with quantity ordered.
- d. Purchase costs per unit differ due to quantity discounts.

56. Ral Co. sells 20,000 radios evenly throughout the year. The cost of carrying one unit in inventory for one year is $8, and the purchase order cost per order is $32. What is the economic order quantity?
- a. 625
- b. 400

- c. 283
- d. 200

57. The following information pertains to material X which is used by Sage Co.:

Annual usage in units	20,000
Working days per year	250
Safety stock in units	800
Normal lead time in working days	30

Units of material X will be required evenly throughout the year. The order point is
- a. 800
- b. 1,600
- c. 2,400
- d. 3,200

OTHER OBJECTIVE QUESTIONS

Problem 1   (15 to 20 minutes)

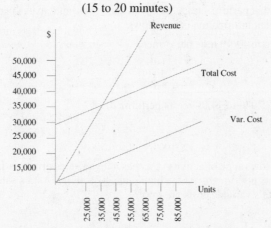

Above is a cost-volume-profit relationship diagram. The contribution margin is 67%.

Required:

For **questions 1 through 3,** a numerical answer is required. The candidate would select an answer from a list of numbers.

1. Breakeven in units from the graph.
2. Fixed costs from the graph.
3. If target NI is $10,000, what is the desired sales level in dollars (rounded to nearest $100)?

For the following assumptions of any CVP analysis, indicate whether the assumption as stated is true or false.

4. Costs cannot be separated into variable and fixed elements.
5. Variable cost per unit decreases as output increases.
6. Selling price will need to change with the activity level.
7. Productivity and efficiency are constant.
8. Labor is the only factor that causes changes in cost.
9. Units produced equals units sold in a given period.
10. Fixed cost per unit remains constant over a relevant range.

Problem 2   (5-10 minutes)

The following information pertains to a product for a ten-week budget period:

• Sales price	$11 per unit	• Manufacturing and sales of 70,000 units are expected to occur evenly over the period.
• Materials	$3 per unit	
• Manufacturing conversion costs—		• Materials are paid for in the week following use.
Fixed	$210,000	• There are no beginning inventories.
Variable	$2 per unit	
• Selling and administrative costs—		
Fixed	$45,000	
Variable	$1 per unit	
• Beginning accounts payable for materials	$40,000	

Required:

For **items 1 through 5,** determine the correct amount using the above information. Any information contained in an item is unique to that item and is **not** to be incorporated in your calculations when answering other items. Since a numerical answer is required, the candidate would be given a list of numbers to choose from.

1. What amount should be budgeted for cash payments to material suppliers during the period?
2. Using variable costing, what is the budgeted income for the period?
3. Using absorption costing, what is the budgeted income for the period?
4. Actual results are as budgeted, except that only 60,000 of the 70,000 units produced were sold. Using absorption costing, what is the difference between the reported income and the budgeted net income?
5. If a special order for 4,000 units would cause the loss of 1,000 regular sales, what minimum amount of revenue must be generated from the special order so that net income is not reduced? (All cost relationships are unchanged.)

Problem 3   (40 to 50 minutes)

Asta, Inc. is a medical laboratory that performs tests for physicians. Asta anticipates performing between 5,000 and 12,000 tests during the month of April. Relevant information is as follows:

At the low range of activity (0 to 4,999 tests performed)

Sales price per test	$ 60
Variable costs per test	20
Fixed costs	160,000

At the high range of activity (5,000 to 14,999 tests performed)

Sales price per test	$ 60
Variable costs per test	20
Fixed costs	200,000

Compared to industry averages, at the low range of activity Asta has a lower sales price per test, higher fixed costs, and the same breakeven point in number of tests performed. At the high range of activity, Asta's sales price per test and fixed costs are the same as industry averages, and Asta's variable costs are lower.

Required:

Part a.

Items 1 through 8. Items 1 through 8 represent costs incurred by Asta. The following two responses are required for each item:

(1) Determine how the cost should be categorized from the list below.

> ### *Categories*
>
> A.   Direct materials cost.
> B.   Direct manufacturing labor cost.
> C.   Overhead cost for testing.
> D.   General and administrative cost.

(2) Indicate (F) if the cost is fixed or (V) if the cost is variable.

Items to be answered

1. Office manager's salary.

2. Cost of electricity to run laboratory equipment.

3. Hourly wages of part-time technicians who perform tests.

4. Cost of lubricant used on laboratory equipment.

5. Cost of distilled water used in tests.

6. Accelerated depreciation on laboratory equipment.

7. Straight-line depreciation on laboratory building.

8. Cost of expensive binders in which test results are given to physicians.

Part b.

Items 9 through 12. Items 9 through 12 require numeric responses. For each item, calculate the numeric amount.

Items to be answered

9. Contribution margin per test.

10. Breakeven point in number of tests at low activity range.

11. Breakeven point in number of tests at high activity range.

12. Number of units sold to achieve a gross profit of $160,000.

Part c.

Items 13 through 15. Items 13 through 15 refer to Asta's costs in comparison to industry averages. For each item, indicate (G) if Asta's costs are greater than the industry average, (L) if Asta's costs are lesser than the industry average, or (S) if Asta's costs are the same as the industry average.

Items to be answered

13. Variable costs at low activity range.

14. Contribution margin at high activity range.

15. Breakeven point at high activity range.

MULTIPLE-CHOICE ANSWERS

1. a __ __	13. d __ __	25. c __ __	37. d __ __	49. c. __ __
2. c __ __	14. c __ __	26. c __ __	38. b __ __	50. d __ __
3. d __ __	15. a __ __	27. b __ __	39. d __ __	51. a __ __
4. a __ __	16. b __ __	28. c __ __	40. c __ __	52. c __ __
5. b __ __	17. c __ __	29. c __ __	41. a __ __	53. c __ __
6. d __ __	18. a __ __	30. d __ __	42. c __ __	54. d __ __
7. c __ __	19. a __ __	31. c __ __	43. d __ __	55. a __ __
8. a __ __	20. d __ __	32. a __ __	44. c __ __	56. b __ __
9. b __ __	21. b __ __	33. a __ __	45. c __ __	57. d __ __
10. b __ __	22. b __ __	34. b __ __	46. b __ __	
11. b __ __	23. a __ __	35. d __ __	47. d __ __	1st: __/57 = __%
12. b __ __	24. c __ __	36. d __ __	48. b __ __	2nd: __/57 = __%

MULTIPLE-CHOICE ANSWER EXPLANATIONS

A. Analyzing Cost Behavior

1. **(a)** The requirement is to determine the variable component of order filling cost per order. The high-low method of analysis should be used to separate the mixed cost into its fixed and variable components. The formula used in developing the variable rate is

$$\frac{\text{Cost at high point} - \text{Cost at low point}}{\text{High activity point} - \text{Low activity point}} = \text{Variable rate}$$

In this problem, order filling costs are given at four levels of activity because the number of order was different in each month. Substituting the highest and lowest cost ($4,320 and $3,120) and activity (1,800 and 1,200) figures into the formula yields the variable cost of order filling per order.

$$\frac{\$4,320 - \$3,120}{1,800 - 1,200} = \$2.00/\text{order}$$

2. **(c)** The graph depicts Sender's fixed and variable parcel mailing costs. Fixed costs total $15,000, since this amount of cost is incurred even when zero parcels are mailed. Variable costs at a mailing volume of 20,000 parcels is $60,000 ($75,000 total cost – $15,000 fixed cost), resulting in a per unit variable cost of $3.00 ($60,000 VC / 20,000 units). Therefore, Sender's estimated cost of mailing 12,000 parcels is $51,000 [$15,000 FC + ($3 VC x 12,000 units)].

3. **(d)** Regression analysis determines the functional relationship between variables and provides a measure of probable error. Multiple regression analysis involves the use of two or more independent variables (such as the number of shipments and the weight of materials handled) to predict one dependent variable (inventory warehouse costs). Economic order quantity analysis determines the amount to be ordered while minimizing the sum of ordering and carrying costs. Probability analysis is an application of statistical decision theory that, under conditions of uncertainty, leads to more reliable decisions. Correlation analysis determines the relationship between variables. The degree and direction of correlation is measured on a 1-to-1 basis.

4. **(a)** The determination that needs to be made is which of the cost drivers would be the best predictor of overhead costs (machine hours or direct materials weight). The information given regarding the coefficient of determination (R^2) measures the correlation between the cost driver and overhead costs. The higher the R^2, the better the corre-

lation. Therefore, machine hours would be the more accurate cost driver.

5. **(b)** The correlation coefficient is a relative measure of the relationship between two variables. The range of the correlation coefficient is from -1 (perfect negative correlation) to +1 (perfect positive correlation). A correlation coefficient of zero means that there is **no** correlation between the two variables. Since the level of sales **increases** as the level of income **decreases**, this relationship represents a strong **negative** correlation. Answer (c) is incorrect because it represents a **positive** correlation. Answers (a) and (d) are incorrect because they lie outside of the range for correlation coefficients.

B. Cost-Volume-Profit (CVP) Analysis

6. **(d)** Any income statement can be expressed as

Sales – Variable costs – Fixed costs = Operating income

At the breakeven point, operating income = $0. In addition, the Contribution margin = Sales – Variable costs. Therefore, the above equation may be restated as

Sales – Variable costs – Fixed costs = 0
Sales – Variable costs = Fixed costs
Contribution margin = Fixed costs

This makes sense because, by definition, the breakeven point is the point at which revenues equal expenses; after variable costs are subtracted from sales, the contribution margin remaining will be just enough to cover fixed costs.

7. **(c)** The short-cut breakeven point formula is calculated as follows:

$$\frac{\text{Breakeven}}{\text{(units)}} = \frac{\text{Fixed costs}}{\text{Contribution margin}}$$

Thus, by decreasing the numerator (fixed costs) and increasing the denominator (contribution margin), the breakeven point will be reduced.

8. **(a)** The solutions approach is to work backward from breakeven sales to determine the contribution margin (CM) ratio. The CM ratio can then be used to determine Del's projected profit at $1,200,000 sales. This is accomplished by plugging fixed costs and breakeven sales into the breakeven equation.

$$\text{Breakeven sales} = \frac{\text{Fixed costs}}{\text{CM ratio}}$$

$$\$800{,}000 = \frac{\$100{,}000}{\text{CM ratio}}$$

$$\text{CM ratio} = 0.125, \text{ or } 12.5\%$$

Therefore, projected total contribution margin from $1,200,000 sales is $150,000 ($1,200,000 x 12.5%), and projected profit is $50,000 ($150,000 CM − $100,000 fixed costs).

9. **(b)** The requirement is to determine the price that Thor Lab should charge to make the same profit with increased fixed costs. The first step in solving this problem is to calculate the variable cost per unit. The variable cost component is determined as follows:

Sales	−	VC	−	FC	=	Profit
(80,000 x $120)	−	(80,000x)	−	$1,000,000	=	$200,000
$9,600,000	−	80,000x	−	$1,000,000	=	$200,000
				$8,400,000	=	80,000x
				$105	=	x

The next step is to substitute the variable cost component and the increased fixed cost amount into the above equation to determine the necessary price. The price can be computed as follows:

$$80{,}000x - (80{,}000 \times \$105) - \$2{,}200{,}000 = \$200{,}000$$
$$80{,}000x = \$10{,}800{,}000$$
$$x = \$135$$

10. **(b)** Breakeven analysis is based on several simplified assumptions. One assumption is that, over the relevant range, variable costs **per unit** remain unchanged. It is assumed that over the relevant range, selling price per unit remains constant. Thus, unit revenues are linear. Total variable costs increase with increases in production; therefore, total costs also increase. Over the relevant range, total fixed costs are always linear since they do not change.

11. **(b)** The requirement is to determine Cott's fixed cost using only sales, contribution margin, and margin of safety. First, Cott's breakeven sales should be determined. Since the margin of safety defines how far revenues can fall before the breakeven point is reached, breakeven sales equal $120,000 ($200,000 sales − $80,000 margin of safety). We also know that Cott's contribution margin is 20% of sales. Contribution margin (CM) equals sales minus all related variable costs (VC), and the contribution margin percentage is calculated as

$$CM\% = \frac{\text{Total CM}}{\text{Revenues}}$$

Or, in this case,

$$20\% = \frac{\text{Total CM}}{\$120{,}000}$$

Total CM at breakeven = ($120,000) (20%) = $24,000

At the breakeven point, no profit exists and Sales − VC = FC. Therefore, the CM at the breakeven point equals fixed costs, and Cott's fixed costs total $24,000.

12. **(b)** The budgeted breakeven point is the volume at which total revenues equal total expenses. An increase in direct manufacturing labor wage rates would result in higher variable expenses and a lower contribution per unit. Accordingly, this **increases** the volume of sales necessary to breakeven. The budgeted margin of safety is the excess of budgeted total revenues minus total revenues at the break-even point. As discussed above, the increase in direct manufacturing labor wages increased the breakeven point. This higher breakeven point **decreases** the budgeted margin of safety.

13. **(d)** To answer this question, an understanding of cost behavior patterns and CVP charts is needed. The CVP chart presented in the problem can be interpreted as follows:

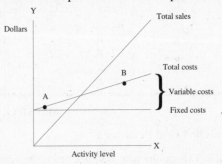

Within a relevant range, **total** variable costs vary directly with the number of units produced and sold. Because these costs remain constant per unit, the variable costs associated with point A and point B will be the same percentage of total sales associated with each point. Total fixed costs remain constant in total at any activity level. Because these costs are allocated evenly to units produced and sold, they represent a higher percentage of lower sales than of higher sales. Point A is to the left of point B, indicating a lower sales level for point A. The fixed costs will, therefore, be a greater percentage of sales at point A than at point B.

14. **(c)** If sales dollars are used to measure activity levels, the various activity levels on the X axis would be expressed in terms of sales. Total costs could be read by comparing a point on the total cost line to the Y axis only, because total costs are a dependent variable, which are measured on the Y axis. Total revenues could be read by comparing a point on the total sales line to either the Y axis or the X axis.

15. **(a)** The profit-volume (P/V) chart provides a quick condensed comparison of how alternatives for pricing, variable costs, and/or fixed costs may affect net income as volume levels change. In this problem, sales prices remain constant and, therefore, are not relevant. In a P/V chart, the vertical (Y) axis represents net income/loss in dollars. The horizontal (X) axis represents volume in units or dollars. Points on the Y axis above the intersection with the X axis represent profits while points below the intersection represent losses. Total fixed costs are represented by the point at which a specific P/V line intersects the Y axis. This point is always below zero on the Y axis. Because point G (where the P/V line for 2002 intersects the Y axis) is closer to zero than point E (where the P/V line for 2001 intersects the Y axis), point G is less negative; therefore, total fixed costs decreased from 2001 levels. The effect of total variable costs on net income is represented by the positive slope of a P/V line. Variable costs stay the same per unit but change in total as volume levels change. Therefore, a higher per unit amount of variable costs causes a lower per unit amount of net income across various volume levels. Because the graph represents changes in levels of totals, a steeper P/V line slope indicates more profit per unit. Because the slope of line GH (the P/V line for 2002) is **less** steep than the slope of line EF (the P/V line for 2001), net income per unit is less in

2002 than in 2001. Variable costs, therefore, rose between 2001 and 2002.

B.2. Breakeven: Multiproduct Firm

16. (b) The requirement is to determine how many units of product X (one of three products) Thomas would sell at the breakeven point. The solutions approach is first to find the number of composite units to breakeven; a composite unit consists of the number of units of each of the three products in the mix. Since Thomas sells three units of X for each unit of Z and two units of Y for each unit of X, they are selling six units of Y for each unit of Z; therefore, a composite unit consists of 3X, 6Y, and 1Z. The total contribution margin for one composite unit is

X (3) ($1.00)	=	$ 3	
Y (6) ($1.50)	=	$ 9	
Z (1) ($3.00)	=	$ 3	
		$15	

The breakeven point in terms of units of the product mix group is

$600,000 ÷ $15 = 40,000 composite units

Since there are three units of X in each composite unit, (40,000) (3) or 120,000 units of X are sold at breakeven.

17. (c) Breakeven analysis is based upon several simplified assumptions. Included in these assumptions is that variable costs are constant per unit and, for a multiproduct company, that a given sales mix is maintained for all volume changes. When absorption costing is used, operating income is a function of **both** production volume and sales volume. This is because an increase in inventory levels causes fixed costs to be held in inventory while a decrease in inventory levels causes fixed costs to be charged to cost of goods sold. These fluctuations can dramatically affect income and the breakeven point. On the other hand, when variable costing is used the same amount of fixed costs will be deducted from income whether or not inventory levels fluctuate. As a result, the breakeven point will be the same even if production does not equal sales. Hence, operating income under variable costing is a function **only** of sales, and assumption I. is incorrect.

18. (a) If sales prices, cost behavior, and actual **total** sales were as budgeted, then the excess profit must have resulted from a departure from budget by the **individual** products. Since the slope of line EH is greater than that of line HG (the slope representing profit per unit), Product 1 had the excess sales. Line OE represents fixed costs & line OF represents quantity sold up to the breakeven point. OE/OF is the contribution margin that may offset fixed costs until the breakeven point, F, is reached.

C. Variable (Direct) and Absorption (Full) Costing

19. (a) The difference between net income under variable costing and net income under full absorption costing is $36,000, which is equal to 20,000 x $180,000/100,000. The difference between the two methods is the fixed cost of manufacturing in the ending inventory that would be capitalized under the full absorption costing method and expensed under the variable costing method. Answer (b) is incorrect because the fixed selling and administration costs would be expensed under either method.

20. (d) Under variable costing, both variable direct and variable indirect manufacturing costs are assigned to inventory. All fixed costs are considered sunk costs and thus are written off as an expense of the period. Additionally, variable selling and administrative costs are also treated as period costs and thus not assigned to inventory.

21. (b) The requirement is to determine the different results obtained using absorption and variable costing. Under absorption costing, fixed costs are applied to units produced and are inventoried as product costs. Variable costing considers fixed costs to be period rather than product costs. Killo Co.'s inventoried costs under both methods are as follows:

	Absorption	Variable
Variable costs	1,000 x $90 = $90,000	1,000 x $90 = $90,000
Fixed costs	1,000 x $20 = 20,000	
Total cost of inventory	$110,000	$90,000

Under the variable method, the $20,000 of fixed cost was charged to income, whereas with absorption costing the fixed costs were absorbed into inventory. Therefore, absorption costing results in a pretax income that is higher by $20,000.

22. (b) The solutions approach is to visualize each income statement as shown below.

Absorption costing IS

	Sales
–	Cost of goods sold
	Gross profit (margin)
–	Selling & Admin. Expenses
	Operating income

Variable costing IS

	Sales
–	Variable expenses
	Contribution margin
–	Fixed expenses
	Operating income

Because the question states that actual sales revenue, total gross profit, and total contribution margin approximated budgeted figures, CGS and variable expenses must have also approximated budgeted figures. Net income is substantially greater, therefore, because selling and administrative fixed expenses had decreased. If manufacturing fixed costs had increased, gross margin would have decreased. If sales prices and variable costs had increased proportionately, the contribution margin would have increased by the same percentage. If sales prices had declined proportionately less than variable costs, the contribution margin would have again increased.

23. (a) The requirement is to determine what situation would cause variable costing net income to be higher than absorption costing net income. Answer (a) is correct because this difference in reported income is explained if units produced in 2002 are less than units sold in 2002. This is true because under variable costing, the amount of overhead included in cost of goods sold is the amount applied in 2002 (since all units produced were sold), whereas under absorption costing the overhead released to cost of goods sold includes that applied in 2002 as well as overhead included in the 2001 year-end inventory. Answer (b) is incorrect since a level of production lower than the activity level used to allocate overhead would result in underapplied overhead. Answer (c) is incorrect because the opposite situation results in overapplied overhead. Answer (d) is incorrect because production in excess of units sold would produce a higher absorption costing income than the variable costing income.

D. Budgeting

24. (c) The requirement is to determine the number of kilos of chemical Loire that Mien is planning to purchase in October. The first step is to prepare a production budget for product Nous.

Sales	53,000
Increase in ending inventory	6,000
Total units needed	59,000

Next, a purchases budget for raw material Loire should be prepared.

Production needs (59,000 x 4)	236,000
Decrease in ending inventory	(50,000)
Total kilos needed	186,000

Note that the production needs for Loire equal the number of units of Nous to be produced times the number of kilos of Loire needed per unit (4).

25. (c) Calculation of the cash payments for components in May is shown below.

Payments for June sales	$1,750 ($7,000 x 25%)
Payment for July sales	$6,000 ($8,000 x 75%)
Total cash payments	$7,750

Answer (a) is incorrect because parts are ordered two months prior to sales. Therefore, costs of components for sales of June and July should be considered. Answer (b) is incorrect because parts are ordered two months prior to sales. Therefore, costs of components for sales of June and July should be considered. Answer (d) is incorrect because parts are ordered two months prior to sales. Therefore, costs of components for sales of June and July should be considered.

26. (c) The requirement is to determine budgeted cash disbursements for purchases for 2002. The solutions approach is to use T-accounts to trace the flow of budgeted costs through the accounts.

Inventory			
Bal. 1/1/02	30,000		
Purchases	?	300,000	CGS
Bal. 12/31/02	42,000		

T-account analysis reveals that total purchases of inventory for the year must be $312,000.

Goods sold or on hand at 12/31	–	Beginning inventory	=	Purchases
($300,000 + $42,000)	–	$30,000	=	$312,000

Payments for purchases are made in the month following purchase. Thus, accounts payable at 1/1/02 will be paid in January 2002 and 1/12 of 2002 purchases (since Toyi is purchased in equal amounts each month) will be paid for in January 2003.

Accounts payable is depicted as follows:

Accounts Payable			
Cash disbursements	306,000*	20,000	Bal. 1/1/02
		312,000	Purchases
		26,000**	Bal. 12/31/02

*   ($312,000 purchases x 11/12) + $20,000 beg. AP
** $312,000 purchases x 1/12

Therefore, budgeted cash payments for Toyi for 2002 is $306,000.

27. (b) The requirement is to find the total budgeted costs for the seven stores in the coming year. Fixed costs last year were $70,000, and therefore variable costs totaled $430,000. The key is to find the variable costs per store. This is calculated by dividing variable costs ($430,000) by the number of stores last year (five), or, $86,000. Therefore, total costs budgeted in the new year is calculated as follows:

Variable cost per store	$86,000
Number of stores	x 7
Total budgeted variable costs	602,000
Add: fixed costs	70,000
Total budgeted costs	$672,000

E. Flexible Budgets

28. (c) A flexible budget is simply a static budget adjusted for various possible volume levels within the relevant range. A master budget or a flexible budget may be used during both the planning phase, when the budget is prepared, and the controlling phase, when actual results are compared to the budget. A flexible budget may be prepared for any unit for which costs vary with changes in activity level. Flexible budgets provide as much cost control as do master budgets because they are based on costs **allowable** at different activity levels. In fact, flexible budgets may offer an even greater degree of control because valid guidelines are available to managers even if output deviates from expectations, whereas static budgets supply information regarding only the planned volume.

29. (c) The requirement is to determine whether a flexible budget is appropriate for a marketing and/or a direct material usage budget. Flexible budgets are used to analyze changes in costs and revenues as changes in activity levels take place. If no changes are expected to occur and thus all amounts in the flexible budget remain constant throughout the relevant range (i.e., all costs are fixed), there is no need for a flexible budget. A marketing budget includes expenses incurred for promotion and sales. Some of these items, such as sales commissions or sample promotional products change with activity level. Direct material usage is directly dependent on activity level. Since a flexible budget would be appropriate for both a marketing and a direct materials usage budget.

30. (d) Within the relevant range, **total** fixed costs remain constant. As production levels increase, the same amount of fixed cost is spread over a greater number of units, and fixed costs **per unit** decrease. In contrast, variable costs **per unit** do not change within the relevant range.

F. Responsibility Accounting

31. (c) Responsibility accounting allocates to responsibility centers those costs, revenues, and/or assets which a manager can control. If a manager is only responsible for costs, the area of responsibility under his/her control is called a cost center. If the manager is responsible for both revenues and costs, his/her area of control is called a profit center. Thus, controllable revenue pertains to the profit center but not the cost center.

32. (a) A manager of a profit center is responsible for both the revenues and the costs of that center. Costs charged directly to a profit center, excluding fixed costs, are subject to the control of the profit center manager. As a result, the profit center's contribution margin (Sales – All variable costs) is controllable by the center manager. In this case, the manager of Carr Co.'s center No. 43 would be most likely to control the center's contribution margin of $70,000. The period expenses shown in the problem would not be subject to the manager's control and thus are irrelevant items.

33. **(a)** Direct manufacturing labor costs are labor costs that can be easily traced to the manufacture of a product. Wages earned by machine operators producing a firm's product are, therefore, direct manufacturing labor costs. Controllable costs are those which can be directly influenced by a given manager within a given time span. Wages earned by machine operators are controllable by the machine operators' foreman.

H. Performance Analysis

34. **(b)** Return on investment (ROI) may be calculated using the following equation:

$$x \; \frac{\text{Net income}}{\text{Sales}} = \text{ROI}$$

Thus, the equation that should be used to compute Bala's return on investment is (6/4) x (1/6) = ROI.

35. **(d)** Return on assets, also referred to as return on investment (ROI), is calculated as follows:

ROI	=	Profit margin	x	Asset turnover
ROI	=	0.02	x	5
ROI	=	0.10, or 10%		

36. **(d)** Residual income equals the net income of a division minus imputed interest on the division's assets. In this problem, we are given Darwin's operating income and imputed interest rate, but Darwin's assets must be derived using sales and capital turnover, as shown below.

$$\text{Capital turnover} = \frac{\text{Sales of division}}{\text{Invested capital of division}}$$

$$4 = \frac{\$400,000}{X}$$

$$X = \frac{\$400,000}{4} = \$100,000$$

Since Darwin's invested capital totals $100,000, its operating income is $40,000, and interest is imputed at 10%, residual income is calculated as follows:

$$= \frac{\text{Division}}{\text{net income}} - \frac{\text{Imputed interest}}{\text{on investment}}$$

RI = $40,000 – ($100,000 x 10%)

RI = $30,000

37. **(d)** Residual income is income minus an imputed interest charge for invested capital. Residual income will be maximized as long as the division earns a rate of return that exceeds the imputed charge. Division A's project will earn a rate of return **greater** than the imputed interest charge, so this project should be accepted. Division B's project will earn a rate of return **less** than the imputed interest charge, so this project should not be accepted.

38. **(b)** The DuPont formula is used to calculate return on investment.

Asset turnover	x	Income as a percentage of sales	=	Return on investment (ROI)
$\dfrac{\text{Revenue}}{\text{Invested capital}}$	x	$\dfrac{\text{Income}}{\text{Revenue}}$	=	$\dfrac{\text{Income}}{\text{Invested capital}}$

The combination of changes which will maximize return on investment are to increase both asset turnover and income as a percentage of sales, since multiplying two larger numbers will result in a larger product.

39. **(d)** All of these nonfinancial measures would be useful in evaluating the performance of a manufacturing system. Throughput (cycle) time measures the total amount of production time required per unit. This measure is important to assess the timeliness of the production process, which is required for on-time delivery of goods. The proportion of total production time consumed by setup activities reflects one aspect of production efficiency. Setup time represents money spent on a non-value-adding activity, and thus should be minimized as much as possible. The proportion of total units completed which require rework is a useful measure of product quality. An excessive rate of rework alerts management that it needs to examine its quality control procedures.

I. Product and Service Pricing

40. **(c)** The solutions approach is to algebraically reconstruct how Cuff Caterers determined the total price per person. Three components comprise the total price: the cost of the food, the service charge, and the sales tax. The 15% service charge is computed on the food (F) only. The 6% sales tax is computed on the food plus the service charge. The following equation is used to compute the price:

$$F + .15F + .06 (F + .15F) = \$60.00$$

Where

F	=	the cost of the food alone
.15F	=	the service charge
.06 (F + .15F)	=	the sales tax

Solving algebraically

1.219F	=	$60.00
F	=	$49.22

41. **(a)** The target price is to be set at a budgeted ratio of operating income to revenue, or a profit margin on sales of 15%. This problem may be solved using the following equation:

Let x	=	Target price
Revenue – Cost	=	Profit
500x – $990,000	=	.15(500x)
.85(500x)	=	$990,000
425x	=	$990,000
x	=	$2,329

42. **(c)** The requirement is to determine the amount that Briar should receive from the contract. This amount can be computed as follows:

Actual costs incurred	$1,920,000
Multiply by 110% (cost + 10%)	x 1.10
Formula price	$2,112,000

The target price of $2,200,000 exceeds the formula price of $2,112,000 by $88,000. Briar is to receive 50% of this amount, or $44,000, in addition to the formula price. Therefore, Briar is to receive a total of $2,156,000 ($2,112,000 + $44,000).

43.   (d)   To determine the price at which expected product sales will yield the greatest profits, many factors such as customer preferences, competitors' reactions, cost structures, etc. must be considered. A customer's perception of the quality and durability (life) of a product affects how much s/he is willing to pay for that product. However, in some cases a customer may prefer to pay less money and receive a product of lesser quality. Therefore, Vince should consider the quality and life of the new device as well as customers' relative preference for quality compared to price.

44.   (c)   Klunker is using a "time and material" pricing approach. The charges for each are calculated below.

Time:

$$\underset{\text{hour}}{\underset{\text{cost per}}{\text{Labor}}} + \frac{\$120,000}{\underset{\text{Total labor hours}}{10,000}} + \underset{\text{per hour}}{\underset{\text{margin}}{\text{Profit}}}$$

$$\$30 + \frac{\$120,000}{10,000} + \$8 = \$50/\text{labor hour}$$

Materials:

$$\left(\underset{\text{cost for job}}{\text{Materials}}\right) + \left(\underset{\text{cost for job}}{\text{Materials}} \times \frac{\underset{\text{handling \& storage}}{\text{Materials}}}{\underset{\text{cost for year}}{\text{Total materials}}}\right)$$

$$\$800 + \left(\$800 \times \frac{\$10,000}{\$500,000}\right) = \$816$$

The total price for the overhaul should therefore be $1,416 [($50/hr. x 12 hrs) + $816)]. Note that materials handling and storage costs are allocated at $0.02 per dollar of materials, and other overhead is allocated at $12 per labor hour.

J.   Transfer Pricing

45.   (c)   The requirement is to determine whether Ajax should take on a new customer and end its sales to the Bradley division and why. As a profit center, Ajax will make the decision independent of the effects on the corporation as a whole. If Ajax sells to the new customer, its revenues will increase to $1,500,000 ($75 x 20,000), but its costs will remain the same at $1,200,000 ($900,000 + $300,000). This results in a positive gross margin of $300,000 ($1,500,000 – $1,200,000). The new gross margin is $600,000 [$300,000 – (–$300,000)] greater than the original gross margin. The shortcut (incremental) approach is to multiply 20,000 units times the $30 increase ($75 – $45) in Ajax's unit selling (transfer) price.

46.   (b)   Negotiated transfer prices should fall within a range limited by a ceiling and a floor. The ceiling is the lowest market price that could be obtained from an external supplier, and the floor equals the outlay costs plus opportunity cost of the transferring division. Since James' MIS department does not have to option to sell services to external customers, its opportunity cost is $0. Since all costs of service departments must be covered by the revenue-producing departments, the MIS department's outlay cost equals its total costs. The department's full capacity level is 1,000 reports per year. However, the user departments will be requesting 1,250 reports (5 user subunits x 250 reports each). Thus, the MIS department will incur costs of $12,000 [$48 x (1,250 – 1,000)] for the 250 reports above capacity, in addition to the $45,000 budgeted costs for full capacity. The total cost of $57,000 ($45,000 + $12,000) is used to calculate the floor. The ceiling is based on the $70,000 that would be incurred to purchase MIS services externally. Since the MIS department will be producing 1,250 reports, the floor is $45.60 ($57,000 ÷ 1,250), and the ceiling is $56.00 ($70,000 ÷ 1,250). At full capacity, any differential costs of additional production are added to the floor. $48.00

represents only the differential cost of producing each report above full capacity, not cost per report for total production. Budgeted costs are based on production of 1,250 reports, not 1,000.

47.   (d)   The goal of transfer pricing is to encourage managers to make transfer decisions which maximize profits of the company as a **whole**. Some transfers may not be profitable to a particular division, but would effect a cost savings to the company by avoiding costs of purchasing externally. For example, when a division is already operating at full capacity and uses variable cost transfer prices, additional production for internal transfer would result in a loss for the transferring division because no contribution margin is earned to cover the differential fixed costs incurred. Conversely, internal production may be cheaper to the corporate entity than purchasing the product, in which case the division should accept the order. However, the division manager is likely to engage in suboptimization by rejecting the order to enhance the division's performance, while adversely affecting overall company performance.

K.   Inventory Models

48.   (b)   In a just-in-time (JIT) purchasing system, orders are placed such that delivery of raw materials occurs just as they are needed for production. This system requires the placement of more frequent, smaller orders and ideally eliminates inventories. Conversely, in a traditional system large orders are placed less frequently and extra inventory is carried to avoid stockouts and the resulting production delays during order lead time. Certain cost changes would encourage managers to switch to a JIT system. One is **decreased** cost per purchase order, which would increase the attractiveness of placing the many more orders required. Another is **increased** inventory unit carrying costs, which would make the elimination of inventories desirable.

49.   (c)   Calculation of the reorder point includes consideration of the average daily usage, average delivery time, and stock-out costs. Answer (a) is incorrect because ordering costs are included in determining the economic order quantity but not the reorder point. Answer (b) is incorrect because carrying cost is considered in determining the economic order quantity but not the reorder point. Answer (d) is incorrect because the economic order quantity is not considered in determining the reorder point.

50.   (d)   The purpose of the just-in-time (JIT) production system is to decrease the size of production runs (and therefore inventory levels) by decreasing set-up costs. Lot **sizes** would decrease as the **number** of lots processed during the year increases. Since inventory levels would decrease with JIT, relevant costs would also drop (i.e., capital invested in inventory could be invested in other assets—a cost savings). The **fixed** facility and administrative costs are irrelevant as fixed costs would remain the same regardless of changes for JIT. The unit costs will increase because fixed costs will be spread over fewer inventory units produced from JIT's eliminating effect on excess inventory production.

51.   (a)   The goal of a just-in-time system is to identify and eliminate all non-value-added activities. One of the major features of a just-in-time system is a decrease in the number of suppliers to build strong relations and ensure quality goods. In a just-in-time system raw material is purchased only as it is needed for production, thereby eliminating the need for costly storage. In a just-in-time system, vendors make more frequent deliveries of small quantities of materials that are placed into production immediately upon receipt.

52. (c)   The purpose of a "just-in-time" production system is to decrease the size of production runs while increasing the number of lots processed during the year. This production philosophy requires that inventory be delivered as it is needed, rather than held in large quantities. Inventory turnover is computed as

$$\frac{\text{Cost of goods sold}}{\text{Average inventory}}$$

As average inventory decreases, inventory turnover increases. As average inventory levels decrease, inventory as a percentage of total assets will also decrease.

53. (c)   Just-in-time (JIT) manufacturing is a pull-through system of production unlike the traditional batch manufacturing push-through system. Answers (a), (b), and (d) are characteristics of a JIT manufacturing system.

54. (d)   The requirement is to determine the effect of a decrease in safety stock on Dee Co.'s economic order quantity (EOQ). The EOQ represents the optimal quantity of inventory to be ordered based on demand and various inventory costs. The formula for computing EOQ is

$$EOQ = \sqrt{\frac{2aD}{k}}, \text{ where}$$

D = Demand (in units) for a specified time period
a = Ordering costs per purchase order
k = Cost of carrying one unit in inventory for the specified time period

Safety stock is a buffer of excess inventory held to guard against stockouts. Safety stock is usually a multiple of demand and has no effect on a company's EOQ.

55. (a)   The economic order quantity (EOQ) formula was developed on the basis of the following assumption:

1. Demand occurs at a constant rate throughout the year and is known with certainty.
2. Lead time on the receipt of orders is constant.
3. The entire quantity ordered is received at one time.
4. The unit costs of the items ordered are constant; thus, there can be no quantity discounts.
5. There are no limitations on the size of the inventory.

Answer (b) is incorrect because it contradicts assumption 5. Answers (c) and (d) are incorrect because they are the opposite of assumption 4.

56. (b)   The requirement is to calculate the economic order quantity (EOQ). The EOQ formula is

$$EOQ = \sqrt{\frac{2aD}{k}}$$

In the above equation, a = cost of placing one order, D = annual demand in units, and k = cost of carrying one unit in inventory for one year. Substituting the given information, the equation becomes

$$EOQ = \sqrt{\frac{(2)(32)(20,000)}{8}} = \sqrt{160,000} = 400 \text{ units}$$

57. (d)   The requirement is to determine the order point for material X. When safety stock is maintained, the order point is computed as follows:

$$\frac{\text{Daily}}{\text{demand}} \times \frac{\text{Lead time}}{\text{in days}} + \frac{\text{Safety}}{\text{stock}}$$

Daily demand is eighty units (20,000 units ÷ 250 days). Therefore, the order point is 3,200 units [(80 x 30) + 800].

OTHER OBJECTIVE ANSWERS AND ANSWER EXPLANATIONS

Problem 1

1.   **(35,000 units)** The breakeven in units is found at the point where the revenue line intersects the total cost line, in this case 35,000 units.

2.   **($30,000)** Fixed costs remain constant over a relevant range and are incurred even if no production occurs. Therefore, when unit production is zero the fixed cost equals total cost because no variable cost has been incurred.

3.   **($59,700)** The desired level of sales in dollars is calculated by adding fixed cost to the target NI, and then dividing by contribution margin % [($30,000 + $10,000) ÷ 0.67 = $59,700 rounded).

4.   **(F)** Variable and fixed elements need to be separated in order to break down cost and analyze the effects of sales volume on profits.

5.   **(F)** For the CVP analysis to provide predictability, the variable cost per unit needs to remain constant while the total variable cost increases as output increases.

6.   **(F)** To provide consistency, the selling price needs to remain constant within any relevant activity range.

7.   **(T)** For variable cost per unit to remain constant within a relevant range, productivity and efficiency must remain constant.

8.   **(F)** Under the CVP model, volume is assumed to be the only factor which causes changes in cost.

9.   **(T)** An underlying principle of the CVP model is that there are no changes in inventory levels.

10. **(F)** The fixed cost per unit varies with volume whereas the total fixed cost remains constant.

Problem 2

1.   **($229,000)** Cash payments for material suppliers would be calculated as follows:

Beginning balance of accounts payable	$ 40,000
Add: Requirements for production during the ten-week	
period (70,000 units x $3 per unit)	210,000
Less: Ending balance of accounts payable	(21,000)
	$229,000

Since materials are paid for in the week following use, the materials used in the last week of production have not been paid for. Therefore, ending accounts payable includes 10% (one week of the ten-week period) of the production requirements for the ten-week period, or $21,000 (10% x $210,000). Ending accounts payable is subtracted from the total of beginning accounts payable plus production requirements for the period, to arrive at the amount that should be budgeted for cash payment to material suppliers during the period.

2.   **($95,000)** The budgeted income for the period, using variable (direct) costing, is determined in the following manner. The budgeted contribution margin per unit is calculated by subtracting the variable costs from the sale price per unit [$11 – ($3 + $2 + $1) = $5]. The budgeted contribution margin per unit is multiplied by the units of production during the period, 70,000 to arrive at $350,000 ($5 x 70,000) total budgeted contribution margin. Finally, fixed costs of $255,000 ($210,000 + $45,000) are subtracted to arrive at $95,000 of budgeted income for the period ($350,000 – $255,000). Remember variable costing considers all fixed manufacturing overhead as a period cost rather than as a product cost.

3.   **($95,000)** The budgeted income for the period under absorption costing would be the same as under variable costing, because there are no beginning or ending inventories. Variable costing considers all fixed manufacturing overhead as a period cost rather than as a product cost, while absorption costing considers fixed manufacturing overhead to be a product cost.

4.   **($20,000)** The 10,000 unit shortage in sales resulted in a decrease in contribution of $50,000 (10,000 x $5 contribution margin per unit). Absorption costing considers fixed manufacturing overhead to be a product cost (not a period cost). Therefore, $30,000 of fixed costs would be placed in ending inventory. The $30,000 is calculated by multiplying the fraction of units remaining in inventory (10,000/70,000) by the fixed manufacturing costs of $210,000. The reported income for the period is $20,000 less than the budgeted net income. This difference is computed as follows:

Decrease in contribution	$(50,000)
Fixed costs inventories	– 30,000
Net decrease in income	$ 20,000

5.   **($29,000)** The loss of 1,000 regular sales multiplied by the $5 contribution margin per unit results in a $5,000 decrease in income. Revenues generated from the special order minus variable costs must equal this decrease in income ($5,000), in order to maintain the net income that would be achieved without the special order. The minimum amount of revenue needed is computed as follows:

Revenue	–	[($3 + $2 + $1) x 4,000]	=	$5,000
Revenue	=	$5,000 + $24,000		
Revenue	=	$29,000		

Problem 3

1.   **(D,F)** An office manager's salary is not directly related to the acquisition or production of goods and cannot logically or easily be allocated to the product. Therefore, this cost would be categorized as fixed general and administrative cost because it does not vary with production levels.

2.   **(C,V)** Manufacturing costs that cannot be specifically traced to the cost object, such as the cost of electricity, are considered to be overhead costs. Asta should classify this as a variable cost because the electricity cost fluctuates in direct proportion to the amount that the lab equipment is used.

3.   **(B,V)** The hourly wages of technicians who perform tests can be identified directly with the product (direct manufacturing labor) and total costs vary in proportion to the number of tests performed (variable cost).

4.   **(C,V)** The cost of lubricants used on lab equipment is insignificant and does not justify the cost of being traced directly to the product. Therefore, it is classified as variable overhead cost because total costs vary with the amount that the lab equipment is used.

5.   **(A,V)** Direct materials cost includes the acquisition costs of materials that comprise the cost object and which can be traced to the cost object in an economically feasible manner. Here, the cost object is tests performed, and thus the cost of distilled water used in tests constitutes direct materials. This cost is variable since it increases with the number of tests performed.

6.   **(C,F)** Depreciation on equipment used in production is always considered an overhead cost. This cost is fixed because it does not fluctuate with production levels (contrast with the units-of-production method of depreciation).

7.   **(C,F)** Depreciation on the laboratory building is a fixed overhead cost because it is not directly traceable to the product and it does not vary with production levels (within the relevant range).

8.   **(A,V)** The cost of materials which become part of the finished product comprise direct materials cost. In some cases, the cost of items such as binders would be considered insignificant and would thus be included in overhead costs. However, in this case the problem states that the binders are expensive, and thus it is worthwhile to trace these costs directly to the product.

9.   **($40)** Contribution margin is calculated as (Sales – All variable costs). For Asta, the sales price per test and variable costs per test remain the same whether the company operates at the high range or the low range of activity. Thus, contribution margin per test equals $40 ($60 sales price per test – $20 variable costs per test).

10.   **(4,000)** The breakeven point in number of tests at the low activity range is calculated as

$$\frac{\text{Fixed costs}}{\text{Unit CM}} = \frac{\$160,000}{\$40} = 4,000 \text{ units}$$

11.   **(5,000)** The breakeven point in number of tests at the high activity range is calculated as

$$\frac{\text{Fixed costs}}{\text{Unit CM}} = \frac{\$200,000}{\$40} = 5,000 \text{ units}$$

Note that the same unit contribution margin may be used as in item 10, because the sales price per unit and variable costs per unit do not vary with the activity level.

12.   **(9,000)** The number of units sold to achieve a gross profit of $160,000 is calculated as

$$\frac{\text{Fixed costs + Profit}}{\text{Unit CM}} = \frac{\$200,000 + \$160,000}{\$40} = 9,000 \text{ units}$$

13.   **(L)** The problem states that in comparison to industry averages, at the low range of activity Asta has a lower sales price per test, higher fixed costs, and the same breakeven point in number of tests performed. It helps to visualize these factors by labeling the breakeven equation.

Sales price per test	x	Number of tests	=	Fixed cost	+	Variable costs/test	x	Number of tests
Lower		Same		Higher		?		Same

This diagram shows that to offset the higher-than-average fixed costs enough to result in a lower sales price than average, the variable costs must be lower than average.

14.   **(G)** Contribution margin is calculated as (Sales – Variable costs). At the high range of activity, Asta's sales price per test is the same as industry averages while its variable costs are lower. Therefore, since less variable cost is being subtracted from the same sales price, the contribution margin must be greater than industry averages.

15.   **(L)** The problem states that at the high range of activity Asta has the same fixed costs as industry averages. In item 14, you determined that the contribution margin was greater than average. To determine the status of the breakeven point, it helps to visualize these factors by labeling the breakeven equation.

Units to breakeven	=	Fixed costs	÷	Unit CM
?		Same		Greater

Since the denominator is increased while the numerator remains unchanged, the quotient (the breakeven point) must be decreased. Therefore, Asta's breakeven point at the high activity range must be lower than industry averages.

STANDARDS AND VARIANCES

Standard costs are predetermined target costs which should be attainable under efficient conditions. The tightness, or attainment difficulty, of standard costs should be determined by the principles of motivation (e.g., excessively tight standards may result in employees feeling that the standards are impossible to achieve; consequently, they may ignore them). Standard costs are used to aid in the budget process, pinpoint trouble areas, and evaluate performance.

The tightness of standards is generally described by one of two terms. **Ideal** standards reflect the absolute minimum costs which could be achieved under perfect operating conditions. **Currently attainable** standards should be achieved under efficient operating conditions. Generally, currently attainable standards are set so they will be difficult, but not impossible, to achieve. Currently attainable standards are most often used since they are more realistic for budgeting purposes and are a better motivational tool than ideal standards.

Variances are differences between actual and standard costs. The total variance is generally broken down into subvariances to further pinpoint the causes of the variance.

A. Variance Analysis

In calculating the variances for direct material and direct manufacturing labor the following symbols will be employed as defined:

AP: Actual price paid per unit of input (e.g., price per foot of lumber, per hour of labor, per ton of steel, etc.)
SP: Standard price per unit of input
AQ: The actual quantity of input (feet, hours, tons, etc.) used in production
SQ: The standard quantity of input that should have been used for the good units produced

Variances can be computed using the diagram approach that follows.

B. Material Variances

The diagram for computing material variances is

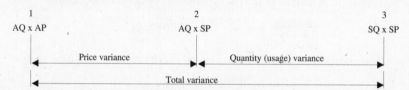

The price variance is unfavorable if AP > SP; the quantity variance is unfavorable if AQ > SQ. Favorable variances arise when actual amounts are less than standard amounts.

The only alternative allowed on the variances above concerns the material price variance. The price variance can be recognized when material is placed in production (as assumed in the previous discussion) or when material is purchased (which is desirable for early identification and control). If the price variance is to be recognized at the time of purchase, AQ (for the price variance **only**) becomes quantity **purchased** rather than quantity **used**.

The materials price variance is generally considered to be the responsibility of the purchasing department, while the materials quantity variance is the responsibility of the production department.

EXAMPLE:

The following data relate to DFW Manufacturing, which produced 5,000 units of product during the period:

Direct materials standard per finished unit: 2 lbs. @ $1.60 per lb.
Actual: 10,100 lbs purchased @ $1.65 per lb., 9,500 lbs. used in production

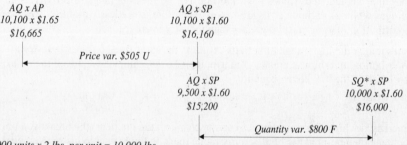

*   *SQ = 5,000 units x 2 lbs. per unit = 10,000 lbs.*

C. Labor Variances

The computational form of the labor variances is similar to the calculation of material variances—except that the price being used changes from price per pound of material to price (rate) per hour of labor, and the quantity changes from pounds, yards, etc., to hours. Therefore, the diagrams are the same, although the terminology differs.

Material variance		Labor variance
Price	——————→	Rate
Quantity	——————→	Efficiency

Both labor variances are usually considered to be the responsibility of the production department.

EXAMPLE:

The following data relate to DFW Manufacturing. Recall that the company produced 5,000 units of product during the period:

Direct labor standard per finished unit: 3 hours @ $2.50 per hour
Actual: 15,400 hours worked @ $2.60 per hour

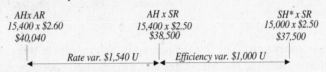

AHx AR	AH x SR	SH* x SR
15,400 x $2.60	15,400 x $2.50	15,000 x $2.50
$40,040	$38,500	$37,500

Rate var. $1,540 U   Efficiency var. $1,000 U

* *SH = 5,000 units x 3 hours = 15,000 hours*

D. Overhead Variances

Overhead variances tend to be more complicated than those computed for direct materials and direct labor, primarily because of the different computation methods that are available. The easier approach to master is a parallel of the variance grids shown earlier, with overhead being subdivided into fixed and variable elements. Variable overhead parallels the calculation of direct labor variances; fixed overhead, in contrast, requires a minor modification. The general setup approach follows:

Variable overhead

Actual VOH	AQ x SR	SQ x SR
	(1)	(2)
	Spending	Efficiency

Fixed overhead

Actual FOH	Budget	SQ x SR
	(3)	(4)
	Budget/spending	Production volume

Notice the use of AQ and SQ. On virtually all CPA exams, direct labor hours is the base used to apply overhead to production.

EXAMPLE:

To illustrate the proper approach, we will continue to focus on DFW Manufacturing, which applies overhead to production on the basis of hours. Recall from the earlier calculations that 5,000 units were manufactured. 15,400 hours were worked, and each unit is supposed to take 3 hours of labor time. Additional data follow.

Estimated (standard) factory overhead based on a "normal capacity" of 16,000 labor hours:

Variable	3 hours @ $1.50
Fixed	3 hours @ $0.50*

Actual overhead cost for the period

Variable	$22,800
Fixed	$ 8,100

* *$8,000 budgeted fixed overhead costs ÷ 16,000 direct labor hours*

Variable Overhead

Actual	AQ x SR	SQ x SR
$22,800	15,400 x $1.50	15,000 x $1.50
	$23,100	$22,500

Spending var. $300 F   Efficiency var. $600 U

Fixed Overhead

This example illustrates several key points.

According to the information presented, DFW has a capacity to work 16,000 hours, which is the equivalent of 5,334 units (16,000 ÷ 3 hours per unit). Since the firm produced only 5,000 units, the production volume variance is unfavorable. Overhead in the SQ x SR column ($22,500 + $7,500 = $30,000) is the amount **applied** to production. Since actual overhead was $30,900 ($22,800 + $8,100), overhead is $900 underapplied. This latter amount will always coincide with the combination of all four variances ($300F – $600U – $100U – $500U = $900U).

The 3-variance approach. The 3-variance method results in the calculation of three variances rather than the four just illustrated. The **only** difference between these two approaches is in the calculation of the spending variance, which is a combination to create a total spending variance as shown below.

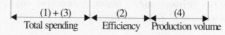

For DFW, the total spending variance is $200F ($300F – $100U).

The 2-variance approach. The 2-variance approach results in the calculation of only two variances: the production volume variance shown earlier and a combined spending/efficiency variance (see the following diagram).

This latter variance for DFW is $400U ($300F – $100U – $600U).

Some computational hints. These variance approaches are fairly straightforward if you start with the 4-variance method and then work backwards to arrive at the 3-variance approach and then work that backwards to arrive at the last method. Occasionally, the exam may not give you enough data to perform all calculations to do this. The following hints have proven to be extremely helpful:

- The production volume variance is the same no matter what approach is used.
- The efficiency variance is the same for the 3- and 4-variance approach.
- When in doubt, you can calculate the total variance (the difference between actual total overhead and applied overhead [SQ x SR]), subtract the variances that you can compute, and the result, a forced figure, will often be the variance that is requested by the examiners.

Miscellaneous. The budget variance (also called the controllable variance) arises when the amount spent on both fixed and variable overhead differs from the amount budgeted for the actual hours worked.

The production volume variance is solely a **fixed** overhead variance. It is caused by under- or over-utilization of capacity. If actual output is less than (more than) capacity activity, an unfavorable (favorable) output level variance results. The capacity volume is the activity level used to set the predetermined fixed overhead rate for product costing purposes (see Module 34).

E. Disposition of Variances

If insignificant, variances are frequently written off to cost of goods sold on grounds of expediency (ARB 43 states that you may report inventories using standard costs if they are based on currently attainable standards). If significant, the variances must be allocated among the inventories and cost of goods sold, usually in proportion to the ending balances.

MULTIPLE-CHOICE QUESTIONS (1-18)

1. Companies in what type of industry may use a standard cost system for cost control?

	Mass production industry	Service industry
a.	Yes	Yes
b.	Yes	No
c.	No	No
d.	No	Yes

2. In connection with a standard cost system being developed by Flint Co., the following information is being considered with regard to standard hours allowed for output of one unit of product:

	Hours
Average historical performance for the past three years	1.85
Production level to satisfy average consumer demand over a seasonal time span	1.60
Engineering estimates based on attainable performance	1.50
Engineering estimates based on ideal performance	1.25

To measure controllable production inefficiencies, what is the best basis for Flint to use in establishing standard hours allowed?

a. 1.25
b. 1.50
c. 1.60
d. 1.85

3. Which of the following standard costing variances would be **least** controllable by a production supervisor?

a. Overhead volume.
b. Overhead efficiency.
c. Labor efficiency.
d. Material usage.

4. The standard direct material cost to produce a unit of Lem is four meters of material at $2.50 per meter. During May 2002, 4,200 meters of material costing $10,080 were purchased and used to produce 1,000 units of Lem. What was the material price variance for May 2002?

a. $400 favorable.
b. $420 favorable.
c. $ 80 unfavorable.
d. $480 unfavorable.

5. Dahl Co. uses a standard costing system in connection with the manufacture of a "one size fits all" article of clothing. Each unit of finished product contains two yards of direct material. However, a 20% direct material spoilage calculated on input quantities occurs during the manufacturing process. The cost of the direct material is $3 per yard. The standard direct material cost per unit of finished product is

a. $4.80
b. $6.00
c. $7.20
d. $7.50

6. Carr Co. had an unfavorable materials usage variance of $900. What amounts of this variance should be charged to each department?

	Purchasing	Warehousing	Manufacturing
a.	$0	$0	$900
b.	$0	$900	$0
c.	$300	$300	$300
d.	$900	$0	$0

7. Yola Co. manufactures one product with a standard direct manufacturing labor cost of four hours at $12.00 per hour. During June, 1,000 units were produced using 4,100 hours at $12.20 per hour. The unfavorable direct labor efficiency variance was

a. $1,220
b. $1,200
c. $ 820
d. $ 400

8. The following direct manufacturing labor information pertains to the manufacture of product Glu:

Time required to make one unit	2 direct labor hours
Number of direct workers	50
Number of productive hours per week, per worker	40
Weekly wages per worker	$500
Workers' benefits treated as direct manufacturing labor costs	20% of wages

What is the standard direct manufacturing labor cost per unit of product Glu?

a. $30
b. $24
c. $15
d. $12

9. On the diagram below, the line OW represents the standard labor cost at any output volume expressed in direct labor hours. Point S indicates the actual output at standard cost, and Point A indicates the actual hours and actual cost required to produce S.

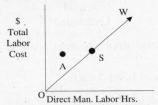

Which of the following variances are favorable or unfavorable?

	Rate variance	Efficiency variance
a.	Favorable	Unfavorable
b.	Favorable	Favorable
c.	Unfavorable	Unfavorable
d.	Unfavorable	Favorable

10. The following were among Gage Co.'s 2002 costs:

Normal spoilage	$ 5,000
Freight out	10,000
Excess of actual manufacturing costs over standard costs	20,000
Standard manufacturing costs	100,000
Actual prime manufacturing costs	80,000

Gage's 2002 actual manufacturing overhead was

a. $ 40,000
b. $ 45,000
c. $ 55,000
d. $120,000

11. Baby Frames, Inc. evaluates manufacturing overhead in its factory by using variance analysis. The following information applies to the month of May:

	Actual	Budgeted
Number of frames manufactured	19,000	20,000
Variable overhead costs	$4,100	$2 per direct labor hour
Fixed overhead costs	$22,000	$20,000
Direct labor hours	2,100	0.1 hour per frame

What is the fixed overhead spending variance?
a. $1,000 favorable.
b. $1,000 unfavorable.
c. $2,000 favorable.
d. $2,000 unfavorable.

12. Under the 2-variance method for analyzing overhead, which of the following variances consists of both variable and fixed overhead elements?

	Controllable (budget) variance	Volume variance
a.	Yes	Yes
b.	Yes	No
c.	No	No
d.	No	Yes

13. During 2002, a department's 3-variance overhead standard costing system reported unfavorable spending and volume variances. The activity level selected for allocating overhead to the product was based on 80% of practical capacity. If 100% of practical capacity had been selected instead, how would the reported unfavorable spending and volume variances be affected?

	Spending variance	Volume variance
a.	Increased	Unchanged
b.	Increased	Increased
c.	Unchanged	Increased
d.	Unchanged	Unchanged

14. The following information pertains to Roe Co.'s 2002 manufacturing operations:

Standard direct manufacturing labor hours per unit	2
Actual direct manufacturing labor hours	10,500
Number of units produced	5,000
Standard variable overhead per standard direct manufacturing labor hour	$3
Actual variable overhead	$28,000

Roe's 2002 unfavorable variable overhead efficiency variance was
a. $0
b. $1,500
c. $2,000
d. $3,500

15. Which of the following variances would be useful in calling attention to a possible short-term problem in the control of overhead costs?

	Spending variance	Volume variance
a.	No	No
b.	No	Yes
c.	Yes	No
d.	Yes	Yes

Items 16 and 17 are based on the following:

The diagram below depicts a factory overhead flexible budget line DB and standard overhead application line OA. Activity is expressed in machine hours with Point V indicating the standard hours required for the actual output in September 2002. Point S indicates the actual machine hours (inputs) and actual costs in September 2002.

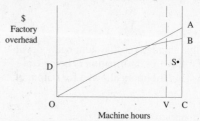

16. Are the following overhead variances favorable or unfavorable?

	Volume (capacity) variance	Efficiency variance
a.	Favorable	Favorable
b.	Favorable	Unfavorable
c.	Unfavorable	Favorable
d.	Unfavorable	Unfavorable

17. The budgeted total variable overhead cost for C machine hours is
a. AB
b. BC
c. AC minus DO
d. BC minus DO

18. Lanta Restaurant compares monthly operating results with a static budget. When actual sales are less than budget, would Lanta usually report favorable variances on variable food costs and fixed supervisory salaries?

	Variable food costs	Fixed supervisory salaries
a.	Yes	Yes
b.	Yes	No
c.	No	Yes
d.	No	No

OTHER OBJECTIVE QUESTIONS

Problem 1 (10 to 15 minutes)

Items 1 through 5 are based on the following:

Bilco Inc. produces bricks and uses a standard costing system. On the diagram below, the line OP represents Bilco's standard material cost at any output volume expressed in direct material pounds to be used. Bilco had identical outputs in each of the first three months of 2002, with a standard cost of V in each month. Points Ja, Fe, and Ma represent the actual pounds used and actual costs incurred in January, February, and March, respectively.

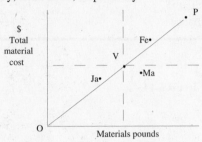

Required:

For **items 1 through 5,** determine whether each variance is Favorable or Unfavorable.

Items to be answered

1. January material price variance.

2. January material usage variance.

3. February material price variance.

4. February material usage variance.

5. March material net variance.

Problem 2 (35 to 45 minutes)

Tredoc Co. is engaged in the business of seasonal tree-spraying and uses chemicals in its operations to prevent disease and bug-infestation. Employees receive wages of $10 per hour. The direct manufacturing labor efficiency variance represents the difference between actual time consumed in spraying a tree and the standard time allowed for the height of the tree (specified in feet), multiplied by the $10 standard hourly wage rate. For budgeting purposes, there is a standard allowance of one hour per customer for travel, setup, and clearup time. However, since several factors are uncontrollable by the employee, this one-hour budget allowance is excluded from the calculation of the direct manufacturing labor efficiency variance. Employees are responsible for keeping their own daily time cards.

Chemical usage should vary directly with the tree-footage sprayed. Variable overhead includes costs that vary directly with the number of customers, as well as costs that vary according to tree-footage sprayed. Customers pay a service charge of $10 per visit and $1 per tree-foot sprayed.

The standard static budget and actual results for June are as follows:

		Static budget		Actual results
Service calls	(190 customers)	$ 1,900	(200 customers)	$ 2,000
Footage sprayed	(18,000 feet)	18,000	(20,000 feet)	20,000
Total revenues		19,900		22,000
Chemicals	(900 gallons)	2,700	(2,000 gallons)	4,000
Direct manuf. labor:				
Travel, setup, and cleanup	(190 hours) $1,900		(300 hours) $3,000	
Tree-spraying	(900 hours) 9,000		(800 hours) 8,000	
Total direct manuf. labor		10,900		11,000
Overhead:				
Variable based on number of customers	950			
Variable based on tree-footage	1,800			
Fixed	2,000			
Total overhead		4,750		6,000
Total costs		18,350		21,000
Gross profit before bonus		$ 1,550		$ 1,000

Required:

Compute the following for June. Indicate whether each variance is favorable (F) or unfavorable (U).

1. Direct materials price variance.

2. Direct materials usage (efficiency) variance.

3. Direct manufacturing labor travel, setup, and cleanup variance.

4. Direct manufacturing labor efficiency variance.

5. Overhead spending (flexible budget) variance.

Problem 3

Return to Module 34 and do Problem 1, **Items 6-11**.

MULTIPLE-CHOICE ANSWERS

1. a __ __	5. d __ __	9. d __ __	13. c __ __	17. d __ __
2. b __ __	6. a __ __	10. a __ __	14. b __ __	18. b __ __
3. a __ __	7. b __ __	11. d __ __	15. c __ __	1st: __/18 = __%
4. b __ __	8. a __ __	12. b __ __	16. b __ __	2nd: __/18 = __%

MULTIPLE-CHOICE ANSWER EXPLANATIONS

A. Variance Analysis

1. **(a)** Many service firms, nonprofit organizations, and governmental units, in addition to manufacturing firms, use standard cost systems. For example, a trucking company may set standards for fuel costs.

2. **(b)** Standard costs are predetermined target costs which should be attainable under **efficient** conditions. Currently attainable standards should be achieved under efficient operating conditions. Therefore, engineering estimates based on attainable performance would provide the best basis for Flint in establishing standard hours allowed.

3. **(a)** The requirement is to determine the standard costing variance which would be **least** controllable by a production supervisor. The overhead output level (volume) variance arises because the **actual** production volume level achieved usually does not coincide with the production level used as a denominator volume for calculating a budgeted overhead **application** rate. The overhead output level variance results from treating a **fixed cost** as if it were a **variable cost**. Answers (b), (c), and (d) are incorrect because all of these variances arise when the quantity of actual inputs used differs from the quantity of inputs that should have been used. A production manager would have more control over inputs to production than over the determination of the denominator volume.

B. Material Variances

4. **(b)** The requirement is to determine Lem's material price variance for May. The direct materials price variance is the difference between actual unit prices and standard unit prices multiplied by the actual quantity, as shown below.

```
                              AQ x SP
                              $10,500
   AQ x AP                 (4,200m x $2.50/m)
   $10,080
            |_____|
            |   Material price variance, $420F   |
```

The $420 price variance is favorable because the actual purchase price of the material was lower than the standard price. Since the material was purchased for only $2.40 per meter ($10,080 cost ÷ 4,200m), Lem saved $.10 per meter compared to the standard price, for a total price savings of $420 (4,200m x $.10/m). Note that the standard quantity of materials is ignored in order to isolate these price differences; differences in quantity are addressed by the materials usage variance.

5. **(d)** Each unit of finished product contains two yards of direct material. However, the problem states that the 20% direct material spoilage is calculated on the quantity of direct material **input**. Although not mentioned, the facts in this question infer that the spoilage is normal and should be

part of the product's standard cost. The solutions approach would be to set up the following formula:

Input quantity	–	Spoilage	=	Output amount
X	–	.2X	=	2 yds.
		.8X	=	2 yds.
		X	=	2.5 yds.

Thus, the standard direct material cost per unit of finished product is $7.50 (2.5 yds. x $3).

6. **(a)** The materials usage variance measures the **actual** amount of materials **used** versus the standard amount that should have been used given the level of output. Normally the only department with controls over usage of materials is the manufacturing department. The purchasing department normally controls the cost of materials **purchased,** and not the amounts used (materials price variance). The warehouse department has little or no control over the materials used.

C. Labor Variances

7. **(b)** The solutions approach to compute the direct manufacturing labor efficiency variance is to set up a diagram as follows:

```
   AH x SR                         SH x SR
 (4,100 x $12)                  (4,000 x $12)
   $49,200                         $48,000
        |_____|
                      ?
              Efficiency variance
               $1,200 unfavorable
```

NOTE: To compute the Standard Hours (SH), multiply the Standard Hours allowed per unit produced (4) by the number of units produced (1,000).

8. **(a)** Standard costs are predetermined target costs which should be attainable under efficient conditions. The standard direct manufacturing labor cost per unit of product Glu is calculated as follows:

Weekly wages per worker	$500
Benefits treated as DML cost	100
Total DML per week per worker	$600
Hours per week	÷40
DML cost per hour	$ 15
Hours required for each unit	x 2
Standard DML cost per unit	$ 30

9. **(d)** A labor rate variance is the difference between budgeted wage rates and the wage rates actually paid. The problem states that line OW represents the standard labor cost at any output volume. Because point A is **above** the line, the actual cost was higher than the standard. The rate variance is, therefore, unfavorable. A labor efficiency variance is the difference between actual hours worked and standard hours allowed for output. On the diagram, point S is further on the X axis (Direct manufacturing labor hours) than point A indicating that the standard hours allowed are higher than the actual hours worked. Because actual hours are less than standard hours, this variance would be favorable.

D. Overhead Variances

10. (a)   To determine Gage's actual manufacturing overhead from the information given, total actual manufacturing costs must first be computed

Standard manufacturing cost	$100,000
Excess of actual manufacturing	
cost over standard costs	20,000
Total actual costs	$120,000

Since prime costs consist of direct materials and direct manufacturing labor, these costs are deducted from total actual costs to derive the portion that are overhead costs. Ordinarily, normal spoilage is not added to actual manufacturing overhead. The cost of normal spoilage should be added to the cost of good units produced. Freight out is also excluded because it is a selling expense.

Total actual costs	$120,000
Prime costs	(80,000)
Actual manufacturing overhead	$ 40,000

11. (d)   The fixed overhead spending variance is calculated as follows:

Budgeted fixed overhead	$20,000
Actual fixed overhead	22,000
Unfavorable fixed overhead spending	
variance	$ 2,000

12. (b)   The requirement is to determine which of the variances given consist of both variable and fixed overhead elements under a two-variance method. As shown in the diagram below, the controllable or budget variance includes both variable and fixed overhead elements, because the actual overhead amount, the first vertical line, includes both elements as does the budgeted overhead amount, the middle vertical line.

Actual	Budget for outputs achieved FOH + (SQ x SVR)	Applied SQ x STR*
	Budget var.	Volume var.

* *STR = Standard variable rate (SVR) + Standard fixed rate (SFR)*

The output level (volume) variance includes only the variance of fixed overhead, because the SQ x SVR is common to both amounts (i.e., it is included in the STR) used to determine the output level variance. The difference in the two amounts is the output level variance. It arises because the middle vertical line includes the total amount of budgeted fixed overhead, whereas the third vertical line includes the amount of fixed overhead applied using a per unit amount based on normal volume or level of activity. Whenever the standard activity level based on good output (SQ) is different than the normal activity level, a volume variance will arise. Therefore, both variable and fixed overhead elements are included in the controllable variance but not in the output level variance.

13. (c)   The requirement is to determine how unfavorable spending and output level (volume) variances computed using the three-variance method would be affected if the estimated activity level were increased. An increase in the activity level used to allocate overhead to the product will lower the standard fixed application rate (SFR). The formula for computing the SFR is

$$\text{Predetermined overhead rate} = \frac{\text{Estimated fixed overhead cost}}{\text{Estimated activity level}}$$

If the denominator in this formula is raised, the SFR is lowered. However, an increase in activity level used to allocate overhead will not affect the standard variable application rate (SVR). This rate is computed using the high-low method or regression analysis. The diagram for the 3-variance method is

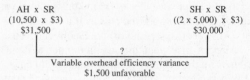

	Budget for actual inputs	Budget for outputs achieved	Applied
Actual	FOH + (AQ x SVR)	FOH + (SQ x SVR)	(SQ x STR)*
	Spending var.	Efficiency var.	Output level var.

:————————Net (overall) overhead variance————————:

**STR = Standard variable rate (SVR) + Standard fixed rate (SFR)*

When computing the standard variance, the SVR is used but the SFR is not. Therefore, this variance will not change with a change in activity level. The output level variance is computed by comparing the budgeted amount of total overhead costs for outputs achieved with the total amount of overhead applied. Both computations use SVR, but only the applied figure uses the SFR. In this problem, the output level variance is unfavorable indicating that the budgeted amount is more than the applied amount. When the SFR is lowered with the increase in activity level, less cost will be applied for every unit produced. The output level variance will therefore be increased and become more unfavorable.

14. (b)   The solutions approach to compute the variable overhead efficiency variance is to set up a diagram as follows:

AH x SR (10,500 x $3) $31,500	SH x SR ((2 x 5,000) x $3) $30,000

?
Variable overhead efficiency variance $1,500 unfavorable

15. (c)   A spending variance is caused by differences between the actual amount spent on fixed and variable overhead items and the amounts budgeted based on actual inputs. An output level variance is the difference between budgeted fixed overhead and applied fixed overhead. It is caused by under- or overutilization of plant capacity. Differences between actual and budgeted amounts (spending variances) occur often and can be corrected by changing the accounting estimates used in the budgeting process or the purchasing policies used. A difference in under- or over-utilization of plant capacity is a complex problem not easily corrected. Spending variances indicate short-term problems dealing with amounts spent on overhead while output level variances indicate long-term problems dealing with plant capacity.

16. (b)   The output level variance is solely a **fixed** overhead variance and is caused by under-/overutilization of capacity. This variance is computed by comparing the amount of fixed overhead budgeted with the amount of fixed overhead applied.

On the graph, line DB represents the flexible budget line for various outputs achieved and line OA represents the standard application line for various outputs achieved. Point V represents the standard quantity allowed for the output achieved. The dashed line extended vertically from V indicates the amount of overhead applied (where dashed line crosses OA) and the flexible budget amount (where dashed line crosses DB). Because the point on DB is below the point on OA, a larger amount was applied than the flexible budget amount. The output level variance is, therefore, favorable.

An overhead efficiency variance is solely a **variable** overhead variance and is caused by more (less) variable overhead being incurred due to inefficient (efficient) use of inputs. This variance is computed by comparing the flexible budget amount for actual inputs (Actual quantity of inputs x Standard variable application rate) with the amount applied (Standard quantity allowed for achieved output x Standard variable application rate). On the graph, Point S indicates the actual hours (inputs) used. Point V indicates the standard quantity allowed for the achieved outputs. Point S falls on the X axis further from zero than does Point V. Therefore, more hours were actually used than budgeted for the output achieved. The efficiency variance is unfavorable.

17.   (d)   On the graph, line DB represents the total factory overhead flexible budget line for various outputs achieved. Point D (the Y intercept) indicates the amount of fixed overhead included in the flexible budget. Line BC represents the total flexible budget amount estimated for the level of inputs used at Point C. Budgeted total variable overhead cost for C machine hours is total overhead budget (BC) less fixed overhead budgeted (DO).

18.   (b)   The requirement is to determine if favorable variances for variable food costs and fixed supervisory salaries would be reported by comparing actual results to amounts in a static budget. A static budget has only one planned volume level. The budget is not adjusted or altered to reflect changes in volume or other conditions during the budget period. In this problem, the actual level of sales was lower than the level used to make the static budget. Because variable costs remain the same per unit but change with levels of activity within the relevant range, actual variable costs would be lower than those in the budget. The variance reported for these costs would therefore be favorable. Fixed costs, however, are assumed to remain the same in total at all activity levels within the relevant range unless a change is specifically indicated. Because no such change is indicated in this problem concerning the fixed supervisory salaries, the actual amount for this cost would be the same as the amount in the static budget. There would be no variance reported for this fixed cost.

OTHER OBJECTIVE ANSWERS AND ANSWER EXPLANATIONS

Problem 1

For the diagram presented, three key elements should be identified. First, line OP represents the standard materials cost at any output volume expressed in direct material pounds to be used. The cost per pound is the same at any point on the line. Any point above the line has a higher materials cost per pound than standard. Conversely, any point below the line has a lower materials cost per pound. The material price variance measures the difference between standard material cost per pound and actual material cost per pound times the actual pounds of material. An unfavorable material price variance is generated when the actual material cost per pound is greater than standard cost per pound. Therefore, any point above line OP yields an unfavorable material price variance. Also, a favorable material price variance is created when the actual material cost per pound is less than the standard material cost per pound, thus, points below line OP yield a favorable material price variance. This relationship can be illustrated graphically:

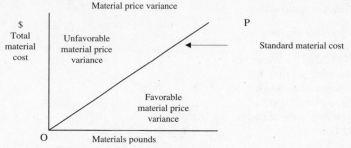

The second key element of the diagram is the vertical broken line. This broken line represents the standard pounds of materials needed for Bilco's output (Bilco had identical output for January, February, and March 2002). The materials usage variance measures the difference between pounds of materials used and the pounds of materials that should have been used at standard. If actual usage is less than standard, a favorable material usage variance is created, and if actual usage exceeds standard an unfavorable variance is generated. Any point to the left of the vertical broken line has used less materials than standard to generate the identical output and thus has a favorable materials usage variance. Points to the right of the vertical broken line have used more materials than standard; this results in an unfavorable usage variance. The following illustration summarizes this relationship:

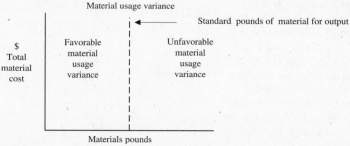

The third key element of the diagram is the horizontal broken line. This broken line represents the total standard materials cost for Bilco's production. Actual costs can be depicted by drawing a horizontal line from the monthly data points to the total materials cost axis. This intersection represents total actual material costs. Comparing total standard material costs with total actual material cost yields the monthly net material variances. Points below the horizontal broken line result in favorable net variances, and points above the line are unfavorable variances. The graph below illustrates the net variances.

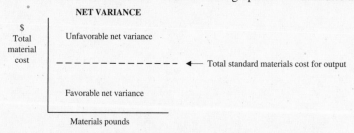

These elements of the diagram should be applied in answering **items 1 through 5**.

1. (U) January's cost per pound is greater than the standard materials cost represented by line OP. Thus, January's material price variance is unfavorable.

2. (F) January has used less material pounds than indicated by the standard (vertical broken line). Therefore, the material usage variance is favorable.

3. (U) February's cost per pound is greater than the standard materials cost represented by line OP. Thus, February's material price variance is unfavorable.

4.   (U) February has used more material pounds than indicated by the standard (vertical broken line). Therefore, the material usage variance is unfavorable.

5.   (F) The horizontal broken line represents the standard total materials cost for Bilco's production. The actual total materials cost for March (represented by point Ma) is below the horizontal broken line. Therefore, the actual total materials cost is less than the standard total materials cost and the material net variance for March is favorable.

Problem 2

1.   ($2,000, F) Computation of the direct materials price variance requires actual quantity (AQ), actual price (AP), and standard price (SP). AQ is given (2,000 gallons). SP is computed by dividing static budget chemicals cost by static budget gallons ($2,700 ÷ 900 = $3.00). AP is computed by dividing actual chemicals cost by actual gallons ($4,000 ÷ 2,000 = $2.00). The price variance is $2,000 favorable, as computed below.

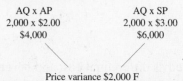

AQ x AP   AQ x SP
2,000 x $2.00   2,000 x $3.00
$4,000 $6,000

Price variance $2,000 F

2.   ($3,000, U) Computation of the direct materials usage (efficiency) variance requires AQ, SP, and standard quantity (SQ). In the static budget, 900 gallons are allowed for 18,000 feet (900 ÷ 18,000 = 1/20 gallon per foot). Therefore, the standard gallons allowed for actual footage sprayed is 1,000 gallons (20,000 x 1/20). The efficiency variance is $3,000 unfavorable, as computed below.

AQ x SP   SQ x SP
2,000 x $3.00   1,000 x $3.00
$6,000 $3,000

Efficiency variance $3,000 U

3.   ($1,000, U) The direct manufacturing labor travel, setup, and clearup variance is an efficiency variance based on the labor required **per customer** rather than **per footage sprayed**. To compute the variance, AQ, SP, and SQ are needed. AQ for travel, setup, and clearup is given as 300 hours. SQ is 200 hours (200 customers x 1 hour each). SP is also given ($10 per hour) or can be computed from the static budget ($1,900 ÷ 190 hours). The variance is $1,000 unfavorable, as computed below.

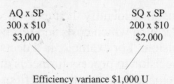

AQ x SP   SQ x SP
300 x $10   200 x $10
$3,000 $2,000

Efficiency variance $1,000 U

4.   ($2,000, F) The direct labor efficiency variance is based on the labor efficiency variance for **footage sprayed,** rather than for **customer calls** as in the previous computation. Again, AQ, SP, and SQ are needed to compute this variance. AQ for tree-spraying is 800 hours (given). SP is $10 per hour, as discussed in 3. SQ for tree-spraying is computed by determining the standard hours per foot from the static budget (900 hours ÷ 18,000 feet = 1/20 hour per foot), and by multiplying that amount by actual footage sprayed (1/20 x 20,000 = 1,000 hours). The efficiency variance is $2,000 favorable, as computed below.

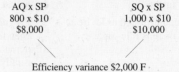

AQ x SP   SQ x SP
800 x $10   1,000 x $10
$8,000 $10,000

Efficiency variance $2,000 F

5.   ($1,000, U) The overhead spending (flexible budget) variance is the difference between actual overhead and budgeted overhead. Actual overhead is $6,000 (given). Budgeted overhead, determined from the static budget, is $2,000 fixed, 10¢ per foot sprayed ($1,800 ÷ 18,000 feet) and $5 per customer ($950 ÷ 190 customers). Therefore, budgeted overhead based on June's actual activity level is $5,000 [$2,000 + (20,000 x 10¢) + (200 x $5)]. The spending (flexible budget) variance is $1,000 unfavorable, as shown below.

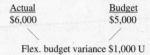

Actual   Budget
$6,000 $5,000

Flex. budget variance $1,000 U

NONROUTINE DECISIONS

The focus of this module is nonroutine decision making, which can be broken down into two broad categories, referred to here as short-term differential (relevant) cost analysis and capital budgeting decisions (or long-term differential cost analysis). The basic difference between these two categories is that capital budgeting decisions usually involve a large initial investment to be returned over a long-term period, while short-term differential cost decisions do not involve such an investment or such a long-term period for the returns.

A. Short-Term Differential Cost Analysis

Differential cost decisions include

1. Sell or process further (see also Section I., Module 34)
2. Special order
3. Outsourcing (make or buy)
4. Closing a department or segment
5. Sale of obsolete inventory
6. Scarce resources

These decisions would better be described as differential cost and **revenue** decisions, since basically the decision maker must consider differences in costs and revenues over various alternatives. All other things being equal, the alternative providing the greatest profit (or cost savings) should be chosen.

Three concepts relate to most differential cost decisions.

1. **The only relevant costs or revenues are those expected future costs and revenues that differ across alternatives.** If an alternative leads to increased revenues (costs) as compared to the present method used or other alternative considered, then these revenues (costs) are **relevant** (i.e., a differential cash flow).
2. **All costs incurred in the past (sunk costs) are irrelevant, unless they have future tax ramifications.** Past costs include joint costs, the cost of obsolete inventory, and fixed costs (in the short run).
3. **Opportunity cost, the income obtainable from an alternative use of a resource, must be considered.** If an alternative is profitable and that alternative is rejected in favor of others, the benefits foregone become a "cost" to be evaluated in the decision-making process.

To work a relevant cost problem, you must first identify the type of decision that is involved. Once you have identified the decision, you can determine which costs and revenues are relevant for accepting or rejecting an alternative and in reaching a decision. For example, in a decision to sell at split-off or process further, joint costs are irrelevant and a decision to process further is made if incremental revenue exceeds incremental cost. Finally, a decision is made based on the benefit or loss that would be derived from each alternative.

The table presented below summarizes various differential cost decisions and includes only **quantitative** factors.

Decision	*Description*	*Decision guideline*
1. Sell or process further	Should joint products be sold at split-off or processed further?	Ignore joint costs. Process further if incremental revenue exceeds incremental cost.
2. Special order	Should a discount-priced order be accepted when there is idle capacity?	If regular sales are not affected, accept order when the revenue from the order exceeds the incremental cost. Fixed production costs are usually irrelevant—they remain the same no matter what the company does.
3. Outsourcing (make or buy)	Should a part be manufactured or bought from a supplier?	Choose lower cost option. Fixed costs usually are irrelevant. Often opportunity costs are present.
4. Closing a department or segment	Should a segment of the company, such as a product line, be terminated?	Compare existing contribution margin with alternative. Consider any changes in future fixed costs.
5. Sale of obsolete inventory	Should obsolete inventory be reworked or junked?	Cost of inventory is sunk and ignored. Choose alternative with greatest excess of future revenue over future cost.
6. Scarce resources	Which products should be emphasized when capacity is limited?	Determine scarce resource (e.g., machine hours). Emphasize products with greatest contribution margin per unit of scarce resource.

Qualitative factors may be equally important in nonroutine decisions. For example, in the outsourcing decision, qualitative factors include

1. Quality of purchased part compared to manufactured part
2. Relationships with suppliers
3. Quickness in obtaining needed parts

Uncertainty also affects decision making. See the probability section at the end of this module for further discussion.

An example of a differential cost decision (special order) is presented below, comparing the simpler, more efficient **incremental** approach with the equally effective but more cumbersome **total** approach. Unless a problem requires the total approach, use of the incremental approach will save valuable exam time.

> EXAMPLE: *Potts Co. manufactures cookware. Expected annual volume of 100,000 sets per year is well below full capacity of 150,000. Normal selling price is $40/set. Manufacturing cost is $30/set ($20 variable and $10 fixed). Total fixed manufacturing cost is $1,000,000. Selling and administrative expenses are expected to be $500,000 ($300,000 fixed and $200,000 variable). A catalog company offers to buy 25,000 sets for $27/set. No extra selling and administrative costs would be caused by the order, and acceptance will not affect regular sales. Should the offer be accepted?*

INCREMENTAL APPROACH

Incremental revenue (25,000 x $27)	$ 675,000
Incremental cost (25,000 x $20)	(500,000)
Benefit of accepting order (contribution margin)	$ 175,000

TOTAL APPROACH

		Without order		*With order*
Sales (100,000 x $40) less Variable costs:		$4,000,000	[+(25,000 x $27)]	$4,675,000
Manufacturing	(100,000 x $20)	(2,000,000)	[+(25,000 x $20)]	(2,500,000)
Sell. and admin.	(100,000 x $2)	(200,000)		(200,000)
		1,800,000		1,975,000
Contribution margin less Fixed costs:				
Manufacturing		(1,000,000)		(1,000,000)
Sell. and admin.		(300,000)		(300,000)
Operating income		$ 500,000		$ 675,000

> At first glance, it may appear that the order should not be accepted because the selling price of $27 is less than the $30 manufacturing cost per set. However, fixed costs do not increase if the order is accepted and are therefore irrelevant to this decision. The result is that, with either the incremental or the total approach, operating income is increased by $175,000. Therefore, Potts Company should accept the order.

B. Capital Budgeting

Capital budgeting is a technique to evaluate long-term investments. Capital budgeting decisions using discounted cash flow techniques involve evaluation of an investment today in terms of the present value of future cash returns from the investment. Note that only **relevant** cash flows, as defined in the previous section, are considered for purposes of capital budgeting. The objective is to identify the most profitable or best investment alternative. The cash returns can take two forms depending on the nature of the project. If the project will produce revenue, the return is the difference between the cash revenues (inflows) and cash expenses (outflows). Other projects generate cost savings (e.g., cash outflows for labor that are not made because a new machine is more efficient). The latter are, in effect, reductions in outflows, which, for simplicity, can be treated as cash inflows. Conceptually, the results of both types of projects are the same. The entity ends up with more cash by making the initial capital investment.

Two terms frequently used on the CPA exam are net cash flow (difference between future annual cash inflows and outflows) and after-tax net cash flow (net cash flow after tax expense).

The choice among alternative investing decisions can be made on the basis of several capital budgeting models: (1) Payback, (2) Net present value, (3) Excess present value index, (4) Internal (time-adjusted) rate of return, and (5) Accounting rate of return.

The **payback** method evaluates investments on the length of time until recapture (return) of the investment. For example, if a $10,000 investment were to return a cash flow of $2,500 a year, the payback period would be four years. If the payback period is to be computed after income taxes, it is necessary to calculate cash flow as shown below, remembering that depreciation itself does not consume cash. Assuming a five-year life with no salvage value and a 40% income tax rate, the after-tax payback period would be computed as follows:

Cash flow: $2,500 x (1 – 40%) = $1,500
Tax savings from depreciation: $2,000 x 40% = $800
$10,000 ÷ $2,300 = 4.35 years

This method ignores total project profitability and the time value of money. The only redeeming aspect of the payback method is that it is an indicator of risk and liquidity. Generally speaking, the shorter the payback period, the faster the investment is returned (liquidity) and the shorter the time the funds are at risk to changes in the environment.

The **net present value** (NPV) method is a discounted cash flow method which calculates the present value of the future cash flows of a project and compares this with the investment outlay required to implement the project. The net present value of a project is defined as

NPV = (Present value of future cash flows) – (Required investment)

The calculation of the present value of the future cash flows requires the selection of a discount rate (also referred to as the target or hurdle rate). The rate used should be the minimum rate of return that management is willing to accept on capital investment projects. The rate used should be no less than the cost of capital—the rate management currently must pay to obtain funds. A project which earns exactly the desired rate of return will have a net present value of 0. A positive net present value identifies projects which will earn in excess of the minimum rate. For example, if a company desires a minimum return of 6% on an investment of $10,000 that has an expected return of $2,500 for five years, the present value of the cash flows is $10,530 ($2,500 x 4.212: 4.212 is the TVMF for the present value of an annuity, n = 5, i = 6%; see Module 26A, Present Value: Fundamentals). The net present value of $530 ($10,530 – $10,000) indicates that the project will earn a return in excess of the 6% minimum desired. If the requirement were for a net-of-tax return of 6%, the net-of-tax cash flow of $2,300 computed in the previous section for the payback method would be multiplied by 4.212. This would result in a present value of $9,687.60 for the cash inflows, which is less than the $10,000 initial outlay. Therefore, this investment should not be made.

The NPV method is based on cash flows and would ignore depreciation if taxes were not considered. As shown earlier, however, depreciation results in a tax savings that must be factored into the evaluation. For example, assume that a company is considering the purchase of equipment costing $20,000 for use in a new project. MACRS is used to depreciate equipment for tax purposes, under which the machine has a useful life of seven years. The required rate of return of the company is 8%. The present value of the tax savings from depreciation would be as follows:

Year	Income tax deduction for depreciation	Income tax savings at 30% tax rate	8% Discount factor	Present value at 8%*
1	$2,858	$ 857	.926	$ 794
2	4,898	1,469	.857	1,259
3	3,498	1,049	.794	833
4	2,498	749	.735	551
5	1,786	536	.681	365
6	1,784	535	.630	337
7	1,786	536	.583	312
8	892	268	.540	145
				$4,596

* *Tax savings x Discount factor*

Therefore, $4,596 would be included in the NPV computation as a cash inflow from the equipment.

The **excess present value (profitability) index** computes the ratio of the present value of the cash inflows to the initial cost of a project. It is used to implement the net present value method when there is a limit on funds available for capital investments. Assuming other factors are equal, this is accomplished by allocating funds to those projects with the highest excess present value indexes.

First, the net present value of each alternative is calculated using the minimum required rate of return. Then the excess present value index is computed

$$\frac{\text{Present value of future net cash inflows}}{\text{Initial investment}} \times 100 = \text{Excess present value index}$$

If the index is equal to or greater than 100%, the project will generate a return equal to or greater than the required rate of return.

The **internal (time-adjusted) rate of return** (IRR) method is another discounted cash flow method. It determines the rate of discount at which the present value of the future cash flows will exactly equal the investment outlay. This rate is compared with the minimum desired rate of return to determine if the investment should be made. The internal rate of return is determined by setting the investment today equal to the discounted value of future cash flows. The discounting factor (rate of return) is the unknown. The TVMF for the previous example is

$$
\begin{array}{rcl}
\text{PV (investment today)} & = & \text{TVMF x Cash flows} \\
\$10,000 & = & \text{TVMF x } \$2,500 \\
\text{TVMF} & = & 4.00
\end{array}
$$

The interest rate of a TVMF of 4.00 where n = 5 is approximately 8%. The after-tax rate of return is determined using the $2,300 after-tax cash inflow amount as follows:

$$
\begin{array}{rcl}
\$10,000 & = & \text{TVMF x } \$2,300 \\
\text{TVMF} & = & 4.35
\end{array}
$$

The interest rate of a TVMF of 4.35 where n = 5 is approximately 5%. CPA exam multiple-choice questions in this area do not require finding the exact rate of return if the exact TVMF falls between two TVMF given in a table. The answers are worded "less than 5%, but greater than 0%," "less than 7%, but greater than 5%," etc.

The relationship between the NPV method and the IRR method can be summarized as follows:

NPV	*IRR*
NPV > 0	IRR > Discount rate
NPV = 0	IRR = Discount rate
NPV < 0	IRR < Discount rate

The internal rate of return method is based upon an important assumption when comparing investments of different lengths. The method implicitly assumes that the cash inflows from the investment with the shorter life can be reinvested at the same internal rate of return. For example, assume a company must choose between two projects, A and B. The IRR of project A is 15% with a life of five years while the IRR of project B is 12% with a life of ten years. Project A may seem like the best choice since it yields the highest return. However, the internal rate of return method assumes that the cash inflows from the project can be reinvested at 15%. If the cash inflows can only be reinvested at 9%, then project B may be the better alternative.

The **accounting rate of return** (ARR) method computes an approximate rate of return which ignores the time value of money. It is computed as follows:

$$
\text{ARR} = \text{Expected increase in annual net income} \div \text{Average (or initial) investment}
$$

Using the same example, the ARR before taxes is

$$
(\$2,500 - \$2,000) \div (\$10,000 \div 2) = 10\%
$$

The ARR after taxes is

$$
[(\$2,500 - \$2,000) \times 60\%] \div (\$10,000 \div 2) = 6\%
$$

Note that the numerator is the increase in **net income**, not **cash flows**, so depreciation is subtracted. The average investment is one-half the initial investment because the initial investment is depreciated down to 0 by the end of the project. If a problem asked for ARR based on **initial** investment, you would not divide the investment by 2.

Two complicating factors often found on the CPA exam are **salvage value** and **uneven cash flows**. The salvage value is a future cash inflow which must be considered. Uneven cash flows mean that the basic payback formula cannot be used; net cash inflows must be accumulated until the investment is returned. For the NPV and IRR methods, each year's net cash inflow must be discounted separately using the present value of $1 table.

C. Probability Analysis

Because it is not always possible to make decisions under conditions of total certainty, decision makers must have a method of determining the best estimate or course of action where uncertainty exists. One method is probability analysis. This is used where there are a number of possible outcomes and the probability of occurrence of each outcome can be estimated by the decision maker.

For example, assume the life of an asset is unknown; however, the decision maker estimates that there is a 30% probability of a four-year life, a 50% probability of a five-year life, and a 20% probability of a six-year life. By multiplying the probability by the number of years for each possible outcome and then summing the results, the expected (weighted-average) life of the asset can be determined as follows:

Years of life	x	Probability	=	Expected value
4		.3		1.2
5		.5		2.5
6		.2		1.2
				4.9 years

Thus, the expected life of the asset is found to be 4.9 years. Notice that because the expected life or value is the weighted-average of the three possible outcomes, it represents the best available estimate.

Another application of probability analysis can be found in question number 35 from Part II of the November 1986 Practice Exam as shown below.

Clay Co. operated three shipping terminals, referred to as X, Y, and Z. Of the total cargo shipped, terminals X, Y, and Z handle approximately 60%, 30%, and 10%, respectively, with error rates of 3%, 4%, and 6%, respectively. Clay's internal auditor randomly selects one shipping document, ascertaining that this document contains an error. The probability that the error occurred in terminal X is

a. 60%
b. 50%
c. 23%
d.   3%

A good solutions approach to this question is to set it up as follows:

Terminal	% of volume	x	Rate of error	=	Expected value
X	60%		3%		1.8%
Y	30		4		1.2
Z	10		6		0.6
					3.6%

Here, the expected value of 3.6% represents the rate of error of all the shipping documents combined. The problem states that an error has been found. You must determine the probability that this error occurred in terminal X. Since the 1.8% expected value for terminal X is equal to 50% of the total expected value (1.8% ÷ 3.6%), the probability that the error occurred at terminal X is 50% which is answer (b).

MULTIPLE-CHOICE QUESTIONS (1-27)

1. Clay Co. has considerable excess manufacturing capacity. A special job order's cost sheet includes the following applied manufacturing overhead costs:

Fixed costs	$21,000
Variable costs	33,000

The fixed costs include a normal $3,700 allocation for in-house design costs, although no in-house design will be done. Instead the job will require the use of external designers costing $7,750. What is the total amount to be included in the calculation to determine the minimum acceptable price for the job?

   a. $36,700
   b. $40,750
   c. $54,000
   d. $58,050

2. For the year ended December 31, 2002, Abel Co. incurred direct costs of $500,000 based on a particular course of action during the year. If a different course of action had been taken, direct costs would have been $400,000. In addition, Abel's 2002 fixed costs were $90,000. The incremental cost was

   a. $ 10,000
   b. $ 90,000
   c. $100,000
   d. $190,000

3. Mili Co. plans to discontinue a division with a $20,000 contribution margin. Overhead allocated to the division is $50,000, of which $5,000 cannot be eliminated. The effect of this discontinuance on Mili's pretax income would be an increase of

   a. $ 5,000
   b. $20,000
   c. $25,000
   d. $30,000

4. Buff Co. is considering replacing an old machine with a new machine. Which of the following items is economically relevant to Buff's decision? (Ignore income tax considerations.)

	Carrying amount of old machine	*Disposal value of new machine*
a.	Yes	No
b.	No	Yes
c.	No	No
d.	Yes	Yes

5. During 2002, Deet Corp. experienced the following power outages:

Number of outages per month	*Number of months*
0	3
1	2
2	4
3	3
	12

Each power outage results in out-of-pocket costs of $400. For $500 per month, Deet can lease an auxiliary generator to provide power during outages. If Deet leases an auxiliary generator in 2003 the estimated savings (or additional expenditures) for 2003 would be

   a. $(3,600)
   b. $(1,200)
   c. $ 1,600
   d. $ 1,900

6. Para Co. is reviewing the following data relating to an energy saving investment proposal:

Cost	$50,000
Residual value at the end of 5 years	10,000
Present value of an annuity of 1 at 12% for 5 years	3.60
Present value of 1 due in 5 years at 12%	0.57

What would be the annual savings needed to make the investment realize a 12% yield?

   a. $ 8,189
   b. $11,111
   c. $12,306
   d. $13,889

7. Jago Co. has two products that use the same manufacturing facilities and cannot be subcontracted. Each product has sufficient orders to utilize the entire manufacturing capacity. For short-run profit maximization, Jago should manufacture the product with the

   a. Lower total manufacturing costs for the manufacturing capacity.
   b. Lower total variable manufacturing costs for the manufacturing capacity.
   c. Greater gross profit per hour of manufacturing capacity.
   d. Greater contribution margin per hour of manufacturing capacity.

8. The discount rate (hurdle rate of return) must be determined in advance for the

   a. Payback period method.
   b. Time-adjusted rate of return method.
   c. Net present value method.
   d. Internal rate of return method.

9. The capital budgeting technique known as payback period uses

	Depreciation expense	*Time value of money*
a.	Yes	Yes
b.	Yes	No
c.	No	No
d.	No	Yes

10. Which of the following is a strength of the payback method?

   a. It considers cash flows for all years of the project.
   b. It distinguishes the source of cash inflows.
   c. It considers the time value of money.
   d. It is easy to understand.

11. Tam Co. is negotiating for the purchase of equipment that would cost $100,000, with the expectation that $20,000 per year could be saved in after-tax cash costs if the equipment were acquired. The equipment's estimated useful life is ten years, with no residual value, and would be depreciated by the straight-line method. The payback period is

   a. 4.0 years.
   b. 4.4 years.
   c. 4.5 years.
   d. 5.0 years.

12. Pole Co. is investing in a machine with a three-year life. The machine is expected to reduce annual cash operating costs by $30,000 in each of the first two years and by $20,000 in year three. Present values of an annuity of $1 at 14% are:

Period 1	0.88
2	1.65
3	2.32

Using a 14% cost of capital, what is the present value of these future savings?

a. $59,600
b. $60,800
c. $62,900
d. $69,500

13. For the next two years, a lease is estimated to have an operating net cash inflow of $7,500 per annum, before adjusting for $5,000 per annum tax basis lease amortization, and a 40% tax rate. The present value of an ordinary annuity of $1 per year at 10% for two years is 1.74. What is the lease's after-tax present value using a 10% discount factor?

a. $ 2,610
b. $ 4,350
c. $ 9,570
d. $11,310

14. A project's net present value, ignoring income tax considerations, is normally affected by the

a. Proceeds from the sale of the asset to be replaced.
b. Carrying amount of the asset to be replaced by the project.
c. Amount of annual depreciation on the asset to be replaced.
d. Amount of annual depreciation on fixed assets used directly on the project.

15. Polo Co. requires higher rates of return for projects with a life span greater than five years. Projects extending beyond five years must earn a higher specified rate of return. Which of the following capital budgeting techniques can readily accommodate this requirement?

	Internal rate of return	Net present value
a.	Yes	No
b.	No	Yes
c.	No	No
d.	Yes	Yes

16. Neu Co. is considering the purchase of an investment that has a positive net present value based on Neu's 12% hurdle rate. The internal rate of return would be

a. 0
b. 12%
c. > 12%
d. < 12%

17. Kern Co. is planning to invest in a two-year project that is expected to yield cash flows from operations, net of income taxes, of $50,000 in the first year and $80,000 in the second year. Kern requires an internal rate of return of 15%. The present value of $1 for one period at 15% is 0.870 and for two periods at 15% is 0.756. The future value of $1 for one period at 15% is 1.150 and for two periods at 15% is 1.323. The maximum that Kern should invest immediately is

a. $ 81,670
b. $103,980
c. $130,000
d. $163,340

18. How are the following used in the calculation of the internal rate of return of a proposed project? Ignore income tax considerations.

	Residual sales value of project	Depreciation expense
a.	Exclude	Include
b.	Include	Include
c.	Exclude	Exclude
d.	Include	Exclude

Items 19 and 20 are based on the following:

Tam Co. is negotiating for the purchase of equipment that would cost $100,000, with the expectation that $20,000 per year could be saved in after-tax cash costs if the equipment were acquired. The equipment's estimated useful life is ten years, with no residual value, and would be depreciated by the straight-line method. Tam's predetermined minimum desired rate of return is 12%. Present value of an annuity of 1 at 12% for ten periods is 5.65. Present value of 1 due in ten periods at 12% is .322.

19. In estimating the internal rate of return, the factors in the table of present values of an annuity should be taken from the columns closest to

a. 0.65
b. 1.30
c. 5.00
d. 5.65

20. Accrual accounting rate of return based on initial investment is

a. 30%
b. 20%
c. 12%
d. 10%

21. Lin Co. is buying machinery it expects will increase average annual operating income by $40,000. The initial increase in the required investment is $60,000, and the average increase in required investment is $30,000. To compute the accrual accounting rate of return, what amount should be used as the numerator in the ratio?

a. $20,000
b. $30,000
c. $40,000
d. $60,000

22. The capital budgeting technique known as accounting rate of return uses

	Revenue over life of project	Depreciation expense
a.	No	Yes
b.	No	No
c.	Yes	No
d.	Yes	Yes

23. Under frost-free conditions, Cal Cultivators expects its strawberry crop to have a $60,000 market value. An unprotected crop subject to frost has an expected market value of $40,000. If Cal protects the strawberries against frost, then the market value of the crop is still expected to be $60,000 under frost-free conditions and $90,000 if there is a frost. What must be the probability of a frost for Cal to be indifferent to spending $10,000 for frost protection?

a. .167
b. .200
c. .250
d. .333

24. Dough Distributors has decided to increase its daily muffin purchases by 100 boxes. A box of muffins costs $2 and sells for $3 through regular stores. Any boxes not sold through regular stores are sold through Dough's thrift store for $1. Dough assigns the following probabilities to selling additional boxes:

Additional sales	Probability
60	.6
100	.4

What is the expected value of Dough's decision to buy 100 additional boxes of muffins?
    a. $28
    b. $40
    c. $52
    d. $68

25. Which tool would most likely be used to determine the best course of action under conditions of uncertainty?
    a. Cost-volume-profit analysis.
    b. Expected value (EV).
    c. Program evaluation and review technique (PERT).
    d. Scattergraph method.

26. To assist in an investment decision, Gift Co. selected the most likely sales volume from several possible outcomes. Which of the following attributes would that selected sales volume reflect?
    a. The midpoint of the range.
    b. The median.
    c. The greatest probability.
    d. The expected value.

27. Probability (risk) analysis is
    a. Used only for situations involving five or fewer possible outcomes
    b. Used only for situations in which the summation of probability weights is greater than one.
    c. An extension of sensitivity analysis.
    d. Incompatible with sensitivity analysis.

OTHER OBJECTIVE QUESTIONS

Problem 1   (10 to 15 minutes)

Items 1 through 4 are based on the following:

A company has two mutually exclusive projects, A and B, which have the same initial investment requirements and lives. Project B has a decrease in estimated net cash inflows each year, and project A has an increase in estimated net cash inflows each year. Project A has a greater total net cash inflow. Diagram I below depicts the net cash inflows of each project by year. Diagram II depicts the net present value (NPV) of each project assuming various discount rates.

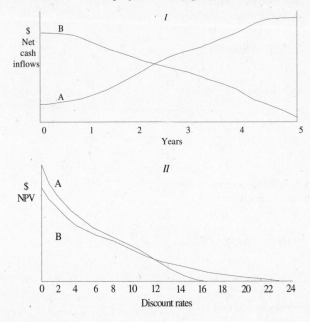

Required:

For items 1 through 4, select your answer from the following list.

A. Project A
B. Project B
C. Both projects equal

1. Which project would be likely to have the shorter payback period?

2. Which project would have the greater average accounting rate of return?

3. Which project would have the greater internal rate of return?

4. Assume, due to innovation, the projects were to terminate at the end of year four with cash flows remaining as projected for the first four years and no cash flows in year five. Which project would have the greater internal rate of return?

Problem 2[1]   (20 to 30 minutes)

Isle, Inc. commenced operations on January 2, 2002. Isle's three products (Aran, Bute, Cilly) are produced in different plants located in the same community. The following selected information is taken from Isle's internal 2002 contribution income statement, based on standard costs:

---

[1]   *This OOAF question is comprehensive over managerial accounting. Thus, we put it in the last managerial module (37).*

Isle, Inc.
2001 CONTRIBUTION INCOME STATEMENT

| | Products | | | |
	Aran	Bute	Cilly	Total
Sales (Aran 80,000 units)	$1,200,000	$800,000	$500,000	$2,500,000
Standard costs:				
Direct materials	180,000			
Direct labor (Aran 20,000 hours)	240,000			
Variable manufacturing overhead	80,000	(Detail omitted)		
Total variable manufacturing costs	500,000			
Less: Finished goods inventory 12/31/02	100,000			
Variable cost of goods sold	400,000			
Variable selling and administrative costs	120,000			
Total variable costs	520,000			
Standard contribution margin	680,000	176,000	144,000	1,000,000
Fixed manufacturing overhead costs	440,000	(Detail omitted)		
Fixed selling and administrative costs	140,000			
Total fixed costs	580,000			
Standard operating income	100,000	35,000	25,000	160,000
Variances—Favorable (F)/Unfavorable (U):				
Direct materials— Price	2,000 (F)			
Usage	16,000 (U)			
Direct labor— Rate	12,000 (F)	(Detail omitted)		
Efficiency	24,000 (U)			
Manufacturing overhead—Total	43,000 (U)			
Selling and administrative—Total	7,000 (U)			
Operating income, Net of variances	$ --	$ 41,000	$ 36,000	$ 77,000

Additional information:

• Manufacturing Capacity Utilization	75%	80%	70%
• Average investment	$1,000,000	$800,000	$400,000
• Demand	Somewhat seasonal and moderately difficult to project more than three years	Constant and easy to project more than three years	Very seasonal and very difficult to project more than three years

- Isle also prepared standard absorption costing statements using full capacity (based on machine hours) to allocate overhead costs.
- Fixed costs are incurred evenly throughout the year.
- There is no ending work in process.
- Material price variances are reported when raw materials are taken from inventory.
- Apart from initial build-ups in raw materials, and finished goods inventories, production schedules are based on sales forecasts.

For **items 1 through 13,** determine whether the statement is yes (Y) or no (N).

1. Does Isle practice a just-in-time philosophy?

2. Should Isle include standard indirect material costs in standard fixed overhead costs?

3. Should Isle categorize the operation of production equipment as a value-adding activity?

4. If Isle's three products were produced in a single plant, would activity-based costing provide more useful total production cost information for Aran, Bute, and Cilly than traditional standard costing?

5. Is the regression analysis technique helpful in determining the variable cost component of Isle's manufacturing overhead costs?

6. In Isle's internal performance reports, should normal spoilage costs be reported in fixed manufacturing overhead costs?

7. The computation of Bute's normal spoilage assumes ten units in 1,000 contain defective materials and, independently, fifteen units in 1,000 contain defective workmanship. Is the probability that is used in computing Bute's normal spoilage less than .025?

8. Isle has contracted to sell units of Aran to a customer in a segregated market during the off-season. Ignore variances and the costs of developing and administering the contract, and assume that standard cost patterns are unchanged except that variable selling and administrative costs are one-half the standard rate. Isle will sell Aran at a price which recoups the variable cost of goods sold at the standard rate, plus variable selling and administrative costs at one-half of the standard rate. Will Isle break even on the contract?

9. Were the actual 2002 direct manufacturing labor hours used in manufacturing Aran less than the standard hours?

10. Would Aran's 2002 operating income reported using absorption cost be lower than the amount reported using variable costing?

11. Was the total amount paid for direct materials put into process for the manufacture of Aran more than the standard cost allowed for the work done?

Items 12 and 13 are based on the following:

Isle is considering investing $60,000 in a ten-year property lease that will reduce Aran's annual selling and administration costs by $12,000. Isle's cost of capital is 12%. The present value factor for a ten-year annuity at 12% is 5.65.

12. Is there a positive net present value for the lease investment?

13. Is the internal rate of return for the lease investment lower than the cost of capital?

For **items 14 through 18**, choose the correct answer.

14. For which product is evaluation of investments by the payback method likely to be more appropriate?
   a. Aran
   b. Bute
   c. Cilly

15. For which product is the economic order quantity formula likely to be most useful when purchasing raw materials to be used in manufacturing?
   a. Aran
   b. Bute
   c. Cilly

16. If Isle sells $10,000 more of Bute and $10,000 less of Cilly, what is the effect on Isle's standard dollar breakeven point?
   a. Increase
   b. Decrease
   c. No effect

17. Which product had the greatest actual return on investment?
   a. Aran
   b. Bute
   c. Cilly

18. Ignore 2002 reported variances and assume that Isle used expected demand to allocate manufacturing overhead costs. Which product would be most likely to have a substantial percentage of underapplied or overapplied fixed manufacturing overhead costs on quarterly statements?
   a. Aran
   b. Bute
   c. Cilly

For **items 19 through 23**, a numerical answer is required. This candidate would select an answer from a list of numbers.

19. What is Aran's budgeted standard per unit cost for variable selling and administrative costs on sales of 75,000 units?

20. What is Aran's budgeted standard fixed selling and administrative costs on sales of 75,000 units?

21. What is Isle's standard breakeven point in sales dollars for the actual sales mix achieved?

22. What amount of Aran's direct material and direct manufacturing labor variances might be regarded, wholly or partially, as direct manufacturing labor employees' responsibility?

23. Isle uses the graph below to estimate Aran's total standard manufacturing cost.

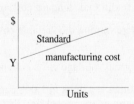

What amount does Y represent?

MULTIPLE-CHOICE ANSWERS

1. b __ __	7. d __ __	13. d __ __	19. c __ __	25. b __ __
2. c __ __	8. c __ __	14. a __ __	20. d __ __	26. c __ __
3. c __ __	9. c __ __	15. d __ __	21. c __ __	27. c __ __
4. b __ __	10. d __ __	16. c __ __	22. d __ __	
5. c __ __	11. d __ __	17. b __ __	23. b __ __	1st: __/27 = __%
6. c __ __	12. c __ __	18. d __ __	24. c __ __	2nd: __/27 = __%

MULTIPLE-CHOICE ANSWER EXPLANATIONS

A. Short-Term Differential Cost Analysis

1. (b) When determining a price for a special order when there is idle capacity, only the differential manufacturing costs are considered. The underlying assumption is that acceptance of the order will not affect regular sales. In the short run, fixed costs are sunk costs and are irrelevant. Since regular sales will not be affected by the special order, fixed and variable costs incurred during normal operations are not considered. Clay Company should consider only the variable costs associated with the order and the differential cost of using the external designers. The costs to be considered total $40,750 ($33,000 + $7,750). The order is accepted if revenue from the order exceeds the differential costs.

2. (c) When deciding between alternatives, the only relevant costs or revenues are those expected future costs and revenues that differ across alternatives. In the short run, fixed costs are sunk costs and are irrelevant. Thus, Abel's 2002 fixed costs are ignored for purposes of short-term differential cost analysis. The incremental cost was $100,000 ($500,000 – $400,000).

3. (c) The requirement is to evaluate the effect on pretax profit if a department is discontinued. The solutions approach is to isolate those revenues and costs that would differ if the department is discontinued. If the department is discontinued, $20,000 of contribution margin would be lost. The $5,000 of allocated overhead will continue regardless of the decision made. Thus, $45,000 ($50,000 – $5,000) of allocated overhead cost would be eliminated or avoided. The net effect on pretax profit would be an increase of $25,000 ($45,000 of cost avoided less $20,000 of contribution margin lost).

4. (b) The requirement is to determine which costs are economically relevant to Buff Co.'s decision of whether to replace an old machine with a new machine. Costs which will not differ among alternatives are not relevant for decision making purposes. Sunk costs are those which are not avoidable and are the result of a past decision. The original cost, accumulated depreciation, and therefore the carrying amount of Buff's old machine are not relevant to the decision because this is a past cost that cannot be changed. The costs associated with the new machine are avoidable. The disposal value of a new machine is relevant to Buff's decision because it represents a cash inflow which differs between the alternatives.

5. (c) The requirement is to calculate Deet's estimated savings for 2003 if it leases an auxiliary generator for use during power outages. In 2002 Deet incurred the following costs due to power outages:

Number of outages per month		Number of months		Number of outages
0	x	3	=	0
1	x	2	=	2
2	x	4	=	8
3	x	3	=	9
		12		19

19 outages x $400/outage = $7,600

The cost of leasing an auxiliary generator is only $6,000 (12 mos. x $500/mo). Therefore, Deet would save $1,600 ($7,600 – $6,000) in 2003 by leasing the generator.

6. (c) The requirement is to determine the annual savings needed for an investment to realize a 12% yield. The internal rate of return method of capital budgeting determines the rate of return at which the present value of the cash flows will exactly equal the investment outlay. In this problem, the desired IRR is given and the cash flows must be determined. The necessary annual savings can be computed as follows:

TVMF X Cash flows = PV (investment today)
$$3.60X = \$50,000 - (.57 \text{ X } \$10,000)$$
$$3.60X = \$44,300$$
$$X = \$12,306$$

If the annual savings equals $12,306, the present value of the cash inflows will exactly equal the cash outflows.

7. (d) The costs relevant to short-term decision making include only those costs that differ among alternatives. Fixed costs are sunk costs; that is, they are already committed and have no bearing on short-run decisions. Both total manufacturing costs and gross profit contain a fixed cost component. A multiproduct firm operating at full capacity should base product mix decisions on profit maximization. However, the product with lower total variable manufacturing costs at full capacity may not necessarily be the product that will optimize income due to differences in sales price. Total revenues for the more costly product may be so much greater that this product still produces more income than the cheaper one. Similarly, the product with the highest contribution margin (CM) per unit may not be the product that will maximize income due to differences in the number of units that can be produced at full capacity. For example, if at full capacity 100 units of Product A could be produced and sold at $20.00 CM per unit or 500 units of Product B could be produced and sold for only $5.00 CM per unit, production of Product B will optimize **total** CM [$2,500 (500 x $5) for B versus $2,000 (100 x $20) for A]. Instead, the relevant figure is the product which yields the highest CM per unit of the **limiting factor**. Since Jago would be operating at full capacity with either product, machine hours is limiting and the product which generates the greater CM per hour of manufacturing capacity is the product which will optimize short-term profits.

B. Capital Budgeting

8. (c) The requirement is to determine when the discount rate (hurdle rate) must be determined before a capital budgeting method can be used. The payback method measures the time it will take to recoup, in the form of cash inflows from operations, the initial dollars invested in a project. The payback method does **not** consider the time value of money. The time-adjusted rate of return method is also called the internal rate of return method. This method computes the rate of interest at which the present value of expected cash inflows from a project equals the present value of expected cash outflows of the project. Here, the discount rate is not determined in advance but is the end result of the calculation. The net present value method is the correct answer because it calculates the expected net monetary gain or loss from a project by discounting all expected future cash inflows and outflows to the present using some predetermined minimum desired rate of return (hurdle rate).

B. Capital Budgeting: Payback

9. (c) The payback period is computed by dividing the initial investment by the annual net cash inflow. Depreciation expense is not subtracted from cash inflow; only the income taxes which are caused by the depreciation deduction are subtracted. One of the weaknesses of the payback period is that it ignores the time value of money.

10. (d) The payback method is easy to understand but it is not very sophisticated. Answer (a) is incorrect because the payback method only considers cash flows until the cost is recovered. Answer (b) is incorrect because the payback method only considers net cash inflows from all sources. Answer (c) is incorrect because the payback method does not consider the time value of money.

11. (d) The payback method evaluates investments on the length of time until total dollars invested are recouped in the form of cash inflow or cash outflows avoided. It is calculated as Initial investment ÷ Annual cash inflow of a project. The payback period of the equipment under consideration by Tam is

$$\$100{,}000 \div \$20{,}000 = 5 \text{ years}$$

B. Capital Budgeting: Net Present Value

12. (c) The requirement is to determine the present value of the future cash savings resulting from purchase of the new machine. The present value of the $30,000 savings per year for the first two years is calculated using the present value of an annuity for two periods. Since the amount of the cash savings drops to $20,000 in year three, this amount must be calculated separately. The PV of an annuity for three periods minus the PV of an annuity for two periods, equals the PV of an amount to be received three years in the future. The total present value of the cash savings is calculated as follows:

PV of $30,000 for 2 periods = $30,000 x 1.65 = $49,500
PV of $20,000 in period 3 = $20,000 x (2.32 – 1.65) =   13,400
    Total present value of cash savings $62,900

Alternatively, $20,000 could have been treated as an annuity for three years and an additional $10,000 for two years.

13. (d) The net present value of a project equals

NPV = (PV future cash flows) – (Investment)

Since this problem involves a lease requiring only annual payments there is no initial investment in this case. Lease amortization must be subtracted from cash inflows to determine income tax expense.

$7,500	Annual cash inflow
– 5,000	Tax basis lease amortization
$2,500	Taxable lease income
x 40%	
$1,000	Tax expense per year

However, lease amortization is **not** a cash outflow and is thus excluded from the calculation of NPV. The after-tax present value of the lease equals:

$ 7,500	Annual cash inflow
– 1,000	Cash outflow for taxes
$6,500	
x 1.74	PV factor for two years at 10%
$11,310	

14. (a) A project's net present value is determined by considering the project's cash inflows and cash outflows discounted to their present values using the required rate of return. The initial outlay for the replacement asset is considered to be the cash outflow reduced by any proceeds from the sale of the asset to be replaced.

B. Capital Budgeting: Internal (Time-Adjusted) Rate of Return

15. (d) The internal rate of return method determines the rate of return at which the present value of the cash flows will exactly equal the investment outlay. It will indicate the rate of return earned over the life of the project. The net present value method determines the present value of all future cash flows at a selected discount rate. If the NPV of the cash flows is positive, the return earned by the project is higher than the selected rate. Both methods will provide the information needed to decide if a project's rate of return will meet Polo Co.'s requirement.

16. (c) The relationship between the NPV method and the IRR method can be summarized as follows:

NPV	IRR
NPV > 0	IRR > Discount rate
NPV = 0	IRR = Discount rate
NPV < 0	IRR < Discount rate

Since the problem states that Neu Co. has a positive net present value on the investment, then the internal rate of return would be > 12%.

17. (b) The maximum amount that Kern Co. should invest now to obtain a 15% internal rate of return is the present value of the project's total net cash flows as computed below.

Year	Net cash flows	x	Present value of an ord. annuity	=	Present value of net cash flows
1	$50,000	x	.870	=	$ 43,500
2	$80,000	x	.756	=	$ 60,480
	Total present value				$103,980

18. (d) The internal rate of return of a proposed project includes the residual sales value of a project but not the depreciation expense. This is true because the residual sales value represents a future cash flow whereas depreciation expense (ignoring income tax considerations) provides no cash inflow or outflow.

19. (c) The internal rate of return (IRR) determines the rate of discount at which the present value of the future cash flows will exactly equal the investment outlay. It is computed by setting up the following equation

Initial investment = TVMF x Cash flows

and solving for the time value of money factor (TVMF). The IRR can then be found by locating the TVMF for (n) periods in the present value of an ordinary annuity table and tracing to the top of that column to find the rate of return. The problem asks for the TVMF for the IRR of the equipment, which is calculated as follows:

$$\$100,000 = TVMF \times \$20,000$$

$$5.00 = TVMF$$

In estimating the IRR, the factors in the table of present values of an annuity should be taken from the columns closest to 5.00.

B.   Capital Budgeting: Accounting Rate of Return

20.   (d)   The accounting rate of return (ARR) computes an approximate rate of return which ignores the time value of money. It is calculated as Expected increase in annual net income ÷ Average investment in a project. Tam's expected increase in annual income is as follows:

Annual savings in after-tax cash costs	$20,000
Annual depreciation on equipment ($100,000 ÷ 10 years)	(10,000)
Increase in annual net income	$10,000

A $100,000 investment is required to purchase the equipment. Thus, the ARR of the equipment under consideration by Tam is

$$\$10,000 \div \$100,000 = 10\%$$

21.   (c)   The **accounting rate of return** method (ARR) computes an approximate rate of return which ignores the time value of money. It is computed as follows:

ARR = Expected increase in annual net income ÷ Average investment

Therefore, $40,000 (as stated in problem) is the expected increase in annual income.

22.   (d)   The accounting rate of return (ARR) is based on financial statements prepared on the accrual basis. The formula to compute the ARR is

$$ARR = \frac{\text{Expected increase in annual net income}}{\text{Initial (or average) investment}}$$

Both the revenue over life of project and depreciation expense are used in the calculation of ARR. Depreciation expense over the project's life and other expenses directly associated with the project under consideration including income tax effects are subtracted from revenue over life of the project to determine net income over life of project. Net income over the project's life is then divided by the economic life to determine annual net income, the numerator of the ARR formula. This is a weakness of the ARR method because it does not consider actual cash flows or the time value of money.

C.   Probability Analysis

23.   (b)   The requirement is to determine what the probability of frost must be if Cal were indifferent to spending $10,000 for frost protection. In other words, you must find the point at which the cost of the frost protection equals the expected value of the loss from frost damage. The table below summarizes the possible outcomes.

	Frost	Frost-free
Protected	$90,000 Market value	$60,000 Market value
Unprotected	$40,000 Market value	$60,000 Market value

The difference between the market value of protected and unprotected strawberries if a frost were to occur is $50,000. Since we want to determine the probability of a frost when the expected value of the loss from frost damage is $10,000, this probability can be calculated as follows:

Loss from frost damage	x	Probability of frost	=	Expected value of the loss
$50,000	x	P	=	$10,000
		P	=	$\dfrac{\$10,000}{\$50,000}$
		P	=	.200

24.   (c)   Expected values are calculated as the weighted-average of all possible outcomes using the probabilities of the outcomes as weights. The expected number of additional muffin sales is

Additional sales		Probability		Expected value
60	x	0.6	=	36
100	x	0.4	=	40
				76

Since Dough earns $1 profit per box ($3 sales price – $2 cost), this represents $76 (76 boxes x $1 profit) of additional profit. However, the twenty-four unsold boxes would have to be sold at a $1 loss per box ($1 sales price – $2 cost) through Dough's thrift store. Therefore, the expected value of the decision to purchase the additional muffins is $52 net profit ($76 profit – $24 loss).

25.   (b)   Because it is not always possible to make decisions under conditions of total certainty, decision making must have a method of determining the best estimate or course of action where uncertainty exists. One method is probability analysis. Probabilities are used to calculate the expected value of each action. The expected value of an action is the weighted-average of the payoffs for that action, where the weights are the probabilities of the various mutually exclusive events that occur. Cost-volume-profit analysis is accurate in predicting profits or providing profitability estimates at all levels of production in the relevant range. Program evaluation and review technique (PERT) is used to estimate, schedule, and manage a network of interdependent project activities. It is useful for managing large-scale, complex projects. The scattergraph method is a graphical approach to computing the relationship between two variables.

26.   (c)   A probability distribution describes the possible outcomes relating to a single action and the likelihood of occurrence of each possible outcome. Gift Co. selected the most likely sales volume from several possible outcomes, which was simply the sales volume with the greatest probability of occurring. Gift Co. did not calculate the weighted-average of the outcomes (the sum of the probability of each outcome occurring times the sales volume of that outcome) to find the expected value.

27.   (c)   Probability analysis is an extension of sensitivity analysis. There is no specified limit on the number of possible outcomes. The summation of the probability weights should always equal one. Probability analysis and sensitivity analysis are not incompatible.

OTHER OBJECTIVE ANSWERS AND ANSWER EXPLANATIONS

Problem 1

1.   (B) The payback method, which does not consider the time value of money, measures the amount of time it takes to recoup an investment in cash inflows. Since the problem states that project B has greater cash inflows than project A in the early years, and the initial investment in each project is the same, the investment in project B would be recovered earlier. Thus, project B would have a shorter payback period, and answer (B) is correct.

2.   (A) The solutions approach is to recall the ARR formula below.

$$ARR = \frac{\text{Expected increase in annual net income}}{\text{Average investment}}$$

Note that the problem asks for the project with the greater **average** ARR. The problem states that over the lives of both projects, project A will have greater total net cash inflows. Since the problem asks for average ARR, timing of the cash flows does not matter. Average investment for each project is the same, thus, over the total lives of the projects, project A will have the greater increase in net income, and the greater average ARR.

3.   (B) The internal rate of return method determines the rate of return at which the present value of the cash flows will exactly equal the investment outlay. This rate of return is defined as the rate at which net present value is equal to 0. Graph II shows that NPV = 0 for project A at a discount rate of 16% and for project B at a discount rate of 22%. Therefore, answer (B) is correct as it would have the greater internal rate of return.

4.   (B) The internal rate of return method determines the rate of return at which the present value of the cash flows will exactly equal the investment outlay. Since IRR considers the time value of money, project B will have a higher rate of return based on the timing of the cash flows. Project B cash inflows are greater in the early years while project A cash inflows are received in later years. Thus, project A cash inflows must be discounted back at a lower interest rate to equal the initial investment.

Problem 2

1.   (N) The requirement is to determine whether Isle practices a just-in-time philosophy. Under a just-in-time philosophy, production is driven by demand for the finished product. Each step in the production process, including the delivery of materials, should occur immediately as needed by the next step in the production process. In addition, one key feature of a just-in-time production system is the elimination of inventory. In this case, Isle built up both its raw materials and its finished goods inventories; therefore, Isle is **not** practicing a just-in-time philosophy.

2.   (N) The requirement is to determine whether indirect material costs should be included in standard fixed overhead costs. Standard indirect material costs are costs related to materials which cannot easily be traced directly to a product, for example, glue. Although the costs of these items are not directly traceable, the amount of indirect material costs varies with the level of production. Therefore, standard indirect material costs should be included in **variable** overhead costs, rather than in **fixed** overhead costs.

3.   (Y) Value-adding activities are those activities which the customer perceives as adding usefulness or quality to a product. Since the operation of production equipment is required to complete a product for sale, the operation of this equipment should be categorized as a value-adding activity.

4.   (Y) The requirement is to determine whether activity-based costing (ABC) would provide more useful total production cost information than traditional standard costing if all three of Isle's products were produced in the same plant. Activity-based costing divides production costs into many cost pools and then allocates those costs to products based on the activities which drive the costs. Traditional standard costing determines standard costs based on inputs allowed at the best level of performance. Since ABC allocates costs based on the activities which cause those costs, this method would provide more useful cost information than traditional standard costing.

5.   (Y) Regression analysis is a statistical model that measures the amount of change in the dependent variable associated with changes in one or more independent variables. Since variable manufacturing overhead is a function of the volume of production, regression analysis can be used to determine the change in variable overhead (the dependent variable) associated with changes in volume (the independent variable).

6.   (N) Normal spoilage occurs under efficient operating conditions and is thus unavoidable; therefore, the cost of normal spoilage is considered a cost of the good units produced. Since spoilage is **detected** at the point of inspection, normal spoilage cost equals all costs incurred for spoiled units prior to inspection. In a process costing environment, two methods exist for handling normal spoilage costs. If normal spoilage occurs consistently, spoiled units are omitted from the calculation of equivalent units of production (EUP) but their cost is not removed from work in process. Hence, normal spoilage costs will automatically be allocated to good production when these units are transferred to finished goods and ending WIP. Conversely, if normal spoilage does not occur consistently, normal spoilage cost must be allocated to good units via a predetermined **variable** factory overhead rate. In this case, normal spoilage cost is calculated based on EUP. This amount is then removed from WIP and debited to factory overhead control. The point is that in either instance, normal spoilage cost is never reported as part of **fixed** manufacturing overhead.

7. **(Y)** Probability analysis is used to determine possible outcomes in an environment of uncertainty. Note that the probability of units containing defective materials is independent of the probability of units containing defective workmanship. This means that the occurrence of a defect in material is not caused by a defect in workmanship or vice versa. The probability used in computing Bute's normal spoilage can be determined by summing the probabilities of each potential defect and deducting the joint probability of the two types of defects occurring together.

	Probability
Defective materials (10/1,000)	0.01000
Defective workmanship (15/1,000)	0.01500
Joint probability	(.00015)
	.02485

8. **(Y)** The breakeven point for a product is determined as follows:

$$\frac{\text{Fixed costs}}{\text{Contribution margin}} = \text{Breakeven point in units}$$

The problem states that the standard cost patterns are unchanged. Since fixed costs will not increase with the additional production, and these fixed costs have already been covered by normal sales, Isle need only earn enough on the sales to cover the variable costs of production. The problem states that Isle will recoup its variable costs; therefore, Isle will break even on the contract.

9. **(N)** The requirement is to determine whether actual direct manufacturing labor hours were less than standard direct manufacturing labor hours. The problem states that the direct manufacturing labor efficiency variance was $24,000 unfavorable. Recall the method for computing variances.

Actual hours	X	Actual rate		Actual hours	X	Standard rate		Standard hours	X	Standard rate
	Rate variance				Efficiency variance					

Since the efficiency variance was unfavorable, actual hours were greater than standard hours.

10. **(N)** Absorption costing differs from variable costing in its treatment of fixed manufacturing overhead costs. Under a variable costing method, only variable costs are deducted from revenue to determine contribution margin, and **all** fixed costs are expensed in the period incurred. In contrast, under absorption costing, fixed manufacturing overhead costs are capitalized in inventory and expensed as finished goods are sold through cost of goods sold. Since Isle had inventory remaining at the end of its first year of operations, production exceeded sales. Since a portion of fixed manufacturing overhead costs remains in inventory at year-end, not all fixed manufacturing overhead is deducted from income, whereas under variable costing all fixed manufacturing overhead would be expensed. Therefore, operating income under the absorption costing method will be higher than income under the variable costing method.

11. **(Y)** The requirement is to determine whether the **total** amount paid for direct materials used in production of Aran was greater than the standard cost allowed for the work done. This total would include the combined effects of price and usage variances. Aran's direct materials variances are diagrammed as follows:

Actual quan.	X	Actual price		Actual quan.	X	Std. price		Std. quan.	X	Std. price
	Price variance = $2,000F				Usage variance = $16,000U					
		Total direct materials variance = $14,000U								

As shown, a total unfavorable direct materials variance of $14,000 resulted from production of Aran. Since the total variance was unfavorable, the actual cost of direct materials was higher than the standard cost.

12. **(Y)** Recall the computation of net present value. Net present value is the difference between total cash inflows and total cash outflows, discounted to the present point in time at the required rate of return. Net present value for the lease investment can be computed as follows:

Total future cash inflows ($12,000 per year for ten years)	$12,000 x 5.65* = $67,800
Total cash outflows	(60,000)
Net present value	$ 7,800

* *Amount represents the present value factor for a ten-year annuity at Isle's cost of capital or required rate of return of 12%.*

13. **(N)** Internal rate of return on a project is defined as the rate at which the present value of cash inflows is equal to the present value of cash outflows (Net present value = 0). Since the net present value of the project is positive, the internal rate of return must be higher than the cost of capital.

14. **(B) or (C)** The payback method evaluates the amount of time it will take to recover the initial cost of a project based on future cash flows. The payback method is most appropriate in situations involving even cash flows. The payback method does not consider the time value of money. The payback formula is as follows:

$$\frac{\text{Initial cash outflow}}{\text{Annual future cash inflows}}$$

The problem states that sales of Bute are constant and easy to project for more than three years. Based on this information, future cash flows from Bute sales should be more level and predictable than the other two products. Therefore, use of the payback method would be most appropriate in evaluating investments for Bute. However, the problem states that sales for Cilly are difficult to project for more than three years. Since the information does not indicate the length of the payback period, if it is three years or less the payback method would also be appropriate for Cilly. As a result of this lack of information, the AICPA accepted either answer (B) or (C).

15. **(B)** The economic order quantity formula determines the most appropriate order size for inventory items by minimizing the costs of obtaining and storing the inventory items. The formula for economic order quantity is as follows:

$$EOQ = \sqrt{\frac{2\,aD}{k}}$$

where

a = ordering costs per purchase order
D = demand in units for a specified time period
k = cost of carrying one unit in stock for the time period used in "D"

Use of EOQ would be most useful when purchasing materials for use in the production of B since sales of B are consistent and easily projected. This allows for more accurate demand projections and carrying cost estimates.

16. **(A)** Standard dollar breakeven point can be computed as follows:

$$\frac{\text{Breakeven}}{\text{point in \$}} = \frac{\text{Fixed costs}}{\text{Contribution margin ratio}}$$

Contribution margin ratio is computed as contribution margin divided by revenues. Contribution margin ratios for Bute and Cilly are shown below.

$$\underset{\text{Bute}}{\frac{\$176}{\$800}} = 0.22 \qquad \underset{\text{Cilly}}{\frac{\$144}{\$500}} = 0.29$$

If the product mix changes to include higher sales of Bute and lower sales of Cilly, the standard dollar breakeven point will **increase**. Because Bute's contribution margin ratio is lower, more dollars will be required to generate the same contribution margin.

17. **(C)** Actual return on investment, ROI, is computed as follows:

$$\frac{\text{Income}}{\text{Average investment}} = \text{ROI}$$

In this case actual income is "operating income, net of variances." Computing the ROI on each of the three products shows that Cilly has the highest actual ROI.

	Aran	*Bute*	*Cilly*
Income	$\dfrac{0}{1,000,000} = 0\%$	$\dfrac{41}{800} = 5.1\%$	$\dfrac{36}{400} = 9\%$
Investment			

18. **(C)** The problem states that sales of Cilly are very seasonal and difficult to project. If fixed manufacturing overhead costs are allocated based on expected demand, Cilly will have underapplied overhead during periods when production is lower than expected and overapplied overhead during periods when production is higher than expected.

19. **($1.50)** The requirement is to determine the budgeted standard per unit cost for variable selling and administrative costs on sales of 75,000 units. Note that the contribution income statement given in the problem is based on standard costs. By using the information given, the standard variable selling and administrative cost per unit of Aran can be computed as follows:

$$\frac{\text{Variable selling \& admin. costs}}{\text{Units sold}} \qquad \frac{\$120,000}{80,000} = \$1.50$$

By nature, variable costs are fixed on a per unit basis and vary only in total with the level of production. Therefore, the 75,000 units produced is irrelevant, and the answer is $1.50 per unit.

20. **($140,000)** The requirement is to determine Aran's budgeted standard fixed selling and administrative costs on sales of 75,000 units. Notice that the income statement given in the problem is based on standard costs. By nature, fixed costs are fixed over a range of production volumes. The problem does not indicate that fixed costs change with a 5,000 unit decrease in production; therefore, fixed costs will equal $140,000.

21. **($2,100,000)** Standard breakeven point in sales dollars can be computed as follows:

$$\frac{\text{Fixed costs}}{\text{Contribution margin ratio}}$$

Contribution margin ratio is computed as contribution margin divided by revenues. The calculation of Isle's standard breakeven point in sales dollars for the current product mix is shown below.

(1)	Total fixed costs	=	CM – Std. operating income
		=	$1,000,000 – $160,000
		=	$840,000
(2)	CM ratio	=	CM/Revenue
		=	$1,000,000/$2,500,000
		=	0.40
(3)	Breakeven point	=	Fixed costs/CM ratio
		=	$840,000/.40
		=	$2,100,000

22.   ($40,000) The requirement is to determine the amount of direct material and direct manufacturing labor variances that might be regarded as direct manufacturing labor employees' responsibility. Recall the variances associated with direct materials and direct manufacturing labor. Direct materials variances include price and usage variances. Price variances are based on actual purchase prices and preestablished standard costs, both of which are beyond the control of direct manufacturing labor employees. The usage variance, however, is based on the actual amount of materials used as compared to a preestablished standard. The usage variance may be affected by direct manufacturing labor employees (e.g., breakage, loss, theft). Direct manufacturing labor variances include the rate variance and the efficiency variance. Like the materials price variance, the rate variance is beyond employees' control. The efficiency variance, however, may be affected by employees since this variance measures actual hours as compared to a preestablished standard. Therefore, the answer is $40,000 ($16,000 materials usage variance + $24,000 labor efficiency variance).

23.   ($440,000) The requirement is to determine what Y represents in the graph. Note that the graph is used to estimate Aran's total standard manufacturing cost. Total standard cost is comprised of both fixed and variable manufacturing costs. By nature, fixed costs are fixed over a range of production while variable costs increase as production volume increases. At zero units of production, point Y represents costs which are unavoidable even though no units were produced. Therefore, Y represents fixed manufacturing overhead costs and the answer is $440,000.

Keep practicing! Wiley's CPA Examination Review Software has over 2,800 questions.

Available at www.wiley.com/cpa

7 GOVERNMENTAL AND NOT-FOR-PROFIT ORGANIZATIONS

Questions on governmental and other not-for-profit entities have appeared on all recent examinations. Questions have dealt with local government and various not-for-profit organizations. The AICPA Content Specification Outline of the coverage of governmental and not-for-profit organizations for the Accounting and Reporting section of the exam appears in Chapter 5 of the four part set and Chapter 8 in Volume 1 of the 2 volume set. As shown in the outline, this area will be weighted 30% of this exam.

Jurisdiction between the FASB and GASB

While the CPA Examination groups governmental and not-for-profit accounting together, jurisdiction over governmental and not-for-profit organizations is split between the FASB and the GASB, both of which set standards under the oversight of the Financial Accounting Foundation.

The FASB has authority to establish accounting and financial reporting standards for all nongovernmental not-for-profit organizations. The GASB has authority to establish accounting and financial reporting standards for all state and local governmental units, including governmental not-for-profit organizations. (Federal Government accounting and reporting standards are being developed by another organization, the Federal Accounting Standards Advisory Board (FASAB), but these standards are not currently on the CPA Examination.)

Not-for-profit organizations have traditionally been categorized in four ways: (1) colleges and universities, (2) health care entities, (3) voluntary health and welfare organizations, and (4) "other not-for-profit" organizations. Not-for-profit organizations in each of these categories can be either governmental or nongovernmental and, thus, can be subject to either GASB or FASB jurisdiction. In recent years, the CPA Examination has tested nongovernmental, not-for-profit organizations under FASB guidance.

Governmental not-for-profit organizations report as special-purpose entities engaged in governmental activities or business-type activities, or both, as appropriate. Governmental not-for-profit organizations are covered in the state and local governmental accounting in Module 38.

Nongovernmental not-for-profit organizations report in accordance with certain FASB and AICPA pronouncements relating to not-for-profit organizations. These entities are covered in Module 39.

Definition of a Government

The FASB and GASB have agreed upon a definition of a government that governs whether a particular organization is either governmental or nongovernmental for purposes of determining where accounting jurisdiction lies. Based on this definition, an entity is under GASB jurisdiction if it meets the definition of a government as outlined below. If not, the entity would be under the jurisdiction of the FASB. The definition which is contained in the AICPA Audit and Accounting Guides, *Health Care Organizations* and *Not-for-Profit Organizations* is as follows:

> *Public corporations and bodies corporate and politic are governmental organizations. Other organizations are governmental organizations if they have one or more of the following characteristics:*
>
> a. *Popular election of officers or appointment (or approval) of a controlling majority of the members of the organization's governing body by officials of one or more state or local governments;*
> b. *The potential for unilateral dissolution by a government with the net assets reverting to the government; or*
> c. *The power to enact and enforce a tax levy.*
>
> *Furthermore, organizations are presumed to be governmental if they have the ability to issue directly (rather than through a state or municipal authority) debt that pays interest exempt from federal taxation. However, organizations possessing only that ability (to issue tax-exempt debt) and none of the other governmental characteristics may rebut the presumption that they are governmental if their determination is supported by compelling, direct evidence.*

Examples of organizations that are either governmental (under GASB) or nongovernmental (under FASB) follow:

Organization Type	Governmental (under GASB)	Nongovernmental (under FASB)
College and University	Northern Illinois University	University of Chicago
Health Care Organization	Cook County Hospital	St. Mary's Hospital (Catholic)
Voluntary Health and Welfare Organization	_____ County Service Agency	American Cancer Society
"Other" Not-for-Profit Organization	_____ County Museum	American Institute of CPAs

GOVERNMENTAL (STATE AND LOCAL) ACCOUNTING

Governmental accounting has many similarities to commercial accounting. For example, governmental accounting uses the double-entry system, journals, ledgers, trial balances, financial statements, internal control, etc. Differences arise due to the objectives and environment of government. The major differences include

1. The absence of a profit motive, except for governmental enterprises, such as utilities
2. A legal emphasis that involves restrictions both in the raising and spending of revenues
3. An inability to "match" revenues with expenditures, as revenues are often provided by persons other than those receiving the services
4. An emphasis on accountability or stewardship of resources entrusted to public officials
5. The use of fund accounting and reporting, as well as government-wide reporting
6. The recording of the budget in some funds
7. The use of modified accrual accounting rather than full accrual accounting in some funds

As mentioned earlier, the Governmental Accounting Standards Board (GASB) has the authority to establish standards of financial reporting for all units of state and local government. The GASB was created in 1984 and replaced the National Council on Governmental Accounting (NCGA). Current pronouncements (level "A" GAAP) are reflected in the *Codification of Governmental Accounting and Financial Reporting Standards*, issued by the GASB each year. Level "B" GAAP are contained in the AICPA Audit and Accounting Guide, *Audits of State and Local Governmental Units*, issued each year. To date, the GASB has issued (as of this writing) 39 Statements, 6 Interpretations, and 2 Concepts Statements. The GASB has authority under the AICPA Ethics Rule 203, *Accounting Principles*.

Recently, the GASB issued three statements that completely transformed the accounting and financial reporting for state and local governments, and public colleges and universities. GASB 33, *Accounting and Financial Reporting for Nonexchange Transactions*, was issued in December 1998 and is required to be followed for fiscal years ending after June 15, 2001. Early implementation is encouraged.

GASB 34, *Basic Financial Statements—and Management's Discussion and Analysis—for State and Local Governments*, was issued in June 1999. Implementation depends upon the size of the government (defined as total annual revenues as of the first fiscal year ending after June 15, 1999).

One of the requirements of GASB 34 is the recording and depreciating of infrastructure, which was optional in the past. Prospective recording is required upon adoption of the statement. Retroactive recording of infrastructure acquired or significantly improved in fiscal years ending after June 30, 1980, is required for years after the dates shown above, except that governments with total revenues less than $10 million are not required to report infrastructure retroactively.

GASB 35, *Basic Financial Statements—and Management's Discussion and Analysis—for Public Colleges and Universities*, incorporates public colleges and universities into GASB 34 reporting requirements for special-purpose entities.

GASB Statements 33, 34, and 35 are now on the CPA Examination. Materials superceded by those pronouncements are no longer on the CPA Exam.

A. The Government Reporting Model

GASB 34 provides requirements that constitute the minimum required to be in compliance with GAAP. These requirements for **general-purpose** governmental units (states, municipalities, counties) are

- Management's Discussion and Analysis (MD&A) (Required Supplementary Information)
- Government-Wide Financial Statements
    Statement of Net Assets
    Statement of Activities
- Fund Financial Statements
    Governmental Funds
        Balance Sheet
        Statement of Revenues, Expenditures, and Changes in Fund Balances
    Proprietary Funds
        Statement of Net Assets (or Balance Sheet)
        Statement of Revenues, Expenses, and Changes in Fund Net Assets (or Fund Equity)
        Statement of Cash Flows
    Fiduciary Funds

Statement of Fiduciary Net Assets
Statement of Changes in Fiduciary Net Assets
* Notes to the Financial Statements
* Required Supplementary Information (RSI) other than Management's Discussion and Analysis
    Schedule of Funding Progress (for Entities Reporting Pension Trust Funds)
    Schedule of Employer Contributions (for Entities Reporting Pension Trust Funds)
    Budgetary Comparison Schedules
    Information about Infrastructure Assets (for Entities Reported Using the Modified Approach)
    Claims Development Information When the Government Sponsors a Public Entity Risk Pool

In addition, general-purpose governments may choose to provide certain **other supplementary information**, including combining statements for nonmajor funds. If a government wishes to prepare a complete **Comprehensive Annual Financial Report (CAFR),** three major sections would be included. First, an **introductory section** (unaudited) would include a letter of transmittal, organization chart, and list of principal officials. Second, a **financial section** would be prepared, including an auditor's report, the required information, and other supplementary information listed above. Finally, a **statistical section** would include a number of schedules such as the revenues by source and expenditures by function for the past ten years, debt per capita, and demographic data.

Special-purpose governments include park districts, tollway authorities, school districts, and sanitation districts. GASB has categorized special-purpose governments as those that are engaged in governmental activities, business-type activities, fiduciary activities, and both governmental and business-type activities. Special-purpose governments that are engaged in governmental activities and have more than one program and special-purpose governments that are engaged in both governmental and business-type activities must prepare both the government-wide and fund financial statements. Special-purpose governments that are engaged in a single governmental activity (such as a cemetery district) may combine the government-wide and fund financial statements or use other methods allowed by GASB. Special-purpose governments that are engaged in only business-type activities or fiduciary activities are not required to prepare the government-wide statements, but only prepare the proprietary or fiduciary fund statements. All governments must include the MD&A, Notes, and RSI.

Public colleges and universities and other governmental not-for-profit organizations may choose to report as special-purpose governments engaged in only business-type activities, engaged in only governmental activities, or engaged in both governmental and business-type activities.

B. The Reporting Entity

The GASB carefully defines the **reporting entity** in an effort to ensure that all boards, commissions, agencies, etc. that are under the control of the reporting entity are included. A **primary government** is either (1) a state government, (2) a general-purpose local government, or (3) a special-purpose local government that has a separately elected governing body, is legally separate, and is fiscally independent of other state or local governments. A **component unit** is a legally separate organization for which the elected officials of a primary government are financially accountable, or for which the nature and significance of their relationships with a primary government is such that omission would cause the primary government's financial statements to be misleading.

Most component units are reported, in the government-wide financial statements, in a separate column or columns to the right of the information related to the primary government **(discretely presented)**. Component units whose activities are so closely tied to the primary government as to be indistinguishable should be **blended** with the primary government figures. Thus, the **primary government** and several additional **component units** may be combined to constitute the **reporting entity**.

GASB 39, *Determining Whether Certain Organizations Are Component Units*, requires that fundraising foundations and similar organizations whose primary purposes is to raise or hold significant resources for the benefit of a specific governmental unit should be reported as a component unit of that government.

C. Management's Discussion and Analysis

The **Management's Discussion and Analysis (MD&A)** provides, in plain English terms, an overview of the government's financial activities. This section is to provide a comparison of the current year results with the results of the prior year, with emphasis on the prior year. Included will be
* A brief discussion of the financial statements

- Condensed financial information from the government-wide financial statements and individual fund statements
- An analysis of significant variations between the original budget, final budget, and actual results for the year
- A description of significant capital asset and long-term debt activity for the year
- A discussion by governments that use the modified approach to report infrastructure assets regarding the condition of these capital assets and changes from the prior year
- A description of any known facts, decisions, or conditions that would have a significant effect on the government's financial position or results of operations.

MD&A is considered to be Required Supplementary Information (RSI). The nature of RSI is described in Section G. Only items required by GASB are included.

D. Government-Wide Financial Statements

The **government-wide** statements include the Statement of Net Assets and the Statement of Activities, both of which are reproduced in this module. The government-wide statements are prepared on the economic resources measurement focus and accrual basis of accounting. All activities of the primary government are included, with the exception of fiduciary activities.

The **Statement of Net Assets** is a type of balance sheet, except that the form, "Assets – Liabilities = Net assets" is used. Full accrual accounting is to be used, including the recording and depreciation of fixed assets, including infrastructure. Note that "net assets" is broken down into three categories: (1) invested in capital assets, net of related debt, (2) restricted, and (3) unrestricted. The term "invested in capital assets, net of related debt" is computed by taking the value of capital (fixed) assets, less accumulated depreciation, less the debt associated with the acquisition of the capital assets. The term "restricted," as defined by GASB means "(a) externally imposed by creditors (such as through debt covenants), grantors, contributors, or laws or regulations of other governments, and (b) imposed by law through constitutional provisions or enabling legislation." Unrestricted net assets is a "plug" figure, computed by taking the total net assets and subtracting the invested in capital assets, net of related debt and the restricted net assets.

Note also that the columns are separated into (1) governmental activities, (2) business-type activities, (3) total primary government, and (4) component units. Governmental activities are those that are financed primarily through taxes and other nonexchange transactions. Business-type activities are those normally financed through user charges. The terms "primary government" and "component units" are described above. If a government has more component units than can be displayed effectively in the Statement of Net Assets, then the detail of each component unit should be disclosed in the notes to the financial statements.

The **Statement of Activities** reports revenues and expenses, on the full accrual basis. This is a consolidated statement except that interfund transactions are not eliminated, when those transactions are between governmental and business-type activities, and between the primary government and discretely presented component units. Expenses are reported by function. Revenues are also reported on the accrual basis and may be exchange revenues or nonexchange revenues. **Exchange revenues** are reported when goods or services are transferred, as is true for business enterprises. **Nonexchange revenues** are reported in accord with Section I below.

Program revenues, those that are directly associated with the functional expense categories, are deducted to arrive at the net expense or revenue. Note that program revenues include (1) charges for services, (2) operating grants and contributions, and (3) capital grants and contributions, although program revenues are not limited to the three categories. Examples of program revenue would be the fees charged for park operations under "culture and recreation," and fines and forfeits. Charges for services are deducted from the function which creates the revenues. Grants and contributions (both operating and capital) are reported in the function to which their use is restricted. The net expense or revenue is broken out between governmental activities, business-type activities, and component units, the same as in the Statement of Net Assets. General revenues are deducted from the net expenses or added to net revenues. General revenues include all taxes levied by the reporting government and other nonexchange revenues not restricted to a particular program. After that, separate additions or deductions are made for special items, extraordinary items, and transfers (between categories). If a government had contributions to term and permanent endowments and contributions to permanent fund principal, these would also be shown after general revenues. Finally, the net assets at the beginning and end of the year are reconciled. (This is called an "all-inclusive activity" statement.)

Extraordinary items are those that are both unusual in nature and infrequent in occurrence (the same as for business enterprises). **Special items** (a new GASB category) are those events within the control of management that are either unusual in nature or infrequent in occurrence. An example of a special item would be the gain on sale of park land.

> Alternatively, the internal balances could be reported on separate lines as assets and liabilities. A notation would need to be added to inform the reader that the "Total" column is adjusted for those amounts.

Sample City
STATEMENT OF NET ASSETS
December 31, 2002

| | Primary government | | | |
	Governmental activities	Business-type activities	Total	Component units
Assets				
Cash and cash equivalents	$ 13,597,899	$ 10,279,143	$ 23,877,042	$ 303,935
Investments	27,365,221	--	27,365,221	7,428,952
Receivables (net)	12,833,132	3,609,615	16,442,747	4,042,290
Internal balances	175,000	(175,000)	--	--
Inventories	322,149	126,674	448,823	83,697
Capital assets, net (Note 1)	170,022,760	151,388,751	321,411,511	37,744,786
Total assets	224,316,161	165,229,183	389,545,344	49,603,660
Liabilities				
Accounts payable	6,783,310	751,430	7,534,740	1,803,332
Deferred revenue	1,435,599	--	1,435,599	38,911
Noncurrent liabilities (Note 2):				
Due within one year	9,236,000	4,426,286	113,662,286	1,426,639
Due in more than one year	83,302,378	74,482,273	157,784,651	27,106,151
Total liabilities	100,757,287	79,659,989	180,417,276	30,375,033
Net assets				
Invested in capital assets, net of related debt	103,711,386	73,088,574	176,799,960	15,906,392
Restricted for:				
Capital projects	11,705,864	--	11,705,864	492,445
Debt service	3,020,708	1,451,996	4,472,704	--
Community development projects	4,811,043	--	4,811,043	--
Other purposes	3,214,302	--	3,214,302	--
Unrestricted (deficit)	(2,904,429)	11,028,624	8,124,195	2,829,790
Total net assets	$123,558,874	$ 85,569,194	$209,128,068	$19,228,627

> *Net assets restricted for capital projects* includes approximately $13 million of capital debt for which the proceeds have not yet been used to construct capital assets.

Source: GASB 34, page 201.

All governments are required to report those expenses that are directly associated with each function on the appropriate line. If a government chooses to allocate some indirect expenses to functions, separate columns should show the direct, indirect, and total costs charged to each function. Direct expenses include depreciation that can be directly charged. Depreciation expense that serves all functions may be allocated as an indirect expense or charged to general government or as unallocated depreciation expense. Depreciation expense for general **infrastructure assets** (roads, bridges, storm sewers, etc.) should not be allocated but shown as an expense of that function that normally is used for capital outlay (public works, for example) or as a separate line. Interest on long-term debt would be included in direct expenses if the interest is due to a single function. Most interest, however, cannot be identified with a single function and should be shown in a separate line. Interest is capitalized for business-type activities but not for governmental activities.

Sample City
STATEMENT OF ACTIVITIES
For the Year Ended December 31, 2002

Functions/Programs	Expenses	Charges for services	Operating grants and Contributions	Capital grants and contributions	Net (expense) revenue and changes in net assets — Primary government — Governmental activities	Business-type activities	Total	Component units
Primary government								
Governmental activities:								
General government	$ 9,571,410	$ 3,146,915	$ 843,617	$ --	$ (5,580,878)	$ --	$ (5,580,878)	$ --
Public safety	34,844,749	1,198,855	1,307,693	62,300	(32,275,901)	--	(32,275,901)	--
Public works	10,128,538	850,000	--	2,252,615	(7,025,923)	--	(7,025,923)	--
Engineering services	1,299,645	704,793	--	--	(594,852)	--	(594,852)	--
Health and sanitation	6,738,672	5,612,267	575,000	--	(551,405)	--	(551,405)	--
Cemetery	735,866	212,496	--	--	(523,370)	--	(523,370)	--
Culture and recreation	11,532,350	3,995,199	2,450,000	--	(5,087,151)	--	(5,087,151)	--
Community development	2,994,389	--	--	2,580,000	(414,389)	--	(414,389)	--
Education (payment to school district)	21,893,273	--	--	--	(21,893,273)	--	(21,893,273)	--
Interest on long-term debt	6,068,121	--	--	--	(6,068,121)	--	(6,068,121)	--
Total governmental activities	105,807,013	15,720,525	5,176,310	4,894,915	(80,015,263)	--	(80,015,263)	--
Business-type activities:								
Water	3,595,733	4,159,350	--	1,159,909	--	1,723,526	1,723,526	--
Sewer	4,912,853	7,170,533	--	486,010	--	2,743,690	2,743,690	--
Parking facilities	2,796,283	1,344,087	--	--	--	(1,452,196)	(1,452,196)	--
Total business-type activities	11,304,869	12,673,970	--	1,645,919	--	3,015,020	3,015,020	--
Total primary government	$117,111,882	$28,394,495	$5,176,310	$6,540,834	(80,015,263)	3,015,020	(77,000,243)	--
Component units								
Landfill	$ 3,382,157	$ 3,857,858	$ --	$ 11,397	--	--	--	487,098
Public school system	31,186,498	705,765	3,937,083	--	--	--	--	(26,543,650)
Total component units	$ 34,568,655	$ 4,563,623	$3,937,083	$ 11,397	--	--	--	(26,056,552)
General revenues:								
Taxes:								
Property taxes, levied for general purposes					51,693,573	--	51,693,573	--
Property taxes, levied for debt service					4,726,244	--	4,726,244	--
Franchise taxes					4,055,505	--	4,055,505	--
Public service taxes					8,969,887	--	8,969,887	--
Payment from Sample City					--	--	--	21,893,273
Grants and contributions not restricted to specific programs					1,457,820	--	1,457,820	6,461,708
Investment earnings					1,958,144	601,349	2,559,493	881,763
Miscellaneous					884,907	104,925	989,832	22,464
Special item—gain on sale of park land					2,653,488	--	2,653,488	--
Transfers					501,409	(501,409)	--	--
Total general revenues, special items, and transfers					76,900,977	204,865	77,105,842	29,259,208
Change in net assets					(3,114,286)	3,219,885	105,599	3,202,656
Net assets—beginning					126,673,160	82,349,309	209,022,469	16,025,971
Net assets—ending					$123,558,874	$85,569,194	$209,128,068	$19,228,627

The detail presented for government activities represents the *minimum* requirement. Governments are encouraged to provide more details—for example, police, fire, EMS, and inspections—rather than simply "public safety."

Source: GASB 34, pp. 208-9.

A government may choose to use a **modified approach for recording charges for infrastructure assets** rather than charge depreciation. Under the modified approach, if a government meets certain criteria for maintaining its infrastructure, expenditures to extend service life would be reported as expenses in lieu of depreciation. A fixed asset management system must be in place that meets certain criteria, and extensive disclosures are required.

E. Fund Financial Statements

In addition to government-wide statements, GASB 34 requires a number of fund financial statements. Most governments use fund accounting internally and prepare the government-wide statements with worksheet adjustments from this fund accounting base. A fund is defined by the GASB as

> A fiscal and accounting entity with a self-balancing set of accounts recording cash and other financial resources, together with all related liabilities and residual equities and balances, and changes therein, which are segregated for the purpose of carrying on specific activities or attaining certain objectives in accordance with special regulations, restrictions, or limitations.

GASB now has 11 fund types, which are classified into three general categories.

Governmental funds	*Proprietary funds*	*Fiduciary funds*
(1) General	(6) Internal service	(8) Agency
(2) Special revenue	(7) Enterprise	(9) Pension and other employee benefit trust funds
(3) Debt service		
(4) Capital projects		(10) Investment trust funds
(5) Permanent		(11) Private-purpose trust funds

Fund financial statements are presented separately for the governmental, proprietary, and fiduciary fund categories. Each government has only one general fund; each other fund type may have any number of individual funds, although GASB encourages having as few funds as possible. Fixed assets and long-term debt are not reported in the fund financial statements, only in the government-wide financial statements.

The fund financial statements for the governmental and enterprise fund categories report **major funds,** not all funds. The general fund is always a major fund. Other funds must be considered major when both of the following conditions exist: (1) total assets, liabilities, revenues, expenditures/expenses of that individual governmental or enterprise fund constitute 10% of the governmental or enterprise category **and** (2) total assets, liabilities, revenues, expenditures/expenses are 5% of the total of the governmental and enterprise category combined. In addition, a government may choose to call any fund major if it feels that reporting that fund would be useful.[1] In governmental and enterprise fund statements, the nonmajor funds are aggregated and reported as a single column. Combining statements for nonmajor funds are shown as "Other supplementary information" later in the financial section of CAFR. Internal service funds are reported in a single column on the proprietary fund statements.

Fiduciary fund financial statements report a separate column for fund type (agency, pension and other employee benefit trust, investment trust, and private purpose). If separate reports are not available for each pension trust fund, then the notes must disclose this information. If separate reports are available, then the notes must disclose how readers can obtain those reports.

A reconciliation between the information presented in the governmental fund financial statements and the governmental activities column of the government-wide financial statements is required either at the bottom of the fund financial statements or in a schedule immediately following the fund financial statements. Explanations should either accompany the reconciliation or be in the notes.

Governmental funds focus on the current financial resources raised and expended to carry out general government purposes. Governmental funds include the general, special revenue, debt service, capital projects, and permanent funds. The **General fund** accounts for all financial resources except those re-

---

[1] *The determination of whether or not a fund is major or nonmajor can be illustrated by the HUD Programs Fund, shown in the governmental funds statements as a major fund. The first step is to determine whether or not the HUD Programs Fund is 10% of the governmental funds assets ($7,504,765/51,705,690 = 14.5%), liabilities ($6,428,389/16,812,584 = 38.3%), revenues ($2,731,473/97,482,467 = 2.80%), or expenditures ($2,954,389/121,332,470 = 2.44%). The first (10%) criterion is met for assets and liabilities but not for revenues and expenditures. As a result, the 5% test will be applied for assets and liabilities only. See the statements for governmental and proprietary funds. The assets do not qualify [$7,504,765/(51,705,690 + 165,404,18) = 3.45%]. However, the liabilities do exceed 5% [$6,428,389/(16,812,584 + 79,834,989) = 6.65%]. Thus, the HUD Programs Fund must be shown as a major fund.*

quired to be accounted for in another fund. The general fund includes expenditures for general government, public safety, culture and recreation, public works and engineering, and other activities not set aside in other funds. **Special revenue funds** account for specific revenue sources that are legally restricted to expenditure for specified current purposes. An example would include a motor fuel tax limited by law to highway and street construction and repair. **Debt service funds** account for the accumulation of resources for, and the payment of, general long-term debt and interest. **Capital projects funds** account for financial resources to be used for the acquisition or construction of major capital facilities, other than those financed by proprietary funds or trust funds. **Permanent funds** are used to report resources that are legally restricted to the extent that only earnings, and not principal, may be used to support government programs.

Two governmental fund financial statements are required: (1) **Balance Sheet** and (2) **Statement of Revenues, Expenditures, and Changes in Fund Balances**. Both of these are illustrated in this module. Governmental fund financial statements are prepared on the current financial resources measurement focus and modified accrual basis of accounting (see Section H., "Measurement Focus and Basis of Accounting"). Note in the Balance Sheet that fund balances are broken down between "reserved" and "unreserved." In fund accounting terminology, a reservation of fund balance represents a commitment that makes that portion unavailable for appropriation. Examples include encumbrances, inventories, and amounts set aside equal to long-term assets in governmental funds. Unreserved fund balance is the amount that is available for appropriation. Note in the Statement of Revenues, Expenditures, and Changes in Fund Balances that revenues are reported by source, expenditures are reported by character (current, debt service, capital outlay) and then by function (general government, public safety, etc.). The category "other financing sources and uses" includes transfers between funds and proceeds from the sale of long-term debt and proceeds from the sale of fixed assets. Special and extraordinary items are reported in this statement in the same manner as in the government-wide Statement of Activities, and a reconciliation between the beginning and ending fund balance completes the statement. Interest related to fixed assets is **not** capitalized.

Proprietary funds focus on total economic resources, income determination, and cash flow presentation. Proprietary funds include internal service funds (which are considered governmental activities in the government-wide statements) and enterprise funds (which are considered business-type activities in the government-wide statements). **Internal service funds** report any activity that provides goods or services to other funds of the primary government on a cost-reimbursement basis. Examples might include print shops, motor pools, and self-insurance activities. Internal service funds may incidentally provide services to other governments on a cost-reimbursement basis. **Enterprise funds** may be used to provide goods or services to external users for a fee. Enterprise funds must be used if (1) the activity is financed with debt that is secured solely by a pledge of the net revenues from fees and charges of that activity, or (2) laws or regulations require that the activity's cost of providing services be recovered with fees and charges, rather than from taxes or similar revenues. Examples of enterprise funds would include water utilities, airports, and swimming pools.

Statements required for proprietary funds include (1) **Statement of Net Assets (or Balance Sheet)**, (2) **Statement of Revenues, Expenses, and Changes in Net Assets (or Fund Equity)**, and (3) **Statement of Cash Flows**. These statements are all included in this module. Note that the Statement of Net Assets is prepared in the same "Assets – Liabilities = Net Assets" format as the Statement of Net Assets in the government-wide statements. GASB permits the more traditional balance sheet format, "Assets = Liabilities + Fund Equity" for this proprietary funds statement. The net asset category has the same breakdown as the government-wide statement of net assets, "invested in capital assets, net of related debt," "restricted," and "unrestricted." Note also that the internal service funds are shown separately to the right as a fund type, with all internal service funds grouped together. A classified format, with current and noncurrent assets and liabilities shown separately, is required by GASB.

The Statement of Revenues, Expenses, and Changes in Fund Net Assets is an all-inclusive operating statement, with a reconciliation of the beginning and ending fund net assets as the last item. Major enterprise funds are shown, along with a total of all enterprise fund activity, and the total of internal service funds is shown separately. GASB requires an operating income figure, with operating revenues and expenses shown separately from nonoperating revenues and expenses. Capital contributions, transfers, extraordinary items, and special items are to be shown after the nonoperating revenues and expenses. GASB requires that depreciation be shown separately as an operating expense and that interest be shown as a nonoperating expense. Interest related to fixed assets is capitalized.

Sample City
BALANCE SHEET
GOVERNMENTAL FUNDS
December 31, 2002

	General	HUD programs	Community redevelopment	Route 7 construction	Other governmental funds	Total governmental funds
Assets						
Cash and cash equivalents	$3,418,485	$1,236,523	$ --	$ --	$5,606,792	$10,261,800
Investments	--	--	13,262,695	10,467,037	3,485,252	27,214,984
Receivables, net	3,644,561	2,953,438	353,340	11,000	10,221	6,972,560
Due from other funds	1,370,757	--	--	--	--	1,370,757
Receivables from other governments	--	119,059	--	--	1,596,038	1,715,097
Liens receivable	791,926	3,195,745	--	--	--	3,987,671
Inventories	182,821	--	--	--	--	182,821
Total assets	$9,408,550	$7,504,765	$13,616,035	$10,478,037	$10,698,303	$51,705,690
Liabilities and fund balances						
Liabilities						
Accounts payable	$3,408,680	$129,975	$190,548	$1,104,632	$1,074,831	$5,908,666
Due to other funds	--	25,369	--	--	--	25,369
Payable to other governments	94,074	--	--	11,000	--	94,074
Deferred revenue	4,250,430	6,273,045	250,000	--	--	10,784,475
Total liabilities	7,753,184	6,428,389	440,548	1,115,632	1,074,831	16,812,584
Fund balances						
Reserved for:						
Inventories	182,821	--	--	--	--	182,821
Liens receivables	791,926	--	--	--	--	791,926
Encumbrances	40,292	41,034	119,314	5,792,587	1,814,122	7,807,349
Debt service	--	--	--	--	3,832,062	3,832,062
Other purposes	--	--	--	--	1,405,300	1,405,300
Unreserved, reported in:						
General fund	640,327	--	--	--	--	640,327
Special revenue funds	--	1,035,342	--	--	1,330,718	2,366,060
Capital projects funds	--	--	13,056,173	3,569,818	1,241,270	17,867,261
Total fund balances	1,655,366	1,076,376	13,175,487	9,362,405	9,623,472	34,893,106
Total liabilities and fund balances	$9,408,550	$7,504,765	$13,616,035	$10,478,037	$10,698,303	

> "Designations" of unreserved fund balances may be displayed or disclosed in the notes.

Amounts reported for governmental activities in the statement of net assets are different because:

Capital assets used in governmental activities are not financial resources and therefore are not reported in the funds. — 161,082,708

Other long-term assets are not available to pay for current-period expenditures and therefore are deferred in the funds. — 9,348,876

Internal service funds are used by management to charge the costs of certain activities, such as insurance and telecommunications, to individual funds. The assets and liabilities of the internal service funds are included in governmental activities in the statement of net assets. — 2,994,691

Long-term liabilities, including bonds payable, are not due and payable in the current period and therefore are not reported in the funds. — (84,760,507)

Net assets of governmental activities — $123,558,874

Source: GASB 34, pp. 220-1.

Sample City
STATEMENT OF REVENUES, EXPENDITURES, AND CHANGES IN FUND BALANCES
GOVERNMENTAL FUNDS
For the Year Ended December 31, 2002

	General	HUD programs	Community redevelopment	Route 7 construction	Other governmental funds	Total governmental funds
Revenues						
Property taxes	$51,173,436	$ --	$ --	$ --	$ 4,680,192	$ 55,853,628
Franchise taxes	4,055,505	--	--	--	--	4,055,505
Public service taxes	8,969,887	--	--	--	--	8,969,887
Fees and fines	606,946	--	--	--	--	606,946
Licenses and permits	2,287,794	--	--	--	--	2,287,794
Intergovernmental	6,119,938	2,578,191	--	--	2,830,916	11,529,045
Charges for services	11,374,460	--	--	--	30,708	11,405,168
Investment earnings	552,325	87,106	549,489	270,161	364,330	1,823,411
Miscellaneous	881,874	66,176	--	2,939	94	951,083
Total Revenues	86,022,165	2,731,473	549,489	273,100	7,906,240	97,482,467
Expenditures						
Current						
General government	8,630,835	--	417,814	16,700	121,052	9,186,401
Public safety	33,729,623	--	--	--	--	33,729,623
Public works	4,975,775	--	--	--	3,721,542	8,697,317
Engineering services	1,299,645	--	--	--	--	1,299,645
Health and sanitation	6,070,032	--	--	--	--	6,070,032
Cemetery	706,305	--	--	--	--	706,305
Culture and recreation	11,411,685	--	--	--	--	11,411,685
Community development	--	2,954,389	--	--	--	2,954,389
Education—payment to school district	21,893,273	--	--	--	--	21,893,273
Debt service						
Principal	--	--	--	--	3,450,000	3,450,000
Interest and other charges	--	--	--	--	5,215,151	5,215,151
Capital outlay	--	--	2,246,671	11,281,769	3,190,209	16,718,649
Total expenditures	88,717,173	2,954,389	2,664,485	11,298,469	15,697,954	121,332,470
Excess (deficiency) of revenues over expenditures	(2,695,008)	(222,916)	(2,114,996)	(11,025,369)	(7,791,714)	(23,850,003)
Other Financing Sources (Uses)						
Proceeds of refunding bonds	--	--	--	--	38,045,000	38,045,000
Proceeds of long-term capital-related debt	--	--	17,529,560	--	1,300,000	18,829,560
Payment to bond refunding escrow agent	--	--	--	--	(37,284,144)	(37,284,144)
Transfers in	129,323	--	--	--	5,551,187	5,680,510
Transfers out	(2,163,759)	(348,046)	(2,273,187)	--	(219,076)	(5,004,068)
Total other financing sources and uses	(2,034,436)	(348,046)	15,256,373	--	7,392,967	20,266,858
Special Item						
Proceeds from sale of park land	3,476,488	--	--	--	--	3,476,488
Net change in fund balances	(1,252,956)	(570,962)	13,141,377	(11,025,369)	(398,747)	(106,657)
Fund balances—beginning	2,908,322	1,647,338	34,110	20,387,774	10,022,219	34,999,763
Fund balances—ending	$ 1,655,366	$1,076,376	$13,175,487	$ 9,362,405	$ 9,623,472	$ 34,893,106

Source: GASB 34, pp. 222-3

The Statement of Cash Flows is prepared in accord with the requirements of GASB 9, as modified by GASB 34, and contains several major differences from the familiar business cash flow statement required by FASB. First, only the direct method is acceptable, and a reconciliation is required. Second, the reconciliation is from operating income to net cash provided by operating activities, not from net income as required by FASB. Third, GASB has four categories instead of the three required by FASB. These are operating, noncapital financing, capital and related financing, and investing. Fourth, cash receipts from interest are classified as investing, not operating activities. Fifth, cash payments for interest are classified as financing (either noncapital or capital and related), not as operating activities. Finally, purchases of capital assets (resources provided by financing activities) are considered financing, not investing, activities.

Sample City
STATEMENT OF NET ASSETS
PROPRIETARY FUNDS
December 31, 2002

> This statement illustrates the "net assets" format; the "balance sheet" format also is permitted. Classification of assets and liabilities is required in either case.

	Business-type activities—enterprise funds			Governmental activities—internal service funds
	Water and sewer	*Parking facilities*	*Totals*	
Assets				
Current assets:				
Cash and cash equivalents	$ 8,416,653	$ 369,168	$ 8,785,821	$ 3,336,099
Investments	--	--	--	150,237
Receivables, net	3,564,586	3,535	3,568,121	157,804
Due from other governments	41,494	--	41,494	--
Inventories	126,674	--	126,674	139,328
Total current assets	12,149,407	372,703	12,522,110	3,783,468
Noncurrent assets:				
Restricted cash and cash equivalents	--	1,493,322	1,493,322	--
Capital assets:				
Land	813,513	3,021,637	3,835,150	--
Distribution and collection systems	39,504,183	--	39,504,183	--
Buildings and equipment	106,135,666	23,029,166	129,164,832	14,721,786
Less accumulated depreciation	(15,328,911)	(5,786,503)	(21,115,414)	(5,781,734)
Total noncurrent assets	131,124,451	21,757,622	152,882,073	8,940,052
Total assets	143,273,858	22,130,325	165,404,183	12,723,520
Liabilities				
Current liabilities:				
Accounts payable	447,427	304,003	751,430	780,570
Due to other funds	175,000	--	175,000	1,170,388
Compensated absences	112,850	8,827	121,677	237,690
Claims and judgments	--	--	--	1,687,975
Bonds, notes, and loans payable	3,944,609	360,000	4,304,609	249,306
Total current liabilities	4,679,886	672,830	5,352,716	4,125,929
Noncurrent liabilities:				
Compensated absences	451,399	35,306	486,705	--
Claims and judgments	--	--	--	5,602,900
Bonds, notes, and loans payable	54,451,549	19,544,019	73,995,568	--
Total noncurrent liabilities	54,902,948	19,579,325	74,482,273	5,602,900
Total liabilities	59,582,834	20,252,155	79,834,989	9,728,829
Net Assets				
Invested in capital assets, net of related debt	72,728,293	360,281	73,088,574	8,690,746
Restricted for debt service	--	1,451,996	1,451,996	--
Unrestricted	10,962,731	65,893	11,028,624	(5,696,055)
Total net assets	$ 83,691,024	$ 1,878,170	$ 85,569,194	$ 2,994,691

Source: GASB 34, p.227.

Fiduciary fund financial statements provide information, based on the economic resources measurement focus and accrual accounting, on resources held and used by governments for the benefit of individuals and entities other than the government. Fiduciary fund statements are the Statement of Fiduciary Net Assets and the Statement of Changes in Fiduciary Net Assets. Unlike the statements for the governmental and enterprise fund categories, fiduciary fund statements report totals for each of the four fund types. The fund types are (1) pension (and other employee benefit) trust funds, (2) investment trust funds, (3) private-purpose trust funds, and (4) agency funds. However, each individual pension or employee benefit trust fund report must be reported in the notes if separate reports have not been issued. If separate reports have been issued, the notes to the financial statement must indicate how the reader might obtain such reports.

Pension (and other employee benefit) trust funds account for funds held in trust for the payment of employee retirement and other benefits. These trust funds exist when the government is the trustee for the pension plan. Accounting for these plans is covered by GASB 25 and 26. **Investment trust funds** are used to report the external portions of investment pools, when the reporting government is trustee. **Private-purpose trust funds** should be used to report all other trust arrangements where the principal and income benefit individuals, private organizations, and other governments. An example would be a fund to report scholarship funds contributed by individuals and businesses, by a public school system. Finally, **agency funds** report resources held by the reporting government in a purely custodial capacity. Agency funds report only assets and liabilities and are not included in the Statement of Changes in Net Assets.

Sample City
STATEMENT OF REVENUES, EXPENSES, AND CHANGES IN FUND NET ASSETS
PROPRIETARY FUNDS
For the Year Ended December 31, 2002

	Business-type activities—enterprise funds			Governmental activities—internal service funds
	Water and sewer	Parking facilities	Totals	
Operating revenues:				
Charges for service	$11,329,883	$1,340,261	$12,670,144	$15,256,164
Miscellaneous	--	3,826	3,826	1,066,761
Total operating revenues	11,329,883	1,344,087	12,673,970	16,322,925
Operating expenses:				
Personal services	3,400,559	762,348	4,162,907	4,157,156
Contractual services	344,422	96,032	440,454	584,396
Utilities	754,107	100,726	854,833	214,812
Repairs and maintenance	747,315	64,617	811,932	1,960,490
Other supplies and expenses	498,213	17,119	515,332	234,445
Insurance claims and expenses	--	--	--	8,004,286
Depreciation	1,163,140	542,049	1,705,189	1,707,872
Total operating expenses	6,907,756	1,582,891	8,490,647	16,863,457
Operating income (loss)	4,422,127	(238,804)	4,183,323	(540,532)
Nonoperating revenues (expenses):				
Interest and investment revenue	454,793	146,556	601,349	134,733
Miscellaneous revenue	--	104,925	104,925	20,855
Interest expense	(1,600,830)	(1,166,546)	(2,767,376)	(41,616)
Miscellaneous expense	--	(46,846)	(46,846)	(176,003)
Total nonoperating revenues (expenses)	(1,146,037)	(961,911)	(2,107,948)	(62,031)
Income (loss) before contributions and transfers	3,276,090	(1,200,715)	2,075,375	(602,563)
Capital contributions	1,645,919	--	1,645,919	18,788
Transfers out	(290,000)	(211,409)	(501,409)	(175,033)
Change in net assets	4,632,009	(1,412,124)	3,219,885	(758,808)
Total net assets—beginning	79,059,015	3,290,294	82,349,309	3,753,499
Total net assets—ending	$83,691,024	$1,878,170	$85,569,194	$ 2,994,691

Source: GASB 34, p.229.

The statements required for fiduciary funds are the **Statement of Fiduciary Net Assets** and **Statement of Changes in Fiduciary Net Assets**. Examples of these statements are reflected in this module. The Statement of Fiduciary Net Assets is prepared in the form "Assets – Liabilities = Net Assets." Columns are included for each fund type. The Statement of Changes in Fiduciary Net Assets uses the terms "additions" and "deductions" instead of revenues and expenses, but the additions and deductions are computed on the full accrual basis. This, like all other GASB operating statements, is an "all-inclusive" statement with a reconciliation of the beginning and ending net assets at the bottom of the statement. Note that agency funds have only assets and liabilities and are not reported in the Statement of Changes in Fiduciary Net Assets.

Sample City
STATEMENT OF CASH FLOWS
PROPRIETARY FUNDS
For the Year Ended December 31, 2002

	Business-type activities—enterprise funds			Governmental activities—internal service funds
	Water and sewer	Parking facilities	Totals	
Cash flows from operating activities				
Receipts from customers	$11,400,200	$ 1,345,292	$12,745,492	$15,326,343
Payments to suppliers	(2,725,349)	(365,137)	(3,090,486)	(2,812,238)
Payments to employees	(3,360,055)	(750,828)	(4,110,883)	(4,209,688)
Internal activity—payments to other funds	(1,296,768)	--	(1,296,768)	--
Claims paid	--	--	--	(8,482,451)
Other receipts (payments)	(2,325,483)	--	(2,325,483)	1,061,118
Net cash provided by operating activities	1,692,545	229,327	1,921,872	883,084
Cash flows from noncapital financing activities				
Operating subsidies and transfers to other funds	(290,000)	(211,409)	(501,409)	(175,033)
Cash flows from capital and related financing activities				
Proceeds from capital debt	4,041,322	8,660,778	12,702,100	--
Capital contributions	1,645,919	--	1,645,919	--
Purchases of capital assets	(4,194,035)	(144,716)	(4,338,751)	(400,086)
Principal paid on capital debt	(2,178,491)	(8,895,000)	(11,073,491)	(954,137)
Interest paid on capital debt	(1,479,708)	(1,166,546)	(2,646,254)	41,616
Other receipts (payments)	--	19,174	19,174	131,416
Net cash (used) by capital and related financing activities	(2,164,993)	(1,526,310)	(3,691,303)	(1,264,423)
Cash flows from investing activities				
Proceeds from sales and maturities of investments	--	--	--	15,684
Interest and dividends	454,793	143,747	598,540	129,550
Net cash provided by investing activities	454,793	143,747	598,540	145,234
Net (decrease) in cash and cash equivalents	(307,655)	(1,364,645)	(1,672,300)	(411,138)
Balances—beginning of the year	8,724,308	3,227,135	11,951,443	3,747,237
Balances—end of the year	$ 8,416,653	$ 1,862,490	$10,279,143	$ 3,336,099
Reconciliation of operating income (loss) to net cash provided (used) by operating activities				
Operating income (loss)	$ 4,422,127	$ (238,804)	$ 4,183,323	$ (540,532)
Adjustments to reconcile operating income to net cash provided (used) by operating activities:				
Depreciation expense	1,163,140	542,049	1,705,189	1,707,872
Change in assets and liabilities:				
Receivables, net	653,264	1,205	654,469	31,941
Inventories	2,829	--	2,829	39,790
Accounts and other payables	(297,446)	(86,643)	(384,089)	475,212
Accrued expenses	(4,251,369)	(11,520)	(4,239,849)	(831,199)
Net cash provided by operating activities	$ 1,692,545	$ 229,327	$ 1,921,872	$ 883,084

Source: GASB 34, pp. 230–231

F. Notes to the Financial Statements

Note disclosure requirements are found in the GASB *Codification* Section 2300 and in GASB Statements 34 and 38. Some of the major disclosures are a summary of accounting policies, a description of the reporting entity, disclosures on cash and investments (including securitization), fixed assets, long-term debt, pensions, commitments and contingencies, information on exceeding the budget at the legal level of control, and disclosures of individual funds with deficit fund balances. Some disclosures brought about by GASB 34 include a description of the government-wide statements, the policy for capitalizing fixed assets and estimating useful lives, segment information for enterprise funds, and the policy for recording infrastructure, including the use of the modified approach, if applicable.

G. Required Supplementary Information (RSI) other than MD&A

GASB requires four types of information that should be included immediately after the notes to the financial statements. These four items, along with MD & A (see Section C) are considered Required Supplementary Information (RSI). RSI is information presented outside the basic financial statements. While RSI is not covered in the audit opinion, omission of RSI, incomplete RSI, or misleading RSI requires a comment by the auditor. However, an auditor may not modify the report on the basic financial statements as a result of problems discovered related to RSI.

The four types of information are (1) two pension schedules, (2) schedules when the government sponsors a public entity risk pool, (3) a budgetary comparison schedule, and (4) certain schedules when using the modified approach for reporting infrastructure. The pension schedules include a **Schedule of Funding Progress** and a **Schedule of Employer Contributions**. These statements are required when a government reports a defined benefit pension plan. The Schedule of Funding Progress provides actuarial information regarding the actuarial value of assets, the actuarial accrued liability, and the unfunded actuarial liability, if any. The Schedule of Employer Contributions reflects the amount contributed compared with the amount required to be contributed.

The second type of schedule required when the government is sponsor of a public entity risk pool provides revenue and claims development information.

Sample City
STATEMENT OF FIDUCIARY NET ASSETS
FIDUCIARY FUNDS
December 31, 2002

	Employee retirement plan	*Private-purpose trusts*	*Agency funds*
Assets			
Cash and cash equivalents	$ 1,973	$ 1,250	$ 44,889
Receivables:			
Interest and dividends	508,475	760	--
Other receivables	6,826	--	183,161
Total receivables	515,301	760	183,161
Investments, at fair value:			
US government obligations	13,056,037	80,000	--
Municipal bonds	6,528,019	--	--
Corporate bonds	16,320,047	--	--
Corporate stocks	26,112,075	--	--
Other investments	3,264,009	--	--
Total investments	65,280,187	80,000	--
Total assets	65,797,461	82,010	$228,050
Liabilities			
Accounts payable	--	1,234	--
Refunds payable and others	1,358	--	228,050
Total liabilities	1,358	1,234	$228,050
Net Assets			
Held in trust for pension benefits and other purposes	$65,796,103	$80,776	

Source: GASB 34, p. 235.

Sample City
STATEMENT OF CHANGES IN FIDUCIARY NET ASSETS
FIDUCIARY FUNDS
For the Year Ended December 31, 2002

	Employee retirement plan	*Private-purpose trusts*
Additions		
Contributions:		
Employer	$ 2,721,341	$ --
Plan members	1,421,233	--
Total contributions	4,142,574	--
Investment earnings:		
Net (decrease) in fair value of investments	(272,522)	--
Interest	2,460,871	4,560
Dividends	1,445,273	--
Total investment earnings	3,633,622	4,560
Less investment expense	216,428	--
Net investment earnings	3,417,194	4,560
Total additions	7,559,768	4,560
Deductions		
Benefits	2,453,047	3,800
Refunds of contributions	464,691	--
Administrative expenses	87,532	678
Total deductions	3,005,270	4,478
Change in net assets	4,554,498	82
Net assets—beginning of the year	61,241,605	80,694
Net assets—end of the year	$65,796,103	$80,776

Source: GASB 34, pp. 235-6.

The third type of information is to provide **budgetary comparison schedules** for the general fund and all major special revenue funds for which an annual budget has been passed by the governmental unit. Prior accounting principles required this as one of the general-purpose financial statements. Current GAAP permits, but does not require, this schedule to be shown as a basic statement. This schedule includes the original budget, the final budget, and the actual revenues and expenditures computed on the budgetary basis. A variance column may or may not be used. The format may be that of the original budget document or in the format, terminology, and classifications in the Statement of Revenues, Expenditures, and Changes in Fund Balances. Information must be provided, either in this schedule or in notes to the RSI, which provides a reconciliation from the budgetary basis to GAAP. An example of a Budget—Actual Statement is included below.

Sample City
STATEMENT OF REVENUES, EXPENDITURES, AND CHANGES IN FUND BALANCES—
BUDGET AND ACTUAL
GENERAL FUND
For the Year Ended December 31, 2002

	Budgeted amounts		*Actual amounts*
	Original	*Final*	*(budgetary basis)*
Revenues			
Property taxes	$52,017,833	$51,853,018	$51,173,436
Other taxes—franchise and public service	12,841,209	12,836,024	13,025,392
Fees and fines	718,800	718,800	606,946
Licenses and permits	2,126,600	2,126,600	2,287,794
Intergovernmental	6,905,898	6,571,360	6,119,938
Charges for services	12,392,972	11,202,150	11,374,460
Interest	1,501,945	550,000	552,325
Miscellaneous	3,024,292	1,220,991	881,874
Total revenues	91,043,549	87,078,943	86,022,165
Expenditures			
Current			
General government (including contingencies and miscellaneous)	11,837,534	9,468,155	8,621,500
Public safety	33,050,966	33,983,706	33,799,709
Public works	5,215,630	5,025,848	4,993,187
Engineering services	1,296,275	1,296,990	1,296,990
Health and sanitation	5,756,250	6,174,653	6,174,653
Cemetery	724,500	724,500	706,305
Culture and recreation	11,059,140	11,368,070	11,289,146
Education—payment to school district	22,000,000	22,000,000	21,893,273
Total expenditures	90,940,295	90,041,922	88,774,763
Excess (deficiency) of revenues over expenditures	103,254	(2,962,979)	(2,752,598)

Other Financing Sources (Uses)

Transfers in	939,525	130,000	129,323
Transfers out	(2,970,256)	(2,163,759)	(2,163,759)
Total other financing sources and uses	(2,030,731)	(2,033,759)	(2,034,436)
Special Item			
Proceeds from sale of park land	1,355,250	3,500,000	3,476,488
Net change in fund balance	(572,227)	(1,496,738)	(1,310,546)
Fund balances—beginning	3,528,750	2,742,799	2,742,799
Fund balances—ending	$ 2,956,523	$ 1,246,061	$ 1,432,253

Source: GASB 34, pp. 272-273. Budget to GAAP Reconciliation Omitted.

The fourth type of information is presented only when the government is using the **modified approach for reporting infrastructure**. Governments have the option of not depreciating their infrastructure assets if they adopt the "modified" approach for recording infrastructure. Two requirements must be met to adopt this approach. First, the government must manage the eligible infrastructure assets using an asset management system that has certain characteristics. These characteristics include (1) keeping an up-to-date inventory of infrastructure assets, (2) performing condition assessments of eligible infrastructure assets, summarizing the results using a measurement scale, and (3) estimating the costs each year to preserve the infrastructure assets at the condition level established and disclosed by the government. Second, the government must document that the infrastructure assets have been preserved at the condition level prescribed by the government. Two schedules are required: (1) a schedule reflecting the condition of the government's infrastructure, and (2) a comparison of the needed and actual expenditures to maintain the government's infrastructure. Certain disclosures are needed to provide explanations, in notes to the RSI.

An example is provided to illustrate the difference between the "depreciation approach" and the "modified approach" to record infrastructure. Assume a government had $1,000,000 in ordinary maintenance expenses, $2,000,000 in expenditures to extend the life of existing infrastructure, and $3,000,000 in expenditures to add to or improve existing infrastructure. Depreciation (if recorded) amounted to $2,500,000. If the "depreciation approach" were used, $3,500,000 would be charged to expense ($1,000,000 + $2,500,000). If the modified approach were used, the amount charged to expense would be $3,000,000 ($1,000,000 + $2,000,000). In both cases, the $1,000,000 would be charged to expense, and the $3,000,000 would be capitalized. Under the "modified approach," the $2,000,000 in expenditures to extend the life of infrastructure is substituted for depreciation expense.

H. Measurement Focus and Basis of Accounting (MFBA)

GASB Standards require two methods of accounting, each used in certain parts of the financial statements. These are described in terms of measurement focus and basis of accounting. The first is the **economic resources measurement focus and accrual basis of accounting**. This method is similar to accounting for business enterprises. The objective is to measure all of the economic resources available to the governmental entity, including fixed assets and subtracting long-term debt. Full accrual accounting is used, where revenues are recognized when earned and expenses are recognized when incurred. Fixed assets are recorded and depreciated. The economic resources measurement focus and accrual basis of accounting is used for the government-wide statements, the proprietary fund statements, and the fiduciary fund statements.

The second is the **current financial resources measurement focus and modified accrual basis of accounting**. The objective is to measure only the current financial resources available to the governmental entity. As a result fixed assets are not accounted for nor is long-term debt. Modified accrual accounting is used. Under modified accrual accounting, revenues are recognized when measurable and available to finance expenditures of the current period. Property taxes may be considered "available" when collected within sixty days of the end of the fiscal year. The recognition of expenditures (not expenses) is modified in the following way. First, expenditures may be recorded for current items (salaries, supplies), capital outlays (purchase of a police car, construction expenditures), or debt service (matured interest, matured principal). Second, payment of principal and interest on long-term indebtedness, including bonds, notes, capital leases, compensated absences, claims and judgments, pensions, special termination benefits, and landfill closure and postclosure care are recorded when due, rather than accrued. However, a government may accrue an additional amount if it has provided financial resources to a debt service fund for payment of liabilities that will mature early in the following period (not more than a month). Otherwise expenditures are accrued and reported as fund liabilities. The current financial resources measurement focus and modified accrual basis of accounting are used in the governmental fund financial statements and will be illustrated later.

I. **Accounting for Nonexchange Transactions**

The previous section indicated that, under the accrual basis of accounting, revenues are recognized when earned. Revenues include **exchange transactions**, in which goods or services of equal or approximately equal values are exchanged, and **nonexchange transactions**. GASB indicates that revenues from exchange transactions are to be recognized in accord with generally accepted accounting principles as those principles have evolved over the years and provides no special guidance. However, GASB 33, *Accounting and Financial Reporting for Nonexchange Transactions*, defines nonexchange transactions as transactions "in which a government gives (or receives) value without directly receiving (or giving) equal value in exchange." GASB 33 is written under the presumption that an entity is following full accrual accounting. When governmental fund financial statements are issued, modified accrual accounting "modifies" the provisions of GASB 33 to require that resources must be measurable and available to finance the expenditures of the current period, as described in Section H. above.

GASB 33 classifies nonexchange transactions into four categories, and revenue recognition depends upon the category. The categories are: (1) derived tax revenues, (2) imposed nonexchange revenues, (3) government-mandated nonexchange transactions, and (4) voluntary nonexchange transactions. For the government-wide financial statements, revenue from nonexchange transactions is considered to be an increase in unrestricted net assets unless the revenue is restricted by the grantor, donor, or legislation. For example, a hotel-motel tax may have to be used, by legislation, for promotion of tourism. Purpose restrictions do not affect the timing of revenue recognition.

In order for a receivable and revenue to be recognized, four types of **eligibility requirements** must be met. First is the **required characteristics of the recipients**. The recipient of resources must have the characteristics required by the provider. For example, the recipient of certain state funds allocated for road repairs may have to be either a county government, a municipality, or a township. Second, **time requirements** must be met, if a provider specifies that resources must be expended in a certain future period. For example, if a state indicates that funds are appropriated for water system improvements for the fiscal year ended June 30, 2004, then neither a receivable nor revenue would be recognized by the local governments receiving the funds until that fiscal year. In the absence of specified time requirements, a receivable and revenue would be recognized when a promise is unconditional. Third, certain grants from one government to another cannot be provided until the receiving government has expended the funds. This is a condition the GASB calls a **reimbursement**. Reimbursement grant revenues are recognized only when expenditures are recognized. Finally, resources pledged that have a **contingency** attached are not to be recognized until that contingency is removed.

Derived tax revenues result from taxes assessed by governments on exchange transactions. Examples include sales taxes, income taxes, and motor fuel taxes. Receivables and revenues are to be recognized when the underlying transaction (the sale, the income, etc.) takes place. For example, under accrual accounting, if a state imposed a sales tax of 6%, the state would record a revenue of $6 when a merchant recorded a sale of $100. If resources are received before the underlying transaction takes place, then the asset would be offset by deferred revenues, a liability.

Imposed nonexchange transactions are taxes and other assessments by governments that are not derived from underlying transactions. Examples include property taxes, special assessments, and fines and forfeits. Assets from imposed nonexchange transactions should be recognized when an enforceable legal claim exists, or when the resources are received, whichever occurs first. In the case of property taxes, this would normally be specified in the enabling legislation, such as the lien or assessment date. Revenues for property taxes should be recognized, net of estimated refunds and estimated uncollectible taxes, in the period for which the taxes are levied, regardless of when the enforcement date or collection date might be. All other imposed nonexchange transactions should be recognized as revenues at the same time as the assets, or as soon as use is first permitted. On the modified accrual basis, property taxes may not be recognized unless collected within sixty days after the end of a fiscal year.

Government-mandated nonexchange transactions exist when the providing government, such as the federal government or a state government, requires the receiving government to expend funds for a specific purpose. For example, a state may require school districts to "mainstream" certain children by including them in regular classes and also to provide additional assistance in the form of extra aides. Funding for this purpose would be considered to be a government-mandated nonexchange transaction. Receiving governments should recognize assets and revenues when all eligibility requirements have been met.

Voluntary nonexchange transactions include grants and entitlements from one government to another where the providing government does not impose specific requirements upon the receiving government. For example, a state provides a grant for new technology for school districts but does not require those school districts to accept the grant or utilize that technology. Even though the use of the grant is restricted, it is a voluntary nonexchange transaction. It also includes voluntary contributions from individuals and other entities to governments. An example of this type of transaction would be the gift of funds from an individual to a school district or a college. Voluntary nonexchange transactions may or may not have purpose restrictions. The recognition of assets and revenues would be when all eligibility requirements have been met, the same as government-mandated nonexchange transactions.

If after a revenue has been recognized by a governmental entity (in a later fiscal year), those funds must be returned to the provider, then the recipient government must record an expense and liability (or reduction of cash). If there is a difference in the provider government's and recipient government's fiscal year, then the provider's fiscal year would govern for purposes of determining eligibility requirements. If the providing government, a state, has a biennial fiscal year, then half of the grant would be recognized by the recipient government in each of the providing government's two fiscal years.

J. Budgetary Accounting for the General and Special Revenue Funds

The GASB, in one of its basic principles, states

1. An annual budget(s) should be adopted by every governmental unit.
2. The accounting system should provide the basis for appropriate budgetary control.
3. A common terminology and classification should be used consistently throughout the budget, the accounts, and the financial reports of each fund.

In accordance with the principle above, budgets should be prepared for each of the fund types used by governmental units. This directive, by itself, does not differentiate governmental from commercial enterprises. What is different, however, is the inclusion of budgetary accounts in the formal accounting system for the general and major special revenue funds. Inclusion of the budgetary accounts facilitates a budget-actual comparison in Required Supplementary Information or as a basic financial statement. The budget-actual comparison is required for the general fund and all major special revenue funds that have a legally adopted annual budget. Budgetary accounts are generally used in those funds for which the budget-actual comparison is made. As a result, CPA examination questions always assume budgetary accounts for the general fund and sometimes, but not always, assume budgetary accounts for special revenue funds.

Budgetary accounts (Estimated Revenues, Appropriations, Estimated Other Financing Sources, Estimated Other Financing Uses, Budgetary Fund Balance) are incorporated into governmental accounting systems to provide legislative control over revenues and other resource inflows and expenditures and other resource outflows. Recording the budget also provides an assessment of management's stewardship by facilitating a comparison of budget vs. actual. The journal entries that follow illustrate the budgetary accounts used by the general and special revenue funds.

Upon adoption of the estimated revenues and appropriations budgets (at the beginning of the period), the following entry is made and posted to the general ledger:

Estimated Revenues Control[1] (individual items are posted to subsidiary ledger)	1,000,000 (anticipated resources/revenues)	
Appropriations Control (individual items are posted to subsidiary ledger)		980,000 (anticipated expenditures/liabilities)
Budgetary Fund Balance		20,000 (surplus is anticipated)

Budgetary Fund Balance is a budgetary account. This budgetary entry is reversed at year-end.

As actual resource inflows and outflows occur during the year, they are recorded in Revenues and Expenditures accounts, and the detail is posted to the revenues and expenditures subsidiary ledgers to facilitate budget vs. actual comparisons. To prevent the overspending of an item in the appropriations budget, an additional budgetary account is maintained during the year. This budgetary account is called Encum-

---

[1] *Throughout this module "Control" has been used in the journal entries. However, to avoid redundancy, "Control" has not been used in this text.*

brances. When goods or services are ordered, appropriations (specific items in the subsidiary ledger) are encumbered (restricted) with the following entry:

Encumbrances Control (detail posted to subsidiary ledger)	5,000 (cost estimate)	
Budgetary Fund Balance—Reserved for Encumbrances		5,000 (cost estimate)

Budgetary Fund Balance—Reserved for Encumbrances is also a budgetary account. When the debit in the entry is posted, the amount that can still be obligated or expended for an individual budget line item is reduced. Thereafter, when the goods or services ordered are received, the encumbrance entry is reversed and the actual resource outflow (expenditures) is recorded.

Budgetary Fund Balance—Reserved for Encumbrances	5,000	
Encumbrances Control (detail posted to subsidiary ledger)		5,000
Expenditures Control (detail posted to subsidiary ledger)	5,200 (actual cost)	
Accounts Payable		5,200 (actual cost)

The Encumbrances account does not represent an expenditure; it is a budgetary account which represents the estimated cost of goods or services which have yet to be received. In effect, the recording of encumbrances represents the recording of executory contracts, which is essential to prevent overspending of an appropriation (normally, an illegal act). Likewise, the account "Budgetary Fund Balance—Reserved for Encumbrances" is not a liability account; it is a budgetary account. If encumbrances are outstanding at the end of a period, that account is closed to the Fund Balance—Reserved for Encumbrances, which is reported in the fund balance section of the balance sheet (similar to an appropriation of retained earnings on a corporation's balance sheet).

At the end of the year, the following closing entries would be recorded, assuming actual revenues for the year totaled $1,005,000, actual expenditures for the year were $950,000, and encumbrances outstanding at year-end were $10,000:

1.	Budgetary Fund Balance	20,000	
	Appropriations Control	980,000	
	Estimated Revenues Control		1,000,000
	To reverse the budgetary entry and close the budgetary accounts		

2.	Revenues Control	1,005,000	
	Expenditures Control		950,000
	Encumbrances Control		10,000
	Fund Balance—Unreserved		45,000
	If Expenditures and Encumbrances had exceeded Revenues, Fund Balance—Unreserved, an equity account, would have been debited in this closing entry.		

3.	Budgetary Fund Balance—Reserved for Encumbrances	10,000	
	Fund Balance—Reserved for Encumbrances		10,000

Fund Balance—Unreserved and Fund Balance—Reserved for Encumbrances are balance sheet equity accounts.

K. Expenditure Classification for Governmental Funds

Expenditure classification. The GASB *Codification* includes guidelines for the classification of governmental fund expenditure data as set forth in GASB Statement 1. Both internal and external management control benefit from multiple classification of expenditures. In addition, multiple classifications prove important from an accountability standpoint. This classification system provides assistance in aggregating data and performing data analysis. Internal evaluations, external reporting, and intergovernmental comparisons can be enhanced by this multiple classification system. The following chart describes each expenditure classification with examples.

Classification	Description	Examples
Function (or program)	• Provides information on the overall purposes or objectives of expenditures • Represents a major service or area of responsibility	Highways and streets Health and welfare Education General government Public safety
Organization unit (department)	• Grouped according to the government's organizational structure • The responsibility for a department is fixed	Police department Fire department Parks and recreational department Personnel department City clerk

Activity	• Specific and distinguishable line of work performed by an organizational unit as part of one of its functions or programs
	• More meaningful if the performance of each activity is fixed
		Police protection function
		Subactivities:
		  Police administration
		  Crime control and investigation
		  Traffic control
		  Police training
		  Support services

Character	• Classifies expenditures by the fiscal period benefited	Current expenditures Capital outlays Debt service
Object	• Classified according to the types of items purchased or services obtained	Personal services Supplies Rent Utilities Buildings

The Statement of Revenues, Expenditures, and Changes in Fund Balances (see page 137) generally reports expenditures by function within character classification. Budgets often report expenditures by object class at the departmental level.

L. Accounting for the General Fund

The general fund is the most significant governmental fund. It accounts for all transactions not accounted for in any other fund. Revenues come from many sources (taxes, licenses and permits, fines and forfeits, charges for services, etc.), and the expenditures cover the major functions of government (public safety, highways and streets, education, etc.). The illustration below presents an overview of the general fund account structure.

GENERAL FUND ACCOUNT STRUCTURE

Real Accounts
Current Assets (DR)
Current Liabilities (CR)
Fund Balance (Fund Equity) (CR)
    Reserved (Encumbrances, Inventories, etc.)
    Unreserved
        Designated
        Undesignated

Nominal Accounts

Revenues Control (CR)

Other Financing Sources Control (CR)
    (Transfers In)
    (Bond Issue Proceeds)

Expenditures Control (DR)

Other Financing Uses Control (DR)
    (Transfers Out)

Budgetary Accounts

Estimated Revenues Control (DR)

Estimated Other Financing
    Sources Control (DR)

Appropriations Control (CR)
Encumbrances Control (DR)

Estimated Other Financing
    Uses Control (CR)
Budgetary Fund Balance (DR) (CR)
Budgetary Fund Balance—Reserved
    for Encumbrances (CR)

The following represents an accounting cycle problem for the general fund. Some of these entries have been illustrated previously.

a. Adoption of a budget where estimated revenues exceed appropriations and planned transfers by $10,000. (First year of existence for this governmental unit.)

Estimated Revenues Control (detail posted to subsidiary ledger)	300,000	
Appropriations Control (detail posted to subsidiary ledger)		240,000
Estimated Other Financing Uses Control		50,000
Budgetary Fund Balance		10,000

b. Transfers to a debt service fund (for general long-term debt payments) amount to $50,000.

Other Financing Uses—Transfers Out	50,000	
Due to Debt Service Fund		50,000

According to the GASB, transfers should be recognized in the accounting period in which the interfund receivable and payable arises. The account "Transfers Out" is a temporary/nominal account that is compared with the budgetary account "Estimated Other Financing Uses." The account "Due to—Fund" is a current liability. Note that the debt service fund would record a receivable as follows:

Debt Service

Due from General Fund	50,000	
Other Financing Sources—Transfers In		50,000

The "Transfers" accounts are closed at the end of the year. It is important to note that the account "Transfers Out" is not an expenditure account, but is an Other Financing Use, and that the account "Transfers In" is not a revenue account, but is an Other Financing Source. (See the combined statement of revenues, expenditures, and changes in fund balance shown previously.) There is a complete discussion of interfund transactions and transfers later in this module.

c. The property tax levy is recorded as revenues, under the modified accrual basis, when the tax levy is enacted by the governmental unit, if collections will be in time to finance expenditures of the current period. The tax bills amount to $250,000, and $20,000 is estimated to be uncollectible.

Property Taxes Receivable—Current	250,000	
Allowance for Uncollectible Taxes—Current		20,000
Revenues Control		230,000

Under the modified accrual basis, revenues should be recorded in the period in which they are both measurable and available. The GASB requires that property taxes be recognized as a revenue if the taxes are

1. Available—collected by year-end or soon enough to pay liabilities of the current period (no more than sixty days after the end of the fiscal year)
2. To finance the budget of the current period

To the extent the modified accrual criteria for recognition are not met, the property tax levy would be recorded with a credit to Deferred Revenues, a liability, instead of Revenues.

If cash is needed to pay for expenditures before the property tax receivables are collected, it is not uncommon for governmental units to borrow on tax anticipation notes. The receivable serves as security for this loan and, as taxes are collected, the anticipation warrants are liquidated (i.e., Tax Anticipation Notes Payable is debited).

Note, also, the treatment of the allowance for uncollectible accounts. Expendable funds account for resource inflows (revenues) and resource outflows (expenditures). Expenses are not recorded. The Allowance for Uncollectible Accounts represents an estimated reduction in a resource inflow and, accordingly, revenues are recorded net of estimated uncollectible taxes.

d. Revenues from fines, licenses, and permits amount to $40,000.

Cash	40,000	
Revenues Control (detail posted)		40,000

Resource inflows from fines, licenses, permits, etc. are usually not measurable until the cash is collected. Sometimes, it is possible to measure the potential resource inflow; however, because the availability is questionable, revenues are recorded when cash is collected.

e. The state owes the city $25,000 for the city's share of the state sales tax. The amount has not been received at year-end, but it is expected within the first few months of the next fiscal year (in time to pay the liabilities as of the current fiscal year).

State Sales Tax Receivable	25,000	
Revenues Control (detail posted)		25,000

Sales taxes, income taxes, etc. may be accrued before collection by a governmental unit, if collection is anticipated in time to pay for current year expenditures. Other firm commitments from the state or other governmental units for grants, etc. are also recorded.

f. Incurred liabilities for salaries, repairs, utilities, rent, and other regularly occurring items for $200,000.

Expenditures Control (detail posted)	200,000	
Accounts Payable		200,000

Note that all resource outflows authorized in the appropriations budget are debited to Expenditures. It makes no difference whether the outflow is for a fire truck or for rent. Remember, expendable funds do not have a capital maintenance objective. Also, note that the encumbrance accounts were not used in this example. There is usually no need to encumber appropriations for items that occur regularly, and which possess a highly predictable amount (e.g., salaries, rent, etc.). It should be pointed out, however, that there is no hard and fast rule for when to use encumbrances, and encumbrance policies do vary tremendously (i.e., from every expenditure being encumbered to virtually no expenditures being encumbered).

g. Ordered one police car; estimated cost is $17,000. One month later, ordered second police car; estimated cost is $16,500.

Encumbrances Control	17,000	
Budgetary Fund Balance—Reserved for Encumbrances		17,000
Encumbrances Control	16,500	
Budgetary Fund Balance—Reserved for Encumbrances		16,500

Recording encumbrances prevents overspending line-item appropriations. In the case of the police cars, assume the appropriations budget authorized $34,000 for police vehicles. After the first police car was ordered, the unencumbered appropriation for police vehicles was reduced to $17,000. This placed a dollar limit on what could be spent on the second car.

h. Police car ordered first was received; actual cost is $16,800.

Budgetary Fund Balance—Reserved for Encumbrances	17,000	
Encumbrances Control		17,000
Expenditures Control	16,800	
Accounts Payable		16,800

i. Property tax collections amounted to $233,000, payments to other funds amounted to $50,000 (see item b.), and payments of vouchers were $190,000.

Cash	233,000	
Property Taxes Receivable—Current		233,000
Due to Debt Service Fund	50,000	
Cash		50,000
Accounts Payable	190,000	
Cash		190,000
Allowance for Uncollectible Taxes—Current	3,000	
Revenues Control		3,000

The last entry above is required because the Allowance for Uncollectible Taxes—Current was overstated. Note that the estimate was $20,000 in entry c. above. Tax revenues were estimated to be $230,000. Since property tax collections exceeded $230,000 for the current year, an increase in revenues is required.

j. Recorded $5,000 inventory of materials and supplies, reduced the allowance for uncollectible property taxes to $10,000, and reclassified uncollected property taxes to delinquent accounts.

Materials and Supplies Inventory[2]	5,000	
Fund Balance—Reserved for Inventory of Materials and Supplies		5,000
Allowance for Uncollectible Taxes—Current	7,000	
Revenues Control		7,000
Property Taxes Receivable—Delinquent	17,000	
Allowance for Uncollectible Taxes—Current	10,000	
Allowance for Uncollectible Taxes—Delinquent		10,000
Property Taxes Receivable—Current		17,000

One of the reasons for recording the inventory of materials and supplies is to inform the preparers of the budget that items purchased during the year and charged to expenditures (item f.) are still unused. The account "Fund Balance—Reserved for Inventory of Materials and Supplies" is a reservation of Fund Balance. In this respect, it is similar to "Fund Balance—Reserved for Encumbrances."

The second entry adjusts the estimate of uncollectible property taxes to $10,000. This is the result of collecting more property taxes than anticipated (see entries made in c. and i. above) and of an estimate that $7,000 will now be collected.

The third entry reclassifies property taxes receivable from current to delinquent at the end of the year. Generally, interest and penalty charges accrue on the unpaid taxes from the date they become delinquent. If these items have accrued at the end of a fiscal period, they would be recorded in the following way:

Interest and Penalties Receivable on Delinquent Taxes	xx	
Allowance for Uncollectible Interest and Penalties		xx
Revenues Control		xx

k. Appropriate closing entries are made.

Budgetary Fund Balance	10,000	
Appropriations Control	240,000	
Estimated Other Financing Uses Control	50,000	
Estimated Revenues Control		300,000
Revenues	305,000	
Expenditures Control		216,800
Encumbrances Control		16,500
Other Financing Uses—Transfers Out		50,000
Fund Balance—Unreserved		21,700
Budgetary Fund Balance—Reserved for Encumbrances	16,500	
Fund Balance—Reserved for Encumbrances		16,500

Financial statements. Under the GASB *Codification*, individual fund statements should not be prepared that simply repeat information found in the basic or combining statements but may be prepared to present individual fund budgetary comparisons (not needed for the general fund), to present prior year comparative data, or to present more detailed information than is found in the basic or combining statements.

The balance sheet below would represent the general fund portion of the governmental funds balance sheet. Note the following points from the balance sheet:

1. The total fund balance (equity) is $43,200, but only $21,700 is unreserved. This $21,700 represents the appropriable component of total fund balance (i.e., the amount that can be used next period to help finance a deficit budget). The $21,700 represents unreserved net liquid resources.

2. The reason for crediting "Fund Balance—Reserved for Inventory of Materials and Supplies" in item j. previously should now be more meaningful. The inventory of materials and supplies is not a liquid resource that can be used to finance future expenditures. Consequently, if this asset is disclosed, it must be disclosed via a fund restriction.

3. The "Fund Balance—Reserved for Encumbrances" which is disclosed on the balance sheet relates to the second police car that was ordered but not delivered at year-end. When the car is received

---

[2] *The illustration covers the "purchases method" for materials and supplies. The "consumption method" is not covered in this illustration. Consult an advanced or governmental text for coverage of the latter method.*

in the next period, the following journal entries could be made, assuming the actual cost is $16,600:

Expenditures—Prior Year	16,500	
Expenditures Control	100	
Accounts Payable		16,600
Fund Balance—Reserved for Encumbrances	16,500	
Expenditures—Prior Year		16,500

The police car would not be recorded in the general fund as a fixed asset; rather it would be displayed as a fixed asset in the government-wide Statement of Net Assets.

City of X
GENERAL FUND
BALANCE SHEET
At June 30, 2003

Assets			Liabilities and Fund Equity		
Cash		$33,000	Liabilities:		
Property Taxes Receivable—Delinquent	$17,000		Accounts Payable		$26,800
Less: Allowance for Uncollectible			Fund Equity:		
Taxes—Delinquent	10,000	7,000	Reserved for Inventory of Materials		
State Sales Tax Receivable		25,000	and Supplies	$ 5,000	
Inventory of Materials and Supplies		5,000	Reserved for Encumbrances	16,500	
			Unreserved Fund Balance	21,700	
			Total Fund Equity		$43,200
Total Assets		$70,000	Total Liabilities and Fund Equity		$70,000

The following would be the general fund portion of the Budgetary Comparison Schedule:

City of X
BUDGETARY COMPARISON SCHEDULE
GENERAL FUND
For the Year Ended June 30, 2003

	Budgeted amounts		Actual amounts	Variances with final budget
	Original	*Final*	*(Budgetary basis)*	*positive (negative)*
Budgetary Fund Balance, July 1, 2002	--	--	--	--
Resources (Inflows)	$300,000	$300,000	$305,000	$ 5,000
Amounts Available for Appropriation	300,000	300,000	305,000	5,000
Charges to Appropriations (Outflows)	240,000	240,000	233,300	6,700
Transfers to Other Funds	50,000	50,000	50,000	--
Total Charges to Appropriations	290,000	290,000	283,300	6,700
Budgetary Fund Balance, June 30, 2003	$ 10,000	$ 10,000	$ 21,700	$11,700

The Budgetary Comparison Schedule is included in Required Supplementary Information (RSI), presented after the notes to the basic statements. The format may be in accord with the budget or in accord with the Statement of Revenues, Expenditures, and Changes in Fund Balances (see page 137). The Budgetary Fund Balance may or may not be the same as the Unreserved Fund Balance reported in the Balance Sheet for the General Fund. (In this example, it is the same.)

One additional point needs to be covered before going to special revenue funds; that is, how to account for the inventory of materials and supplies in the second or any subsequent year. Accordingly, assume that at the end of the second year, $4,000 of materials and supplies were unused. The adjusting entry would appear as follows:

Fund Balance—Reserved for Inventory of Materials and Supplies	1,000	
Materials and Supplies Inventory		1,000

This entry, when posted, will result in a balance of $4,000 in the inventory and reserve accounts. Note the entry at the end of the first year established a $5,000 balance in these accounts. Thereafter, the inventory and reserve accounts are adjusted upward or downward to whatever the balance is at the end of the year.[3]

---

[3] *Again, this entry illustrates the "purchases method" of accounting for inventories. Consult a governmental or advanced text for illustration of the "consumption method."*

M. Accounting for Special Revenue Funds

Special revenue funds account for earmarked revenue as opposed to the many revenue sources that are accounted for in the general fund. The earmarked revenue is then used to finance various authorized expenditures. For example, a city might place its share of the state's gasoline tax revenues into a State Gasoline Tax Fund, which could then be used to maintain streets. Note that a governmental unit has some discretion in terms of how many special revenue funds it creates. Sometimes separate funds are required by law or grant requirements. Many federal and state grants are reported in special revenue funds.

The accounting for special revenue funds parallels that of the general fund. One type of transaction that often takes place in a special revenue fund is a "reimbursement" grant from a federal or state government. **GASB Statement 33** lists reimbursement grant requirements as one of the conditions that must be satisfied before a revenue can be recognized, either for accrual or modified accrual accounting. With a reimbursement grant, the granting government will not provide resources unless the receiving government provides evidence that an appropriate expenditure has taken place; **GASB 33** requires that the expenditure must be recognized prior to a revenue being recognized.

For example, assume a municipality with a calendar fiscal year receives a grant award on November 1, 2003, in the amount of $30,000. No entry would be recorded (either a receivable or revenue) until the expenditure takes place.

Assume the expenditure takes place on March 1, 2004. The entries would be (for accrual accounting)

Expenditures Control	30,000	
Cash		30,000
Grants Receivable	30,000	
Revenues Control—Grants		30,000

Assume cash is received on April 1, 2004; the entry would be

Cash	30,000	
Grants Receivable		30,000

The budgetary comparison schedule in RSI must include "major" special revenue funds for which annual budgets have been legally adopted.

N. Accounting for Capital Projects Funds

Capital projects funds account for the acquisition and use of resources for the construction or purchase of major, long-lived fixed assets, except for those that are financed by internal service, enterprise, and trust funds. Resources for construction or purchase normally come from the issuance of general long-term debt, from government grants (federal, state, and local), and from interfund transfers.

Project budgets for estimated resources and expenditures must be approved before the project can begin. However, unlike the budgets of general and special revenue funds, an annual budget for capital projects funds may not be legally adopted and need not be recorded formally in the accounts.

The following transactions illustrate the entries encountered in a capital projects fund:

a. City Council approved the construction of a new city hall at an estimated cost of $10,000,000. General obligation long-term serial bonds were authorized for issuance in the face amount of $10,000,000. (No entries are required.)

b. $10,000,000 in 8% general obligation serial bonds were issued for $10,100,000. Assume that the premium is transferred to a debt service fund for the eventual payment of the debt. (Premiums and discounts in governmental funds are not amortized in the fund financial statements.)

Cash	10,100,000	
Other Financing Sources—Proceeds of Bonds		10,100,000
Other Financing Uses—Transfers Out	100,000	
Cash		100,000

Note the credit to Proceeds of Bonds. This is an Other Financing Source on the operating statement, whereas the Transfers Out is an Other Financing Use. Both accounts are temporary accounts that are closed to Unreserved Fund Balance at year-end.

The transfer requires an entry in the debt service fund.

Debt Service Fund

Cash	100,000	
Other Financing Sources—Transfer In		100,000

This entry will be explained in more detail later.

c. The bond issue proceeds are temporarily invested in a Certificate of Deposit (CD) and earn $50,000. The earnings are authorized to be sent to the debt service fund for the payment of bonds.

Capital Projects Fund

Investment in CD	10,000,000	
Cash		10,000,000
Cash	50,000	
Revenues—Interest		50,000

Debt Service Fund

Other Financing Uses—			Cash	50,000	
Transfers Out	50,000		Other Financing Sources—		
Cash		50,000	Transfers In		50,000

d. The lowest bid, $9,800,000, is accepted from a general contractor.

Encumbrances Control	9,800,000	
Fund Balance—Reserved for Encumbrances[4]		9,800,000

e. $2,000,000 of the temporary investments are liquidated.

Cash	2,000,000	
Investment in CD		2,000,000

f. Progress billings due to the general contractor for work performed amount to $2,000,000. The contract allows 10% of the billings to be retained until final inspection and approval of the building. The contractor was paid $1,800,000.

Fund Balance—Reserved for Encumbrances	2,000,000	
Encumbrances Control		2,000,000
Expenditures—Construction	2,000,000	
Contracts Payable		2,000,000
Contracts Payable	2,000,000	
Cash		1,800,000
Contracts Payable—Retained Percentage		200,000

The account "Contracts Payable—Retained Percentage" is a liability account. Note, also, that the fixed asset is not recorded in the capital projects fund because this fund is expendable and does not have a capital maintenance objective.

g. Interest accrued on a CD at the end of the year amounted to $40,000. This was authorized to be sent to the debt service fund for the payment of debt.

Capital Projects Fund

Interest Receivable	40,000	
Revenues—Interest		40,000

Debt Service Fund

Other Financing Uses—			Due from Other Funds	40,000	
Transfers Out	40,000		Other Financing Sources—		
Due to Other Funds		40,000	Transfers In		40,000

The interest is recognized because it is measurable and will soon be available to finance debt service fund expenditures.

h. Closing entries for the capital projects fund would appear as follows:

(1)

Revenues—Interest	90,000	
Other Financing Sources—Proceeds of Bonds	10,100,000	
Fund Balance—Unreserved		10,190,000

(2)

Fund Balance—Unreserved	9,800,000	
Encumbrances Control		7,800,000
Expenditures—Construction		2,000,000

(3)

Fund Balance—Unreserved	190,000	
Other Financing Uses—Transfers Out		190,000

The GASB requires that the totals for "major" capital projects funds appear in the balance sheet and the Statement of Revenues, Expenditures, and Changes in Fund Balances, for governmental funds. Combin-

---

[4] *Since an annual budget is not assumed in this example, the credit is taken directly to the fund equity account.*

ing statements are required in the CAFR for nonmajor capital projects funds along with other nonmajor governmental funds.

A "stand-alone" Statement of Revenues, Expenditures, and Changes in Fund Balances appears for the capital projects fund example.

City of X
Capital Projects Fund
STATEMENT OF REVENUES, EXPENDITURES, AND CHANGES
IN FUND BALANCES
Year Ended June 30, 2003

Revenues:		
Interest on Temporary Investments		$ 90,000
Expenditures:		
Construction of City Hall		2,000,000
Excess of Expenditures over Revenues		(1,910,000)
Other Financing Sources and Uses:		
Proceeds of General Obligation Bonds	$10,100,000	
Transfer to Debt Service Fund	(190,000)	9,910,000
Excess of Revenues and Other Financing Sources over Expenditures		
and Other Financing Uses		8,000,000
Fund Balance—Beginning of Year		--
Fund Balance—End of Year		$8,000,000

At the beginning of the second year, the following entry would be made to reestablish the Encumbrances balance:

Encumbrances Control	7,800,000	
Fund Balance—Unreserved		7,800,000

The purpose of this entry is to permit the recording of expenditures in the normal manner (i.e., reverse the encumbrances before recording the expenditures).

When the city hall project is finished, the capital projects fund should be terminated. Assuming there are no cost overruns, the excess cash left in the fund upon project completion must be transferred to some other fund, normally a debt service fund. This entry is described along with other interfund transactions and transfers in Section S.

O. Debt Service Funds

Debt service funds usually handle the repayment of general obligation long-term debt and interest. This type of debt is secured by the good faith and taxing power of the governmental unit. Repayment of internal service and enterprise long-term debt is accounted for in those individual funds. Consequently, debt service funds are normally established as the result of issuing general obligation bonds for capital projects. The bond liability to be extinguished is not recorded in the debt service fund until it matures. General long-term debt is reported only in the government-wide financial statements.

Assume the City of X authorizes a debt service fund for the general obligation serial bonds issued to finance the city hall project. The debt service fund is also authorized to pay the 8% interest on the $10,000,000 of debt on December 31 and June 30. The fiscal year-end is June 30. Note that the debt service fund has received resources from the general and capital projects funds. Transactions showing recognition and receipt of these resources were illustrated in the discussions of the general and capital projects funds. They are repeated below as follows:

(1)	Due from General Fund	50,000		(Transaction b.
	Other Financing Sources—Transfers In		50,000	in Section L.)
(2)	Cash	50,000		(Transaction i.
	Due from General Fund		50,000	in Section L.)
(3)	Cash	100,000		(Transaction b.
	Other Financing Sources—Transfers In		100,000	in Section N.)
(4)	Cash	50,000		(Transaction c.
	Other Financing Sources—Transfers In		50,000	in Section N.)
(5)	Due from Capital Projects Fund	40,000		(Transaction g.
	Other Financing Sources—Transfers In		40,000	in Section N.)

Assume the bonds were issued on July 1. In addition, assume that $250,000 of the bonds mature each six months, starting June 30.

a. The property tax levy contains $870,000 portion allocable to the debt service fund. $20,000 of this amount is estimated to be uncollectible.

Property Taxes Receivable—Current	870,000	
Allowance for Uncollectible Taxes—Current		20,000
Revenues—Property Taxes		850,000

b. $840,000 of property taxes are collected during the year. The remainder of the property taxes is reclassified as delinquent.

Cash	840,000	
Property Taxes Receivable—Current		840,000
Property Taxes Receivable—Delinquent	30,000	
Allowance for Uncollectible Taxes—Current	20,000	
Property Taxes Receivable—Current		30,000
Allowance for Uncollectible Taxes—Delinquent		20,000

c.   The semiannual interest is paid on December 31 and June 30. The following entries are made on December 31:

Expenditures—Interest	400,000	
Matured Interest Payable		400,000
Matured Interest Payable	400,000	
Cash		400,000

The following entries are made on June 30:

Expenditures—Interest	400,000	
Matured Interest Payable		400,000
Matured Interest Payable	400,000	
Cash		400,000

Note that if interest were paid on dates other than December 31 and June 30, interest would not be accrued to the end of the fiscal year.

d.   On June 30, the first $250,000 principal payment became due, and $200,000 was paid. The following entries would be made in the debt service fund:

Expenditures—Principal	250,000	
Matured Bonds Payable		250,000
Matured Bonds Payable	200,000	
Cash		200,000

If a bank were used as the fiscal agent, cash would first be transferred to a "Cash with Fiscal Agent" account, and payment would then be made from that account.

e.   Appropriate closing entries are made based upon all information presented.

Revenues—Property Taxes	850,000	
Other Financing Sources—Transfers In	240,000	
Expenditures—Interest		800,000
Expenditures—Principal		250,000
Fund Balance—Designated for Debt Service		40,000

The balance sheet for the debt service fund would appear as follows:

City of X
DEBT SERVICE FUND
BALANCE SHEET
June 30, 2003

Assets		*Liabilities and Fund Equity*	
Cash	$40,000	*Liabilities:*	
Due from Capital Projects Fund	40,000	Matured Bonds Payable	$50,000
Property taxes receivable—Delinquent (net of		*Fund Equity:*	
$20,000 allowance for uncollectible taxes)	10,000	Fund Balance—Designated for Debt Service	40,000
Total Assets	$90,000	Total Liabilities and Fund Equity	$90,000

Under modified accrual accounting, expenditures for principal and interest are generally not accrued but recorded when due. GASB 36 provides that if resources are available at year-end and payment is to be made within one month after year-end, an accrual may be made, if a debt service fund is used.

P. Permanent Funds

A fifth category of governmental funds, introduced by GASB 34, is the **permanent fund** type. Permanent funds account for nonexpendable funds provided and held for some governmental purpose. The income from those investments will be recorded as revenues and expenditures.

A common example would be a cemetery perpetual care fund. Assume a local citizen was concerned about the deplorable condition of the city cemetery and on January 2, 2003, contributed $500,000 with the stipulation that the funds be invested and held; the income is to be used for the purpose of maintaining the city cemetery. On January 2, the cash was received and invested.

Cash	500,000	
Revenues—Additions to Permanent Endowments		500,000
Investments	500,000	
Cash		500,000

During 2003, $30,000 was earned on the investment, and $25,000 was expended.

Cash (and/or interest receivable)	30,000	
Revenues—Investment Income		30,000
Expenditures	25,000	
Cash (or Accounts Payable)		25,000

Q. Accounting for Special Assessments

GASB 6, *Accounting and Reporting for Special Assessments,* outlines the accounting and financial reporting for special assessments. Special assessments are levied for projects to be paid primarily by the property owners who benefited (for example, a street lighting or sidewalk project).

Under GASB 6, the accounting for special assessment capital projects depends on the liability of the governmental unit for the special assessment debt. If the governmental unit is not obligated in any way for the debt, the special assessment activities will be accounted for in an agency fund. However, if the governmental unit is either **primarily** or **potentially liable** for the debt, the accounting will take place as if it were any other capital improvement and financing transaction. Construction activities will be recorded in a capital projects fund and debt principal and interest activities would be recorded in a debt service fund.

R. Accounting for Proprietary Funds

Internal service funds are established to account for the provision of goods and services by one department of the government to other departments within the government, generally on a cost-reimbursement basis. Uses of internal service fund services are budgeted through the budgets of the user departments. Internal service funds are normally established for the following types of activities: central garages, motor pools, central printing and duplicating, stores departments, self-insurance, etc. **Enterprise funds,** on the other hand, account for activities for which the government provides goods and services that are (1) rendered primarily to the general public, (2) financed substantially or entirely through user charges, and (3) intended to be self-supporting. Enterprise funds are usually established for public utilities, airports, toll roads and bridges, transit systems, golf courses, solid waste landfills, etc.

Proprietary funds use the accrual basis of accounting and are nonexpendable; capital is to be maintained. Revenues and expenses are recorded generally as they would be in commercial enterprises. Fixed assets are recorded in proprietary funds, and depreciation expense is deducted from revenues. These funds also report their own long-term liabilities. The GASB has provided a special rule regarding the use of FASB pronouncements in enterprise funds of state and local government. That rule has two parts.

1. Enterprise funds should follow FASB pronouncements issued prior to November 30, 1989, unless those FASB pronouncements conflict with GASB pronouncements.
2. Enterprise funds may or may not follow FASB pronouncements issued after November 30, 1989, that do not conflict with GASB pronouncements. The decision regarding whether or not to follow such FASB pronouncements must be applied consistently to all FASB pronouncements, and the choice must be disclosed.

An example of a FASB pronouncement that does conflict would be SFAS 35 regarding pensions, which has different conclusions than GASB reached in its pension standards.

When proprietary funds are initially established, a contribution or advance is usually received from the general fund. A contribution is a transfer and would be recorded by the internal service or enterprise fund as follows:

Cash	xx	
Capital Contributions		xx

The Capital Contributions account is a separate category in the statement of Revenues, Expenses, and Changes in Net Assets. On the other hand, an advance from the general fund is a long-term loan and would be recorded by an internal service or enterprise fund as follows:

Cash	xx	
Advance from General Fund		xx

The advance is a long-term liability on the proprietary fund's balance sheet. It is a long-term asset on the general fund's balance sheet, which requires a reservation of Fund Balance.

Accounting entries for proprietary funds are similar to those for business enterprises. "Operating Revenues—Charges for Services" is a common operating revenue account for both internal service and enterprise funds. As indicated earlier, revenues and expenses are recognized on the full accrual basis and are classified as operating and nonoperating. Some features that distinguish the accounting for proprietary funds are

1. Long-term debt is recorded directly in internal service and enterprise funds. Revenue bonds are those that are backed only by the revenues of the proprietary activity. However, revenue bonds with general obligation backing and general obligation bonds that are to be paid with revenues of the proprietary activities are also recorded in the proprietary funds.

2. Interest on long-term debt is accrued as an expense, unlike interest on general long-term debt (see debt service funds). Premiums and discounts on debt issuances, as well as debt issue costs, are recorded with the debt and amortized over the life of the bonds.

3. Fixed assets are capitalized and depreciated, using one of the generally accepted methods used by business enterprises.

4. Revenues, expenses, capital contributions, and transfers are closed out to net assets at year-end. Three categories of net assets exist, as indicated earlier: (a) invested in capital assets, net of related debt, (b) restricted, and (c) unrestricted. These are the same asset categories as are used in the government-wide Statement of Net Assets.

5. Net assets—invested in capital assets, net of related debt, would be the net of fixed assets, less accumulated depreciation, less any long-term debt issued to finance capital assets. Net assets—restricted would offset, for example, any resources held for future debt service in accord with bond indenture requirements.

6. A special problem exists with self-insurance funds, which are often classified as internal service funds.[5] Governments transfer resources from other funds to self-insurance funds, from which claims are paid. To the extent that the transfers do not exceed the actuarially determined liability of the government, they are recorded as expenditures or expenses. Any transfers in addition to the actuarially determined liability are classified as transfers.

7. Another special problem exists with municipal waste landfills, which are often classified as enterprise funds. Many of the solid waste landfills in the US are operated by local governmental units. The problem which arises in accounting for municipal landfills is that most revenue is earned early in the useful life of the landfill, as various persons and organizations pay to dispose of waste; conversely, a significant portion of the costs, termed closure and postclosure care costs as defined by US Government regulations, occur up to twenty to thirty years later. The GASB requires that these future costs be estimated and charged against periodic revenues on a "units of production" basis according to the amount of landfill capacity consumed during each period. If a municipal waste landfill is operated as an enterprise fund, expenses and liabilities are accounted for on a full accrual basis and recorded directly in the enterprise fund. If the municipal waste landfill is operated through a governmental fund, the expenditure and fund liability would be limited to the amount that will be paid with currently available resources, and the remaining liability would be reported in the government-wide statements.

CPA exam questions sometimes portray a situation, such as a federal government grant for bus purchases, and ask candidates to provide accounting treatment for when the transaction is recorded in a governmental fund (record a revenue if expended, defer revenue if not), and for when the transaction is re-

---

[5] *GASB requires that, if self-insurance is to be recorded in a single fund, that fund must be an internal service or the general fund.*

corded in a proprietary fund (record as capital contributions). When uncertain, candidates should generally recall business accounting principles to record the proprietary fund transaction.

S. Accounting for Fiduciary Funds

Fiduciary funds (trust and agency) account for resources invested or to be expended for the benefit of other governments, private organizations, or individuals. (Resources held and invested for the benefit of the reporting government are classified as permanent funds, a governmental fund category.) Included in the fiduciary fund category are pension (and other employee benefit) trust funds, investment trust funds, private-purpose trust funds, and agency funds.

Pension (and other employee benefit) trust funds are maintained when the governmental unit is trustee for the pension (or other employee benefit) plan. In addition, many state governments operate statewide Public Employee Retirement Systems (PERS) for local governments, teachers, university employees, judges, etc. These PERS are normally a part of the state government reporting entity. Full accrual accounting is used for pension trust funds, and investments are reported at fair value. Pension trust funds are required to have two statements and two schedules (included as required supplementary information; see the contents of the CAFR). The pension trust funds are included in the (1) Statement of Fiduciary Net Assets and the (2) Statement of Changes in Fiduciary Net Assets. The two RSI schedules are the (1) Schedule of Funding Progress (which illustrates actuarial status) and the (2) Schedule of Employer Contributions.

Government pension plans do not include the required actuarial liability in the statement of fiduciary net assets. Rather, the actuarial liability is reported in the schedule of funding progress and in the notes. Extensive note disclosures are required, both for the PERS and for the government as employer, whether or not it is trustee of the pension plan.

The above requirements relate to **defined benefit** pension plans. Under **defined contribution** plans, the government is liable only for the required contributions not made.

Employer accounting for defined benefit plans is the same, regardless of whether or not the government is the trustee for the pension plan. Expenditures (or expenses) are charged in the appropriate funds (especially the general, special revenue, and enterprise funds) in an amount equal to the amount provided to the pension plan. The pension trust fund (or statewide PERS) would record those contributions as additions. Other additions for the pension trust fund would include employee contributions, investment income, and gains in the market value of investments. Deductions would include retirement benefit payments, disability payments, refunds to terminated (nonvested) employees, and losses in the market value of investments.

Statewide PERS may be **agency** defined benefit, **cost-sharing** defined benefit, or defined contribution. **Agency** plans maintain separate balances for each participating government so that it is possible to determine its unfunded actuarial liability (or assets in excess of accrued actuarial benefits). **Cost-sharing** plans normally compute balances on a statewide basis only; it is not the responsibility of each participating government to fund its own liability.

A final use for pension trust funds is IRS Sec. 457 Deferred Compensation Plans (tax-deferred annuities for government employees). In many cases, these plans will not be recorded. However, when the plan meets the criteria for inclusion in a government financial statement, GASB 34 requires that a pension trust fund be used.

Investment trust funds are required when a government sponsors an external investment pool; for example, when a county sponsors an investment pool for all cities, school districts, and other governments within its borders. The **external portion** of investment pools are to be reported (by the county) in a manner similar to pension trust funds. Statements of Net Fiduciary Assets and of Changes in Fiduciary Net Assets are required. Statements of Cash Flows are not required.

Private-purpose trust funds represent all other trust arrangements under which principal and income benefit other governments, private organizations, or individuals. Private-purpose trust funds may be **nonexpendable** or **expendable**. A nonexpendable trust fund is one in which the principal cannot be expended but which provide that income may be expended for some agreed-upon purpose. Sometimes, this is called an endowment. For example, a donor gives $500,000 to a city with instructions that the principal be invested permanently and that the income be used to provide scholarships for low-income children to attend a private, not-for-profit day care program. The receipt and investment of the gift would be recorded as

Cash	500,000	
Additions—Contributions		500,000

Investments	500,000	
Cash		500,000

Assume $30,000 is received in investment income and expended.

Cash	30,000	
Additions—Investment Income		30,000
Deductions—Awarding of Scholarships	30,000	
Cash		30,000

Expendable private-purpose trust funds are accounted for in the same manner, except that the principal as well as investment income may be expended. For example, a donor may give $10,000 to a school district with instructions that each year $2,000 plus investment income be awarded to the top student in the senior class, as a scholarship.

Another use of private-purpose trust funds, in some cases, is for **escheat property**. Escheat property is property taken over by a government, usually state government, when the property is abandoned and the legal owners cannot be found. GASB 37 concluded that escheat property generally is recorded in the governmental or proprietary fund to which the property ultimately escheats (e.g., an educational fund). A liability is recorded for estimated amounts to potential claimants. A private-purpose trust fund is used when resources are held for individuals, private organizations, or another government.

Agency funds are used to account for activities where the government is acting as an agent for others. Agency funds have only assets and liabilities; no fund equity, revenue, or expenditure accounts are used. The GASB requires the use of agency funds for special assessments where the government is not liable in any way for the debt.

Another common use of agency funds is to account for property taxes. Property taxes are usually remitted to a county treasurer who places the monies in a county Tax Agency Fund. The taxes are held until such time as they are remitted to each of the other local governments located within the county. Often, a fee is charged, which decreases the amount that is distributed to the other local governments and increases the amount that is distributed to the County General Fund.

T. Reporting Interfund Activity

Under GASB 34, interfund activity is shown between individual funds in fund financial statements and between business-type and governmental-type activities in the government-wide financial statements. GASB provides for two major types of interfund activity, each with two subtypes:

1. Reciprocal interfund activity

    a. Interfund loan and advances
    b. Interfund services provided and used

2. Nonreciprocal interfund activity

    a. Interfund transfers
    b. Interfund reimbursements

Interfund loans and advances are transactions in which one fund provides resources with a requirement for repayment. Short-term loans are recorded with "Due from" and "Due to" accounts. For example, if an enterprise fund made a short-term loan to the general fund, the entry would be

Enterprise Fund			*General Fund*		
Due from General Fund	100,000		Cash	100,000	
Cash		100,000	Due to Enterprise Fund		100,000

Long-term interfund receivables and payables use the terms "Advance to" and "Advance from." If a governmental fund makes a long-term loan to another fund, it is necessary to reserve fund balances, as the resources are not "available" for expenditure. For example, assume the general fund advances $50,000 to an internal service fund. The entries would be

General Fund			*Internal Service Fund*		
Advance to Internal Service Fund	50,000		Cash	50,000	
Cash		50,000	Advance from General Fund		50,000
Fund Balance—Unreserved	50,000				
Fund Balance—Reserved for Long-Term Advances		50,000			

Loans and advances to and from component units are to be separately identified in the government-wide financial statements.

Interfund services provided and used represent transactions in which sales and purchases of goods and services between funds are made at prices approximating their external exchange price. Examples would include the sale of water from an enterprise fund to the general fund, the provision of services by an internal service fund to a governmental fund, a payment in lieu of taxes from an enterprise fund to the general fund (where payment is approximately equal to services provided), and the payment of a retirement fund contribution from the general fund to a pension trust fund. Revenues (or additions) are recognized by one fund, and an expenditure or expense is recorded by another fund. As a result, the operating statements will include these revenues and expenditures/expenses. For example, assume an internal services fund provides $30,000 in service to the general fund.

Internal Service Fund			*General Fund*		
Due from General Fund	30,000		Expenditures Control	30,000	
Operating Revenues—			Due to Internal Service Fund		30,000
Charges for Services		30,000			

Prior to GASB 34, these were known as quasi-external transactions.

Interfund transfers are nonreciprocal transfers between funds, where payment is not expected. Examples would include an annual subsidy from an enterprise fund to the general fund or an annual transfer from the general fund to a debt service fund. To illustrate the latter in the amount of $300,000

General Fund			*Debt Service Fund*		
Other Financing Uses—Transfer to			Cash	300,000	
Debt Service Fund	300,000		Other Financing Sources—		
Cash		300,000	Transfer from General Fund		300,000

Transfers are reported as "Other Financing Sources/Uses" in the governmental fund operating statements.

Interfund reimbursements are repayments from funds responsible for expenditures or expenses to those funds that initially paid for them. For example, assume the general fund paid an enterprise fund for a consultant's fee that was initially paid by the enterprise fund and charged to expense.

General Fund			*Enterprise Fund*		
Expenditures Control	50,000		Cash	50,000	
Cash		50,000	Consultant Fee Expense		50,000

U. Accounting for Investments

GASB's rules for investment accounting are contained in Statement 31, *Accounting and Financial Reporting for Certain Investments and for External Investment Pools.* GASB 31 provides that investments in debt securities and in equity securities with determinable fair values be reported at fair value. Changes in fair value should be reported as a part of operations, using modified accrual or accrual accounting, as appropriate. No distinction is to be made on the face of the financial statements between realized and unrealized gains and losses, although disclosure may be made of realized gains in the notes. Investment income should be reported in the fund holding the investments.

V. Conversion from Fund Financial Statements to Government-Wide Financial Statements

Most state and local governments will keep their books on a fund basis in order to facilitate the preparation of fund financial statements and to prepare the budget-actual schedule as a part of RSI. This will mean that governments will record transactions on the modified accrual basis for governmental funds and on the accrual basis for proprietary and fiduciary funds. Many governments will make changes, on a worksheet basis, in order to prepare the government-wide financial statements. The following are the major changes that will be necessary to convert from governmental fund statements to the governmental activities portion of the government-wide statements.

1. General fixed assets

When general fixed assets are acquired through governmental funds, the account expenditures is debited. Governmental funds do not record fixed assets. It will be necessary to eliminate the expenditure accounts in the governmental funds and record fixed assets. These fixed assets will increase the net assets of the governmental activities. Assuming the amount is $10 million the entry would be

Fixed Assets (Land, Buildings, Equipment, etc.)	10,000,000	
Expenditures Control		10,000,000

In addition, a depreciation charge will be required for the equipment.

2. **Issuance of general long-term debt**

When general long-term debt is issued, governmental funds credit Proceeds of Debt, which is an Other Financing Source. Also, premiums and discounts are not amortized but simply add to or deduct from the amount of resources available. It will be necessary to eliminate those entries and record the debt as a liability, to be shown as a reduction of net assets in the governmental activities column of the Statement of Net Assets. Moreover, any premium or discount must be associated with the liability and amortized over the life of the bonds. The worksheet entry to convert the sale of bonds from governmental fund accounting to government-wide statements, assuming a sale of $5 million at par, would be

Other Financing Sources—Proceeds of Bonds	5,000,000	
Bonds Payable		5,000,000

3. **Debt service payments**

When making principal payments on long-term debt, governmental funds debit expenditures. Those expenditures will need to be eliminated and replaced with a debit to the debt principal when preparing the government-wide statements. In addition, governmental funds do not accrue interest payable but record expenditures on the maturity date. Accrual of interest payable will be required for the government-wide statements, including adjustments for amortization of premiums and discounts. The worksheet entry to convert a $100,000 principal payment from governmental fund accounting to government-wide statements would be

Bonds Payable	100,000	
Expenditures—Principal		100,000

4. **Adjustment of revenue recognition**

Governmental funds recognize revenues only when measurable and available to finance expenditures of the current period. In the case of property taxes, revenues cannot be recognized if those revenues will be collected more than sixty days after the end of the fiscal year. When preparing the government-wide financial statements, some adjustments will be required to recognize all revenues, net of uncollectible receivables, in accord with revenue accounting for exchange and nonexchange transactions, as described earlier in this module. Assume a government levied $10 million in property taxes for the year 2003 with 2% uncollectible. The amount to be recognized on the government-wide statements is $9,800,000. Assume that during 2003 and the first sixty days of 2004, $9,600,000 had been and was expected to be collected, limiting the amount reported as revenues in the governmental funds Statement of Revenues, Expenditures, and Changes in Fund Balances to $9,600,000. The $200,000 would have been shown as a deferred revenue (liability) in the Governmental Funds Balance Sheet. The worksheet entry would be

Deferred Revenues	200,000	
Revenues Control		200,000

5. **Accrual of expenses**

Under modified accrual accounting, expenditures are recorded for items that are current, capital outlay, and debt service. As indicated earlier, adjustments must be made to reduce expenditures for capital outlay payments and debt service principal payments. In addition, adjustments must be made to record the noncurrent portion of certain liabilities (claims and judgments, compensated absences, etc.). These worksheet entries would debit expenses and credit liabilities.

6. **Other**

Some governments use the purchases method to record governmental fund inventories, and these must be changed to the consumption method when using accrual accounting. Other governments do not record and amortize certain prepaid items, such as prepaid insurance and prepaid rent. Adjustments must also be made for these items.

7. **Reclassifications**

Fund financial statements are presented separately for governmental, proprietary, and fiduciary fund categories. Government-wide financial statements have columns for governmental activities, business-type activities, and component units. In order to make the transition from fund financial statements, the fiduciary funds will be eliminated. Internal service funds, which are proprietary funds, are to be classified as governmental activities in the government-wide statements. Discretely presented component units, which are not presented at all in the fund financial statements, will be added when preparing the government-wide financial statements.

W. College and University Accounting—Public (Governmental)—GASB 35

GASB 35, *Basic Financial Statements—and Management's Discussion and Analysis—for Public Colleges and Universities,* becomes effective in three phases for public institutions that are not component units of another reporting entity based on total revenues in the first fiscal year ending after June 15, 1999.

- Institutions with total annual revenues of $100 million or more—for periods beginning after June 15, 2001.
- Institutions with total annual revenues of $10 million or more but less than $100 million—for periods beginning after June 15, 2002.
- Institutions with annual revenues of less than $10 million—for periods beginning after June 15, 2003.

These are the same dates as required for state and local governments outlined in GASB 34. As is true for state and local governments, retroactive adoption of infrastructure reporting is deferred a few years. Public colleges that are component units of other reporting entities (states, for example) must adopt the provisions of GASB 35 at the same time as their primary government.

GASB 35 requires that public colleges follow the standards for special purpose governments outlined in GASB 34. This means that public colleges may choose to use the guidance for special purpose governments engaged in (1) only business-type activities, (2) engaged in only governmental activities, or (3) engaged in both governmental and business-type activities.

Public colleges that choose to report as special purpose governments that are engaged in only governmental activities or in governmental and business-type activities are required to follow the reporting model presented earlier in this module for state and local governments. This model requires (1) a Management's Discussion and Analysis (MD&A), (2) Government-Wide Financial Statements, (3) Fund Financial Statements, (4) Notes to the Financial Statements, and (5) Required Supplementary Information (CRSI) other than MD&A.

While a number of community colleges may choose to report in the manner described in the previous paragraph, most public colleges and universities will choose to report as special entities engaged only in **business-type** activities. In this case, proprietary fund statements only are required. These institutions will report (1) an MD&A, (2) a Statement of Net Assets, (3) a Statement of Revenues, Expenses, and Changes in Net Assets, (4) a Statement of Cash Flows, and (5) Required Supplementary Information other than MD&A. Public colleges reporting in this format present statements using the **economic resources measurement focus and the accrual basis of accounting**.

The **Statement of Net Assets** (as illustrated) may be presented in the format: Assets – Liabilities = Net Assets. Alternatively, a balance sheet format (Assets = Liabilities + Net Assets) may be presented. In either case, a classified statement must be presented, distinguishing between current and long-term assets and between current and long-term liabilities. As is the case for state and local governments, net assets must be segregated between (1) invested in capital assets, net of related debt, (2) restricted, and (3) unrestricted. Restricted net assets should show major categories of restrictions. It is **not** permissible to show designations of unrestricted net assets.

The **Statement of Revenues, Expenses, and Changes in Net Assets** is reported in an "all-inclusive" format that reconciles to the ending total net assets. GASB requires that revenues be reported by major source and that a distinction be made between operating and nonoperating revenues and expenses. The general format is

	Operating Revenues
−	Operating Expenses
=	Operating Income (Loss)
+	Nonoperating Revenues and Expenses
=	Income Before Other Revenues, Expenses Gains, Losses, and Transfers
±	Capital Contributions, Additions to Permanent and Term Endowments, Special and Extraordinary Items, and Transfers
=	Increase (Decrease in Net Assets)
+	Net Assets, Beginning of Period
=	Net Assets, End of Period

GASB Statement 35 requires that state appropriations for operating purposes be shown as a nonoperating revenue. State appropriations for capital outlay are shown separately as capital appropriation. Capital grants and gifts, additions to permanent endowments, extraordinary items, and special items are also displayed separately.

The **Statement of Cash Flows** is prepared using the GASB format described earlier in this module. The direct method must be used, along with a reconciliation between net operating income (loss) and net cash provided (used) by operating activities. Four categories are used: (1) operating activities, (2) non-capital financing activities, (3) capital and related financing activities, and (4) investing activities. Note that interest paid is classified as a (capital or noncapital) financing activity and interest received is classified as cash flows from investing activities.

GASB Statement 35 requires that cash flows from state appropriations for operations be reported as cash flows from noncapital financing activities. It also requires that cash flows from state appropriations for construction be reported as cash flows from capital and related financing activities.

ABC University
STATEMENT OF NET ASSETS
June 30, 2003

	Primary institution	Component unit hospital
Assets		
Current assets:		
Cash and cash equivalents	$ 4,571,218	$ 977,694
Short-term investments	15,278,981	2,248,884
Accounts receivable, net	6,412,520	9,529,196
Inventories	585,874	1,268,045
Deposit with bond trustee	4,254,341	--
Notes and mortgages receivable, net	359,175	--
Other assets	432,263	426,427
Total current assets	$31,894,372	$14,450,246
Noncurrent assets:		
Restricted cash and cash equivalents	24,200	18,500
Endowment investments	21,548,723	--
Notes and mortgages receivable, net	2,035,323	--
Other long-term investments	--	6,441,710
Investments in real estate	6,426,555	
Capital assets, net	158,977,329	32,602,940
Total noncurrent assets	189,012,130	39,063,150
Total assets	$220,906,502	$53,513,396
Liabilities		
Current liabilities:		
Accounts payable and accrued liabilities	4,897,470	2,911,419
Deferred revenue	3,070,213	--
Long-term liabilities—current portion	4,082,486	989,321
Total current liabilities	$12,050,169	$3,900,740
Noncurrent liabilities:		
Deposits	1,124,128	--
Deferred revenue	1,500,000	--
Long-term liabilities	31,611,427	2,194,236
Total noncurrent liabilities	34,235,555	2,194,236
Total liabilities	$46,285,724	$6,094,976
Net Assets		
Invested in capital assets, net of related debt	$126,861,400	$32,199,938
Restricted for:		
Nonexpendable:		
Scholarships and fellowships	10,839,473	--
Research	3,767,564	2,286,865
Expendable:		
Scholarships and fellowships	2,803,756	--
Research	5,202,732	--
Instructional department uses	938,571	--
Loans	2,417,101	--
Capital projects	4,952,101	913,758
Debt service	4,254,341	152,947
Other	403,632	--
Unrestricted	12,180,107	11,864,912
Total net assets	$174,620,778	$47,418,420

Source: *GASB 35, p. 27.*

ABC University
STATEMENT OF REVENUES, EXPENSES, AND CHANGES IN NET ASSETS
For the Year Ended June 30, 2003

> Operating expense may be displayed using either object or functional classification.

	Primary institution	Component unit hospital
Revenues		
Operating revenues:		
Student tuition and fees (net of scholarship allowances of $3,214,454)	$ 36,913,194	$ --
Patient services (net of charity care of $5,114,352)	--	46,296,957
Federal grants and contracts	10,614,660	--
State and local grants and contracts	3,036,953	7,475,987
Nongovernmental grants and contracts	873,740	
Sales and services of educational departments	19,802	--
Auxiliary enterprises:		
Residential life (net of scholarship allowances of $428,641)	28,079,274	--
Bookstore (net of scholarship allowances of $166,279)	9,092,363	--
Other operating revenues	143,357	421,571
Total operating revenues	88,773,343	54,194,515
Expenses		
Operating expenses:		
Salaries:		
Faculty (physicians for the hospital)	34,829,499	16,703,805
Exempt staff	29,597,676	8,209,882
Nonexempt wages	5,913,762	2,065,267
Benefits	18,486,559	7,752,067
Scholarships and fellowships	3,809,374	--
Utilities	16,463,492	9,121,352
Supplies and other services	12,451,064	7,342,009
Depreciation	6,847,377	2,976,212
Total operating expenses	128,398,803	54,170,594
Operating income (loss)	(39,625,460)	23,921
Nonoperating Revenues (Expenses)		
State appropriations	39,760,508	--
Gifts	1,822,442	--
Investment income (net of investment expense of $87,316 for the primary institution and $19,823 for the hospital)	2,182,921	495,594
Interest on capital asset—related debt	(1,330,126)	(34,538)
Other nonoperating revenues	313,001	321,449
Net operating revenues	42,748,746	782,505
Income before other revenues, expenses, gains, or losses	3,123,286	806,426
Capital appropriations	2,075,750	--
Capital grants and gifts	690,813	711,619
Additions to permanent endowments	85,203	--
Increase in net assets	5,975,052	1,518,045
Net Assets		
Net assets—beginning of year	168,645,726	45,900,375
Net assets—end of year	$174,620,778	$47,418,420

Source: *GASB 35, page 28.*

GASB Statement 39 provides guidance relating to whether or not certain legally separate tax-exempt entities are to be reported in the financial statements of governments. These provisions are especially important to public colleges and universities, many of which have legally separate foundations. GASB Statement 39 will result in many of these foundations being reported as discretely presented component units in public college and university financial statements. All three of the following criteria must be met before these foundations are included:

1. The economic resources received or held by the separate organization are entirely or almost entirely for the benefit of the primary government, its component units, or its constituents.
2. The primary government or its component units is entitled to, or has the ability to otherwise access a majority of the economic resources received or held by the separate organization.
3. The economic resources received or held by an individual organization that the specific primary government is entitled to, or has the ability to otherwise access are significant to that primary government.

ABC University
STATEMENT OF CASH FLOWS
For the Year Ended June 30, 2003

The direct method of reporting cash flows is required.	*Primary institution*	*Component unit hospital*
Cash Flows from Operating Activities		
Tuition and fees	$ 33,628,945	$ --
Research grants and contracts	13,884,747	--
Payments from insurance and patients	--	18,582,530
Medicaid and Medicare	--	31,640,524
Payments to suppliers	(28,175,500)	(13,084,643)
Payments to employees	(87,233,881)	(32,988,044)
Loans issued to students and employees	(384,628)	--
Collection of loans to students and employees	291,642	--
Auxiliary enterprise charges:		
Residence halls	26,327,644	--
Bookstore	8,463,939	--
Other receipts (payments)	1,415,502	(997,502)
Net cash provided (used) by operating activities	(31,781,590)	3,152,865
Cash Flows from Noncapital Financing Activities		
State appropriations	39,388,534	--
Gifts and grants received for other than capital purposes:		
Private gifts for endowment purposes	85,203	--
Net cash flows provided by noncapital financing activities	39,473,737	--
Cash Flows from Capital and Related Financing Activities		
Proceeds from capital debt	4,125,000	--
Capital appropriations	1,918,750	--
Capital grants and gifts received	640,813	711,619
Proceeds from sale of capital assets	22,335	5,066
Purchases of capital assets	(8,420,247)	(1,950,410)
Principal paid on capital debt and lease	(3,788,102)	(134,095)
Interest paid on capital debt and lease	(1,330,126)	(34,538)
Net cash used by capital and related financing activities	(6,831,577)	(1,402,358)
Cash Flows from Investing Activities		
Proceeds from sales and maturities of investments	16,741,252	2,843,124
Interest on investments	2,111,597	70,501
Purchase of investments	(17,680,113)	(4,546,278)
Net cash provided (used) by investing activities	1,172,736	(1,632,653)
Net increase in cash	2,033,306	117,854
Cash—beginning of year	2,562,112	878,340
Cash—end of year	$ 4,595,418	$ 996,194
Reconciliation of net operating revenues (expenses) to net cash provided (used) by operating activities:		
Operating income (loss)	$(39,625,460)	$ 23,921
Adjustments to reconcile net income (loss) to net cash provided (used) by operating activities:		
Depreciation expense	6,847,377	2,976,212
Change in assets and liabilities:		
Receivables, net	1,295,704	330,414
Inventories	37,284	(160,922)
Deposit with bond trustee	67,115	--
Other assets	(136,229)	75,456
Accounts payable	(323,989)	(75,973)
Deferred revenue	217,630	--
Deposits held for others	(299,428)	--
Compensated absences	138,406	(16,243)
Net cash provided (used) by operating activities	$(31,781,590)	$3,152,865

NOTE: *The required information about noncash investing, capital, and financing activities is not illustrated.*

Source: *GASB 35, pp. 29-30.*

MULTIPLE-CHOICE QUESTIONS (1-113)

1. Which of the following statements about the statistical section of the Comprehensive Annual Financial Report (CAFR) of a governmental unit is true?
- a. Statistical tables may **not** cover more than two fiscal years.
- b. Statistical tables may **not** include nonaccounting information.
- c. The statistical section is **not** part of the basic financial statements.
- d. The statistical section is an integral part of the basic financial statements.

2. What is the basic criterion used to determine the reporting entity for a governmental unit?
- a. Special financing arrangement.
- b. Geographic boundaries.
- c. Scope of public services.
- d. Financial accountability.

3. South City School District has a separately elected governing body that administers the public school system. The district's budget is subject to the approval of the city council. The district's financial activity should be reported in the City's financial statements by
- a. Blending only.
- b. Discrete presentation.
- c. Inclusion as a footnote only.
- d. Either blending or inclusion as a footnote.

4. Marta City's school district is a legally separate entity, but two of its seven board members are also city council members and the district is financially dependent on the city. The school district should be reported as a
- a. Blended unit.
- b. Discrete presentation.
- c. Note disclosure.
- d. Primary government.

5. Darien Village adopted the provision of GASB 34, *Basic Financial Statements—and Management's Discussion and Analysis—for State and Local Governments*, for its financial statements issued for 2003. As of December 31, 2003, Darien determined that it had spent $5,000,000 on infrastructure assets since the village was incorporated in 1980, and that infrastructure had an expected life of fifty years. These infrastructure assets consist primarily of roads and bridges that were financed with general long-term debt. Darien decided to use the modified approach for reporting its infrastructure assets on its government-wide financial statements for 2003. During 2003, Darien spent $250,000 maintaining and preserving its roads and bridges, and $500,000 to extend the life of existing infrastructure. On the statement of net assets at December 31, 2003, what amount should Darien report for infrastructure under the governmental activities column?
- a. $5,000,000
- b. $0
- c. $4,900,000
- d. $5,500,000

6. Hunt Community Development Agency (HCDA), a financially independent authority, provides loans to commercial businesses operating in Hunt County. This year, HCDA made loans totaling $500,000. How should HCDA

classify the disbursements of loans on the cash flow statement?
- a. Operating activities.
- b. Noncapital financing activities.
- c. Capital and related financing activities.
- d. Investing activities.

7. The statement of activities of the government-wide financial statements is designed primarily to provide information to assess which of the following?
- a. Operational accountability.
- b. Financial accountability.
- c. Fiscal accountability.
- d. Functional accountability.

Items 8 and 9 are based on the following:

Fullerton City adopted the provisions of GASB 34, *Basic Financial Statements—and Management's Discussion and Analysis—for State and Local Governments,* for its financial statements issued for 2003. As of December 31, 2003, the city compiled the information below for its capital assets, exclusive of infrastructure assets.

Cost of capital assets financed with general obligation debt and tax revenues	$3,500,000
Accumulated depreciation on the capital assets	750,000
Outstanding debt related to the capital assets	1,250,000

8. On the government-wide statement of net assets at December 31, 2003, under the governmental activities column, what amount should be reported for capital assets?
- a. $3,500,000
- b. $1,500,000
- c. $2,250,000
- d. $2,750,000

9. On the government-wide statement of net assets at December 31, 2003, under the governmental activities column, the information related to capital assets should be reported in the net assets section at which of the following amounts?
- a. $3,500,000
- b. $1,500,000
- c. $2,250,000
- d. $2,750,000

10. In accordance with GASB 34, *Basic Financial Statements—and Management's Discussion and Analysis—for State and Local Governments*, which of the following statements is correct about the accounting for infrastructure assets using the modified approach?

- I. Depreciation expense on the infrastructure assets should be reported on the government-wide statement of activities, under the governmental activities column.
- II. Certain information about infrastructure assets reported using the modified approach is required supplementary information in the annual report.

- a. I only.
- b. II only.
- c. Both I and II.
- d. Neither I nor II.

11. In accordance with GASB 34, *Basic Financial Statements—and Management's Discussion and Analysis—for State and Local Governments*, depreciation expense would be reported on which of the following financial statements?

I.   The government-wide statement of activities.
II. The statement of revenues, expenses, and changes in fund net assets prepared for proprietary funds.

    a. I only.
    b. II only.
    c. Both I and II.
    d. Neither I nor II.

12. In accordance with GASB 34, *Basic Financial Statements—and Management's Discussion and Analysis— for State and Local Governments*, governments should prepare
    a. Combined financial statements, using the modified accrual basis of accounting and the flow of economic resources.
    b. Combined financial statements, using the accrual basis of accounting and the flow of financial resources.
    c. Government-wide financial statements, using the accrual basis of accounting and the flow of financial resources.
    d. Government-wide financial statements, using the accrual basis of accounting and the flow of economic resources.

13. In accordance with GASB 34, *Basic Financial Statements—and Management's Discussion and Analysis— for State and Local Governments*, which of the following statements is true?

I.   Infrastructure assets do not need to be reported on the government-wide statement of net assets if the government decides to use the modified approach in its accounting for infrastructure.
II. Component units are reported on the financial statements for governmental funds.

    a. I only.
    b. II only.
    c. Both I and II.
    d. Neither I nor II.

14. Fund accounting is used by governmental units with resources that must be
    a. Composed of cash or cash equivalents.
    b. Incorporated into combined or combining financial statements.
    c. Segregated for the purpose of carrying on specific activities or attaining certain objectives.
    d. Segregated physically according to various objectives.

15. Dogwood City's water enterprise fund received interest of $10,000 on long-term investments. How should this amount be reported on the Statement of Cash Flows?
    a. Operating activities.
    b. Noncapital financing activities.
    c. Capital and related financing activities.
    d. Investing activities.

16. The primary authoritative body for determining the measurement focus and basis of accounting standards for governmental fund operating statements is the
    a. Governmental Accounting Standards Board (GASB).
    b. National Council on Governmental Accounting (NCGA).

    c. Governmental Accounting and Auditing Committee of the AICPA (GAAC).
    d. Financial Accounting Standards Board (FASB).

17. Governmental financial reporting should provide information to assist users in which situation(s)?

I.   Making social and political decisions.
II. Assessing whether current-year citizens received services but shifted part of the payment burden to future-year citizens.

    a. I only.
    b. II only.
    c. Both I and II.
    d. Neither I nor II.

18. Which event(s) should be included in a statement of cash flows for a governmental entity?

I.   Cash inflow from issuing bonds to finance city hall construction.
II. Cash outflow from a city utility representing payments in lieu of property taxes.

    a. I only.
    b. II only.
    c. Both I and II.
    d. Neither I nor II.

19. The following transactions were among those reported by Corfe City's electric utility enterprise fund for 2002:

Capital contributed by subdividers	$ 900,000
Cash received from customer households	2,700,000
Proceeds from sale of revenue bonds	4,500,000

In the electric utility enterprise fund's statement of cash flows for the year ended December 31, 2002, what amount should be reported as cash flows from capital and related financing activities?
    a. $4,500,000
    b. $5,400,000
    c. $7,200,000
    d. $8,100,000

20. For which of the following governmental entities that use proprietary fund accounting should a statement of cash flows be presented?

	Tollway authorities	*Governmental utilities*
a.	No	No
b.	No	Yes
c.	Yes	Yes
d.	Yes	No

21. In accordance with GASB 34, *Basic Financial Statements—and Management's Discussion and Analysis— for State and Local Governments*, which of the following financial statements should be prepared for proprietary funds?
    a. Statement of revenues, expenditures, and changes in fund balances.
    b. Statement of activities.
    c. Statement of changes in proprietary net assets.
    d. Statement of cash flows.

22. In accordance with GASB 34, *Basic Financial Statements—and Management's Discussion and Analysis— for State and Local Governments*, which of the following statements is correct about the information reported on the balance sheet prepared for the governmental funds?

I.   The focus is on reporting major funds, with all nonmajor funds aggregated and reported in a single column.
II. Fund balances are reported in two amounts—restricted and unrestricted.

   a.   I only.
   b.   II only.
   c.   Both I and II.
   d.   Neither I nor II.

23. In accordance with GASB 34, *Basic Financial Statements—and Management's Discussion and Analysis—for State and Local Governments*, which of the following statements is correct about the information reported on the statement of net assets for the proprietary funds?

I.   Assets and liabilities are classified into current and noncurrent classifications.
II. All activities of internal service funds are aggregated and reported in a single column.

   a.   I only.
   b.   II only.
   c.   Both I and II.
   d.   Neither I nor II.

24. In accordance with GASB 34, *Basic Financial Statements—and Management's Discussion and Analysis—for State and Local Governments*, which of the following financial statements is prepared using the accrual basis of accounting and the economic resources measurement focus?

I.   The statement of net assets for proprietary funds.
II. The statement of revenues, expenditures, and changes in fund balances for the governmental funds.

   a.   I only.
   b.   II only.
   c.   Both I and II.
   d.   Neither I nor II.

25. In accordance with GASB 34, *Basic Financial Statements—and Management's Discussion and Analysis—for State and Local Governments*, agency funds are reported on which of the following financial statements?

I.   Statement of fiduciary net assets.
II. Statement of changes in fiduciary net assets.

   a.   I only.
   b.   II only.
   c.   Both I and II.
   d.   Neither I nor II.

26. In accordance with GASB 34, *Basic Financial Statements—and Management's Discussion and Analysis—for State and Local Governments*, private-purpose trust funds are reported on which of the following financial statements?

I.   Government-wide statement of net assets.
II. Statement of changes in fiduciary net assets.

   a.   I only.
   b.   II only.
   c.   Both I and II.
   d.   Neither I nor II.

27. In accordance with GASB 34, *Basic Financial Statements—and Management's Discussion and Analysis—for State and Local Governments*, which fund type(s) is(are) reported on the statement of cash flows?

   a.   Governmental and fiduciary fund types.
   b.   Governmental and proprietary fund types.
   c.   Fiduciary and proprietary fund types.
   d.   Proprietary fund type only.

28. In accordance with GASB 34, *Basic Financial Statements—and Management's Discussion and Analysis—for State and Local Governments*, which of the following statements is(are) true regarding the statement of cash flows?

I.   The statement of cash flows is a government-wide financial statement.
II. The statement of cash flows reports cash flows from three activities—operating, investing, and financing.

   a.   I only.
   b.   II only.
   c.   Both I and II.
   d.   Neither I nor II.

29. In accordance with GASB 34, *Basic Financial Statements—and Management's Discussion and Analysis—for State and Local Governments*, a reconciliation must be shown of the items that cause the difference between (1) the total of the fund balances that appears on the balance sheet for the governmental funds and (2) the total net assets that are disclosed for governmental activities on the government-wide statement of net assets. Which of the following items would be disclosed in this reconciliation?

I.   Capital assets used in governmental activities.
II. The assets and liabilities of internal service funds included in governmental activities.

   a.   I only.
   b.   II only.
   c.   Both I and II.
   d.   Neither I nor II.

30. In accordance with GASB 34, *Basic Financial Statements—and Management's Discussion and Analysis—for State and Local Governments*, a reconciliation must be shown of the items that cause the difference between (1) the net change in fund balances for the governmental funds on the statement of revenues, expenditures, and changes in fund balances, and (2) the change in net assets of governmental activities on the statement of activities. Which of the following items would be disclosed in this reconciliation?

I.   Revenues and expenses of internal service funds that were reported in proprietary funds.
II. The amount by which capital outlays exceeded depreciation expense for the period.

   a.   I only.
   b.   II only.
   c.   Both I and II.
   d.   Neither I nor II.

31. In accordance with GASB 34, *Basic Financial Statements—and Management's Discussion and Analysis—for State and Local Governments*, what measurement focus should be used for the preparation of the following financial statements?

	Statement of changes in fiduciary net assets	Government-wide statement of net assets
a.	Financial resources	Economic resources
b.	Economic resources	Financial resources
c.	Economic resources	Economic resources
d.	Financial resources	Financial resources

32. In accordance with GASB 34, *Basic Financial Statements—and Management's Discussion and Analysis—for State and Local Governments*, which of the following statement is(are) true?

  I. Pension trust funds are reported on the statement of changes in fiduciary net assets.

  II. Retained earnings is reported in the net assets section of the statement of net assets for proprietary funds.

    a. I only.
    b. II only.
    c. Both I and II.
    d. Neither I nor II.

33. In accordance with GASB 34, *Basic Financial Statements—and Management's Discussion and Analysis—for State and Local Governments*, which of the following statements is correct concerning the statement of cash flows prepared for proprietary funds?

    a. The statement format is the same as that of a business enterprise's statement of cash flows.
    b. Cash flows from capital financing activities are reported separately from cash flows from noncapital financing activities.
    c. Cash flows from operating activities may not be reported using the direct method.
    d. Cash received from interest revenue and cash paid for interest expense are both reported as operating activities.

34. For governmental fund reporting, which item is considered the primary measurement focus?

    a. Income determination.
    b. Flows and balances of current financial resources.
    c. Capital maintenance.
    d. Cash flows and balances.

35. Which of the following funds of a governmental unit recognizes revenues in the accounting period in which they become available and measurable?

	General fund	*Enterprise fund*
a.	Yes	No
b.	No	Yes
c.	Yes	Yes
d.	No	No

36. Property taxes and fines represent which of the following classes of nonexchange transactions for governmental units?

    a. Derived tax revenues.
    b. Imposed nonexchange revenues.
    c. Government-mandated nonexchange transactions.
    d. Voluntary nonexchange transactions.

37. In accordance with GASB 33, *Accounting and Financial Reporting for Nonexchange Transactions*, which of the following transactions would qualify as a nonexchange transaction in the City of Geneva?

    a. The water utility (enterprise) fund billed the general fund for water usage.
    b. Property taxes were levied by the general fund.
    c. The motor pool (internal service) fund billed other departments for services rendered.
    d. The general fund sold police cars for their estimated residual value.

Items 38 and 39 are based on the following:

    The general fund of Elizabeth City received a $100,000 grant from the state to be used for retraining its police force in modern crime-fighting methods. The state recently passed legislation that requires retraining for all police departments in the state. The grant was received in cash on June 15, 2003, and was used for retraining seminars during July 2003. The state mandated that the grant be spent in the fiscal year ending June 30, 2004. Elizabeth's fiscal year ends on June 30. Answer each of the questions below based upon the guidance provided by GASB 33, *Accounting and Financial Reporting for Nonexchange Transactions*.

38. What account should be credited in the general fund on the date the grant was received?
    a. Restricted revenue.
    b. Deferred revenue.
    c. Revenue.
    d. Unreserved fund balance.

39. The grant from the state is an example of what type of nonexchange transaction?
    a. Government-mandated.
    b. Imposed.
    c. Voluntary.
    d. Derived.

Items 40 and 41 are based on the following:

    The merchants of Eldorado City collect a sales tax of 5% on retail sales. The sales taxes are remitted by retailers to the state and distributed by the state to the various governmental units that are within the boundaries of Eldorado City. During the month of June 2003, the state received $50,000 of sales taxes form merchants in Eldorado. As of June 30, 2003, none of the sales taxes had been remitted to Eldorado or to any of the other governments that were within the boundaries of Eldorado. However, Eldorado estimated that its share of the sales taxes would be received in early July 2003, and would be used to pay for expenditures incurred during the year ended June 30, 2003. Eldorado's fiscal year ends on June 30. Answer both of the questions below using the guidance provided in GASB 33, *Accounting and Financial Reporting for Nonexchange Transactions*.

40. From the perspective of Eldorado City, the sales taxes are an example of what type of nonexchange transaction?
    a. Imposed.
    b. Voluntary.
    c. Derived.
    d. Government-mandated

41. On the statement of revenues, expenditures, and changes in fund balance for the year ended June 30, 2003, how should the general fund of Eldorado report its share of the sales taxes that will be received in July 2003?
    a. Deferred revenue.
    b. Restricted revenue.
    c. Revenue.
    d. Unreserved fund balance.

42. On July 1, 2003, the general fund of Sun City levied property taxes for the fiscal year ending June 30, 2004. According to GASB 33, *Accounting and Financial Reporting for Nonexchange Transactions*, property taxes are an example of what type of nonexchange transaction?

  a. Voluntary.
  b. Government-mandated.
  c. Imposed.
  d. Derived.

43. For the year ended December 31, 2003, the general fund of Karsten City levied property taxes of $1,000,000. The city estimated that $10,000 of the levy would not be collectible. By December 31, 2003, the city had collected $850,0000 of property taxes and expected to collect the remainder of the taxes as follows:

- $100,000 by March 1, 2004
- $ 40,000 during the remainder of 2004

In accordance with GASB 33, *Accounting and Reporting for Nonexchange Transactions*, how much property tax revenue should be reported by the general fund on the statement of revenues, expenditures, and changes in fund balances prepared for the year ended December 31, 2003?

  a. $ 850,000
  b. $ 950,000
  c. $ 990,000
  d. $1,000,000

44. For the year ended December 31, 2003, the general fund of Ward Village reported revenues from the following sources on the statement of revenues, expenditures, and changes in fund balances:

Sales taxes	$ 25,000
Property taxes	125,000
Income taxes	15,000
Fines	10,000

In accordance with GASB 33, *Accounting and Reporting for Nonexchange Transactions*, what is the amount of revenues that came from imposed nonexchange transactions?

  a. $175,000
  b. $150,000
  c. $140,000
  d. $135,000

45. In December 2003, the general fund of Millard City received $25,000 from the state as an advance on the city's portion of sales tax revenues, and it received $20,000 from property owners for property taxes to be levied in 2004. The advance payment of sales taxes represented the amount that the state collected in 2003 that would have been distributed to Millard in the early part of 2004. Millard used the advance to pay for expenditures incurred by the general fund in 2003. The cash received from property owners for property taxes to be levied in 2004 will be used to pay for expenditures incurred in 2004. In accordance with GASB 33, *Accounting and Reporting for Nonexchange Transactions*, what amount of revenue from these transactions should be reported by Millard's general fund on the statement of revenues, expenditures, and changes in fund balances for the year ended December 31, 2003?

  a. $25,000
  b. $20,000
  c. $0
  d. $45,000

46. In accordance with GASB 33, *Accounting and Reporting for Nonexchange Transactions*, which of the following revenues results from taxes assessed by a government on exchange transactions (a derived tax revenue)?

  a. Property tax revenues.
  b. Fines and forfeits.
  c. Motor fuel taxes.
  d. Unrestricted government grants.

47. In accordance with GASB 33, *Accounting and Reporting for Nonexchange Transactions*, which of the following revenues results from taxes and other assessments imposed by governments that are not derived from underlying transactions?

  a. Income taxes.
  b. Sales taxes.
  c. Motor fuel taxes.
  d. Fines and forfeits.

Items 48 and 49 are based on the following:

    Ridge Township's governing body adopted its general fund budget for the year ended July 31, 2003, comprised of Estimated Revenues of $100,000 and Appropriations of $80,000. Ridge formally integrates its budget into the accounting records.

48. To record the appropriations of $80,000, Ridge should
  a. Credit Appropriations Control.
  b. Debit Appropriations Control.
  c. Credit Estimated Expenditures Control.
  d. Debit Estimated Expenditures Control.

49. To record the $20,000 budgeted excess of estimated revenues over appropriations, Ridge should
  a. Credit Estimated Excess Revenues Control.
  b. Debit Estimated Excess Revenues Control.
  c. Credit Budgetary Fund Balance.
  d. Debit Budgetary Fund Balance.

50. For the budgetary year ending December 31, 2003, Maple City's general fund expects the following inflows of resources:

Property Taxes, Licenses, and Fines	$9,000,000
Proceeds of Debt Issue	5,000,000
Interfund Transfers for Debt Service	1,000,000

In the budgetary entry, what amount should Maple record for estimated revenues?

  a. $ 9,000,000
  b. $10,000,000
  c. $14,000,000
  d. $15,000,000

51. In 2003, New City issued purchase orders and contracts of $850,000 that were chargeable against 2003 budgeted appropriations of $1,000,000. The journal entry to record the issuance of the purchase orders and contracts should include a
  a. Credit to Vouchers Payable of $1,000,000.
  b. Credit to Budgetary Fund Balance—Reserved for Encumbrances of $850,000.
  c. Debit to Expenditures of $1,000,000.
  d. Debit to Appropriations of $850,000.

52. During its fiscal year ended June 30, 2003, Cliff City issued purchase orders totaling $5,000,000, which were properly charged to Encumbrances at that time. Cliff received goods and related invoices at the encumbered amounts totaling $4,500,000 before year-end. The remaining goods of $500,000 were not received until after year-end. Cliff paid $4,200,000 of the invoices received during the year. What amount of Cliff's encumbrances were outstanding at June 30, 2003?

a. $0
b. $300,000
c. $500,000
d. $800,000

53. Elm City issued a purchase order for supplies with an estimated cost of $5,000. When the supplies were received, the accompanying invoice indicated an actual price of $4,950. What amount should Elm debit (credit) to Budgetary Fund Balance—Reserved for Encumbrances after the supplies and invoice were received?

a. $ (50)
b. $ 50
c. $4,950
d. $5,000

54. A budgetary fund balance reserved for encumbrances in excess of a balance of encumbrances indicates

a. An excess of vouchers payable over encumbrances.
b. An excess of purchase orders over invoices received.
c. An excess of appropriations over encumbrances.
d. A recording error.

55. Encumbrances outstanding at year-end in a state's general fund should be reported as a

a. Liability in the general fund.
b. Fund balance reserve in the general fund.
c. Liability in the General Long-Term Debt Account Group.
d. Fund balance designation in the general fund.

56. When Rolan County adopted its budget for the year ending June 30, 2003, $20,000,000 was recorded for Estimated Revenues Control. Actual revenues for the year ended June 30, 2003, amounted to $17,000,000. In closing the budgetary accounts at June 30, 2003,

a. Revenues Control should be debited for $3,000,000.
b. Estimated Revenues Control should be debited for $3,000,000.
c. Revenues Control should be credited for $20,000,000.
d. Estimated Revenues Control should be credited for $20,000,000.

57. The budget of a governmental unit, for which the appropriations exceed the estimated revenues, was adopted and recorded in the general ledger at the beginning of the year. During the year, expenditures and encumbrances were less than appropriations, whereas revenues equaled estimated revenues. The Budgetary Fund Balance account is

a. Credited at the beginning of the year and debited at the end of the year.
b. Credited at the beginning of the year and **not** changed at the end of the year.
c. Debited at the beginning of the year and credited at the end of the year.
d. Debited at the beginning of the year and **not** changed at the end of the year.

58. The following information pertains to Park Township's general fund at December 31, 2003:

Total assets, including $200,000 of cash	$1,000,000
Total liabilities	600,000
Fund balance—Reserved for encumbrances	100,000

Appropriations do not lapse at year-end. At December 31, 2003, what amount should Park report as unreserved fund balance in its general fund balance sheet?

a. $200,000
b. $300,000
c. $400,000
d. $500,000

59. The following information pertains to Pine City's general fund for 2003:

Appropriations Control	$6,500,000
Expenditures Control	5,000,000
Other Financing Sources Control	1,500,000
Other Financing Uses Control	2,000,000
Revenues Control	8,000,000

After Pine's general fund accounts were closed at the end of 2003, the fund balance increased by

a. $3,000,000
b. $2,500,000
c. $1,500,000
d. $1,000,000

60. Cedar City issues $1,000,000, 6% revenue bonds at par on April 1 to build a new water line for the water enterprise fund. Interest is payable every six months. What amount of interest expense should be reported for the year ended December 31?

a. $0
b. $30,000
c. $45,000
d. $60,000

61. The expenditure element "salaries and wages" is an example of which type of classification?

a. Object.
b. Program.
c. Function.
d. Activity.

Items 62 and 63 are based on the following information for Oak City for the calendar year 2003:

Collections during 2003	$500,000
Expected collections during the first sixty days of 2004	100,000
Expected collections during the balance of 2004	60,000
Expected collections during January 2005	30,000
Estimated to be uncollectible	10,000
Total levy	$700,000

62. What amount should Oak City report for 2003 property tax revenues in the Statement of Revenues, Expenditures, and Changes in Fund Balances prepared for governmental funds?

a. $700,000
b. $690,000
c. $600,000
d. $500,000

63. What amount should Oak City report for 2003 property tax revenues in the government-wide Statement of Activities?

a. $700,000
b. $690,000
c. $600,000
d. $500,000

64. Which of the following transactions is an expenditure of a governmental unit's general fund?
- a. Contribution of enterprise fund capital by the general fund.
- b. Transfer from the general fund to a capital projects fund.
- c. Operating subsidy transfer from the general fund to an enterprise fund.
- d. Routine employer contributions from the general fund to a pension trust fund.

65. During the year, a city's electric utility, which is operated as an enterprise fund, rendered billings for electricity supplied to the general fund. Which of the following accounts should be debited by the general fund?
- a. Appropriations.
- b. Expenditures
- c. Due to Electric Utility Enterprise Fund.
- d. Transfers.

66. Which of the following fund types used by a government most likely would have a Fund Balance—Reserved for Inventory of Supplies?
- a. General.
- b. Internal service.
- c. Enterprise.
- d. Debt service.

67. The following revenues were among those reported by Ariba Township in 2003:

Net rental revenue (after depreciation) from a parking garage owned by Ariba	$ 40,000
Interest earned on investments held for employees' retirement benefits	100,000
Property taxes	6,000,000

What amount of the foregoing revenues should be accounted for in Ariba's governmental-type funds?
- a. $6,140,000
- b. $6,100,000
- c. $6,040,000
- d. $6,000,000

Items 68 through 70 are based on the following:

The general fund of Cliff Township acquired two police cars at the beginning of January 2003, at a total cost of $40,000. The cars are expected to last for four years and have a $10,000 residual value. Straight-line depreciation is used. Cliff adopted the provisions of GASB 34, *Basic Financial Statements—and Management's Discussion and Analysis—for State and Local Governments,* for its financial statements issued for 2003.

68. On the balance sheet for the governmental funds at December 31, 2003, the police cars will be reported under assets in the general fund column at which of the following amounts?
- a. $40,000
- b. $32,500
- c. $0
- d. $22,500

69. On the government-wide statement of net assets at December 31, 2003, the police cars will be reported under assets in the governmental activities column at which of the following amounts?

- a. $40,000
- b. $32,500
- c. $0
- d. $22,500

70. On the statement of revenues, expenditures, and changes in fund balances prepared for the governmental funds for the year ended December 31, 2003, the police cars will be reported as
- a. Expenditures of $40,000.
- b. Expense of $7,500.
- c. Expenditures of $7,500.
- d. Expense of $40,000.

Items 71 through 74 are based on the following:

The City of Vicksburg adopted the provisions of GASB 34, *Basic Financial Statements—and Management's Discussion and Analysis—for State and Local Governments,* for its financial statements issued for the year ended December 31, 2003. During the year ended December 31, 2003, the general fund of Vicksburg has the following selected transactions:

- Acquired police cars for $75,000 in January 2003. The cars have an estimated five-year useful life and a $15,000 salvage value. The City uses the straight-line method to depreciate all of its capital assets.
- Transferred $30,000 to the pension trust fund. The amount represented the employer's contribution.
- Levied property taxes in the amount of $800,000. Two percent of the levy was not expected to be collected. At December 31, 2003, $750,000 of the property taxes were collected, but the remainder was not expected to be collected within sixty days after the end of 2003.
- Received $100,000 of sales tax revenues from the state and was owed another $25,000 by the state for sales taxes collected in 2003 that will not be remitted to Vicksburg until mid-March 2004. The sales taxes expected to be received in March will be used to pay for expenditures incurred in 2004.

71. On the statement of revenues, expenditures, and changes in fund balances prepared for the governmental funds for the year ended December 31, 2003, what amount should be reported for expenditures in Vicksburg's general fund related to the acquisition of police cars and to the pension transfer?
- a. $ 42,000
- b. $105,000
- c. $ 75,000
- d. $ 30,000

72. On the statement of revenues, expenditures, and changes in fund balances prepared for the governmental funds for the year ended December 31, 2003, what amount should be reported for revenues in Vicksburg's general fund related to property taxes and sales taxes?
- a. $884,000
- b. $909,000
- c. $850,000
- d. $875,000

73. On the government-wide statement of activities prepared for the year ended December 31, 2003, what amount should be reported for expenses for governmental activities related to the acquisition of the police cars and to the pension transfer?

a. $ 42,000
b. $105,000
c. $ 75,000
d. $ 30,000

74. On the government-wide statement of activities prepared for the year ended December 31, 2003, what amount should be reported for revenues from governmental activities related to the property taxes and the sales taxes?

a. $884,000
b. $909,000
c. $850,000
d. $875,000

75. In November 2003, Maple Township received an unexpected state grant of $100,000 to finance the purchase of school buses, and an additional grant of $5,000 was received for bus maintenance and operations. According to the terms of the grant, the State reimbursed Maple Township for $60,000 for the purchase of school buses and an additional $5,000 for bus maintenance during the year ended June 30, 2004. The remaining $40,000 of the capital grant is expected to be spent during the next fiscal year June 30, 2005. Maple's school bus system is appropriately accounted for in a special revenue fund. In connection with the grants for the purchase of school buses and bus maintenance, what amount should be reported as grant revenues for the year ending June 30, 2004, when using modified accrual accounting?

a. $ 5,000
b. $ 60,000
c. $ 65,000
d. $100,000

76. Lake County received the following proceeds that are legally restricted to expenditure for specified purposes:

Levies on affected property owners to install sidewalks	$500,000
Gasoline taxes to finance road repairs	900,000

What amount should be accounted for in Lake's special revenue funds?

a. $1,400,000
b. $ 900,000
c. $ 500,000
d. $0

77. Should a special revenue fund with a legally adopted budget maintain its accounts on an accrual basis and integrate budgetary accounts into its accounting system?

	Maintain on accrual basis	Integrate budgetary accounts
a.	Yes	Yes
b.	Yes	No
c.	No	Yes
d.	No	No

78. In 2003, Menton City received $5,000,000 of bond proceeds to be used for capital projects. Of this amount, $1,000,000 was expended in 2003. Expenditures for the $4,000,000 balance were expected to be incurred in 2004. These bond proceeds should be recorded in capital projects funds for

a. $5,000,000 in 2003.
b. $5,000,000 in 2004.
c. $1,000,000 in 2003 and $4,000,000 in 2004.
d. $1,000,000 in 2003 and in the general fund for $4,000,000 in 2003.

79. Financing for the renovation of Fir City's municipal park, begun and completed during 2003, came from the following sources:

Grant from state government	$400,000
Proceeds from general obligation bond issue	500,000
Transfer from Fir's general fund	100,000

In its 2003 capital projects fund operating statement, Fir should report these amounts as

	Revenues	Other financing sources
a.	$1,000,000	$0
b.	$ 900,000	$ 100,000
c.	$ 400,000	$ 600,000
d.	$0	$1,000,000

80. In which of the following fund types of a city government are revenues and expenditures recognized on the same basis of accounting as the general fund?

a. Pension trust.
b. Internal service.
c. Enterprise.
d. Debt service.

81. Japes City issued $1,000,000 general obligation bonds at 101 to build a new city hall. As part of the bond issue, the city also paid a $500 underwriter fee and $2,000 in debt issue costs. What amount should Japes City report as other financing sources?

a. $1,010,000
b. $1,008,000
c. $1,007,500
d. $1,000,000

82. Dale City is accumulating financial resources that are legally restricted to payments of general long-term debt principal and interest maturing in future years. At December 31, 2003, $5,000,000 has been accumulated for principal payments and $300,000 has been accumulated for interest payments. These restricted funds should be accounted for in the

	Debt service fund	General fund
a.	$0	$5,300,000
b.	$ 300,000	$5,000,000
c.	$5,000,000	$ 300,000
d.	$5,300,000	$0

83. On April 1, 2003, Oak County incurred the following expenditures in issuing long-term bonds:

Issue costs	$400,000
Debt insurance	90,000

Oak County has established a debt service fund for the payment of interest and principal of its long-term bonds. Assuming Oak County's fiscal year ends of June 30, what amount of issue costs and debt insurance costs should be reported as an asset on the governmental funds' balance sheet at June 30, 2003?

a. $0
b. $ 90,000
c. $400,000
d. $490,000

84. Receipts from a special tax levy to retire and pay interest on general obligation bonds should be recorded in which fund?

a. General.
b. Capital projects.

c.   Debt service.
d.   Special revenue.

85. Wood City, which is legally obligated to maintain a debt service fund, issued the following general obligation bonds on July 1, 2003:

Term of bonds	10 years
Face amount	$1,000,000
Issue price	101
Stated interest rate	6%

Interest is payable January 1 and July 1. What amount of bond premium should be amortized in Wood's debt service fund for the year ended December 31, 2003?
   a. $1,000
   b. $ 500
   c. $ 250
   d. $0

86. The debt service fund of a governmental unit is used to account for the accumulation of resources for, and the payment of, principal and interest in connection with a

	Trust fund	*Proprietary fund*
a.	No	No
b.	No	Yes
c.	Yes	Yes
d.	Yes	No

87. Tott City's serial bonds are serviced through a debt service fund with cash provided by the general fund. In a debt service fund's statements, how are cash receipts and cash payments reported?

	Cash receipts	*Cash payments*
a.	Revenues	Expenditures
b.	Revenues	Other Financing Use
c.	Other Financing Source	Expenditures
d.	Other Financing Source	Other Financing Use

88. On March 2, 2003, Finch City issued ten-year general obligation bonds at face amount, with interest payable March 1 and September 1. The proceeds were to be used to finance the construction of a civic center over the period April 1, 2003, to March 31, 2004. During the fiscal year ended June 30, 2003, no resources had been provided to the debt service fund for the payment of principal and interest.
   On June 30, 2003, Finch's debt service fund should include interest payable on the general obligation bonds for
   a.   0 months.
   b.   Three months.
   c.   Four months.
   d.   Six months.

89. Fish Road property owners in Sea County are responsible for special assessment debt that arose from a storm sewer project. If the property owners default, Sea has no obligation regarding debt service, although it does bill property owners for assessments and uses the monies it collects to pay debt holders. What fund type should Sea use to account for these collection and servicing activities?
   a.   Agency.
   b.   Debt service.
   c.   Investment trust funds.
   d.   Capital projects.

90. Cy City's Municipal Solid Waste Landfill Enterprise Fund was established when a new landfill was opened Janu-

ary 3, 2003. The landfill is expected to reach capacity and close December 31, 2023. Cy's 2003 expenses would include a portion of which of the year 2024 expected disbursements?
  I.   Cost of a final cover to be applied to the landfill.
  II. Cost of equipment to be installed to monitor methane gas buildup.
   a.   I only.
   b.   II only.
   c.   Both I and II.
   d.   Neither I nor II.

91. Chase City uses an internal service fund for its central motor pool. The assets and liabilities account balances for this fund that are not eliminated normally should be reported in the government-wide statement of net assets as
   a.   Governmental activities.
   b.   Business-type activities.
   c.   Fiduciary activities.
   d.   Note disclosures only.

92. The billings for transportation services provided to other governmental units are recorded by an internal service fund as
   a.   Transportation appropriations.
   b.   Operating revenues.
   c.   Interfund exchanges.
   d.   Intergovernmental transfers.

93. The following information for the year ended June 30, 2003, pertains to a proprietary fund established by Burwood Village in connection with Burwood's public parking facilities:

Receipts from users of parking facilities	$400,000
Expenditures	
Parking meters	210,000
Salaries and other cash expenses	90,000
Depreciation of parking meters	70,000

For the year ended June 30, 2003, this proprietary fund should report net income of
   a. $0
   b. $ 30,000
   c. $100,000
   d. $240,000

94. A state government had the following activities:
  I.   State-operated lottery $10,000,000
  II. State-operated hospital   3,000,000

Which of the above activities should be accounted for in an enterprise fund?
   a.   Neither I nor II.
   b.   I only.
   c.   II only.
   d.   Both I and II.

95. For governmental units, depreciation expense on assets acquired with capital grants externally restricted for capital acquisitions should be reported in which type of fund?

	Governmental fund	*Proprietary fund*
a.	Yes	No
b.	Yes	Yes
c.	No	No
d.	No	Yes

96. An enterprise fund would be used when the governing body requires that

I. Accounting for the financing of an agency's services to other government departments be on a cost-reimbursement basis.

II. User charges cover the costs of general public services.

III. Net income information be reported for an activity.

a. I only.
b. I and II.
c. I and III.
d. II and III.

97. The following transactions were among those reported by Cliff County's water and sewer enterprise fund for 2003:

Proceeds from sale of revenue bonds	$5,000,000
Cash received from customer households	3,000,000
Capital contributed by subdividers	1,000,000

In the water and sewer enterprise fund's statement of cash flows for the year ended December 31, 2003, what amount should be reported as cash flows from capital and related financing activities?

a. $9,000,000
b. $8,000,000
c. $6,000,000
d. $5,000,000

98. The orientation of accounting and reporting for all proprietary funds of governmental units is

a. Income determination.
b. Project.
c. Flow of funds.
d. Program.

Items 99 through 101 are based on the following:

Rock County has acquired equipment through a noncancelable lease-purchase agreement dated December 31, 2002. This agreement requires no down payment and the following minimum lease payments:

December 31	Principal	Interest	Total
2003	$50,000	$15,000	$65,000
2004	50,000	10,000	60,000
2005	50,000	5,000	55,000

99. What account should be debited for $150,000 in the general fund at inception of the lease if the equipment is a general fixed asset and Rock does **not** use a capital projects fund?

a. Other Financing Uses Control.
b. Equipment.
c. Expenditures Control.
d. Memorandum entry only.

100. If the equipment is used in enterprise fund operations and the lease payments are to be financed with enterprise fund revenues, what account should be debited for $150,000 in the enterprise fund at the inception of the lease?

a. Expenses Control.
b. Expenditures Control.
c. Other Financing Sources Control.
d. Equipment.

101. If the equipment is used in internal service fund operations and the lease payments are financed with internal service fund revenues, what account or accounts should be debited in the internal service fund for the December 31, 2003 lease payment of $65,000?

a.	Expenditures Control	$65,000
b.	Expenses Control	$65,000
c.	Capital Lease Payable	$50,000
	Expenses Control	15,000
d.	Expenditures Control	$50,000
	Expenses Control	15,000

102. Hill City's water utility fund held the following investments in US Treasury securities at June 30, 2003:

Investment	Date purchased	Maturity date	Carrying amount
Three-month T-bill	5/31/03	7/31/03	$30,000
Three-year T-note	6/15/03	8/31/03	50,000
Five-year T-note	10/1/99	9/30/04	100,000

In the fund's balance sheet, what amount of these investments should be reported as cash and cash equivalents at June 30, 2003?

a. $0
b. $ 30,000
c. $ 80,000
d. $180,000

103. The following fund types used by Green Township had total assets at June 30, 2003, as follows:

Agency funds	$ 300,000
Debt service funds	1,000,000

Total fiduciary fund assets amount to

a. $0
b. $ 300,000
c. $1,000,000
d. $1,300,000

104. Grove County collects property taxes levied within its boundaries and receives a 1% fee for administering these collections on behalf of the municipalities located in the county. In 2003, Grove collected $1,000,000 for its municipalities and remitted $990,000 to them after deducting fees of $10,000. In the initial recording of the 1% fee, Grove's agency fund should credit

a. Net Assets—Agency Fund, $10,000.
b. Fees Earned—Agency Fund, $10,000.
c. Due to Grove County General Fund, $10,000.
d. Revenues Control, $10,000.

Items 105 and 106 are based on the following:

Elm City contributes to and administers a single-employer defined benefit pension plan on behalf of its covered employees. The plan is accounted for in a pension trust fund. For the year ended December 31, 2003, employer contributions to the pension trust fund amounted to $11,000.

105. What account should be credited in the pension trust fund to record the 2003 employer contribution of $11,000?

a. Additions.
b. Other Financing Sources Control.
c. Due from Special Revenue Fund.
d. Pension Benefit Obligation.

106. To record the 2003 pension contribution of $11,000, what debit is required in the governmental-type fund used in connection with employer pension contributions?

a. Other Financing Uses Control.
b. Expenditures Control.
c. Expenses Control.
d. Due to Pension Trust Fund.

107. In accordance with GASB 34, *Basic Financial Statements—and Management's Discussion and Analysis—*

for State and Local Governments, what types of interfund transactions are included in the amount reported for transfers on the government-wide statement of activities?

I. Yearly operating subsidies from the general fund to an enterprise fund.

II. Billings from an enterprise fund to an internal service fund for services rendered.

a. I only.
b. II only.
c. Both I and II.
d. Neither I nor II.

108. Jamestown adopted the provisions of GASB 34, *Basic Financial Statements—and Management's Discussion and Analysis—for State and Local Governments*, for its financial statements issued for the year ended December 31, 2003. During the year ended December 31, 2003, Jamestown had the following selected transactions:

- The general fund made a $100,000 advance to an internal service fund. The internal service fund will repay the advance in 2006.
- The water utility enterprise fund billed the general fund $25,000 for water usage.
- The general fund transferred $30,000 to a debt service fund to pay interest on general obligation bonds.

On Jamestown's government-wide statement of activities for the year ended December 31, 2003, what amount should be reported for transfers?

a. $125,000
b. $ 55,000
c. $0
d. $130,000

109. The town of Harrisville adopted the provisions of GASB 34, *Basic Financial Statements—and Management's Discussion and Analysis—for State and Local Governments*, for its financial statements issued for the year ended December 31, 2003. During the year ended December 31, 2003, Harrisville had the following selected transactions:

- The general fund made a permanent transfer of $100,000 to an enterprise fund. The enterprise fund used the amount transferred to acquire capital assets.
- The general fund transferred $1,000,000 to a capital projects fund for the town's portion of the cost for the renovation of the town hall.
- The general fund was reimbursed $5,000 by an enterprise fund for expenses paid by the general fund that were properly charged as operating expenses of the enterprise fund.

On Harrisville's government-wide statement of activities for the year ended December 31, 2003, what amount should be reported as transfers?

a. $ 100,000
b. $1,100,000
c. $1,005,000
d. $ 105,000

110. In accordance with GASB 35, a public college or university that chooses to report only business-type activities should present only the financial statements required for

a. Enterprise funds.
b. Government funds.
c. Internal service funds.
d. Enterprise and internal service funds.

111. In accordance with GASB 35, a public college or university that chooses to report both governmental and business-type activities should report

	Fund financial statements	Government-wide financial statements
a.	No	Yes
b.	Yes	No
c.	Yes	Yes
d.	No	No

112. A public college had tuition and fees of $20,000,000. Scholarships, for which no services were required, amounted to $1,000,000. Employee discounts, which were provided in exchange for services, amounted to $2,000,000. The amount to be reported as net tuition and fees by the public college would be

a. $20,000,000.
b. $19,000,000.
c. $18,000,000.
d. $17,000,000.

113. Which of the following is true regarding the Statement of Revenues, Expenses, and Changes in Net Assets for a public college choosing to report as a special-purpose entity engaged in business-type activities only?

a. State appropriations should be reported as nonoperating income.
b. An operating income figure must be displayed.
c. Both contributions for plant and for endowment purposes must be reported separately after both operating and nonoperating revenues and expenses.
d. All of the above.

OTHER OBJECTIVE QUESTIONS

Problem 1   (25 to 40 minutes)

Jefferson City was incorporated as a municipality and began operations on January 1, 2003. The budget approved by the City Council was recorded, and the City used the modified accrual basis of accounting to record its general fund transactions in 2003. Jefferson has decided to use encumbrance accounting, and its outstanding encumbrances at year-end do not lapse. Jefferson's general fund trial balance, before any adjusting and closing entries were made is presented below at December 31, 2003.

	Debits
Cash	$ 48,000
Property taxes receivable—current	19,300
Expenditures control	160,000
Other financial uses control—transfers out	40,000
Encumbrances control	10,000
Estimated revenues control	233,700
Total	$511,500

	Credits
Appropriations control	$174,000
Estimated other financing uses control—transfers out	40,000
Allowance for uncollectible taxes—current	4,300
Accounts payable	18,000
Deferred revenue	10,000
Revenues control	235,500
Budgetary fund balance reserved for encumbrances	10,000
Budgetary fund balance	19,700
Total	$511,500

Additional information:

	Estimated revenues	*Actual revenues*
Property taxes	$210,700	$210,700
Licenses	14,800	15,800
Sales taxes	8,200	9,000
Totals	$233,700	$235,500

	Appropriations	*Expenditures*	*Estimated other financing uses—transfers out*	*Other financing uses—transfers out*
Current outlay—services	$90,000	$87,000		
Current outlay—supplies	38,000	35,000		
Capital expenditures—equipment	46,000	38,000		
Transfer to debt service fund			$40,000	$40,000
Totals	$174,000	$160,000	$40,000	$40,000

It was estimated that 2% of the property taxes would not be collected. Accordingly, property taxes were levied to yield the budgeted amount of $210,700. Property taxes of $195,700 had been collected by December 31, 2003. It was expected that $6,000 of the remaining collectible property taxes would be received by March 1, 2004, and that any remaining collectible property taxes would be received after March 1, 2004.

Supplies of $3,000 and equipment of $15,000 were received before the end of 2003, but the vouchers were unpaid at December 31, 2003. As of December 31, 2003, purchase orders were outstanding for supplies and equipment not yet received, in the amounts of $2,500 and $7,500, respectively. Jefferson depreciates equipment over a five-year useful life using the straight-line method and $0 salvage value. One-half year's depreciation is taken in the year of acquisition.

Jefferson decided to record $5,000 of supplies on hand at December 31, 2003. In conformity with a city ordinance, expenditures are based on purchases rather than usage.

During the year ended December 31, 2003, Jefferson received $9,000 of sales taxes from the state. The state owes Jefferson another of $1,000 of sales taxes as a result of retail transactions that occurred during 2003. However, this amount will not be remitted until March of 2004.

On November 1, 2003, Jefferson issued, at face amount, $800,000 of 6% general obligation serial bonds. Interest is payable each May 1 and November 1. $80,000 of bonds mature and come due each year, beginning on November 1, 2004. The bonds were issued to finance the construction of an addition to city hall, but no contracts had been executed by December 31, 2003.

Jefferson established a debt service fund in November 2003, to pay the interest and the principal of the general obligation bonds. The city council of Jefferson authorized the general fund to transfer $40,000 to the debt service fund. The transfer was required by the bond ordinance. The transfer, which was made in November, will be used by the debt service fund to pay the principal of the bonds.

In November 2003, Jefferson received notification of a $10,000 grant from the state to be used for retraining its fire departments in modern fire fighting methods. The state passed legislation in 2003 that required retraining for all fire departments in the state. The grant is a reimbursement grant and Jefferson plans to spend the grant on training seminars in February of 2004. The general fund accounts for the grant.

For items 1 through 23, determine various amounts that would be reported on Jefferson's financial statements for 2003. On the CPA exam, a list of amounts would be provided, and candidates would be instructed to blacken the oval of the letter for an amount that best answers each question.

Required:

Items 1 through 10 relate to amounts that are reported on the balance sheet prepared for the governmental funds at December 31, 2003. Assume the capital projects and the debt service funds are major funds.

1. What amount should be reported for cash in the capital projects fund?

2. What amount should be reported for property taxes receivable, net of allowance for uncollectible taxes, in the general fund?

3. What amount should be reported for deferred revenue in the general fund?

4. What amount should be reported for fund balance reserved for encumbrances in the general fund?

5. What amount should be reported for fund balance reserved for supplies in the general fund?

6. What amount should be reported for unreserved fund balance in the general fund?

7. What amount should be reported for unreserved fund balance in the capital projects fund?

8. What amount should be reported for bonds payable in the debt service fund?

9. What amount should be reported for interest payable related to the general obligation bonds in the debt service fund?

10. What amount should be reported for equipment, net of accumulated depreciation, in the general fund?

Required:

Items 11 through 16 relate to amounts that are reported on the Statement of Revenues, Expenditures, and Changes in Fund Balances prepared for the governmental funds for the year ended December 31, 2003. Assume the capital projects and debt service funds are major funds.

11. What amount should be reported for other financing uses for the general fund?

12. What amount should be reported for property tax revenues for the general fund?

13. What amount should be reported for total expenditures for the general fund?

14. What amount should be reported for other financing sources for the capital projects fund?

15. What amount should be reported for other financing sources for the debt service fund?

16. What amount should be reported for depreciation expense for the equipment acquired by the general fund?

Required:

Items 17 through 23 relate to amounts that are reported on the Statement of Net Assets prepared for Jefferson's governmental activities at December 31, 2003.

17. What amount should be reported for property taxes receivable?

18. What amount should be reported for sales taxes receivable?

19. What amount should be reported for deferred revenue?

20. What amount should be reported for equipment net of accumulated depreciation?

21. What amount should be reported for net assets invested in capital assets? Assume no debt was incurred in the acquisition of the equipment.

22. What amount should be reported for restricted net assets?

23. What amount should be reported for interest payable related to the general obligation bonds?

MULTIPLE-CHOICE ANSWERS

1. c __ __	24. a __ __	47. d __ __	70. a __ __	93. d __ __
2. d __ __	25. a __ __	48. a __ __	71. b __ __	94. d __ __
3. b __ __	26. b __ __	49. c __ __	72. c __ __	95. d __ __
4. b __ __	27. d __ __	50. a __ __	73. a __ __	96. d __ __
5. a __ __	28. d __ __	51. b __ __	74. b __ __	97. c __ __
6. a __ __	29. c __ __	52. c __ __	75. c __ __	98. a __ __
7. a __ __	30. c __ __	53. d __ __	76. b __ __	99. c __ __
8. d __ __	31. c __ __	54. d __ __	77. c __ __	100. d __ __
9. b __ __	32. a __ __	55. b __ __	78. a __ __	101. c __ __
10. b __ __	33. b __ __	56. d __ __	79. c __ __	102. c __ __
11. c __ __	34. b __ __	57. c __ __	80. d __ __	103. b __ __
12. d __ __	35. a __ __	58. b __ __	81. a __ __	104. c __ __
13. d __ __	36. b __ __	59. b __ __	82. d __ __	105. a __ __
14. c __ __	37. b __ __	60. c __ __	83. a __ __	106. b __ __
15. d __ __	38. b __ __	61. a __ __	84. c __ __	107. a __ __
16. a __ __	39. a __ __	62. c __ __	85. d __ __	108. c __ __
17. c __ __	40. c __ __	63. b __ __	86. a __ __	109. a __ __
18. b __ __	41. c __ __	64. d __ __	87. c __ __	110. a __ __
19. b __ __	42. c __ __	65. b __ __	88. a __ __	111. c __ __
20. c __ __	43. b __ __	66. a __ __	89. a __ __	112. b __ __
21. d __ __	44. d __ __	67. d __ __	90. c __ __	113. d __ __
22. a __ __	45. a __ __	68. c __ __	91. a __ __	1st: __/113 = __%
23. c __ __	46. c __ __	69. b __ __	92. b __ __	2nd: __/113 = __%

MULTIPLE-CHOICE ANSWER EXPLANATIONS

B. The Reporting Entity

1. (c) GASB 34 indicates that the basic financial statements include only the government-wide statements, the fund statements, and the notes to the financial statements.

2. (d) The concept underlying the definition of the financial reporting entity is that elected officials are accountable to their constituents for their actions. Accordingly, the financial reporting entity consists of (1) the primary government, (2) organizations for which the primary government is **financially accountable**, and (3) other organizations for which the nature and significance of their relationship with the primary government is such that exclusion would cause the reporting entity's financial statements to be misleading or incomplete. Thus, the basic criterion used to determine the reporting entity is financial accountability.

3. (b) The requirement is to determine how the school district's financial activity should be reported. The school district is a component unit, which means it is a legally separate organization for which the elected officials of a primary government are financially accountable. Component units can be presented either discretely or blended. If the component unit is so closely tied to the primary government that the activities seem to be indistinguishable, the presentation should be blended. The school district's budget requires separate approval of the city council, so it is not indistinguishable. The activities of the component unit are distinguishable from the primary government, and therefore should be shown discretely.

4. (b) The requirement is to determine how the school district should be reported. A component unit is a legally separate organization for which the elected officials of a primary government are financially accountable. The school district is a component unit, which can be presented either

discretely or blended. The unit is blended if the activities of the unit are so closely tied to the primary government as to be indistinguishable. Even though two of the district's members are city council members, the activities of the school district are distinct from the primary government and should be presented discretely.

D. Government-Wide Financial Statements

5. (a) In accordance with GASB 34, state and local governments are required to report infrastructure assets on the government-wide statement of net assets. However, GASB 34 does not require infrastructure assets to be depreciated. GASB 34 permits governments to use a modified approach in its accounting for infrastructure assets. The modified approach results in the government reporting expense for the maintenance costs related to infrastructure assets (on the government-wide statement of activities) and in its reporting no depreciation expense, if certain conditions are met by the government as specified in GASB 34. Therefore, on the statement of net assets for Darien Village at December 31, 2003, infrastructure assets would be reported at $5,000,000 without any reduction for accumulated depreciation.

6. (a) GASB 9, para 19, indicates that "cash flows from operating activities include transactions of certain loan programs." These include "program loan" programs that are undertaken to fulfill a governmental responsibility, such as the loan program mentioned in this problem.

7. (a) GASB 34, para 296, (part of the basis of conclusions) indicates that "The Board concluded that a government's basic financial statements should provide operational accountability information for the government as a whole, including information about the cost of services, operating results, and financial position."

8. (d) In accordance with GASB 34, capital assets, exclusive of infrastructure assets, are reported on the government-wide statement of net assets at cost less accumulated depreciation. In the case involving Fullerton City, the amount reported under assets is $2,750,000, computed by subtracting $750,000 of accumulated depreciation from the $3,500,000 cost of the capital assets.

9. (b) In the net assets section of the government-wide statement of net assets, GASB 34 requires that the amount invested in capital assets be reported net of related debt. In the case of Fullerton City, the amount reported would be $1,500,000, computed by subtracting $1,250,000 from $2,750,000, the amount reported for capital assets in the asset section of the statement of net assets.

10. (b) In accordance with GASB 34, depreciation expense on infrastructure assets is not required if the government chooses the modified approach. Under the modified approach, infrastructure assets are reported on the government-wide statement of net assets at their cost without reduction for accumulated depreciation. On the government-wide statement of activities, the cost to extend the life of the infrastructure assets is reported as an expense, and certain information about infrastructure assets is disclosed as required supplementary information.

11. (c) According to GASB 34, the government-wide statement of activities should be prepared using the accrual basis of accounting and the flow of economic resources measurement focus. As a result, capital assets are reported as assets and depreciated over their useful lives, and depreciation expense should be reported on the statement of activities. The statement of revenues, expenses, and changes in fund net assets prepared for the proprietary funds is also prepared using the accrual basis of accounting and the flow of economic resources measurement focus. Therefore, capital assets are depreciated over their useful lives, and depreciation expense is reported on the statement of revenues, expenses, and changes in fund net assets.

12. (d) According to GASB 34, governments should prepare government-wide financial statements based upon the accrual basis of accounting and the economic resources measurement focus. In addition to the government-wide financial statements, governments are also required to report financial statements for governmental funds, proprietary funds, and fiduciary funds. The financial statements for governmental funds are based upon the modified accrual basis and the financial resources measurement focus, while the financial statements for proprietary and fiduciary funds are based upon the accrual basis of accounting and the flow of economic resources measurement focus.

13. (d) According to GASB 34, infrastructure assets are required to be reported on the government-wide statement of net assets. The use of the modified approach for infrastructure assets means that these assets are not depreciated if certain conditions are satisfied. However, infrastructure assets are reported on the statement of net assets, even if they are not depreciated. According to GASB 34, component units are reported on the entity-wide financial statements. They are not reported on the financial statements of the governmental funds

E. Fund Financial Statements

14. (c) A fund is defined as a fiscal and accounting entity with a self balancing set of accounts. These funds record cash and other financial resources, together with all related liabilities and residual equities or balances, and changes therein, **and are segregated for the purpose of carrying on specific activities or attaining certain objectives** in accordance with special regulations, restrictions, or limitations.

15. (d) GASB 9, para 27, indicates that cash flows from investing activities includes interest received as returns on investments. The candidate should note that this is different from SFAS 95, which classifies interest on investments as cash flows from operating activities.

16. (a) The Governmental Accounting Standards Board (GASB) has the authority to establish standards of financial reporting for all units of state and local government. Upon its formation in 1984, GASB adopted the past pronouncements of its predecessor organization, the National Council on Governmental Accounting (NCGA), and guidelines in the AICPA *Audits of State and Local Governmental Units*, which the GASB later modified. The FASB sets standards for profit-seeking businesses, and not governmental units.

17. (c) Financial reporting by state and local governments is used in making economic, social, and political decisions and in assessing accountability. Additionally, current year citizens need information concerning when costs of current services are actually paid for. Thus, both items I and II are provided to the users of governmental reporting.

18. (b) The requirement is to determine which event(s) should be included in a statement of cash flows for a government entity. Governmental funds do not have a statement of cash flows because they are accounted for on the modified accrual basis. A statement of cash flows is included for proprietary funds because they are accounted for on the accrual basis. The cash inflow from issuing bonds to finance city hall construction is accounted for in the governmental funds. The cash outflow from a city utility representing payments in lieu of property taxes is accounted for in the proprietary funds.

19. (b) Cash flows from sale of revenue bonds and capital contributed by subdividers are classified as cash flows from capital and related financing activities. Both the $4,500,000 proceeds from sale of revenue bonds and $900,000 capital contributed by subdividers would be reported as cash flows from capital and related financing activities. Cash flows from customer households are operating cash flows.

20. (c) The statement of cash flows is applicable to proprietary funds, nonexpendable trust funds, and governmental entities that use proprietary fund accounting, including public benefit corporations and authorities, governmental utilities, and governmental hospitals. PERS (Public Employee Retirement Systems) and pension trust funds are exempt from this requirement.

21. (d) In accordance with GASB 34, there are three financial statements that should be prepared for proprietary funds. The financial statements for proprietary funds include

1. The statement of net assets
2. The statement of revenues, expenses, and changes in fund net assets
3. The statement of cash flows

22. **(a)** In accordance with GASB 34, the focus of fund financial statements is on major and nonmajor funds, not on fund types. On the balance sheet for the governmental funds, the general fund is always reported as a major fund, while other funds are evaluated as major or nonmajor based upon criteria specified in GASB 34. A separate column is required for each major fund, while all nonmajor funds are aggregated in a single column. On the balance sheet for the governmental funds, fund balances are reported in two categories—reserved and unreserved. The terms restricted and unrestricted are not used on the balance sheet for the governmental funds.

23. **(c)** In accordance with GASB 34, the statement of net assets for proprietary funds should (1) report assets and liabilities in current and noncurrent classifications, and (2) report all the activities of internal service funds in a single column.

24. **(a)** According to GASB 34, the financial statements of proprietary funds should be based upon the accrual basis of accounting and the economic resources measurement focus. Therefore, the statement of net assets for proprietary funds is prepared on the accrual basis and the economic resources measurement focus. On the other hand, the financial statements prepared for governmental funds should be based upon the modified accrual basis of accounting and the financial resources measurement focus. Therefore, the statement of revenues, expenditures, and changes in fund balances prepared for governmental funds is not prepared on the accrual basis and the economic resources measurement focus.

25. **(a)** According to GASB 34, two financial statements should be prepared for fiduciary funds—the statement of fiduciary net assets and the statement of changes in fiduciary net assets. Fiduciary funds include pension trust, investment trust, private-purpose trust, and agency funds. Agency funds should be reported on the statement of fiduciary net assets, but not on the statement of changes in fiduciary net assets. Since agency funds report only assets and liabilities, they are reported on the statement of fiduciary net assets, but they are not reported on the statement of changes in fiduciary net assets.

26. **(b)** According to GASB 34, private-purpose trust funds are fiduciary funds that should be reported on two fiduciary fund financial statements: (1) the statement of fiduciary net assets and (2) the statement of changes in fiduciary net assets. Therefore, private-purpose trust funds are reported on the statement of changes in fiduciary net assets. According to GASB 34, the government-wide statement of net assets discloses information about governmental activities, business-type activities, and component units. Fiduciary activities are not disclosed on the government-wide financial statements. This means that private-purpose trust funds would not be reported on the statement of net assets for governmental and business-type activities.

27. **(d)** According to GASB 34, the statement of cash flows is prepared only for the proprietary funds. The state-ment of cash flows is not a government-wide financial statement. Therefore, governmental and fiduciary fund types are not reported on the statement of cash flows.

28. **(d)** According to GASB 34, the statement of cash flows is prepared only for the proprietary funds. The statement of cash flows is not a government-wide financial statement. The format of the statement of cash flows consists of four sections. The sections include cash flows from (1) operating activities, (2) noncapital financing activities, (3) capital and related financing activities, and (4) investing activities. This format for the statement of cash flows is different from the format used by business enterprises that discloses operating, investing, and financing activities.

29. **(c)** According to GASB 34, the balance sheet prepared for the governmental funds is based on the modified accrual basis of accounting and financial resources measurement focus. However, the government-wide statement of net assets is prepared based on the accrual basis of accounting and the economic resources measurement focus. The differences between these two financial statements result in a difference between the amount reported for net assets for governmental activities on the statement of net assets and the amount reported for fund balances on the balance sheet for the governmental funds. GASB 34 requires that the reasons for this difference be reported in a reconciliation schedule. One of the reasons for the difference is the acquisition of capital assets by governmental funds during the year. These capital assets do not appear under assets on the balance sheet of the governmental funds because they are recorded as expenditures using the modified accrual basis of accounting and the financial resources measurement focus. Therefore, the acquisition of capital assets has the effect of reducing the fund balances of governmental funds on the balance sheet. However, capital assets are reported as assets on the government-wide statement of net assets. Capital assets acquired by governmental funds are reported on this statement as assets under governmental activities. Therefore, total net assets related to governmental activities are not affected on the statement of net assets when capital assets are acquired. Accordingly, capital assets used in governmental activities are items that are reported in the schedule that reconciles the net assets of governmental activities with the fund balances of the governmental funds. The assets and liabilities of internal service funds are additional items that cause a difference between the fund balances of the government funds and the net assets of governmental activities. The reason that the assets and liabilities of internal service funds cause a difference is that they are included with governmental activities on the statement of net assets, thereby causing net assets of governmental activities to increase. However, internal service fund assets and liabilities are not reported in the governmental fund financial statements; rather, they are included in the proprietary fund financial statements. Therefore, the fund balances of the governmental funds do not include these items. Accordingly, the assets and liabilities of internal service funds are reported in the schedule that reconciles the net assets of governmental activities with the fund balances of the governmental funds.

30. **(c)** According to GASB 34, the statement of revenues, expenditures, and changes in fund balances prepared for the governmental funds is prepared using the modified accrual basis of accounting and the financial resources measurement focus. However, the government-wide statement of activities is prepared using the accrual basis of accounting and the economic resources measurement focus. The differences between these two financial statements result in a difference between the amount reported for the change in net assets for governmental activities on the statement of activities, and the amount reported for the net change in fund balances on the statement of revenues, expenditures, and changes in fund balances for the governmental funds. GASB 34 requires that the reasons for this difference be reported in a reconciliation schedule. One of the reasons for the difference is capital assets that were acquired by governmental funds during the year. On the statement of revenues, expenditures, and changes in fund balances, capital assets are reported as expenditures, using the modified accrual basis of accounting and the financial resources measurement focus. However, capital assets acquired by governmental funds are reported as assets and are depreciated on the government-wide statement of activities. Therefore, the difference between capital expenditures and depreciation expense is reported as a reconciling item. On the other hand, the revenues and expenses of internal service funds are additional items that cause a difference between the net change in the fund balances reported on the statement of revenues, expenditures, and changes in fund balances of the governmental funds and the change in the net assets of governmental activities reported on the statement of activities. The reason that the revenues and expenses of internal service funds cause a difference is that they are included with governmental activities on the statement of activities, thereby causing the net change in fund balances of governmental activities to increase. However, internal service fund revenues and expenses are not reported in the governmental fund financial statements; rather, they are included in the proprietary fund financial statements. Therefore, the net change in fund balances of the governmental funds do not include internal service fund revenues and expenses. Accordingly, the revenues and expenses of internal service funds should be reported in the schedule that reconciles the change in net assets of governmental activities with the net change in the fund balances of the governmental funds.

31. (c) According to GASB 34, the accrual basis of accounting and the economic resources measurement focus are concepts that go together. This means that financial statements prepared using the accrual basis also are based upon the economic resources measurement focus. Both the government-wide statement of net assets and the statement of changes in fiduciary net assets are prepared using the accrual basis of accounting and the economic resources measurement focus. The only financial statements that use the financial resources measurement focus are those prepared for governmental funds—the balance sheet and the statement of revenues, expenditures, and changes in fund balances.

32. (a) According to GASB 34, pension trust funds are fiduciary funds that are reported on the statement of changes in fiduciary net assets. On the statement of net assets for proprietary funds, net assets are disclosed in three classifications: (1) invested in capital assets, net of related debt, (2) restricted, and (3) unrestricted. Retained earnings is not disclosed on the statement of net assets for proprietary funds; the term "net assets" is used as the equity account.

33. (b) According to GASB 34, the statement of cash flows is prepared for proprietary funds. The statement format is not the same as that for business enterprises. The format for the statement of cash flows for proprietary funds contains four sections: (1) cash flows from operating activities, (2) cash flows from noncapital financing activities, (3) cash flows from capital and related financing activities, and (4) cash flows from investing activities. The cash flows from operating activities can be presented using either the direct method or the indirect method. Cash paid for interest is not reported in the operating activities section. It would be disclosed either in the noncapital financing activities' section or the capital and related financing activities' section, depending upon where the debt that caused the interest payments was reported. Interest revenue received in cash is not reported in the operating activities' section. It is reported in the investing activities' section because this is where the investments were reported that resulted in the interest revenue.

H. Measurement Focus and Basis of Accounting

34. (b) The governmental fund measurement focus is on determination of financial position (sources, uses, and balances of financial resources), rather than upon income determination.

35. (a) Governmental fund revenues should be recognized in the accounting period in which they become available and measurable. Governmental funds include the general fund, special revenue funds, capital projects funds, debt service funds, and permanent funds. Proprietary fund revenues should be recognized in the accounting period in which they are earned and become measurable. Proprietary funds include the enterprise and internal service funds. As the question requires the funds in which revenue is recognized in the period it becomes available and measurable, this would include the general fund but not the enterprise fund.

I. Accounting for Nonexchange Transactions

36. (b) GASB 33, para 7, indicates that "imposed nonexchange revenues result from assessments by governments on nongovernmental entities, including individuals, other than assessments on nonexchange transactions. Examples include property (ad valorem) taxes; fines and penalties...."

37. (b) The levy of property taxes is a nonexchange transaction. GASB 33 defines nonexchange transactions as transactions "in which a government gives (or receives) value without directly receiving (or giving) equal value in exchange." Exchange transactions are transactions "in which each party receives and gives up essentially equal values." In the case of a property tax levy, the government is receiving value, the right to receive payments from property owners, without directly giving equal value in return. The government services that are financed from a property tax levy are not provided to individual taxpayers in proportion to the amount of property taxes that are paid. The other answers are incorrect because they are examples of exchange transactions.

38. (b) Deferred revenue should be credited upon receipt of the grant. According to the guidance provided in GASB 33, cash received from government-mandated grants should be reported as deferred revenue when cash is received prior to all eligibility requirements being met. A time restriction is one example of eligibility requirements not being met before the end of the fiscal period. Note that, if there was no time restriction placed on the government-mandated grant by the state, Elizabeth City would have reported revenue for the year ended June 30, 2003.

39. **(a)** According to the guidance provided in GASB 33, the grant from the state is an example of a government-mandated type of nonexchange transaction. Government-mandated nonexchange transactions exists when the providing government, such as a state government, requires the receiving government to expend the funds for a specific purpose.

40. **(c)** According to the guidance provided by GASB 33, sales tax revenues are an example of a derived tax revenue. Derived tax revenues result from taxes assessed by government on exchange transactions. In the case of sales taxes, exchange transactions between merchants and consumers provide the basis for the collection of the sales tax revenues.

41. **(c)** The general fund of Eldorado should report the sales taxes to be received in July 2003 as revenue for the year ended June 30, 2003. Under the modified accrual measurement focus, the sales taxes should be reported as revenue for the year ended June 30, 2003 because the sales taxes are available to finance expenditures made in the year ended June 30, 2003.

42. **(c)** According to the guidance provided by GASB 33, property tax revenues are an example of an imposed tax revenue. Imposed revenues result from taxes and other assessments imposed by governments that are not derived from underlying transactions.

43. **(b)** In accordance with GASB 33, the modified accrual basis of accounting should be used for recording and reporting property tax revenues for the general fund on the statement of revenues, expenditures, and changes in fund balances. Under the modified accrual basis of accounting, revenues are recognized in the period when they are both measurable and available to pay for expenditures incurred during the current fiscal period. With respect to property tax revenues, "available" means collected during the year and within the first sixty days after the end of the year. For the general fund of Karsten City, the property taxes collected in 2003 of $850,000 as well as the $100,000 expected to be collected by March 1 of 2004 would be added to get the property tax revenues recognized in 2003. The sum of $950,000 of property tax revenues would be reported by the general fund on the statement of revenues, expenditures, and changes in fund balances for the year ended December 31, 2003. The journal entries to record the property tax levy and collections for 2003 appear below.

Property taxes receivable—Current	1,000,000	
Property tax revenues ($850,000 + 100,000)		950,000
Deferred revenues (report as a liability on the balance sheet)		40,000
Allowance for estimated uncollectible property taxes—Current		10,000
Cash	850,000	
Property taxes receivable—Current		850,000

The deferred revenue account of $40,000 represents the property taxes expected to be collected after March 1, 2004.

Because the taxes are expected to be collected after sixty days from the end of 2003, the taxes are not considered available to pay for expenditures incurred in 2003. This is the reason for crediting deferred revenue in 2003.

44. **(d)** In accordance with GASB 33, imposed nonexchange transactions include taxes and other assessments derived from underlying transactions. Examples include property taxes, special assessments, and fines and forfeits. For the general fund of Ward Village, imposed nonexchange transactions would include property tax revenues of $125,000 and fines of $10,000. Sales taxes and income taxes would be classified as derived tax revenues.

45. **(a)** In accordance with GASB 33, the modified accrual basis of accounting should be used for recording and reporting revenues reported by the general fund on the Statement of Revenues, Expenditures, and Changes in Fund Balances. The modified accrual basis of accounting for revenues results in revenues being recognized in the period in which they are both measurable and available to pay for expenditures incurred during the current fiscal period. The sales tax advance of $25,000 should be reported as revenue in 2003 because it was available to pay for expenditures incurred by the general fund in 2003. On the other hand, the cash received from property owners of $20,000 should not be reported as revenue in 2003 because the money cannot be used to pay for expenditures incurred by the general fund in 2003. The property taxes received in December 2003 should be reported as deferred revenue on the December 31, 2003 balance sheet for the general fund. Deferred revenue would appear under the liabilities classification. The entry to record both of the cash receipts in the general fund in December 2003 appears below.

Cash	45,000	
Sales tax revenues		25,000
Deferred revenue		20,000

46. **(c)** According to GASB 33, revenues that result from taxes assessed by government on exchange transactions are classified as derived tax revenues. Examples of derived tax revenue include sales taxes, income taxes, and motor fuel taxes. Property tax revenues and fines and forfeits are examples of revenues that come from imposed nonexchange transactions. Imposed nonexchange transactions are taxes and other assessments imposed by governments that are not derived from underlying transactions. Unrestricted government grants are an example of voluntary nonexchange transactions. This category includes grants and entitlements from one government to another where the providing government does not impose certain requirements on the receiving government.

47. **(d)** According to GASB 33, revenues that result from taxes and other assessments imposed by governments that are not derived from underlying transactions are categorized as imposed nonexchange transactions. Examples include property taxes, special assessments, and fines and forfeits. Income taxes, sales taxes, and motor fuel taxes are examples of derived tax revenues. Derived tax revenues result from taxes assessed by government on exchange transactions.

J. Budgetary Accounting for the General and Special Revenue Funds

48. **(a)** To record the budget, Ridge would make the following journal entry:

Estimated Revenues	100,000	
Appropriations		80,000
Budgetary Fund Balance		20,000

Therefore, as the Appropriations account is credited for the anticipated expenditures.

49.   (c)   To record the budget, Ridge would make the following journal entry:

Estimated Revenues	100,000	
Appropriations		80,000
Budgetary Fund Balance		20,000

Therefore, the Budgetary Fund Balance account is credited for the anticipated surplus of revenues over expenditures.

50.   (a)   Revenues to the general fund are defined as "increases in fund financial resources other than from interfund transfers and debt issue proceeds." Transfers to a fund and debt issue proceeds received by a fund are classified as other financing sources of the fund. Therefore, in Maple's budgetary entry, estimated revenues would be debited for the $9,000,000 expected from property taxes, licenses, and fines. The Estimated Other Financing Sources account would be debited for the $6,000,000, consisting of the debt issue proceeds and the interfund transfers.

51.   (b)   Assuming that encumbrance accounting is utilized by the city, the journal entry to record the issuance of purchase orders and contracts is a debit to Encumbrances Control and a credit to Budgetary Fund Balance—Reserved for Encumbrances for the amount of the purchase order or estimated cost of the contracts.

52.   (c)   As Cliff approves and issues its purchase orders, the purchase order amount ($5,000,000) is recorded in the Encumbrances Control account. As the goods are received, the related purchase order amount of these goods (i.e., the amount that was originally recorded, $4,500,000) is removed from the Encumbrances Control account. Therefore, at year-end, the amount of outstanding encumbrances is $500,000. Keep in mind that the actual invoice amount is not the amount removed from the Encumbrances Control account. The invoice amount will be vouchered and charged to Expenditures Control.

53.   (d)   When Elm issued its purchase order, the following journal entry would have been made to encumber the amount:

Encumbrances Control	5,000	
Budgetary Fund Balance—Reserved for		
Encumbrances		5,000

When the supplies were received the following journal entries would have been made:

Budgetary Fund Balance—Reserved		
for Encumbrances	5,000	
Encumbrances Control		5,000
Expenditures Control	4,950	
Vouchers Payable		4,950

54.   (d)   When purchase orders for goods or services are approved and issued, the Encumbrances Control account is debited and the Budgetary Fund Balance—Reserved for Encumbrances is credited for the amount of the purchase orders. As goods are received or services are rendered the above encumbrance entry is reversed. Thus, the amount left in each would be zero. Note that the same amount is initially recorded in each of the accounts (i.e., the debit equals

the credit). The same amount is also relieved from both accounts. A Budgetary Fund Balance—Reserved for Encumbrances in excess of a balance in the Encumbrances Control account indicates there has been a recording error. An excess of vouchers payable over encumbrances means that not all anticipated expenditures are being encumbered. This is often the case for salaries and wages. However, the Budgetary Fund Balance—Reserved for Encumbrances would still equal the Encumbrances Control account. An excess of appropriations over encumbrances indicates that there are more anticipated expenditures than there are approved and issued purchase orders that have been encumbered. However, the Budgetary Fund Balance—Reserved for Encumbrances would still be equal to the Encumbrances Control account.

55.   (b)   Encumbrances outstanding at year-end represent the estimated amount of the expenditures that could result if unperformed contracts in process at year-end are computed. Encumbrances outstanding at year-end are not expenditures or liabilities. Where appropriations do not lapse at year-end, encumbrances outstanding at year-end should be reported as reservations of fund balance for the subsequent year expenditures. Where appropriations lapse at year-end, the governmental unit may honor the contracts in progress at year-end or cancel them. If the governmental unit intends to honor them, the encumbrances outstanding at year-end should be disclosed by reservation of fund balance.

56.   (d)   When closing entries are made for a governmental unit, Estimated Revenues Control is credited for the same amount that it was debited for in the beginning of the period budget/entry. Also, Revenues Control is debited in the amount of recorded revenue for the year. In this case, Estimated Revenues Control would be credited for $20,000,000 and Revenues Control would be debited for $17,000,000 to close the books. Revenues Control and Estimated Revenues Control are not netted in the closing entry.

57.   (c)   The Budgetary Fund Balance account is debited upon budget adoption when the appropriations exceed the estimated revenues. The following entry is made when the budget is adopted:

Estimated Revenues Control	xx	
Budgetary Fund Balance	xx	
Appropriations Control		xx

At the end of the year, the budgetary accounts must be closed out. The budgetary closing entry is simply a reverse of the adoption entry.

Appropriations Control	xx	
Estimated Revenues Control		xx
Budgetary Fund Balance		xx

The Budgetary Fund Balance is debited at the beginning of the year when appropriations exceed the estimated revenues. An entry must be made to close the Budgetary Fund Balance account at the end of the year. Note that any differences between the budgetary revenues and appropriations and the actual revenues and expenditures and encumbrances do not affect the **Budgetary** Fund Balance account. They would, however, affect the Unreserved Fund Balance account when the operations accounts are closed out.

58.   (b)   The $100,000 balance in the Fund Balance—Reserved for Encumbrances account indicates that there were open purchase orders at year-end. Since the appropriations do not lapse at year-end, the Fund Balance—

Reserved for Encumbrances account will not be closed but will be reported as a separate line item in the fund balance section of the balance sheet. The term "reserve" indicates that the funds are not available for expenditure. Therefore, the $100,000 cannot be included in the unreserved fund balance amount. Therefore, the amount of the Unreserved Fund Balance in the 2003 balance sheet would be $300,000 ($1,000,000 – $600,000 – $100,000).

59. (b) The closing of the general fund accounts is done by closing the budgetary accounts against each other and the actual revenue, expenditure and other accounts to the Unreserved Fund Balance. This is done most easily by reversing the beginning of the year budget entry in one entry and then using a separate entry to close the actual accounts to fund balance. The following entry would therefore be made to close the actual accounts to obtain the amount of increase in the fund balance:

General Fund

Other Financing Sources Control	1,500,000	
Revenues Control	8,000,000	
Expenditures Control		5,000,000
Other Financing Uses Control		2,000,000
Fund Balance—Unreserved		2,500,000

The Appropriations account would be closed in the reversal of the budget entry and has no effect on fund balance.

K. Expenditure Classification for Governmental Funds

60. (c) GASB 34, para 92, indicates that proprietary funds (including enterprise funds) are to use accrual accounting. Paragraph 93 indicates that FASB pronouncements issued on or before November 30, 1989, are to be followed unless superceded by a GASB pronouncement. Accrual accounting recognizes interest revenue over time; in this case, interest revenue would be $1,000,000 x .06 x 9/12 = $45,000.

61. (a) Expenditure classification by object is based upon the type of items purchased or services obtained. Examples of "Current Operations" object of expenditure classifications are personal services, supplies, and other services and charges. Salaries are an example of classification by object. Function or program classifications provide information regarding the overall purpose or objectives of expenditures (i.e., police protection, sanitation, highways and streets, etc.). Activity classification provides data for calculating expenditures per unit of activity (i.e., street resurfacing).

L. Accounting for the General Fund

62. (c) "When a property tax assessment is made, it is to finance the budget of a particular period, and the revenue produced from any property tax assessment should be recognized in the fiscal period for which it was levied, provided the 'available' criteria are met. 'Available' means then due, or past due and receivable within the current period, and collected within the current period or expected to be collected soon enough thereafter to pay liabilities of the current period. Such time thereafter shall not exceed sixty days." This is how property tax revenues are reported on the Statement of Revenues, Expenditures, and Changes in Fund Balances for governmental funds. Therefore, both the collections during 2003 of $500,000 and the expected collections during the first sixty days of 2004 of $100,000 would be reported as property tax revenues for 2003. Remember that

the estimated uncollectible amounts are not reported on the operating statement as an offset to revenues, but rather are reported as a contra asset account. The governmental unit, in calculating the amount of the levy, factors in what has historically been uncollectible, so that the revenues in effect have already been adjusted.

63. (b) Under GASB Statement 33, imposed nonexchange revenues, including property taxes, should be recorded in the year for which budgeted. In this case, the amount would be $690,000, the total levy less the estimated uncollectible amount.

64. (d) Interfund services provided and used are transactions that would be treated as revenues or expenditures/expenses if they involved organizations external to the government (i.e., **routine employer contributions from a general fund to a pension trust fund**, internal service fund billings to departments, enterprise funds billing for services provided to the general fund). The proper accounting for interfund services provided and used is to treat them as revenues in the fund providing the goods or services and **as expenditures/ expenses in the fund receiving the goods or services,** exactly as if the transactions involved parties external to the government. Thus, answer (d) is correct because the general fund should record an expenditure for routine employer contributions to the pension trust fund. Answer (a) is incorrect because the contribution of enterprise fund capital by the general fund should be recorded in the general fund as a transfer. Answers (b) and (c) are incorrect because routine transfers between funds should also be recorded as transfers.

65. (b) Interfund services provided and used are treated as revenues or expenditures/expenses if they involved organizations external to the government (i.e., a city's electric utility providing electricity to the general fund, internal service fund billings to departments, routine employer contributions from a general fund to a pension trust fund). The proper accounting for interfund services provided and used transactions is to treat them as revenues in the fund providing the goods or services and as expenditures/expenses in the fund receiving the goods or services, exactly as if the transactions involved parties external to the government. The general fund should recognize an expenditure for the amount billed by the city's electric utility.

66. (a) The internal service fund and the enterprise fund use the accrual basis of accounting and both report net assets, not fund balances. Net assets are reported in the following manner: (1) invested in capital assets, net of related debt, (2) restricted, and (3) unrestricted. The capital projects fund does not keep an inventory of supplies and therefore would not have a Fund Balance—Reserved for Inventory of Supplies. The general fund does maintain an inventory of supplies and would therefore have a Fund Balance—Reserved for Inventory of Supplies.

67. (d) The $6,000,000 in property taxes would be accounted for in Ariba's general fund, which is a governmental fund. The $40,000 of net rental revenue (after depreciation) from a parking garage would be accounted for in an enterprise fund, which is a proprietary fund. An enterprise fund provides products or services to the public, such as the use of the parking garage. The $100,000 interest earned on investments held for employees' retirement benefits would be included in a trust fund (more than likely a pension trust fund).

68. **(c)** In accordance with GASB 34, the balance sheet prepared for the governmental funds should be based on the current financial resources measurement focus and the modified accrual basis of accounting. This means that capital assets, such as police cars, are not reported on the balance sheet for governmental funds. Instead, the police cars are reported as expenditures on the statement of revenues, expenditures, and changes in fund balances for the year ended December 31, 2003.

69. **(b)** In accordance with GASB 34, the government-wide statement of net assets is prepared using the economic resources measurement focus and the full accrual basis of accounting. In the column for governmental activities, the police cars would be reported at $32,500. This amount is the original cost of $40,000 less accumulated depreciation of $7,500. The use of full accrual accounting means that the police cars are depreciated. The depreciation expense is reported on the government-wide statement of activities. Depreciation expense would be $7,500, computed by taking $40,000 less the salvage value of $10,000, and dividing by the useful life of four years.

70. **(a)** GASB 34 requires use of the current financial resources measurement focus and the modified accrual basis of accounting for governmental funds. On the statement of revenues, expenditures, and changes in fund balances prepared for 2003 for the governmental funds, the acquisition of the police cars is reported as expenditures of $40,000.

71. **(b)** According to GASB 34, the statement of revenues, expenditures, and changes in fund balances prepared for governmental funds is based upon the modified accrual basis of accounting and the financial resources measurement focus. On the statement of revenues, expenditures, and changes in fund balances, the acquisition of police cars is reported as expenditures of $75,000. The $30,000 payment by the general fund to the pension trust fund is reported as an interfund services provided and used transaction. On the statement of revenues, expenditures, and changes in fund balances, the $30,000 should be reported as expenditures. Therefore, the acquisition of the police cars and the pension transfer result in $105,000 of expenditures being reported on the statement of revenues, expenditures, and changes in fund balances for the governmental funds.

72. **(c)** According to GASB 34, the statement of revenues, expenditures, and changes in fund balances prepared for governmental funds is based upon the modified accrual basis of accounting and the financial resources measurement focus. On the statement of revenues, expenditures, and changes in fund balances, the revenue from property taxes should be reported at $750,000. The levy of $800,000 less the 2% that was not expected to be collected results in $784,000, of which $750,000 was collected in 2003. Because the remaining $34,000 was not expected to be collected within sixty days of the end of 2003, the $34,000 is not considered available in 2003, and, therefore, it is not reported as revenue in 2003. At December 31, 2003, the $34,000 should be reported as deferred revenue on the balance sheet prepared for the governmental funds. Deferred revenues are reported as liabilities on this balance sheet. On the other hand, sales tax revenues for 2003 would be

$100,000. The amount of sales taxes that are expected to be received in mid-March of 2004 is not considered available in 2003, and should not be included in revenues on the statement of revenues, expenditures, and changes in fund balances prepared for the governmental funds for the year ended December 31, 2003. Therefore, property tax revenues and sales tax revenues for 2003 would be reported at $850,000.

73. **(a)** According to GASB 34, the government-wide statement of activities should be prepared based upon the accrual basis of accounting and the economic resources measurement focus. The statement of activities reports governmental activities, business-type activities, and component units. For the police cars that were purchased in 2003, this means that depreciation expense of $12,000 would be reported under governmental activities. The police cars would be reported as assets on the government-wide statement of net assets, and the depreciation expense for 2003 would be computed by dividing five years into $75,000 less the salvage value of $15,000. The transfer to the pension trust fund would be reported under governmental activities as an expense of $30,000. The transfer is accounted for as an interfund services provided and used transaction in 2003. This means that the transfer would be reported in expenses under governmental activities for the year ended December 31, 2003. Therefore, $42,000 of expenses result from the acquisition of the police cars and the pension transfer in 2003. These expenses would be reported on the government-wide statement of activities for 2003.

74. **(b)** According to GASB 34, the government-wide statement of activities should be prepared based upon the accrual basis of accounting and the economic resources measurement focus. The statement of activities reports governmental activities, business-type activities, and component units. For 2003, property tax revenues should be reported at the full amount of the levy of $800,000 less the 2% that was not expected to be collected. This means that $784,000 would be reported for property tax revenues in 2003. The $34,000 of property taxes that were not collected in 2003 are reported as revenues in 2003 because the statement of activities is based upon accrual accounting. For 2003, sales tax revenues should be reported at $125,000. Sales tax revenues reported for 2002 include the $100,000 collected during 2003 as well as the $25,000 that will be collected in mid-March of 2004. The $25,000 of sales taxes that will be collected in mid-March 2004 are reported as revenues in 2003 on the statement of activities because the sales taxes were collected by the state in 2003. Therefore, the accrual basis of accounting mandates that the $25,000 be reported as revenue under governmental activities in 2003. Therefore, for the year ended December 31, 2003, a total of $909,000 of revenues are reported for property taxes ($784,000) and sales taxes ($125,000) on the government-wide statement of activities.

M. Accounting for Special Revenue Funds

75. **(c)** According to GASB 33, the grant received by Maple Township is an example of a voluntary nonexchange transaction in which the providing State government imposes purpose restrictions on the grant to Maple Township. Under modified accrual accounting, grant revenue should be recognized when it is both measurable and available. Applying these criteria to the grant, revenues should be recognized in the period that Maple received reimbursement from the state for the purchase of buses ($60,000) and for bus maintenance ($5,000). It is at the point of reimbursement that the grant becomes available.

76. (b) Special revenue funds are used to account for the proceeds of specific revenue sources (other than expendable trusts or for major capital projects) that are legally restricted to expenditures for specified purposes. Thus, the gasoline taxes to finance road repairs should be accounted for in a special revenue fund. The levies to property owners to install sidewalks would be recorded either in an agency fund (if special assessment debt is not backed by the government) or by a debt service fund (if the debt is backed by the government).

77. (c) A special revenue fund is a governmental fund and therefore uses the modified accrual basis of accounting, not the accrual basis. Budgetary accounts should be used in the general fund and special revenue fund.

N. Accounting for Capital Projects Funds

78. (a) The objective of a capital projects fund is to account for the financial resources to be used for the acquisition or construction of major capital facilities. The inflow of bond proceeds should be accounted for in the year received, regardless of when the bond proceeds are expended. Therefore, the $5,000,000 of bond proceeds should be recorded in the capital projects fund in 2003, the year received. They should be treated as an "other financing source" in the operating statement of the fund. Note that the servicing of the debt will be accounted for in the debt service fund.

79. (c) Grants received by the capital projects fund from another governmental unit are considered revenues of the capital projects fund. Also, taxes or other revenues raised specifically for the capital projects fund are recorded as revenues of the fund. However, proceeds of debt issues should be recorded as proceeds of bonds/long-term debt and should be reported as an other financing source in the operating statement. Similarly, resources transferred to the capital projects fund generally from the general or special revenue fund are recorded as transfers in and reported in the other financing sources section of the operating statement. Thus, Fir should report only the $400,000 from the grant as a revenue. The $600,000 consisting of the bond issue proceeds and general fund transfer should be reported as other financing sources.

O. Debt Service Funds

80. (d) Governmental fund revenues and expenditures should be recognized on the modified accrual basis. Governmental funds include the general fund, special revenue funds, capital projects funds, debt service funds, and permanent funds. Proprietary fund revenues and expenses should be recognized on the accrual basis. Proprietary funds include enterprise funds and internal service funds. Fiduciary fund additions and deductions should be recognized on the accrual basis. Pension trust funds should be accounted for on the accrual basis.

81. (a) GASB 37, para 16, indicates that proceeds of long-term issues not recorded as fund liabilities should be reported as other financing sources in governmental funds.

In addition, general long-term debt issue premiums should also be reported as other financing sources. Paragraph 87 of GASB 34 indicates that debt issue costs, including underwriter fees, should be reported as expenditures.

82. (d) Debt service funds are to account for the accumulation of resources for and payment of, general long-term debt principal and interest. The general fund does not account for resources restricted for payment of general long-term debt principal and interest.

83. (a) According to GASB 34, the balance sheet prepared for governmental funds is prepared using the modified accrual basis of accounting and the flow of financial resources measurement focus. Under the modified accrual basis of accounting and the financial resources measurement focus, the bond issue costs of $400,000 and the debt insurance costs of $90,000 should be charged to expenditures in the debt service fund on June 30, 2003. This means that none of the costs will be reported as an asset on the governmental funds' balance sheet prepared at June 30, 2003.

84. (c) The requirement is to determine which fund should record receipts from a special tax levy to retire and pay interest on general obligation bonds. The correct answer is (c) because the debt service fund usually handles the repayment of general obligation long-term debt interest. A levy allocable to the debt service fund is recorded in the fund. Answer (a) is incorrect because levies for the purpose of paying interest do not get recorded in the general fund. The general fund records levies that do not have a specific purpose. Answer (b) is incorrect because capital projects funds are for construction or the purchase of fixed assets. Answer (d) is incorrect because special revenue funds are for earmarked revenue that is not to pay interest on general obligation debt.

85. (d) The bond premium amount is usually deemed to be another financing source in the debt service fund and is recorded as such when the bonds are sold. The premium is not capitalized and amortized.

86. (a) The GASB classifies three types of funds used in governmental accounting: governmental, proprietary, and fiduciary. Debt service funds are used to accumulate resources to pay general long-term debt of governmental funds. The debt service fund is not used in connection with either a trust fund or a proprietary fund.

87. (c) Cash received in the debt service fund from the general fund for debt service is recorded as a transfer. Cash payments of principal and interest on the debt are then recorded as expenditures in the debt service fund. The following entries would be made in the debt service fund:

Cash	xx	
Transfers In—General Fund		xx
Expenditures—Principal	xx	
Expenditures—Interest	xx	
Cash (Payable)		xx

88. (a) Interest on the general obligation bonds is payable on March 1 and September 1. The debt service fund accounts for the accumulation of cash to pay the interest and principal on general obligation bonds. However, interest on the bonds is not recorded until it is legally payable. On June 30, 2003, no interest is legally payable, so there would be no accrual of interest to be paid as of that date.

Q. Accounting for Special Assessments

89. **(a)** The debt service transactions of a special assessment issue for which the government is not obligated in any manner should be reported in an agency fund, rather than a debt service fund. The government's duties are limited to acting as an agent for the assessed property owners and the bondholders.

R. Accounting for Proprietary Funds

90. **(c)** Municipal solid waste landfills that use proprietary accounting (i.e., enterprise fund) should recognize as expense (and liability) a portion of the estimated total cost of closure and post closure in each period that the landfill accepts solid waste. Estimated total costs should be assigned to periods based on use rather than on the passage of time, using a formula based on the percentage of capacity used each period. Because Cy City's landfill operates as an enterprise fund, the city's 2003 expenses should include a portion of the year 2024 expected disbursements for both the final cover (I) and cost of equipment to monitor methane gas buildup (II).

91. **(a)** GASB 34, para 13, clearly states that, in the government-wide statements, governmental activities normally include transactions that are reported in governmental and internal service funds.

92. **(b)** Internal service funds account for activities that produce goods or services to be provided to other departments or governmental units on a cost reimbursement basis. Internal service funds also use the full accrual method of accounting. When the governmental units are billed, the internal service fund would record the following entry:

Billings to Departments	xx	
Operating Revenues		xx

93. **(d)** A proprietary fund is created to account for goods or services the governmental unit provides to benefit the general public. It uses the accrual basis of accounting and the flow of economic resources measurement focus (i.e., capital maintenance is an objective). Fixed assets and depreciation expense on them are recorded in such funds. Therefore, the $210,000 expenditure for the parking meters would be capitalized and shown net of accumulated depreciation on Burwood's June 30, 2003 balance sheet. Burwood's net income for the year ending June 30, 2003, would be $240,000 calculated as

Receipts from users	$400,000
Expenses	
Depreciation—Parking meters	(70,000)
Salaries and other	(90,000)
Net income	$240,000

94. **(d)** Enterprise funds are used to account for operations that are financed and operated in a manner similar to private business enterprises—where the intent of the government is that costs of providing goods or services to the general public on a continuing basis be financed or recovered primarily through user charges; or where the government has decided that periodic determination of net income is appropriate for accountability purposes. Accordingly, revenues from lotteries need to be matched with related expenses for prizes. Thus, lotteries should be accounted for in a fund type that uses full accrual accounting, most commonly an enterprise fund. In addition, the GASB *Codifica-*

tion, Section H05, requires that hospitals be reported as a single enterprise fund when they are included as part of another government's reporting entity.

95. **(d)** Depreciation of general fixed assets should **not** be recorded in the accounts of governmental funds. Depreciation of fixed assets accounted for in a proprietary fund should be recorded in the accounts of that fund. The determination of recording depreciation expense in a governmental unit's fund does not change as a result of the funding source used to acquire the asset.

96. **(d)** An enterprise fund is used to account for operations where the intent of the governing body is to finance the cost of the operations through user charges or where the governing body has decided revenue, expenses, and net income information is necessary. A fund that accounts for the financing of an agency's services to other government departments on a cost-reimbursement basis is an internal service fund.

97. **(c)** Cash flows from sale of revenue bonds and capital contributed by subdividers are classified as cash flows from capital and related financing activities. Both the $5,000,000 proceeds from sale of revenue bonds and $1,000,000 capital contributed by subdividers would be reported as cash flows from capital and related financing activities. Cash flows from customer households are operating cash flows.

98. **(a)** Proprietary funds are used to account for a government's ongoing organizations and activities that are similar to those often found in the private sector. The generally accepted accounting principles here are those applicable to similar businesses in the private sector; and the measurement focus is on **determination of net income,** financial position, and cash flows.

99. **(c)** As described in the GASB *Codification,* the aggregate lease liability is recorded as an expenditure and an "Other Financing Source" in the general fund. Therefore, Expenditures Control is debited. Answer (b) is incorrect because capital assets are not reported in the general fund. Answer (d) is incorrect because an entry needs to be recorded and posted on the books when equipment is acquired through noncancelable lease-purchase agreement. A memorandum entry is not sufficient. Answer (a) is incorrect because "Other Financing Uses" account is used for transfers out of a fund.

100. **(d)** The enterprise fund is a proprietary fund and all assets and liabilities of proprietary funds are accounted for and reported in their respective funds. Therefore, transactions for enterprise fund capital leases are accounted for and reported entirely within the enterprise fund. Equipment would be debited for $150,000 in the enterprise fund.

101. **(c)** All assets and liabilities of proprietary funds are accounted for and reported in their respective funds. The entry to establish the capital lease in the internal service fund would include a debit to Equipment for $150,000 and a credit to Capital Lease Payable for $150,000. Using general business accounting, the entry to make the December 31, 2003 payment of $65,000 would debit Capital Lease Payable for the principal of $50,000 and Expenses Control for the interest of $15,000, and credit Cash for $65,000. The internal service fund is nonexpendable and **expenses** (**not** expenditures) are recognized on the full accrual basis. Expenses should only be debited for the interest of $15,000, not for the principal of $50,000.

102. (c) Per the GASB *Codification*, cash includes both cash and cash equivalents. Cash equivalents are highly liquid investments readily convertible into cash, usually maturing within three months (ninety days) or less from the date the entity **purchased** the security. Maturity is not measured from the original issuance date. Therefore, in this question, the three-month treasury bill would be included in cash and cash equivalents as well as the three-year treasury note. The three-year treasury note was purchased on 6/15/03 and matures 8/31/03. Therefore, it will be held less than ninety days. The correct answer is (c), $80,000 ($30,000 + $50,000).

S. Accounting for Fiduciary Funds

103. (b) Fiduciary funds are used to account for assets held by a governmental unit in a trustee capacity or as an agent for individuals, private organizations, other governmental units, and/or other funds. They include investment trust, private-purpose trust, pension trust, and agency funds. Therefore, the total fiduciary fund assets of Green Township at June 30, 2003, is $300,000. The debt service fund is a governmental-type fund.

104. (c) Fiduciary funds (i.e., agency funds and trust funds) are used to account for assets held by a governmental unit in a trustee capacity or as an agent for individuals, private organizations, other governmental units, and/or other funds. The entry to record the 1% fee and the disbursement to the municipalities would be as follows:

Due to Various Municipalities	1,000,000	
Due to Grove County		10,000
General Fund Cash		990,000

Note that the general fund would make the following entry:

Due from Agency Fund	xxx	
Revenue from Tax Collec. Serv.		xxx

Agency funds have only assets and liabilities as accounts and do not record revenues, expenditures, or transfers. In addition, agency funds do not have net assets.

105. (a) The entry to record the 2003 employer contribution in the Pension Trust Fund consists of a debit to Cash (or a "Due From" account) and a credit to Additions—Employer Contributions, both for $11,000. The GASB *Codification* classifies this contribution as an interfund services provided and used transaction that would be treated as an addition if it involved organizations external to the governmental unit. Therefore, the GASB states that it should be accounted for as an addition for the pension trust fund. Answer (b) is incorrect because Other Financing Sources include transfers to a fund which are recurring, routine transfers from one fund to another. The employer contribution is not a transfer. Answer (c) is incorrect because "Due From" is a debit account and the question asks for the credit account. Answer (d) is incorrect because Pension Benefit Obligation is the actuarial present value of credited projected benefits. It measures the present value of pension benefits adjusted for the effects of projected salary increases and any step-rate benefits estimated to be payable in the future as a result of employer service to date. The employer contribution is not included in this definition.

106. (b) The employer pension contribution is an interfund services provided and used transaction, one that would be treated as an addition, revenue, expense, or expenditure if it involved organizations external to the governmental unit. In this case, the entry for the governmental-type fund would include a debit to Expenditures Control for $11,000 and a credit to Cash (or a "Due To" account) for $11,000. Answer (a) is incorrect because Other Financing Uses include transfers out of a fund, which are routine recurring transfers of resources from one fund to another. Consequently, the employer contribution does not fall under the category of an Other Financing Use. Answer (c) is incorrect because governmental funds use modified accrual accounting and report expenditures, not expenses. Answer (d) is incorrect because Due To Pension Trust Fund could be the credit entry, and not the debit entry asked for in the question.

T. Reporting Interfund Activity

107. (a) On the government-wide statement of activities, transfers are reported between government activities and business-type activities. The business-type activities include the activities of enterprise funds, while the governmental activities include those of governmental funds and internal service funds. Transfers that are made to establish enterprise funds as well as yearly transfers to help subsidize enterprise funds are both reported as transfers, according to the guidance provided by GASB 34. On the other hand, billings by an enterprise fund to an internal service fund for services rendered are not reported as transfers on the statement of activities. This transition is a quasi-external transaction that should be reported on the statement of activities as an expense of governmental activities and as an operating revenue for business-type activities. The revenues and expenses of internal service funds are reported as governmental activities on the government-wide statement of activities.

108. (c) According to GASB 34, the amount reported for transfers on the government-wide statement of activities represents transfers between governmental activities and business-type activities. Examples of transfers would be permanent transfers from governmental activities to business-type activities in order to establish enterprise funds and annual transfers from governmental activities to help subsidize enterprise fund activities. The activities of internal service funds are included with governmental activities, while the activities of enterprise funds are reported under business-type activities. The $100,000 advance to an internal service fund constitutes a loan, and the general fund asset and internal service fund liability that result would be eliminated in preparing the government-wide statement of net assets. Therefore, the advance would not be reported in transfers on the statement of activities. The $25,000 billing by the enterprise fund to the general fund is recorded as a quasi-external transaction. Under governmental activities, $25,000 would be included in expenses, while, under business-type activities, the $25,000 would be reported as revenues. Therefore, the quasi-external transaction would not be reported in transfers. Finally, the $30,000 transferred by the general fund to a debt service fund is recorded as a transfer in by the debt service fund and as a transfer out by the general fund. However, because both of these funds are reported in governmental activities, the transfer in and transfer out are eliminated in preparing the statement of activities and are not reported in the governmental activities column on the statement of activities. Therefore, the general fund transfer to the debt service fund would not be reported as a transfer on the statement of activities.

109. **(a)**   According to GASB 34, transfers are reported on the government-wide statement of activities. For transfers to be reported, they must be between governmental activities and business-type activities. Governmental activities include the activities of internal service funds, while business-type activities include the activities of enterprise funds. Two kinds of transfers that are reported on the statement of activities include (1) permanent transfers either from governmental activities to business-type activities or from business-type activities to governmental activities and (2) recurring transfers from governmental activities to business-type activities or from business-type activities to governmental activities. Permanent transfers are typically made once, while the recurring transfers are typically made annually. The $100,000 transfer from the general fund to an enterprise fund would be reported as a transfer on the statement of activities because it is an example of a permanent transfer. The $1,000,000 transfer from the general fund to a capital project fund is a transfer made within governmental activities and, therefore, would not be disclosed as a transfer on the statement of activities. The $5,000 reimbursement from the enterprise fund to the general fund is not reported as a transfer on the statement of activities. The effect of this transaction is to increase expenses under business-type activities and to decrease expenses under governmental activities.

W. College and University Accounting—Public (Governmental)—GASB 35

110. **(a)**   According to GASB 35, public colleges and universities that choose to report only business-type activities should present only the financial statements required for enterprise funds.

111. **(c)**   According to GASB 35, public colleges and universities that choose to report both governmental and business-type activities should report both government-wide and fund financial statements.

112. **(b)**   Both public and private colleges report tuition and fee income net of the amount provided for scholarships, for which no services are provided. On the other hand, scholarships provided in exchange for services are reported as an expense and are not deducted from revenues. As a result, the net tuition and fees would be the $20,000,000 less the $1,000,000 scholarships provided, not in exchange for services, or $19,000,000.

113. **(d)**   GASB Statement 35 provides that public colleges may choose to report as special-purpose entities engaged in business-type activities. GASB Statement 34 requires that special-purpose entities engaged only in business-type activities should prepare the statements required for enterprises funds, including a Statement of Revenues, Expenses, and Changes in Net Assets. One requirement for that statement is that an operating income figure must be displayed (answer b). GASB Statement 34 also indicates that contributions for plant and endowment purposes are not recorded as revenues but in separate categories; GASB Statement 35 illustrations show those items listed after revenues and expenses (answer c). GASB

Statement 35 specifically requires that state appropriations must be reported as nonoperating income (answer a). Since answers (a), (b), and (c) are correct, answer (d) is the choice.

OTHER OBJECTIVE ANSWERS AND ANSWER EXPLANATIONS

Problem 1

1. **($800,000)** The proceeds of the general obligation bonds are reported in the capital projects fund.

2. **($15,000)** $19,300 less the allowance of $4,300 = $15,000.

3. **($19,000)** The collectible taxes at 12/31/03 amount to $15,000. Of this amount $6,000 are collectible within sixty days of the end of the year. The amount collectible within sixty days of the end of the year are revenues of 2002 using the modified accrual basis of accounting. The other $9,000 that are collectible after sixty days of the year-end are considered deferred revenues at December 31, 2003. In addition to the deferred revenues from property taxes, deferred revenues of $10,000 are also reported from the state grant. Under modified accrual accounting, reimbursement grants are not reported as revenue until the year in which they are expended. For Jefferson, grant revenues will be reported in 2004 because this is the year that the state grant will be expended. The entry to record deferred revenues from property taxes is shown below.

Revenues	9,000	
Deferred revenues		9,000

4. **($10,000)** Fund balance reserved for encumbrances would be reported at $10,000, the sum of purchase orders that are outstanding at December 31, 2003. The purchase orders outstanding at 12/31/03 include $2,500 for supplies and $7,500 for equipment.

5. **($5,000)** Fund balance reserved for supplies would be reported at $5,000 at December 31, 2003. The entry to record the supplies is

Inventory of supplies	5,000	
Fund balance reserved for supplies inventory		5,000

6. **($16,500)** Unreserved fund balance at December 31, 2003, for the general fund is $16,500. This amount results from making the following closing entries:

Revenues control ($235,500 less $9,000 classified to deferred revenue)	226,500	
Expenditures control		160,000
Other financing uses control—transfers out		40,000
Encumbrances control		10,000
Fund balance—unreserved		16,500
Budgetary fund balance reserved for encumbrances	10,000	
Fund balance reserved for encumbrances		10,000

The sales taxes of $1,000 owed by the state to Jefferson at December 31, 2003, are not reportable as revenue in 2003 under the modified accrual basis of accounting because they are not available until March 2004.

7. **($800,000)** This is the same as the amount of cash in the capital projects fund.

8. **($0)** The bonds payable are not reported in the debt service fund until they mature and the debt service fund has the resource to pay them. However, the bonds payable are reported in the government-wide Statement of Net Assets.

9. **($0)** Unmatured interest payable is not reported in the debt service fund. Interest payable is not accrued when using modified accrual accounting.

10. **($0)** Equipment is not reported as an asset in the general fund. The modified accrual basis of accounting along with the financial resources measurement focus results in the acquisition of fixed assets being recorded as expenditures.

11. **($40,000)** The $40,000 transfer to the debt service fund is reported by the general fund as an other financing use on the Statement of Revenues, Expenditures, and Changes in Fund Balances.

12. **($201,700)** Property tax revenues are determined by taking $210,700 and subtracting $9,000, the amount not expected to be collected until after March 1, 2004.

13. **($160,000)** This is the amount reported in the trial balance for Jefferson's general fund.

14. **($800,000)** Jefferson's capital projects fund should report the proceeds of the general obligation bonds as other financing sources on the Statement of Revenues, Expenditures, and Changes in Fund Balances.

15. **($40,000)** Jefferson's debt service fund should report the $40,000 transfer from the general fund as other financing sources on the Statement of Revenues, Expenditures, and Changes in Fund Balances.

16. **($0)** The general fund does not depreciate fixed assets on governmental fund financial statements because governmental fund financial statements are prepared using a financial resources measurement focus and the modified accrual basis of accounting.

17. **($15,000)** This is the same amount that is reported on the balance sheet of the governmental funds.

18. **($1,000)** Sales taxes receivable would be reported at $1,000 on the government-wide Statement of Net Assets. The sales taxes owed to Jefferson at December 31, 2003, would be reported as follows:

Sales taxes receivable	1,000	
Revenues control		1,000

The above entry is made because the government-wide Statement of Net Assets is based on the economic resources measurement focus and accrual accounting.

19. **($10,000)** The government-wide Statement of Net Assets is prepared using the economic resources measurement focus and the accrual basis of accounting. The sixty day rule that applies to the recognition of property tax revenues for modified accrual accounting does not apply to accrual based financial statements. Property tax revenues under accrual accounting include the entire amount that was expected to be collected—$210,700. None of this amount should be deferred revenue at December 31, 2003. The state grant of $10,000 is not reported as revenue in 2003 under accrual accounting. Under GASB 34, reimbursement grants cannot be reported as revenue until the expenditure is recognized, due to GASB 33's classification as an eligibility requirement.

20. **($34,200)** The Statement of Net Assets reports fixed assets, net of accumulated depreciation. $38,000 less one-half year's depreciation for 2002 of $3,800, results in $34,200 being reported for equipment, net on the December 31, 2003 Statement of Net Assets.

21. **($34,200)** On the Statement of Net Assets, net assets invested in capital assets are reported at cost less accumulated depreciation less any debt that was incurred to purchase the fixed assets. In the case at hand, $38,000 less $3,800 of accumulated depreciation, or $34,200, is the amount reported as net assets invested in capital assets. This amount would be reduced for any related debt, but there is none in this case.

22. **($40,000)** Restricted net assets consist of the $800,000 of assets restricted for the construction of the addition to city hall less the bonds payable of $800,000 that are reported under long-term liabilities on the Statement of Net Assets. In addition, restricted net assets include the $40,000 in the debt service fund that is restricted for principal of the general obligation bonds. Restricted assets of $840,000 ($800,000 + $40,000) less the bonds payable of $800,000 equal restricted net assets of $40,000 at December 31, 2003.

23. **($8,000)** Interest payable is reported under current liabilities on the Statement of Net Assets because the statement is prepared using the accrual basis of accounting. The amount is determined in the following manner:

$$\$800,000 \times .06 \times 2/12 = \$8,000.$$

NOT-FOR-PROFIT ACCOUNTING

Nonprofit[1] organizations provide socially desirable services without the intention of realizing a profit. Nonprofit organizations are financed by user charges, contributions from donors and/or foundations, investment income, and government grants. The nature and extent of support depends upon the type of nonprofit organization.

As mentioned in the introduction to Module 38, nonprofit organizations are either in the private sector (nongovernmental) or in the public sector (governmental). Examples of private sector nonprofits would be private colleges (University of Chicago), private sector health care entities operated by religious or other non-profit organizations, voluntary health and welfare organizations, and various "other" nonprofits, such as performing arts companies. Examples of government nonprofits would be public colleges (Northern Illinois University), government hospitals, and government museums. Private sector nonprofit organizations have GAAP set primarily by the FASB; governmental nonprofit organizations have GAAP set primarily by the GASB.

In June of 1993, the FASB issued SFAS 116, *Accounting for Contributions Received and Contributions Made,* and SFAS 117, *Financial Statements of Not-for-Profit Organizations.* These standards are applicable to private sector not-for-profit organizations of all types. This module presents GAAP for private sector non-profits under SFAS 116 and 117. The AICPA has developed two *Audit Guides* that correspond and add to the new FASB principles: (1) Not-for-Profit Organizations, and (2) Health Care Organizations. The *Not-for-Profit Guide* applies only to private sector not-for-profits. The *Health Care Guide* applies to all health care entities, private for-profit, private not-for-profit, and governmental.

Governmental nonprofits are not permitted to follow SFAS 116 and 117. (The definition of a government is provided in the introductory section of Module 38.) As applied to colleges, health care entities, and other not-for-profit organizations, that guidance has been outlined through different pronouncements.

First, in November 1999, the GASB issued Statement 35, *Basic Financial Statements—and Management's Discussion and Analysis—for Public Colleges and Universities.* GASB 35 permits public colleges to report as special-purpose entities engaged in governmental or business-type activities, or both. Most four-year institutions are expected to report as special-purpose entities engaged only in business-type activities. Some community colleges may choose to report as special-purpose entities engaged in governmental activities due to the extent of state and local government tax support. The provisions of GASB 35 are outlined in Module 38.

Second, GASB 34 indicates that hospitals and other health care providers may be considered special-purpose entities that may be engaged in either governmental or business-type activities, or both. Most health care organizations will choose to report as special-purpose entities that are engaged in business-type activities. As a result, proprietary fund statements will be required for those health care entities. The AICPA Audit and Accounting Guide, *Health Care Organizations,* contains guidance for both private sector and governmental health care organizations; both are presented in this module.

Third, other governmental not-for-profit organizations (essentially governmental voluntary health and welfare and "other" not-for-profit organizations) also may be considered special-purpose entities that may be engaged in either governmental or business-type activities, or both. However, GASB 34 specifically permits these organizations that were using the "AICPA Not-for-Profit Model" upon adoption of GASB 34 to report as special-purpose entities engaged in business-type activities. These entities will present proprietary fund statements. The AICPA Audit and Accounting Guide, *Not-for-Profit Organizations,* applies only to private sector organizations and these principles are contained in this module; governmental not-for-profits are less significant and are not illustrated in this module.

The first section of this module presents the FASB and AICPA standards for all nongovernmental non-profits, including private sector colleges, universities, and health care entities. The second section presents standards that apply primarily to private colleges and universities. The third and fourth sections present standards for health care entities; first for private sector health care entities; next for governmental health care entities. Module 38 presents standards for public colleges and universities.

A. FASB and AICPA Standards for Private Sector Nonprofits

SFAS 116, *Accounting for Contributions Received and Contributions Made,* and SFAS 117, *Financial Statements of Not-for-Profit Organizations,* apply to private sector nonprofits subject to FASB guidance; they do not apply to governmental nonprofits subject to GASB guidance.

More recently, FASB issued Statement 124, *Accounting for Certain Investments Held by Not-for-Profit Organizations.* This statement requires fair value accounting for most equity and debt investments

---

[1] *The terms not-for-profit and nonprofit are used interchangeably here and in practice.*

by not-for-profit organizations and requires reporting of realized and unrealized gains and losses directly in the Statement of Activities.

Most recently, FASB issued Statement 136, *Transfers of Assets to a Not-for-Profit Organization or Charitable Trust That Raises or Holds Contributions for Others.* This statement provides guidance regarding proper reporting by foundations and similar not-for-profits when funds are raised for others, as described in 1.m. and n. below.

The FASB guidance is intended to eliminate the differences in accounting and reporting standards that existed previously between four types of not-for-profit organizations. While some differences exist, for example, in functional categories reported, private sector nonprofit colleges and universities, health care entities, voluntary health and welfare organizations, and "other" organizations follow the basic guidance in the FASB standards; some differences between health care entities and other private sector not-for-profits will be illustrated later. The section lists a number of basic requirements, illustrates financial statements, and presents a few journal entries as required by SFAS 116, 117, 124, and 136. All illustrations are for a general nongovernmental not-for-profit organization, but remember that the principles apply to all four types (colleges and universities, health care organizations, voluntary health and welfare organizations, and "other" not-for-profit organizations).

1. **Important Features of the FASB Guidance**

   a. The standards apply to **all** nongovernmental nonprofit organizations, except those that operate for the direct economic benefit of members (such as mutual insurance companies). General FASB standards, unless specifically prohibited by those standards or do not apply because of their nature (capital stock, etc.) or unless modified by these standards, are presumed to apply.

   b. Net assets are divided into three classes: unrestricted, temporarily restricted, and permanently restricted. Fund classifications are not reported, unless the information can be shown as subdivisions of the three major classes. To be restricted, resources must be restricted by donors or grantors; internally designated resources are unrestricted. Only contributed resources may be restricted.

   c. Permanently restricted resources include (1) certain assets, such as artwork, etc. that must be maintained or used in a certain way, and (2) endowments, which represent resources that must be invested permanently with income to be used for either restricted or unrestricted purposes, and (3) land, when that land must be held in perpetuity.

   d. Temporarily restricted resources include unexpended resources that are to be used for a particular purpose, at a time in the future, or are to be invested for a period of time (a term endowment). Temporarily restricted resources might also be used for the acquisition or receipt of a gift of plant and would represent the undepreciated amount. As the plant is depreciated, the amount depreciated would be reclassified from temporarily restricted net assets to unrestricted net assets and shown as a deduction from unrestricted revenues, gains, and other support on the statement of activities. Alternatively, plant may be initially recorded as unrestricted.

   e. Unrestricted resources include all other resources including unrestricted contributions, the net amount from providing services, unrestricted income from investments, etc. Resources are presumed to be unrestricted, unless evidence exists that donor-imposed restrictions exist. As mentioned above, undepreciated plant may be included as unrestricted or temporarily restricted.

   f. Statements required are (1) Statement of Financial Position, (2) Statement of Activities, and (3) Statement of Cash Flows. Certain note disclosures are also required and others recommended. In addition, voluntary health and welfare organizations are required to report a Statement of Functional Expenses that show expenses by function and by natural classifications.

   g. The Statement of Financial Position reports assets, liabilities, and net assets. Organization-wide totals must be provided for assets, liabilities and net assets, and net assets must be broken down between unrestricted, temporarily restricted, and permanently restricted.

   h. The Statement of Activities reports revenues, expenses, gains, losses, and reclassifications (between classes of net assets). Organization-wide totals must be provided. Separate revenues, expenses, gains, losses, and reclassifications for each class may or may not be reported, but the changes in net assets for each class must be reported.

   i. Revenues, expenses, gains, and losses are reported on the full accrual basis. A revenue is presumed to be unrestricted unless donor-imposed restrictions apply, either permanent or temporary. A presumption is made, in the absence of contrary information, that a given expense would use restricted resources first, rather than unrestricted resources. Revenues and expenses should be reported at gross amounts; gains and losses are often reported net. Investment gains and losses may be reported net.

j.   Unconditional contributions are to be recorded as assets (contributions receivable) and as revenues (contribution revenue). However, a donor-imposed **condition** causes a not-for-profit organization to not recognize either a receivable or a revenue. A donor-imposed condition specifies a future or uncertain event whose occurrence or failure to occur gives the promisor a right of return of the assets transferred or releases the promisor from its obligation to transfer the assets promised. For example, a not-for-profit organization receives a pledge from a donor that she will transfer $1,000,000 if matching funds can be raised within a year. The $1,000,000 would not be recognized as a revenue until the possibility of raising the matching funds is reasonably certain.

k.   Multiyear contributions receivable would be recorded at the present value of the future collections. Moneys to be collected in future years would be presumed to be temporarily restricted revenues (based on time restrictions) and then reclassified in the year of receipt. The difference between the previously recorded temporarily restricted revenue at present value amounts and the current value would be recorded as contribution revenue, not interest. **All** contributions are to be recorded at fair market value as of the date of the contribution.

l.   Organizations making the contributions, including businesses and other nonprofits, would recognize contribution expense using the same rules as followed by the receiving organization.

m.   Contributions are to be distinguished from exchange revenues. The *Not-for-Profit Guide* indicates criteria that indicate when an increase in net assets is a contribution and when it is an exchange revenue; the most important rule is that if nothing is given by the not-for-profit organization in exchange in a transaction, that transaction would be considered a contribution. Contributions are recognized as additions to any of the net asset classifications. Exchange revenues (tuition, membership dues, charges for services, etc.) are increases in unrestricted net assets and are recognized in accordance with GAAP as applied to business enterprises.

n.   SFAS 136 requires that when a not-for-profit organization (such as a foundation) is an **intermediary** or an **agent** for the transfer of assets to another not-for-profit organization, that intermediary or agent would not recognize a contribution. Unless the intermediary or agent not-for-profit organization is granted **variance power** to redirect the resources, or unless it is financially interrelated, the receipt of resources would be offset with the recognition of a liability to the recipient organization. If variance power exists, the recipient organization would recognize contribution revenue.

o.   SFAS 136 also requires that the recipient organization recognize a revenue when the intermediary or agent recognizes a liability. When the intermediary or agent and the beneficiary are **financially interrelated**, the intermediary or agent would recognize contribution revenue; the beneficiary would recognize its interest in the net assets of the intermediary or agent.

p.   Expenses are to be reported by function either in the statements or in the notes. The FASB does not prescribe functional classifications but does describe functions as program and supporting. Major program classifications should be shown. Supporting activities include management and general, fund raising, and membership development. Other classifications may be included, such as operating income, but are not required, except for health care entities. All expenses are reported as decreases in unrestricted net assets.

q.   Plant is recorded, as mentioned above, either as temporarily restricted or unrestricted, and depreciated. Depreciation is to be charged for exhaustible fixed assets.

r.   An entity may or may not capitalize "collections." "Collections" are works of art, historical treasures, and similar assets if those assets meet all of the following conditions:

    (1) They are held for public exhibition, education, or research in furtherance of public service rather than financial gain;

    (2) They are protected, kept encumbered, cared for, and preserved;

    (3) They are subject to an organizational policy that requires the proceeds from sales of collection items to be used to acquire other items for collections.

    If collections are not capitalized, revenues (contributions) would not be recognized for donated collections. Extensive note disclosure regarding accessions, disposals, etc. are required.

s.   Investments in all debt securities and investments in equity securities that have readily determinable fair values (except equity securities accounted for under the equity method and investments in consolidated subsidiaries) are to be reported at fair value in the Statements of Net Assets. Unlike SFAS 115 for business enterprises, all unrealized gains and losses are to be reflected in the Statement of Activities along with realized gains and losses, in the appropriate net asset class.

t.   Contributed services, when recognized, are recognized as both revenue and expense. However, contributed services should be recognized only when the services: (a) create or enhance nonfinancial assets, or (b) require specialized skills, are provided by individuals possessing those skills, and would typically be purchased if not provided by donation.

u.   All expenses are reported as unrestricted. Expenses using resources that are temporarily restricted, including depreciation of plant, would be matched by a reclassification of resources from temporarily restricted to unrestricted net assets.

v.   The "Reclassification" category of the Statement of Activities is unique. Sometimes "Reclassifications" are called "Net Assets Released from Restrictions." Reclassifications generally include (a) satisfaction of program restrictions (a purpose restriction by a donor), (b) satisfaction of equipment acquisition restrictions (depreciation of assets classified as temporarily restricted), (c) satisfaction of time restrictions (donor actual or implied restrictions as to when funds be used), and (d) expiration of term endowment.

w.   Cash Flow statements are required for nonprofit organizations. The three FASB categories (operating, investing, and financing) are to be used. As is true for business organizations, either the direct or indirect method may be used. The indirect method, or reconciliation schedule for the direct method, will reconcile the change in **total** net assets to the net cash used by operating activities. Restricted contributions for long term purposes (endowments, plant, future program purposes, etc.) are reported as financing activities.

x.   Note disclosures are required for all items required for generally accepted accounting principles that are relevant to nonprofit organizations. In addition, specific requirements of SFAS 117 include (a) policy disclosures related to choices related to restricted contributions received and expended in the same period, and to the recording of plant as temporarily restricted or unrestricted, and (b) more detailed information regarding the nature of temporarily and permanently restricted resources.

y.   The FASB specifically encourages note disclosures on (a) detail of the reclassification, (b) detail of investments and (c) breakdown of expenses by function and natural classifications (except for Voluntary Health and Welfare Organizations, which must include this information in a Statement of Functional Expenses).

z.   The *Not-for-Profit Guide* provides guidance for **split-interest agreements**, such as charitable lead trusts and charitable remainder trusts. Split-interest agreements represent arrangements whereby both a donor (or beneficiary) and a not-for-profit organization receive benefits, often at different times in a multiyear arrangement. Specific rules exist for each type of split-interest agreement. The general rule is that the not-for-profit will record revenues in an amount equal to the present value of anticipated receipts.

aa. FASB requires that fund-raising expenses be reported either on the face of the financial statements or in the notes. AICPA Statement of Position 98-2 indicates that when an activity, such as a mailing, might involve fund-raising and either program or management and general activities, it is presumed to be fund-raising unless three criteria exist. Those criteria are

(1) **Purpose.** The activity has more than one purpose, as evidenced by whether compensation or fees for performing the activity are based strictly on the amount raised or on the performance of some program and/or management and general activity.

(2) **Audience.** If the audience is selected on the basis of its likelihood to contribute to the not-for-profit, this criterion is not met.

(3) **Content.** In order for this criterion to be met, the mailing or event must include a call to action other than raising money. For example, a mailing from the American Cancer Society might call for recipients to have regular check-ups, to exercise, to eat the right kinds of food, etc.

2. **Illustrative Financial Statements**

The FASB requires three financial statements for nongovernmental, not-for-profit organizations, including (1) Statement of Financial Position, (2) Statement of Activities, and (3) Statement of Cash

Flows. Voluntary health and welfare organizations (such as the American Red Cross, a mental health association, or a Big Brothers/Big Sisters organization) are required to prepare a fourth statement, a Statement of Functional Expenses. The first three of these statements are described and illustrated below.

a.   **Statement of Financial Position.** A Balance Sheet or Statement of Financial Position must show total assets, total liabilities, and total net assets. Net assets must be broken down between those that are unrestricted, temporarily restricted, and permanently restricted. Assets and liabilities may be classified or reported in order of liquidity and payment date. Assets restricted for long-term purposes must be reported separately from those that are not. The comparative format illustrated is optional; entities may report only balances for one year. Contributions receivable are to be reported at the present value of future receipts. Investments in securities with determinable fair values are to be reported at fair value. The following reflects one of the permissible formats in SFAS 117:

Not-for-Profit Organization
STATEMENTS OF FINANCIAL POSITION
June 30, 20X1 and 20X0
(in thousands)

	20X1	*20X0*
Assets		
Cash and cash equivalents	$ 75	$ 460
Accounts and interest receivable	2,130	1,670
Inventories and prepaid expenses	610	1,000
Contributions receivable	3,025	2,700
Short-term investments	1,400	1,000
Assets restricted to investment		
in land, buildings, and equipment	5,210	4,560
Land, buildings, and equipment	61,700	63,590
Long-term investments	218,070	203,500
Total assets	$292,220	$278,480
Liabilities and net assets		
Accounts payable	$ 2,570	$ 1,050
Refundable advance		650
Grants payable	875	1,300
Notes payable		1,140
Annuity obligations	1,685	1,700
Long-term debt	5,500	6,500
Total liabilities	10,630	12,340
	20X1	*20X0*
Net assets		
Unrestricted	115,228	103,670
Temporarily restricted	24,342	25,470
Permanently restricted	142,020	137,000
Total net assets	281,590	266,140
Total liabilities and net assets	$292,220	$278,480

Source: *SFAS 117, p.56*

b.   **Statement of Activities.** Note the following from the example Statement of Activities:

(1) Contributions, income on long-term investments, and net unrealized and realized gains on long-term investments may increase unrestricted, temporarily restricted, and permanently restricted net assets. All of these revenue sources increase unrestricted net assets unless restricted by donors.

(2) Fees increase unrestricted net assets. All exchange revenues increase unrestricted net assets. Exchange revenues include admissions charges, fees, and membership dues.

(3) Net unrealized gains are shown together with realized gains and investments. FASB prohibits displaying net unrealized and realized gains separately.

(4) All expenses decrease unrestricted net assets. (Losses, such as the actuarial loss, may decrease restricted net assets.)

(5) At some point net assets are released from restrictions (reclassified) from temporarily restricted to unrestricted net assets. This might be for satisfaction of program restrictions, satisfaction of equipment acquisition restrictions, expiration of time restrictions, or expiration of

term endowments. Note that when net assets are released from restrictions, temporarily restricted net assets decrease and unrestricted net assets increase.

(6) Expenses are broken down between programs (A, B, C) and supporting (management and general, fund-raising). While the FASB does not require these functional breakdowns, the FASB does have two requirements.

(a) Expenses must be reported by function in the notes if not in this statement, and
(b) Fund-raising expenses must be disclosed in the notes, if not in this statement.

The FASB permits other formats. For example, some entities prepare two statements.

(a) Statement of Revenues, Expenses, and Changes in Unrestricted Net Assets, and
(b) Statement of Changes in Net Assets.

Regardless of the format used, the change in net assets must be reported, by net asset class and in total.

Not-for-Profit Organization
STATEMENT OF ACTIVITIES
Year Ended June 30, 20X1
(in thousands)

	Unrestricted	Temporarily restricted	Permanently restricted	Total
Revenues, gains, and other support:				
Contributions	$ 8,640	$ 8,110	$ 280	$ 17,030
Fees	5,400			5,400
Income on long-term investments	5,600	2,580	120	8,300
Other investment income	850			850
Net unrealized and realized gains on long-term investments	8,228	2,952	4,620	15,800
Other	150			150
Net assets released from restrictions:				
Satisfaction of program restrictions	11,990	(11,990)		
Satisfaction of equipment acquisition restrictions	1,500	(1,500)		
Expiration of time restrictions	1,250	(1,250)		
Total revenues, gains, and other support	43,608	(1,098)	5,020	47,530
Expenses and losses:				
Program A	13,100			13,100
Program B	8,540			8,540
Program C	5,760			5,760
Management and general	2,420			2,420
Fund raising	2,150			2,150
Total expenses	31,970			31,970
Fire loss	80			80
Actuarial loss on annuity obligations		30		30
Total expenses and losses	32,050	30		32,080
Change in net assets	11,558	(1,128)	5,020	15,450
Net assets at beginning of year	103,670	25,470	137,000	266,140
Net assets at end of year	$115,228	$24,342	$142,020	$281,590

Source: *SFAS 117, p.59.*

c. **Statement of Cash Flows.** In general, the FASB rules for cash flow statements, required by FASB Statement 95, apply to not-for-profit organizations. Note that GASB rules, illustrated in Module 38, do not apply. The only major difference is that cash receipts for contributions restricted for long-term purposes are classified as financing activities.

Not-for-Profit Organization
STATEMENT OF CASH FLOWS
Year Ended June 30, 20X1
(in thousands)

Cash flows from operating activities:	
Cash received from service recipients	$ 5,220
Cash received from contributors	8,030
Cash collected on contributions receivable	2,615
Interest and dividends received	8,570
Miscellaneous receipts	150
Interest paid	(382)
Cash paid to employees and suppliers	(23,808)
Grants paid	(425)
Net cash used by operating activities	(30)
Cash flows from investing activities:	
Insurance proceeds from fire loss on building	250
Purchase of equipment	(1,500)
Proceeds from sale of investments	76,100
Purchase of investments	(74,900)
Net cash used by investing activities	(50)
Cash flows from financing activities:	
Proceeds from contributions restricted for:	
Investment in endowment	200
Investment in term endowment	70
Investment in plant	1,210
Investment subject to annuity agreements	200
	1,680
Other financing activities:	
Interest and dividends restricted for reinvestment	300
Payments of annuity obligations	(145)
Payments on notes payable	(1,140)
Payments on long-term debt	(1,000)
	(1,985)
Net cash used by financing activities	(305)
Net decrease in cash and cash equivalents	(385)
Cash and cash equivalents at beginning of year	460
Cash and cash equivalents at end of year	$ 75
Reconciliation of change in net assets to net cash used by operating activities:	
Change in net assets	$ 15,450
Adjustments to reconcile change in net assets to net cash used by operating activities:	
Depreciation	3,200
Fire loss	80
Actuarial loss on annuity obligations	30
Increase in accounts and interest receivable	(460)
Decrease in inventories and prepaid expenses	390
Increase in contributions receivable	(325)
Increase in accounts payable	1,520
Decrease in refundable advance	(650)
Decrease in grants payable	(425)
Contributions restricted for long-term investment	(2,740)
Interest and dividends restricted for long-term investment	(300)
Net unrealized and realized gains on long-term investments	(15,800)
Net cash used by operating activities	$ (30)
Supplemental data for noncash investing and financing activities:	
Gifts of equipment	$140
Gift of paid-up life insurance, cash surrender value	$80

Source: *SFAS 117, pp.64-65.*

3. Illustrative Transactions

a. Unrestricted revenues and expenses.

Under FASB guidance, full accrual accounting is used. A look at the Statement of Activities indicates that revenues might include contributions, fees, investment income, and realized and unrealized gains on investments. Expenses must be reported as unrestricted and reported by function, either in the statements or in the notes.

Assume the following unrestricted revenues:

Cash	1,000,000	
Contributions Receivable	200,000	
Accounts Receivable	100,000	
Interest Receivable	50,000	
Contributions—Unrestricted		700,000
Fees—Unrestricted		300,000
Income on Long-Term Investments—Unrestricted		350,000

Income earned from investments can be unrestricted, temporarily restricted, or permanently restricted depending on the wishes of the donor. If the donor does not specify, the investment income is unrestricted, even if the investment principal itself is permanently restricted.

Assume the following expenses, reported by function:

Program A Expense	400,000	
Program B Expense	300,000	
Program C Expense	200,000	
Management and General Expense	100,000	
Fund Raising Expense	200,000	
Cash		900,000
Accounts Payable		300,000

b. Purpose restrictions—temporarily restricted resources

Temporarily restricted resources are generally restricted by purpose, by time, and for the acquisition of plant. Assume that in 20X0 a donor gives $100,000 in cash for cancer research and that the funds are expended in 20X1. In 20X0, the following entry would be made:

Cash	100,000	
Contributions—Temporarily Restricted		100,000

At the end of 20X0 the $100,000 would be a part of the net assets of the temporarily restricted net asset class. In 20X1, the following entries would be made, assuming the funds are expended for cancer research.

Program A Expense (Research)	100,000	
Cash		100,000
Reclassifications from Temporarily Restricted Net Assets—		
Satisfaction of Program Restrictions	100,000	
Reclassifications to Unrestricted Net Assets—Satisfaction of		
Program Restrictions		100,000

Note that the assets are released from restriction by the expense, by conducting the research. Looking at the example statement of activities, the $100,000 would be included as a part of the $11,990,000 in program reclassifications.

c. Time restrictions—temporarily restricted resources

If a donor makes a contribution and indicates that the contribution should be used in a future period, that contribution would be recorded as a revenue in the temporarily restricted net asset class and then transferred to the unrestricted net asset class in the time period specified by the donor. In the absence of other information, if a pledge is made, the schedule of anticipated receipts would determine when the net assets are reclassified. Assume a $100,000 pledge in late 20X0, intended to be used by the nonprofit organization in 20X1; the entry in 20X0 would be

Pledges receivable	100,000	
Contributions—Temporarily Restricted		100,000

At the end of 20X0, the $100,000 would be reflected in the net assets of the temporarily restricted in class. In 20X1, the following entries would be made:

Cash	100,000	
Pledges receivable		100,000
Reclassifications from Temporarily Restricted Net Assets—		
Satisfaction of Time Restrictions	100,000	
Reclassifications to Unrestricted Net Assets—Satisfaction of		
Time Restrictions		100,000

The $100,000 above would be a part of the $1,500,000 in reclassifications for satisfaction of time restrictions in the statement of activities. Note that time, not an expense, determines when the asset is released from restrictions. In the special case of multiyear pledges, the present value of the future payments should be recorded as a revenue in the year of the pledge. In future years, the increase in the present value, due to the passage of time, is to be recorded as contribution revenue, not interest.

Finally, note that a time restriction might be explicit or implicit. An explicit time restriction would occur when a donor states specifically that the funds are for a certain year (this might be printed on pledge cards). An implicit time restriction reflects the provision that cash must be received from a donor during an accounting period, or the pledge will be assumed to carry a time restriction. The idea is that, if a donor wished a nonprofit to spend the money this year, the donor would have contributed the cash.

d. Plant acquisition restrictions—temporarily restricted resources

Sometimes donors give moneys restricted for the acquisition of plant, often in connection with a fund drive. The resources, whether in the form of pledges, cash, or investments, would be held in the temporarily restricted net asset class until expended. When expended, the nonprofit organization has a choice of two options: (1) reclassify the resources to the unrestricted class and record the entire plant as unrestricted, or (2) record the plant as temporarily restricted and reclassify to unrestricted in accordance with the depreciation schedule. Under the first option, assume that a donor gives $50,000 to a nonprofit organization in 20X0 for the purchase of equipment. The equipment is purchased in 20X1. The following entry would be made in the temporarily restricted class in 20X0:

Cash	50,000	
Contributions		50,000

In 20X1, the following entries would be made:

Equipment	50,000	
Cash		50,000
Reclassifications from Temporarily Restricted Net Assets—		
Satisfaction of Equipment Acquisition Restrictions	50,000	
Reclassification to Unrestricted Net Assets—Satisfaction of		
Equipment Acquisition Restrictions		50,000

The equipment would then be depreciated as a charge to expense in the unrestricted class as would be normal in business accounting. Remember that depreciation may be allocated to functional categories. Assume a ten-year life and that the equipment was purchased at the beginning of the year and that the equipment was used solely for Program A.

Program A Expense	5,000	
Accumulated Depreciation—Equipment		5,000

The above alternative has normally been used in the CPA Examination. When this is the case, the problem often states that, "the Not-for-Profit Organization implies no restriction on the acquisition of fixed assets."

The second alternative is to record the equipment as an increase in temporarily restricted net assets and reclassify it over time. The entries are illustrated below. Assume the contribution was received but unexpended in 20X0.

Cash	50,000	
Contributions—Temporarily Restricted		50,000

Assume the equipment was acquired early in 20X1.

Equipment	50,000	
Cash		50,000

Note that the $50,000 remains in temporarily restricted net assets. At the end of 20X1, the depreciation entry is made, and $5,000 is reclassified.

Program A Expense	5,000	
Accumulated Depreciation—Equipment		5,000
Reclassification from Temporarily Restricted Net Assets—		
Satisfaction of Equipment Acquisition Restrictions	5,000	
Reclassification to Unrestricted Net Assets—Satisfaction of		
Equipment Acquisition Restrictions		5,000

Note that, using the first alternative, at the end of 20X1, the net asset balance of $45,000 would be in the unrestricted net asset class; in the second alternative, the $45,000 net asset balance would be in the temporarily restricted net asset class.

e. Permanently restricted resources

Resources in the permanently restricted class are held permanently. An example would be an endowment, where a donor makes a contribution with the instructions that the amount be permanently invested. The income might be unrestricted or restricted for a particular activity or program. Assume that in 20X1 a donor gave $100,000 for the purpose of creating an endowment. An entry would be made in the permanently restricted class (this would be part of the $280,000 shown in the Statement of Activities).

Cash	100,000	
Contributions—Permanently Restricted		100,000

Note that revenues can be recorded in any of the three net asset classes but that expenses are recorded only in the unrestricted class. Note also that the expiration of restrictions is recorded by reclassifications.

B. College and University Accounting—Private Sector Institutions

Private colleges and universities are subject to the same guidance as other not-for-profit organizations that are included under the *Not-for-Profit Guide*. However, a few comments that specifically impact colleges and universities are in order.

1. Student tuition and fees are reported net of those scholarships and fellowships that are provided not in return for compensation. For example, a scholarship provided by an institution based on grades, entering ACT or SAT, etc., would be debited to a revenue deduction account.

Cash	8,000	
Revenue Deduction—Student Scholarships	2,000	
Revenue—Student Tuition and Fees		10,000

2. Student graduate assistantships and other amounts given as tuition remissions (for example for full-time employees) that are given in return for services provided to the institution are charged as expenses, to the department and function where the services are provided. For example, assume the services were provided to the Biology Department.

Cash	8,000	
Expense—Instruction (Biology Department)	2,000	
Revenue—Student Tuition and Fees		10,000

3. The AICPA *Not-for-Profit Guide* specifically states that operation and maintenance of physical plant is not to be reported as a functional expense. Those costs, including depreciation, are to be allocated to other functions.

4. The *Not-for-Profit Guide* does not include examples of financial statements for colleges and universities, or other not-for-profit organizations. The illustrative statement of activities for an educational institution is taken from the *Financial Accounting and Reporting Manual for Higher Education* published by the National Association of College and University Business Officers. Many other formats are possible, as long as the changes in net assets are shown separately for unrestricted, temporarily restricted, and permanently restricted net assets. Note that all expenses are reported as decreases in unrestricted net assets; losses may be reported as decreases in any of the net asset classes.

Educational Institution
ILLUSTRATIVE STATEMENT OF ACTIVITIES
Multicolumn Format

	Unrestricted	Temporarily Restricted	Permanently Restricted	Total
Revenues and gains:				
Tuition and fees	$xxx	--	--	$xxx
Contributions	xxx	$xxx	$xxx	xxx
Contracts and other exchange transactions	xxx	--	--	xxx
Investment income on life income and annuity agreements	--	xxx	--	xxx
Investment income on endowment	xxx	xxx	xxx	xxx
Other investment income	xxx	xxx	xxx	xxx
Net realized gains on endowment	xxx	xxx	xxx	xxx
Net realized gains on other investments	xxx	xxx	xxx	xxx
Sales and services of auxiliary enterprises	xxx	--	--	xxx
Total revenues and gains	xxx	xxx	xxx	xxx
Net assets released from restrictions	xxx	(xxx)	--	--
Total revenues and gains and other support	xxx	xxx	xxx	xxx
Expenses and losses:				
Educational and general:				
Instruction	xxx	--	--	xxx
Research	xxx	--	--	xxx
Public service	xxx	--	--	xxx
Academic support	xxx	--	--	xxx
Student services	xxx	--	--	xxx
Institutional support	xxx	--	--	xxx
Total educational and general expenses	xxx	--	--	xxx
Auxiliary enterprises	xxx	--	--	xxx
Total expenses	xxx	--	--	xxx
Fire loss	xxx	--	--	xxx
Payments to life income beneficiaries	--	xxx	--	xxx
Actuarial loss on annuity obligations	xxx	--	--	xxx
Total expenses and losses	xxx	--	--	xxx
Increase (decrease) in net assets	xxx	xxx	xxx	xxx
Net assets at beginning of year	xxx	xxx	xxx	xxx
Net assets at end of year	$xxx	$xxx	$xxx	$xxx

Source: *National Association of College and University Business Officers,* **Financial Accounting and Reporting Manual for Higher Education**, *Chapter 500, as modified with the exclusion of Operation and Maintenance of Physical Plant and Scholarships and Fellowships as functional expenses.*

C. Health Care Organization Accounting—Private Sector

The AICPA has issued an AICPA Audit and Accounting Guide, *Health Care Organizations*. This *Guide* applies both to private sector and governmental health care organizations; separate illustrative statements are presented for each. This section of the module presents private sector health care principles, first by indicating the unique features (beyond part A of this module) that apply and second by presenting illustrative statements. A few of the major features are as follows:

1. Requirements of the *Guide* apply to clinics, medical group practices, individual practice associations, individual practitioners, emergency care facilities, laboratories, surgery centers, other ambulatory care organizations, continuing care retirement communities, health maintenance organizations, home health agencies, hospitals, nursing homes, and rehabilitation centers. Sometimes, a fine line is drawn between those organizations that are considered health care entities and those that are considered voluntary health and welfare organizations, which are not covered by this *Guide*. The distinction is made by the source of revenues, not by the services provided. A nonprofit organization providing health care service in return for payment (an exchange transaction) by the recipient of the service, by a third-party payor, or a government program would be considered a health care organization. A nonprofit organization providing health care service funded primarily by voluntary contributions (from persons or organizations not receiving the service) would be considered a voluntary health and welfare organization.

2. Health care organizations may be not-for-profit, investor owned, or governmental. When possible, accounting and reporting for all types should be similar.

3. Financial statements include a balance sheet, a statement of operations, a statement of changes in net assets, a cash flow statement, and notes to the financial statements.

4. The statement of operations should include a performance indicator, such as operating income, revenues over expenses, etc. The *Guide* specifically indicates that the following must be reported separately from (underneath) that performance indicator (this is a partial list):

    a. Equity transfers involving other entities that control the reporting entity, are controlled by the reporting entity, or are under the common control of the reporting entity.
    b. Receipt of restricted contributions.
    c. Contributions of (and assets released from donor restrictions related to) long-lived assets.
    d. Unrealized gains and losses on investments not restricted by donors or by law, except for those investments classified as trading securities.
    e. Investment returns restricted by donors or by law.
    f. Other items that are required by GAAP to be reported separately (such as extraordinary items, the effect of discontinued operations, accounting changes).

5. Note disclosure must indicate the policies adopted by the entity to determine what is and what is not included in the performance indicator.

6. Patient service revenue is to be reported on the accrual basis net of adjustments for contractual and other adjustments in the operating statement. Provisions recognizing contractual adjustments and other adjustments (for example, hospital employee discounts) are deducted from gross patient revenue to determine **net patient** revenue. Significant revenue under capitation agreements (revenues from third party payors based on number of employees to be covered, etc. instead of services performed) is to be reported separately. Note disclosure should indicate the methods of revenue recognition and description of the types and amounts of contractual adjustments.

7. Patient service revenue does not include charity care. Management's policy for providing charity care and the level of charity care provided should be disclosed in the notes.

8. "Other revenues, gains, and losses" (included in operative revenues) include items such as

    a. Investment income
    b. Fees from educational programs
    c. Proceeds from sale of cafeteria meals
    d. Proceeds from gift shop, parking lot revenue, etc.

9. As is true for other not-for-profit organizations, contributions restricted to long-term purposes (plant acquisition, endowment, term endowment, etc.) would not be reported in the Statement of Operations (as unrestricted revenue) but would be reported in the Statement of Changes in Net Assets as a revenue increasing temporarily restricted or permanently restricted net assets, as appropriate.

10. Expenses are decreases in unrestricted net assets. Expenses may be reported by either natural (salaries, supplies, etc.) or functional classification. Not-for-profit health care entities must disclose expenses in the notes by function if functional classification is not presented on the operating statement. Functional classifications should be based on full cost allocations. Unlike organizations subject to the *Not-for-Profit Guide,* health care organizations may report depreciation, interest, and bad debt expense along with functional categories.

11. Health care organizations, except for continuing care retirement communities, are to present a classified balance sheet, with current assets and current liabilities shown separately. Continuing care retirement communities may sequence assets in terms of nearness to cash and liabilities in accordance with the maturity date.

Two statements are presented for a private sector not-for-profit hospital, both taken from the *Guide.* The statement of operations is presented with one line shown for "excess of revenues over expenses." This is the performance indicator. Note the separation of items above and below that line. Also note the presentation separately for depreciation, interest, and provision for bad debts. In addition, note that the net assets released from restrictions includes separate amounts for those net assets released for operations and those released for other items. The statement of changes in net assets presents the other changes required by SFAS 116 and 117.

Sample Not-for-Profit Hospital
STATEMENTS OF OPERATIONS
Years Ended December 31, 20X7 and 20X6
(in thousands)

	20X7	20X6
Unrestricted revenues, gains and other support:		
Net patient service revenue	$85,156	$78,942
Premium revenue	11,150	10,950
Other revenue	2,601	5,212
Net assets released from restrictions used for operations	300	--
Total revenues, gains and other support	99,207	95,104
Expenses:		
Operating expenses	88,521	80,585
Depreciation and amortization	4,782	4,280
Interest	1,752	1,825
Provision for bad debts	1,000	1,300
Other	2,000	1,300
Total expenses	98,055	89,290
Operating income	1,152	5,814
Other income:		
Investment income	3,900	3,025
Excess of revenues over expenses	5,052	8,839
Change in net unrealized gains and losses on other than trading securities	300	375
Net assets released from restrictions used for purchase of property and equipment	200	
Change in interest in net assets of Sample Hospital Foundation	283	536
Transfers to parent	(688)	(3,051)
Increase in unrestricted net assets, before extraordinary item	5,147	6,699
Extraordinary loss from extinguishment of debt	(500)	--
Increase in unrestricted net assets	$ 4,647	$ 6,699

See accompanying notes to financial statements.

Source: AICPA Audit and Accounting Guide, **Health Care Organizations**, 2001, p. 161.

Sample Not-for-Profit Hospital
STATEMENTS OF CHANGES IN NET ASSETS
Years Ended December 31, 20X7 and 20X6
(in thousands)

	20X7	20X6
Unrestricted net assets:		
Excess of revenues over expenses	$ 5,052	$ 8,839
Net unrealized gains on investments, other than trading securities	300	375
Change in interest in net assets of Sample Hospital Foundation	283	536
Transfers to parent	(688)	(3,051)
Net assets released from restrictions used for purchase of property and equipment	200	--
Increase in unrestricted net assets before extraordinary item	5,147	6,699
Extraordinary loss from extinguishment of debt	(500)	--
Increase in unrestricted net assets	4,647	6,699
Temporarily restricted net assets:		
Contributions for charity care	140	996
Net realized and unrealized gains on investments	5	8
Net assets released from restrictions	(500)	--
Increase (decrease) in temporarily restricted net assets	(355)	1,004
Permanently restricted net assets:		
Contributions for endowment funds	50	411
Net realized and unrealized gains on investments	5	2
Increase in permanently restricted net assets	55	413
Increase in net assets	4,347	8,116
Net assets, beginning of year	72,202	64,086
Net assets, end of year	$76,549	$72,202

See accompanying notes to financial statements.

Source: *AICPA Audit and Accounting Guide,* **Health Care Organizations**, *2001, p.163.*

D. Health Care Organization Accounting—Governmental

Governmental health care organizations, as mentioned earlier, are not allowed to use the principles established in SFAS 116 and 117 for not-for-profit organizations. The AICPA *Health Care Guide*, however, attempts to present accounting and reporting principles allowed by the GASB in as close a fashion as possible to private sector health care entities. A few major observations should be noted.

1. Governmental health care organizations are permitted by GASB 34 to report as special-purpose entities engaged in governmental or business-type activities, or both. Most will choose to report as special-purpose entities engaged in business-type activities.

2. Governmental health care organizations reporting as special-purpose entities engaged in business-type activities will prepare the statements required for proprietary funds. These are the (1) Balance Sheets, (2) Statement of Revenues, Expenses, and Changes in Net Assets, and (3) Statement of Cash Flows

3. GASB principles must be followed in the separate reports of governmental health care organizations. For example, net assets are to be categorized as (a) invested in capital assets, net of related debt; (b) restricted, and (c) unrestricted. The GASB cash flow format should be used. Refer to the proprietary fund example statements in Module 38.

4. To the extent possible, AICPA *Health Care Guide* principles should also be followed. For example, the items listed above in Section C.4. should be reported below the performance indicator, net patient revenue should be calculated in the same manner as described in C.6. above and should not include charity care cases (see above).

5. The AICPA has not, as of the date of this writing, issued a revision to the *Health Care Guide* to incorporate the provisions of GASB 34.

MULTIPLE-CHOICE QUESTIONS (1-83)

1. A statement of functional expenses is required for which one of the following private nonprofit organizations?
a. Colleges.
b. Hospitals.
c. Voluntary health and welfare organizations.
d. Performing arts organizations.

2. The statement of financial position (balance sheet) for Founders Library, a private nonprofit organization, should report separate dollar amounts for the library's net assets according to which of the following classifications?
a. Unrestricted and permanently restricted.
b. Temporarily restricted and permanently restricted.
c. Unrestricted and temporarily restricted.
d. Unrestricted, temporarily restricted, and permanently restricted.

3. Chicago Museum, a private nonprofit organization, has both regular and term endowments. On the museum's statement of financial position (balance sheet), how should the net assets of each type of endowment be reported?

	Term endowments	Regular endowments
a.	Temporarily restricted	Permanently restricted
b.	Permanently restricted	Permanently restricted
c.	Unrestricted	Temporarily restricted
d.	Temporarily restricted	Temporarily restricted

4. Kerry College, a private not-for-profit college, received $25,000 from Ms. Mary Smith on April 30, 2003. Ms. Smith stipulated that her contribution be used to support faculty research during the fiscal year beginning on July 1, 2003. On July 15, 2003, administrators of Kerry awarded research grants totaling $25,000 to several faculty in accordance with the wishes of Ms. Smith. For the year ended June 30, 2003, Kerry College should report the $25,000 contribution as
a. Temporarily restricted revenues on the statement of activities.
b. Unrestricted revenue on the statement of activities.
c. Temporarily restricted deferred revenue on the statement of activities.
d. An increase in fund balance on the statement of financial position.

5. Good Hope, a private not-for-profit voluntary health and welfare organization, received a cash donation of $500,000 from Mr. Charles Peobody on November 15, 2003. Mr. Peobody directed that his donation be used to acquire equipment for the organization. Good Hope used the donation to acquire equipment costing $500,000 in January of 2004. For the year ended December 31, 2003, Good Hope should report the $500,000 contribution on its
a. Statement of activities as unrestricted revenue.
b. Statement of financial position as temporarily restricted deferred revenue.
c. Statement of financial position as unrestricted deferred revenue.
d. Statement of activities as temporarily restricted revenue.

6. On the statement of activities for a private not-for-profit performing arts center, expenses should be deducted from

I. Unrestricted revenues.
II. Temporarily restricted revenues.
III. Permanently restricted revenues.

a. I, II, and III.
b. Both I and II.
c. I only.
d. II only.

7. Albert University, a private not-for-profit university, had the following cash inflows during the year ended June 30, 2003:

I. $500,000 from students for tuition.
II. $300,000 from a donor who stipulated that the money be invested indefinitely.
III. $100,000 from a donor who stipulated that the money be spent in accordance with the wishes of Albert's governing board.

On Albert University's statement of cash flows for the year ended June 30, 2003, what amount of these cash flows should be reported as operating activities?
a. $900,000
b. $400,000
c. $800,000
d. $600,000

8. Gamma Pi, a private nonprofit fraternal organization, should prepare a statement of financial position and which of the following financial statements?

I. Statement of activities.
II. Statement of changes in fund balances.
III. Statement of cash flows.

a. I, II, and III.
b. III only.
c. II and III.
d. I and III.

9. Save the Planet, a private nonprofit research organization, received a $500,000 contribution from Ms. Susan Clark. Ms. Clark stipulated that her donation be used to purchase new computer equipment for Save the Planet's research staff. The contribution was received in August of 2003, and the computers were acquired in January of 2004. For the year ended December 31, 2003, the $500,000 contribution should be reported by Save the Planet on its
a. Statement of activities as unrestricted revenue.
b. Statement of activities as deferred revenue.
c. Statement of activities as temporarily restricted revenue.
d. Statement of financial position as deferred revenue.

10. United Ways, a private not-for-profit voluntary health and welfare organization, received a contribution of $10,000 from a donor in 2003. The donor did not specify any use restrictions on the contribution; however, the donor specified that the donation should not be used until 2004. The governing board of United Ways spent the contribution in 2004 for fund-raising expenses. For the year ended December 31, 2003, United Ways should report the contribution on its
a. Statement of financial position as deferred revenue.
b. Statement of activities as unrestricted revenue.
c. Statement of financial position as an increase in fund balance.
d. Statement of activities as temporarily restricted revenue.

11. The statement of cash flows for a private not-for-profit hospital should report cash flows according to which of the following classifications?

I. Operating activities.
II. Investing activities.
III. Financing activities.

    a. I, II, and III.
    b. II and III.
    c. I only.
    d. I and III.

12. Pharm, a nongovernmental not-for-profit organization, is preparing its year-end financial statements. Which of the following statements is required?

    a. Statement of changes in financial position.
    b. Statement of cash flows.
    c. Statement of changes in fund balance.
    d. Statement of revenue, expenses and changes in fund balance.

13. Stanton College, a not-for-profit organization, received a building with no donor stipulations as to its use. Stanton does not have an accounting policy implying a time restriction on donated assets. What type of net assets should be increased when the building is received?

I. Unrestricted.
II. Temporarily restricted.
III. Permanently restricted.

    a. I only.
    b. II only.
    c. III only.
    d. II or III.

14. Sea Lion Park, a private not-for-profit zoological society, received contributions restricted for research totaling $50,000 in 2003. None of the contributions were spent on research in 2003. In 2004, $35,000 of the contributions were used to support the research activities of the society. The net effect on the statement of activities for the year ended December 31, 2004, for Sea Lion Park would be a

    a. $15,000 increase in temporarily restricted net assets.
    b. $35,000 decrease in temporarily restricted net assets.
    c. $35,000 increase in unrestricted net assets.
    d. $35,000 decrease in unrestricted net assets.

15. Clara Hospital, a private not-for-profit hospital, earned $250,000 of gift shop revenues and spent $50,000 on research during the year ended December 31, 2003. The $50,000 spent on research was part of a $75,000 contribution received during December of 2002 from a donor who stipulated that the donation be used for medical research. Assume none of the gift shop revenues were spent in 2003. For the year ended December 31, 2003, what was the increase in unrestricted net assets from the events occurring during 2003?

    a. $300,000
    b. $200,000
    c. $250,000
    d. $275,000

16. Which of the following transactions of a private not-for-profit voluntary health and welfare organization would increase temporarily restricted net assets on the statement of activities for the year ended June 30, 2003?

I. Received a contribution of $10,000 from a donor on May 15, 2003, who stipulated that the donation not be spent until August of 2003.
II. Spent $25,000 for fund-raising on June 20, 2003. The amount expended came from a $25,000 contribution on March 12, 2003. The donor stipulated that the contribution be used for fund-raising activities.

    a. Both I and II.
    b. Neither I nor II.
    c. I only.
    d. II only.

17. Catherine College, a private not-for-profit college, received the following contributions during 2003:

I. $5,000,000 from alumni for construction of a new wing on the science building to be constructed in 2003.
II. $1,000,000 from a donor who stipulated that the contribution be invested indefinitely and that the earnings be used for scholarships. As of December 31, 2003, earnings from investments amounted to $50,000.

For the year ended December 31, 2003, what amount of these contributions should be reported as temporarily restricted revenues on the statement of activities?

    a. $ 50,000
    b. $5,050,000
    c. $5,000,000
    d. $6,050,000

18. On December 31, 2003, Hope Haven, a private not-for-profit voluntary health and welfare organization, received a pledge from a donor who stipulated that $1,000 would be given to the organization each year for the next five years, starting on December 31, 2004. Present value factors at 6% for five periods are presented below.

Present value of an ordinary annuity for 5 periods at 6%   4.21236
Present value of an annuity due for 5 periods at 6%   4.46511

For the year ended December 31, 2003, Hope Haven should report, on its statement of activities,

    a. Unrestricted revenues of $5,000.
    b. Temporarily restricted revenues of $4,465.
    c. Unrestricted revenues of $4,465.
    d. Temporarily restricted revenues of $4,212.

19. For Guiding Light, a nongovernmental nonprofit religious organization, net assets that can be expended in accordance with the wishes of the governing board of the organization should be reported as

I. Unrestricted.
II. Temporarily restricted.
III. Permanently restricted.

    a. I only.
    b. Both I and II.
    c. I, II, and III.
    d. Either I or II.

20. The Jackson Foundation, a not-for-profit private organization, had the following cash contributions and expenditures in 2003:

Unrestricted cash contributions of $500,000.

Cash contributions of $200,000 restricted by the donor to the acquisition of property.

Cash expenditures of $200,000 to acquire property with the donation in the above item.

Jackson's statement of cash flows should include which of the following amounts?

	Operating activities	Investing activities	Financing activities
a.	$700,000	$(200,000)	$0
b.	$500,000	$0	$0
c.	$500,000	$(200,000)	$200,000
d.	$0	$500,000	$200,000

21. United Hope, a private not-for-profit voluntary health and welfare organization, received the following contributions in 2003:

I. $500 from donors who stipulated that the money not be spent until 2004.
II. $1,000 from donors who stipulated that the contributions be used for the acquisition of equipment, none of which was acquired in 2003.

Which of the above events increased temporarily restricted net assets for the year ending December 31, 2003?

    a. I only.
    b. Both I and II.
    c. II only.
    d. Neither I nor II.

22. A statement of financial position (balance sheet), which reports unrestricted, temporarily restricted, and permanently restricted net assets, is required for which one of the following organizations?

I. A public university.
II. A private, not-for-profit hospital.

    a. Both I and II.
    b. I only.
    c. Neither I nor II.
    d. II only.

23. A storm broke glass windows in the building of Lea Meditators, a not-for-profit religious organization. A member of Lea's congregation, a professional glazier, replaced the windows at no charge. In Lea's statement of activities, the breakage and replacement of the windows should

    a. Not be reported.
    b. Be reported by note disclosure only.
    c. Be reported as an increase in both expenses and contributions.
    d. Be reported as an increase in both net assets and contributions.

24. SFAS 117, *Financial Statements of Not-for-Profit Organizations,* focuses on

    a. Basic information for the organization as a whole.
    b. Standardization of funds nomenclature.
    c. Inherent differences of not-for-profit organizations that impact reporting presentations.
    d. Distinctions between current fund and noncurrent fund presentations.

25. On December 30, 2003, Leigh Museum, a not-for-profit organization, received a $7,000,000 donation of Day Co. shares with donor-stipulated requirements as follows:

Shares valued at $5,000,000 are to be sold, with the proceeds used to erect a public viewing building.

Shares valued at $2,000,000 are to be retained, with the dividends used to support current operations.

As a consequence of the receipt of the Day shares, how much should Leigh report as temporarily restricted net assets on its 2003 statement of financial position (balance sheet)?

    a. $0
    b. $2,000,000
    c. $5,000,000
    d. $7,000,000

26. The Jones family lost its home in a fire. On December 25, 2003, a philanthropist sent money to the Amer Benevolent Society, a not-for-profit organization, to purchase furniture for the Jones family. During January 2004, Amer purchased this furniture for the Jones family. How should Amer report the receipt of the money in its 2003 financial statements?

    a. As an unrestricted contribution.
    b. As a temporarily restricted contribution.
    c. As a permanently restricted contribution.
    d. As a liability.

27. If the Pel Museum, a not-for-profit organization, received a contribution of historical artifacts, it need **not** recognize the contribution if the artifacts are to be sold and the proceeds used to

    a. Support general museum activities.
    b. Acquire other items for collections.
    c. Repair existing collections.
    d. Purchase buildings to house collections.

28. A large not-for-profit organization's statement of activities should report the net change for net assets that are

	Unrestricted	Permanently restricted
a.	Yes	Yes
b.	Yes	No
c.	No	No
d.	No	Yes

29. Which of the following classifications is required for reporting of expenses by all not-for-profit organizations?

    a. Natural classification in the statement of activities or notes to the financial statements.
    b. Functional classification in the statement of activities or notes to the financial statements.
    c. Functional classification in the statement of activities and natural classification in a matrix format in a separate statement.
    d. Functional classification in the statement of activities and natural classification in the notes to the financial statements.

30. Rosary Botanical Gardens, a private not-for-profit organization, established a $500,000 quasi endowment on September 1, 2003. On the garden's statement of financial position at December 31, 2003, the assets in this quasi endowment should be included in which of the following classifications?

    a. Temporarily restricted net assets.
    b. Unrestricted net assets.
    c. Permanently restricted net assets.

d.   Either temporarily or permanently restricted net assets, depending on the expected term of the quasi endowment.

31. During 2003, an alumnus of Smith College, a private not-for-profit college, transferred $100,000 to the college with the stipulation that it be spent for library acquisitions. However, the alumnus specified that none of the cash transferred could be spent until the college had matched the entire amount transferred with donations from other alumni by December 31, 2004. As of December 31, 2003, the college had received matching cash donations of only $5,000 from other alumni, and the college estimated that it was reasonably possible that it would not reach the goal of $100,000 by December 31, 2004. If the funds are not matched by December 31, 2004, the cash will be returned to the alumnus. On the college's statement of financial position at December 31, 2003, the cash transfer of $100,000 would be included in the amount reported for

a.   Liabilities.
b.   Unrestricted net assets.
c.   Temporarily restricted net assets.
d.   Permanently restricted net assets.

32. During the year ended December 31, 2003, a not-for-profit performing arts entity received the following donor-restricted contribution and investment income:

I. Cash contribution of $100,000 to be permanently invested.
II. Cash dividends and interest of $6,000 to be used for the acquisition of theater equipment.

As a result of these cash receipts, the statement of cash flows for the year ended December 31, 2003, would report an increase of

a. $106,000 from operating activities.
b. $106,000 from financing activities.
c. $6,000 from operating activities and an increase of $100,000 from financing activities.
d. $100,000 from operating activities and an increase of $6,000 from financing activities.

33. Which of the following private, nonprofit entities is required to report expenses both by function and by natural classification?

a.   Hospitals.
b.   Colleges and universities.
c.   Voluntary health and welfare organizations.
d.   Performing arts organizations.

34. On December 5, 2003, Jones Heating and Air Conditioning Service repaired the heating system in the building occupied by Good Hope, a private not-for-profit voluntary health and welfare organization. An invoice for $1,500 was received by Good Hope for the repairs on December 15, 2003. On December 30, 2003, Jones notified Good Hope that the invoice was canceled and that the repairs were being donated without charge. For the year ended December 31, 2003, how should Good Hope report these contributed services?

a.   Only in the notes to the financial statements.
b.   No disclosure is required either in the financial statements or in the notes.
c.   As an increase in unrestricted revenues and as an increase in expenses on the statements of activities.

d.   As an increase in temporarily restricted net assets on the statement of activities.

35. During the year ended December 31, 2003, the James Community Foundation, a private not-for-profit organization, received the following contributed services:

I. Anderson & Anderson, attorneys-at-law, contributed their services which involved advice related to the foundation's regular endowments.
II. Senior citizens participated in a telethon to raise money for a new music building.

Which of these contributed services should be included in unrestricted revenues, gains, and other support on James Community Foundation's statement of activities for the year ended December 31, 2003?

a.   Both I and II.
b.   Neither I nor II.
c.   II only.
d.   I only.

36. Child Care Centers, Inc., a not-for-profit organization, receives revenue from various sources during the year to support its day care centers. The following cash amounts were received during 2003:

$2,000 restricted by the donor to be used for meals for the children.
$1,500 received for subscriptions to a monthly child-care magazine with a fair market value to subscribers of $1,000.
$10,000 to be used only upon completion of a new playroom that was only 50% complete at December 31, 2003.

What amount should Child Care Centers record as contribution revenue in its 2003 Statement of Activities?

a. $ 2,000
b. $ 2,500
c. $10,000
d. $11,000

37. On December 20, 2003, United Appeal, a private not-for-profit voluntary health and welfare organization, received a donation of computer equipment valued at $25,000 from a local computer retailer. The equipment is expected to have a useful life of three years. The donor placed no restrictions on how long the computer equipment was to be used, and United has an accounting policy that does not imply a time restriction on gifts of long-lived assets. On United's statement of activities prepared for the year ended December 31, 2003, the donation of computer equipment should be reported

a.   As an increase in temporarily restricted net assets.
b.   Only in the notes to the financial statements.
c.   As an increase in unrestricted net assets.
d.   As either an increase in temporarily restricted net assets or as an increase in unrestricted net assets.

38. On December 30, 2003, the Board of Trustees of Henry Museum, a private not-for-profit organization, designated $4,000,000 of unrestricted net assets for the construction of an addition to its building. What effect does this designation have on the museum's unrestricted and temporarily restricted net assets which are reported on the statement of financial position (balance sheet) at December 31, 2003?

	Unrestricted *net assets*	*Temporarily restricted* *net assets*
a.	No effect	Increase
b.	Decrease	Increase
c.	Decrease	No effect
d.	No effect	No effect

39. Darlin Hospital, a private not-for-profit hospital, had the following cash receipts for the year ended December 31, 2003:

Patient service revenue	$300,000
Gift shop revenue	25,000
Interest revenue restricted by donor stipulation for acquisition of equipment	50,000

As a result of these cash receipts, the hospital's statement of cash flows for the year ended December 31, 2003, would report an increase in operating activities of

- a. $325,000
- b. $375,000
- c. $350,000
- d. $300,000

40. For a private, not-for-profit organization, when is a donor's conditional promise to give considered to be unconditional?

- a. When the condition is partially met.
- b. When the possibility that the condition will not be met is remote.
- c. When the conditional promise is made.
- d. When cash or other assets promised are received.

41. A not-for-profit organization receives $150 from a donor. The donor receives two tickets to a theater show and an acknowledgment in the theater program. The tickets have a fair market value of $100. What amount is recorded as contribution revenue?

- a. $0
- b. $ 50
- c. $100
- d. $150

42. On November 30, 2002, Justin Barlow, an alumnus of Murry School, a private, not-for-profit high school, contributed $15,000, with the stipulation that the donation be used for faculty travel expenses during 2003. During 2003, Murry spent all of the donation in accordance with Mr. Barlow's wishes. For the year ended December 31, 2003, what was the effect of the donation on unrestricted and temporarily restricted net assets?

	Unrestricted *net assets*	*Temporarily restricted* *net assets*
a.	Increase	Decrease
b.	No effect	Decrease
c.	Increase	No effect
d.	No effect	No effect

43. A private not-for-profit voluntary health and welfare organization received a cash donation in 2002 that contained a donor-imposed restriction that stipulated that the donation could not be spent until 2003. The voluntary health and welfare organization spent the donation in 2003 on fundraising activities. On the statement of activities prepared for the year ended December 31, 2003, the expiration of the time restriction would result in reporting a(n)

- a. Increase in temporarily restricted net assets.

- b. Reclassification that decreased temporarily restricted net assets.
- c. Increase in unrestricted net assets.
- d. Expense that decreased temporarily restricted net assets.

44. According to SFAS 117, which prescribes the financial statements of not-for-profit organizations, reporting reclassifications is caused by which of the following?

- I. Expiration of donor-imposed conditions.
- II. Expiration of donor-imposed restrictions.

- a. I only.
- b. Both I and II.
- c. II only.
- d. Neither I nor II.

45. Which of the following transactions would result in an increase in unrestricted net assets for the year ended December 31, 2003?

- I. A private, not-for-profit hospital earned interest on investments that were board-designated.
- II. A private, not-for-profit voluntary health and welfare organization received unconditional promises to give (pledges) which will not be received until the beginning of 2004. The donors placed no restrictions on their donations.

- a. Both I and II.
- b. I only.
- c. II only.
- d. Neither I nor II.

46. Benevolent Society, a private not-for-profit organization, should recognize contributed services on its statement of activities if which of the following conditions is(are) met?

- I. The contributed services create or enhance nonfinancial assets.
- II. The contributed services require specialized skills, are provided by individuals possessing those skills, and would typically need to be purchased if not provided by donation.

- a. Both I and II.
- b. Neither I nor II.
- c. I only.
- d. Either I or II.

47. During 2003, Margaret Billingsley, a prominent art collector, donated several items in her collection to the Darwin Museum, a private, not-for-profit organization. Ms. Billingsley stipulated that her contribution be shown to the public, that it should be preserved, and not be sold. Darwin's accounting policy is to capitalize all donations of art, historical treasures, and similar items. On the date of donation, what was the effect of Ms. Billingsley's donation on Darwin's financial statements?

- a. Temporarily restricted net assets increased.
- b. Reclassifications caused a simultaneous increase in permanently restricted net assets and a decrease in temporarily restricted net assets.
- c. There was no effect on any class of Darwin's net assets.
- d. Permanently restricted net assets increased.

48. Which of the following transactions or events would cause an increase in unrestricted net assets for the year ended December 31, 2002?

  I. A private not-for-profit voluntary health and welfare organization spent a restricted donation that was received in 2001. In accordance with the donor's wishes, the donation was spent on public health education during 2002.

  II. During 2003, a private, not-for-profit college earned dividends and interest on term endowments. Donors placed no restrictions on the earnings of term endowments. The governing board of the college intends to use this investment income to fund undergraduate scholarships for 2004.

    a.   II only.
    b.   I only.
    c.   Neither I nor II.
    d.   Both I and II.

49. Mary Egbart promised Columbus College, a private, not-for-profit college, that she would provide 80% of the funds needed to construct a new performing arts center, if the college could get the remaining 20% of the funds needed from other donors by July 1, 2004. The promise was made in 2003. At December 31, 2003, the governing board of the college had received donations from other donors for approximately 15% of the cost of the new center and believed that the probability of not getting the remaining 5% of the necessary funds was remote. For the year ended December 31, 2003, Ms. Egbart's promise would

    a.   Be reported as an increase in permanently restricted net assets on the statement of activities.
    b.   Not be reported on the statement of activities.
    c.   Be reported as an increase in deferred support on the statement of financial position.
    d.   Be reported as an increase in temporarily restricted net assets on the statement of activities.

50. A private, not-for-profit hospital adopted SFAS 124, *Accounting for Certain Investments Held by Not-for-Profit Organizations*. For the year ended December 31, 2003, how should the hospital report its investments in debt securities that are classified as current assets and noncurrent assets on its statement of financial position (balance sheet)?

	Debt securities in current assets	*Debt securities in noncurrent assets*
a.	Fair value	Amortized cost
b.	Amortized cost	Fair value
c.	Fair value	Fair value
d.	Amortized cost	Amortized cost

51. The governing board of Crestfallen, a private not-for-profit voluntary health and welfare organization, acquired equity securities of BMZ Company at a cost of $35,000 on May 1, 2003. The governing board used unrestricted net assets to acquire this investment, and it intends to use the income from its investment in BMZ, as well as other investments, to acquire much needed computer equipment for the organization. The investment in the equity securities of BMZ Company, which is listed on a national stock exchange, represents less than a 1% interest in the company. On November 15, 2003, Crestfallen received $1,000 of dividends from BMZ, and the fair value of the BMZ equity securities was $42,000 on December 31, 2003. Assume

Crestfallen adopted SFAS 124, *Accounting for Certain Investments Held by Not-for-Profit Organizations*. As a result of Crestfallen's investment in BMZ Company, the statement of activities for the year ended December 31, 2003 would report an increase of

    a. $8,000 in unrestricted net assets.
    b. $8,000 in temporarily restricted net assets.
    c. $1,000 in unrestricted net assets.
    d. $7,000 in unrestricted net assets.

52. Jazz Planners, a private not-for-profit performing arts organization, has donor-restricted permanent endowment funds which include investments in equity securities. These equity securities all have readily determinable fair values because they are all traded on national security exchanges. Most of the equity investments represent between 1% and 3% of the common stock of the investee companies; however, a few of Jazz Planner's investments permit the organization significant influence over the operating and financing policies of the investee companies. Jazz Planner's adopted SFAS 124, *Accounting for Certain Investments Held by Not-for-Profit Organizations*. How should the organization report these equity securities on its statement of financial position (balance sheet)?

	Equity securities: 1% to 3% ownership	*Equity securities: significant influence*
a.	Fair value	Fair value
b.	Fair value	Use equity method
c.	Lower of cost or market	Fair value
d.	Fair value	Lower of cost or market

53. Rose Smith made a cash donation for a specific purpose in December 2002, to United Ways, a nongovernmental, nonprofit organization that raises contributions for others. Assume United Ways was (1) not granted variance power by Rose Smith over her donation and (2) the beneficiaries of the donation are not financially related to United Ways. According to SFAS 136, *Transfer of Assets to a Not-for-Profit Organization or Charitable Trust That Raises or Holds Contributions for Others*, how should United Ways account for Rose's cash donation?

    a.   As an increase in contribution revenue.
    b.   As an increase in liabilities.
    c.   As either an increase in contribution revenue or liabilities.
    d.   As neither an increase in contribution revenue nor liabilities.

54. World-Wide Helpers Foundation, a nonprofit entity, received a cash donation in 2003 from Herold Smith. World-Wide Helpers Foundation is controlled by World-Wide Helpers, a nonprofit entity that raises resources for others. The resources of World-Wide Helpers Foundation are used for the benefit of World-Wide Helpers. World-Wide Helpers and its foundation have adopted SFAS 136, *Transfer of Assets to a Not-for-Profit Organization or Charitable Trust That Raises or Holds Contributions for Others*, for its 2003 financial statements. How should World-Wide Helpers Foundation account for the cash donation?

    a.   As an increase in contribution revenues.
    b.   As an increase in liabilities.
    c.   As either an increase in contribution revenue or liabilities.
    d.   As neither an increase in contribution revenue or liabilities.

55. In accordance with SFAS 136, *Transfer of Assets to a Not-for-Profit Organization or Charitable Trust That Raises or Holds Contributions for Others*, a cash donation from a resource provider should be reported as contribution revenue by a recipient organization when which of the following exists?

- a. The recipient organization and beneficiary are **not** financially interrelated.
- b. The resource provider does **not** allow the recipient organization to use the donation for beneficiaries other than those specified by the resource provider.
- c. The resource provider does **not** grant variance power to the recipient organization to redirect the donation to other beneficiaries.
- d. The resource provider grants variance power to the recipient organization to redirect the donation to other beneficiaries.

56. Peter Smith made a cash donation in January 2003, to World-Wide Helpers, a nongovernmental, nonprofit organization that raises contributions for others. Peter specified the beneficiaries for his contribution, but provided variance power to World-Wide Helpers to use the donation for beneficiaries not specified by Peter. According to SFAS 136, *Transfer of Assets to a Not-for-Profit Organization or Charitable Trust That Raises or Holds Contributions for Others*, how should World-Wide Helpers account for Peter's cash donation?

- a. As an increase in contribution revenue.
- b. As an increase in liabilities.
- c. As either an increase in contribution revenue or liabilities.
- d. As neither an increase in contribution revenue nor liabilities.

57. The Taft family lost its home in a flood in October 2003. In November of 2003, Mary Wilson donated cash to Goodbody Benevolent Society to purchase furniture for the Taft family. In December 2003, Goodbody purchased this furniture for the Taft family. Goodbody has adopted SFAS 136, *Transfer of Assets to a Not-for-Profit Organization or Charitable Trust That Raises or Holds Contributions for Others*. How should Goodbody report the receipt of the cash donation in its 2003 financial statements?

- a. As an unrestricted contribution.
- b. As a temporarily restricted contribution.
- c. As a liability.
- d. As either a liability or as a temporarily restricted contribution.

58. An arrangement where a donor makes an initial gift to a trust or directly to the not-for-profit organization, in which the not-for-profit organization has a beneficial interest but is not the sole beneficiary is known as a

- a. Donor-imposed condition.
- b. Donor-imposed restriction.
- c. Share-the-wealth agreement.
- d. Split-interest agreement.

59. Under which of the following cases should joint costs be allocated between fund-raising and the appropriate program or management and general function?

- a. An appeal for funds accompanied by a statement of the mission of the not-for-profit entity.
- b. An appeal for funds accompanied by a brochure explaining why funds are needed and how they will be used.

- c. An organization seeks the involvement of the public in the attainment of their missions by telling people what they should do about particular issues in addition to fund-raising appeals.
- d. An appeal for funds and education materials sent to a person based on his/her presumed ability to provide financial support.

60. Which of the following are considered to be capital additions in the statement of activity of a not-for-profit organization?

- I. Nonexpendable gifts, grants, and bequests restricted by donors to endowment funds.
- II. Legally restricted investment income on investments held in endowment funds that must be added to the principal.
- III. Donor-restricted gifts for program or supporting services.

- a. I, II, and III.
- b. I and III only.
- c. I and II only.
- d. III only.

61. Depending on the extent of discretion that the not-for-profit recipient has over the use or subsequent disposition of the assets, gifts in kind may be treated as

	Agency transactions	*Contributions*
a.	No	No
b.	No	Yes
c.	Yes	Yes
d.	Yes	No

62. A not-for-profit organization receives an asset for which they have little or no discretion over the use of the asset. The organization should report the asset as a(n)

- a. Contribution.
- b. Agency transaction.
- c. Exchange.
- d. Conditional transfer.

63. Elizabeth Hospital, a nonprofit hospital affiliated with a religious group, should prepare which of the following financial statements?

	Statement of changes in net assets	*Statement of operations*
a.	Yes	No
b.	No	Yes
c.	Yes	Yes
d.	No	No

64. Williams Hospital, a nonprofit hospital affiliated with a religious group, reported the following information for the year ended December 31, 2003:

Gross patient service revenue at the hospital's full established rates	$980,000
Bad debts expense	10,000
Contractual adjustments with third-party payors	100,000
Allowance for discounts to hospital employees	15,000

On the hospital's statement of operations for the year ended December 31, 2003, what amount should be reported as net patient service revenue?

- a. $865,000
- b. $880,000

c. $855,000
d. $955,000

65. For private sector health care organizations, which of the following is included in patient service revenue?
    a. Contractual adjustments.
    b. Charity care.
    c. Significant revenue under capitation agreements (premium revenue).
    d. Unrestricted contributions.

66. Which of the following is **not** covered by the AICPA Audit and Accounting Guide, *Health Care Organizations*?
    a. Nursing homes.
    b. Home health agencies.
    c. Hospitals.
    d. Voluntary health and welfare organizations.

67. Which of the following can be included in the performance indicator on the statement of operations for private sector health care organizations?
    a. Extraordinary items.
    b. Premium revenue from capitation agreements.
    c. Equity transfers.
    d. Contributions of long-lived assets.

68. If not-for-profit health care entities do not use this expense classification on the operating statement, they must provide it in the notes.
    a. Natural.
    b. Character.
    c. Functional.
    d. Object.

69. When functional classifications are used by private sector health care organizations, they should be based on
    a. Net present value.
    b. Full cost allocations.
    c. Percentage allocations.
    d. Resale value.

70. Which of the following would be acceptable as a performance indicator on a private sector health care entity's statement of operations?
    a. Increase in unrestricted net assets.
    b. Net income.
    c. Increase in net assets.
    d. Excess of revenues over expenses.

71. How is charity care accounted for on the financial statements of a not-for-profit private sector health care organization?
    a. As patient service revenue.
    b. As bad debt expense.
    c. As a separate component of revenue.
    d. Not included on the financial statements.

72. How are nonrefundable advance fees representing payments for future services to be accounted for by nonprofit continuing care retirement communities?
    a. As revenue.
    b. As a liability.
    c. As other financing sources.
    d. In a trust fund.

73. Kash Hospital, a private sector, not-for-profit organization, has gross patient service revenues of $750,000, charity care of $75,000, amounts disallowed by third-party payors

of $63,000, and donor-unrestricted contributions of $110,000. What is the amount of net patient service revenue?
    a. $687,000
    b. $722,000
    c. $785,000
    d. $797,000

74. James Hospital, a nonprofit hospital affiliated with a private university, provided $200,000 of charity care for patients during the year ended December 31, 2003. The hospital should report this charity care
    a. As net patient service revenue of $200,000 on the statement of operations.
    b. As net patient service revenue of $200,000 and as an operating expense of $200,000 on the statement of operations.
    c. As accounts receivable of $200,000 on the balance sheet at December 31, 2003.
    d. Only in the notes to the financial statements for 2003.

75. Michael Hospital, a nonprofit hospital affiliated with a private university, reported the following information for the year ended December 31, 2003:

Cash contributions received from donors for capital additions to be acquired in 2004	$150,000
Proceeds from sales at hospital gift shop and snack bar	75,000
Dividend revenue not restricted by donors or by law	25,000

Using the information provided, what amount should be reported as "other revenue and gains" on the hospital's statement of operations for the year ended December 31, 2003?
    a. $ 25,000
    b. $ 75,000
    c. $100,000
    d. $250,000

76. Swathmore Hospital, a nonprofit hospital affiliated with Swathmore University, received the following cash contributions from donors during the year ended December 31, 2002:

Contributions restricted by donors for research	$ 50,000
Contributions restricted by donors for capital acquisitions	250,000

Neither of the contributions was spent during 2002; however, during 2003, the hospital spent the entire $50,000 contribution on research and the entire $250,000 contribution on a capital asset that was placed into service during the year. The hospital has adopted an accounting policy that does not imply a time restriction on gifts of long-lived assets. On the hospital's statement of operations for the year ended December 31, 2003, what total amount should be reported for "net assets released from restrictions?"
    a. $ 50,000
    b. $300,000
    c. $250,000
    d. $0

77. The governing board of Smithson Hospital, a nonprofit hospital affiliated with a religious organization, acquired 100 BMI Company bonds for $103,000 on June 30, 2003. The bonds pay interest on June 30 and December 30. On December 31, 2003, interest of $3,000 was received from BMI, and the fair value of the BMI bonds was $105,000. The governing board acquired the BMI bonds with cash which was unrestricted, and it classified the bonds as trading securities at December 31, 2003, since it intends to sell all of the bonds in January 2004. As a result of the investment in BMI bonds, what amount should be included in revenue, gains, and other support on the statement of operations for the year ended December 31, 2003?

    a. $0
    b. $3,000
    c. $2,000
    d. $5,000

78. On the statement of operations for a nonprofit, nongovernmental hospital, which of the items below is included in the amount reported for "revenue and gains over expenses and losses" (the performance indicator)?

  I. Unrealized loss on other than trading securities. The securities are included in unrestricted net assets.
  II. Contribution received from a donor that cannot be used until next year.

    a. I only.
    b. II only.
    c. Both I and II.
    d. Neither I nor II.

79. Tucker Hospital, a nonprofit hospital affiliated with Tucker University, received a donation of medical supplies during the year ended December 31, 2003. The supplies cost the vendor $10,000 and had a selling price of $15,000 on the date they were donated. The vendor did not place any restrictions on how the supplies were to be used. During 2003, all of the donated medical supplies were used. On the hospital's statement of operations for the year ended December 31, 2003, how should the donation be reported?

    a. The donation should be included in both revenue and operating expenses in the amount of $10,000.
    b. The donation should be excluded from the statement of operations.
    c. The donation should be included in both revenue and operating expenses in the amount of $15,000.
    d. The donation should be included in revenue in the amount of $15,000 and in operating expenses in the amount of $10,000.

80. Wilson Hospital, a nonprofit hospital affiliated with Wilson College, had the following cash receipts for the year ended December 31, 2003:

Collections of health care receivables	$750,000
Contribution from donor to establish a term endowment	250,000
Tuition from nursing school	50,000
Dividends received from investments in permanent endowment	80,000

The dividends received are restricted by the donor for hospital building improvements. No improvements were made during 2003. On the hospital's statement of cash flows for the year ended December 31, 2003, what amount of these cash receipts would be included in the amount reported for net cash provided (used) by operating activities?

    a. $ 880,000
    b. $ 800,000
    c. $1,050,000
    d. $ 750,000

81. Which of the following financial statements of a private, nonprofit hospital reports the changes in unrestricted, temporarily restricted, and permanently restricted net assets for a time period?

	Balance sheet	*Statement of operations*
a.	Yes	Yes
b.	Yes	No
c.	No	Yes
d.	No	No

82. Unrealized gains on investments which are permanently restricted as to use by donors are reported by a private, nonprofit hospital on the

    a. Statement of operations.
    b. Statement of cash flows.
    c. Statement of changes in net assets.
    d. Statement of operations and statement of cash flows.

83. The statement of operations for a private, nonprofit hospital should include a performance indicator that indicates the results of operations for a period. Which of the following items would be included in a hospital's performance indicator reported on the statement of operations?

  I. Proceeds from sales of cafeteria meals and guest trays to employees, medical staff, and visitors.
  II. Net assets released from restrictions used for operating expenses.

    a. I only.
    b. Both I and II.
    c. II only.
    d. Neither I nor II.

OTHER OBJECTIVE QUESTIONS

Problem 1   (30 to 40 minutes)

Items 1 through 10 in the left-hand column represent various transactions pertaining to Brown University, a private university, for the year ended December 31, 2003. To the right of these transactions is a listing of how transactions could affect the statement of activities (List A effects) and the statement of cash flows (List B effects).

Required:

Indicate how each transaction should be reported by Brown University on (1) the statement of activities and (2) the statement of cash flows prepared for the year ended December 31, 2003. Brown reports separate columns for changes in unrestricted, temporarily restricted, and permanently restricted net assets on its statement of activities. In addition, Brown uses the direct method of reporting its cash flows from operating activities. Brown has a policy of not restricting net assets related to plant. A List A or List B effect may be used once, more than once, or not at all.

	Transactions	*Statement of activities* *List A effects*	*Statement of cash flows* *List B effects*
1.	A donor contributed $100,000 and stipulated that it be invested permanently.	A. Increases unrestricted net assets	H. Increases cash flows from operating activities
2.	Donors contributed $500,000 for the acquisition of equipment.	B. Increases temporarily restricted net assets	I. Decreases cash flows from operating activities
3.	Depreciation expense of $750,000 was recorded for 2003.	C. Increases permanently restricted net assets	J. Increases cash flows from investing activities
4.	$3,000,000 was received, representing tuition for the spring, summer, and fall semesters.	D. Decreases unrestricted net assets	K. Decreases cash flows from investing activities
5.	Investments of $100,000 were acquired with the cash received from the donor in transaction 1.	E. Decreases temporarily restricted net assets	L. Increases cash flows from financing activities
6.	Interest and dividends of $8,000 were received from the investments acquired in transaction 5. The donor stipulated that the earnings be used for student scholarships in 2003.	F. Decreases permanently restricted net assets	M. Decreases cash flows from financing activities
7.	$75,000 was received from donors who had pledged that amount in 2002. The cash will be used to pay for a marketing campaign that aimed at increasing enrollment. The marketing cost was incurred in 2003 and will be paid in 2004.	G. Transaction not reported on the statement of activities	N. Transaction not reported on the statement of cash flows
8.	$900,000 was paid to faculty for salaries incurred during the year.		O. Transaction reported in the schedule reconciling change in net assets to net cash provided from operating activities
9.	$25,000 was given to faculty for summer research grants. The grants came from donations made by alumni in 2002.		
10.	$40,000 of donations were received from alumni who did **not** stipulate how their donations were to be used.		

Problem 2   (15 to 20 minutes)

This problem consists of 3 parts concerning nongovernmental not-for-profit organizations. Part **a.** consists of 3 items, Part **b.** consists of 6 items, and Part **c.** consists of 8 items.

Items 1 through 3 are based on the following:

Community Service, Inc. is a nongovernmental not-for-profit voluntary health and welfare calendar-year organization that began operations on January 1, 2002. It performs voluntary services and derives its revenue from the general public. Community implies a time restriction on all promises to contribute cash in future periods. However, no such policy exists with respect to gifts of long-lived assets. Contributions restricted as to purpose received and expended in the same year are reported first as an increase in temporarily restricted net assets.

Selected transactions occurred during Community's 2003 calendar year.

Unrestricted written promises to contribute cash—2002 and 2003

2002 promises (collected in 2003)	$22,000
2003 promises (collected in 2003)	95,000
2003 promises (uncollected)	28,000

Written promises to contribute cash restricted to use for community college scholarships—2002 and 2003

2002 promises (collected and expended in 2003)	10,000
2003 promises (collected and expended in 2003)	20,000
2003 promises (uncollected)	12,000

Written promise to contribute $25,000 if matching funds are raised for the capital campaign during 2003

Cash received in 2003 from contributor as good-faith advance	25,000
Matching funds received in 2003	0

Cash received in 2002 with donor's only stipulation that a bus be purchased

Expenditure of full amount of donation 7/1/02	37,000

Required:

a. Items 1 through 3 represent the 2002 amounts that Community reported for selected financial statement elements in its December 31, 2003 statement of financial position and 2003 statement of activities. For each item, indicate whether the amount was overstated, understated, or correctly stated. Select your answer from the list below. An answer may be selected once, more than once, or not at all.

<u>List</u>
O. Overstated.
U. Understated.
C. Correctly stated.

1. Community reported $28,000 as contributions receivable.

2. Community reported $37,000 as net assets released from restrictions (satisfaction of use restrictions).

3. Community reported $22,000 as net assets released from restrictions (due to the lapse of time restrictions).

Items 4 through 9 are based on the following:

Community Service, Inc. is a nongovernmental not-for-profit voluntary health and welfare calendar-year organization that began operations on January 1, 2002. It performs voluntary services and derives its revenue from the general public. Community implies a time restriction on all promises to contribute cash in future periods. However, no such policy exists with respect to gifts of long-lived assets.

Selected transactions occurred during Community's 2003 calendar year.

Debt security endowment received in 2003; income to be used for community services

Face value	$90,000
Fair value at time of receipt	88,000
Fair value at 12/31/03	87,000
Interest earned in 2003	9,000

Ten concerned citizens volunteered to serve meals to the homeless (400 hours; fair market value of services $5 per hour)   2,000

Short-term investment in equity securities in 2003

Cost	10,000
Fair value12/31/03	12,000
Dividend income	1,000

Music festival to raise funds for a local hospital

Admission fees	5,000
Sales on food and drinks	14,000
Expenses	4,000

Reading materials donated to Community and distributed to the children in 2003

Fair market value	8,000

Federal youth training fee for service grant

Cash received during 2003	30,000
Instructor salaries paid	26,000

Other cash operating expenses

Business manager salary	60,000
General bookkeeper salary	40,000
Director of community activities salary	50,000
Space rental (75% for community activities, 25% for office activities)	20,000
Printing and mailing costs for pledge cards	2,000

Interest payment on short-term bank loan in 2003	1,000
Principal payment on short-term bank loan in 2003	20,000

Required:

b.   For items **4 through 9**, determine the amounts for the following financial statements elements in the 2003 statement of activities. Select your answer from the following list of amounts. An amount may be selected once, more than once, or not at all.

<u>Selections</u>

A.	$0	I.	$26,000
B.	$ 2,000	J.	$50,000
C.	$ 3,000	K.	$87,000
D.	$ 5,000	L.	$88,000
E.	$ 8,000	M.	$90,000
F.	$ 9,000	N.	$94,000
G.	$14,000	O.	$99,000
H.	$16,000		

4.   Contributions—permanently restricted.

5.   Revenues—fees.

6.   Program expenses.

7.   General fund-raising expenses (excludes special events).

8.   Income on long-term investments—unrestricted.

9.   Contributed voluntary services.

   Items 10 through 17 are based on the fact pattern and financial information found in **both part a. and part b.**

Required:

c.   **Items 10 through 17** represent Community's transactions reportable in the statement of cash flows. For each of the items listed, select the classification that best described the item. A classification may be selected once, more than once, or not at all.

<u>Classifications</u>

O.   Cash flows from operating activities.
I.   Cash flows from investing activities.
F.   Cash flows from financing activities.

10.   Unrestricted 2003 promises collected.

11.   Cash received from a contributor as a good-faith advance on a promise to contribute matching funds.

12.   Purchase of bus.

13.   Principal payment on short-term bank loan.

14.   Purchase of equity securities.

15.   Dividend income earned on equity securities.

16.   Interest payment on short-term bank loan.

17.   Interest earned on endowment.

MULTIPLE-CHOICE ANSWERS

1.	c	__ __	19.	a	__ __	37.	c	__ __	55.	d	__ __	73.	a	__ __
2.	d	__ __	20.	c	__ __	38.	d	__ __	56.	a	__ __	74.	d	__ __
3.	a	__ __	21.	b	__ __	39.	a	__ __	57.	c	__ __	75.	c	__ __
4.	a	__ __	22.	d	__ __	40.	b	__ __	58.	d	__ __	76.	b	__ __
5.	d	__ __	23.	c	__ __	41.	b	__ __	59.	c	__ __	77.	d	__ __
6.	c	__ __	24.	a	__ __	42.	b	__ __	60.	c	__ __	78.	d	__ __
7.	d	__ __	25.	c	__ __	43.	b	__ __	61.	c	__ __	79.	c	__ __
8.	d	__ __	26.	d	__ __	44.	c	__ __	62.	b	__ __	80.	b	__ __
9.	c	__ __	27.	b	__ __	45.	b	__ __	63.	c	__ __	81.	d	__ __
10.	d	__ __	28.	a	__ __	46.	d	__ __	64.	a	__ __	82.	c	__ __
11.	a	__ __	29.	b	__ __	47.	d	__ __	65.	a	__ __	83.	b	__ __
12.	b	__ __	30.	b	__ __	48.	a	__ __	66.	d	__ __			
13.	a	__ __	31.	a	__ __	49.	d	__ __	67.	b	__ __			
14.	b	__ __	32.	b	__ __	50.	c	__ __	68.	c	__ __			
15.	c	__ __	33.	c	__ __	51.	a	__ __	69.	b	__ __			
16.	c	__ __	34.	c	__ __	52.	b	__ __	70.	d	__ __	1st:	__/83 = __%	
17.	b	__ __	35.	d	__ __	53.	b	__ __	71.	d	__ __	2nd:	__/83 = __%	
18.	d	__ __	36.	b	__ __	54.	a	__ __	72.	b	__ __			

MULTIPLE-CHOICE ANSWER EXPLANATIONS

A. FASB and AICPA Standards for Private Sector Nonprofits

1. **(c)** According to SFAS 117, a statement of functional expenses is required for voluntary health and welfare organizations. Other private nonprofit organizations are encouraged to disclose this information, but they are not required to.

2. **(d)** According to SFAS 117, a statement of financial position for a nongovernmental nonprofit entity, like a library, should report net assets according to whether the net assets are unrestricted, temporarily restricted, or permanently restricted.

3. **(a)** According to SFAS 117, the net assets of term endowments should be reported as temporarily restricted, while the net assets of regular endowments should be reported as permanently restricted. The net assets of term endowments are temporarily restricted because the donor of a term endowment stipulates that the endowment last only a specific number of years. Donors of regular endowments intend that these endowments last indefinitely; hence, the net assets are permanently restricted.

4. **(a)** According to SFAS 116, contributions are reported as revenue in the year received even though there are donor-imposed use or time restrictions on the donation. Since Ms. Smith's donation was use and time restricted, the donation should be reported as a temporarily restricted revenue on the statement of activities for the year ended June 30, 2002. This reporting is in accordance with SFAS 117.

5. **(d)** According to SFAS 116, contributions are reported as revenue in the year received even though there are donor-imposed use or time restrictions on the contribution. Since Mr. Peobody's contribution was use restricted, the contribution would be reported as temporarily restricted revenue on the statement of activities for the year ended December 31, 2003. This reporting is in accordance with SFAS 117.

6. **(c)** According to SFAS 117, all expenses are reported as unrestricted on the statement of activities. This means that expenses are deducted only from unrestricted revenues.

7. **(d)** In accordance with SFAS 117, nongovernmental not-for-profit organizations are required to report a statement of cash flows. On this statement, cash flows are reported using the classifications of operating, investing, and financing activities. Cash flows related to revenues and expenses that are unrestricted should be reported in the operating activities section. The cash inflows from both tuition ($500,000) and the unrestricted contribution ($100,000) are both unrestricted and should be reported as operating activities. Restricted contributions for long-term purposes, like the $300,000 endowment, are reported as financing activities on the statement of cash flows.

8. **(d)** According to SFAS 117, nongovernmental, not-for-profit entities should prepare the following financial statements:

1. Statement of financial position
2. Statement of activities
3. Statement of cash flows

In addition, a voluntary health and welfare organization should also prepare a statement of functional expenses.

9. **(c)** According to SFAS 116, donor restricted contributions should be reported as revenue in the period received. According to SFAS 117, donor restricted contributions which are restricted according to use should be reported as either temporarily restricted revenues or as permanently restricted revenues, depending on the restriction. In the case of Save the Planet, the restriction is temporary, not permanent. Therefore, Ms. Clark's contribution should be reported as temporarily restricted revenue on the statement of activities for the year ended December 31, 2003.

10. **(d)** According to SFAS 116, donor restricted contributions are revenues in the year the contribution is made, not in the year the contribution is spent. According to SFAS 117, contributions that are restricted temporarily should be reported on the statement of activities as temporarily restricted revenues.

11.   (a)   According to SFAS 117, the statement of cash flows for a nongovernmental not-for-profit entity should report its cash flows from operating, investing, and financing activities.

12.   (b)   SFAS 117, para 6, indicates that "a complete set of financial statements of not-for-profit organization shall include a statement of financial position as of the end of the reporting period, a statement of activities and a statement of cash flows for the reporting period, and accompanying notes to financial statements."

13.   (a)   SFAS 116, para 16, states

"gifts of long-lived assets received without stipulations about how long the donated asset must be used shall be reported as restricted support if it is an organization's accounting policy to imply a time restriction that expires over the useful life of the donated assets...In the absence of that policy and other donor-imposed restrictions on use of the asset, gifts of long-lived assets shall be reported as unrestricted support."

14.   (b)   For the year ended December 31, 2003, the contributions received for research would be reported on the statement of activities as an increase of $50,000 in temporarily restricted net assets. According to SFAS 116, contributions received from outside donors for use in research are reported as temporarily restricted net assets. For the year ended December 21, 2004, a reclassification of net assets would be reported on the statement of activities. A reclassification of $35,000 would be reported as both a decrease in temporarily restricted net assets and an increase in unrestricted net assets. In addition, research expense of $35,000 would be reported as a decrease in unrestricted net assets on the statement of activities for the year ended December 31, 2004. Therefore, as a result of the transactions in 2004, there was a decrease of $35,000 in temporarily restricted net assets and no effect on unrestricted net assets (the $35,000 reclassification to unrestricted net assets is offset by a $35,000 increase in research expense).

15.   (c)   Unrestricted net assets increased $250,000 for the year ended December 31, 2003. According to SFAS 117, the $50,000 spent on research during 2003 would be reclassified (added) to unrestricted net assets when the money was spent for research. The $50,000 addition to unrestricted revenues, gains, and other support would be accompanied by a $50,000 reclassification (deduction) from temporarily restricted revenues. The expenses of $50,000 for research are deducted from unrestricted revenues, etc., which include the $50,000 reclassification. Therefore, the net effect on unrestricted net assets of spending $50,000 on research is zero. The $250,000 of gift shop revenue is unrestricted revenue because the governing board has control of this revenue.

16.   (c)   According to SFAS 116, contributions should be reported as revenue in the period of contribution, even though a donor has placed a time or use restriction on the contribution. According to SFAS 117, the $10,000 and the $25,000 contributions should be reported as temporarily restricted revenues on the statement of activities for the year ended June 30, 2003. When the $25,000 is spent on fund-raising, a reclassification of $25,000 should be reported as a deduction from temporarily restricted revenues. This $25,000 deduction results in a net increase in temporarily restricted net assets of $10,000 on the statement of activities

for the year ended June 30, 2003. The deduction of $25,000 from temporarily restricted revenues also results in an increase in unrestricted revenues, gains, and other support of $25,000. According to SFAS 117, expenses can only be deducted from unrestricted revenues on the statement of activities. Therefore, the fund-raising expenses of $25,000 will be deducted from unrestricted revenues, gains, and other support that includes the $25,000 reclassification from temporarily restricted revenues. Alternatively, SFAS 117 also permits temporarily restricted revenues to be reported as unrestricted revenues in the year the resources are received. This alternative is allowed only for the amount of temporarily restricted revenues that are spent during the year. In the situation presented, $25,000 would be disclosed as both an unrestricted revenue and expense for 2003. There would be no need for a reclassification; however, the answer would not change because temporarily restricted net assets increase $10,000 as a result of the contribution that was not spent in 2002.

17.   (b)   According to SFAS 116, contributions should be reported as revenues in the period received, even though donors have placed time or use restrictions on the contributions. According to SFAS 117, the $5,000,000 contribution from alumni for a new wing for the science building should be reported as a temporarily restricted revenue on the statement of activities for the year ended December 31, 2003. Also, the $50,000 of earnings related to the investments should also be reported as temporarily restricted revenues on the statement of activities for the year ended December 31, 2003. The $1,000,000 contribution from the donor, who stipulated that the contribution be invested indefinitely, should be reported as a permanently restricted revenue on the statement of activities for the year ended December 31, 2003.

18.   (d)   According to SFAS 116, a multiyear pledge should be reported at its present value. According to SFAS 117, if there is a time restriction on the pledge, the pledge should be reported as a temporarily restricted revenue in the year the pledge is given. In Hope Haven's situation, the pledge should be reported as temporarily restricted revenue in 2003. The pledge should be reported at its present value. This amount is calculated by using the present value of an ordinary annuity factor for five periods at 6% ($1,000 x 4.21236 = $4,212 rounded).

19.   (a)   According to SFAS 117, net assets under the control of the governing board are reported as unrestricted net assets.

20.   (c)   The requirement is to determine how to report three cash flows on the statement of cash flows for a nongovernmental, nonprofit entity, the Jackson Foundation. According to the guidance provided in SFAS 117, the $500,000 cash inflow from unrestricted contributions should be reported as an increase in the operating activities section. The $200,000 cash inflow restricted for the acquisition of property should be reported as an increase in the financing activities section, while the use of the $200,000 to acquire property should be shown as a decrease in the investing activities section.

21.   (b)   According to SFAS 116, contributions are reported as revenue in the year received, whether the donors place time or use restrictions on the resources. According to

SFAS 117, net assets should be disclosed according to whether they are unrestricted, temporarily restricted, and permanently restricted. Both of the events listed would increase temporarily restricted net assets for the year ending December 31, 2003.

22.   (d)   SFAS 117 requires a statement of financial position which reports unrestricted, temporarily restricted, and permanently restricted net assets for nongovernmental, not-for-profit organizations. Therefore, the statement of financial position is required for a private, not-for-profit hospital, but not for a public university, which is supported by government.

23.   (c)   Per SFAS 116, contributed services which would be purchased if not donated, and which require performance by a specialist, shall be recorded as an increase in both expenses and contributions. In this case, the requirements of SFAS 116 are met since the window needs to be replaced and the work is performed by a professional glazier (specialist).

24.   (a)   SFAS 117 establishes standards for general-purpose external financial statements. This statement focuses on the basic information of the organization as a whole so as to enhance the relevance, understandability, and comparability of the financial statements by the external users. Thus, answer (a) is correct since the overall objective is the enhancement of the basic information, while answers (b), (c), and (d) address factors that are taken into consideration to achieve the objective.

25.   (c)   SFAS 117 requires classification of an organization's net assets and its revenues, expenses, gains, and losses based on the existence or absence of donor-imposed restrictions. It requires that the amount for **each** of three classes of net assets—permanently restricted, temporarily restricted, and unrestricted—be displayed in a statement of financial position and that the amounts of change in each of those classes of net assets be displayed in a statement of activities.

A temporary restriction is a donor-imposed restriction that permits the donee organization to use up or expend the donated assets as specified; it is satisfied either by the passage of time or by actions of the organizations involved. Accordingly, the $5,000,000 contribution of Day Co. shares represents temporarily restricted net assets until the shares are sold and the proceeds used to erect a public viewing building. The $2,000,000 contribution of Day Co. shares represents permanently restricted net assets because the shares are to be retained permanently.

26.   (d)   A liability (not revenue) is recorded when the reporting entity acts as an agent or trustee. A recipient of assets who is an agent or trustee has little or no discretion in determining how the assets transferred will be used. The receipt of cash to purchase furniture specifically for the Jones family would constitute a "transfer" of assets. Upon receipt of the asset (cash), the Amer Benevolent society must expend (i.e., purchase furniture) the contribution to comply with the restrictions of the donor. Answer (a) is incorrect because the donee restricted the use of the contribution. Answer (c) is incorrect because a permanent restriction stipulates that the resources be maintained permanently (but permits the donee organization to expend part or all of the income or other economic benefits derived from the donated assets).

27.   (b)   Per SFAS 116, an entity need not recognize the contributions of works of art and historical artifacts if the collection is held for public exhibition rather than financial profit, cared for and preserved, and, if sold, the proceeds are used to acquire other items for collections.

28.   (a)   A Statement of Activities reports revenues, expenses, gains, losses, and reclassifications. Resources are divided into three classes: unrestricted, temporarily restricted, and permanently restricted. Separate revenues, expenses, gains, losses, and reclassifications for each class may or may not be reported, but the change in net assets for each class **must** be reported.

29.   (b)   The requirement is to determine what classification is required to report expenses of all not-for-profit organizations. All not-for-profit organizations must classify expenses according to their function in either the financial statement or in the notes to the financial statements.

30.   (b)   Quasi endowment funds are established by the governing board of an organization using unrestricted net assets. Therefore, the assets in the quasi endowment would be included in the unrestricted net assets category.

31.   (a)   According to SFAS 116, a transfer of assets with a conditional promise to contribute them shall be accounted for as a refundable advance until the conditions have been substantially met. The conditions have been substantially met when the possibility that they will not be met is remote. In this question, the chance that the condition will not be met is reasonably possible, which is a higher level of doubt than remote and thus results in reporting the cash transfer as a liability at December 31, 2003.

32.   (b)   According to SFAS 117, the receipt of cash from a donor to establish a permanent endowment should be reported as a financing activity on the statement of cash flows. This same paragraph also states that receipts from investment income that by donor stipulation are restricted for the purposes of acquiring plant, equipment, and other long-lived assets should also be reported as a financing activity.

33.   (c)   According to SFAS 117, voluntary health and welfare organizations should provide a statement of functional expenses. This statement reports expenses by both function (program and supporting) and by their natural classification (salaries expense, depreciation expense, etc.).

34.   (c)   According to SFAS 116, donations of services are recognized on the statement of activities if either of the following two conditions are met: (1) the services create or enhance a nonfinancial asset, or (2) the services require specialized skills, are provided by individuals possessing those skills, and would typically need to be purchased if not provided by donation. The services provided by Jones Heating and Air Conditioning would clearly meet the second criterion. Good Hope would record the invoice in the following manner:

Supporting Expenses	1,500	
Accounts Payable		1,500

Upon notification that the invoice was canceled, Good Hope would make the following journal entry:

Accounts Payable	1,500	
Unrestricted Revenues		1,500

Therefore, the net effect of the contributed services is an increase in expenses and an increase in unrestricted revenues.

35: **(d)** According to SFAS 116, donations of services are recognized on the statement of activities if either of the following conditions are met: (1) the services create or enhance a nonfinancial asset, or (2) the services require specialized skills, are provided by individuals possessing those skills, and would typically need to be purchased if not provided by donation. The services of Anderson and Anderson, attorneys-at-law, clearly meet criterion 2 and should be reported as unrestricted revenues on James' statement of activities. However, the services provided by the senior citizens do not meet either criterion, and should not be reported on the foundation's statement of activities.

36. **(b)** The requirement is to determine what amount should be reported as contribution revenue in the 2003 statement of activities. The $2,000 restricted for meals is considered contribution revenue even though it is restricted. The amount received over the fair market value of the subscriptions is considered to be contribution revenue, which is $500 ($1,500 – $1,000). The $10,000 to be used upon completion of a new playroom is not part of 2003 revenue contribution because a condition, completion of a new playroom, has not been fulfilled. The money is only available upon completion, and the building is not complete in 2003. What is included in contribution revenue is $2,500 ($2,000 + $500).

37. **(c)** According to SFAS 116, gifts of long-lived assets should be reported as unrestricted support if the organization has an accounting policy which does not imply a time restriction on such gifts.

38. **(d)** The designation of unrestricted net assets by the board of Henry Museum for the building addition does not change the classification of the net assets which were designated. The assets designated were unrestricted before the designation, and they remain unrestricted after the designation.

39. **(a)** Cash flows from operating activities would include both the cash received from patient service revenue of $300,000 and the cash received from gift shop sales of $25,000. According to SFAS 117, cash received from investment income that is restricted by donors for the acquisition of long-lived fixed assets should be reported as financing activities.

40. **(b)** According to SFAS 116, a conditional promise to give is considered unconditional if the possibility that the condition will not be met is remote.

41. **(b)** The requirement is to determine how much of the $150 from a donor in exchange for theater tickets and an acknowledgment is considered contribution revenue. Contribution revenue is the amount given above the fair market value. The amount given, $150, is $50 more than fair market value of the tickets, which is $100.

42. **(b)** The use of the cash donation for faculty travel in 2003 is reported as a reclassification on the high school's statement of activities for 2003. Reclassifications are reported on the statement of activities as "net assets released from restrictions." Net assets released from restrictions of $15,000 are reported as a negative amount for temporarily restricted net assets in 2003, while net assets released from restrictions of $15,000 are reported as a positive amount for unrestricted net assets for 2003. However, the $15,000 of travel expense is reported on the statement of activities as an expense for 2003. According to SFAS 117, all expenses are reported on the statement of activities as decreases in unrestricted net assets. This means that the use of the donation for faculty travel had no effect on unrestricted net assets in 2003. Note that, when the donation was received in 2002, temporarily restricted net assets increased by $15,000 on the statement of activities prepared for 2002.

43. **(b)** According to SFAS 117, expiration of donor-imposed restrictions that simultaneously increase one class of net assets and decrease another should be reported as reclassifications on the statement of activities. Reclassifications are reported as "net assets released from restrictions." When the time restriction on the donation expired in 2003, unrestricted net assets increased while temporarily restricted net assets decreased. The spending of the donation on fund-raising should be reported as an expense, which, according to SFAS 117, is a deduction from unrestricted net assets. Therefore, the net effect of the reclassification and the use of the donation is zero on unrestricted net assets. However, the reclassification decreased temporarily restricted net assets for 2003.

44. **(c)** According to SFAS 117, reclassifications result from expirations of donor-imposed restrictions. The donor-imposed restrictions may be either time or purpose related. When a donor-imposed condition is satisfied, the conditional promise to give assets becomes unconditional, and there is an increase in the appropriate classification of net assets, depending on the restrictions placed upon the assets by the donors. However, this increase is reported as either revenue or support at the time the promise becomes unconditional.

45. **(b)** Interest earned on board-designated investments is reported as unrestricted revenue. When the governing board of a not-for-profit organization places restrictions on assets, they are restricting the use of unrestricted net assets. Therefore, income earned on board-designated investments represents an increase in unrestricted net assets. Unconditional promises to give are reported in the period the pledges are made, not in the period of cash collection. However, since the contributions will not be received until 2004, the contributions should be reported as an increase in temporarily restricted net assets on the statement of activities for 2003 because of this time restriction.

46. **(d)** According to SFAS 116, contributed services should be recognized if either of the following conditions is met: (1) the services create or enhance nonfinancial assets, or (2) the services require specialized skills, are provided by individuals possessing those skills, and would typically need to be purchased if not provided by donation.

47. **(d)** According to SFAS 117, donations of works of art for which the donor stipulated a specified purpose and which are to be preserved and not be sold, represent permanently restricted net assets. Since the museum's policy is to capitalize all donations of art, Ms. Billingsley's donation would be reported as an increase in permanently restricted net assets on the statement of activities.

48. **(a)** The restricted donation of the voluntary health and welfare organization is reported as a reclassification on the statement of activities for 2003. The net effect of the re-classification and the recognition of the expense is zero. The reclassification resulting from the expiration of the donor-imposed restriction increases unrestricted net assets; however, the expense resulting from using the funds for public health education is subtracted from this increase, causing no effect on unrestricted net assets. The interest and dividends earned on the term endowments are unrestricted, and should be reported as an increase in unrestricted revenue for 2003. Since no expenses have been incurred from the use of the investment income for 2003, the net effect is an increase in unrestricted net assets for 2003.

49. (d) According to SFAS 116, a conditional promise to give is considered unconditional if the possibility that the condition will not be met is remote. At December 31, 2003, Ms. Egbart's promise would be considered unconditional. This means that the college should report the funds that Ms. Egbart promised as an increase in temporarily restricted net assets on its statement of activities prepared for the year ended December 31, 2003.

50. (c) According to SFAS 124, all investments in debt securities should be measured at fair value in the statement of financial position.

51. (a) According to SFAS 124, the investment in BMZ is covered by the standard, since the standard does not apply to investments in equity securities which are accounted for under the equity method or are consolidated. Since Crestfallen owns less than 1% of BMZ Company, the equity method cannot be used to account for the investment. Therefore, the provisions of paragraph 7 apply to the investment in BMZ.

According to SFAS 124, investments in equity securities with readily determinable market values should be reported at fair value in the statement of financial position. In order to report BMZ's equity securities at their market value of $42,000, a gain of $7,000 should be recognized on the statement of activities. This gain represents an increase in unrestricted net assets, since the gain is related to an investment made by the governing board with unrestricted net assets. In addition, the dividends of $1,000 would also be reported as an increase in unrestricted net assets, since the dividends were earned on unrestricted net assets. Therefore, the investment in BMZ would result in an $8,000 increase in unrestricted net assets on the statement of activities prepared for the year ended December 31, 2003.

52. (b) According to SFAS 124, investments in equity securities that are accounted for under the equity method are not covered by the standard. Therefore, Jazz Planners' investments that permit it to have significant influence over the operating and financing policies of the investee companies should be reported on the statement of financial position using the equity method. On the other hand, the investments that represent 1% to 3% ownership interests would be covered by SFAS 124. According to of SFAS 124, these investments in equity securities should be reported on the statement of financial position at fair value.

53. (b) According to SFAS 136, when a resource provider transfers assets to a nonprofit entity and (1) does not grant the recipient organization variance power and (2) the recipient organization and the beneficiaries are not financially interrelated, the recipient entity should record an in-crease in assets and liabilities as a result of the donation. In the case at hand, United Ways is the recipient entity that should record the cash donation by increasing both assets and liabilities.

54. (a) According to SFAS 136, when the recipient organization and the beneficiary are financially interrelated organizations, and the resources held by the recipient organization must be used for the benefit of the beneficiary, the recipient entity should account for the asset transfer as an increase in assets and as an increase in contribution revenue. In the case at hand, World-Wide Helpers Foundation is the recipient entity that should record the asset transfer by increasing cash and increasing contribution revenue.

55. (d) According to SFAS 136, a contribution from a resource provider is reported as contribution revenue if (1) the recipient organization is granted variance power by the resource provider or (2) the recipient organization and the beneficiary are financially interrelated organizations. In the case at hand, answer (d) is correct because the resource provider granted variance power to the recipient organization. Answers (b) and (c) are incorrect because the resource provider designates the beneficiaries and does not grant the recipient organization the ability to redirect the donation to other than the specified beneficiaries. For both situations (b) and (c), the recipient organization should record the donation by increasing both assets and liabilities. Answer (a) is incorrect because contribution revenue is reported by a recipient organization if the recipient organization and the beneficiary are financially interrelated. If they are not financially interrelated, the recipient organization should report the donation as an increase in assets and an increase in liabilities.

56. (a) According to SFAS 136, when the resource provider provides variance power over transferred assets, the recipient entity should account for the assets donated as an increase in assets and an increase in contribution revenue. Variance power means the ability of the recipient organization to redirect the resources transferred to it by a resource provider. In case at hand, World-Wide Helpers is the recipient entity that should record the cash donation by increasing both assets and contribution revenue.

57. (c) According to SFAS 136, a recipient organization that receives a contribution from a resource provider is required to report the contribution as an asset and a liability unless one of two condition exist (1) the recipient organization is granted variance power to redirect the resources, or (2) the recipient organization and the beneficiary are financially interrelated organizations. Since Mary Wilson did not grant variance power to Goodbody to redirect her donation to other flood victims, and the Taft family and Goodbody are not financially interrelated organizations, the cash donation should be reported as a liability in Goodbody's 2003 financial statements.

58. (d) According to the AICPA Audit and Accounting Guide, *Not-for-Profit Organizations*,

> Under a split-interest agreement, a donor makes an initial gift to a trust or directly to the not-for-profit organization, in which the not-for-profit organization has a beneficial interest but is not the sole beneficiary....The assets are invested and administered by the organization, a trustee, or a fiscal agent, and distributions are made to a beneficiary or beneficiaries during the term of the

agreement. At the end of the agreement's term, the remaining assets covered by the agreement are distributed to or retained by either the not-for-profit organization or another beneficiary or beneficiaries.

59. **(c)** According to the Not-for-Profit Guide, all joint costs of informational materials or activities that include a fund-raising appeal should be reported as fund-raising expense unless an appeal is designed to motivate its audience to action other than providing financial support. Answer (c) is the only alternative that requires both other action and financial support.

60. **(c)** According to the Not-for-Profit Guide, capital additions include nonexpendable gifts restricted to endowment, plant, or loan funds and the legally restricted investment income on investments in such funds. Donor-restricted gifts for programs or supporting services are not capital additions.

61. **(c)** According to the Not-for-Profit Guide, gifts in kind are noncash assets received by not-for-profit organizations from resource providers. These gifts in kind are reported as agency transactions or as contributions depending on the extent of discretion that the not-for-profit recipient has over the use or subsequent disposition of the assets.

62. **(b)** According to the Not-for-Profit Guide, when a not-for-profit organization has little or no discretion over the use of the asset, the transaction is an agency transaction.

C. Health Care Organization Accounting—Private Sector

63. **(c)** According to the AICPA Audit and Accounting Guide, *Health Care Organizations*, the basic financial statements for a hospital include a balance sheet, a statement of operations, a statement of changes in net assets, and a statement of cash flows. Accordingly, Elizabeth Hospital should prepare both a statement of changes in net assets as well as a statement of operations.

64. **(a)** According to the AICPA Audit and Accounting Guide, *Health Care Organizations*, the provision for contractual adjustments and discounts is recognized on the accrual basis and deducted from gross patient service revenue to determine net patient revenue. Bad debts expense is reported as an operating expense, not as a contra to gross patient service revenue. Accordingly, net patient service revenue for 2003 is $865,000. This amount is determined by subtracting the contractual adjustments of $100,000 and the discounts of $15,000 from gross patient service revenue of $980,000.

65. **(a)** Patient service revenue is to be reported net of adjustments for contractual and other adjustments in the operating statement. Provisions recognizing contractual adjustments and other adjustments are recorded on an accrual basis and deducted from gross service revenue to determine net service revenue.

66. **(d)** Voluntary health and welfare organizations are categorized as not-for-profit, nonbusiness-oriented organizations that are covered by the AICPA Audit and Accounting Guide, *Not-for-Profit Organizations*. Nursing home, home health agencies, and hospitals are all considered health care entities and are covered in the AICPA Audit and Accounting Guide, *Health Care Organizations*.

67. **(b)** The AICPA Audit and Accounting Guide, *Health Care Organizations* lists the items that must be reported separately from the performance indicator. Among these are extraordinary items (and other items required by GAAP to be reported separately), equity transfers, receipt of restricted contributions, contributions of long-lived assets, restricted investment returns, and unrealized gains/losses of unrestricted investments (except trading securities). Premium revenue is included in the performance indicator.

68. **(c)** The AICPA Audit and Accounting Guide, *Health Care Organizations* states that expenses may be reported on the face of the financial statements using either a natural classification or functional presentation. Not-for-profit organizations that report using a natural classification of expenses are required to disclose expenses by functional classification in the notes.

69. **(b)** Functional classifications should be based on full cost allocations. Health care organizations may report depreciation, interest, and bad debts along with functions.

70. **(d)** The performance indicator should report the results of operations. However, it should not include such items as extraordinary items, unrealized gains and losses on nontrading securities, and contributions of long-lived assets. Increase in unrestricted net assets and increase in net assets include these items and so cannot be performance indicators. Net income is a term associated with for-profit enterprises and so is not used by health care entities.

71. **(d)** According to the AICPA Audit and Accounting Guide, *Health Care Organizations*,

> *Charity care represents health care services that are provided but are never expected to result in cash flows. As a result, charity care does not qualify for recognition as receivables or revenue in the financial statements. Distinguishing charity care from bad-debt expense requires the exercise of judgment. Charity care is provided to a patient with demonstrated inability to pay. Each organization establishes its own criteria for charity care consistent with its mission statement and financial ability. Only the portion of a patient's account that meets the organization's charity care criteria is recognized as charity. Although it is not necessary for the entity to make this determination upon admission or registration of an individual, at some point the entity must determine that the individual meets the established criteria for charity care.*

Therefore, charity care is not included on the financial statements.

72. **(b)** According to the AICPA Audit and Accounting Guide, *Health Care Organizations*, "Under provisions of continuing-care contracts entered into by a CCRC and residents, nonrefundable advance fees represent payment for future services and should be accounted for as deferred revenue." Deferred revenue is classified as a liability.

73. **(a)** Patient service revenue is to be reported net of contractual adjustments. Contractual adjustments are the difference between revenue at established rates and the amounts realizable from third-party payors under contractual agreements. Charity care is not part of patient service revenue, and donor contributions are reported separately. Therefore,

Gross patient service revenue	$750,000
− Contractual adjustments	− 63,000
= Net patient service revenue	$687,000

74. **(d)** According to the AICPA Audit and Accounting Guide, *Health Care Organizations*, charity care does not qualify for recognition as receivables or revenue in the financial statements. According to the AICPA Audit and Accounting Guide, *Health Care Organizations,* management's policy for providing charity care, as well as the level of charity care provided, should be disclosed in the financial statements. Such disclosure generally is made in the notes to the financial statement and is measured based on the providers' rates, costs, units of service, or other statistical measure.

75. **(c)** According to the AICPA Audit and Accounting Guide, *Health Care Organizations*, a hospital's other revenue, gains, and losses are derived from services other than providing health care services or coverage to patients. Other revenue, gains, and losses typically include interest and dividends that are unrestricted as well as proceeds from sales at gift shops and snack bars. Cash contributions from donors that are restricted to the acquisition of capital assets during 2004 are not reported on the statement of operations for 2003. The capital contribution should be reported on the statement of changes in net assets for the year ended December 31, 2003, as an increase in temporarily restricted net assets. Therefore, the amount that Michael should report as other revenue and gains on its statement of operations for 2003 is $100,000.

76. **(b)** According to the AICPA Audit and Accounting Guide, *Health Care Organizations*, expirations of donor restrictions on temporarily restricted net assets should be reported on the statement of operations as net assets released from restrictions. On Swathmore's statement of operations for 2003, the use of the $50,000 contribution for research in 2003 should be reported as "net assets released from restrictions." This amount should be included in revenues, gains, and other support on the statement of operations, and it is also included in the "performance indicator" reported on the statement of operations. The use of the $250,000 contribution to acquire a capital asset placed into service during 2003 is also reported as "net assets released from restrictions" on the 2003 statement of operations. This results because the hospital adopted an accounting policy that did not imply a time restriction on gifts of long-lived assets. However, this amount is reported after the performance indicator on the statement of operations. Accordingly, the total amount reported as net assets released from restrictions on the 2003 statement of operations is $300,000.

77. **(d)** According to the AICPA Audit and Accounting Guide, *Health Care Organizations*, unrealized gains on trading securities should be included as part of the amount reported for revenue, gains, and other support on the statement of operations. These unrealized gains are included in the performance indicator. Likewise, unrestricted revenues from interest and dividends are included as part of the amount reported for revenue, gains, and other support on the statement of operations. Therefore, Smithson Hospital should report both the $3,000 of interest revenue and the $2,000 unrealized holding gain ($105,000 less $103,000) in the amount reported for revenue, gains, and other support on its statement of operations for the year ended December 31, 2003.

78. **(d)** According to the AICPA Audit and Accounting Guide, *Health Care Organizations*, unrealized gains and

losses from other than trading securities, which are not restricted by donors, are reported after the performance indicator on the statement of operations. Therefore, the unrealized loss in item I is reported on the statement of operations, but it is not included in the amount reported for revenue and gains over expenses and losses, the performance indicator. The donor contribution that cannot be used until next year is not reported on the statement of operations. The contribution represents an increase in temporarily restricted net assets and is reported on the statement of changes in net assets.

79. **(c)** According to the AICPA Audit and Accounting Guide, *Health Care Organizations*, a donation of noncash assets should be reported at fair value and reported as an increase in the appropriate net asset class. If there are no donor-imposed restrictions on the donation, the donation increases unrestricted net assets on the statement of operations. More specifically, the donation is included in the amount reported for revenue, gains, and other support if the donation is used for the operations of the hospital. The use of the donation in the operations of the hospital is reported as part of the operations expenses for the period. The donation of medical supplies to Tucker Hospital should be reported as both a revenue and as an operating expense in the amount of $15,000 on the statement of operations for the year ended December 31, 2003.

80. **(b)** The cash flows from revenues, gains, and other support, which are reported on the hospital's statement of operations, would be included in the net cash provided (used) by operating activities on the statement of cash flows. Both net patient service revenue and tuition revenue are included in the amount reported for revenue, gains, and other support on the hospital's statement of operations. Accordingly, cash received from patient service revenue and from tuition revenue are both included in the amount reported for cash flows from operating activities. The cash received for the term endowment as well as the cash received from dividends would not be included in the amount reported for net cash provided (used) by operating activities. Both of these cash receipts would be reported as increases in cash flows provided by financing activities. According to SFAS 117, cash contributions that are donor-restricted for long-term purposes are reported as financing activities on the statement of cash flows. In addition, the AICPA Audit and Accounting Guide, *Health Care Organizations*, states that cash received for long-term purposes, for example, the cash received for the term endowment and the building improvements, is not reported as a current asset. So that the statement of cash flows will reconcile with the change in cash and cash equivalents reported as current assets on the balance sheet, an amount equal to the cash received for the two financing activities is included in the amount reported for cash flows from investing activities. For Wilson Hospital, this would mean that $330,000, the sum of the $250,000 for the term endowment and the $80,000 of restricted dividends, is reported as a negative amount in the investing activities' section of the statement of cash flows. Note that both of these amounts are reported as investing activities whether the cash was spent this period or in subsequent period(s).

81. **(d)** The statement of changes in net assets reports the changes in the hospital's unrestricted, temporarily restricted, and permanently restricted net assets for a time period. The statement of operations discloses only the

changes in unrestricted net assets for a time period, while
the balance sheet discloses the amounts of unrestricted, temporarily restricted, and permanently restricted net assets as
of a specific date. Therefore, neither the balance sheet nor
the statement of operations discloses the changes in unrestricted, temporarily restricted, and permanently restricted
net assets for a time period.

82. (c)   According to the AICPA Audit and Accounting
Guide, *Health Care Organizations*, investment returns not
restricted by donors are reported on the statement of operations. The statement of operations explains the change in
the hospital's unrestricted net assets for a period. Consequently, investment returns that are permanently restricted
would not be reported on the statement of operations. Investment returns that are realized in cash are reported on the
statement of cash flows. However, investment returns that
are not realized in cash are not reported on the statement of
cash flows. Investment returns, whether realized or unrealized, that are restricted by donors are reported on the statement of changes in net assets. Unrealized gains on investments that are permanently restricted represent investment
returns which would be reported as an increase in permanently restricted net assets on the statement of changes in net
assets.

83. (b)   The AICPA Audit and Accounting Guide,
Health Care Organizations, lists proceeds from sales of
cafeteria meals and guest trays to employees, medical staff,
and visitors as one of the items reported as other revenue on
the statement of operations. Other revenue is included in the
performance indicator on the statement of operations. Net
assets released from restrictions are also reported in the performance indicator if the net assets are used for operating
expenses.

OTHER OBJECTIVE ANSWERS AND ANSWER EXPLANATIONS

Problem 1

1. (C, L) In accordance with SFAS 117, contributions from donors who stipulate that the donation be invested permanently are reported as increases in permanently restricted net assets on the statement of activities. On the statement of cash flows for 2003, cash inflows from contributions restricted for an endowment are reported as cash inflows from financing activities.

2. (B, L) In accordance with SFAS 117, contributions from donors for the acquisition of plant assets are reported as increases in temporarily restricted net assets on the statement of activities. In accordance with SFAS 116, the contributions are reported as revenues in the year received, not in the year they are used. On the statement of cash flows, cash inflows from contributions restricted for plant assets are reported as cash inflows from financing activities.

3. (D, O) In accordance with SFAS 117, all expenses are decreases in unrestricted net assets on the statement of activities. On the statement of cash flows, depreciation expense would be reported in the schedule that reconciles the change in net assets to net cash provided from operating activities.

4. (A, H) In accordance with SFAS 117, revenues that are under the control of the governing board are increases in unrestricted net assets on the statement of activities. Tuition revenues are an example of resources that are under the control of the governing board. On the statement of cash flows, the cash received from tuition is reported as an increase in cash flows from operating activities.

5. (G, K) The acquisition of investments does not affect the permanently restricted net assets. The receipt of cash increased unrestricted net assets in 2003; however, the acquisition of investments simply increases one asset (investments) and decreases another (cash). Therefore, the acquisition of investments would not be reported on the statement of activities for 2003. On the statement of cash flows, the acquisition of the investments would represent a decrease in the cash flows from investing activities.

6. (B, H) In accordance with SFAS 117, the $8,000 of dividends and interest is reported as an increase in temporarily restricted net assets on the statement of activities for 2003. Since the donor stipulated that the earnings be used for scholarships, the earnings are reported as temporarily restricted. On the statement of cash flows, the cash received for interest and dividends would be reported as an increase in the cash flows from operating activities.

7. (E, H) In accordance with SFAS 116, contributions are reported as revenues in the year the pledges are made, not in the year the pledges are received. Thus, the pledges were reported as revenues on the statement of activities for 2002. The pledges increased temporarily restricted net assets on the statement of activities in 2002. In 2003, the receipt and use of the cash for the marketing campaign resulted in a reclassification from temporarily restricted net assets to unrestricted net assets. This reclassification resulted in a decrease in temporarily restricted net assets. The expense for the marketing campaign is reported as a decrease in unrestricted net assets. Therefore, there was no effect in unrestricted net asset in 2003 as a result of this event. In accordance with SFAS 117, the cash received for the marketing campaign should be reported as an increase in the cash flows from operating activities.

8. (D, I) In accordance with SFAS 117, all expenses are reported as reductions of unrestricted net assets. The expense for faculty salaries would be reported as an expense on the statement of activities for 2003, and it would be deducted from unrestricted revenues, gains, and other support. On the statement of cash flows for 2003, the cash paid for faculty salaries would be reported as a decrease in the cash flows from operating activities.

9. (E, I) In accordance with SFAS 116, the cash used for faculty research grants in 2003 was reported as an increase in temporarily restricted net assets on the statement of activities in 2002. In 2003, the use of the donations for faculty research grants requires a reclassification of net assets from temporarily restricted net assets to unrestricted net assets. This reclassification decreases temporarily restricted net assets. However, the reclassification has no effect on unrestricted net assets because research expense is deducted from unrestricted revenues, gains, and other support, which includes the amount reclassified from temporarily restricted net assets. On the statement of cash flows for 2003, the cash spent for research is reported as a decrease in cash flows from operating activities.

10. (A, H) In accordance with SFAS 117, contributions from donors who do not stipulate how their donations are to be used are reported as increases in unrestricted net assets on the statement of activities. Whenever the governing board has control over how donations are to be used, the donations represent unrestricted net assets. On the statement of cash flows for 2003, the donations are reported as increases in the cash flows from operating activities.

Problem 2

1. (U) Contributions receivable should be the $28,000 from the unrestricted written promises to contribute cash made in 2003 and the $12,000 of written promises uncollected to contribute cash restricted to use for community scholarships.

2. (U) Net assets released from restrictions (satisfaction of use restrictions) includes the $37,000 expended for a bus with the $30,000 expended for scholarships for a total of $67,000 released from use restrictions.

3. (C) Only the unrestricted written promises to contribute cash are restricted by time. The amount promised in 2002 and collected in 2003 has had the time restriction lapse.

4. (L) The only contribution that is permanently restricted is the principal of the debt security endowment. The contribution is booked at fair value at the time of receipt.

5. (D) The only fees are the admission fees of the music festival of $5,000

6. (O) Program expenses include the costs of the reading materials donated ($8,000), the instructor salaries ($26,000), the salary of the director of community activities ($50,000), and the space rental used for community activities ($15,000). The expenses for the music festival are fund-raising expenses. The other operating expenses are general, management, and fund-raising.

7. (B) The only general fund-raising expenses are printing and mailing costs for pledge cards ($2,000). The expenses for the music festival are for a special event.

8. (A) The only income from long-term investment is the income from the debt security, but that income is restricted for use.

9. (A) No services were received that create or enhance nonfinancial assets or require specialized skills that would have been purchased; therefore, no services are recorded.

10. (O) Unrestricted promises collected are part of the operating section of the statement of cash flows.

11. (O) Cash received as a good-faith advance on a promise to contribute matching funds is an operating activity.

12. (I) The purchase of a bus is equipment, which is classified as an investing activity.

13. (F) Paying part of the principal of a loan is a financing activity.

14. (I) Purchasing equity securities is an investment, which is an investing activity.

15. (O) Income earned on investments is an operating activity.

16. (O) The payment of interest is an operating activity.

17. (O) Interest income from an endowment is an operating activity.

8 FEDERAL TAXATION

Introduction

Module 40/Individual Taxation (ITAX)

TAXES ON THE ACCOUNTING AND REPORTING EXAMINATION

Federal taxation is tested in the Accounting and Reporting section of the exam. According to the AICPA's Content Specification Outline, federal taxation should account for a total of 60% of the Accounting and Reporting section. Of this 60%, 20% will test the federal income taxation of individuals, 20% will test the federal income taxation of corporations, 10% will test partnerships, and 10% will test the income taxation of estates and trusts, federal gift and estate taxation, exempt organizations, and preparers' responsibilities.

You will want to note that the Accounting and Reporting section will contain only multiple-choice questions and other objective format (OOAF) problems; no essays will appear in this section of the exam. An other objective format problem for taxes appeared for the first time on the May 1992 exam, and a similar problem appeared on the May 1993 examination. In both cases, these OOAF problems provided a list of transactions pertaining to a self-employed taxpayer together with a list of possible alternative tax treatments. A corporate OOAF problem appeared on the May 1994, May 1995, and May 1996 examinations and consisted of several parts including items regarding the corporate alternative minimum tax. Generally, May examinations contain an OOAF problem concerning corporate taxation, while November examinations contain an OOAF problem concerning individual taxation.

The multiple-choice questions test detailed application of the Internal Revenue Code and tax regulations. The instructions indicate that "answers should be based on the Internal Revenue Code and Tax Regulations in effect for the tax period specified in the item. If no tax period is specified, use the current Internal Revenue Code and Tax Regulations." On recent examinations, approximately 60% of the multiple-choice questions have specified the preceding taxable year, while the remaining 40% have no year specified.

As a practical matter, the examiners generally avoid testing on recent tax law changes, and have indicated that the **exam will generally cover federal tax regulations in effect 6 months before the date of the exam**. Also note that you are not expected to know amounts that change between years because of being indexed for inflation (e.g., the dollar amount of personal exemption, standard deduction, etc.).

The AICPA Content Specification Outline of the coverage of taxes for the Accounting and Reporting section of the exam appears in Chapter 5 of the 4-part set and Chapter 8 of Volume 1 in the 2-volume set. As shown in the outline, taxation will be weighted 60% of this exam.

The summary tax outlines presented in this chapter begin by emphasizing individual taxation. Because of numerous common concepts, partnership and corporate taxation are later presented in terms of their differences from individual taxation (i.e., learn individual taxes thoroughly and then learn the special rules of partnership and corporate taxation). Interperiod and intraperiod tax allocation questions are presented in Module 27, Deferred Taxes, of the Financial Accounting and Reporting Volume.

The property transactions outline has been inserted between individual taxation and the partnership and corporate tax outlines because property transactions are common to all types of taxpayers, and generally are tested within every tax problem, both PTAX and CTAX, as well as ITAX.

The next section presents a detailed outline of the individual tax formula, and outlines of two basic federal income tax returns: Form 1065—Partnership; and Form 1120—Corporation. These outlines are an intermediary step between the simple formula outline (below) and the outlines of the detailed rules.

Formula Outline for Individuals
Gross income
  − "above the line" deductions
Adjusted gross income
  − total itemized deductions (or standard deduction)
  − exemptions
Taxable income
  x tax rates
  − tax credits
Tax liability

OVERVIEW OF FEDERAL TAX RETURNS

Problems requiring computation of taxable income require that you be familiar with the outlines below. The tax return outlines help you "pull together" all of the detailed tax rules. The schedule and form identification numbers are provided for reference only; they are not tested on the examination.

Review the outlines presented below. The outlines will introduce you to the topics tested on the exam and their relationship to final "tax liability."

Form 1040—Individuals

A. Income

1. Wages, salaries, tips, etc.
2. Interest (Sch. B)
3. Dividend income (Sch. B)
4. Income other than wages, dividends, and interest (The gross income reported on the schedules below is already reduced by corresponding deductible expenses. Only the net income [or loss] is reported on Form 1040.)

   a. State and local income tax refunds
   b. Alimony received
   c. Business income or loss (Sch. C)
   d. Capital gain or loss (Sch. D)
   e. Other gains or losses (Form 4797)
   f. Taxable IRA distributions, pensions, and annuities
   g. Rents, royalties, partnerships, S corporations, estates, trusts, etc. (Sch. E)
   h. Unemployment compensation, social security
   i. Other

B. Less "Above the Line" Deductions (also known as "Deductions **for** AGI")

1. One-half of self-employment tax
2. Moving expenses
3. Self-employed health insurance deduction
4. Medical savings account deduction
5. Payments to an individual retirement arrangement (IRA)
6. Payments to a Keogh retirement plan
7. Penalty on early withdrawal of savings
8. Student loan interest deduction
9. Alimony paid

C. Adjusted Gross Income

D. Less Itemized Deductions (Sch. A), (or standard deduction), including

1. Medical and dental expenses
2. Taxes
3. Interest expense
4. Contributions
5. Casualty and theft losses
6. Miscellaneous

   a. Subject to 2% of AGI limitation
   b. Not subject to 2% of AGI limitation

E. Less Exemptions

F. Taxable Income

1. Find your tax in the tables, or
2. Use tax rate schedules

G. Additional Taxes

1. Alternative minimum tax (Form 6251)
2. Parents' election to report child's interest and dividends (Form 8814)
3. Lump-sum distribution from qualified retirement plans (Form 4972)

H. Less Tax Credits

1. General business credit

    a. Investment credit (Form 3468)
    b. Alcohol fuels credit
    c. Low-income housing credit
    d. Disabled access credit
    e. Employer social security credit

2. Credit for the elderly or the disabled (Sch. R)
3. Credit for child and dependent care expenses (Form 2441)
4. Child tax credit
5. Education credits (Form 8863)
6. Adoption credit (Form 8839)
7. Foreign tax credit (Form 1116)
8. Credit for prior year minimum tax

I. Tax Liability
J. Other Taxes

1. Self-employment tax (Sch. SE)
2. Advance earned income credit payments
3. Social security tax on unreported tip income (Form 4137)
4. Tax on IRAs and other retirement plans (Form 5329)
5. Household employment taxes (Sch. H)

K. Less Payments

1. Tax withheld on wages
2. Estimated tax payments
3. Earned income credit
4. Amount paid with an extension
5. Excess FICA paid
6. Credit for federal tax on special fuels (Form 4136)
7. Credit from a regulated investment company (Form 2439)

L. Amount Overpaid or Balance Due

Form 1065—Partnerships

A. Income

1. Gross sales less returns and allowances
2. Less cost of goods sold
3. Gross profit
4. Ordinary income from other partnerships and fiduciaries
5. Net farm profit
6. Ordinary gain or loss (including depreciation recapture)
7. Other

B. Less Deductions

1. Salaries and wages (other than to partners)
2. Guaranteed payments to partners
3. Rents
4. Interest expense

5. Taxes
6. Bad debts
7. Repairs
8. Depreciation
9. Depletion
10. Retirement plans
11. Employee benefit program contributions
12. Other

C. Ordinary Income (Loss) from trade or business activity
D. Schedule K (on partnership return) and Schedule K-1 to be prepared for each partner

1. Ordinary income (loss) from trade or business activity
2. Income (loss) from rental real estate activity
3. Income (loss) from other rental activity
4. Portfolio income (loss)

   a. Interest
   b. Dividends
   c. Royalties
   d. Net short-term capital gain (loss)
   e. Net long-term capital gain (loss)
   f. Other portfolio income (loss)

5. Guaranteed payments
6. Net gain (loss) under Sec. 1231 (other than casualty or theft)
7. Other
8. Charitable contributions
9. Sec. 179 expense deduction
10. Deductions related to portfolio income
11. Other
12. Credits

   a. Credit for income tax withheld
   b. Low-income housing credit
   c. Qualified rehabilitation expenditures related to rental real estate
   d. Credits related to rental real estate activities

13. Other
14. a. Net earnings (loss) from self-employment
    b. Gross farming or fishing income
    c. Gross nonfarm income

15. Tax preference items

    a. Depreciation adjustment on property placed in service after 12/31/86
    b. Tax-exempt private activity bond interest

16. Investment interest expense
17. Foreign income taxes

Form 1120—Corporations

A. Gross Income
1. Gross sales less returns and allowances
2. Less cost of goods sold
3. Gross profit
4. Dividends
5. Interest
6. Gross rents
7. Gross royalties

    8. Net capital gains
    9. Ordinary gain or loss
  10. Other income

B. Less Deductions

    1. Compensation of officers
    2. Salaries and wages (net of jobs credit)
    3. Repairs
    4. Bad debts
    5. Rents
    6. Taxes
    7. Interest
    8. Charitable contributions
    9. Depreciation
  10. Depletion
  11. Advertising
  12. Pension, profit-sharing plan contributions
  13. Employee benefit programs
  14. Other
  15. Net operating loss deduction
  16. Dividends received deduction

C. TAXABLE INCOME times tax rates
D. Less tax credits equals TAX LIABILITY

I. GROSS INCOME ON INDIVIDUAL RETURNS

This section outlines (1) gross income in general, (2) exclusions from gross income, (3) items to be included in gross income, (4) tax accounting methods, and (5) items to be included in gross income net of deductions (e.g., business income, sales and exchanges).

A. In General

1. **Gross income** includes all income from whatever source derived, unless specifically excluded

   a. Does not include a return of capital (e.g., if a taxpayer loans $6,000 to another and is repaid $6,500 at a later date, only the $500 difference is included in gross income)

   b. The income must be **realized** (i.e., there must be a transaction which gives rise to the income)

      (1) A mere appreciation in the value of property is not income (e.g., value of one's home increases $2,000 during year. Only if the house is sold will the increase in value be realized)

      (2) A transaction may be in the form of actual receipt of cash or property, accrual of a receivable, or sale or exchange

   c. The income must also be **recognized** (i.e., the transaction must be a taxable event, and not a transaction for which nonrecognition is provided in the Internal Revenue Code)

   d. An **assignment of income** will not be recognized for tax purposes

      (1) If income from property is assigned, it is still taxable to the owner of the property.

      EXAMPLE: X owns a building and assigns the rents to Y. The rents remain taxable to X, even though the rents are received by Y.

      (2) If income from services is assigned, it is still taxable to the person who earns it.

      EXAMPLE: X earns $200 per week. To pay off a debt owed to Y, he assigns half of it to Y. $200 per week remains taxable to X.

2. Distinction between exclusions, deductions, and credits

   a. **Exclusions**—income items which are not included in gross income

      (1) Exclusions must be specified by law. Remember, gross income includes all income except that specifically excluded.

      (2) Although exclusions are exempt from income tax, they may still be taxed under other tax rules (e.g., gifts may be subject to the gift tax).

   b. **Deductions**—amounts that are subtracted from income to arrive at adjusted gross income or taxable income

      (1) Deductions for adjusted gross income (above the line deductions)—amounts deducted from gross income to arrive at adjusted gross income

      (2) Itemized deductions (below the line deductions)—amounts deducted from adjusted gross income to arrive at taxable income

   c. **Credits**—amounts subtracted from the computed tax to arrive at taxes payable

B. Exclusions from Gross Income (not reported)

1. Payments received for **support** of minor children

   a. Must be children of the parent making the payments

   b. Decree of divorce or separate maintenance generally must specify the amount to be treated as child support, otherwise payments may be treated as alimony

2. **Property settlement** (division of capital) received in a divorce

3. **Annuities** and pensions are excluded to the extent they represent a return of capital

   a. Excluded portion of each payment is

   $$\frac{\text{Net cost of annuity}}{\text{Expected total annuity payments}} \times \text{Payment received}$$

   b. "Expected total annuity payments" is calculated by multiplying the annual return by

      (1) The number of years receivable if it is an annuity for a definite period

      (2) A life expectancy multiple (from IRS tables) if it is an annuity for life

    c.   Once this exclusion ratio is determined, it remains constant until the cost of the annuity is completely recovered. Any additional payments will be fully taxable.

> *EXAMPLE: Mr. Jones purchased an annuity contract for $3,600 that will pay him $1,500 per year beginning in 2002. His expected return under the contract is $10,800. Mr. Jones' exclusion ratio is $3,600 ÷ $10,800 = 1/3. For 2002, Mr. Jones will exclude $1,500 x 1/3 = $500; and will include the remaining $1,000 in gross income.*

    d.   If the taxpayer dies before total cost is recovered, unrecovered cost is allowed as a miscellaneous itemized deduction on the taxpayer's final tax return.

4. **Life insurance proceeds** (face amount of policy) are generally excluded if paid by reason of death

    a.   If proceeds are received in **installments**, amounts received in excess of pro rata part of face amount are taxable as interest

    b.   **Dividends** on unmatured insurance policies are excluded to the extent not in excess of cumulative premiums paid.

    c.   **Accelerated death benefits** received under a life insurance policy by a *terminally or chronically ill* individual are generally excluded from gross income

        (1) Similarly, if a portion of a life insurance contract on the life of a terminally or chronically ill individual is assigned or sold to a viatical settlement provider, proceeds received from the provider are excluded.

        (2) For a chronically ill individual, the exclusion is limited to the amount paid by the individual for unreimbursed long-term care costs. Payments made on a per diem basis, up to $175 per day, are excludable regardless of actual long-term care costs incurred.

    d.   All interest is taxable if proceeds are left with insurance company under agreement to pay only interest.

    e.   If insurance proceeds are paid for reasons other than death or under c. above, all proceeds in excess of cost are taxable. Annuity rules apply to installment payments.

5. Certain **employee benefits** are excluded

    a.   **Group-term life insurance** premiums paid by employer (the **cost of up to $50,000** of insurance coverage is excluded). Exclusion not limited if beneficiary is the employer or a qualified charity.

    b.   Insurance premiums employer pays to fund an accident or health plan for employees are excluded.

    c.   **Accident and health benefits** provided by employer are excluded if benefits are for

        (1) Permanent injury or loss of bodily function

        (2) Reimbursement for medical care of employee, spouse, or dependents

            (a) Employee cannot take itemized deduction for reimbursed medical expenses

            (b) Exclusion may not apply to highly compensated individuals if reimbursed under a discriminatory self-insured medical plan

    d.   Employees of small businesses (50 or fewer employees) and self-employed individuals may qualify for a **medical savings account** (MSA) if covered under a high-deductible health insurance plan. An MSA is similar to an IRA, except used for health care.

        (1) Employer contributions to an employee's MSA are excluded from gross income (except if made through a cafeteria plan), and employee contributions are deductible for AGI.

        (2) Contributions are limited to 65% (75% for family coverage) of the annual health insurance deductible amount.

        (3) Earnings of an MSA are not subject to tax; distributions from an MSA used to pay qualified medical expenses are excluded from gross income.

    e.   **Meals or lodging** furnished for the convenience of the employer on the employer's premises are excluded.

        (1) For the convenience of the employer means there must be a noncompensatory reason such as the employee is required to be on duty during this period.

        (2) In the case of lodging, it also must be a condition of employment.

    f.   Employer-provided educational assistance (e.g., payment of tuition, books, fees) derived from an employer's qualified **educational assistance program** is excluded up to maximum of **$5,250** per year. The exclusion applies to both undergraduate as well as graduate-level courses, but does not apply to assistance payments for courses involving sports, games, or hobbies, unless they involve the employer's business or are required as part of a degree program. Excludable assistance does not include tools or supplies that the employee retains after completion of the course, nor the cost of meals, lodging, or transportation.

g. Employer payments to an employee for **dependent care assistance** are excluded from an employee's income if made under a written, nondiscriminatory plan. Maximum exclusion is **$5,000** per year ($2,500 for a married person filing a separate return).

h. **Qualified adoption expenses** paid or incurred by an employer in connection with an employee's adoption of a child are excluded from the employee's gross income. For tax years beginning after December 31, 2001, the maximum exclusion is **$10,000** per eligible child (including special needs children) and the exclusion is ratably phased out for modified AGI between $150,000 and $190,000.

i. **Employee fringe benefits** are generally excluded if

   (1) **No additional-cost services**—for example, airline pass
   (2) **Employee discount** that is nondiscriminatory
   (3) **Working condition fringes**—excluded to the extent that if the amount had been paid by the employee, the amount would be deductible as an employee business expense
   (4) **De minimis fringes**—small value, impracticable to account for (e.g., coffee, personal use of copying machine)
   (5) **Qualified transportation fringes**

      (a) Up to $100 per month for 2002 can be excluded for employer-provided transit passes and transportation in a commuter highway vehicle if the transportation is between the employee's home and work place.
      (b) Up to $185 per month for 2002 can be excluded for employer-provided parking on or near the employer's place of business.

   (6) **Qualified moving expense reimbursement**—an individual can exclude any amount received from an employer as payment for (or reimbursement of) expenses which would be deductible as moving expenses if directly paid or incurred by the individual. The exclusion does not apply to any payment (or reimbursement of) an expense actually deducted by the individual in a prior taxable year.

j. **Workers' compensation** is fully excluded if received for an occupational sickness or injury and is paid under a workers' compensation act or statute.

6. Accident and health insurance benefits derived from policies **purchased by the taxpayer** are excluded, but not if the medical expenses were deducted in a prior year and the tax benefit rule applies.

7. **Damages for physical injury or physical sickness** are excluded.

   a. If an action has its origin in a physical injury or physical sickness, then all damages therefrom (other than punitive damages) are excluded (e.g., damages received by an individual on account of a claim for loss due to a physical injury to such individual's spouse are excludible from gross income).

   b. Damages (other than punitive damages) received on account of a claim of wrongful death, and damages that are compensation for amounts paid for medical care (including medical care for emotional distress) are excluded.

   c. Emotional distress is not considered a physical injury or physical sickness. No exclusion applies to damages received from a claim of employment discrimination, age discrimination, or injury to reputation (even if accompanied by a claim of emotional distress).

   d. Punitive damages generally must be included in gross income, even if related to a physical injury or physical sickness.

8. **Gifts, bequests, devises, or inheritances** are excluded.

   a. Income subsequently derived from property so acquired is not excluded (e.g., interest or rent).
   b. "Gifts" from employer except for noncash holiday presents are generally not excluded.

9. The receipt of **stock dividends** (or stock rights) is generally excluded from income (see page 347 for basis and holding period), but the FMV of the stock received will be included in income if the distribution

a. Is on preferred stock

b. Is payable, at the election of any shareholder, in stock or property

c. Results in the receipt of preferred stock by some common shareholders, and the receipt of common stock by other common shareholders

d. Results in the receipt of property by some shareholders, and an increase in the proportionate interests of other shareholders in earnings or assets of the corporation

10. Certain **interest income** is excluded.

a. Interest on obligations of a **state** or one of its political subdivisions (e.g., **municipal** bonds), the District of Columbia, and US possessions is generally **excluded** from income if the bond proceeds are used to finance traditional governmental operations.

b. Other state and local government-issued obligations (private activity bonds) are generally fully taxable. An obligation is a private activity bond if (1) more than 10% of the bond proceeds are used (directly or indirectly) in a private trade or business and more than 10% of the principal or interest on the bonds is derived from, or secured by, money or property used in the trade or business, or (2) the lesser of 5% or $5 million of the bond proceeds is used (directly or indirectly) to make or finance loans to private persons or entities.

c. The following bonds are **excluded from the private activity bond category** even though their proceeds are not used in traditional government operations. The interest from these bonds is excluded from income.

   (1) Qualified bonds issued for the benefit of schools, hospitals, and other charitable organizations

   (2) Bonds used to finance certain exempt facilities, such as airports, docks, wharves, mass commuting facilities, etc.

   (3) Qualified redevelopment bonds, small-issue bonds (i.e., bonds not exceeding $1 million), and student loan bonds

   (4) Qualified mortgage and veterans' mortgage bonds

d. Interest on **US obligations** is **included** in income.

11. **Savings bonds for higher education**

a. The accrued interest on Series EE US savings bonds that are redeemed by the taxpayer is excluded from gross income to the extent that the aggregate redemption proceeds (principal plus interest) are used to finance the higher education of the taxpayer, taxpayer's spouse, or dependents.

   (1) The bonds must be issued after December 31, 1989, to an individual age twenty-four or older at the bond's issue date.

   (2) The purchaser of the bonds must be the sole owner of the bonds (or joint owner with his or her spouse). Married taxpayers must file a joint return to qualify for the exclusion.

   (3) The redemption proceeds must be used to pay qualified higher education expenses (i.e., tuition and required fees less scholarships, fellowships, and employer-provided educational assistance) at an accredited university, college, junior college, or other institution providing postsecondary education, or at an area vocational education school.

   (4) If the redemption proceeds exceed the qualified higher education expenses, only a pro rata amount of interest can be excluded.

   > EXAMPLE: During 2002, a married taxpayer redeems Series EE bonds receiving $6,000 of principal and $4,000 of accrued interest. Assuming qualified higher education expenses total $9,000, accrued interest of $3,600 ($9,000/$10,000 x $4,000) can be excluded from gross income.

b. If the taxpayer's modified AGI exceeds a specified level, the exclusion is subject to phaseout as follows:

Filing status	2002 AGI phaseout range
Married filing jointly	$86,400 – $116,400
Single (including head of household)	$57,600 – $ 72,600

   (1) The reduction of the exclusion is computed as

$$\left(\frac{\text{Excess AGI}}{\begin{array}{c}\$15,000 \\ (\$30,000 \text{ for joint returns})\end{array}} \right) \times \left(\begin{array}{c}\text{Otherwise} \\ \text{excludable} \\ \text{interest}\end{array} \right) = \text{Reduction}$$

(2) If the taxpayer's modified AGI exceeds the applicable phaseout range, no exclusion is available.

> *EXAMPLE: Assume the joint return of the married taxpayer in the above example has modified AGI of $106,400 for 2002. The reduction would be ($20,000/$30,000) x $3,600 = $2,400. Thus, of the $4,000 of interest received, a total of $1,200 could be excluded from gross income.*

12. **Scholarships and fellowships**

   a. A **degree candidate** can exclude the amount of a scholarship or fellowship that is used for tuition and course-related fees, books, supplies, and equipment. Amounts used for other purposes including room and board are included in income.

   b. Amounts received as a grant or a tuition reduction that represent payment for teaching, research, or other services are not excludable.

   c. Nondegree students may not exclude any part of a scholarship or fellowship grant.

13. Political contributions received by candidates' campaign funds are excluded from income, but included if put to personal use.

14. Rental value of parsonage or cash rental allowance for a parsonage is excluded by a minister.

15. **Discharge of indebtedness** normally results in income to debtor, but may be **excluded** if

   a. A discharge of certain student loans pursuant to a loan provision providing for discharge if the individual works in a certain profession for a specified period of time

   b. A discharge of a corporation's debt by a shareholder (treated as a contribution to capital)

   c. The discharge is a gift

   d. The discharge is a purchase money debt reduction (treat as a reduction of purchase price)

   e. Debt is discharged in a bankruptcy proceeding, or debtor is insolvent both before and after discharge

   (1) If debtor is insolvent before but solvent after discharge of debt, income is recognized to the extent that the FMV of assets exceeds liabilities after discharge

   (2) The amount excluded from income in e. above must be applied to reduce tax attributes in the following order

   (a) NOL for taxable year and loss carryovers to taxable year
   (b) General business credit
   (c) Minimum tax credit
   (d) Capital loss of taxable year and carryovers to taxable year
   (e) Reduction of the basis of property
   (f) Passive activity loss and credit carryovers
   (g) Foreign tax credit carryovers to or from taxable year

   (3) Instead of reducing tax attributes in the above order, taxpayer may elect to first reduce the basis of depreciable property

16. **Lease improvements.** Increase in value of property due to improvements made by lessee are excluded from lessor's income unless improvements are made in lieu of fair value rent.

17. **Foreign earned income exclusion.** An individual meeting either a bona fide residence test or a physical presence test may elect to exclude up to $80,000 of income earned in a foreign country for calendar year 2002. Qualifying taxpayers also may elect to exclude additional amounts based on foreign housing costs.

   a. To qualify, an individual must be a (1) US citizen who is a foreign resident for an uninterrupted period that includes an entire taxable year (bona fide residence test), or (2) US citizen or resident present in a foreign country for at least 330 full days in any twelve-month period (physical presence test).

   b. An individual who elects to exclude the housing cost amount can exclude only the lesser of (1) the housing cost amount attributable to employer-provided amounts, or (2) the individual's foreign earned income for the year.

   c. Housing cost amounts not provided by an employer can be deducted for AGI, but deduction is limited to the excess of the taxpayer's foreign earned income over the applicable foreign earned income exclusion.

C. Items to Be Included in Gross Income

Gross income includes all income from any source except those specifically excluded. The more common items of gross income are listed below. Those items requiring a detailed explanation are discussed on the following pages.

1. Compensation for services, including wages, salaries, bonuses, commissions, fees, and tips

   a. Property received as compensation is included in income at FMV on date of receipt.
   b. Bargain purchases by an employee from an employer are included in income at FMV less price paid.
   c. Life insurance premiums paid by employer must be included in an employee's gross income except for group-term life insurance coverage of $50,000 or less.
   d. Employee expenses paid or reimbursed by the employer unless the employee has to account to the employer for these expenses and they would qualify as deductible business expenses for employee.
   e. **Tips** must be included in gross income

      (1) If an individual receives less than $20 in tips while working for one employer during one month, the tips do not have to be reported to the employer, but the tips must be included in the individual's gross income when received
      (2) If an individual receives $20 or more in tips while working for one employer during one month, the individual must report the total amount of tips to the employer by the tenth day of the following month for purposes of withholding of income tax and social security tax. Then the total amount of tips must be included in the individual's gross income for the month in which reported to the employer.

2. Gross income derived from business or profession
3. Distributive share of partnership or S corporation income
4. Gain from the sale or exchange of real estate, securities, or other property
5. Rents and royalties
6. Dividends
7. **Interest** including

   a. Earnings from savings and loan associations, mutual savings banks, credit unions, etc.
   b. Interest on bank deposits, corporate or US government bonds, and treasury bills

      (1) Interest from US obligations is included, while interest on state and local obligations is generally excluded.
      (2) If a taxpayer elects to amortize the bond premium on taxable bonds acquired after 1987, any bond premium amortization is treated as an offset against the interest earned on the bond. The amortization of bond premium reduces taxable income (by offsetting interest income) as well as the bond's basis.

   c. **Interest on tax refunds**
   d. Imputed interest from interest-free and low-interest loans

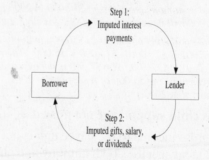

      (1) Borrower is treated as making imputed interest payments (subject to the same deduction restrictions as actual interest payments) which the lender reports as interest income.
      (2) Lender is treated as making gifts (for personal loans) or paying salary or dividends (for business-related loans) to the borrower.

(3) Rate used to impute interest is tied to average yield on certain federal securities; if the federal rate is greater than the interest rate charged on a loan (e.g., a low-interest loan), impute interest only for the excess.

    (a) For demand loans, the deemed transfers are generally treated as occurring at the end of each year, and will fluctuate with interest rates.

    (b) For term loans, the interest payments are determined at the date of the loan and then allocated over the term of the loan; lender's payments are treated as made on date of loan.

(4) No interest is imputed to either the borrower or the lender for any day on which the aggregate amount of loans between such individuals (and their spouses) does not exceed $10,000.

(5) For any day that the aggregate amount of loans between borrower and lender (and their spouses) does not exceed $100,000, imputed interest is limited to borrower's "net investment income"; no interest is imputed if borrower's net investment income does not exceed $1,000.

EXAMPLE: Parents make a $200,000 interest-free demand loan to their unmarried daughter on January 1, 2002. Assume the average federal short-term rate is 6% for 2002. If the loan is outstanding for the entire year, under Step 1, the daughter is treated as making a $12,000 ($200,000 x 6%) interest payment on 12/31/02, which is included as interest income on the parents' 2002 tax return. Under Step 2, the parents are treated as making a $12,000 gift to their daughter on 12/31/02. (Note that the gift will be offset by annual exclusions totaling $22,000 for gift tax purposes as discussed in Module 44.)

8. **Alimony** and separate maintenance payments

  a. Alimony is included in the recipient's gross income and is deductible toward AGI by the payor. In order for a payment to be considered as alimony, the payment must

    (1) Be made **pursuant to a decree** of divorce or written separation instrument

    (2) Be made in **cash** and received **by or on behalf** of the payee's spouse

    (3) **Terminate upon death** of the recipient

    (4) Not be made to a member of the same household at the time the payments are made

    (5) Not be made to a person with whom the taxpayer is filing a joint return

    (6) Not be characterized in the decree or written instrument as other than alimony

  b. **Alimony recapture** may occur if payments sharply decline in the second or third years. This is accomplished by making the payor report the recaptured alimony from the first and second years as income (and allowing the payee to deduct the same amount) in the third year.

    (1) Recapture for the second year occurs to the extent that the alimony paid in the second year exceeds the third-year alimony by more than $15,000.

    (2) Recapture for the first year occurs to the extent that the alimony paid in the first year exceeds the average alimony paid in the second year (reduced by the recapture for that year) and third year by more than $15,000.

    (3) Recapture will not apply to any year in which payments terminate as a result of the death of either spouse or the remarriage of the payee.

    (4) Recapture does not apply to payments that may fluctuate over three years or more and are not within the control of the payor spouse (e.g., 20% of the net income from a business).

EXAMPLE: If a payor makes alimony payments of $50,000 in 2000 and no payments in 2001 or 2002, $50,000 – $15,000 = $35,000 will be recaptured in 2002 (assuming none of the exceptions apply).

EXAMPLE: If a payor makes alimony payments of $50,000 in 2000, $20,000 in 2001, and nothing in 2002, the recapture amount for 2001 is $20,000 – $15,000 = $5,000. The recapture amount for 2000 is $50,000 – ($15,000 + $7,500) = $27,500. The $7,500 is the average payments for 2001 and 2002 after reducing the $20,000 year 2001 payment by the $5,000 of recapture for 2001. The recapture amounts for 2000 and 2001 total $32,500 and are reported in 2002.

  c. Any amounts specified as **child support** are not treated as alimony.

    (1) Child support is not gross income to the payee and is not deductible by the payor.

    (2) If the decree or instrument specifies both alimony and child support, but **less is paid than required,** then amounts are first allocated to child support, with any remainder allocated to alimony.

    (3) If a specified amount of alimony is to be reduced upon the happening of some **contingency relating to a child,** then an amount equal to the specified reduction will be treated as child support rather than alimony.

> *EXAMPLE: A divorce decree provides that payments of $1,000 per month will be reduced by $400 per month when a child reaches age twenty-one. Here, $400 of each $1,000 monthly payment will be treated as child support.*

9. **Social security,** pensions, annuities (other than excluded recovery of capital)

   a. Up to 50% of social security retirement benefits may be included in gross income if the taxpayer's provisional income (AGI + tax-exempt income + 50% of the social security benefits) exceeds a threshold that is $32,000 for a joint return, $0 for married taxpayers filing separately, and $25,000 for all other taxpayers. The amount to be included in gross income is the lesser of

      (1) 50% of the social security benefits, or
      (2) 50% of the excess of the taxpayer's provisional income over the base amount.

      > *EXAMPLE: A single taxpayer with AGI of $20,000 received tax-exempt interest of $2,000 and social security benefits of $7,000. The social security to be included in gross income is the lesser of*
      >
      > *1/2 ($ 7,000) = $3,500; or*
      > *1/2 ($25,500 − $25,000) = $250.*

   b. **Up to 85%** of social security retirement benefits may be included in gross income for taxpayers with provisional income above a higher second threshold that is $44,000 for a joint return, $0 for married taxpayers filing separately, and $34,000 for all other taxpayers. The amount to be included in gross income is the lesser of

      (1) 85% of the taxpayer's social security benefits, or
      (2) The sum of (a) 85% of the excess of the taxpayer's provisional income above the applicable higher threshold amount plus (b) the smaller of (i) the amount of benefits included under a. above, or (ii) $4,500 for single taxpayers or $6,000 for married taxpayers filing jointly.

   c. **Rule of thumb:** Social security retirement benefits are fully excluded by low-income taxpayers (i.e., provisional income less than $25,000); 85% of benefits must be included in gross income by high-income taxpayers (i.e., provisional income greater than $60,000).

   d. **Lump-sum distributions** from qualified pension, profit-sharing, stock bonus, and Keogh plans (but not IRAs) may be eligible for special tax treatment.

      (1) The portion of the distribution allocable to pre-1974 years is eligible for long-term capital gain treatment.
      (2) If the employee was born before 1936, the employee may elect ten-year averaging.
      (3) Alternatively, the distribution may be rolled over tax-free (within sixty days) to a traditional IRA, but subsequent distributions from the IRA will be treated as ordinary income.

10. **Income in respect of a decedent** is income that would have been income of the decedent before death but was not includible in income under the decedent's method of accounting (e.g., installment payments that are paid to a decedent's estate after his/her death). Such income has the same character as it would have had if the decedent had lived and must be included in gross income by the person who receives it.

11. Employer supplemental unemployment benefits or strike benefits from union funds

12. Fees, including those received by an executor, administrator, director, or for jury duty or precinct election board duty

13. Income from discharge of indebtedness unless specifically excluded (see page 240)

14. **Stock options**

   a. An **incentive stock option** receives favorable tax treatment.

      (1) The option must meet certain technical requirements to qualify.
      (2) No income is recognized by employee when option is granted or exercised.
      (3) If employee holds the stock acquired through exercise of the option at least two years from the date the option was granted, and holds the stock itself at least one year, the

         (a) Employee's realized gain will be long-term capital gain
         (b) Employer receives no deduction

      (4) If the holding period requirements above are not met, the employee has ordinary income to the extent that the FMV at date of exercise exceeds the option price.

         (a) Remainder of gain is short-term or long-term capital gain.
         (b) Employer receives a deduction equal to the amount employee reports as ordinary income.

(5) An incentive stock option may be treated as a nonqualified stock option if a corporation so elects at the time the option is issued.

b. A **nonqualified stock option** is included in income when received if option has a determinable FMV.

(1) If option has no ascertainable FMV when received, then income arises when option is exercised; to the extent of the difference between the FMV when exercised and the option price.

(2) Amount recognized (at receipt or when exercised) is treated as ordinary income to employee; employer is allowed a deduction equal to amount included in employee's income.

c. An **employee stock purchase plan** that does not discriminate against rank and file employees

(1) No income when employee receives or exercises option

(2) If the employee holds the stock at least two years after the option is granted and at least one year after exercise, then

(a) Employee has ordinary income to the extent of the lesser of

1] FMV at time option granted over option price, or
2] FMV at disposition over option price

(b) Capital gain to the extent realized gain exceeds ordinary income

(3) If the stock is not held for the required time, then

(a) Employee has ordinary income at the time of sale for the difference between FMV when exercised and the option price. This amount also increases basis.

(b) Capital gain or loss for the difference between selling price and increased basis

15. **Prizes and awards** are generally taxable.

a. Prizes and awards received for religious, charitable, scientific, educational, artistic, literary, or civic achievement can be excluded only if the recipient

(1) Was selected without any action on his/her part,

(2) Is not required to render substantial future services, and

(3) Designates that the prize or award is to be transferred by the payor to a governmental unit or a tax-exempt charitable, educational, or religious organization

(4) The prize or award is excluded from the recipient's income, but no charitable deduction is allowed for the transferred amount.

b. **Employee achievement awards** are excluded from an employee's income if the cost to the employer of the award does not exceed the amount allowable as a deduction (generally from $400 to $1,600; see page 249).

(1) The award must be for length of service or safety achievement and must be in the form of tangible personal property (cash does not qualify).

(2) If the cost of the award exceeds the amount allowable as a deduction to the employer, the employee must include in gross income the greater of

(a) The portion of cost not allowable as a deduction to the employer, or

(b) The excess of the award's FMV over the amount allowable as a deduction.

16. **Tax benefit rule.** A recovery of an item deducted in an earlier year must be included in gross income to the extent that a tax benefit was derived from the prior deduction of the recovered item.

a. A tax benefit was derived if the previous deduction reduced the taxpayer's income tax.

b. A recovery is excluded from gross income to the extent that the previous deduction did not reduce the taxpayer's income tax.

(1) A deduction would not reduce a taxpayer's income tax if the taxpayer was subject to the alternative minimum tax in the earlier year and the deduction was not allowed in computing AMTI (e.g., state income taxes).

(2) A recovery of state income taxes, medical expenses, or other items deductible on Schedule A (Form 1040) will be excluded from gross income if an individual did not itemize deductions for the year the item was paid.

> EXAMPLE: *Individual X, a single taxpayer, did not itemize deductions but instead used the standard deduction of $4,700 for 2002. In 2003, a refund of $300 of 2002 state income taxes is received. X would exclude the $300 refund from income in 2003.*

> EXAMPLE: *Individual Y, a single taxpayer, had total itemized deductions of $4,800 for 2002, including $800 of state income taxes. In 2003, a refund of $400 of 2002 state income taxes is received. Y must include $100 ($4,800 – $4,700) of the refund in income for 2003.*

17. Embezzled or other illegal income
18. **Gambling winnings**
19. **Unemployment compensation** is fully included in gross income by the recipient.

D. Tax Accounting Methods

Tax accounting methods often affect the period in which an item of income or deduction is recognized. Note that the classification of an item is not changed, only the time for its inclusion in the tax computation.

1. Cash method or accrual method is commonly used.

   a. **Cash method** recognizes income when first received or constructively received; expenses are deductible when paid.

      (1) **Constructive receipt** means that an item is unqualifiedly available without restriction (e.g., interest on bank deposit is income when credited to account).

      (2) Not all receipts are income (e.g., loan proceeds, return of investment); not all payments are deductible (e.g., loan repayment, expenditures benefiting future years generally must be capitalized and deducted over cost recovery period).

   b. The cash method cannot generally be used if inventories are necessary to clearly reflect income, and cannot generally be used by C corporations, partnerships that have a C corporation as a partner, tax shelters, and certain tax-exempt trusts. However, the following may use the cash method:

      (1) A qualified personal service corporation (e.g., corporation performing services in health, law, engineering, accounting, actuarial science, performing arts, or consulting) if at least 95% of stock is owned by specified shareholders including employees.

      (2) An entity (other than a tax shelter) if for every year it has average annual gross receipts of **$5 million or less** for any prior three-year period and provided it does not have inventories for sale to customers.

      (3) A **small business taxpayer** with average annual gross receipts of **$1 million or less** for any prior three-year period (ending after December 17, 1998) can use the cash method and is excepted from the requirements to account for inventories and use the accrual method for purchases and sales of merchandise.

      (4) A **small business taxpayer** is eligible to use the cash method of accounting if, in addition to having average gross receipts of more than $1 million and less than $10 million, the business meets any one of three requirements.

         (a) The principal business activity is **not** retailing, wholesaling, manufacturing, mining, publishing, or sound recording;

         (b) The principal business activity is the provision of services, or custom manufacturing; or

         (c) Regardless of the principal business activity, a taxpayer may use the cash method with respect to any separate business that satisfies (a) or (b) above.

      (5) A taxpayer using the accrual method who meets the requirements in (3) or (4) can change to the cash method but must treat merchandise inventory as a material or supply that is not incidental (i.e., only deductible in the year actually consumed or used in the taxpayer's business).

   c. **Accrual method** must be used by taxpayers (other than small business taxpayers) for purchases and sales when inventories are required to clearly reflect income.

      (1) **Income** is recognized when "all events" have occurred that fix the taxpayer's right to receive the item of income and the amount can be determined with reasonable accuracy.

      (2) An **expense** is deductible when "all events" have occurred that establish the fact of the liability and the amount can be determined with reasonable accuracy. The all-events test is not satisfied until **economic performance** has taken place.

(a) For property or services to be provided **to the taxpayer,** economic performance occurs when the property or services are actually provided by the other party.

(b) For property or services to be provided **by the taxpayer,** economic performance occurs when the property or services are physically provided by the taxpayer.

(3) An exception to the economic performance rule treats certain **recurring items of expense** as incurred in advance of economic performance provided

(a) The all-events test, without regard to economic performance, is satisfied during the tax year;

(b) Economic performance occurs within a reasonable period (but in no event more than 8.5 months after the close of the tax year);

(c) The item is recurring in nature and the taxpayer consistently treats items of the same type as incurred in the tax year in which the all-events test is met; and

(d) Either the amount is not material or the accrual of the item in the year the all-events test is met results in a better matching against the income to which it relates.

2. **Special rules** regarding methods of accounting

a. **Rents and royalties received in advance** are included in gross income in the year received under both the cash and accrual methods.

(1) A **security deposit** is included in income when not returned to tenant.

(2) An amount called a "security deposit" that may be used as final payment of rent is considered to be advance rent and included in income when received.

> EXAMPLE: *In 2002, a landlord signed a five-year lease. During 2002, the landlord received $5,000 for that year's rent, and $5,000 as advance rent for the last year (2006) of the lease. All $10,000 will be included in income for 2002.*

b. Dividends are included in gross income in the year received under both the cash and accrual methods.

c. No advance deduction is generally allowed for accrual method taxpayers for estimated or contingent expenses; the obligation must be "fixed and determinable."

3. The **installment method** applies to gains (not losses) from the disposition of property where at least one payment is to be received after the year of sale. The installment method does not change the character of the gain to be reported (e.g., ordinary, capital, etc.), and is required unless the taxpayer makes a negative election to report the full amount of gain in year of sale.

a. The installment method **cannot be used** for property held for sale in the ordinary course of business (except time-share units, residential lots, and property used or produced in farming), and cannot be used for sales of stock or securities traded on an established securities market.

b. The amount to be reported in each year is determined by the formula

$$\frac{\text{Gross profit}}{\text{Total contract price}} \times \text{Amount received in year}$$

(1) **Contract price** is the selling price reduced by the seller's liabilities that are assumed by the buyer, to the extent not in excess of the seller's basis in the property.

> EXAMPLE: *Taxpayer sells property with a basis of $80,000 to buyer for a selling price of $150,000. As part of the purchase price, buyer agrees to assume a $50,000 mortgage on the property and pay the remaining $100,000 in 10 equal annual installments together with adequate interest.*
>
> *The contract price is $100,000 ($150,000 – $50,000); the gross profit is $70,000 ($150,000 – $80,000); and the gross profit ratio is 70% ($70,000 ÷ $100,000). Thus, $7,000 of each $10,000 payment is reported as gain from the sale.*

> EXAMPLE: *Assume the same facts as above except that the seller's basis is $30,000. The contract price is $120,000 ($150,000 – mortgage assumed but only to extent of seller's basis of $30,000); the gross profit is $120,000 ($150,000 – $30,000); and the gross profit ratio is 100% ($120,000 ÷ $120,000). Thus, 100% of each $10,000 payment is reported as gain from the sale. In addition, the amount by which the assumed mortgage exceeds the seller's basis ($20,000) is deemed to be a payment in year of sale. Since the gross profit ratio is 100%, all $20,000 is reported as gain in the year the mortgage is assumed.*

(2) Any depreciation recapture under Secs. 1245, 1250, and 291 must be included in income in the year of sale. Amount of recapture included in income is treated as an increase in the basis

of the property for purposes of determining the gross profit ratio. Remainder of gain is spread over installment payments.

    (3) If installment obligations are pledged as security for a loan, the net proceeds of the loan are treated as payments received on the installment obligations.

    (4) Installment obligations arising from nondealer sales of property used in the taxpayer's trade or business or held for the production of rental income (e.g., factory building, warehouse, office building, apartment building) are subject to an interest charge on the tax that is deferred on such sales to the extent that the amount of deferred payments arising from all dispositions of such property during a taxable year and outstanding as of the close of the taxable year exceeds $5,000,000. This provision does not apply to installment sales of property if the sales price does not exceed $150,000, to sales of personal use property, and to sales of farm property.

4. **Percentage-of-completion** method can be used for contracts that are not completed within the year they are started.

    a. Percentage-of-completion method recognizes income each year based on the percentage of the contract completed that year.

    b. Taxpayer may elect not to recognize income or account for costs from a contract for a tax year if less than 10% of the estimated total contract costs have been incurred as of the end of the year.

E. Business Income and Deductions

1. **Gross income** for a business includes sales less cost of goods sold plus other income. In computing cost of goods sold

    a. Inventory is generally valued at (1) cost, or (2) market, whichever is lower

    b. Specific identification, FIFO, and LIFO are allowed

    c. If LIFO is used for taxes, it must also be used on books

    d. Lower of cost or market cannot be used with LIFO

2. All **ordinary** (customary and not a capital expenditure) and **necessary** (appropriate and helpful) **expenses** incurred in a trade or business are deductible.

    a. Business expenses that violate public policy (fines or illegal kickbacks) are not deductible.

    b. No deduction or credit is allowed for any amount paid or incurred in carrying on a trade or business that consists of trafficking in controlled substances. However, this limitation does not alter the definition of gross income (i.e., sales less cost of goods sold).

    c. Business expenses must be reasonable.

        (1) If salaries are excessive (unreasonable compensation), they may be disallowed as a deduction to the extent unreasonable.

        (2) Reasonableness of compensation issue generally arises only when the relationship between the employer and employee exceeds that of the normal employer-employee relationship (e.g., employee is also a shareholder).

        (3) Use test of what another enterprise would pay under similar circumstances to an unrelated employee.

    d. In the case of an individual, any charge (including taxes) for basic local telephone service with respect to the **first telephone line** provided to any residence of the taxpayer shall be treated as a nondeductible personal expense. Disallowance does not apply to charges for long-distance calls, charges for equipment rental, and optional services provided by a telephone company, or charges attributable to additional telephone lines to a taxpayer's residence other than the first telephone line.

    e. **Uniform capitalization rules** generally require that all costs incurred (both direct and indirect) in manufacturing or constructing real or personal property, or in purchasing or holding property for sale, must be capitalized as part of the cost of the property.

        (1) These costs become part of the basis of the property and are recovered through depreciation or amortization, or are included in inventory and recovered through cost of goods sold as an offset to selling price.

(2) The rules apply to inventory, noninventory property produced or held for sale to customers, and to assets or improvements to assets constructed by a taxpayer for the taxpayer's own use in a trade or business or in an activity engaged in for profit.

(3) Taxpayers subject to the rules are required to capitalize not only direct costs, but also most indirect costs that benefit the assets produced or acquired for resale, including general, administrative, and overhead costs.

(4) Retailers and wholesalers must include in inventory all costs incident to purchasing and storing inventory such as wages of employees responsible for purchasing inventory, handling, processing, repackaging and assembly of goods, and off-site storage costs. These rules do not apply to "small retailers and wholesalers" (i.e., a taxpayer who acquires personal property for resale if the taxpayer's average annual gross receipts for the three preceding taxable years do not exceed $10,000,000).

(5) Interest must be capitalized if the debt is incurred or continued to finance the construction or production of real property, property with a recovery period of twenty years, property that takes more than two years to produce, or property with a production period exceeding one year and a cost exceeding $1 million.

(6) The capitalization rules do not apply to research and experimentation expenditures, property held for personal use, and to free-lance authors, photographers, and artists.

f. **Business meals, entertainment, and travel**

(1) Receipts must be maintained for all lodging expenditures and for other expenditures of **$75** or more except transportation expenditures where receipts are not readily available.

(2) Adequate contemporaneous records must be maintained for business meals and entertainment to substantiate the amount of expense, for example, who, when, where, and why (the 4 W's).

(3) Business meals and entertainment must be directly related or associated with the active conduct of a trade or business to be deductible. The taxpayer or a representative must be present to satisfy this requirement.

(4) The amount of the otherwise allowable deduction for business meals or entertainment must be reduced by 50%. This **50% reduction rule** applies to all food, beverage, and entertainment costs (even though incurred in the course of travel away from home) after determining the amount otherwise deductible. The 50% reduction rule will not apply if

　(a) The full value of the meal or entertainment is included in the recipient's income or excluded as a fringe benefit.

　(b) An employee is reimbursed for the cost of a meal or entertainment (the 50% reduction rule applies to the party making the reimbursement).

　(c) The cost is for a traditional employer-paid employee recreation expense (e.g., a company Christmas party).

　(d) The cost is for samples and other promotional activities made available to the public.

　(e) The expense is for a sports event that qualifies as a charitable fund-raising event.

　(f) The cost is for meals or entertainment sold for full consideration.

(5) The cost of a ticket to any entertainment activity is limited (prior to the 50% reduction rule) to its face value.

(6) No deduction is generally allowed for expenses with respect to an entertainment, recreational, or amusement facility.

　(a) Entertainment facilities include yachts, hunting lodges, fishing camps, swimming pools, etc.

　(b) If the facility or club is used for a business purpose, the related out-of-pocket expenditures are deductible even though depreciation, etc. of the facility is not deductible.

(7) No deduction is allowed for dues paid to country clubs, golf and athletic clubs, airline clubs, hotel clubs, and luncheon clubs. Dues are generally deductible if paid to professional organizations (accounting, medical, and legal associations), business leagues, trade associations, chambers of commerce, boards of trade, and civic and public service organizations (Kiwanis, Lions, Elks).

(8) **Transportation and travel expenses** are deductible if incurred in the active conduct of a trade or business.

(a) Deductible transportation expenses include local transportation between two job locations, but excludes commuting expenses between residence and job.

(b) Deductible travel expenses are those incurred while temporarily "away from tax home" overnight including meals, lodging, transportation, and expenses incident to travel (clothing care, etc.).

1] Travel expenses to and from domestic destination are fully deductible if business is the primary purpose of trip.

2] Actual automobile expenses can be deducted, or for calendar year 2002, taxpayers can use standard mileage rate of 36.5¢/mile for all business miles (plus parking and tolls). This rate decreases to 36¢/mile beginning January 1, 2003.

3] No deduction is allowed for travel as a form of education. This rule applies when a travel expense would otherwise be deductible only on the ground that the travel itself serves educational purposes.

4] No deduction is allowed for expenses incurred in attending a convention, seminar, or similar meeting for investment purposes.

g. Deductions for **business gifts** are limited to **$25** per recipient each year.

(1) Advertising and promotional gifts costing $4 or less are not limited.

(2) Gifts of tangible personal property costing $400 or less are deductible if awarded as an employee achievement award for length of service or safety achievement.

(3) Gifts of tangible personal property costing $1,600 or less are deductible if awarded as an employee achievement award under a qualified plan for length of service or safety achievement.

(a) Plan must be written and nondiscriminatory.

(b) Average cost of all items awarded under the plan during the tax year must not exceed $400.

h. **Bad debts** are generally deducted in the year they become worthless.

(1) There must have been a valid "debtor-creditor" relationship.

(2) A **business bad debt** is one that is incurred in the trade or business of the lender.

(a) Deductible against ordinary income (toward AGI)

(b) Deduction allowed for partial worthlessness

(3) Business bad debts must be deducted under the specific charge-off method (the reserve method generally cannot be used).

(a) A deduction is allowed when a specific debt becomes partially or totally worthless.

(b) A bad debt deduction is available for accounts or notes receivable only if the amount owed has already been included in gross income for the current or a prior taxable year. Since receivables for services rendered of a **cash method** taxpayer have not yet been included in gross income, the receivables cannot be deducted when they become uncollectible.

(4) A **nonbusiness bad debt** (not incurred in trade or business) can only be deducted

(a) If totally worthless

(b) As a short-term capital loss

(5) Guarantor of debt who has to pay takes same deduction as if the loss were from a direct loan

(a) Business bad debt if guarantee related to trade, business, or employment

(b) Nonbusiness bad debt if guarantee entered into for profit but not related to trade or business

i. A **hobby** is an activity not engaged in for profit (e.g., stamp or card collecting engaged in for recreation and personal pleasure).

(1) Special rules generally limit the deduction of hobby expenses to the amount of hobby gross income. No net loss can generally be deducted for hobby activities.

(2) Hobby expenses are deductible as itemized deductions in the following order:

(a) First deduct taxes, interest, and casualty losses pertaining to the hobby.

(b) Then other hobby operating expenses are deductible to the extent they do not exceed hobby gross income reduced by the amounts deducted in (a). Out-of-pocket expenses are deducted before depreciation. These hobby expenses are aggregated with other miscellaneous itemized deductions that are subject to the 2% of AGI floor.

(3) An activity is presumed to be for profit (not a hobby) if it produces a net profit in at least three out of five consecutive years (two out of seven years for horses).

3. Net operating loss (NOL)

a. A net operating loss is generally a business loss but may occur even if an individual is not engaged in a separate trade or business (e.g., a NOL created by a personal casualty loss).

b. A NOL may be carried **back two years** and carried **forward twenty years** to offset taxable income in those years.

(1) Carryback is first made to the second preceding year.

(2) Taxpayer may elect not to carryback and only carryforward twenty years.

(3) A three-year carryback period is permitted for the portion of the NOL that relates to casualty and theft losses of individual taxpayers, and to NOLs that are attributable to presidentially declared disasters and are incurred by taxpayers engaged in farming or by a small business.

(4) A *small business* is any trade or business (including one conducted by a corporation, partnership, or sole proprietorship) with average annual gross receipts of $5 million or less for the three-year tax period preceding the loss year.

c. For NOLs arising in tax years ending in 2001 and 2002, the two-year (or three-year) carryback is extended to five years. However, a taxpayer may make an irrevocable election to waive the five-year carryback period, and carry back only two years (or three years if applicable).

d. The following cannot be included in the computation of a NOL:

(1) Any NOL carryforward or carryback from another year

(2) Excess of capital losses over capital gains. Excess of nonbusiness capital losses over nonbusiness capital gains even if overall gains exceed losses

(3) Personal exemptions

(4) Excess of nonbusiness deductions (usually itemized deductions) over nonbusiness income

    (a) The standard deduction is treated as a nonbusiness deduction.

    (b) Contributions to a self-employed retirement plan are considered nonbusiness deductions.

    (c) Casualty losses (even if personal) are considered business deductions.

    (d) Dividends and interest are nonbusiness income; salary and rent are business income.

(5) Any remaining loss is a NOL and must be carried back first, unless election is made to carryforward only.

EXAMPLE: George, single with no dependents, started his own delivery business and incurred a loss from the business for 2002. In addition, he earned interest on personal bank deposits of $1,800. After deducting his itemized deductions for interest and taxes of $9,000, and his personal exemption of $3,000, the loss shown on George's Form 1040 was $20,250. George's net operating loss would be computed as follows:

Taxable income		*$(20,250)*
Nonbusiness deductions	*$9,000*	
Nonbusiness income	*–1,800*	*7,200*
Personal exemption		*3,000*
Net operating loss		*$(10,050)*

4. Limitation on deductions for **business use of home**. To be deductible

a. A portion of the home must be used exclusively and regularly as the *principal place of business*, or as a meeting place for patients, clients, or customers.

(1) Exclusive use rule does not apply to the portion of the home used as a day care center and to a place of regular storage of business inventory or product samples if the home is the sole fixed location of a trade or business selling products at retail or wholesale.

(2) If an employee, the exclusive use must be for the convenience of the employer.

(3) A home office qualifies as a taxpayer's *principal place of business* if

    (a) It is the place where the primary income-generating functions of the trade or business are performed; or

(b) The office is used to conduct administrative or management activities of the taxpayer's business, and there is no other fixed location of the business where substantial administrative or management activities are performed. Activities that are administrative or managerial in nature include billing customers, clients, or patients; keeping books and records; ordering supplies; setting up appointments; and forwarding orders or writing reports.

b. Deduction is limited to the excess of gross income derived from the business use of the home over deductions otherwise allowable for taxes, interest, and casualty losses.

c. Any business expenses not allocable to the use of the home (e.g., wages, transportation, supplies) must be deducted before home use expenses.

d. Any business use of home expenses that are disallowed due to the gross income limitation can be carried forward and deducted in future years subject to the same restrictions.

EXAMPLE: Taxpayer uses 10% of his home exclusively for business purposes. Gross income from his business totaled $750, and he incurred the following expenses:

	Total	*10% Business*
Interest	*4,000*	*$400*
Taxes	*2,500*	*250*
Utilities, insurance	*1,500*	*150*
Depreciation	*2,000*	*200*

Since total deductions for business use of the home are limited to business gross income, the taxpayer can deduct the following for business use of his home: $400 interest; $250 taxes; $100 utilities and insurance; and $0 depreciation (operating expenses such as utilities and insurance must be deducted before depreciation). The remaining $50 of utilities and insurance, and $200 of depreciation can be carried forward and deducted in future years subject to the same restrictions.

5. Loss deductions incurred in a trade or business, or in the production of income, are limited to the amount a taxpayer has "**at risk**."

a. Applies to all activities except the leasing of personal property by a closely held corporation (5 or fewer individuals own more than 50% of stock)

b. Applies to individuals and closely held regular corporations

c. Amount "at risk" includes

(1) The cash and adjusted basis of property contributed by the taxpayer, and
(2) Liabilities for which the taxpayer is personally liable; excludes nonrecourse debt.

d. For real estate activities, a taxpayer's amount at risk includes "qualified" nonrecourse financing secured by the real property used in the activity.

(1) Nonrecourse financing is qualified if it is borrowed from a lender engaged in the business of making loans (e.g., bank, savings and loan) provided that the lender is not the promoter or seller of the property or a party related to either; or is borrowed from or guaranteed by any federal, state, or local government or instrumentality thereof.
(2) Nonrecourse financing obtained from a qualified lender who has an equity interest in the venture is treated as an amount at risk, as long as the terms of the financing are commercially reasonable.
(3) The nonrecourse financing must not be convertible, and no person can be personally liable for repayment.

e. Excess losses can be carried over to subsequent years (no time limit) and deducted when the "at risk" amount has been increased.

f. Previously allowed losses will be recaptured as income if the amount at risk is reduced below zero.

6. **Losses and credits from passive activities** may generally only be used to offset income from (or tax allocable to) passive activities. Passive losses may not be used to offset active income (e.g., wages, salaries, professional fees, etc.) or portfolio income (e.g., interest, dividends, annuities, royalties, etc.).

EXAMPLE: Ken has salary income, a loss from a partnership in whose business Ken does not materially participate, and income from a limited partnership. Ken may offset the partnership loss against the income from the limited partnership, but not against his salary income.

EXAMPLE: Robin has dividend and interest income of $40,000 and a passive activity loss of $30,000. The passive activity loss cannot be offset against the dividend and interest income.

a. Applies to individuals, estates, trusts, closely held C corporations, and personal service corporations

   (1) A closely held C corporation is one with five or fewer shareholders owning more than 50% of stock.

   (2) Personal service corporation is an incorporated service business with more than 10% of its stock owned by shareholder-employees.

b. **Passive activity** is any activity that involves the conduct of a trade or business in which the taxpayer does "not materially participate," any rental activity, and any limited partnership interest.

   (1) Material participation is the taxpayer's involvement in an activity on a regular, continuous, and substantial basis considering such factors as time devoted, physical duties performed, and knowledge of or experience in the business.

   (2) Passive activity does not include (1) a working interest in any oil or gas property that a taxpayer owns directly or through an entity that does not limit the taxpayer's liability, (2) operating a hotel or transient lodging if significant services are provided, or (3) operating a short-term equipment rental business.

c. **Losses** from passive activities may be deducted only against income from passive activities.

   (1) If there is insufficient passive activity income to absorb passive activity losses, the excess losses are carried forward indefinitely to future years.

   (2) If there is insufficient passive activity income in subsequent years to fully absorb the loss carryforwards, the unused losses from a passive activity may be deducted when the taxpayer's entire interest in the activity that gave rise to the unused losses is finally disposed of in a fully taxable transaction.

   (3) Other dispositions

      (a) A transfer of a taxpayer's interest in a passive activity by reason of the taxpayer's death results in suspended losses being allowed (to the decedent) to the extent they exceed the amount of the step-up in basis allowed.

      (b) If the disposition is by gift, the suspended losses are added to the basis of the gift property. If less than 100% of an interest is transferred by gift, an allocable portion of the suspended losses is added to the basis of the gift.

      (c) An installment sale of a passive interest triggers the recognition of suspended losses in the ratio that the gain recognized in each year bears to the total gain on sale.

      (d) If a formerly passive activity becomes an active one, suspended losses are allowed against income from the now active business (if the activity remains the same).

d. **Credits** from passive activities can only be used to offset the tax liability attributable to passive activity income.

   (1) Excess credits are carried forward indefinitely (subject to limited carryback during the phase-in period).

   (2) Excess credits (unlike losses) cannot be used in full in the year in which the taxpayer's entire passive activity interest is disposed of. Instead, excess credits continue to be carried forward.

   (3) Credits allowable under the passive activity limitation rules are also subject to the general business credit limitation.

e. Although a **rental activity** is defined as a passive activity regardless of the property owner's participation in the operation of the rental property, a special rule permits an individual to offset up to $25,000 of income that is **not** from passive activities by losses or credits from rental real estate if the individual **actively participates** in the rental real estate activity.

   (1) "Active participation" is less stringent than "material participation" and is met if the taxpayer personally operates the rental property; or, if a rental agent operates the property, the taxpayer participates in management decisions or arranges for others to provide services.

   (2) An individual is not considered to actively participate in a rental real estate activity unless the individual's interest in the activity (including any interest owned by the individual's spouse) was at least 10% of the value of all interests in the activity throughout the year.

(3) The active participation requirement must be met in both the year that the loss arises and the year in which the loss is allowed.

(4) For losses, the $25,000 amount is reduced by 50% of AGI in excess of $100,000 and fully phased out when AGI exceeds $150,000. For this purpose, AGI is computed before including taxable social security, before deducting IRA contributions, and before the exclusion of interest from Series EE bonds used for higher education.

(5) For low-income housing and rehabilitation credits, the $25,000 amount is reduced by 50% of AGI in excess of $200,000 and fully phased out when AGI exceeds $250,000.

    f.   If a taxpayer meets certain eligibility requirements, losses and credits from rental real estate activities in which the taxpayer materially participates are not subject to the passive loss limitations. This provision applies to individuals and closely held C corporations.

(1) Individuals are eligible if (a) more than half of all the personal services they perform during the year are for real property trades or businesses in which they materially participate, and (b) they perform more than 750 hours of service per year in those real estate activities. On a joint return, this relief is available if either spouse separately satisfies the requirements.

(2) Closely held C corporations are eligible if more than 50% of their gross receipts for the taxable year are derived from real property trades or businesses in which the corporation materially participated.

(3) Suspended losses from any rental real property that is not treated as passive by the above provision are treated as losses from a former passive activity. The deductibility of these suspended losses is limited to income from the activity; they are not allowed to offset other income.

    g.   The passive activity limitation rules do not apply to losses disallowed under the at risk rules.

F. Depreciation, Depletion, and Amortization

Depreciation is an allowance for the exhaustion, wear and tear of property used in a trade or business, or of property held for the production of income. The depreciation class of property is generally determined by reference to its Asset Depreciation Range (ADR) guideline class. Taxpayers must determine annual deductions based on the applicable property class, depreciation method, and averaging convention.

1.   For property placed in service prior to 1981, the basis of property reduced by salvage value was recovered over its useful life using the straight-line, declining balance, or sum-of-the-years' digits method. Whether an accelerated method of depreciation could be used depended on the classification and useful life of the property, and whether it was new or used when acquired. The Accelerated Cost Recovery System (ACRS) was used to recover the basis of depreciable property placed in service after 1980 and before 1987.

2.   **Modified Accelerated Cost Recovery System (MACRS)**

    a.   MACRS is **mandatory** for most depreciable property placed in service **after 1986**.

    b.   Salvage value is completely ignored under MACRS; the method of cost recovery and the recovery period are the same for both new and used property.

    c.   **Recovery property** includes all property other than land, intangible assets, and property the taxpayer elects to depreciate under a method not expressed in terms of years (e.g., units of production or income forecast methods). Recovery property placed in service after 1986 is divided into six classes of personal property based on ADR midpoint life and into two classes of real property. Each class is assigned a recovery period and a depreciation method. Recovery deductions for the first six classes are based on the declining balance method, switching to the straight-line method to maximize deductions.

(1) **3-year, 200% class.** Includes property with an ADR midpoint of four years or less (except for autos and light trucks) and certain horses

(2) **5-year, 200% class.** Includes property with an ADR midpoint of more than four and less than ten years. Also included are autos and light trucks, computers and peripheral equipment, office machinery (typewriters, calculators, copiers, etc.)

(3) **7-year, 200% class.** Includes property with an ADR midpoint of at least ten and less than sixteen years. Also included are property having no ADR midpoint and not classified elsewhere, and office furniture and fixtures (desks, files, etc.)

    (4) **10-year, 200% class.** Includes property with an ADR midpoint of at least sixteen and less than twenty years

    (5) **15-year, 150% class.** Includes property with an ADR midpoint of at least twenty years and less than twenty-five years

    (6) **20-year, 150% class.** Includes property with an ADR midpoint of twenty-five years or more, other than real property with an ADR midpoint of 27.5 years or more

    (7) **27 1/2-year, straight-line class.** Includes residential rental property (i.e., a building or structure with 80% or more of its rental income from dwelling units)

    (8) **39-year, straight-line class.** Includes any property that is neither residential real property nor property with a class life of less than 27.5 years

d. Instead of using the declining balance method for three-year through twenty-year property, taxpayers can elect to use the straight-line method over the MACRS class life. This is an annual class-by-class election.

e. Instead of using the 200% declining balance method for three-year through ten-year property, taxpayers can elect to use the 150% declining balance method. This is an annual class-by-class election.

f. An **alternative depreciation system** (ADS) provides for straight-line depreciation over the property's ADS class life (twelve years for personal property with no ADS class life, and forty years for real property).

    (1) A taxpayer may elect to use the alternative system for any class of property placed in service during a taxable year. For real property, the election is made on a property-by-property basis.

    (2) Once made, the election is irrevocable and continues to apply to that property for succeeding years, but does not apply to similar property placed in service in a subsequent year, unless a new election is made.

    (3) The alternative system must be used for foreign use property, property used 50% or more for personal use, and for purposes of computing earnings and profits.

g. An **averaging convention** is used to compute depreciation for the taxable year in which property is placed in service or disposed of under both the regular MACRS and alternative depreciation system.

    (1) **Personal property** is treated as placed in service or disposed of at the midpoint of the taxable year, resulting in a **half-year** of depreciation for the year in which the property is placed in service or disposed of. However, no depreciation is allowed for personal property disposed of in the same taxable year in which it was placed in service.

    EXAMPLE: A calendar-year taxpayer purchased machinery (5-year, 200% class) for $10,000 in January 2002. Because of the averaging convention, the depreciation for 2002 will be ($10,000 x 40% x 1/2) = $2,000.

    (2) A **midquarter** convention must be used if more than 40% of all personal property is placed in service during the last quarter of the taxpayer's taxable year. Under this convention, property is treated as placed in service (or disposed of) in the middle of the quarter in which placed in service (or disposed of).

    EXAMPLE: In January 2002 a calendar-year taxpayer purchased machinery for $10,000. In December 2002 the taxpayer purchased additional machinery for $30,000. All machinery was assigned to the 5-year, 200% class. No other depreciable assets were purchased during the year.

    Since the machinery placed in service during the last three months of the year exceeded 40% of the depreciable basis of all personal property placed in service during the taxable year, all machinery is depreciated under the midquarter convention. The taxpayer may claim 3.5 quarters depreciation on the machinery acquired in January ($10,000 x 40% x 3.5/4 = $3,500), and only 1/2 quarter of depreciation for the machinery acquired in December ($30,000 x 40% x .5/4 = $1,500).

    (3) **Real property** is treated as placed in service or disposed of in the middle of a month, resulting in a **half-month** of depreciation for the month disposed of or placed in service.

    EXAMPLE: A calendar-year taxpayer purchased a warehouse (39-year property) for $150,000 and placed it in service on March 26, 2002. Because of the mid-month convention, the depreciation for 2002 will be ($150,000 x 9.5/468 months) = $3,045.

h. The cost of **leasehold improvements** made by a lessee must be recovered over the MACRS recovery period of the underlying property without regard to the lease term. Upon the expiration of the lease, any unrecovered adjusted basis in abandoned leasehold improvements will be treated as a loss.

i. **Sec. 179 expense election.** A taxpayer (other than a trust or estate) may annually elect to treat the cost of qualifying depreciable property as an expense rather than a capital expenditure.

(1) Qualifying property is generally recovery property that is tangible personal property acquired by purchase from an unrelated party for use in the active conduct of a trade or business.

(2) The maximum cost that can be expensed is **$24,000 for 2002** but is reduced dollar-for-dollar by the cost of qualifying property that is placed in service during the taxable year that exceeds $200,000.

(3) The amount of expense deduction is further limited to the taxable income derived from the active conduct by the taxpayer of any trade or business. Any expense deduction disallowed by this limitation is carried forward to the succeeding taxable year.

(4) If property is converted to nonbusiness use at any time, the excess of the amount expensed over the MACRS deductions that would have been allowed must be recaptured as ordinary income in the year of conversion.

j. **Additional first-year depreciation.** Taxpayers may take additional first-year depreciation equal to 30% of the adjusted basis of specified property placed in service after September 10, 2001, and before September 11, 2004.

(1) Original use of the property must begin with the taxpayer and eligible property includes property with a recovery period of twenty years or less, non-Sec. 197 computer software, and qualified leasehold improvements.

(2) The Sec. 179 expense election is computed prior to the additional first-year depreciation allowance. The regular MACRS deduction is computed after reducing adjusted basis by any Sec. 179 expense election and the additional first-year depreciation allowance.

(3) Additional first-year depreciation is allowed for both regular tax and alternative minimum tax (AMT) in the year the property is placed in service, and no AMT depreciation adjustment is necessary.

> EXAMPLE: A calendar-year taxpayer purchases new machinery (7-year, 200% class) for $203,000 during August 2002 and elects to take the maximum Sec. 179 expense deduction and additional first-year depreciation. The Sec. 179 expense deduction would be computed first and would total $24,000 – ($203,000 – $200,000) = $21,000. Second, additional first-year depreciation would be computed and would total ($203,000 – $21,000) x 30% = $54,600. Third, regular MACRS depreciation would be computed and would total [$203,000 – ($21,000 + $54,600)] x 2/7 x 1/2 = $18,200

k. For a passenger automobile first placed in service during calendar year 2001, the amount of MACRS (including expensing) deductions is limited to $3,060 in the year placed in service ($7,660 if additional first-year depreciation is taken), $4,900 for the second year, $2,950 for the third year, and $1,775 for each year thereafter. These amounts are indexed for inflation.

(1) These limits are reduced to reflect personal use [e.g., if auto is used 30% for personal use and 70% for business use, limits are (70% x $3,060) = $2,142 for the year of acquisition, (70% x $4,900) = $3,430 for the second year, etc.].

(2) If automobile is not used more than 50% for business use, MACRS is limited to straight-line depreciation over five years.

(a) Use of the automobile for income-producing purposes is not counted in determining whether the more than 50% test is met, but is considered in determining the amount of allowable depreciation.

> EXAMPLE: An automobile is used 40% in a business, 35% for production of income, and 25% for personal use. The 200% declining balance method cannot be used because business use is not more than 50%. However, depreciation limited to the straight-line method is allowed based on 75% of use.

(b) If the more than 50% test is met in year of acquisition, but business use subsequently falls to 50% or less, MACRS deductions in excess of five-year straight-line method are recaptured.

l. Transportation property other than automobiles (e.g., airplanes, trucks, boats, etc.), entertainment property (including real property), any computer or peripheral equipment not used exclusively at a regular business establishment, and cellular telephones and similar telecommunications equipment are subject to the same more than 50% business use requirement and consequent restrictions on depreciation as are applicable to automobiles.

    (1) Failure to use these assets more than 50% for business purposes will limit the deductions to the straight-line method.

    (2) If the more than 50% test is met in year of acquisition, but business use subsequently falls to 50% or less, MACRS deductions in excess of the applicable straight-line method are recaptured.

3. **Depletion**

  a. Depletion is allowed on timber, minerals, oil, and gas, and other exhaustible natural resources or wasting assets.

  b. There are 2 basic methods to compute depletion for the year.

    (1) **Cost** method divides the adjusted basis by the total number of recoverable units and multiplies by the number of units sold (or payment received for, if cash basis) during the year.

      (a) Adjusted basis is cost less accumulated depletion (not below zero).

        EXAMPLE: Land cost $10,050,000 of which $50,000 is the residual value of the land. There are 1,000,000 barrels of oil recoverable. If 10,000 barrels were sold, cost depletion would be ($10,000,000 ÷ 1,000,000 barrels) x 10,000 = $100,000.

    (2) **Percentage** method uses a specified percentage of gross income from the property during the year.

      (a) Deduction may not exceed 50% of the taxable income (before depletion) from the property.

      (b) May be taken even after costs have been recovered and there is no basis

      (c) May be used for domestic oil and gas wells by "independent producer" or royalty owner; cannot be used for timber

      (d) The percentage is a statutory amount and generally ranges from 5% to 20% depending on the mineral.

4. **Amortization** is allowed for several special types of capital expenditures.

  a. A corporation's or partnership's organizational expenses can be amortized over sixty or more months. Otherwise deductible only when corporation or partnership is dissolved.

  b. **Business investigation and start-up costs** are deductible in the year paid or incurred if the taxpayer is currently in a similar line of business as the start-up business. If not in a similar line of business and the new business is

    (1) Acquired by the taxpayer, then investigation and start-up costs are capitalized and may be amortized over not less than sixty months beginning with the month that business begins

    (2) Not acquired by the taxpayer, then investigation costs are not deductible

  c. Pollution control facilities can be amortized over sixty months if installed on property that was placed in operation prior to 1976. The pollution control investment must not increase output, capacity, or the useful life of the asset.

  d. Patents and copyrights may be amortized over their useful life.

    (1) Seventeen years for patents; life of author plus fifty years for copyrights

    (2) If become obsolete early, deduct in that year

  e. Research and experimental expenses may be amortized over sixty months or more. Alternatively, may be expensed at election of taxpayer if done so for year in which such expenses are first incurred or paid.

  f. Intangible assets for which the Code does not specifically provide for amortization are amortizable over their useful lives.

5. **Sec. 197 intangibles**

  a. Most **acquired intangible assets** are to be amortized over a fifteen-year period, beginning with the month in which the intangible is acquired (the treatment of self-created intangible assets is not affected). Sec. 197 applies to most intangibles acquired either in stand-alone transactions or as part of the acquisition of a trade or business.

b. An amortizable Sec. 197 intangible is any qualifying intangible asset which is acquired by the taxpayer, and which is held in connection with the conduct of a trade or business. Qualifying intangibles include goodwill, going concern value, workforce, information base, know-how, customer-based intangibles, government licenses and permits, franchises, trademarks, and trade names.

c. Certain assets qualify as Sec. 197 intangibles only if acquired in connection with the acquisition of a trade or business or substantial portion thereof. These include covenants not to compete, computer software, film, sound recordings, video tape, patents, and copyrights.

d. Certain intangible assets are expressly excluded from the definition of Sec. 197 intangibles including many types of financial interests, instruments, and contracts; interests in a corporation, partnership, trust, or estate; interests in land; professional sports franchises; and leases of tangible personal property.

e. No loss can be recognized on the disposition of a Sec. 197 intangible if the taxpayer retains other Sec. 197 intangibles acquired in the same transaction or a series of transactions. Any disallowed loss is added to the basis of remaining Sec. 197 intangibles and recovered through amortization.

II. "ABOVE THE LINE" DEDUCTIONS

"Above the line" deductions are taken from gross income to determine adjusted gross income. Adjusted gross income is important, because it may affect the amount of allowable charitable contributions, medical expenses, casualty losses, and miscellaneous itemized deductions. The deductions that reduce gross income to arrive at adjusted gross income are

1. Business deductions of a self-employed person (see Business Income and Deductions, page 247)
2. Losses from sale or exchange of property (discussed in Sales and Other Dispositions and in Capital Gains and Losses, pages 346 and 353)
3. Deductions attributable to rents and royalties
4. One-half of self-employment tax
5. Moving expenses
6. Contributions to self-employed retirement plans and IRAs
7. Deduction for interest on education loans
8. Penalties for premature withdrawals from time deposits
9. Alimony payments
10. Jury duty pay remitted to employer

A. The treatment of **reimbursed employee business expenses** depends on whether the employee makes an adequate accounting to the employer and returns amounts in excess of substantiated expenses.

1. Per diem reimbursements at a rate not in excess of the federal per diem rate and 34.5 cents per mile are deemed to satisfy the substantiation requirement if employee provides time, place, and business purpose of expenses.

2. If the employee **makes an adequate accounting** to employer and reimbursements equal expenses, or if the employee substantiates expenses and returns any excess reimbursement, the reimbursements are excluded from gross income and the expenses are not deductible.

3. If the employee **does not make an adequate accounting** to the employer or does not return excess reimbursements, the total amount of reimbursement is included in the employee's gross income and the related employee expenses are deductible as miscellaneous itemized deductions subject to the 50% limitation for business meals and entertainment and the 2% of AGI floor (same as for unreimbursed employee business expenses).

B. Expenses attributable to **property held for the production of rents or royalties** are deductible "above the line."

1. **Rental of vacation home**

a. If there is any personal use, the **amount deductible** is

(1) $\dfrac{\text{No. of days rented}}{\text{Total days used}} \times \text{Total expenses} = \text{Amount deductible}$

(2) Personal use is by taxpayer or any other person to whom a fair rent is not charged.

b. **If used as a residence,** amount deductible is further limited to rental income less deductions otherwise allowable for interest, taxes, and casualty losses.

    (1) Used as a residence if personal use exceeds greater of fourteen days or 10% of number of days rented

    (2) These limitations do not apply if rented or held for rental for a continuous twelve-month period with no personal use.

      EXAMPLE: Use house as a principal residence and then begin to rent in June. As long as rental continues for twelve consecutive months, limitations do not apply in year converted to rental.

c. If used as a residence (above) and **rented for less than fifteen days** per year, then income therefrom is not reported and rental expense deductions are not allowed.

    EXAMPLE: Taxpayer rents his condominium for 120 days for $2,000 and uses it himself for 60 days. The rest of the year it is vacant. His expenses are

Mortgage interest	*$1,800*
Real estate taxes	*600*
Utilities	*300*
Maintenance	*300*
Depreciation	*2,000*
	$5,000

Taxpayer may deduct the following expenses:

	Rental expense	*Itemized deduction*
Mortgage interest	*$1,200*	*$600*
Real estate taxes	*400*	*200*
Utilities	*200*	*--*
Maintenance	*200*	*--*
Depreciation	*--*	*--*
	$2,000	*$800*

Taxpayer may not deduct any depreciation because his rental expense deductions are limited to rental income when he has made personal use of the condominium in excess of the fourteen-day or 10% rule.

C. A **self-employed** individual can **deduct one-half of the self-employment tax paid** for the taxable year (e.g., if the amount of self-employment tax that an individual taxpayer must pay for 2002 is $7,710, the individual can deduct 50% x $7,710 = $3,855 in arriving at AGI).

D. A **self-employed** individual can **deduct 70%** for 2002 (100% for 2003) of the **premiums for medical insurance** for the individual, spouse, and dependents in arriving at AGI.

  1. This deduction cannot exceed the individual's net earnings from the trade or business with respect to which the plan providing for health insurance was established. For purposes of this limitation, an S corporation more-than-two-percent shareholder's earned income is determined exclusively by reference to the shareholder's wages received from the S corporation.

  2. No deduction is allowed if the self-employed individual or spouse is eligible to participate in an employer's subsidized health plan. The determination of whether self-employed individuals or their spouses are eligible for employer-paid health benefits is to be made on a calendar month basis.

  3. Any medical insurance premiums not deductible under the above rules are deductible as an itemized medical expense deduction from AGI.

  4. The deduction does not reduce the income base for purposes of the self-employment tax.

E. Moving Expenses

  1. The distance between the former residence and new job (d_2) must be **at least fifty miles** farther than from the former residence to the former job (d_1) (i.e., $d_2 - d_1 \geq 50$ miles). If no former job, new job must be at least fifty miles from former residence.

  2. Employee must be **employed** at least thirty-nine weeks out of the twelve months following the move. Self-employed individual must be employed seventy-eight weeks out of the twenty-four months following the move (in addition to thirty-nine weeks out of first twelve months). Time test does not have to be met in case of death, taxpayer's job at new location ends because of disability, or taxpayer is laid off for other than willful misconduct.

  3. **Deductible** moving expenses include the costs of moving household goods and personal effects from the old to the new residence, and the costs of traveling (including lodging) from the old residence to the new residence.

  4. **Nondeductible** moving expenses include the costs of meals, househunting trips, temporary lodging in the general location of the new work site, expenses incurred in selling an old house or buying a new house, and expenses in settling a lease on an old residence or acquiring a lease on a new residence.

F. Contributions to Certain Retirement Plans

1. Contributions to an **Individual Retirement Account** (IRA)

    a. If neither the taxpayer nor the taxpayer's spouse is an active participant in an employer-sponsored retirement plan or a Keogh plan, there is no phaseout of IRA deductions.

    (1) The maximum deduction for an individual's contributions to an IRA is generally the lesser of

    (a) **$3,000,** or
    (b) 100% of compensation (including alimony)

    (2) For married taxpayers filing a joint return, up to $3,000 can be deducted for contributions to the IRA of each spouse (even if one spouse is not working), provided that the combined earned income of both spouses is at least equal to the amounts contributed to the IRAs.

    b. For 2002, the IRA deduction for individuals who are active participants in an employer retirement plan or a Keogh plan is proportionately phased out for married individuals filing jointly with AGI between $54,000 and $64,000, and for single individuals with AGI between $34,000 and $44,000.

    (1) An individual will not be considered an active participant in an employer plan merely because the individual's spouse is an active participant for any part of the plan year.
    (2) The maximum deductible IRA contribution for an individual who is not an active participant, but whose spouse is, will be proportionately phased out at a combined AGI between $150,000 and $160,000.

    c. Under the **phaseout rule,** the $3,000 maximum deduction is reduced by a percentage equal to adjusted gross income in excess of the lower AGI amount (above) divided by $10,000. The deduction limit is rounded to the next lowest multiple of $10.

    (1) A taxpayer whose AGI is not above the applicable phaseout range can make a $200 deductible contribution regardless of the proportional phaseout rule. This $200 minimum applies separately to taxpayer and taxpayer's spouse.
    (2) A taxpayer who is partially or totally prevented from making deductible IRA contributions can make **nondeductible IRA contributions**.
    (3) Total IRA contributions (whether deductible or not) are subject to the $3,000 or 100% of compensation limit.

    EXAMPLE: For 2002, a single individual who has compensation income (and AGI) of $40,000 and who is an active participant in an employer-sponsored retirement plan would be subject to a limit reduction of $1,800 computed as follows: $3,000 x [($40,000 – $34,000) ÷ $10,000)] = $1,800. Thus, the individual's deductible IRA contribution would be limited to $3,000 – $1,800 = $1,200. However, the individual could make nondeductible IRA contributions of up to $1,800 more.

    EXAMPLE: For 2002, a single individual who has compensation income (and AGI) of $43,600 and who is an active participant in an employer-sponsored retirement plan would normally be limited to an IRA deduction of $3,000 – [($43,600 – $34,000) ÷ $10,000] x $3,000 = $120. However, because of the special rule in (2) above, a $200 IRA contribution deduction is allowable.

    d. For tax years 2002 through 2005, an individual at least age 50 before the close of the taxable year can make an additional "catch-up" contribution of $500 to an IRA. Thus, for 2002, the maximum IRA contribution and deduction for an individual at least age 50 is $3,000 + $500 = $3,500.

    e. The 10% penalty tax on early withdrawals (pre-age 59 1/2) does not apply to amounts withdrawn for "qualified higher education expenses" and "first-time homebuyer expenses" ($10,000 lifetime cap).

    (1) Qualified higher education expenses include tuition, fees, books, supplies, and equipment for postsecondary education for the taxpayer, taxpayer's spouse, or any child or grandchild of the taxpayer or the taxpayer's spouse
    (2) Qualified first-time homebuyer distributions must be used in 120 days to buy, build, or rebuild a first home that is a principal residence for the taxpayer or taxpayer's spouse. Acquisition costs include reasonable financing or other closing costs.

2. Contributions to a **Roth IRA** are not deductible, but qualified distributions of earnings are tax-free. Individuals making contributions to a Roth IRA can still make contributions to a deductible or nondeductible IRA, but maximum contributions to all IRAs is limited to $3,000 for 2002. ($3,500 if the individual is at least age 50).

a. Eligibility for a Roth IRA is phased out for single taxpayers with AGI between $95,000 and $110,000, and for joint filers with AGI between $150,000 and $160,000.

b. Unlike traditional IRAs contributions may be made to Roth IRAs even after the individual reaches age 70 1/2.

c. Qualified distributions from a Roth IRA are not included in gross income and are not subject to the 10% early withdrawal penalty. A qualified distribution is a distribution that is made after the five-year period beginning with the first tax year for which a contribution was made and the distribution is made (1) after the individual reaches age 59 1/2, (2) to a beneficiary (or the individual's estate) after the individual's death, (3) after the individual becomes disabled, or (4) for the first-time homebuyer expenses of the individual, individual's spouse, children, grandchildren, or ancestors ($10,000 lifetime cap).

d. Nonqualified distributions are includible in income to the extent attributable to earnings and generally subject to the 10% early withdrawal penalty. Distributions are deemed to be made from contributed amounts first.

e. Taxpayers with AGI of less than $100,000 can convert assets in traditional IRAs to a Roth IRA at any time without paying the 10% tax on early withdrawals, although the deemed distributions of IRA assets will be included in income.

3. Contributions can be made to an **education IRA** (Coverdell Education Savings Account) of up to $2,000 per beneficiary (until the beneficiary reaches age eighteen), to pay the costs of a beneficiary's higher education.

a. Contributions are not deductible, but withdrawals to pay the cost of a beneficiary's education expenses are tax-free.

b. Any earnings of an education IRA that are distributed but are not used to pay a beneficiary's education expenses must be included in the distributee's gross income and are subject to a 10% penalty tax.

c. Under a special rollover provision, the amount left in an education IRA before the beneficiary reaches age 30 can be rolled over to another family member's education IRA without triggering income taxes or penalties.

d. Eligibility is phased out for single taxpayers with modified AGI between $95,000 and $110,000, and for married taxpayers with modified AGI between $190,000 and $220,000.

e. For tax years beginning after December 31, 2001, expenses that may be paid tax-free from an education IRA have been expanded to include expenses for enrollment (including room and board, uniforms, transportation, computers, and Internet access services) in elementary or secondary schools, whether public, private, or religious. Furthermore, taxpayers may take advantage of the exclusion for distributions from education IRAs, the Hope and lifetime learning credits, and the qualified tuition program in the same year.

4. **Self-employed** individuals (sole proprietors and partners) may contribute to a qualified retirement plan (called H.R.-10 or Keogh Plan).

a. The maximum contribution and deduction to a defined-contribution self-employed retirement plan is the lesser of

(1) $40,000, or 100% of earned income for 2002

(2) The definition of "earned income" includes the retirement plan and self-employment tax deductions (i.e., earnings from self-employment must be reduced by the retirement plan contribution and the self-employment tax deduction for purposes of determining the maximum deduction).

b. A taxpayer may elect to treat contributions made up until the due date of the tax return (including extensions) as made for the taxable year for which the tax return is being filed, if the retirement plan was established by the end of that year.

5. An employer's contributions to an employee's **simplified employee pension (SEP) plan** are deductible by the employer, limited to the lesser of 15% of compensation (up to a compensation ceiling of $200,000 for 2002) or $40,000. Thus, an employer's maximum contribution to, and deduction for, an employee's SEP for 2002 is $200,000 x 15% = $30,000.

a. SEP may contain a salary reduction provision allowing an employee to take a reduced salary and to have the reduction (up to $11,000 for 2002) deposited in the plan as an employer contribution.

b. The employer's SEP contributions (including up to $11,000 of employee salary reduction contributions) are excluded from the employee's gross income.

c. In addition, the employee may make deductible IRA contributions subject to the IRA phaseout rules (discussed in 2.c. above).

6. A **savings incentive match plan for employees (SIMPLE)** is not subject to the nondiscrimination rules (including top-heavy provisions) and certain other complex requirements generally applicable to qualified plans, and may be structured as an IRA or as a 401(k) plan.

   a. Limited to employers with 100 or fewer employees who received at least $5,000 in compensation from the employer in the preceding year.

      (1) Plan allows employees to make elective contributions of up to $6,500 of their pretax salaries per year (expressed as a percentage of compensation, not a fixed dollar amount) and requires employers to match a portion of the contributions.

      (2) Eligible employees are those who earned at least $5,000 in any two prior years and who may be expected to earn at least $5,000 in the current year.

   b. Employers must satisfy one of two contribution formulas.

      (1) Matching contribution formula generally requires an employer to match the employee contribution dollar-for-dollar up to 3% of the employee's compensation for the year.

      (2) Alternatively, an employer can make a nonelective contribution of 2% of compensation for each eligible employee who has at least $5,000 of compensation from the employer during the year.

   c. Contributions to the plan are immediately vested, but a 25% penalty applies to employee withdrawals made within two years of the date the employee began participating in the plan.

G. Deduction for Interest on Education Loans

1. An individual is allowed to deduct **up to $2,500** for interest on qualified education loans. However, the deduction is not available if the individual is claimed as a dependent on another taxpayer's return.

2. A *qualified education loan* is any debt incurred to pay the qualified higher education expenses of the taxpayer, taxpayer's spouse, or dependents (as of the time the debt was incurred), and the education expenses must relate to a period when the student was enrolled on at least a half-time basis. However, any debt owed to a related party is not a qualified educational loan (e.g., education debt owed to family member).

3. Qualified education expenses include such costs as tuition, fees, room, board, and related expenses.

4. The deduction is phased out for single taxpayers with modified AGI between $50,000 and $65,000, and for married taxpayers with modified AGI between $100,000 and $130,000.

H. Deduction for Qualified Tuition and Related Expenses

1. For tax years beginning after 2001, individuals will be allowed to deduct qualified higher education expenses in arriving at AGI. For 2002 and 2003, the maximum deduction is limited to $3,000.

2. Taxpayers with AGI up to $65,000 ($130,000 for married filing jointly) can claim the deduction. Taxpayers with AGI above these levels, married individuals filing separately, and an individual who can be claimed as a dependent are not entitled to any deduction.

3. *Qualified tuition and related expenses* means tuition and fees required for enrollment of the taxpayer, taxpayer's spouse, or dependent at a postsecondary educational institution. Such term does not include expenses with respect to any course involving sports, games, or hobbies, unless such course is part of the individual's degree program. Also excluded are nonacademic fees such as student activity fees, athletic fees, and insurance expenses.

4. The deduction is allowed for expenses paid during the tax year, in connection with enrollment during the year or in connection with an academic term beginning during the year or the first three months of the following year.

5. If a taxpayer takes a Hope credit or lifetime learning credit with respect to a student, the qualified higher education expenses of that student for the year are not deductible under this provision.

I. Penalties for Premature Withdrawals from Time Deposits

1. Full amount of interest is included in gross income.
2. Forfeited interest is then subtracted "above the line."

J. Alimony or Separate Maintenance Payments Are Deducted "Above the Line."

K. Jury Duty Pay Remitted to Employer

1. An employee is allowed to deduct the amount of jury duty pay that was surrendered to an employer in return for the employer's payment of compensation during the employee's jury service period.
2. Both regular compensation and jury duty pay must be included in gross income.

III. ITEMIZED DEDUCTIONS FROM ADJUSTED GROSS INCOME

Itemized deductions reduce adjusted gross income, and are sometimes referred to as "below the line" deductions because they are deducted from adjusted gross income. Itemized deductions (or a standard deduction) along with personal exemptions are subtracted from adjusted gross income to arrive at taxable income.

A taxpayer will itemize deductions only if the taxpayer's total itemized deductions exceed the applicable standard deduction that is available to nonitemizers. The amount of the standard deduction is based on the filing status of the taxpayer, whether the taxpayer is a dependent, and is indexed for inflation. Additional standard deductions are allowed for age and blindness.

Filing status	Basic standard deduction 2002
a) Married, filing jointly; or surviving spouse	$7,850
b) Married, filing separately	3,925
c) Head of household	6,900
d) Single	4,700

A dependent's basic standard deduction is limited to the lesser of (1) the basic standard deduction for single taxpayers of $4,700 for 2002; or (2) the greater of (a) $750, or (b) the dependent's earned income plus $250.

An unmarried individual who is not a surviving spouse, and is either age sixty-five or older or blind, receives an additional standard deduction of $1,150 for 2002. The standard deduction is increased by $2,300 for 2002 if the individual is both elderly and blind. The increase is $900 for 2002 for each married individual who is age sixty-five or older or blind. The increase for a married individual who is both elderly and blind is $1,800 for 2002. An elderly or blind individual who may be claimed as a dependent on another taxpayer's return may claim the basic standard deduction plus the additional standard deduction(s). For example, for 2002 an unmarried dependent, age sixty-five, with only unearned income would have a standard deduction of $750 + $1,150 = $1,900.

The major itemized deductions are outlined below. It should be remembered that some may be deducted in arriving at AGI if they are incurred by a self-employed taxpayer in a trade or business, or for the production of rents or royalties.

A. Medical and Dental Expenses

1. Medical and dental expenses paid by taxpayer for himself, spouse, or dependent (relationship, support, and citizenship tests are met) are deductible in year of payment, if not reimbursed by insurance, employer, etc. A child of divorced or separated parents is treated as a dependent of both parents for this purpose.
2. Computation—unreimbursed medical expenses (including *prescribed* medicine and insulin, and medical insurance premiums) are deducted to the extent **in excess of 7.5%** of adjusted gross income.

   EXAMPLE: Ralph and Alice Jones, who have Adjusted Gross Income of $20,000, paid the following medical expenses: $900 for hospital and doctor bills (above reimbursement), $250 for prescription medicine, and $600 for medical insurance. The Joneses would compute their medical expense deduction as follows:

Prescribed medicine	*$ 250*
Hospital, doctors	*900*
Medical insurance	*600*
	$1,750
Less 7.5% of AGI	*−1,500*
Medical expense deduction	*$250*

3. Deductible medical care does not include **cosmetic surgery** or other procedures, unless the surgery or procedure is necessary to ameliorate a deformity arising from, or directly related to, a congenital abnormality, a personal injury resulting from an accident or trauma, or a disfiguring disease.

   a. Cosmetic surgery is defined as any procedure directed at improving the patient's appearance and does not meaningfully promote the proper function of the body or prevent or treat illness or disease.

   b. If expenses for cosmetic surgery are not deductible under this provision, then amounts paid for insurance coverage for such expenses are not deductible, and an employer's reimbursement of such expenses under a health plan is not excludable from the employee's gross income.

4. Expenses incurred by physically handicapped individuals for **removal of structural barriers** in their residences to accommodate their handicapped condition are fully deductible as medical expenses. Qualifying expenses include constructing entrance or exit ramps, widening doorways and hallways, the installation of railings and support bars, and other modifications.

5. **Capital expenditures** for special equipment (other than in 4. above) installed for medical reasons in a home or automobile are deductible as medical expenses to the extent the expenditures exceed the increase in value of the property.

6. **Deductible** medical expenses include

   a. Fees for doctors, surgeons, dentists, osteopaths, ophthalmologists, optometrists, chiropractors, chiropodists, podiatrists, psychiatrists, psychologists, and Christian Science practitioners

   b. Fees for hospital services, therapy, nursing services (including nurses' meals you pay for), ambulance hire, and laboratory, surgical, obstetrical, diagnostic, dental, and X-ray services

   c. Meals and lodging provided by a hospital during medical treatment, and meals and lodging provided by a center during treatment for alcoholism or drug addiction

   d. Amounts paid for lodging (but not meals) while away from home primarily for medical care provided by a physician in a licensed hospital or equivalent medical care facility. Limit is $50 per night for each individual.

   e. Medical and hospital insurance premiums

   f. *Prescribed* medicines and insulin

   g. Transportation for needed medical care (actual expenses for calendar-year 2002, 13¢/mile if you use your car). This standard rate decreases to 12¢/mile beginning January 1, 2003.

   h. Special items and equipment, including false teeth, artificial limbs, eyeglasses, hearing aids, crutches, guide dogs, motorized wheelchairs, hand controls on a car, and special telephones for deaf

7. Items **not deductible** as medical expenses include

   a. Bottled water, maternity clothes, and diaper service

   b. Household help, and care of a normal and healthy baby by a nurse (but a portion may qualify for child or dependent care tax credit)

   c. Toothpaste, toiletries, cosmetics, etc.

   d. Program to stop smoking or lose weight (unless prescribed to alleviate a specific illness)

   e. Trip, social activities, or health club dues for general improvement of health

   f. Nonprescribed medicines and drugs (e.g., over-the-counter medicines)

   g. Illegal operation or treatment

   h. Funeral and burial expenses

8. Reimbursement of expenses deducted in an earlier year may have to be included in gross income in the period received under the tax benefit rule.

9. Reimbursement in excess of expenses is includible in income to the extent the excess reimbursement was paid by policies provided by employer.

B. Taxes

1. The following taxes are **deductible as a tax** in year paid if they are imposed on the taxpayer:

   a. **Income tax** (state, local, or foreign)

      (1) The deduction for state and local taxes includes amounts withheld from salary, estimated payments made during the year, and payments made during the year on a tax for a prior year.

(2) A refund of a prior year's taxes is not offset against the current year's deduction, but is generally included in income under the tax benefit rule.

b. **Real property taxes** (state, local, or foreign) are deductible by the person on whom the taxes are imposed.

   (1) When real property is sold, the deduction is apportioned between buyer and seller on a daily basis within the real property tax year, even if parties do not apportion the taxes at the closing.
   (2) **Assessments** for improvements (e.g., special assessments for streets, sewers, sidewalks, curbing) are generally not deductible, but instead must be added to the basis of the property. However, the portion of an assessment that is attributable to repairs or maintenance, or to meeting interest charges on the improvements, is deductible as taxes.

c. **Personal property taxes** (state or local, not foreign) are deductible if ad valorem (i.e., assessed in relation to the value of property). A motor vehicle tax based on horsepower, weight, or model year is not deductible.

2. The following taxes are **deductible only as an expense** incurred in a trade or business or in the production of income (above the line):

   a. Social security and other employment taxes paid by employer
   b. Federal excise taxes on automobiles, tires, telephone service, and air transportation
   c. Customs duties and gasoline taxes
   d. State and local taxes not deductible as such (stamp or cigarette taxes) or charges of a primarily regulatory nature (licenses, etc.)
   e. Sales taxes incurred on the acquisition or disposition of property are treated as part of the cost of the acquired property or as a reduction in the amount realized on the disposition.

3. The following taxes are **not deductible:**

   a. Federal income taxes
   b. Federal, state, or local estate or gift taxes
   c. Social security and other federal employment taxes paid by employee (including self-employment taxes)
   d. Social security and other employment taxes paid by an employer on the wages of an employee who only performed domestic services (i.e., maid, etc.)

C. Interest Expense

1. The classification of interest expense is generally determined by tracing the use of the borrowed funds. Interest expense is not deductible if loan proceeds were used to produce tax-exempt income (e.g., purchase municipal bonds).
2. No deduction is allowed for prepaid interest; it must be capitalized and deducted in the future period(s) to which it relates. However, an individual may elect to deduct *mortgage points* when paid if the points represent interest and mortgage proceeds were used to buy, build, or substantially improve a principal residence. Otherwise points must be capitalized and deducted over the term of the mortgage.
3. **Personal interest.** No deduction is allowed for personal interest.

   a. Personal interest **includes** interest paid or incurred to purchase an asset for personal use, credit card interest for personal purchases, interest incurred as an employee, and interest on income tax underpayments.
   b. Personal interest **excludes** qualified residence interest, investment interest, interest allocable to a trade or business (other than as an employee), interest incurred in a passive activity, and interest on deferred estate taxes.

   *EXAMPLE: X, a **self-employed** consultant, finances a new automobile used 80% for business and 20% for personal use. X would treat 80% of the interest as deductible business interest expense (toward AGI), and 20% as nondeductible personal interest.*

   *EXAMPLE: Y, an **employee**, finances a new automobile used 80% for use in her employer's business and 20% for personal use. All of the interest expense on the auto loan would be considered nondeductible personal interest.*

4. **Qualified residence interest.** The disallowance of personal interest above does not apply to interest paid or accrued on acquisition indebtedness or home equity indebtedness secured by a security interest

perfected under local law on the taxpayer's principal residence or a second residence owned by the taxpayer.

a. **Acquisition indebtedness.** Interest is deductible on up to $1,000,000 ($500,000 if married filing separately) of loans secured by the residence if such loans were used to acquire, construct, or substantially improve the home.

(1) Acquisition indebtedness is reduced as principal payments are made and cannot be restored or increased by refinancing the home.

(2) If the home is refinanced, the amount qualifying as acquisition indebtedness is limited to the amount of acquisition debt existing at the time of refinancing plus any amount of the new loan that is used to substantially improve the home.

b. **Home equity indebtedness.** Interest is deductible on up to $100,000 ($50,000 if married filing separately) of loans secured by the residence (other than acquisition indebtedness) regardless of how the loan proceeds are used (e.g., automobile, education expenses, medical expenses, etc.). The amount of home equity indebtedness cannot exceed the FMV of the home as reduced by any acquisition indebtedness.

EXAMPLE: Allan purchased a home for $380,000, borrowing $250,000 of the purchase price that was secured by a fifteen-year mortgage. In 2002, when the home was worth $400,000 and the balance of the first mortgage was $230,000, Allan obtained a second mortgage on the home in the amount of $120,000, using the proceeds to purchase a car and to pay off personal loans. Allan may deduct the interest on the balance of the first mortgage acquisition indebtedness of $230,000. However, Allan can deduct interest on only $100,000 of the second mortgage as qualified residence interest because it is considered home equity indebtedness (i.e., the loan proceeds were not used to acquire, construct, or substantially improve a home). The interest on the remaining $20,000 of the second mortgage is nondeductible personal interest.

c. The term "residence" includes houses, condominiums, cooperative housing units, and any other property that the taxpayer uses as a dwelling unit (e.g., mobile home, motor home, boat, etc.).

d. In the case of a residence used partly for rental purposes, the interest can only be qualified residence interest if the taxpayer's personal use during the year exceeds the greater of fourteen days or 10% of the number of days of rental use (unless the residence was not rented at any time during the year).

e. Qualified residence interest does not include interest on unsecured home improvement loans, but does include mortgage prepayment penalties.

5. **Investment interest.** The deduction for investment interest expense for noncorporate taxpayers is limited to the amount of net investment income. Interest disallowed is carried forward indefinitely and is allowed only to the extent of net investment income in a subsequent year.

EXAMPLE: For 2002, a single taxpayer has investment interest expense of $40,000 and net investment income of $24,000. The deductible investment interest expense for 2002 is limited to $24,000, with the remaining $16,000 carried forward and allowed as a deduction to the extent of net investment income in subsequent years.

a. Investment interest expense is interest paid or accrued on indebtedness properly allocable to property held for investment, including

(1) Interest expense allocable to portfolio income, and

(2) Interest expense allocable to a trade or business in which the taxpayer does not materially participate, if that activity is not treated as a passive activity

b. Investment interest expense excludes interest expense taken into account in determining income or loss from a passive activity, interest allocable to rental real estate in which the taxpayer actively participates, qualified residence interest, and personal interest.

c. Net investment income includes

(1) Interest, dividends, rents, and royalties in excess of any related expenses, and

(2) The net gain (all gains minus all losses) on the sale of investment property, but only to the extent that the net gain exceeds the net capital gain (i.e., net LTCG in excess of net STCL).

d. Although a taxpayer's **net capital gain** (i.e., an excess of net LTCG over net STCL) is generally **excluded** from the computation of investment income above, a taxpayer may elect to include any amount of net capital gain in investment income. However, if this election is made, a taxpayer must reduce the amount of net capital gain otherwise eligible for reduced maximum tax rates by the amount included as investment income.

> *EXAMPLE: Assume a taxpayer has the following items of income and expense for 2002:*
>
> | | |
> |---|---:|
> | Interest income | $ 6,000 |
> | Dividend income | 9,000 |
> | Net long-term capital gain | 18,000 |
> | Investment interest expense | 25,000 |
>
> *The taxpayer's deduction for investment interest expense is generally limited to $15,000 for 2002 unless the taxpayer elects to include a portion of the net LTCG in the determination of the investment interest expense limitation. If the taxpayer elects to treat $10,000 of the net LTCG as investment income, all of the taxpayer's investment interest expense will be deductible. But by doing this, $10,000 of the net LTCG will be taxed at ordinary tax rates, leaving only the remaining $8,000 of net LTCG to be taxed at preferential rates.*

  e. Only investment expenses (e.g., rental fees for safety deposit box rental, investment counseling fees, subscriptions to investment periodicals) remaining after the 2% of AGI limitation are used in computing net investment income.

  f. Income and expenses taken into account in computing the income or loss from a passive activity are excluded from net investment income.

D. Charitable Contributions

Contributions to qualified domestic charitable organizations are deductible in the year actually paid or donated (for both accrual- and cash-basis taxpayers) with some carryover allowed. A "pledge" is *not* a payment. Charging the contribution on your credit card *does constitute payment*.

1. **Qualified organizations** include

   a. A state, a US possession or political subdivision, or the District of Columbia if made exclusively for public purposes

   b. A community chest, corporation, foundation, etc., operated exclusively for charitable, religious, educational, scientific, or literary purposes, or for the prevention of cruelty to children or animals, or for fostering national or international amateur sports competition (unless they provide facilities or equipment)

      (1) No part of the earnings may inure to any individual's benefit
      (2) May not attempt to influence legislation or intervene in any political campaign

   c. Church, synagogue, or other religious organizations

   d. War veterans' organizations

   e. Domestic fraternal societies operating under the lodge system (only if contribution used exclusively for the charitable purposes listed in b. above)

   f. Nonprofit cemetery companies if the funds are irrevocably dedicated to the perpetual care of the cemetery as a whole, and not a particular lot or mausoleum crypt

2. Dues, fees, or assessments paid to qualified organizations are deductible to the extent that payments exceed benefits received. Dues, fees, or assessments are not deductible if paid to veterans' organizations, lodges, fraternal organizations, and country clubs

3. Out-of-pocket expenses to maintain a **student** (domestic or foreign) in a taxpayer's home are deductible (limited to $50/month for each month the individual is a full-time student) if

   a. Student is in 12th or lower grade and not a dependent or relative

   b. Based on written agreement between taxpayer and qualified organization

   c. Taxpayer receives no reimbursement

4. Payments to qualified organizations for goods or services are deductible to the extent the amount paid exceeds the fair market value of benefits received.

5. A taxpayer who makes a payment to or for the benefit of a college or university and is thereby entitled to purchase tickets to athletic events is allowed to deduct 80% of the payment as a charitable contribution. Any payment that is attributable to the actual cost of tickets is not deductible as a charitable contribution.

6. Unreimbursed out-of-pocket expenses incurred while rendering services to a charitable organization without compensation are deductible, including actual auto expenses or a standard rate of 14¢ per mile may be used for 2002 and 2003.

7. No charitable deduction is allowed for any **contribution of $250 or more** unless the donor obtains written acknowledgment from the donee including a good faith estimate of the value of any goods or services provided to the donor in exchange for the contribution. Canceled checks are not sufficient substantiation for contributions of $250 or more.

8. **Nondeductible** contributions include contributions to/for/of

   a. Civic leagues, social clubs, and foreign organizations
   b. Communist organizations, chambers of commerce, labor unions
   c. The value of the taxpayer's time or services
   d. The use of property, or less than an entire interest in property
   e. Blood donated
   f. Tuition or amounts in place of tuition
   g. Payments to a hospital for care of particular patients
   h. "Sustainer's gift" to retirement home
   i. Raffles, bingo, etc. (but may qualify as gambling loss)
   j. Fraternal societies if the contributions are used to defray sickness or burial expenses of members
   k. Political organizations
   l. Travel, including meals and lodging (e.g., trip to serve at charity's national meeting), if there is any significant element of personal pleasure, recreation, or vacation involved

9. Contributions of property to qualified organizations are **deductible**

   a. At fair market value when FMV is below basis
   b. At basis when fair market value exceeds basis and property would result in short-term capital gain or ordinary income if sold (e.g., gain would be ordinary because of depreciation recapture or if property is inventory)
   c. If contributed property is *capital gain property* that would result in LTCG if sold (i.e., generally investment property and personal-use property held more than one year), the amount of contribution is the property's FMV. However, if the contributed property is *tangible personal capital gain property* and its use is unrelated to the charity's activity, the amount of contribution is restricted to the property's basis.
   d. Appraisal fees on donated property are a miscellaneous itemized deduction.

10. The overall limitation for contribution deductions is **50%** of adjusted gross income (before any net operating loss carryback). A second limitation is that contributions of long-term capital gain property to charities in Section 10.a. below (where gain is not reduced) are limited to **30%** of AGI. A third limitation is that some contributions to certain charities are limited to **20%** of AGI or a lesser amount.

   a. Contributions to the following are taken first and may be taken up to **50%** of AGI limitation

      (1) Public charities

         (a) Churches
         (b) Educational organizations
         (c) Tax-exempt hospitals
         (d) Medical research
         (e) States or political subdivisions
         (f) US or District of Columbia

      (2) All private operating foundations, that is, foundations that spend their income directly for the active conduct of their exempt activities (e.g., public museums)
      (3) Certain private nonoperating foundations that distribute proceeds to public and private operating charities

   b. Deductions for contributions of **long-term capital gain property** (when the gain is not to be reduced) to organizations in Section 10.a. above are limited to **30%** of adjusted gross income; but, taxpayer may elect to reduce all appreciated long-term capital gain property by the potential gain and not be subject to this 30% limitation.

   c. Deductions for contributions to charities that do not qualify in Section 10.a. above (generally private nonoperating foundations) are subject to special limitations.

      (1) The deduction limitation for gifts of

(a) Ordinary income property is the lesser of (1) 30% of AGI, or (2) (50% x AGI) – gifts to charities in Section 10.a. above

(b) Capital gain property is lesser of (1) 20% of AGI, or (2) (30% x AGI) – gifts of long-term capital gain property to charities in Section 10.a. above where no reduction is made for appreciation

(2) These deductions are taken after deductions to organizations in Section 10.a. above without the 30% limitation on capital gain property in Section 10.b. above.

EXAMPLE: An individual with AGI of $9,000 made a contribution of capital gain appreciated property with a FMV of $5,000 to a church, and gave $2,000 cash to a private nonoperating foundation. Since the contribution to the church (before the 30% limit) exceeds 50% of AGI, no part of the contribution to the foundation is deductible this year. Assuming no election is made to reduce the contribution of the capital gain property by the amount of its appreciation, the current deduction for the contribution to the church is limited to 30% x $9,000 = $2,700.

11. Contributions in excess of the 50%, 30%, or 20% limitation can be carried forward for **five years** and remain subject to the 50%, 30%, or 20% limitation in the carryforward years.

EXAMPLE: Ben's adjusted gross income is $50,000. During the year he gave his church $2,000 cash and land (held for investment more than one year) having a fair market value of $30,000 and a basis of $22,000. Ben also gave $5,000 cash to a private foundation to which a 30% limitation applies.

Since Ben's contributions to an organization to which the 50% limitation applies (disregarding the 30% limitation for capital gain property) exceed $25,000 (50% of $50,000), his contribution to the private foundation is not deductible this year. The $2,000 cash donated to the church is deducted first. The donation for the gift of land is not required to be reduced by the appreciation in value, but is limited to $15,000 (30% x $50,000). Thus, Ben may deduct only $17,000 ($2,000 + $15,000). The unused portion of the land contribution ($15,000) and the gift to the private foundation ($5,000) are carried over to the next year, still subject to their respective 30% limitations.

Alternatively, Ben may elect to reduce the value of the land by its appreciation of $8,000 and not be subject to the 30% limitation for capital gain property. In such case, his current deduction would be $25,000 ($2,000 cash + $22,000 land + $1,000 cash to private foundation), but only the remaining $4,000 cash to the private foundation would be carried over to the next year.

E. Personal Casualty and Theft Gains and Losses

Gains and losses from casualties and thefts of **property held for personal use** are not subject to the Sec. 1231 netting process. Instead, personal casualty and theft gains and losses are **separately netted**, without regard to the holding period of the converted property.

1. A **casualty loss** must be identifiable, damaging to property, and sudden, unexpected, or unusual. Casualty losses **include**

   a. Damage from a fire, storm, accident, mine cave-in, sonic boom, or loss from vandalism
   b. Damage to trees and shrubs if there is a decrease in the total value of the real estate
   c. A loss on personal residence that has been rendered unsafe by reason of a disaster declared by the President and has been ordered demolished or relocated by a state or local government.

2. Losses **not deductible** as casualties include

   a. Losses from the breakage of china or glassware through handling or by a family pet
   b. Disease, termite, or moth damage
   c. Expenses incident to casualty (temporary quarters, etc.)
   d. Progressive deterioration through a steadily operating cause and damage from normal process. Thus, the steady weakening of a building caused by normal or usual wind and weather conditions is not a casualty loss.
   e. Losses from nearby disaster (property value reduced due to location near a disaster area)
   f. Loss of future profits from, for example, ice storm damage to standing timber that reduces the rate of growth or the quality of future timber. To qualify as a casualty, the damage must actually result in existing timber being rendered unfit for use.

3. Casualty loss is deductible in the year the loss occurs.

   a. Theft loss is deductible in the year the loss is discovered.
   b. Loss in a federally declared disaster area is deductible either in the year loss occurs or the preceding year (by filing an amended return).

A CHARITABLE CONTRIBUTION FLOWCHART FOR INDIVIDUALS

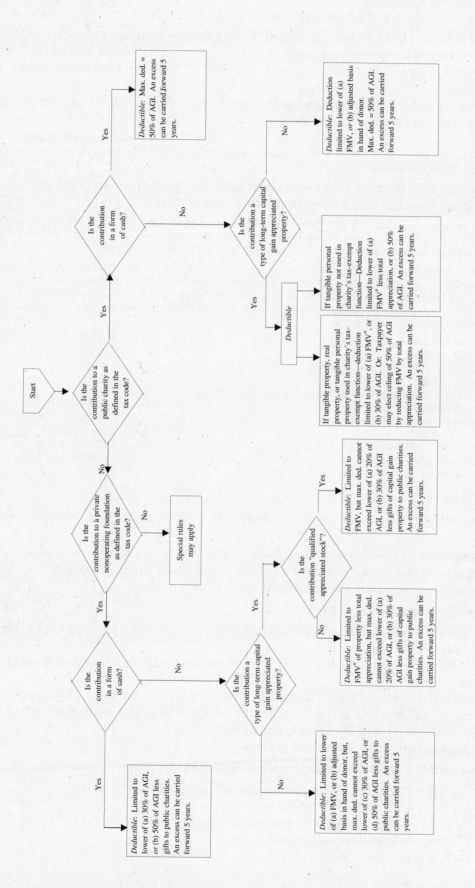

Start

Is the contribution to a public charity as defined in the tax code?

Yes → Is the contribution in a form of cash?

Yes → *Deductible:* Max. ded. = 50% of AGI. An excess can be carried forward 5 years.

No → Is the contribution a type of long-term capital gain appreciated property?

No → *Deductible:* Deduction limited to lower of (a) FMV, or (b) adjusted basis in hand of donor. Max. ded. = 50% of AGI. An excess can be carried forward 5 years.

Yes → *Deductible*

If tangible personal property not used in charity's tax-exempt function—Deduction limited to lower of (a) FMV* less total appreciation, or (b) 50% of AGI. An excess can be carried forward 5 years.

If tangible property, real property, or tangible personal property used in charity's tax-exempt function—deduction limited to lower of (a) FMV*, or (b) 30% of AGI. Or: Taxpayer may elect ceiling of 50% of AGI by reducing FMV by total appreciation. An excess can be carried forward 5 years.

No → Is the contribution to a private nonoperating foundation as defined in the tax code?

No → Special rules may apply

Yes → Is the contribution in a form of cash?

Yes → *Deductible:* Limited to lower of (a) 30% of AGI, or (b) 50% of AGI less gifts to public charities. An excess can be carried forward 5 years.

No → Is the contribution a type of long-term capital gain appreciated property?

Yes → Is the contribution "qualified appreciated stock"?

Yes → *Deductible:* Limited to FMV, but max. ded. cannot exceed lower of (a) 20% of AGI, or (b) 30% of AGI less gifts of capital gain property to public charities. An excess can be carried forward 5 years.

No → *Deductible:* Limited to FMV† of property less total appreciation, but max. ded. cannot exceed lower of (a) 20% of AGI, or (b) 30% of AGI less gifts of capital gain property to public charities. An excess can be carried forward 5 years.

No → *Deductible:* Limited to lower of (a) FMV, or (b) adjusted basis in hand of donor, but, max. ded. cannot exceed lower of (c) 30% of AGI, or (d) 50% of AGI less gifts to public charities. An excess can be carried forward 5 years.

AGI = adjusted gross income.
FMV = fair market value.
*The FMV of depreciable property given to a charitable organization must be reduced by the potential ordinary gain generated by depreciation recapture.

4. The **amount of loss** is the lesser of (1) the decrease in the FMV of the property resulting from the casualty, or (2) the adjusted basis of the property. The amount of loss must be reduced by

   a. Any insurance or reimbursement, and
   b. $100 floor for each separate nonbusiness casualty

5. An individual is not permitted to deduct a casualty loss for damage to **insured property** not used in a trade or business or in a transaction entered into for profit unless the individual files a timely insurance claim with respect to the loss. Casualty insurance premiums are considered a personal expense and are not deductible.

6. If personal casualty and theft **gains exceed losses** (after the $100 floor for each loss), then all gains and losses are treated as capital gains and losses.

   EXAMPLE: An individual incurred a $5,000 personal casualty gain, and a $1,000 personal casualty loss (after the $100 floor) during the current taxable year. Since there was a net gain, the individual will report the gain and loss as a $5,000 capital gain and a $1,000 capital loss.

7. If **losses (after the $100 floor for each loss) exceed gains,** the losses (1) offset gains, and (2) are an ordinary deduction from AGI to the extent **in excess of 10% of AGI**.

   EXAMPLE: An individual had AGI of $40,000 (before casualty gains and losses), and also had a personal casualty loss of $12,000 (after the $100 floor) and a personal casualty gain of $3,000. Since there was a personal casualty net loss, the net loss will be deductible as an itemized deduction of [$12,000 – $3,000 – (10% x $40,000)] = $5,000.

   EXAMPLE: Frank Jones' lakeside cottage, which cost him $13,600 (including $1,600 for the land) on April 30, 1987, was partially destroyed by fire on July 12, 2002. The value of the property immediately before the fire was $46,000 ($24,000 for the building and $22,000 for the land), and the value immediately after the fire was $36,000. He collected $7,000 from the insurance company. It was Jones' only casualty for 2002 and his AGI was $25,000. Jones' casualty loss deduction from the fire would be $400, computed as follows:

Value of entire property before fire	*$46,000*
Value of entire property after fire	*–36,000*
Decrease in fair market value of entire property	*$10,000*
Adjusted basis (cost in this case)	*$13,600*
Loss sustained (lesser of decrease in FMV or adjusted basis)	*$10,000*
Less insurance recovery	*–7,000*
Casualty loss	*$ 3,000*
Less $100 limitation	*– 100*
Loss after $100 limitation	*$ 2,900*
Less 10% of AGI	*2,500*
Casualty loss deduction	*$ 400*

F. Miscellaneous Deductions

1. The following miscellaneous expenses are only deductible to the extent they (in the aggregate) **exceed 2% of AGI.**

   a. **Outside salesman expenses** include all business expenses of an employee who principally solicits business for his/her employer while away from the employer's place of business.

   b. All **unreimbursed employee expenses** including

      (1) Employee **education** expenses if

         (a) Incurred to maintain or improve skills required in employee's present job, or to meet requirements to keep job
         (b) Deductible expenses include unreimbursed transportation, travel, tuition, books, supplies, etc.
         (c) Education expenses are not deductible if required to meet minimum educational requirements in employee's job, or the education qualifies the employee for a new job (e.g., CPA review course) even if a new job is not sought
         (d) Travel as a form of education is not deductible

      (2) **Other deductible unreimbursed employee expenses** include

         (a) Transportation and travel (including 50% of meals and entertainment)
         (b) Uniforms not adaptable to general use
         (c) Employment agency fees to secure employment in same occupation
         (d) Subscription to professional journals
         (e) Dues to professional societies, union dues, and initiation fees

(f) Physical examinations required by employer
(g) A college professor's research, lecturing, and writing expenses
(h) Amounts teacher pays to a substitute
(i) Surety bond premiums
(j) Malpractice insurance premiums
(k) A research chemist's laboratory breakage fees
(l) Small tools and supplies

c. Tax counsel, assistance, and tax return preparation fees
d. Expenses for the production of income other than those incurred in a trade or business or for production of rents and royalties (e.g., investment counsel fees, clerical help, safe-deposit box rent, legal fees to collect alimony, etc.)

2. The following miscellaneous expenses are **not subject to the 2% floor,** but instead are **deductible in full**.

   a. Gambling losses to the extent of gambling winnings
   b. Impairment-related work expenses for handicapped employees
   c. Estate tax related to income in respect of a decedent
   d. Certain adjustments when a taxpayer restores amounts held under a claim of right
   e. Certain costs of cooperative housing corporations
   f. Certain expenses of short sales
   g. The balance of an employee's investment in an annuity contract where the employee dies before recovering the entire investment

3. Examples of **nondeductible expenses** include

   a. Fees and licenses, such as auto licenses, marriage licenses, and dog tags
   b. Home repairs, insurance, rent
   c. Personal legal expenses
   d. Life insurance
   e. Burial expenses
   f. Capital expenditures
   g. Illegal bribes and kickbacks
   h. Fines and tax penalties
   i. Collateral
   j. Commuting to and from work
   k. Professional accreditation fees
   l. Bar examination fees and incidental expenses in securing admission to the bar
   m. Medical and dental license fees paid to obtain initial licensing
   n. Campaign expenses of a candidate for any office are not deductible, nor are registration fees for primary elections, even if taxpayer is the incumbent of the office to be contested.
   o. Cost of midday meals while working late (except while traveling away from home)
   p. Political contributions

G. An individual whose AGI exceeds a threshold amount of $137,300 for 2002 is required to reduce the amount of allowable itemized deductions by 3% of the excess over the threshold amount. The threshold amount is $68,650 for 2002 for a married person filing separately.

1. Itemized deductions **subject to reduction** include taxes, qualified residence interest, charitable contributions, miscellaneous itemized deductions (other than gambling).
2. The reduction is determined after first taking into account the other limitations that determine how much of a particular type of expense may be deducted (e.g., the 2% floor for miscellaneous itemized deductions).
3. Itemized deductions **not subject to reduction** include medical, investment interest, casualty and theft losses, and gambling losses.
4. The **reduction cannot exceed 80%** of allowable itemized deductions, not counting medical expenses, investment interest, casualty losses, and gambling losses (to the extent of gambling income).
5. This limitation does not apply for purposes of computing the alternative minimum tax (i.e., itemized deductions that are otherwise allowed in computing AMTI are not reduced by this limitation).

EXAMPLE:

	Allen	Baker
Adjusted gross income for 2002	$230,000	$230,000
Medical expenses	$ 0	$ 17,000
State income tax	6,000	3,000
Real estate taxes	10,000	0
Charitable contributions	4,000	0
Reduction limitation, lesser of [($230,000 – $137,300) x 3%] or ($20,000 x 80%)	(2,781)	
($3,000 x 80%)		(2,400)
Total itemized deductions	$ 17,219	17,600
Taxable income before personal exemptions	$212,781	$212,400

IV. EXEMPTIONS

Personal exemptions are similar to itemized deductions in that they are deducted from adjusted gross income. Personal exemptions are allowed for the taxpayer, spouse, and dependent if the dependent is a US citizen or resident.

1. The personal exemption amount is $3,000 for 2002.
2. The deduction for personal exemptions is reduced or even eliminated if AGI exceeds certain threshold amounts. Once AGI exceeds these thresholds, personal exemptions are reduced by 2% for each $2,500 ($1,250 for a married person filing separately) or fraction thereof by which AGI exceeds the thresholds.

    a. The AGI threshold amounts are as follows:

	2002
Joint return; or surviving spouse	$206,000
Married filing separately	103,000
Head of household	171,650
Single	137,300

    b. Since the reduction is 2% for each $2,500 ($1,250 for a married person filing separately) or fraction thereof by which AGI exceeds the threshold, all personal exemptions are completely eliminated when AGI exceeds the thresholds by more than $122,500.

    EXAMPLE

	Single	Joint return
Adjusted gross income for 2002	$ 230,000	$ 230,000
Threshold	(137,300)	(206,000)
Excess	$ 92,700	$ 24,000
Personal exemption(s) before phaseout	$ 3,000	$6,000
Percentage reduction	76%	
$92,700/$2,500 x 2%		
$24,000/$2,500 x 2%		20%
Phaseout	(2,280)	(1,200)
Personal exemption(s) after phaseout	$ 720	$ 4,800

3. Personal exemption for **taxpayer**

    a. Full exemption even if birth or death occurred during the year
    b. No personal exemption for taxpayer if eligible to be claimed as a dependent on another taxpayer's return

4. Exemption for **spouse**

    a. Exemption on joint return
    b. Not allowed if divorced or legally separated at end of year
    c. If a separate return is filed, taxpayer may claim spouse exemption only if the spouse had no gross income and was not the dependent of another taxpayer.

5. Exemptions for **dependents**

    a. Full exemption even if death or birth occurred during the year
    b. Each dependent must meet **five tests**.

(1) **Joint return.** Dependent cannot file a joint return, unless filed solely for refund of tax withheld.
(2) **Member of household or related.** Dependent must either live with the taxpayer for the entire year or be related (closer than cousin).

  (a) *Related* includes ancestors, descendants, brothers and sisters, uncles and aunts, nephews and nieces, half and step relationships, and in-laws.
  (b) Relationships established by marriage are not ended by death or divorce.
  (c) A person temporarily absent for vacation, school, or sickness, or indefinitely confined in a nursing home meets the member of household test.
  (d) A person who died during the year but was a member of household until death, and a child who is born during the year and is a member of household for the rest of year, meet the member of household requirement.

(3) **Citizenship.** Dependent must be a citizen, resident, or national of US, or a resident of Canada or Mexico.
(4) **Gross income.** Dependent had less than $3,000 for 2002 of gross income.

  (a) Does not apply to child of taxpayer under the age of nineteen at end of year.
  (b) Does not apply to child of taxpayer if a full-time student at least five months during year and under age twenty-four at end of year.
  (c) Gross income does not include tax-exempt income (e.g., nontaxable social security).

(5) **Support.** Taxpayer must furnish over one-half of support.

  (a) Includes food, clothing, FMV of lodging, medical, education, recreation, and certain capital expenses.
  (b) Excludes life insurance premiums, funeral expenses, nontaxable scholarships, income and social security taxes paid from a dependent's own income.

*NOTE: A phrase that may be used as a device to remember the five dependency tests is—Joe **M**ust **C**ome **G**et **S**upper.*

  c. A **multiple support agreement** can be used if no single taxpayer furnishes more than 50% of the support of a dependent. Then any taxpayer (who meets the other requirements) contributing **more than 10%** can claim the dependent provided others furnishing more than 10% agree not to claim the dependent as an exemption.
  d. Child of divorced or separated parents

  (1) Treated as receiving over one-half of support from custodial parent (i.e., parent who has custody for the greater part of the year)
  (2) Noncustodial parent will be treated as providing over one-half of support if

    (a) Custodial parent signs a written declaration waiving the right to claim such child as a dependent, and the written declaration is attached to the noncustodial parent's return, or
    (b) Pre–1985 divorce decree or written agreement entitles that parent to the exemptions and that parent provides $600 or more for the child's support.

V. TAX COMPUTATION

A. Tax Tables

1. Tax tables contain precomputed tax liability based on taxable income.

  a. AGI less itemized deductions and exemptions
  b. Filing status

  (1) Single
  (2) Head of household
  (3) Married filing separately
  (4) Married filing joint return (even if only one had income)
  (5) Surviving spouse (qualifying widow[er] with dependent child)

2. Tax tables must be used by taxpayers unless taxable income is $100,000 or more.

B. Tax Rate Schedules

1. For 2002 the tax rates for individuals are as follows:

Tax rate	Joint return surviving spouse		Married filing separately	
10%	$ 0	– $ 12,000	$ 0	– $ 6,000
15%	$ 12,001	– $ 46,700	$ 6,001	– $ 23,350
27%	$ 46,701	– $112,850	$ 23,351	– $ 56,425
30%	$112,851	– $171,950	$ 56,426	– $ 85,975
35%	$171,951	– $307,050	$ 85,976	– $153,525
38.6%	$307,051 and over		$153,526 and over	

Tax rate	Head of household		Single	
10%	$ 0	– $ 10,000	$ 0	– $ 6,000
15%	$ 10,001	– $ 37,450	$ 6,001	– $ 27,950
27%	$ 37,451	– $ 96,700	$ 27,951	– $ 67,700
30%	$ 96,701	– $156,600	$ 67,701	– $141,250
35%	$156,601	– $307,050	$141,251	– $307,050
38.6%	$307,051 and over		$307,051 and over	

2. **Income of children under age fourteen.** The earned income of a child of any age and the unearned income of a child fourteen years or older as of the end of the taxable year is taxed at the child's own marginal rate. However, the **unearned income in excess of $1,500** (for 2002) of a child under age fourteen is generally taxed at the rates of the child's parents.

a. The amount taxed at the parents' rates equals the child's unearned income less the sum of (1) any penalty for early withdrawal of savings, (2) $750, and (3) the greater of $750 or the child's itemized deductions directly connected with the production of unearned income.

   (1) Directly connected itemized deductions are those expenses incurred to produce or collect income, or maintain property that produces unearned income, including custodian fees, service fees to collect interest and dividends, and investment advisory fees. These are deductible as miscellaneous itemized deductions subject to a 2% of AGI limitation.

   (2) The amount taxed at the parents' rates cannot exceed the child's taxable income.

   EXAMPLE: Janie (age 11) is claimed as a dependent on her parents' return and in 2002 receives dividend income of $10,000, and has no itemized deductions. The amount of Janie's income taxed at her parents' tax rates is $8,500 [$10,000 – ($750 + $750)].

   EXAMPLE: Brian (age 12) is claimed as a dependent on his parents' return and in 2002 receives interest income of $15,000 and has itemized deductions of $1,200 that are directly connected to the production of the interest income. The amount of Brian's income taxed at his parents' tax rates is $13,050 [$15,000 – ($750 + $1,200)].

   EXAMPLE: Kerry (age 10) is claimed as a dependent on her parents' return and in 2002 receives interest income of $12,000, has an early withdrawal penalty of $350, and itemized deductions of $400 that are directly connected to the production of the interest income. The amount of Kerry's income taxed at her parents' tax rates is $10,150 [$12,000 – ($350 + $750 + $750)].

b. A child's tax liability on unearned income taxed at the parents' rates is the child's share of the increase in tax (including alternative minimum tax) that would result from adding to the parents' taxable income the unearned income of their children under age fourteen.

c. If the child's parents are divorced, the custodial parent's taxable income will be used in determining the child's tax liability.

d. If child's parents are divorced and both parents have custody, the taxable income of the parent having custody for the greater portion of the calendar year will be used in determining the child's tax liability.

3. **Reporting unearned income of a child on parent's return.** Parents may elect to include on their return the unearned income of their child under age fourteen whose income consists solely of interest and dividends and is between $750 and $7,500 (for 2002).

a. The child is treated as having no gross income and does not have to file a tax return for the year the election is made.

b. The electing parents must include the child's gross income in excess of $1,500 on their return for the tax year, resulting in the taxation of that income at the parents' highest marginal rate. Also, the parents must report additional tax liability equal to the lesser of (1) $112.50, or (2) 15% of the child's income in excess of $750.

c. The election cannot be made if estimated tax payments were made for the tax year in the child's name and social security number, or if the child is subject to backup withholding.

C. Filing Status

1. Married persons (married at year-end or at time of death of spouse) can file joint return or separate returns.

2. **Qualifying widow(er) with dependent child** (i.e., surviving spouse) may use joint tax rates for the two years following the year in which the spouse died.

    a. Surviving spouse must have been eligible to file a joint return in the year of the spouse's death.
    b. Dependent child, stepchild, adopted child, or foster child must live in household with surviving spouse.
    c. Surviving spouse must provide more than 50% of costs of maintaining household that was the main home of the child for the entire year.

3. **Head of household** status applies to an unmarried person (other than a qualifying widow(er) with dependent child) who provides more than 50% of costs of maintaining household for more than one-half the year for

    a. Taxpayer's unmarried child, stepchild, grandchild, or adopted child (who need not be a dependent), or
    b. Relative (closer than cousin) who is a dependent; including a married child or married descendant
    c. Parents need not live with head of household, but parents' household must be maintained by taxpayer (e.g., nursing home) and parents must qualify as taxpayer's dependents
    d. Unmarried requirement is satisfied if spouses are living apart under a separate maintenance decree.

4. **Cost of maintaining household**

    a. *Includes* rent, mortgage interest, taxes, insurance on home, repairs, utilities, and food eaten in the home.
    b. *Excludes* the cost of clothing, education, medical expenses, vacations, life insurance, transportation, rental value of home, value of taxpayer's services.

D. Alternative Minimum Tax (AMT)

1. The alternative minimum tax for noncorporate taxpayers is computed by applying a two-tiered rate schedule to a taxpayer's alternative minimum tax base. A 26% rate applies to the first $175,000 of a taxpayer's alternative minimum taxable income (AMTI) in excess of the exemption amount. A 28% rate applies to AMTI greater than $175,000 ($87,500 for married taxpayers filing separately) above the exemption amount. This tax applies to the extent that a taxpayer's AMT exceeds the amount of regular tax.

2. A taxpayer's AMT is generally the amount by which the applicable percentage (26% or 28%) of AMTI as reduced by an exemption amount and reduced by the AMT foreign tax credit exceeds the amount of a taxpayer's regular tax as reduced by the regular tax foreign tax credit.

3. AMT computation formula

    ```
                Regular taxable income
             +  (–)  Adjustments
             +       Tax preferences
          =  Alternative minimum taxable income
             –       Exemption amount
          =  Alternative minimum tax base
             x        26% or 28%
          =  Tentative before foreign tax credit
             –        AMT foreign tax credit
          =  Tentative minimum tax
             –        Regular tax liability (reduced by regular tax foreign tax credit)
          =  AMT (if positive)
    ```

4. **Exemption.** AMTI is offset by an exemption. However, the AMT exemption amount is phased out at the rate of 25% of AMTI between certain specified levels.

Filing status	AMT exemption	Phaseout range
Married filing jointly;		
Surviving Spouse	$49,000	$150,000 – $346,000
Single; Head of Household	$35,750	$112,500 – $255,500
Married filing separately	$24,500	$ 75,000 – $173,000

5. **Adjustments.** In determining AMTI, taxable income must be computed with various adjustments. Example of adjustments include

a. For real property placed in service after 1986 and before 1999, the difference between regular tax depreciation and straight-line depreciation over forty years.

b. For personal property placed in service after 1986, the difference between regular tax depreciation and depreciation using the 150% declining balance method (switching to straight-line when necessary to maximize the deduction)

c. For long-term contracts, the excess of income under the percentage-of-completion method over the amount reported using the completed-contract method

d. The installment method cannot be used for sales of dealer property

e. The medical expense deduction is computed using a 10% floor (instead of the 7.5% floor used for regular tax)

f. No deduction is allowed for home mortgage interest if the loan proceeds were not used to buy, build, or improve the home

g. No deduction is allowed for personal, state, and local taxes, and for miscellaneous itemized deductions subject to the 2% floor for regular tax purposes

h. No deduction is allowed for personal exemptions and the standard deduction

6. **Preference items.** The following are examples of preference items added to taxable income (as adjusted above) in computing AMTI:

a. Tax-exempt interest on certain private activity bonds reduced by related interest expense that is disallowed for regular tax purposes

b. Accelerated depreciation on real property and leased personal property placed in service before 1987—excess of accelerated depreciation over straight-line

c. The excess of percentage of depletion over the property's adjusted basis

d. 42% of the amount of excluded gain from Sec. 1202 small business stock

7. **Regular tax credits.** Generally, an individual's tax credits are allowed to reduce regular tax liability, but only to the extent that regular income tax liability exceeds tentative minimum tax liability.

a. However, personal nonrefundable credits are allowed to the extent of the sum of (1) regular tax liability (reduced by the foreign tax credit), plus (2) the alternative minimum tax (i.e., the excess of the tentative minimum tax over the regular tax) determined without regard to the AMT foreign tax credit.

b. These nonrefundable personal credits include the dependent care credit, the credit for the elderly and disabled, the adoption credit, the child tax credit, and the HOPE and lifetime learning credits.

> *EXAMPLE: For 2002, the Millers' regular tax liability (before credits) is $3,000, and their tentative minimum tax is $4,000. The Millers may claim up to $4,000 of nonrefundable personal credits to offset both their regular tax and their AMT.*

8. **Minimum tax credit.** The amount of AMT paid (net of exclusion preferences) is allowed as a credit against regular tax liability in future years.

a. The amount of the AMT credit to be carried forward is the excess of the AMT paid over the AMT that would be paid if AMTI included only exclusion preferences (e.g., disallowed itemized deductions and the preferences for excess percentage of depletion, tax-exempt interest, and charitable contributions).

b. The credit can be carried forward indefinitely, but not carried back.

c. The AMT credit can only be used to reduce regular tax liability, **not** future AMT liability.

E. Other Taxes

1. **Social security** (FICA) tax is imposed on both employers and employees (withheld from wages). The FICA tax has two components: old age, survivor, and disability insurance (OASDI) and medicare hospital insurance (HI). The OASDI rate is 6.2% and the HI rate is 1.45%, resulting in a combined rate of 7.65%. For 2002, the OASDI portion (6.2%) is capped at $84,900, while the HI portion (1.45%) applies to all wages.

2. **Federal unemployment** (FUTA) tax is imposed only on employers at a rate of 6.2% of the first $7,000 of wages paid to each employee. A credit of up to 5.4% is available for unemployment taxes paid to a state, leaving a net federal tax of 0.8%.

3. **Self-employment** tax is imposed on individuals who work for themselves (e.g., sole proprietor, independent contractor, partner). The combined self-employment tax rate is 15.3%, of which the medicare portion is 2.9%.

   a. The full self-employment tax (15.3%) is capped at $84,900 for 2002, while the medicare portion (2.9%) applies to all self-employment earnings.

   b. Income from self-employment generally includes all items of business income less business deductions. Does not include personal interest, dividends, rents, capital gains and losses, and gains and losses on the disposition of business property.

   c. Wages subject to FICA tax are deducted from $84,900 for 2002 in determining the amount of income subject to self-employment tax.

   d. No tax if net earnings from self-employment are less than $400.

   e. A deduction equal to one-half of the self-employment tax rate (7.65%) multiplied by the taxpayer's self-employment income (without regard to this deduction) is allowed in computing the taxpayer's net earnings from self-employment.

      (1) This deemed deduction is allowed in place of deducting one-half of the amount of self-employment tax that is actually paid.

      (2) The purpose of this deduction is to allow the amount on which the self-employment tax is based to be adjusted downward to reflect the fact that employees do not pay FICA tax on the amount of the FICA tax that is paid by their employers.

EXAMPLE: A taxpayer has self-employment income of $50,000 before the deemed deduction for 2002. The deemed deduction is $50,000 x 7.65% = $3,825, resulting in net earnings from self-employment of $50,000 − $3,825 = $46,175 and a self-employment tax of $46,175 x 15.30% = $7,065. In computing AGI, the taxpayer is allowed to deduct one-half of the self-employment tax actually paid, $7,065 x 50% = $3,533.

EXAMPLE: A taxpayer has self-employment income of $100,000 before the deemed deduction for 2002. The deemed deduction is $100,000 x 7.65% = $7,650, resulting in net earnings from self-employment of $100,000 − $7,650 = $92,350. The taxpayer's self-employment tax will be ($84,900 x 15.3%) + [($92,350 − $84,900) x 2.9%] = $13,206. In computing AGI, the taxpayer is allowed to deduct one-half of the self-employment tax actually paid, $13,206 x 50% = $6,603.

VI. TAX CREDITS/ESTIMATED TAX PAYMENTS

Tax credits directly reduce tax liability. The tax liability less tax credits equals taxes payable. Taxes that have already been withheld on wages and estimated tax payments are credited against tax liability without limitation, even if the result is a refund due to the taxpayer.

A. General Business Credit

1. It is comprised of the (1) investment credit (energy, rehabilitation, and reforestation), (2) work opportunity credit, (3) welfare-to-work credit, (4) alcohol fuels credit, (5) research credit, (6) low-income housing credit, (7) enhanced oil recovery credit, (8) disabled access credit, (9) renewable resources electricity production credit, (10) empowerment zone employment credit, (11) Indian employment credit, (12) employer social security credit, (13) orphan drug credit, (14) new markets tax credit, (15) small-employer pension plan startup cost credit, and (16) the employer-provided child care credit.

2. The general business credit is allowed to the extent of "net income tax" less the greater of (1) the tentative minimum tax or (2) 25% of "net regular tax liability" above $25,000.

   a. "Net income tax" means the amount of the regular income tax plus the alternative minimum tax, and minus nonrefundable tax credits (except the alternative minimum tax credit).

   b. "Net regular tax liability" is the taxpayer's regular tax liability reduced by nonrefundable tax credits (except the alternative minimum tax credit).

EXAMPLE: An individual (not subject to the alternative minimum tax) has a net income tax of $65,000. The individual's general business credit cannot exceed $65,000 − [25% x ($65,000 − $25,000)] = $55,000.

3. A general business credit in excess of the limitation amount is carried back one year and forward twenty years.

B. Business Energy Credit

1. The business energy credit is **10%** for qualified investment in property that uses solar, geothermal, or ocean thermal energy. The property must be constructed by the taxpayer, or if acquired, the taxpayer must be the first person to use the property.
2. The recoverable basis of energy property must be reduced by 50% of the amount of business energy credit.

C. Credit for Rehabilitation Expenditures

1. Special investment credit (in lieu of regular income tax credits and energy credits) for qualified expenditures incurred to substantially rehabilitate old buildings. Credit percentages are (1) 10% for nonresidential buildings placed in service before 1936 (other than certified historic structures), and (2) 20% for residential and nonresidential certified historic structures.
2. **To qualify** for credit on other than certified historic structures

   a. 75% of external walls must remain in place as external or internal walls
   b. 50% or more of existing external walls must be retained in place as external walls
   c. 75% or more of existing internal structural framework must be retained in place

3. A building's recoverable basis must be reduced by 100% of the amount of rehabilitation credit.

D. Work Opportunity Credit

1. Credit is generally 40% of the first $6,000 of qualified first year wages paid to each qualified new employee who begins work before January 1, 2002. For qualified summer youth employees, the credit is 40% of the first $3,000 of wages for services performed during any ninety-day period between May 1 and September 15.
2. Qualified new employees include a (1) qualified IV-A recipient, (2) qualified veteran, (3) qualified exfelon, (4) high-risk youth, (5) vocational rehabilitation referral, (6) qualified summer youth employee, and, (7) qualified food stamp recipient.
3. Employer's deduction for wages is reduced by the amount of credit.
4. Taxpayer may elect not to claim credit (to avoid reducing wage deduction).

E. Welfare-to-Work Credit

1. Credit is available for wages paid to long-term family assistance recipients who begin work before January 1, 2002.
2. The amount of credit is 35% of the first $10,000 of qualified first-year wages and 50% of the first $10,000 of qualified second-year wages.
3. The employer's deduction for wages is reduced by the amount of credit.
4. The work opportunity credit is not available for an employee in the same year that the welfare-to-work credit is taken with respect to the employee.

F. Alcohol Fuels Credit

1. A ten cents per gallon tax credit is allowed for the production of up to fifteen million gallons per year of ethanol by an eligible small ethanol producer (i.e., one having a production capacity of up to thirty million gallons of alcohol per year).
2. The tax credit for ethanol blenders is sixty cents per gallon for 190 or greater proof ethanol and forty cents per gallon for 150 to 190 proof ethanol.

G. Low-Income Housing Credit

1. The amount of credit for owners of low-income housing projects depends upon (1) whether the taxpayer acquires existing housing or whether the housing is newly constructed or rehabilitated, and (2) whether or not the housing project is financed by tax-exempt bonds or other federally subsidized financing. The applicable credit rates are the appropriate percentages issued by the IRS for the month in which the building is placed in service.
2. The amount on which the credit is computed is the portion of the total depreciable basis of a qualified housing project that reflects the portion of the housing units within the project that are occupied by qualified low-income individuals.
3. The credit is claimed each year (for a ten-year period) beginning with the year that the property is placed in service. The first-year credit is prorated to reflect the date placed in service.

H. Disabled Access Credit

1. A tax credit is available to an eligible small business for expenditures incurred to make the business accessible to disabled individuals. The amount of this credit is equal to 50% of the amount of the eligible access expenditures for a year that exceed $250 but do not exceed $10,250.
2. An eligible small business is one that either (1) had gross receipts for the preceding tax year that did not exceed $1 million, or (2) had no more than 30 full-time employees during the preceding tax year, and (3) elects to have this credit apply.
3. Eligible access expenditures are amounts incurred to comply with the requirements of the Americans with Disabilities Act of 1990 and include amounts incurred for the purpose of removing architectural, communication, physical, or transportation barriers that prevent a business from being accessible to, or usable by, disabled individuals; amounts incurred to provide qualified readers to visually impaired individuals, and amounts incurred to acquire or modify equipment or devices for disabled individuals. Expenses incurred in connection with new construction are not eligible for the credit.
4. This credit is included as part of the general business credit; no deduction or credit is allowed under any other Code provision for any amount for which a disabled access credit is allowed.

I. Empowerment Zone Employment Credit

1. The credit is generally equal to 20% of the first $15,000 of wages paid to each employee who is a resident of a designated empowerment zone and performs substantially all services within the zone in an employer's trade or business.
2. The deduction for wages must be reduced by the amount of credit.

J. Employer Social Security Credit

1. Credit allowed to food and beverage establishments for the employer's portion of FICA tax (7.65%) attributable to reported tips in excess of those tips treated as wages for purposes of satisfying the minimum wage provisions of the Fair Labor Standards Act.
2. No deduction is allowed for any amount taken into account in determining the credit.

K. Employer-Provided Child Care Credit

1. For tax years beginning after December 31, 2001, employers who provide child care facilities to their employees during normal working hours are eligible for a credit equal to 25% of qualified child care expenditures, and 10% of qualified child care resource and referral expenditures. The maximum credit is $150,000 per year, and is subject to a ten-year recapture rule.
2. *Qualified child care expenditures* include amounts paid to acquire, construct, and rehabilitate property which is to be used as a qualified child care facility (e.g., training costs of employees, scholarship programs, compensation for employees with high levels of child care training).
3. To prevent a double benefit, the basis of qualifying property is reduced by the amount of credit, and the amount of qualifying expenditures that would otherwise be deductible must be reduced by the amount of credit.

L. Credit for the Elderly and the Disabled

1. Eligible taxpayers are those who are either (1) 65 or older or (2) permanently and totally disabled.
    a. Permanent and total disability is the inability to engage in substantial gainful activity for a period that is expected to last for a continuous twelve-month period.
    b. Married individuals must file a joint return to claim the credit unless they have not lived together at all during the year.
    c. Credit cannot be claimed if Form 1040A or 1040EZ is filed.
2. Credit is **15%** of an initial amount reduced by certain amounts excluded from gross income and AGI in excess of certain levels. The amount of credit is limited to the amount of tax liability.
    a. Initial amount varies with filing status.
        (1) $5,000 for single or joint return where only one spouse is 65 or older
        (2) $7,500 for joint return where both spouses are 65 or older
        (3) $3,750 for married filing a separate return
        (4) Limited to disability income for taxpayers under age 65

    b. Reduced by annuities, pensions, social security, or disability income that is excluded from gross income

    c. Also reduced by 50% of the excess of AGI over

        (1) $7,500 if single

        (2) $10,000 if joint return

        (3) $5,000 for married individual filing separate return

EXAMPLE: H, age 67, and his wife, W, age 65, file a joint return and have adjusted gross income of $12,000. H received social security benefits of $2,000 during the year. The computation of their credit would be as follows:

Initial amount		*$7,500*
Less: social security	*$2,000*	
50% of AGI over $10,000	*1,000*	*3,000*
Balance		*4,500*
		x 15%
Amount of credit (limited to tax liability)		*$ 675*

M. Child Care Credit

1. The credit may vary from **20% to 30%** of the amount paid for qualifying household and dependent care expenses incurred to enable taxpayer to be gainfully employed or look for work. Credit is 30% if AGI is $10,000 or less, but is reduced by 1 percentage point for each $2,000 (or portion thereof) of AGI in excess of $10,000 (but not reduced below 20%).

EXAMPLE: Able, Baker, and Charlie have AGIs of $10,000, $20,000, and $40,000 respectively, and each incurs child care expenses of $2,000. Able's child care credit is $600 (30% x $2,000); Baker's credit is $500 (25% x $2,000); and Charlie's credit is $400 (20% x $2,000).

2. **Eligibility** requirements include

    a. Expenses must be incurred to enable taxpayer to be gainfully employed

    b. Married taxpayer must file joint return. If divorced or separated, credit available to parent having custody longer time during year

    c. Taxpayer must furnish more than half the cost of maintaining a household that is the principal residence of both taxpayer and **qualifying individual,** who is

        (1) Dependent under thirteen years of age, or

        (2) Dependent or spouse who is physically or mentally incapable of self-care

    d. **Qualifying expenses** are those incurred for care of qualifying individual and for household services that were partly for care of qualifying individual to enable taxpayer to work or look for work

        (1) Expenses incurred outside taxpayer's household qualify only if incurred for a qualifying individual who regularly spends at least eight hours each day in taxpayer's household

        (2) Payments to taxpayer's child under age nineteen do not qualify

        (3) Payments to a relative do not qualify if taxpayer is entitled to a dependency exemption for that relative

3. **Maximum amount of expenses** that qualify for credit is the least of

    a. Actual expenses incurred, or

    b. **$2,400** for one, **$4,800** for two or more qualifying individuals, or

    c. Taxpayer's earned income (or spouse's earned income if smaller)

    d. If spouse is a student or incapable of self-care and thus has little or no earned income, spouse is treated as being gainfully employed and having earnings of not less than $200 per month for one, $400 per month for two or more qualifying individuals

EXAMPLE: Husband and wife have earned income of $10,000 each, resulting in AGI of $20,000. They have one child, age 3. They incurred qualifying household service expenses of $1,500 and child care expenses at a nursery school of $1,200.

Household expenses	*$1,500*
Add child care outside home	*1,200*
Total employment-related expenses	*$2,700*
Maximum allowable expenses	*$2,400*
Credit = 25% x $2,400	*$ 600*

4. For tax years beginning after December 31, 2002, the credit varies from 20% to 35% of qualifying expenditures which are limited to $3,000 for one qualifying individual, and $6,000 for two or more qualifying individuals.

N. Foreign Tax Credit

1. Foreign income taxes on US taxpayers can either be deducted or used as a credit at the option of the taxpayer each year.
2. The credit is limited to the overall limitation of

$$\frac{\text{TI from all foreign countries}}{\text{Taxable income} + \text{Exemptions}} \text{ x } (\text{US tax} - \text{Credit for elderly})$$

3. The limitation must be computed separately for passive income (i.e., dividends, interest, royalties, rents, and annuities).
4. Foreign tax credit in excess of the overall limitation is subject to a two-year carryback and a five-year carryforward.
5. There is no limitation if foreign taxes are used as a deduction.

O. Earned Income Credit

1. The earned income credit is a **refundable** tax credit for eligible low-income workers. Earned income includes wages, salaries, and other employee compensation (including union strike benefits), plus earnings from self-employment (after the deduction for one-half self-employment taxes). Earned income excludes income from pensions and annuities, and investment income such as interest and dividends.
2. For 2002, the earned income credit is allowed at a rate of 34% of the first $7,370 of earned income for an individual with one qualifying child, and is allowed at a rate of 40% on the first of $10,350 of earned income for an individual with two or more qualifying children. The maximum credit is reduced by 15.98% (21.06% for an individual with two or more qualifying children) of the amount of which earned income (or AGI if greater) exceeds $14,520.
3. To be eligible for the credit an individual must

   a. Have earned income and a return that covers a twelve-month period
   b. Maintain a household for more than half the year for a qualifying child in the US
   c. Have a filing status other than married filing a separate return
   d. Not be a qualifying child of another person
   e. Not claim the exclusion for foreign earned income
   f. Not have disqualified income in excess of $2,550

4. A **qualifying child** must be

   a. The individual's son, daughter, adopted child, grandchild, stepson, stepdaughter, descendant of a stepchild, or foster child.
   b. Under age nineteen, or a full-time student under age twenty-four, or permanently and totally disabled.

5. **Disqualified income** includes both taxable and tax-exempt interest, dividends, net rental and royalty income, net capital gain income, and net passive income.
6. A **reduced earned income credit** is available to an individual who does not have qualifying children if (1) the individual's principal place of abode for more than half the tax year is in the US, (2) the individual (or spouse) is at least age twenty-five (but under sixty-five) at the end of the tax year, and (3) the individual does not qualify as a dependency exemption on another taxpayer's return. For 2002, the maximum credit is 7.65% of the first $4,910 of earned income, and is reduced by 7.65% of earned income (or AGI if greater) in excess of $7,150.
7. The earned income credit is refundable if the amount of credit exceeds the taxpayer's tax liability. Individuals with qualifying children who expect a refund because of the earned income credit may arrange to have up to 60% of the credit added to paychecks.

P. Credit for Adoption Expenses

1. A nonrefundable credit of up to $10,000 for qualified adoption expenses incurred for each eligible child (including a child with special needs).

    a.   An *eligible child* is an individual who has not attained the age of 18 as of the time of the adoption, or who is physically or mentally incapable of self-care. A *child with special needs* must be a citizen or resident of the US.

    b.   Married taxpayers generally must file a joint return to claim the credit.

    c.   The credit is phased out ratably for modified AGI between $150,000 and $190,000.

2.   *Qualified adoption expenses* are taken into account in the year the adoption becomes final and include all reasonable and necessary adoption fees, court costs, attorney fees, and other expenses that are directly related to the legal adoption by the taxpayer of an eligible child. However, expenses incurred in carrying out a surrogate parenting arrangement or in adopting a spouse's child do not qualify for the credit.

3.   Any portion of the credit not allowed because of the limitation based on tax liability may be carried forward for up to five years.

Q. Child Tax Credit (CTC)

1.   The amount of the credit is $600 per qualifying child.

2.   A *qualifying child* is a US citizen or resident who is a child, descendant, stepchild, or eligible foster child for whom the taxpayer may claim a dependency exemption and who is less than seventeen years old as of the close of the calendar year in which the tax year of the taxpayer begins.

3.   The child tax credit begins to phase out when modified adjusted gross income reaches $110,000 for joint filers, $55,000 for married taxpayers filing separately, and $75,000 for single taxpayers. The credit is reduced by $50 for each $1,000, or fraction thereof, of modified AGI above the thresholds.

4.   The CTC is refundable to the extent of 10% of the taxpayer's earned income in excess of $10,000, up to the per child credit amount of $600 per child. Taxpayers with more than two children may calculate the refundable portion of the credit using the excess of their social security taxes (i.e., taxpayer's share of FICA taxes and one-half of self-employment taxes) over their earned income credit, if it results in a larger amount. The amount of refundable CTC reduces the amount of nonrefundable CTC.

R. Hope Scholarship Credit

1.   For the *first two years* of a postsecondary school program, qualifying taxpayers may elect to take a nonrefundable tax credit of 100% for the first $1,000 of qualified tuition and related expenses (not room and board), and a 50% credit for the next $1,000 of such expenses, for a total credit of up to $1,500 a year per student.

2.   The credit is available on a *per student basis* and covers tuition payments for the taxpayer as well as the taxpayer's spouse and dependents.

    a.   To be eligible for the credit, the student must be enrolled on at least a half-time basis for one academic period during the year.

    b.   If a student is claimed as a dependent of another taxpayer, only that taxpayer may claim the education credit for the student's qualified tuition and related expenses. However, if the taxpayer is eligible to, but does **not** claim the student as a dependent, only the student may claim the education credit for the student's qualified tuition and related expenses.

3.   The credit is phased out for single taxpayers with modified AGI between $41,000 and $51,000, and for joint filers with a modified AGI between $82,000 and $102,000.

4.   For a tax year, a taxpayer may elect only one of the following with respect to one student: (1) the Hope credit, (2) the lifetime learning credit, or (3) the exclusion for distributions from a Coverdell education savings account (i.e., education IRA).

S. Lifetime Learning Credit

1.   A nonrefundable 20% tax credit is available for up to $5,000 ($10,000 for tax years beginning after 12/32/02) of qualified tuition and related expenses per year for graduate and undergraduate courses at an eligible educational institution.

2.   The credit may be claimed for an unlimited number of years, is available on a *per taxpayer basis*, covers tuition payments for the taxpayer, spouse, and dependents.

3.   Similar to the Hope credit, if a student is claimed as a dependent of another taxpayer, only that taxpayer may claim the education credit for the student's qualified tuition and related expenses. However, if the taxpayer is eligible to, but does **not** claim the student as a dependent, only the student may claim the education credit for the student's qualified tuition and related expenses.

4. The credit is phased out for single taxpayers with a modified AGI between $41,000 and $51,000, and for joint filers with modified AGI between $82,000 and $102,000.

5. For a tax year, a taxpayer may elect only one of the following with respect to one student: (1) the Hope credit, (2) the lifetime learning credit, or (3) the exclusion for distributions from a Coverdell education savings account (i.e., education IRA).

> *EXAMPLE: Alan paid qualified tuition and related expenses for his dependent, Betty, to attend college. Assuming all other relevant requirements are met, Alan may claim either a Hope Scholarship credit or lifetime learning credit with respect to his dependent, Betty, but not both.*

> *EXAMPLE: Cathy paid $2,000 in qualified tuition and related expenses for her dependent, Doug, to attend college. Also during the year, Cathy paid $600 in qualified tuition to attend a continuing education course to improve her job skills. Assuming all relevant requirements are met, Cathy may claim the Hope Scholarship credit for the $2,000 paid for her dependent, Doug, and a lifetime learning credit for the $600 of qualified tuition that she paid for the continuing education course to improve her job skills.*

> *EXAMPLE: The facts are the same as in the preceding example, except that Cathy paid $3,500 in qualified tuition and related expenses for her dependent, Doug, to attend college. Although a Hope Scholarship credit is available only with respect to the first $2,000 of qualified tuition and related expenses paid with respect to Doug, Cathy **cannot** add the $1,500 of excess expenses to her $600 of qualified tuition in computing the amount of her lifetime learning credit.*

> *EXAMPLE: Ernie has one dependent, Frank. During the current year, Ernie paid qualified tuition and related expenses for Frank to attend college. Although Ernie is eligible to claim Frank as a dependent on Ernie's federal income tax return, Ernie does **not** do so. Therefore, assuming all other relevant requirements are met, Frank is allowed an education credit on Frank's federal income tax return for his qualified tuition and related expenses paid by Ernie, and Ernie is not allowed an education credit with respect to Frank's education expenses. The result would be the same if Frank had paid his qualified tuition expenses himself.*

T. Estimated Tax Payments

1. An individual whose regular and alternative minimum tax liability is not sufficiently covered by withholding on wages must pay estimated tax in quarterly installments or be subject to penalty.

2. Quarterly payments of estimated tax are due by the 15th day of the 4th, 6th, and 9th month of the taxable year, and by the 15th day of the 1st month of the following year.

3. For 2002, individuals (other than high-income individuals) will incur no penalty if the amount of tax withheld plus estimated payments are at least equal to the lesser of

    a. 90% of the current year's tax,
    b. 90% of the tax determined by annualizing current-year taxable income through each quarter, or
    c. 100% of the prior year's tax

4. For 2002, high-income individuals must use 112% (instead of 100%) if they base their estimates on their prior year's tax. A person is a high-income individual if the AGI shown on the individual's return for the preceding tax year exceeds $150,000 ($75,000 for a married individual filing separately).

5. The penalty is based on the difference between the required annual payment (i.e., lesser of a., b., or c. above) and the amount paid.

6. Generally no penalty if

    a. Total tax due was less than $1,000;
    b. Taxpayer had no tax liability for prior year (i.e., total tax was zero), prior year was a twelve-month period, and taxpayer was a US citizen or resident for entire year; or,
    c. IRS waives penalty because failure to pay was the result of casualty, disaster, or other unusual circumstances.

VII. FILING REQUIREMENTS

A. Form 1040 must generally be filed if gross income at least equals the sum of the taxpayer's standard deduction plus personal exemptions allowable (e.g., generally $4,700 + $3,000 = $7,700 for single taxpayer for 2002).

1. The additional standard deduction for age ($1,150 for 2002) is included in determining an individual's filing requirement; the additional standard deduction for blindness and dependency exemptions are not included.

> *EXAMPLE: A single individual age 65 and blind who **cannot** be claimed as a dependency exemption by another taxpayer must file a return for 2002 if the individual's gross income is at least $4,700 + $3,000 + $1,150 = $8,850*

2. An individual who can be claimed as a dependency exemption by another taxpayer must file a return if the individual either has (1) unearned income in excess of the sum of $750 plus any additional stan-

dard deductions allowed for age and blindness, or (2) total gross income in excess of the individual's standard deduction (i.e., earned income plus $250 up to the normal amount of the basic standard deduction—$4,700 for single taxpayer—plus additional standard deductions for age and blindness).

EXAMPLE: A single individual age 65 who can be claimed as a dependency exemption by another taxpayer must file a return for 2002 if the individual has unearned income (e.g., interest and dividends) in excess of $750 + $1,150 = $1,900.

3. Self-employed individual must file if net earnings from self-employment are **$400** or more.
4. A married individual filing separately must file if gross income is $3,000 or more.

B. Return must be filed by 15th day of 4th calendar month following close of taxable year.
C. An automatic four-month extension of time for filing the return can be obtained by filing Form 4868 by the due date of the return, and paying any estimated tax due.

VIII. TAX PROCEDURES

A. Audit and Appeal Procedures

1. Taxpayer makes determination of tax when return is filed.
2. Examination of questionable returns may be conducted by correspondence, in an IRS office (i.e., office audit), or at taxpayer's place of business (i.e., field audit).
3. If taxpayer does not agree with the changes proposed by the examiner and the examination was made in an IRS office or by correspondence, the taxpayer may request a meeting with the examiner's supervisor.
4. If no agreement is reached, or if the examination was conducted in the field, the IRS will send the taxpayer a copy of the examination report and a letter stating the proposed changes (**thirty-day letter**).
5. A taxpayer has thirty days to (1) accept deficiency, (2) appeal the examiner's findings, or (3) may disregard the thirty-day letter and wait for a statutory notice of deficiency (**ninety-day letter**).
6. If taxpayer has appealed and agreement is not reached at appellate level of IRS, a ninety-day letter is sent.
7. Taxpayer has ninety days to file a petition in the Tax Court.

    a. Assessment and collection are prohibited so long as the taxpayer can petition the Tax Court. Payment of deficiency is not required before going to Tax Court.
    b. If a petition is not filed within ninety days, the tax deficiency is assessed and the amount is subject to collection if not paid within ten days.

B. Assessments

1. The normal period for assessment of a tax deficiency is **three years** after the due date of the return or three years after the return is filed, whichever is later.
2. The assessment period is extended to **six years** if gross income omissions exceed 25% of the gross income stated on the return.
3. There is no time limit for assessment if no return is filed, if the return is fraudulent, or if there is a willful attempt to evade taxes.
4. Assessment period (normally three years) is suspended for 150 days after timely mailing of deficiency notice (ninety-day letter) to taxpayer.
5. Within sixty days after making the assessment, the IRS is required to provide a notice and demand for payment. If tax is not paid, the tax may be collected by levy or by court proceedings started within ten years of assessment.

C. Collection from Transferees and Fiduciaries

1. Transferee provisions are a method of collecting a predetermined tax that the transferor taxpayer cannot pay.
2. Generally transferor must be insolvent, or no longer in existence (e.g., corporation was dissolved).
3. Generally transferees are liable only to the extent of property received from the transferor taxpayer.

D. Closing Agreement and Compromise

1. A closing agreement is a final determination of tax liability that is binding on both the IRS and taxpayer.

2. A compromise is a writing-down of the tax liability. The IRS has broad authority to compromise in the event that doubt exists as to the existence of actual tax liability or because of the taxpayer's inability to pay.

E. Claims for Refund

1. An income tax refund claim is made on Form 1040X. Form 843 should be used to file a refund claim for taxes other than income taxes. Form 1045 may be used to file for a tentative adjustment or refund of taxes when an overpayment of taxes for a prior year results from the carryback of a current year's net operating loss.

2. Period for filing refund claims

   a. Refund claim must be filed within **three years** from date return was filed, or **two years** from payment of tax, whichever is later. If return filed before due date, the return is treated as filed on due date.

   b. Three-year period is extended to seven years for claims resulting from bad debts or worthless securities.

   c. If refund claim results from a carryback (e.g., NOL), the three-year period begins with the return for the year in which the carryback arose.

3. Suit for refund

   a. Only recourse from IRS's disallowance of refund claim is to begin suit in court within two years of notice of disallowance.

   b. If IRS fails to act on refund claim within six months, the taxpayer may treat it as disallowed.

F. Interest

1. Interest is allowed on overpayments from date of overpayment to thirty days before date of refund check.

   a. If an overpayment, amounts of tax withheld and estimated payments are deemed paid on due date of return.

   b. No interest is allowed if refund is made within forty-five days of later of (1) return due date or (2) actual filing of return.

2. For underpayments of tax, the interest rate is equal to the three-month Treasury bill rate plus three percentage points. For overpayments, the interest rate is equal to the federal short-term rate plus two percentage points.

G. Taxpayer Penalties

1. Penalties may be imposed for late filing or failure to file, and late payment of tax.

   a. **Late filing** or failure to file penalty is 5% of the net tax due per month (up to 25%).

   b. **Late payment** of tax penalty is 1% of the net tax due per month (up to 25%).

      (1) For any month to which both of the above apply, the late filing penalty is reduced by the late payment penalty so that the maximum is 5% per month (up to 25%).

      (2) For returns not filed within sixty days of due date (including extensions), the IRS may assess a minimum late filing penalty which is the lesser of $100 or the amount of net tax due.

2. An **accuracy-related penalty of 20%** of the underpayment applies if the underpayment of tax is attributable to one or more of the following: (1) negligence or disregard of rules and regulations, (2) any substantial understatement of income tax, (3) any substantial valuation overstatement, (4) any substantial overstatement of pension liabilities, or (5) any substantial gift or estate tax valuation understatement.

   a. Accuracy-related penalty does not apply if the underpayment is due to reasonable cause, or there is adequate disclosure and the position has a reasonable basis for being sustained.

   b. **Negligence penalty** applies to any careless, reckless, or intentional disregard of rules or regulations, and any failure to make a reasonable attempt to comply with the provisions of the tax law. Penalty is imposed only on the portion of tax liability due to negligence, and can be avoided by adequate disclosure of a position that has a reasonable basis.

   c. **Substantial understatement of income tax penalty** applies if the understatement exceeds the greater of (1) 10% of the tax due, or (2) $5,000 ($10,000 for most corporations). Penalty can be avoided by adequate disclosure of a position that has a reasonable basis, or if there is substantial authority for the position taken.

d. **Substantial overstatement penalty** may be imposed if the value (or adjusted basis) of property stated on the return is 200% or more of the amount determined to be correct.

    (1) Penalty applies to the extent resulting income tax underpayment exceeds $5,000 ($10,000 for most corporations).

    (2) Penalty is applied at a 40% rate if gross overvaluation is 400% or more of the amount determined to be correct.

e. **Substantial overstatement of pension liabilities penalty** applies if the amount of stated pension liabilities is 200% or more of the amount determined to be correct. Penalty is 40% if misstatement is 400% or more, but penalty is not applicable if resulting underpayment is $1,000 or less.

f. **Gift or estate tax valuation misstatement penalty** applies if the value of property on a gift or estate return is 50% or less of the amount determined to be correct.

    (1) Penalty is 40% if valuation used is 25% or less of amount determined to be correct.

    (2) No penalty if resulting understatement of tax is $5,000 or less.

3. **Civil fraud penalty** is 75% of the portion of underpayment attributable to fraud. The accuracy-related penalty does not apply to the portion of underpayment subject to the fraud penalty.

MULTIPLE-CHOICE QUESTIONS (1-217)

1. Richard Brown, who retired on May 31, 2002, receives a monthly pension benefit of $700 payable for life. His life expectancy at the date of retirement is ten years. The first pension check was received on June 15, 2002. During his years of employment, Brown contributed $12,000 to the cost of his company's pension plan. How much of the pension amounts received may Brown exclude from taxable income for the years 2002, 2003, and 2004?

	2002	2003	2004
a.	$0	$0	$0
b.	$4,900	$4,900	$4,900
c.	$ 700	$1,200	$1,200
d.	$4,900	$8,400	$8,400

2. Seymour Thomas named his wife, Penelope, the beneficiary of a $100,000 (face amount) insurance policy on his life. The policy provided that upon his death, the proceeds would be paid to Penelope with interest over her present life expectancy, which was calculated at twenty-five years. Seymour died during 2002, and Penelope received a payment of $5,200 from the insurance company. What amount should she include in her gross income for 2002?
- a. $ 200
- b. $1,200
- c. $4,200
- d. $5,200

3. Under a "cafeteria plan" maintained by an employer,
- a. Participation must be restricted to employees, and their spouses and minor children.
- b. At least three years of service are required before an employee can participate in the plan.
- c. Participants may select their own menu of benefits.
- d. Provision may be made for deferred compensation other than 401(k) plans.

4. David Autrey was covered by an $80,000 group-term life insurance policy of which his wife was the beneficiary. Autrey's employer paid the entire cost of the policy, for which the uniform annual premium was $8 per $1,000 of coverage. Autrey died during 2002, and his wife was paid the $80,000 proceeds of the insurance policy. What amount of group-term life insurance proceeds must be included in gross income by Autrey's widow?
- a. $0
- b. $30,000
- c. $50,000
- d. $80,000

5. Howard O'Brien, an employee of Ogden Corporation, died on June 30, 2002. During July, Ogden made employee death payments (which do not represent the proceeds of life insurance) of $10,000 to his widow, and $10,000 to his fifteen-year-old son. What amounts should be included in gross income by the widow and son in their respective tax returns for 2002?

	Widow	Son
a.	$ 5,000	$ 5,000
b.	$ 5,000	$10,000
c.	$ 7,500	$ 7,500
d.	$10,000	$10,000

6. John Budd files a joint return with his wife. Budd's employer pays 100% of the cost of all employees' group-term life insurance under a qualified plan. Under this plan, the maximum amount of tax-free coverage that may be provided for Budd by his employer is
- a. $100,000
- b. $ 50,000
- c. $ 10,000
- d. $ 5,000

7. During the current year Hal Leff sustained a serious injury in the course of his employment. As a result of this injury, Hal received the following payments during the year:

Workers' compensation	$2,400
Reimbursement from his employer's accident and health plan for medical expenses paid by Hal and not deducted by him	1,800
Damages for physical injuries	8,000

The amount to be included in Hal's gross income for the current year should be
- a. $12,200
- b. $ 8,000
- c. $ 1,800
- d. $0

8. James Martin received the following compensation and fringe benefits from his employer during 2002:

Salary	$50,000
Year-end bonus	10,000
Medical insurance premiums paid by employer	1,000
Reimbursement of qualified moving expenses	5,000

What amount of the preceding payments should be included in Martin's 2002 gross income?
- a. $60,000
- b. $61,000
- c. $65,000
- d. $66,000

9. On February 1, 2002, Hall learned that he was bequeathed 500 shares of common stock under his father's will. Hall's father had paid $2,500 for the stock in 1998. Fair market value of the stock on February 1, 2002, the date of his father's death, was $4,000 and had increased to $5,500 six months later. The executor of the estate elected the alternate valuation date for estate tax purposes. Hall sold the stock for $4,500 on June 1, 2002, the date that the executor distributed the stock to him. How much income should Hall include in his 2002 individual income tax return for the inheritance of the 500 shares of stock that he received from his father's estate?
- a. $5,500
- b. $4,000
- c. $2,500
- d. $0

10. In 2002, Gail Judd received the following dividends from:

Benefit Life Insurance Co., on Gail's life insurance policy (Total dividends received have not yet exceeded accumulated premiums paid)	$100
Safe National Bank, on bank's common stock	300
Roe Mfg. Corp., a Delaware corporation, on preferred stock	500

What amount of dividend income should Gail report in her 2002 income tax return?
- a. $900
- b. $800

c. $500
d. $300

11. Amy Finch had the following cash receipts during 2002:

Dividend from a mutual insurance company on a life insurance policy	$500
Dividend on listed corporation stock; payment date by corporation was 12/30/01, but Amy received the dividend in the mail on 1/2/02	875

Total dividends received to date on the life insurance policy do not exceed the aggregated premiums paid by Amy. How much should Amy report for dividend income for 2002?

a. $1,375
b. $ 875
c. $ 500
d. $0

12. Jack and Joan Mitchell, married taxpayers and residents of a separate property state, elect to file a joint return for 2002 during which they received the following dividends:

	Received by	
	Jack	Joan
Alert Corporation (a qualified, domestic corporation)	$400	$ 50
Canadian Mines, Inc. (a Canadian company)		300
Eternal Life Mutual Insurance Company (dividends on life insurance policy)	200	

Total dividends received to date on the life insurance policy do not exceed cumulative premiums paid. For 2002, what amount should the Mitchells report on their joint return as dividend income?

a. $550
b. $600
c. $750
d. $800

13. During 1999, Karen purchased 100 shares of preferred stock of Boling Corp. for $5,500. During 2002, Karen received a stock dividend of ten additional shares of Boling Corp. preferred stock. On the date the preferred stock was distributed, it had a fair market value of $60 per share. What is Karen's basis in the ten shares of preferred stock that she received as a dividend?

a. $0
b. $500
c. $550
d. $600

14. Micro Corp., a calendar-year accrual-basis corporation, purchased a five-year, 8%, $100,000 taxable corporate bond for $108,530 on July 1, 2002, the date the bond was issued. The bond paid interest semiannually. Micro elected to amortize the bond premium. For Micro's 2002 tax return, the bond premium amortization for 2002 should be

I. Computed under the constant yield to maturity method.
II. Treated as an offset to the interest income on the bond.

a. I only.
b. II only.
c. Both I and II.
d. Neither I nor II.

15. In a tax year where the taxpayer pays qualified education expenses, interest income on the redemption of qualified US Series EE Bonds may be excluded from gross in-

come. The exclusion is subject to a modified gross income limitation and a limit of aggregate bond proceeds in excess of qualified higher education expenses. Which of the following is(are) true?

I. The exclusion applies for education expenses incurred by the taxpayer, the taxpayer's spouse, or any person whom the taxpayer may claim as a dependent for the year.
II. "Otherwise qualified higher education expenses" must be reduced by qualified scholarships not includible in gross income.

a. I only.
b. II only.
c. Both I and II.
d. Neither I nor II.

16. During 2002 Kay received interest income as follows:

On US Treasury certificates	$4,000
On refund of 2000 federal income tax	500

The total amount of interest subject to tax in Kay's 2002 tax return is

a. $4,500
b. $4,000
c. $ 500
d. $0

17. Charles and Marcia are married cash-basis taxpayers. In 2002, they had interest income as follows:

- $500 interest on federal income tax refund.
- $600 interest on state income tax refund.
- $800 interest on federal government obligations.
- $1,000 interest on state government obligations.

What amount of interest income is taxable on Charles and Marcia's 2002 joint income tax return?

a. $ 500
b. $1,100
c. $1,900
d. $2,900

18. Clark bought Series EE US Savings Bonds in 2002. Redemption proceeds will be used for payment of college tuition for Clark's dependent child. One of the conditions that must be met for tax exemption of accumulated interest on these bonds is that the

a. Purchaser of the bonds must be the sole owner of the bonds (or joint owner with his or her spouse).
b. Bonds must be bought by a parent (or both parents) and put in the name of the dependent child.
c. Bonds must be bought by the owner of the bonds before the owner reaches the age of twenty-four.
d. Bonds must be transferred to the college for redemption by the college rather than by the owner of the bonds.

19. Daniel Kelly received interest income from the following sources in 2002:

New York Port Authority bonds	$1,000
Puerto Rico Commonwealth bonds	1,800

What portion of such interest is tax exempt?

a. $0
b. $1,000
c. $1,800
d. $2,800

20. In 2002 Uriah Stone received the following interest payments:

  • Interest of $400 on refund of federal income tax for 2000.

  • Interest of $300 on award for personal injuries sustained in an automobile accident during 1999.

  • Interest of $1,500 on municipal bonds.

  • Interest of $1,000 on United States savings bonds (Series HH).

What amount, if any, should Stone report as interest income on his 2002 tax return?

    a. $0
    b. $ 700
    c. $1,700
    d. $3,200

21. For the year ended December 31, 2002, Don Raff earned $1,000 interest at Ridge Savings Bank on a certificate of deposit scheduled to mature in 2004. In January 2003, before filing his 2002 income tax return, Raff incurred a forfeiture penalty of $500 for premature withdrawal of the funds. Raff should treat this $500 forfeiture penalty as a

    a.   Reduction of interest earned in 2002, so that only $500 of such interest is taxable on Raff's 2002 return.
    b.   Deduction from 2003 adjusted gross income, deductible only if Raff itemizes his deductions for 2003.
    c.   Penalty **not** deductible for tax purposes.
    d.   Deduction from gross income in arriving at 2003 adjusted gross income.

22. Which payment(s) is(are) included in a recipient's gross income?

 I. Payment to a graduate assistant for a part-time teaching assignment at a university. Teaching is not a requirement toward obtaining the degree.
 II. A grant to a Ph.D. candidate for his participation in a university-sponsored research project for the benefit of the university.

    a.   I only.
    b.   II only.
    c.   Both I and II.
    d.   Neither I nor II.

23. Majors, a candidate for a graduate degree, received the following scholarship awards from the university in 2002:

  • $10,000 for tuition, fees, books, and supplies required for courses.

  • $2,000 stipend for research services required by the scholarship.

What amount of the scholarship awards should Majors include as taxable income in 2002?

    a. $12,000
    b. $10,000
    c. $ 2,000
    d. $0

24. In July 1987, Dan Farley leased a building to Robert Shelter for a period of fifteen years at a monthly rental of $1,000 with no option to renew. At that time the building had a remaining estimated useful life of twenty years.

Prior to taking possession of the building, Shelter made improvements at a cost of $18,000. These improvements had an estimated useful life of twenty years at the commencement of the lease period. The lease expired on June 30, 2002, at which point the improvements had a fair market value of $2,000. The amount that Farley, the landlord, should include in his gross income for 2002 is

    a. $ 6,000
    b. $ 8,000
    c. $10,000
    d. $18,500

25. Bob and Sue Stewart were divorced in 2000. Under the terms of their divorce decree, Bob paid alimony to Sue at the rate of $50,000 in 2000, $20,000 in 2001, and nothing in 2002. What amount of alimony recapture must be included in Bob's gross income for 2002?

    a. $0
    b. $23,283
    c. $30,000
    d. $32,500

26. Which of the following conditions must be present in a post-1984 divorce agreement for a payment to qualify as deductible alimony?

 I. Payments must be in cash.
 II. The payment must end at the recipient's death

    a.   I only.
    b.   II only.
    c.   Both I and II.
    d.   Neither I nor II.

27. Darr, an employee of Sorce C corporation, is not a shareholder. Which of the following would be included in a taxpayer's gross income?

    a.   Employer-provided medical insurance coverage under a health plan.
    b.   A $10,000 gift from the taxpayer's grandparents.
    c.   The fair market value of land that the taxpayer inherited from an uncle.
    d.   The dividend income on shares of stock that the taxpayer received for services rendered.

28. With regard to the inclusion of social security benefits in gross income for the 2002 tax year, which of the following statements is correct?

    a.   The social security benefits in excess of modified adjusted gross income are included in gross income.
    b.   The social security benefits in excess of one half the modified adjusted gross income are included in gross income.
    c.   Eighty-five percent of the social security benefits is the maximum amount of benefits to be included in gross income.
    d.   The social security benefits in excess of the modified adjusted gross income over $32,000 are included in gross income.

29. Perle, a dentist, billed Wood $600 for dental services. Wood paid Perle $200 cash and built a bookcase for Perle's office in full settlement of the bill. Wood sells comparable bookcases for $350. What amount should Perle include in taxable income as a result of this transaction?

    a. $0

b. $200
c. $550
d. $600

30. John and Mary were divorced in 2001. The divorce decree provides that John pay alimony of $10,000 per year, to be reduced by 20% on their child's 18th birthday. During 2002, John paid $7,000 directly to Mary and $3,000 to Spring College for Mary's tuition. What amount of these payments should be reported as income in Mary's 2002 income tax return?

    a. $ 5,600
    b. $ 8,000
    c. $ 8,600
    d. $10,000

31. Clark filed Form 1040EZ for the 2001 taxable year. In July 2002, Clark received a state income tax refund of $900, plus interest of $10, for overpayment of 2001 state income tax. What amount of the state tax refund and interest is taxable in Clark's 2002 federal income tax return?

    a. $0
    b. $ 10
    c. $900
    d. $910

32. Hall, a divorced person and custodian of her twelve-year-old child, submitted the following information to the CPA who prepared her 2002 return:

The divorce agreement, executed in 1999, provides for Hall to receive $3,000 per month, of which $600 is designated as child support. After the child reaches age eighteen, the monthly payments are to be reduced to $2,400 and are to continue until remarriage or death. However, for the year 2002, Hall received a total of only $5,000 from her former husband. Hall paid an attorney $2,000 in 2002 in a suit to collect the alimony owed.

What amount should be reported in Hall's 2002 return as alimony income?

    a. $28,800
    b. $ 5,000
    c. $ 3,000
    d. $0

33. Lee, an attorney, uses the cash receipts and disbursements method of reporting. In 2002, a client gave Lee 500 shares of a listed corporation's stock in full satisfaction of a $10,000 legal fee the client owed to Lee. This stock had a fair market value of $8,000 on the date it was given to Lee. The client's basis for this stock was $6,000. Lee sold the stock for cash in January 2003. In Lee's 2002 income tax return, what amount of income should be reported in connection with the receipt of the stock?

    a. $10,000
    b. $ 8,000
    c. $ 6,000
    d. $0

34. In 1998, Ross was granted an incentive stock option (ISO) by her employer as part of an executive compensation package. Ross exercised the ISO in 2000 and sold the stock in 2002 at a gain. Ross was subject to regular tax for the year in which the

    a.   ISO was granted.
    b.   ISO was exercised.

    c.   Stock was sold.
    d.   Employer claimed a compensation deduction for the ISO.

35. Ed and Ann Ross were divorced in January 2002. In accordance with the divorce decree, Ed transferred the title in their home to Ann in 2002. The home, which had a fair market value of $150,000, was subject to a $50,000 mortgage that had twenty more years to run. Monthly mortgage payments amount to $1,000. Under the terms of settlement, Ed is obligated to make the mortgage payments on the home for the full remaining twenty-year term of the indebtedness, regardless of how long Ann lives. Ed made twelve mortgage payments in 2002. What amount is taxable as alimony in Ann's 2002 return?

    a. $0
    b. $ 12,000
    c. $100,000
    d. $112,000

36. Income in respect of a cash-basis decedent

    a.   Covers income earned and collected after a decedent's death.
    b.   Receives a stepped-up basis in the decedent's estate.
    c.   Includes a bonus earned before the taxpayer's death but not collected until after death.
    d.   Must be included in the decedent's final income tax return.

37. The following information is available for Ann Drury for 2002:

Salary	$36,000
Premiums paid by employer on group-term life insurance in excess of $50,000	500
Proceeds from state lottery	5,000

How much should Drury report as gross income on her 2002 tax return?

    a. $36,000
    b. $36,500
    c. $41,000
    d. $41,500

38. Mr. and Mrs. Alvin Charak took a foster child, Robert, into their home in 2002. A state welfare agency paid the Charaks $3,900 during the year for related expenses. Actual expenses incurred by the Charaks during 2002 in caring for Robert amounted to $3,000. The remaining $900 was spent by the Charaks in 2002 towards their own personal expenses. How much of the foster child payments is taxable income to the Charaks in 2002?

    a. $0
    b. $ 900
    c. $2,900
    d. $3,900

39. Pierre, a headwaiter, received tips totaling $2,000 in December 2002. On January 5, 2003, Pierre reported this tip income to his employer in the required written statement. At what amount, and in which year, should this tip income be included in Pierre's gross income?

    a. $2,000 in 2002.
    b. $2,000 in 2003.
    c. $1,000 in 2002, and $1,000 in 2003.
    d. $ 167 in 2002, and $1,833 in 2003.

40. With regard to the alimony deduction in connection with a 2002 divorce, which one of the following statements is correct?

    a. Alimony is deductible by the payor spouse, and includible by the payee spouse, to the extent that payment is contingent on the status of the divorced couple's children.

    b. The divorced couple may be members of the same household at the time alimony is paid, provided that the persons do not live as husband and wife.

    c. Alimony payments must terminate on the death of the payee spouse.

    d. Alimony may be paid either in cash or in property.

41. In 2002, Joan accepted and received a $10,000 award for outstanding civic achievement. Joan was selected without any action on her part, and no future services are expected of her as a condition of receiving the award. What amount should Joan include in her 2002 adjusted gross income in connection with this award?

    a. $0
    b. $ 4,000
    c. $ 5,000
    d. $10,000

42. In 2002, Emil Gow won $5,000 in a state lottery. Also in 2002, Emil spent $400 for the purchase of lottery tickets. Emil elected the standard deduction on his 2002 income tax return. The amount of lottery winnings that should be included in Emil's 2002 taxable income is

    a. $0
    b. $2,000
    c. $4,600
    d. $5,000

43. Lake Corp., an accrual-basis calendar-year corporation, had the following 2002 receipts:

2003 advanced rental payments where the lease ends in 2004	$125,000
Lease cancellation payment from a five-year lease tenant	50,000

Lake had no restrictions on the use of the advanced rental payments and renders no services. What amount of income should Lake report on its 2002 tax return?

    a. $0
    b. $ 50,000
    c. $125,000
    d. $175,000

44. Paul Bristol, a cash-basis taxpayer, owns an apartment building. The following information was available for 2002:

- An analysis of the 2002 bank deposit slips showed recurring monthly rents received totaling $50,000.
- On March 1, 2002, the tenant in apartment 2B paid Bristol $2,000 to cancel the lease expiring on December 31, 2002.
- The lease of the tenant in apartment 3A expired on December 31, 2002, and the tenant left improvements valued at $1,000. The improvements were not in lieu of any rent required to have been paid.

In computing net rental income for 2002, Bristol should report gross rents of

    a. $50,000
    b. $51,000

    c. $52,000
    d. $53,000

45. Emil Gow owns a two-family house that has two identical apartments. Gow lives in one apartment and rents out the other. In 2002, the rental apartment was fully occupied and Gow received $7,200 in rent. During the year ended December 31, 2002, Gow paid the following:

Real estate taxes	$6,400
Painting of rental apartment	800
Annual fire insurance premium	600

In 2002, depreciation for the entire house was determined to be $5,000. What amount should Gow include in his adjusted gross income for 2002?

    a. $2,900
    b. $ 800
    c. $ 400
    d. $ 100

46. Amy Finch had the following cash receipts during 2002:

Net rent on vacant lot used by a car dealer (lessee pays all taxes, insurance, and other expenses on the lot)	$6,000
Advance rent from lessee of above vacant lot, such advance to be applied against rent for the last two months of the five-year lease in 2006	1,000

How much should Amy include in her 2002 taxable income for rent?

    a. $7,000
    b. $6,800
    c. $6,200
    d. $6,000

47. Royce Rentals, Inc., an accrual-basis taxpayer, reported rent receivable of $25,000 and $35,000 in its 2002 and 2001 balance sheets, respectively. During 2002, Royce received $50,000 in rent payments and $5,000 in nonrefundable rent deposits. In Royce's 2002 corporate income tax return, what amount should Royce include as rent revenue?

    a. $45,000
    b. $50,000
    c. $55,000
    d. $65,000

48. John Budd is single, with no dependents. During 2002, John received wages of $11,000 and state unemployment compensation benefits of $2,000. He had no other source of income. The amount of state unemployment compensation benefits that should be included in John's 2002 adjusted gross income is

    a. $2,000
    b. $1,000
    c. $ 500
    d. $0

49. A cash-basis taxpayer should report gross income

    a. Only for the year in which income is actually received in cash.

    b. Only for the year in which income is actually received whether in cash or in property.

    c. For the year in which income is either actually or constructively received in cash only.

    d. For the year in which income is either actually or constructively received, whether in cash or in property.

50. Which of the following taxpayers may use the cash method of accounting?
- a. A tax shelter.
- b. A qualified personal service corporation.
- c. A C corporation with annual gross receipts of $50,000,000.
- d. A manufacturer with annual gross receipts of $3,000,000.

51. In 2001, Stewart Corp. properly accrued $5,000 for an income item on the basis of a reasonable estimate. In 2002, after filing its 2001 federal income tax return, Stewart determined that the exact amount was $6,000. Which of the following statements is correct?
- a. No further inclusion of income is required as the difference is less than 25% of the original amount reported and the estimate had been made in good faith.
- b. The $1,000 difference is includible in Stewart's 2002 income tax return.
- c. Stewart is required to notify the IRS within 30 days of the determination of the exact amount of the item.
- d. Stewart is required to file an amended return to report the additional $1,000 of income.

52. Axis Corp. is an accrual-basis calendar-year corporation. On December 13, 2002, the Board of Directors declared a 2% of profits bonus to all employees for services rendered during 2002 and notified them in writing. None of the employees own stock in Axis. The amount represents reasonable compensation for services rendered and was paid on March 13, 2003. Axis' bonus expense may
- a. Not be deducted on Axis' 2002 tax return because the per share employee amount **cannot** be determined with reasonable accuracy at the time of the declaration of the bonus.
- b. Be deducted on Axis' 2002 tax return.
- c. Be deducted on Axis' 2003 tax return.
- d. Not be deducted on Axis' tax return because payment is a disguised dividend.

53. On December 1, 2001, Michaels, a self-employed cash-basis taxpayer, borrowed $100,000 to use in her business. The loan was to be repaid on November 30, 2002. Michaels paid the entire interest of $12,000 on December 1, 2001. What amount of interest was deductible on Michaels' 2002 income tax return?
- a. $12,000
- b. $11,000
- c. $ 1,000
- d. $0

54. Blair, CPA, uses the cash receipts and disbursements method of reporting. In 2002, a client gave Blair 100 shares of a listed corporation's stock in full satisfaction of a $5,000 accounting fee the client owed Blair. This stock had a fair market value of $4,000 on the date it was given to Blair. The client's basis for this stock was $3,000. Blair sold the stock for cash in January 2003. In Blair's 2002 return, what amount of income should be reported in connection with the receipt of the stock?
- a. $0
- b. $3,000
- c. $4,000
- d. $5,000

55. Unless the Internal Revenue Service consents to a change of method, the accrual method of tax reporting is generally mandatory for a sole proprietor when there are

	Accounts receivable for services rendered	Year-end merchandise inventories
a.	Yes	Yes
b.	Yes	No
c.	No	No
d.	No	Yes

56. Alex Burg, a cash-basis taxpayer, earned an annual salary of $80,000 at Ace Corp. in 2002, but elected to take only $50,000. Ace, which was financially able to pay Burg's full salary, credited the unpaid balance of $30,000 to Burg's account on the corporate books in 2002, and actually paid this $30,000 to Burg on January 30, 2003. How much of the salary is taxable to Burg in 2002?
- a. $50,000
- b. $60,000
- c. $65,000
- d. $80,000

57. Dr. Berger, a physician, reports on the cash basis. The following items pertain to Dr. Berger's medical practice in 2002:

Cash received from patients in 2002	$200,000
Cash received in 2002 from third-party reimbursers for services provided by Dr. Berger in 2001	30,000
Salaries paid to employees in 2002	20,000
Year-end 2002 bonuses paid to employees in 2002	1,000
Other expenses paid in 2002	24,000

What is Dr. Berger's net income for 2002 from his medical practice?
- a. $155,000
- b. $156,000
- c. $185,000
- d. $186,000

58. Which of the following taxpayers may use the cash method of accounting for tax purposes?
- a. Partnership that is designated as a tax shelter.
- b. Retail store with $2 million inventory, and $9 million average annual gross receipts.
- c. An international accounting firm.
- d. C corporation manufacturing exercise equipment with average annual gross receipts of $8 million.

59. The uniform capitalization method must be used by
- I. Manufacturers of tangible personal property.
- II. Retailers of personal property with $2 million dollars in average annual gross receipts for the three preceding years.

- a. I only.
- b. II only.
- c. Both I and II.
- d. Neither I nor II.

60. Mock operates a retail business selling illegal narcotic substances. Which of the following item(s) may Mock deduct in calculating business income?
- I. Cost of merchandise.
- II. Business expenses other than the cost of merchandise.

- a. I only.
- b. II only.

c. Both I and II.

d. Neither I nor II.

61. Banks Corp., a calendar-year corporation, reimburses employees for properly substantiated qualifying business meal expenses. The employees are present at the meals, which are neither lavish nor extravagant, and the reimbursement is not treated as wages subject to withholdings. For 2002, what percentage of the meal expense may Banks deduct?

a. 0%

b. 50%

c. 80%

d. 100%

62. Which of the following costs is not included in inventory under the Uniform Capitalization rules for goods manufactured by the taxpayer?

a. Research.

b. Warehousing costs.

c. Quality control.

d. Taxes excluding income taxes.

63. Under the uniform capitalization rules applicable to property acquired for resale, which of the following costs should be capitalized with respect to inventory if **no** exceptions are met?

	Marketing costs	*Off-site storage costs*
a.	Yes	Yes
b.	Yes	No
c.	No	No
d.	No	Yes

64. In the case of a corporation that is **not** a financial institution, which of the following statements is correct with regard to the deduction for bad debts?

a. Either the reserve method or the direct charge-off method may be used, if the election is made in the corporation's first taxable year.

b. On approval from the IRS, a corporation may change its method from direct charge-off to reserve.

c. If the reserve method was consistently used in prior years, the corporation may take a deduction for a reasonable addition to the reserve for bad debts.

d. A corporation is required to use the direct charge-off method rather than the reserve method.

65. Ram Corp.'s operating income for the year ended December 31, 2002, amounted to $100,000. Included in Ram's 2002 operating expenses is a $6,000 insurance premium on a policy insuring the life of Ram's president. Ram is beneficiary of this policy. In Ram's 2002 tax return, what amount should be deducted for the $6,000 life insurance premium?

a. $6,000

b. $5,000

c. $1,000

d. $0

66. Jason Budd, CPA, reports on the cash basis. In April 2001, Budd billed a client $3,500 for the following professional services:

Personal estate planning	$2,000
Personal tax return preparation	1,000
Compilation of business financial statements	500

No part of the $3,500 was ever paid. In April 2002, the client declared bankruptcy, and the $3,500 obligation became totally uncollectible. What loss can Budd deduct on his 2002 tax return for this bad debt?

a. $0

b. $ 500

c. $1,500

d. $3,500

67. Earl Cook, who worked as a machinist for Precision Corp., loaned Precision $1,000 in 1999. Cook did not own any of Precision's stock, and the loan was not a condition of Cook's employment by Precision. In 2002, Precision declared bankruptcy, and Cook's note receivable from Precision became worthless. What loss can Cook claim on his 2002 income tax return?

a. $0

b. $ 500 long-term capital loss.

c. $1,000 short-term capital loss.

d. $1,000 business bad debt.

68. During the 2002 holiday season, Palo Corp. gave business gifts to seventeen customers. These gifts, which were not of an advertising nature, had the following fair market values:

4	at	$ 10
4	at	25
4	at	50
5	at	100

How much of these gifts was deductible as a business expense for 2002?

a. $840

b. $365

c. $140

d. $0

69. Jennifer, who is single, has the following items of income and deduction for 2002:

Salary	$30,000
Itemized deductions (all attributable to a personal casualty loss when a hurricane destroyed her residence)	45,000
Personal exemption	3,000

What is the amount of Jennifer's net operating loss for 2002?

a. $0

b. $15,000

c. $18,000

d. $45,000

70. Robin Moore, a self-employed taxpayer, reported the following information for 2002:

Income:	Dividends from investments	$ 500
	Net short-term capital gain on sale of investment	1,000
Deductions:	Net loss from business	(6,000)
	Personal exemption	(3,000)
	Standard deduction	(4,700)

What is the amount of Moore's net operating loss for 2002?

a. $4,500

b. $5,000

c. $6,000

d. $9,200

71. Destry, a single taxpayer, reported the following on his US Individual Income Tax Return Form 1040:

Income

Wages	$ 5,000
Interest on savings account	1,000
Net rental income	4,000

Deductions

Personal exemption	$ 3,000
Standard deduction	4,700
Net business loss	16,000
Net short-term capital loss	2,000

What is Destry's net operating loss that is available for carryback or carryforward?

- a. $ 7,000
- b. $ 9,000
- c. $12,700
- d. $16,000

72. Cobb, an unmarried individual, had an adjusted gross income of $200,000 in 2002 before any IRA deduction, taxable social security benefits, or passive activity losses. Cobb incurred a loss of $30,000 in 2002 from rental real estate in which he actively participated. What amount of loss attributable to this rental real estate can be used in 2002 as an offset against income from nonpassive sources?

- a. $0
- b. $12,500
- c. $25,000
- d. $30,000

73. The rule limiting the allowability of passive activity losses and credits applies to

- a. Partnerships.
- b. S corporations.
- c. Personal service corporations.
- d. Widely held C corporations.

74. Don Wolf became a general partner in Gata Associates on January 1, 2002, with a 5% interest in Gata's profits, losses, and capital. Gata is a distributor of auto parts. Wolf does not materially participate in the partnership business. For the year ended December 31, 2002, Gata had an operating loss of $100,000. In addition, Gata earned interest of $20,000 on a temporary investment. Gata has kept the principal temporarily invested while awaiting delivery of equipment that is presently on order. The principal will be used to pay for this equipment. Wolf's passive loss for 2002 is

- a. $0
- b. $4,000
- c. $5,000
- d. $6,000

75. With regard to the passive loss rules involving rental real estate activities, which one of the following statements is correct?

- a. The term "passive activity" includes any rental activity without regard as to whether or not the taxpayer materially participates in the activity.
- b. Gross investment income from interest and dividends **not** derived in the ordinary course of a trade or business is treated as passive activity income that can be offset by passive rental activity losses when the "active participation" requirement is **not** met.

- c. Passive rental activity losses may be deducted only against passive income, but passive rental activity credits may be used against tax attributable to nonpassive activities.
- d. The passive activity rules do **not** apply to taxpayers whose adjusted gross income is $300,000 or less.

76. If an individual taxpayer's passive losses and credits relating to rental real estate activities cannot be used in the current year, then they may be carried

- a. Back two years, but they cannot be carried forward.
- b. Forward up to a maximum period of twenty years, but they cannot be carried back.
- c. Back two years or forward up to twenty years, at the taxpayer's election.
- d. Forward indefinitely or until the property is disposed of in a taxable transaction.

77. Aviation Corp. manufactures model airplanes for children. During 2002, Aviation purchased $203,000 of production machinery to be used in its business. For 2002, Aviation's taxable income before any Sec. 179 expense deduction was $7,000. What is the maximum amount of Sec. 179 expense election Aviation will be allowed to deduct for 2002 and the maximum amount of Sec. 179 expense election that can carryover to 2003?

		Expense	*Carryover*
a.		$ 7,000	$14,000
b.		$ 7,000	$17,000
c.		$21,000	$0
d.		$24,000	$0

78. Which of the following conditions must be satisfied for a taxpayer to expense, in the year of purchase, under Internal Revenue Code Section 179, the cost of new or used tangible depreciable personal property?

I. The property must be purchased for use in the taxpayer's active trade or business.
II. The property must be purchased from an unrelated party.

- a. I only.
- b. II only.
- c. Both I and II.
- d. Neither I nor II.

79. Krol Corp., a calendar-year taxpayer, purchased furniture and fixtures for use in its business and placed the property in service on November 1, 2002. The furniture and fixtures cost $56,000 and represented Krol's only acquisition of depreciable property during the year. Krol did **not** take additional first-year depreciation and did **not** elect to expense any part of the cost of the property under Sec. 179. What is the amount of Krol Corp.'s depreciation deduction for the furniture and fixtures under the Modified Accelerated Cost Recovery System (MACRS) for 2002?

- a. $ 2,000
- b. $ 2,667
- c. $ 8,000
- d. $16,000

80. On June 29, 2002, Sullivan purchased and placed into service an apartment building costing $360,000 including

$30,000 for the land. What was Sullivan's MACRS deduction for the apartment building in 2002?

- a. $7,091
- b. $6,500
- c. $6,000
- d. $4,583

81. Data Corp., a calendar-year corporation, purchased and placed into service office equipment during November 2002. No other equipment was placed into service during 2002. Under the general MACRS depreciation system, what convention must Data use?

- a. Full-year.
- b. Half-year.
- c. Midquarter.
- d. Midmonth.

82. Under the modified accelerated cost recovery system (MACRS) of depreciation for property placed in service after 1986,

- a. Used tangible depreciable property is excluded from the computation.
- b. Salvage value is ignored for purposes of computing the MACRS deduction.
- c. No type of straight-line depreciation is allowable.
- d. The recovery period for depreciable realty must be at least 27.5 years.

83. With regard to depreciation computations made under the general MACRS method, the half-year convention provides that

- a. One-half of the first year's depreciation is allowed in the year in which the property is placed in service, regardless of when the property is placed in service during the year, and a half-year's depreciation is allowed for the year in which the property is disposed of.
- b. The deduction will be based on the number of months the property was in service, so that one-half month's depreciation is allowed for the month in which the property is placed in service and for the month in which it is disposed of.
- c. Depreciation will be allowed in the first year of acquisition of the property only if the property is placed in service **no** later than June 30 for calendar-year corporations.
- d. Depreciation will be allowed in the last year of the property's economic life only if the property is disposed of after June 30 of the year of disposition for calendar-year corporations.

84. In 2002, Roe Corp. purchased and placed in service a machine to be used in its manufacturing operations. This machine cost $201,000. What portion of the cost may Roe elect to treat as an expense rather than as a capital expenditure?

- a. $19,000
- b. $20,000
- c. $23,000
- d. $24,000

85. Easel Co. has elected to reimburse employees for business expenses under a nonaccountable plan. Easel does not require employees to provide proof of expenses and allows employees to keep any amount not spent. Under the plan, Mel, an Easel employee for a full year, gets $400 per month

for business automobile expenses. At the end of the year Mel informs Easel that the only business expense incurred was for business mileage of 12,000 at a rate of 34.5 cents per mile, the IRS standard mileage rate at the time. Mel encloses a check for $660 to refund the overpayment to Easel. What amount should be reported in Mel's gross income for the year?

- a. $0
- b. $660
- c. $4,140
- d. $4,800

86. Adams owns a second residence that is used for both personal and rental purposes. During 2002, Adams used the second residence for 50 days and rented the residence for 200 days. Which of the following statements is correct?

- a. Depreciation may not be deducted on the property under any circumstances.
- b. A rental loss may be deducted if rental-related expenses exceed rental income.
- c. Utilities and maintenance on the property must be divided between personal and rental use.
- d. All mortgage interest and taxes on the property will be deducted to determine the property's net income or loss

87. Charles Gilbert, a corporate executive, incurred business-related unreimbursed expenses in 2002 as follows:

Entertainment	$900
Travel	700
Education	400

Assuming that Gilbert does not itemize deductions, how much of these expenses should he deduct on his 2002 tax return?

- a. $0
- b. $ 700
- c. $1,300
- d. $1,600

88. James, a calendar-year taxpayer, was employed and resided in Boston. On February 4, 2002, James was permanently transferred to Florida by his employer. James worked full-time for the entire year. In 2002, James incurred and paid the following unreimbursed expenses in relocating.

Lodging and travel expenses while moving	$1,000
Meals while in route to Florida	300
Cost of insuring household goods and personal effects during move	200
Cost of shipping household pets to new home	100
Costs of moving household furnishings and personal effects	3,000

What amount was deductible as moving expenses on James' 2002 tax return?

- a. $4,600
- b. $4,500
- c. $4,300
- d. $4,000

89. Martin Dawson, who resided in Detroit, was unemployed for the last six months of 2001. In January 2002, he moved to Houston to seek employment, and obtained a full-time job there in February. He kept this job for the balance of the year. Martin paid the following expenses in 2002 in connection with his move:

Rental of truck to move his personal belongings to	
Houston	$ 800
Penalty for breaking the lease on his Detroit apartment	300
Total	$1,100

How much can Martin deduct in 2002 for moving expenses?
a. $0
b. $ 300
c. $ 800
d. $1,100

90. Richard Putney, who lived in Idaho for five years, moved to Texas in 2002 to accept a new position. His employer reimbursed him in full for all direct moving costs, but did not pay for any part of the following indirect moving expenses incurred by Putney:

Househunting trips to Texas	$800
Temporary housing in Texas	900

How much of the indirect expenses can be deducted by Putney as moving expenses?
a. $0
b. $ 900
c. $1,500
d. $1,700

91. Which one of the following statements concerning Roth IRAs is **not** correct?
a. The maximum annual contribution to a Roth IRA is reduced if adjusted gross income exceeds certain thresholds.
b. Contributions to a Roth IRA are not deductible.
c. An individual is allowed to make contributions to a Roth IRA even after age 70½.
d. A contribution to a Roth IRA can be made by the due date for filing the individual's tax return for the year (including extensions).

92. What is the maximum amount of adjusted gross income that a taxpayer may have and still qualify to roll over the balance from a traditional individual retirement account (IRA) into a Roth IRA?
a. $ 50,000
b. $ 80,000
c. $100,000
d. $150,000

93. Which one of the following statements concerning an education IRA (Coverdell Education Savings Account) is **not** correct?
a. Contributions to an education IRA are not deductible.
b. A taxpayer may contribute up to $2,000 in 2002 to an education IRA to pay the costs of the designated beneficiary's higher education.
c. Eligibility for an education IRA is phased out if adjusted gross income exceeds certain threshold levels.
d. Contributions can be made to an education IRA on behalf of a beneficiary until the beneficiary reaches age twenty-one.

94. For 2002, Val and Pat White (both age 40) filed a joint return. Val earned $35,000 in wages and was covered by his employer's qualified pension plan. Pat was unemployed and received $5,000 in alimony payments for the first four months of the year before remarrying. The couple had no other income. Each contributed $3,000 to an IRA account.

The allowable IRA deduction on their 2002 joint tax return is
a. $6,000
b. $4,000
c. $3,000
d. $2,000

95. Davis, a sole proprietor with no employees, has a Keogh profit-sharing plan to which he may contribute 15% of his annual earned income. For this purpose, "earned income" is defined as net self-employment earnings reduced by the
a. Deductible Keogh contribution.
b. Self-employment tax.
c. Self-employment tax and one-half of the deductible Keogh contribution.
d. Deductible Keogh contribution and one-half of the self-employment tax.

96. Ronald Birch, who is single and age 28, earned a salary of $40,000 in 2002 as a plumber employed by Lupo Company. Birch was covered for the entire year 2002 under Lupo's qualified pension plan for employees. In addition, Birch had a net income of $15,000 from self-employment in 2002. What is the maximum amount that Birch can deduct in 2002 for contributions to an individual retirement account (IRA)?
a. $3,000
b. $2,000
c. $1,500
d. $0

97. Sol and Julia Crane (both age 43) are married and filed a joint return for 2002. Sol earned a salary of $80,000 in 2002 from his job at Troy Corp., where Sol is covered by his employer's pension plan. In addition, Sol and Julia earned interest of $3,000 in 2002 on their joint savings account. Julia is not employed, and the couple had no other income. On July 15, 2002, Sol contributed $3,000 to an IRA for himself, and $3,000 to an IRA for his spouse. The allowable IRA deduction in the Cranes' 2002 joint return is
a. $0
b. $3,000
c. $4,000
d. $6,000

98. Paul and Lois Lee, both age fifty, are married and filed a joint return for 2002. Their 2002 adjusted gross income was $80,000, including Paul's $75,000 salary. Lois had no income of her own. Neither spouse was covered by an employer-sponsored pension plan. What amount could the Lees contribute to IRAs for 2002 to take advantage of their maximum allowable IRA deduction in their 2002 return?
a. $3,000
b. $3,500
c. $6,000
d. $7,000

99. In 2002, deductible contributions to a defined contribution qualified retirement plan on behalf of a self-employed individual whose income from self-employment is $50,000 are limited to
a. $ 2,000
b. $11,000
c. $40,000
d. $50,000

100. Which allowable deduction can be claimed in arriving at an individual's 2002 adjusted gross income?

    a. Charitable contribution.
    b. Foreign income taxes.
    c. Tax return preparation fees.
    d. Self-employed health insurance deduction.

101. Which one of the following statements concerning the deduction for interest on qualified education loans is **not** correct?

    a. The deduction is available even if the taxpayer does not itemize deductions.
    b. The deduction only applies to the first sixty months of interest payments.
    c. Qualified education expenses include tuition fees, room, and board.
    d. The educational expenses must relate to a period when the student was enrolled on at least a half-time basis.

102. Dale received $1,000 in 2002 for jury duty. In exchange for regular compensation from her employer during the period of jury service, Dale was required to remit the entire $1,000 to her employer in 2002. In Dale's 2002 income tax return, the $1,000 jury duty fee should be

    a. Claimed in full as an itemized deduction.
    b. Claimed as an itemized deduction to the extent exceeding 2% of adjusted gross income.
    c. Deducted from gross income in arriving at adjusted gross income.
    d. Included in taxable income without a corresponding offset against other income.

103. During 2002, George (age ten and claimed as a dependency exemption by his parents) received dividend income of $3,700, and had wages from an after-school job of $1,700. What is the amount that will be reported as George's taxable income for 2002?

    a. $1,000
    b. $2,600
    c. $3,450
    d. $4,700

104. Which of the following requirements must be met in order for a single individual to qualify for the additional standard deduction?

	Must be age 65 or older or blind	*Must support dependent child or aged parent*
a.	Yes	Yes
b.	No	No
c.	Yes	No
d.	No	Yes

105. Carroll, an unmarried taxpayer with an adjusted gross income of $100,000, incurred and paid the following unreimbursed medical expenses for the year:

Doctor bills resulting from a serious fall	$5,000
Cosmetic surgery that was necessary to correct a congenital deformity	$15,000

Carroll had no medical insurance. For regular income tax purposes, what was Carroll's maximum allowable medical expense deduction, after the applicable threshold limitation, for the year?

    a. $0
    b. $12,500
    c. $15,000
    d. $20,000

106. Charlene and Gene Blair are married and filed a joint return for 2002. Their medical related expenditures for 2002 included the following:

Medical insurance premiums	$ 800
Medicines prescribed by doctors	450
Aspirin and over-the-counter cold capsules	80
Unreimbursed doctor fees	1,000
Transportation to and from doctors	150
Emergency room fee	500

The emergency room fee related to an injury incurred by the Blair's son, Eric, during a visit to their home. The Blairs graciously paid the bill; however, they provided no other support for Eric during the year. For 2002, Eric earned $12,000 as a self-employed house painter. Assuming the Blairs' adjusted gross income was $30,000, what amount of medical expenses can the Blairs deduct as an itemized deduction for 2002?

    a. $0
    b. $ 150
    c. $ 650
    d. $1,750

107. Tom and Sally White, married and filing joint income tax returns, derive their entire income from the operation of their retail stationery shop. Their 2002 adjusted gross income was $100,000. The Whites itemized their deductions on Schedule A for 2002. The following unreimbursed cash expenditures were among those made by the Whites during 2002:

Repair and maintenance of motorized wheelchair for physically handicapped dependent child	$ 600
Tuition, meals, lodging at special school for physically handicapped dependent child in an institution primarily for the availability of medical care, with meals and lodging furnished as necessary incidents to that care	8,000

Without regard to the adjusted gross income percentage threshold, what amount may the Whites claim in their 2002 return as qualifying medical expenses?

    a. $8,600
    b. $8,000
    c. $ 600
    d. $0

108. In 2002, Wells paid the following expenses:

Premiums on an insurance policy against loss of earnings due to sickness or accident	$3,000
Physical therapy after spinal surgery	2,000
Premium on an insurance policy that covers reimbursement for the cost of prescription drugs	500

In 2002, Wells recovered $1,500 of the $2,000 that she paid for physical therapy through insurance reimbursement from a group medical policy paid for by her employer. Disregarding the adjusted gross income percentage threshold, what amount could be claimed on Wells' 2002 income tax return for medical expenses?

    a. $4,000
    b. $3,500
    c. $1,000
    d. $ 500

109. Mr. and Mrs. Sloan incurred the following expenses on December 15, 2002, when they adopted a child:

Child's medical expenses	$5,000
Legal expenses	8,000
Agency fee	3,000

Before consideration of any "floor" or other limitation on deductibility, what amount of the above expenses may the Sloans deduct on their 2002 joint income tax return?

- a. $16,000
- b. $13,000
- c. $11,000
- d. $ 5,000

110. Ruth and Mark Cline are married and will file a joint 2002 income tax return. Among their expenditures during 2002 were the following discretionary costs that they incurred for the sole purpose of improving their physical appearance and self-esteem:

Face-lift for Ruth, performed by a licensed surgeon	$5,000
Hair transplant for Mark, performed by a licensed surgeon	3,600

Disregarding the adjusted gross income percentage threshold, what total amount of the aforementioned doctors' bills may be claimed by the Clines in their 2002 return as qualifying medical expenses?

- a. $0
- b. $3,600
- c. $5,000
- d. $8,600

111. During 2002, Scott charged $4,000 on his credit card for his dependent son's medical expenses. Payment to the credit card company had not been made by the time Scott filed his income tax return in 2003. However, in 2002, Scott paid a physician $2,800 for the medical expenses of his wife, who died in 2001. Disregarding the adjusted gross income percentage threshold, what amount could Scott claim in his 2002 income tax return for medical expenses?

- a. $0
- b. $2,800
- c. $4,000
- d. $6,800

112. Which one of the following expenditures qualifies as a deductible medical expense for tax purposes?

- a. Diaper service.
- b. Funeral expenses.
- c. Nursing care for a healthy baby.
- d. Premiums paid for Medicare B supplemental medical insurance.

113. Jon Stenger, a cash-basis taxpayer, had adjusted gross income of $35,000 in 2002. During the year he incurred and paid the following medical expenses:

Drugs and medicines prescribed by doctors	$ 300
Health insurance premiums	750
Doctors' fees	2,550
Eyeglasses	75
	$3,675

Stenger received $900 in 2002 as reimbursement for a portion of the doctors' fees. If Stenger were to itemize his deductions, what would be his allowable net medical expense deduction?

- a. $0
- b. $ 150
- c. $1,050
- d. $2,475

114. During 2002, Mr. and Mrs. Benson provided substantially all the support, in their own home, for their son John, age twenty-six, and for Mrs. Benson's cousin Nancy, age seventeen. John had $3,900 of income for 2002, and Nancy's income was $2,500. The Bensons paid the following medical expenses during the year:

Medicines and drugs:	
For themselves	$400
For John	500
For Nancy	100
Doctors:	
For themselves	600
For John	900
For Nancy	200

What is the total amount of medical expenses (before application of any limitation rules), that would enter into the calculation of itemized deductions on the Bensons' 2002 tax return?

- a. $1,000
- b. $1,300
- c. $2,400
- d. $2,700

115. All of the following taxes are deductible as itemized deductions by a self-employed taxpayer **except:**

- a. Foreign real estate taxes
- b. Foreign income taxes
- c. Personal property taxes
- d. One-half of self-employment taxes

116. Matthews was a cash-basis taxpayer whose records showed the following:

2002 state and local income taxes withheld	$1,500
2002 state estimated income taxes paid December 30, 2002	400
2002 federal income taxes withheld	2,500
2002 state and local income taxes paid April 17, 2002	300

What total amount was Matthews entitled to claim for taxes on her 2002 Schedule A of Form 1040?

- a. $4,700
- b. $2,200
- c. $1,900
- d. $1,500

117. In 2001, Farb, a cash-basis individual taxpayer, received an $8,000 invoice for personal property taxes. Believing the amount to be overstated by $5,000, Farb paid the invoiced amount under protest and immediately started legal action to recover the overstatement. In June 2002, the matter was resolved in Farb's favor, and he received a $5,000 refund. Farb itemizes his deductions on his tax returns. Which of the following statements is correct regarding the deductibility of the property taxes?

- a. Farb should deduct $8,000 in his 2001 income tax return and should report the $5,000 refund as income in his 2002 income tax return.
- b. Farb should **not** deduct any amount in his 2001 income tax return and should deduct $3,000 in his 2002 income tax return.
- c. Farb should deduct $3,000 in his 2001 income tax return.

d. Farb should **not** deduct any amount in his 2001 income tax return when originally filed, and should file an amended 2001 income tax return in 2002.

118. In 2002, Burg paid $8,000 to the tax collector of Sun City for realty taxes on a two-family house owned in joint-tenancy between Burg and his mother. Of this amount, $3,800 covered back taxes for 2001, and $4,200 covered 2002 taxes. Burg resides on the second floor of the house, and his mother resides on the first floor. In Burg's itemized deductions on his 2002 return, what amount was Burg entitled to claim for realty taxes?

   a. $0
   b. $4,000
   c. $4,200
   d. $8,000

119. Sara Harding is a cash-basis taxpayer who itemized her deductions. The following information pertains to Sara's state income taxes for the taxable year 2002:

Withheld by employer in 2002		$2,000
Payments on 2002 estimate:		
4/15/02	$300	
6/15/02	300	
9/15/02	300	
1/15/03	300	1,200
Total paid and withheld		$3,200
Actual tax, per state return		3,000
Overpayment		$ 200

There was no balance of tax or refund due on Sara's 2001 state tax return. How much is deductible for state income taxes on Sara's 2002 federal income tax return?

   a. $2,800
   b. $2,900
   c. $3,000
   d. $3,200

120. During 2002, Jack and Mary Bronson paid the following taxes:

Taxes on residence (for period January 1 to September 30, 2002)	$2,700
State motor vehicle tax on value of the car	360

The Bronsons sold their house on June 30, 2002, under an agreement in which the real estate taxes were not prorated between the buyer and sellers. What amount should the Bronsons deduct as taxes in calculating itemized deductions for 2002?

   a. $1,800
   b. $2,160
   c. $2,700
   d. $3,060

121. George Granger sold a plot of land to Albert King on July 1, 2002. Granger had not paid any realty taxes on the land since 2000. Delinquent 2001 taxes amounted to $600, and 2002 taxes amounted to $700. King paid the 2001 and 2002 taxes in full in 2002, when he bought the land. What portion of the $1,300 is deductible by King in 2002?

   a. $ 353
   b. $ 700
   c. $ 962
   d. $1,300

122. During 2002 Mr. and Mrs. West paid the following taxes:

Property taxes on residence	$1,800
Special assessment for installation of a sewer system in their town	1,000
State personal property tax on their automobile	600
Property taxes on land held for long-term appreciation	300

What amount can the Wests deduct as property taxes in calculating itemized deductions for 2002?

   a. $2,100
   b. $2,700
   c. $3,100
   d. $3,700

123. Alex and Myra Burg, married and filing joint income tax returns, derive their entire income from the operation of their retail candy shop. Their 2002 adjusted gross income was $50,000. The Burgs itemized their deductions on Schedule A for 2002. The following unreimbursed cash expenditures were among those made by the Burgs during 2002:

State income tax	$1,200
Self-employment tax	7,650

What amount should the Burgs deduct for taxes in their itemized deductions on Schedule A for 2002?

   a. $1,200
   b. $3,825
   c. $5,025
   d. $7,650

124. The 2002 deduction by an individual taxpayer for interest on investment indebtedness is

   a. Limited to the investment interest paid in 2002.
   b. Limited to the taxpayer's 2002 interest income.
   c. Limited to the taxpayer's 2002 net investment income.
   d. Not limited.

125. The Browns borrowed $20,000, secured by their home, to purchase a new automobile. At the time of the loan, the fair market value of their home was $400,000, and it was unencumbered by other debt. The interest on the loan qualifies as

   a. Deductible personal interest.
   b. Deductible qualified residence interest.
   c. Nondeductible interest.
   d. Investment interest expense.

126. On January 2, 1999, the Philips paid $50,000 cash and obtained a $200,000 mortgage to purchase a home. In 2002 they borrowed $15,000 secured by their home, and used the cash to add a new room to their residence. That same year they took out a $5,000 auto loan.

The following information pertains to interest paid in 2002:

Mortgage interest	$17,000
Interest on room construction loan	1,500
Auto loan interest	500

For 2002, how much interest is deductible, prior to any itemized deduction limitations?

   a. $17,000
   b. $17,500
   c. $18,500
   d. $19,000

127. Jackson owns two residences. The second residence, which has never been used for rental purposes, is the only residence that is subject to a mortgage. The following expenses were incurred for the second residence in 2002:

Mortgage interest	$5,000
Utilities	1,200
Insurance	6,000

For regular income tax purposes, what is the maximum amount allowable as a deduction for Jackson's second residence in 2002?

     a. $6,200 in determining adjusted gross income.
     b. $11,000 in determining adjusted gross income.
     c. $5,000 as an itemized deduction.
     d. $12,200 as an itemized deduction.

128. Robert and Judy Parker made the following payments during 2002:

Interest on a life insurance policy loan (the loan proceeds were used for personal use)	$1,200
Interest on home mortgage for period January 1 to October 4, 2002	3,600
Penalty payment for prepayment of home mortgage on October 4, 2002	900

How much can the Parkers utilize as interest expense in calculating itemized deductions for 2002?

     a. $5,700
     b. $4,620
     c. $4,500
     d. $3,600

129. Charles Wolfe purchased the following long-term investments at par during 2002:

$20,000 general obligation bonds of Burlington County (wholly tax-exempt)
$10,000 debentures of Arrow Corporation

Wolfe financed these purchases by obtaining a $30,000 loan from the Union National Bank. For the year 2002, Wolfe made the following interest payments:

Union National Bank	$3,600
Interest on home mortgage	3,000
Interest on credit card charges (items purchased for personal use)	500

What amount can Wolfe utilize as interest expense in calculating itemized deductions for 2002?

     a. $3,000
     b. $4,200
     c. $5,400
     d. $7,100

130. During 2002, William Clark was assessed a deficiency on his 2000 federal income tax return. As a result of this assessment he was required to pay $1,120 determined as follows:

Additional tax	$900
Late filing penalty	60
Negligence penalty	90
Interest	70

What portion of the $1,120 would qualify as itemized deductions for 2002?

     a. $0
     b. $ 14
     c. $150
     d. $220

131. Stein, an unmarried taxpayer, had adjusted income of $80,000 for the year and qualified to itemize deductions. Stein had no charitable contribution carryovers and only made one contribution during the year. Stein donated stock, purchased seven years earlier for $17,000, to a tax-exempt educational organization. The stock was valued at $25,000 when it was contributed. What is the amount of charitable contributions deductible on Stein's current year income tax return?

     a. $17,000
     b. $21,000
     c. $24,000
     d. $25,000

132. Moore, a single taxpayer, had $50,000 in adjusted gross income for 2002. During 2002 she contributed $18,000 to her church. She had a $10,000 charitable contribution carryover from her 2001 church contributions. What was the maximum amount of properly substantiated charitable contributions that Moore could claim as an itemized deduction for 2002?

     a. $10,000
     b. $18,000
     c. $25,000
     d. $28,000

133. Spencer, who itemizes deductions, had adjusted gross income of $60,000 in 2002. The following additional information is available for 2002:

Cash contribution to church	$4,000
Purchase of art object at church bazaar (with a fair market value of $800 on the date of purchase)	1,200
Donation of used clothing to Salvation Army (fair value evidenced by receipt received)	600

What is the maximum amount Spencer can claim as a deduction for charitable contributions in 2002?

     a. $5,400
     b. $5,200
     c. $5,000
     d. $4,400

134. Ruth Lewis has adjusted gross income of $100,000 for 2002 and itemizes her deductions. On September 1, 2002, she made a contribution to her church of stock held for investment for two years that cost $10,000 and had a fair market value of $70,000. The church sold the stock for $70,000 on the same date. Assume that Lewis made no other contributions during 2002 and made no special election in regard to this contribution on her 2002 tax return. How much should Lewis claim as a charitable contribution deduction for 2002?

     a. $50,000
     b. $30,000
     c. $20,000
     d. $10,000

135. On December 15, 2002, Donald Calder made a contribution of $500 to a qualified charitable organization, by charging the contribution on his bank credit card. Calder paid the $500 on January 20, 2003, upon receipt of the bill from the bank. In addition, Calder issued and delivered a promissory note for $1,000 to another qualified charitable organization on November 1, 2002, which he paid upon maturity six months later. If Calder itemizes his deductions, what portion of these contributions is deductible in 2002?

     a. $0
     b. $ 500
     c. $1,000
     d. $1,500

136. Under a written agreement between Mrs. Norma Lowe and an approved religious exempt organization, a ten-year-old girl from Vietnam came to live in Mrs. Lowe's home on August 1, 2002, in order to be able to start school in the US on September 3, 2002. Mrs. Lowe actually spent $500 for food, clothing, and school supplies for the student during 2002, without receiving any compensation or reimbursement of costs. What portion of the $500 may Mrs. Lowe deduct on her 2002 income tax return as a charitable contribution?

    a. $0
    b. $200
    c. $250
    d. $500

137. During 2002, Vincent Tally gave to the municipal art museum title to his private collection of rare books that was assessed and valued at $60,000. However, he reserved the right to the collection's use and possession during his lifetime. For 2002, he reported an adjusted gross income of $100,000. Assuming that this was his only contribution during the year, and that there were no carryovers from prior years, what amount can he deduct as contributions for 2002?

    a. $0
    b. $30,000
    c. $50,000
    d. $60,000

138. Jimet, an unmarried taxpayer, qualified to itemize 2002 deductions. Jimet's 2002 adjusted gross income was $30,000 and he made a $2,000 cash donation directly to a needy family. In 2002, Jimet also donated stock, valued at $3,000, to his church. Jimet had purchased the stock four months earlier for $1,500. What was the maximum amount of the charitable contribution allowable as an itemized deduction on Jimet's 2002 income tax return?

    a. $0
    b. $1,500
    c. $2,000
    d. $5,000

139. Taylor, an unmarried taxpayer, had $90,000 in adjusted gross income for 2002. During 2002, Taylor donated land to a church and made no other contributions. Taylor purchased the land in 1991 as an investment for $14,000. The land's fair market value was $25,000 on the day of the donation. What is the maximum amount of charitable contribution that Taylor may deduct as in itemized deduction for the land donation for 2002?

    a. $25,000
    b. $14,000
    c. $11,000
    d. $0

140. In 2002, Joan Frazer's residence was totally destroyed by fire. The property had an adjusted basis and a fair market value of $130,000 before the fire. During 2002, Frazer received insurance reimbursement of $120,000 for the destruction of her home. Frazer's 2002 adjusted gross income was $70,000. Frazer had no casualty gains during the year. What amount of the fire loss was Frazer entitled to claim as an itemized deduction on her 2002 tax return?

    a. $ 2,900
    b. $ 8,500
    c. $ 8,600
    d. $10,000

141. Alex and Myra Burg, married and filing joint income tax returns, derive their entire income from the operation of their retail candy shop. Their 2002 adjusted gross income was $50,000. The Burgs itemized their deductions on Schedule A for 2002. The following unreimbursed cash expenditures were among those made by the Burgs during 2002:

> Repair of glass vase accidentally broken in home by dog;
> vase cost $500 in 1999; fair value $600 before accident
> and $200 after accident $90

Without regard to the $100 "floor" and the adjusted gross income percentage threshold, what amount should the Burgs deduct for the casualty loss in their itemized deductions on Schedule A for 2002?

    a. $0
    b. $ 90
    c. $300
    d. $400

142. Hall, a divorced person and custodian of her twelve-year-old child, filed her 2002 federal income tax return as head of a household. During 2002 Hall paid a $490 casualty insurance premium on her personal residence. Hall does not rent out any portion of the home, nor use it for business.

The casualty insurance premium of $490 is

    a. Allowed as an itemized deduction subject to the $100 floor and the 10% of adjusted gross income floor.
    b. Allowed as an itemized deduction subject to the 2% of adjusted gross income floor.
    c. Deductible in arriving at adjusted gross income.
    d. Not deductible in 2002.

Items 143 and 144 are based on the following selected 2002 information pertaining to Sam and Ann Hoyt, who filed a joint federal income tax return for the calendar year 2002. The Hoyts had adjusted gross income of $34,000 and itemized their deductions for 2002. Among the Hoyts' cash expenditures during 2002 were the following:

> $2,500 repairs in connection with 2002 fire damage to the Hoyt residence. This property has a basis of $50,000. Fair market value was $60,000 before the fire and $55,000 after the fire. Insurance on the property had lapsed in 2001 for nonpayment of premium.
> $800 appraisal fee to determine amount of fire loss.

143. What amount of fire loss were the Hoyts entitled to deduct as an itemized deduction on their 2002 return?

    a. $5,000
    b. $2,500
    c. $1,600
    d. $1,500

144. The appraisal fee to determine the amount of the Hoyts' fire loss was

    a. Deductible from gross income in arriving at adjusted gross income.
    b. Subject to the 2% of adjusted gross income floor for miscellaneous itemized deductions.
    c. Deductible after reducing the amount by $100.
    d. Not deductible.

145. Which of the following is **not** a miscellaneous itemized deduction?

    a. Legal fee for tax advice related to a divorce.

    b.   IRA trustee's fees that are separately billed and paid.

    c.   Appraisal fee for a charitable contribution.

    d.   Check-writing fees for a personal checking account.

146. Hall, a divorced person and custodian of her twelve-year-old child, submitted the following information to the CPA who prepared her 2002 return:

The divorce agreement, executed in 1999, provides for Hall to receive $3,000 per month, of which $600 is designated as child support. After the child reaches eighteen, the monthly payments are to be reduced to $2,400 and are to continue until remarriage or death. However, for the year 2002, Hall received a total of only $5,000 from her former husband. Hall paid an attorney $2,000 in 2002 in a suit to collect the alimony owed.

The $2,000 legal fee that Hall paid to collect alimony should be treated as

    a.   A deduction in arriving at adjusted gross income.

    b.   An itemized deduction subject to the 2% of adjusted gross income floor.

    c.   An itemized deduction **not** subject to the 2% of adjusted gross income floor.

    d.   A nondeductible personal expense.

147. Hall, a divorced person and custodian of her twelve-year-old child, submitted the following information to the CPA who prepared her 2002 return:

During 2002, Hall spent a total of $1,000 for state lottery tickets. Her lottery winnings in 2002 totaled $200. Hall's lottery transactions should be reported as follows:

| | | *Schedule A—itemized deductions* | |
| | | *Other miscellaneous deductions* | |
	Other income on page 1	*Subject to 2% AGI floor*	*Not subject to 2% AGI floor*
a.	$0	$0	$0
b.	$200	$0	$200
c.	$200	$200	$0
d.	$200	$0	$0

148. Joel Rich is an outside salesman, deriving his income solely from commissions, and personally bearing all expenses without reimbursement of any kind. During 2002, Joel paid the following expenses pertaining directly to his activities as an outside salesman:

Travel	$10,000
Secretarial	7,000
Telephone	1,000

How should these expenses be deducted in Joel's 2002 return?

	From gross income, in arriving at adjusted gross income	*As itemized deductions*
a.	$18,000	$0
b.	$11,000	$ 7,000
c.	$10,000	$ 8,000
d.	$0	$18,000

149. Magda Micale, a public school teacher with adjusted gross income of $10,000, paid the following items in 2002 for which she received no reimbursement:

Initiation fee for membership in teachers' union	$100
Dues to teachers' union	180
Voluntary unemployment benefit fund contributions to union-established fund	72

How much can Magda claim in 2002 as allowable miscellaneous deductions on Schedule A of Form 1040?

    a. $ 80

    b. $280

    c. $252

    d. $352

150. Harold Brodsky is an electrician employed by a contracting firm. His adjusted gross income is $25,000. During the current year he incurred and paid the following expenses:

Use of personal auto for company business (reimbursed by employer for $200)	$300
Specialized work clothes	550
Union dues	600
Cost of income tax preparation	150
Preparation of will	100

If Brodsky were to itemize his personal deductions, what amount should he claim as miscellaneous deductible expenses?

    a. $ 800

    b. $ 900

    c. $1,500

    d. $1,700

151. Which items are **not** subject to the phaseout of the amount of certain itemized deductions that may be claimed by high-income individuals?

    a.   Qualified residence interest.

    b.   Charitable contributions.

    c.   Investment interest expenses.

    d.   Real estate taxes.

152. For 2002, Dole's adjusted gross income exceeds $500,000. After the application of any other limitation, itemized deductions are reduced by

    a.   The **lesser** of 3% of the excess of adjusted gross income over the applicable amount or 80% of **certain** itemized deductions.

    b.   The **lesser** of 3% of the excess of adjusted gross income over the applicable amount or 80% of **all** itemized deductions.

    c.   The **greater** of 3% of the excess of adjusted gross income over the applicable amount or 80% of **certain** itemized deductions.

    d.   The **greater** of 3% of the excess of adjusted gross income over the applicable amount or 80% of **all** itemized deductions.

153. Which one of the following is **not** included in determining the total support of a dependent?

    a.   Fair rental value of dependent's lodging.

    b.   Medical insurance premiums paid on behalf of the dependent.

    c.   Birthday presents given to the dependent.

    d.   Nontaxable scholarship received by the dependent.

154. In 2002, Smith, a divorced person, provided over one-half the support for his widowed mother, Ruth, and his son, Clay, both of whom are US citizens. During 2002, Ruth did not live with Smith. She received $9,000 in social security benefits. Clay, a full-time graduate student, and his wife lived with Smith. Clay had no income but filed a joint return for 2002, owing an additional $500 in taxes on his wife's income. How many exemptions was Smith entitled to claim on his 2002 tax return?

a. 4
b. 3
c. 2
d. 1

155. Jim and Kay Ross contributed to the support of their two children, Dale and Kim, and Jim's widowed parent, Grant. For 2002, Dale, a twenty-year-old full-time college student, earned $4,500 from a part-time job. Kim, a twenty-three-year-old bank teller, earned $12,000. Grant received $5,000 in dividend income and $4,000 in nontaxable social security benefits. Grant, Dale, and Kim are US citizens and were over one-half supported by Jim and Kay. How many exemptions can Jim and Kay claim on their 2002 joint income tax return?

a. Two
b. Three
c. Four
d. Five

156. Joe and Barb are married, but Barb refuses to sign a 2002 joint return. On Joe's separate 2002 return, an exemption may be claimed for Barb if

a. Barb was a full-time student for the entire 2002 school year.
b. Barb attaches a written statement to Joe's income tax return, agreeing to be claimed as an exemption by Joe for 2002.
c. Barb was under the age of nineteen.
d. Barb had **no** gross income and was **not** claimed as another person's dependent in 2002.

157. Al and Mary Lew are married and filed a joint 2002 income tax return in which they validly claimed the $3,000 personal exemption for their dependent seventeen-year-old daughter, Doris. Since Doris earned $5,400 in 2002 from a part-time job at the college she attended full-time, Doris was also required to file a 2002 income tax return. What amount was Doris entitled to claim as a personal exemption in her 2002 individual income tax return?

a. $0
b. $ 750
c. $2,900
d. $4,550

158. During 2002 Robert Moore, who is fifty years old and unmarried, maintained his home in which he and his widower father, age seventy-five, resided. His father had $3,500 interest income from a savings account and also received $2,400 from social security during 2002. Robert provided 60% of his father's total support for 2002. What is Robert's filing status for 2002, and how many exemptions should he claim on his tax return?

a. Head of household and two exemptions.
b. Single and two exemptions.
c. Head of household and one exemption.
d. Single and one exemption.

159. John and Mary Arnold are a childless married couple who lived apart (alone in homes maintained by each) the entire year 2002. On December 31, 2002, they were legally separated under a decree of separate maintenance. Which of the following is the only filing status choice available to them when filing for 2002?

a. Single.
b. Head of household.
c. Married filing separate return.
d. Married filing joint return.

160. Albert and Lois Stoner, age sixty-six and sixty-four, respectively, filed a joint tax return for 2002. They provided all of the support for their blind nineteen-year-old son, who has no gross income. Their twenty-three-year-old daughter, a full-time student until her graduation on June 14, 2002, earned $3,000, which was 40% of her total support during 2002. Her parents provided the remaining support. The Stoners also provided the total support of Lois' father, who is a citizen and lifelong resident of Peru. How many exemptions can the Stoners claim on their 2002 income tax return?

a. 4
b. 5
c. 6
d. 7

161. Jim Planter, who reached age sixty-five on January 1, 2002, filed a joint return for 2002 with his wife Rita, age fifty. Mary, their twenty-one-year-old daughter, was a full-time student at a college until her graduation on June 2, 2002. The daughter had $6,500 of income and provided 25% of her own support during 2002. In addition, during 2002 the Planters were the sole support for Rita's niece, who had no income. How many exemptions should the Planters claim on their 2002 tax return?

a. 2
b. 3
c. 4
d. 5

162. In 2002, Sam Dunn provided more than half the support for his wife, his father's brother, and his cousin. Sam's wife was the only relative who was a member of Sam's household. None of the relatives had any income, nor did any of them file an individual or a joint return. All of these relatives are US citizens. Which of these relatives should be claimed as a dependent or dependents on Sam's 2002 return?

a. Only his wife.
b. Only his father's brother.
c. Only his cousin.
d. His wife, his father's brother, and his cousin.

163. In 2002, Alan Kott provided more than half the support for his following relatives, none of whom qualified as a member of Alan's household:

Cousin
Niece
Foster parent

None of these relatives had any income, nor did any of these relatives file an individual or joint return. All of these relatives are US citizens. Which of these relatives could be claimed as a dependent on Alan's 2002 return?

a. No one.
b. Niece.
c. Cousin.
d. Foster parent.

164. Sara Hance, who is single and lives alone in Idaho, has no income of her own and is supported in full by the following persons:

	Amount of support	Percent of total
Alma (an unrelated friend)	$2,400	48
Ben (Sara's brother)	2,150	43
Carl (Sara's son)	450	9
	$5,000	100

Under a multiple support agreement, Sara's dependency exemption can be claimed by
     a. No one.
     b. Alma.
     c. Ben.
     d. Carl.

165. Mr. and Mrs. Vonce, both age sixty-two, filed a joint return for 2002. They provided all the support for their daughter, who is nineteen, legally blind, and who has no income. Their son, age twenty-one and a full-time student at a university, had $6,200 of income and provided 70% of his own support during 2002. How many exemptions should Mr. and Mrs. Vonce have claimed on their 2002 joint income tax return?
     a. 2
     b. 3
     c. 4
     d. 5

166. Which of the following is(are) among the requirements to enable a taxpayer to be classified as a "qualifying widow(er)"?

     I. A dependent has lived with the taxpayer for six months.
     II. The taxpayer has maintained the cost of the principal residence for six months.

     a. I only.
     b. II only.
     c. Both I and II.
     d. Neither I nor II.

167. For head of household filing status, which of the following costs are considered in determining whether the taxpayer has contributed more than one-half the cost of maintaining the household?

	Insurance on the home	Rental value of home
a.	Yes	Yes
b.	No	No
c.	Yes	No
d.	No	Yes

168. A husband and wife can file a joint return even if
     a. The spouses have different tax years, provided that both spouses are alive at the end of the year.
     b. The spouses have different accounting methods.
     c. Either spouse was a nonresident alien at any time during the tax year, provided that at least one spouse makes the proper election.
     d. They were divorced before the end of the tax year.

169. Emil Gow's wife died in 2000. Emil did not remarry, and he continued to maintain a home for himself and his dependent infant child during 2001 and 2002, providing full support for himself and his child during these years. For 2000, Emil properly filed a joint return. For 2002, Emil's filing status is
     a. Single.
     b. Head of household.
     c. Qualifying widower with dependent child.
     d. Married filing joint return.

170. Nell Brown's husband died in 1999. Nell did not remarry, and continued to maintain a home for herself and her dependent infant child during 2000, 2001, and 2002, providing full support for herself and her child during these three years. For 1999, Nell properly filed a joint return. For 2002, Nell's filing status is
     a. Single.
     b. Married filing joint return.
     c. Head of household.
     d. Qualifying widow with dependent child.

171. Mrs. Irma Felton, by herself, maintains her home in which she and her unmarried son reside. Her son, however, does not qualify as her dependent. Mrs. Felton's husband died in 2001. What is Mrs. Felton's filing status for 2002?
     a. Single.
     b. Qualifying widow with dependent child.
     c. Head of household.
     d. Married filing jointly.

172. Poole, forty-five years old and unmarried, is in the 15% tax bracket. He had 2002 adjusted gross income of $20,000. The following information applies to Poole:

Medical expenses	$6,500
Standard deduction	4,700
Personal exemption	3,000

Poole wishes to minimize his income tax. What is Poole's 2002 total income tax?
     a. $3,000
     b. $1,845
     c. $1,800
     d. $1,575

173. Which of the following itemized deductions are deductible when computing the alternative minimum tax for individuals?
     a. State income taxes
     b. Home equity mortgage interest when the loan proceeds were used to purchase an auto
     c. Unreimbursed employee expenses in excess of 2% of adjusted gross income
     d. Gambling losses.

174. Randy Lowe reported the following items in computing his regular federal income tax for 2002:

Personal exemption	$3,000
Itemized deduction for state taxes	1,500
Cash charitable contributions	1,250
Net long-term capital gain	700
Excess of accelerated depreciation over straight-line depreciation on real property placed in service prior to 1987	600
Tax-exempt interest from private activity bonds	400

What are the amounts of tax preference items and adjustments that must be added to or subtracted from regular taxable income in order to compute Lowe's alternative minimum taxable income for 2002?

	Preferences	Adjustments
a.	$1,000	$4,500
b.	$1,000	$5,750
c.	$1,700	$4,500
d.	$2,250	$5,200

175. In 2001, Karen Miller had an alternative minimum tax liability of $20,000. This was the first year that she paid an alternative minimum tax. When she recomputed her 2001 alternative minimum tax using only exclusion preferences and adjustments, her alternative minimum tax was $9,000. For 2002, Karen had a regular tax liability of $50,000 and a tentative minimum tax of $45,000. What is the amount of Karen's unused minimum tax credit from 2002 that will carry over to 2003?

    a. $0
    b. $4,000
    c. $5,000
    d. $6,000

176. In 2002, Don Mills, a single taxpayer, had $70,000 in taxable income before personal exemptions. Mills had no tax preferences. His itemized deductions were as follows:

State and local income taxes	$5,000
Home mortgage interest on loan to acquire residence	6,000
Miscellaneous deductions that exceed 2% of adjusted gross income	2,000

What amount did Mills report as alternative minimum taxable income before the AMT exemption?

    a. $72,000
    b. $75,000
    c. $77,000
    d. $83,000

177. An individual's alternative minimum tax adjustments include

	Net long-term capital gain in excess of net short-term capital loss	Home equity interest expense where loan proceeds not used to buy, build, or improve home
a.	Yes	Yes
b.	Yes	No
c.	No	Yes
d.	No	No

178. The credit for prior year alternative minimum tax liability may be carried

    a. Forward for a maximum of five years.
    b. Back to the three preceding years or carried forward for a maximum of five years.
    c. Back to the three preceding years.
    d. Forward indefinitely.

179. The alternative minimum tax (AMT) is computed as the

    a. Excess of the regular tax over the tentative AMT.
    b. Excess of the tentative AMT over the regular tax.
    c. The tentative AMT plus the regular tax.
    d. Lesser of the tentative AMT or the regular tax.

180. The following information pertains to Joe Diamond, a cash-method sole proprietor for 2002:

Gross receipts from business	$150,000
Interest income from personal investments	10,000
Cost of goods sold	80,000
Other business operating expenses	40,000

What amount of net self-employment earnings would be multiplied by the applicable self-employment tax rate to compute Diamond's self-employment tax for 2002?

    a. $25,410
    b. $27,705
    c. $30,000
    d. $40,000

181. Freeman, a single individual, reported the following income in the current year:

Guaranteed payment from services rendered to a partnership	$50,000
Ordinary income from an S corporation	$20,000

What amount of Freeman's income is subject to self-employment tax?

    a. $0
    b. $20,000
    c. $50,000
    d. $70,000

182. Rich is a cash-basis self-employed air-conditioning repairman with 2002 gross business receipts of $20,000. Rich's cash disbursements were as follows:

Air conditioning parts	$2,500
Yellow Pages listing	2,000
Estimated federal income taxes on self-employment income	1,000
Business long-distance telephone calls	400
Charitable contributions	200

What amount should Rich report as net self-employment income?

    a. $15,100
    b. $14,900
    c. $14,100
    d. $13,900

183. The self-employment tax is

    a. Fully deductible as an itemized deduction.
    b. Fully deductible in determining net income from self-employment.
    c. One-half deductible from gross income in arriving at adjusted gross income.
    d. Not deductible.

184. An employee who has had social security tax withheld in an amount greater than the maximum for a particular year, may claim

    a. Such excess as either a credit or an itemized deduction, at the election of the employee, if that excess resulted from correct withholding by two or more employers.
    b. Reimbursement of such excess from his employers, if that excess resulted from correct withholding by two or more employers.
    c. The excess as a credit against income tax, if that excess resulted from correct withholding by two or more employers.
    d. The excess as a credit against income tax, if that excess was withheld by one employer.

185. Alex Berger, a retired building contractor, earned the following income during 2002:

Director's fee received from Keith Realty Corp.	$ 600
Executor's fee received from the estate of his deceased sister	7,000

Berger's gross income from self-employment for 2002 is

    a. $0
    b. $ 600
    c. $7,000
    d. $7,600

186. Smith, a retired corporate executive, earned consulting fees of $8,000 and director's fees of $2,000 in 2002. Smith's gross income from self-employment for 2002 is
    a. $0
    b. $ 2,000
    c. $ 8,000
    d. $10,000

187. Which one of the following credits is not a component of the general business credit?
    a. Disabled access credit.
    b. Employer social security credit.
    c. Foreign tax credit.
    d. Welfare-to-work credit.

188. Which of the following credits is a combination of several tax credits to provide uniform rules for the current and carryback-carryover years?
    a. General business credit.
    b. Foreign tax credit.
    c. Minimum tax credit.
    d. Enhanced oil recovery credit.

189. Melvin Crane is sixty-six years old, and his wife, Matilda, is sixty-five. They filed a joint income tax return for 2002, reporting an adjusted gross income of $15,600, on which they paid a tax of $60. They received $3,000 from social security benefits in 2002. How much can they claim on Form 1040 in 2002, as a credit for the elderly?
    a. $0
    b. $ 60
    c. $255
    d. $675

190. Nora Hayes, a widow, maintains a home for herself and her two dependent preschool children. In 2002, Nora's earned income and adjusted gross income was $29,000. During 2002, Nora paid work-related expenses of $3,000 for a housekeeper to care for her children. How much can Nora claim for child care credit in 2002?
    a. $0
    b. $480
    c. $600
    d. $900

191. Robert and Mary Jason, filing a joint tax return for 2002, had a tax liability of $9,000 based on their tax table income and three exemptions. Robert and Mary had earned income of $20,000 and $12,000, respectively, during 2002. In order for Mary to be gainfully employed, the Jasons incurred the following employment-related expenses for their four-year-old son John in 2002:

Payee	Amount
Union Day Care Center	$1,500
Acme Home Cleaning Service	500
Wilma Jason, babysitter (Robert Jason's mother)	1,000

Assuming that the Jasons do not claim any other credits against their tax, what is the amount of the child care tax credit they should report on their tax return for 2002?
    a. $300
    b. $480

    c. $500
    d. $600

192. To qualify for the child care credit on a joint return, at least one spouse must

	Have an adjusted gross income of $10,000 or less	Be gainfully employed when related expenses are incurred
a.	Yes	Yes
b.	No	No
c.	Yes	No
d.	No	Yes

193. Sunex Co., an accrual-basis, calendar-year domestic C corporation, is taxed on its worldwide income. In the current year, Sunex's US tax liability on its domestic and foreign-source income is $60,000 and no prior year foreign income taxes have been carried forward. Which factor(s) may affect the amount of Sunex's foreign tax credit available in its current year corporate income tax return?

	Income source	The foreign tax rate
a.	Yes	Yes
b.	Yes	No
c.	No	Yes
d.	No	No

194. The following information pertains to Wald Corp.'s operations for the year ended December 31, 2002:

Worldwide taxable income	$300,000
US source taxable income	180,000
US income tax before foreign tax credit	96,000
Foreign nonbusiness-related interest earned	30,000
Foreign income taxes paid on nonbusiness-related interest earned	12,000
Other foreign source taxable income	90,000
Foreign income taxes paid on other foreign source taxable income	27,000

What amount of foreign tax credit may Wald claim for 2002?
    a. $28,800
    b. $36,600
    c. $38,400
    d. $39,000

195. Foreign income taxes paid by a corporation
    a. May be claimed either as a deduction or as a credit, at the option of the corporation.
    b. May be claimed only as a deduction.
    c. May be claimed only as a credit.
    d. Do **not** qualify either as a deduction or as a credit.

196. Which of the following credits can result in a refund even if the individual had **no** income tax liability?
    a. Credit for prior year minimum tax.
    b. Credit for the elderly or the disabled.
    c. Earned income credit.
    d. Child and dependent care credit.

197. Kent qualified for the earned income credit in 2002. This credit could result in a
    a. Refund even if Kent had no tax withheld from wages.
    b. Refund only if Kent had tax withheld from wages.
    c. Carryback or carryforward for any unused portion.

d. Subtraction from adjusted gross income to arrive at taxable income.

198. Which one of the following statements is correct with regard to the earned income credit?

a. The credit is available only to those individuals whose earned income is equal to adjusted gross income.

b. For purposes of the earned income test, "earned income" includes workers' compensation benefits.

c. The credit can result in a refund even if the individual had **no** tax withheld from wages.

d. The credit is available on a tax return that covers less than twelve months.

199. Which of the following tax credits **cannot** be claimed by a corporation?

a. Foreign tax credit.

b. Earned income credit.

c. Alternative fuel production credit.

d. General business credit.

200. Which one of the following statements is correct regarding the credit for adoption expenses?

a. The credit for adoption expenses is a refundable credit.

b. The maximum credit is $5,000 for the adoption of a child with special needs.

c. Qualified adoption expenses are taken into account in the year that the adoption becomes final.

d. An eligible child is an individual who has not attained the age of twenty-one as of the time of adoption.

201. Which one of the following statements is **not** correct with regard to the child tax credit?

a. The credit is $600 per qualifying child for tax years beginning in 2002.

b. The amount of credit is reduced if modified adjusted gross income exceeds certain thresholds.

c. To qualify for the credit, a dependent child must be less than sixteen years old.

d. A qualifying child must be a US citizen or resident.

202. Which one of the following statements concerning the Hope scholarship credit is **not** correct?

a. The credit is available for the first two years of postsecondary education program.

b. The credit is available on a per student basis.

c. To be eligible for the credit, the student must be enrolled full-time for at least one academic period during the year.

d. If a parent claims a child as a dependent, any qualified expenses paid by the child are deemed to be paid by the parent.

203. Which one of the following statements concerning the lifetime learning credit is **not** correct?

a. The credit is 20% of the first $5,000 of qualified tuition and related expenses per year.

b. Qualifying expenses include the cost of tuition for graduate courses at an eligible educational institution.

c. The credit may be claimed for an unlimited number of years.

d. The credit is available on a per student basis.

204. Chris Baker's adjusted gross income on her 2001 tax return was $160,000. The amount covered a twelve-month period. For the 2002 tax year, Baker may avoid the penalty for the underpayment of estimated tax if the timely estimated tax payments equal the required annual amount of

I. 90% of the tax on the return for the current year, paid in four equal installments.

II. 100% of prior year's tax liability, paid in four equal installments.

a. I only.

b. II only.

c. Both I and II.

d. Neither I nor II.

205. Krete, an unmarried taxpayer, had income exclusively from wages. By December 31, 2001, Krete's employer had withheld $16,000 in federal income taxes and Krete had made no estimated tax payments. On April 15, 2002, Krete timely filed an extension request to file her individual tax return and paid $300 of additional taxes. Krete's 2001 income tax liability was $16,500 when she timely filed her return on April 30, 2002, and paid the remaining income tax liability balance. What amount would be subject to the penalty for the underpayment of estimated taxes?

a. $0

b. $ 200

c. $ 500

d. $16,500

206. John Smith is the executor of his father's estate. His father, a calendar-year taxpayer, died on July 15, 2002. As executor of his father's estate, John is required to file a final income tax return Form 1040 for his father's 2002 tax year. What is the due date of his father's 2002 federal income tax return assuming John does not file for an extension?

a. November 1, 2002.

b. November 15, 2002.

c. March 15, 2002.

d. April 15, 2002.

207. Ray Birch, age sixty, is single with no dependents. Birch's only income is from his occupation as a self-employed plumber. Birch must file a return for 2002 if his net earnings from self-employment are at least

a. $ 400

b. $ 750

c. $2,900

d. $4,550

208. Jackson Corp., a calendar-year corporation, mailed its 2001 tax return to the Internal Revenue Service by certified mail on Tuesday, March 13, 2002. The return, postmarked March 13, 2002, was delivered to the Internal Revenue Service on March 18, 2002. The statute of limitations on Jackson's corporate tax return begins on

a. December 31, 2001.

b. March 13, 2002.

c. March 16, 2002.

d. March 18, 2002.

209. A calendar-year taxpayer files an individual tax return for 2001 on March 20, 2002. The taxpayer neither committed fraud nor omitted amounts in excess of 25% of gross income on the tax return. What is the latest date that the Internal Revenue Service can assess tax and assert a notice of deficiency?

    a.   March 20, 2005.
    b.   March 20, 2004.
    c.   April 15, 2005.
    d.   April 15, 2004.

210. Harold Thompson, a self-employed individual, had income transactions for 2001 (duly reported on his return filed in April 2002) as follows:

Gross receipts	$400,000
Less cost of goods sold and deductions	320,000
Net business income	$ 80,000
Capital gains	36,000
Gross income	$116,000

In November 2002, Thompson discovers that he had inadvertently omitted some income on his 2001 return and retains Mann, CPA, to determine his position under the statute of limitations. Mann should advise Thompson that the six-year statute of limitations would apply to his 2001 return only if he omitted from gross income an amount in excess of

    a. $ 20,000
    b. $ 29,000
    c. $100,000
    d. $109,000

211. If a taxpayer omits from his or her income tax return an amount that exceeds 25% of the gross income reported on the return, the Internal Revenue Service can issue a notice of deficiency within a maximum period of

    a.   Three years from the date the return was filed, if filed before the due date.
    b.   Three years from the date the return was due, if filed by the due date.
    c.   Six years from the date the return was filed, if filed before the due date.
    d.   Six years from the date the return was due, if filed by the due date.

212. A claim for refund of erroneously paid income taxes, filed by an individual before the statute of limitations expires, must be submitted on Form

    a.   1139
    b.   1045
    c.   1040X
    d.   843

213. If an individual paid income tax in 2002 but did **not** file a 2002 return because his income was insufficient to require the filing of a return, the deadline for filing a refund claim is

    a.   Two years from the date the tax was paid.
    b.   Two years from the date a return would have been due.
    c.   Three years from the date the tax was paid.
    d.   Three years from the date a return would have been due.

214. A married couple filed their joint 2000 calendar-year return on March 15, 2001, and attached a check for the balance of tax due as shown on the return. On June 15, 2002, the couple discovered that they had failed to include $2,000 of home mortgage interest in their itemized deductions. In order for the couple to recover the tax that they would have

saved by using the $2,000 deduction, they must file an amended return no later than

    a.   December 31, 2003.
    b.   March 15, 2004.
    c.   April 15, 2004.
    d.   June 15, 2004.

215. Richard Baker filed his 2001 individual income tax return on April 15, 2002. On December 31, 2002, he learned that 100 shares of stock that he owned had become worthless in 2001. Since he did not deduct this loss on his 2001 return, Baker intends to file a claim for refund. This refund claim must be filed not later than April 15,

    a.   2003
    b.   2005
    c.   2008
    d.   2009

216. A taxpayer filed his income tax return after the due date but neglected to file an extension form. The return indicated a tax liability of $50,000 and taxes withheld of $45,000. On what amount would the penalties for late filing and late payment be computed?

    a. $0
    b. $ 5,000
    c. $45,000
    d. $50,000

217. An accuracy-related penalty applies to the portion of tax underpayment attributable to

I.   Any substantial gift or estate tax valuation understatement

II.   Any substantial income tax valuation overstatement.

    a.   I only.
    b.   II only.
    c.   Both I and II.
    d.   Neither I nor II.

OTHER OBJECTIVE QUESTIONS

Problem 1   (45 to 55 minutes)

Cole, a newly licensed CPA, opened an office in 2002 as a sole practitioner engaged in the practice of public accountancy. Cole reports on the cash basis for income tax purposes. Listed below are Cole's 2002 business and nonbusiness transactions, as well as possible tax treatments.

Required:

For each of Cole's transactions (**Items 1 through 20**), select the appropriate tax treatment. A tax treatment may be selected once, more than once, or not at all.

Items to be answered

Transactions

1. Fees received for jury duty.

2. Interest income on mortgage loan receivable.

3. Penalty paid to bank on early withdrawal of savings.

4. Write-offs of uncollectible accounts receivable from accounting practice.

5. Cost of attending review course in preparation for the Uniform CPA Examination.

6. Fee for the biennial permit to practice as a CPA.

7. Costs of attending CPE courses in fulfillment of state board requirements.

8. Contribution to a qualified Keogh retirement plan.

9. Loss sustained from nonbusiness bad debt.

10. Loss sustained on sale of "Small Business Corporation" (Section 1244) stock.

11. Taxes paid on land owned by Cole and rented out as a parking lot.

12. Interest paid on installment purchases of household furniture.

13. Alimony paid to former spouse who reports the alimony as taxable income.

14. Personal medical expenses charged on credit card in December 2002 but not paid until January 2003.

15. Personal casualty loss sustained.

16. State inheritance tax paid on bequest received.

17. Foreign income tax withheld at source on dividend received.

18. Computation of self-employment tax.

19. One-half of self-employment tax paid with 2002 return filed in April 2003.

20. Insurance premiums paid on Cole's life.

Tax treatments

A. Taxable as interest income in Schedule B—Interest and Dividend Income.

B. Taxable as other income on page 1 of Form 1040.

C. Not taxable.

D. Deductible on page 1 of Form 1040 to arrive at adjusted gross income.

E. Deductible in Schedule A—Itemized Deductions, subject to threshold of 7.5% of adjusted gross income.

F. Deductible in Schedule A—Itemized Deductions, subject to threshold of 10% of adjusted gross income and additional threshold of $100.

G. Deductible in full in Schedule A—Itemized Deductions (cannot be claimed as a credit).

H. Deductible in Schedule B—Interest and Dividend Income.

I. Deductible in Schedule C—Profit or Loss from Business.

J. Deductible in Schedule D—Capital Gains or Losses.

K. Deductible in Schedule E—Supplemental Income and Loss.

L. Deductible in Form 4797—Sales of Business Property.

M. Claimed in Form 1116—Foreign Tax Credit, or in Schedule A—Itemized Deductions, at taxpayer's option.

N. Based on gross self-employment income.

O. Based on net earnings from self-employment.

P. Not deductible.

Problem 2   (40 to 50 minutes)

Green is self-employed as a human resources consultant and reports on the cash basis for income tax purposes. Listed below are Green's 2002 business and nonbusiness transactions, as well as possible tax treatments.

Required:

For each of Green's transactions (**Items 1 through 25**), select the appropriate tax treatment. A tax treatment may be selected once, more than once, or not at all.

Items to be answered

Transactions

1. Retainer fees received from clients.

2. Oil royalties received.

3. Interest income on general obligation state and local government bonds.

4. Interest on refund of federal taxes.

5. Death benefits from term life insurance policy on parent.

6. Interest income on US Treasury bonds.

7. Share of ordinary income from an investment in a limited partnership reported in Form 1065, Schedule K-1.

8. Taxable income from rental of a townhouse owned by Green.

9. Prize won as a contestant on a TV quiz show.

10. Payment received for jury service.

11. Dividends received from mutual funds that invest in tax-free government obligations.

12. Qualifying medical expenses not reimbursed by insurance.

13. Personal life insurance premiums paid by Green.

14. Expenses for business-related meals where clients were present.

15. Depreciation on personal computer purchased in 2002 used for business.

16. Business lodging expenses, while out of town.

17. Subscriptions to professional journals used for business.

18. Self-employment taxes paid.

19. Qualifying contributions to a simplified employee pension plan.

20. Election to expense business equipment purchased in 2002.

21. Qualifying alimony payments made by Green.

22. Subscriptions for investment-related publications.

23. Interest expense on a home-equity line of credit for an amount borrowed to finance Green's business.

24. Interest expense on a loan for an auto used 75% for business.

25. Loss on sale of residence.

Tax treatments

A. Taxable as other income on Form 1040.

B. Reported in Schedule B—Interest and Dividend Income.

C. Reported in Schedule C as trade or business income.

D. Reported in Schedule E—Supplemental Income and Loss.

E. Not taxable.

F. Fully deductible on Form 1040 to arrive at adjusted gross income.

G. Fifty percent deductible on Form 1040 to arrive at adjusted gross income.

H. Reported in Schedule A—Itemized Deductions (deductibility subject to threshold of 7.5% of adjusted gross income).

I. Reported in Schedule A—Itemized Deductions (deductibility subject to threshold of 2% of adjusted gross income).

J. Reported in Form 4562—Depreciation and Amortization and deductible in Schedule A—Itemized Deductions (deductibility subject to threshold of 2% of adjusted gross income).

K. Reported in Form 4562—Depreciation and Amortization, and deductible in Schedule C—Profit or Loss from Business.

L. Fully deductible in Schedule C—Profit or Loss from Business.

M. Partially deductible in Schedule C—Profit or Loss from Business.

N. Reported in Form 2119—Sale of Your Home, and deductible in Schedule D—Capital Gains and Losses.

O. Not deductible.

Problem 3   (15 to 25 minutes)

Facts: Mark Smith is an employee of Patton Corporation. Additionally, Smith operates a consulting business as a sole proprietor and owns an apartment building. Smith made the expenditures listed below during 2002.

Required:

For each of the following items, mark the appropriate column of your Objective Answer Sheet to indicate whether each expenditure is deductible for AGI, from AGI (not subject to 2% limitation), from AGI (subject to 2% limitation), or not deductible.

	(A) For AGI	(B) From AGI (No 2%)	(C) From AGI (2% Floor)	(D) Not ded.
1. Smith paid the medical expenses of his mother-in-law. Although Smith provided more than half of her support, she does not qualify as Smith's dependent because she had gross income of $5,000.				
2. Smith paid the real estate taxes on his rental apartment building.				
3. Smith paid state sales taxes of $1,500 on an automobile that he purchased for personal use.				
4. Smith paid the real estate taxes on his mother-in-law's home. She is the owner of the home.				
5. Smith paid $1,500 of interest on credit card charges. The charges were for items purchased for personal use.				
6. Smith paid an attorney $500 to prepare Smith's will.				
7. Smith incurred $750 of expenses for business meals and entertainment in his position as an employee of Patton Corporation. Smith's expenses were not reimbursed.				
8. Smith paid self-employment taxes of $3,000 as a result of earnings from the consulting business that he conducts as a sole proprietor.				
9. Smith made a contribution to his self-employed retirement plan (Keogh Plan).				
10. Smith had gambling losses totaling $2,500 for the year. He is including a lottery prize of $5,000 in his gross income this year.				

Problem 4   (25 to 40 minutes)

Mrs. Vick, a forty-year-old cash-basis taxpayer, earned $45,000 as a teacher and $5,000 as a part-time real estate agent in 2002. Mr. Vick, who died on July 1, 2002, had been permanently disabled on his job and collected state disability benefits until his death. For all of 2002 and 2003, the Vicks' residence was the principal home of both their eleven-year-old daughter Joan and Mrs. Vick's unmarried cousin, Fran Phillips, who had no income in either year. During 2002, Joan received $200 a month in survivor social security benefits that began on August 1, 2002, and will continue at least until her eighteenth birthday. In 2002 and 2003, Mrs. Vick provided over one-half the support for Joan and Fran, both of whom were US citizens. Mrs. Vick did not remarry. Mr. and Mrs. Vick received the following in 2002:

Earned income	$50,000
State disability benefits	1,500
Interest on:	
Refund from amended tax return	50
Savings account and certificates of deposit	350
Municipal bonds	100
Gift	3,000
Pension benefits	900
Jury duty pay	200
Gambling winnings	450
Life insurance proceeds	5,000

Additional information:

- Mrs. Vick received the $3,000 cash gift from her uncle.
- Mrs. Vick received the pension distributions from a qualified pension plan, paid for exclusively by her husband's employer.
- Mrs. Vick had $100 in gambling losses in 2002.
- Mrs. Vick was the beneficiary of the life insurance policy on her husband's life. She received a lump-sum distribution. The Vicks had paid $500 in premiums.
- Mrs. Vick received Mr. Vick's accrued vacation pay of $500 in 2003.

For **items 1 and 2,** determine and select from the choices below, **BOTH** the filing status and the number of exemptions for each item.

Filing Status	*Exemptions*
S. Single	1
M. Married filing joint	2
H. Head of household	3
Q. Qualifying widow with dependent child	4

1. Determine the filing status and the number of exemptions that Mrs. Vick can claim on the 2002 federal income tax return, to get the most favorable tax results.

2. Determine the filing status and the number of exemptions that Mrs. Vick can claim on the 2002 federal income tax return to get the most favorable tax results, if she solely maintains the costs of her home.

For **items 3 through 9,** determine the amount, if any, that is taxable and should be included in Adjusted Gross Income (AGI) on the 2002 federal income tax return filed by Mrs. Vick. Since a numerical answer is required, candidates would be given a list of numeric answers to choose from.

3. State disability benefits

4. Interest income

5. Pension benefits

6. Gift

7. Life insurance proceeds

8. Jury duty pay

9. Gambling winnings

During 2002 the following payments were made or losses were incurred. For **items 10 through 23,** select the appropriate tax treatment. A tax treatment may be selected once, more than once, or not at all.

Payments and losses

10. Premiums on Mr. Vick's personal life insurance policy.

11. Penalty on Mrs. Vick's early withdrawal of funds from a certificate of deposit.

12. Mrs. Vick's substantiated cash donation to the American Red Cross.

13. Payment of estimated state income taxes.

14. Payment of real estate taxes on the Vick home.

15. Loss on the sale of the family car.

16. Cost in excess of the increase in value of residence, for the installation of a stairlift in January 2002, related directly to the medical care of Mr. Vick.

17. The Vicks' health insurance premiums for hospitalization coverage.

18. CPA fees to prepare the 2001 tax return.

19. Amortization over the life of the loan of points paid to refinance the mortgage at a lower rate on the Vick home.

20. One-half the self-employment tax paid by Mrs. Vick.

21. Mrs. Vick's $100 in gambling losses.

22. Mrs. Vick's union dues.

23. 2001 federal income tax paid with the Vicks' tax return on April 15, 2002.

Tax treatment

A. Not deductible.

B. Deductible in Schedule A—Itemized Deductions, subject to threshold of 7.5% of adjusted gross income.

C. Deductible in Schedule A—Itemized Deductions, subject to threshold of 2% of adjusted gross income.

D. Deductible on page 1 of Form 1040 to arrive at adjusted gross income.

E. Deductible in full in Schedule A—Itemized Deductions.

F. Deductible in Schedule A—Itemized Deductions, subject to maximum of 50% of adjusted gross income.

For **items 24 through 31,** determine whether the statement is true (T) or false (F) regarding the Vicks' 2002 income tax return.

24. The funeral expenses paid by Mr. Vick's estate is a 2002 itemized deduction.

25. Any federal estate tax on the income in respect of decedent, to be distributed to Mrs. Vick, may be taken as a miscellaneous itemized deduction **not** subject to the 2% of adjusted gross income floor.

26. A casualty loss deduction on property used in Mrs. Vick's part-time real estate business is reported as an itemized deduction.

27. The Vicks' income tax liability will be reduced by the credit for the elderly or disabled.

28. The CPA preparer is required to furnish a completed copy of the 2002 income tax return to Mrs. Vick.

29. Since Mr. Vick died during the year, the income limitation for the earned income credit does **not** apply.

30. Mr. Vick's accrued vacation pay, at the time of his death, is to be distributed to Mrs. Vick in 2003. This income should be included in the 2002 Federal income tax return.

31. The Vicks paid alternative minimum tax in 2001. The amount of alternative minimum tax that is attributable to "deferral adjustments and preferences" can be used to offset the alternative minimum tax in the following years.

Problem 5
(25 to 40 minutes)

Tom and Joan Moore, both CPAs, filed a joint 2002 federal income tax return showing $70,000 in taxable income. During 2002, Tom's daughter Laura, age sixteen, resided with Tom's former spouse. Laura had no income of her own and was not Tom's dependent.

Required:

a. For **items 1 through 10,** determine the amount of income or loss, if any, that should be included on page one of the Moores' 2002 Form 1040. On the CPA exam, a list of numeric answers would be provided for the candidate to choose from.

1. The Moores had no capital loss carryovers from prior years. During 2002 the Moores had the following stock transactions that resulted in a net capital loss:

	Date acquired	Date sold	Sales price	Cost
Revco	2/1/01	3/17/02	$15,000	$25,000
Abbco	2/18/02	4/1/02	8,000	4,000

2. In 1999, Joan received an acre of land as an inter vivos gift from her grandfather. At the time of the gift, the land had a fair market value of $50,000. The grandfather's adjusted basis was $60,000. Joan sold the land in 2002 to an unrelated third party for $56,000.

3. The Moores received a $500 security deposit on their rental property in 2002. They are required to return the amount to the tenant.

4. Tom's 2002 wages were $53,000. In addition, Tom's employer provided group-term life insurance on Tom's life in excess of $50,000. The value of such excess coverage was $2,000.

5. During 2002, the Moores received a $2,500 federal tax refund and a $1,250 state tax refund for 2001 overpayments. In 2001, the Moores were not subject to the alternative minimum tax and were not entitled to any credit against income tax. The Moores' 2001 adjusted gross income was $80,000 and itemized deductions were $1,450 in excess of the standard deduction. The state tax deduction for 2001 was $2,000.

6. In 2002, Joan received $1,300 in unemployment compensation benefits. Her employer made a $100 contribution to the unemployment insurance fund on her behalf.

7. The Moores received $8,400 in gross receipts from their rental property during 2002. The expenses for the residential rental property were

Bank mortgage interest	$1,200
Real estate taxes	700
Insurance	500
MACRS depreciation	3,500

8. The Moores received a stock dividend in 2002 from Ace Corp. They had the option to receive either cash or Ace stock with a fair market value of $900 as of the date of distribution. The par value of the stock was $500.

9. In 2002, Joan received $3,500 as beneficiary of the death benefit that was provided by her brother's employer. Joan's brother did not have a nonforfeitable right to receive the money while living, and the death benefit does not represent the proceeds of life insurance.

10. Tom received $10,000, consisting of $5,000 each of principal and interest, when he redeemed a Series EE savings bond in 2002. The bond was issued in his name in 1993 and the proceeds were used to pay for Laura's college tuition. Tom had not elected to report the yearly increases in the value of the bond.

Required:

b. For **item 11,** determine the amount of the adjustment, if any, to arrive at adjusted gross income.

11. As required by a 1997 divorce agreement, Tom paid an annual amount of $8,000 in alimony and $10,000 in child support during 2002.

Required:

c. During 2002, the following events took place. For **items 12 through 23,** select the appropriate tax treatment. A tax treatment may be selected once, more than once, or not at all.

Tax treatment

A.　Not deductible on Form 1040.

B.　Deductible in full in Schedule A—Itemized Deductions.

C.　Deductible in Schedule A—Itemized Deductions, subject to a threshold of 7.5% of adjusted gross income.

D.　Deductible in Schedule A—Itemized Deductions, subject to a limitation of 50% of adjusted gross income.

E.　Deductible in Schedule A—Itemized Deductions, subject to a $100 floor and a threshold of 10% of adjusted gross income.

F.　Deductible in Schedule A—Itemized Deductions, subject to a threshold of 2% of adjusted gross income.

12.　On March 23, 2002, Tom sold fifty shares of Zip stock at a $1,200 loss. He repurchased fifty shares of Zip on April 15, 2002.

13.　Payment of a personal property tax based on the value of the Moores' car.

14.　Used clothes were donated to church organizations.

15.　Premiums were paid covering insurance against Tom's loss of earnings.

16.　Tom paid for subscriptions to accounting journals.

17.　Interest was paid on a $10,000 home-equity line of credit secured by the Moores' residence. The fair market value of the home exceeded the mortgage by $50,000. Tom used the proceeds to purchase a sailboat.

18.　Amounts were paid in excess of insurance reimbursement for prescription drugs.

19.　Funeral expenses were paid by the Moores for Joan's brother.

20.　Theft loss was incurred on Joan's jewelry in excess of insurance reimbursement. There were no 2002 personal casualty gains.

21.　Loss on the sale of the family's sailboat.

22.　Interest was paid on the $300,000 acquisition mortgage on the Moores' home. The mortgage is secured by their home.

23.　Joan performed free accounting services for the Red Cross. The estimated value of the services was $500.

Required:

d.　For **items 24 through 29,** indicate if the statement is true (T) or false (F) regarding the Moores' 2002 tax return.

24.　For 2002, the Moores were subject to the phaseout of half their allowable itemized deductions for regular tax because their adjusted gross income was $75,000.

25.　The Moores' unreimbursed medical expenses for AMT had to exceed 10% of adjusted gross income.

26.　The Moores' personal exemption amount for regular tax was not permitted for determining 2002 AMT.

27.　The Moores paid $1,200 in additional 2002 taxes when they filed their return on Monday, April 15, 2002. Their 2002 federal tax withholdings equaled 100% of 2001 tax liability. Therefore, they were not subject to the underpayment of tax penalty.

28.　The Moores, both being under age fifty, were not subject to an early withdrawal penalty on their IRA withdrawals to pay for medical expenses in excess of 7.5% of their adjusted gross income.

29.　The Moores were allowed an earned income credit against their 2002 tax liability equal to a percentage of their wages.

Problem 6　　　　　　　　　　　　(25 to 40 minutes)

a.　The Internal Revenue Service is auditing Oate's 2002 Form 1040—Individual Income Tax Return. During 2002, Oate, an unmarried custodial parent, had one dependent three-year-old child and worked in a CPA firm. For 2002, Oate, who had adjusted gross income of $40,000, qualified to itemize deductions and was subject to federal income tax liability.

Required:

For **items 1 through 9,** select from the following list of tax treatments the appropriate tax treatment. A tax treatment may be selected once, more than once, or not at all.

1.　In 2002, Oate paid $2,000 interest on the $25,000 home equity mortgage on her vacation home, which she used exclusively for personal use. The mortgage is secured by Oate's vacation home, and the loan proceeds were used to purchase an automobile.

2.　For 2002, Oate had a $30,000 cash charitable contribution carryover from her 2001 cash donation to the American Red Cross. Oate made no additional charitable contributions in 2002.

3. During 2002, Oate had investment interest expense that did not exceed her net investment income.

4. Oate's 2002 lottery ticket losses were $450. She had no gambling winnings.

5. During 2002, Oate paid $2,500 in real property taxes on her vacation home, which she used exclusively for personal use.

6. In 2002, Oate paid a $500 premium for a homeowner's insurance policy on her principal residence.

7. For 2002, Oate paid $1,500 to an unrelated babysitter to care for her child while she worked.

8. In 2002, Oate paid $4,000 interest on the $60,000 acquisition mortgage of her principal residence. The mortgage is secured by Oate's home.

9. During 2002, Oate paid $3,600 real property taxes on residential rental property in which she actively participates. There was no personal use of the rental property.

Selections
A. Not deductible on Form 1040.
B. Deductible in full on Schedule A—Itemized Deductions.
C. Deductible in Schedule A—Itemized Deductions subject to a limitation of 50% of adjusted gross income.
D. Deductible in Schedule A—Itemized Deductions as miscellaneous deduction subject to a threshold of 2% of adjusted gross income.
E. Deductible in Schedule A—Itemized Deductions as miscellaneous deductions not subject to a threshold of 2% adjusted gross income.
F. Deductible on Schedule E—Supplemental Income and Loss.
G. A credit is allowable.

b. Frank and Dale Cumack are married and filing a joint 2002 income tax return. During 2002, Frank, sixty-five, was retired from government service and Dale, fifty-five, was employed as a university instructor. In 2002, the Cumacks contributed all of the support to Dale's father, Jacques, an unmarried French citizen and French resident who had no gross income.

Required:

For **items 10 through 19,** select the correct amount of income, loss, or adjustment to income that should be recognized on page 1 of the Cumacks' 2002 Form 1040—Individual Income Tax Return to arrive at the adjusted gross income for each separate transaction. A tax treatment may be selected once, more than once, or not at all.

Any information contained in an item is unique to that item and is not to be incorporated in your calculations when answering other items.

Selections

A.	$0	H.	$ 9,000
B.	$1,000	I.	$ 10,000
C.	$2,000	J.	$ 25,000
D.	$2,250	K.	$ 30,000
E.	$3,000	L.	$125,000
F.	$4,000	M.	$150,000
G.	$5,000		

10. During 2002, Dale received a $30,000 cash gift from her aunt.

11. Dale contributed $3,500 to her traditional Individual Retirement Account (IRA) on January 15, 2002. In 2002, she earned $60,000 as a university instructor. During 2002 the Cumacks were not active participants in an employer's qualified pension or annuity plan.

12. In 2002, the Cumacks received a $1,000 federal income tax refund.

13. During 2002, Frank, a 50% partner in Diske General Partnership, received a $4,000 guaranteed payment from Diske for services that he rendered to the partnership that year.

14. In 2002, Frank received $10,000 as beneficiary of his deceased brother's life insurance policy.

15. Dale's employer pays 100% of the cost of all employees' group-term life insurance under a qualified plan. Policy cost is $5 per $1,000 of coverage. Dale's group-term life insurance coverage equals $450,000.

16. In 2002, Frank won $5,000 at a casino and had $2,000 in gambling losses.

17. During 2002, the Cumacks received $1,000 interest income associated with a refund of their prior years' federal income tax.

18. In 2002, the Cumacks sold their first and only residence for $400,000. They purchased their home in 1988 for $50,000 and have lived there since then. There were no other capital gains, losses, or capital loss carryovers. The Cumacks do not intend to buy another residence.

19. In 2002, Zeno Corp. declared a stock dividend and Dale received one additional share of Zeno common stock for three shares of Zeno common stock that she held. The stock that Dale received had a fair market value of $9,000. There was no provision to receive cash instead of stock.

c.   Frank and Dale Cumack are married and filing a joint 2002 income tax return. During 2002, Frank, sixty-five, was retired from government service and Dale, fifty-five, was employed as a university instructor. In 2002, the Cumacks contributed all of the support to Dale's father, Jacques, an unmarried French citizen and French resident who had no gross income.

Required:

For **item 20,** determine whether the Cumacks overstated, understated, or correctly determined the number of both personal and dependency exemptions.

<u>Selections</u>

O. Overstated the number of both personal and dependency exemptions.
U. Understated the number of both personal and dependency exemptions.
C. Correctly determined the number of both personal and dependency exemptions.

20. The Cumacks claimed three exemptions on their 2002 joint income tax return.

MULTIPLE-CHOICE ANSWERS

1. c __ __	45. c __ __	89. c __ __	133. c __ __	177. c __ __
2. b __ __	46. a __ __	90. a __ __	134. b __ __	178. d __ __
3. c __ __	47. a __ __	91. d __ __	135. b __ __	179. b __ __
4. a __ __	48. a __ __	92. c __ __	136. b __ __	180. b __ __
5. d __ __	49. d __ __	93. d __ __	137. a __ __	181. c __ __
6. b __ __	50. b __ __	94. a __ __	138. b __ __	182. a __ __
7. d __ __	51. b __ __	95. d __ __	139. a __ __	183. a __ __
8. a __ __	52. b __ __	96. d __ __	140. a __ __	184. c __ __
9. d __ __	53. b __ __	97. b __ __	141. a __ __	185. b __ __
10. b __ __	54. c __ __	98. d __ __	142. d __ __	186. d __ __
11. b __ __	55. d __ __	99. c __ __	143. d __ __	187. c __ __
12. c __ __	56. d __ __	100. d __ __	144. b __ __	188. a __ __
13. d __ __	57. d __ __	101. b __ __	145. d __ __	189. b __ __
14. c __ __	58. c __ __	102. c __ __	146. b __ __	190. c __ __
15. c __ __	59. a __ __	103. c __ __	147. b __ __	191. b __ __
16. a __ __	60. a __ __	104. c __ __	148. d __ __	192. b __ __
17. c __ __	61. b __ __	105. b __ __	149. a __ __	193. a __ __
18. a __ __	62. a __ __	106. b __ __	150. b __ __	194. b __ __
19. d __ __	63. d __ __	107. a __ __	151. c __ __	195. a __ __
20. c __ __	64. d __ __	108. c __ __	152. c __ __	196. c __ __
21. d __ __	65. d __ __	109. d __ __	153. d __ __	197. a __ __
22. c __ __	66. a __ __	110. a __ __	154. c __ __	198. c __ __
23. c __ __	67. c __ __	111. d __ __	155. b __ __	199. b __ __
24. a __ __	68. b __ __	112. d __ __	156. d __ __	200. c __ __
25. d __ __	69. b __ __	113. b __ __	157. a __ __	201. c __ __
26. c __ __	70. c __ __	114. d __ __	158. d __ __	202. c __ __
27. d __ __	71. a __ __	115. d __ __	159. a __ __	203. d __ __
28. c __ __	72. a __ __	116. c __ __	160. a __ __	204. a __ __
29. c __ __	73. c __ __	117. a __ __	161. c __ __	205. a __ __
30. b __ __	74. c __ __	118. d __ __	162. b __ __	206. d __ __
31. b __ __	75. a __ __	119. b __ __	163. b __ __	207. a __ __
32. d __ __	76. d __ __	120. b __ __	164. c __ __	208. c __ __
33. b __ __	77. a __ __	121. a __ __	165. b __ __	209. c __ __
34. c __ __	78. c __ __	122. b __ __	166. d __ __	210. d __ __
35. a __ __	79. a __ __	123. a __ __	167. c __ __	211. d __ __
36. c __ __	80. b __ __	124. c __ __	168. b __ __	212. c __ __
37. d __ __	81. c __ __	125. b __ __	169. c __ __	213. a __ __
38. b __ __	82. b __ __	126. c __ __	170. c __ __	214. c __ __
39. b __ __	83. a __ __	127. c __ __	171. c __ __	215. d __ __
40. c __ __	84. c __ __	128. c __ __	172. c __ __	216. b __ __
41. d __ __	85. d __ __	129. a __ __	173. d __ __	217. c __ __
42. d __ __	86. c __ __	130. a __ __	174. a __ __	
43. d __ __	87. a __ __	131. c __ __	175. d __ __	1st: __/217 = __%
44. c __ __	88. c __ __	132. c __ __	176. c __ __	2nd: __/217 = __%

MULTIPLE-CHOICE ANSWER EXPLANATIONS

I.B.3. Annuities

1.   (c)   The requirement is to determine the pension (annuity) amounts excluded from income during 2002, 2003, and 2004. Brown's contribution of $12,000 will be recovered pro rata over the life of the annuity. Under this rule, $100 per month (12,000 ÷ 120 months) is excluded from income.

	Received	*Excluded*	*Included*
2002	$4,900	$ 700	$4,200
2003	8,400	1,200	7,200
2004	8,400	1,200	7,200

I.B.4. Life Insurance Proceeds

2.   (b)   The requirement is to determine the amount of life insurance payments to be included in a widow's gross income. Life insurance proceeds paid by reason of death are excluded from income if paid in a lump sum or in installments. If the payments are received in installments, the principal amount of the policy divided by the number of annual payments is excluded each year. Therefore, $1,200 of the $5,200 insurance payment is included in Penelope's gross income.

Annual installment	$ 5,200
Principal amount ($100,000 ÷ 25)	− 4,000
Gross income	$ 1,200

I.B.5. Employee Benefits

3.   (c)   The requirement is to determine the correct statement regarding a "cafeteria plan" maintained by an employer. Cafeteria plans are employer-sponsored benefit packages that offer employees a choice between taking cash and receiving qualified benefits (e.g., accident and health insurance, group-term life insurance, coverage under a dependent care or group legal services program). Thus, employees "may select their own menu of benefits." If an employee chooses qualified benefits, they are excluded from the employee's gross income to the extent allowed by law. If an employee chooses cash, it is includible in the employee's gross income as compensation. Answer (a) is incorrect because participation is restricted to employees only. Answer (b) is incorrect because there is no minimum service requirement that must be met before an employee can participate in a plan. Answer (d) is incorrect because deferred compensation plans other than 401(k) plans are not included in the definition of a cafeteria plan.

4.   (a)   The requirement is to determine the amount of group-term life insurance proceeds that must be included in gross income by Autrey's widow. Life insurance proceeds paid by reason of death are generally excluded from gross income. Note that although only the cost of the first $50,000 of group-term insurance coverage can be excluded from gross income during the employee's life, the entire amount of insurance proceeds paid by reason of death will be excluded from the beneficiary's income.

5.   (d)   The requirement is to determine the amount of employee death payments to be included in gross income by the widow and the son. The $5,000 employee death benefit exclusion was repealed for decedents dying after August 20, 1996.

6.   (b)   The requirement is to determine the maximum amount of tax-free group-term life insurance coverage that can be provided to an employee by an employer. The cost of the first $50,000 of group-term life insurance coverage provided by an employer will be excluded from an employee's income.

7.   (d)   The requirement is to determine the amount to be included in Hal's gross income for the current year. All three amounts that Hal received as a result of his injury are excluded from gross income. Benefits received as workers' compensation and compensation for damages for physical injuries are always excluded from gross income. Amounts received from an employer's accident and health plan as reimbursement for medical expenses are excluded so long as the medical expenses are not deducted as itemized deductions.

8.   (a)   James Martin's gross income consists of

Salary	$50,000
Bonus	10,000
	$60,000

Medical insurance premiums paid by an employer are excluded from an employee's gross income. Additionally, qualified moving expense reimbursements are an employee fringe benefit and can be excluded from gross income. This means that an employee can exclude an amount paid by an employer as payment for (or reimbursement of) expenses that would be deductible as moving expenses if directly paid or incurred by the employee.

I.B.8. Gifts and Inheritances

9.   (d)   The requirement is to determine how much income Hall should include in his 2002 tax return for the inheritance of stock which he received from his father's estate.

Since the definition of gross income excludes property received as a gift, bequest, devise, or inheritance, Hall recognizes no income upon receipt of the stock. Since the executor of his father's estate elected the alternate valuation date (August 1), and the stock was distributed to Hall before that date (June 1), Hall's basis for the stock would be its $4,500 FMV on June 1. Since Hall also sold the stock on June 1 for $4,500, Hall would have no gain or loss resulting from the sale.

I.B.9. Stock Dividends

10.   (b)   The requirement is to determine the amount of dividend income that should be reported by Gail Judd. The $100 dividend on Gail's life insurance policy is treated as a reduction of the cost of insurance (because total dividends have not yet exceeded accumulated premiums paid) and is excluded from gross income. Thus, Gail will report the $300 dividend on common stock and the $500 dividend on preferred stock, a total of $800 as dividend income for 2002.

11.   (b)   The requirement is to determine the amount of dividend income to be reported on Amy's 2002 return. Dividends are included in income at earlier of actual or constructive receipt. When corporate dividends are paid by mail, they are included in income for the year in which received. Thus, the $875 dividend received 1/2/02 is included in income for 2002. The $500 dividend on a life insurance policy from a mutual insurance company is treated as a reduction of the cost of insurance and is excluded from gross income.

12.   (c)   The requirement is to determine the amount of dividends to be reported by the Mitchells on a joint return. The amount of dividends would be ($400 + $50 + $300) = $750. The $200 dividend on the life insurance policy is not gross income, but is considered a reduction of the cost of the policy.

13.   (d)   The requirement is to determine Karen's basis in the 10 shares of preferred stock received as a stock dividend. Generally, stock dividends are nontaxable, and a taxpayer's basis for original stock is allocated to the dividend stock in proportion to fair market values. However, any stock that is distributed **on** preferred stock results in a taxable stock dividend. The amount to be included in the shareholder's income is the stock's fair market value on date of distribution. Similarly, the shareholder's basis for the dividend shares will be equal to their fair market value on date of distribution (10 x $60 = $600).

I.B.10. Interest Income

14.   (c)   The requirement is to determine the correct statement(s) regarding the amortization of bond premium on a taxable bond. The amount of premium amortization on taxable bonds acquired by the taxpayer after 1987 is treated as an offset to the amount of interest income reported on the bond. The method of calculating the annual amortization is determined by the date the bond was issued, as opposed to the acquisition date. If the bond was issued after September 27, 1985, the amortization must be calculated under the constant yield to maturity method. Otherwise, the amortization must be made ratably over the life of the bond. Under the constant yield to maturity method, the amortizable bond premium is computed on the basis of the taxpayer's yield to maturity, using the taxpayer's basis for the bond, and compounding at the close of each accrual period.

15. (c) The requirement is to determine whether two statements are true concerning the exclusion of interest income on US Series EE Bonds that are redeemed to pay for higher education. The accrued interest on US Series EE savings bonds that are redeemed by a taxpayer is excluded from gross income to the extent that the aggregate redemption proceeds (principal plus interest) are used to finance the higher education of the taxpayer, taxpayer's spouse, or dependents. Qualified higher educational expenses include tuition and fees, but not room and board or the cost of courses involving sports, games, or hobbies that are not part of a degree program. In determining the amount of available exclusion, qualified educational expenses must be reduced by qualified scholarships that are exempt from tax, and any other nontaxable payments such as veteran's educational assistance and employer-provided educational assistance.

16. (a) The requirement is to determine the amount of interest subject to tax in Kay's 2002 tax return. Interest must generally be included in gross income, unless a specific statutory provision provides for its exclusion (e.g., interest on municipal bonds). Interest on US Treasury certificates and on a refund of federal income tax would be subject to tax on Kay's 2002 tax return.

17. (c) The requirement is to determine the amount of interest income taxable on Charles and Marcia's joint income tax return. A taxpayer's income includes interest on state and federal income tax refunds and interest on federal obligations, but excludes interest on state obligations. Here, their joint taxable income must include the $500 interest on federal income tax refund, $600 interest on state income tax refund, and $800 interest on federal government obligations, but will exclude the $1,000 tax-exempt interest on state government obligations. Although a refund of federal income tax would be excluded from gross income, any interest on a refund must be included in gross income.

18. (a) The requirement is to determine the condition that must be met for tax exemption of accumulated interest on Series EE US Savings Bonds. An individual may be able to exclude from income all or a part of the interest received on the redemption of Series EE US Savings Bonds. To qualify, the bonds must be issued after December 31, 1989, the purchaser of the bonds must be the sole owner of the bonds (or joint owner with his or her spouse), and the owner(s) must be at least twenty-four years old before the bond's issue date. To exclude the interest the redemption proceeds must be used to pay the tuition and fees incurred by the taxpayer, spouse, or dependents to attend a college or university or certain vocational schools.

19. (d) The requirement is to determine the amount of tax-exempt interest. Interest on obligations of a state or one of its political subdivisions (e.g., New York Port Authority bonds), or a possession of the US (e.g., Puerto Rico Commonwealth bonds) is tax-exempt.

20. (c) Stone will report $1,700 of interest income. Interest on FIT refunds, personal injury awards, US savings bonds, and most other sources is fully taxable. However, interest on state or municipal bonds is generally not taxable.

21. (d) The requirement is to determine how Don Raff's $500 interest forfeiture penalty should be reported. An interest forfeiture penalty for making a premature withdrawal from a certificate of deposit should be deducted from gross income in arriving at adjusted gross income in the year in which the penalty is incurred, which in this case is 2003.

I.B.12. Scholarships and Fellowships

22. (c) The requirement is to determine which payment(s) must be included in a recipient's gross income. A candidate for a degree can exclude amounts received as a scholarship or fellowship if, according to the conditions of the grant, the amounts are used for the payment of tuition and fees, books, supplies, and equipment required for courses at an educational institution. All payments received for services must be included in income, even if the services are a condition of receiving the grant or are required of all candidates for the degree. Here, the payment to a graduate assistant for a part-time teaching assignment and the grant to a Ph.D. candidate for participation in research are payments for services and must be included in income.

23. (c) The requirement is to determine the amount of scholarship awards that Majors should include as taxable income in 2002. Only a candidate for a degree can exclude amounts received as a scholarship award. The exclusion available to degree candidates is limited to amounts received for the payment of tuition and fees, books, supplies, and equipment required for courses at the educational institution. Since Majors is a candidate for a graduate degree, Majors can exclude the $10,000 received for tuition, fees, books, and supplies required for courses. However, the $2,000 stipend for research services required by the scholarship must be included in taxable income for 2002.

I.B.16. Lease Improvements

24. (a) The requirement is to determine a lessor's 2002 gross income. A lessor excludes from income any increase in the value of property caused by improvements made by the lessee, unless the improvements were made in lieu of rent. In this case, there is no indication that the improvements were made in lieu of rent. Therefore, for 2002, Farley should only include the six rent payments in income: 6 × $1,000 = $6,000.

I.C. Items to Be Included in Gross Income

25. (d) The requirement is to determine the amount of alimony recapture that must be included in Bob's gross income for 2002. Alimony recapture may occur if alimony payments sharply decline in the second and third years that payments are made. The payor must report the recaptured alimony as gross income in the third year, and the payee is allowed a deduction for the same amount. Recapture for the second year (2001) occurs to the extent that the alimony paid in the second year ($20,000) exceeds the alimony paid in the third year ($0) by more than $15,000 [i.e., $20,000 – ($0 + $15,000) = $5,000 of recapture].

Recapture for the first year (2000) occurs to the extent that the alimony paid in the first year ($50,000) exceeds the *average alimony* paid in the second and third years by more than $15,000. For this purpose, the alimony paid in the second year ($20,000) must be reduced by the amount of recapture for that year ($5,000).

First year (2000) payment	$50,000
Second year (2001) payment	
($20,000 – $5,000)	$15,000
Third year (2002) payment	+ 0
Total	$15,000
÷ 2	(7,500)
	(15,000)
Recapture for first year (2000)	$ 27,500

Thus, the total recapture to be included in Bob's gross income for 2002 is $5,000 + $27,500 = $32,500.

26. (c)   The requirement is to determine which conditions must be present in a post-1984 divorce agreement for a payment to qualify as deductible alimony. In order for a payment to be deductible by the payor as alimony, the payment must be made in cash or its equivalent, the payment must be received by or on behalf of a spouse under a divorce or separation instrument, the payments must terminate at the recipient's death, and must not be designated as other than alimony (e.g., child support).

27. (d)   The requirement is to determine which of the following would be included in gross income by Darr who is an employee of Sorce C corporation. The definition of gross income includes income from whatever source derived and would include the dividend income on shares of stock that Darr received for services rendered. However, items specifically excluded from gross income include amounts received as a gift or inheritance, as well as employer-provided medical insurance coverage under a health plan.

28. (c)   The requirement is to determine the correct statement regarding the inclusion of social security benefits in gross income for 2002. A maximum of 85% of social security benefits may be included in gross income for high-income taxpayers. Thus, no matter how high a taxpayer's income, 85% of the social security benefits is the maximum amount of benefits to be included in gross income.

29. (c)   The requirement is to determine the amount that Perle should include in taxable income as a result of performing dental services for Wood. An exchange of services for property or services is sometimes called bartering. A taxpayer must include in income the amount of cash and the fair market value of property or services received in exchange for the performance of services. Here, Perle's taxable income should include the $200 cash and the bookcase with a comparable value of $350, a total of $550.

30. (b)   The requirement is to determine the amount of payments to be included in Mary's income tax return for 2002. Alimony must be included in gross income by the payee and is deductible by the payor. In order to be treated as alimony, a payment must be made in cash and be received by or paid on behalf of the former spouse. Amounts treated as child support are not alimony; they are neither deductible by the payor, nor taxable to the payee. Payments will be treated as child support to the extent that payments will be reduced upon the happening of a contingency relating to a child (e.g., the child attaining a specified age, marrying, becoming employed). Here, since future payments will be reduced by 20% on their child's 18th birthday, the total cash payments of $10,000 ($7,000 paid directly to Mary plus the $3,000 of tuition paid on Mary's behalf) must be reduced by 20% and result in $8,000 of alimony income for Mary. The

remaining $2,000 is treated as child support and is not taxable.

31. (b)   The requirement is to determine the amount of interest for overpayment of 2001 state income tax and state income tax refund that is taxable in Clark's 2002 federal income tax return. The $10 of interest income on the tax refund is taxable and must be included in gross income. On the other hand, a state income tax refund is included in gross income under the "tax benefit rule" only if the refunded amount was deducted in a prior year and the deduction provided a benefit because it reduced the taxpayer's federal income tax. The payment of state income taxes will not result in a "benefit" if an individual does not itemize deductions, or is subject to the alternative minimum tax for the year the taxes are paid. Individuals who file Form 1040EZ are not allowed to itemize deductions and must use the standard deduction. Since state income taxes are only allowed as an itemized deduction and Clark did not itemize for 2001 (he used Form 1040EZ), his $900 state income tax refund is nontaxable and is excluded from taxable income.

32. (d)   The requirement is to determine the amount to be reported in Hall's 2002 return as alimony income. If a divorce agreement specifies both alimony and child support, but less is paid than required, then payments are first allocated to child support, with only the remainder in excess of required child support to be treated as alimony. Pursuant to Hall's divorce agreement, $3,000 was to be paid each month, of which $600 was designated as child support, leaving a balance of $2,400 per month to be treated as alimony. However, during 2002, only $5,000 was paid to Hall by her former husband which was less than the $36,000 required by the divorce agreement. Since required child support payments totaled $600 x 12 = $7,200 for 2002, all $5,000 of the payments actually received by Hall during 2002 is treated as child support, with nothing remaining to be reported as alimony.

33. (b)   The requirement is to determine the amount of income to be reported by Lee in connection with the receipt of stock for services rendered. Compensation for services rendered that is received by a cash method taxpayer must be included in income at its fair market value on the date of receipt.

34. (c)   The requirement is to determine when Ross was subject to "regular tax" with regard to stock that was acquired through the exercise of an incentive stock option. There are no tax consequences when an incentive stock option is granted to an employee. When the option is exercised, any excess of the stock's FMV over the option price is a tax preference item for purposes of the employee's alternative minimum tax. However, an employee is not subject to regular tax until the stock acquired through exercise of the option is sold.

If the employee holds the stock acquired through exercise of the option at least two years from the date the option was granted (and holds the stock itself at least one year), the employee's realized gain is treated as long-term capital gain in the year of sale, and the employer receives no compensation deduction. If the preceding holding period rules are not met at the time the stock is sold, the employee must report ordinary income to the extent that the stock's FMV at date of exercise exceeded the option price, with any remaining gain reported as long-term or short-term capital gain. As a result, the employer receives a compensation deduction equal to the amount of ordinary income reported by the employee.

35. **(a)** The requirement is to determine the amount that is taxable as alimony in Ann's return. In order to be treated as alimony, a payment must be made in cash and be received by or on behalf of the payee spouse. Furthermore, cash payments must be required to terminate upon the death of the payee spouse to be treated as alimony. In this case, the transfer of title in the home to Ann is not a cash payment and cannot be treated as alimony. Although the mortgage payments are cash payments made on behalf of Ann, the payments are not treated as alimony because they will be made throughout the full twenty-year mortgage period and will not terminate in the event of Ann's death.

36. **(c)** The requirement is to determine the correct statement with regard to income in respect of a cash basis decedent. Income in respect of a decedent is income earned by a decedent before death that was not includible in the decedent's final income tax return because of the decedent's method of accounting (e.g., receivables of a cash basis decedent). Such income must be included in gross income by the person who receives it and has the same character (e.g., ordinary or capital) as it would have had if the decedent had lived.

37. **(d)** The requirement is to determine the amount of gross income. Drury's gross income includes the $36,000 salary, the $500 of premiums paid by her employer for group-term life insurance coverage in excess of $50,000, and the $5,000 proceeds received from a state lottery.

38. **(b)** The requirement is to determine the amount of foster child payments to be included in income by the Charaks. Foster child payments are excluded from income to the extent they represent reimbursement for expenses incurred for care of the foster child. Since the payments ($3,900) exceeded the expenses ($3,000), the $900 excess used for the Charaks' personal expenses must be included in their gross income.

39. **(b)** The requirement is to determine the amount and the year in which the tip income should be included in Pierre's gross income. If an individual receives less than $20 in tips during one month while working for one employer, the tips do not have to be reported to the employer and the tips are included in the individual's gross income when received. However, if an individual receives $20 or more in tips during one month while working for one employer, the individual must report the total amount of tips to that employer by the tenth day of the next month. Then the tips are included in gross income for the month in which they are reported to the employer. Here, Pierre received $2,000 in tips during December 2002 that he reported to his employer in January 2003. Thus, the $2,000 of tips will be included in Pierre's gross income for 2003.

40. **(c)** The requirement is to determine the correct statement regarding the alimony deduction in connection with a 2002 divorce. To be considered alimony, cash payments must terminate on the death of the payee spouse. Answer (a) is incorrect because alimony payments cannot be contingent on the status of the divorced couple's children.

Answer (b) is incorrect because the divorced couple cannot be members of the same household at the time the alimony is paid. Answer (d) is incorrect because only cash payments can be considered alimony.

41. **(d)** The requirement is to determine the amount of a $10,000 award for outstanding civic achievement that Joan should include in her 2002 adjusted gross income. An award for civic achievement can be excluded from gross income only if the recipient was selected without any action on his/her part, is not required to render substantial future services as a condition of receiving the award, and designates that the award is to be directly transferred by the payor to a governmental unit or a tax-exempt charitable, educational, or religious organization. Here, since Joan accepted and actually received the award, the $10,000 must be included in her adjusted gross income.

42. **(d)** The requirement is to determine the amount of lottery winnings that should be included in Gow's taxable income. Lottery winnings are gambling winnings and must be included in gross income. Gambling losses are deductible from AGI as a miscellaneous deduction (to the extent of winnings) not subject to the 2% of AGI floor if a taxpayer itemizes deductions. Since Gow elected the standard deduction for 2002, the $400 spent on lottery tickets is not deductible. Thus, all $5,000 of Gow's lottery winnings are included in his taxable income.

I.C.5. Rents and Royalties

43. **(d)** The requirement is to determine the amount of advance rents and lease cancellation payments that should be reported on Lake Corp.'s 2002 tax return. Advance rental payments must be included in gross income when received, regardless of the period covered or whether the taxpayer uses the cash or accrual method. Similarly, lease cancellation payments are treated as rent and must be included in income when received, regardless of the taxpayer's method of accounting.

44. **(c)** The requirement is to determine the amount to be reported as gross rents. Gross rents include the $50,000 of recurring rents plus the $2,000 lease cancellation payment. The $1,000 of lease improvements are excluded from income since they were **not** required in lieu of rent.

45. **(c)** The requirement is to determine the amount of net rental income that Gow should include in his adjusted gross income. Since Gow lives in one of two identical apartments, only 50% of the expenses relating to both apartments can be allocated to the rental unit.

Rent	$7,200
Less:	
Real estate taxes (50% x $6,400)	(3,200)
Painting of rental apartment	(800)
Fire insurance (50% x $600)	(300)
Depreciation (50% x $5,000)	(2,500)
Net rental income	$ 400

46. **(a)** The requirement is to determine the amount of rent income to be reported on Amy's 2002 return. Both the $6,000 of rent received for 2002, as well as the $1,000 of advance rent received in 2002 for the last two months of the lease must be included in income for 2002. Advance rent must be included in income in the year received regardless of the period covered or the accounting method used.

47. **(a)** The requirement is to determine the amount to be reported as rent revenue in an accrual-basis taxpayer's tax return for 2002. An accrual-basis taxpayer's rent revenue would consist of the amount of rent earned during the taxable year plus any advance rent received. Advance rents must be included in gross income when received under both the cash and accrual methods, even though they have not yet been earned. In this case, Royce's rent revenue would be determined as follows:

Rent receivable 12/31/01	$35,000
Rent receivable 12/31/02	25,000
Decrease in receivables	(10,000)
Rent collections during 2002	50,000
Rent deposits	5,000
Rent revenue for 2002	$45,000

The rent deposits must be included in gross income for 2002 because they are nonrefundable deposits.

I.C.19. Unemployment Compensation

48. **(a)** The requirement is to determine the amount of state unemployment benefits that should be included in adjusted gross income. All unemployment compensation benefits received must be included in gross income.

I.D. Tax Accounting Methods

49. **(d)** The requirement is to determine the correct statement regarding the reporting of income by a cash-basis taxpayer. A cash-basis taxpayer should report gross income for the year in which income is either actually or constructively received, whether in cash or in property. Constructive receipt means that an item of income is unqualifiedly available to the taxpayer without restriction (e.g., interest on bank deposit is income when credited to account).

50. **(b)** The requirement is to determine which taxpayer may use the cash method of accounting. The cash method cannot generally be used if inventories are necessary to clearly reflect income, and cannot generally be used by C corporations, partnerships that have a C corporation as a partner, tax shelters, and certain tax-exempt trusts. Taxpayers permitted to use the cash method include a qualified personal service corporation, an entity (other than a tax shelter) if for every year it has average gross receipts of $5 million or less for any prior three-year period (and provided it does not have inventories), and a small taxpayer with average annual gross receipts of $1 million or less for any prior three-year period may use the cash method and is excepted from the requirement to account for inventories

51. **(b)** The requirement is to select the correct statement regarding the $1,000 of additional income determined by Stewart, an accrual method corporation. Under the accrual method, income generally is reported in the year earned. If an amount is included in gross income on the basis of a reasonable estimate, and it is later determined that the exact amount is more, then the additional amount is included in income in the tax year in which the determination of the exact amount is made. Here, Stewart properly accrued $5,000 of income for 2001, and discovered that the exact amount was $6,000 in 2002. Therefore, the additional $1,000 of income is properly includible in Stewart's 2002 income tax return.

52. **(b)** The requirement is to determine the correct statement regarding Axis Corp.'s deduction for its employees bonus expense. An accrual-method taxpayer can deduct compensation (including a bonus) when there is an obligation to make payment, the services have been performed, and the amount can be determined with reasonable accuracy. It is not required that the exact amount of compensation be determined during the taxable year. As long as the computation is known and the liability is fixed, accrual is proper even though the profits upon which the compensation are based are not determined until after the end of the year.

Although compensation is generally deductible only for the year in which the compensation is paid, an exception is made for accrual method taxpayers so long as payment is made within 2 1/2 months after the end of the year. Here, since the services were performed, the method of computation was known, the amount was reasonable, and payment was made by March 15, 2003, the bonus expense may be deducted on Axis Corp.'s 2002 tax return. Note that the bonus could not be a disguised dividend because none of the employees were shareholders.

53. **(b)** The requirement is to determine the amount of the 2001 interest payment of $12,000 that was deductible on Michaels' 2002 income tax return. Generally, there is no deduction for prepaid interest. When a taxpayer pays interest for a period that extends beyond the end of the tax year, the interest paid in advance must be spread over the period to which it applies. Michaels paid $12,000 of interest during 2001 that relates to the period beginning December 1, 2001, and ending November 30, 2002. Therefore, 1/12 x $12,000 = $1,000 of interest was deductible for 2001, and 11/12 x $12,000 = $11,000 was deductible for 2002.

54. **(c)** The requirement is to determine the amount of income to be reported in Blair's 2002 return for the stock received in satisfaction of a client fee owed to Blair. Since Blair is a cash method taxpayer, the amount of income to be recognized equals the $4,000 fair market value of the stock on date of receipt. Note that the $4,000 of income is reported by Blair in 2002 when the stock is received; not in 2002 when the stock is sold.

55. **(d)** The requirement is to determine whether the accrual method of tax reporting is mandatory for a sole proprietor when there are accounts receivable for services rendered, or year-end merchandise inventories. A taxpayer's taxable income should be computed using the method of accounting by which the taxpayer regularly computes income in keeping the taxpayer's books. Either the cash or the accrual method generally can be used so long as the method is consistently applied and clearly reflects income. However, when the production, purchase, or sale of merchandise is an income producing factor, inventories must be maintained to clearly reflect income. If merchandise inventories are necessary to clearly determine income, only the accrual method of tax reporting can be used for purchases and sales.

56. **(d)** The requirement is to determine the amount of salary taxable to Burg in 2002. Since Burg is a cash-basis taxpayer, salary is taxable to Burg when actually or constructively received, whichever is earlier. Since the $30,000 of unpaid salary was unqualifiedly available to Burg during 2002, Burg is considered to have constructively received it. Thus, Burg must report a total of $80,000 of salary for 2002; the $50,000 actually received plus $30,000 constructively received.

57. **(d)** The requirement is to determine the 2002 medical practice net income for a cash basis physician. Dr. Berger's income consists of the $200,000 received from patients and the $30,000 received from third-party reimbursers during 2002. His 2002 deductions include the $20,000 of salaries and $24,000 of other expenses paid in 2002. The year-end bonuses will be deductible for 2003.

58. **(c)** The requirement is to determine which taxpayer may use the cash method of accounting for tax purposes. The cash method generally cannot be used (and the accrual method must be used to measure sales and cost of goods sold) if inventories are necessary to clearly determine income. Additionally, the cash method generally cannot generally be used by (1) a corporation (other than an S corporation), (2) a partnership with a corporation as a partner, and (3) a tax shelter. However, this prohibition against the use of the cash method in the preceding sentence does not apply to a farming business, a qualified personal service corporation (e.g., a corporation performing services in health, law, engineering, architecture, accounting, actuarial science, performing arts, or consulting), and a corporation or partnership (that is not a tax shelter) that does not have inventories and whose average annual gross receipts for the most recent three-year period do not exceed $5 million.

I.E. Business Income and Deductions

59. **(a)** Uniform capitalization rules generally require that all costs incurred (both direct and indirect) in manufacturing or constructing real or personal property, or in purchasing or holding property for sale, must be capitalized as part of the cost of the property. However, these rules do not apply to a "small retailer or wholesaler" who acquires personal property for resale if the retailer's or wholesaler's average annual gross receipts for the three preceding taxable years do not exceed $10 million.

60. **(a)** The requirement is to determine whether the cost of merchandise, and business expenses other than the cost of merchandise, can be deducted in calculating Mock's business income from a retail business selling illegal narcotic substances. Generally, business expenses that are incurred in an illegal activity are deductible if they are ordinary and necessary, and reasonable in amount. Under a special exception, no deduction or credit is allowed for any amount that is paid or incurred in carrying on a trade or business which consists of trafficking in controlled substances. However, this limitation that applies to expenditures in connection with the illegal sale of drugs does not alter the normal definition of gross income (i.e., sales minus cost of goods sold). As a result, in arriving at gross income from the business, Mock may reduce total sales by the cost of goods sold, and thus is allowed to deduct the cost of merchandise in calculating business income.

61. **(b)** The requirement is to determine the percentage of business meals expense that Banks Corp. can deduct for 2002. Generally, only 50% of business meals and entertainment is deductible. When an employer reimburses its employees' substantiated qualifying business meal expenses, the 50% limitation on deductibility applies to the employer.

62. **(a)** The requirement is to determine which of the costs is **not** included in inventory under the Uniform Capitalization (UNICAP) rules for goods manufactured by a taxpayer. UNICAP rules require that specified overhead items must be included in inventory including factory repairs and maintenance, factory administration and officers' salaries related to production, taxes (other than income taxes), the costs of quality control and inspection, current and past service costs of pension and profit-sharing plans, and service support such as purchasing, payroll, and warehousing costs. Nonmanufacturing costs such as selling, advertising, and research and experimental costs are not required to be included in inventory.

63. **(d)** If no exceptions are met, the uniform capitalization rules generally require that all costs incurred in purchasing or holding inventory for resale must be capitalized as part of the cost of the inventory. Costs that must be capitalized with respect to inventory include the costs of purchasing, handling, processing, repackaging and assembly, and off-site storage. An off-site storage facility is one that is not physically attached to, and an integral part of, a retail sales facility. Service costs such as marketing, selling, advertising, and general management are immediately deductible and need not be capitalized as part of the cost of inventory.

64. **(d)** The requirement is to determine the correct statement regarding the deduction for bad debts in the case of a corporation that is not a financial institution. Except for certain small banks that can use the experience method of accounting for bad debts, all taxpayers (including those that previously used the reserve method) are required to use the direct charge-off method of accounting for bad debts.

65. **(d)** The requirement is to determine the amount of life insurance premium that can be deducted in Ram Corp.'s income tax return. Generally, no deduction is allowed for expenditures that produce tax-exempt income. Here, no deduction is allowed for the $6,000 life insurance premium because Ram is the beneficiary of the policy, and the proceeds of the policy will be excluded from Ram's income when the officer dies.

66. **(a)** The requirement is to determine the amount of bad debt deduction for a cash-basis taxpayer. Accounts receivable resulting from services rendered by a cash-basis taxpayer have a zero tax basis, because the income has not yet been reported. Thus, failure to collect the receivable results in a nondeductible loss.

67. **(c)** The requirement is to determine the loss that Cook can claim as a result of the worthless note receivable in 2002. Cook's $1,000 loss will be treated as a nonbusiness bad debt, deductible as a short-term capital loss. The loss is **not** a business bad debt because Cook was not in the business of lending money, nor was the loan required as a condition of Cook's employment. Since Cook owned no stock in Precision, the loss could **not** be deemed to be a loss from worthless stock, deductible as a long-term capital loss.

68. **(b)** The requirement is to determine the amount of gifts deductible as a business expense. The deduction for business gifts is limited to $25 per recipient each year. Thus, Palo Corporation's deduction for business gifts would be [(4 x $10) + (13 x $25)] = $365.

I.E.3 Net Operating Loss (NOL)

69. **(b)** The requirement is to determine Jennifer's net operating loss (NOL) for 2002. Jennifer's personal casualty loss of $45,000 incurred as a result of the destruction of her personal residence is allowed as a deduction in the computation of her NOL and is subtracted from her salary income of $30,000, to arrive at a NOL of $15,000. No deduction is allowed for personal and dependency exemptions in the computation of a NOL.

70. **(c)** The requirement is to determine the amount of net operating loss (NOL) for a self-employed taxpayer for 2002. A NOL generally represents a loss from the conduct of a trade or business and can generally be carried back two years and forward twenty years to offset income in the carryback and carryforward years. Since a NOL generally represents a business loss, an individual taxpayer's personal exemptions and an excess of nonbusiness deductions over nonbusiness income cannot be subtracted in computing the NOL. Nonbusiness deductions generally include itemized deductions as well as the standard deduction if the taxpayer does not itemize. In this case, the $4,700 standard deduction offsets the $1,500 of nonbusiness income received in the form of dividends and short-term capital gain, but the excess ($3,200) cannot be included in the NOL computation. Thus, the taxpayer's NOL simply consists of the $6,000 business loss.

71. **(a)** The requirement is to determine Destry's net operating loss (NOL). A net operating loss generally represents a loss from the conduct of a trade or business and can generally be carried back two years and forward twenty years to offset income in the carryback and carryforward years. Since a NOL generally represents a business loss, an individual taxpayer's personal exemption and an excess of nonbusiness deductions (e.g., standard deduction) over nonbusiness income (e.g., interest from savings account) cannot be subtracted in computing the NOL. Similarly, no deduction is allowed for a net capital loss. As a result, Destry's NOL consists of his net business loss of $16,000 reduced by his business income of $5,000 from wages and $4,000 of net rental income, resulting in a NOL of $7,000.

I.E.6. Losses and Credits from Passive Activities

72. **(a)** The requirement is to determine the amount of Cobb's rental real estate loss that can be used as an offset against income from nonpassive sources. Losses from passive activities may generally only be used to offset income from other passive activities. Although a rental activity is defined as a passive activity regardless of the owner's participation in the operation of the rental property, a special rule permits an individual to offset up to $25,000 of income that is not from passive activities by losses from a rental real estate activity if the individual actively participates in the rental real estate activity. However, this special $25,000 allowance is reduced by 50% of the taxpayer's AGI in excess of $100,000, and is fully phased out when AGI exceeds $150,000. Since Cobb's AGI is $200,000, the special $25,000 allowance is fully phased out and no rental loss can be offset against income from nonpassive sources.

73. **(c)** The requirement is to determine the entity to which the rules limiting the allowability of passive activity losses and credits applies. The passive activity limitations apply to individuals, estates, trusts, closely held C corporations, and personal service corporations. Application of the passive activity loss limitations to personal service corporations is intended to prevent taxpayers from sheltering personal service income by creating personal service corporations and acquiring passive activity losses at the corporate level. A personal service corporation is a corporation (1) whose principal activity is the performance of personal services, and (2) such services are substantially performed by owner-employees. Since passive activity income, losses, and credits from partnerships and S corporations flow through to be reported on the tax returns of the owners of such entities, the passive activity limitations are applied at the partner and shareholder level, rather than to partnerships and S corporations themselves.

74. **(c)** The requirement is to determine Wolf's passive loss resulting from his 5% general partnership interest in Gata Associates. A partnership is a pass-through entity and its items of income and loss pass through to partners to be included on their tax returns. Since Wolf does not materially participate in the partnership's auto parts business, Wolf's distributable share of the loss from the partnership's auto parts business is classified as a passive activity loss. Portfolio income or loss must be excluded from the computation of the income or loss resulting from a passive activity, and must be separately passed through to partners.

Portfolio income includes all interest income, other than interest income derived in the ordinary course of a trade or business. Interest income derived in the ordinary course of a trade or business includes only interest income on loans and investments made in the ordinary course of a trade or business of lending money, and interest income on accounts receivable arising in the ordinary course of a trade or business. Since the $20,000 of interest income derived by the partnership resulted from a temporary investment, the interest income must be classified as portfolio income and cannot be netted against the $100,000 operating loss from the auto parts business. Thus, Wolf will report a passive activity loss of $100,000 x 5% = $5,000; and will report portfolio income of $20,000 x 5% = $1,000.

75. **(a)** The requirement is to determine the correct statement regarding the passive loss rules involving rental real estate activities. By definition, any rental activity is a passive activity without regard as to whether or not the taxpayer materially participates in the activity. Answer (b) is incorrect because interest and dividend income not derived in the ordinary course of business is treated as **portfolio** income, and **cannot** be offset by passive rental activity losses when the "active participation" requirement is **not** met. Answer (c) is incorrect because passive rental activity credits **cannot** be used to offset the tax attributable to **nonpassive** activities. Answer (d) is incorrect because the passive activity rules contain no provision that excludes taxpayers below a certain income level from the limitations imposed by the passive activity rules.

76. **(d)** The requirement is to determine the correct statement regarding an individual taxpayer's passive losses and credits relating to rental real estate activities that cannot be currently deducted. Generally, losses and credits from passive activities can only be used to offset income from (or tax allocable to) passive activities. If there is insufficient passive activity income (or tax) to absorb passive activity losses and credits, the unused losses and credits are carried forward indefinitely or until the property is disposed of in a taxable transaction. Answers (a) and (c) are incorrect because unused passive losses and credits are never carried back to prior taxable years. Answer (b) is incorrect because there is no maximum carryforward period.

I.F.   Depreciation, Depletion, and Amortization

77.   (a)   The requirement is to determine the maximum amount of Sec. 179 expense election that Aviation Corp. will be allowed to deduct for 2002, and the maximum amount of expense election that it can carry over to 2003. Sec. 179 permits a taxpayer to elect to treat up to $24,000 of the cost of qualifying depreciable personal property as an expense rather than as a capital expenditure. However, the $24,000 maximum is reduced dollar-for-dollar by the cost of qualifying property placed in service during the taxable year that exceeds $200,000. Here, the maximum amount that can be expensed is $24,000 – ($203,000 – $200,000) = $21,000 for 2002. However, this amount is further limited as a deduction for 2002 to Aviation's taxable income of $7,000 before the Sec. 179 expense deduction. The remainder ($21,000 – $7,000 = $14,000) that is not currently deductible because of the taxable income limitation can be carried over and will be deductible subject to the taxable income limitation in 2003.

78.   (c)   The requirement is to determine which conditions must be satisfied to enable a taxpayer to expense the cost of new or used tangible depreciable personal property under Sec. 179. Taxpayers may elect to expense up to $24,000 of the cost of new or used tangible depreciable personal property placed in service during the taxable year. To qualify, the property must be acquired by purchase from an unrelated party for use in the taxpayer's active trade or business. The maximum cost that can be expensed ($24,000 for 2002) is reduced dollar-for-dollar by the cost of qualifying property that is placed in service during the year that exceeds $200,000. Additionally, the amount that can be expensed is further limited to the aggregate taxable income derived from the active conduct of any trade or business of the taxpayer.

79.   (a)   The requirement is to determine the MACRS deduction for the furniture and fixtures placed in service during 2002. The furniture and fixtures qualify as seven-year property and under MACRS will be depreciated using the 200% declining balance method. Normally, a half-year convention applies to the year of acquisition. However, the midquarter convention must be used if more than 40% of all personal property is placed in service during the last quarter of the taxpayer's taxable year. Since this was Krol's only acquisition of personal property and the property was placed in service during the last quarter of Krol's calendar year, the mid-quarter convention must be used. Under this convention, property is treated as placed in service during the middle of the quarter in which placed in service. Since the furniture and fixtures were placed in service in November, the amount of allowable MACRS depreciation is limited to $56,000 x 2/7 x 1/8 = $2,000.

80.   (b)   The requirement is to determine Sullivan's MACRS deduction for the apartment building in 2002. The MACRS deduction for residential real property placed in service during 2002 must be determined using the mid-month convention (i.e., property is treated as placed in service at the midpoint of the month placed in service) and the straight-line method of depreciation over a 27.5-year recovery period. Here, the $360,000 cost must first be reduced by the $30,000 allocated to the land, to arrive at a basis for depreciation of $330,000. Since the building was placed in service on June 29, the mid-month convention results in 6.5 months of depreciation for 2002. The MACRS deduction for 2002 is [$330,000 x (6.5 months)/(27.5 x 12 months)] = $6,500.

81.   (c)   The requirement is to determine the depreciation convention that must be used when a calendar-year taxpayer's only acquisition of equipment during the year occurs during November. Generally, a half-year convention applies to depreciable personal property, and a mid-month convention applies to depreciable real property. Under the half-year convention, a half-year of depreciation is allowed for the year in which property is placed in service, regardless of when the property is placed in service during the year, and a half-year of depreciation is allowed for the year in which the property is disposed of. However, a taxpayer must instead use a mid-quarter convention if more than 40% of all depreciable personal property acquired during the year is placed in service during the last quarter of the taxable year. Under this convention, property is treated as placed in service (or disposed of) in the middle of the quarter in which placed in service (or disposed of). Since Data Corp. is a calendar-year taxpayer and its only acquisition of depreciable personal property was placed in service during November (i.e., the last quarter of its taxable year), it must use the midquarter convention, and will only be allowed a half-quarter of depreciation of its office equipment for 2002.

82.   (b)   The requirement is to determine the correct statement regarding the modified accelerated cost recovery system (MACRS) of depreciation for property placed in service after 1986. Under MACRS, salvage value is completely ignored for purposes of computing the depreciation deduction, which results in the recovery of the entire cost of depreciable property. Answer (a) is incorrect because used tangible depreciable property is depreciated under MACRS. Answer (c) is incorrect because the cost of some depreciable realty must be depreciated using the straight-line method. Answer (d) is incorrect because the cost of some depreciable realty is included in the ten-year (e.g., single purpose agricultural and horticultural structures) and twenty-year (e.g., farm buildings) classes.

83.   (a)   The requirement is to determine the correct statement regarding the half-year convention under the general MACRS method. Under the half-year convention that generally applies to depreciable personal property, one-half of the first year's depreciation is allowed in the year in which the property is placed in service, regardless of when the property is placed in service during the year, and a half-year's depreciation is allowed for the year in which the property is disposed of, regardless of when the property is disposed of during the year. Answer (b) is incorrect because allowing one-half month's depreciation for the month that property is placed in service or disposed of is known as the "midmonth convention."

84.   (c)   The requirement is to determine the portion of the $201,000 cost of the machine that can be treated as an expense for 2002. Sec. 179 permits a taxpayer to elect to treat up to $24,000 of the cost of qualifying depreciable personal property as an expense rather than as a capital expenditure. However, the $24,000 maximum is reduced dollar-for-dollar by the cost of qualifying property placed in service during the taxable year that exceeds $200,000. Here, the maximum amount that can be expensed is [$24,000 − ($201,000 − $200,000)] = $23,000.

II. "Above the Line" Deductions

85. (d)   The requirement is to determine the amount to be reported in Mel's gross income for the $400 per month received for business automobile expenses under a nonaccountable plan from Easel Co. Reimbursements and expense allowances paid to an employee under a nonaccountable plan must be included in the employee's gross income and are reported on the employee's W-2. The employee must then complete Form 2106 and itemize to deduct business-related expenses such as the use of an automobile.

86. (c)   The requirement is to determine the correct statement regarding a second residence that is rented for 200 days and used 50 days for personal use. Deductions for expenses related to a dwelling that is also used as a residence by the taxpayer may be limited. If the taxpayer's personal use exceeds the greater of 14 days, or 10% of the number of days rented, deductions allocable to rental use are limited to rental income. Here, since Adams used the second residence for 50 days and rented the residence for 200 days, no rental loss can be deducted. All expenses related to the property, including utilities and maintenance, must be allocated between personal use and rental use. Answer (d) is incorrect because only the mortgage interest and taxes allocable to rental use would be deducted in determining the property's net rental income or loss. Answer (a) is incorrect, since depreciation on the property could be deducted if Adams' gross rental income exceeds allocable out-of-pocket rental expenses.

87. (a)   The requirement is to determine the amount of unreimbursed employee expenses that can be deducted by Gilbert if he does not itemize deductions. Gilbert cannot deduct any of the expenses listed if he does not itemize deductions. The unreimbursed employee business expenses are deductible only as itemized deductions, subsequent to the 2% of AGI floor.

II.E. Moving Expenses

88. (c)   The requirement is to determine the amount of moving expense that James can deduct for 2002. Direct moving expenses are deductible if closely related to the start of work at a new location and a distance test (i.e., distance from new job to former residence is at least fifty miles further than distance from old job to former residence) and a time test (i.e., employed at least thirty-nine weeks out of twelve months following move) are met. Since both tests are met, James' unreimbursed lodging and travel expenses ($1,000), cost of insuring household goods and personal effects during move ($200), cost of shipping household pets ($100), and cost of moving household furnishings and personal effects ($3,000) are deductible. Indirect moving expenses such as premove househunting, temporary living expenses, and meals while moving are not deductible.

89. (c)   The requirement is to determine Martin's deductible moving expenses. Moving expenses are deductible

if closely related to the start of work at a new location and a distance (i.e., new job must be at least fifty miles from former residence) and time (i.e., employed at least thirty-nine weeks out of twelve months following move) tests are met. Here, both tests are met and Martin's $800 cost of moving his personal belongings is deductible. However, the $300 penalty for breaking his lease is not deductible.

90. (a)   Only the direct costs incurred for transporting a taxpayer, his or her family, and their household goods and personal effects from their former residence to their new residence can qualify as deductible moving expenses. The indirect moving expense costs incurred for meals while in transit, house hunting, temporary lodging, to sell or purchase a home, and to break or acquire a lease are not deductible.

II.F. Contributions to Certain Retirement Plans

91. (d)   The requirement is to determine the incorrect statement concerning a Roth IRA. The maximum annual contribution to a Roth IRA is subject to reduction if the taxpayer's adjusted gross income exceeds certain thresholds. Unlike a traditional IRA, contributions are not deductible and can be made even after the taxpayer reaches age 70½. The contribution must be made by the due date of the taxpayer's tax return (**not** including extensions).

92. (c)   The requirement is to determine the maximum amount of adjusted gross income that a taxpayer may have and still qualify to roll over a traditional IRA into a Roth IRA. A conversion or rollover of a traditional IRA to a Roth IRA can occur if the taxpayer's AGI does not exceed $100,000, the taxpayer is not married filing a separate return, and the rollover occurs within sixty days of the IRA distribution. For purposes of the determining eligibility, the $100,000 AGI ceiling is determined by including taxable social security and is determined before the exclusions for interest on Series EE bonds used for higher education, employer provided adoption assistance, and foreign earned income. The IRA conversion or rollover amount is not taken into account in determining the $100,000 AGI ceiling.

93. (d)   The requirement is to determine which statement concerning an education IRA is not correct. Contributions to an education IRA are not deductible, but withdrawals of earnings will be tax-free if used to pay the qualified higher education expenses of the designated beneficiary. The maximum amount that can be contributed to an education IRA for 2002 is limited to $2,000, but the annual contribution is phased out by adjusted gross income in excess of certain thresholds. Contributions generally cannot be made to an education IRA after the date on which the designated beneficiary reaches age eighteen.

94. (a)   The requirement is to determine the Whites' allowable IRA deduction on their 2002 joint return. For married taxpayers filing a joint return for 2002, up to $3,000 can be deducted for contributions to the IRA of each spouse (even if one spouse is not working), provided that the combined earned income of both spouses is at least equal to the amounts contributed to the IRAs. Even though Val is covered by his employer's qualified pension plan, the Whites are eligible for the maximum deduction because their gross income of $35,000 + $5,000 = $40,000 does not exceed the base amount at which the maximum $3,000 deduction would be reduced. Also note that Pat's $5,000 of taxable alimony payments is treated as compensation for purposes of qualifying for an IRA deduction. Since they each contributed $3,000 to an IRA account, the allowable deduction on their joint return is $6,000.

95. **(d)** The requirement is to determine the definition of "earned income" for purposes of computing the annual contribution to a Keogh profit-sharing plan by Davis, a sole proprietor. A self-employed individual may contribute to a qualified retirement plan called a Keogh plan. The maximum contribution to a Keogh profit-sharing plan is the lesser of $40,000 or 25% of earned income. For this purpose, "earned income" is defined as net earnings from self-employment (i.e., business gross income minus allowable business deductions) reduced by the deduction for one-half of the self-employment tax, and the deductible Keogh contribution itself.

96. **(d)** A single individual with AGI over $44,000 for 2002 would only be entitled to an IRA deduction if the taxpayer is not covered by a qualified employee pension plan.

97. **(b)** The requirement is to determine the allowable IRA deduction on the Cranes' 2002 joint return. Since Sol is covered by his employer's pension plan, Sol's contribution of $3,000 is proportionately phased out as a deduction by AGI between $54,000 and $64,000. Since the Cranes' AGI exceeded $64,000, no deduction is allowed for Sol's contribution. Although Julia is not employed, $3,000 can be contributed to her IRA because the combined earned income on the Cranes' return is at least $6,000. The maximum IRA deduction for an individual who is not covered by an employer plan, but whose spouse is, is proportionately phased out for AGI between $150,000 and $160,000. Since Julia is not covered by an employer plan and the Cranes' AGI is below $150,000, the $3,000 contribution to Julia's IRA is fully deductible for 2002.

98. **(d)** The requirement is to determine the Lees' maximum IRA contribution and deduction on a joint return for 2002. Since neither taxpayer was covered by an employer-sponsored pension plan, there is no phaseout of the maximum deduction due to the level of their adjusted gross income. For married taxpayers filing a joint return, up to $3,000 can be deducted for contributions to the IRA of each spouse (even if one spouse is not working), provided that the combined earned income of both spouses is at least equal to the amounts contributed to the IRAs. Additionally, an individual at least age 50 can make a special catch-up contribution of $500 for 2002, resulting in an increased maximum contribution and deduction of $3,500 for 2002. Thus, the Lees may contribute and deduct a maximum of $7,000 to their individual retirement accounts for 2002, with a maximum of $3,500 placed into each account.

99. **(c)** The maximum deduction for contributions to a defined contribution self-employed retirement plan is limited to the lesser of $40,000, or 100% of self-employment income for 2002.

100. **(d)** The requirement is to determine which allowable deduction can be claimed in arriving at an individual's adjusted gross income. Seventy percent of a self-employed individual's health insurance premiums are deductible in arriving at an individual's adjusted gross income for 2002. Charitable contributions, foreign income taxes (if not used

as a credit), and tax return preparation fees can be deducted only from adjusted gross income if an individual itemizes deductions.

II.G. Deduction for Interest on Education Loan

101. **(b)** The requirement is to determine the incorrect statement concerning the deduction for interest on qualified education loans. For a tax year beginning in 2002, an individual is allowed to deduct up to $2,500 for interest on qualified education loans in arriving at AGI. The deduction is subject to an income phase-out and the loan proceeds must have been used to pay for the qualified higher education expenses (e.g., tuition, fees, room, board) of the taxpayer, spouse, or a dependent (at the time the debt was incurred). The education expenses must relate to a period when the student was enrolled on at least a half-time basis. The sixty-month limitation was repealed for tax years beginning after 2001.

102. **(c)** The requirement is to determine how Dale should treat her $1,000 jury duty fee that she remitted to her employer. Fees received for serving on a jury must be included in gross income. If the recipient is required to remit the jury duty fees to an employer in exchange for regular compensation, the remitted jury duty fees are allowed as a deduction from gross income in arriving at adjusted gross income.

III.   Itemized Deductions from Adjusted Gross Income

103. **(c)** The requirement is to determine George's taxable income. George's adjusted gross income consists of $3,700 of dividends and $1,700 of wages. Since George is eligible to be claimed as a dependency exemption by his parents, there will be no personal exemption on George's return and his basic standard deduction is limited to the greater of $750, or George's earned income of $1,700, plus $250. Thus, George's taxable income would be computed as follows:

Dividends	$ 3,700
Wages	1,700
AGI	$ 5,400
Exemption	0
Std. deduction	(1,950)
Taxable income	$ 3,450

104. **(c)** The item asks you to determine the requirements that must be met in order for a single individual to qualify for the additional standard deduction. A single individual who is age sixty-five or older or blind is eligible for an additional standard deduction ($1,150 for 2002). Two additional standard deductions are allowed for an individual who is age sixty-five or older **and** blind. It is not required that an individual support a dependent child or aged parent in order to qualify for an additional standard deduction.

III.A.   Medical and Dental Expenses

105. **(b)** The requirement is to determine Carroll's maximum medical expense deduction after the applicable threshold limitation for the year. An individual taxpayer's unreimbursed medical expenses are deductible to the extent in excess of 7.5% of the taxpayer's adjusted gross income. Although the cost of cosmetic surgery is generally not deductible, the cost is deductible if the cosmetic surgery or procedure is necessary to ameliorate a deformity related to a congenital abnormality or personal injury resulting from an accident, trauma, or disfiguring disease. Here, Carroll's deduction is ($5,000 + $15,000) – ($100,000 x 7.5%) = $12,500.

106. (b) The requirement is to determine the Blairs' itemized deduction for medical expenses for 2002. A taxpayer can deduct the amounts paid for the medical care of himself, spouse, or dependents. The Blairs' qualifying medical expenses include the $800 of medical insurance premiums, $450 of prescribed medicines, $1,000 of unreimbursed doctor's fees, and $150 of transportation related to medical care. These expenses, which total $2,400, are deductible to the extent they exceed 7.5% of adjusted gross income, and result in a deduction of $150. Note that nonprescription medicines, including aspirin and over-the-counter cold capsules, are not deductible. Additionally, the Blairs cannot deduct the emergency room fee they paid for their son because they did not provide more than half of his support and he therefore does not qualify as their dependent.

107. (a) The requirement is to determine the amount the Whites may deduct as qualifying medical expenses without regard to the adjusted gross income percentage threshold. The Whites' deductible medical expenses include the $600 spent on repair and maintenance of the motorized wheelchair and the $8,000 spent for tuition, meals, and lodging at the special school for their physically handicapped dependent child. Payment for meals and lodging provided by an institution as a necessary part of medical care is deductible as a medical expense if the main reason for being in the institution is to receive medical care. Here, the item indicates that the Whites' physically handicapped dependent child was in the institution primarily for the availability of medical care, and that meals and lodging were furnished as necessary incidents to that care.

108. (c) The requirement is to determine the amount Wells can deduct as qualifying medical expenses without regard to the adjusted gross income percentage threshold. Wells' deductible medical expenses include the $500 premium on the prescription drug insurance policy and the $500 unreimbursed payment for physical therapy. The earnings protection policy is not considered medical insurance because payments are not based on the amount of medical expenses incurred. As a result, the $3,000 premium is a nondeductible personal expense.

109. (d) The requirement is to determine the amount of expenses incurred in connection with the adoption of a child that can be deducted by the Sloans on their 2002 joint return. A taxpayer can deduct the medical expenses paid for a child at the time of adoption if the child qualifies as the taxpayer's dependent when the medical expenses are paid. Additionally, if a taxpayer pays an adoption agency for medical expenses the adoption agency already paid, the taxpayer is treated as having paid those expenses. Here, the Sloans can deduct the child's medical expenses of $5,000 that they paid. On the other hand, the legal expenses of $8,000 and agency fee of $3,000 incurred in connection with the adoption are treated as nondeductible personal expenses. However, the Sloans will qualify to claim a nonrefundable tax credit of up to $10,000 for these qualified adoption expenses.

110. (a) The requirement is to determine the amount that can be claimed by the Clines in their 2002 return as qualifying medical expenses. No medical expense deduction is allowed for cosmetic surgery or similar procedures, unless the surgery or procedure is necessary to ameliorate a deformity related to a congenital abnormality or personal injury resulting from an accident, trauma, or disfiguring disease. Cosmetic surgery is defined as any procedure that is directed at improving a patient's appearance and does not meaningfully promote the proper function of the body or prevent or treat illness or disease. Thus, Ruth's face-lift and Mark's hair transplant do not qualify as deductible medical expenses in 2002.

111. (d) The requirement is to determine the amount that Scott can claim as deductible medical expenses. The medical expenses incurred by a taxpayer for himself, spouse, or a dependent are deductible when paid or charged to a credit card. The $4,000 of medical expenses for his dependent son are deductible by Scott in 2002 when charged on Scott's credit card. It does not matter that payment to the credit card issuer had not been made when Scott filed his return. Expenses paid for the medical care of a decedent by the decedent's spouse are deductible as medical expenses in the year they are paid, whether the expenses are paid before or after the decedent's death. Thus, the $2,800 of medical expenses for his deceased spouse are deductible by Scott when paid in 2002, even though his spouse died in 2001.

112. (d) The requirement is to determine which expenditure qualifies as a deductible medical expense. Premiums paid for Medicare B supplemental medical insurance qualify as a deductible expense. Diaper service, funeral expenses, and nursing care for a healthy baby are not deductible as medical expenses.

113. (b) The requirement is to determine Stenger's net medical expense deduction for 2002. It would be computed as follows:

Prescription drugs	$ 300
Medical insurance premiums	750
Doctors ($2,550 – $900)	1,650
Eyeglasses	75
	$2,775
Less 7.5% of AGI ($35,000)	2,625
Medical expense deduction for 2002	$ 150

114. (d) The requirement is to determine the total amount of deductible medical expenses for the Bensons before the application of any limitation rules. Deductible medical expenses include those incurred by a taxpayer, taxpayer's spouse, dependents of the taxpayer, or any person for whom the taxpayer could claim a dependency exemption except that the person had gross income of $3,000 or more, or filed a joint return. Thus, the Bensons may deduct medical expenses incurred for themselves, for John (i.e., no dependency exemption only because his gross income is $3,000 or more), and for Nancy (i.e., a dependent of the Bensons).

III.B.   Taxes

115. (d) The requirement is to determine the tax that is not deductible as an itemized deduction. One-half of a self-employed taxpayer's self-employment tax is deductible from gross income in arriving at adjusted gross income. Foreign real estate taxes, foreign income taxes, and personal property taxes can be deducted as itemized deductions from adjusted gross income.

116. (c)   The requirement is to determine the amount that Matthews can deduct as taxes on her 2002 Schedule A of Form 1040. An individual's state and local income taxes are deductible as an itemized deduction, while federal income taxes are not deductible. For a cash-basis taxpayer, state and local taxes are deductible for the year in which paid or withheld. As a result, Matthew's deduction for 2002 consists of her state and local taxes withheld of $1,500 and the December 30 estimated payment of $400. The state and local income taxes that Matthews paid in April 2003 will be deductible for 2003.

117. (a)   The requirement is to determine the correct statement regarding Farb, a cash-basis individual taxpayer who paid an $8,000 invoice for personal property taxes under protest in 2001, and received a $5,000 refund of the taxes in 2002. If a taxpayer receives a refund or rebate of taxes deducted in an earlier year, the taxpayer must generally include the refund or rebate in income for the year in which received. Here, Farb should deduct $8,000 in his 2001 income tax return and should report the $5,000 refund as income in his 2002 income tax return.

118. (d)   The requirement is to determine the amount of itemized deduction for realty taxes that can be deducted by Burg. Generally, an individual's payment of state, local, or foreign real estate taxes is deductible as an itemized deduction if the individual is the owner of the property on which the taxes are imposed. Because the property is jointly-owned by Burg, he is individually liable for the entire amount of realty taxes and may deduct the entire payment on his return. Even back taxes can be deducted by Burg as long as he was the owner of the property during the period of time to which the back taxes are related.

119. (b)   The requirement is to determine Sara's deduction for state income taxes in 2002. Sara's deduction would consist of the $2,000 withheld by her employer in 2002, plus the three estimated payments (3 x $300 = $900) actually paid during 2002, a total of $2,900. Note that the 1/15/03 estimated payment would be deductible for 2003.

120. (b)   The requirement is to determine the amount of **taxes** deductible as an itemized deduction. The $360 vehicle tax based on value is deductible as a personal property tax. The real property tax of $2,700 must be apportioned between the Bronsons and the buyer for tax purposes even though they did not actually make an apportionment. Since the house was sold June 30, while the taxes were paid to September 30, the Bronsons would deduct 6/9 x $2,700 = $1,800. The buyer would deduct the remaining $900.

121. (a)   The requirement is to determine what portion of the $1,300 of realty taxes is deductible by King in 2002. The $600 of delinquent taxes charged to the seller and paid by King are not deductible, but are added to the cost of the property. The $700 of taxes for 2002 are apportioned between the seller and King according to the number of days that each held the property during the year. King's deduction would be

$$\frac{184}{365} \times \$700 = \$353$$

122. (b)   The requirement is to determine the amount of property taxes deductible as itemized deductions. The property taxes on the residence and the land held for appreciation, together with the personal property taxes on the auto are deductible. The special assessment is not deductible, but would be added to the basis of the residence.

123. (a)   The requirement is to determine the amount the Burgs should deduct for taxes in their itemized deductions. The $1,200 of state income tax paid by the Burgs is deductible as an itemized deduction. However, the $7,650 of self-employment tax is not deductible as an itemized deduction. Instead, 50% x $7,650 = $3,825 of self-employment tax is deductible from gross income in arriving at the Burgs' adjusted gross income.

III.C.   Interest Expense

124. (c)   The requirement is to determine the correct statement regarding an individual taxpayer's deduction for interest on investment indebtedness. The deduction for interest expense on investment indebtedness is limited to the taxpayer's net investment income. Net investment income includes such income as interest, dividends, and short-term capital gains, less any related expenses.

125. (b)   The requirement is to determine the correct statement regarding the interest on the Browns' $20,000 loan that was secured by their home and used to purchase an automobile. Qualified residence interest consists of interest on acquisition indebtedness and home equity indebtedness. Interest on home equity indebtedness loans of up to $100,000 is deductible as qualified residence interest if the loans are secured by a taxpayer's principal or second residence regardless of how the loan proceeds are used. The amount of home equity indebtedness cannot exceed the fair market value of a home as reduced by any acquisition indebtedness. Since the Browns' home had a FMV of $400,000 and was unencumbered by other debt, the interest on the $20,000 home equity loan is deductible as qualified residence interest.

126. (c)   The requirement is to determine how much interest is deductible by the Philips for 2002. Qualified residence interest includes the interest on acquisition indebtedness. Such interest is deductible on up to $1 million of loans secured by a principal or second residence if the loans were used to purchase, construct, or substantially improve a home. Here, the Philips' original mortgage of $200,000 as well as the additional loan of $15,000 qualify as acquisition indebtedness, and the resulting $17,000 + $1,500 = $18,500 of interest is deductible. On the other hand, the $500 of interest on the auto loan is considered personal interest and not deductible.

127. (c)   The requirement is to determine the maximum amount allowable as a deduction for Jackson's second residence. Qualified residence interest includes acquisition indebtedness and home equity indebtedness on the taxpayer's principal residence and a second residence. Here, the $5,000 of mortgage interest on the second residence is qualified residence interest and is deductible as an itemized deduction. In contrast, the $1,200 of utilities expense and $6,000 of insurance expense are nondeductible personal expenses.

128. **(c)**   The requirement is to determine the amount of interest expense deductible as an itemized deduction. The $3,600 of home mortgage interest, and the $900 mortgage prepayment penalty are fully deductible as interest expense in computing itemized deductions. The $1,200 interest on the life insurance policy is not deductible since it is classified as personal interest.

129. **(a)**   The requirement is to determine the amount of interest deductible as an itemized deduction. Since 2/3 of the loan proceeds were used to purchase tax-exempt bonds, 2/3 of the bank interest is nondeductible. The remaining 1/3 of the bank interest ($1,200) is related to the purchase of the Arrow debentures and is classified as investment interest deductible to the extent of net investment income ($0). The $3,000 of home mortgage interest is fully deductible as qualified residence interest. The interest on credit card charges is personal interest and is not deductible.

130. **(a)**   None of the items listed relating to the tax deficiency for 2000 are deductible. The interest on the tax deficiency is considered personal interest and is not deductible. The additional federal income tax, the late filing penalty, and the negligence penalty are also not deductible.

III.D.   Charitable Contributions

131. **(c)**   The requirement is to determine the amount of charitable contributions deductible on Stein's current year income tax return. The donation of appreciated stock held more than twelve months is a contribution of intangible, long-term capital gain appreciated property. The amount of contribution is the stock's FMV of $25,000, but is limited in deductibility for the current year to 30% of AGI. Thus, the current year deduction is limited to 30% x $80,000 = $24,000. The remaining $1,000 of contributions can be carried forward for up to five years, subject to the 30% limitation in the carryforward years.

132. **(c)**   The requirement is to determine the maximum amount of properly substantiated charitable contributions that Moore could claim as an itemized deduction for 2002. Moore gave $18,000 to her church during 2002 and had a $10,000 charitable contribution carryover from 2001, resulting in a total of $28,000 of contributions. Since an individual's deduction for charitable contributions cannot exceed an overall limitation of 50% of adjusted gross income, Moore's charitable contribution deduction for 2002 is limited to ($50,000 AGI x 50%) = $25,000. Since Moore's 2002 contributions will be deducted before her carryforward from 2001, Moore will carry over $3,000 of her 2001 contributions to 2003.

133. **(c)**   The requirement is to determine the maximum amount that Spencer can claim as a deduction for charitable contributions in 2002. The cash contribution of $4,000 to church and the $600 fair market value of the used clothing donated to Salvation Army are fully deductible. However, the deduction for the art object is limited to the $400 excess of its cost ($1,200) over its fair market value ($800).

134. **(b)**   The requirement is to determine Lewis' charitable contribution deduction. The donation of appreciated stock held more than twelve months is a contribution of intangible, long-term capital gain appreciated property. The amount of contribution is the stock's FMV of $70,000, but is limited in deductibility for 2002 to 30% of AGI. Thus,

the 2002 deduction is $100,000 x 30% = $30,000. The amount of contribution in excess of the 30% limitation ($70,000 – $30,000 = $40,000) can be carried forward for up to five years, subject to the 30% limitation in the carryforward years.

135. **(b)**   The requirement is to determine the amount of contributions deductible in 2002. Charitable contributions are generally deductible in the year actually paid. The $500 charge to his bank credit card made on December 15, 2002, is considered a payment, and is deductible for 2002. The $1,000 promissory note delivered on November 1, 2002, is not considered a contribution until payment of the note upon maturity in 2003.

136. **(b)**   The requirement is to determine the amount of student expenses deductible as a charitable contribution. A taxpayer may deduct as a charitable contribution up to $50 per **school month** of unreimbursed expenses incurred to maintain a student (in the 12th or lower grade) in the taxpayer's home pursuant to a written agreement with a qualified organization. Since the student started school in September, the amount deductible as a charitable contribution is $50 x 4 = $200.

137. **(a)**   Vincent Tally is not entitled to a deduction for contributions in 2002 because he did not give up his entire interest in the book collection. By reserving the right to use and possess the book collection for his lifetime, Vincent Tally has not made a completed gift. Therefore, no deduction is available. The contribution will be deductible when his entire interest in the books is transferred to the art museum.

138. **(b)**   The requirement is to determine the maximum amount of charitable contribution allowable as an itemized deduction on Jimet's 2002 income tax return. If appreciated property is contributed, the amount of contribution is generally the property's FMV if the property would result in a long-term capital gain if sold. If not, the amount of contribution for appreciated property is generally limited to the property's basis. Here, the stock worth $3,000 was purchased for $1,500 just four months earlier. Since its holding period did not exceed twelve months, a sale of the stock would result in a short-term capital gain, and the amount of allowable contribution deduction is limited to the stock's basis of $1,500. Additionally, to be deductible, a contribution must be made to a qualifying **organization**. As a result, the $2,000 cash given directly to a needy family is not deductible.

139. **(a)**   The requirement is to determine the maximum amount of charitable contribution deductible as an itemized deduction on Taylor's tax return for 2002. The donation of appreciated land purchased for investment and held for more than twelve months is a contribution of real capital gain property (property that would result in long-term capital gain if sold). The amount of contribution is the land's FMV of $25,000, limited in deductibility for the current year to 30% of AGI. In this case, since 30% of AGI would be 30% x $90,000 = $27,000, the full amount of the land contribution ($25,000) is deductible for 2002.

III.E.   Personal Casualty and Theft Gains and Losses

140. **(a)**   The requirement is to determine the amount of the fire loss to her personal residence that Frazer can claim as an itemized deduction. The amount of a personal casualty loss is computed as the lesser of (1) the adjusted basis of the property ($130,000), or (2) the decline in the property's fair market value resulting from the casualty ($130,000 – $0 = $130,000); reduced by any insurance recovery ($120,000), and a $100 floor. Since Frazer had no casualty gains during the year, the net casualty loss is then deductible as an itemized deduction to the extent that it exceeds 10% of adjusted gross income.

Fire loss	$ 130,000
Insurance proceeds	(120,000)
$100 floor	(100)
10% of $70,000 AGI	(7,000)
Casualty loss itemized deduction	$ 2,900

141. (a) The requirement is to determine the amount the Burgs should deduct for the casualty loss (repair of glass vase accidentally broken by their dog) in their itemized deductions. A casualty is the damage, destruction, or loss of property resulting from an identifiable event that is sudden, unexpected, or unusual. Deductible casualty losses may result from earthquakes, tornadoes, floods, fires, vandalism, auto accidents, etc. However, a loss due to the accidental breakage of household articles such as glassware or china under normal conditions is not a casualty loss. Neither is a loss due to damage caused by a family pet.

142. (d) The requirement is to determine the proper treatment of the $490 casualty insurance premium. Casualty insurance premiums on an individual's personal residence are considered nondeductible personal expenses. Even though a casualty is actually incurred during the year, no deduction is available for personal casualty insurance premiums.

143. (d) The requirement is to determine the amount of the fire loss damage to their personal residence that the Hoyts can deduct as an itemized deduction. The amount of a nonbusiness casualty loss is computed as the lesser of (1) the adjusted basis of the property, or (2) the property's decline in FMV; reduced by any insurance recovery, and a $100 floor. If an individual has a net casualty loss for the year, it is then deductible as an itemized deduction to the extent that it exceeds 10% of adjusted gross income.

Lesser of:			
Adjusted basis	=	$50,000	
Decline in FMV			
($60,000 – $55,000)	=	$ 5,000	$ 5,000
Reduce by:			
Insurance recovery			(0)
$100 floor			(100)
10% of $34,000 AGI			(3,400)
Casualty loss itemized deduction			$ 1,500

Note that the $2,500 spent for repairs is not included in the computation of the loss.

144. (b) The requirement is to determine the proper treatment for the $800 appraisal fee that was incurred to determine the amount of the Hoyts' fire loss. The appraisal fee is considered an expense of determining the Hoyts' tax liability; it is not a part of the casualty loss itself. Thus, the appraisal fee is deductible as a miscellaneous itemized deduction subject to a 2% of adjusted gross income floor.

III.F. Miscellaneous Deductions

145. (d) The requirement is to determine which item is **not** a miscellaneous itemized deduction. A legal fee for tax advice related to a divorce, IRA trustee's fees that are separately billed and paid, and an appraisal fee for valuing a charitable contribution qualify as miscellaneous itemized deductions subject to the 2% of AGI floor. On the other hand, the check writing fees for a personal checking account are a personal expense and not deductible.

146. (b) The requirement is to determine the proper treatment of the $2,000 legal fee that was incurred by Hall in a suit to collect the alimony owed her. The $2,000 legal fee is considered an expenditure incurred in the production of income. Expenses incurred in the production of income are deductible as miscellaneous itemized deductions subject to the 2% of adjusted gross income floor.

147. (b) The requirement is to determine the proper reporting of Hall's lottery transactions. Hall's lottery winnings of $200 must be reported as other income on page 1 of Hall's Form 1040. Hall's $1,000 expenditure for state lottery tickets is deductible as a miscellaneous itemized deduction not subject to the 2% of AGI floor, but is limited in amount to the $200 of lottery winnings included in Hall's gross income.

148. (d) The requirement is to determine how expenses pertaining to business activities should be deducted by an outside salesman. An outside salesman is an employee who principally solicits business for his employer while away from the employer's place of business. All unreimbursed business expenses of an outside salesman are deducted as miscellaneous itemized deductions, subject to a 2% of AGI floor. Deductible expenses include business travel, secretarial help, and telephone expenses.

149. (a) The requirement is to determine the amount that can be claimed as miscellaneous itemized deductions. Both the initiation fee and the union dues are fully deductible. The voluntary benefit fund contribution is not deductible. Miscellaneous itemized deductions are generally deductible only to the extent they exceed 2% of AGI. In this case the deductible amount is $80 [$280 – (.02 x $10,000)].

150. (b) The requirement is to compute the amount of miscellaneous itemized deductions. The cost of uniforms not adaptable to general use (specialized work clothes), union dues, unreimbursed auto expenses, and the cost of income tax preparation are all miscellaneous itemized deductions. The preparation of a will is personal in nature, and is not deductible. Thus, the computation of Brodsky's miscellaneous itemized deductions in excess of the 2% of AGI floor is as follows:

Unreimbursed auto expenses	$ 100
Specialized work clothes	550
Union dues	600
Cost of income tax preparation	150
	$1,400
Less (2% x $25,000)	(500)
Deduction allowed	$ 900

III.G.   Reduction of Itemized Deductions

151. (c) The requirement is to determine the item that is not subject to the phaseout of itemized deductions for high-income individuals. An individual whose adjusted gross income exceeds a threshold amount ($137,300 for 2002) is required to reduce the amount of allowable itemized deductions by 3% of the excess of adjusted gross income over the threshold amount. All itemized deductions are subject to this reduction **except** medical expenses, nonbusiness casualty losses, investment interest expense, and gambling losses.

152. (a) The requirement is to determine the correct statement regarding the reduction in itemized deductions. For an individual whose AGI exceeds a threshold amount, the amount of otherwise allowable itemized deductions is reduced by the lesser of (1) 3% of the excess of AGI over the threshold amount, or (2) 80% of certain itemized deductions. The itemized deductions that are subject to reduction include taxes, qualified residence interest, charitable contributions, and miscellaneous itemized deductions (other than gambling losses). The reduction of these itemized deductions can not exceed 80% of the amount that is otherwise allowable.

IV. Exemptions

153. (d) The requirement is to determine which item is not included in determining the total support of a dependent. Support includes food, clothing, FMV of lodging, medical, recreational, educational, and certain capital expenditures made on behalf of a dependent. Excluded from support is life insurance premiums, funeral expenses, nontaxable scholarships, and income and social security taxes paid from a dependent's own income.

154. (c) The requirement is to determine the number of exemptions that Smith was entitled to claim on his 2002 tax return. Smith will be allowed one exemption for himself and one exemption for his dependent mother. Smith is entitled to an exemption for his mother because he provided over half of her support, and her gross income ($0) was less than $3,000. Note that her $9,000 of social security benefits is excluded from her gross income, and that she did not have to live with Smith because she is related to him. No exemption is available to Smith for his son, Clay, because his son filed a joint return on which there was a tax liability.

155. (b) The requirement is to determine how many exemptions Jim and Kay can claim on their 2002 joint income tax return. Jim and Kay are entitled to one personal exemption each on their joint return. They also are entitled to one exemption for Dale since they provided more than half of Dale's support, and Dale was a full-time student under age twenty-four not subject to the $3,000 gross income test. However, no dependency exemptions are available for Kim and Grant because they each had gross income of at least $3,000.

156. (d) The requirement is to determine the requirements which must be satisfied in order for Joe to claim an exemption for his spouse on Joe's separate return for 2002. An exemption can be claimed for Joe's spouse on Joe's separate 2002 return only if the spouse had **no** gross income and was **not** claimed as another person's dependent in 2002.

157. (a) The requirement is to determine the amount of personal exemption on a dependent's tax return. No personal exemption is allowed on an individual's tax return if the individual can be claimed as a dependency exemption by another taxpayer.

158. (d) The requirement is to determine Robert's filing status and the number of exemptions that he should claim. Robert's father does not qualify as Robert's dependent because his father's gross income (interest income of $3,500) was not less than $3,000. Social security is not included in the gross income test. Since his father does not qualify as his dependent, Robert does not qualify for head-of-household filing status. Thus, Robert will file as single with one exemption.

159. (a) The requirement is to determine the filing status of the Arnolds. Since they were legally separated under a decree of separate maintenance on the last day of the taxable year and do not qualify for head-of-household status, they must each file as single.

160. (a) Mr. and Mrs. Stoner are entitled to one exemption each. They are entitled to one exemption for their daughter since they provided over 50% of her support, and she was a full-time student under age twenty-four not subject to the $3,000 gross income test. An exemption can be claimed for their son because they supported him, and he made less than $3,000 in gross income. No exemption is allowable for Mrs. Stoner's father since he was neither a US citizen nor resident of the US, Canada, or Mexico. There is no additional exemption for being age sixty-five or older.

161. (c) The requirement is to determine the number of exemptions the Planters may claim on their joint tax return. There is one exemption for Mr. Planter, and one exemption for his spouse. In addition there is one dependency exemption for their daughter, and one dependency exemption for the niece. The dependency gross income test does not apply to their daughter since she was under age twenty-four and a full-time student for at least some part of at least five calendar months. There is no additional exemption for being age sixty-five or older.

162. (b) The requirement is to determine which of the relatives can be claimed as a dependent (or dependents) on Sam's 2002 return. A taxpayer's own spouse is never a dependent of the taxpayer. Although a personal exemption is generally available for a taxpayer's spouse on the taxpayer's return, it is not a "dependency exemption." Generally, a dependency exemption is available for a dependent if (1) the taxpayer furnishes more than 50% of the dependent's support, (2) the dependent's gross income is less than $3,000, (3) the dependent is of specified relationship to the taxpayer or lives in the taxpayer's household for the entire year, (4) the dependent is a US citizen or resident of the US, Canada, or Mexico, and (5) the dependent does not file a joint return. Here, the support, gross income, US citizen, and joint return tests are met with respect to both Sam's cousin and his father's brother (i.e., Sam's uncle). However, Sam's cousin is not of specified relationship to Sam as defined in the IRC, and could only be claimed as a dependent if the cousin lived in Sam's household for the entire year. Since Sam's cousin did not live in Sam's household, Sam cannot claim a dependency exemption for his cousin. On the other hand, Sam's uncle is of specified relationship to Sam as defined in the IRC and can be claimed as a dependency exemption by Sam.

163. (b) The requirement is to determine which relative could be claimed as a dependent. One of the requirements that must be satisfied to claim a person as a dependent is that the person must be (1) of specified relationship to the taxpayer, or (2) a member of the taxpayer's household. Cousins and foster parents are not of specified relationship and only qualify if a member of the taxpayer's household. Since Alan's cousin and foster parent do not qualify as members of Alan's household, only Alan's niece can be claimed as a dependent.

164. (c) The requirement is to determine who can claim Sara's dependency exemption under a multiple support agreement. A multiple support agreement can be used if (1) no single taxpayer furnishes more than 50% of a dependent's support, and (2) two or more persons, each of whom would be able to take the exemption but for the support test, together provide more than 50% of the dependent's support. Then, any taxpayer who provides more than 10% of the dependent's support can claim the dependent if (1) the other persons furnishing more than 10% agree not to claim the dependent as an exemption, and (2) the other requirements for a dependency exemption are met. One of the other requirements that must be met is that the dependent be related to the taxpayer or live in the taxpayer's household. Alma is not eligible for the exemption because Sara is unrelated to Alma and did not live in Alma's household. Carl is not eligible for the exemption because he provided only 9% of Sara's support. Ben is eligible to claim the exemption for Sara under a multiple support agreement because Ben is related to Sara and has provided more than 10% of her support.

165. (b) The requirement is to determine the number of exemptions allowable in 2002. Mr. and Mrs. Vonce are entitled to one exemption each. They are also entitled to one exemption for their dependent daughter since they provided over one half of her support and she had less than $3,000 of gross income. An exemption is not available for their son because he provided over one half of his own support.

V.C.   Filing Status

166. (d) The requirement is to determine which statements (if any) are among the requirements to enable a taxpayer to be classified as a "qualifying widow(er)." Qualifying widow(er) filing status is available for the two years following the year of a spouse's death if (1) the surviving spouse was eligible to file a joint return in the year of the spouse's death, (2) does not remarry before the end of the current year, and (3) the surviving spouse pays **over 50%** of the cost of maintaining a household that is the principal home for the **entire year** of the surviving spouse's dependent child.

167. (c) The requirement is to determine which items are considered in determining whether an individual has contributed more than one half the cost of maintaining the household for purposes of head of household filing status. The cost of maintaining a household includes such costs as rent, mortgage interest, taxes, insurance on the home, repairs, utilities, and food eaten in the home. The cost of maintaining a household does **not** include the cost of clothing, education, medical treatment, vacations, life insurance, transportation, the rental value of a home an individual

owns, or the value of an individual's services or those of any member of the household.

168. (b) The requirement is to determine the correct statement regarding the filing of a joint tax return. A husband and wife can file a joint return even if they have different accounting methods. Answer (a) is incorrect because spouses must have the same tax year to file a joint return. Answer (c) is incorrect because if either spouse was a nonresident alien at any time during the tax year, **both** spouses must elect to be taxed as US citizens or residents for the entire tax year. Answer (d) is incorrect because taxpayers cannot file a joint return if divorced before the end of the year.

169. (c) The requirement is to determine Emil Gow's filing status for 2002. Emil should file as a "Qualifying widower with dependent child" (i.e., surviving spouse) which will entitle him to use the joint return tax rates. This filing status is available for the two taxable years following the year of a spouse's death if (1) the surviving spouse was eligible to file a joint return in the year of the spouse's death, (2) does not remarry before the end of the current tax year, and (3) the surviving spouse pays over 50% of the cost of maintaining a household that is the principal home for the entire year of the surviving spouse's dependent child.

170. (c) The requirement is to determine Nell's filing status for 2002. Nell qualifies as a head of household because she is unmarried and maintains a household for her infant child. Answer (a) is incorrect because although Nell is single, head of household filing status provides for lower tax rates. Answer (b) is incorrect because Nell is unmarried at the end of 2002. Since Nell's spouse died in 1999, answer (d) is incorrect because the filing status of a "qualifying widow" is only available for the two years following the year of the spouse's death.

171. (c) Mrs. Felton qualifies as a head of household because she is both unmarried and maintains a household for her unmarried child. The unmarried child for whom she maintains a household need not qualify as her dependent in order for Mrs. Felton to claim the head-of-household status. Answer (b) is incorrect because in order for Mrs. Felton to qualify, her son must qualify as a dependent, which he does not. Although Mrs. Felton would have qualified as married filing jointly, answer (d), in 2001 (the year of her husband's death), the problem requirement is her 2002 status. Answer (a), single, is incorrect because although the widow is single, head of household filing status provides for lower tax rates.

172. (c) The requirement is to determine the 2002 income tax for Poole, an unmarried taxpayer in the 15% bracket with $20,000 of adjusted gross income. To determine Poole's taxable income, his adjusted gross income must be reduced by the greater of his itemized deductions or a standard deduction, and a personal exemption. Since Poole's medical expenses of $6,500 are deductible to the extent in excess of 7.5% of his AGI of $20,000, his itemized deductions of $5,000 exceed his available standard deduction of $4,700. Poole's tax computation is as follows:

Adjusted gross income		$20,000
Less:		
Itemized deductions	$5,000	
Personal exemption	3,000	8,000
Taxable income		$12,000
Tax rate		x 15%
Income tax		$ 1,800

V.D.   Alternative Minimum Tax (AMT)

173. (d)   The requirement is to determine the itemized deduction that is deductible when computing an individual's alternative minimum tax (AMT). For purposes of computing an individual's AMT, no deduction is allowed for personal, state, and local income taxes, and miscellaneous itemized deductions subject to the 2% of adjusted gross income threshold. Similarly, no deduction is allowed for home mortgage interest if the loan proceeds were not used to buy, build, or substantially improve the home.

174. (a)   The requirement is to determine the amount of tax preferences and adjustments that must be included in the computation of Randy's alternative minimum tax. The tax preferences include the $600 of excess depreciation on real property placed in service prior to 1987, and the $400 of tax-exempt interest on private activity bonds. These must be added to regular taxable income in arriving at alternative minimum taxable income (AMTI). The adjustments include the $3,000 personal exemption and $1,500 of state income taxes that are deductible in computing regular taxable income but are not deductible in computing AMTI.

175. (d)   The requirement is to determine the amount of Karen's unused alternative minimum tax credit that will carry over to 2003. The amount of alternative minimum tax paid by an individual that is attributable to timing preferences and adjustments is allowed as a tax credit (i.e., minimum tax credit) that can be applied against regular tax liability in future years. The minimum tax credit is computed as the excess of the AMT actually paid over the AMT that would have been paid if AMTI included only exclusion preferences and adjustments (e.g., disallowed itemized deductions, excess percentage depletion, tax-exempt private activity bond interest). Since the minimum tax credit can only be used to reduce future regular tax liability, the credit can only reduce regular tax liability to the point at which it equals the taxpayer's tentative minimum tax. In this case, Karen's payment of $20,000 of alternative minimum tax in 2001 generates a minimum tax credit of $20,000 – $9,000 = $11,000 which is carried forward to 2002. Since Karen's 2002 regular tax liability of $50,000 exceeded her tentative minimum tax of $45,000, $5,000 of Karen's minimum tax credit would be used to reduce her 2002 tax liability to $45,000. Therefore, $11,000 – $5,000 = $6,000 of unused minimum tax credit would carry over to 2003.

176. (c)   The requirement is to determine the amount that Mills should report as alternative minimum taxable income (AMTI) before the AMT exemption. Certain itemized deductions, although allowed for regular tax purposes, are not deductible in computing an individual's AMTI. As a result, no AMT deduction is allowed for state, local, and foreign income taxes, real and personal property taxes, and miscellaneous itemized deductions subject to the 2% of AGI floor. Also, the deduction for medical expenses is computed using a 10% floor (instead of the 7.5% floor used for regular tax), and no deduction is allowed for qualified residence interest

if the mortgage proceeds were **not** used to buy, build, or substantially improve the taxpayer's principal residence or a second home. Additionally, no AMT deduction is allowed for personal exemptions and the standard deduction.

Here, Mills' $5,000 of state and local income taxes and $2,000 of miscellaneous itemized deductions that were deducted for regular tax purposes must be added back to his $70,000 of regular taxable income before personal exemption to arrive at Mills' AMTI before AMT exemption of ($70,000 + $5,000 + $2,000)= $77,000. Note that no adjustment was necessary for the mortgage interest because the mortgage loan was used to acquire his residence.

177. (c)   The requirement is to determine whether a net capital gain and home equity interest expense are adjustments for purposes of computing the alternative minimum tax. Although an excess of net long-term capital gain over net short-term capital loss may be subject to a reduced maximum tax rate, the excess is neither a tax preference nor an adjustment in computing the alternative minimum tax. On the other hand, home equity interest expense where the home equity loan proceeds were not used to buy, build, or improve the home is an adjustment because the interest expense, although deductible for regular tax purposes, is not deductible for purposes of computing an individual's alternative minimum tax.

178. (d)   The requirement is to determine the proper treatment for the credit for prior year alternative minimum tax (AMT). The amount of AMT paid by an individual taxpayer that is attributable to timing differences can be carried forward indefinitely as a minimum tax credit to offset the individual's future regular tax liability (not future AMT liability). The amount of AMT credit to be carried forward is the excess of the AMT actually paid over the AMT that would have been paid if AMTI included only exclusion preferences (e.g., disallowed itemized deductions, preferences for excess percentage depletion, and tax-exempt private activity bond interest).

179. (b)   The requirement is to determine the correct statement regarding the computation of the alternative minimum tax (AMT). A taxpayer is subject to the AMT only if the taxpayer's tentative AMT exceeds the taxpayer's regular tax. Thus, the alternative minimum tax is computed as the excess of the tentative AMT over the regular tax.

V.E.   Other Taxes

180. (b)   The requirement is to determine the amount of net self-employment earnings that would be multiplied by the self-employment tax rate to compute Diamond's self-employment tax for 2002. Since self-employment earnings generally represent earnings derived from a trade or business carried on as a sole proprietor, the $10,000 of interest income from personal investments would be excluded from the computation. On the other hand, a self-employed taxpayer is allowed a deemed deduction equal to 7.65% of self-employment earnings in computing the amount of net earnings upon which the tax is based. The purpose of this deemed deduction is to reflect the fact that employees do not pay FICA tax on the corresponding 7.65% FICA tax paid by their employers.

Gross receipts from business	$150,000
Cost of goods sold	(80,000)
Operating expenses	(40,000)
Self-employment earnings	$ 30,000
Less deemed deduction (100%- 7.65%)	x 92.35%
Net earnings to be multiplied by self-employment tax rate	$ 27,705

181. (c) The requirement is to determine the amount of Freeman's income that is subject to self-employment tax. The self-employment tax is imposed on self-employment income to provide Social Security and Medicare benefits for self-employed individuals. Self-employment income includes an individual's net earnings from a trade or business carried on as sole proprietor or as an independent contractor. The term also includes a partner's distributive share of partnership ordinary income or loss from trade or business activities, as well as guaranteed payments received by a partner for services rendered to a partnership. Self-employment income excludes gains and losses from the disposition of property used in a trade or business, as well as a shareholder's share of ordinary income from an S corporation

182. (a) The requirement is to determine the amount of Rich's net self-employment income. Income from self-employment generally includes all items of business income less business deductions. Excluded from the computation would be estimated income taxes on self-employment income, charitable contributions, investment income, and gains and losses on the disposition of property used in a trade or business. An individual's charitable contributions can only be deducted as an itemized deduction. Rich's net self-employment income would be

Business receipts	$20,000
Air conditioning parts	(2,500)
Yellow Pages listing	(2,000)
Business telephone calls	(400)
	$15,100

183. (c) The requirement is to determine the correct statement regarding the self-employment tax. The self-employment tax is imposed at a rate of 15.3% on individuals who work for themselves (e.g., sole proprietor, independent contractor, partner). One-half of an individual's self-employment tax is deductible from gross income in arriving at adjusted gross income.

184. (c) The requirement is to determine the correct statement with regard to social security tax (FICA) withheld in an amount greater than the maximum for a particular year. If an individual works for more than one employer, and combined wages exceed the maximum used for FICA purposes, too much FICA tax will be withheld. In such case, since the excess results from correct withholding by two or more employers, the excess should be claimed as a credit against income tax. Answer (a) is incorrect because the excess cannot be used as an itemized deduction. Answer (b) is incorrect because if employers withhold correctly, no reimbursement can be obtained from the employers. Answer (d) is incorrect because if the excess FICA tax withheld results from incorrect withholding by any one employer, the employer must reimburse the excess and it cannot be claimed as a credit against tax.

185. (b) The requirement is to determine Berger's gross income from self-employment for 2002. Self-employment income represents the net earnings of an individual from a

trade or business carried on as a proprietor or partner, or from rendering services as an independent contractor. The director's fee is self-employment income since it is related to a trade or business, and Berger is not an employee. Fees received by a fiduciary (e.g., executor) are generally not related to a trade or business and not self-employment income. However, executor's fees may constitute self-employment if the executor is a professional fiduciary or carries on a trade or business in the administration of an estate.

186. (d) The requirement is to determine Smith's gross income from self-employment. Self-employment income represents the net earnings of an individual from a trade or business carried on as a sole proprietor or partner, or from rendering services as an independent contractor (i.e., not an employee). The $8,000 consulting fee and the $2,000 of director's fees are self-employment income because they are related to a trade or business and Smith is not an employee.

VI.A. General Business Credit

187. (c) The requirement is to determine which credit is not a component of the general business credit. The general business credit is a combination of several credits that provide uniform rules for current and carryback-carryover years. The general business credit is composed of the investment credit, work opportunity credit, welfare-to-work credit, alcohol fuels credit, research credit, low-income housing credit, enhanced oil recovery credit, disabled access credit, renewable electricity production credit, empowerment zone employment credit, Indian employment credit, employer social security credit, orphan drug credit, and the new markets credit. A general business credit in excess of the limitation amount is carried back one year and forward twenty years to offset tax liability in those years.

188. (a) The requirement is to determine which tax credit is a combination of credits to provide for uniform rules for the current and carryback-carryover years. The general business credit is composed of the investment credit, work opportunity credit, welfare-to-work credit, alcohol fuels credit, research credit, low-income housing credit, enhanced oil recovery credit, disabled access credit, renewable electricity production credit, empowerment zone employment credit, Indian employment credit, employer social security credit, orphan drug credit, and the new markets credit. A general business credit in excess of the limitation amount is carried back one year and forward twenty years to offset tax liability in those years.

VI.K. Credit for the Elderly and the Disabled

189. (b) The requirement is to determine the amount that can be claimed as a credit for the elderly. The amount of credit (limited to tax liability) is 15% of an initial amount reduced by social security and 50% of AGI in excess of $10,000. Here, the credit is the lesser of (1) the taxpayers' tax liability of $60, or (2) 15% [$7,500 – $3,000 – (.50)($15,600 – $10,000)] = $255.

VI.L. Child Care Credit

190. (c) The requirement is to compute Nora's child care credit for 2002. Since she has two dependent preschool children, all $3,000 paid for child care qualifies for the credit. The credit is 30% of qualified expenses, but is reduced by one percentage point for each $2,000 (or fraction thereof) of AGI over $10,000 down to a minimum of 20%. Since Nora's AGI is $29,000, her credit is 20% x $3,000 = $600.

191. (b)   The requirement is to determine the amount of the child care credit allowable to the Jasons. The credit is from 20% to 30% of certain dependent care expenses limited to the lesser of (1) $2,400 for one qualifying individual, $4,800 for two or more; (2) taxpayer's earned income, or spouse's if smaller; or (3) actual expenses. The $1,500 paid to the Union Day Care Center qualifies, as does the $1,000 paid to Wilma Jason. Payments to relatives qualify if the relative is not a dependent of the taxpayer. Since Robert and Mary Jason only claimed three exemptions, Wilma was not their dependent. The $500 paid to Acme Home Cleaning Service does not qualify since it is *completely* unrelated to the care of their child. To qualify, expenses must be at least partly for the care of a qualifying individual. Since qualifying expenses exceed $2,400, the Jasons' credit is 20% x $2,400 = $480.

192. (b)   The requirement is to determine the qualifications for the child care credit that at least one spouse must satisfy on a joint return. The child care credit is a percentage of the amount paid for qualifying household and dependent care expenses incurred to enable an individual to be gainfully employed or look for work. To qualify for the child care credit on a joint return, at least one spouse must be gainfully employed or be looking for work when the related expenses are incurred. Note that it is not required that at least one spouse be gainfully employed, but only needs to be looking for work when the expenses are incurred. Additionally, at least one spouse must have earned income during the year. However, there is no limit as to the maximum amount of earned income or adjusted gross income reported on the joint return.

VI.M. Foreign Tax Credit

193. (a)   The requirement is to determine which factor(s) may affect the amount of Sunex's foreign tax credit available in its current year corporate income tax return. Since US taxpayers are subject to US income tax on their worldwide income, they are allowed a credit for the income taxes paid to foreign countries. The applicable foreign tax rate will affect the amount of foreign taxes paid, and thereby affect the amount available as a foreign tax credit. Additionally, since the amount of credit that can be currently used cannot exceed the amount of US tax attributable to the foreign-source income, the income source will affect the amount of available foreign tax credit for the current year if the limitation based on the amount of US tax is applicable.

194. (b)   The requirement is to determine the amount of foreign tax credit that Wald Corp. may claim for 2002. Since US taxpayers are subject to US income tax on their worldwide income, they are allowed a credit for the income taxes paid to foreign countries. However, the amount of credit that can be currently used cannot exceed the amount of US tax that is attributable to the foreign income. This foreign tax credit limitation can be expressed as follows:

$$\frac{\text{Foreign TI}}{\text{Worldwide TI}} \times (\text{US tax}) = \text{Foreign tax credit limitation}$$

One limitation must be computed for foreign source passive income (e.g., interest, dividends, royalties, rents, annuities), with a separate limitation computed for all other foreign source taxable income.

In this case, the foreign income taxes paid on other foreign source taxable income of $27,000 is fully usable as a credit in 2002 because it is less than the applicable limitation amount (i.e., the amount of US tax attributable to the income).

$$\frac{\$90,000}{\$300,000} \times (\$96,000) = \$28,800$$

On the other hand, the credit for the $12,000 of foreign income taxes paid on non-business-related interest is limited to the amount of US tax attributable to the foreign interest income, $9,600.

$$\frac{\$30,000}{\$300,000} \times (\$96,000) = \$9,600$$

Thus, Wald Corp.'s foreign tax credit for 2002 totals $27,000 + $9,600 = $36,600. The $12,000 – $9,600 = $2,400 of unused foreign tax credit resulting from the application of the limitation on foreign taxes attributable to foreign source interest income can be carried back two years and forward five years to offset US income tax in those years.

195. (a)   The requirement is to determine the correct statement regarding a corporation's foreign income taxes. Foreign income taxes paid by a corporation may be claimed either as a credit or as a deduction, at the option of the corporation.

VI.N. Earned Income Credit

196. (c)   The requirement is to determine the credit that can result in a refund even if an individual had no income tax liability. The earned income credit is a refundable credit and can result in a refund even if the individual had no tax withheld from wages.

197. (a)   The requirement is to choose the correct statement regarding Kent's earned income credit. The earned income credit could result in a refund even if Kent had no tax withheld from wages. Since the credit is refundable, answer (c) is incorrect because there will never be any unused credit to carry back or forward. Answer (d) is incorrect because the credit is a direct subtraction from the computed tax.

198. (c)   The requirement is to determine the correct statement regarding the earned income credit. The earned income credit is a refundable credit and can result in a refund even if the individual had no tax withheld from wages. To qualify, an individual must have earned income, but the amount of earned income does not have to equal adjusted gross income. For purposes of the credit, earned income excludes workers' compensation benefits. Additionally, the credit is available only if the tax return covers a full twelve-month period.

199. (b)   The requirement is to determine the tax credit that cannot be claimed by a corporation. The foreign tax credit, alternative fuel production credit, and general business credit may be claimed by a corporation. The earned income credit cannot be claimed by a corporation; it is available only to individuals.

VI.O. Credit for Adoption Expenses

200. (c) The requirement is to determine the correct statement regarding the credit for adoption expenses. The adoption expenses credit is a nonrefundable credit for up to $10,000 of expenses (including special needs children) incurred to adopt an eligible child. An eligible child is one who is under eighteen years of age at time of adoption, or physically or mentally incapable of self-care. Qualified adoption expenses are taken as a credit in the year the adoption becomes final.

VI.P. Child Tax Credit

201. (c) The requirement is to determine the incorrect statement concerning the child tax credit. Individual taxpayers are permitted to take a tax credit based solely on the number of their dependent children under age seventeen. The amount of the credit is $600 per qualifying child, but is subject to reduction if adjusted gross income exceeds certain income levels. A qualifying child must be a US citizen or resident.

VI.Q. Hope Scholarship Credit

202. (c) The requirement is to determine the incorrect statement concerning the Hope scholarship credit. The Hope scholarship credit provides for a maximum credit of $1,500 per year (100% of the first $1,000, plus 50% of the next $1,000 of tuition expenses) for the first two years of postsecondary education. The credit is available on a per student basis and covers tuition paid for the taxpayer, spouse, and dependents. To be eligible, the student must be enrolled on at least a part-time basis for one academic period during the year. If a parent claims a child as a dependent, only the parent can claim the credit and any qualified expenses paid by the child are deemed paid by the parent.

VI.R. Lifetime Learning Credit

203. (d) The requirement is to determine the incorrect statement concerning the lifetime learning credit. The lifetime learning credit provides a credit of 20% of up to $5,000 of tuition and fees paid by a taxpayer for one or more students for graduate and undergraduate courses at an eligible educational institution. The credit may be claimed for an unlimited number of years, is available on a per taxpayer basis, and covers tuition paid for the taxpayer, spouse, and dependents.

VI.S. Estimated Tax Payments

204. (a) The requirement is to determine which statement(s) describe how Baker may avoid the penalty for the underpayment of estimated tax for the 2002 tax year. An individual whose regular and alternative minimum tax liability is not sufficiently covered by withholding from wages must pay estimated tax in quarterly installments or be subject to penalty. Individuals will incur no underpayment penalty for 2002 if the amount of tax withheld plus estimated payments are at least equal to the lesser of (1) 90% of the current year's tax; (2) 100% of the prior year's tax; or (3) 90% of the tax determined by annualizing current year taxable income through each quarter. However, note that for 2002, high-income individuals (i.e., individuals whose adjusted gross income for the preceding year exceeds $150,000) must use 112% (instead of 100%) if they wish to base their estimated tax payments on their prior year's tax liability.

205. (a) The requirement is to determine what amount would be subject to penalty for the underpayment of estimated taxes. A taxpayer will be subject to an underpayment of estimated tax penalty if the taxpayer did not pay enough tax either through withholding or by estimated tax payments. For 2001, there will be no penalty if the total tax shown on the return less the amount paid through withholding (including excess social security tax withholding) is less than $1,000. Additionally, for 2001, individuals will incur no penalty if the amount of tax withheld plus estimated payments are at least equal to the lesser of (1) 90% of the current year's tax (determined on the basis of actual income or annualized income), or (2) 100% of the prior year's tax. In this case, since the tax shown on Krete's return ($16,500) less the tax paid through withholding ($16,000) was less than $1,000, there will be no penalty for the underpayment of estimated taxes.

VII. Filing Requirements

206. (d) The requirement is to determine the original due date for a decedent's federal income tax return. The final return of a decedent is due on the same date the decedent's return would have been due had death not occurred. An individual's federal income tax return is due on the 15th day of the fourth calendar month following the close of the tax year (e.g., April 15 for a calendar-year taxpayer).

207. (a) The requirement is to determine Birch's filing requirement. A self-employed individual must file an income tax return if net earnings from self-employment are $400 or more.

VIII.B. Assessments

208. (c) The requirement is to determine the date on which the statute of limitations begins for Jackson Corp.'s 2001 tax return. Generally, any tax that is imposed must be assessed within three years of the filing of the return, or if later, the due date of the return. Since Jackson Corp.'s 2001 return was filed on March 13, 2002, and the return was due on March 15, 2002, the statute of limitations expires on March 15, 2005. This means that the statute of limitations begins on March 16, 2002.

209. (c) The requirement is to determine the latest date that the IRS can assert a notice of deficiency for a 2001 calendar-year return if the taxpayer neither committed fraud nor omitted amounts in excess of 25% of gross income. The normal period for assessment is the later of three years after a return is filed, or three years after the due date of the return. Since the 2001 calendar-year return was filed on March 20, 2002, and was due on April 15, 2002, the IRS must assert a deficiency no later than April 15, 2005.

210. (d) A six-year statute of limitations applies if gross income omitted from the return exceeds 25% of the gross income reported on the return. For this purpose, gross income of a business includes total gross receipts before subtracting cost of goods sold and deductions. Thus, a six-year statute of limitations will apply to Thompson if he omitted from gross income an amount in excess of ($400,000 + $36,000) x 25% = $109,000.

211. (d)   The requirement is to determine the maximum period during which the IRS can issue a notice of deficiency if the gross income omitted from a taxpayer's return exceeds 25% of the gross income reported on the return. A **six-year** statute of limitations applies if gross income omitted from the return exceeds 25% of the gross income reported on the return. Additionally, a tax return filed **before** its due date is treated as filed **on** its due date. Thus, if a return is filed before its due date, and the gross income omitted from the return exceeds 25% of the gross income reported on the return, the IRS has **six** years from the due date of the return to issue a notice of deficiency.

VIII.E.   Claims for Refund

212. (c)   The requirement is to determine the form that must be filed by an individual to claim a refund of erroneously paid income taxes. Form 1040X, Amended US Individual Income Tax Return, should be used to claim a refund of erroneously paid income taxes. Form 843 should be used to file a refund claim for taxes other than income taxes. Form 1139 may be used by a corporation to file for a tentative adjustment or refund of taxes when an overpayment of taxes for a prior year results from the carryback of a current year's net operating loss or net capital loss. Form 1045 may be used by taxpayers other than corporations to apply for similar adjustments.

213. (a)   The requirement is to determine the date by which a refund claim must be filed if an individual paid income tax during 2002 but did not file a tax return. An individual must file a claim for refund within three years from the date a return was filed, or two years from the date of payment of tax, whichever is later. If no return was filed, the claim for refund must be filed within two years from the date that the tax was paid.

214. (c)   The requirement is to determine the date by which a taxpayer must file an amended return to claim a refund of tax paid on a calendar-year 2000 return. A taxpayer must file an amended return to claim a refund within three years from the date a return was filed, or two years from the date of payment of tax, whichever is later. If a return is filed before its due date, it is treated as filed on its due date. Thus, the taxpayer's 2000 calendar-year return that was filed on March 15, 2001, is treated as filed on April 15, 2001. Therefore, an amended return to claim a refund must be filed not later than April 15, 2004.

215. (d)   The requirement is to determine the date by which a refund claim due to worthless security must be filed. The normal three-year statute of limitations is extended to seven years for refund claims resulting from bad debts or worthless securities. Since the securities became worthless during 2001, and Baker's 2001 return was filed on April 15, 2002, Baker's refund claim must be filed no later than April 15, 2009.

VIII.G.   Taxpayer Penalties

216. . (b)   The requirement is to determine the amount on which the penalties for late filing and late payment would be computed. The late filing and late payment penalties are based on the amount of net tax due. If a taxpayer's tax return indicated a tax liability of $50,000, and $45,000 of taxes were withheld, the late filing and late payment penalties would be based on the $5,000 of tax that is owed.

217. (c)   An accuracy-related penalty equal to 20% of the underpayment of tax may be imposed if the underpayment of tax is attributable to one or more of the following: (1) negligence or disregard of the tax rules and regulations; (2) any substantial understatement of income tax; (3) any substantial valuation overstatement; (4) any substantial overstatement of pension liabilities; or (5) any substantial gift or estate tax valuation understatement. The penalty for gift or estate tax valuation understatement may apply if the value of property on a gift or estate tax return is 50% or less of the amount determined to be correct. The penalty for a substantial income tax valuation overstatement may apply if the value (or adjusted basis) of property is 200% or more of the amount determined to be correct.

OTHER OBJECTIVE ANSWERS AND ANSWER EXPLANATIONS

Problem 1

1. **(B)** Fees received for jury duty represent compensation for services and must be included in gross income. Since there is no separate line for jury duty fees, they are taxable as other income on page 1 of Form 1040.

2. **(A)** Interest income on a mortgage loan receivable must be included in gross income and is taxable as interest income in Schedule B—Interest and Dividend Income.

3. **(D)** An interest forfeiture penalty for making an early withdrawal from a certificate of deposit is deductible on page 1 of Form 1040 to arrive at adjusted gross income.

4. **(P)** The problem indicates that Cole is a CPA reporting on the cash basis. Accounts receivable resulting from services rendered by a cash-basis taxpayer have a zero tax basis, because the income has not yet been reported. Therefore, the write-offs of zero basis uncollectible accounts receivable from Cole's accounting practice are not deductible.

5. **(P)** An educational expense that is part of a program of study that can qualify an individual for a new trade or business is not deductible. This is true even if the individual is not seeking a new job. In this case, the cost of attending a review course in preparation for the CPA examination is a nondeductible personal expense since it qualifies Cole for a new profession.

6. **(I)** Licensing and regulatory fees paid to state or local governments are an ordinary and necessary trade or business expense and are deductible by a sole proprietor on Schedule C—Profit or Loss from Business. Since Cole is a cash method taxpayor, he can deduct the fee for the biennial permit to practice when paid in 2002.

7. **(I)** All trade or business expenses of a self-employed individual are deductible on Schedule C—Profit or Loss from Business. Education must meet certain requirements before the related expenses can be deducted. Generally, deductible education expenses must not be a part of a program that will qualify the individual for a new trade or business and must (1) be required by an employer or by law to keep the individual's present position, or (2) maintain or improve skills required in the individual's present work. In this case, Cole already is a CPA and is fulfilling state CPE requirements, so his education costs of attending CPE courses are deductible in Schedule C—Profit or Loss from Business.

8. **(D)** Contributions to a self-employed individual's qualified Keogh retirement plan are deductible on page 1 of Form 1040 to arrive at adjusted gross income. The maximum deduction for contributions to a defined contribution Keogh retirement plan is limited to the lesser of $40,000, or 100 % of self-employment income.

9. **(J)** A loss sustained from a nonbusiness bad debt is always classified as a short-term capital loss. Therefore, Cole's nonbusiness bad debt is deductible in Schedule D—Capital Gains or Losses.

10. **(L)** A loss sustained on the sale of Sec. 1244 stock is generally deductible as an ordinary loss, with the amount of ordinary loss deduction limited to $50,000. On a joint return, the limit is increased to $100,000, even if the stock was owned by only one spouse. The ordinary loss resulting from the sale of Sec. 1244 stock is deductible in Form 4797—Sales of Business Property. To the extent that a loss on Sec. 1244 stock exceeds the applicable $50,000 or $100,000 limit, the loss is deductible as a capital loss in Schedule D—Capital Gains or Losses. Similarly, if Sec. 1244 stock is sold at a gain, the gain would be reported as a capital gain in Schedule D if the stock is a capital asset.

11. **(K)** Rental income and expenses related to rental property are generally reported in Schedule E. Here, the taxes paid on land owned by Cole and rented out as a parking lot are deductible in Schedule E—Supplemental Income and Loss. Schedule E also is used to report the income or loss from royalties, partnerships, S corporations, estates, and trusts.

12. **(P)** The interest paid on installment purchases of household furniture is considered personal interest and is not deductible. Personal interest is any interest that is not qualified residence interest, investment interest, passive activity interest, or business interest. Personal interest generally includes interest on car loans, interest on income tax, installment plan interest, credit card finance charges, and late payment charges by a utility.

13. **(D)** Alimony paid to a former spouse who reports the alimony as taxable income is deductible on page 1 of Form 1040 to arrive at adjusted gross income.

14. **(E)** Personal medical expenses are generally deductible as an itemized deduction subject to a 7.5% of AGI threshold for the year in which they are paid. Additionally, an individual can deduct medical expenses charged to a credit card in the year the charge is made. It makes no difference when the amount charged is actually paid. Here, Cole's personal medical expenses charged on a credit card in December 2002 but not paid until January 2003 are deductible for 2002 in Schedule A—Itemized Deductions, subject to a threshold of 7.5% of adjusted gross income.

15. **(F)** If an individual sustains a personal casualty loss, it is deductible in Schedule A—Itemized Deductions subject to a threshold of $100 and an additional threshold of 10% of adjusted gross income.

16. **(P)** State inheritance taxes paid on a bequest that was received are not deductible. Other taxes not deductible in computing an individual's federal income tax include federal estate and gift taxes, federal income taxes, and social security and other employment taxes paid by an employee.

17. **(M)** An individual can deduct foreign income taxes as an itemized deduction or can deduct foreign income taxes as a tax credit. Cole's foreign income tax withheld at source on foreign dividends received can be claimed in Form 1116—Foreign Tax Credit, or in Schedule A—Itemized Deductions, at Cole's option.

18.   (O) A self-employed individual is subject to a self-employment tax if the individual's net earnings from self-employment are at least $400.

19.   (D) An individual's self-employment tax is computed in Schedule SE and is added as an additional tax in arriving at the individual's total tax. One-half of the computed self-employment tax is allowed as a deduction in arriving at adjusted gross income. Here, one-half of Cole's self-employment tax for 2002 is deductible for 2002 on page 1 of Form 1040 to arrive at adjusted gross income, even though the tax was not paid until the return was filed in April 2003.

20.   (P) Insurance premiums paid on Cole's life are classified as a personal expense and are not deductible.

Problem 2

1.   (C) All trade or business income and deductions of a self-employed individual are reported on Schedule C—Profit or Loss from Business. Retainer fees received from clients is reported in Schedule C as trade or business income.

2.   (D) Income derived from royalties is reported in Schedule E—Supplemental Income and Loss. Schedule E also is used to report the income or loss from rental real estate, partnerships, S corporations, estates, and trusts.

3.   (E) Interest from general obligation state and local government bonds is tax-exempt and is excluded from gross income.

4.   (B) The interest income on a refund of federal income taxes must be included in gross income and is reported in Schedule B—Interest and Dividend Income. The actual refund of federal income taxes itself is excluded from gross income.

5.   (E) Life insurance proceeds paid by reason of death are generally excluded from gross income. Here, the death benefits received by Green from a term life insurance policy on the life of Green's parent are not taxable.

6.   (B) Interest income from US Treasury bonds and treasury bills must be included in gross income and is reported in Schedule B—Interest and Dividend Income.

7.   (D) A partner's share of a partnership's ordinary income that is reported to the partner on Form 1065, Schedule K-1 must be included in the partner's gross income and is reported in Schedule E—Supplemental Income and Loss.

8.   (D) The taxable income from the rental of a townhouse owned by Green must be included in gross income and is reported in Schedule E—Supplemental Income and Loss.

9.   (A) A prize won as a contestant on a TV quiz show must be included in gross income. Since there is no separate line on Form 1040 for prizes, they are taxable as other income on Form 1040.

10.   (A) Fees received for jury duty represent compensation for services and must be included in gross income. Since there is no separate line for jury duty fees, they are taxable as other income on Form 1040.

11.   (E) An investor in a mutual fund may receive several different kinds of distributions including ordinary dividends, capital gain distributions, tax-exempt interest dividends, and return of capital distributions. A mutual fund may pay tax-exempt interest dividends to its shareholders if it meets certain requirements. These dividends are paid from the tax-exempt state and local obligation interest earned by the fund and retain their tax-exempt character when reported by the shareholder. Thus, Green's dividends received from mutual funds that invest in tax-free government obligations are not taxable.

12.   (H) Qualifying medical expenses not reimbursed by insurance are deductible in Schedule A as an itemized deduction to the extent in excess of 7.5% of adjusted gross income.

13.   (O) Personal life insurance premiums paid on Green's life are classified as a personal expense and not deductible.

14.   (M) All trade or business expenses of a self-employed individual are deductible on Schedule C—Profit or Loss from Business. However, only 50% of the cost of business meals and entertainment is deductible. Therefore, Green's expenses for business-related meals where clients were present are partially deductible in Schedule C.

15.   (K) The deduction for depreciation on listed property (e.g., automobiles, cellular telephones, computers, and property used for entertainment etc.) is computed on Form 4562—Depreciation and Amortization. Since Green's personal computer was used in his business as a self-employed consultant, the amount of depreciation computed on Form 4562 is then deductible in Schedule C—Profit or Loss from Business.

16.   (L) Lodging expenses while out of town on business are an ordinary and necessary business expense and are fully deductible by a self-employed individual in Schedule C—Profit or Loss from Business.

17.   (L) The cost of subscriptions to professional journals used for business are an ordinary and necessary business expense and are fully deductible by a self-employed individual in Schedule C—Profit or Loss from Business.

18.   (G) An individual's self-employment tax is computed in Schedule SE and is added as an additional tax in arriving at the individual's total tax liability. One-half of the computed self-employment tax is then allowed as a deduction on Form 1040 in arriving at adjusted gross income.

19.   (F) Qualifying contributions to a self-employed individual's simplified employee pension plan are deductible on page 1 of Form 1040 to arrive at adjusted gross income.

20.   (K) For 2002, Sec. 179 permits a taxpayer to elect to treat up to $24,000 of the cost of qualifying depreciable personal business property as an expense rather than as a capital expenditure. In this case, Green's election to expense business equipment would be computed on Form 4562—Depreciation and Amortization, and then would be deductible in Schedule C—Profit or Loss from Business.

21. (**F**) Qualifying alimony payments made by Green to a former spouse are fully deductible on Form 1040 to arrive at adjusted gross income.

22. (**I**) The costs of subscriptions for investment publications are not related to Green's trade or business, but instead are considered expenses incurred in the production of portfolio income and are reported as miscellaneous itemized deductions in Schedule A—Itemized Deductions. These investment expenses are deductible to the extent that the aggregate of expenses in this category exceed 2% of adjusted gross income.

23. (**L**) The nature of interest expense is determined by using a tracing approach (i.e., the nature depends upon how the loan proceeds were used). Since the interest expense on Green's home-equity line of credit was for a loan to finance Green's business, the best answer is to treat the interest as a business expense fully deductible in Schedule C—Profit or Loss from Business.

24. (**M**) The interest expense on a loan for an auto used by a self-employed individual in a trade or business is deductible as a business expense. Since Green's auto was used 75% for business, only 75% of the interest expense is deductible in Schedule C—Profit or Loss from Business. The remaining 25% is considered personal interest expense and is not deductible.

25. (**O**) The loss resulting from the sale of Green's personal residence is not deductible because the property was held for personal use. Only losses due to casualty or theft are deductible for personal use property.

Problem 3

1. (**B**) Deductible medical expenses include amounts paid for the diagnosis, cure, relief, treatment or prevention of disease of the taxpayer, spouse, and dependents. The term **dependent** includes any person who qualifies as a dependency exemption, or would otherwise qualify as a dependency exemption except that the gross income and joint return tests are not met. Therefore, the medical expenses of Smith's mother-in-law are properly deductible from Smith's AGI and are not subject to the 2% limitation.

2. (**A**) Expenses attributable to property held for the production of rents or royalties are properly deductible "above the line." "Above the line" deductions are subtracted from gross income to determine adjusted gross income. Therefore, expenses incurred from a passive activity such as Smith's rental apartment building are deductible for AGI.

3. (**D**) State sales tax paid on an automobile purchased for personal use is not deductible. However, if the automobile had been purchased for business use, the sales tax incurred in its acquisition would be treated as part of the cost of the automobile and could be recovered through depreciation.

4. (**D**) Real estate (real property) taxes are deductible only if imposed on property owned by the taxpayer. Since Smith's mother-in-law is the legal owner of the house, Smith cannot deduct his payment of those real estate taxes.

5. (**D**) No deduction is allowed for personal interest.

6. (**D**) Personal legal expenses are not a deductible expense. Only legal counsel obtained for advice concerning tax matters or incurred in the production of income are deductible. Therefore, Smith cannot deduct the $500 incurred to prepare his will.

7. (**C**) Unreimbursed employee expenses including business meals and entertainment (subject to the 50% rule) are deductible to the extent they exceed 2% of AGI. Therefore, $375 ($750 x 50%) is deductible from AGI, subject to the 2% floor.

8. (**A**) An individual is allowed to deduct one half of the self-employment tax paid for the taxable year in the computation of AGI. Therefore, $1,500 is deductible for AGI.

9. (**A**) Contributions by self-employed individuals to a qualified retirement plan (Keogh Plan) are a deduction for AGI.

10. (**B**) Gambling losses to the extent of gambling winnings are categorized as miscellaneous deductions not subject to the 2% floor. Therefore, the $2,500 of Smith's gambling losses would be deductible in full since he properly included his $5,000 winnings in his gross income for 2002.

Problem 4

For **items 1 and 2,** candidates were asked to determine the filing status and number of exemptions for Mrs. Vick.

1. (**M,4**) Since Mr. Vick died during the year, Mrs. Vick is considered married for the entire year for filing status purposes. There would be four exemptions on the Vicks' joint return—one each for Mr. and Mrs. Vick, one for their 11-year-old daughter Joan, and one for Mrs. Vick's unmarried cousin Fran Phillips. Although Fran is treated as unrelated to the Vicks for dependency exemption purposes, Fran qualifies as a dependency exemption because the Vicks' residence was Fran's principal home for 2002.

2. (**Q,3**) Mrs. Vick will file as a "qualifying widow with dependent child" which will entitle her to use the joint return rates for 2002. This filing status is available for the two years following the year of the spouse's death if (1) the surviving spouse was eligible to file a joint return in the year of the spouse's death, (2) does not remarry before the end of the taxable year, and (3) the surviving spouse pays over 50% of the cost of maintaining a household that is the principal home for the entire year of the surviving spouse's dependent child. There will be three exemptions on the return—one for Mrs. Vick, a dependency exemption for her daughter Joan, and a dependency exemption for her cousin Fran.

For **items 3 through 9,** candidates were asked to determine the amount that is taxable and should be included in Adjusted Gross Income (AGI) on the 2002 federal income tax return filed by Mrs. Vick.

3. **($0)** State disability benefits are excluded from gross income.

4. **($400)** The $50 interest on the tax refund and $350 interest from a savings account and certificates of deposit are taxable; the $100 interest on municipal bonds is excluded from gross income.

5. **($900)** The pension benefits are fully taxable because it was paid for exclusively by Mr. Vick's employer.

6. **($0)** Property received as a gift is always excluded from gross income.

7. **($0)** The proceeds of life insurance paid because of Mr. Vick's death are excluded from gross income, without regard to the amount of premiums paid.

8. **($200)** Jury duty pay represents compensation for services and must be included in gross income.

9. **($450)** The $450 of gambling winnings must be included in gross income. Mrs. Vick's $100 of gambling losses are deductible only from AGI as a miscellaneous itemized deduction.

For **items 10 through 23,** candidates were asked to select the appropriate tax treatment for the payments made or losses incurred by Mrs. Vick for 2002.

10. **(A)** Life insurance premiums are considered a personal expense and are not deductible.

11. **(D)** An interest forfeiture penalty for making an early withdrawal from a certificate of deposit is deductible on page 1 of Form 1040 to arrive at adjusted gross income.

12. **(F)** Charitable contributions are generally deductible as an itemized deduction up to a **maximum of 50% of AGI**.

13. **(E)** Estimated state income tax payments are deductible in full as an itemized deduction on Schedule A.

14. **(E)** Real estate taxes on a principal residence are deductible in full as an itemized deduction on Schedule A.

15. **(A)** A family car is a personal use asset and a loss from its sale is not deductible. The only type of loss that can be deducted on a personal use asset is a casualty or theft loss.

16. **(B)** A capital expenditure made for medical reasons that improves a residence is deductible as a medical expense to the extent that the expenditure exceeds the increase in value of the residence. As a medical expense, the excess expenditure is deductible as an itemized deduction on Schedule A subject to a 7.5% of AGI threshold.

17. **(B)** Health insurance premiums qualify as a medical expense and are deductible as an itemized deduction on Schedule A subject to a 7.5% of AGI threshold.

18. **(C)** Tax return preparation fees are deductible as an itemized deduction on Schedule A subject to a 2% of AGI threshold.

19. **(E)** Points paid to refinance a mortgage are deductible as interest expense over the term of the loan. Interest expense on a personal residence is deductible as an itemized deduction on Schedule A.

20. **(D)** One-half of a self-employed taxpayer's self-employment tax is deductible on page 1 of Form 1040 to arrive at AGI.

21. **(E)** Gambling losses are deductible as a miscellaneous itemized deduction on Schedule A to the extent that the taxpayer's gambling winnings are included in gross income. Since Mrs. Vick reported $450 of gambling winnings, her $100 of gambling losses are deductible.

22. **(C)** Unreimbursed employee expenses (including union dues) are generally deductible as miscellaneous itemized deductions on Schedule A subject to a 2% of AGI threshold.

23. **(A)** A payment of federal income tax is not deductible in computing a taxpayer's taxable income.

For **items 24 through 31,** candidates were asked to determine whether each statement regarding the Vicks' 2002 income tax return is true (T) or false (F).

24. **(F)** Funeral expenses are not deductible for federal income tax purposes.

25. **(T)** Income in respect of a decedent must be included in gross income by its recipient, and is also includible in the decedent's gross estate and subject to the federal estate tax. As a result, any estate tax attributable to its inclusion in the decedent's gross estate can be deducted by the income recipient as a miscellaneous itemized deduction not subject to the 2% of AGI threshold.

26. **(F)** A casualty loss deduction on property used in a trade or business of a self-employed taxpayer is deductible from gross income in arriving at AGI.

27. **(F)** The credit for the elderly and disabled is 15% of an initial amount reduced by certain amounts excluded from gross income and AGI in excess of specified levels. In the case of taxpayers under age 65, the initial amount is limited to disability income. Since Mr. Vick's initial amount (disability income of $1,500) would be reduced by 50% of AGI in excess of $10,000, no credit for the elderly and disabled would be available to the Vicks for 2002.

28. **(T)** A tax return preparer must furnish a copy of the return to the taxpayer no later than when the original return is presented to the taxpayer for signing.

29. **(F)** Mr. Vick's death does not affect the income phase out of the earned income credit.

30. **(F)** Mr. Vick's accrued vacation pay is considered income in respect of a decedent and is includible in income by Mrs. Vick when received.

31. **(F)** The amount of alternative minimum tax paid that is attributable to deferral adjustments and preferences results in a minimum tax credit that can be carried forward indefinitely to offset future regular income tax.

Problem 5

For **items 1 through 10,** candidates were required to determine the amount of income or loss, if any, that should be included on page one of the Moores' 2002 Form 1040.

1. **($3,000)** The Moores have a net capital loss of $6,000, of which $3,000 can be currently deducted, with the remaining $3,000 carried forward as a LTCL.

2. **($0)** Joan received the land as a gift, and her basis for gain is the land's adjusted basis of $60,000, while her basis for loss is the land's $50,000 fair market value on date of gift. Joan recognizes no gain or loss on the sale because she sold the land for $56,000 and the use of her basis for gain ($60,000) does not result in a gain, and the use of her basis for loss ($50,000) does not result in a loss.

3. **($0)** The security deposit is not treated as rent and only will be included in gross income when not returned to the tenant.

4. **($55,000)** Tom's compensation consists of the wages of $53,000 plus the $2,000 value of group-term life insurance coverage in excess of $50,000.

5. **($1,250)** Since the Moores' itemized deductions exceeded their available standard deduction by $1,450, all $1,250 of the state income tax refund must be included in gross income for 2002 because its deduction in 2001 reduced the Moores' federal income tax.

6. **($1,300)** Unemployment compensation is fully includible in gross income.

7. **($2,500)** The net rental income is computed on Schedule E and reported on page 1 of Form 1040.

8. **($900)** Although generally nontaxable, a stock dividend will be taxable if any shareholder can elect to receive the distribution in either stock or in property. The amount of dividend is equal to the stock's $900 fair market value on date of distribution.

9. **($3,500)** The $5,000 employee death benefit exclusion was repealed for decedents dying after August 20, 1996.

10. **($5,000)** The accrued interest on redeemed Series EE US savings bonds can be excluded from gross income to the extent that the aggregate redemption proceeds (principal plus interest) are used to finance the higher education expenses (tuition and fees) of the taxpayer, taxpayer's spouse, or dependents. Here, there is no interest exclusion available for Tom because the proceeds were used to pay for Laura's tuition, and Laura does not qualify as Tom's dependent.

For **item 11,** candidates were required to determine the amount of the adjustment, if any, to arrive at the Moores' adjusted gross income (AGI).

11. **($8,000)** The alimony is deductible in arriving at AGI, but child support is not deductible.

For the events described in **items 12 through 23,** candidates were required to select the appropriate tax treatment.

12. **(A)** No loss is deductible if stock is sold at a loss and within thirty days before or after the sale, substantially identical stock in the same corporation is purchased. Here, the loss on the March 23 sale of 50 shares of Zip stock cannot be recognized because Tom repurchased fifty shares of Zip stock on April 15. The $1,200 loss not recognized is added to the basis of the newly acquired stock.

13. **(B)** Personal property taxes based on value are fully deductible as an itemized deduction.

14. **(D)** The fair market value of used clothing donated to a qualified charitable organization is deductible as an itemized deduction subject to a 50% of AGI limitation.

15. **(A)** Premiums on insurance against the loss of earnings in the event of disability are a nondeductible personal expense.

16. **(F)** Since Tom is a CPA working as an employee, the unreimbursed cost of subscriptions to accounting journals is deductible as an itemized deduction subject to a threshold of 2% of AGI.

17. **(B)** Interest on home-equity indebtedness of up to $100,000 is fully deductible as an itemized deduction regardless of how the proceeds of the loan were used.

18. **(C)** The unreimbursed cost of prescriptions qualify as a medical expense deductible as an itemized deduction subject to a threshold of 7.5% of AGI.

19. **(A)** Funeral expenses are a nondeductible personal expense.

20. **(E)** A theft loss on personal use property is deductible as an itemized deduction subject to a $100 floor and a threshold of 10% of AGI.

21. **(A)** A loss resulting from the sale of personal use property is not deductible.

22. **(B)** Interest on acquisition indebtedness of up to $1 million is fully deductible as an itemized deduction if the mortgage is secured by the taxpayer's principal or second residence.

23. **(A)** No charitable deduction is allowable for the value of a taxpayer's services performed for a charitable organization.

For the events described in items **24 through 29,** candidates were required to indicate if the statement is true (T) or false (F) regarding the Moores' 2002 tax return.

24. **(F)** For 2002, an individual whose AGI exceeds a threshold amount of $137,300 is required to reduce the amount of allowable itemized deductions by 3% of the excess over the threshold amount. All itemized deductions are subject to reduction except for medical expenses, investment interest, casualty losses, and gambling losses.

25. **(T)** Although a 7.5% threshold applies for regular tax purposes, the threshold is increased to 10% for alternative minimum tax purposes.

26. **(T)** Personal exemptions and the standard deduction are not permitted in computing an individual's alternative minimum tax.

27. **(T)** Individuals are generally not subject to an underpayment penalty if the amount of tax withheld plus estimated tax payments are at least equal to the amount of tax shown on the prior year's return.

28. **(T)** Generally a 10% penalty tax is imposed on an IRA withdrawal made before an individual reaches age 59 1/2 regardless of the use of the withdrawal. However, individuals may qualify for penalty-free early withdrawals from IRAs if the distributions are used to pay certain medical expenses or medical insurance premiums.

29. **(F)** A reduced earned income credit is available to low-income individuals without a qualifying child, but is phased out by earned income and AGI in excess of specified levels, and is completely eliminated if earned income or AGI exceeds $12,060.

Problem 6

For **items 1 through 9,** candidates were asked to select the appropriate tax treatment from a list of tax treatments.

1. **(B)** Interest expense on home equity indebtedness is deductible on up to $100,000 of home equity loans secured by a first or second residence regardless of how the loan proceeds were used.

2. **(C)** Contributions in excess of applicable percentage limitations can be carried forward for up to five tax years. Here, the $30,000 of charitable contribution carryover from 2001 is deductible as an itemized deduction for 2002 subject to a limitation of 50% of AGI.

3. **(B)** Investment interest expense is deductible as an itemized deduction to the extent of net investment income. Since Oate's investment interest expense did not exceed her net investment income, it is deductible in full.

4. **(A)** Gambling losses (including lottery ticket losses) are deductible as an itemized deduction to the extent of the gambling winnings included in gross income. Since Oate had no gambling winnings, the losses are not deductible.

5. **(B)** State, local, or foreign real estate taxes imposed on the taxpayer for property held for personal use are fully deductible as an itemized deduction.

6. **(A)** A premium for a homeowner's insurance policy on a principal residence is a nondeductible personal expense.

7. **(G)** Payments to an unrelated babysitter to care for her child while Oate worked would qualify for the child and dependent care credit. Generally, the credit may vary from 20% to 30% of up to $2,400 ($4,800 for two or more qualifying individuals) of qualifying household and dependent care expenses incurred to enable the taxpayer to be gainfully employed or look for work.

8. **(B)** Interest expense on acquisition indebtedness is deductible on up to $1 million of loans secured by the residence if such loans were used to acquire, construct, or substantially improve a principal residence or a second residence.

9. **(F)** An expense incurred in the production of rental income (e.g., interest, taxes, depreciation, insurance, utilities) are deductible on Schedule E and are included in the computation of net rental income or loss.

For **items 10 through 19,** candidates were asked to select the correct amount of income, loss, or adjustment to income that should be recognized on page 1 of the Cumacks' 2002 Form 1040 to arrive at the adjusted gross income for each separate transaction.

10. **($0)** Amounts received as a gift are fully excluded from gross income.

11. **($2,000)** The maximum deduction for contributions to a traditional IRA by an individual at least age 50 is the lesser of $3,500, or 100% of compensation for 2002. Since the Cumacks were not active participants in an employer's qualified pension or annuity plan, there is no phaseout of the maximum deduction based on AGI.

12. **($0)** Since federal income taxes are not deductible in computing a taxpayer's federal income tax liability, a refund of federal income taxes is excluded from gross income.

13. **($4,000)** Guaranteed payments are partnership payments to partners for services rendered or for the use of capital without regard to partnership income. A guaranteed payment is deductible by the partnership, and the receipt of a guaranteed payment must be included in the partner's gross income, and is reported as self-employment income in the computation of the partner's self-employment tax.

14. **($0)** The proceeds of life insurance policies paid by reason of death of the insured are generally excluded from the beneficiary's gross income.

15. **($2,000)** An employer's payment of the cost of the first $50,000 of coverage for group-term life insurance can be excluded from an employee's gross income. Since Dale's employer provided group-term insurance of $450,000, and the cost of coverage was $5 per $1,000 of coverage, $5 x 400 = $2,000, must be included in Dale's gross income.

16. **($5,000)** Gambling winnings must be included in gross income. Gambling losses cannot be offset against gambling winnings, but instead are deducted from AGI as a miscellaneous itemized deduction limited in amount to the gambling winnings included in gross income.

17. **($1,000)** Although a federal income tax refund can be excluded from gross income, interest on the refund must be included in gross income.

18. **($0)** Up to $250,000 of gain can be excluded from gross income if an individual owned and occupied a residence as a principal residence for an aggregate of at least two of the five years preceding sale. The excludable gain is increased to $500,000 for married individuals filing jointly if either spouse meets the ownership requirement, and both spouses meet the use requirement.

19. **($0)** Stock dividends are generally excluded from gross income because a shareholder's relative interest in earnings and assets is unaffected.

For **item 20,** candidates were asked to determine whether the Cumacks overstated, understated, or correctly determined the number of personal and dependency exemptions.

20. **(O)** To qualify as a dependency exemption, a dependent must be a US citizen or resident of the US, Canada, or Mexico. Since Dale's father, Jacques, is both a French citizen and French resident, he does not qualify as a dependency exemption even though the Cumacks provided all of his support.

TRANSACTIONS IN PROPERTY

A. Sales and Other Dispositions

A sale or other disposition is a transaction that generally gives rise to the recognition of gain or loss. Gains or losses may be categorized as ordinary or capital. If an exchange is nontaxable, the recognition of gain or loss is generally deferred until a later sale of the newly acquired property. This is accomplished by giving the property received the basis of the old property exchanged.

1. The **basis of property** to determine gain or loss is generally its cost or purchase price.

   a. The **cost** of property is the amount paid for it in cash or the FMV of other property, plus expenses connected with the purchase such as abstract of title fees, installation of utility services, legal fees (including title search, contract, and deed fees), recording fees, surveys, transfer taxes, owner's title insurance, and any amounts the seller owes that the buyer agrees to pay (e.g., back taxes and interest, recording or mortgage fees, charges for improvements or repairs, sales commissions).

   b. If property is acquired subject to a debt, or the purchaser assumes a debt, this debt is also included in cost.

   EXAMPLE: Susan purchased a parcel of land by paying cash of $30,000 and assuming a mortgage of $60,000. She also paid $400 for a title insurance policy on the land. Susan's basis for the land is $90,400.

   c. If **acquired by gift**, the basis for gain is the basis of the donor (transferred basis) increased by any gift tax paid attributable to the net appreciation in the value of the gift.

      (1) Basis for loss is lesser of gain basis (above), or FMV on date of gift.
      (2) Because of this rule, no gain or loss is recognized when use of the basis for computing loss results in a gain, and use of the basis for computing gain results in a loss.

      EXAMPLE: Jill received a boat from her father as a gift. Father's adjusted basis was $10,000 and FMV was $8,000 at date of gift. Jill's basis for gain is $10,000, while her basis for loss is $8,000. If Jill later sells the boat for $9,200, no gain or loss will be recognized.

      (3) The increase in basis for gift tax paid is limited to the amount (not to exceed the gift tax paid) that bears the same ratio to the amount of gift tax paid as the net appreciation in value of the gift bears to the amount of the gift.

         (a) The amount of gift is reduced by any portion of the $11,000 annual exclusion allowable with respect to the gift.
         (b) Where more than one gift of a present interest is made to the same donee during a calendar year, the $11,000 exclusion is applied to gifts in chronological order.

      EXAMPLE: Tom received a gift of property with a FMV of $100,001 and an adjusted basis of $71,000. The donor paid a gift tax of $18,000 on the transfer. Tom's basis for the property would be $77,000 determined as follows:

      $$\$71,000 \text{ basis} + \left[\$18,000 \text{ gift tax} \times \frac{(\$100,000 \ FMV - \$70,000 \ basis)}{(\$100,000 \ FMV - \$10,000 \ exclusion)} \right] = \$77,000$$

   d. If **acquired from decedent**, basis is property's FMV on date of decedent's death, or alternate valuation date (generally six months after death).

      (1) Use FMV on date of disposition if alternate valuation is elected and property is distributed, sold, or otherwise disposed of during six-month period following death.

      EXAMPLE: Ann received 100 shares of stock as an inheritance from her uncle Henry, who died January 20, 2002. The stock had a FMV of $40,000 on January 20, and a FMV of $30,000 on July 20, 2002. The stock's FMV was $34,000 on June 15, 2002, the date the stock was distributed to Ann.

      If the alternate valuation is not elected, or no estate tax return is filed, Ann's basis for the stock is its FMV of $40,000 on the date of Henry's death. If the alternate valuation is elected, Ann's basis will be the stock's $34,000 FMV on June 15 (the date of distribution) since the stock was distributed to Ann within six months after the decedent's death.

      (2) FMV rule not applicable to appreciated property acquired by the decedent by gift within one year before death if such property then passes from the donee-decedent to the original donor or donor's spouse. The basis of such property to the original donor (or spouse) will be the adjusted basis of the property to the decedent immediately before death.

e. The basis of **stock received as a dividend** depends upon whether it was included in income when received.

    (1) If included in income, basis is its FMV at date of distribution.

    (2) If nontaxable when received, the basis of shareholder's original stock is allocated between the dividend stock and the original stock in proportion to their relative FMVs. The holding period of the dividend stock includes the holding period of the original stock.

       EXAMPLE: T owns 100 shares of XYZ Corp. common stock that was acquired in 1999 for $12,000. In 2002, T received a nontaxable distribution of 10 XYZ Corp. preferred shares. At date of distribution the FMV of the 100 common shares was $15,000, and the FMV of the 10 preferred shares was $5,000. The portion of the $12,000 basis allocated to the preferred and common shares would be

$$Preferred = \frac{\$5,000}{\$20,000} \ (\$12,000) \ = \ \$3,000$$

$$Common = \frac{\$15,000}{\$20,000} \ (\$12,000) \ = \ \$9,000$$

f. The basis of **stock rights** depends upon whether they were included in income when received.

    (1) If rights were nontaxable and allowed to expire, they are deemed to have no basis and no loss can be deducted.

    (2) If rights were nontaxable and exercised or sold

        (a) Basis is zero if FMV of rights is less than 15% of FMV of stock, unless taxpayer elects to allocate basis

        (b) If FMV of rights at date of receipt is at least 15% of FMV of stock, or if taxpayer elects, basis is

$$\frac{\text{FMV of rights}}{\text{FMV of rights + FMV stock}} \quad \text{x} \quad \left(\begin{array}{c} \text{Basis in} \\ \text{stock} \end{array} \right)$$

    (3) If rights were taxable and included in income, basis is their FMV at date of distribution.

g. Detailed rules for basis are included in following discussions of exchanges and involuntary conversions.

2. In a **sale**, the gain or loss is generally the difference between

    a. The cash or fair market value received, and the adjusted basis of the property sold

    b. If the property sold is mortgaged (or encumbered by any other debt) and the buyer assumes or takes the property subject to the debt

        (1) Include the amount of the debt in the amount realized because the seller is relieved of the obligation

        EXAMPLE: Property with a $10,000 mortgage, and a basis of $15,000, is sold for $10,000 cash and buyer assumes the mortgage. The amount realized is $20,000, and the gain is $5,000.

        (2) If the amount of the mortgage exceeds basis, use the same rules.

        EXAMPLE: Property with a $15,000 mortgage, and a basis of $10,000, is given away subject to the mortgage. The amount realized is $15,000, and the gain is $5,000.

    c. Casual sellers of property (as opposed to dealers) reduce selling price by any selling expenses.

3. In a **taxable exchange**, the gain or loss is the difference between the adjusted basis of the property exchanged and the FMV of the property received. The basis of property received in a taxable exchange is its FMV.

4. **Nontaxable exchanges** generally are not taxed in the current period. Questions concerning nontaxable exchanges often require a determination of the basis of property received, and the effect of boot on the recognition of gain.

    a. **Like-kind exchange**—an exchange of business or investment property for property of a like-kind

        (1) Does not apply to property held for personal use, inventory, stocks, bonds, notes, intangible evidences of ownership, and interests in a partnership

(2) Property held for business use may be exchanged for investment property or vice versa.

(3) Like-kind means "same class of property."

    (a) Real property must be exchanged for real property; personal property must be exchanged for personal property within the same General Asset Class or within the same Product Class. For example

        1] Land held for investment exchanged for apartment building

        2] Real estate exchanged for a lease on real estate to run thirty years or more

        3] Truck exchanged for a truck

    (b) Exchange of personal property for real property does not qualify.

    (c) Exchange of US real property for foreign real property does not qualify.

(4) To qualify as a like-kind exchange (1) the property to be received must be identified within forty-five days after the date on which the old property is relinquished, and (2) the exchange must be completed within 180 days after the date on which the old property is relinquished, but not later than the due date of the tax return (including extensions) for the year that the old property is relinquished.

(5) The **basis of like-kind property received** is the basis of like-kind property given.

    (a) + Gain recognized

    (b) + Basis of boot given (money or property not of a like-kind)

    (c) − Loss recognized

    (d) − FMV of boot received

(6) If unlike property (i.e., boot) is received, its basis will be its FMV on the date of the exchange.

(7) If property is exchanged solely for other like-kind property, no gain or loss is recognized. The basis of the property received is the same as the basis of the property transferred.

(8) If boot (money or property not of a like-kind) is given, no gain or loss is generally recognized. However, gain or loss is recognized if the boot given consists of property with a FMV different from its basis.

EXAMPLE: Land held for investment plus shares of stock are exchanged for investment real estate with a FMV of $13,000. The land transferred had an adjusted basis of $10,000 and FMV of $11,000; the stock had an adjusted basis of $5,000 and FMV of $2,000. A $3,000 loss is recognized on the transfer of stock. The basis of the acquired real estate is $12,000 ($10,000 + $5,000 basis of boot given − $3,000 loss recognized).

(9) **If boot is received**

    (a) Any realized gain is recognized to the extent of the lesser of (1) the realized gain, or (2) the FMV of the boot received

    (b) No loss is recognized due to the receipt of boot

EXAMPLE: Land held for investment with a basis of $10,000 was exchanged for other investment real estate with a FMV of $9,000, an automobile with a FMV of $2,000, and $1,500 in cash. The realized gain is $2,500. Even though $3,500 of "boot" was received, the recognized gain is only $2,500 (limited to the realized gain). The basis of the automobile (unlike property) is its FMV $2,000; while the basis of the real estate acquired is $9,000 ($10,000 + $2,500 gain recognized − $3,500 boot received).

(10) **Liabilities** assumed (or liabilities to which property exchanged is subject) on either or both sides of the exchange are treated as boot.

    (a) Boot received—if the liability was assumed by the other party

    (b) Boot given—if the taxpayer assumed a liability on the property acquired

    (c) If liabilities are assumed on both sides of the exchange, they are offset to determine the net amount of boot given or received.

EXAMPLE: A owns investment land with an adjusted basis of $50,000, FMV of $70,000, but which is subject to a mortgage of $15,000. B owns investment land with an adjusted basis of $60,000, FMV of $65,000, but which is subject to a mortgage of $10,000. A and B exchange real estate investments with A assuming B's $10,000 mortgage, and B assuming A's $15,000 mortgage. The computation of realized gain, recognized gain, and basis for the acquired real estate for both A and B is as follows:

	A		*B*
FMV of real estate received	$65,000		$70,000
+ Liability on old real estate assumed by other party (boot received)	15,000	*(1)*	10,000
Amount realized on the exchange	$80,000		$80,000
– Adjusted basis of old real estate transferred	–50,000		–60,000
– Liability assumed by taxpayer on new real estate (boot given)	–10,000	*(2)*	–15,000
Gain realized	$20,000		$5,000
Gain recognized (1) minus (2)	$ 5,000		$ --
Basis of old real estate transferred	$50,000		$60,000
+ Gain recognized	5,000		--
– Liability on old real estate assumed by other party (boot received)	–15,000		–10,000
Basis of new real estate acquired	$50,000		$65,000

(d) Boot given in the form of an assumption of a liability does **not** offset boot received in the form of cash or unlike property; however, boot given in the form of cash or unlike property does offset boot received in the form of a liability assumed by the other party.

EXAMPLE: Assume the same facts as above except that the mortgage on B's old real estate was $6,000, and that A paid B cash of $4,000 to make up the difference. The tax effects to A remain unchanged. However, since the $4,000 cash cannot be offset by the liability assumed by B, B must recognize a gain of $4,000, and will have a basis of $69,000 for the new real estate.

(11) If within two years after a like-kind exchange between related persons [as defined in Sec. 267(b)] either person disposes of the property received in the exchange, any gain or loss that was not recognized on the exchange must be recognized (subject to the loss limitation rules for related persons) as of the date that the property was disposed of. This gain recognition rule does not apply if the subsequent disposition was the result of the death of one of the persons, an involuntary conversion, or where neither the exchange nor the disposition had tax avoidance as one of its principal purposes.

b. **Involuntary conversions**

(1) Occur when money or other property is received for property that has been destroyed, damaged, stolen, or condemned (even if property is transferred only under threat or imminence of condemnation).

(2) If payment is received and gain is realized, taxpayer may **elect not to recognize gain** if converted property is replaced with property of similar or related use.

(a) Gain is recognized only to the extent that the amount realized exceeds the cost of the replacement.

(b) The **replacement** must be purchased within a **period** beginning with the earlier of the date of disposition or the date of threat of condemnation, and ending two years after the close of the taxable year in which gain is first **realized** (three years for condemned business or investment real property, other than inventory or property held primarily for resale).

(c) **Basis of replacement property** is the cost of the replacement decreased by any gain not recognized.

EXAMPLE: Taxpayer had unimproved real estate (with an adjusted basis of $20,000) which was condemned by the county. The county paid him $24,000 and he reinvested $21,000 in unimproved real estate. $1,000 of the $4,000 realized gain would not be recognized. His tax basis in the new real estate would be $20,000 ($21,000 cost – $1,000 deferred gain).

EXAMPLE: Assume the same facts as above except the taxpayer reinvested $25,000 in unimproved real estate. None of the $4,000 realized gain would be recognized. His basis in the new real estate would be $21,000 ($25,000 cost – $4,000 deferred gain).

(3) If property is converted directly into property similar or related in service or use, complete nonrecognition of gain is mandatory. The basis of replacement property is the same as the property converted.

(4) The meaning of **property similar or related in service or use** is more restrictive than "like-kind."

(a) For an owner-user—property must be functionally the same and have same end use (business vehicle must be replaced by business vehicle that performs same function).

(b) For a lessor—property must perform same services for **lessor** (lessor could replace a rental manufacturing plant with a rental-wholesale grocery warehouse even though tenant's functional use differs).

(c) A purchase of at least 80% of the stock of a corporation whose property is similar or related in service or use also qualifies.

(d) More liberal "like-kind" test applies to real property held for business or investment (other than inventory or property held primarily for sale) that is converted by seizure, condemnation, or threat of condemnation (e.g., improved real estate could be replaced with unimproved real estate).

(5) If property is not replaced within the time limit, an amended return is filed to recognize gain in the year realized.

(6) Losses on involuntary conversions are recognized whether the property is replaced or not. However, a loss on condemnation of property held for personal use (e.g., personal residence) is not deductible.

c. **Sale or exchange of principal residence**

(1) An individual may **exclude** from income up to **$250,000** of gain that is realized on the sale or exchange of a residence, if the individual owned and occupied the residence as a principal residence for an aggregate of *at least two of the five years* preceding the sale or exchange. The amount of excludable gain is increased to **$500,000** for married individuals filing jointly if either spouse meets the ownership requirement, and both spouses meet the use requirement.

(a) The exclusion replaces the gain rollover rules and the one-time $125,000 exclusion formerly available to eligible individuals age fifty-five or older.

(b) Gain in excess of the $250,000 (or $500,000) exclusion must be included in income even though the sale proceeds are reinvested in another principal residence.

(2) The exclusion is determined on an individual basis.

(a) A single individual who otherwise qualifies for the exclusion is entitled to exclude up to $250,000 of gain even though the individual marries someone who has used the exclusion within two years before the marriage.

(b) In the case of married taxpayers who do not share a principal residence but file joint returns, a $250,000 exclusion is available for a qualifying sale or exchange of each spouse's principal residence.

(3) Special rules apply to divorced taxpayers.

(a) If a residence is transferred to a taxpayer incident to a divorce, the time during which the taxpayer's spouse or former spouse owned the residence is added to the taxpayer's period of ownership.

(b) A taxpayer who owns a residence is deemed to use it as a principal residence while the taxpayer's spouse or former spouse is given use of the residence under the terms of a divorce or separation.

(4) A taxpayer's period of ownership of a residence includes the period during which the taxpayer's deceased spouse owned the residence.

(5) Tenant-stockholders in a cooperative housing corporation can qualify to exclude gain from the sale of the stock.

(6) If the taxpayer does not meet the two-year ownership or use requirements, a pro rata amount of the $250,000 or $500,000 exclusion applies if the sale or exchange is due to a change in place of employment, health, or unforeseen circumstances.

EXAMPLE: Harold, an unmarried taxpayer, purchased a home in a suburb of Chicago on October 1, 2000. Eighteen months later his employer transferred him to St. Louis and Harold sold his home for a gain of $200,000. Since Harold sold his home because of a change in place of employment and had owned and used the home as a principal residence for eighteen months, the exclusion of his gain is limited to $250,000 x 18/24 = $187,500.

(7) A loss from the sale of personal residence is not deductible.

d. **Exchange of insurance policies.** No gain or loss is recognized on an exchange of certain life, endowment, and annuity contracts to allow taxpayers to obtain better insurance.

5. **Sales and exchanges of securities**

a. Stocks and bonds are not included under like-kind exchanges

b. Exchange of stock of same corporation

    (1) Common for common, or preferred for preferred is nontaxable

    (2) Common for preferred, or preferred for common is taxable, unless exchange qualifies as a recapitalization (see page 1104)

c. Exercise of conversion privilege in convertible stock or bond is generally nontaxable.

d. The first-in, first-out (FIFO) method is used to determine the basis of securities sold unless the taxpayer can specifically identify the securities sold and uses specific identification.

e. **Capital gains exclusion for small business stock**

    (1) A noncorporate taxpayer can exclude 50% of capital gains resulting from the sale of qualified small business stock held for more than five years.

    (2) To qualify, the stock must be acquired directly (or indirectly through a pass-through entity) at its original issuance.

    (3) A qualified small business is a C corporation with $50 million or less of capitalization. Generally, personal service, banking, leasing, investing, real estate, farming, mineral extraction, and hospitality businesses do not qualify as eligible small businesses.

    (4) Gains eligible for exclusion are limited to the greater of $10 million, or 10 times the investor's stock basis.

        (a) 42% of the excluded gain is treated as a tax preference item for AMT purposes.

        (b) Only gains net of exclusion are included in determining the investment interest expense and capital loss limitations.

f. **Rollover of capital gain from publicly traded securities**

    (1) An individual or C corporation may elect to roll over an otherwise currently taxable capital gain from the sale of publicly traded securities if the sale proceeds are used to purchase common stock or a partnership interest in a specialized small business investment company (SSBIC) within sixty days of the sale of the securities.

    (2) An SSBIC is a partnership or corporation licensed by the Small Business Administration under the Small Business Investment Act of 1958 as in effect on May 13, 1993.

    (3) The amount of gain eligible for rollover is limited to $50,000 per year for individuals (lifetime cap of $500,000) and $250,000 per year for corporations (lifetime cap of $1 million).

    (4) The taxpayer's basis in the SSBIC stock or partnership interest must be reduced by the gain that is rolled over.

g. **Market discount bonds**

    (1) Gain on the disposition of a bond (including a tax-exempt bond) that was acquired for a price that was less than the principal amount of the bond is treated as taxable interest income to the extent of the accrued market discount for bonds purchased after April 30, 1993.

    (2) Accrued market discount is the difference between the bond's cost basis and its redemption value at maturity amortized over the remaining life of the bond.

h. **Wash sales**

    (1) Wash sale occurs when stock or securities (or options to acquire stock or securities) are sold at a loss and within **thirty days before or after the sale**, substantially identical stock or securities (or options to acquire them) in the same corporation are purchased.

    (2) Wash sale loss is not deductible, but is added to the basis of the new stock.

    (3) Wash sale rules do not apply to gains.

EXAMPLE: C purchased 100 shares of XYZ Corporation stock for $1,000. C later sold the stock for $700, and within thirty days acquired 100 shares of XYZ Corporation stock for $800. The loss of $300 on the sale of stock is not recognized. However, the unrecognized loss of $300 is added to the $800 cost of the new stock to arrive at the basis for the new stock of $1,100. The holding period of the new stock includes the period of time the old stock was held.

    (4) Does not apply to dealers in stock and securities where loss is sustained in ordinary course of business.

  i. **Worthless stock and securities**

    (1) Treated as a capital loss as if sold on the last day of the taxable year they become worthless.

    (2) Treated as an ordinary loss if stock and securities are those of an **80% or more owned corporate subsidiary** that derived more than 90% of its gross receipts from active-type sources.

6. **Losses on deposits in insolvent financial institutions**

  a. Loss resulting from a nonbusiness deposit in an insolvent financial institution is generally treated as a nonbusiness bad debt deductible as a short-term capital loss (STCL) in the year in which a final determination of the amount of loss can be made.

  b. As an alternative, if a reasonable estimate of the amount of loss can be made, an individual may elect to

    (1) Treat the loss as a personal casualty loss subject to the $100 floor and 10% of AGI limitation. Then no bad debt deduction can be claimed.

    (2) In lieu of (1) above, treat up to $20,000 as a miscellaneous itemized deduction subject to the 2% of AGI floor if the deposit was not federally insured. Then remainder of loss is treated as a STCL.

*EXAMPLE: An individual with no capital gains and an AGI of $70,000, incurred a loss on a federally insured deposit in a financial institution of $30,000. The individual may treat the loss as a $30,000 STCL subject to the $3,000 net capital loss deduction limitation, with the remaining $27,000 carried forward as a STCL; or, may treat the loss as a personal casualty loss and an itemized deduction of [($30,000 – $100) – (10% x $70,000)] = $22,900. If the deposit had **not** been federally insured, the individual could also have taken a miscellaneous itemized deduction of [$20,000 – (2% x $70,000)] = $18,600, with the remaining $10,000 treated as a STCL (i.e., $3,000 net capital loss deduction and a $7,000 STCL carryover).*

7. **Losses, expenses, and interest between related taxpayers**

  a. **Loss is disallowed** on the sale or exchange of property to a related taxpayer.

    (1) Transferee's basis is cost; holding period begins when transferee acquires property.

    (2) On a later resale, any gain recognized by the transferee is reduced by the disallowed loss (unless the transferor's loss was from a wash sale, in which case no reduction is allowed).

    (3) **Related taxpayers** include

      (a) Members of a family, including spouse, brothers, sisters, ancestors, and lineal descendents

      (b) A corporation and a more than 50% shareholder

      (c) Two corporations which are members of the same controlled group

      (d) A person and an exempt organization controlled by that person

      (e) Certain related individuals in a trust, including the grantor or beneficiary and the fiduciary

      (f) A C corporation and a partnership if the same persons own more than 50% of the corporation, and more than 50% of the capital and profits interest in the partnership

      (g) Two S corporations if the same persons own more than 50% of each

      (h) An S corporation and a C corporation if the same persons own more than 50% of each

EXAMPLE: During August 2001, Bob sold stock with a basis of $4,000 to his brother Ray for $3,000, its FMV. During June 2002, Ray sold the stock to an unrelated taxpayer for $4,500. Bob's loss of $1,000 is disallowed; Ray recognizes a STCG of ($4,500 – $3,000) – $1,000 disallowed loss = $500.

    (4) **Constructive stock ownership rules** apply in determining if taxpayers are related. For purposes of determining stock ownership

      (a) Stock owned, directly or indirectly, by a corporation, partnership, estate, or trust is considered as being owned proportionately by its shareholders, partners, or beneficiaries.

      (b) An individual is considered as owning the stock owned, directly or indirectly, by his brothers and sisters (whole or half blood), spouse, ancestors, and lineal descendents.

(c) An individual owning stock in a corporation [other than by (b) above] is considered as owning the stock owned, directly or indirectly, by his partner.

b. The disallowed loss rule in a. above does not apply to transfers between spouses, or former spouses incident to divorce, as discussed below.

c. Any loss from the sale or exchange of property between corporations that are members of the same **controlled group** is deferred (instead of disallowed) until the property is sold outside the group. Use controlled group definition found in Module 43, D.2., but substitute "more than 50%" for "at least 80%."

EXAMPLE: Mr. Gudjob is the sole shareholder of X Corp. and Y Corp. During 2001, X Corp. sold nondepreciable property with a basis of $8,000 to Y Corp. for $6,000, its FMV. During 2002, Y Corp. sold the property to an unrelated taxpayer for $6,500. X Corp.'s loss in 2001 is deferred. In 2002, X Corp. recognizes the $2,000 of deferred loss, and Y Corp. recognizes a gain of $500.

d. An accrual-basis payor is effectively placed on the cash method of accounting for purposes of deducting accrued interest and other expenses owed to a related cash-basis payee.

(1) No deduction is allowable until the year the amount is actually paid.

(2) This rule applies to pass-through entities (e.g., a partnership and **any** partner; two partnerships if the same persons own more than 50% of each; an S corporation and **any** shareholder) in addition to the related taxpayers described in a.(3) above, but does not apply to guaranteed payments to partners. This rule also applies to a personal service corporation and **any** employee-owner.

EXAMPLE: A calendar-year S corporation accrued a $500 bonus owed to an employee-shareholder in 2002 but did not pay the bonus until February 2003. The $500 bonus will be deductible by the S corporation in 2003, when the employee-shareholder reports the $500 as income.

8. **Transfer between spouses**

a. No gain or loss is generally recognized on the transfer of property from an individual to (or in trust for the benefit of)

(1) A spouse (other than a nonresident alien spouse), or

(2) A former spouse (other than a nonresident alien former spouse), if the transfer is related to the cessation of marriage, or occurs within one year after marriage ceases

b. Transfer is treated as if it were a gift from one spouse to the other.

c. Transferee's basis in the property received will be the transferor's basis (even if FMV is less than the property's basis).

EXAMPLE: H sells property with a basis of $6,000 to his spouse, W, for $8,000. No gain is recognized to H, and W's basis for the property is $6,000. W's holding period includes the period that H held the property.

d. If property is transferred to a **trust** for the benefit of a spouse or former spouse (incident to divorce)

(1) Gain is recognized to the extent that the amount of liabilities assumed exceeds the total adjusted basis of property transferred.

(2) Gain or loss is recognized on the transfer of installment obligations.

9. Gain from the sale or exchange of property will be entirely ordinary gain (no capital gain) if the property is depreciable in hands of transferee and the sale or exchange is between

a. A person and a more than 50% owned corporation or partnership

b. A taxpayer and any trust in which such taxpayer or spouse is a beneficiary, unless such beneficiary's interest is a remote contingent interest

c. Constructive ownership rules apply; use rules in Section 7.a.(4)(a) and (b) above

B. Capital Gains and Losses

1. Capital gains and losses result from the "sale or exchange of capital assets." The term **capital assets** includes investment property and property held for personal use. The term specifically **excludes**

a. Stock in trade, inventory, or goods held primarily for sale to customers in the normal course of business

   b. Depreciable or real property used in a trade or business

   c. Copyrights or artistic, literary, etc., compositions created by the taxpayer

     (1) They are capital assets only if purchased by the taxpayer.

     (2) Patents are generally capital assets in the hands of the inventor.

   d. Accounts or notes receivable arising from normal business activities

   e. US government publications acquired other than by purchase at regular price

   f. Supplies of a type regularly used or consumed by a taxpayer in the ordinary course of the taxpayer's trade or business

2. Whether short-term or long-term depends upon the **holding period**

   a. Long-term if held more than one year

   b. The day property was acquired is excluded and the day it is disposed of is included.

   c. Use calendar months (e.g., if held from January 4 to January 4 it is held exactly one year)

   d. If stock or securities which are traded on an established securities market (or other property regularly traded on an established market) are sold, any resulting gain or loss is recognized on the date the trade is executed (transaction date) by both cash and accrual taxpayers.

   e. The holding period of property received in a nontaxable exchange (e.g., like-kind exchange, involuntary conversion) includes the holding period of the property exchanged, if the property that was exchanged was a capital asset or Sec. 1231 asset.

   f. If the basis of property to a prior owner carries over to the present owner (e.g., gift), the holding period of the prior owner "tacks on" to the present owner's holding period.

   g. If using the lower FMV on date of gift to determine loss, then holding period begins when the gift is received.

     EXAMPLE: X purchased property on July 14, 2001, for $10,000. X made a gift of the property to Z on June 10, 2002, when its FMV was $8,000. Since Z's basis for gain is $10,000, Z's holding period for a disposition at a gain extends back to July 14, 2001. Since Z's $8,000 basis for loss is determined by reference to FMV at June 10, 2002, Z's holding period for a disposition at a loss begins on June 11.

   h. Property acquired from a decedent is always given long-term treatment, regardless of how long the property was held by the decedent or beneficiary, and is treated as property held more than twelve months.

3. Computation of capital gains and losses for **all taxpayers**

   a. First net STCG with STCL and net LTCG with LTCL to determine

     (1) Net short-term capital gain or loss (NSTCG or NSTCL)

     (2) Net long-term capital gain or loss (NLTCG or NLTCL)

   b. Then net these two together to determine whether there is a net capital gain or loss (NCG or NCL)

4. The following rules apply to **individuals**:

   a. Capital gains offset capital losses, with any remaining net capital gains included in gross income.

   b. Net capital gains are subject to tax at various rates, depending on the type of assets sold or exchanged and length of time the assets were held.

     (1) Capital gain from assets held one year or less is taxed at the taxpayer's regular tax rates (up to 38.6%).

     (2) Capital gain from the sale of collectibles held more than twelve months (e.g., antiques, metals, gems, stamps, coins) is taxed at a maximum rate of 28%.

     (3) Capital gain attributable to unrecaptured depreciation on Sec. 1250 property held more than twelve months is taxed at a maximum rate of 25%.

     (4) Capital gain from assets held more than twelve months (other than collectibles and Sec. 1250 property) is taxed at a rate of 20% (or 10% for individuals in the 10% or 15% tax brackets).

     (5) For tax years beginning after December 31, 2000, a lower rate of 18% (8% for individuals in the 10% or 15% tax bracket) may be applied if the individual held the asset more than five years.

(a) If the individual is in the 10% or 15% tax bracket, all assets qualify for the five-year holding period.

(b) If the individual is in a tax bracket higher than 15%, the five-year holding period only applies to assets acquired after December 31, 2000.

c. Gains and losses (including carryovers) within each of the rate groups are netted to arrive at a net gain or loss. A net loss in any rate group is applied to reduce the net gain in the highest rate group first (e.g., a net short-term capital loss is applied to reduce any net gain from the 28% group, then the 25% group, and finally to reduce gain from the 20% group).

EXAMPLE: Kim, who is in the 31% tax bracket, had the following capital gains and losses for calendar-year 2002:

Net short-term capital loss	*$(1,500)*
28% group—collectibles net gain	*900*
25% group—unrecaptured Sec. 1250 net gain	*2,000*
20% group—net gain	*5,000*
Net capital gain	*$ 6,400*

In this case, the NSTCL of $1,500 first offsets the $900 of collectibles gain, and then offsets $600 of the unrecaptured Sec. 1250 gain. As a result of this netting procedure, Kim has $1,400 of unrecaptured Sec. 1250 gain that will be taxed at a rate of 25%, and $5,000 of capital gain that will be taxed at a rate of 20%.

d. If there is a **net capital loss** the following rules apply:

(1) A net capital loss is a deduction in arriving at AGI, but limited to the lesser of

(a) $3,000 ($1,500 if married filing separately), or

(b) The excess of capital losses over capital gains

(2) Both a NSTCL and a NLTCL are used dollar-for-dollar in computing the capital loss deduction.

EXAMPLE: An individual had $2,000 of NLTCL and $500 of NSTCL for 2002. The capital losses are combined and the entire net capital loss of $2,500 is deductible in computing the individual's AGI.

(3) Short-term losses are used before long-term losses. The amount of net capital loss that exceeds the allowable deduction may be carried over for an unlimited period of time. Capital loss carryovers retain their identity; short-term losses carry over as short-term losses, and long-term losses carry over as long-term losses in the 28% group. Losses remaining unused on a decedent's final return are extinguished and provide no tax benefit.

EXAMPLE: An individual has a $4,000 STCL and a $5,000 LTCL for 2002. The $9,000 net capital loss results in a capital loss deduction of $3,000 for 2002, while the remainder is a carryover to 2003. Since $3,000 of the STCL would be used to create the capital loss deduction, there is a $1,000 STCL carryover and a $5,000 LTCL carryover to 2003. The $5,000 LTCL carryover would first offset gains in the 28% group.

(4) For purposes of determining the amount of excess net capital loss that can be carried over to future years, the taxpayer's net capital loss for the year is reduced by the lesser of (1) $3,000 ($1,500 if married filing separately), or (2) adjusted taxable income.

(a) Adjusted taxable income is taxable income increased by $3,000 ($1,500 if married filing separately) and the amount allowed for personal exemptions.

(b) An excess of deductions allowed over gross income is taken into account as negative taxable income.

EXAMPLE: For 2002, a single individual with no dependents had a net capital loss of $8,000, and had allowable deductions that exceeded gross income by $4,000. For 2002, the individual is entitled to a net capital loss deduction of $3,000, and will carry over a net capital loss of $6,000 to 2003. This amount represents the 2002 net capital loss of $8,000 reduced by the lesser of (1) $3,000, or (2) – $4,000 + $3,000 + $3,000 personal exemption = $2,000.

5. **Corporations** have special capital gain and loss rules.

a. Capital losses are only allowed to offset capital gains, not ordinary income.

b. A **net capital loss** is carried back three years, and forward five years to offset capital gains in those years. All capital loss carrybacks and carryovers are treated as **short-term** capital losses.

EXAMPLE: A corporation has a NLTCL of $8,000 and a NSTCG of $2,000, resulting in a net capital loss of $6,000 for 2002. The $6,000 NLTCL is not deductible for 2002, but is first carried back as a STCL to 1999 to offset capital gains. If not used up in 1999, the STCL is carried to 2000 and 2001, and then forward to 2003, 2004, 2005, 2006, and 2007 to offset capital gains in those years.

c. Although an alternative tax computation still exists for a corporation with a net capital gain, the alternative tax computation applies the highest corporate rate (35%) to a net capital gain and thus provides no benefit.

C. Personal Casualty and Theft Gains and Losses

Gains and losses from casualties and thefts of property held for personal use are separately netted, without regard to the holding period of the converted property.

1. If gains exceed losses (after the $100 floor for each loss), then all gains and losses are treated as capital gains and losses, short-term or long-term depending upon holding period.

   EXAMPLE: An individual incurred a $25,000 personal casualty gain, and a $15,000 personal casualty loss (after the $100 floor) during the current taxable year. Since there was a net gain, the individual will report the gain and loss as a $25,000 capital gain and a $15,000 capital loss.

2. If losses (after the $100 floor for each loss) exceed gains, the losses (1) offset gains, and (2) are an ordinary deduction from AGI to the extent in excess of 10% of AGI.

   EXAMPLE: An individual had AGI of $40,000 (before casualty gains or losses), and also had a personal casualty loss of $25,000 (after the $100 floor) and a personal casualty gain of $15,000. Since there was a net personal casualty loss, the net loss will be deductible as an itemized deduction of [$25,000 – $15,000 – (10% x $40,000)] = $6,000.

D. Gains and Losses on Business Property

Although property used in a business is excluded from the definition of "capital assets," Sec. 1231 extends capital gain and loss treatment to business assets if the gains from these assets exceed losses. However, before Sec. 1231 becomes operative, Sections 1245, 1250, and 291 provide for recapture of depreciation (i.e., gain is taxed as ordinary income to the extent of certain depreciation previously deducted).

1. All gains and losses are **ordinary** on business property **held one year or less**.

2. **Section 1231**

   a. All property included must have been held for **more than one year**.

      (1) Section 1231 gains and losses include those from

          (a) Sale or exchange of property used in trade or business (or held for production of rents or royalties) and which is not

              1] Inventory
              2] A copyright or artistic composition

          (b) Casualty, theft, or condemnation of

              1] Property used in trade or business
              2] Capital assets held in connection with a trade or business, or a transaction entered into for profit

          (c) Infrequently encountered items such as cut timber, coal and domestic iron ore, livestock, and unharvested crop

   b. The combining of Sec. 1231 gains and losses is accomplished in **two steps**. **First**, net all casualty and theft gains and losses on property held for more than one year.

      (1) If the losses exceed gains, treat them all as ordinary losses and gains and do not net them with other Sec. 1231 gains and losses.
      (2) If the gains exceed losses, the net gain is combined with other Sec. 1231 gains and losses.

   c. **Second**, net all other Sec. 1231 gains and losses (except casualty and theft net loss per above).

      (1) Include casualty and theft net gain
      (2) Include gains and losses from condemnations (other than condemnations on nonbusiness, non-income-producing property)
      (3) Include gains and losses from the sale or exchange of property used in trade or business

   d. If losses exceed gains, treat all gains and losses as ordinary.
   e. If gains exceed losses, treat the Sec. 1231 net gain as a long-term capital gain.

EXAMPLE: Taxpayer has a gain of $10,000 from the sale of land used in his business, a loss of $4,000 on the sale of depreciable property used in his business, and a $2,000 (noninsured) loss when a car used in his business was involved in a collision.

The net gain or loss from casualty or theft is the $2,000 loss. The net casualty loss of $2,000 is treated as an ordinary loss and not netted with other Sec. 1231 gains and losses.

The $10,000 gain is netted with the $4,000 loss resulting in a net Sec. 1231 gain of $6,000, which is then treated as a long-term capital gain.

f. Net Sec. 1231 gain will be treated as ordinary income (instead of LTCG) to the extent of nonrecaptured net Sec. 1231 losses for the five most recent taxable years.

   (1) Losses are deemed recaptured in the chronological order in which they arose
   (2) Any Sec. 1231 gain recharacterized as ordinary income consists first of gain in the 28% group, then gain in the 25% group, and finally gain the 20% group

EXAMPLE: Corp. X, on a calendar year, has a net Sec. 1231 gain of $10,000 for 2002. For the years 1997 through 2001, Corp. X had net Sec. 1231 losses totaling $8,000. Of the $10,000 net Sec. 1231 gain for 2002, the first $8,000 will be treated as ordinary income, with only the remaining $2,000 treated as long-term capital gain.

3. **Section 1245 Recapture**

   a. Requires the recapture as **ordinary income** of all gain attributable to

      (1) **Post-1961 depreciation** on the disposition of Sec. 1245 property
      (2) **Post-1980 recovery deductions** on the disposition of Sec. 1245 recovery property (including amount expensed under Sec. 179 expense election)

   b. **Sec. 1245 property** generally includes depreciable tangible and intangible **personal property**, for example

      (1) Desks, machines, equipment, cars, and trucks
      (2) Special purpose structures, storage facilities, and other property (but not buildings and structural components); for example, oil and gas storage tanks, grain storage bins and silos, and escalators and elevators

   c. **Sec. 1245 recovery property** means **all** ACRS recovery property placed in service after 1980 and **before 1987** other than nineteen-year real property that is classified as real residential rental property, real property used outside the US, subsidized low-income housing, and real property for which a straight-line election was made.

   NOTE: If the cost of nineteen-year nonresidential real property placed in service before 1987 was recovered using the prescribed percentages of ACRS, the gain on disposition is ordinary income to extent of all ACRS deductions. Such recapture is not limited to the excess of accelerated depreciation over straight-line. However, if the straight-line method was elected for nineteen-year real property, there is no recapture and all gain is Sec. 1231 gain.

   d. Sec. 1245 does not apply to real residential rental property and nonresidential real property placed in service after 1986 because only straight-line depreciation is allowable.

   e. Upon the disposition of property subject to Sec. 1245, any recognized gain will be ordinary income to the extent of all depreciation or post-1980 cost recovery deductions.

      (1) Any remaining gain after recapture will be Sec. 1231 gain if property held more than one year.

      EXAMPLE: Megan sold equipment used in her business for $11,000. The equipment had cost $10,000 and $6,000 of depreciation had been taken, resulting in an adjusted basis of $4,000. Megan's recognized gain is $11,000 – $4,000 = $7,000. Since the equipment was Sec. 1245 property, the gain must be recognized as Sec. 1245 ordinary income to the extent of the $6,000 of depreciation deducted. The remaining $1,000 gain ($7,000 gain – $6,000 ordinary income) is recognized as Sec. 1231 gain.

      EXAMPLE: Assume the same facts as in the preceding example, except the equipment was sold for $9,000. Megan's recognized gain would be $9,000 – $4,000 = $5,000. Now, since the $6,000 of depreciation deducted exceeds the recognized gain of $5,000, the amount of Sec. 1245 ordinary income would be limited to the recognized gain of $5,000. There would be no Sec. 1231 gain.

      EXAMPLE: Assume the same facts as in the first example, except the equipment was sold for only $3,500. Megan's sale of the equipment now results in a recognized loss of $3,500 – $4,000 = ($500). Since there is loss, there would be no Sec. 1245 depreciation recapture and the $500 loss would be classified as a Sec. 1231 loss.

      (2) If the disposition is not by sale, use FMV of property (instead of selling price) to determine gain.

(a) When boot is received in a like-kind exchange, Sec. 1245 will apply to the recognized gain.

> *EXAMPLE: Taxpayer exchanged his old machine (adjusted basis of $2,500) for a smaller new machine worth $5,000 and received $1,000 cash. Depreciation of $7,500 had been taken on the old machine. The realized gain of $3,500 ($6,000 – $2,500) will be recognized to the extent of the $1,000 boot, and will be treated as ordinary income as the result of Sec. 1245.*

(b) Sec. 1245 recapture does not apply to transfers by gift (including charitable contributions) or transfers at death.

4. **Section 1250 Recapture**

   a. Applies to all real property (e.g., buildings and structural components) that is not Sec. 1245 recovery property.

      (1) If Sec. 1250 property was held twelve months or less, gain on disposition is recaptured as ordinary income to extent of all depreciation (including straight-line).

      (2) If Sec. 1250 property was held more than twelve months, gain is recaptured as ordinary income to the extent of post-1969 **additional depreciation** (generally depreciation in excess of straight-line).

> *EXAMPLE: An office building with an adjusted basis of $200,000 was sold by **individual X** in 2002 for $350,000. The property had been purchased for $300,000 in 1980 and $100,000 of depreciation had been deducted. Straight-line depreciation would have totaled $70,000.*

Total gain ($350,000 – $200,000)	*$150,000*
Post-1969 additional depreciation recaptured as ordinary income	*(30,000)*
Remainder is Sec. 1231 gain	*$120,000*

5. **Section 291 Recapture**

   a. The ordinary income element on the disposition of Sec. 1250 property by **corporations** is increased by 20% of the additional amount that would have been ordinary income if the property had instead been Sec. 1245 property or Sec. 1245 recovery property.

> *EXAMPLE: Assuming the same facts as in the above example except that the building was sold by **Corporation X** in 2002, the computation of gain would be*

Total gain ($350,000 – $200,000)	*$150,000*
Post-1969 additional depreciation recaptured as ordinary income	*(30,000)**
Additional ordinary income—20% of $70,000 (the additional amount that would have been ordinary income if the property were Sec. 1245 property)	*(14,000)**
Remainder is Sec. 1231 gain	*$106,000*

> * *All $44,000 ($30,000 + $14,000) of recapture is referred to as Sec. 1250 ordinary income.*

6. **Summary of Gains and Losses on Business Property.** The treatment of gains and losses (other than personal casualty and theft) on property held for **more than one year** is summarized in the following **four steps** (also enumerated on flowchart at end of this section):

   a. Separate all recognized gains and losses into four categories

      (1) Ordinary gain and loss
      (2) Sec. 1231 casualty and theft gains and losses
      (3) Sec. 1231 gains and losses other than by casualty or theft
      (4) Gains and losses on capital assets (other than by casualty or theft)

> *NOTE: (2) and (3) are only temporary classifications and all gains and losses will ultimately receive ordinary or capital treatment.*

   b. Any gain (casualty or other) on Sec. 1231 property is treated as ordinary income to extent of Sec. 1245, 1250, and 291 depreciation recapture.

   c. After depreciation recapture, any remaining Sec. 1231 casualty and theft gains and losses on business property are netted.

      (1) If losses exceed gains—the losses and gains receive ordinary treatment
      (2) If gains exceed losses—the net gain is combined with other Sec. 1231 gains and losses in d. below

   d.   After recapture, any remaining Sec. 1231 gains and losses (other than by casualty or theft), are combined with any net casualty or theft gain from c. above.

     (1) If losses exceed gains—the losses and gains receive ordinary treatment

     (2) If gains exceed losses—the net gain receives LTCG treatment (except ordinary income treatment to extent of nonrecaptured net Sec. 1231 losses for the five most recent tax years)

       EXAMPLE: *Taxpayer incurred the following transactions during the current taxable year:*

Loss on condemnation of land used in business held fifteen months	$ (500)
Loss on sale of machinery used in business held two months	(1,000)
Bad debt loss on loan made three years ago to friend	(2,000)
Gain from insurance reimbursement for tornado damage to business property held ten years	3,000
Loss on sale of business equipment held three years	(4,000)
Gain on sale of land held four years and used in business	5,000

The gains and losses would be treated as follows: Note that the loss on machinery is ordinary because it was not held more than one year.

Ordinary	Sec. 1231 Casualty	Other Sec. 1231	Capital L-T	Capital S-T
$(1,000)	$3,000	$ (500)		$(2,000)*
		(4,000)		
		5,000		
	$3,000 →	3,000		
		$3,500		
$(1,000)		$3,500 →	$3,500	
			$3,500	$(2,000)

      * A nonbusiness bad debt is always treated as a STCL.*

TAX TREATMENT OF GAINS AND LOSSES (OTHER THAN PERSONAL CASUALTY AND THEFT) ON PROPERTY HELD MORE THAN ONE YEAR

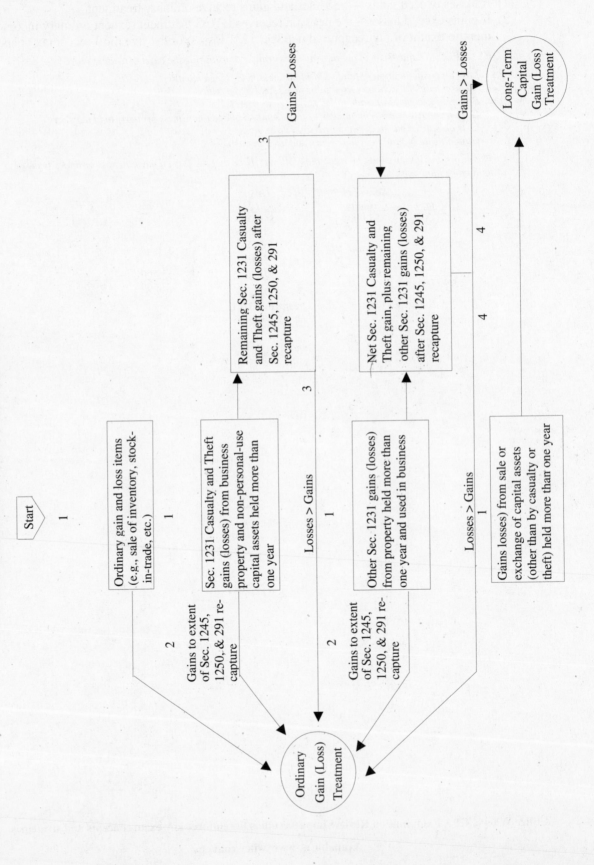

MULTIPLE-CHOICE QUESTIONS (1-62)

1. Ralph Birch purchased land and a building which will be used in connection with Birch's business. The costs associated with this purchase are as follows:

Cash down payment	$ 40,000
Mortgage on property	350,000
Survey costs	2,000
Title and transfer taxes	2,500
Charges for hookup of gas, water, and sewer lines	3,000
Back property taxes owed by the seller that were paid by Birch	5,000

What is Birch's tax basis for the land and building?

- a. $ 44,500
- b. $394,500
- c. $397,500
- d. $402,500

2. Fred Berk bought a plot of land with a cash payment of $40,000 and a purchase money mortgage of $50,000. In addition, Berk paid $200 for a title insurance policy. Berk's basis in this land is

- a. $40,000
- b. $40,200
- c. $90,000
- d. $90,200

3. Julie received a parcel of land as a gift from her Aunt Agnes. At the time of the gift, the land had a fair market value of $81,000 and an adjusted basis of $21,000. This was the only gift that Julie received from Agnes during 2002. If Agnes paid a gift tax of $14,000 on the transfer of the gift to Julie, what tax basis will Julie have for the land?

- a. $21,000
- b. $31,000
- c. $33,000
- d. $80,000

Items 4 and 5 are based on the following data:

In 1999 Iris King bought shares of stock as an investment, at a cost of $10,000. During 2002, when the fair market value was $8,000, Iris gave the stock to her daughter, Ruth.

4. If Ruth sells the shares of stock in 2003 for $7,000, Ruth's recognized loss would be

- a. $3,000
- b. $2,000
- c. $1,000
- d. $0

5. Ruth's holding period of the stock for purposes of determining her loss

- a. Started in 1999.
- b. Started in 2002.
- c. Started in 2003.
- d. Is irrelevant because Ruth received the stock for no consideration of money or money's worth.

Items 6 through 8 are based on the following data:

Laura's father, Albert, gave Laura a gift of 500 shares of Liba Corporation common stock in 2002. Albert's basis for the Liba stock was $4,000. At the date of this gift, the fair market value of the Liba stock was $3,000.

6. If Laura sells the 500 shares of Liba stock in 2002 for $5,000, her basis is

- a. $5,000
- b. $4,000
- c. $3,000
- d. $0

7. If Laura sells the 500 shares of Liba stock in 2002 for $2,000, her basis is

- a. $4,000
- b. $3,000
- c. $2,000
- d. $0

8. If Laura sells the 500 shares of Liba stock in 2002 for $3,500, what is the reportable gain or loss in 2002?

- a. $3,500 gain.
- b. $ 500 gain.
- c. $ 500 loss.
- d. $0.

9. On June 1, 2002, Ben Rork sold 500 shares of Kul Corp. stock. Rork had received this stock on May 1, 2002, as a bequest from the estate of his uncle, who died on March 1, 2002. Rork's basis was determined by reference to the stock's fair market value on March 1, 2002. Rork's holding period for this stock was

- a. Short-term.
- b. Long-term.
- c. Short-term if sold at a gain; long-term if sold at a loss.
- d. Long-term if sold at a gain; short-term if sold at a loss.

10. Fred Zorn died on January 5, 2002, bequeathing his entire $2,000,000 estate to his sister, Ida. The alternate valuation date was validly elected by the executor of Fred's estate. Fred's estate included 2,000 shares of listed stock for which Fred's basis was $380,000. This stock was distributed to Ida nine months after Fred's death. Fair market values of this stock were

At the date of Fred's death	$400,000
Six months after Fred's death	450,000
Nine months after Fred's death	480,000

Ida's basis for this stock is

- a. $380,000
- b. $400,000
- c. $450,000
- d. $480,000

Items 11 and 12 are based on the following data:

On March 1, 2002, Lois Rice learned that she was bequeathed 1,000 shares of Elin Corp. common stock under the will of her uncle, Pat Prevor. Pat had paid $5,000 for the Elin stock in 1997. Fair market value of the Elin stock on March 1, 2002, the date of Pat's death, was $8,000 and had increased to $11,000 six months later. The executor of Pat's estate elected the alternative valuation for estate tax purposes. Lois sold the Elin stock for $9,000 on May 1, 2002, the date that the executor distributed the stock to her.

11. Lois' basis for gain or loss on sale of the 1,000 shares of Elin stock is

- a. $ 5,000
- b. $ 8,000
- c. $ 9,000
- d. $11,000

12. Lois should treat the 1,000 shares of Elin stock as a
- a. Short-term Section 1231 asset.
- b. Long-term Section 1231 asset.
- c. Short-term capital asset.
- d. Long-term capital asset.

Items 13 and 14 are based on the following data:

In January 2002, Joan Hill bought one share of Orban Corp. stock for $300. On March 1, 2002, Orban distributed one share of preferred stock for each share of common stock held. This distribution was nontaxable. On March 1, 2002, Joan's one share of common stock had a fair market value of $450, while the preferred stock had a fair market value of $150.

13. After the distribution of the preferred stock, Joan's bases for her Orban stocks are

	Common	Preferred
a.	$300	$0
b.	$225	$ 75
c.	$200	$100
d.	$150	$150

14. The holding period for the preferred stock starts in
- a. January 2002.
- b. March 2002.
- c. September 2002.
- d. December 2002.

15. On July 1, 1998, Lila Perl paid $90,000 for 450 shares of Janis Corp. common stock. Lila received a nontaxable stock dividend of 50 new common shares in August 2002. On December 20, 2002, Lila sold the 50 new shares for $11,000. How much should Lila report in her 2002 return as long-term capital gain?
- a. $0
- b. $ 1,000
- c. $ 2,000
- d. $11,000

16. Tom Gow owned a parcel of investment real estate that had an adjusted basis of $25,000 and a fair market value of $40,000. During 2002, Gow exchanged his investment real estate for the items of property listed below.

Land to be held for investment (fair market value)	$35,000
A small sailboat to be held for personal use (fair market value)	3,000
Cash	2,000

What is Tom Gow's recognized gain and basis in his new investment real estate?

	Gain recognized	Basis for real estate
a.	$2,000	$22,000
b.	$2,000	$25,000
c.	$5,000	$25,000
d.	$5,000	$35,000

17. In a "like-kind" exchange of an investment asset for a similar asset that will also be held as an investment, no taxable gain or loss will be recognized on the transaction if both assets consist of
- a. Convertible debentures.
- b. Convertible preferred stock.
- c. Partnership interests.
- d. Rental real estate located in different states.

18. Leker exchanged a van that was used exclusively for business and had an adjusted tax basis of $20,000 for a new van. The new van had a fair market value of $15,000, and Leker also received $3,000 in cash. What was Leker's tax basis in the acquired van?
- a. $20,000
- b. $17,000
- c. $12,000
- d. $ 5,000

19. Pat Leif owned an apartment house that he bought in 1989. Depreciation was taken on a straight-line basis. In 2002, when Pat's adjusted basis for this property was $200,000, he traded it for an office building having a fair market value of $600,000. The apartment house has 100 dwelling units, while the office building has 40 units rented to business enterprises. The properties are **not** located in the same city. What is Pat's reportable gain on this exchange?
- a. $400,000 Section 1250 gain.
- b. $400,000 Section 1231 gain.
- c. $400,000 long-term capital gain.
- d. $0.

20. On July 1, 2002, Riley exchanged investment real property, with an adjusted basis of $160,000 and subject to a mortgage of $70,000, and received from Wilson $30,000 cash and other investment real property having a fair market value of $250,000. Wilson assumed the mortgage. What is Riley's recognized gain in 2002 on the exchange?
- a. $ 30,000
- b. $ 70,000
- c. $ 90,000
- d. $100,000

21. On October 1, 2002, Donald Anderson exchanged an apartment building having an adjusted basis of $375,000 and subject to a mortgage of $100,000 for $25,000 cash and another apartment building with a fair market value of $550,000 and subject to a mortgage of $125,000. The property transfers were made subject to the outstanding mortgages. What amount of gain should Anderson recognize in his tax return for 2002?
- a. $0
- b. $ 25,000
- c. $125,000
- d. $175,000

22. The following information pertains to the acquisition of a six-wheel truck by Sol Barr, a self-employed contractor:

Cost of original truck traded in	$20,000
Book value of original truck at trade-in date	4,000
List price of new truck	25,000
Trade-in allowance for old truck	6,000
Business use of both trucks	100%

The basis of the new truck is
- a. $27,000
- b. $25,000
- c. $23,000
- d. $19,000

23. An office building owned by Elmer Bass was condemned by the state on January 2, 2001. Bass received the condemnation award on March 1, 2002. In order to qualify for nonrecognition of gain on this involuntary conversion, what is the last date for Bass to acquire qualified replacement property?

a. August 1, 2003.
b. January 2, 2004.
c. March 1, 2005.
d. December 31, 2005.

24. In March 2002, Davis, who is single, purchased a new residence for $200,000. During that same month he sold his former residence for $380,000 and paid the realtor a $20,000 commission. The former residence, his first home, had cost $65,000 in 1979. Davis added a bathroom for $5,000 in 1998. What amount of gain is recognized from the sale of the former residence on Davis' 2002 tax return?
a. $160,000
b. $ 90,000
c. $ 40,000
d. $0

25. The following information pertains to the sale of Al and Beth Oran's principal residence:

Date of sale	February 2002
Date of purchase	October 1985
Net sales price	$760,000
Adjusted basis	$170,000

Al and Beth owned their home jointly and had occupied it as their principal residence since acquiring the home in 1984. In June 2002, the Orans bought a condo for $190,000 to be used as their principal residence. What amount of gain must the Orans recognize on their 2002 joint return from the sale of their residence?
a. $ 90,000
b. $150,000
c. $340,000
d. $400,000

26. Ryan, age fifty-seven, is single with no dependents. In January 2002, Ryan's principal residence was sold for the net amount of $400,000 after all selling expenses. Ryan bought the house in 1989 and occupied it until sold. On the date of sale, the house had a basis of $180,000. Ryan does not intend to buy another residence. What is the maximum exclusion of gain on sale of the residence that may be claimed in Ryan's 2002 income tax return?
a. $250,000
b. $220,000
c. $125,000
d. $0

27. Miller, an individual calendar-year taxpayer, purchased 100 shares of Maples Inc. common stock for $10,000 on July 10, 2001, and an additional fifty shares of Maples Inc. common stock for $4,000 on December 24, 2001. On January 8, 2002, Miller sold the 100 shares purchased on July 10, 2001, for $7,000. What is the amount of Miller's recognized loss for 2002 and what is the basis for her remaining fifty shares of Maples Inc. stock?
a. $3,000 recognized loss; $4,000 basis for her remaining stock.
b. $1,500 recognized loss; $5,500 basis for her remaining stock.
c. $1,500 recognized loss; $4,000 basis for her remaining stock.
d. $0 recognized loss; $7,000 basis for her remaining stock.

28. Smith, an individual calendar-year taxpayer, purchased 100 shares of Core Co. common stock for $15,000 on De-

cember 15, 2002, and an additional 100 shares for $13,000 on December 30, 2002. On January 3, 2003, Smith sold the shares purchased on December 15, 2002, for $13,000. What amount of loss from the sale of Core stock is deductible on Smith's 2002 and 2003 income tax returns?

	2002	*2003*
a.	$0	$0
b.	$0	$2,000
c.	$1,000	$1,000
d.	$2,000	$0

29. On March 10, 2002, James Rogers sold 300 shares of Red Company common stock for $4,200. Rogers acquired the stock in 1999 at a cost of $5,000.

On April 4, 2002, he repurchased 300 shares of Red Company common stock for $3,600 and held them until July 18, 2002, when he sold them for $6,000.

How should Rogers report the above transactions for 2002?
a. A long-term capital loss of $800.
b. A long-term capital gain of $1,000.
c. A long-term capital gain of $1,600.
d. A long-term capital loss of $800 and a short-term capital gain of $2,400.

30. Murd Corporation, a domestic corporation, acquired a 90% interest in the Drum Company in 1998 for $30,000. During 2002, the stock of Drum was declared worthless. What type and amount of deduction should Murd take for 2002?
a. Long-term capital loss of $1,000.
b. Long-term capital loss of $15,000.
c. Ordinary loss of $30,000.
d. Long-term capital loss of $30,000.

31. If an individual incurs a loss on a nonbusiness deposit as the result of the insolvency of a bank, credit union, or other financial institution, the individual's loss on the non-business deposit may be deducted in any one of the following ways **except**:
a. Miscellaneous itemized deduction
b. Casualty loss
c. Short-term capital loss
d. Long-term capital loss

Items 32 and 33 are based on the following:

Conner purchased 300 shares of Zinco stock for $30,000 in 1998. On May 23, 2002, Conner sold all the stock to his daughter Alice for $20,000, its then fair market value. Conner realized no other gain or loss during 2002. On July 26, 2002, Alice sold the 300 shares of Zinco for $25,000.

32. What amount of the loss from the sale of Zinco stock can Conner deduct in 2002?
a. $0
b. $ 3,000
c. $ 5,000
d. $10,000

33. What was Alice's recognized gain or loss on her sale?
a. $0.
b. $5,000 long-term gain.
c. $5,000 short-term loss.
d. $5,000 long-term loss.

34. In 2002, Fay sold 100 shares of Gym Co. stock to her son, Martin, for $11,000. Fay had paid $15,000 for the stock in 1999. Subsequently in 2002, Martin sold the stock to an unrelated third party for $16,000. What amount of gain from the sale of the stock to the third party should Martin report on his 2002 income tax return?

    a. $0
    b. $1,000
    c. $4,000
    d. $5,000

35. Among which of the following related parties are losses from sales and exchanges not recognized for tax purposes?

    a.   Mother-in-law and daughter-in-law.
    b.   Uncle and nephew.
    c.   Brother and sister.
    d.   Ancestors, lineal descendants, and all in-laws.

36. On May 1, 2002, Daniel Wright owned stock (held for investment) purchased two years earlier at a cost of $10,000 and having a fair market value of $7,000. On this date he sold the stock to his son, William, for $7,000. William sold the stock for $6,000 to an unrelated person on July 1, 2002. How should William report the stock sale on his 2002 tax return?

    a.   As a short-term capital loss of $1,000.
    b.   As a long-term capital loss of $1,000.
    c.   As a short-term capital loss of $4,000.
    d.   As a long-term capital loss of $4,000.

37. Al Eng owns 50% of the outstanding stock of Rego Corp. During 2002, Rego sold a trailer to Eng for $10,000, the trailer's fair value. The trailer had an adjusted tax basis of $12,000, and had been owned by Rego and used in its business for three years. In its 2002 income tax return, what is the allowable loss that Rego can claim on the sale of this trailer?

    a. $0
    b. $2,000 capital loss.
    c. $2,000 Section 1231 loss.
    d. $2,000 Section 1245 loss.

38. For a cash basis taxpayer, gain or loss on a year-end sale of listed stock arises on the

    a.   Trade date.
    b.   Settlement date.
    c.   Date of receipt of cash proceeds.
    d.   Date of delivery of stock certificate.

39. Lee qualified as head of a household for 2002 tax purposes. Lee's 2002 taxable income was $100,000, exclusive of capital gains and losses. Lee had a net long-term loss of $8,000 in 2002. What amount of this capital loss can Lee offset against 2002 ordinary income?

    a. $0
    b. $3,000
    c. $4,000
    d. $8,000

40. For the year ended December 31, 2002, Sol Corp. had an operating income of $20,000. In addition, Sol had capital gains and losses resulting in a net short-term capital gain of $2,000 and a net long-term capital loss of $7,000. How much of the excess of net long-term capital loss over net short-term capital gain could Sol offset against ordinary income for 2002?

    a. $5,000
    b. $3,000
    c. $1,500
    d. $0

41. In 2002, Nam Corp., which is not a dealer in securities, realized taxable income of $160,000 from its business operations. Also, in 2002, Nam sustained a long-term capital loss of $24,000 from the sale of marketable securities. Nam did not realize any other capital gains or losses since it began operations. In Nam's income tax returns, what is the proper treatment for the $24,000 long-term capital loss?

    a.   Use $3,000 of the loss to reduce 2002 taxable income, and carry $21,000 of the long-term capital loss forward for five years.
    b.   Use $6,000 of the loss to reduce 2002 taxable income by $3,000, and carry $18,000 of the long-term capital loss forward for five years.
    c.   Use $24,000 of the long-term capital loss to reduce 2002 taxable income by $12,000.
    d.   Carry the $24,000 long-term capital loss forward for five years, treating it as a short-term capital loss.

42. For assets acquired in 2002, the holding period for determining long-term capital gains and losses is more than

    a.   18 months.
    b.   12 months.
    c.   9 months.
    d.   6 months.

43. On July 1, 2002, Kim Wald sold an antique for $12,000 that she had bought for her personal use in 2000 at a cost of $15,000. In her 2002 return, Kim should treat the sale of the antique as a transaction resulting in

    a.   A nondeductible loss.
    b.   Ordinary loss.
    c.   Short-term capital loss.
    d.   Long-term capital loss.

44. Paul Beyer, who is unmarried, has taxable income of $30,000 exclusive of capital gains and losses and his personal exemption. In 2002, Paul incurred a $1,000 net short-term capital loss and a $5,000 net long-term capital loss. His capital loss carryover to 2003 is

    a. $0
    b. $1,000
    c. $3,000
    d. $5,000

45. Capital assets include

    a.   A corporation's accounts receivable from the sale of its inventory.
    b.   Seven-year MACRS property used in a corporation's trade or business.
    c.   A manufacturing company's investment in US Treasury bonds.
    d.   A corporate real estate developer's unimproved land that is to be subdivided to build homes, which will be sold to customers.

46. Joe Hall owns a limousine for use in his personal service business of transporting passengers to airports. The limousine's adjusted basis is $40,000. In addition, Hall owns his personal residence and furnishings, that together cost him $280,000. Hall's capital assets amount to

a. $320,000
b. $280,000
c. $ 40,000
d. $0

47. In 2002, Ruth Lee sold a painting for $25,000 that she had bought for her personal use in 1996 at a cost of $10,000. In her 2002 return, Lee should treat the sale of the painting as a transaction resulting in
a.   Ordinary income.
b.   Long-term capital gain.
c.   Section 1231 gain.
d.   No taxable gain.

48. In 2002, a capital loss incurred by a married couple filing a joint return
a.   Will be allowed only to the extent of capital gains.
b.   Will be allowed to the extent of capital gains, plus up to $3,000 of ordinary income.
c.   Will be allowed to the extent of capital gains, plus up to $6,000 of ordinary income.
d.   Is **not** an allowable loss.

49. Platt owns land that is operated as a parking lot. A shed was erected on the lot for the related transactions with customers. With regard to capital assets and Section 1231 assets, how should these assets be classified?

	Land	Shed
a.	Capital	Capital
b.	Section 1231	Capital
c.	Capital	Section 1231
d.	Section 1231	Section 1231

50. In 1998, Iris King bought a diamond necklace for her own use, at a cost of $10,000. In 2002, when the fair market value was $12,000, Iris gave this necklace to her daughter, Ruth. No gift tax was due. This diamond necklace is a
a.   Capital asset.
b.   Section 1231 asset.
c.   Section 1245 asset.
d.   Section 1250 asset.

51. Which of the following is a capital asset?
a.   Delivery truck.
b.   Personal-use recreation equipment.
c.   Land used as a parking lot for customers.
d.   Treasury stock, at cost.

52. Don Mott was the sole proprietor of a high-volume drug store which he owned for fifteen years before he sold it to Dale Drug Stores, Inc. in 2002. Besides the $900,000 selling price for the store's tangible assets and goodwill, Mott received a lump sum of $30,000 in 2002 for his agreement not to operate a competing enterprise within ten miles of the store's location for a period of six years. The $30,000 will be taxed to Mott as
a. $30,000 ordinary income in 2002.
b. $30,000 short-term capital gain in 2002.
c. $30,000 long-term capital gain in 2002.
d.   Ordinary income of $5,000 a year for six years.

53. In June 2002, Olive Bell bought a house for use partially as a residence and partially for operation of a retail gift shop. In addition, Olive bought the following furniture:

Kitchen set and living room pieces for the residential
   portion $ 8,000
Showcases and tables for the business portion   12,000

How much of this furniture comprises capital assets?
a. $0
b. $ 8,000
c. $12,000
d. $20,000

54. An individual's losses on transactions entered into for personal purposes are deductible only if
a.   The losses qualify as casualty or theft losses.
b.   The losses can be characterized as hobby losses.
c.   The losses do not exceed $3,000 ($6,000 on a joint return).
d.   No part of the transactions was entered into for profit.

55. Evon Corporation, which was formed in 1999, had $50,000 of net Sec. 1231 gain for its 2002 calendar year. Its net Sec. 1231 gains and losses for its three preceding tax years were as follows:

Year	Sec. 1231 results
1999	Gain of $10,000
2000	Loss of $15,000
2001	Loss of $20,000

As a result, Evon Corporation's 2002 net Sec. 1231 gain would be characterized as
a.   A net long-term capital gain of $50,000.
b.   A net long-term capital gain of $35,000 and ordinary income of $15,000.
c.   A net long-term capital gain of $25,000 and ordinary income of $25,000.
d.   A net long-term capital gain of $15,000 and ordinary income of $35,000.

56. Which one of the following would **not** be Sec. 1231 property even though held for more than twelve months?
a.   Business inventory.
b.   Unimproved land used for business.
c.   Depreciable equipment used in a business.
d.   Depreciable real property used in a business.

57. Vermont Corporation distributed packaging equipment that it no longer needed to Michael Jason who owns 20% of Vermont's stock. The equipment, which was acquired in 1997, had an adjusted basis of $2,000 and a fair market value of $9,000 at the date of distribution. Vermont had properly deducted $6,000 of straight-line depreciation on the equipment while it was used in Vermont's manufacturing activities. What amount of ordinary income must Vermont recognize as a result of the distribution of the equipment?
a. $0
b. $3,000
c. $6,000
d. $7,000

58. Tally Corporation sold machinery that had been used in its business for a loss of $22,000 during 2002. The machinery had been purchased and placed in service sixteen months earlier. For 2002, the $22,000 loss will be treated as a
a   Capital loss.
b.   Sec. 1245 loss.
c.   Sec. 1231 loss.
d.   Casualty loss because the machinery was held less than two years.

59. On January 2, 2000, Bates Corp. purchased and placed into service seven-year MACRS tangible property costing $100,000. On July 31, 2002, Bates sold the property for

$102,000, after having taken $47,525 in MACRS depreciation deductions. What amount of the gain should Bates recapture as ordinary income?

a. $0
b. $ 2,000
c. $47,525
d. $49,525

60. Thayer Corporation purchased an apartment building on January 1, 1999, for $200,000. The building was depreciated using the straight-line method. On December 31, 2002, the building was sold for $220,000, when the asset balance net of accumulated depreciation was $170,000. On its 2002 tax return, Thayer should report

a. Section 1231 gain of $42,500 and ordinary income of $7,500.
b. Section 1231 gain of $44,000 and ordinary income of $6,000.
c. Ordinary income of $50,000.
d. Section 1231 gain of $50,000.

61. For the year ended December 31, 2002, McEwing Corporation, a calendar-year corporation, reported book income before income taxes of $120,000. Included in the determination of this amount were the following gain and losses from property that had been held for more than one year:

Loss on sale of building depreciated on the straight-line method	$(7,000)
Gain on sale of land used in McEwing's business	16,000
Loss on sale of investments in marketable securities	(8,000)

For the year ended December 31, 2002, McEwing's taxable income was

a. $113,000
b. $120,000
c. $125,000
d. $128,000

62. David Price owned machinery which he had acquired in 2001 at a cost of $100,000. During 2002, the machinery was destroyed by fire. At that time it had an adjusted basis of $86,000. The insurance proceeds awarded to Price amounted to $125,000, and he immediately acquired a similar machine for $110,000.

What should Price report as ordinary income resulting from the involuntary conversion for 2002?

a. $14,000
b. $15,000
c. $25,000
d. $39,000

OTHER OBJECTIVE QUESTIONS

Problem 1

Required:

Classify the gains and losses resulting from the following independent transactions. For each transaction (**Items 1 through 12**), select the appropriate tax treatment. A tax treatment may be selected once, more than once, or not at all.

<table>
<tr><td colspan="2">Transaction</td><td colspan="2">Tax treatment</td></tr>
<tr><td>1.</td><td>Gain from sale of business inventory held thirteen months.</td><td>A.</td><td>Long-term capital gain</td></tr>
<tr><td></td><td></td><td>B.</td><td>Long-term capital loss</td></tr>
<tr><td>2.</td><td>Gain from sale of personal residence held three years.</td><td>C.</td><td>Short-term capital gain</td></tr>
<tr><td></td><td></td><td>D.</td><td>Short-term capital loss</td></tr>
<tr><td>3.</td><td>Gain from sale of unimproved land used as business parking lot and held seventeen months.</td><td>E.</td><td>Sec. 1231 gain</td></tr>
<tr><td></td><td></td><td>F.</td><td>Sec. 1231 loss</td></tr>
<tr><td>4.</td><td>Loss from sale of eight-year old boat held for personal use.</td><td>G.</td><td>Ordinary income</td></tr>
<tr><td></td><td></td><td>H.</td><td>Ordinary loss</td></tr>
<tr><td>5.</td><td>Gain from sale of lot held as investment for eleven months.</td><td>I.</td><td>Not deductible</td></tr>
</table>

6. Casualty gain on personal residence held ten years (this was taxpayer's only casualty during year).

7. Casualty loss on truck used in business and held seven months.

8. Loss from nonbusiness bad debt that was outstanding two years.

9. Loss from sale of factory building held twenty-two months.

10. Loss from sale of business warehouse held four months.

11. Collection of cash method taxpayer's accounts receivable.

12. Gain from sale of unimproved land used as parking lot for business and held nine months.

MULTIPLE-CHOICE ANSWERS

1. d __ __	14. a __ __	27. b __ __	40. d __ __	53. b __ __
2. d __ __	15. c __ __	28. a __ __	41. d __ __	54. a __ __
3. c __ __	16. c __ __	29. c __ __	42. b __ __	55. d __ __
4. c __ __	17. d __ __	30. c __ __	43. a __ __	56. a __ __
5. b __ __	18. b __ __	31. d __ __	44. c __ __	57. c __ __
6. b __ __	19. d __ __	32. a __ __	45. c __ __	58. c __ __
7. b __ __	20. d __ __	33. a __ __	46. b __ __	59. c __ __
8. d __ __	21. b __ __	34. b __ __	47. b __ __	60. b __ __
9. b __ __	22. c __ __	35. c __ __	48. b __ __	61. b __ __
10. c __ __	23. d __ __	36. a __ __	49. d __ __	62. a __ __
11. c __ __	24. c __ __	37. c __ __	50. a __ __	
12. d __ __	25. a __ __	38. a __ __	51. b __ __	1st: __/62 = __%
13. b __ __	26. b __ __	39. b __ __	52. a __ __	2nd: __/62 = __%

MULTIPLE-CHOICE ANSWER EXPLANATIONS

A.1. Basis of Property

1. **(d)** The requirement is to determine Birch's tax basis for the purchased land and building. The basis of property acquired by purchase is a cost basis and includes not only the cash paid and liabilities incurred, but also includes certain settlement fees and closing costs such as abstract of title fees, installation of utility services, legal fees (including title search, contract, and deed fees), recording fees, surveys, transfer taxes, owner's title insurance, and any amounts the seller owes that the buyer agrees to pay, such as back taxes and interest, recording or mortgage fees, charges for improvements or repairs, and sales commissions.

2. **(d)** The requirement is to determine the basis for the purchased land. The basis of the land consists of the cash paid ($40,000), the purchase money mortgage ($50,000), and the cost of the title insurance policy ($200), a total of $90,200.

A.1.c. Acquired by Gift

3. **(c)** The requirement is to determine Julie's basis for the land received as a gift. A donee's basis for gift property is generally the same as the donor's basis, increased by any gift tax paid that is attributable to the property's net appreciation in value. That is, the amount of gift tax that can be added is limited to the amount that bears the same ratio as the property's net appreciation bears to the amount of taxable gift. For this purpose, the amount of gift is reduced by any portion of the $11,000 annual exclusion that is allowable with respect to the gift. Thus, Julie's basis is $21,000 + [$14,000 ($81,000 – 21,000) / ($81,000 – $11,000)] = $33,000.

4. **(c)** The requirement is to determine Ruth's recognized loss if she sells the stock received as a gift for $7,000. Since the stock's FMV ($8,000) was less than its basis ($10,000) at date of gift, Ruth's basis for computing a loss is the stock's FMV of $8,000 at date of gift. As a result, Ruth's recognized loss is $8,000 – $7,000 = $1,000.

5. **(b)** The requirement is to determine Ruth's holding period for stock received as a gift. If property is received as a gift, and the property's FMV on date of gift is used to determine a loss, the donee's holding period begins when the gift was received. Thus, Ruth's holding period starts in 2002.

6. **(b)** The requirement is to determine the basis of the Liba stock if it is sold for $5,000. If property acquired by gift is sold at a gain, its basis is the donor's basis ($4,000), increased by any gift tax paid attributable to the net appreciation in value of the gift ($0).

7. **(b)** The requirement is to determine the basis of the Liba stock if it is sold for $2,000. If property acquired by gift is sold at a loss, its basis is the lesser of (1) its gain basis ($4,000 above), or (2) its FMV at date of gift ($3,000).

8. **(d)** The requirement is to determine the amount of reportable gain or loss if the Liba stock is sold for $3,500. No gain or loss is recognized on the sale of property acquired by gift if the basis for loss ($3,000 above) results in a gain and the basis for gain ($4,000 above) results in a loss.

A.1.d. Acquired from Decedent

9. **(b)** The requirement is to determine the holding period for stock received as a bequest from the estate of a deceased uncle. Property received from a decedent is deemed to be held long-term regardless of the actual period of time that the decedent or beneficiary actually held the property and is treated as held for more than twelve months.

10. **(c)** The requirement is to determine Ida's basis for stock inherited from a decedent. The basis of property received from a decedent is generally the property's FMV at date of the decedent's death, or FMV on the alternate valuation date (six months after death). Since the executor of Zorn's estate elected to use the alternate valuation for estate tax purposes, the stock's basis to Ida is its $450,000 FMV six months after Zorn's death.

NOTE: If the stock had been distributed to Ida within six months of Zorn's death, the stock's basis would be its FMV on date of distribution.

11. **(c)** The requirement is to determine Lois' basis for gain or loss on the sale of Elin stock acquired from a decedent. Since the alternate valuation was elected for Prevor's estate, but the stock was distributed to Lois within six months of date of death, Lois' basis is the $9,000 FMV of the stock on date of distribution (5/1/02).

12. **(d)** The requirement is to determine how Lois should treat the shares of Elin stock. The stock should be treated as a capital asset held long-term since (1) property acquired from a decedent is considered to be held for more than twelve months regardless of its actual holding period, and (2) the stock is an investment asset in Lois' hands. The stock is not a Sec. 1231 asset because it was not held for use in Lois' trade or business.

A.1.e. Stock Received as a Dividend

13. (b) The requirement is to determine the basis for the common stock and the preferred stock after the receipt of a nontaxable preferred stock dividend. Joan's original common stock basis must be allocated between the common stock and the preferred stock according to their relative fair market value.

Common stock (FMV)	$450
Preferred stock (FMV)	150
Total value	$600

The ratio of the common stock to total value is $450/$600 or 3/4. This ratio multiplied by the original common stock basis of $300 results in a basis for the common stock of $225. The basis of the preferred stock would be ($150/$600 x $300) = $75.

14. (a) The requirement is to determine the holding period for preferred stock that was received in a nontaxable distribution on common stock. Since the tax basis of the preferred stock is determined in part by the basis of the common stock, the holding period of the preferred stock includes the holding period of the common stock (i.e., the holding period of the common stock tacks on to the preferred stock). Thus, the holding period of the preferred stock starts when the common stock was acquired, January 2002.

15. (c) The requirement is to determine the amount of long-term capital gain to be reported on the sale of fifty shares of stock received as a nontaxable stock dividend. After the stock dividend, the basis of each share would be determined as follows:

$$\frac{\$90,000}{450 + 50} = \$180 \text{ per share}$$

Since the holding period of the new shares includes the holding period of the old shares, the sale of the fifty new shares for $11,000 results in a LTCG of $2,000 [$11,000 – (50 shares x $180)].

A.4.a. Like-Kind Exchange

16. (c) The requirement is to determine Gow's recognized gain and basis for the investment real estate acquired in a like-kind exchange. In a like-kind exchange of property held for investment, a realized gain ($15,000 in this case) will be recognized only to the extent of unlike property (i.e., boot) received. Here the unlike property consists of the $2,000 cash and $3,000 FMV of the sailboat received, resulting in the recognition of $5,000 of gain. The basis of the acquired like-kind property reflects the deferred gain resulting from the like-kind exchange, and is equal to the basis of the property transferred ($25,000), increased by the amount of gain recognized ($5,000), and decreased by the amount of boot received ($2,000 + $3,000), or $25,000.

17. (d) The requirement is to determine which exchange qualifies for nonrecognition of gain or loss as a like-kind exchange. The exchange of business or investment property solely for like-kind business or investment property is treated as a nontaxable exchange. Like-kind means "the same class of property." Real property must be exchanged for real property, and personal property must be exchanged for personal property. Here, the exchange of rental real estate is an exchange of like-kind property, even though the real estate is located in different states. The like-kind exchange provisions do not apply to exchanges of stocks, bonds, notes, convertible securities, the exchange of partnership interests, and property held for personal use.

18. (b) The requirement is to determine the basis for Leker's new van. The exchange of Leker's old van with a basis of $20,000 that was used exclusively for business, for a new van worth $15,000 plus $3,000 cash qualified as a like-kind exchange. Since it is a like-kind exchange, Leker's realized loss of $20,000 – ($15,000 + $3,000) = $2,000 cannot be recognized, but instead is reflected in the basis of the new van. The new van's basis is the adjusted basis of Leker's old van of $20,000 reduced by the $3,000 of cash boot received, resulting in a basis of $17,000.

19. (d) The requirement is to determine the reportable gain resulting from the exchange of an apartment building for an office building. No gain or loss is recognized on the exchange of business or investment property for property of a like-kind. The term "like-kind" means the same class of property (i.e., real estate must be exchanged for real estate, personal property exchanged for personal property). Thus, the exchange of an apartment building for an office building qualifies as a like-kind exchange. Since no boot (money or unlike property) was received, the realized gain of $600,000 – $200,000 = $400,000 is not recognized.

20. (d) The requirement is to determine the amount of recognized gain resulting from a like-kind exchange of investment property. In a like-kind exchange, gain is recognized to the extent of the lesser of (1) "boot" received, or (2) gain realized.

FMV of property received	$ 250,000
Cash received	30,000
Mortgage assumed	70,000
Amount realized	$ 350,000
Basis of property exchanged	(160,000)
Gain realized	$ 190,000

Since the "boot" received includes both the cash and the assumption of the mortgage, gain is recognized to the extent of the $100,000 of "boot" received.

21. (b) The requirement is to determine the amount of gain recognized to Anderson on the like-kind exchange of apartment buildings. Anderson's realized gain is computed as follows:

FMV of building received		$550,000
Mortgage on old building		100,000
Cash received		25,000
Amount realized		$675,000
Less:		
Basis of old building	$375,000	
Mortgage on new building	125,000	500,000
Realized gain		$175,000

Since the boot received in the form of cash cannot be offset against boot given in the form of an assumption of a mortgage, the realized gain is recognized to the extent of the $25,000 cash received.

22. (c) The requirement is to determine the basis of a new truck acquired in a like-kind exchange. The basis of the new truck is the book value (i.e., adjusted basis) of the old truck of $4,000 plus the additional cash paid of $19,000 (i.e., the list price of the new truck of $25,000 less the trade-in allowance of $6,000).

A.4.b.   Involuntary Conversions

23.   (d)   The requirement is to determine the end of the replacement period for nonrecognition of gain following the condemnation of real property. For a condemnation of real property held for productive use in a trade or business or for investment, the replacement period ends three years after the close of the taxable year in which the gain is first realized. Since the gain was realized in 2002, the replacement period ends December 31, 2005.

A.4.c.   Sale or Exchange of Residence

24.   (c)   The requirement is to determine the amount of gain from the sale of the former residence that is recognized on Davis' 2002 return. An individual may exclude from income up to $250,000 of gain that is realized on the sale or exchange of a residence, if the individual owned and occupied the residence as a principal residence for an aggregate of at least two of the five years preceding the sale or exchange. Davis' former residence cost $65,000 and he had made improvements costing $5,000, resulting in a basis of $70,000. Since Davis sold his former residence for $380,000 and paid a realtor commission of $20,000, the net amount realized from the sale was $360,000. Thus, Davis realized a gain of $360,000 – $70,000 = $290,000. Since Davis qualifies to exclude $250,000 of the gain from income, the remaining $40,000 of gain is recognized and included in Davis' income for 2002.

25.   (a)   The requirement is to determine the amount of gain to be recognized on the Orans' 2002 joint return from the sale of their residence. An individual may exclude from income up to $250,000 of gain that is realized on the sale or exchange of a residence, if the individual owned and occupied the residence as a principal residence for an aggregate of at least two of the five years preceding the sale or exchange. The amount of excludable gain is increased to $500,000 for married individuals filing jointly if either spouse meets the ownership requirement, and both spouses meet the use requirement. Here, the Orans realized a gain of $760,000 – $170,000 = $590,000, and qualify to exclude $500,000 of the gain from income. The remaining $90,000 of gain is recognized and taxed to the Orans for 2002.

26.   (b)   The requirement is to determine the maximum exclusion of gain on the sale of Ryan's principal residence. An individual may exclude from income up to $250,000 of gain that is realized on the sale or exchange of a residence, if the individual owned and occupied the residence as a principal residence for an aggregate of at least two of the five years preceding the sale or exchange. Since Ryan meets the ownership and use requirements, and realized a gain of $400,000 – $180,000 = $220,000, all of Ryan's gain will be excluded from his gross income.

A.5.   Sales and Exchanges of Securities

27.   (b)   The requirement is to determine Miller's recognized loss and the basis for her remaining fifty shares of Maples Inc. stock. No loss can be deducted on the sale of stock if substantially identical stock is purchased within

thirty days before or after the sale. Any loss that is not deductible because of this rule is added to the basis of the new stock. If the taxpayer acquires less than the number of shares sold, the amount of loss that cannot be recognized is determined by the ratio of the number of shares acquired to the number of shares sold. Miller purchased 100 shares of Maples stock for $10,000 and sold the stock on January 8, 2002, for $7,000, resulting in a loss of $3,000. However, only half of the loss can be deducted by Miller because on December 24, 2001 (within thirty days before the January 8, 2002 sale), Miller purchased an additional 50 shares of Maples stock. Since only $1,500 of the loss can be recognized, the $1,500 of loss not recognized is added to the basis of Miller's remaining 50 shares resulting in a basis of $4,000 + $1,500 = $5,500.

28.   (a)   The requirement is to determine the amount of loss from the sale of Core stock that is deductible on Smith's 2002 and 2003 income tax returns. No loss can be deducted on the sale of stock if substantially identical stock is purchased within thirty days before or after the sale. Any loss that is not deductible because of this rule is added to the basis of the new stock. In this case, Smith purchased 100 shares of Core stock for $15,000 and sold the stock on January 3, 2003 , for $13,000, resulting in a loss of $2,000. However, the loss cannot be deducted by Smith because on December 30, 2002 (within thirty days prior to the January 3, 2003 sale), Smith purchased an additional 100 shares of Core stock. Smith's disallowed loss of $2,000 is added to the $13,000 cost of the 100 Core shares acquired on December 30 resulting in a tax basis of $15,000 for those shares.

29.   (c)   The purchase of substantially identical stock within thirty days of the sale of stock at a loss is known as a wash sale. The $800 loss incurred in the wash sale ($5,000 basis less $4,200 amount realized) is disallowed. The basis of the replacement (substantially identical) stock is its cost ($3,600) plus the disallowed wash sale loss ($800). The holding period of the replacement stock includes the holding period of the wash sale stock. The amount realized ($6,000) less the basis ($4,400) results in a long-term gain of $1,600.

30.   (c)   Worthless securities generally receive capital loss treatment. However, if the loss is incurred by a corporation on its investment in an affiliated corporation (80% or more ownership), the loss is treated as an ordinary loss.

A.6.   Losses on Deposits in Insolvent Financial Institutions

31.   (d)   A loss resulting from a nonbusiness deposit in an insolvent financial institution is generally treated as a nonbusiness bad debt deductible as a short-term capital loss. However, subject to certain limitations, an individual may elect to treat the loss as a casualty loss or as a miscellaneous itemized deduction.

A.7.   Losses, Expenses, and Interest between Related Taxpayers

32.   (a)   The requirement is to determine the amount of the $10,000 loss that Conner can deduct from the sale of stock to his daughter, Alice. Losses are disallowed on sales or exchanges of property between related taxpayers, including members of a family. For this purpose, the term *family* includes an individual's spouse, brothers, sisters, ancestors, and lineal descendants (e.g., children, grandchildren, etc.).

Since Conner sold the stock to his daughter, no loss can be deducted.

33. **(a)** The requirement is to determine the recognized gain or loss on Alice's sale of the stock that she had purchased from her father. Losses are disallowed on sales or exchanges of property between related taxpayers, including family members. Any gain later realized by the related transferee on the subsequent disposition of the property is not recognized to the extent of the transferor's disallowed loss. Here, her father's realized loss of $30,000 – $20,000 = $10,000 was disallowed because he sold the stock to his daughter, Alice. Her basis for the stock is her cost of $20,000. On the subsequent sale of the stock, Alice realizes a gain of $25,000 – $20,000 = $5,000. However, this realized gain of $5,000 is not recognized because of her father's disallowed loss of $10,000.

34. **(b)** The requirement is to determine the amount of gain from the sale of stock to a third party that Martin should report on his 2002 income tax return. Losses are disallowed on sales of property between related taxpayers, including family members. Any gain later realized by the transferee on the disposition of the property is not recognized to the extent of the transferor's disallowed loss. Here, Fay's realized loss of $15,000 – $11,000 = $4,000 is disallowed because she sold the stock to her son, Martin. Martin's basis for the stock is his cost of $11,000. On the subsequent sale of the stock to an unrelated third party, Martin realizes a gain of $16,000 – $11,000 = $5,000. However, this realized gain of $5,000 is recognized only to the extent that it exceeds Fay's $4,000 disallowed loss, or $1,000.

35. **(c)** The requirement is to determine among which of the related individuals are losses from sales and exchanges not recognized for tax purposes. No loss deduction is allowed on the sale or exchange of property between members of a family. For this purpose, an individual's *family* includes only brothers, sisters, half-brothers and half-sisters, spouse, ancestors (parents, grandparents, etc.) and lineal descendants (children, grandchildren, etc.) Since in-laws and uncles are excluded from this definition of a family, a loss resulting from a sale or exchange with an uncle or between in-laws would be recognized.

36. **(a)** Losses are disallowed on sales between related taxpayers, including family members. Thus, Daniel's loss of $3,000 is disallowed on the sale of stock to his son, William. William's basis for the stock is his $7,000 cost. Since William's stock basis is determined by his cost (not by reference to Daniel's cost), there is no "tack-on" of Daniel's holding period. Thus, a later sale of the stock for $6,000 on July 1 generates a $1,000 STCL for William.

37. **(c)** The requirement is to determine the amount of loss that Rego Corp. can deduct on a sale of its trailer to a 50% shareholder. Losses are disallowed on transactions between related taxpayers, including a corporation and a shareholder owning more than 50% of its stock. Since Al Eng owns only 50% (not more than 50%), the loss is recognized by Rego. Since the trailer was held for more than one year and used in Rego's business, the $2,000 loss is a Sec. 1231 loss. Answer (d) is incorrect because Sec. 1245 only applies to gains.

B. Capital Gains and Losses

38. **(a)** The requirement is to determine when gain or loss on a year-end sale of listed stock arises for a cash basis taxpayer. If stock or securities that are traded on an established securities market are sold, any resulting gain or loss is recognized on the trade date (i.e., the date on which the trade is executed) by both cash and accrual method taxpayers.

39. **(b)** The requirement is to determine the amount of an $8,000 net long-term capital loss that can be offset against Lee's taxable income of $100,000. An individual's net capital loss can be offset against ordinary income up to a maximum of $3,000 ($1,500 if married filing separately). Since a net capital loss offsets ordinary income dollar for dollar, Lee has a $3,000 net capital loss deduction for 2002 and a long-term capital loss carryover of $5,000 to 2003.

40. **(d)** The requirement is to determine the amount of excess of net long-term capital loss over net short-term capital gain that Sol Corp. can offset against ordinary income. A corporation's net capital loss cannot be offset against ordinary income. Instead, a net capital loss is generally carried back three years and forward five years as a STCL to offset capital gains in those years.

41. **(d)** The requirement is to determine the proper treatment for a $24,000 NLTCL for Nam Corp. A corporation's capital losses can only be used to offset capital gains. If a corporation has a net capital loss, the net capital loss cannot be currently deducted, but must be carried back three years and forward five years as a STCL to offset capital gains in those years. Since Nam had not realized any capital gains since it began operations, the $24,000 LTCL can only be carried forward for five years as a STCL.

42. **(b)** The requirement is to determine the holding period for determining long-term capital gains and losses. Long-term capital gains and losses result if capital assets are held more than twelve months.

43. **(a)** The requirement is to determine the treatment for the sale of the antique by Wald. Since the antique was held for personal use, the sale of the antique at a loss is not deductible.

44. **(c)** The requirement is to determine the capital loss carryover to 2003. The NSTCL and the NLTCL result in a net capital loss of $6,000. LTCLs are deductible dollar for dollar, the same as STCLs. Since an individual can deduct a net capital loss up to a maximum of $3,000, the net capital loss of $6,000 results in a capital loss deduction of $3,000 for 2002, and a long-term capital loss carryover to 2003 of $3,000.

B.1. Capital Assets

45. **(c)** The requirement is to determine the item that is included in the definition of capital assets. The definition of capital assets includes property held as an investment and would include a manufacturing company's investment in US Treasury bonds. In contrast, the definition specifically excludes accounts receivable arising from the sale of inventory, depreciable property used in a trade or business, and property held primarily for sale to customers in the ordinary course of a trade or business.

46. **(b)** The requirement is to determine the amount of Hall's capital assets. The definition of capital assets includes investment property and property held for personal use (e.g., personal residence and furnishings), but excludes property used in a trade or business (e.g., limousine).

47. **(b)** The requirement is to determine the proper treatment for the gain recognized on the sale of a painting that was purchased in 1996 and held for personal use. The definition of "capital assets" includes investment property and property held for personal use (if sold at a gain). Because the painting was held for more than one year, the gain from the sale of the painting must be reported as a long-term capital gain. Note that if personal-use property is sold at a loss, the loss is not deductible.

48. **(b)** The requirement is to determine the correct treatment for a capital loss incurred by a married couple filing a joint return for 2002. Capital losses first offset capital gains, and then are allowed as a deduction of up to $3,000 against ordinary income, with any unused capital loss carried forward indefinitely. Note that a married taxpayer filing separately can only offset up to $1,500 of net capital loss against ordinary income.

49. **(d)** The requirement is to determine the proper classification of land used as a parking lot and a shed erected on the lot for customer transactions. The definition of capital assets includes investment property and property held for personal use, but excludes any property used in a trade or business. The definition of Sec. 1231 assets generally includes business assets held more than one year. Since the land and shed were used in conjunction with a parking lot business, they are properly classified as Sec. 1231 assets.

50. **(a)** The requirement is to determine the classification of Ruth's diamond necklace. The diamond necklace is classified as a capital asset because the definition of "capital asset" includes investment property and *property held for personal use.* Answers (b), (c), and (d) are incorrect because Sec. 1231 generally includes only assets used in a trade or business, while Sections 1245 and 1250 only include depreciable assets.

51. **(b)** The requirement is to determine which asset is a capital asset. The definition of capital assets includes personal-use property, but excludes property used in a trade or business (e.g., delivery truck, land used as a parking lot). Treasury stock is not considered an asset, but instead is treated as a reduction of stockholders' equity.

52. **(a)** The requirement is to determine how a lump sum of $30,000 received in 2002, for an agreement not to operate a competing enterprise, should be treated. A covenant not to compete is not a capital asset. Thus, the $30,000 received as consideration for such an agreement must be reported as ordinary income in the year received.

53. **(b)** The requirement is to determine the amount of furniture classified as capital assets. The definition of capital assets includes investment property and property held for personal use (e.g., kitchen and living room pieces), but excludes property used in a trade or business (e.g., showcases and tables).

C. Personal Casualty and Theft Gains and Losses

54. **(a)** The requirement is to determine the correct statement regarding the deductibility of an individual's losses on transactions entered into for personal purposes. An individual's losses on transactions entered into for personal purposes are deductible only if the losses qualify as casualty or theft losses. Answer (b) is incorrect because hobby losses are not deductible. Answers (c) and (d) are incorrect because losses (other than by casualty or theft) on transactions entered into for personal purposes are not deductible.

D. Gains and Losses on Business Property

55. **(d)** The requirement is to determine the characterization of Evon Corporation's $50,000 of net Sec. 1231 gain for its 2002 tax year. Although a net Sec. 1231 gain is generally treated as a long-term capital gain, it instead must be treated as ordinary income to the extent of the taxpayer's nonrecaptured net Sec. 1231 losses for its five preceding taxable years. Here, since the nonrecaptured net Sec. 1231 losses for 2000 and 2001 total $35,000, only $15,000 of the $50,000 net Sec. 1231 gain will be treated as a long-term capital gain.

56. **(a)** The requirement is to determine which item would not be characterized as Sec. 1231 property. Sec. 1231 property generally includes both depreciable and nondepreciable property used in a trade or business or held for the production of income if held for more than twelve months. Specifically excluded from Sec. 1231 is inventory and property held for sale to customers, as well as accounts and notes receivable arising in the ordinary course of a trade or business.

57. **(c)** The requirement is to determine the amount of ordinary income that must be recognized by Vermont Corporation from the distribution of the equipment to a shareholder. When a corporation distributes appreciated property, it must recognize gain just as if it had sold the property for its fair market value. As a result Vermont must recognize a gain of $9,000 – $2,000 = $7,000 on the distribution of the equipment. Since the distributed property is depreciable personality, the gain is subject to Sec. 1245 recapture as ordinary income to the extent of the $6,000 of straight-line depreciation deducted by Vermont. The remaining $1,000 of gain would be treated as Sec. 1231 gain.

58. **(c)** The requirement is to determine the nature of a loss resulting from the sale of business machinery that had been held sixteen months. Property held for use in a trade or business is specifically excluded from the definition of capital assets, and if held for more than one year is considered Sec. 1231 property. Answer (b) is incorrect because Sec. 1245 only applies to gains.

59. **(c)** The requirement is to determine the amount of gain from the sale of property that must be recaptured as ordinary income. A gain from the disposition of seven-year tangible property is subject to recapture under Sec. 1245 which recaptures gain to the extent of all depreciation previously deducted. Here, Bates' gain from the sale of the property is determined as follows:

Selling price		$102,000
Cost	$100,000	
Depreciation	– 47,525	
Adjusted basis		– 52,475
Gain		$ 49,525

Under Sec. 1245, Bates Corp's gain is recaptured as ordinary income to the extent of the $47,525 deducted as depreciation. The remaining $2,000 of gain would be classified as Sec. 1231 gain.

60. (b) The requirement is to determine the proper treatment of the $50,000 gain on the sale of the building, which is Sec. 1250 property. Sec. 1250 recaptures gain as ordinary income to the extent of "excess" depreciation (i.e., depreciation deducted in excess of straight-line). The total gain less any depreciation recapture is Sec. 1231 gain. Since straight-line depreciation was used, there is no recapture under Sec. 1250. However, Sec. 291 requires that the amount of ordinary income on the disposition of Sec. 1250 property by corporations be increased by 20% of the additional amount that would have been ordinary income if the property had instead been Sec. 1245 property. If the building had been Sec. 1245 property the amount of recapture would have been $30,000 ($200,000 – $170,000). Thus, the Sec. 291 ordinary income is $30,000 x 20% = $6,000. The remaining $44,000 is Sec. 1231 gain.

61. (b) The requirement is to determine McEwing Corporation's taxable income given book income plus additional information regarding items that were included in book income. The loss on sale of the building ($7,000) and gain on sale of the land ($16,000) are Sec. 1231 gains and losses. The resulting Sec. 1231 net gain of $9,000 is then treated as LTCG and will be offset against the LTCL of $8,000 resulting from the sale of investments. Since these items have already been included in book income, McEwing's taxable income is the same as its book income, $120,000.

62. (a) The realized gain resulting from the involuntary conversion ($125,000 insurance proceeds – $86,000 adjusted basis = $39,000) is recognized only to the extent that the insurance proceeds are not reinvested in similar property ($125,000 – $110,000 = $15,000). Since the machinery was Sec. 1245 property, the recognized gain of $15,000 is recaptured as ordinary income to the extent of the $14,000 of depreciation previously deducted. The remaining $1,000 is Sec. 1231 gain.

OTHER OBJECTIVE ANSWER EXPLANATIONS

Problem 1

1. **(G)** Inventory is neither a Sec. 1231 asset nor a capital asset.

2. **(A)** Capital assets include personal use property.

3. **(E)** Sec. 1231 includes gain from nondepreciable business property held more than one year.

4. **(I)** Loss from sale of personal use property is not deductible.

5. **(C)** Capital assets include investment property.

6. **(A)** A net personal casualty gain is treated as a capital gain.

7. **(H)** Ordinary loss because the business truck was not held for more than one year.

8. **(D)** Loss from nonbusiness bad debt is always treated as a short-term capital loss.

9. **(F)** Business property held more than one year.

10. **(H)** Ordinary because property must be held more than one year to be a Sec. 1231 loss.

11. **(G)** Accounts receivable are neither Sec. 1231 assets nor capital assets.

12. **(G)** Ordinary loss because business land not held for more than one year.

PARTNERSHIPS

Partnerships are organizations of two or more persons to carry on business activities for profit. For tax purposes, partnerships also include a syndicate, joint venture, or other unincorporated business through which any business or financial operation is conducted. Partnerships do not pay any income tax, but instead act as a conduit to pass-through tax items to the partners. Partnerships file an informational return (Form 1065), and partners report their share of partnership ordinary income or loss and other items on their individual returns. The nature or character (e.g., taxable, nontaxable) of income or deductions is not changed by the pass-through nature of the partnership.

A. Entity Classification

1. **Check-the-box regulations** permit an unincorporated entity to choose to be taxed as a partnership or a corporation by simply checking a box on Form 8832.

2. To be eligible to make an election, a business entity must have at least two members that carry on a business and divide the profits.

   a. Trusts and corporations are not eligible to make an election. A publicly traded partnership generally must be treated as a corporation.

   b. A one-member business entity (e.g., sole proprietorship) may elect to be treated as an association (taxed as a corporation), or disregarded and not treated as separate from its owner; but cannot be treated as a partnership.

3. Under default rules, unless an election is made to the contrary, an entity with only a single member will be disregarded as an entity separate from its owner.

4. Once a newly formed entity makes an election, a different election cannot be made for sixty months unless there is more than a 50% ownership change and the IRS consents.

B. Partnership Formation

1. As a general rule, **no gain or loss** is recognized by a partner when there is a contribution of property to the partnership in exchange for an interest in the partnership. There are three situations where gain must be recognized.

   a. A partner must recognize gain when property is contributed which is subject to a liability, and the resulting decrease in the partner's individual liability exceeds the partner's partnership basis.

      (1) The excess of liability over adjusted basis is generally treated as a capital gain from the sale or exchange of a partnership interest.

      (2) The gain will be treated as ordinary income to the extent the property transferred was subject to depreciation recapture under Sec. 1245 or 1250.

      EXAMPLE: A partner acquires a 20% interest in a partnership by contributing property worth $10,000 but with an adjusted basis of $4,000. There is a mortgage of $6,000 that is assumed by the partnership. The partner must recognize a gain of $800, and has a zero basis for the partnership interest, calculated as follows:

Adjusted basis of contributed property	$ 4,000
Less: portion of mortgage allocated to other partners (80% x $6,000)	(4,800)
Partner's basis (not reduced below 0)	$ 0

   b. Gain will be recognized on a contribution of property to a partnership in exchange for an interest therein if the partnership would be an investment company if incorporated.

   c. Partner must recognize compensation income when an interest in partnership capital is received in exchange for **services rendered**.

      EXAMPLE: X received a 10% capital interest in the ABC Partnership in exchange for services rendered. On the date X was admitted to the partnership, ABC's net assets had a basis of $30,000 and a FMV of $50,000. X must recognize compensation income of $5,000.

2. Property contributed to the partnership has the same **basis** as it had in the contributing partner's hands (a transferred basis).

   a. The basis for the partner's partnership interest is increased by the adjusted basis of property contributed.

   b. No gain or loss is generally recognized by the partnership upon the contribution.

3. The **partnership's holding period** for contributed property includes the period of time the property was held by the partner.

4. A **partner's holding period** for a partnership interest includes the holding period of property contributed, if the contributed property was a capital asset or Sec. 1231 asset in the contributing partner's hands.

C. Partnership Income and Loss

1. Since a partnership is not a separate taxable entity, but instead acts as a conduit to pass-through items of income and deduction to individual partners, the partnership's reporting of income and deductions requires a two-step approach.

   a. **First,** all items having special tax characteristics (i.e., subject to partial or full exclusion, % or dollar limitation, etc.) must be segregated and taken into account separately by each partner so that any special tax characteristics are preserved.

      (1) These special items are listed separately on Schedule K of the partnership return and include

         (a) Capital gains and losses
         (b) Sec. 1231 gains and losses
         (c) Charitable contributions
         (d) Foreign income taxes
         (e) Sec. 179 expense deduction for recovery property (limited to $24,000 for 2002)
         (f) Interest, dividend, and royalty income
         (g) Interest expense on investment indebtedness
         (h) Net income (loss) from rental real estate activity
         (i) Net income (loss) from other rental activity

   b. **Second,** all remaining items (since they have no special tax characteristics) are ordinary in nature and are netted in the computation of partnership ordinary income or loss from trade or business activities

      (1) Frequently encountered ordinary income and deductions include

         (a) Sales less cost of goods sold
         (b) Business expenses such as wages, rents, bad debts, and repairs
         (c) Guaranteed payments to partners
         (d) Depreciation
         (e) Amortization (over sixty months or more) of partnership organization expenses—Note that syndication fees (expenses of selling partnership interests) are neither deductible nor amortizable
         (f) Sec. 1245, 1250, etc., recapture
         (g) See Form 1065 outline at beginning of chapter for more detail

2. The **character** of any gain or loss recognized on the disposition of property is generally determined by the nature of the property in the hands of the partnership. However, for contributed property, the character may be based on the nature of the property to the contributing partner before contribution.

   a. If a partner contributes **unrealized receivables,** the partnership will recognize ordinary income or loss on the subsequent disposition of the unrealized receivables.

   b. If the property contributed was **inventory** property to the contributing partner, any gain or loss recognized by the partnership on the disposition of the property within five years will be treated as ordinary income or loss.

   c. If the contributed property was a **capital asset,** any loss later recognized by the partnership on the disposition of the property within five years will be treated as a capital loss to the extent of the contributing partner's unrecognized capital loss at the time of contribution. This rule applies to losses only, not to gains.

3. A person sitting for the examination should be able to calculate a partnership's ordinary income by adjusting partnership book income (or partnership book income by adjusting ordinary income).

EXAMPLE: A partnership's accounting income statement discloses net income of $75,000 (i.e., book income). The three partners share profit and losses equally. Supplemental data indicate the following information has been included in the computation of net income:

	DR.	CR.
Net sales		$160,000
Cost of goods sold	$ 88,000	
Tax-exempt income		1,500
Sec. 1231 casualty gain		9,000
Section 1231 gain (other than casualty)		6,000
Section 1250 gain		20,000
Long-term capital gain		7,500
Short-term capital loss	6,000	
Guaranteed payments ($8,000 per partner)	24,000	
Charitable contributions	9,000	
Advertising expense	2,000	
	$129,000	$204,000

Partnership ordinary income is $66,000, computed as follows:

Book income		$ 75,000
Add:		
Charitable contributions	$ 9,000	
Short-term capital loss	6,000	15,000
		$ 90,000
Deduct:		
Tax-exempt income	$ 1,500	
Sec. 1231 casualty gain	9,000	
Section 1231 gain (other than casualty)	6,000	
Long-term capital gain	7,500	24,000
Partnership ordinary income		$ 66,000

Each partner's share of partnership ordinary income is $22,000.

4. Three sets of rules may limit the amount of partnership loss that a partner can deduct.

   a. A partner's distributive share of partnership ordinary loss and special loss items is deductible by the partner only to the extent of the **partner's basis** for the partnership interest at the end of the taxable year [Sec. 704(d)].

      (1) The pass-through of loss is considered to be the last event during the partnership's taxable year; all positive basis adjustments are made prior to determining the amount of deductible loss.

      (2) Unused losses are carried forward and can be deducted when the partner obtains additional basis for the partnership interest.

      EXAMPLE: A partner who materially participates in the partnership's business has a distributive share of partnership capital gain of $200 and partnership ordinary loss of $3,000, but the partner's basis in the partnership is only $2,400 before consideration of these items. The partner can deduct $2,600 of the ordinary loss ($2,400 of beginning basis + $200 net capital gain). The remaining $400 of ordinary loss must be carried forward.

   b. The deductibility of partnership losses is also limited to the amount of the partner's **at-risk basis** [Sec. 465].

      (1) A partner's at-risk basis is generally the same as the partner's regular partnership basis with the exception that liabilities are included in at-risk basis only if the partner is personally liable for such amounts.

      (2) Nonrecourse liabilities are generally excluded from at-risk basis.

      (3) Qualified nonrecourse real estate financing is included in at-risk basis.

   c. The deductibility of partnership losses may also be subject to the **passive activity loss limitations** [Sec. 469]. Passive activity losses are deductible only to the extent of the partner's income from other passive activities (see Module 40).

      (1) Passive activities include (a) any partnership trade or business in which the partner does not materially participate, and (b) any rental activity.

      (2) A limited partnership interest generally fails the material participation test.

      (3) To qualify for the $25,000 exception for active participation in a rental real estate activity, a partner (together with spouse) must own at least 10% of the value of the partnership interests.

D. Partnership Agreements

1. A partner's distributive share of income or loss is generally determined by the partnership agreement. Such agreement can have different ratios for income or loss, and may agree to allocate other items (e.g., credits and deductions) in varying ratios

    a. Special allocations must have **substantial economic effect**.

        (1) Economic effect is measured by an analysis of the allocation on the partners' capital accounts. The special allocation (a) must be reflected in the partners' capital accounts, (b) liquidation distributions must be based upon the positive capital account balances of partners, and (c) there must be a deficit payback agreement wherein partners agree to restore any deficit capital account balances.

        (2) An allocation's economic effect will **not** be substantial if the net change recorded in the partners' capital accounts does not differ substantially from what would have been recorded without the special allocation, and the total tax liability of all partners is less.

    b. If no allocation is provided, or if the allocation of an item does not have substantial economic effect, the partners' distributive shares of that item shall be determined by the ratio in which the partners generally divide the income or loss of the partnership.

    c. **If property is contributed** by a partner to a partnership, related items of income, deduction, gain, or loss must be allocated among partners in a manner that reflects the difference between the property's tax basis and its fair market value at the time of contribution.

        EXAMPLE: Partner X contributes property with a tax basis of $1,000 and a fair market value of $10,000 to the XYZ Partnership. If the partnership subsequently sells the property for $12,000, the first $9,000 of gain must be allocated to X, with the remaining $2,000 of gain allocated among partners according to their ratio for sharing gains.

        (1) If property contributed to a partnership is distributed within seven years to a partner other than the partner who contributed such property, the contributing partner must recognize gain or loss equal to the amount that would have been recognized if the partnership had sold the property for its fair market value at the time of distribution.

        (2) The above recognition rule will not generally apply if other property of a like-kind to the contributed property is distributed to the contributing partner no later than the earlier of (1) the 180th day after the date on which the originally contributed property was distributed to another partner, or (2) the due date (without extension) for the contributing partner's return for the tax year in which the original distribution of property occurred.

    d. If there was any change in the ownership of partnership interests during the year, distributive shares of partnership interest, taxes, and payments for services or for the use of property must be allocated among partners by assigning an appropriate share of each item to each day of the partnership's taxable year.

        EXAMPLE: Z becomes a 40% partner in calendar-year Partnership XY on December 1. Previously, X and Y each had a 50% interest. Partnership XY uses the cash method of accounting and on December 31 pays $10,000 of interest expense that relates to its entire calendar year. Z's distributive share of the interest expense will be ($10,000 ÷ 365 days) x 31 days x 40% = $340.

2. **Distributable shares** of income and guaranteed payments are reported by partners for their taxable year during which the end of the partnership fiscal year occurs. All items, including guaranteed payments, are deemed to pass-through on the last day of the partnership's tax year.

    a. **Guaranteed payments** are payments to a partner determined without regard to income of the partnership. Guaranteed payments are deductible by the partnership and reported as income by the partners.

        EXAMPLE: Z (on a calendar-year) has a 20% interest in a partnership that has a fiscal year ending May 31. Z received a guaranteed payment for services rendered of $1,000 a month from 6/1/01 to 12/31/01 and $1,500 a month from 1/1/02 to 5/31/02. After deducting the guaranteed payment, the partnership had ordinary income of $50,000 for its fiscal year ended 5/31/02. Z must include $24,500 in income on Z's calendar-year 2002 return ($50,000 x 20%) + ($1,000 x 7) + ($1,500 x 5).

    b. Partners are generally not considered to be employees for purposes of employee fringe benefits (e.g., cost of $50,000 of group-term life insurance, exclusion of premiums or benefits under an employer accident or health plan, etc.). A partner's fringe benefits are deductible by the partnership as guaranteed payments and must be included in a partner's gross income.

3. **Family partnerships** are subject to special rules because of their potential use for tax avoidance.

   a. If the business is primarily service oriented (capital is not a material income-producing factor), a family member will be considered a partner only if the family member shares in the management or performs needed services.

   b. Capital is not a material income-producing factor if substantially all of the gross income of the business consists of fees, commissions, or other compensation for personal services (e.g., accountants, architects, lawyers).

   c. A family member is generally considered a partner if the family member actually owns a capital interest in a business in which capital is a material income-producing factor.

   d. Where a capital interest in a partnership in which capital is a material income-producing factor is treated as created by gift, the distributive shares of partnership income of the donor and donee are determined by first making a reasonable allowance for services rendered to the partnership, and then allocating the remainder according to the relative capital interests of the donor and donee.

E. Partner's Basis in Partnership

1. A partner's **original basis** is generally determined by the manner in which the partnership interest was acquired (e.g., contribution of property, compensation for services, purchase, gift, received from decedent).

2. As the partnership operates, the partner's basis for the partnership interest increases or decreases.

    a. A partner's basis is increased by the adjusted basis of any subsequent capital contributions.

    b. Also, a partner's basis is **increased** by any distributive share of

      (1) Partnership ordinary income
      (2) Capital gains and other special income items
      (3) Tax-exempt income of the partnership
      (4) The excess of the deduction for depletion over the partnership's basis of the property subject to depletion

    c. A partner's basis is **decreased** (but not below zero) by

      (1) The amount of money and the adjusted basis of other property distributed to the partner
      (2) The partner's distributive share of partnership ordinary loss and special expense items, as well as nondeductible items not properly chargeable to capital
      (3) The amount of the partner's deduction for depletion on oil and gas wells

      EXAMPLE: In the example in Section 3. on page 377, one partner's tax basis (who had a $15,000 tax basis at the beginning of the year) would be $40,000 at the end of the year, calculated as shown below.

Beginning partnership basis		*$15,000*
Add:		
Distributive share of partnership ordinary income	*22,000*	
Tax-exempt income	*500*	
Sec. 1231 casualty gain	*3,000*	
Section 1231 gain (other than casualty)	*2,000*	
Long-term capital gain	*2,500*	*30,000*
		$45,000
Less:		
Short-term capital loss	*$ 2,000*	
Charitable contributions	*3,000*	*5,000*
Ending partnership basis		*$40,000*

    d. **Changes in liabilities** affect a partner's basis.

      (1) An **increase** in the **partnership's liabilities** (e.g., loan from a bank, increase in accounts payable) increases each partner's basis in the partnership by each partner's share of the increase.

      (2) Any **decrease** in the **partnership's liabilities** is considered to be a distribution of money to each partner and reduces each partner's basis in the partnership by each partner's share of the decrease.

(3) Any **decrease** in a partner's **individual liability** by reason of the assumption by the partnership of such individual liabilities is considered to be a distribution of money to the partner by the partnership (i.e., partner's basis is reduced).

(4) Any **increase** in a partner's **individual liability** by reason of the assumption by the partner of partnership liabilities is considered to be a contribution of money to the partnership by the partner. Thus, the partner's basis is increased.

EXAMPLE: The XYZ partnership owns a warehouse with an adjusted basis of $120,000 subject to a mortgage of $90,000. Partner X (one of three equal partners) has a basis for his partnership interest of $75,000. If the partnership transfers the warehouse and mortgage to Partner X as a current distribution, X's basis for his partnership interest immediately following the distribution would be $15,000, calculated as follows:

Beginning basis	$ 75,000
Individual assumption of mortgage	+ 90,000
	$165,000
Distribution of warehouse	−120,000
Partner's share of decrease in partnership's liabilities	− 30,000
Basis after distribution	$ 15,000

EXAMPLE: Assume in the example above that one of the other one-third partners had a basis of $75,000 immediately before the distribution. What would the partner's basis be immediately after the distribution to Partner X? $45,000 (i.e., $75,000 less 1/3 of the $90,000 decrease in partnership liabilities).

F. Transactions with Controlled Partnerships

1. If a person engages in a transaction with a partnership other than as a member of such partnership, any resulting gain or loss is generally recognized. However, if the transaction involves a **more than 50% owned partnership**, one of three special rules may apply. Constructive ownership rules [page 352, Sections 7.a.(4)(a) and (b)] apply in determining whether a transaction involves a more than 50% owned partnership.

a. **No losses** are deductible from sales or exchanges of property between a partnership and a person owning (directly or indirectly) more than 50% of the capital or profits interests in such partnership, or between two partnerships in which the same persons own (directly or indirectly) more than 50% of the capital or profits interests. A gain later realized on a subsequent sale by the transferee will not be recognized to the extent of the disallowed loss.

EXAMPLE: Partnership X is owned by three equal partners, A, B, and C, who are brothers. Partnership X sells property at a loss of $5,000 to C. Since C owns a more than 50% interest in the partnership (i.e., C constructively owns his brothers' partnership interests), the $5,000 loss is disallowed to Partnership X.

EXAMPLE: Assume the same facts as in the above example. C later resells the property to Z, an unrelated taxpayer, at a gain of $6,000. C's realized gain of $6,000 will not be recognized to the extent of the $5,000 disallowed loss to the Partnership X.

b. If a person related to a partner does not indirectly own a more than 50% partnership interest, a transaction between the related person and the partnership is treated as occurring between the related person and the partners individually.

EXAMPLE: X owns 100% of X Corp. and also owns a 25% interest in WXYZ Partnership. X Corp. sells property at a $1,200 loss to the WXYZ Partnership. Since X Corp. is related to partner X (i.e., X owns more than 50% of X Corp.), the transaction is treated as if it occurred between X Corp. and partners W, X, Y, and Z individually. Therefore, the loss disallowed to X Corp. is $1,200 x 25% = $300.

c. A **gain** recognized on a sale or exchange of property between a partnership and a person owning (directly or indirectly) more than 50% of the capital or profits interests in such partnership, or between two partnerships in which the same persons own (directly or indirectly) more than 50% of the capital or profits interests, will be treated as **ordinary income** if the property is **not a capital asset** in the hands of the transferee.

EXAMPLE: Assume the same facts as in the preceding example. Further assume that F is the father of W, Y, and Z. F sells investment property to Partnership WXYZ at a gain of $10,000. If the property will not be a capital asset to Partnership WXYZ, F must report the $10,000 gain as ordinary income because F constructively owns a more than 50% partnership interest (i.e., F constructively owns his children's partnership interests).

d. A **gain** recognized on a sale or exchange of property between a partnership and a person owning (directly or indirectly) more than 50% of the capital or profits interests in such partnership will be treated as **ordinary income** if the property is **depreciable property** in the hands of the transferee.

G. Taxable Year of Partnership

1. When a partnership adopts (or attempts to change) its taxable year, it is subject to the following restrictions:

   a. A partnership must adopt the taxable year used by one or more of its partners owning an aggregate interest of more than 50% in profits and capital (but only if the taxable year used by such partners has been the same for the lesser of three taxable years or the period the partnership has existed).

      EXAMPLE: A partnership is formed by a corporation (which receives a 55% partnership interest) and five individuals (who each receive a 9% partnership interest). The corporation has a fiscal year ending June 30, while the individuals have a calendar year. The partnership must adopt a fiscal year ending June 30.

   b. If partners owning a more than 50% interest in partnership profits and capital do not have the same year-end, the partnership must adopt the same taxable year as used by all of its principal partners (i.e., a partner with a 5% or more interest in capital or profits).

   c. If its principal partners have different taxable years, the partnership must adopt the taxable year that results in the least aggregate deferral of income to partners.

2. A different taxable year than the year determined above can be used by a partnership if a **valid business purpose** can be established and IRS permission is received. The business purpose test will be met if a partnership receives at least 25% of its gross receipts in the last two months of a twelve-month period, and this "25% test" has been satisfied for three consecutive years.

   EXAMPLE: Partnership X is owned by three equal partners—A, B, and C, who use a calendar year. Partnership X has received at least 25% of its gross receipts during the months of June and July for each of the last three years. Partnership X may be allowed to change to a fiscal year ending July 31.

3. A partnership that otherwise would be required to adopt or change its tax year (normally to the calendar year) may **elect to use a fiscal year if the election does not result in a deferral period longer than three months**, or, if less, the deferral period of the year currently in use.

   a. The "deferral period" is the number of months between the close of the fiscal year elected and the close of the required year (e.g., if a partnership elects a tax year ending September 30 and a tax year ending December 31 is required, the deferral period of the year ending September 30 is three months).

   b. A partnership that elects a tax year other than a required year must make a "required payment" which is in the nature of a refundable, noninterest-bearing deposit that is intended to compensate the government for the revenue lost as a result of tax deferral. The required payment is due on May 15 each year and is recomputed for each subsequent year.

4. The **taxable year** of a partnership ordinarily **will not close** as a result of the death or entry of a partner, or the liquidation or sale of a partner's interest. But the partnership's taxable year closes as to **the partner** whose **entire interest** is sold or liquidated. Additionally, the partnership tax year closes with respect to a deceased partner as of date of death.

   EXAMPLE: A partner sells his entire interest in a calendar-year partnership on March 31. His pro rata share of partnership income up to March 31 is $15,000. Since the partnership year closes with respect to him at the time of sale, the $15,000 is includible in his income and increases the basis of his partnership interest for purposes of computing gain or loss on the sale. However, the partnership's taxable year does not close as to its remaining partners.

   EXAMPLE: X (on a calendar year) is a partner in the XYZ Partnership that uses a June 30 fiscal year. X died on April 30, 2002. Since the partnership year closes with respect to X at his death, X's final return for the period January 1 through April 30 will include his share of partnership income for the period beginning July 1, 2001, and ending April 30, 2002. His share of partnership income for May and June 2002 will be reported by his estate or other successor in interest.

H. Partnership's Use of Cash Method

1. The cash method cannot generally be used if inventories are necessary to clearly reflect income and cannot generally be used by tax shelters and partnerships that have a C corporation as a partner.

2. Any partnership (other than a tax shelter) can use the cash method if for every year it has average gross receipts of **$5 million or less** for any prior three-year period and does not have inventories for sale to customers.

3. A small partnership with average annual gross receipts of **$1 million or less** for any prior three-year period (ending after December 17, 1998) can use the cash method and is excepted from the requirements to account for inventories and use the accrual method for purchases and sales of merchandise.

I. Termination or Continuation of Partnership

1. A partnership will terminate when it no longer has at least two partners.
2. A partnership and its taxable year will terminate for all partners if there is a sale or exchange of 50% or more of the **total interests** in partnership capital and profits within a twelve-month period.

   a. Sales or exchanges of at least 50% during any twelve-month period cause a termination.

   > *EXAMPLE: The calendar-year ABC Partnership has three equal partners, A, B, and C. B sold his interest to D on November 1, 2001, and C sold his interest to E on April 1, 2002. The ABC Partnership is considered terminated on April 1 because at least 50% of the total interests have been sold within a twelve-month period.*

   b. If the same partnership interest is sold more than once during a twelve-month period, the sale is counted only once.

   > *EXAMPLE: The calendar-year RST Partnership has three equal partners, R, S, and T. T sold his interest to X on December 1, 2001, and X sold his interest to Y on May 1, 2002. The RST Partnership is not terminated because multiple sales of the same partnership interest are counted only once.*

3. In a **merger** of partnerships, the resulting partnership is a continuation of the merging partnership whose partners have a more than 50% interest in the resulting partnership.

   > *EXAMPLE: Partnerships AB and CD merge on April 1, forming the ABCD Partnership in which the partners' interests are as follows: Partner A, 30%; B, 30%; C, 20%; and D, 20%. Partnership ABCD is a continuation of the AB Partnership. The CD Partnership is considered terminated and its taxable year closed on April 1.*

4. In a **division** of a partnership, a resulting partnership is a continuation of the prior partnership if the resulting partnership's partners had a more than 50% interest in the prior partnership.

   > *EXAMPLE: Partnership ABCD is owned as follows: A, 40%; and B, C, and D each own a 20% interest. The partners agree to separate and form two partnerships—AC and BD. Partnership AC is a continuation of ABCD. BD is considered a new partnership and must adopt a taxable year, as well as make any other necessary tax accounting elections.*

J. Sale of a Partnership Interest

1. Since a partnership interest is usually a capital asset, the sale of a partnership interest generally results in **capital gain or loss**.

   a. Gain is excess of amount realized over the adjusted basis for the partnership interest.

   b. Include the selling partner's share of partnership liabilities in the amount realized because the selling partner is relieved of them.

   > *EXAMPLE: Miller sold her partnership interest to Carter for $150,000 cash, plus Carter's assumption of Miller's $60,000 share of partnership liabilities. The amount realized by Miller on the sale of her partnership interest is $150,000 + $60,000 = $210,000.*

2. **Gain is ordinary** (instead of capital) to extent attributable to unrealized receivables or appreciated inventory (Sec. 751 items).

   a. The term **unrealized receivables** generally refers to the accounts receivable of a cash method taxpayer, but for this purpose also includes any potential recapture under Secs. 1245, 1250, and 1252.

   b. The term **inventory** includes all assets except capital assets and Section 1231 assets.

   > *EXAMPLE: X has a 40% interest in the XY Partnership. Partner X sells his 40% interest to Z for $50,000. X's basis in his partnership is $22,000 and the cash-method partnership had the following receivables and inventory:*

	Adjusted basis	Fair market value
Accounts receivable	0	$10,000
Inventory	4,000	10,000
Potential Sec. 1250 recapture	0	10,000
	$4,000	$30,000

   > *X's total gain is $28,000 (i.e., $50,000 – $22,000). Since the Sec. 1250 recapture is treated as "unrealized receivables" and the inventory is appreciated, X will recognize ordinary income to the extent that his selling price attributable to Sec. 751 items ($30,000 x 40% = $12,000) exceeds his basis in those items ($4,000 x 40% = $1,600), that is, $10,400. The remainder of X's gain ($28,000 – $10,400 = $17,600) will be treated as capital gain.*

K. Pro Rata Distributions from Partnership

1. Partnership recognizes no gain or loss on a distribution.
2. If a single distribution consists of **multiple items of property,** the distributed property reduces the partner's basis for the partnership interest in the **following order:**

    a. Money,

    b. Adjusted basis of unrealized receivables and inventory, and

    c. Adjusted basis of other property.

3. Partner recognizes **gain** only to the extent **money received exceeds the partner's partnership basis**.

    a. Relief from liabilities is deemed a distribution of money.

    b. Gain is capital except for gain attributable to unrealized receivables and substantially appreciated inventory.

    c. The receipt of property (other than money) will not cause the recognition of gain.

    EXAMPLE: Casey had a basis of $9,000 for his partnership interest at the time that he received a nonliquidating partnership distribution consisting of $5,000 cash and other property with a basis of $3,000 and a FMV of $8,000. No gain is recognized by Casey since the cash received did not exceed his partnership basis. Casey's $9,000 basis for his partnership interest is first reduced by the $5,000 cash, and then reduced by the $3,000 basis of other property, to $1,000. Casey will have a basis for the other property received of $3,000.

4. Partner recognizes **loss** only upon **complete liquidation** of a partnership interest through receipt of only money, unrealized receivables, or inventory.

    a. The amount of loss is the basis for the partner's partnership interest less the money and the partnership's basis in the unrealized receivables and inventory received by the partner.

    b. The loss is generally treated as a capital loss.

    c. If property other than money, unrealized receivables, or inventory is distributed in complete liquidation of a partner's interest, no loss can be recognized.

EXAMPLE: Day had a basis of $20,000 for his partnership interest before receiving a distribution in complete liquidation of his interest. The liquidating distribution consisted of $6,000 cash and inventory with a basis of $11,000. Since Day's liquidating distribution consisted of only money and inventory, Day will recognize a loss on the liquidation of his partnership interest. The amount of loss is the $3,000 difference between the $20,000 basis for his partnership interest, and the $6,000 cash and the $11,000 basis for the inventory received. Day will have an $11,000 basis for the inventory.

EXAMPLE: Assume the same facts as in the preceding example except that Day's liquidating distribution consists of $6,000 cash and a parcel of land with a basis of $11,000. Since the liquidating distribution now includes property other than money, receivables, and inventory, no loss can be recognized on the liquidation of Day's partnership interest. The basis for Day's partnership interest is first reduced by the $6,000 cash to $14,000. Since no loss can be recognized, the parcel of land must absorb all of Day's unrecovered partnership basis. As a result, the land will have a basis of $14,000.

5. In **nonliquidating (current) distributions**, a partner's basis in distributed property is generally the same as the partnership's former basis in the property; but is **limited** to the basis for the partner's partnership interest less any money received.

EXAMPLE: Sara receives a current distribution from her partnership at a time when the basis for her partnership interest is $10,000. The distribution consists of $7,000 cash and Sec. 1231 property with an adjusted basis of $5,000 and a FMV of $9,000. No gain is recognized by Sara since the cash received did not exceed her basis. After being reduced by the cash, her partnership basis of $3,000 is reduced by the basis of the property (but not below zero). Her basis for the property is limited to $3,000.

6. **If multiple properties are distributed** in a liquidating distribution, or if the partnership's basis for distributed properties exceed the partner's basis for the partnership interest, the partner's basis for the partnership interest is allocated in the following order:

    a. Basis is first allocated to unrealized receivables and inventory items in an amount equal to their adjusted basis to the partnership. If the basis for the partner's interest to be allocated to the assets is less than the total basis of these properties to the partnership, a **basis decrease** is required and is determined under (1) below.

    b. To the extent a partner's basis is not allocated to assets under a. above, basis is allocated to other distributed properties by assigning to each property its adjusted basis in the hands of the partnership, and then increasing or decreasing the basis to the extent required in order for the adjusted basis of the distributed properties to equal the remaining basis for the partner's partnership interest.

        (1) A **basis decrease** is allocated

            (a) First to properties with unrealized depreciation in proportion to their respective amounts of unrealized depreciation (but only to the extent of each property's unrealized depreciation), and

            (b) Then in proportion to the respective adjusted basis of the distributed properties.

EXAMPLE: A partnership distributes two items of property (A and B) that are neither unrealized receivables nor inventory to Baker in liquidation of his partnership interest that has a basis of $20.

	Partnership basis	*FMV*
Property A	$15	$15
Property B	15	5
Total	$30	$20

Basis is first allocated $15 to A and $15 to B (their adjusted bases to the partnership). A $10 basis decrease is required because the assets' bases of $30 exceeds Baker's basis for his partnership interest of $20. The $10 decrease is allocated to B to the extent of its unrealized depreciation. Thus, Baker has a basis of $15 for property A and a basis of $5 for property B.

    (2) A **basis increase** is allocated

        (a) First to properties with unrealized appreciation in proportion to their respective amounts of unrealized appreciation (but only to the extent of each property's unrealized appreciation), and

        (b) Then in proportion to the relative FMVs of the distributed properties.

EXAMPLE: A partnership distributes two items of property (C and D) that are neither unrealized receivables nor inventory to Alan in liquidation of his partnership interest that has a basis of $55.

	Partnership basis	*FMV*
Property C	$ 5	$40
Property D	10	10
Total	$15	$50

Basis is first allocated $5 to C and $10 to D (their adjusted bases to the partnership). The $40 basis increase (Alan's $55 basis less the partnership's basis for the assets $15) is then allocated to C to the extent of its unrealized appreciation of $35, with the remaining $5 of basis adjustment allocated according to the relative FMV of C and D [i.e., $4 to C (for a total basis of $44) and $1 to D (for a total basis of $11)]

7. Payments made in liquidation of the interest of a retiring or deceased partner are generally treated as partnership distributions made in exchange for the partner's interest in partnership property. Such payments generally result in capital gain or loss to the retiring or deceased partner.

    a. However, payments made to a retiring or deceased general partner in a partnership in which capital is **not** a material income-producing factor must be reported as ordinary income by the partner to the extent such payments are for the partner's share of unrealized receivables or goodwill (unless the partnership agreement provides for a payment with respect to goodwill).

    b. Amounts treated as ordinary income by the retiring or deceased partner are either deductible by the partnership (treated as guaranteed payments), or reduce the income allocated to remaining partners (treated as a distributive share of partnership income).

    c. Capital is **not** a material income-producing factor if substantially all of the gross income of the business consists of fees, commissions, or other compensation for personal services (e.g., accountants, doctors, dentists, lawyers).

L. Non-Pro-Rata Distributions from Partnership

1. A non-pro-rata (disproportionate) distribution occurs when

    a. A distribution is disproportionate as to a partner's share of unrealized receivables or substantially appreciated inventory. Inventory is **substantially appreciated** if its FMV exceeds 120% of its basis.

        (1) Partner may receive more than the partner's share of these assets, or

        (2) Partner may receive more than the partner's share of other assets, in effect giving up a share of unrealized receivables or substantially appreciated inventory

    b. The partner may recognize gain or loss.

        (1) The gain or loss is the difference between the FMV of what is received and the basis of what is given up.

        (2) The gain or loss is limited to the disproportionate amount of unrealized receivables or substantially appreciated inventory that is received or given up.

        (3) The character of the gain or loss depends upon the character of the property given up.

c. The partnership may similarly recognize gain or loss when there is a disproportionate distribution with respect to substantially appreciated inventory or unrealized receivables.

EXAMPLE: A, B, and C each own a one-third interest in a partnership. The partnership has the following assets:

	Adjusted basis	*FMV*
Cash	$ 6,000	$ 6,000
Inventory	6,000	12,000
Land	9,000	18,000
	$21,000	$36,000

Assume that A has a $7,000 basis for his partnership interest and that all inventory is distributed to A in liquidation of his partnership interest. He is treated as having exchanged his 1/3 interest in the cash and the land for a 2/3 increased interest in the substantially appreciated inventory. He has a gain of $3,000. He received $8,000 (2/3 x $12,000) of inventory for his basis of $2,000 (1/3 x $6,000) in cash and $3,000 (1/3 x $9,000) of land. The gain is capital if the land was a capital asset. The partnership is treated as having received $8,000 (FMV of A's 1/3 share of cash and land) in exchange for inventory with a basis of $4,000 (basis of inventory distributed in excess of A's 1/3 share). Thus, the partnership will recognize ordinary income of $4,000.

M. Optional Adjustment to Basis of Partnership Property

1. On a distribution of property to a partner, or on a sale by a partner of a partnership interest, the partnership may elect to adjust the basis of its assets to **prevent any inequities** that otherwise might occur. Once an election is made, it applies to all similar transactions unless IRS approves revocation of the election.

2. Upon the **distribution of partnership property**, the basis of remaining partnership property will be adjusted for **all** partners.

   a. Increased by

   (1) The amount of gain recognized to a distributee partner, and
   (2) The excess of the partnership's basis in the property distributed over the basis of that property in the hands of distributee partner

   EXAMPLE: If election were made under facts in the example on page 382, $2,000 of basis that otherwise would be lost will be allocated to remaining partnership Sec. 1231 property.

   b. Decreased by

   (1) The amount of loss recognized to a distributee partner, and
   (2) The excess of basis of property in hands of distributee over the prior basis of that property in the partnership

3. Upon the **sale or exchange of a partnership interest**, the basis of partnership property to the **transferee** (not other partners) will be

   a. Increased by the excess of the basis of the transferee's partnership interest over the transferee's share of the adjusted basis of partnership property
   b. Decreased by the excess of transferee's share of adjusted basis of partnership property over the basis for the transferee's partnership interest

   EXAMPLE: Assume X sells his 40% interest to Z for $80,000 when the partnership balance sheet reflects the following

   XY Partnership

Assets	*Basis*	*FMV*
Accounts Receivable	$ 0	$100,000
Real Property	30,000	100,000
Capital		
X (40%)		$ 80,000
Y (60%)		120,000

Z will have a basis for his partnership interest of $80,000, while his share of the adjusted basis of partnership property will only be $12,000. If the partnership elects to adjust the basis of partnership property, it will increase the basis of its assets by $68,000 ($80,000 – $12,000) solely for the benefit of Z. The basis of the receivables will increase from 0 to $40,000 with the full adjustment allocated to Z. When the receivables are collected, Y will have $60,000 of income and Z will have none. The basis of the real property will increase by $28,000 to $58,000, so that Z's share of the basis will be $40,000 (i.e., $12,000 + $28,000).

Utilize Wiley's CPA Examination Review Impact Audios to reinforce key exam concepts and strategies.

Available at www.wiley.com/cpa

MULTIPLE-CHOICE QUESTIONS (1-67)

1. At partnership inception, Black acquires a 50% interest in Decorators Partnership by contributing property with an adjusted basis of $250,000. Black recognizes a gain if

I. The fair market value of the contributed property exceeds its adjusted basis.
II. The property is encumbered by a mortgage with a balance of $100,000.

    a.   I only.
    b.   II only.
    c.   Both I and II.
    d.   Neither I nor II.

2. On June 1, 2002, Kelly received a 10% interest in Rock Co., a partnership, for services contributed to the partnership. Rock's net assets at that date had a basis of $70,000 and a fair market value of $100,000. In Kelly's 2002 income tax return, what amount must Kelly include as income from transfer of the partnership interest?

    a. $ 7,000 ordinary income.
    b. $ 7,000 capital gain.
    c. $10,000 ordinary income.
    d. $10,000 capital gain.

3. Ola Associates is a limited partnership engaged in real estate development. Hoff, a civil engineer, billed Ola $40,000 in 2002 for consulting services rendered. In full settlement of this invoice, Hoff accepted a $15,000 cash payment plus the following:

	Fair market value	Carrying amount on Ola's books
3% limited partnership interest in Ola	$10,000	N/A
Surveying equipment	7,000	$3,000

What amount should Hoff, a cash-basis taxpayer, report in his 2002 return as income for the services rendered to Ola?

    a. $15,000
    b. $28,000
    c. $32,000
    d. $40,000

4. The following information pertains to property contributed by Gray on July 1, 2002, for a 40% interest in the capital and profits of Kag & Gray, a partnership:

As of June 30, 2002	
Adjusted basis	Fair market value
$24,000	$30,000

After Gray's contribution, Kag & Gray's capital totaled $150,000. What amount of gain was reportable in Gray's 2002 return on the contribution of property to the partnership?

    a. $0
    b. $ 6,000
    c. $30,000
    d. $36,000

5. The holding period of a partnership interest acquired in exchange for a contributed capital asset begins on the date

    a.   The partner is admitted to the partnership.
    b.   The partner transfers the asset to the partnership.
    c.   The partner's holding period of the capital asset began.
    d.   The partner is first credited with the proportionate share of partnership capital.

6. The following information pertains to Carr's admission to the Smith & Jones partnership on July 1, 2002:

Carr's contribution of capital: 800 shares of Ed Corp. stock bought in 1989 for $30,000; fair market value $150,000 on July 1, 2002.

Carr's interest in capital and profits of Smith & Jones: 25%.

Fair market value of net assets of Smith & Jones on July 1, 2002, after Carr's admission: $600,000.

Carr's gain in 2002 on the exchange of the Ed Corp. stock for Carr's partnership interest was

    a. $120,000 ordinary income.
    b. $120,000 long-term capital gain.
    c. $120,000 Section 1231 gain.
    d. $0.

7. The holding period of property acquired by a partnership as a contribution to the contributing partner's capital account

    a.   Begins with the date of contribution to the partnership.
    b.   Includes the period during which the property was held by the contributing partner.
    c.   Is equal to the contributing partner's holding period prior to contribution to the partnership.
    d.   Depends on the character of the property transferred.

8. On September 1, 2002, James Elton received a 25% capital interest in Bredbo Associates, a partnership, in return for services rendered plus a contribution of assets with a basis to Elton of $25,000 and a fair market value of $40,000. The fair market value of Elton's 25% interest was $50,000. How much is Elton's basis for his interest in Bredbo?

    a. $25,000
    b. $35,000
    c. $40,000
    d. $50,000

9. Basic Partnership, a cash-basis calendar-year entity, began business on February 1, 2002. Basic incurred and paid the following in 2002:

Filing fees incident to the creation of the partnership	$ 3,600
Accounting fees to prepare the representations in offering materials	12,000

Basic elected to amortize costs. What was the maximum amount that Basic could deduct on the 2002 partnership return?

    a. $11,000
    b. $ 3,300
    c. $ 2,860
    d. $ 660

10. In computing the ordinary income of a partnership, a deduction is allowed for

    a.   Contributions to recognized charities.
    b.   The first $100 of dividends received from qualifying domestic corporations.
    c.   Short-term capital losses.
    d.   Guaranteed payments to partners.

11. Which of the following limitations will apply in determining a partner's deduction for that partner's share of partnership losses?

	At-risk	Passive loss
a.	Yes	No
b.	No	Yes
c.	Yes	Yes
d.	No	No

12. Dunn and Shaw are partners who share profits and losses equally. In the computation of the partnership's 2002 book income of $100,000, guaranteed payments to partners totaling $60,000 and charitable contributions totaling $1,000 were treated as expenses. What amount should be reported as ordinary income on the partnership's 2002 return?

    a. $100,000
    b. $101,000
    c. $160,000
    d. $161,000

13. The partnership of Martin & Clark sustained an ordinary loss of $84,000 in 2002. The partnership, as well as the two partners, are on a calendar-year basis. The partners share profits and losses equally. At December 31, 2002, Clark, who materially participates in the partnership's business, had an adjusted basis of $36,000 for his partnership interest, before consideration of the 2002 loss. On his individual income tax return for 2002, Clark should deduct a(n)

    a. Ordinary loss of $36,000.
    b. Ordinary loss of $42,000.
    c. Ordinary loss of $36,000 and a capital loss of $6,000.
    d. Capital loss of $42,000.

14. The partnership of Felix and Oscar had the following items of income during the taxable year ended December 31, 2002.

Income from operations	$156,000
Tax-exempt interest income	8,000
Dividends from foreign corporations	6,000
Net rental income	12,000

What is the total ordinary income of the partnership for 2002?

    a. $156,000
    b. $174,000
    c. $176,000
    d. $182,000

15. A guaranteed payment by a partnership to a partner for services rendered, may include an agreement to pay

I. A salary of $5,000 monthly without regard to partnership income.
II. A 25% interest in partnership profits.

    a. I only.
    b. II only.
    c. Both I and II.
    d. Neither I nor II.

16. Chris, a 25% partner in Vista partnership, received a $20,000 guaranteed payment in 2002 for deductible services rendered to the partnership. Guaranteed payments were not made to any other partner. Vista's 2002 partnership income consisted of

Net business income before guaranteed payments	$80,000
Net long-term capital gains	10,000

What amount of income should Chris report from Vista Partnership on her 2002 tax return?

    a. $37,500
    b. $27,500

    c. $22,500
    d. $20,000

17. On January 2, 2002, Arch and Bean contribute cash equally to form the JK Partnership. Arch and Bean share profits and losses in a ratio of 75% to 25%, respectively. For 2002, the partnership's ordinary income was $40,000. A distribution of $5,000 was made to Arch during 2002. What amount of ordinary income should Arch report from the JK Partnership for 2002?

    a. $ 5,000
    b. $10,000
    c. $20,000
    d. $30,000

18. Guaranteed payments made by a partnership to partners for services rendered to the partnership, that are deductible business expenses under the Internal Revenue Code, are

I. Deductible expenses on the US Partnership Return of Income, Form 1065, in order to arrive at partnership income (loss).
II. Included on Schedule K-1 to be taxed as ordinary income to the partners.

    a. I only.
    b. II only.
    c. Both I and II.
    d. Neither I nor II.

19. The method used to depreciate partnership property is an election made by

    a. The partnership and must be the same method used by the "principal partner."
    b. The partnership and may be any method approved by the IRS.
    c. The "principal partner."
    d. Each individual partner.

20. Under the Internal Revenue Code sections pertaining to partnerships, guaranteed payments are payments to partners for

    a. Payments of principal on secured notes honored at maturity.
    b. Timely payments of periodic interest on bona fide loans that are **not** treated as partners' capital.
    c. Services or the use of capital without regard to partnership income.
    d. Sales of partners' assets to the partnership at guaranteed amounts regardless of market values.

21. Dale's distributive share of income from the calendar-year partnership of Dale & Eck was $50,000 in 2002. On December 15, 2002, Dale, who is a cash-basis taxpayer, received a $27,000 distribution of the partnership's 2002 income, with the $23,000 balance paid to Dale in May 2003. In addition, Dale received a $10,000 interest-free loan from the partnership in 2002. This $10,000 is to be offset against Dale's share of 2003 partnership income. What total amount of partnership income is taxable to Dale in 2002?

    a. $27,000
    b. $37,000
    c. $50,000
    d. $60,000

22. At December 31, 2001, Alan and Baker were equal partners in a partnership with net assets having a tax basis and fair market value of $100,000. On January 1, 2002,

Carr contributed securities with a fair market value of $50,000 (purchased in 2000 at a cost of $35,000) to become an equal partner in the new firm of Alan, Baker, and Carr. The securities were sold on December 15, 2002, for $47,000. How much of the partnership's capital gain from the sale of these securities should be allocated to Carr?

    a.　$0
    b.　$ 3,000
    c.　$ 6,000
    d.　$12,000

23. Gilroy, a calendar-year taxpayer, is a partner in the firm of Adams and Company which has a fiscal year ending June 30. The partnership agreement provides for Gilroy to receive 25% of the ordinary income of the partnership. Gilroy also receives a guaranteed payment of $1,000 monthly which is deductible by the partnership. The partnership reported ordinary income of $88,000 for the year ended June 30, 2002, and $132,000 for the year ended June 30, 2003. How much should Gilroy report on his 2002 return as total income from the partnership?

    a.　$25,000
    b.　$30,500
    c.　$34,000
    d.　$39,000

24. On December 31, 2001, Edward Baker gave his son, Allan, a gift of a 50% interest in a partnership in which capital is a material income-producing factor. For the year ended December 31, 2002, the partnership's ordinary income was $100,000. Edward and Allan were the only partners in 2002. There were no guaranteed payments to partners. Edward's services performed for the partnership were worth a reasonable compensation of $40,000 for 2002. Allan has never performed any services for the partnership. What is Allan's distributive share of partnership income for 2002?

    a.　$20,000
    b.　$30,000
    c.　$40,000
    d.　$50,000

Items 25 and 26 are based on the following:

Jones and Curry formed Major Partnership as equal partners by contributing the assets below.

	Asset	Adjusted basis	Fair market value
Jones	Cash	$45,000	$45,000
Curry	Land	30,000	57,000

The land was held by Curry as a capital asset, subject to a $12,000 mortgage, that was assumed by Major.

25. What was Curry's initial basis in the partnership interest?

    a.　$45,000
    b.　$30,000
    c.　$24,000
    d.　$18,000

26. What was Jones' initial basis in the partnership interest?

    a.　$51,000
    b.　$45,000
    c.　$39,000
    d.　$33,000

Items 27 and 28 are based on the following:

Flagg and Miles are each 50% partners in Decor Partnership. Each partner had a $200,000 tax basis in the partnership on January 1, 2002. Decor's 2002 net business income before guaranteed payments was $45,000. During 2002, Decor made a $7,500 guaranteed payment to Miles for deductible services rendered.

27. What total amount from Decor is includible in Flagg's 2002 tax return?

    a.　$15,000
    b.　$18,750
    c.　$22,500
    d.　$37,500

28. What is Miles's tax basis in Decor on December 31, 2002?

    a.　$211,250
    b.　$215,000
    c.　$218,750
    d.　$222,500

29. Peters has a one-third interest in the Spano Partnership. During 2002, Peters received a $16,000 guaranteed payment, which was deductible by the partnership, for services rendered to Spano. Spano reported a 2002 operating loss of $70,000 before the guaranteed payment. What is(are) the net effect(s) of the guaranteed payment?

  I. The guaranteed payment decreases Peters' tax basis in Spano by $16,000.
  II. The guaranteed payment increases Peters' ordinary income by $16,000.

    a.　I only.
    b.　II only.
    c.　Both I and II.
    d.　Neither I nor II.

30. Dean is a 25% partner in Target Partnership. Dean's tax basis in Target on January 1, 2002, was $20,000. At the end of 2002, Dean received a nonliquidating cash distribution of $8,000 from Target. Target's 2002 accounts recorded the following items:

Municipal bond interest income	$12,000
Ordinary income	40,000

What was Dean's tax basis in Target on December 31, 2002?

    a.　$15,000
    b.　$23,000
    c.　$25,000
    d.　$30,000

31. On January 4, 2002, Smith and White contributed $4,000 and $6,000 in cash, respectively, and formed the Macro General Partnership. The partnership agreement allocated profits and losses 40% to Smith and 60% to White. In 2002, Macro purchased property from an unrelated seller for $10,000 cash and a $40,000 mortgage note that was the general liability of the partnership. Macro's liability

    a.　Increases Smith's partnership basis by $16,000.
    b.　Increases Smith's partnership basis by $20,000.
    c.　Increases Smith's partnership basis by $24,000.
    d.　Has **no** effect on Smith's partnership basis.

32. Gray is a 50% partner in Fabco Partnership. Gray's tax basis in Fabco on January 1, 2002, was $5,000. Fabco made no distributions to the partners during 2002, and recorded the following:

Ordinary income	$20,000
Tax exempt income	8,000
Portfolio income	4,000

What is Gray's tax basis in Fabco on December 31, 2002?

    a. $21,000
    b. $16,000
    c. $12,000
    d. $10,000

33. On January 1, 2002, Kane was a 25% equal partner in Maze General Partnership, which had partnership liabilities of $300,000. On January 2, 2002, a new partner was admitted and Kane's interest was reduced to 20%. On April 1, 2002, Maze repaid a $100,000 general partnership loan. Ignoring any income, loss, or distributions for 2002, what was the **net** effect of the two transactions for Kane's tax basis in Maze partnership interest?

    a.   Has **no** effect.
    b.   Decrease of $35,000.
    c.   Increase of $15,000.
    d.   Decrease of $75,000.

34. Lee inherited a partnership interest from Dale. The adjusted basis of Dale's partnership interest was $50,000, and its fair market value on the date of Dale's death (the estate valuation date) was $70,000. What was Lee's original basis for the partnership interest?

    a. $70,000
    b. $50,000
    c. $20,000
    d. $0

35. Which of the following should be used in computing the basis of a partner's interest acquired from another partner?

	Cash paid by transferee to transferor	Transferee's share of partnership liabilities
a.	No	Yes
b.	Yes	No
c.	No	No
d.	Yes	Yes

36. Hall and Haig are equal partners in the firm of Arosa Associates. On January 1, 2002, each partner's adjusted basis in Arosa was $40,000. During 2002 Arosa borrowed $60,000, for which Hall and Haig are personally liable. Arosa sustained an operating loss of $10,000 for the year ended December 31, 2002. The basis of each partner's interest in Arosa at December 31, 2002, was

    a. $35,000
    b. $40,000
    c. $65,000
    d. $70,000

37. Doris and Lydia are sisters and also are equal partners in the capital and profits of Agee & Nolan. The following information pertains to 300 shares of Mast Corp. stock sold by Lydia to Agee & Nolan.

Year of purchase	1997
Year of sale	2002
Basis (cost)	$9,000
Sales price (equal to fair market value)	$4,000

The amount of long-term capital loss that Lydia recognized in 2002 on the sale of this stock was

    a. $5,000
    b. $3,000
    c. $2,500
    d. $0

38. In March 2002, Lou Cole bought 100 shares of a listed stock for $10,000. In May 2002, Cole sold this stock for its fair market value of $16,000 to the partnership of Rook, Cole & Clive. Cole owned a one-third interest in this partnership. In Cole's 2002 tax return, what amount should be reported as short-term capital gain as a result of this transaction?

    a. $6,000
    b. $4,000
    c. $2,000
    d. $0

39. Kay Shea owns a 55% interest in the capital and profits of Dexter Communications, a partnership. In 2002, Kay sold an oriental lamp to Dexter for $5,000. Kay bought this lamp in 1996 for her personal use at a cost of $1,000 and had used the lamp continuously in her home until the lamp was sold to Dexter. Dexter purchased the lamp as an investment. What is Kay's reportable gain in 2002 on the sale of the lamp to Dexter?

    a. $4,000 ordinary income.
    b. $4,000 long-term capital gain.
    c. $2,200 ordinary income.
    d. $1,800 long-term capital gain.

40. Gladys Peel owns a 50% interest in the capital and profits of the partnership of Peel and Poe. On July 1, 2002, Peel bought land the partnership had used in its business for its fair market value of $10,000. The partnership had acquired the land five years ago for $16,000. For the year ended December 31, 2002, the partnership's net income was $94,000 after recording the $6,000 loss on the sale of land. Peel's distributive share of ordinary income from the partnership for 2002 was

    a. $47,000
    b. $48,500
    c. $49,000
    d. $50,000

41. Under Section 444 of the Internal Revenue Code, certain partnerships can elect to use a tax year different from their required tax year. One of the conditions for eligibility to make a Section 444 election is that the partnership must

    a.   Be a limited partnership.
    b.   Be a member of a tiered structure.
    c.   Choose a tax year where the deferral period is **not** longer than three months.
    d.   Have less than seventy-five partners.

42. Which one of the following statements regarding a partnership's tax year is correct?

    a.   A partnership formed on July 1 is required to adopt a tax year ending on June 30.
    b.   A partnership may elect to have a tax year other than the generally required tax year if the deferral period for the tax year elected does **not** exceed three months.
    c.   A "valid business purpose" can **no** longer be claimed as a reason for adoption of a tax year other than the generally required tax year.

   d.   Within thirty days after a partnership has established a tax year, a form must be filed with the IRS as notification of the tax year adopted.

43. Without obtaining prior approval from the IRS, a newly formed partnership may adopt

   a.   A taxable year which is the same as that used by one or more of its partners owning an aggregate interest of more than 50% in profits and capital.

   b.   A calendar year, only if it comprises a twelve-month period.

   c.   A January 31 year-end if it is a retail enterprise, and all of its principal partners are on a calendar year.

   d.   Any taxable year that it deems advisable to select.

44. Irving Aster, Dennis Brill, and Robert Clark were partners who shared profits and losses equally. On February 28, 2002, Aster sold his interest to Phil Dexter. On March 31, 2002, Brill died, and his estate held his interest for the remainder of the year. The partnership continued to operate and for the fiscal year ending June 30, 2002, it had a profit of $45,000. Assuming that partnership income was earned on a pro rata monthly basis and that all partners were calendar-year taxpayers, the distributive shares to be included in 2002 gross income should be

   a.   Aster $10,000, Brill $0, Estate of Brill $15,000, Clark $15,000, and Dexter $5,000.

   b.   Aster $10,000, Brill $11,250, Estate of Brill $3,750, Clark $15,000, and Dexter $5,000.

   c.   Aster $0, Brill $11,250, Estate of Brill $3,750, Clark $15,000, and Dexter $15,000.

   d.   Aster $0, Brill $0, Estate of Brill $15,000, Clark $15,000, and Dexter $15,000.

45. On January 3, 2002, the partners' interests in the capital, profits, and losses of Able Partnership were

	% of capital profits and losses
Dean	25%
Poe	30%
Ritt	45%

On February 4, 2002, Poe sold her entire interest to an unrelated party. Dean sold his 25% interest in Able to another unrelated party on December 20, 2002. No other transactions took place in 2002. For tax purposes, which of the following statements is correct with respect to Able?

   a.   Able terminated as of February 4, 2002.

   b.   Able terminated as of December 20, 2002.

   c.   Able terminated as of December 31, 2002.

   d.   Able did **not** terminate.

46. Curry's sale of her partnership interest causes a partnership termination. The partnership's business and financial operations are continued by the other members. What is(are) the effect(s) of the termination?

   I.   There is a deemed distribution of assets to the remaining partners and the purchaser.

   II.   There is a hypothetical recontribution of assets to a new partnership.

   a.   I only.

   b.   II only.

   c.   Both I and II.

   d.   Neither I nor II.

47. Cobb, Danver, and Evans each owned a one-third interest in the capital and profits of their calendar-year partnership. On September 18, 2002, Cobb and Danver sold their partnership interests to Frank, and immediately withdrew from all participation in the partnership. On March 15, 2003, Cobb and Danver received full payment from Frank for the sale of their partnership interests. For tax purposes, the partnership

   a.   Terminated on September 18, 2002.

   b.   Terminated on December 31, 2002.

   c.   Terminated on March 15, 2003.

   d.   Did **not** terminate.

48. Partnership Abel, Benz, Clark & Day is in the real estate and insurance business. Abel owns a 40% interest in the capital and profits of the partnership, while Benz, Clark, and Day each owns a 20% interest. All use a calendar year. At November 1, 2002, the real estate and insurance business is separated, and two partnerships are formed: Partnership Abel & Benz takes over the real estate business, and Partnership Clark & Day takes over the insurance business. Which one of the following statements is correct for tax purposes?

   a.   Partnership Abel & Benz is considered to be a continuation of Partnership Abel, Benz, Clark & Day.

   b.   In forming Partnership Clark & Day, partners Clark and Day are subject to a penalty surtax if they contribute their entire distributions from Partnership Abel, Benz, Clark & Day.

   c.   Before separating the two businesses into two distinct entities, the partners must obtain approval from the IRS.

   d.   Before separating the two businesses into two distinct entities, Partnership Abel, Benz, Clark & Day must file a formal dissolution with the IRS on the prescribed form.

49. Under which of the following circumstances is a partnership that is not an electing large partnership considered terminated for income tax purposes?

   I.   Fifty-five percent of the total interest in partnership capital and profits is sold within a twelve-month period.

   II.   The partnership's business and financial operations are discontinued.

   a.   I only.

   b.   II only.

   c.   Both I and II.

   d.   Neither I nor II.

50. David Beck and Walter Crocker were equal partners in the calendar-year partnership of Beck & Crocker. On July 1, 2002, Beck died. Beck's estate became the successor in interest and continued to share in Beck & Crocker's profits until Beck's entire partnership interest was liquidated on April 30, 2003. At what date was the partnership considered terminated for tax purposes?

   a.   April 30, 2003.

   b.   December 31, 2002.

   c.   July 31, 2002.

   d.   July 1, 2002.

51. On December 31, 2002, after receipt of his share of partnership income, Clark sold his interest in a limited partnership for $30,000 cash and relief of all liabilities. On that date, the adjusted basis of Clark's partnership interest was $40,000, consisting of his capital account of $15,000 and his share of the partnership liabilities of $25,000. The partnership has no unrealized receivables or appreciated inventory. What is Clark's gain or loss on the sale of his partnership interest?

    a. Ordinary loss of $10,000.
    b. Ordinary gain of $15,000.
    c. Capital loss of $10,000.
    d. Capital gain of $15,000.

Items 52 and 53 are based on the following:

The personal service partnership of Allen, Baker & Carr had the following cash basis balance sheet at December 31, 2002:

Assets	Adjusted basis per books	Market value
Cash	$102,000	$102,000
Unrealized accounts receivable	--	420,000
Totals	$102,000	$522,000
Liability and Capital		
Note payable	$ 60,000	$ 60,000
Capital accounts:		
Allen	14,000	154,000
Baker	14,000	154,000
Carr	14,000	154,000
Totals	$102,000	$522,000

Carr, an equal partner, sold his partnership interest to Dole, an outsider, for $154,000 cash on January 1, 2003. In addition, Dole assumed Carr's share of the partnership's liability.

52. What was the total amount realized by Carr on the sale of his partnership interest?

    a. $174,000
    b. $154,000
    c. $140,000
    d. $134,000

53. What amount of ordinary income should Carr report in his 2003 income tax return on the sale of his partnership interest?

    a. $0
    b. $ 20,000
    c. $ 34,000
    d. $140,000

54. On April 1, 2002, George Hart, Jr. acquired a 25% interest in the Wilson, Hart and Company partnership by gift from his father. The partnership interest had been acquired by a $50,000 cash investment by Hart, Sr. on July 1, 1996. The tax basis of Hart, Sr.'s partnership interest was $60,000 at the time of the gift. Hart, Jr. sold the 25% partnership interest for $85,000 on December 17, 2002. What type and amount of capital gain should Hart, Jr. report on his 2002 tax return?

    a. A long-term capital gain of $25,000.
    b. A short-term capital gain of $25,000.
    c. A long-term capital gain of $35,000.
    d. A short-term capital gain of $35,000.

55. On June 30, 2002, James Roe sold his interest in the calendar-year partnership of Roe & Doe for $30,000. Roe's adjusted basis in Roe & Doe at June 30, 2002, was $7,500 before apportionment of any 2002 partnership income. Roe's distributive share of partnership income up to June 30, 2002, was $22,500. Roe acquired his interest in the

partnership in 1996. How much long-term capital gain should Roe report in 2002 on the sale of his partnership interest?

    a. $0
    b. $15,000
    c. $22,500
    d. $30,000

56. Curry's adjusted basis in Vantage Partnership was $5,000 at the time he received a nonliquidating distribution of land. The land had an adjusted basis of $6,000 and a fair market value of $9,000 to Vantage. What was the amount of Curry's basis in the land?

    a. $9,000
    b. $6,000
    c. $5,000
    d. $1,000

57. Hart's adjusted basis in Best Partnership was $9,000 at the time he received the following nonliquidating distribution of partnership property:

Cash	$ 5,000
Land	
Adjusted basis	7,000
Fair market value	10,000

What was the amount of Hart's basis in the land?

    a. $0
    b. $ 4,000
    c. $ 7,000
    d. $10,000

58. Day's adjusted basis in LMN Partnership interest is $50,000. During the year Day received a nonliquidating distribution of $25,000 cash plus land with an adjusted basis of $15,000 to LMN, and a fair market value of $20,000. How much is Day's basis in the land?

    a. $10,000
    b. $15,000
    c. $20,000
    d. $25,000

Items 59 and 60 are based on the following:

The adjusted basis of Jody's partnership interest was $50,000 immediately before Jody received a current distribution of $20,000 cash and property with an adjusted basis to the partnership of $40,000 and a fair market value of $35,000.

59. What amount of taxable gain must Jody report as a result of this distribution?

    a. $0
    b. $ 5,000
    c. $10,000
    d. $20,000

60. What is Jody's basis in the distributed property?

    a. $0
    b. $30,000
    c. $35,000
    d. $40,000

61. On June 30, 2002, Berk retired from his partnership. At that time, his capital account was $50,000 and his share of the partnership's liabilities was $30,000. Berk's retirement payments consisted of being relieved of his share of the partnership liabilities and receipt of cash payments of

$5,000 per month for eighteen months, commencing July 1, 2002. Assuming Berk makes no election with regard to the recognition of gain from the retirement payments, he should report income of

	2002	2003
a.	$13,333	$26,667
b.	20,000	20,000
c.	40,000	--
d.	--	40,000

62. The basis to a partner of property distributed "in kind" in complete liquidation of the partner's interest is the

    a. Adjusted basis of the partner's interest increased by any cash distributed to the partner in the same transaction.

    b. Adjusted basis of the partner's interest reduced by any cash distributed to the partner in the same transaction.

    c. Adjusted basis of the property to the partnership.

    d. Fair market value of the property.

Items 63 and 64 are based on the following data:

Mike Reed, a partner in Post Co., received the following distribution from Post:

	Post's basis	Fair market value
Cash	$11,000	$11,000
Inventory	5,000	12,500

Before this distribution, Reed's basis in Post was $25,000.

63. If this distribution were nonliquidating, Reed's basis for the inventory would be

    a. $14,000

    b. $12,500

    c. $ 5,000

    d. $ 1,500

64. If this distribution were in complete liquidation of Reed's interest in Post, Reed's recognized gain or loss resulting from the distribution would be

    a. $7,500 gain.

    b. $9,000 loss.

    c. $1,500 loss.

    d. $0

65. In 1997, Lisa Bara acquired a one-third interest in Dee Associates, a partnership. In 2002, when Lisa's entire interest in the partnership was liquidated, Dee's assets consisted of the following: cash, $20,000 and tangible property with a basis of $46,000 and a fair market value of $40,000. Dee has no liabilities. Lisa's adjusted basis for her one-third interest was $22,000. Lisa received cash of $20,000 in liquidation of her entire interest. What was Lisa's recognized loss in 2002 on the liquidation of her interest in Dee?

    a. $0.

    b. $2,000 short-term capital loss.

    c. $2,000 long-term capital loss.

    d. $2,000 ordinary loss.

66. For tax purposes, a retiring partner who receives retirement payments ceases to be regarded as a partner

    a. On the last day of the taxable year in which the partner retires.

    b. On the last day of the particular month in which the partner retires.

    c. The day on which the partner retires.

    d. Only after the partner's entire interest in the partnership is liquidated.

67. John Albin is a retired partner of Brill & Crum, a personal service partnership. Albin has not rendered any services to Brill & Crum since his retirement in 2001. Under the provisions of Albin's retirement agreement, Brill & Crum is obligated to pay Albin 10% of the partnership's net income each year. In compliance with this agreement, Brill & Crum paid Albin $25,000 in 2002. How should Albin treat this $25,000?

    a. Not taxable.

    b. Ordinary income.

    c. Short-term capital gain.

    d. Long-term capital gain.

OTHER OBJECTIVE QUESTIONS

Problem 1   (30 to 40 minutes)

On January 2, 2002, Rashid and Hughes established and began operating Madison Restaurant, in which both actively participate as equal partners. Madison's income statement for the year ended December 31, 2002, is presented below.

Sales			$980,000
Cost of sales			460,000
Gross profit			520,000
Operating expenses:			
(1) Salaries and wages (excluding partners)	$190,000		
(2) Less welfare-to-work credit	20,000	$170,000	
(3) Guaranteed payments to partners		110,000	
(4) Amortization of permanent liquor license		2,000	
(5) Annual liquor license fee		1,000	
(6) Depreciation		49,000	
(7) Section 179 deduction		0	
(8) Partners' health insurance premiums		18,000	
(9) Contributions to defined benefit (Keogh) pension plan		14,000	
(10) Charitable contribution		30,000	394,000
Operating (ordinary) income			126,000
Other income (loss):			
(11) Dividends		4,000	
(12) Rental		(2,000)	
Total		2,000	
Other expense:			
(13) Interest on investment debt		(2,000)	0
Total income			$126,000

Additional information

- Rashid and Hughes share profits and losses equally.
- The welfare-to-work credit pertains to qualified wages paid to an approved target group.
- Guaranteed payments to partners are for services rendered and are determined without regard to partnership income.
- In addition to the guaranteed payments, Rashid and Hughes each drew $29,000. These drawings were unrelated to the guaranteed payments.
- The permanent liquor license was purchased for $10,000 from a cafe that had gone out of business. This license, which is renewable for an indefinite period, is being amortized over the five-year term of Madison's lease.
- The cost of depreciable personal property used in the restaurant operations was $200,000. Madison elected to expense the maximum amount allowable for these Section 179 assets. The $36,000 depreciation includes the Section 179 deduction.
- The health insurance premiums were paid for services rendered by the partners without regard to partnership income. The value of the premiums equaled the cost of this coverage.
- Guaranteed payments to partners and partners' health insurance premiums are divided equally between Rashid and Hughes.
- Of the $14,000 contributions to the defined benefit (Keogh) pension plan, $8,000 was paid on behalf of the partners.
- The $30,000 charitable contribution is the adjusted basis of stock that had been bought as an investment. Its fair market value was $33,000 when it was donated to a qualified charitable organization.
- Madison sustained a $2,000 net loss on the rental of a vacant lot unrelated to the restaurant operations.

Required:

For each numbered item listed above, indicate the appropriate amount of income, deduction, or credit, **if any**, which should be recorded on the following:

Madison's Income and Deductions on page 1 of Form 1065, Partnership Return.

Madison's Schedule K, Partners' Shares of Income, Credits, Deductions, Etc.

Rashid's Schedule K-1, Partner's Share of Income, Credits, Deductions, Etc.

NOTE: On the CPA exam, a list of numeric answers would be provided for the candidate to select from.

Problem 2   (5 to 10 minutes)

During 2002, Adams, a general contractor, Brinks, an architect, and Carson, an interior decorator, formed the Dex Home Improvement General Partnership by contributing the assets below.

	Asset	Adjusted basis	Fair market value	% of partner share in capital, profits & losses
Adams	Cash	$40,000	$40,000	50%
Brinks	Land	$12,000	$21,000	20%
Carson	Inventory	$24,000	$24,000	30%

The land was a capital asset to Brinks, subject to a $5,000 mortgage, which was assumed by the partnership.

Required:

For items 1 and 2, determine and select the initial basis of the partner's interest in Dex.

1. Brinks' initial basis in Dex is
   a. $21,000
   b. $12,000
   c. $ 8,000

2. Carson's initial basis in Dex is
   a. $25,500
   b. $24,000
   c. $19,000

During 2002, the Dex Partnership breaks even but decides to make distributions to each partner.

Required:

For items 3 through 8, determine whether the statement is true (T) of false (F).

3. A nonliquidating cash distribution may reduce the recipient partner's basis in his partnership interest below zero.

4. A nonliquidating distribution of unappreciated inventory reduces the recipient partner's basis in his partnership interest.

5. In a liquidating distribution of property other than money, where the partnership's basis of the distributed property exceeds the basis of the partner's interest, the partner's basis in the distributed property is limited to his predistribution basis in the partnership interest.

6. Gain is recognized by the partner who receives a nonliquidating distribution of property, where the adjusted basis of the property exceeds his basis in the partnership interest before the distribution.

7. In a nonliquidating distribution of inventory, where the partnership has no unrealized receivables or appreciated inventory, the basis of inventory that is distributed to a partner cannot exceed the inventory's adjusted basis to the partnership.

8. The partnership's nonliquidating distribution of encumbered property to a partner who assumes the mortgage, does not affect the other partners' bases in their partnership interests.

MULTIPLE-CHOICE ANSWERS

1. d __ __	15. a __ __	29. b __ __	43. a __ __	57. b __ __
2. c __ __	16. a __ __	30. c __ __	44. b __ __	58. b __ __
3. c __ __	17. d __ __	31. a __ __	45. b __ __	59. a __ __
4. a __ __	18. c __ __	32. a __ __	46. c __ __	60. b __ __
5. c __ __	19. b __ __	33. b __ __	47. a __ __	61. d __ __
6. d __ __	20. c __ __	34. a __ __	48. a __ __	62. b __ __
7. b __ __	21. c __ __	35. d __ __	49. c __ __	63. c __ __
8. b __ __	22. d __ __	36. c __ __	50. a __ __	64. b __ __
9. d __ __	23. c __ __	37. d __ __	51. d __ __	65. c __ __
10. d __ __	24. b __ __	38. a __ __	52. a __ __	66. d __ __
11. c __ __	25. c __ __	39. b __ __	53. d __ __	67. b __ __
12. b __ __	26. a __ __	40. d __ __	54. a __ __	
13. a __ __	27. b __ __	41. c __ __	55. a __ __	1st: __/67= __%
14. a __ __	28. c __ __	42. b __ __	56. c __ __	2nd: __/67= __%

MULTIPLE-CHOICE ANSWER EXPLANATIONS

B. Partnership Formation

1. (d) The requirement is to determine which statements are correct regarding Black's recognition of gain on transferring property with an adjusted basis of $250,000 in exchange for a 50% partnership interest. Generally, no gain is recognized when appreciated property is transferred to a partnership in exchange for a partnership interest. However, gain will be recognized if the transferred property is incumbered by a mortgage, and the partnership's assumption of the mortgage results in a decrease in the transferor's individual liabilities that exceeds the basis of the property transferred. Here, the basis of the property transferred is $250,000, and the net decrease in Black's individual liabilities is $50,000 (i.e., $100,000 x 50%), so no gain is recognized.

2. (c) The requirement is to determine the amount that must be included on Kelly's 2002 income tax return as the result of the receipt of a 10% partnership interest in exchange for services. A taxpayer must recognize ordinary income when a capital interest in a partnership is received as compensation for services rendered. The amount of ordinary income to be included on Kelly's 2002 return is the fair market value of the partnership interest received ($100,000 x 10% = $10,000).

3. (c) The requirement is to determine the amount that Hoff, a cash-basis taxpayer, should report as income for the services rendered to Ola Associates. A cash-basis taxpayer generally reports income when received, unless constructively received at an earlier date. The amount of income to be reported is the amount of money, plus the fair market value of other property received. In this case, Hoff must report a total of $32,000, which includes the $15,000 cash, the $10,000 FMV of the limited partnership interest, and the $7,000 FMV of the surveying equipment received. Note that since Hoff is a cash-basis taxpayer, he would not report income at the time that he billed Ola $40,000, nor would he be entitled to a bad debt deduction when he accepts $32,000 of consideration in full settlement of his $40,000 invoice.

4. (a) The requirement is to determine the amount of gain reportable in Gray's return as a result of Gray's contribution of property in exchange for a 40% partnership interest. Generally, no gain or loss is recognized on the contribution of property in exchange for a partnership interest. Note that this nonrecognition rule applies even though the

value of the partnership capital interest received (40% x $150,000 = $60,000) exceeds the fair market value of the property contributed ($30,000).

5. (c) The requirement is to determine the correct statement regarding the holding period for a partnership interest acquired in exchange for a contributed capital asset. The holding period for a partnership interest that is acquired through a contribution of property depends upon the nature of the contributed property. If the contributed property was a capital asset or Sec. 1231 asset to the contributing partner, the holding period of the acquired partnership interest includes the period of time that the capital asset or Sec. 1231 asset was held by the partner. For all other contributed property, a partner's holding period for a partnership interest begins when the partnership interest is acquired.

6. (d) The requirement is to determine the amount of gain recognized on the exchange of stock for a partnership interest. Generally no gain or loss is recognized on the transfer of property to a partnership in exchange for a partnership interest. Since Carr's gain is not recognized, there will be a carryover basis of $30,000 for the stock to the partnership, and Carr will have a $30,000 basis for the 25% partnership interest received.

7. (b) The requirement is to determine the holding period for property acquired by a partnership as a contribution to the contributing partner's capital account. Generally no gain or loss is recognized on the contribution of property to a partnership in exchange for a capital interest. Since the partnership's basis for the contributed property is determined by reference to the contributing partner's former basis for the property (i.e., a transferred basis), the partnership's holding period includes the period during which the property was held by the contributing partner.

8. (b) The requirement is to determine Elton's basis for his 25% interest in the Bredbo partnership. Since Elton received a capital interest with a FMV of $50,000 in exchange for property worth $40,000 and services, Elton must recognize compensation income of $10,000 ($50,000 – $40,000) on the transfer of services for a capital interest. Thus, Elton's basis for his partnership interest consists of the $25,000 basis of assets transferred plus the $10,000 of income recognized on the transfer of services, a total of $35,000.

9.   **(d)**   The requirement is to determine the maximum amount of filing fees and accounting fees that Basic could deduct on the 2002 partnership return. The filing fees incident to the creation of the partnership are *organizational expenditures* that can be amortized over not less than sixty months beginning with the month that business begins if an election is made with the partnership's first tax return. Since Basic is a calendar-year partnership and began business in February, there would be eleven months of amortization for 2002, resulting in a maximum deduction of $3,600 x 11/60 = $660. The accounting fees to prepare the representations in offering materials are considered syndication fees. *Syndication fees* include the costs connected with the issuing and marketing of partnership interests such as commissions, professional fees, and printing costs. These costs must be capitalized and can neither be amortized nor depreciated.

C. Partnership Income and Loss

10.   **(d)**   The requirement is to determine the item that is deductible in the computation of the ordinary income of a partnership. Guaranteed payments to partners are always deductible in computing a partnership's ordinary income. Contributions to recognized charities and short-term capital losses cannot be deducted in computing a partnership's ordinary income because they are subject to special limitations and must be separately passed through so that any applicable limitations can be applied at the partner level. Similarly, dividends are an item of portfolio income and must be separately passed through to partners in order to retain its character as portfolio income when reported on partners' returns.

11.   **(c)**   The requirement is to determine whether the at-risk and passive activity loss limitations apply in determining a partner's deduction for that partner's share of partnership losses. A partner's distributive share of partnership losses is generally deductible by the partner to the extent of the partner's basis in the partnership at the end of the taxable year. Additionally, the deductibility of partnership losses is limited to the amount of the partner's at-risk basis, and will also be subject to the passive activity loss limitations if they are applicable. Note that the at-risk and passive activity loss limitations apply at the partner level, rather than at the partnership level.

12.   **(b)**   The requirement is to determine the amount to be reported as ordinary income on the partnership's return given partnership book income of $100,000. The $60,000 of guaranteed payments to partners were deducted in computing partnership book income and are also deductible in computing partnership ordinary income. However, the $1,000 charitable contribution deducted in arriving at partnership book income must be separately passed through to partners on Schedule K-1 and cannot be deducted in computing partnership ordinary income. Thus, the partnership's ordinary income is $100,000 + $1,000 = $101,000.

13.   **(a)**   The requirement is to determine the amount and type of partnership loss to be deducted on Clark's individual return. Since a partnership functions as a pass-through entity, the nature of a loss as an ordinary loss is maintained when passed through to partners. However, the amount of partnership loss that can be deducted by a partner is limited to a partner's tax basis in the partnership at the end of the partnership taxable year. Thus, Clark's distributive share of the ordinary loss ($42,000) is only deductible to the extent

of $36,000. The remaining $6,000 of loss would be carried forward by Clark and could be deducted after his partnership basis has been increased.

14.   **(a)**   The requirement is to determine the ordinary income of the partnership. Income from operations is considered ordinary income. The net rental income and the dividends from foreign corporations are separately allocated to partners and must be excluded from the computation of the partnership's ordinary income. Tax-exempt income remains tax-exempt and must also be excluded from the computation of ordinary income. Thus, ordinary income only consists of the income from operations of $156,000.

D. Partnership Agreements

15.   **(a)**   The requirement is to determine the correct statement(s) concerning agreements for guaranteed payments. Guaranteed payments are payments made to a partner for services or for the use of capital if the payments are determined *without regard to the amount of partnership income*. Guaranteed payments are deductible by a partnership in computing its ordinary income or loss from trade or business activities, and must be reported as self-employment income by the partner receiving payment. A payment that represents a 25% interest in partnership profits could not be classified as a guaranteed payment because the payment is conditioned on the partnership having profits.

16.   **(a)**   The requirement is to determine the amount of income that Chris should report as a result of her 25% partnership interest. A partnership is a pass-through entity and its items of income and deduction pass through to be reported on partners' returns even though not distributed. The amount to be reported by Chris consists of her guaranteed payment, plus her 25% share of the partnership's business income and capital gains. Since Chris's $20,000 guaranteed payment is for deductible services rendered to the partnership, it must be subtracted from the partnership's net business income before guaranteed payments of $80,000 to determine the amount of net business income to be allocated among partners. Chris's reportable income from the partnership includes

Guaranteed payment	$20,000
Business income [($80,000 – $20,000) x 25%]	15,000
Net long-term capital gain ($10,000 x 25%)	2,500
	$37,500

17.   **(d)**   The requirement is to determine Arch's share of the JK Partnership's ordinary income for 2002. A partnership functions as a pass-through entity and its items of income and deduction are passed through to partners according to their profit and loss sharing ratios, which may differ from the ratios used to divide capital. Here, Arch's distributive share of the partnership's ordinary income is $40,000 x 75% = $30,000. Note that Arch will be taxed on his $30,000 distributive share of ordinary income even though only $5,000 was distributed to him.

18.   **(c)**   The requirement is to determine whether the statements regarding partners' guaranteed payments are correct. Guaranteed payments made by a partnership to partners for services rendered are an ordinary deduction in computing a partnership's ordinary income or loss from trade or business activities on page 1 of Form 1065. Partners must report the receipt of guaranteed payments as ordinary income (self-employment income) and that is why the payments also must be separately listed on Schedule K and Schedule K-1.

19. (b) The requirement is to determine the correct statement regarding a partnership's election of a depreciation method. The method used to depreciate partnership property is an election made by the partnership and may be any method approved by the IRS. The partnership is not restricted to using the same method as used by its "principal partner." Since the election is made at the partnership level, and not by each individual partner, partners are bound by whatever depreciation method that the partnership elects to use.

20. (c) The requirement is to determine the correct statement regarding guaranteed payments to partners. Guaranteed payments are payments made to partners for their services or for the use of capital without regard to the amount of the partnership's income. Guaranteed payments are deductible by the partnership in computing its ordinary income or loss from trade of business activities, and must be reported as self-employment income by the partners receiving payment.

21. (c) The requirement is to determine the total amount of partnership income that is taxable to Dale in 2002. A partnership functions as a pass-through entity and its items of income and deduction are passed through to partners on the last day of the partnership's taxable year. Income and deduction items pass through to be reported by partners even though not actually distributed during the year. Here, Dale is taxed on his $50,000 distributive share of partnership income for 2002, even though $23,000 was not received until 2003. The $10,000 interest-free loan does not effect the pass-through of income for 2002, and the $10,000 offset against Dale's distributive share of partnership income for 2003 will not effect the pass-through of that income in 2003.

22. (d) The requirement is to determine the amount of the partnership's capital gain from the sale of securities to be allocated to Carr. Normally, the entire amount of precontribution gain would be allocated to Carr. However, in this case the allocation to Carr is limited to the partnership's recognized gain resulting from the sale, $47,000 selling price – $35,000 basis = $12,000.

23. (c) The requirement is to determine the amount that Gilroy should report for 2002 as total income from the partnership. Gilroy's income will consist of his share of the partnership's ordinary income for the fiscal year ending June 30, 2002 (the partnership year that ends within his year), plus the twelve monthly guaranteed payments that he received for that period of time.

25% x $88,000	=	$22,000
12 x $ 1,000	=	12,000
Total income	=	$34,000

24. (b) The requirement is to determine Allan's distributive share of the partnership income. In a family partnership, services performed by family members must first be reasonably compensated before income is allocated according to the capital interests of the partners. Since Edward's services were worth $40,000, Allan's distributive share of partnership income is ($100,000 – $40,000) x 50% = $30,000.

25. (c) The requirement is to determine Curry's initial basis for the 50% partnership interest received in exchange for a contribution of property subject to a $12,000 mortgage that was assumed by the partnership. Generally, no gain or loss is recognized on the contribution of property in exchange for a partnership interest. As a result, Curry's initial basis for the partnership interest received consists of the $30,000 adjusted basis of the land contributed to the partnership, less the net reduction in Curry's individual liability resulting from the partnership's assumption of the $12,000 mortgage. Since Curry received a 50% partnership interest, the net reduction in Curry's individual liability is $12,000 x 50% = $6,000. As a result, Curry's basis for the partnership interest is $30,000 – $6,000 = $24,000.

26. (a) The requirement is to determine Jones' initial basis for the 50% partnership interest received in exchange for a contribution of cash of $45,000. Since partners are individually liable for their share of partnership liabilities, an increase in partnership liabilities increases a partner's basis in the partnership by the partner's share of the increase. Jones' initial basis consists of the $45,000 of cash contributed, increased by the increase in Jones' individual liability resulting from the partnership's assumption of Curry's mortgage ($12,000 x 50% = $6,000). Thus, Jones' initial basis for the partnership interest is $45,000 + $6,000 = $51,000.

27. (b) The requirement is to determine the total amount includible in Flagg's 2002 tax return as a result of Flagg's 50% interest in the Decor Partnership. Decor's net business income of $45,000 would be reduced by the guaranteed payment of $7,500, resulting in $37,500 of ordinary income that would pass through to be reported on partners' returns. Here, Flagg's share of the includible income would be $37,500 x 50% = $18,750.

28. (c) The requirement is to determine Miles's tax basis for his 50% interest in the Decor Partnership on December 31, 2002. The basis for a partner's partnership interest is increased by the partner's distributive share of partnership income that is taxed to the partner. Here, Decor's net business income of $45,000 would be reduced by the guaranteed payment of $7,500, resulting in $37,500 of ordinary income that would pass through to be reported on partners' returns and increase the basis of their partnership interests. Here, Miles's beginning tax basis for the partnership interest of $200,000 would be increased by Miles's distributive share of ordinary income ($37,500 x 50% = $18,750), to $218,750.

29. (b) The requirement is to determine the net effect(s) of the $16,000 guaranteed payment made to Peters by the Spano Partnership who reported an operating loss of $70,000 before deducting the guaranteed payment. A guaranteed payment is a partnership payment made to a partner for services or for the use of capital if the payment is determined without regard to the amount of partnership income. A guaranteed payment is deductible by a partnership in computing its ordinary income or loss from trade or business activities and must be reported as self-employment income by the partner receiving the payment, thereby increasing Peters' ordinary income by $16,000. However, since Peters has only a one-third interest in the Spano Partnership, the $16,000 of guaranteed payment deducted by Spano would have the effect of reducing Peters' tax basis in Spano by only one-third of $16,000.

E. Partner's Basis in Partnership

30. (c)   The requirement is to determine the basis for Dean's 25% partnership interest at December 31, 2002. A partner's basis for a partnership interest is increased or decreased by the partner's distributive share of all partnership items. Basis is increased by the partner's distributive share of all income items (including tax-exempt income) and is decreased by all loss and deduction items (including nondeductible items) and distributions received from the partnership. In this case, Dean's beginning basis of $20,000 would be increased by the pass-through of his distributive share of the partnership's ordinary income ($40,000 x 25% = $10,000) and municipal bond interest income ($12,000 x 25% = $3,000), and would be decreased by the $8,000 cash nonliquidating distribution that he received.

31. (a)   The requirement is to determine the effect of a $40,000 increase in partnership liabilities on the basis for Smith's 40% partnership interest. Since partners are individually liable for their share of partnership liabilities, a change in the amount of partnership liabilities affects a partner's basis for a partnership interest. When partnership liabilities increase, it is effectively treated as if each partner individually borrowed money and then made a capital contribution of the borrowed amount. As a result, an increase in partnership liabilities increases each partner's basis in the partnership by each partner's share of the increase. Here, Smith's basis is increased by his 40% share of the mortgage (40% x $40,000 = $16,000).

32. (a)   The requirement is to determine Gray's tax basis for a 50% interest in the Fabco Partnership. The basis for a partner's partnership interest is increased by the partner's distributive share of all partnership items of income and is decreased by the partner's distributive share of all loss and deduction items. Here, Gray's beginning basis of $5,000 would be increased by Gray's 50% distributive share of ordinary income ($10,000), tax-exempt income ($4,000), and portfolio income ($2,000), resulting in an ending basis of $21,000 for Gray's Fabco partnership interest.

33. (b)   The requirement is to determine the net effect of the two transactions on Kane's tax basis for his Maze partnership interest. A partner's basis for a partnership interest consists of the partner's capital account plus the partner's share of partnership liabilities. A decrease in a partner's share of partnership liabilities is considered to be a deemed distribution of money and reduces a partner's basis for the partnership interest. Here, Kane's partnership interest was reduced from 25% to 20% on January 2, resulting in a reduction in Kane's share of liabilities of 5% x $300,000 = $15,000. Subsequently, on April 1, when there was a $100,000 repayment of partnership loans, there was a further reduction in Kane's share of partnership liabilities of 20% x $100,000 = $20,000. Thus, the net effect of the reduction of Kane's partnership interest to 20% from 25%, and the repayment of $100,000 of partnership liabilities would be to reduce Kane's basis for the partnership interest by $15,000 + $20,000 = $35,000.

34. (a)   The requirement is to determine the original basis of Lee's partnership interest that was received as an inheritance from Dale. The basis of property received from a decedent is generally its fair market value as of date of death. Since fair market value on the date of Dale's death was used for estate tax purposes, Lee's original basis is $70,000.

35. (d)   The requirement is to determine whether cash paid by a transferee, and the transferee's share of partnership liabilities are to be included in computing the basis of a partner's interest acquired from another partner. When an existing partner sells a partnership interest, the consideration received by the transferor partner, and the basis of the transferee's partnership interest includes both the cash actually paid by the transferee to the transferor, as well as the transferee's assumption of the transferor's share of partnership liabilities.

36. (c)   The requirement is to determine the basis of each partner's interest in Arosa at December 31, 2002. Since there are two equal partners, each partner's adjusted basis in Arosa of $40,000 on January 1, 2002, would be increased by 50% of the $60,000 loan and would be decreased by 50% of the $10,000 operating loss. Thus, each partner's basis in Arosa at December 31, 2002, would be $40,000 + $30,000 liability – $5,000 loss = $65,000.

F. Transactions with Controlled Partnerships

37. (d)   The requirement is to determine the amount of long-term capital loss recognized by Lydia from the sale of stock to Agee & Nolan. A loss is disallowed if incurred in a transaction between a partnership and a person owning (directly or constructively) more than a 50% capital or profits interest. Although Lydia directly owns only a 50% partnership interest, she constructively owns her sister's 50% partnership interest. Since Lydia directly and constructively has a 100% partnership interest, her $5,000 loss is disallowed.

38. (a)   The requirement is to determine the amount to be reported as short-term capital gain on Cole's sale of stock to the partnership. If a person engages in a transaction with a partnership other than as a partner of such partnership, any resulting gain is generally recognized just as if the transaction had occurred with a nonpartner. Here, Cole's gain of $16,000 – $10,000 = $6,000 is fully recognized. Since the stock was not held for more than twelve months, Cole's $6,000 gain is treated as a short-term capital gain.

39. (b)   The requirement is to determine the amount and nature of Kay's gain from the sale of the lamp to Admor. A gain that is recognized on a sale of property between a partnership and a person owning a more than 50% partnership interest will be treated as ordinary income if the property is not a capital asset in the hands of the transferee. Although Kay has a 55% partnership interest, the partnership purchased the lamp as an investment (i.e., a capital asset), and Kay's gain will solely depend on how she held the lamp. Since she used the lamp for personal use, Kay has a $5,000 – $1,000 = $4,000 long-term capital gain.

40. (d)   The requirement is to determine Peel's distributive share of ordinary income from the partnership. Although the $6,000 loss that was deducted in arriving at the partnership's net income would also be deductible for tax purposes, it must be separately passed through to partners because it is a Sec. 1231 loss. Thus, the $6,000 loss must be added back to the $94,000 of partnership net income and results in partnership ordinary income of $100,000. Peel's share is $100,000 x 50% = $50,000.

G. Taxable Year of Partnership

41. (c) The requirement is to determine the correct statement regarding a partnership's eligibility to make a Sec. 444 election. A partnership must generally adopt the same taxable year as used by its one or more partners owning an aggregate interest of more than 50% in partnership profits and capital. However, under Sec. 444, a partnership can instead elect to adopt a fiscal year that does not result in a deferral period of longer than three months. The deferral period is the number of months between the end of its selected year and the year that it generally would be required to adopt. For example, a partnership that otherwise would be required to adopt a taxable year ending December 31, could elect to adopt a fiscal year ending September 30. The deferral period would be the months of October, November, and December. The partnership is not required to be a limited partnership, be a member of tiered structure, or have less than seventy-five partners.

42. (b) The requirement is to determine the correct statement regarding a partnership's tax year. A partnership must generally determine its taxable year in the following order: (1) it must adopt the taxable year used by its one or more partners owning an aggregate interest of more than 50% in profits and capital; (2) if partners owning a more than 50% interest in profits and capital do not have the same year-end, the partnership must adopt the same taxable year as used by all of its principal partners; and (3) if principal partners have different taxable years, the partnership must adopt the taxable year that results in the least aggregate deferral of income to partners.

A different taxable year other than the year determined above can be used by a partnership if a valid business purpose can be established and IRS permission is received. Alternatively, a partnership can elect to use a tax year (other than one required under the general rules in the first paragraph), if the election does not result in a deferral of income of more than three months. The deferral period is the number of months between the close of the elected tax year and the close of the year that would otherwise be required under the general rules. Thus, a partnership that would otherwise be required to adopt a tax year ending December 31 could elect to adopt a fiscal year ending September 30 (three-month deferral), October 31 (two-month deferral), or November 30 (one-month deferral). Note that a partnership that makes this election must make "required payments" which are in the nature of refundable, noninterest-bearing deposits that are intended to compensate the Treasury for the revenue lost as a result of the deferral period.

43. (a) A newly formed partnership must adopt the same taxable year as is used by its partners owning a more than 50% interest in profits and capital. If partners owning more than 50% do not have the same taxable year, a partnership must adopt the same taxable year as used by all of its principal partners (i.e., partners with a 5% or more interest in capital and profits). If its principal partners have different taxable years, a partnership must adopt the tax year that results in the least aggregate deferral of income to partners.

44. (b) The requirement is to determine the distributive shares of partnership income for the partnership fiscal year

ended June 30, 2002, to be included in gross income by Aster, Brill, Estate of Brill, Clark, and Dexter. Clark was a partner for the entire year and is taxed on his distributive 1/3 share ($45,000 x 1/3 = $15,000). Since Aster sold his entire partnership interest to Dexter, the partnership tax year closes with respect to Aster on February 28. As a result, Aster's distributive share is $45,000 x 1/3 x 8/12 = $10,000. Dexter's distributive share is $45,000 x 1/3 / 4/12 = $5,000.

Additionally, partnership tax year closes with respect to a deceased partner as of date of death. Since Brill died on March 31, the distributive share to be included in Brill's 2002 Form 1040 would be $45,000 x 1/3 x 9/12 = $11,250. Since Brill's estate held his partnership interest for the remainder of the year, the estate's distributive share of income is $45,000 x 1/3 x 3/12 = $3,750.

I. Termination or Continuation of Partnership

45. (b) The requirement is to determine the correct statement regarding the termination of the Able Partnership. A partnership is terminated for tax purposes when there is a sale or exchange of 50% or more of the total interests in partnership capital and profits within any twelve-month period. Since Poe sold her 30% interest on February 4, 2002, and Dean sold his 25% partnership interest on December 20, 2002, there has been a sale of 55% of the total interests within a twelve-month period and the Able Partnership is terminated on December 20, 2002.

46. (c) The requirement is to determine which statements are correct concerning the termination of a partnership. A partnership will terminate when there is a sale of 50% or more of the total interests in partnership capital and profits within any twelve-month period. When this occurs, there is a deemed distribution of assets to the remaining partners and the purchaser, and a hypothetical recontribution of these same assets to a new partnership.

47. (a) The requirement is to determine the date on which the partnership terminated for tax purposes. The partnership was terminated on September 18, 2002, the date on which Cobb and Danver sold their partnership interests to Frank, since on that date there was a sale of 50% or more of the total interests in partnership capital and profit.

48. (a) The requirement is to determine the correct statement concerning the division of Partnership Abel, Benz, Clark, & Day into two partnerships. Following the division of a partnership, a resulting partnership is deemed to be a continuation of the prior partnership if the resulting partnership's partners had a more than 50% interest in the prior partnership. Here, as a result of the division, Partnership Abel & Benz is considered to be a continuation of the prior partnership because its partners (Abel and Benz) owned more than 50% of the interests in the prior partnership (i.e., Abel 40% and Benz 20%).

49. (c) The requirement is to determine under which circumstances a partnership, other than an electing large partnership, is considered terminated for income tax purposes. A partnership will be terminated when (1) there are no longer at least two partners, (2) no part of any business, financial operation, or venture of the partnership continues to be carried on by any of its partners in a partnership, or (3) within a twelve-month period there is a sale or exchange of

50% or more of the total interest in partnership capital and profits.

50. (a) The requirement is to determine the date on which the partnership was terminated. A partnership generally does not terminate for tax purposes upon the death of a partner, since the deceased partner's estate or successor in interest continues to share in partnership profits and losses. However, the Beck and Crocker Partnership was terminated when Beck's entire partnership interest was liquidated on April 30, 2003, since there no longer were at least two partners and the business ceased to exist as a partnership.

J.   Sale of a Partnership Interest

51. (d) The requirement is to determine the amount and character of gain or loss recognized on the sale of Clark's partnership interest. A partnership interest is a capital asset and a sale generally results in capital gain or loss, except that ordinary income must be reported to the extent of the selling partner's share of unrealized receivables and appreciated inventory. Here, Clark realized $55,000 from the sale of his partnership interest ($30,000 cash + relief from his $25,000 share of partnership liabilities). Since the partnership had no unrealized receivables or appreciated inventory and the basis of Clark's interest was $40,000, Clark realized a capital gain of $55,000 – $40,000 = $15,000 from the sale.

52. (a) The requirement is to determine the total amount realized by Carr on the sale of his partnership interest. The total amount realized consists of the amount of cash received plus the buyer's assumption of Carr's share of partnership liabilities. Thus, the total amount realized is $154,000 + ($60,000 x 1/3) = $174,000.

53. (d) The requirement is to determine the amount of ordinary income that Carr should report on the sale of his partnership interest. Although the sale of a partnership interest generally results in capital gain or loss, ordinary income must be recognized to the extent of the selling partner's share of unrealized receivables and appreciated inventory. Here, Carr must report ordinary income to the extent of his 1/3 share of the unrealized accounts receivable of $420,000, or $140,000.

54. (a) The requirement is to determine the amount and type of capital gain to be reported by Hart, Jr. from the sale of his partnership interest. Since the partnership interest was acquired by gift from Hart, Sr., Jr.'s basis would be the same as Sr.'s basis at date of gift, $60,000. Since Jr.'s basis is determined from Sr.'s basis, Jr.'s holding period includes the period the partnership interest was held by Sr. Thus, Hart, Jr. will report a LTCG of $85,000 – $60,000 = $25,000.

55. (a) The requirement is to determine the amount of LTCG to be reported by Roe on the sale of his partnership interest. Roe's basis for his partnership interest of $7,500 must first be increased by his $22,500 distributive share of partnership income, to $30,000. Since the selling price also was $30,000, Roe will report no gain or loss on the sale of his partnership interest.

K.   Pro Rata Distributions from Partnership

56. (c) The requirement is to determine the basis for land acquired in a nonliquidating partnership distribution. Generally, no gain or loss is recognized on the distribution

of partnership property to a partner. As a result, the partner's basis for distributed property is generally the same as the partnership's former basis for the property (a transferred basis). However, since the distribution cannot reduce the basis for the partner's partnership interest below zero, the distributed property's basis to the partner is limited to the partner's basis for the partnership interest before the distribution. In this case, Curry's basis for the land will be limited to the $5,000 basis for his partnership interest before the distribution.

57. (b) The requirement is to determine Hart's basis for the land received in a nonliquidating partnership distribution. If both cash and noncash property are received in a single distribution, the basis for the partner's partnership interest is first reduced by the cash, before being reduced by noncash property. Although a partner's basis for noncash property is generally the same as the partnership's basis for the property ($7,000 in this case), the partner's basis for distributed property will be limited to the partner's basis for the partnership interest reduced by any cash received in the same distribution. Here, the $9,000 basis of Hart's partnership interest is first reduced by the $5,000 cash received, with the remaining basis of $4,000 allocated as basis for the land received.

58. (b) The requirement is to determine Day's basis in the land received in a nonliquidating distribution. If both cash and noncash property are received in a single distribution, the basis for the partner's partnership interest is first reduced by the cash, before the noncash property. Since partnership distributions are generally nontaxable, a distributee partner's basis for distributed property is generally the same as the partnership's former basis for the property (a transferred basis). Here, the basis of Day's partnership interest of $50,000 is first reduced by the $25,000 of cash received, and then reduced by the $15,000 adjusted basis of the land, to $10,000. Day's basis for the land received is $15,000.

59. (a) The requirement is to determine the amount of taxable gain that Jody must report as the result of a current distribution of cash and property from her partnership. No loss can be recognized as a result of a proportionate current (nonliquidating) distribution, and gain will be recognized only if the amount of cash received exceeds the basis for the partner's partnership interest. If both cash and noncash property are received in a single distribution, the basis for the partner's interest is first reduced by the cash, before noncash property. Since the $20,000 cash received does not exceed the $50,000 basis of Jody's partnership interest immediately before the distribution, no gain is recognized.

60. (b) The requirement is to determine the basis of property received in a current distribution. If both cash and noncash property are received in a single distribution, the basis for the partner's partnership interest is first reduced by the cash, before being reduced by noncash property. Although a partner's basis for distributed property is generally the same as the partnership's basis for the property ($40,000 in this case), the partner's basis for distributed property will be limited to the partner's basis for the partnership interest reduced by any money received in the same distribution. Here, the $50,000 basis of Jody's partnership interest is first reduced by the $20,000 of cash received, with the remaining basis of $30,000 allocated as the basis for the property received.

61. **(d)** The requirement is to determine the amount of income from the receipt of retirement payments to be reported by Berk in 2002 and 2003. Payments to a retiring partner are generally treated as received in exchange for the partner's interest in partnership property. As such, they are generally treated under the rules that apply to liquidating distributions. Retirement payments are not deductible by the partnership as guaranteed payments and are not treated as distributive shares of income. Under the rules for liquidating distributions, the $5,000 per month cash payments are treated as a reduction of the basis for Berk's partnership interest, and result in gain to the extent in excess of basis. Berk's $80,000 basis for his partnership interest ($50,000 capital + $30,000 share of liabilities) would first be reduced by the relief from $30,000 of liabilities to $50,000. Next, the $30,000 of cash payments received during 2002 (6 x $5,000) would reduce Berk's basis to $20,000 and result in no gain to be reported for 2002. Finally, the $60,000 of payments for 2003 (12 x $5,000) would exceed his remaining basis and result in Berk's reporting of $40,000 of capital gain for 2003.

62. **(b)** The requirement is to determine the correct statement regarding the basis of property to a partner that is distributed "in-kind" in complete liquidation of the partner's interest. In a complete liquidation of a partner's interest in a partnership, the in-kind property distributed will have a basis equal to the adjusted basis of the partner's partnership interest reduced by any money received in the same distribution. Generally, in a liquidating distribution, the basis for a partnership interest is (1) first reduced by the amount of money received, (2) then reduced by the partnership's basis for any unrealized receivables and inventory received, (3) with any remaining basis for the partnership interest allocated to other property received in proportion to their adjusted bases (not FMV) to the partnership.

63. **(c)** The requirement is to determine the basis of the inventory received in a nonliquidating partnership distribution of cash and inventory. Here, the $25,000 basis of Reed's partnership interest would first be reduced by the $11,000 of cash received, and then reduced by the $5,000 basis of the inventory to $9,000. Reed's basis for the inventory received is $5,000.

64. **(b)** The requirement is to determine Reed's recognized gain or loss resulting from the cash and inventory received in complete liquidation of Reed's partnership interest. A distributee partner can recognize loss only upon the complete liquidation of the partner's interest through the receipt of only money, unrealized receivables, or inventory. Since Reed received only money and inventory, the amount of recognized loss is the $9,000 difference between the $25,000 basis of his partnership interest and the $11,000 of cash and $5,000 basis for the inventory received.

65. **(c)** The requirement is to determine the amount of loss recognized by Lisa on the complete liquidation of her one-third partnership interest. A distributee partner can recognize loss only upon the complete liquidation of the partner's interest through receipt of only money, unrealized receivables, or inventory. Since Lisa only received cash, the amount of recognized loss is the $2,000 difference between

the $22,000 adjusted basis of her partnership interest and the $20,000 of cash received. Since a partnership interest is a capital asset and Lisa acquired her one-third interest in 1997, Lisa has a $2,000 long-term capital loss.

66. **(d)** The requirement is to determine when a retiring partner who receives retirement payments ceases to be regarded as a partner. A retiring partner continues to be a partner for income tax purposes until the partner's entire interest has been completely liquidated through distributions or payments.

67. **(b)** The requirement is to determine the treatment for the payments received by Albin. Payments made by a personal service partnership to a retired partner that are determined by partnership income are distributive shares of partnership income, regardless of the period over which they are paid. Thus, they are taxable to Albin as ordinary income.

OTHER OBJECTIVE ANSWERS AND ANSWER EXPLANATIONS

Problem 1

	Form 1065	Schedule K	Schedule K-1
(1)	170,000	0	0
(2)	0	20,000	10,000
(3)	110,000	110,000	55,000
(4)	0	0	0
(5)	1,000	0	0
(6)	25,000	0	0
(7)	0	24,000	12,000
(8)	18,000	18,000	9,000
(9)	6,000	8,000	4,000
(10)	0	30,000	15,000
(11)	0	4,000	2,000
(12)	0	2,000	1,000
(13)	0	2,000	1,000

This problem requires the candidate to indicate the appropriate amount that should appear for (a) Madison's Income and Deductions on page 1 of Form 1065 (Partnership Return), (b) Madison's Schedule K on page 3 of Form 1065 (Partners Shares of Income, Credits, Deductions, Etc.), and (c) Rashid's Schedule K-1 (Partner's Share of Income, Credits, Deductions, Etc.).

A partnership is a pass-through entity acting as a conduit to pass-through items of income, deduction, and credit to be reported on the tax returns of its partners. Partnership items having special tax characteristics (e.g., passive activity income, deductions subject to dollar or percentage limitations, etc.) must be separately listed and shown on Schedules K and K-1 so that their special characteristics are preserved when reported on partners' tax returns. In contrast, partnership ordinary income and deduction items having no special tax characteristics can be netted together in the computation of a partnership's ordinary income and deductions from trade or business activities on page 1 of Form 1065.

The solutions approach is to analyze each item appearing in the "Income Statement" column of Madison's tax worksheet to determine whether the item can be included in the computation of Madison's ordinary income and deductions on page 1 of Form 1065, or should be separately shown on Madison's Schedule K and Rashid's Schedule K-1 to retain any special tax characteristics that the item may have.

Schedule K is a summary schedule, listing the total of all partners' shares of income, deductions, and credits, including the net amount of a partnership's ordinary income and deductions that is computed on page 1 of Form 1065.

A Schedule K-1 is prepared for each partner listing only that particular partner's share of partnership income, deductions, credits, etc. Since Rashid and Hughes share profits and losses of the Madison partnership equally, Rashid's Schedule K-1 will generally reflect a 50% share of the amounts reported on Madison's Schedule K.

1.   The salaries and wages of $190,000 paid to employees reduced by the $20,000 of wages qualifying for the welfare-to-work credit are deductible in the computation of Madison's ordinary income and do not require adjustment.

2.   Since the welfare-to-work credit is part of the general business credit and is subject to limitation, the $20,000 of qualified wages must be separately listed on Schedules K and K-1 so that the welfare-to-work credit and any applicable limitation can be computed at the partner level. Rashid's Schedule K-1 would reflect 50% x $20,000 = $10,000.

3.   Guaranteed payments made to a partner for services or for the use of capital are determined without regard to the income of the partnership. The $110,000 of guaranteed payments are deductible by the partnership in computing its ordinary income, and must also be separately listed on Schedules K and K-1 because the receipt of guaranteed payments by partners must be reported as ordinary income. The amount of guaranteed payments received by Rashid totals $55,000 and is shown on Rashid's Schedule K-1. The amount of guaranteed payments would be increased by the health insurance premiums paid on behalf of partners in item 8. below.

4.   No amortization of the permanent liquor license is allowed for tax purposes because the license is renewable for an indefinite period.

5.   The $1,000 annual liquor license fee does not require adjustment and is included in the computation of Madison's ordinary income.

6., 7.   The cost of qualifying property did not exceed $200,000 for 2002, so the maximum Sec. 179 expense deduction of $24,000 is available on Madison's return. Since this $24,000 limitation applies at both the partnership and partner levels, the Sec. 179 expense deduction must be separately shown on Schedules K and K-1. Since the depreciation deducted in the income statement column already includes the $24,000 expense deduction, the income statement depreciation of $49,000 must be reduced by $24,000, which results in $25,000 of depreciation that is deductible in computing Madison's ordinary income. The $24,000 Sec. 179 expense deduction must be separately shown on Madison's Schedule K. $24,000 x 50% = $12,000 of Sec. 179 expense deduction is separately shown on Rashid's Schedule K-1.

8.   The $18,000 of health insurance premiums paid by the partnership on behalf of its partners were paid for services rendered by the partners and are treated as guaranteed payments. As such, they are deductible in computing the partnership's ordinary income, and are includible in the partners' gross income as ordinary income. The $18,000 of premiums also are shown as guaranteed payments on Madison's Schedule K, with Rashid's share ($9,000) shown on Rashid's Schedule K-1.

9.   The $14,000 of contributions to a defined benefit pension plan must be reduced by the $8,000 that was paid on behalf of the partners to arrive at the $6,000 paid for the benefit of employees that is deductible in computing Madison's ordinary income. The $8,000 paid on behalf of partners is separately shown on Madison's Schedule K, with Rashid's share ($4,000) shown on Rashid's Schedule K-1 so that the limitations that apply to contributions to defined benefit plans can be applied at the partner level.

10.   Charitable contributions are not deductible in the computation of a partnership's ordinary income. Instead, they are separately shown on a partnership's Schedule K and a partner's Schedule K-1 so that the appropriate percentage limitations can be applied on partners' returns. Here the contribution represents stock purchased as an investment that had an adjusted basis of $30,000 and a fair market value of $33,000 when donated to a qualified charitable organization. Since the Madison partnership was first established on January 2, 2002, it is reasonable to assume that the stock had not been held for more than one year and therefore does not qualify as capital gain property (i.e., property which if sold would generate a long-term capital gain). Since the stock fails to qualify as capital gain property, the amount of contribution is limited to the stock's adjusted basis of $30,000.

11.   The dividends of $4,000 represent portfolio income and cannot be included in the computation of Madison's ordinary income from trade or business activities. Instead, the $4,000 of dividends must be separately shown as portfolio income on Madison's Schedule K, with Rashid's 50% share ($2,000) shown on Rashid's Schedule K-1.

12.   The rental loss of $2,000 is a passive activity loss and cannot be included in the computation of Madison's ordinary income. The $2,000 rental loss must be separately shown on Madison's Schedule K, and Rashid's 50% share ($1,000) separately shown on Rashid's Schedule K-1 in order to pass-through as a passive activity loss so that the passive activity loss limitations can be applied at the partner level.

13.   The $2,000 of interest expense on investment debt cannot be deducted in computing Madison's ordinary income. Instead, $2,000 must be separately shown on Madison's Schedule K, and $1,000 separately shown on Rashid's Schedule K-1 in order that the limitation that applies to the deduction of investment interest expense can be applied at the partner level.

Problem 2

1.   **(c)** The requirement is to determine Brinks' initial basis for his 20% partnership interest received in exchange for a contribution of property subject to a $5,000 mortgage. Generally, no gain or loss is recognized on the contribution of property in exchange for a partnership interest. As a result, Brinks' initial basis for the partnership interest received consists of the $12,000 basis of the land contributed to the partnership, less the net reduction in Brinks' individual liability resulting from the partnership's assumption of the mortgage. Since Brinks received a 20% partnership interest, the net reduction in Brinks' individual liability equals $5,000 x 80% = $4,000. As a result, Brinks' basis for the partnership interest is $12,000 – $4,000 = $8,000.

2.   **(a)** The requirement is to determine Carson's initial basis for his 30% partnership interest received in exchange for a contribution of inventory. Since partners are individually liable for their share of partnership liabilities, an increase in partnership liabilities increases a partner's basis in the partnership by the partner's share of the increase. Carson's initial basis is the $24,000 adjusted basis of the inventory contributed, increased by the increase in his individual liability resulting from the partnership's assumption of Brinks' mortgage ($5,000 x 30% = $1,500). Thus, Carson's initial basis for the partnership interest is $24,000 + $1,500 = $25,500.

For items 3 through 8, candidates were asked to determine whether each statement concerning partnership distributions to partners is true (T) or false (F).

3.   **(F)** A partner can never have a negative basis for a partnership interest. Partnership distributions can only reduce a partner's basis to zero.

4.   **(T)** Partnership distributions are generally nontaxable and reduce the recipient partner's basis by the adjusted basis of the property distributed.

5.   **(T)** A liquidating distribution of property other than money generally does not cause the distributee partner to recognize gain. As a result, the distributee partner's basis in the distributed property is limited to the partner's predistribution basis for the partnership interest.

6.   **(F)** Gain is recognized by a distributee partner only if the amount of money distributed exceeds the partner's predistribution basis for the partnership interest. Distributions of property other than money never result in the recognition of gain by the distributee partner.

7.   **(T)** Generally, a nonliquidating distribution of inventory is not taxable, and the adjusted basis for the inventory carries over to the distributee partner. As a result, the distributee partner's basis for the inventory cannot exceed the inventory's adjusted basis to the partnership.

8.   **(F)** Since partners are individually liable for partnership liabilities, a decrease in partnership liabilities will decrease the basis for a partner's partnership interest by the partner's share of the decrease. Thus, if a distributee partner assumes a mortgage on encumbered property, the other partners' bases in their partnership interests will be decreased by their share of the decrease in partnership liabilities.

CORPORATIONS

Corporations are separate taxable entities, organized under state law. Although corporations may have many of the same income and deduction items as individuals, corporations are taxed at different rates and some tax rules are applied differently. There also are special provisions applicable to transfers of property to a corporation, and issuance of stock.

A. Transfers to a Controlled Corporation (Sec. 351)

1. **No gain or loss** is recognized if property is transferred to a corporation solely in exchange for stock and immediately after the exchange those persons transferring property control the corporation.

    a. **Property** includes everything but services.
    b. **Control** means ownership of at least 80% of the total combined voting power and 80% of each class of nonvoting stock.
    c. **Receipt of boot** (e.g., cash, short-term notes, securities, etc.) will cause recognition of gain (but not loss).

    (1) Corporation's assumption of liabilities is treated as boot only if there is a tax avoidance purpose, or no business purpose.
    (2) Shareholder recognizes gain if liabilities assumed by corporation exceed the total basis of property transferred by the shareholder.

2. **Shareholder's basis for stock** = Adjusted basis of property transferred

    a. + Gain recognized
    b. – Boot received (assumption of liability always treated as boot for purposes of determining stock basis)

3. **Corporation's basis for property** = Transferor's adjusted basis + Gain recognized to transferor.

    EXAMPLE: *Individuals A, B, & C form ABC Corp. and make the following transfer to their corporation:*

Item transferred	A	B	C
Property – FMV	$10,000	$8,000	$ --
– Adjusted basis	1,500	3,000	--
Liability assumed by ABC Corp.	2,000	--	--
Services	--	--	1,000
Consideration received			
Stock (FMV)	$ 8,000	$7,600	$1,000
Two-year note (FMV)	--	400	--
Gain recognized to shareholder	$ 500[a]	$ 400[b]	$1,000[c]
Basis of stock received	--	3,000	1,000
Basis of property to corp.	2,000	3,400	1,000[d]

    a *Liability in excess of basis: $2,000 – $1,500 = $500*
    b *Assumes B elects out of the installment method*
    c *Ordinary compensation income*
    d *Expense or asset depending on nature of services rendered*

B. Section 1244—Small Business Corporation (SBC) Stock

1. Sec. 1244 stock permits shareholders to deduct an **ordinary loss** on sale or worthlessness of stock.

    a. Shareholder must be the original holder of stock, and an individual or partnership.
    b. Stock can be common or preferred, voting or nonvoting, and must have been issued for money or property (other than stock or securities)
    c. Ordinary loss limited to **$50,000 ($100,000** on joint return); any excess is treated as a capital loss.
    d. The corporation during the five-year period before the year of loss, received less than 50% of its total gross receipts from royalties, rents, dividends, interest, annuities, and gains from sales or exchanges of stock or securities.

    EXAMPLE: *Jim (married and filing a joint return) incurred a loss of $120,000 from the sale of Sec. 1244 stock during 2002. $100,000 of Jim's loss is deductible as an ordinary loss, with the remaining $20,000 treated as a capital loss.*

2. If Sec. 1244 stock is received in exchange for property whose FMV is less than its adjusted basis, the stock's basis is reduced to the FMV of the property to determine the amount of ordinary loss.

3. For purposes of determining the amount of ordinary loss, increases in basis through capital contributions or otherwise are treated as allocable to stock which is not Sec. 1244 stock.

EXAMPLE: Joe made a Sec. 351 transfer of a truck to a corporation in exchange for Sec. 1244 stock. The truck had a basis of $20,000 and a FMV of $16,000 at date of transfer. Joe subsequently made a $5,000 capital contribution to the corporation before his stock became worthless. Although Joe's stock basis was $25,000 ($20,000 basis of truck + $5,000 capital contribution), his ordinary loss is limited to $16,000. His remaining loss of $9,000 consisting of the $4,000 built-in loss at time of transfer plus the $5,000 capital contribution, is treated as a capital loss.

4. SBC is any domestic corporation whose aggregate amount of money and adjusted basis of other property received for stock, as a contribution to capital, and as paid-in surplus, does not exceed $1,000,000. If more than $1 million of stock is issued, up to $1 million of qualifying stock can be designated as Sec. 1244 stock.

C. Variations from Individual Taxation

1. Filing and payment of tax

   a. A corporation generally must file a Form 1120 every year even though it has no taxable income. A short-form Form 1120-A may be filed if gross receipts, total income, and total assets are each less than $500,000.

   b. The return must be filed by the fifteenth day of the third month following the close of its taxable year (e.g., March 15 for calendar-year corporation).

      (1) An automatic six-month extension may be obtained by filing Form 7004.
      (2) Any balance due on the corporation's tax liability must be paid with the request for extension.

   c. Estimated tax payments must be made by every corporation whose estimated tax is expected to be $500 or more. A corporation's estimated tax is its expected tax liability (including alternative minimum tax) less its allowable tax credits.

      (1) Quarterly payments are due on the fifteenth day of the fourth, sixth, ninth, and twelfth months of its taxable year (April 15, June 15, September 15, and December 15 for a calendar-year corporation). Any balance due must be paid by the due date of the return.
      (2) No penalty for underpayment of estimated tax will be imposed if payments at least equal the lesser of

         (a) 100% of the current year's tax (determined on the basis of actual income or annualized income), or
         (b) 100% of the preceding year's tax (if the preceding year was a full twelve months and showed a tax liability).

      (3) A corporation with $1 million or more of taxable income in any of its three preceding tax years (i.e., **large corporation**) can use its preceding year's tax only for its first installment and must base its estimated payments on 100% of its current year's tax to avoid penalty.
      (4) If any amount of tax is not paid by the original due date, interest must be paid from the due date until the tax is paid.
      (5) A failure-to-pay tax delinquency penalty will be owed if the amount of tax paid by the original due date of the return is less than 90% of the tax shown on the return. The failure-to-pay penalty is imposed at a rate of 0.5% per month (or fraction thereof), with a maximum penalty of 25%.

2. Corporations are subject to

   a. **Regular tax rates**

	Taxable income	Rate
(1)	$0-$50,000	15%
(2)	$50,001-$75,000	25
(3)	$75,001-$10 million	34
(4)	Over $10 million	35

      (5) The less-than-34% brackets are phased out by adding an additional tax of 5% of the excess of taxable income over $100,000, up to a maximum additional tax of $11,750.
      (6) The 34% bracket is phased out for corporations with taxable income in excess of $15 million by adding an additional 3% of the excess of taxable income over $15 million, up to a maximum additional tax of $100,000.

b. Certain personal service corporations are not eligible to use the less-than-35% brackets and their taxable income is taxed at a flat 35% rate.

c. **Alternative minimum tax (AMT)**

(1) **Computation.** The AMT is generally the amount by which 20% of alternative minimum taxable income (AMTI) as reduced by an exemption and the alternative minimum tax foreign tax credit, exceeds the regular tax (i.e., regular tax liability reduced by the regular tax foreign tax credit). AMTI is equal to taxable income computed with specified adjustments and increased by tax preferences.

(2) **Exemption.** AMTI is offset by a $40,000 exemption. However, the exemption is reduced by 25% of AMTI over $150,000, and completely phased out once AMTI reaches $310,000.

(3) **AMT formula**

```
        Regular taxable income before NOL deduction
   +    Tax preference items
  +(–)  Adjustments (other than ACE and NOL deduction)
        Pre-ACE alternative minimum taxable income (AMTI)
  +(–)  ACE adjustment [75% of difference between pre-ACE AMTI and adjusted current earnings (ACE)]
   –    AMT NOL deduction [limited to 90% of pre-NOL AMTI]
        Alternative minimum taxable income (AMTI)
   –    Exemption ($40,000 less 25% of AMTI over $150,000)
        Alternative minimum tax base
   x    20% rate
        Tentative AMT before foreign tax credit
   –    AMT foreign tax credit (limited to 90% of pre-credit AMT)
        Tentative minimum tax (TMT)
   –    Regular income tax (less regular tax foreign tax credit)
        Alternative minimum tax (if positive)
```

(4) **Preference items.** The following are examples of items added to regular taxable income in computing pre-ACE AMTI:

(a) Tax-exempt interest on private activity bonds (net of related expenses)

(b) Excess of accelerated over straight-line depreciation on real property and leased personal property placed in service before 1987

(c) The excess of percentage depletion deduction over the property's adjusted basis

(d) The excess of intangible drilling costs using a ten-year amortization over 65% of net oil and gas income

(5) **Adjustments.** The following are examples of adjustments to regular taxable income in computing pre-ACE AMTI:

(a) For real property placed in service after 1986 and before 1999, the difference between regular tax depreciation and straight-line depreciation over forty years

(b) For personal property placed in service after 1986, the difference between regular tax depreciation and depreciation using the 150% declining balance method

(c) The installment method cannot be used for sales of inventory-type items

(d) Income from long-term contracts must be determined using the percentage of completion method

(6) **Adjusted current earnings (ACE).** ACE is a concept based on a corporation's earnings and profits, and is calculated by making adjustments to pre-ACE AMTI.

```
AMTI before ACE adjustment and NOL deduction
Add:     Tax-exempt income on municipal bonds (less expenses)
         Tax-exempt life insurance death benefits (less expenses)
         70% dividends-received deduction
Deduct:  Depletion using cost depletion method
         Depreciation using ADS straight-line for all property (this adjustment eliminated for property
             placed in service after 1993)
Other:   Capitalize organizational expenditures and circulation expenses
         Add increase (subtract decrease) in LIFO recapture amount (i.e., excess of FIFO value over
             LIFO basis)
         Installment method cannot be used for nondealer sales of property
         Amortize intangible drilling costs over five years
Adjusted current earnings (ACE)
– Pre-ACE AMTI
Balance (positive or negative)
x 75%
ACE adjustment (positive or negative)
```

EXAMPLE: Acme, Inc. has adjusted current earnings of $100,000 and alternative minimum taxable income (before this adjustment) of $60,000. Since adjusted current earnings exceeds pre-ACE AMTI by $40,000, 75% of this amount must be added to Acme's AMTI. Thus, Acme's AMTI for the year is $90,000 [$60,000 + ($40,000 x 75%)].

(a) The ACE adjustment can be positive or negative, but a negative ACE adjustment is limited in amount to prior years' net positive ACE adjustments.

(b) The computation of ACE is not the same as the computation of a corporation's E&P. For example, federal income taxes, penalties and fines, and the disallowed portion of business meals and entertainment would be deductible in computing E&P, but are not deductible in computing ACE.

(7) **Minimum tax credit.** The amount of AMT paid is allowed as a credit against regular tax liability in future years.

(a) The credit can be carried forward indefinitely, but not carried back.

(b) The AMT credit can only be used to reduce regular tax liability, not future AMT liability.

(8) **Small corporation exemption.** A corporation is exempt from the corporate AMT for its first tax year (regardless of income levels). After the first year, it is exempt from AMT if it passes a gross receipts test. It is exempt for its second year if its first year's gross receipts do not exceed $5 million. To be exempt for its third year, the corporation's average gross receipts for the first two years must not exceed $7.5 million. To be exempt for the fourth year (and subsequent years), the corporation's average gross receipts for all prior three-year periods must not exceed $7.5 million.

EXAMPLE: Zero Corp., a calendar-year corporation, was formed on January 2, 1999 and had gross receipts for its first four taxable years as follows:

Year	Gross receipts
1999	$ 4,500,000
2000	9,000,000
2001	8,000,000
2002	6,500,000

Zero is automatically exempt from AMT for 1999. It is exempt for 2000 because its gross receipts for 1999 do not exceed $5 million. Zero also is exempt for 2001 because its average gross receipts for 1999-2000 do not exceed $7.5 million. Similarly, it is exempt for 2002 because its average gross receipts for 1999-2001 do not exceed $7.5 million. However, Zero will lose its exemption from AMT for 2003 and all subsequent years because its average gross receipts for 2000-2002 exceed $7.5 million.

d. See subsequent discussion for penalty taxes on

(1) Accumulated earnings

(2) Personal holding companies

3. **Gross income** for a corporation is quite similar to the rules for an individual taxpayer. However, there are a few differences.

a. A corporation does not recognize gain or loss on the **issuance of its own stock** (including treasury stock), or on the lapse or acquisition of an option to buy or sell its stock (including treasury stock).

    (1) It generally recognizes gain (but not loss) if it distributes appreciated property to its shareholders.

    (2) **Contributions to capital** are excluded from a corporation's gross income, whether received from shareholders or nonshareholders.

        (a) If property is received from a shareholder, the shareholder recognizes no gain or loss, and the shareholder's basis for the contributed property transfers to the corporation.

        (b) If property is received as a capital contribution from a nonshareholder, the corporation's basis for the contributed property is zero.

            1] If money is received, the basis of property purchased within one year afterwards is reduced by the money contributed.

            2] Any money not used reduces the basis of the corporation's existing property beginning with depreciable property.

b. No gain or loss is recognized on the **issuance of debt**.

    (1) Premium or discount on bonds payable is amortized as income or expense over the life of bonds.

    (2) Ordinary income/loss is recognized by a corporation on the repurchase of its bonds, determined by the relationship of the repurchase price to the net carrying value of the bonds (issue price plus or minus the discount or premium amortized).

    (3) Interest earned and gains recognized in a bond sinking fund are income to the corporation.

c. Gains are treated as ordinary income on sales to or from a more than 50% shareholder, or between corporations which are more than 50% owned by the same individual, if the property is subject to depreciation in the hands of the buyer.

4. Deductions for a corporation are much the same as for individuals. However, there are some major differences.

    a. Adjusted gross income is not applicable to corporations.

    b. **Organizational expenditures** may be amortized over **sixty months** or longer if elected in the tax return for the year in which the corporation begins business, otherwise deductible only in the year of liquidation.

    (1) The election must be made by the due date for filing the tax return (including extensions) for the tax year in which the corporation begins business, and applies to expenditures incurred before the end of the tax year in which the corporation begins business (even if the amounts have not yet been paid by a cash-method corporation).

    (2) Amortization period starts with the month that the corporation begins business.

    (3) Organizational expenditures include expenses of temporary directors and organizational meetings, state fees for incorporation, accounting and legal service costs incident to incorporation (e.g., drafting bylaws, minutes of organizational meetings, and terms of original stock certificates).

    (4) Expenditures connected with issuing or selling shares of stock, or listing stock on an exchange are neither deductible nor amortizable. Expenditures connected with the transfer of an asset to the corporation must be capitalized as part of the cost of the asset.

    c. The deduction for **charitable contributions** is **limited to 10% of taxable income** before the contributions deduction, the dividends received deduction, a net operating loss carryback (but after carryover), and a capital loss carryback (but after carryover).

    (1) Generally the same rules apply for valuation of contributed property as for individuals except

        (a) Deduction for donations of inventory and other appreciated ordinary income-producing property is the donor's basis plus one-half of the unrealized appreciation but limited to twice the basis, provided

            1] Donor is a corporation (but not an S corporation)

            2] Donee must use property for care of ill, needy, or infants

3] Donor must obtain a written statement from the donee that the use requirement has been met

4] No deduction allowed for unrealized appreciation that would be ordinary income under recapture rules

(b) Deduction for donation of appreciated scientific personal property to a college or university is the donor's basis plus one-half the unrealized appreciation but limited to twice the basis, provided

1] Donor is a corporation (but not an S corporation, personal holding company, or service organization)

2] Property was constructed by donor and contributed within two years of substantial completion, and donee is original user of property

3] Donee must use property for research or experimentation

4] Donor must obtain a written statement from the donee that the use requirement has been met

5] No deduction allowed for unrealized appreciation that would be ordinary income under recapture rules

(2) Contributions are deductible in period paid (subject to 10% limitation) unless corporation is an accrual method taxpayer and then deductible (subject to 10% limitation) when authorized by board of directors if payment is made within 2 1/2 months after tax year end, and corporation elects to deduct contributions when authorized.

(3) Excess contributions over the 10% limitation may be carried forward for up to five years.

> EXAMPLE: The books of a calendar-year, accrual-method corporation for 2002 disclose net income of $350,000 after deducting a charitable contribution of $50,000. The contribution was authorized by the Board of Directors on December 24, 2002, and was actually paid on January 31, 2003. The allowable charitable contribution deduction for 2002 (if the corporation elects to deduct it when accrued) is $40,000, calculated as follows: ($350,000 + $50,000) x .10 = $40,000. The remaining $10,000 is carried forward for up to five years.

d. A **100% DRD** may be elected for dividends received from affiliated (i.e., at least 80% owned) corporations if a consolidated tax return is not filed.

(1) If a consolidated tax return is filed, intercompany dividends are eliminated and not included in consolidated gross income.

(2) See Section D. for discussion of affiliated corporations

e. An **80% dividends received deduction** (DRD) is allowed for qualified dividends from taxable domestic unaffiliated corporations that are **at least 20% owned**.

(1) DRD may be **limited to 80% of taxable income** before the dividends received deduction, the net operating loss deduction, and a capital loss carryback.

> EXAMPLE: A corporation has income from sales of $20,000 and dividend income of $10,000, along with business expenses of $22,000. Since taxable income before the DRD would be $8,000 (less than the dividend income), the DRD is limited to $6,400 (80% x $8,000). Thus, taxable income would be $1,600 ($8,000 – $6,400).

(2) Exception: The 80% of **taxable income limitation does not apply** if the full 80% DRD creates or increases a net operating loss.

> EXAMPLE: In the example above, assume that all facts are the same except that business expenses are $22,001. Since the full DRD ($8,000) would create a $1 net operating loss ($7,999 – $8,000), the taxable income limitation would not apply and the full DRD ($8,000) would be allowed.

f. Only a **70% dividends received deduction** (instead of 80%) is allowed for qualified dividends from taxable domestic unaffiliated corporations that are **less than 20% owned**.

(1) A 70% of taxable income limitation (instead of 80%) and a limitation exception for a net operating loss apply as in e.(1) and (2) above.

(2) If dividends are received from both 20% owned corporations and corporations that are less than 20% owned, the 80% DRD and 80% DRD limitation for dividends received from 20% owned corporations is computed first. Then the 70% DRD and 70% DRD limitation is computed for dividends received from less than 20% owned corporations. For purposes of com-

puting the 70% DRD limitation, taxable income is reduced by the total amount of dividends received from 20% owned corporations.

> *EXAMPLE: A corporation has taxable income before the dividends received deduction of $100,000. Included in taxable income are $65,000 of dividends from a 20% owned corporation and $40,000 of dividends from a less than 20% owned corporation. First, the 80% DRD for dividends received from the 20% owned corporation is computed. That deduction equals $52,000 [i.e., the lesser of 80% of the dividends received (80% x $65,000), or 80% of taxable income (80% x $100,000)].*
>
> *Second, the 70% DRD for the dividends received from the less than 20% owned corporation is computed. That deduction is $24,500 [i.e., the lesser of 70% of the dividends received (70% x $40,000), or 70% of taxable income after deducting the amount of dividends from the 20% owned corporation (70% x [$100,000 – $65,000])].*
>
> *Thus, the total dividends received deduction is $52,000 + $24,500 = $76,500.*

g. A portion of a corporation's 80% (or 70%) DRD will be disallowed if the dividends are directly attributable to **debt-financed portfolio stock**.

   (1) "Portfolio stock" is any stock (except stock of a corporation if the taxpayer owns at least 50% of the voting power and at least 50% of the total value of such corporation).

   (2) The DRD percentage for debt-financed portfolio stock = [80% (or 70%) x (100% – average % of indebtedness on the stock)].

   > *EXAMPLE: P, Inc. purchased 25% of T, Inc. for $100,000, paying with $50,000 of its own funds and $50,000 borrowed from its bank. During the year P received $9,000 in dividends from T, and paid $5,000 in interest expense on the bank loan. No principal payments were made on the loan during the year. If the stock were not debt financed, P's DRD would be $9,000 x 80% = $7,200. However, because half of the stock investment was debt financed, P's DRD is $9,000 x [80% x (100% – 50%)] = $3,600.*

   (3) The reduction in the DRD cannot exceed the interest deduction allocable to the portfolio stock indebtedness.

   > *EXAMPLE: Assume the same facts as above except that the interest expense on the bank loan was only $3,000. The reduction in the DRD would be limited to the $3,000 interest deduction on the loan. The DRD would be ($9,000 x 80%) – $3,000 = $4,200.*

h. **No DRD** is allowed if the dividend paying stock is held **less than forty-six days** during the ninety-day period that begins forty-five days before the stock becomes ex-dividend. In the case of preferred stock, no DRD is allowed if the dividends received are for a period or periods in excess of 366 days and the stock has been held for less than ninety-one days during the 180-day period that begins ninety days before the stock becomes ex-dividend.

i. The **basis of stock** held by a corporation must be reduced by the nontaxed portion of a nonliquidating **extraordinary dividend** received with respect to the stock, unless the corporation has held the stock for more than two years before the dividend is announced. To the extent the nontaxed portion of an extraordinary dividend exceeds the adjusted basis of the stock, the excess is recognized as gain for the taxable year in which the extraordinary dividend is received.

   (1) The nontaxed portion of a dividend is generally the amount that is offset by the DRD.

   (2) A dividend is considered "extraordinary" when it equals or exceeds 10% (5% for preferred stock) of the stock's adjusted basis (or FMV if greater on the day preceding the ex-dividend date).

   (3) Aggregation of dividends

      (a) All dividends received that have ex-dividend dates that occur within a period of 85 consecutive days are treated as one dividend.

      (b) All dividends received within 365 consecutive days are treated as extraordinary dividends if they in total exceed 20% of the stock's adjusted basis.

   (4) This provision is not applicable to dividends received from an affiliated corporation, and does not apply if the stock was held during the entire period the paying corporation (and any predecessor) was in existence.

   > *EXAMPLE: Corporation X purchased 30% of the stock of Corporation Y for $10,000 during June 2002. During December 2002, X received a $20,000 dividend from Y. X sold its Y stock for $5,000 in March 2003.*
   >
   > *Because the dividend from Y is an extraordinary dividend, the nontaxed portion (equal to the DRD allowed to X) $20,000 x 80% = $16,000 has the effect of reducing the Y stock basis from $10,000 to $0, with the remaining $6,000 recognized as gain for 2002. At time of sale, the excess of sale proceeds over the reduced stock basis $5,000 – $0 = $5,000 is also recognized as gain.*

j. **Losses** in the ordinary course of business are deductible.

    (1) Loss is **disallowed** if the sale or exchange of property is between

        (a) A corporation and a more than 50% shareholder,

        (b) A C corporation and an S corporation if the same persons own more than 50% of each, or

        (c) A corporation and a partnership if the same persons own more than 50% of the corporation, and more than 50% of the capital and profits interest in the partnership.

        (d) In the event of a disallowed loss, the transferee on subsequent disposition only recognizes gain to the extent it exceeds the disallowed loss.

    (2) Any loss from the sale or exchange of property between corporations that are members of the same **controlled group** is **deferred** (instead of disallowed) until the property is sold outside the group. See controlled group definition in Section D.2., except substitute "more than 50%" for "at least 80%."

    (3) An accrual method C corporation is effectively placed on the cash method of accounting for purposes of deducting accrued interest and other expenses owed to a related cash-method payee. No deduction is allowable until the year the amount is actually paid.

        EXAMPLE: A calendar-year corporation accrues $10,000 of salary to an employee (a 60% shareholder) during 2002, but does not make payment until February 2003. The $10,000 will be deductible by the corporation and reported as income by the employee-shareholder in 2003.

    (4) **Capital losses** are deductible only to the extent of capital gains (i.e., may not offset ordinary income).

        (a) Unused capital losses are carried back three years and then carried forward five years to offset capital gains.

        (b) All corporate capital loss carrybacks and carryforwards are treated as **short-term**.

    (5) Bad debt losses are treated as ordinary deductions.

    (6) Casualty losses are treated the same as for an individual except

        (a) There is no $100 floor

        (b) If property is completely destroyed, the amount of loss is the property's adjusted basis

        (c) A partial loss is measured the same as for an individual's nonbusiness loss (i.e., the lesser of the decrease in FMV, or the property's adjusted basis)

    (7) A corporation's **net operating loss** is computed the same way as its taxable income.

        (a) The dividends received deduction is allowed without limitation.

        (b) No deduction is allowed for a NOL carryback or carryover from other years.

        (c) A NOL is generally carried back two years and forward twenty years to offset taxable income in those years. However, a three-year carryback is permitted for the portion of a NOL that is attributable to a presidentially declared disaster and is incurred by a small business corporation (i.e., a corporation whose average annual gross receipts are $5 million or less for the three-tax-year period preceding the loss year). A corporation may elect to forego carryback and only carry forward twenty years.

        (d) For NOLs arising in tax years ending in 2001 and 2002, the carryback period is extended to five years. However, a corporation can make an irrevocable election to waive the five-year carryback period, and carryback only 2 years (or three years if applicable).

k. Depreciation and depletion computations are same as for individuals.

l. Research and development expenditures of a corporation (or individual) may be treated under one of three alternatives

    (1) Currently expensed in year paid or incurred

    (2) Amortized over a period of sixty months or more if life not determinable

    (3) Capitalized and depreciated over determinable life

m. Contributions to a pension or profit sharing plan

    (1) Defined benefit plans

(a) Maximum deductible contribution is actuarially determined.

(b) There also are minimum funding standards.

(2) Defined contribution plans

(a) **Maximum deduction** for contributions to qualified profit-sharing or stock bonus plans is generally limited to 25% (after 2001) of the compensation paid or accrued during the year to covered employees.

(b) If more than 25% is paid, the excess can be carried forward as part of the contributions of succeeding years to the extent needed to bring the deduction up to 25%.

5. In working a corporate problem, certain calculations must be made in a specific order [e.g., charitable contributions (CC) must be computed before the dividends received deduction (DRD)]. The following memory device is quite helpful:

Gross income
  – Deductions (except CC and DRD)
Taxable income before CC and DRD
    – CC (limited to 10% of TI before CC, DRD,
      capital loss carryback, and NOL carryback)
Taxable income before DRD
    – DRD (may be limited* to 80% (or 70%) of TI before
      DRD, capital loss carryback, and NOL carryover or carryback)
Taxable income
  x Applicable rates
Tax liability before tax credits
  – Tax credits
Tax liability

   * *Limitation not applicable if full 80% (or 70%) of dividends received creates or increases a NOL.*

6. A person sitting for the CPA examination should be able to **reconcile book and taxable income**.

a. If you begin with book income to calculate taxable income, make the following adjustments:

(1) **Increase book income** by

(a) Federal income tax expense

(b) Excess of capital losses over capital gains because a net capital loss is not deductible

(c) Income items in the tax return not included in book income (e.g., prepaid rents, royalties, interest)

(d) Charitable contributions in excess of the 10% limitation

(e) Expenses deducted on the books but not on the tax return (e.g., amount of business gifts in excess of $25, nondeductible life insurance premiums paid, 50% of business meals and entertainment)

(2) **Deduct from book income**

(a) Income reported on the books but not on the tax return (e.g., tax exempt interest, life insurance proceeds)

(b) Expenses deducted on the tax return but not on the books (e.g., MACRS depreciation above straight-line, charitable contribution carryover)

(c) The dividends received deduction

b. When going from taxable income to book income, the above adjustments would be reversed.

c. **Schedule M-1** of Form 1120 provides a reconciliation of income per books with taxable income before the NOL and DRD. There are two types of Schedule M-1 items:

(1) Permanent differences (e.g., tax-exempt interest)

(2) Temporary differences—items reflected in different periods (e.g., accelerated depreciation on tax return and straight-line on books)

   EXAMPLE: A corporation discloses that it had net income after taxes of $36,000 per books. Included in the computation were deductions for charitable contributions of $10,000, a net capital loss of $5,000, and federal income taxes paid of $9,000. What is the corporation's TI?

Net income per books after tax	$36,000
Nondeductible net capital loss	+ 5,000
Federal income tax expense	+ 9,000
Charitable contributions	+10,000
Taxable income before CC	$60,000
CC (limited to 10% x 60,000)	- 6,000
Taxable income	$54,000

d. **Schedule M-2** of Form 1120 analyzes changes in a corporation's Unappropriated Retained Earnings per books between the beginning and end of the year.

Balance at beginning of year
Add: Net income per books
            Other increases
Less: Dividends to shareholders
            Other decreases (e.g., addition to reserve for contingencies)
Balance at end of year

D. Affiliated and Controlled Corporations

1. An **affiliated group** is a parent-subsidiary chain of corporations in which **at least 80%** of the combined voting power and total value of all stock (except nonvoting preferred) are owned by includible corporations.

   a. They may elect to file a consolidated return. Election is binding on all future returns.
   b. If affiliated corporations file a consolidated return, intercompany dividends are eliminated in the consolidation process. If separate tax returns are filed, dividends from affiliated corporations are eligible for a 100% dividends received deduction.
   c. Possible advantages of a consolidated return include the deferral of gain on intercompany transactions and offsetting operating/capital losses of one corporation against the profits/capital gains of another.

   EXAMPLE: P Corp. owns 80% of the stock of A Corp., 40% of the stock of B Corp., and 45% of the stock of C Corp. A Corp. owns 40% of the stock of B Corp. A consolidated tax return could be filed by P, A, and B.

   EXAMPLE: Parent and Subsidiary file consolidated tax returns using a calendar year. During 2002, Subsidiary paid a $10,000 dividend to Parent. Also during 2002, Subsidiary sold land with a basis of $20,000 to Parent for its FMV of $50,000. During 2003, Parent sold the land to an unrelated taxpayer for $55,000.

   *   The intercompany dividend is eliminated in the consolidation process and is excluded from consolidated taxable income. Additionally, Subsidiary's $30,000 of gain from the sale of land to Parent is deferred for 2002. The $30,000 will be included in consolidated taxable income for 2003 when Parent reports $5,000 of income from the sale of that land to the unrelated taxpayer.*

2. A **controlled group** of corporations is limited to an aggregate of $75,000 of taxable income taxed at less than 35%, one $250,000 accumulated earnings credit, one $24,000 Sec. 179 expense deduction, etc. There are three basic types of controlled groups.

   a. **Parent-subsidiary**—Basically same as P-S group eligible to file consolidated return, except ownership requirement is 80% of combined voting power **or** total value of stock. Affiliated corporations are subject to the controlled group limitations if the corporations file separate tax returns.
   b. **Brother-sister**—Two or more corporations at least 80% owned by five or fewer individuals, estates, or trusts, who also own more than 50% of each corporation when counting only identical ownership in each corporation. The 80% test is applied by including only the shares of those shareholders that hold stock in each corporation of the group being tested. The percentage tests are based on voting power **or** total value.

EXAMPLE:

Individual shareholder	Corporations W	X	Stock considered for 50% test
A	30%	20%	20%
B	5	40	5%
C	30	35	30%
D	15	5	5%
E	20	--	--
	100%	100%	60%

Corporations W and X are a controlled group since five or fewer individuals own at least 80% of each, and also own more than 50% when counting only identical ownership.

EXAMPLE:	Individual	Corporations		Stock considered
	shareholder	Y	Z	for 50% test
	F	79%	100%	79%
	G	21%	--	--
		100%	100%	79%

Y and Z are not a controlled group because the 80% test is not met for Corporation Y. Since G owns no stock in Z, G's stock in Y cannot be added to F's Y stock for purposes of applying the 80% test.

c. **Combined**—The parent in a P-S group is also a member of a brother-sister group of corporations.

EXAMPLE: Individual H owns 100% of the stock of Corporations P and Q. Corporation P owns 100% of the stock of Corporation S. P, S, and Q are members of one controlled group.

E. Dividends and Distributions

1. **Ordinary corporate distributions**

   a. Corporate distributions of property to shareholders on their stock are subject to a **three-step** treatment.

   (1) Dividend—to be included in gross income
   (2) Return of stock basis—nontaxable and reduces shareholder's basis for stock
   (3) Gain—to extent distribution exceeds shareholder's stock basis

   b. The **amount** of distribution to a shareholder is the cash plus the FMV of other property received, reduced by liabilities assumed.

   c. A shareholder's tax **basis** for distributed property is the property's FMV at date of distribution (not reduced by liabilities).

   d. A **dividend** is a distribution of property by a corporation to its shareholders out of

   (1) Earnings and profits of the current taxable year (CEP), computed at the end of the year, without regard to the amount of earnings and profits at the date of distribution; or,
   (2) Earnings and profits accumulated after February 28, 1913 (AEP).

   EXAMPLE: Corporation X has earnings and profits of $6,000 and makes a $10,000 distribution to its sole shareholder, A, who has a stock basis of $3,000. The $10,000 distribution to A will be treated as a dividend of $6,000, a nontaxable return of stock basis of $3,000, and a capital gain of $1,000.

   e. The **distributing corporation recognizes gain** on the distribution of appreciated property as if such property were sold for its FMV.

   EXAMPLE: A corporation distributes property with a FMV of $10,000 and a basis of $3,000 to a shareholder. The corporation recognizes a gain of $10,000 – $3,000 = $7,000.

   (1) If the distributed property is subject to a liability (or if the distributee assumes a liability) and the FMV of the distributed property is less than the amount of liability, then the gain is the difference between the amount of liability and the property's basis.

   EXAMPLE: A corporation distributes property with a FMV of $10,000 and a basis of $3,000 to a shareholder, who assumes a liability of $12,000 on the property. The corporation recognizes a gain of $12,000 – $3,000 = $9,000.

   (2) The type of gain recognized (e.g., ordinary, Sec. 1231, capital) depends on the nature of the property distributed (e.g., recapture rules may apply).

2. **Earnings and profits**

   a. **Current earnings and profits** (CEP) are **similar to book income**, but are computed by making adjustments to taxable income.

   (1) Add—tax-exempt income, dividends received deduction, excess of MACRS depreciation over depreciation computed under ADS, etc..
   (2) Deduct—federal income taxes, net capital loss, excess charitable contributions, expenses relating to tax-exempt income, penalties, etc.

   b. **Accumulated earnings and profits** (AEP) represent the sum of prior years' CEP, reduced by distributions and net operating loss of prior years.

   c. CEP are increased by the gain recognized on a distribution of appreciated property (excess of FMV over basis).

d. Distributions reduce earnings and profits (but not below zero) by

(1) The amount of money
(2) The face amount (or issue price if less) of obligations of the distributing corporation, and
(3) The adjusted basis (or FMV if greater) of other property distributed
(4) Above reductions must be adjusted by any liability assumed by the shareholder, or the amount of liability to which the property distributed is subject.

> *EXAMPLE: Z Corp. has two 50% shareholders, B Corp. and Mr. C. Z Corp. distributes a parcel of land (held for investment) to each shareholder. Each parcel of land has a FMV of $12,000 with a basis of $8,000 and each shareholder assumes a liability of $3,000 on the property received. Z Corp. will recognize a gain of $4,000 on the distribution of each property.*

	B Corp.	*Mr. C*
Dividend ($12,000 – $3,000)	*$ 9,000*	*$ 9,000*
Tax basis for property received	*12,000*	*12,000*
Effect (before tax) on Z's earnings & profits:		
Increased by gain (FMV-basis)	*4,000*	*4,000*
Increased by liabilities distributed	*3,000*	*3,000*
Decreased by FMV of property distributed	*(12,000)*	*(12,000)*

3. **Stock redemptions**

a. A stock redemption is **treated as an exchange**, generally resulting in capital gain or loss treatment to the shareholder if at least one of the following five tests is met. Constructive stock ownership rules generally apply in determining whether the following tests are met:

(1) The redemption is not essentially equivalent to a dividend (this has been interpreted by Revenue Rulings to mean that a redemption must reduce a shareholder's right to vote, share in earnings, and share in assets upon liquidation; and after the redemption the shareholder's stock ownership [both direct and constructive] must not exceed 50%), or
(2) The redemption is substantially disproportionate (i.e., after redemption, shareholder's percentage ownership is less than 80% of shareholder's percentage ownership prior to redemption, and less than 50% of shares outstanding), or
(3) All of the shareholder's stock is redeemed, or
(4) The redemption is from a noncorporate shareholder in a partial liquidation, or
(5) The distribution is a redemption of stock to pay death taxes under Sec. 303.

b. If none of the above tests are met, the redemption proceeds are treated as an ordinary Sec. 301 distribution, **taxable as a dividend** to the extent of the distributing corporation's earnings and profits.

c. A corporation cannot deduct amounts paid or incurred in connection with a redemption of its stock (except for interest expense on loans used to purchase stock).

4. **Complete liquidations**

a. Amounts received by **shareholders** in liquidation of a corporation are treated as received in exchange for stock, generally resulting in capital gain or loss. Property received will have a basis equal to FMV.

b. A **liquidating corporation** generally recognizes gain or loss on the sale or distribution of its assets in complete liquidation.

(1) If a distribution, gain or loss is computed as if the distributed property were sold to the distributee for FMV.
(2) If distributed property is subject to a liability (or a shareholder assumes a liability) in excess of the basis of the distributed property, FMV is deemed to be not less than the amount of liability.

c. **Distributions to related persons**

(1) No loss is generally recognized to a liquidating corporation on the distribution of property to a related person if

(a) The distribution is not pro rata, or
(b) The property was acquired by the liquidating corporation during the five-year period ending on the date of distribution in a Sec. 351 transaction or as a contribution to capital.

This includes any property whose basis is determined by reference to the adjusted basis of property described in the preceding sentence.

(2) Related person is a shareholder who owns (directly or constructively) more than 50% of the corporation's stock.

d. Carryover basis property

(1) If a corporation acquires property in a Sec. 351 transaction or as a contribution to capital at any time after the date that is two years before the date of the adoption of the plan of complete liquidation, any loss resulting from the property's sale, exchange, or distribution can be recognized only to the extent of the decline in value that occurred subsequent to the date that the corporation acquired the property.

(2) The above rule applies only where the loss is not already completely disallowed by c.(1) above, and is intended to apply where there is no clear and substantial relationship between the contributed property and the conduct of the corporation's business. If the contributed property is actually used in the corporation's business, the above rule should not apply if there is a business purpose for placing the property in the corporation.

EXAMPLE: A shareholder makes a capital contribution of property unrelated to the corporation's business with a basis of $15,000 and a FMV of $10,000 on the contribution date. Within two years the corporation adopts a plan of liquidation and sells the property for $8,000. The liquidating corporation's recognized loss will be limited to $10,000 – $8,000 = $2,000.

e. Liquidation of subsidiary

(1) **No gain or loss** is recognized to a **parent corporation** under Sec. 332 on the receipt of property in complete liquidation of an **80% or more owned subsidiary**. The subsidiary's basis for its assets along with all tax accounting attributes (e.g., earnings and profits, NOL and charitable contribution carryforwards) will transfer to the parent corporation.

(2) **No gain or loss** is recognized to a **subsidiary corporation** on the distribution of property to its parent if Sec. 332 applies to the parent corporation.

(a) If the subsidiary has debt outstanding to the parent, nonrecognition also applies to property distributed in satisfaction of the debt.

(b) Gain (but not loss) is recognized on the distribution of property to minority (20% or less) shareholders.

(3) Nonrecognition does not extend to minority shareholders. A minority shareholder's gain or loss will be recognized under the general rule at 4.a. on the preceding page.

EXAMPLE: Parent Corp. owns 80% of Subsidiary Corp., with the remaining 20% of Subsidiary stock owned by Alex. Parent's basis in its Subsidiary stock is $100,000, while Alex has a basis for her Subsidiary stock of $15,000. Subsidiary Corp. is to be liquidated and will distribute to Parent Corp. assets with a FMV of $200,000 and a basis of $150,000, and will distribute to Alex assets with a FMV of $50,000 and a basis of $30,000. Subsidiary has an unused capital loss carryover of $10,000. The tax effects of the liquidation will be as follows:

Parent Corp. will not recognize gain on the receipt of Subsidiary's assets in complete liquidation, since Subsidiary is an at least 80%-owned corporation. The basis of Subsidiary's assets to Parent will be their transferred basis $150,000, and Parent will inherit Subsidiary's unused capital loss carryover of $10,000.

Alex will recognize a gain of $35,000 ($50,000 FMV – $15,000 stock basis) from the liquidation. Alex's tax basis for Subsidiary's assets received in the liquidation will be their FMV of $50,000.

Subsidiary Corp. will not recognize gain on the distribution of its asses to Parent Corp., but will recognize a gain of $20,000 ($50,000 FMV – $30,000 basis) on the distribution of its assets to Alex.

5. Stock purchases treated as asset acquisitions

a. An acquiring corporation that has purchased at least 80% of a target corporation's stock within a twelve-month period may elect under Sec. 338 to have the purchase of stock treated as an acquisition of assets.

b. Old target corporation is deemed to have sold all its assets on the acquisition date, and is treated as a new corporation that has purchased those assets on the day after the acquisition date.

(1) Acquisition date is the date on which at least 80% of the target's stock has been acquired by purchase within a twelve-month period.

(2) Gain or loss is generally recognized to old target corporation on deemed sale of assets.

(3) The deemed sales price for the target corporation's assets is generally the FMV of the target's assets as of the close of the acquisition date.

F. Collapsible Corporations

1. Rules to prevent taxpayers from using corporations to convert ordinary income into capital gain by

    a. Forming or using an existing corporation to construct or produce property

    b. Before corporation realizes **two-thirds** of the taxable income from the property, shareholders sell stock.

    c. Thus, shareholders attempt to realize a capital gain on the sale of stock instead of recognizing ordinary income through continued operation of the corporation.

2. If a corporation is collapsible, a shareholder's gain may have to be reported as ordinary income instead of capital gain.

G. Personal Holding Company and Accumulated Earnings Taxes

1. Personal holding companies (PHC) are subject to a penalty tax on undistributed PHC income to discourage taxpayers from accumulating their investment income in a corporation taxed at lower than individual rates.

    a. A **personal holding company** is any corporation (except certain banks, financial institutions, and similar corporations) that meets two requirements.

        (1) During anytime in the last half of the tax year, five or fewer individuals own more than 50% of the value of the outstanding **stock** directly or indirectly, **and**

        (2) The corporation receives at least 60% of its adjusted ordinary gross **income** as "personal holding company income" (e.g., dividends, interest, rents, royalties, and other passive income)

    b. Taxed

        (1) At ordinary corporate rates on taxable income, plus

        (2) At highest individual tax rate on undistributed PHC income (38.6% for 2002)

    c. The PHC tax

        (1) Is **self-assessing** (i.e., computed on Sch. PH and attached to Form 1120); a six-year statute of limitations applies if no Sch. PH is filed

        (2) May be avoided by dividend payments sufficient in amount to reduce undistributed PHC income to zero

    d. The PHC tax is computed as follows:

> Taxable Income
>   + Dividends-received deduction
>   + Net operating loss deduction (except NOL of immediately preceding year allowed without a dividends-received deduction)
>   − Federal and foreign income taxes
>   − Charitable contributions in excess of 10% limit
>   − Net capital loss
>   − Net LTCG over NSTCL (net of tax)
> Adjusted Taxable Income
>   − Dividends paid during taxable year
>   − Dividends paid within 2 1/2 months after close of year (limited to 20% of dividends actually paid during year)
>   − Dividend carryover
>   − Consent dividends
> Undistributed PHC Income
>   x   38.6% (for 2002)
> Personal Holding Company Tax

    e. **Consent dividends** are hypothetical dividends that are treated as if they were paid on the last day of the corporation's taxable year. Since they are not actually distributed, shareholders increase their stock basis by the amount of consent dividends included in their gross income.

f.   PHC tax liability for a previous year (but not interest and penalties) may be avoided by payment of a deficiency dividend within ninety days of a "determination" by the IRS that the corporation was a PHC for a previous year.

2.   Corporations may be subject to an **accumulated earnings tax** (AET), in addition to regular income tax, if they accumulate earnings beyond reasonable business needs in order to avoid a shareholder tax on dividend distributions.

a.   The tax is not self-assessing, but is based on the IRS' determination of the existence of tax avoidance intent.

b.   AET may be imposed without regard to the number of shareholders of the corporation, but does not apply to personal holding companies.

c.   **Accumulated earnings credit** is allowed for greater of

(1) $250,000 ($150,000 for personal service corporations) minus the accumulated earnings and profits at end of prior year, or

(2) Reasonable needs of the business (e.g., expansion, working capital, to retire debt, etc.).

d.   Balance of accumulated taxable income is taxed at the highest individual tax rate (38.6% for 2002)

e.   The AET may be avoided by dividend payments sufficient in amount to reduce accumulated taxable income to zero.

f.   The accumulated earnings tax is computed as follows:

```
Taxable Income
    +   Dividends-received deduction
    +   NOL deduction
    -   Federal and foreign income taxes
    -   Excess charitable contributions (over 10% limit)
    -   Net capital loss
    -   Net LTCG over net STCL (net of tax)
Adjusted Taxable Income
    -   Dividends paid during last 9 1/2 months of tax year and 2 1/2 months after close
    -   Consent dividends
    -   Accumulated earnings credit
Accumulated Taxable Income
    x   38.6% (for 2002)
Accumulated Earnings Tax
```

H. S Corporations

An S corporation generally pays no corporate income taxes. Instead, it functions as a pass-through entity (much like a partnership) with its items of income, gain, loss, deduction, and credit passed through and directly included in the tax computations of its shareholders. Electing small business corporations are designated as S corporations; all other corporations are referred to as C corporations.

1.   **Eligibility** requirements for S corporation status

a.   Domestic corporation

b.   An S corporation may own any percent of the stock of a C corporation, and 100% of the stock of a qualified subchapter S subsidiary.

(1) An S corporation cannot file a consolidated return with an affiliated C corporation.

(2) A *qualified subchapter S subsidiary* (QSSS) is any domestic corporation that qualifies as an S corporation and is 100% owned by an S corporation parent, which elects to treat it as a QSSS. A QSSS is not treated as a separate corporation and all of its assets, liabilities, and items of income, deduction, and credit are treated as belonging to the parent S corporation.

c.   Only **one class of stock** issued and outstanding. A corporation will not be treated as having more than one class of stock solely because of differences in voting rights among the shares of common stock (i.e., both voting and nonvoting common stock may be outstanding).

d.   **Shareholders** must be individuals, estates, or trusts created by will (only for a two-year period), voting trusts, an Electing Small Business Trust (ESBT), a Qualified Subchapter S Trust (QSST), or a trust all of which is treated as owned by an individual who is a citizen or resident of the US (i.e., Subpart E trust).

(1) A QSST and a Subpart E trust may continue to be a shareholder for two years beginning with the date of death of the deemed owner.

(2) Code Sec. 401(a) qualified retirement plan trusts and Code Sec. 501(c) charitable organizations that are exempt from tax under Code Sec. 501(a) are eligible to be shareholders of an S corporation. The S corporation's items of income and deduction will flow through to the tax-exempt shareholder as unrelated business taxable income (UBIT).

e. No nonresident alien shareholders

f. Number of shareholders **limited to 75**

(1) Husband and wife (and their estates) are counted as one shareholder.

(2) Each beneficiary of a voting trust is considered a shareholder.

(3) If a trust is treated as owned by an individual, that individual (not the trust) is treated as the shareholder.

2. An **election must be filed** anytime in the preceding taxable year or on or before the fifteenth day of the third month of the year for which effective.

a. All shareholders on date of election, plus any shareholders who held stock during the taxable year but before the date of election, must consent to the election.

(1) If an election is made on or before the fifteenth day of the third month of taxable year, but either (1) a shareholder who held stock during the taxable year and before the date of election does not consent to the election, or (2) the corporation did not meet the eligibility requirements during the part of the year before the date of election, then the election is treated as made for the following taxable year.

(2) An election made after the fifteenth day of the third month of the taxable year is treated as made for the following year.

b. A newly formed corporation's election will be timely if made within two and one-half months of the first day of its taxable year (e.g., a calendar-year corporation formed on August 6, 2002, could make an S corporation election that would be effective for its 2002 calendar year if the election is filed on or before October 20, 2002).

c. A valid election is effective for all succeeding years until terminated.

d. The IRS has the authority to waive the effect of an invalid election caused by a corporation's inadvertent failure to qualify as a small business corporation or to obtain required shareholder consents (including elections regarding qualified subchapter S trusts), or both. Additionally, the IRS may treat late-filed subchapter S elections as timely filed if there is reasonable cause justifying the late filing.

3. **LIFO recapture.** A C corporation using LIFO that converts to S status must recapture the excess of the inventory's value using a FIFO cost flow assumption over its LIFO tax basis as of the close of its last tax year as a C corporation.

a. The LIFO recapture is included in the C corporation's gross income and the tax attributable to its inclusion is payable in four equal installments.

b. The first installment must be paid by the due date of the tax return for the last C corporation year, with the three remaining installments due by the due dates of the tax returns for the three succeeding taxable years.

4. A corporation making an S election is generally required to **adopt or change to (1) a year ending December 31**, or (2) a fiscal year that is the same as the fiscal year used by shareholders owning more than 50% of the corporation's stock.

a. An S corporation may use a different fiscal year if a valid business purpose can be established (i.e., natural business year) and IRS permission is received. The business purpose test will be met if an S corporation receives at least 25% of its gross receipts in the last two months of the selected fiscal year, and this 25% test has been satisfied for three consecutive years.

EXAMPLE: An S corporation, on a calendar year, has received at least 25% of its gross receipts during the months of May and June for each of the last three years. The S corporation may be allowed to change to a fiscal year ending June 30.

b. An S corporation that otherwise would be required to adopt or change its tax year (normally to the calendar year) may elect to use a fiscal year if the election does not result in a deferral period longer than three months, or, if less, the deferral period of the year currently in use.

   (1) The "deferral period" is the number of months between the close of the fiscal year elected and the close of the required year (e.g., if an S corporation elects a tax year ending September 30 and a tax year ending December 31 is required, the deferral period of the year ending September 30 is three months).

   (2) An S corporation that elects a tax year other than a required year must make a "required payment" which is in the nature of a refundable, non-interest-bearing deposit that is intended to compensate the government for the revenue lost as a result of tax deferral. The required payment is due on May 15 each year and is recomputed for each subsequent year.

5. An S corporation must **file Form 1120S** by the fifteenth day of the third month following the close of its taxable year (e.g., March 15 for a calendar-year S corporation).

  (a) An automatic six-month extension may be obtained by filing Form 7004.

  (b) Estimated tax payments must be made if estimated tax liability (e.g., built-in gains tax, excess net passive income tax) is expected to be $500 or more.

6. **Termination** of S corporation status may be caused by

  a. Shareholders owning **more than 50%** of the shares of stock of the corporation consent to **revocation** of the election.

   (1) A revocation made on or before the fifteenth day of the third month of the taxable year is generally effective on the first day of such taxable year.

   (2) A revocation made after the fifteenth day of the third month of the taxable year is generally effective as of the first day of the following taxable year.

   (3) Instead of the dates mentioned above, a revocation may specify an effective date on or after the date on which the revocation is filed.

    EXAMPLE: For a calendar-year S corporation, a revocation not specifying a revocation date that is made on or before 3/15/02 is effective as of 1/1/02. A revocation not specifying a revocation date that is made after 3/15/02 is effective as of 1/1/03. If a revocation is filed 3/11/02 and specifies a revocation date of 7/1/02, the corporation ceases to be an S corporation on 7/1/02.

  b. The corporation's **failing to satisfy any of the eligibility requirements** listed in 1. Termination is effective on the date an eligibility requirement is failed.

    EXAMPLE: A calendar-year S corporation with common stock outstanding issues preferred stock on April 1, 2002. Since its S corporation status terminates on April 1, it must file an S corporation tax return (Form 1120S) for the period January 1 through March 31, and a C corporation tax return (Form 1120) for the period April 1 through December 31, 2002. Both tax returns would be due by March 15, 2003.

  c. Passive investment income exceeding 25% of gross receipts for three consecutive taxable years if the corporation has subchapter C earnings and profits at the end of each of those years.

   (1) Subchapter C earnings and profits are earnings and profits accumulated during a taxable year for which the corporation was a C corporation.

   (2) Termination is effective as of the first day of the taxable year beginning after the third consecutive year of passive investment income in excess of 25% of gross receipts.

    EXAMPLE: An S corporation with subchapter C earnings and profits had passive investment income in excess of 25% of its gross receipts for its calendar years 2000, 2001, and 2002. Its S corporation status would terminate 1/1/03.

  d. Generally once terminated, S corporation status can be reelected only after five non-S-corporation years.

   (1) The corporation can request IRS for an earlier reelection.

   (2) IRS may treat an inadvertent termination as if it never occurred.

7. An **S corporation** generally pays no federal income taxes, but may have to pay a tax on its built-in gain, or on its excess passive investment income if certain conditions are met (see page 424).

a. The S corporation is treated as a **pass-through entity**; the character of any item of income, expense, gain, loss, or credit is determined at the corporate level, and passes through to shareholders, retaining its identity.

b. An S corporation must recognize gain on the distribution of appreciated property (other than its own obligations) to its shareholders. Gain is recognized in the same manner as if the property had been sold to the distributee at its FMV.

EXAMPLE: An S corporation distributes property with a FMV of $900 and an adjusted basis of $100 to its sole shareholder. Gain of $800 will be recognized by the corporation. The character of the gain will be determined at the corporate level, and passed through and reported by its shareholder. The shareholder is treated as receiving a $900 distribution, subject to the distribution rules discussed on page 423.

c. Expenses and interest owed to any cash-method shareholder are deductible by an accrual-method S corporation only when paid.

EXAMPLE: An accrual-method calendar-year S corporation accrues $2,000 of salary to a cash-method employee (a 1% shareholder) during 2002, but does not make payment until February 2003. The $2,000 will be deductible by the corporation in 2003, and reported by the shareholder-employee as income in 2003.

d. An S corporation will not generate any earnings and profits. All items are reflected in adjustments to the basis of shareholders' stock and/or debt.

e. S corporations must make estimated tax payments for the tax liability attributable to the built-in gains tax, excess passive investment income tax, and the tax due to investment credit recapture.

f. The provisions of subchapter C apply to an S corporation, except where inconsistent with subchapter S. For example, an S corporation can use Secs. 332 and 337 to liquidate an acquired subsidiary, and can make a Sec. 338 election if otherwise qualified.

8. A **shareholder** of an S corporation must separately take into account (for the shareholder's taxable year in which the taxable year of the S corporation ends) (1) the shareholder's pro rata share of the corporation's items of income (including tax-exempt income), loss, deduction, or credit the separate treatment of which could affect the tax liability of **any** shareholder, plus (2) the shareholder's pro rata share of all remaining items which are netted together into "ordinary income (loss) from trade or business activity."

a. Some of the **items which must be separately passed through** to retain their identity include

    (1) Net long-term capital gain (loss)
    (2) Net short-term capital gain (loss)
    (3) Net gain (loss) from Sec. 1231 casualty or theft
    (4) Net gain (loss) from other Sec. 1231 transactions
    (5) Tax-exempt interest
    (6) Charitable contributions
    (7) Foreign income taxes
    (8) Depletion
    (9) Investment interest expense
    (10) Dividend, interest, and royalty income
    (11) Net income (loss) from real estate activity
    (12) Net income (loss) from other rental activity

b. All separately stated items plus the ordinary income or loss are allocated on a **per share, per day basis** to anyone who was a shareholder during the year. Items are allocated to shareholders' stock (both voting and nonvoting) but not to debt.

EXAMPLE: Alan owned 100% of a calendar-year S corporation's stock on January 1, 2002. Alan sold all his stock to Betty on January 31. Assuming the S corporation had $365,000 of ordinary income for the entire 2002 calendar year, the amount allocated to Alan would be $31,000 (31 days x $1,000 per day), and the amount allocated to Betty would be $334,000 (334 days x $1,000 per day).

    (1) The per share, per day rule will not apply if

        (a) A shareholder's interest is completely terminated and all affected shareholders consent to allocate items as if the corporation's taxable year consisted of two years, the first of which ends on the date the shareholder's interest was terminated. The closing of the books method applies only to the affected shareholders. *Affected shareholders* include the shareholder whose interest was terminated and shareholders to whom the terminating shareholder transferred shares during the year.

> *EXAMPLE: Assume in the above example that the S corporation had net income of $40,000 for the month of January. If both Alan and Betty consent, $40,000 would be allocated to Alan, and $325,000 would be allocated to Betty.*

    (b) An S corporation's election is terminated on other than the first day of the taxable year, and all shareholders during the S short year and all persons who were shareholders on the first day of the C short year consent to allocate items using the corporation's financial accounting records.

(2) The per share, per day rule **cannot** be used if

    (a) There is a sale or exchange of 50% or more of the stock of the corporation during an S termination year. Financial accounting records must be used to allocate items.

    (b) A Sec. 338 election is made. Then the gains and losses resulting from the Sec. 338 election must be reported on a C corporation return.

c.   A shareholder who disposes of stock in an S corporation is treated as the shareholder for the day of disposition. A shareholder who dies is treated as the shareholder for the day of the shareholder's death.

9.   Three sets of rules may limit the amount of S corporation loss that a shareholder can deduct.

a.   A shareholder's allocation of the aggregate **losses and deductions** of an S corporation can be deducted by the shareholder to the extent of the **shareholder's basis for stock plus basis of any debt** owed the shareholder by the corporation [Sec. 1366 (d)].

(1) An excess of loss over combined basis for stock and debt can be carried forward indefinitely and deducted when there is basis to absorb it.

> *EXAMPLE: An S corporation incurred losses totaling $50,000. Its sole shareholder (who materially participates in the business and is at-risk) had a stock basis of $30,000 and debt with a basis of $15,000. The shareholder's loss deduction is limited to $45,000. The losses first reduce stock basis to zero, then debt basis is reduced to zero. The excess loss of $5,000 can be carried forward and deducted when there is basis to absorb it.*

(2) Once reduced, the basis of debt is later increased (but not above its original basis) by *net undistributed income.*

> *EXAMPLE: An S corporation incurred a loss of $20,000 for 2001. Its sole shareholder (who materially participates in the business and is at-risk) had a stock basis of $10,000 and debt with a basis of $15,000. The pass-through of the $20,000 loss would first reduce stock basis to zero, and then reduce debt basis to $5,000.*
>
>   *Assume that for 2002, the same S corporation had ordinary income of $10,000, and made a $4,000 cash distribution to its shareholder during the year. The first $4,000 of basis increase resulting from the pass-through of income would be allocated to stock in order to permit the $4,000 distribution to be nontaxable. The remaining basis increase (net **un**distributed income of $6,000) would restore debt basis to $11,000 (from $5,000).*

b.   The deductibility of S corporation losses is also limited to the amount of the shareholder's **at-risk basis** at the end of the taxable year [Sec. 465].

(1) A shareholder's amount at-risk includes amounts borrowed and reloaned to the S corporation if the shareholder is personally liable for repayment of the borrowed amount, or has pledged property not used in the activity as security for the borrowed amount.

(2) A shareholder's amount at-risk does not include any debt of the S corporation to any person other than the shareholder, even if the shareholder guarantees the debt.

c.   The deductibility of S corporation losses may also be subject to the **passive activity loss limitations** [Sec. 469]. Passive activity losses are deductible only to the extent of the shareholder's income from other passive activities (See Module 40).

(1) Passive activities include (a) any S corporation trade or business in which the shareholder does not materially participate, and (b) any rental activity.

(2) If a shareholder "actively participates" in a rental activity and owns (together with spouse) at least 10% of the value of an S corporation's stock, up to $25,000 of rental losses may be deductible against earned income and portfolio income.

10. A shareholder's S corporation **stock basis** is **increased** by all income items (including tax-exempt income), plus depletion in excess of the basis of the property subject to depletion; **decreased** by all loss and deduction items, nondeductible expenses not charged to capital, and the shareholder's deduction for depletion on oil and gas wells; and **decreased** by distributions that are excluded from gross income. Stock basis is **adjusted in the following order:**

    a. Increased for all income items

    b. Decreased for distributions that are excluded from gross income

    c. Decreased for nondeductible, noncapital items

    d. Decreased for deductible expenses and losses

> *EXAMPLE: An S corporation has tax-exempt income of $5,000, and an ordinary loss from business activity of $6,000 for calendar year 2002. Its sole shareholder had a stock basis of $2,000 on January 1, 2002. The $5,000 of tax-exempt income would pass through to the shareholder, increasing the shareholder's stock basis to $7,000, and would permit the pass-through and deduction of the $6,000 of ordinary loss, reducing the shareholder's stock basis to $1,000.*

> *EXAMPLE: An S corporation had an ordinary loss from business activity of $6,000 and made a $7,000 cash distribution to its sole shareholder during calendar year 2002. The sole shareholder had a stock basis of $8,000 on January 1, 2002. The $7,000 cash distribution would be nontaxable and would reduce stock basis to $1,000. As a result, only $1,000 of the $6,000 ordinary loss would be allowable as a deduction to the shareholder for 2002. The remaining $5,000 of ordinary loss would be carried forward and deducted by the shareholder when there is stock basis to absorb it.*

11. The **treatment of distributions** (Cash + FMV of other property) to shareholders is determined as follows:

    a. Distributions are **nontaxable** to the extent of the Accumulated Adjustments Account (AAA) and are applied to **reduce the AAA and the shareholder's stock basis**.

        (1) The AAA represents the cumulative total of undistributed net income items for S corporation taxable years beginning after 1982.

        (2) If there is more than one distribution during the year, a pro rata portion of each distribution is treated as made from the AAA.

        (3) The AAA can have a negative balance if expenses and losses exceed income.

        (4) No adjustment is made to the AAA for tax-exempt income and related expenses, and Federal taxes attributable to a year in which the corporation was a C corporation. Tax-exempt income and related expenses are reflected in the corporation's Other Adjustments Account (OAA).

        (5) For purposes of determining the treatment of a distribution, the amount in the AAA at the close of any taxable year is determined without regard to any **net negative adjustment** (i.e., the excess of reductions over increases to the AAA for the taxable year) for such taxable year.

    b. Distributions in excess of the AAA are treated as **ordinary dividends** to the extent of the corporation's **accumulated earnings and profits (AEP).** These amounts represent earnings and profits that were accumulated (and never taxed to shareholders) during C corporation taxable years.

    c. Distributions are next **nontaxable** to the extent of **remaining stock basis** and are applied to reduce the OAA and paid-in capital.

    d. Distributions **in excess of stock basis** are treated as **gain** from the sale of stock.

> *EXAMPLE: A calendar-year S corporation had subchapter C accumulated earnings and profits of $10,000 at December 31, 2001. During calendar year 2002, the corporation had net income of $20,000, and distributed $38,000 to its sole shareholder on June 20, 2002. Its shareholder had a stock basis of $15,000 at January 1, 2002.*
>
> *The $20,000 of net income passes through and is includible in gross income by the shareholder for 2002. The shareholder's stock basis is increased by the $20,000 of income (to $35,000), as is the AAA which is increased to $20,000. Of the $38,000 distribution, the first $20,000 is nontaxable and (1) reduces stock basis to $15,000, and (2) the AAA to zero; the next $10,000 of distribution is reported as dividend income (no effect on stock basis); while the remaining $8,000 of distribution is nontaxable and reduces stock basis to $7,000.*

12. Health and accident insurance premiums and other **fringe benefits** paid by an S corporation on behalf of a more than 2% shareholder-employee are deductible by the S corporation as compensation and includible in the shareholder-employee's gross income on Form W-2.

13. An S corporation (that previously was a C corporation) is taxed on its **net recognized built-in gain** if the gain is (1) attributable to an excess of the FMV of its assets over their aggregate adjusted basis as of the beginning of its first taxable year as an S corporation, and (2) is recognized within **ten years** after the effective date of its S corporation election.

a. This provision generally applies to C corporations that make an S corporation election after December 31, 1986.

b. To determine the tax, (1) take the lesser of (a) the net recognized built-in gain for the taxable year, or (b) taxable income determined as if the corporation were a C corporation (except the NOL and dividends-received deductions are not allowed); (2) subtract any NOL and capital loss carryforwards from C corporation years; (3) multiply the resulting amount by the highest corporate tax rate (currently 35%); and (4) subtract any general business credit carryovers from C corporation years and the special fuels tax credit.

c. Any net recognized built-in gain that escapes the built-in gains tax because of the taxable income limitation is carried forward and is subject to the built-in gains tax to the extent the corporation subsequently has other taxable income (that is not already subject to the built-in gains tax) for any taxable year within the ten-year recognition period.

d. Recognized built-in gain **does not include** gain from the disposition of an asset if

    (1) The asset was not held by the corporation when its S election became effective (e.g., an asset was purchased after the first day of its S election), or

    (2) The gain is attributable to appreciation that occurred after the S election became effective (e.g., an asset is sold for a gain of $1,000, but $600 of its appreciation occurred after the first day of its S election; the corporation would be taxed on only $400 of gain).

e. The total amount of net recognized built-in gain that will be taxed to an S corporation is limited to the aggregate net unrealized built-in gain when the S election became effective.

f. The **built-in gains tax** that is paid by an S corporation is **treated as a loss** sustained by the S corporation during the taxable year. The character of the loss is determined by allocating the loss proportionately among the recognized built-in gains giving rise to such tax.

EXAMPLE: For 2002, an S corporation has taxable income of $100,000, which includes a $40,000 long-term capital gain that is also a recognized built-in gain. Since its recognized built-in gain of $40,000 is less than its taxable income, its built-in gains tax for 2002 is $40,000 x 35% = $14,000. Since the built-in gain was a long-term capital gain, the built-in gains tax paid of $14,000 is treated as a long-term capital loss. As a result, a net long-term capital gain of $26,000 ($40,000 LTCG – $14,000 LTCL) passes through to shareholders for 2002.

EXAMPLE: For 2002, an S corporation has taxable income of $10,000, which includes a $40,000 long-term capital gain that is also a recognized built-in gain. Since its taxable income of $10,000 is less than its recognized built-in gain of $40,000, its built-in gains tax for 2002 is limited to $10,000 x 35% = $3,500. As a result, a net long-term capital gain of $40,000 – $3,500 = $36,500 passes through to shareholders for 2002.

The remaining $30,000 of untaxed recognized built-in gain would be suspended and carried forward to 2003, where it would again be treated as a recognized built-in gain. If the S corporation has at least $30,000 of taxable income in 2003 that is not already subject to the built-in gains tax, the suspended gain from 2002 will be taxed. As a result, the amount of built-in gains tax paid by the S corporation for 2003 will be $30,000 x 35% = $10,500, and will pass through to shareholders as a long-term capital loss, since the original gain in 2002 was a long-term capital gain.

14. If an S corporation has subchapter C accumulated earnings and profits, and its **passive investment income exceeds 25% of gross receipts**, a tax is imposed at the highest corporate rate on the lesser of (1) excess net passive income (ENPI), or (2) taxable income.

    a. $$\text{ENPI} = \left(\begin{array}{c}\text{Net passive}\\\text{income}\end{array}\right) \times \left(\frac{\text{Passive investment income} - (25\% \text{ of Gross receipts})}{\text{Passive investment income}}\right)$$

    b. **Passive investment income** means gross receipts derived from dividends, interest, royalties, rents, annuities, and gains from the sale or exchange of stock or securities. However, dividends from an affiliated C corporation subsidiary are not treated as passive investment income to the extent the dividends are attributable to the earnings and profits derived from the active conduct of a trade or business by the C corporation.

    c. The tax paid reduces the amount of passive investment income passed through to shareholders

    EXAMPLE: An S corporation has gross receipts of $80,000, of which $50,000 is interest income. Expenses incurred in the production of this passive income total $10,000. The ENPI is $24,000.

    $$\text{ENPI} = (\$50,000 - \$10,000) \times \left(\frac{\$50,000 - (25\% \times \$80,000)}{\$50,000}\right) = \$24,000$$

I. Corporate Reorganizations

Certain exchanges, usually involving the exchange of one corporation's stock for the stock or property of another, result in deferral of gain or loss.

1. There are seven different **types** of reorganizations which generally result in nonrecognition treatment.

   a. Type A—statutory mergers or consolidations

      (1) Merger is one corporation absorbing another by operation of law
      (2) Consolidation is two corporations combining in a new corporation, the former ones dissolving

   b. Type B—the use of solely voting stock of the acquiring corporation (or its parent) to acquire at least 80% of the voting power and 80% of each class of nonvoting stock of the target corporation

      (1) No boot can be used by the acquiring corporation to acquire the target's stock
      (2) Results in the acquisition of a controlled subsidiary

   c. Type C—the use of solely voting stock of the acquiring corporation (or its parent) to acquire substantially all of the target's properties

      (1) In determining whether the acquisition is made for solely voting stock, the assumption by the acquiring corporation of a liability of the target corporation, or the fact that the property acquired is subject to a liability is disregarded.
      (2) "Substantially all" means at least 90% of the FMV of the target's net assets, and at least 70% of its gross assets.
      (3) The target (acquired) corporation must distribute the consideration it receives, as well as all of its other properties, in pursuance of the plan of reorganization.

   d. Type D—a transfer by a corporation of part or all of its assets to another if immediately after the transfer the transferor corporation, or its shareholders, control the transferee corporation (i.e., own at least 80% of the voting power and at least 80% of each class of nonvoting stock)

      (1) Although it may be acquisitive, this type of reorganization is generally used to divide a corporation.
      (2) Generally results in a spin-off, split-off, or split-up.

   e. Type E—a recapitalization to change the capital structure of a single corporation (e.g., bondholders exchange old bonds for new bonds or stock)

   f. Type F—a mere change in identity, form, or place of organization (e.g., name change, change of state of incorporation)

   g. Type G—a transfer of assets by an insolvent corporation or pursuant to bankruptcy proceedings, with the result that former creditors often become the owners of the corporation

2. For the reorganization to be tax-free, it must meet one of the above definitions and the exchange must be made under a plan or reorganization involving the affected corporations as parties to the reorganization. It generally must satisfy the judicial doctrines of continuity of shareholder interest, business purpose, and continuity of business enterprise.

   a. **Continuity of shareholder interest**—The shareholders of the transferor (acquired) corporation must receive stock in the transferee (acquiring) corporation at least equal in value to 50% of the value of all of the transferor's formerly outstanding stock.

   b. **Continuity of business enterprise**—The transferor's historic business must be continued, or a significant portion (e.g., 1/3) of the transferor's historic assets must be used in a business.

3. **No gain or loss** is generally recognized to a **transferor corporation** on the transfer of its property pursuant to a plan of reorganization.

   a. The **transferee corporation's basis for property** received equals the transferor's basis plus gain recognized (if any) to the transferor.

   b. Gain is recognized on the distribution to shareholders of any property other than stock or securities of a party to the reorganization (e.g., property the transferor retained and did not transfer to the acquiring corporation), as if such property were sold for its FMV.

4. No gain or loss is recognized by a corporation on the disposition of stock or securities in another corporation that is a party to the reorganization.

    a. No gain or loss is generally recognized on the distribution of stock or securities of a controlled subsidiary in a qualifying spin-off, split-off, or split-up. However, the distributing corporation must recognize gain on the distribution of its subsidiary's stock if immediately after the distribution, any person holds a 50% or greater interest in the distributing corporation or a distributed subsidiary that is attributable to stock acquired by purchase during the five-year period ending on date of distribution.

    b. Gain is recognized on the distribution of appreciated boot property.

5. If a **shareholder receives boot** in a reorganization, gain is recognized (but not loss).

    a. Boot includes the FMV of an excess of principal (i.e., face) amount of securities received over the principal amount of securities surrendered.

      EXAMPLE: In a recapitalization, a bondholder exchanges a bond with a face amount and basis of $1,000, for a new bond with a face amount of $1,500 and a fair market value of $1,575. Since an excess face amount of security ($500) has been received, the bondholder's realized gain of $575 will be recognized to the extent of the fair market value of the excess [($500/$1,500) x $1,575] = $525.

    b. Recognized gain will be treated as a dividend to the extent of the shareholder's ratable share of earnings and profits of the acquired corporation if the receipt of boot has the effect of the distribution of a dividend.

      (1) Whether the receipt of boot has the effect of a dividend is determined by applying the Sec. 302(b) redemption tests based on the shareholder's stock interest in the acquiring corporation (i.e., as if only stock had been received, and then the boot was used to redeem the stock that was not received).

      (2) The receipt of boot will generally not have the effect of a dividend, and will thus result in capital gain.

6. A shareholder's **basis for stock and securities received** equals the basis of stock and securities surrendered, plus gain recognized, and minus boot received.

    EXAMPLE: Pursuant to a merger of Corporation T into Corporation P, Smith exchanged 100 shares of T that he had purchased for $1,000, for 80 shares of P having a FMV of $1,500 and also received $200 cash. Smith's realized gain of $700 is recognized to the extent of the cash received of $200, and is treated as a capital gain. Smith's basis for his P stock is $1,000 ($1,000 + $200 recognized gain – $200 cash received).

7. **Carryover of tax attributes**

    a. The tax attributes of the acquired corporation (e.g., NOL carryovers, earnings and profits, accounting methods, etc.) generally carry over to the acquiring corporation in an acquisitive reorganization.

    b. The amount of an **acquired corporation's NOL** carryovers that can be utilized by the acquiring corporation for its first taxable year ending after the date of acquisition is **limited by Sec. 381** to

$$\begin{array}{c}\text{Acquiring} \\ \text{corporation's} \\ \text{TI before} \\ \text{NOL deduction}\end{array} \quad \text{x} \quad \frac{\text{Days after acquisition date}}{\text{Total days in taxable year}}$$

    EXAMPLE: Corporation P (on a calendar year) acquired Corporation T in a statutory merger on October 19, 2002, with the former T shareholders receiving 60% of P's stock. If T had a NOL carryover of $70,000, and P has taxable income (before a NOL deduction) of $91,500, the amount of T's $70,000 NOL carryover that can be deducted by P for 2002 would be

$$\$91,500 \ x \ \frac{73}{365} = \$18,300$$

    c. If there is a **more than 50% change in ownership** of a loss corporation, the taxable income for any year of the new loss (or surviving) corporation may be reduced by a NOL carryover from the old loss corporation only to the extent of the value of the old loss corporation's stock on the date of the ownership change multiplied by the "long-term tax-exempt rate" (**Sec. 382 limitation**).

      (1) An ownership change has occurred when the percentage of stock owned by an entity's 5% or more shareholders has increased by more than 50 percentage points relative to the lowest per-

centage owned by such shareholders at any time during the preceding three-year testing period.

(2) For the year of acquisition, the Sec. 382 limitation amount is available only to the extent allocable to days after the acquisition date.

$$\text{Sec. 382 limitation} \quad x \quad \frac{\text{Days after acquisition date}}{\text{Totals days in taxable year}}$$

EXAMPLE: *If T's former shareholders received only 30% of P's stock in the preceding example, there would be a more than 50 percentage point change in ownership of T Corporation, and T's NOL carryover would be subject to a Sec. 382 limitation. If the FMV of T's stock on October 19, 2002, was $500,000 and the long-term tax-exempt rate were 5%, the Sec. 382 limitation for 2002 would be ($500,000 x 5%) x (73/365 days) = $5,000.*

Thus, only $5,000 of T's NOL carryover could be deducted by P for 2002. The remaining $70,000 – $5,000 = $65,000 of T's NOL would be carried forward by P and could be used to offset P's taxable income for 2003 to the extent of the Sec. 382 limitation (i.e., $500,000 x 5% = $25,000).

MULTIPLE-CHOICE QUESTIONS (1-161)

1. Alan, Baker, and Carr formed Dexter Corporation during 2002. Pursuant to the incorporation agreement, Alan transferred property with an adjusted basis of $30,000 and a fair market value of $45,000 for 450 shares of stock, Baker transferred cash of $35,000 in exchange for 350 shares of stock, and Carr performed services valued at $25,000 in exchange for 250 shares of stock. Assuming the fair market value of Dexter Corporation stock is $100 per share, what is Dexter Corporation's tax basis for the property received from Alan?

    a. $0
    b. $30,000
    c. $45,000
    d. $65,000

2. Clark and Hunt organized Jet Corp. with authorized voting common stock of $400,000. Clark contributed $60,000 cash. Both Clark and Hunt transferred other property in exchange for Jet stock as follows:

| | *Other property* | | |
	Adjusted basis	*Fair market value*	*Percentage of Jet stock acquired*
Clark	$ 50,000	$100,000	40%
Hunt	120,000	240,000	60%

What was Clark's basis in Jet stock?

    a. $0
    b. $100,000
    c. $110,000
    d. $160,000

3. Adams, Beck, and Carr organized Flexo Corp. with authorized voting common stock of $100,000. Adams received 10% of the capital stock in payment for the organizational services that he rendered for the benefit of the newly formed corporation. Adams did not contribute property to Flexo and was under no obligation to be paid by Beck or Carr. Beck and Carr transferred property in exchange for stock as follows:

	Adjusted basis	*Fair market value*	*Percentage of Flexo stock acquired*
Beck	5,000	20,000	20%
Carr	60,000	70,000	70%

What amount of gain did Carr recognize from this transaction?

    a. $40,000
    b. $15,000
    c. $10,000
    d. $0

4. Jones incorporated a sole proprietorship by exchanging all the proprietorship's assets for the stock of Nu Co., a new corporation. To qualify for tax-free incorporation, Jones must be in control of Nu immediately after the exchange. What percentage of Nu's stock must Jones own to qualify as "control" for this purpose?

    a.   50.00%
    b.   51.00%
    c.   66.67%
    d.   80.00%

5. Feld, the sole stockholder of Maki Corp., paid $50,000 for Maki's stock in 1996. In 2002, Feld contributed a parcel of land to Maki but was not given any additional stock for this contribution. Feld's basis for the land was $10,000, and its fair market value was $18,000 on the date of the transfer of title. What is Feld's adjusted basis for the Maki stock?

    a. $50,000
    b. $52,000
    c. $60,000
    d. $68,000

6. Rela Associates, a partnership, transferred all of its assets, with a basis of $300,000, along with liabilities of $50,000, to a newly formed corporation in return for all of the corporation's stock. The corporation assumed the liabilities. Rela then distributed the corporation's stock to its partners in liquidation. In connection with this incorporation of the partnership, Rela recognizes

    a.   No gain or loss on the transfer of its assets nor on the assumption of Rela's liabilities by the corporation.
    b.   Gain on the assumption of Rela's liabilities by the corporation.
    c.   Gain or loss on the transfer of its assets to the corporation.
    d.   Gain, but **not** loss, on the transfer of its assets to the corporation.

7. Roberta Warner and Sally Rogers formed the Acme Corporation on October 1, 2002. On the same date Warner paid $75,000 cash to Acme for 750 shares of its common stock. Simultaneously, Rogers received 100 shares of Acme's common stock for services rendered. How much should Rogers include as taxable income for 2002 and what will be the basis of her stock?

	Taxable income	*Basis of stock*
a.	$0	$0
b.	$0	$10,000
c.	$10,000	$0
d.	$10,000	$10,000

8. Which of the following is **not** a requirement for stock to qualify as Sec. 1244 small business corporation stock?

    a.   The stock must be issued to an individual or to a partnership.
    b.   The stock was issued for money or property (other than stock and securities).
    c.   The stock must be common stock.
    d.   The issuer must be a domestic corporation.

9. During the current year, Dinah sold Sec. 1244 small business corporation stock that she owned for a loss of $125,000. Assuming Dinah is married and files a joint income tax return for 2002, what is the character of Dinah's recognized loss from the sale of the stock?

    a. $125,000 capital loss.
    b. $25,000 capital loss; $100,000 ordinary loss.
    c. $75,000 capital loss; $50,000 ordinary loss.
    d. $0 capital loss; $125,000 ordinary loss.

10. Nancy, who is single, formed a corporation during 1998 using a tax-free asset transfer that qualified under Sec. 351. She transferred property having an adjusted basis of $80,000 and a fair market value of $60,000, and in exchange received Sec. 1244 small business corporation stock. During February 2002, Nancy sold all of her stock for $35,000. What is the amount and character of Nancy's recognized loss resulting from the sale of the stock in 2002?

a. $0 ordinary loss; $45,000 capital loss.
b. $25,000 ordinary loss; $10,000 capital loss.
c. $25,000 ordinary loss; $20,000 capital loss.
d. $45,000 ordinary loss; $0 capital loss.

11. A civil fraud penalty can be imposed on a corporation that underpays tax by
  a. Omitting income as a result of inadequate record-keeping.
  b. Failing to report income it erroneously considered **not** to be part of corporate profits.
  c. Filing an incomplete return with an appended statement, making clear that the return is incomplete.
  d. Maintaining false records and reporting fictitious transactions to minimize corporate tax liability.

12. Bass Corp., a calendar-year C corporation, made qualifying 2002 estimated tax deposits based on its actual 2001 tax liability. On March 15, 2003, Bass filed a timely automatic extension request for its 2002 corporate income tax return. Estimated tax deposits and the extension payment totaled $7,600. This amount was 95% of the total tax shown on Bass' final 2002 corporate income tax return. Bass paid $400 additional tax on the final 2002 corporate income tax return filed before the extended due date. For the 2002 calendar year, Bass was subject to pay

I. Interest on the $400 tax payment made in 2003.
II. A tax delinquency penalty.

  a. I only.
  b. II only.
  c. Both I and II.
  d. Neither I nor II.

13. Edge Corp., a calendar-year C corporation, had a net operating loss and zero tax liability for its 2002 tax year. To avoid the penalty for underpayment of estimated taxes, Edge could compute its first quarter 2003 estimated income tax payment using the

	Annualized income method	Preceding year method
a.	Yes	Yes
b.	Yes	No
c.	No	Yes
d.	No	No

14. A corporation's tax year can be reopened after all statutes of limitations have expired if

I. The tax return has a 50% nonfraudulent omission from gross income.
II. The corporation prevails in a determination allowing a deduction in an open tax year that was taken erroneously in a closed tax year.

  a. I only.
  b. II only.
  c. Both I and II.
  d. Neither I nor II.

15. A corporation's penalty for underpaying federal estimated taxes is
  a. Not deductible.
  b. Fully deductible in the year paid.
  c. Fully deductible if reasonable cause can be established for the underpayment.
  d. Partially deductible.

16. Blink Corp., an accrual-basis calendar-year corporation, carried back a net operating loss for the tax year ended December 31, 2002. Blink's gross revenues have been under $500,000 since inception. Blink expects to have profits for the tax year ending December 31, 2003. Which method(s) of estimated tax payment can Blink use for its quarterly payments during the 2003 tax year to avoid underpayment of federal estimated taxes?

I. 100% of the preceding tax year method
II. Annualized income method

  a. I only.
  b. Both I and II.
  c. II only.
  d. Neither I nor II.

17. When computing a corporation's income tax expense for estimated income tax purposes, which of the following should be taken into account?

	Corporate tax credits	Alternative minimum tax
a.	No	No
b.	No	Yes
c.	Yes	No
d.	Yes	Yes

18. Finbury Corporation's taxable income for the year ended December 31, 2002, was $2,000,000 on which its tax liability was $680,000. In order for Finbury to escape the estimated tax underpayment penalty for the year ending December 31, 2003, Finbury's 2003 estimated tax payments must equal at least
  a. 90% of the 2003 tax liability.
  b. 93% of the 2003 tax liability.
  c. 100% of the 2003 tax liability.
  d. The 2002 tax liability of $680,000.

19. Kisco Corp.'s taxable income for 2002 before taking the dividends received deduction was $70,000. This includes $10,000 in dividends from a 15%-owned taxable domestic corporation. Given the following tax rates, what would Kisco's income tax be before any credits?

Taxable income partial rate table	Tax rate
Up to $50,000	15%
Over $50,000 but not over $75,000	25%

  a. $10,000
  b. $10,750
  c. $12,500
  d. $15,750

20. Green Corp. was incorporated and began business in 2000. In computing its alternative minimum tax for 2001, it determined that it had adjusted current earnings (ACE) of $400,000 and alternative minimum taxable income (prior to the ACE adjustment) of $300,000. For 2002, it had adjusted current earnings of $100,000 and alternative minimum taxable income (prior to the ACE adjustment) of $300,000. What is the amount of Green Corp.'s adjustment for adjusted current earnings that will be used in calculating its alternative minimum tax for 2002?
  a. $ 75,000
  b. $ (75,000)
  c. $(100,000)
  d. $(150,000)

21. Eastern Corp., a calendar-year corporation, was formed during 2001. On January 3, 2002, Eastern placed five-year property in service. The property was depreciated under the general MACRS system. Eastern did not elect to use the straight-line method. The following information pertains to Eastern:

Eastern's 2002 taxable income	$300,000
Adjustment for the accelerated depreciation taken on 2002 5-year property	1,000
2002 tax-exempt interest from private activity bonds	5,000

What was Eastern's 2002 alternative minimum taxable income before the adjusted current earnings (ACE) adjustment?

    a. $306,000
    b. $305,000
    c. $304,000
    d. $301,000

22. If a corporation's tentative minimum tax exceeds the regular tax, the excess amount is

    a.   Carried back to the first preceding taxable year.
    b.   Carried back to the third preceding taxable year.
    c.   Payable in addition to the regular tax.
    d.   Subtracted from the regular tax.

23. Rona Corp.'s 2002 alternative minimum taxable income was $200,000. The exempt portion of Rona's 2002 alternative minimum taxable income was

    a. $0
    b. $12,500
    c. $27,500
    d. $52,500

24. A corporation's tax preference items that must be taken into account for 2002 alternative minimum tax purposes include

    a.   Use of the percentage-of-completion method of accounting for long-term contracts.
    b.   Casualty losses.
    c.   Tax-exempt interest on private activity bonds.
    d.   Capital gains.

25. In computing its 2002 alternative minimum tax, a corporation must include as an adjustment

    a.   The dividends received deduction.
    b.   The difference between regular tax depreciation and straight-line depreciation over forty years for real property placed in service in 1998.
    c.   Charitable contributions.
    d.   Interest expense on investment property.

26. A corporation will not be subject to the alternative minimum tax for calendar year 2002 if

    a.   The corporation's net assets do not exceed $7.5 million.
    b.   The corporation's average annual gross receipts do not exceed $10 million.
    c.   The corporation has less then ten shareholders.
    d.   2002 is the corporation's first tax year.

27. Bradbury Corp., a calendar-year corporation, was formed on January 2, 1999, and had gross receipts for its first four taxable years as follows:

Year	Gross receipts
1999	$4,500,000
2000	9,000,000
2001	9,500,000
2002	6,500,000

What is the first taxable year that Bradbury Corp. is **not exempt** from the alternative minimum tax (AMT)?

    a.   2000
    b.   2001
    c.   2002
    d.   Bradbury is exempt from AMT for its first four taxable years.

28. Which of the following entities must include in gross income 100% of dividends received from unrelated taxable domestic corporations in computing regular taxable income?

	Personal service corporations	Personal holding companies
a.	Yes	Yes
b.	No	No
c.	Yes	No
d.	No	Yes

29. Andi Corp. issued $1,000,000 face amount of bonds in 1994 and established a sinking fund to pay the debt at maturity. The bondholders appointed an independent trustee to invest the sinking fund contributions and to administer the trust. In 2002, the sinking fund earned $60,000 in interest on bank deposits and $8,000 in net long-term capital gains. All of the trust income is accumulated with Andi's periodic contributions so that the aggregate amount will be sufficient to pay the bonds when they mature. What amount of trust income was taxable to Andi in 2002?

    a. $0
    b. $ 8,000
    c. $60,000
    d. $68,000

30. The following information pertains to treasury stock sold by Lee Corp. to an unrelated broker in 2002:

Proceeds received	$50,000
Cost	30,000
Par value	9,000

What amount of capital gain should Lee recognize in 2002 on the sale of this treasury stock?

    a. $0
    b. $ 8,000
    c. $20,000
    d. $30,500

31. During 2002, Ral Corp. exchanged 5,000 shares of its own $10 par common stock for land with a fair market value of $75,000. As a result of this exchange, Ral should report in its 2002 tax return

    a. $25,000 Section 1245 gain.
    b. $25,000 Section 1231 gain.
    c. $25,000 ordinary income.
    d.   No gain.

32. Pym, Inc., which had earnings and profits of $100,000, distributed land to Kile Corporation, a stockholder, as a dividend in kind. Pym's adjusted basis for this land was $3,000. The land had a fair market value of $12,000 and was subject to a mortgage liability of $5,000, which was assumed by Kile Corporation. The dividend was declared and paid during November 2002.

How much of the distribution would be reportable by Kile as a dividend, before the dividends received deduction?

- a. $0
- b. $ 3,000
- c. $ 7,000
- d. $12,000

33. Which of the following costs are amortizable organizational expenditures?

- a. Professional fees to issue the corporation's stock.
- b. Commissions paid by the corporation to underwriters for stock issue.
- c. Printing costs to issue the corporation's stock.
- d. Expenses of temporary directors meetings.

34. Brown Corp., a calendar-year taxpayer, was organized and actively began operations on July 1, 2002, and incurred the following costs:

Legal fees to obtain corporate charter	$40,000
Commission paid to underwriter	25,000
Other stock issue costs	10,000

Brown wishes to amortize its organizational costs over the shortest period allowed for tax purposes. In 2002, what amount should Brown deduct for the amortization of organizational expenses?

- a. $8,000
- b. $7,500
- c. $5,000
- d. $4,000

35. The costs of organizing a corporation

- a. May be deducted in full in the year in which these costs are incurred even if paid in later years.
- b. May be deducted only in the year in which these costs are paid.
- c. May be amortized over a period of not less than sixty months even if these costs are capitalized on the company's books.
- d. Are nondeductible capital expenditures.

36. Silo Corp. was organized on March 1, 2002, began doing business on September 1, 2002, and elected to file its income tax return on a calendar-year basis. The following qualifying organizational expenditures were incurred in organizing the corporation:

July 1, 2002	$3,000
September 3, 2002	6,000

The maximum allowable deduction for amortization of organizational expenditures for 2002 is

- a. $ 600
- b. $ 700
- c. $ 900
- d. $1,500

37. During 2002, Jackson Corp. had the following income and expenses:

Gross income from operations	$100,000
Dividend income from taxable domestic 20%-owned corporations	10,000
Operating expenses	35,000
Officers' salaries	20,000
Contributions to qualified charitable organizations	8,000
Net operating loss carryforward from 2001	30,000

What is the amount of Jackson Corp.'s charitable contribution carryover to 2003?

- a. $0
- b. $2,500
- c. $5,500
- d. $6,300

38. In 2002, Cable Corp., a calendar-year C corporation, contributed $80,000 to a qualified charitable organization. Cable's 2002 taxable income before the deduction for charitable contributions was $820,000 after a $40,000 dividends received deduction. Cable also had carryover contributions of $10,000 from the prior year. In 2002, what amount can Cable deduct as charitable contributions?

- a. $90,000
- b. $86,000
- c. $82,000
- d. $80,000

39. If a corporation's charitable contributions exceed the limitation for deductibility in a particular year, the excess

- a. Is **not** deductible in any future or prior year.
- b. May be carried back or forward for one year at the corporation's election.
- c. May be carried forward to a maximum of five succeeding years.
- d. May be carried back to the third preceding year.

40. Tapper Corp., an accrual-basis calendar-year corporation, was organized on January 2, 2002. During 2002, revenue was exclusively from sales proceeds and interest income. The following information pertains to Tapper:

Taxable income before charitable contributions for the year ended December 31, 2002	$500,000
Tapper's matching contribution to employee-designated qualified universities made during 2002	10,000
Board of Directors' authorized contribution to a qualified charity (authorized December 1, 2002, made February 1, 2003)	30,000

What is the maximum allowable deduction that Tapper may take as a charitable contribution on its tax return for the year ended December 31, 2002?

- a. $0
- b. $10,000
- c. $30,000
- d. $40,000

41. Lyle Corp. is a distributor of pharmaceuticals and sells only to retail drug stores. During 2002, Lyle received unsolicited samples of nonprescription drugs from a manufacturer. Lyle donated these drugs in 2002 to a qualified exempt organization and deducted their fair market value as a charitable contribution. What should be included as gross income in Lyle's 2002 return for receipt of these samples?

- a. Fair market value.
- b. Net discounted wholesale price.
- c. $25 nominal value assigned to gifts.
- d. $0.

42. During 2002, Nale Corp. received dividends of $1,000 from a 10%-owned taxable domestic corporation. When Nale computes the maximum allowable deduction for contributions in its 2002 return, the amount of dividends to be included in the computation of taxable income is

- a. $0
- b. $ 200

c. $ 300
d. $1,000

43. Gero Corp. had operating income of $160,000, after deducting $10,000 for contributions to State University, but not including dividends of $2,000 received from nonaffiliated taxable domestic corporations.

In computing the maximum allowable deduction for contributions, Gero should apply the percentage limitation to a base amount of

a. $172,000
b. $170,400
c. $170,000
d. $162,000

44. Norwood Corporation is an accrual-basis taxpayer. For the year ended December 31, 2002, it had book income before tax of $500,000 after deducting a charitable contribution of $100,000. The contribution was authorized by the Board of Directors in December 2002, but was not actually paid until March 1, 2003. How should Norwood treat this charitable contribution for tax purposes to minimize its 2002 taxable income?

a.   It cannot claim a deduction in 2002, but must apply the payment against 2003 income.
b.   Make an election claiming a deduction for 2002 of $50,000 and carry the remainder over a maximum of five succeeding tax years.
c.   Make an election claiming a deduction for 2002 of $60,000 and carry the remainder over a maximum of five succeeding tax years.
d.   Make an election claiming a 2002 deduction of $100,000.

45. In 2002, Best Corp., an accrual-basis calendar-year C corporation, received $100,000 in dividend income from the common stock that it held in a 15%-owned domestic corporation. The stock was not debt-financed, and was held for over a year. Best recorded the following information for 2002:

Loss from Best's operations	$ (10,000)
Dividends received	100,000
Taxable income (before dividends received deduction)	$ 90,000

Best's dividends received deduction on its 2002 tax return was

a. $100,000
b. $ 80,000
c. $ 70,000
d. $ 63,000

46. In 2002, Acorn, Inc. had the following items of income and expense:

Sales	$500,000
Cost of sales	250,000
Dividends received	25,000

The dividends were received from a corporation of which Acorn owns 30%. In Acorn's 2002 corporate income tax return, what amount should be reported as income before special deductions?

a. $525,000
b. $505,000
c. $275,000
d. $250,000

47. The corporate dividends received deduction

a.   Must exceed the applicable percentage of the recipient shareholder's taxable income.
b.   Is affected by a requirement that the investor corporation must own the investee's stock for a specified minimum holding period.
c.   Is unaffected by the percentage of the investee's stock owned by the investor corporation.
d.   May be claimed by S corporations.

48. In 2002, Ryan Corp. had the following income:

Income from operations	$300,000
Dividends from unrelated taxable domestic corporations less than 20% owned	2,000

Ryan had no portfolio indebtedness. In Ryan's 2002 taxable income, what amount should be included for the dividends received?

a. $ 400
b. $ 600
c. $1,400
d. $1,600

49. In 2002, Daly Corp. had the following income:

Profit from operations	$100,000
Dividends from 20%-owned taxable domestic corporation	1,000

In Daly's 2002 taxable income, how much should be included for the dividends received?

a. $0
b. $ 200
c. $ 800
d. $1,000

50. Cava Corp., which has **no** portfolio indebtedness, received the following dividends in 2002:

From a mutual savings bank	$1,500
From a 20%-owned unaffiliated domestic taxable corporation	7,500

How much of these dividends qualifies for the 80% dividends received deduction?

a. $9,000
b. $7,500
c. $1,500
d. $0

51. During 2002, Stark Corp. reported gross income from operations of $350,000 and operating expenses of $400,000. Stark also received dividend income of $100,000 (not included in gross income from operations) from an investment in a taxable domestic corporation in which it owns 10% of the stock. Additionally, Stark had a net operating loss carryover from 2001 of $30,000. What is the amount of Stark Corp.'s net operating loss for 2002?

a. $0
b. $(20,000)
c. $(30,000)
d. $(50,000)

52. A C corporation's net capital losses are

a.   Carried forward indefinitely until fully utilized.
b.   Carried back three years and forward five years.
c.   Deductible in full from the corporation's ordinary income.
d.   Deductible from the corporation's ordinary income only to the extent of $3,000.

53. For the year ended December 31, 2002, Taylor Corp. had a net operating loss of $200,000. Taxable income for the earlier years of corporate existence, computed without reference to the net operating loss, was as follows:

	Taxable income
1997	$ 5,000
1998	$10,000
1999	$20,000
2000	$30,000
2001	$40,000

If Taylor makes **no** special election to waive a net operating loss carryback period, what amount of net operating loss will be available to Taylor for the year ended December 31, 2003?

a. $200,000
b. $130,000
c. $110,000
d. $ 95,000

54. When a corporation has an unused net capital loss that is carried back or carried forward to another tax year,

a. It retains its original identity as short-term or long-term.
b. It is treated as a short-term capital loss whether or not it was short-term when sustained.
c. It is treated as a long-term capital loss whether or not it was long-term when sustained.
d. It can be used to offset ordinary income up to the amount of the carryback or carryover.

55. For the year ended December 31, 2002, Haya Corp. had gross business income of $600,000 and expenses of $800,000. Contributions of $5,000 to qualified charities were included in expenses. In addition to the expenses, Haya had a net operating loss carryover of $9,000. What was Haya's net operating loss for 2002?

a. $209,000
b. $204,000
c. $200,000
d. $195,000

56. Dorsett Corporation's income tax return for 2002 shows deductions exceeding gross income by $56,800. Included in the tax return are the following items:

Net operating loss deduction (carryover from 2001)	$15,000
Dividends received deduction	6,800

What is Dorsett's net operating loss for 2002?

a. $56,800
b. $50,000
c. $41,800
d. $35,000

57. Ram Corp.'s operating income for the year ended December 31, 2002, amounted to $100,000. Also in 2002, a machine owned by Ram was completely destroyed in an accident. This machine's adjusted basis immediately before the casualty was $15,000. The machine was not insured and had no salvage value.

In Ram's 2002 tax return, what amount should be deducted for the casualty loss?

a. $ 5,000
b. $ 5,400
c. $14,900
d. $15,000

58. For the first taxable year in which a corporation has qualifying research and experimental expenditures, the corporation

a. Has a choice of either deducting such expenditures as current business expenses, or capitalizing these expenditures.
b. Has to treat such expenditures in the same manner as they are accounted for in the corporation's financial statements.
c. Is required to deduct such expenditures currently as business expenses or lose the deductions.
d. Is required to capitalize such expenditures and amortize them ratably over a period of not less than sixty months.

59. For the year ended December 31, 2002, Kelly Corp. had net income per books of $300,000 before the provision for federal income taxes. Included in the net income were the following items:

Dividend income from a 5%-owned domestic taxable corporation (taxable income limitation does not apply and there is no portfolio indebtedness)	$50,000
Bad debt expense (represents the increase in the allowance for doubtful accounts)	80,000

Assuming no bad debt was written off, what is Kelly's taxable income for the year ended December 31, 2002?

a. $250,000
b. $330,000
c. $345,000
d. $380,000

60. For the year ended December 31, 2002, Maple Corp.'s book income, before federal income tax, was $100,000. Included in this $100,000 were the following:

Provision for state income tax	$1,000
Interest earned on US Treasury Bonds	6,000
Interest expense on bank loan to purchase US Treasury Bonds	2,000

Maple's taxable income for 2002 was

a. $ 96,000
b. $ 97,000
c. $100,000
d. $101,000

61. For the year ended December 31, 2002, Dodd Corp. had net income per books of $100,000. Included in the computation of net income were the following items:

Provision for federal income tax	$27,000
Net long-term capital loss	5,000
Keyman life insurance premiums (corporation is beneficiary)	3,000

Dodd's 2002 taxable income was

a. $127,000
b. $130,000
c. $132,000
d. $135,000

62. For the year ended December 31, 2002, Bard Corp.'s income per accounting records, before federal income taxes, was $450,000 and included the following:

State corporate income tax refunds	$ 4,000
Life insurance proceeds on officer's death	15,000
Net loss on sale of securities bought for investment in 2000	20,000

Bard's 2002 taxable income was

    a. $435,000
    b. $451,000
    c. $455,000
    d. $470,000

63. Dewey Corporation's book income before federal income taxes was $520,000 for the year ended December 31, 2002. Dewey was incorporated during 2002 and began business in June. Organization costs of $260,000 were expensed for financial statement purposes during 2002. For tax purposes these costs are being written off over the minimum allowable period. For the year ended December 31, 2002, Dewey's taxable income was

    a. $520,000
    b. $489,900
    c. $747,900
    d. $778,000

64. Bishop Corporation reported taxable income of $700,000 on its federal income tax return for calendar year 2002. Selected information for 2002 is available from Bishop's records as follows:

Provision for federal income tax per books	$280,000
Depreciation claimed on the tax return	130,000
Depreciation recorded in the books	75,000
Life insurance proceeds on death of corporate officer	100,000

Bishop reported net income per books for 2002 of

    a. $855,000
    b. $595,000
    c. $575,000
    d. $475,000

65. For the year ended December 31, 2002, Ajax Corporation had net income per books of $1,200,000. Included in the determination of net income were the following items:

Interest income on municipal bonds	$ 40,000
Damages received from settlement of patent infringement lawsuit	200,000
Interest paid on loan to purchase municipal bonds	8,000
Provision for federal income tax	524,000

What should Ajax report as its taxable income for 2002?

    a. $1,492,000
    b. $1,524,000
    c. $1,684,000
    d. $1,692,000

66. For its taxable year 2002, Farve Corp. had net income per books of $80,000, which included municipal bond interest of $5,000, dividend income of $10,000, a deduction for a net capital loss of $6,000, a deduction for business meals of $4,000, and a deduction for federal income taxes of $18,000. What is the amount of income that would be shown on the last line of Schedule M-1 (Reconciliation of Income [Loss] Per Books with Income [Loss] Per Return) of Farve Corp.'s corporate income tax return for 2002?

    a. $ 90,000
    b. $ 93,000
    c. $ 99,000
    d. $101,000

67. In 2002, Starke Corp., an accrual-basis calendar-year corporation, reported book income of $380,000. Included in that amount was $50,000 municipal bond interest income, $170,000 for federal income tax expense, and $2,000 interest expense on the debt incurred to carry the municipal

bonds. What amount should Starke's taxable income be as reconciled on Starke's Schedule M-1 of Form 1120, US Corporation Income Tax Return?

    a. $330,000
    b. $500,000
    c. $502,000
    d. $550,000

68. Would the following expense items be reported on Schedule M-1 of the corporation income tax return (Form 1120) showing the reconciliation of income per books with income per return?

	Lodging expenses for executive out-of-town travel	Deduction for a net capital loss
a.	Yes	Yes
b.	No	No
c.	Yes	No
d.	No	Yes

69. In the reconciliation of income per books with income per return

    a. Only temporary differences are considered.
    b. Only permanent differences are considered.
    c. Both temporary and permanent differences are considered.
    d. Neither temporary nor permanent differences are considered.

70. Media Corp. is an accrual-basis, calendar-year C corporation. Its 2002 reported book income included $6,000 in municipal bond interest income. Its expenses included $1,500 of interest incurred on indebtedness used to carry municipal bonds and $8,000 in advertising expense. What is Media's net M-1 adjustment on its 2002 Form 1120, US Corporation Income Tax Return, to reconcile to its 2002 taxable income?

    a. $(4,500)
    b. $ 1,500
    c. $ 3,500
    d. $ 9,500

71. Barbaro Corporation's retained earnings at January 1, 2002, was $600,000. During 2002 Barbaro paid cash dividends of $150,000 and received a federal income tax refund of $26,000 as a result of an IRS audit of Barbaro's 1999 tax return. Barbaro's net income per books for the year ended December 31, 2002, was $274,900 after deducting federal income tax of $183,300. How much should be shown in the reconciliation Schedule M-2, of Form 1120, as Barbaro's retained earnings at December 31, 2002?

    a. $443,600
    b. $600,900
    c. $626,900
    d. $750,900

72. Olex Corporation's books disclosed the following data for the calendar year 2002:

Retained earnings at beginning of year	$50,000
Net income for year	70,000
Contingency reserve established at end of year	10,000
Cash dividends paid during year	8,000

What amount should appear on the last line of reconciliation Schedule M-2 of Form 1120?

    a. $102,000
    b. $120,000

c. $128,000
d. $138,000

73. Bank Corp. owns 80% of Shore Corp.'s outstanding capital stock. Shore's capital stock consists of 50,000 shares of common stock issued and outstanding. Shore's 2002 net income was $140,000. During 2002, Shore declared and paid dividends of $60,000. In conformity with generally accepted accounting principles, Bank recorded the following entries in 2002:

	Debit	Credit
Investment in Shore Corp. common stock	$112,000	
Equity in earnings of subsidiary		$112,000
Cash	48,000	
Investment in Shore Corp. common stock		48,000

In its 2002 consolidated tax return, Bank should report dividend revenue of

a. $48,000
b. $14,400
c. $ 9,600
d. $0

74. In 2002, Portal Corp. received $100,000 in dividends from Sal Corp., its 80%-owned subsidiary. What net amount of dividend income should Portal include in its 2002 consolidated tax return?

a. $100,000
b. $ 80,000
c. $ 70,000
d. $0

75. Potter Corp. and Sly Corp. file consolidated tax returns. In January 2001, Potter sold land, with a basis of $60,000 and a fair value of $100,000, to Sly for $100,000. Sly sold the land in June 2002 for $125,000. In its 2002 and 2001 tax returns, what amount of gain should be reported for these transactions in the consolidated return?

	2002	2001
a.	$25,000	$40,000
b.	$25,000	$0
c.	$40,000	$25,000
d.	$65,000	$0

76. When a consolidated return is filed by an affiliated group of includible corporations connected from inception through the requisite stock ownership with a common parent

a.   Intercompany dividends are excludable to the extent of 80%.
b.   Operating losses of one member of the group offset operating profits of other members of the group.
c.   Each of the subsidiaries is entitled to an alternative minimum tax exemption.
d.   Each of the subsidiaries is entitled to an accumulated earnings tax credit.

77. Dana Corp. owns stock in Seco Corp. For Dana and Seco to qualify for the filing of consolidated returns, at least what percentage of Seco's total voting power and total value of stock must be directly owned by Dana?

	Total voting power	Total value of stock
a.	51%	51%
b.	51%	80%
c.	80%	51%
d.	80%	80%

78. Consolidated returns may be filed

a.   Either by parent-subsidiary corporations or by brother-sister corporations.
b.   Only by corporations that formally request advance permission from the IRS.
c.   Only by parent-subsidiary affiliated groups.
d.   Only by corporations that issue their financial statements on a consolidated basis.

79. Parent Corporation and Subsidiary Corporation file consolidated returns on a calendar-year basis. In January 2001, Subsidiary sold land, which it had used in its business, to Parent for $50,000. Immediately before this sale, Subsidiary's basis for the land was $30,000. Parent held the land primarily for sale to customers in the ordinary course of business. In July 2002, Parent sold the land to Adams, an unrelated individual. In determining consolidated taxable income for 2002, how much should Subsidiary take into account as a result of the 2001 sale of the land from Subsidiary to Parent?

a. $0
b. $20,000
c. $30,000
d. $50,000

80. On January 1, 2002, Locke Corp., an accrual-basis, calendar-year C corporation, had $30,000 in accumulated earnings and profits. For 2002, Locke had current earnings and profits of $20,000 and made two $40,000 cash distributions to its shareholders, one in April and one in September of 2002. What amount of the 2002 distributions is classified as dividend income to Locke's shareholders?

a. $0
b. $20,000
c. $50,000
d. $80,000

81. Chicago Corp., a calendar-year C corporation, had accumulated earnings and profits of $100,000 as of January 1, 2002 and had a **deficit** in its current earnings and profits for the entire 2002 tax year in the amount of $140,000. Chicago Corp. distributed $30,000 cash to its shareholders on December 31, 2002. What would be the balance of Chicago Corp.'s accumulated earnings and profits as of January 1, 2003?

a. $0
b. $(30,000)
c. $(40,000)
d. $(70,000)

82. Salon, Inc. distributed cash and personal property to its sole shareholder. Using the following facts, determine the amount of gain that would be recognized by Salon, Inc. as the result of making the distribution to its shareholder?

Item	Amount
Cash	$20,000
Personal property:	
Fair market value	6,000
Adjusted basis	3,000
Liability on property assumed by shareholder	10,000

a. $ 3,000
b. $ 4,000
c. $ 7,000
d. $23,000

83. Kent Corp. is a calendar-year, accrual-basis C corporation. In 2002, Kent made a nonliquidating distribution of property with an adjusted basis of $150,000 and a fair market value of $200,000 to Reed, its sole shareholder. The following information pertains to Kent:

Reed's basis in Kent stock at January 1, 2002	$500,000
Accumulated earnings and profits at January 1, 2002	125,000
Current earnings and profits for 2002	60,000

What was taxable as dividend income to Reed for 2002?

- a. $ 60,000
- b. $150,000
- c. $185,000
- d. $200,000

84. Ridge Corp., a calendar-year C corporation, made a nonliquidating cash distribution to its shareholders of $1,000,000 with respect to its stock. At that time, Ridge's current and accumulated earnings and profits totaled $750,000 and its total paid-in capital for tax purposes was $10,000,000. Ridge had no corporate shareholders. Ridge's cash distribution

I.   Was taxable as $750,000 of dividend income to its shareholders.
II. Reduced its shareholders' adjusted bases in Ridge stock by $250,000.

- a.   I only.
- b.   II only.
- c.   Both I and II.
- d.   Neither I nor II.

85. Tour Corp., which had earnings and profits of $400,000, made a nonliquidating distribution of property to its shareholders in 2002 as a dividend in kind. This property, which had an adjusted basis of $30,000 and a fair market value of $20,000 at date of distribution, did not constitute assets used in the active conduct of Tour's business. How much loss did Tour recognize on this distribution?

- a. $30,000
- b. $20,000
- c. $10,000
- d. $0

86. On January 1, 2002, Kee Corp., a C corporation, had a $50,000 deficit in earnings and profits. For 2002 Kee had current earnings and profits of $10,000 and made a $30,000 cash distribution to its stockholders. What amount of the distribution is taxable as dividend income to Kee's stockholders?

- a. $30,000
- b. $20,000
- c. $10,000
- d. $0

87. Dahl Corp. was organized and commenced operations in 1993. At December 31, 2002, Dahl had accumulated earnings and profits of $9,000 before dividend declaration and distribution. On December 31, 2002, Dahl distributed cash of $9,000 and a vacant parcel of land to Green, Dahl's only stockholder. At the date of distribution, the land had a basis of $5,000 and a fair market value of $40,000. What was Green's taxable dividend income in 2002 from these distributions?

- a. $ 9,000
- b. $14,000

- c. $44,000
- d. $49,000

88. Pym, Inc. which had earnings and profits of $100,000, distributed land to Alex Rowe, a stockholder, as a dividend in kind. Pym's adjusted basis for this land was $3,000. The land had a fair market value of $12,000 and was subject to a mortgage liability of $5,000, which was assumed by Rowe. The dividend was declared and paid during November 2002. How much of the distribution was taxable to Rowe as a dividend?

- a. $9,000
- b. $7,000
- c. $4,000
- d. $3,000

89. On June 30, 2002, Ral Corporation had retained earnings of $100,000. On that date, it sold a plot of land to a noncorporate stockholder for $50,000. Ral had paid $40,000 for the land in 1994, and it had a fair market value of $80,000 when the stockholder bought it. The amount of dividend income taxable to the stockholder in 2002 is

- a. $0
- b. $10,000
- c. $20,000
- d. $30,000

90. On December 1, 2002, Gelt Corporation declared a dividend and distributed to its sole shareholder, as a dividend in kind, a parcel of land that was not an inventory asset. On the date of the distribution, the following data were available:

Adjusted basis of land	$ 6,500
Fair market value of land	14,000
Mortgage on land	5,000

For the year ended December 31, 2002, Gelt had earnings and profits of $30,000 without regard to the dividend distribution. By how much should the dividend distribution reduce the earnings and profits for 2002?

- a. $ 1,500
- b. $ 6,500
- c. $ 9,000
- d. $14,000

91. Two unrelated individuals, Mark and David, each own 50% of the stock of Pike Corporation, which has accumulated earnings and profits of $250,000. Because of his inactivity in the business in recent years, Mark has decided to retire from the business and wishes to sell his stock. Accordingly, Pike will distribute cash of $500,000 in redemption of all of the stock owned by Mark. If Mark's adjusted basis for his stock at date of redemption is $300,000, what will be the tax effect of the redemption to Mark?

- a. $125,000 dividend
- b. $200,000 dividend
- c. $200,000 capital gain
- d. $250,000 dividend

92. How does a noncorporate shareholder treat the gain on a redemption of stock that qualifies as a partial liquidation of the distributing corporation?

- a.   Entirely as capital gain.
- b.   Entirely as a dividend.
- c.   Partly as capital gain and partly as a dividend.
- d.   As a tax-free transaction.

93. In 2002, Kara Corp. incurred the following expenditures in connection with the repurchase of its stock from shareholders to avert a hostile takeover:

Interest on borrowings used to repurchase stock	$100,000
Legal and accounting fees in connection with the repurchase	400,000

The total of the above expenditures deductible in 2002 is
   a. $0
   b. $100,000
   c. $400,000
   d. $500,000

94. A corporation was completely liquidated and dissolved during 2002. The filing fees, professional fees, and other expenditures incurred in connection with the liquidation and dissolution are
   a. Deductible in full by the dissolved corporation.
   b. Deductible by the shareholders and not by the corporation.
   c. Treated as capital losses by the corporation.
   d. Not deductible either by the corporation or shareholders.

95. What is the usual result to the shareholders of a distribution in complete liquidation of a corporation?
   a. No taxable effect.
   b. Ordinary gain to the extent of cash received.
   c. Ordinary gain or loss.
   d. Capital gain or loss.

96. Par Corp. acquired the assets of its wholly owned subsidiary, Sub Corp., under a plan that qualified as a tax-free complete liquidation of Sub. Which of the following of Sub's unused carryovers may be transferred to Par?

	Excess charitable contributions	Net operating loss
a.	No	Yes
b.	Yes	No
c.	No	No
d.	Yes	Yes

97. Kappes Corp. distributed marketable securities in a pro rata redemption of its stock in a complete liquidation. These securities, which had been purchased in 1995 for $150,000, had a fair market value of $100,000 when distributed. What loss does Kappes recognize as a result of the distribution?
   a. $0.
   b. $50,000 long-term capital loss.
   c. $50,000 Section 1231 loss.
   d. $50,000 ordinary loss.

98. When a parent corporation completely liquidates its 80%-owned subsidiary, the parent (as stockholder) will ordinarily
   a. Be subject to capital gains tax on 80% of the long-term gain.
   b. Be subject to capital gains tax on 100% of the long-term gain.
   c. Have to report any gain on liquidation as ordinary income.
   d. Not recognize gain or loss on the liquidating distributions.

99. Lark Corp. and its wholly owned subsidiary, Day Corp., both operated on a calendar year. In January 2002, Day adopted a plan of complete liquidation. Two months

later, Day paid all of its liabilities and distributed its remaining assets to Lark. These assets consisted of the following:

Cash	$50,000
Land (at cost)	10,000

Fair market value of the land was $30,000. Upon distribution of Day's assets to Lark, all of Day's capital stock was canceled. Lark's basis for the Day stock was $7,000. Lark's recognized gain in 2002 on receipt of Day's assets in liquidation was
   a. $0
   b. $50,000
   c. $53,000
   d. $73,000

100. On June 1, 2002, Green Corp. adopted a plan of complete liquidation. The liquidation was completed within a twelve-month period. On August 1, 2002, Green distributed to its stockholders installment notes receivable that Green had acquired in connection with the sale of land in 2001. The following information pertains to these notes:

Green's basis	$ 90,000
Fair market value	162,000
Face amount	185,000

How much gain must Green recognize in 2002 as a result of this distribution?
   a. $0
   b. $23,000
   c. $72,000
   d. $95,000

101. Carmela Corporation had the following assets on January 2, 2002, the date on which it adopted a plan of complete liquidation:

	Adjusted basis	Fair market value
Land	$ 75,000	$150,000
Inventory	43,500	66,000
Totals	$118,500	$216,000

The land was sold on June 30, 2002, to an unrelated party at a gain of $75,000. The inventory was sold to various customers during 2002 at an aggregate gain of $22,500. On December 10, 2002, the remaining asset (cash) was distributed to Carmela's stockholders, and the corporation was liquidated. What is Carmela's recognized gain in 2002?
   a. $0
   b. $22,500
   c. $75,000
   d. $97,500

102. Mintee Corp., an accrual-basis calendar-year C corporation, had no corporate shareholders when it liquidated in 2002. In cancellation of all their Mintee stock, each Mintee shareholder received in 2002 a liquidation distribution of $2,000 cash and land with a tax basis of $5,000 and a fair market value of $10,500. Before the distribution, each shareholder's tax basis in Mintee stock was $6,500. What amount of gain should each Mintee shareholder recognize on the liquidating distribution?
   a. $0
   b. $ 500
   c. $4,000
   d. $6,000

103. For the collapsible corporation provisions to be imposed, the holding period of the corporation's stock
   a. Must be a minimum of six months.

b. Must be a minimum of twelve months.
c. Depends on the stockholder's basis for gain or loss.
d. Is irrelevant.

104. Will Benton owned all of the stock of a corporation that has been determined to be collapsible. The basis of the stock to Benton was $25,000, and the corporation had accumulated earnings and profits of $1,000. Benton sold his stock for $40,000. As a result of the sale, Benton must report

a. $15,000 ordinary gain.
b. $1,000 ordinary income and $14,000 capital gain.
c. $14,000 capital gain.
d. $15,000 capital gain.

105. Edge Corp. met the stock ownership requirements of a personal holding company. What sources of income must Edge consider to determine if the income requirements for a personal holding company have been met?

I. Interest earned on tax-exempt obligations.
II. Dividends received from an unrelated domestic corporation.

a. I only.
b. II only.
c. Both I and II.
d. Neither I nor II.

106. Kane Corp. is a calendar-year domestic personal holding company. Which deduction(s) must Kane make from 2002 taxable income to determine undistributed personal holding company income prior to the dividend-paid deduction?

	Federal income taxes	Net long-term capital gain less related federal income taxes
a.	Yes	Yes
b.	Yes	No
c.	No	Yes
d.	No	No

107. Dart Corp., a calendar-year domestic C corporation, is not a personal holding company. For purposes of the accumulated earnings tax, Dart has accumulated taxable income for 2002. Which step(s) can Dart take to eliminate or reduce any 2002 accumulated earnings tax?

I. Demonstrate that the "reasonable needs" of its business require the retention of all or part of the 2002 accumulated taxable income.
II. Pay dividends by March 15, 2003.

a. I only.
b. II only.
c. Both I and II.
d. Neither I nor II.

108. The accumulated earnings tax can be imposed

a. On both partnerships and corporations.
b. On companies that make distributions in excess of accumulated earnings.
c. On personal holding companies.
d. Regardless of the number of stockholders in a corporation.

109. Zero Corp. is an investment company authorized to issue only common stock. During the last half of 2002, Ed-

wards owned 240 of the 1,000 outstanding shares of stock in Zero. Another 560 shares of stock outstanding were owned, twenty shares each, by twenty-eight shareholders who are neither related to each other nor to Edwards. Zero could be a personal holding company if the remaining 200 shares of common stock were owned by

a. An estate where Edwards is the beneficiary.
b. Edwards' brother-in-law.
c. A partnership where Edwards is not a partner.
d. Edwards' cousin.

110. Arbor Corp. has nine common stockholders. Arbor derives all of its income from investments in stocks and securities, and regularly distributes 51% of its taxable income as dividends to its stockholders. Arbor is a

a. Regulated investment company.
b. Personal holding company.
c. Corporation subject to the accumulated earnings tax.
d. Corporation subject to tax on income not distributed to stockholders.

111. Kari Corp., a manufacturing company, was organized on January 2, 2002. Its 2002 federal taxable income was $400,000 and its federal income tax was $100,000. What is the maximum amount of accumulated taxable income that may be subject to the accumulated earnings tax for 2002 if Kari takes only the minimum accumulated earnings credit?

a. $300,000
b. $150,000
c. $ 50,000
d. $0

112. The following information pertains to Hull, Inc., a personal holding company, for the year ended December 31, 2002:

Undistributed personal holding company income	$100,000
Dividends paid during 2002	20,000
Consent dividends reported in the 2002 individual income tax returns of the holders of Hull's common stock, but **not** paid by Hull to its stockholders	10,000

In computing its 2002 personal holding company tax, what amount should Hull deduct for dividends paid?

a. $0
b. $10,000
c. $20,000
d. $30,000

113. Benson, a singer, owns 100% of the outstanding capital stock of Lund Corp. Lund contracted with Benson, specifying that Benson was to perform personal services for Magda Productions, Inc., in consideration of which Benson was to receive $50,000 a year from Lund. Lund contracted with Magda, specifying that Benson was to perform personal services for Magda, in consideration of which Magda was to pay Lund $1,000,000 a year. Personal holding company income will be attributable to

a. Benson only.
b. Lund only.
c. Magda only.
d. All three contracting parties.

114. The personal holding company tax

a. Qualifies as a tax credit that may be used by partners or stockholders to reduce their individual income taxes.

b. May be imposed on both corporations and partnerships.

c. Should be self-assessed by filing a separate schedule with the regular tax return.

d. May be imposed regardless of the number of equal stockholders in a corporation.

115. The accumulated earnings tax does **not** apply to

a. Corporations that have more than 100 stockholders.

b. Personal holding companies.

c. Corporations filing consolidated returns.

d. Corporations that have more than one class of stock.

116. The personal holding company tax may be imposed

a. As an alternative tax in place of the corporation's regularly computed tax.

b. If more than 50% of the corporation's stock is owned, directly or indirectly, by more than ten stockholders.

c. If at least 60% of the corporation's adjusted ordinary gross income for the taxable year is personal holding company income, and the stock ownership test is satisfied.

d. In conjunction with the accumulated earnings tax.

117. The accumulated earnings tax

a. Should be self-assessed by filing a separate schedule along with the regular tax return.

b. Applies only to closely held corporations.

c. Can be imposed on S corporations that do not regularly distribute their earnings.

d. Cannot be imposed on a corporation that has undistributed earnings and profits of less than $150,000.

118. Kee Holding Corp. has eighty unrelated equal stockholders. For the year ended December 31, 2002, Kee's income comprised the following:

Net rental income	$ 1,000
Commissions earned on sales of franchises	3,000
Dividends from taxable domestic corporations	90,000

Deductible expenses for 2002 totaled $10,000. Kee paid no dividends for the past three years. Kee's liability for personal holding company tax for 2002 will be based on

a. $12,000

b. $11,000

c. $ 9,000

d. $0

119. The accumulated earnings tax

a. Depends on a stock ownership test based on the number of stockholders.

b. Can be avoided by sufficient dividend distributions.

c. Is computed by the filing of a separate schedule along with the corporation's regular tax return.

d. Is imposed when the entity is classified as a personal holding company.

120. Where passive investment income is involved, the personal holding company tax may be imposed

a. On both partnerships and corporations.

b. On companies whose gross income arises solely from rentals, if the lessors render no services to the lessees.

c. If more than 50% of the company is owned by five or fewer individuals.

d. On small business investment companies licensed by the Small Business Administration.

121. In determining accumulated taxable income for the purpose of the accumulated earnings tax, which one of the following is allowed as a deduction?

a. Capital loss carryover from prior year.

b. Dividends received deduction.

c. Net operating loss deduction.

d. Net capital loss for current year.

122. The minimum accumulated earnings credit is

a. $150,000 for all corporations.

b. $150,000 for nonservice corporations only.

c. $250,000 for all corporations.

d. $250,000 for nonservice corporations only.

123. Daystar Corp. which is not a mere holding or investment company, derives its income from consulting services. Daystar had accumulated earnings and profits of $45,000 at December 31, 2001. For the year ended December 31, 2002, it had earnings and profits of $115,000 and a dividends-paid deduction of $15,000. It has been determined that $20,000 of the accumulated earnings and profits for 2002 is required for the reasonable needs of the business. How much is the allowable accumulated earnings credit at December 31, 2002?

a. $105,000

b. $205,000

c. $150,000

d. $250,000

124. Lane Inc., an S corporation, pays single coverage health insurance premiums of $4,800 per year and family coverage premiums of $7,200 per year. Mill is a 10% shareholder-employee in Lane. On Mill's behalf, Lane pays Mill's family coverage under the health insurance plan. What amount of insurance premiums is includible in Mill's gross income?

a. $0

b. $ 720

c. $4,800

d. $7,200

125. Beck Corp. has been a calendar-year S corporation since its inception on January 2, 1998. On January 1, 2002, Lazur and Lyle each owned 50% of the Beck stock, in which their respective tax bases were $12,000 and $9,000. For the year ended December 31, 2002, Beck had $81,000 in ordinary business income and $10,000 in tax-exempt income. Beck made a $51,000 cash distribution to each shareholder on December 31, 2002. What was Lazur's tax basis in Beck after the distribution?

a. $ 1,500

b. $ 6,500

c. $52,500

d. $57,500

126. Graphite Corp. has been a calendar-year S corporation since its inception on January 2, 1998. On January 1, 2002, Smith and Tyler each owned 50% of the Graphite stock, in

which their respective bases were $12,000 and $9,000. For the year ended December 31, 2002, Graphite had $80,000 in ordinary business income and $6,000 in tax-exempt income. Graphite made a $53,000 cash distribution to each shareholder on December 31, 2002. What total amount of income from Graphite is includible in Smith's 2002 adjusted gross income?

    a. $96,000
    b. $93,000
    c. $43,000
    d. $40,000

127. Dart Corp., a calendar-year S corporation, had 60,000 shares of voting common stock and 40,000 shares of nonvoting common stock issued and outstanding. On February 23, 2002, Dart filed a revocation statement with the consent of shareholders holding 30,000 shares of its voting common stock and 5,000 shares of its nonvoting common stock. Dart's S corporation election

    a.   Did not terminate.
    b.   Terminated as of January 1, 2002.
    c.   Terminated on February 24, 2002.
    d.   Terminated as of January 1, 2003.

128. Which one of the following statements concerning the eligibility requirements for S corporations is **not** correct?

    a.   An S corporation is permitted to own 90% of the stock of a C corporation.
    b.   An S corporation is permitted to own 100% of the stock of another S corporation.
    c.   An S corporation is permitted to be a partner in a partnership.
    d.   A partnership is permitted to be a shareholder of an S corporation.

129. Dart Corp., a calendar-year corporation, was formed in 1992 and made an S corporation election in 1995 that is still in effect. Its books and records for 2002 reflect the following information:

Accumulated earnings and profits at 1/1/02	$90,000
Accumulated adjustments account at 1/1/02	50,000
Ordinary income for 2002	200,000

Dart Corp. is solely owned by Robert, whose basis in Dart's stock was $100,000 on January 1, 2002. During 2002, Dart distributed $310,000 to Robert. What is the amount of the $310,000 distribution that Robert must report as dividend income for 2002 assuming no special elections were made with regard to the distribution?

    a. $0
    b. $ 60,000
    c. $ 90,000
    d. $140,000

130. Village Corp., a calendar-year corporation, began business in 1995. Village made a valid S Corporation election on September 5, 2002, with the unanimous consent of its shareholders. The eligibility requirements for S status continued to be met throughout 2002. On what date did Village's S status become effective?

    a.   January 1, 2002.
    b.   January 1, 2003.
    c.   September 5, 2002.
    d.   September 5, 2003.

131. A shareholder's basis in the stock of an S corporation is increased by the shareholder's pro rata share of income from

	Tax-exempt interest	Taxable interest
a.	No	No
b.	No	Yes
c.	Yes	No
d.	Yes	Yes

132. Zinco Corp. was a calendar-year S corporation. Zinco's S status terminated on April 1, 2002, when Case Corp. became a shareholder. During 2002 (365-day calendar year), Zinco had nonseparately computed income of $310,250. If no election was made by Zinco, what amount of the income, if any, was allocated to the S short year for 2002?

    a. $77,563
    b. $77,350
    c. $76,500
    d. $0

133. Bristol Corp. was formed as a C corporation on January 1, 1991, and elected S corporation status on January 1, 1999. At the time of the election, Bristol had accumulated C corporation earnings and profits that have not been distributed. Bristol has had the same twenty-five shareholders throughout its existence. In 2002 Bristol's S election will terminate if it

    a.   Increases the number of shareholders to seventy-five.
    b.   Adds a decedent's estate as a shareholder to the existing shareholders.
    c.   Takes a charitable contribution deduction.
    d.   Has passive investment income exceeding 90% of gross receipts in each of the three consecutive years ending December 31, 2001.

134. As of January 1, 2002, Kane owned all the 100 issued shares of Manning Corp., a calendar-year S corporation. On the 40th day of 2002, Kane sold twenty-five of the Manning shares to Rodgers. For the year ended December 31, 2002 (a 365-day calendar year), Manning had $73,000 in nonseparately stated income and made no distributions to its shareholders. What amount of nonseparately stated income from Manning should be reported on Kane's 2002 tax return?

    a. $56,900
    b. $56,750
    c. $54,750
    d. $48,750

135. On February 10, 2002, Ace Corp., a calendar-year corporation, elected S corporation status and all shareholders consented to the election. There was no change in shareholders in 2002. Ace met all eligibility requirements for S status during the preelection portion of the year. What is the earliest date on which Ace can be recognized as an S corporation?

    a.   February 10, 2003.
    b.   February 10, 2002.
    c.   January 1, 2003.
    d.   January 1, 2002.

136. An S corporation has 30,000 shares of voting common stock and 20,000 shares of nonvoting common stock issued and outstanding. The S election can be revoked voluntarily with the consent of the shareholders holding, on the day of the revocation,

	Shares of voting stock	Shares of nonvoting stock
a.	0	20,000
b.	7,500	5,000
c.	10,000	16,000
d.	20,000	0

137. The Haas Corp., a calendar-year S corporation, has two equal shareholders. For the year ended December 31, 2002, Haas had income of $60,000, which included $50,000 from operations and $10,000 from investment interest income. There were no other transactions that year. Each shareholder's basis in the stock of Haas will increase by
- a. $50,000
- b. $30,000
- c. $25,000
- d. $0

138. Which of the following conditions will prevent a corporation from qualifying as an S Corporation?
- a. The corporation owns 100% of the stock of a C corporation.
- b. The corporation is a partner in a partnership.
- c. 30% of the corporation's stock is held by a voting trust.
- d. The corporation has common voting stock and preferred nonvoting stock outstanding.

139. If an S corporation has **no** accumulated earnings and profits, the amount distributed to a shareholder
- a. Must be returned to the S corporation.
- b. Increases the shareholder's basis for the stock.
- c. Decreases the shareholder's basis for the stock.
- d. Has no effect on the shareholder's basis for the stock.

140. A corporation that has been an S corporation from its inception may

	Have both passive and nonpassive income	Be owned by a bankruptcy estate
a.	No	Yes
b.	Yes	No
c.	No	No
d.	Yes	Yes

141. Bern Corp., an S corporation, had an ordinary loss of $36,500 for the year ended December 31, 2002. At January 1, 2002, Meyer owned 50% of Bern's stock. Meyer held the stock for forty days in 2002 before selling the entire 50% interest to an unrelated third party. Meyer's basis for the stock was $10,000. Meyer was a full-time employee of Bern until the stock was sold. Meyer's share of Bern's 2002 loss was
- a. $0
- b. $ 2,000
- c. $ 4,000
- d. $18,300

142. A calendar-year corporation whose status as an S corporation was terminated during 2002 must wait how many years before making a new S election, in the absence of IRS consent to an earlier election?
- a. Can make a new S election for calendar year 2002.

- b. Must wait three years.
- c. Must wait five years.
- d. Must wait six years.

143. Which one of the following will render a corporation ineligible for S corporation status?
- a. One of the stockholders is a decedent's estate.
- b. One of the stockholders is a bankruptcy estate.
- c. The corporation has both voting and nonvoting common stock issued and outstanding.
- d. The corporation has eighty stockholders.

144. With regard to S corporations and their stockholders, the "at risk" rules applicable to losses
- a. Depend on the type of income reported by the S corporation.
- b. Are subject to the elections made by the S corporation's stockholders.
- c. Take into consideration the S corporation's ratio of debt to equity.
- d. Apply at the shareholder level rather than at the corporate level.

145. An S corporation may deduct
- a. Foreign income taxes.
- b. A net Section 1231 loss.
- c. Investment interest expense.
- d. The amortization of organizational expenditures.

146. An S corporation's accumulated adjustments account, which measures the amount of earnings that may be distributed tax-free
- a. Must be adjusted downward for the full amount of federal income taxes attributable to any taxable year in which the corporation was a C corporation.
- b. Must be adjusted upward for the full amount of federal income taxes attributable to any taxable year in which the corporation was a C corporation.
- c. Must be adjusted upward or downward for only the federal income taxes affected by capital gains or losses, respectively, for any taxable year in which the corporation was a C corporation.
- d. Is not adjusted for federal income taxes attributable to a taxable year in which the corporation was a C corporation.

147. If a calendar-year S corporation does **not** request an automatic six-month extension of time to file its income tax return, the return is due by
- a. January 31.
- b. March 15.
- c. April 15.
- d. June 30.

148. An S corporation is **not** permitted to take a deduction for
- a. Compensation of officers.
- b. Interest paid to individuals who are not stockholders of the S corporation.
- c. Charitable contributions.
- d. Employee benefit programs established for individuals who are not stockholders of the S corporation.

149. An S corporation may
    a. Have both common and preferred stock outstanding.
    b. Have a partnership as a shareholder.
    c. Have a nonresident alien as a shareholder.
    d. Have as many as seventy-five shareholders.

150. Which of the following is **not** a requirement for a corporation to elect S corporation status (Subchapter S)?
    a. Must be a member of a controlled group.
    b. Must confine stockholders to individuals, estates, and certain qualifying trusts.
    c. Must be a domestic corporation.
    d. Must have only one class of stock.

151. Brooke, Inc., an S corporation, was organized on January 2, 2002, with two equal stockholders who materially participate in the S corporation's business. Each stockholder invested $5,000 in Brooke's capital stock, and each loaned $15,000 to the corporation. Brooke then borrowed $60,000 from a bank for working capital. Brooke sustained an operating loss of $90,000 for the year ended December 31, 2002. How much of this loss can each stockholder claim on his 2002 income tax return?
    a. $ 5,000
    b. $20,000
    c. $45,000
    d. $50,000

152. Jaxson Corp. has 200,000 shares of voting common stock issued and outstanding. King Corp. has decided to acquire 90% of Jaxson's voting common stock solely in exchange for 50% of its voting common stock and retain Jaxson as a subsidiary after the transaction. Which of the following statements is true?
    a. King must acquire 100% of Jaxson stock for the transaction to be a tax-free reorganization.
    b. The transaction will qualify as a tax-free reorganization.
    c. King must issue at least 60% of its voting common stock for the transaction to qualify as a tax-free reorganization.
    d. Jaxson must surrender assets for the transaction to qualify as a tax-free reorganization.

153. Ace Corp. and Bate Corp. combine in a qualifying reorganization and form Carr Corp., the only surviving corporation. This reorganization is tax-free to the

	Shareholders	Corporations
a.	Yes	Yes
b.	Yes	No
c.	No	Yes
d.	No	No

154. In a type B reorganization, as defined by the Internal Revenue Code, the

  I. Stock of the target corporation is acquired solely for the voting stock of either the acquiring corporation or its parent.
  II. Acquiring corporation must have control of the target corporation immediately after the acquisition.

    a. I only.
    b. II only.
    c. Both I and II.
    d. Neither I nor II.

155. Pursuant to a plan of corporate reorganization adopted in July 2002, Gow exchanged 500 shares of Lad Corp. common stock that he had bought in January 2000 at a cost of $5,000 for 100 shares of Rook Corp. common stock having a fair market value of $6,000. Gow's recognized gain on this exchange was
    a. $1,000 long-term capital gain.
    b. $1,000 short-term capital gain.
    c. $1,000 ordinary income.
    d. $0

156. Which one of the following is a corporate reorganization as defined in the Internal Revenue Code?
    a. Mere change in place of organization of one corporation.
    b. Stock redemption.
    c. Change in depreciation method from accelerated to straight-line.
    d. Change in inventory costing method from FIFO to LIFO.

157. With regard to corporate reorganizations, which one of the following statements is correct?
    a. A mere change in identity, form, or place of organization of one corporation does **not** qualify as a reorganization.
    b. The reorganization provisions **cannot** be used to provide tax-free treatment for corporate transactions.
    c. Securities in corporations **not** parties to a reorganization are always "boot."
    d. A "party to the reorganization" does **not** include the consolidated company.

158. Which one of the following is **not** a corporate reorganization as defined in the Internal Revenue Code?
    a. Stock redemption.
    b. Recapitalization.
    c. Mere change in identity.
    d. Statutory merger.

159. Claudio Corporation and Stellar Corporation both report on a calendar-year basis. Claudio merged into Stellar on June 30, 2002. Claudio had an allowable net operating loss carryover of $270,000. Stellar's taxable income for the year ended December 31, 2002, was $360,000 before consideration of Claudio's net operating loss carryover. Claudio's fair market value before the merger was $1,500,000. The federal long-term tax-exempt rate is 5%. As a result of the merger, Claudio's former shareholders own 10% of Stellar's outstanding stock. How much of Claudio's net operating loss carryover can be used to offset Stellar's 2002 taxable income?
    a. $ 38,014
    b. $ 75,000
    c. $180,000
    d. $181,967

160. In 1999, Celia Mueller bought a $1,000 bond issued by Disco Corporation for $1,100. Instead of paying off the bondholders in cash, Disco issued 100 shares of preferred stock in 2002 for each bond outstanding. The preferred stock had a fair market value of $15 per share. What is the recognized gain to be reported by Mueller in 2002?
    a. $0.
    b. $400 dividend.

    c. $400 long-term capital gain.

    d. $500 long-term capital gain.

161. On April 1, 2002, in connection with a recapitalization of Oakbrook Corporation, Mary Roberts exchanged 500 shares that cost her $95,000 for 1,000 shares of new stock worth $91,000 and bonds in the principal amount of $10,000 with a fair market value of $10,500. What is the amount of Roberts' recognized gain during 2002?

    a. $0

    b. $ 6,500

    c. $10,000

    d. $10,500

OTHER OBJECTIVE QUESTIONS

Problem 1
(10 to 15 minutes)

The following statements relate to the federal income tax treatment of S corporations and their shareholders. For items 1 through 10, indicate if the statement is true (T) or false (F).

1. A C corporation will **not** be eligible to make a subchapter S election if one of its shareholders is a resident alien.

2. Only corporations having $1 million or less of paid-in capital can qualify for a subchapter S election.

3. The election of subchapter S status by a corporation is valid only if all shareholders on the date of election consent to the election.

4. The number of shareholders that an S corporation can have is limited to sixty-five.

5. An S corporation may issue both voting and nonvoting common stock.

6. A revocation of an S election can be made by shareholders owning 60% of the S corporation's stock.

7. Dividend income is included in the computation of an S corporation's nonseparately computed income or loss (i.e., ordinary income or loss).

8. A shareholder's stock basis is increased by an S corporation's taxable income, but is not affected by the S corporation's tax-exempt income.

9. The pass through of an S corporation's deductions and losses to a shareholder first reduces the shareholder's basis for debt (but not below zero), then the basis for the shareholder's stock is reduced.

10. A corporation will not be subject to the built-in gains tax if it is formed in 2002 and makes an S election that is effective for its first taxable year.

Problem 2
(45 to 55 minutes)

The following adjusted accounts appeared in the records of Oak Corp., an accrual-basis corporation, for the year ended December 31, 2002. Numbers in brackets refer to the items in *Additional information*.

Revenues and gains		
Net sales	$900,000	[1]
Dividends	20,000	[2]
Interest	8,000	[3]
Gain on sale of stock	10,000	[4]
Equity in earnings of Tech Partnership	60,000	[5]
Keyman life insurance proceeds	250,000	[6]
Tax refund	5,000	[7]
Total	1,253,000	

Costs and expenses		
Cost of goods sold	525,000	[8]
Salaries and wages	200,000	[9]
Doubtful accounts	20,000	[10]
Taxes	90,000	[11]
Interest	25,000	[12]
Contributions	18,000	[13]
Depreciation	80,000	[14]
Other	33,000	[15]
Federal income tax	65,000	[16]
Total	1,056,000	
Net income	$ 197,000	

Additional information

[1] Trade accounts receivable at December 31, 2002, and at December 31, 2001, amounted to $330,000 and $200,000, respectively.

[2] Dividends were declared and paid in 2002 by an unrelated taxable domestic corporation whose securities are traded on a major stock exchange.

[3] Interest revenue comprises interest on municipal bonds issued in 1989 and purchased by Oak in the open market in 2001.

[4] Gain on sale of stock arose from the following purchase and sale of stock in an unrelated corporation listed on a major stock exchange:

Bought in 1999	Cost	$12,000
Sold in 2002	Proceeds of sale	22,000

[5] Oak owns 50% of Tech Partnership. The other 50% is owned by an unrelated individual. Tech reported the following tax information to Oak:

Oak's share of:

Partnership ordinary income	$ 79,000
Net long-term capital loss	(19,000)

[6] Oak owned the keyman life insurance policy, paid the premiums, and was the direct beneficiary. The proceeds were collected on the death of Oak's controller.
[7] The tax refund arose from Oak's overpayment of federal income tax on the 2001 return.
[8] Cost of goods sold relates to Oak's net sales.
[9] Salaries and wages includes officers' compensation of $75,000.
[10] Doubtful accounts expense represents an addition to Oak's allowance for doubtful accounts based on an aging schedule whereby Oak "reserves" all accounts receivable over 120 days for book purposes. The balance in Oak's allowance for doubtful accounts was $142,000 at December 31, 2002. Actual bad debts written off in 2002 amounted to $11,000.
[11] Taxes comprise payroll taxes and property taxes.
[12] Interest expense resulted from borrowing for working capital purposes.
[13] Contributions were all paid in 2002 to State University, specifically designated for the purchase of lab equipment.
[14] Oak has always used straight-line depreciation for both book and tax purposes.
[15] Other expenses include premiums of $15,000 on the keyman life insurance policy covering the controller.
[16] Federal income tax is the amount estimated and accrued before preparation of the return.

Required:

For **items 1 through 16,** indicate the amount, **if any,** that should be included in the computation of Oak's 2002 federal taxable income. Any possible optional treatment should be resolved in a manner that will minimize Oak's 2002 taxable income. On the CPA exam, a list of numeric answers would be provided for the candidate to select from.

Problem 3   (45 to 55 minutes)

Eve, Inc., a wholesaler, commenced operations on January 2, 2002. Eve is an accrual-basis, calendar-year corporation that made a timely and proper election to be treated as an S corporation.

Eve's income statement for the year ended December 31, 2002, is presented below.

Sales			$500,000
Cost of goods sold			281,000
Gross profit			219,000
Operating expenses			
(1)	Compensation to officer	$80,000	
(2)	Uncollectible accounts	6,000	
(3)	Taxes	27,000	
(4)	Depreciation	15,000	
(5)	Contributions	9,000	
(6)	Employee benefit programs	19,000	
(7)	Amortization of organization costs	10,000	
(8)	Other	21,000	187,000
Operating income			32,000
(9)	Net rental revenue		18,000
Portfolio revenue			
(10)	Interest	6,000	
(11)	Dividends	4,000	
(12)	Short-term capital gain	8,000	18,000
Total income			$ 68,000

Additional information

• The officer's compensation of $80,000 was received in 2002 by Carl Loreck, Eve's president and sole stockholder.
• Eve used the "reserve" method in computing uncollectible accounts expense of $6,000. Actual customers' accounts receivable written off in 2002 because of uncollectibility amounted to $2,000.
• Included in the $27,000 expense for taxes are $800 in parking fines incurred while Eve's trucks were making deliveries to customers, and $2,200 in income taxes paid to a foreign country where Eve has a sales outlet.
• The depreciation of $15,000 was computed under the straight-line method for book purposes. For tax purposes, depreciation was $25,000, including the full $24,000 expense deduction claimed by Eve under Section 179.
• The contributions of $9,000 were made to recognized charitable organizations.
• Included in the employee benefit programs of $19,000 are Loreck's medical expenses amounting to $6,000.
• Eve's organization costs of $50,000 are being amortized over a period of sixty months.
• Included in the other operating expenses of $21,000 is insurance expense of $10,000 in connection with establishment of a reserve for self-insurance.
• The interest revenue of $6,000 was earned on US Government obligations.
• The dividends of $4,000 were received from unrelated taxable domestic corporations.
• The short-term capital gain of $8,000 was realized on the sale of an investment in an unrelated taxable domestic corporation.
• Eve's only payment to Loreck during 2002 was Loreck's salary of $80,000. No other distributions were made.

Required:

For **items 1 through 12** indicate the appropriate amount, **if any,** that would be separately shown on the following:

Eve, Inc.'s Income and Deductions on page 1 of Form 1120-S, S Corporation Return
Loreck's Schedule K-1, Shareholder's Share of Income, Credits, Deductions, etc.

On the CPA exam, a list of numeric answers would be presented for the candidate to select from.

Problem 4   (10 to 15 minutes)

Given below are terms appearing in the federal income tax code, regulations and explanations.

A. Accumulated earnings tax	J. Dividends received deduction	S. Personal holding company tax
B. Capital assets	K. Earned income	T. Personal service corporation
C. Capital contribution	L. Exchanged basis	U. Portfolio income
D. Claim of right	M. Excise tax	V. Regulated investment company
E. Consent divided	N. Fair market value	W. Sec. 1231 assets
F. Constructive dividend	O. Head of household	X. Surviving spouse
G. Constructive receipt	P. Nontaxable exchange	Y. Taxable exchange
H. Deficiency dividend	Q. Passive income	Z. Transferred basis
I. Dividends paid deduction	R. Personal holding company	

Required:

Indicate your choice of the best term applying to each of the statements below. Each term may be selected once, more than once, or not at all.

1.   A corporation whose income was derived solely from dividends, interest, and royalties, and during the last six months of its year more than 50% of the value of its outstanding stock is owned by five or fewer individuals.

2.   The basis used to determine gain on sale of property that was received as a gift.

3.   The trade-in of production machinery for new production machinery by a corporation, when the corporation pays additional cash.

4.   An unmarried individual whose filing status enables the taxpayer to use a set of income tax rates that are lower than those applicable to other unmarried individuals, but are higher than those applicable to married persons filing a joint return.

5.   If income is unqualifiedly available, it will be subject to the income tax even though it is not physically in the taxpayer's possession.

6.   A special tax imposed on corporations that accumulate their earnings beyond the reasonable needs of the business.

7.   The classification of income from interest, dividends, annuities, and certain royalties.

8.   The classification of depreciable assets and real estate used in a trade or business and held for more than one year.

9.   This deduction attempts to mitigate the triple taxation that would occur if one corporation paid dividends to a corporate shareholder who, in turn, distributed such amounts to its individual shareholders.

10.   Sale of property to a corporation by a shareholder for a selling price that is in excess of the property's fair market value.

Problem 5   (15 to 25 minutes)

The following adjusted revenue and expense accounts appeared in the accounting records of Aviator, Inc., an accrual-basis taxpayer, for the year ended December 31, 2002:

Revenues	
Net sales	$2,000,000
Dividends	50,000
Interest	22,000
Gains on the sale of stock	20,000
Total	$2,092,000
Expenses	
Cost of goods sold	$1,000,000
Salaries and wages	400,000
Interest	25,000
Contributions	40,000
Depreciation (see note)	260,000
Losses on the sale of stock	30,000
Total	$1,755,000
Net Income	$ 337,000

NOTE: *There is no Sec. 1245, Sec. 1250, or Sec. 291 recapture.*

Additional information

(1)   The dividends were received from a taxable domestic corporation, whose stock is traded on a major stock exchange.

(2) Interest expense consists of: $20,000 interest on funds borrowed for working capital and $5,000 interest on funds borrowed to purchase municipal bonds.

(3) Interest revenue consists of interest earned on

Corporate bonds purchased in 2001	$20,000
Municipal bonds purchased in 2002	2,000

(4) Contributions of $40,000 were made to qualified charitable organizations.

(5) On January 2, 2002, Aviator, Inc. commenced active operations. In connection with creating the business, Aviator incurred the following organizational expenditures:

Legal fees	$30,000
State incorporation fees	20,000
Brokers commission on the sale of stock	15,000

Aviator is amortizing the deductible expenses over the minimum allowable period. The amortization was erroneously excluded from the accounts shown above.

(6) Gains from the sale of stock arose from the following sales of stock of unrelated corporations:

Tech. Corp (bought February 2002; sold April 2002)	$15,000
Major Corp (bought June 1998; sold September 2002)	5,000

(7) All losses from the sale of stock are classified as long-term capital losses.

Part a.
Required:

For **items 1 through 7** record the appropriate amount as it would appear on the Aviator, Inc. corporate tax return. On the exam, a list of numeric answers would be presented for the candidate to select from.

1. What is the amount of interest expense that Aviator, Inc. can deduct on its tax return?

2. What is the amount of interest income that must be included in Aviator's gross income?

3. What is the allowable amount of organizational expenditures that is deductible on Aviator's tax return?

4. How much of the capital gains must be included in Aviator's gross income?

5. How much of the capital losses can be deducted on Aviator's tax return?

6. What is the amount of Aviator's dividends received deduction?

7. What is Aviator's maximum charitable contributions deduction?

Part b.

Part b. is unrelated to Part a.

Required:

For **items 8 through 12** indicate whether each item would (Y) or would not (N) be included in gross income or deductible on the corporate tax return. Assume that the corporation is an accrual-basis taxpayer.

8. Life insurance proceeds collected as the result of the death of a corporate officer. Aviator, Inc. owned the keyman life insurance policy, paid all premiums and was the sole beneficiary.

9. Life insurance premiums paid on the keyman life insurance policy. Aviator, Inc. was the sole beneficiary.

10. A gain realized from the sale of stock that had been owned by the corporation for a total of thirty days.

11. A dividends received deduction for dividends received from stock owned by the corporation for a total of forty days.

12. Dividends received by Aviator, Inc. **from** a subsidiary which is 85% owned by the corporation. A consolidated tax return is being filed by Aviator, Inc. that includes the dividend paying subsidiary.

Problem 6   (10 to 20 minutes)

Required:

Each of the numbered statements presented below gives a conclusion in relation to the following facts. For **items 1 through 10** indicate if the statement is true (T) or false (F).

On January 2, 2002, Fred Brewer formed Silver Corporation. Brewer contributed $50,000 cash and transferred equipment with an adjusted basis of $100,000 and a fair market value of $175,000, in return for all of Silver's stock. The transferred equipment was subject to liabilities of $30,000, which the corporation assumed.

The following information is available for the dates indicated in 2002:

March 2	Silver Corporation received a $2,000 dividend from stock that it owned in a listed and publicly traded taxable domestic corporation.
April 1	Silver Corporation paid insurance premiums that included: (1) $3,000 for a keyman life insurance policy on Brewer's life (Silver is the beneficiary of this policy); and (2) $15,000 for group-term life insurance on employees' lives (employees' dependents are the beneficiaries of these policies).

July 14	A condemnation award of $20,000 was received by Silver Corporation as consideration for land held primarily as an investment. The land had an adjusted basis of $22,500.
July 31	Silver Corporation exchanged a machine used in its business with an adjusted basis of $8,000 for another machine with a fair market value of $6,000 and received cash of $3,500.
October 20	Silver Corporation distributed property as a dividend to Brewer. This equipment had an adjusted basis of $4,000 and a fair market value of $12,000 on date of distribution. The equipment was subject to liabilities of $5,000, which Brewer assumed.
December 31	The stock that Silver owned in Green Corporation was declared worthless. The investment represented ownership of 100% of the stock of Green, which had always derived all of its gross income from manufacturing operations.

Items to be answered

1. The equipment transferred on January 2 has a tax basis to Silver Corporation of $145,000.

2. The stock received by Fred Brewer on January 2 has a tax basis of $120,000.

3. No gain was recognized by Silver Corporation when it issued its stock in exchange for the cash and equipment received from Fred Brewer.

4. The dividend received on March 2 will increase Silver's taxable income by $2,000.

5. In computing its taxable income for 2002, Silver Corporation can deduct $18,000 for the keyman and group life insurance premiums.

6. The condemnation award received on July 14 results in the recognition of a $2,500 capital loss.

7. The exchange of machines on July 31 results in the recognition of a $3,500 gain to Silver Corporation.

8. The distribution of property on October 20 results in the recognition of an $8,000 gain to Silver Corporation.

9. Brewer's tax basis for the equipment that he receives on October 20 is $12,000.

10. Silver Corporation can deduct an ordinary loss as a result of the worthlessness of its stock investment in Green Corporation.

Problem 7   (40 to 50 minutes)

Following is Ral Corp.'s condensed income statement, before federal income tax, for the year ended December 31, 2002:

Sales		$1,000,000
Cost of sales		700,000
Gross profit		300,000
Operating expenses		220,000
Operating income		80,000
Other income (loss):		
Interest	$ 5,200	
Dividends	19,200	
Net long-term capital loss	(6,400)	18,000
Income before federal income tax		$ 98,000

Additional information
Interest arose from the following sources:

US Treasury notes	$ 3,000
Municipal arbitrage bonds	2,000
Other municipal bonds	200
Total interest	$5,200

Dividends arose from the following sources:

Taxable domestic corporation	Date stock acquired	Percent owned by Ral	
Clove Corp.	7/1/96	30.0	$ 7,000
Ramo Corp.	9/1/98	10.0	6,000
Sol Corp. (stock sold 1/10/03)	12/1/02	5.0	1,000
Real Estate Investment Trust	6/1/01	1.0	2,700
Mutual Fund Corp. (capital gains dividends only)	4/1/00	0.1	400
Money Market Fund (invests only in interest/paying securities)	3/1/99	0.1	2,100
Total dividends			$19,200

Operating expenses include the following:

Bonus of $5,000 paid to Ral's sales manager on January 31, 2003. This bonus was based on a percentage of Ral's 2002 sales and was computed on January 25, 2003, under a formula in effect in 2002.
Estimate of $10,000 for bad debts. Actual bad debts for the year amounted to $8,000.
Keyman life insurance premiums of $4,000. Ral is the beneficiary of the policies.
State income taxes of $12,000.

During 2002, Ral made estimated federal income tax payments of $25,000. These payments were debited to prepaid tax expense on Ral's books.

Ral does not exercise significant influence over Clove and accordingly did **not** use the equity method of accounting for this investment.

Ral declared and paid dividends of $11,000 during 2002.

Corporate income tax rates are as follows:

Taxable income over	but not over	Pay		% on excess	Of the amount over/
$ 0 /	$ 50,000	$ 0	+	15%	$ 0
50,000 /	75,000	7,500		25	50,000
75,000 /	100,000	13,750		34	75,000
100,000 /	335,000	22,250		39	100,000

Ral was not subject to the alternative minimum tax in 2002.

Required:

Items 1 through 14 below pertain to the computation of Ral Corp.'s 2002 federal income tax. For each item, select the appropriate amount. An amount may be selected once, more than once, or not at all.

Item for Ral's 2002 Federal Income Tax

1. Amount of deduction for manager's $5,000 bonus for 2002.
2. Deduction for bad debts for 2002.
3. Deduction for keyman life insurance premiums for 2002.
4. Deduction for state income taxes for 2002.
5. Amount of interest to be included in gross income for 2002.
6. Dividends received deduction for dividends received from Clove Corp.
7. Dividends received deduction for dividends received from Ramo Corp.
8. Dividends received deduction for dividends received from Sol Corp.
9. Dividends received deduction for dividends received from Real Estate Investment Trust.
10. Dividends received deduction for dividends received from Mutual Fund Corp.
11. Dividends received deduction for dividends received from Money Market Fund.
12. Deduction for the $11,000 of dividends paid by Ral to its shareholders.
13. Deduction for net capital loss for 2002.
14. Ral's federal income tax for 2002 if taxable income were $100,000.

Amount

A.	$0	N.	$ 4,800	
B.	$ 280	O.	$ 4,900	
C.	$ 320	P.	$ 5,000	
D.	$ 1,000	Q.	$ 5,200	
E.	$ 1,470	R.	$ 5,600	
F.	$ 1,680	S.	$ 6,400	
G.	$ 1,890	T.	$ 7,000	
H.	$ 2,000	U.	$ 8,000	
I.	$ 2,200	V.	$10,000	
J.	$ 3,000	W.	$11,000	
K.	$ 3,200	X.	$12,000	
L.	$ 4,000	Y.	$13,750	
M.	$ 4,200	Z.	$22,250	

Problem 8
(25 to 40 minutes)

Kimberly Corp. is a calendar-year accrual-basis corporation that commenced operations on January 1, 1999. The following adjusted accounts appear on Kimberly's records for the year ended December 31, 2002. Kimberly is not subject to the uniform capitalization rules.

Revenues and gains	
Gross sales	$2,000,000
Dividends:	
20%-owned domestic corporation	10,000
XYZ Corp.	10,000
Interest:	
US treasury bonds	26,000
Municipal bonds	25,000
Insurance proceeds	40,000
Gain on sale:	
Unimproved lot (1)	20,000
XYZ stock (2)	5,000
State franchise tax refund	14,000
Total	2,150,000

Costs and expenses	
Cost of goods sold	350,000
Salaries and wages	470,000
Depreciation:	
Real property	50,000
Personal property (3)	100,000
Bad debt (4)	10,000
State franchise tax	25,000
Vacation expense	10,000
Interest expense (5)	16,000
Life insurance premiums	20,000
Federal income taxes	200,000
Entertainment expense	20,000
Other expenses	29,000
Total	1,300,000
Net income	$ 850,000

Additional information

(1) Gain on the sale of unimproved lot: Purchased in 2000 for use in business for $50,000. Sold in 2002 for $70,000. Kimberly has never had any Sec. 1231 losses.

(2) Gain on sale of XYZ Stock: Purchased in 1999.

(3) Personal Property: The book depreciation is the same as tax depreciation for all the property that was placed in service before January 1, 2002. The book depreciation is straight-line over the useful life, which is the same as class life. Company policy is to use the half-year convention per books for personal property. Furniture and fixtures costing $56,000 were placed in service on January 2, 2002.

(4) Bad Debt: Represents the increase in the allowance for doubtful accounts based on an aging of accounts receivable. Actual bad debts written off were $7,000.

(5) Interest expense on

Mortgage loan	$10,000
Loan obtained to purchase municipal bonds	4,000
Line of credit loan	2,000

Required:

For **items 1 through 5,** determine the amount that should be reported on Kimberly corporation's 2002 Federal income tax return. On the CPA exam, a list of numeric answers would be presented for the candidate to select from.

Items to be answered

1. What amount of interest income is taxable from the US Treasury bonds?

2. Determine the tax depreciation expense under the Modified Accelerated Cost Recovery System (MACRS), for the furniture and fixtures that were placed in service on January 2, 2002. Assume that no irrevocable depreciation election is made. Round the answer to the nearest thousand. Kimberly did not use the alternative depreciation system (ADS) or a straight-line method of depreciation. No election was made to expense part of the cost of the property, and no additional first-year depreciation was taken.

3. Determine the amount of bad debt to be included as an expense item.

4. Determine Kimberly's net long-term capital gain.

5. What amount of interest expense is deductible?

Required:

For **items 6 through 10,** select whether the following expenses are (F) fully deductible, (P) partially deductible, or (N) nondeductible, for regular tax purposes, on Kimberly's 2002 federal income tax return.

Items to be answered

6. Organization expense incurred at corporate inception in 1999 to draft the corporate charter. No deduction was taken for the organization expense in 1999.

7. Life insurance premiums paid by the corporation for its executives as part of their compensation for services rendered. The corporation is neither the direct nor the indirect beneficiary of the policy and the amount of compensation is reasonable.

8. Vacation pay earned by employees which vested under a plan by December 31, 2002, and was paid February 1, 2003.

9. State franchise tax liability that has accrued during the year and was paid on March 15, 2003.

10. Entertainment expense to lease a luxury skybox during football season to entertain clients. A bona fide business discussion precedes each game. The cost of regular seats would have been one half the amount paid.

Required:

For **items 11 through 15,** select whether the following revenue items are (F) fully taxable, (P) partially taxable, or (N) nontaxable on Kimberly Corp.'s 2002 federal income tax return for regular tax purposes.

Items to be answered

11. Dividends from the 20%-owned domestic corporation. The taxable income limitation does not apply. Kimberly does not have the ability to exercise significant influence.

12. Recovery of an account from prior year's bad debts. Kimberly uses an estimate of uncollectibles based on an aging of accounts receivable for book purposes. The account was written off for tax purposes and reduced Kimberly's income tax liability.

13. Refund of state franchise tax overpayment, previously expensed on Kimberly's 2000 federal tax return, thereby reducing federal taxes that year.

14. Interest income from municipal bonds purchased by Kimberly in 2001 on the open market.

15. Proceeds paid to Kimberly by reason of death, under a life insurance policy that Kimberly had purchased on the life of one of its vice-presidents. Kimberly was the beneficiary and used the proceeds to pay the premium charges for the group term insurance policy for its other employees.

Required:

Items 16 through 24 refer to Kimberly's need to determine if it will be subject to the alternative minimum tax. Determine whether the statement is true (T) or false (F).

Items to be answered

16. The method of depreciation for commercial real property to arrive at alternative minimum taxable income before the adjusted current earnings (ACE) adjustment, is the straight-line method.

17. The corporate exemption amount reduces the alternative minimum taxable income.

18. The ACE adjustment can be a positive or negative amount.

19. Depreciation on personal property to arrive at alternative minimum taxable income before the ACE adjustment is straight-line over the MACRS recovery period.

20. The alternative minimum tax is the excess of the tentative minimum tax over the regular tax liability.

21. Municipal bond interest, other than from private activity bonds, is includible income to arrive at alternative minimum taxable income before the ACE adjustment.

22. The maximum corporate exemption amount for minimum tax purposes is $150,000.

23. The 70% dividends received deduction is available to determine ACE.

24. Municipal bond interest is includible income to determine ACE.

Problem 9   (25 to 40 minutes)

Reliant Corp., an accrual-basis calendar-year C corporation, filed its 2002 federal income tax return on March 15, 2003.

Required:

The following **two** responses are required for each of the **items 1 through 6**.

a. Determine the amount of Reliant's 2002 Schedule M-1 adjustment.

b. Indicate if the adjustment (I) increases, (D) decreases, or (N) has no effect, on Reliant's 2002 taxable income.

1. Reliant's disbursements included reimbursed employees' expenses in 2002 for travel of $100,000, and business meals of $30,000. The reimbursed expenses met the conditions of deductibility and were properly substantiated under an accountable plan. The reimbursement was not treated as employee compensation.

2. Reliant's books expensed $7,000 in 2002 for the term life insurance premiums on the corporate officers. Reliant was the policy owner and beneficiary.

3. Reliant's books indicated an $18,000 state franchise tax expense for 2002. Estimated state tax payments for 2002 were $15,000.

4. Book depreciation on computers for 2002 was $10,000. These computers, which cost $50,000, were placed in service on January 2, 2001. Tax depreciation used MACRS with the half-year convention. No election was made to expense part of the computer cost or to use a straight-line method or the alternative depreciation system.

5. For 2002, Reliant's books showed a $4,000 short-term capital gain distribution from a mutual fund corporation and a $5,000 loss on the sale of Retro stock that was purchased in 2000. The stock was an investment in an unrelated corporation. There were no other 2002 gains or losses and no loss carryovers from prior years.

6. Reliant's 2002 taxable income before the charitable contribution and the dividends received deductions was $500,000. Reliant's books expensed $15,000 in board of director authorized charitable contributions that were paid on January 5, 2003. Charitable contributions paid and expensed during 2002 were $35,000. All charitable contributions were properly substantiated. There were no net operating losses or charitable contributions that were carried forward.

Required:

c.   For **items 7 through 11,** indicate if the expenses are (F) fully deductible, (P) partially deductible, or (N) nondeductible for regular tax purposes on Reliant's 2002 federal income tax return.

7.   Reliant purchased theater tickets for its out of town clients. The performances took place after Reliant's substantial and bona fide business negotiations with its clients.

8.   Reliant accrued advertising expenses to promote a new product line. Ten percent of the new product line remained in ending inventory.

9.   Reliant incurred interest expense on a loan to purchase municipal bonds.

10. Reliant paid a penalty for the underpayment of 2001 estimated taxes.

11. On December 9, 2002, Reliant's board of directors voted to pay a $500 bonus to each nonstockholder employee for 2002. The bonuses were paid on February 3, 2003.

Required:

d.   For **items 12 through 16,** indicate if the following items are (F) fully taxable, (P) partially taxable, or (N) nontaxable for regular tax purposes on Reliant's 2002 federal income tax return. All transactions occurred during 2002.

Items 12 and 13 are based on the following:

Reliant filed an amended federal income tax return for 2000 and received a refund that included both the overpayment of the federal taxes and interest.

12. The portion of Reliant's refund that represented the overpayment of the 2000 federal taxes.

13. The portion of Reliant's refund that is attributable to the interest on the overpayment of federal taxes.

14. Reliant received dividend income from a mutual fund that solely invests in municipal bonds.

15. Reliant, the lessor, benefited from the capital improvements made to its property by the lessee in 2002. The lease agreement is for one year ending December 31, 2002, and provides for a reduction in rental payments by the lessee in exchange for the improvements.

16. Reliant collected the proceeds on the term life insurance policy on the life of a debtor who was not a shareholder. The policy was assigned to Reliant as collateral security for the debt. The proceeds exceeded the amount of the debt.

Required:

e.   For **items 17 through 21,** indicate if the following (I) increase, (D) decrease, or (N) have no effect on Reliant's 2002 alternative minimum taxable income (AMTI) **prior to** the adjusted current earnings adjustment (ACE).

17. Reliant used the 70% dividends received deduction for regular tax purposes.

18. Reliant received interest from a state's general obligation bonds.

19. Reliant used MACRS depreciation on seven-year personal property placed into service January 3, 2002, for regular tax purposes. No expense or depreciation election was made.

20. Depreciation on nonresidential real property placed into service on January 3, 2002, was under the general MACRS depreciation system for regular tax purposes.

21. Reliant had only cash charitable contributions for 2002.

Required:

f.   For **items 22 through 28,** indicate if the statement is true (T) or false (F) regarding Reliant's compliance with tax procedures, tax credits and the alternative minimum tax.

22. Reliant's exemption for alternative minimum tax is reduced by 20% of the excess of the alternative minimum taxable income over $150,000.

23. The statute of limitations on Reliant's fraudulent 1999 federal income tax return expires six years after the filing date of the return.

24. The statute of limitations on Reliant's 2000 federal income tax return, which omitted 30% of gross receipts, expires two years after the filing date of the return.

25. The welfare-to-work tax credit may be combined with other business credits to form part of Reliant's general business credit.

26. Reliant incurred qualifying expenditures to remove existing access barriers at the place of employment in 2002. As a small business, Reliant qualifies for the disabled access credit.

27. Reliant's tax preparer, a CPA firm, may use the 2002 corporate tax return information to prepare corporate officers' tax returns without the consent of the corporation.

28. Reliant must file an amended return for 2002 within one year of the filing date.

Problem 10   (5 to 10 minutes)

Lan Corp., an accrual-basis calendar-year repair service corporation, was formed and began business on January 6, 2002. Lan's valid S corporation election took effect retroactively on January 6, 2002. Since the question requires a numeric answer, a list of numeric amounts would be provided for the candidate to select from.

Required:

a. For **items 1 through 4,** determine the amount, if any, using the fact pattern for each item.

1. Assume the following facts:

Lan's 2002 books recorded the following items:

Gross receipts	$7,260
Interest income on investments	50
Charitable contributions	1,000
Supplies	1,120

What amount of net business income should Lan report on its 2002 Form 1120S, US Income Tax Return for an S Corporation, Schedule K?

2. Assume the following facts:

As of January 6, 2002, Taylor and Barr each owned 100 shares of the 200 issued shares of Lan stock. On January 31, 2002, Taylor and Barr each sold twenty shares to Pike. No election was made to terminate the tax year. Lan had net business income of $14,400 for the year ended December 31, 2002, and made no distributions to its shareholders. Lan's 2002 calendar year had 360 days.

What amount of net business income should have been reported on Pike's 2002 Schedule K-1 from Lan? (2002 is a 360-day tax year.) Round the answer to the nearest hundred.

3. Assume the following facts:

Pike purchased forty Lan shares on January 31, 2002, for $4,000. Lan made no distributions to shareholders, and Pike's 2002 Schedule K-1 from Lan reported

Ordinary business loss	$(1,000)
Municipal bond interest income	150

What was Pike's basis in his Lan stock at December 31, 2002?

4. Assume the following facts:

On January 6, 2002, Taylor and Barr each owned 100 shares of the 200 issued shares of Lan stock. Taylor's basis in Lan shares on that date was $10,000. Taylor sold all of his Lan shares to Pike on January 31, 2002, and Lan made a valid election to terminate its tax year. Taylor's share of ordinary income from Lan prior to the sale was $2,000. Lan made a cash distribution of $3,000 to Taylor on January 30, 2002.

What was Taylor's basis in Lan shares for determining gain or loss from the sale to Pike?

Required:

b. For **items 5 and 6,** indicate if the statement is true (T) or false (F) regarding Lan's S corporation status.

5. Lan issues shares of both preferred and common stock to shareholders at inception on January 6, 2002. This will not affect Lan's S corporation eligibility.

6. Lan, an S corporation since inception, has passive investment income for three consecutive years following the year a valid S corporation election takes effect. Lan's S corporation election is terminated as of the first day of the fourth year.

Problem 11   (25 to 40 minutes)

Capital Corp., an accrual-basis calendar-year C corporation, began operations on January 2, 1999. Capital timely filed its 2002 federal income tax return on March 15, 2003.

Required:

Items 1 through 4 each require **two** responses:

a. For each item below, determine the amount of Capital's 2002 Schedule M-1 adjustment necessary to reconcile book income to taxable income. On the CPA exam, a list of numeric answers would be presented for the candidate to select from.

b.   In addition, determine if the Schedule M-1 adjustment necessary to reconcile book income to taxable income increases, decreases, or has no effect on Capital's 2002 taxable income. An answer may be selected once, more than once, or not at all.

Selections

I.   Increases Capital's 2002 taxable income.
D.   Decreases Capital's 2002 taxable income.
N.   Has no effect on Capital's 2002 taxable income.

1.   At its corporate inception in 1999, Capital incurred and paid $40,000 in organizational costs for legal fees to draft the corporate charter. In 1999, Capital correctly elected, for book purposes, to amortize the organizational expenditures over forty years and for the minimum required period on its federal income tax return. For 2002, Capital amortized $1,000 of the organizational costs on its books.

2.   Capital's 2002 disbursements included $10,000 for reimbursed employees' expenses for business meals and entertainment. The reimbursed expenses met the conditions of deductibility and were properly substantiated under an accountable plan. The reimbursement was not treated as employee compensation.

3.   Capital's 2002 disbursements included $15,000 for life insurance premium expense paid for its executives as part of their taxable compensation. Capital is neither the direct nor the indirect beneficiary of the policy, and the amount of the compensation is reasonable.

4.   In 2002, Capital increased its allowance for uncollectible accounts by $10,000. No bad debt was written off in 2002.

Sunco Corp., an accrual-basis calendar-year C corporation, timely filed its 2002 federal income tax return on March 15, 2003.

Required:

c.   For **Items 5 and 6,** determine if the following items are fully taxable, partially taxable, or nontaxable for regular income tax purposes on Sunco's 2002 federal income tax return. An answer may be selected once, more than once, or not at all.

Selections

F.   Fully taxable for regular income tax purposes on Sunco's 2002 federal income tax return.
P.   Partially taxable for regular income tax purposes on Sunco's 2002 federal income tax return.
N.   Nontaxable for regular income tax purposes on Sunco's 2002 federal income tax return.

5.   In 2002, Sunco received dividend income from a 35%-owned domestic corporation. The dividends were not from debt-financed portfolio stock, and the taxable income limitation did not apply.

6.   In 2002, Sunco received a $2,800 lease cancellation payment from a three-year lease tenant.

Quest Corp., an accrual-basis calendar-year C corporation, timely filed its 2002 federal income tax return on March 15, 2003.

Required:

d.   For **Items 7 and 8,** determine if the following items are fully deductible, partially deductible, or nondeductible for regular income tax purposes on Quest's 2002 federal income tax return. An answer may be selected once, more than once, or not at all.

Selections

F.   Fully deductible for regular income tax purposes on Quest's 2002 federal income tax return.
P.   Partially deductible for regular income tax purposes on Quest's 2002 federal income tax return.
N.   Nondeductible for regular income tax purposes on Quest's 2002 federal income tax return.

7.   Quest's 2002 taxable income before charitable contributions and dividends received deduction was $200,000. Quest's Board of Directors authorized a $38,000 contribution to a qualified charity on December 1, 2002. The payment was made on February 1, 2003. All charitable contributions were properly substantiated.

8.   During 2002 Quest was assessed and paid a $300 uncontested penalty for failure to pay its 2001 federal income taxes on time.

On its 2002 federal income tax return, Gelco Corp., an accrual-basis calendar-year C corporation, reported the same amounts for regular income tax and alternative minimum tax purposes.

Required:

e.   For **Items 9 through 11,** determine if each item, taken separately, contributes to overstating, understating, or correctly stating Gelco's 2002 alternative minimum taxable income (AMTI) prior to the adjusted current earnings adjustment (ACE). An answer may be selected once, more than once, or not at all.

<u>Selections</u>

      O.   Overstating Gelco's 2002 AMTI prior to the ACE.
      U.   Understating Gelco's 2002 AMTI prior to the ACE.
      C.   Correctly stating Gelco's 2002 AMTI prior to the ACE.

 9.   For regular tax purposes, Gelco deducted the maximum MACRS depreciation on seven-year personal property placed in service on January 2, 2002. Gelco made no Internal Revenue Code Section 179 election to expense the property in 2002.

10.   For regular income tax purposes, Gelco depreciated nonresidential real property placed in service on January 2, 1998, under the general MACRS depreciation system for a thirty-nine-year depreciable life.

11.   Gelco excluded state highway construction general obligation bond interest income earned in 2002 for regular income tax and alternative minimum tax (AMT) purposes.

MULTIPLE-CHOICE ANSWERS

1. c	29. d	57. d	85. d	113. b	141. b
2. c	30. a	58. a	86. c	114. c	142. c
3. d	31. d	59. c	87. c	115. b	143. d
4. d	32. c	60. c	88. b	116. c	144. d
5. c	33. d	61. d	89. d	117. d	145. d
6. a	34. d	62. c	90. a	118. d	146. d
7. d	35. c	63. c	91. c	119. b	147. b
8. c	36. a	64. c	92. a	120. c	148. c
9. b	37. c	65. d	93. b	121. d	149. d
10. c	38. b	66. d	94. a	122. d	150. a
11. d	39. c	67. c	95. d	123. a	151. b
12. a	40. d	68. d	96. d	124. d	152. b
13. b	41. a	69. c	97. b	125. b	153. a
14. b	42. d	70. a	98. d	126. d	154. c
15. a	43. a	71. d	99. a	127. a	155. d
16. c	44. c	72. a	100. c	128. d	156. a
17. d	45. d	73. d	101. d	129. b	157. c
18. c	46. c	74. d	102. d	130. b	158. a
19. b	47. b	75. d	103. d	131. d	159. a
20. b	48. b	76. b	104. a	132. c	160. a
21. a	49. b	77. d	105. b	133. d	161. b
22. c	50. b	78. c	106. a	134. b	
23. c	51. b	79. b	107. c	135. d	
24. c	52. b	80. c	108. d	136. c	
25. b	53. d	81. c	109. a	137. b	
26. d	54. b	82. c	110. b	138. d	
27. c	55. d	83. c	111. c	139. c	1st: __/161 = __%
28. a	56. c	84. c	112. d	140. d	2nd: __/161= __%

MULTIPLE-CHOICE ANSWER EXPLANATIONS

A. Transfers to a Controlled Corporation

1. **(c)** The requirement is to determine Dexter Corporation's tax basis for the property received in the incorporation from Alan. Since Alan and Baker are the only transferors of property and they, in the aggregate, own only 800 of the 1,050 shares outstanding immediately after the incorporation, Sec. 351 does not apply to provide nonrecognition treatment for Alan's transfer of property. As a result, Alan is taxed on his realized gain of $15,000, and Dexter Corporation has a cost (i.e., FMV) basis of $45,000 for the transferred property.

2. **(c)** The requirement is to determine Clark's basis for the Jet Corp. stock received in exchange for a contribution of cash and other property. Generally, no gain or loss is recognized if property is transferred to a corporation solely in exchange for stock, if immediately after the transfer, the transferors of property are in control of the corporation. Since Clark and Hunt both transferred property solely in exchange for stock, and together own all of the corporation's stock, their realized gains on the "other property" transferred are not recognized. As a result, Clark's basis for his Jet stock is equal to the $60,000 of cash plus the $50,000 adjusted basis of other property transferred, or $110,000. Hunt's basis for his Jet stock is equal to the $120,000 adjusted basis of the other property that he transferred.

3. **(d)** The requirement is to determine Carr's recognized gain on the transfer of appreciated property in connection with the organization of Flexo Corp. No gain or loss is recognized if property is transferred to a corporation solely in exchange for stock, if the transferors of property are in

control of the corporation immediately after the exchange. "Control" means that the transferors of property must, in the aggregate, own at least 80% of the corporation's stock immediately after the exchange. Since both Beck and Carr transferred property in exchange for stock, and in the aggregate they own 90% of Flexo's stock immediately after the exchange, the requirements for nonrecognition are met.

4. **(d)** The requirement is to determine the percentage of Nu's stock that Jones must own to qualify for a tax-free incorporation. No gain or loss is recognized if property is transferred to a corporation solely in exchange for stock and the transferor(s) are in control of the corporation immediately after the exchange. For this purpose, the term "control" means the ownership of at least 80% of the combined voting power of stock entitled to vote, and at least 80% of each class of nonvoting stock.

5. **(c)** The requirement is to determine Feld's stock basis following the contribution of a parcel of land to his solely owned corporation. When a shareholder makes a contribution to the capital of a corporation, no gain or loss is recognized to the shareholder, the corporation has a transferred (carryover) basis for the property, and the shareholder's original stock basis is increased by the adjusted basis of the additional property contributed. Here, Feld's beginning stock basis of $50,000 is increased by the $10,000 basis for the contributed land, resulting in a stock basis of $60,000.

6. **(a)** The requirement is to determine whether gain or loss is recognized on the incorporation of Rela Associates (a partnership). No gain or loss is recognized if property is transferred to a corporation solely in exchange for stock, if immediately after the transfer, the transferor is in control of the corporation. For purposes of determining whether consideration other than stock (boot) has been received, the assumption of liabilities by the transferee corporation is not to be treated as the receipt of money or other property by the transferor. Thus, Rela Associates recognizes no gain or loss on the transfer of its assets and liabilities to a newly formed corporation in return for all of the corporation's stock.

Also note that no gain or loss will be recognized by Rela Associates on the distribution of the corporation's stock to its partners in liquidation, and no gain or loss will be recognized by the partners when they receive the corporation's stock in liquidation of their partnership interests.

7.   (d)   The requirement is to determine the taxable income to Rogers and the basis of her stock. Since services are excluded from the definition of "property," Rogers' transfer does not fall under the nonrecognition provision of Sec. 351. Rogers must report $10,000 of compensation income and the basis for the stock is $10,000, the amount reported as income.

B.   Sec. 1244 Stock

8.   (c)   The requirement is to determine which statement is **not** a requirement for stock to qualify as Sec. 1244 small business corporation stock. To qualify as Sec. 1244 small business corporation stock, the stock must be issued by a domestic corporation to an individual or partnership in exchange for money or property (other than stock or securities). Any type of stock can qualify, whether common or preferred, voting or nonvoting.

9.   (b)   The requirement is to determine the character of Dinah's recognized loss from the sale of Sec. 1244 stock to be reported on her joint income tax return for 2002. Sec. 1244 permits an individual to deduct an ordinary loss on the sale or worthlessness of stock. The amount of ordinary loss deduction is annually limited to $50,000 ($100,000 for a married taxpayer filing a joint return), with any excess loss treated as a capital loss. Since Dinah is married filing a joint return, her ordinary loss is limited to $100,000, with the remaining $25,000 recognized as a capital loss.

10.   (c)   The requirement is to determine the amount and character of Nancy's recognized loss resulting from the sale of Sec. 1244 stock for $35,000 in 2002. Sec. 1244 permits a single individual to annually deduct up to $50,000 of ordinary loss from the sale or exchange of small business corporation stock. Since Nancy acquired her stock in a tax-free asset transfer under Sec. 351, her stock's basis is $80,000 and the sale of the stock for $35,000 results in a loss of $45,000. However, because the property that Nancy transferred in exchange for the stock had an adjusted basis ($80,000) in excess of its fair market value ($60,000), the stock's basis must be reduced by the excess ($20,000) for purposes of determining the amount that can be treated as an ordinary loss. Thus, the amount of ordinary loss is limited to $60,000 – $35,000=$25,000, with the remaining loss ($45,000 – $25,000 = $20,000) treated as a capital loss.

C.1.   Filing and Payment of Tax

11.   (d)   The requirement is to determine the correct statement concerning the imposition of a civil fraud penalty on a corporation. If part of a tax underpayment is the result of fraud, a fraud penalty equal to 75% of the portion of the underpayment attributable to fraud will be assessed. Fraud differs from simple, honest mistakes and negligence. Fraud involves a taxpayer's actual, deliberate, or intentional wrongdoing with the specific purpose to evade a tax believed to be owing. Examples of conduct from which fraud may be inferred include keeping a double set of books; making false entries or alterations, false invoices or documents; destroying books or records; and, concealing assets or covering up sources of income. Answers (a), (b), and (c) are incorrect because omitting income as a result of inadequate recordkeeping, erroneously failing to report income, and filing an incomplete return with a statement attached making clear that the return is incomplete, do not constitute deliberate actions with the specific intent of evading tax.

12.   (a)   The requirement is to determine whether Bass Corp. has to pay interest on the $400 tax payment made in 2003 and/or a tax delinquency penalty. A corporation is generally required to make estimated tax payments and to pay all of its remaining tax liability on or before the original due date of its tax return. Filing for an extension of time to file the tax return does not extend the time to pay the tax liability. If any amount of tax is not paid by the original due date, interest must be paid from the due date until the tax is paid. Additionally, a failure-to-pay tax delinquency penalty will be owed if the amount of tax paid by the original due date of the return is less than 90% of the tax shown on the return. The failure-to-pay penalty is imposed at a rate of 0.5% per month (or fraction thereof), with a maximum penalty of 25%. The penalty is imposed on the amount of unpaid tax at the beginning of the month for which the penalty is being computed. Bass Corp. is not subject to the failure-to-pay delinquency penalty because it paid in 95% of the total tax shown on its return by the original due date of the return.

13.   (b)   The requirement is to determine whether Edge Corp. could compute its first quarter 2003 estimated income tax payment using the annualized income method and/or the preceding year method. A corporation generally must pay four installments of estimated tax, each equal to 25% of its required annual payment. A penalty for the underpayment of estimated taxes can be avoided if a corporation's quarterly estimated payments are at least equal to the least of (1) 100% of the tax shown on the current year's tax return, (2) 100% of the tax that would be due by placing the current year's income for specified monthly periods on an annualized basis, or (3) 100% of the tax shown on the corporation's return for the preceding year. However, the preceding year's tax liability cannot be used to determine estimated payments if no tax liability existed in the preceding year or a short-period tax return was filed for the preceding year.

14.   (b)   The requirement is to determine which statements are correct in regard to the reopening of a tax year after the statute of limitations have expired. The statute of limitations stipulate a time limit for the government's assessment of tax or a taxpayer's claim for refund. The normal period for the statute of limitations is the later of three years after a return is filed, or three years after the due date of the return. A six-year statute of limitations will apply if the gross income omitted from the return exceeds 25% of the gross income reported on the return. If a taxpayer's return was false or fraudulent with the intent to evade tax, or the taxpayer engaged in a willful attempt to evade tax, there is no statute of limitations. If a tax return has a 50% non-fraudulent omission from gross income, there would be a six-year statute of limitations. However, once the six-year period expired, the year could not be reopened. In contrast, a closed year can be reopened if a corporation prevails in a determination allowing a deduction in an open year that the taxpayer erroneously had taken in a closed tax year. This special rule for the reopening of a tax year is intended to prevent the double inclusion of an item of income, or the double allowance of a deduction or credit that would otherwise occur.

15. (a)   Even though a corporation's penalty for underpaying federal estimated taxes is in the nature of interest, it is treated as an addition to tax, and as such, the penalty is not deductible.

16. (c)   The requirement is to determine which methods of estimated tax payment can be used by Blink Corp. to avoid the penalty for underpayment of federal estimated taxes. Generally, to avoid a penalty for the underpayment of estimated taxes a corporation's quarterly estimated payments must be at least equal to the least of (1) 100% of the tax shown on the current year's tax return, (2) 100% of the tax that would be due by placing income for specified monthly periods on an annualized basis, or (3) 100% of the tax shown on the corporation's return for the preceding year, provided the preceding year showed a positive tax liability and consisted of twelve months. In this case, Blink cannot base its estimated payments on its preceding year because Blink had a net operating loss for 2002.

17. (d)   The requirement is to indicate whether corporate tax credits and the alternative minimum tax must be taken into account for purposes of computing a corporation's estimated income tax payments. A corporation must make estimated tax payments unless its tax liability can reasonably be expected to be less than $500. A corporation's estimated tax is its expected tax liability (including the alternative minimum tax) less its allowable tax credits.

18. (c)   The requirement is to determine the minimum estimated tax payments that must be made by Finbury Corporation to avoid the estimated tax underpayment penalty for 2003. Since Finbury is a large corporation (i.e., a corporation with taxable income of $1,000,000 or more in any of its three preceding tax years), its estimated tax payments must be at least equal to 100% of its 2003 tax liability.

C.2.a.   Corporate Tax Rates

19. (b)   The requirement is to determine Kisco's income tax before credits given $70,000 of taxable income before a dividends received deduction that included a $10,000 dividend from a 15%-owned taxable domestic corporation. Since the $10,000 dividend would be eligible for a 70% dividends received deduction, Kisco's taxable income would be reduced by $7,000, resulting in taxable income of $63,000. The computation of tax would be

$50,000	x	15%	=	$ 7,500
$13,000	x	25%	=	3,250
		Tax	=	$10,750

C.2.c.   Alternative Minimum Tax (AMT)

20. (b)   The requirement is to determine the adjustment for adjusted current earnings (ACE) that will be used in the computation of Green Corp.'s alternative minimum tax for 2002. The ACE adjustment is equal to 75% of the difference between ACE and pre-ACE alternative minimum taxable income (AMTI). The ACE adjustment can be positive or negative, but a negative ACE adjustment is limited in amount to prior years' net positive ACE adjustments. For 2001, Green had a positive ACE adjustment of ($400,000 – $300,000) x 75% = $75,000. For 2002, Green's ACE is less than its pre-ACE AMTI leading to a negative ACE adjustment of ($100,000 – $300,000) x 75% = $150,000. However, this negative ACE adjustment is allowed only to the extent of $75,000, the amount of Green's net positive adjustment for prior years.

21. (a)   The requirement is to determine Eastern's alternative minimum taxable income before the adjusted current earnings (ACE) adjustment. The starting point for computing a corporation's alternative minimum taxable income (AMTI) is its regular taxable income, which is then increased by tax preferences, and increased or decreased by specified adjustments. One tax preference that must be added to a corporation's regular taxable income is the amount of tax-exempt interest from private activity bonds. One adjustment that must be made to convert regular taxable income to AMTI is the adjustment for depreciation on personal business property placed in service after 1986. For regular tax purposes, Eastern utilized the general MACRS depreciation system and would have used the 200% declining balance method for computing regular tax depreciation on the five-year property placed in service during 2002. However, for AMT purposes, depreciation on five-year property must be computed using the 150% declining balance method. In this case, it means that Eastern's regular tax depreciation exceeded its allowable AMT depreciation by $1,000, and this amount must be added back to regular taxable income to arrive at AMTI. Thus, Eastern's AMTI (before ACE adjustment) is its regular taxable income of $300,000, plus its $5,000 of tax-exempt interest from private activity bonds and $1,000 of depreciation adjustment, or $306,000.

22. (c)   The requirement is to determine the correct statement regarding the amount of excess of a corporation's tentative minimum tax over its regular tax. If a corporation's tentative minimum tax exceeds its regular tax, the excess represents the corporation's alternative minimum tax and is payable in addition to its regular tax.

23. (c)   The requirement is to determine the exempt portion of Rona Corp.'s alternative minimum taxable income (AMTI). A corporation is allowed an exemption of $40,000 in computing its AMTI. However, the $40,000 exemption is reduced by 25% of the corporation's AMTI in excess of $150,000. Here, the amount of exemption is $40,000 – [($200,000 – $150,000) x 25%] = $27,500.

24. (c)   The requirement is to determine which item is a tax preference that must be included in the computation of a corporation's alternative minimum tax (AMT) for 2002. Tax-exempt interest on private activity bonds is a tax preference item. Answer (a) is incorrect because it is the excess of income under the percentage-of-completion method over the amount reported using the completed-contract method that is a positive adjustment in computing the AMT. Answer (b) is incorrect because a deduction for casualty losses is allowed in the computation of AMT. Answer (d) is incorrect because capital gains are not a preference item in computing the AMT.

25. **(b)** For real property that was placed in service before January 1, 1999, an AMT adjustment is necessary because for AMT purposes, real property must be depreciated using the straight-line method over a forty-year recovery period, rather than the thirty-nine year or twenty-seven and one-half year recovery period used for regular tax purposes. However, note that this *adjustment has been eliminated for real property first placed in service after December 31, 1998.* The dividends received deduction, charitable contributions, and investment interest expense are neither adjustments nor tax preference items.

26. **(d)** The requirement is to determine when a corporation will not be subject to the alternative minimum tax (AMT) for 2002. A corporation is exempt from AMT for its first tax year. After the first year, a corporation is exempt from AMT for each year that it passes a gross receipts test. A corporation is exempt for its second year if its gross receipts for the first year did not exceed $5 million. For all subsequent years, a corporation is exempt if its average annual gross receipts for the testing period do not exceed $7.5 million. Exemption from the AMT is not based on asset size nor number of shareholders.

27. **(c)** A corporation is exempt from the corporate AMT for its first tax year. It is exempt for its second year if its first year's gross receipts were $5 million or less. To be exempt for its third year, the corporation's average gross receipts for the first two years must be $7.5 million or less. To be exempt for the fourth year (and subsequent years), the corporation's average gross receipts for all prior three-year periods also must be $7.5 million or less. Here, Bradbury is exempt for 2001 because its average gross receipts for 1999-2000 were $6.75 million. However, Bradbury loses its exemption for 2002 and all subsequent years because its average gross receipts for 1999-2001 exceed $7.5 million ($7.67 million).

C.3. Gross Income

28. **(a)** The requirement is to indicate whether personal service corporations and personal holding companies must include 100% of dividends received from unrelated taxable domestic corporations in gross income in computing regular taxable income. Since the question concerns **gross income,** not taxable income, no part of the dividend income would be offset by a dividends received deduction. Therefore, both personal service corporations and personal holding companies must include 100% of dividends received from unrelated taxable domestic corporations in gross income.

29. **(d)** The requirement is to determine the amount of bond sinking fund trust income taxable to Andi Corp. in 2002. Since the trust income will be accumulated and benefit Andi Corp. by reducing the amount of future contributions that Andi must make to the bond sinking fund, all of the trust income, consisting of $60,000 of interest and $8,000 of long-term capital gain, is taxable to Andi Corp.

30. **(a)** The requirement is to determine the amount of capital gain recognized by Lee Corp. on the sale of its treasury stock. A corporation will never recognize gain or loss on the receipt of money or other property in exchange for its stock, including treasury stock.

31. **(d)** The requirement is to determine the amount of gain to be recognized by Ral Corp. when it issues its stock in exchange for land. No gain or loss is ever recognized by a corporation on the receipt of money or other property in exchange for its own stock (including treasury stock).

32. **(c)** The requirement is to determine the amount of dividend reportable by a corporate distributee on a property distribution. The amount of dividend to be reported by a corporate distributee is the FMV of the property less any liability assumed. Kile's dividend would be $12,000, reduced by the liability of $5,000 = $7,000.

C.4.b. Organizational Expenditures

33. **(d)** The requirement is to determine which costs are amortizable organizational expenditures. A corporation's organizational expenditures can be amortized over a period of not less than sixty months, beginning with the month that business begins. Organizational expenditures include fees for accounting and legal services incident to incorporation (e.g., fees for drafting corporate charter, bylaws, terms of stock certificates), expenses of organizational meetings and of temporary directors meetings, and fees paid to the state of incorporation. However, the costs incurred in issuing and selling stock and securities (e.g., professional fees to issue stock, printing costs, underwriting commissions) do not qualify as organizational expenditures and are not tax deductible.

34. **(d)** The requirement is to determine the maximum amount of Brown Corp.'s deduction for the amortization of organizational expenditures. A corporation's organizational expenditures can be amortized over a period of not less than sixty months, beginning with the month that the corporation begins business. Brown's amortizable organizational expenditures include the $40,000 of legal fees to obtain a corporate charter, but exclude underwriting commissions and other stock issue costs. These underwriting commissions and other stock issue costs are not deductible, and merely reduce Brown's paid-in capital. Since Brown began active business operations in July, Brown's maximum amortization deduction is $40,000 x 6/60 = $4,000.

35. **(c)** The requirement is to determine the correct statement regarding the costs of organizing a corporation. A corporation's organizational expenditures (e.g., legal fees for drafting the corporate charter, bylaws, and terms of original stock certificates, necessary accounting services, expenses of temporary directors, fees paid to the state of incorporation) are incidental to the creation of the corporation and have value throughout the life of the corporation. For tax purposes, a corporation may elect to amortize its organization costs over a period of not less than sixty months even if those costs are capitalized on the corporation's books. The election is made by attaching a statement to the corporation's tax return for the tax year in which the corporation begins business, and amortization begins with the month that the corporation begins business.

36. **(a)** The requirement is to determine the maximum deduction for amortization of organizational expenditures for a calendar-year corporation. A corporation's organizational expenditures can be amortized ratably over a period of not less than sixty months, beginning with the month in which the corporation begins business. Since the organizational expenditures total $9,000 and the corporation began business in September, the maximum amount of amortization for 2002 would be ($9,000 x 4/60) = $600.

C.4.c.   Charitable Contributions

37.   (c)   The requirement is to determine the amount of Jackson Corp.'s charitable contributions carryover to 2003. A corporation's charitable contributions deduction is limited to 10% of its taxable income computed before the deduction for charitable contributions, the dividends received deduction, and before deductions for a NOL carryback and capital loss carryback. Although the limitation is computed before deducting NOL and capital loss carrybacks, NOL and capital loss carryforwards are deducted in arriving at the contribution base amount. Thus, of the $8,000 given to charitable organizations during 2002, $2,500 can be currently deducted, leaving $5,500 to be carried over to 2003.

Gross income from operations	$100,000
Dividend income	10,000
Operating expenses	(35,000)
Officers' salaries	(20,000)
NOL carryover from 2001	(30,000)
TI before contributions and DRD	$ 25,000
	x 10%
Contributions deduction for 2002	$ 2,500

38.   (b)   The requirement is to determine the amount that Cable Corp. can deduct for charitable contributions for 2002. A corporation's charitable contribution deduction is limited to 10% of its taxable income computed before the charitable contribution and dividends received deductions. Since Cable's taxable income of $820,000 already included a $40,000 dividends received deduction, $40,000 must be added back to arrive at Cable's contribution base of $860,000. Thus, Cable's maximum contribution deduction for 2002 would be limited to $860,000 x 10% = $86,000. Cable would deduct the $80,000 contributed during 2002, plus $6,000 of its $10,000 carryover from 2001. This means that Cable will have a $4,000 contributions carryover from 2001 to 2003.

39.   (c)   The requirement is to select the correct statement regarding a corporation's charitable contributions in excess of the limitation for deductibility in a particular year. Charitable contributions in excess of the 10% of taxable income limitation may be carried forward to a maximum of five succeeding years. The contributions actually made during a later year plus any carryforwards are also subject to a 10% limitation. Contributions actually made during a taxable year are deducted before carryforwards.

40.   (d)   The requirement is to determine the **maximum** charitable contribution deduction that Tapper Corp. may take on its 2002 return. Since Tapper is an accrual method calendar-year corporation, it can deduct contributions actually made during 2002, plus Tapper can elect to deduct any contribution authorized by its board of directors during 2002, so long as the contribution is subsequently made no later than 2 1/2 months after the end of the tax year. Thus, to maximize its deduction for 2002, Tapper can deduct both the $10,000 contribution made during 2002 as well as the $30,000 contribution authorized during 2002 and paid on February 1, 2003. The total ($40,000) is deductible for 2002 since it is less than the limitation amount ($500,000 x 10% = $50,000).

41.   (a)   The requirement is to determine the amount to be included as gross income in Lyle Corp.'s 2002 return for the receipt of nonprescription drug samples that were later

donated to an exempt organization. When unsolicited samples of items that are normally inventoried and sold in the ordinary course of business are received from a supplier, and later donated as a charitable contribution, the fair market value of the items received must be included in gross income. The taxpayer is then allowed a charitable contribution deduction equal to the fair market value of the items donated.

42.   (d)   The requirement is to determine the portion of the dividends received of $1,000 that is to be included in taxable income when Nale Corp. computes its maximum allowable deduction for contributions. A corporation's maximum allowable deduction for charitable contributions is limited to 10% of its taxable income before the charitable contributions and dividends received deductions. Thus, Nale must include all $1,000 of dividends in its taxable income for purposes of computing its maximum allowable deduction for contributions.

43.   (a)   The requirement is to determine the contribution base for purposes of computing Gero Corp.'s charitable contributions deduction. A corporation's contribution base is its taxable income before the charitable contributions deduction, the dividends received deduction, and before deductions for NOL and capital loss carrybacks. Since Gero had operating income of $160,000 after deducting $10,000 of contributions, its contribution base would be $160,000 + $10,000 + $2,000 dividends = $172,000.

44.   (c)   The requirement is to determine the maximum charitable contribution deduction for 2002. Since Norwood is an accrual-basis calendar-year corporation, it can elect to deduct a contribution authorized by its board of directors during 2002, so long as the contribution is subsequently paid no later than two and one-half months after year-end (i.e., by March 15th). Thus, to maximize its deduction for 2002, Norwood can elect to deduct the $10,000 contribution authorized during 2002 and paid on March 1, 2003, but its deduction is limited to 10% of taxable income before the charitable contribution deduction. The maximum amount deductible for 2002 is

Book income	$500,000
+ Charitable contribution	100,000
TI before CC deduction	$600,000
	x 10%
Maximum CC deduction	$ 60,000

The remaining $40,000 can be carried over a maximum of five years.

C.4.e.   Dividends Received Deduction (DRD)

45.   (d)   The requirement is to determine Best Corp.'s dividends received deduction for the $100,000 of dividends received from an unrelated domestic corporation. Dividends received from less than 20%-owned corporations are generally eligible for a 70% DRD (i.e., 70% x dividend). However, if the corporation's taxable income before the DRD is less than the amount of dividend, the DRD will be limited to 70% of taxable income, unless the full DRD (70% x dividend) creates or increases a net operating loss. Here, since taxable income before the DRD ($90,000) is less than the amount of dividends ($100,000), and the full DRD (70% x $100,000 = $70,000) would not create a NOL, the DRD is limited to 70% x $90,000 = $63,000.

46.   (c)   The requirement is to determine the amount to be reported as income before special deductions on Acorn's tax return. A corporation's taxable income before special deductions generally includes all income and all deductions except for the dividends received deduction. Thus, Acorn's income before special deductions would include the sales of $500,000 and dividend income of $25,000, less the cost of sales of $250,000, a total of $275,000.

47.   (b)   The requirement is to determine the correct statement regarding the corporate dividends received deduction (DRD). To qualify for a DRD, the investor corporation must own the investee's stock for more than forty-five days (ninety days for preferred stock if the dividends received are in arrears for more than one year). Answer (a) is incorrect because the DRD may be limited to the applicable percentage of the investor corporation's taxable income. Answer (c) is incorrect because a 70% DRD applies to dividends from less-than-20%-owned corporations, an 80% DRD applies to dividends from unaffiliated corporations that are at least 20%-owned, while a 100% DRD applies to dividends from corporations that are at least 80%-owned when a consolidated tax return is not filed.

48.   (b)   The requirement is to determine the amount of dividends to be included in Ryan Corp.'s taxable income. Since the dividends were received from less than 20%-owned taxable domestic corporations, they are eligible for a 70% dividends received deduction. Thus, the amount of dividends to be included in taxable income is $2,000 – (70% x $2,000) = $600.

49.   (b)   The requirement is to determine the amount of dividends to be included in Daly Corp.'s **taxable income** for 2002. Since the dividends were received from 20%-owned taxable domestic corporations, they are eligible for an 80% dividends received deduction. Thus, the amount of dividends to be included in taxable income is $1,000 – (80% x $1,000) = $200.

50.   (b)   The requirement is to determine the amount of dividends that qualifies for the 80% dividends received deduction. Only dividends received from taxable domestic unaffiliated corporations that are at least 20%-owned qualify for the 80% dividends received deduction ($7,500). So-called "dividends" paid by mutual savings banks are reported as interest, and are not eligible for the dividends received deduction.

C.4.j.   Losses

51.   (b)   The requirement is to determine Stark Corp.'s net operating loss (NOL) for 2002. A NOL carryover from 2001 would not be allowed in computing the 2002 NOL. In contrast, a dividends received deduction (DRD) is allowed in computing a NOL since a corporation's DRD is not subject to limitation if it creates or increases a NOL. Stark Corp.'s NOL would be computed as follows:

Gross income from operations	$ 350,000
Dividend income	100,000
Less operating expenses	(400,000)
TI before DRD	$ 50,000
DRD (70% x $100,000)	(70,000)
Net operating loss for 2002	$ (20,000)

52.   (b)   The requirement is to determine the proper treatment of a C corporation's net capital losses. A corporation's capital losses can only be used to offset capital gains. If a corporation has a net capital loss, it cannot be currently deducted, but instead must be carried back three years and forward five years as a STCL to offset capital gains in those years.

53.   (d)   The requirement is to determine the amount of Taylor Corp.'s 2002 net operating loss (NOL) that is available for use in its 2003 return. A net operating loss is generally carried back two years and forward twenty years to offset taxable income in the carryback and carryforward years. However, for NOLs arising in tax years ending in 2001 and 2002, a five-year carryback is available. Since Taylor Corp. made no election to waive a carryback period, the 2002 NOL would be used to offset Taylor's 1997 through 2001 taxable income in the five carryback years (a total of $105,000) leaving $200,000 – $105,000 = $95,000 to be carried forward as an NOL deduction in its 2003 return.

54.   (b)   The requirement is to determine the correct statement regarding the carryback or carryforward of an unused net capital loss. A corporation's unused net capital loss is carried back three years and forward for up to five years to offset capital gains in the carryback and carryforward years. An unused net capital loss is always carried back and forward as a short-term capital loss whether or not it was short-term when sustained.

55.   (d)   The requirement is to determine Haya Corporation's net operating loss (NOL) for 2002. A deduction for a net operating loss carryover is not allowed in computing a NOL. Furthermore, a deduction for charitable contributions is generally not allowed, since the charitable contributions deduction is limited to 10% of taxable income before the charitable contributions and dividends received deductions. Thus, Haya's NOL for 2002 would be computed as follows:

Gross income	$ 600,000
Less expenses	(800,000)
	$(200,000)
Add back contributions included in expenses	5,000
NOL for 2002	$(195,000)

56.   (c)   The requirement is to determine the NOL for 2002 given that deductions in the tax return exceed gross income by $56,800. In computing the NOL for 2002, the DRD of $6,800 would be fully allowed, but the $15,000 NOL deduction (carryover from 2001) would not be allowed. $56,800 – $15,000 = $41,800.

57.   (d)   The requirement is to determine the amount of casualty loss deduction available to Ram Corp. due to the complete destruction of its machine. If business property is completely destroyed, the amount of casualty loss deduction is the property's adjusted basis immediately before the casualty. Note that the "$100 floor" and "10% of adjusted gross income" limitations that apply to personal casualty losses, do not apply to business casualty losses.

C.4.l.   R&D Expenditures

58.   (a)   The requirement is to determine the proper treatment for qualifying research and experimentation expenditures. A taxpayer can elect to deduct qualifying research and experimentation expenditures as a current expense if the taxpayer so elects for the first taxable year in which the expenditures are incurred. Otherwise, the taxpayer must capitalize the expenditures. Then, if the capitalized costs are not subject to depreciation (because there is no determinable life), the taxpayer can amortize them over a period of sixty months or longer.

C.6. Reconcile Book and Taxable Income

59. **(c)** The requirement is to determine Kelly Corp.'s taxable income given net income per books of $300,000, that included $50,000 of dividend income and an $80,000 deduction for bad debt expense. Since the dividends were received from a 5%-owned taxable domestic corporation, they are eligible for a 70% dividends received deduction ($50,000 x 70% = $35,000). Since no bad debts were actually written off and the reserve method cannot be used for tax purposes, the $80,000 of bad debt expense per books is not deductible for tax purposes and must be added back to book income to arrive at taxable income. Kelly's taxable income is $300,000 – $35,000 + $80,000 = $345,000.

60. **(c)** The requirement is to determine Maple Corp.'s taxable income given book income before federal income taxes of $100,000. The provision for state income taxes of $1,000 that was deducted per books is also an allowable deduction in computing taxable income. The interest earned on US Treasury Bonds of $6,000 that was included in book income must also be included in computing taxable income. The $2,000 of interest expense on the bank loan to purchase the US Treasury Bonds was deducted per books and is also an allowable deduction in computing taxable income, because the interest income from the obligations is taxable. Since there are no differences between the book and tax treatment of these items, taxable income is the same as book income before federal income taxes, $100,000.

61. **(d)** The requirement is to determine Dodd Corp.'s taxable income given net income per books of $100,000. The $27,000 provision for federal income tax deducted per books is not deductible in computing taxable income. The $5,000 net capital loss deducted per books is not deductible in computing taxable income because a corporation can only use capital losses to offset capital gains. The life insurance premiums of $3,000 deducted per books are not deductible in computing taxable income because life insurance proceeds are excluded from gross income. Thus, Dodd Corp.'s taxable income is $100,000 + $27,000 + $5,000 + $3,000 = $135,000.

62. **(c)** The requirement is to determine Bard Corp.'s taxable income given book income of $450,000. No adjustment is necessary for the $4,000 of state corporate income tax refunds since they were included in book income and would also be included in taxable income due to the "tax benefit rule" (i.e., an item of deduction that reduces a taxpayer's income tax for a prior year must be included in gross income if later recovered). The life insurance proceeds of $15,000 must be subtracted from book income because they were included in book income, but would be excluded from taxable income. The net capital loss of $20,000 that was subtracted in computing book income must be added back to book income because a net capital loss is not deductible in computing taxable income. Thus, Bard Corp.'s taxable income would be $450,000 – $15,000 + $20,000 = $455,000.

63. **(c)** The requirement is to determine Dewey Corporation's taxable income, given that organization costs of $258,000 were deducted as an expense in arriving at book

income of $520,000. For tax purposes, organizational expenditures can be amortized over a minimum period of sixty months, beginning with the month in which the corporation begins business. Since Dewey began business in June, the allowable amortization for 2002 would be $258,000 x 7/60 = $30,100. Thus, adding back the $258,000 deduction for organization expense to book income, and subtracting the $30,100 of allowable amortization for tax purposes results in taxable income of $520,000 + $258,000 – $30,100 = $747,900.

64. **(c)** The requirement is to determine net income per books given TI of $700,000.

Taxable income	$700,000
Provision for federal income tax	– 280,000
Depreciation on tax return	+ 130,000
Depreciation per books	– 75,000
Life insurance proceeds	+ 100,000
Net income per books	$575,000

The provision for federal income tax is not deductible in computing TI but must be deducted per books. The life insurance proceeds are tax exempt, but must be included per books.

65. **(d)** The requirement is to compute Ajax's taxable income given book income of $1,200,000 and items included in the computation of book income. Book income must be adjusted for the tax-exempt interest (net of related expenses) and the provision for federal income tax:

Book income	$1,200,000
Municipal bond interest	(40,000)
Nondeductible interest expense (to produce tax-exempt interest income)	8,000
Provision for federal income tax	524,000
Taxable income	$1,692,000

The damages received for patent infringement that were included in book income are similarly included in taxable income, so no adjustment is necessary.

C.6.c. Schedule M-1

66. **(d)** The requirement is to determine the amount of income to be shown on the last line of Farve Corp.'s Schedule M-1 for 2002. Schedule M-1 provides a reconciliation of income reported per books with income reported on the tax return. Generally, items of income and deduction whose book and tax treatment differ, result in Schedule M-1 items. However, since Schedule M-1 reconciles to taxable income before the dividends received and net operating loss deductions, the dividends received deduction will not be a reconciling item on Schedule M-1. In this case, Farve Corp.'s $80,000 of book income would be increased by the $18,000 of federal income tax, $6,000 of net capital loss, and 50% of the $4,000 of business meals which were deducted per books, but are not deductible for tax purposes. Book income would be reduced by the $5,000 of municipal bond interest that is tax-exempt.

67. **(c)** The requirement is to determine Starke Corp.'s taxable income as reconciled on Schedule M-1 of Form 1120. Schedule M-1 provides a reconciliation of a corporation's book income with its taxable income before the dividends received and net operating loss deductions. Starke reported book income of $380,000 that included $50,000 of municipal bond interest income, and deductions for $170,000 of federal income tax expense and $2,000 of interest expense incurred to carry the municipal bonds. Since municipal bond interest is tax-exempt, the $50,000 of interest income must be subtracted from book income, and the $2,000 of interest expense incurred to carry the municipal bonds is not deductible and must be added back to book income. Similarly, the $170,000 of federal income tax expense is not deductible and must be added back to book income. Thus, Starke's taxable income is $380,000 – $50,000 + $2,000 + $170,000 = $502,000.

68. (**d**)   The requirement is to determine whether lodging expenses for out-of-town travel and the deduction of a net capital loss would be reported on Schedule M-1 of the US corporate income tax return (Form 1120). Schedule M-1 generally provides a reconciliation of a corporation's income per books with the corporation's taxable income before the NOL and dividends received deductions. Since a net capital loss deducted per books would not be deductible for tax purposes, the net capital loss would be added back to book income on Schedule M-1. However, since out-of-town lodging expenses are deductible for both book and tax purposes, the expenses would not appear on Schedule M-1.

69. (**c**)   The reconciliation of income per books with income per return is accomplished on Schedule M-1 of Form 1120. Both temporary differences (e.g., accelerated depreciation on tax return and straight-line on books) and permanent differences (e.g., tax-exempt interest) must be considered to convert book income to taxable income.

70. (**a**)   The requirement is to determine Media Corporation's net M-1 adjustment on its 2002 Form 1120. Generally, items of income and deduction whose book and tax treatment differ result in Schedule M-1 adjustments that reconcile income reported per books with taxable income. Media reported book income that included $6,000 in municipal bond interest income, and deductions that included $1,500 of interest expense incurred on debt to carry the municipal bonds, and $8,000 in advertising expense. Since municipal bond interest is tax-exempt, the $6,000 of interest income must be subtracted from book income. Additionally, since the $1,500 of interest expense to carry the municipal bonds is an expense incurred in the production of exempt income, it is not tax deductible and must be added back to book income. On the other hand, the $8,000 of advertising expense is deductible for book as well as taxable income purposes, and no Schedule M-1 adjustment is necessary. Thus, Media's net Schedule M-1 adjustment to reconcile book income to taxable income is $1,500 – $6,000 = ($4,500).

C.6.d.   Schedule M-2

71. (**d**)   The requirement is to determine the amount to be shown on Schedule M-2 of Form 1120 as Barbaro's retained earnings at December 31, 2002. Beginning with the balance at January 1, 2002, the end of year balance would be computed as follows:

Balance, 1/1/02	$600,000
Net income for year	+ 274,900
Federal income tax refund	+ 26,000
Cash dividends	– 150,000
Balance, 12/31/02	$750,900

72. (**a**)   The requirement is to determine the amount that should appear on the last line of Schedule M-2 of Form 1120. Schedule M-2 is an "Analysis of Unappropriated

Retained Earnings Per Books." Its first line is the balance at the beginning of the year and its last line is the balance at the end of the year. The end-of-year balance would be computed as follows:

Retained earnings, beginning	$ 50,000
Net income for year	+ 70,000
Contingency reserve	– 10,000
Cash dividends	– 8,000
Retained earnings, end of year	$102,000

D.   Affiliated and Controlled Corporations

73. (**d**)   The requirement is to determine the amount of dividend revenue to be reported on Bank Corp.'s consolidated tax return for the $48,000 of dividends received from Bank Corp.'s 80%-owned subsidiary, Shore Corp. Instead of filing separate tax returns, an affiliated group of corporations (i.e., corporations connected through 80% or more stock ownership) can elect to file a consolidated tax return. If a consolidated return is filed, dividends received from affiliated group members are eliminated in the consolidation process, and are not reported on the consolidated tax return.

74. (**d**)   The requirement is to determine the amount of net dividend income received from an affiliated corporation that should be included in Portal Corporation's 2002 consolidated tax return. When dividends are received from an affiliated corporation (i.e., at least 80%-owned subsidiary) during a consolidated return year, the intercompany dividends are eliminated in the consolidation process and are not included in gross income.

75. (**d**)   The requirement is to determine the amount of gain to be reported in the 2002 and 2001 consolidated tax returns. Generally, gains and losses on intercompany transactions during consolidated return years are deferred and reported in subsequent years when a restoration event occurs. Since Potter and Sly filed a consolidated tax return for 2001, Potter's gain on the sale of land to Sly in 2001 is deferred and will be reported when Sly sells the land outside of the affiliated group in 2002. Thus, the 2001 consolidated return will report no gain with regard to the land, while the 2002 consolidated return will report the aggregate amount of gain, $125,000 – $60,000 = $65,000.

76. (**b**)   The requirement is to determine the correct statement regarding an affiliated group of includible corporations filing a consolidated return. One of the advantages of filing a consolidated return is that operating losses of one member of the group offset operating profits of other members of the group. Answer (a) is incorrect because intercompany dividends are eliminated in the consolidation process and are excluded from the return. Answers (c) and (d) are incorrect because an affiliated group of includible corporations is also a controlled group and is therefore limited to one alternative minimum tax exemption and one accumulated earnings credit.

77. (**d**)   The requirement is to determine the stock ownership requirement that must be satisfied to enable Dana Corp. to elect to file a consolidated tax return that includes Seco Corp. For Dana and Seco to qualify for filing a consolidated tax return, Dana must directly own stock possessing at least 80% of the total voting power, and at least 80% of the total value of Seco stock.

78. (c) The requirement is to determine the correct statement regarding the filing of consolidated returns. The election to file consolidated returns is limited to affiliated corporations. Affiliated corporations are parent-subsidiary corporations that are connected through stock ownership wherein at least 80% of the combined voting power and value of all stock (except the common parent's) is directly owned by other includible corporations. Answer (a) is incorrect because brother-sister corporations are not affiliated corporations. Answer (b) is incorrect because no advance permission is required. Answer (d) is incorrect because an affiliated group's election to file consolidated returns is independent of its issuing financial statements on a consolidated basis.

79. (b) The requirement is to determine the amount of gain for 2002 that Subsidiary should take into account as a result of the 2001 sale of land to Parent. Since Parent and Subsidiary are filing consolidated tax returns, the $20,000 of gain to Subsidiary in 2001 is not recognized, but instead is deferred and recognized when the land is sold outside the affiliated group in 2002.

E. Dividends and Distributions

80. (c) The requirement is to determine the amount of the 2002 distributions classified as dividend income to Locke's shareholders. A corporation's distributions to shareholders on their stock are treated as a dividend to the extent of a corporation's current earnings and profits and/or accumulated earnings and profits. Here, the $80,000 distributed to shareholders would be treated as a dividend to the extent of Locke's current ($20,000) and accumulated ($30,000) earnings and profits, or $50,000.

81. (c) The requirement is to determine the balance of Chicago Corp.'s accumulated earnings and profits (AEP) at January 1, 2003. The AEP beginning balance of $100,000 would be reduced by the 2002 deficit of ($140,000), resulting in a deficit of ($40,000). Since distributions only pay out a corporation's positive AEP, and neither create nor increase a deficit in AEP, the AEP deficit of ($40,000) is not affected by the $30,000 distributed to shareholders.

82. (c) The requirement is to determine the amount of gain recognized by Salon, Inc. as a result of the distribution of property and liability to its sole shareholder. Generally, a corporation must recognize gain when it distributes appreciated property to a shareholder. The gain is measured by treating the corporation as if it had sold the property to the shareholder for its fair market value. However, if there is a liability on the property that is assumed by the shareholder and the amount of liability exceeds the property's fair market value, then the amount of liability is used to measure the gain. Here, Salon's recognized gain would total $10,000 liability – $3,000 basis = $7,000.

83. (c) The requirement is to determine the amount received from Kent Corp. that is taxable as dividend income to Reed for 2002. The term "dividend" means any distribution of property made by a corporation to its shareholders out of its current earnings and profits and/or accumulated earnings and profits. For distributions of property other than cash, the amount of distribution is the property's fair market value reduced by any liabilities that are assumed or liabilities to which the property is subject. In this case, the amount

of distribution made by Kent Corp. to Reed is the property's fair market value of $200,000. This $200,000 of distribution is taxable as dividend income to Reed to the extent of Kent Corp.'s current earnings and profits ($60,000) and accumulated earnings and profits ($125,000), a total of $185,000. Note that this answer assumes that the gain that was recognized by Kent Corp. on the distribution ($200,000 FMV – $150,000 adjusted basis = $50,000) has already been included in the amount provided as Kent's current earnings and profits for 2002. This assumption can be made because the item indicates "Current earnings and profits for 2002," not "Current earnings and profits before the distribution." Also, note that the portion of the distribution that is not a dividend ($200,000 – $185,000 = $15,000) is a nontaxable return of Reed's stock basis, and reduces stock basis from $500,000 to $485,000.

84. (c) The requirement is to determine which statements are correct concerning Ridge Corp.'s cash distribution of $1,000,000 to its shareholders with respect to its stock. A corporation's distributions to shareholders on their stock will be taxed as dividend income to the extent of the corporation's current and accumulated earnings and profits. Any distributions in excess of earnings and profits are treated as a nontaxable return of stock basis, with any distributions in excess of a shareholder's stock basis treated as capital gain. Therefore, $750,000 of the distribution to Ridge's shareholders was taxable as a dividend, with the remaining $250,000 treated as a nontaxable return of stock basis.

85. (d) The requirement is to determine the amount of loss recognized by Tour Corporation on the nonliquidating distribution of property to shareholders. Although a gain would be recognized, no loss can be recognized on nonliquidating corporate distributions to shareholders.

86. (c) The requirement is to determine the amount taxable as a dividend to Kee's shareholders for 2002. Corporate distributions of property to shareholders on their stock are taxed as dividends to the extent of accumulated and/or current earnings and profits. Even though a corporation has an accumulated deficit in earnings and profits for prior years ($50,000 in this case), a distribution will nevertheless be taxed as a dividend to the extent of the corporation's earnings and profits for the current taxable year when measured at the end of the year. Thus, the $30,000 distribution will be taxed as a dividend to the extent of the current earnings and profits for 2002 of $10,000.

87. (c) The requirement is to determine the amount of taxable dividend income resulting from Dahl Corp.'s distribution of cash and land to Green. The amount of distribution received by Green equals the amount of cash ($9,000) plus the FMV of the land ($40,000), a total of $49,000. This $49,000 will be taxable as dividend income to Green to the extent that it is paid out of Dahl Corp.'s current and accumulated earnings and profits. Dahl had accumulated earnings and profits of $9,000 before consideration of the dividend declaration and distribution. Since a distributing corporation recognizes gain on the distribution of appreciated property, Dahl must recognize a gain of $40,000 – $5,000 = $35,000 on the distribution of the land. This $35,000 of gain increases Dahl Corp.'s available earnings and profits from $9,000 to $44,000. Thus, Green's $49,000 distribution will be taxed as a dividend to the extent of $44,000.

88. (b) The requirement is to determine the amount of the taxable dividend for an individual shareholder on a property distribution. A distributee shareholder is considered to have received a dividend equal to the fair market value of the property distributed less any liabilities assumed. In this case, Rowe received a taxable dividend of $7,000 ($12,000 – $5,000).

89. (d) The requirement is to determine the amount of dividend income taxable to the shareholder. If a corporation sells property to a shareholder for less than fair market value, the shareholder is considered to have received a constructive dividend to the extent of the difference between the fair market value of the property and the price paid. Thus, the shareholder's dividend income is $80,000 – $50,000 = $30,000.

90. (a) Distributions of property to shareholders reduce earnings and profits (E&P) by the greater of the property's adjusted basis, or its FMV at date of distribution. E&P must be adjusted by any gain recognized to the distributing corporation, and any liabilities to which the property being distributed is subject. Gelt Corporation would recognize a gain of $7,500 on the distribution (i.e., $14,000 FMV – $6,500 basis). The adjustments to E&P (before tax) would be

	E&P
Gain recognized	$ 7,500
Distribution of property (FMV)	(14,000)
Distribution of liability	5,000
Net decrease in E&P (before tax)	$ (1,500)

E.3. Stock Redemptions

91. (c) The requirement is to determine the tax effect of Mark's stock redemption. Since the redemption is a complete redemption of all of Mark's stock ownership, the redemption proceeds of $500,000 qualify for exchange treatment. Thus, Mark will report a capital gain of $500,000 – $300,000 = $200,000.

92. (a) The requirement is to determine how the gain resulting from a stock redemption should be treated by a noncorporate shareholder if the redemption qualifies as a partial liquidation of the distributing corporation. A corporate stock redemption is treated as an exchange, generally resulting in capital gain or loss treatment to a shareholder if the redemption meets any one of five tests. Redemptions qualifying for exchange treatment include (1) a redemption that is not essentially equivalent to a dividend, (2) a redemption that is substantially disproportionate, (3) a redemption that completely terminates a shareholder's interest, (4) a redemption of a noncorporate shareholder in a partial liquidation, and (5) a redemption to pay death taxes. If none of the above five tests are met, the redemption proceeds are generally treated as a dividend.

93. (b) The requirement is to determine the amount of interest and legal and accounting fees that were incurred in connection with Kara Corp.'s stock repurchase that is deductible for 2002. No deduction is allowed for any amount paid or incurred by a corporation in connection with the redemption of its stock, except for interest expense on loans to repurchase stock. Thus, the $100,000 of interest expense on loans used to repurchase stock is deductible, while the $400,000 of legal and accounting fees incurred in connection with the repurchase of stock is not deductible.

E.4. Complete Liquidations

94. (a) The requirement is to determine the correct statement regarding the expenses incurred in completely liquidating and dissolving a corporation. The general expenses incurred in the complete liquidation and dissolution of a corporation are deductible by the corporation as ordinary and necessary business expenses. These expenses include filing fees, professional fees, and other expenditures incurred in connection with the liquidation and dissolution.

95. (d) The requirement is to determine the usual result to the shareholders of a distribution in complete liquidation of a corporation. Amounts received by shareholders in complete liquidation of a corporation are treated as received in exchange for stock, generally resulting in capital gain or loss because the stock was held as an investment. Because liquidating distributions are generally treated as received in a taxable exchange, any property received by shareholders will have a basis equal to fair market value.

96. (d) The requirement is to determine whether the unused carryovers for excess charitable contributions and net operating loss of a wholly owned subsidiary carryover to a parent corporation as a result of a tax-free complete liquidation of the subsidiary. When a parent corporation completely liquidates its 80% or more owned subsidiary under Sec. 332, the liquidation is treated as a mere change in form and the parent corporation will not recognize any gain or loss on the receipt of liquidating distributions from its subsidiary. Similarly, the subsidiary corporation will not recognize any gain or loss on distributions to its parent corporation. As a result, there will be a carryover basis for all of the subsidiary's assets that are received by the parent corporation, as well as a carryover of all of the subsidiary's tax attributes to the parent corporation. The subsidiary's tax attributes that carryover to the parent include such items as earnings and profits, capital loss carryovers, accounting methods, and tax credit carryovers, as well as unused excess charitable contributions, and net operating losses.

97. (b) The requirement is to determine the amount of Kappes Corp.'s recognized loss resulting from the distribution of marketable securities in complete liquidation. Generally, a corporation will recognize gain or loss on the distribution of its property in complete liquidation just as if the property were sold to the distributee for its fair market value. Since the marketable securities were a capital asset and held for more than one year, the distribution results in a long-term capital loss of $150,000 – $100,000 = $50,000.

98. (d) When a parent corporation liquidates its 80% or more owned subsidiary, the parent corporation (as stockholder) will ordinarily not recognize any gain or loss on the receipt of liquidating distributions from its subsidiary.

99. (a) The requirement is to determine the recognized gain to Lark Corp. on the complete liquidation of its wholly owned subsidiary, Day Corp. No gain or loss will be recognized by a parent corporation (Lark Corp.) on the receipt of property in complete liquidation of an 80% or more owned subsidiary (Day Corp.).

100. (c) The requirement is to determine the amount of gain to be recognized by Green Corp. as a result of the distribution of installment notes in the process of liquidation. A corporation generally recognizes gain on the distribution of appreciated property in the process of liquidation. Thus, Green Corp. must recognize gain on the distribution of the notes to the extent that the FMV of the notes ($162,000) exceeds the basis of the notes ($90,000), or $72,000.

101. (d) The requirement is to determine Carmela's recognized gain from the sale of assets during a complete liquidation. Gain or loss is generally recognized by a corporation on the sale of property following the adoption of a plan of complete liquidation even if the corporation then distributes all of its assets within twelve months after the plan of liquidation is adopted. Carmela would recognize gain on the land of $75,000 ($150,000 – $75,000) and on the inventory of $22,500 ($66,000 – $43,500).

102. (d) The requirement is to determine the amount of gain that each Mintee Corp. shareholder should recognize as a result of a liquidating distribution from Mintee. Amounts received by noncorporate shareholders in complete liquidation of a corporation are treated as received in exchange for stock, generally resulting in capital gain or loss because the stock was held as an investment. Here the amount realized by each shareholder consists of $2,000 cash plus the $10,500 FMV of the land, for a total of $12,500. Since each shareholder's stock basis was $6,500, each shareholder has a gain of $12,500 – $6,500 = $6,000.

F.　Collapsible Corporations

103. (d) The requirement is to determine the necessary holding period for a corporation's stock in order for the collapsible corporation provisions to be imposed. If a corporation is collapsible, Sec. 341 may apply and require a shareholder to report ordinary income instead of capital gain regardless of how long the shareholder has held the corporation's stock.

104. (a) A shareholder owning more than 5% of the stock of a corporation that has been determined to be collapsible is generally denied capital gain treatment on a sale of stock. Instead, the shareholder must report all gain as ordinary income.

Sale price	$40,000
Basis	– 25,000
Ordinary income	$15,000

G.　Personal Holding Company and Accumulated Earnings Taxes

105. (b) The requirement is to determine what sources of income that Edge Corp. must consider to determine whether the income requirements for a personal holding company have been met. A corporation is a personal holding company if (1) five or fewer individuals own more than 50% of its stock at any time during the last half of its taxable year, and (2) at least 60% of its adjusted gross income is personal holding company income (e.g., dividends, interest, rent). The computation of the personal holding company income requirement includes only items that are included in gross income. Since interest on tax-exempt obligations would be excluded from gross income, tax-exempt interest would not be considered in determining whether the income requirement is met.

106. (a) The requirement is to determine which deduction(s) can be subtracted from taxable income in arriving at a corporation's undistributed personal holding company in-

come (UPHCI). A series of adjustments must be made to a corporation's taxable income in order to arrive at UPHCI. These adjustments include the deduction of federal income taxes (including AMT and foreign income taxes), and the deduction for a net capital gain (i.e., the excess of NLTCG over NSTCL) less the amount of federal income taxes attributable to the net capital gain. This deduction prevents a personal holding company from paying the PHC tax on its net long-term capital gains.

107. (c) The requirement is to determine which step(s) Dart Corp. can take to eliminate or reduce any 2002 accumulated earnings tax (AET). The AET is a penalty tax that can be imposed (in addition to regular income tax) on a corporation if it accumulates earnings in excess of reasonable business needs. To avoid the AET, Dart can demonstrate that the reasonable needs of its business require the retention of all or part of the 2002 accumulated taxable income. Additionally, Dart can reduce its accumulated taxable income by paying a dividend to its shareholders. For this purpose, any dividends paid within the first 2 1/2 months of the tax year are treated as if paid on the last day of the preceding tax year. Thus, Dart's payment of dividends by March 15, 2003, would reduce its exposure to the AET for 2002.

108. (d) The requirement is to determine the correct statement regarding the accumulated earnings tax (AET). The AET is a penalty tax that can be imposed on a corporation if it accumulates earnings in excess of reasonable business needs, regardless of the number of shareholders that the corporation has. Answer (a) is incorrect because the AET cannot be imposed on partnerships. Answer (b) is incorrect because a corporation that distributes all of its accumulated earnings would not be subject to the AET. Answer (c) is incorrect because the AET cannot be imposed on personal holding companies.

109. (a) The requirement is to determine whose ownership of the remaining 200 shares of common stock could make Zero Corp. (with 1,000 outstanding shares) a personal holding company. A corporation is a personal holding company if (1) at least 60% of its adjusted ordinary gross income is derived from investment sources (e.g., interest, dividends, royalties), and (2) five or fewer individuals own more than 50% of the value of its stock at any time during the last half of its taxable year. In determining whether the more than 50% stock ownership requirement is met, the constructive ownership rules of Sec. 544 apply. Under these rules, an individual is considered as owning the stock owned by his family including only brothers and sisters, spouse, ancestors, and lineal descendants. Additionally, stock owned by a corporation, partnership, estate, or trust is considered as being owned proportionately by its shareholders, partners, or beneficiaries. Here, Edwards directly owns 240 shares and if he were the beneficiary of an estate that owned 200 shares, Edwards would directly and constructively own 440 shares. Then with four other unrelated shareholders, each owning twenty shares, there would be five shareholders who directly or constructively own 520 shares, more than 50% of the corporation's outstanding stock.

110. (b) The requirement is to determine the status of Arbor Corp. A corporation is a personal holding company (PHC) if (1) five or fewer individuals own more than 50% of its stock during the last half of its taxable year, and (2) at least 60% of its adjusted gross income is derived from investment sources (e.g., dividends, interest, rents). Although the amount of dividends paid to its shareholders may affect the computation of the PHC tax, the amount of dividends paid has no effect on the determination of PHC status. Answer (a) is incorrect because a regulated investment company is a status obtained by registering under the Investment Company Act of 1940, and is not determined by the facts and circumstances present for any given year. Answer (c) is incorrect because the accumulated earnings tax does not apply to personal holding companies. Answer (d) is incorrect because all of Arbor's taxable income is subject to regular federal income tax.

111. (c)   The requirement is to determine the maximum amount of accumulated taxable income that may be subject to the accumulated earnings tax for 2002 if Kari Corp. takes only the minimum accumulated earnings credit. Since Kari is a manufacturing company that was first organized in 2002, it is entitled to a minimum accumulated earnings credit of $250,000. To determine its potential exposure to the accumulated earnings tax, its 2002 taxable income of $400,000 must be reduced by its federal income taxes of $100,000 and its minimum accumulated earnings credit of $250,000, to arrive at its maximum exposure of $50,000.

112. (d)   The requirement is to determine the amount that Hull, Inc. can deduct for dividends paid in the computation of its personal holding company (PHC) tax. The PHC tax is a penalty tax imposed at the highest individual tax rate on a corporation's undistributed personal holding company income. A PHC is allowed a dividends paid deduction that is subtracted from its adjusted taxable income in arriving at its undistributed personal holding company income. Hull's dividends paid deduction consists of the $20,000 of dividends actually paid to its shareholders during 2002, plus the $10,000 of consent dividends reported in its shareholders' individual income tax returns for 2002.

Consent dividends are hypothetical dividends that are treated as if they were paid on the last day of the corporation's tax year. Since consent dividends are taxable to shareholders but not actually distributed, shareholders increase their stock basis by the amount of consent dividends included in their gross income. The consent dividend procedure has the same result as an actual dividend distribution, followed by the shareholders making a capital contribution of the dividend back to the corporation.

113. (b)   The requirement is to determine the taxpayer to whom the personal holding company (PHC) income will be attributed. A corporation will be classified as a personal holding company if (1) it is more than 50% owned by five or fewer individuals, and (2) at least 60% of the corporation's adjusted ordinary gross income is PHC income. PHC income is generally passive income and includes dividends, interest, adjusted rents, adjusted royalties, compensation for the use of corporate property by a 25% or more shareholder, and certain personal service contracts involving a 25% or more shareholder. An amount received from a personal service contract is classified as PHC income if (1) some person other than the corporation has the right to designate, by name or by description, the individual who is to perform the services, and (2) the person so designated is (directly or constructively) a 25% or more shareholder. Here, since Benson owns 100% of Lund Corp. and Lund Corp. contracted with Magda specifying that Benson is to perform

personal services for Magda, the income from the personal service contract will be personal holding company income to Lund Corp.

114. (c)   The requirement is to determine the correct statement regarding the personal holding company (PHC) tax. The PHC tax should be self-assessed by filing a separate schedule 1120-PH along with the regular tax return Form 1120. Answer (a) is incorrect because the PHC tax is a penalty tax imposed in addition to regular federal income taxes. Answer (b) is incorrect because the PHC tax can only be imposed on corporations. Answer (d) is incorrect because the PHC tax can only be imposed if five or fewer individuals own more than 50% of the value of a corporation's stock. Thus, if a corporation's stock is owned by ten or more equal unrelated shareholders, the corporation cannot be a PHC.

115. (b)   The requirement is to determine the correct statement regarding the accumulated earnings tax (AET). The AET does not apply to corporations that are personal holding companies. Answer (a) is incorrect because the AET can apply regardless of the number of shareholders that a corporation has. Answers (c) and (d) are incorrect because the AET applies to corporations that accumulate earnings in excess of their reasonable business needs and is not dependent upon whether a corporation files a consolidated return or the number of classes of stock that a corporation has.

116. (c)   The requirement is to determine the correct statement concerning the personal holding company (PHC) tax. The personal holding company tax may be imposed if at least 60% of the corporation's adjusted ordinary gross income for the taxable year is personal holding company income, and the stock ownership test is satisfied. Answer (b) is incorrect because the stock ownership test is met if more than 50% of the corporation's stock is owned, directly or indirectly, by **five or fewer** stockholders. Answer (a) is incorrect because the PHC tax is a penalty tax imposed in addition to the regular corporate income tax. Answer (d) is incorrect because the PHC tax takes precedent over the accumulated earnings tax. The accumulated earnings tax does not apply to a personal holding company.

117. (d)   The requirement is to determine the correct statement concerning the accumulated earnings tax (AET). Answer (d), "The accumulated earnings tax can **not** be imposed on a corporation that has undistributed earnings and profits of less than $150,000," is correct because every corporation (even a personal service corporation) is eligible for an accumulated earnings credit of at least $150,000. Answer (a) is incorrect because the AET is not self-assessing, but instead is assessed by the IRS after finding a tax avoidance intent on the part of the taxpayer. Answer (b) is incorrect because the AET may be imposed regardless of the number of shareholders that a corporation has. Answer (c) is incorrect because the AET cannot be imposed on a corporation for any year in which an S corporation election is in effect because an S corporation's earnings pass through and are taxed to shareholders regardless of whether the earnings are actually distributed.

118. (d)   The requirement is to determine the amount on which Kee Holding Corp.'s liability for personal holding company (PHC) tax will be based. To be classified as a personal holding company, a corporation must meet both a "stock ownership test" and an "income test." The "stock ownership test" requires that more than 50% of the stock must be owned (directly or indirectly) by five or fewer individuals. Since Kee has eighty unrelated equal shareholders, the stock ownership test is not met. Thus, Kee is not a personal holding company and has no liability for the PHC tax.

119. (b) The accumulated earnings tax (AET) can be avoided by sufficient dividend distributions. The imposition of the AET does not depend on a stock ownership test, nor is it self-assessing requiring the filing of a separate schedule attached to the regular tax return. The AET cannot be imposed on personal holding companies.

120. (c) The personal holding company (PHC) tax may be imposed if more than 50% of a corporation's stock is owned by five or fewer individuals. The PHC tax cannot be imposed on partnerships. Additionally, small business investment companies licensed by the Small Business Administration are excluded from the tax. If a corporation's gross income arises solely from rents, the rents will not be PHC income (even though no services are rendered to lessees) and thus, the PHC tax cannot be imposed.

121. (d) A net capital loss for the current year is allowed as a deduction in determining accumulated taxable income for purposes of the accumulated earnings tax. A capital loss carryover from a prior year, a dividends received deduction, and a net operating loss deduction would all be added back to taxable income in arriving at accumulated taxable income.

122. (d) The minimum accumulated earnings credit is $250,000 for nonservice corporations; $150,000 for service corporations.

123. (a) The requirement is to determine Daystar's allowable accumulated earnings credit for 2002. The credit is the greater of (1) the earnings and profits of the tax year retained for reasonable business needs of $20,000; or (2) $150,000 less the accumulated earnings and profits at the end of the preceding year of $45,000. Thus, the credit is $150,000 – $45,000 = $105,000.

H. S Corporations

124. (d) The requirement is to determine the amount of the $7,200 of health insurance premiums paid by Lane, Inc. (an S corporation) to be included in gross income by Mill. Compensation paid by an S corporation includes fringe benefit expenditures made on behalf of officers and employees owning more than 2% of the S corporation' stock. Since Mill is a 10% shareholder-employee, Mill's compensation income reported on his W-2 from Lane must include the $7,200 of health insurance premiums paid by Lane for health insurance covering Mill, his spouse, and dependents. Note that Mill may qualify to deduct 70% of the $7,200 for AGI as a self-employed health insurance deduction, with the remainder of the health insurance premium deductible on Schedule A with other medical expenses if Mill itemizes deductions.

125. (b) The requirement is to determine Lazur's tax basis for the Beck Corp. stock after the distribution. A shareholder's basis for stock of an S corporation is increased by the pass-through of all income items (including tax-exempt income) and is decreased by distributions that are excluded from the shareholder's gross income. Here,

Lazur's beginning basis of $12,000 is increased by his 50% share of Beck's ordinary business income ($40,500) and tax-exempt income ($5,000) and is decreased by the $51,000 cash distribution excluded from his gross income, resulting in a stock basis of $6,500.

126. (d) The requirement is to determine the amount of income from Graphite Corp. (an S corporation) that should be included in Smith's 2002 adjusted gross income. An S corporation is a pass-through entity and its items of income and deduction flow through to be reported on shareholders' returns. Since Smith is a 50% shareholder, half of the ordinary business income ($80,000 x 50% = $40,000) and half of the tax-exempt interest ($6,000 x 50% = $3,000) would pass through to Smith. Since the income passed through to Smith would retain its character, Smith must include the $40,000 of ordinary income in gross income, while the $3,000 of tax-exempt interest retains its exempt characteristic and would be excluded from Smith's gross income. Smith's $12,000 of stock basis at the beginning of the year would be increased by the pass-through of the $40,000 of ordinary income as well as the $3,000 of tax-exempt income, to $55,000. As a result, the $53,000 cash distribution received by Smith would be treated as a nontaxable return of stock basis and would reduce the basis of Smith's stock to $2,000.

127. (a) The requirement is to determine the effect of the revocation statement on Dart Corp.'s S corporation election. A revocation of an S election will be effective if it is signed by shareholders owning more than 50% of the S corporation's outstanding stock. For this purpose, both voting and nonvoting shares are counted. Here Dart Corp. has a total of 100,000 shares outstanding. As a result, the revocation statement consented to by shareholders holding a total of 40,000 shares, would not be effective and would not terminate Dart Corp.'s S corporation election.

128. (d) The requirement is to determine the incorrect statement regarding S corporation eligibility requirements. The eligibility requirements restrict S corporation shareholders to individuals (other than nonresident aliens), estates, and certain trusts. Partnerships and C corporations are not permitted to own stock in an S corporation. However, an S corporation is permitted to be a partner in a partnership, and may own any percentage of stock of a C corporation, as well as own 100% of the stock of a qualified subchapter S subsidiary.

129. (b) The requirement is to determine the portion of the $310,000 distribution that must be reported as dividend income by Robert. Distributions from an S corporation are generally treated as first coming from its accumulated adjustment account (AAA), and then are treated as coming from its accumulated earnings and profits (AEP). A positive balance in an S corporation's AAA is generally nontaxable when distributed because it represents amounts that have already been taxed to shareholders during S years. In contrast, an S corporation's AEP represents earnings accumulated during C years that have never been taxed to shareholders, and must be reported as dividend income when received. In this case, the beginning balance in the AAA and shareholder stock basis must first be increased by the pass through of the $200,000 of ordinary income that is taxed to Robert for 2002. This permits the first $250,000 of the distribution to be nontaxable and will reduce the balance in the AAA to zero and Robert's stock basis to $50,000. The remaining $60,000 of distribution is a distribution of the corporation's AEP and must be reported as dividend income by Robert.

130. (b) The requirement is to determine the date on which Village Corp.'s S status became effective. A subchapter S election that is filed on or before the 15th day of the third month of a corporation's taxable year is generally effective as of the beginning of the taxable year in which filed. If the S election is filed after the 15th day of the third month, the election is generally effective as of the first day of the corporation's next taxable year. Here, Village Corp. uses a calendar year and its S election was filed on September 5, 2002, which is beyond the 15th day of the third month of the taxable year (March 15). As a result, Village's subchapter S status becomes effective as of the first day of its next taxable year, January 1, 2003.

131. (d) The requirement is to determine whether a shareholder's basis in the stock of an S corporation is increased by the shareholder's pro rata share of tax-exempt interest and taxable interest. An S corporation is a pass through entity and its items of income and deduction pass through to be reported on shareholder returns. As a result, a shareholder's S corporation stock basis is increased by the pass through of all items of income, including both taxable as well as tax-exempt interest. An S shareholder's stock basis must be increased by tax-exempt interest in order to permit a later distribution of that interest to be nontaxable.

132. (c) The requirement is to determine the amount of income that should be allocated to Zinco Corp.'s short S year when its S election is terminated on April 1, 2002. When a corporation's subchapter S election is terminated during a taxable year, its income for the entire year must be allocated between the resulting S short year and C short year. If no special election is made, the income must be allocated on a daily basis between the S and C short years. In this case, the daily income equals $310,250/365 days = $850 per day. Since the election was terminated on April 1, there would be ninety days in the S short year, and $850 x 90 = $76,500 of income would be allocated to the tax return for the S short year to be passed through and taxed to shareholders.

133. (d) The requirement is to determine the correct statement regarding the termination of an S election. Answer (d) is correct because an S election will be terminated if an S corporation has passive investment income in excess of 25% of gross receipts for three consecutive taxable years, if the corporation also has subchapter C accumulated earnings and profits at the end of each of those three years. Answer (a) is incorrect because an S corporation is permitted to have a maximum of seventy-five shareholders. Answer (b) is incorrect because a decedent's estate may be a shareholder of an S corporation. Answer (c) is incorrect because S corporations are allowed to make charitable contributions. Contributions separately pass through to shareholders and can be deducted as charitable contributions on shareholder returns.

134. (b) The requirement is to determine the amount of income from Manning (an S corporation) that should be reported on Kane's 2002 tax return. An S corporation's tax items are allocated to shareholders on a per share, per day

basis. Since Manning had income of $73,000 for its entire year, its per day income is $73,000/365 = $200. Since there are 100 shares outstanding, Manning's daily income per share is $200/100 = $2. Since Kane sold twenty-five of his shares on the 40th day of 2002 and held his remaining seventy-five shares throughout the year, the amount of income to be reported on Kane's 2002 return would be determined as follows:

75 shares	x	$2	x	365 days	=	$54,750
25 shares	x	$2	x	40 days	=	2,000
						$56,750

135. (d) The requirement is to determine the earliest date on which Ace Corp. (a calendar-year corporation) can be recognized as an S corporation. Generally, an S election will be effective as of the first day of a taxable year if the election is made on or before the 15th day of the third month of the taxable year. Since there was no change in shareholders during the year, all of Ace's shareholders consented to the election, and Ace met all eligibility requirements during the preelection portion of the year, its election filed on February 10, 2002, is effective as of January 1, 2002. Note that if either a shareholder who held stock during the taxable year and before the date of election did not consent to the election, or the corporation did not meet the eligibility requirements before the date of election, then an otherwise valid election would be treated as made for the following taxable year.

136. (c) The requirement is to determine the number of shares of voting and nonvoting stock that must be owned by shareholders making a revocation of an S election. A revocation of an S election may be filed by shareholders owning more than 50% of an S corporation's outstanding stock. For this purpose, both voting and nonvoting shares are counted. In this case, since the S corporation has a total of 50,000 voting and nonvoting shares outstanding, the shareholders consenting to the revocation must own more than 25,000 shares.

137. (b) The requirement is to determine the amount of increase for each shareholder's basis in the stock of Haas Corp., a calendar-year S corporation, for the year ended December 31, 2002. An S corporation shareholder's basis for stock is increased by the pass through of all S corporation income items (including tax-exempt income), and is decreased by all loss and deduction items, as well as nondeductible expenses not charged to capital. Since Haas has two equal shareholders, each shareholder's stock basis will be increased by 50% of the operating income of $50,000, and 50% of the interest income of $10,000, resulting in an increase for each shareholder of $30,000.

138. (d) The requirement is to determine the condition that will prevent a corporation from qualifying as an S corporation. Certain eligibility requirements must be satisfied before a corporation can make a subchapter S election. Generally, in order to be an S corporation, a corporation must have only one class of stock outstanding and have no more than seventy-five shareholders, who are either individuals, estates, or certain trusts. An S corporation may own any percentage of the stock of a C corporation, and 100% of the stock of a qualified subchapter S subsidiary.

139. (c) The requirement is to determine the correct statement regarding distributions to shareholders by an S corporation that has no accumulated earnings and profits.

S corporations do not generate any earnings and profits, but may have accumulated earnings and profits from prior years as a C corporation. If accumulated earnings and profits are distributed to shareholders, the distributions will be taxed as dividend income to the shareholders. However, if an S corporation has no accumulated earnings and profits, distributions are generally nontaxable and reduce a shareholder's basis for stock. To the extent distributions exceed stock basis, they result in capital gain.

140. (d) The requirement is to determine whether a corporation that has been an S corporation from its inception may have both passive and nonpassive income, and be owned by a bankruptcy estate. To qualify as an S corporation, a corporation must have seventy-five or fewer shareholders who are individuals (other than nonresident aliens), certain trusts, or estates (including bankruptcy estates). If a corporation has been an S corporation since its inception, there is no limitation on the amount or type of income that it generates, and it can have both passive and nonpassive income.

141. (b) The requirement is to determine Meyer's share of an S corporation's $36,500 ordinary loss. An S corporation's items of income and deduction are allocated on a daily basis to anyone who was a shareholder during the taxable year. Here, the $36,500 ordinary loss would be divided by 365 days to arrive at a loss of $100 per day. Since Meyer held 50% of the S corporation's stock for forty days, Meyer's share of the loss would be ($100 x 50%) x 40 days = $2,000.

142. (c) The requirement is to determine the period that a calendar-year corporation must wait before making a new S election following the termination of its S status during 2002. Generally, following the revocation or termination of an S election, a corporation must wait five years before reelecting subchapter S status unless the IRS consents to an earlier election.

143. (d) The requirement is to determine which will render a corporation ineligible for S corporation status. Answer (d) is correct because an S corporation is limited to seventy-five shareholders. Answers (a) and (b) are incorrect because a decedent's estate and a bankruptcy estate are allowed as S corporation shareholders. Although an S corporation may only have one class of stock issued and outstanding, answer (c) is incorrect because a difference in voting rights among outstanding common shares is not treated as having more than one class of stock outstanding.

144. (d) The requirement is to determine the correct statement with regard to the application of the "at-risk" rules to S corporations and their shareholders. The at-risk rules limit a taxpayer's deduction of losses to the amount that the taxpayer can actually lose (i.e., generally the amount of cash and the adjusted basis of property invested by the taxpayer, plus any liabilities for which the taxpayer is personally liable). The at-risk rules apply to S corporation shareholders rather than at the corporate level, with the result that the deduction of S corporation losses is limited to the amount of a shareholder's at-risk investment. The application of the at-risk rules does not depend on the type of income reported by the S corporation, are not subject to any elections made by S corporation shareholders, and are applied without regard to the S corporation's ratio of debt to equity.

145. (d) The requirement is to determine the item that may be deducted by an S corporation. Items having no special tax characteristics can be netted together in the computation of the S corporation's ordinary income or loss, with only the net amount passed through to shareholders. Thus, only ordinary items (e.g., amortization of organizational expenditures) can be deducted by an S corporation. Answer (a) is incorrect because foreign income taxes must be separately passed through to shareholders so that the shareholders can individually elect to treat the payment of foreign income taxes as a deduction or as a credit. Answer (b) is incorrect because a net Sec. 1231 loss must be separately passed through to shareholders so that the Sec. 1231 netting process can take place at the shareholder level. Answer (c) is incorrect because investment interest expense must be separately passed through to shareholders so the deduction limitation (i.e., limited to net investment income) can be applied at the shareholder level.

146. (d) The requirement is to determine the correct statement regarding an S corporation's Accumulated Adjustments Account (AAA). An S corporation that has accumulated earnings and profits must maintain an AAA. The AAA represents the cumulative balance of all items of the undistributed net income and deductions for S corporation years beginning after 1982. The AAA is generally increased by all income items and is decreased by distributions and all loss and deduction items except no adjustment is made for tax-exempt income and related expenses, and no adjustment is made for federal income taxes attributable to a taxable year in which the corporation was a C corporation. The payment of federal income taxes attributable to a C corporation year would decrease an S corporation's accumulated earnings and profits (AEP). Note that the amounts represented in the AAA differ from AEP. A positive AEP balance represents earnings and profits accumulated in C corporation years that have never been taxed to shareholders. A positive AAA balance represents income from S corporation years that has already been taxed to shareholders but not yet distributed. An S corporation will not generate any earnings and profits for taxable years beginning after 1982.

147. (b) The requirement is to determine the due date of a calendar-year S corporation's tax return. An S corporation must file its federal income tax return (Form 1120-S) by the 15th day of the third month following the close of its taxable year. Thus, a calendar-year S corporation must file its tax return by March 15, if an automatic six-month extension of time is not requested.

148. (c) The requirement is to determine the item for which an S corporation is not permitted a deduction. Compensation of officers, interest paid to nonshareholders, and employee benefits for nonshareholders are deductible by an S corporation in computing its ordinary income or loss. However, charitable contributions, since they are subject to percentage limitations at the shareholder level, must be separately stated and are not deductible in computing an S corporation's ordinary income or loss.

149. (d) An S corporation may have as many as seventy-five shareholders. However, an S corporation cannot have both common and preferred stock outstanding because an S corporation is limited to a single class of stock. Similarly, a partnership is not permitted to be a shareholder in an S corporation because all S corporation shareholders must be individuals, estates, or certain trusts. Additionally, an S corporation cannot have a nonresident alien as a shareholder.

150. (a) The requirement is to determine which is **not** a requirement for a corporation to elect S corporation status. An S corporation must generally have only one class of stock, be a domestic corporation, and confine shareholders to individuals, estates, and certain trusts. An S corporation need **not** be a member of a controlled group.

151. (b) The requirement is to determine the amount of loss from an S corporation that can be deducted by each of two equal shareholders. An S corporation loss is passed through to shareholders and is deductible to the extent of a shareholder's basis for stock plus the basis for any debt owed the shareholder by the corporation. Here, each share-holder's allocated loss of $45,000 ($90,000 ÷ 2) is deducti-ble to the extent of stock basis of $5,000 plus debt basis of $15,000, or $20,000. The remainder of the loss ($25,000 for each shareholder) can be carried forward indefinitely by each shareholder and deducted when there is basis to absorb it.

I. Corporate Reorganizations

152. (b) The requirement is to determine the correct statement regarding King Corp.'s acquisition of 90% of Jax-son Corp.'s voting common stock solely in exchange for 50% of King Corp.'s voting common stock. The acquisition by one corporation, in exchange **solely** for part of its voting stock, of stock of another corporation qualifies as a tax-free type B reorganization if immediately after the acquisition, the acquiring corporation is in control of the acquired corpo-ration. The term **control** means the ownership of at least 80% of the acquired corporation's stock. Since King Corp. will use solely its voting stock to acquire 90% of Jaxson Corp. the acquisition will qualify as a tax-free type B reor-ganization. Answer (c) is incorrect because there is no re-quirement concerning the minimum percentage of King Corp. stock that must be used. Answer (d) is incorrect be-cause a type B reorganization involves the acquisition of stock, not assets.

153. (a) The requirement is to determine whether a quali-fying reorganization is tax-free to the corporations and their shareholders. Corporate reorganizations are generally non-taxable. As a result, a corporation will not recognize gain or loss on the transfer of its assets, and shareholders do not recognize gain or loss when they exchange stock and securi-ties in parties to the reorganization. Here, Ace and Bate combine and form Carr, the only surviving corporation. This qualifies as a consolidation (Type A reorganization) and is tax-free to Ace and Bate on the transfer of their assets to Carr, and also is tax-free to the shareholders when they exchange their Ace and Bate stock for Carr stock. Similarly, the reorganization is tax-free to Carr when it issues its shares to acquire the Ace and Bate assets.

154. (c) The requirement is to determine whether the statements are applicable to type B reorganizations. In a type B reorganization, the acquiring corporation must use solely voting stock to acquire control of the target corpora-tion immediately after the acquisition. The stock that is used to make the acquisition can be solely voting stock of the acquiring corporation, or solely voting stock of the parent corporation that is in control of the acquiring corporation,

but not both. If a subsidiary uses its parent's stock to make the acquisition, the target corporation becomes a second-tier subsidiary of the parent corporation.

155. (d) The requirement is to determine Gow's recog-nized gain resulting from the exchange of Lad Corp. stock for Rook Corp. stock pursuant to a plan of corporate reor-ganization. No gain or loss is recognized to a shareholder if stock in one party to a reorganization (Lad Corp.) is ex-changed **solely** for stock in another corporation (Rook Corp.) that is a party to the reorganization.

156. (a) The requirement is to determine the item that is defined in the Internal Revenue Code as a corporate reor-ganization. Corporate reorganizations generally receive nonrecognition treatment. Sec. 368 of the Internal Revenue Code defines seven types of reorganization, one of which is listed. An "F" reorganization is a mere change in identity, form, or place of organization of one corporation. A stock redemption is not a reorganization but instead results in dividend treatment or qualifies for exchange treatment. A change of depreciation method or inventory method is a change of an accounting method.

157. (c) The requirement is to determine the correct statement concerning corporate reorganizations. Answer (b) is incorrect because the reorganization provisions do provide for tax-free treatment for certain corporate transactions. Specifically, shareholders will not recognize gain or loss when they exchange stock or securities in a corporation that is a party to a reorganization solely for stock or securities in such corporation, or in another corporation that is also a party to the reorganization. Thus, securities in corporations not parties to the reorganization are always treated as "boot." Answer (d) is incorrect because the term "a party to the re-organization" includes a corporation resulting from the reor-ganization (i.e., the consolidated company). Answer (a) is incorrect because a mere change in identity, form, or place of organization of one corporation qualifies as a Type F reorganization.

158. (a) The requirement is to determine which is not a corporate reorganization. A corporate reorganization is spe-cifically defined in Sec. 368 of the Internal Revenue Code. Sec. 368 defines seven types of reorganization, of which 3 are present in this item: Type A, a statutory merger; Type E, a recapitalization; and, Type F, a mere change in identity, form, or place of organization. Answer (a), a stock redemp-tion, is the correct answer because it is not a reorganization as defined by Sec. 368 of the Code.

159. (a) The requirement is to determine the amount of Claudio's net operating loss (NOL) carryover that can be used to offset Stellar's 2002 taxable income. The amount of Claudio's NOL ($270,000) that can be utilized by Stellar for 2002 is limited by Sec. 381 to the taxable income of Stellar for its full taxable year (before a NOL deduction) multiplied by the fraction

$$\frac{\text{Days after acquisition date}}{\text{Total days in the taxable year}}$$

This limitation is 185/365 days x $360,000 = $182,466. Additionally, since there was a more than fifty percentage point change in the ownership of Claudio, Sec. 382 limits the amount of Claudio's NOL carryover that can be utilized by Stellar to the fair market value of Claudio multiplied by the federal long-term tax-exempt rate. $1,500,000 \times 5\% =$ $75,000. However, for purposes of applying this limitation for the year of acquisition, the limitation amount is only available to the extent allocable to the days in Stellar's taxable year after the acquisition date.

$$\$75,000 \times 185/365 \text{ days} = \$38,014$$

NOTE: *The remainder of Claudio's NOL ($270,000 – $38,014 = $231,986) can be carried forward and used to offset Stellar's taxable income (subject to the Sec. 382 limitation) in carryforward years.*

160. (a)   The requirement is to determine the recognized gain to be reported by Mueller on the exchange of her Disco bond for Disco preferred stock. The issuance by Disco Corporation of its preferred stock in exchange for its bonds is a nontaxable "Type E" reorganization (i.e., a recapitalization). Since Mueller did not receive any boot, no part of her $400 realized gain is recognized.

161. (b)   The requirement is to determine the amount of recognized gain in a recapitalization. Since a recapitalization is a reorganization, a realized gain will be recognized to the extent that consideration other than stock or securities is received, including the FMV of an excess principal amount of securities received over the principal amount of securities surrendered. Since no securities were surrendered, the entire $10,500 FMV of the securities received by Roberts is treated as boot. However, in this case, Roberts recognized gain is limited to her realized gain ($91,000 + $10,500) – $95,000 = $6,500.

OTHER OBJECTIVE ANSWERS AND ANSWER EXPLANATIONS

Problem 1

1. **(F)** Eligibility requirements for a subchapter S corporation include the requirement that there can be no **nonresident** alien shareholder. However, eligibility requirements can be met if a shareholder is a resident alien.

2. **(F)** Eligibility requirements for S corporation status do not include size limitations based on assets, income, paid-in capital, or any other measure of size with the single exception of the seventy-five shareholder limit.

3. **(T)** For an election of subchapter S corporation status to be valid, all shareholders on the date of election, plus any shareholder who held stock during the taxable year but before the date of election, must consent to the election.

4. **(F)** Eligibility requirements for S corporation status limit the number of shareholders to seventy-five.

5. **(T)** To be eligible for S corporation status, a corporation can have only one class of stock issued and outstanding. A corporation will not be treated as having more than one class of stock solely because of differences in voting rights among the shares of common stock.

6. **(T)** Revocation of the S election may be caused by the consent of shareholders holding more than **50%** of the shares of stock of the corporation.

7. **(F)** Dividend income represents an item of income which must be separately passed through to shareholders to retain its identity as portfolio income.

8. **(F)** A shareholder's stock basis is increased by both an S corporation's taxable income and tax-exempt income.

9. **(F)** The pass-through of an S corporation's deductions and losses will first reduce the shareholder's stock basis to zero, and then the shareholder's basis for debt is reduced (but not below zero).

10. **(T)** A corporation that makes an S election that is effective for its first taxable year will not be subject to the built-in gains tax. The built-in gains tax is applicable to C corporations which later make an S corporation election.

Problem 2

1. **($900,000)** The problem states that Oak Corp. is an accrual-basis corporation. Since the net sales are already stated on an accrual basis, no adjustment is necessary for beginning and ending trade accounts receivable.

2. **($6,000)** The $20,000 of dividends received from an unrelated taxable domestic corporation are eligible for a dividends received deduction. Since the stock was traded on a "major stock exchange," it should be assumed that Oak owned less than 20% of the dividend-paying corporation and that the dividends qualify for a 70% DRD ($20,000 x 70% = $14,000).

3. **($0)** The $8,000 of interest income from municipal bonds is excluded from Oak's gross income.

4. **($0)** Oak's $10,000 of LTCG is offset by Oak's share of the partnership's LTCL.

5. **($79,000)** The $60,000 of earnings from the Tech Partnership represents the netting of Oak's share of the partnership's ordinary income of $79,000 and LTCL of $19,000. Since the $19,000 LTCL is a special loss item, it cannot be netted against ordinary income but instead must be reported as LTCL and be combined with Oak's $10,000 of LTCG. The resulting net LTCL of $9,000 ($19,000 LTCL – $10,000 LTCG) is not currently deductible, but instead must be carried back three years and forward five years to offset capital gains in the carryback and carryforward years.

6. **($0)** The $250,000 of life insurance proceeds resulting from the death of Oak's controller are excluded from Oak's gross income.

7. **($0)** The $5,000 refund of Oak's 2001 federal income tax is excluded from Oak's gross income because Oak's payment of federal income tax was not deductible.

8. **($525,000)** The cost of goods sold is already stated on the accrual basis and no adjustment is necessary.

9. **($125,000)** Since officers' compensation must be separately stated on Oak's tax return, the $75,000 of officers' compensation must be subtracted from salaries and wages, and separately deducted.

10. **($11,000)** Oak's deduction for bad debts is limited to the $11,000 of accounts receivable actually written off during the year.

11. **($90,000)** The payroll taxes and property taxes are fully deductible and no adjustment is necessary.

12. **($25,000)** The interest expense incurred for working capital purposes is fully deductible and no adjustment is necessary.

13. **($5,000)** The deduction for the $18,000 of charitable contributions is limited to 10% of Oak's taxable income before the charitable contributions and dividends received deductions. Before computing this limitation, it is necessary to first consider any remaining adjustments. After considering all remaining adjustments, the calculation of the charitable contributions deduction is computed as follows:

(1)	Sales (net)	$900,000	
	Dividends	20,000	
(5)	Partnership ordinary income	79,000	
	Total income		$999,000
(8)	Cost of goods sold	525,000	
(9)	Salaries and wages	125,000	
(9)	Officers' compensation	75,000	
(10)	Bad debts	11,000	
(11)	Taxes	90,000	
(12)	Interest	25,000	
(14)	Depreciation	80,000	
(15)	Other Expenses	18,000	
	Total deductions		(949,000)
	Taxable income before charitable contributions and dividends received deductions		$ 50,000

The maximum deduction allowed for charitable contributions is limited to 10% of taxable income before the charitable contribution deduction and the dividends received deduction. Therefore, $5,000 will be the maximum deduction allowed for Oak Corp. in 2002. The excess contributions ($18,000 – $5,000 = $13,000) will be carried forward for a period of five years.

14. ($80,000) Since straight-line depreciation is used for both book and tax purposes, no adjustment is necessary.

15. ($18,000) The $33,000 of other expenses must be reduced by the $15,000 of premiums paid on the keyman life insurance policy covering Oak's controller. No deduction is allowed for life insurance premiums on a policy for which Oak is the beneficiary.

16. ($0) The provision for federal income tax is not deductible in computing taxable income.

Problem 3

Reminder to Candidates:

Recall that an S corporation is a pass-through entity acting as a conduit to pass through items of income, deduction, and credit to be reported on the tax returns of its shareholders. S corporation items having special tax characteristics (e.g., portfolio income, deductions subject to percentage or dollar limitations, etc.) must be separately stated and listed on Schedule K and Schedule K-1 so that their special characteristics are preserved when reported on shareholder tax returns. Ordinary income and deduction items having no special tax characteristics are netted together in the computation of an S corporation's ordinary income or loss on page 1 of Form 1120-S.

Answers	Page 1 Form 1120-S	Schedule K-1
(1)	86,000	0
(2)	2,000	0
(3)	24,000	2,200
(4)	1,000	24,000
(5)	0	9,000
(6)	13,000	0
(7)	10,000	0
(8)	11,000	0
(9)	0	18,000
(10)	0	6,000
(11)	0	4,000
(12)	0	8,000

1. ($86,000; $0) Compensation paid to shareholder-employees is deductible in computing an S corporation's ordinary income or loss. Thus, the officer's compensation of $80,000 received by Carl Loreck (Eve's sole stockholder) is deductible in computing Eve's ordinary income. It is increased by the $6,000 of Loreck's medical expenses paid by Eve in item 6 below.

2. ($2,000; $0) The $6,000 of uncollectible accounts reflects the use of the reserve method per books. Since the specific charge-off method must be used for tax purposes, only the $2,000 of uncollectible accounts actually written off is deductible in computing Eve's ordinary income.

3. ($24,000; $2,200) Penalties or fines paid to any government agency or instrumentality because of a violation of law are not deductible. Since the $800 of parking fines resulted from the violation of law, the $800 is not deductible. On the other hand, the $2,200 of foreign income taxes must be shown separately on Schedule K-1 because Loreck may either deduct the taxes as an itemized deduction or may use the taxes as a foreign tax credit on his own return. Therefore, the $27,000 of taxes per books must be reduced by the $800 of parking fines and the $2,200 of foreign income taxes to arrive at the $24,000 of taxes that are deductible in computing Eve's ordinary income.

4. ($1,000; $24,000) The maximum Sec. 179 expense election is $24,000 for 2002. Since this limitation applies at both the S corporation and shareholder levels, the $24,000 of Sec. 179 expense election must be separately shown on Schedule K-1, and will pass through as $24,000 of Sec. 179 expense election to Loreck. Thus, the $25,000 of depreciation must be reduced by $24,000 to arrive at the $1,000 of depreciation deductible in computing Eve's ordinary income.

5. **($0; $9,000)** An S corporation's charitable contributions are not subject to percentage limitations at the corporate level. Instead, charitable contributions must be separately shown on Schedule K-1, and will pass through as charitable contributions so that percentage limitations can be applied on Loreck's return.

6. **($13,000; $0)** The medical expenses and other fringe benefits paid on behalf of a more than 2% shareholder are deductible by the S corporation as compensation and are includible in the shareholder-employee's gross income. Since Loreck is the sole shareholder of Eve, the $19,000 of fringe benefits per books must be reduced by Loreck's $6,000 of medical expenses. These $6,000 of medical expenses are then deductible by Eve as compensation and included in Loreck's gross income on Form W-2.

7. **($10,000; $0)** Eve's organizational costs of $50,000 are being amortized over sixty months per books. Since organizational costs can also be amortized over sixty months for tax purposes, no adjustment is necessary and the $10,000 of organizational costs is deductible in computing Eve's ordinary income.

8. **($11,000; $0)** No tax deduction is allowed for amounts credited to a reserve for self-insurance. Here, the $21,000 of other operating expenses per books must be reduced by the $10,000 of insurance expense in connection with the establishment of a reserve for self-insurance.

9. **($0; $18,000)** Net rental revenue is passive activity income and cannot be included in the computation of ordinary income. Instead, net rental revenue must be separately shown on Schedule K of the S corporation tax return. The net rental revenue passes through to Loreck on Schedule K-1 and will be reported as passive activity income on Loreck's return.

10. **($0; $6,000)** The interest is a component of portfolio income and cannot be included in the computation of Eve's ordinary income. Instead, the $6,000 of interest income must be separately shown and passed through to Loreck retaining its characteristic as interest reported on Loreck's Schedule K-1.

11. **($0; $4,000)** The dividends are portfolio income and cannot be included in the computation of Loreck's ordinary income. Instead, the $4,000 of dividends must be separately shown and pass through to Loreck retaining their characteristic as dividends, when reported on Schedule K-1.

12. **($0; $8,000)** The short-term capital gain is portfolio income and cannot be included in the computation of ordinary income. Instead, as with interest and dividends, the $8,000 of short-term capital gain must be separately shown and passed through to Loreck. Therefore, the $8,000 is reported on Schedule K-1.

Problem 4

1. **(R)** To be classified as a personal holding company, a corporation must meet two requirements: (1) the corporation must receive at least 60% of its adjusted ordinary gross income as "personal holding company income" such as dividends, interest, rents, royalties, and other passive income; and (2) the corporation must have more than 50% of the value of its outstanding stock directly or indirectly owned by five or fewer individuals during any time in the last half of the tax year.

2. **(Z)** The transferred basis, equal to the basis of the donor plus any gift tax paid attributable to the net appreciation in the value of the gift, is the basis used to determine gain on sale of property that was received as a gift.

3. **(P)** A like-kind exchange, the exchange of business or investment property for property of a like-kind, qualifies as a nontaxable exchange. Thus, the exchange of production machinery for new production machinery when boot (money) is given is a nontaxable exchange.

4. **(O)** Head of household filing status applies to unmarried persons not qualifying for surviving spouse status who maintain a household for more than one-half of the taxable year for a dependent. The tax rates applicable to the head of household status are lower than those applicable to individuals filing as single, but are higher than rates applicable to married individuals filing a joint return.

5. **(G)** Under the doctrine of constructive receipt, income is includable in gross income and subject to income tax for the taxable year in which that income is made unqualifiedly available to the taxpayer without restriction, even though not physically in the taxpayer's possession.

6. **(A)** Corporations may be subject to an accumulated earnings tax, in addition to regular income tax, if a corporation accumulates earnings beyond reasonable business needs in order to avoid shareholder tax on dividend distributions.

7. **(U)** Portfolio income is defined as income from interest, dividends, annuities, and certain royalties.

8. **(W)** Section 1231 assets include depreciable assets and real estate used in a trade or business and held for more than one year.

9. **(J)** The dividends received deduction was enacted by Congress to mitigate the triple taxation that occurs when one corporation pays dividends to a corporate stockholder who, in turn, distributes such amounts to its individual stockholders.

10. **(F)** A constructive dividend results when a shareholder is considered to have received a dividend from a corporation, although the corporation did not specifically declare a dividend. This situation may occur when a shareholder/employee receives an excessive salary from a corporation, when there is a loan to a shareholder where there is no intent to repay the amount loaned, or when a corporation purchases shareholder property for an amount in excess of the property's fair market value. Constructive dividends often result when a transaction between a shareholder and corporation is not an arm's-length transaction.

Problem 5

Part a.

1. (**$20,000**) Interest on funds borrowed for working capital is deductible. However, interest incurred on borrowed funds to purchase municipal bonds is not deductible because the resulting income is exempt from tax.

2. (**$20,000**) Interest earned on corporate bonds must be included in gross income. However, interest earned on municipal bonds is excluded.

3. (**$10,000**) Expenditures incurred in creating a corporation may be amortized over a period of not less than sixty months. However, expenditures connected with selling or issuing stock are neither deductible nor amortizable. Therefore, only the legal fees and state incorporation fees are amortized over not less than sixty months. The amount to be deducted on the corporate tax return will equal $10,000 (30,000 + 20,000)/60 x 12 months.

4. (**$20,000**) All of the capital gains would be included in Aviator's gross income.

5. (**$20,000**) Corporate capital losses can only be deducted to the extent of capital gains. Therefore, only $20,000 of capital losses can be deducted on the Aviator, Inc. tax return. Since this is Aviator's first year of existence, the excess of capital losses over capital gains ($10,000) will then be carried forward five years as a short-term capital loss, to offset capital gains.

6. (**$35,000**) The dividends received deduction will be based on 70% of its dividends received, since Aviator, Inc. owns less than 20% of the dividend-paying corporation.

7. (**$38,000**) A charitable contributions deduction is limited to a maximum of 10% of taxable income before the dividends received deduction and a charitable contributions deduction. Therefore, taxable income before these deductions needs to be calculated to determine the maximum allowable deduction. Taxable income is computed as follows:

Sales	$2,000,000
Dividends	50,000
Interest revenue	20,000
Gains on the sale of stock	20,000
Cost of goods sold	(1,000,000)
Salaries and wages	(400,000)
Depreciation	(260,000)
Losses on the sale of stock	(20,000)
Organizational expenditures	(10,000)
Interest expense	(20,000)
	$ 380,000

The charitable contributions deduction will be limited to $38,000 ($380,000 x 10%). The excess not allowed ($40,000 – $38,000 = $2,000) will be carried forward for up to five years.

Part b.

8. (**N**) Life insurance proceeds paid at death are generally excluded from gross income.

9. (**N**) Insurance premiums on a life insurance policy for which the company is the beneficiary are not deductible.

10. (**Y**) Capital gains that result from the sale of stock must be included in gross income, regardless of the length of time that the stock was held.

11. (**N**) No dividends received deduction is allowed if the stock has been held for forty-five days or less. In this case, Aviator, Inc. has only owned the stock a total of forty days. Therefore, no dividends received deduction can be taken for this particular investment.

12. (**N**) When a consolidated return is filed, intercompany dividends received from affiliated group members (i.e., corporations at least 80% owned) are eliminated and not included in consolidated gross income.

Problem 6

1. (**F**) This transaction qualifies as a transfer to a controlled corporation since property was transferred to Silver in exchange for stock **and** Brewer (the transferor) controlled the corporation immediately after the exchange. In such a transfer, the corporation computes its basis in the property received as follows:

$$\text{BASIS TO CORPORATION} = \text{TRANSFEROR'S ADJUSTED BASIS} + \text{GAIN RECOGNIZED TO TRANSFEROR}$$

Receipt of boot will cause recognition of gain. However, the corporation's assumption of liabilities is treated as boot to the transferor only if the liabilities have a tax avoidance purpose or no business purpose. Since no such purpose was mentioned, no gain is recognized to Brewer, and Silver Corporation has a basis for the property of $100,000 ($100,000 + $0).

2. (**T**) The tax basis of the stock received by Brewer may be computed using the following equation:

$$\text{SHAREHOLDER'S BASIS IN STOCK} = \text{ADJUSTED BASIS OF PROPERTY GIVEN} + \text{GAIN RECOGNIZED} - \text{BOOT RECEIVED}$$

For purposes of determining stock basis, the assumption of a liability by the corporation is always treated as boot received by the transferor. Therefore, the basis of Brewer's stock is $120,000, computed as follows:

$$\$150,000 \text{ Adjusted basis } + \ \$0 \text{ Gain } - \ \$30,000 \text{ Liability } = \ \$120,000$$

3. **(T)** A corporation never recognizes gain or loss when it issues its stock (including treasury stock) in exchange for cash or property.

4. **(F)** A 70% dividends received deduction is allowed for qualified dividends from taxable domestic unaffiliated corporations that are less than 20% owned. Therefore, Silver Corporation will receive a DRD of $1,400 ($2,000 x 70%), resulting in a net increase in taxable income of only $600 ($2,000 – $1,400).

5. **(F)** Silver can only deduct the $15,000 in premiums paid for the employee group term insurance. Since Silver Corporation is the beneficiary of the keyman life insurance policy, the $3,000 in premiums paid for this policy may not be deducted.

6. **(T)** A realized loss from an involuntary conversion of business or investment property is recognized whether or not the property is replaced. Although the loss is recognized, a corporation cannot deduct a net capital loss, and Silver's $2,500 capital loss can only be used to offset capital gains.

7. **(F)** In a like-kind exchange such as this one, gain is recognized to the extent of the **lesser** of

      (1)   Realized gain, or
      (2)   FMV of boot received

The realized gain is computed as the value of the property received less the basis of the property given, in this case

$9,500	($6,000 FMV + $3,500 Cash) Received
– 8,000	Given
$1,500	Realized gain

The $1,500 realized gain is less than the $3,500 cash boot received, so Silver Corporation must recognize a gain of $1,500.

8. **(T)** The distributing corporation recognizes a gain on the distribution of appreciated property **as if such property were sold at its FMV**. Thus, the gain to Silver is simply the property's FMV less its adjusted basis.

$$\$12,000 \ - \ \$4,000 \ = \ \$8,000 \text{ Gain}$$

9. **(T)** In the case of property distributed as a dividend, the distributee's tax basis for the property received will be the property's FMV at the date of distribution (not reduced by any liabilities assumed). Therefore, Brewer's tax basis would simply be the $12,000 FMV of the equipment.

10. **(T)** A corporation can deduct an ordinary loss for the worthless stock that it owns in a subsidiary if the corporation owns at least 80% of the subsidiary's stock, and the subsidiary derived more than 90% of its gross receipts from nonpassive sources.

Problem 7

1. **(P; $5,000)** Ral is an accrual method taxpayer, the payment was based on a formula in effect for 2002, and the sales manager had performed the services in 2002.

2. **(U; $8,000)** Since taxpayers are required to use the direct charge-off method in computing taxable income, only the $8,000 of actual bad debts for 2002 can be deducted.

3. **(A; $0)** Since Ral is the beneficiary of the policies and the eventual proceeds will be excluded from gross income, the premium cannot be deducted in computing taxable income.

4. **(X; $12,000)** State income taxes are deductible in computing federal taxable income.

5. **(P; $5,000)** The $3,000 interest on US Treasury notes and $2,000 interest on municipal arbitrage bonds is taxable, while the $200 interest on municipal bonds is nontaxable.

6. **(R; $5,600)** Since Clove is at least 20% owned, the $7,000 of dividends are eligible for an 80% dividends received deduction.

7. **(M; $4,200)** Since Ramo is less than 20% owned, the $6,000 of dividends are eligible for an 70% dividends received deduction.

8. **(A; $0)** No dividends received deduction is allowed because the stock was not held for more than forty-five days.

9. **(A; $0)** No dividends received deduction is allowed because a real estate investment trust (REIT) is a pass-through entity with only one level of tax paid (by its shareholders).

10. **(A; $0)** The $400 of capital gains dividends pass through as capital gains and are not eligible for a dividends received deduction.

11. **(A; $0)** No dividends received deduction is allowed because Money Market Fund derived all of its income from investments in "interest paying securities," not dividend paying stocks.

12. **(A; $0)** No federal income tax deduction is allowed for corporate dividend payments to its own shareholders.

13. **(A; $0)** Ral's net capital loss is $6,400 – $400 capital gains dividends = $6,000. However, a corporation cannot deduct a net capital loss. Instead, it is carried back three years and forward five years to offset capital gains in those years.

14.   (**Z; $22,250**) The tax rate schedule indicates that the tax on $100,000 of taxable income is $22,250.

Problem 8

For **items 1 through 5,** candidates were required to determine the amount that should be reported on Kimberly Corp.'s 2002 Federal income tax return.

1.   (**$26,000**) All $26,000 of interest income from US Treasury bonds is taxable.

2.   (**$8,000**) The furniture and fixtures are classified as seven-year recovery property. Under MACRS, their cost of $56,000 will be recovered using the 200% declining balance method of depreciation and the half-year convention. Thus, the amount of depreciation for the year of acquisition would be $56,000 x 2/7 x 1/2 = $8,000.

3.   (**$7,000**) The bad debt deduction consists of the $7,000 of bad debts actually written off during the year. The reserve method, using the increase in the allowance for doubtful accounts based on an aging of accounts receivable, cannot be used for tax purposes.

4.   (**$25,000**) Since the unimproved lot was used in the business and held for more than one year, the $20,000 gain on its sale is classified as a Sec. 1231 gain. Since Kimberly had no previous nonrecaptured Sec. 1231 losses, the net Sec. 1231 gain is treated as a LTCG. Combining this $20,000 LTCG with the $5,000 LTCG from the sale of XYZ stock results in a net LTCG of $25,000.

5.   (**$12,000**) Deductible interest expense consists of the $10,000 interest on the mortgage loan and the $2,000 interest on the line of credit loan. The $4,000 of interest expense on the loan obtained to purchase municipal bonds is not deductible because the municipal bonds produce tax-exempt income.

For **items 6 through 10,** candidates were required to select whether the expenses are (F) fully deductible, (P) partially deductible, or (N) nondeductible, for regular tax purposes on Kimberly's 2002 federal income tax return.

6.   (**N**) Corporate organizational expenditures may be amortized over a period of sixty months or longer, beginning with the month that business begins, if a proper election statement is attached to the corporate return for the year that business begins. If no election is made, the expenditure must be capitalized and can only be deducted when the corporation is liquidated. Here, the problem indicates that Kimberly was formed and commenced operations during 1999, and further states that no deduction was taken for the organization expense in 1999. Although not specifically stated, this would indicate that no election was made to amortize the organization expense for 1999 and, as a result, no amortization deduction would be available for 2002.

7.   (**F**) The life insurance premiums are fully deductible because Kimberly is neither the direct nor indirect beneficiary of the policy. The life insurance premiums are deductible as part of the reasonable compensation paid to its executives.

8.   (**F**) An accrual method taxpayer can deduct vacation pay for employees **in the year earned** if (1) it is paid during the year, or (2) the vacation pay is vested and paid no later than 2 1/2 months after the end of the year. Here, the vacation pay was vested and paid on February 1, 2003.

9.   (**F**) Corporate franchise taxes are deductible as a business expense. An accrual method corporation can take a deduction for franchise taxes in the year it becomes legally liable to pay the tax regardless of the year that the tax is based on, or the year it is paid. The item indicates that the franchise tax liability accrued during the year (2002).

10.   (**P**) The cost to lease a skybox is disallowed as an entertainment expense to the extent that the amount paid exceeds the cost of the highest-priced nonluxury box seat tickets multiplied by the number of seats in the skybox. Since the item indicates that the cost of regular seats would have been one half the amount paid, only 50% of the cost of the skybox would qualify as an entertainment expense. Of this amount only 50% would be deductible for 2002.

For **items 11 through 15,** candidates were required to select whether the revenue items are (F) fully taxable, (P) partially taxable, or (N) nontaxable on Kimberly Corp.'s 2002 federal income tax return for regular tax purposes.

11.   (**P**) The item is somewhat ambiguous. 100% of the dividends that Kimberly received from a 20%-owned taxable domestic corporation must be included in gross income and therefore, they are fully taxable. However, because the dividends would be eligible for an 80% dividends received deduction, Kimberly's taxable income would include only the remaining 20%.

12.   (**F**) The recovery of a receivable that had been deducted as a bad debt in a prior year must be included in gross income if the deduction reduced the amount of taxes paid that year.

13.   (**F**) Under the tax benefit rule, a refund of a state franchise tax overpayment previously expensed in a prior year must be fully included in gross income if the deduction reduced the amount of income taxes paid that year.

14.   (**N**) Interest income from municipal bonds is excluded from gross income.

15.   (**N**) The proceeds of life insurance paid by reason of death of the insured is generally excluded from gross income. The use of the proceeds does not affect the amount excluded.

For **items 16 through 25,** refer to Kimberly's need to determine if it will be subject to the alternative minimum tax. Candidates were asked to determine whether the statement is true (T) or false (F).

16.   (**T**) The straight-line method of depreciation must be used for depreciable real property acquired after 1986 for both regular tax and alternative minimum tax purposes. For real property placed in service before January 1, 1999, an AMT adjustment

results because for AMT purposes, real property must be depreciated straight-line over forty years. However, for real property placed in service after December 31, 1998, the AMT adjustment has been eliminated because for AMT purposes, the recovery period is the same as that used for regular tax MACRS depreciation (e.g., thirty-nine years or twenty-seven and one-half years).

17. **(T)** AMTI is reduced by a $40,000 exemption. The exemption is reduced by 25% of AMTI over $150,000, and is completely phased out if AMTI is at least $310,000.

18. **(T)** The ACE adjustment is for 75% of the difference between the corporation's adjusted current earnings before this adjustment and its AMTI before the alternative tax NOL deduction. The adjustment will be positive if ACE exceeds AMTI, and will be negative if ACE is less than AMTI.

19. **(F)** Depreciation on personal property to arrive at AMTI is generally computed using the 150% declining balance method. For personalty placed in service before January 1, 1999, AMT depreciation is computed using the property's class life under ADS. For personalty placed in service after December 31, 1998, AMT depreciation is computed using the same MACRS recovery period that is used for regular tax purposes.

20. **(T)** If a corporation's tentative minimum tax exceeds its regular tax, the excess represents the corporation's alternative minimum tax and is payable in addition to its regular tax liability.

21. **(F)** Tax-exempt municipal bond interest other than private activity bond interest is not included in computing AMTI before the ACE adjustment.

22. **(F)** A corporation is allowed a $40,000 exemption in computing its AMTI. The maximum $40,000 exemption is phased out by 25% of the corporation's AMTI in excess of $150,000.

23. **(F)** Although the 100% and 80% dividends received deductions are allowed in computing ACE, the 70% dividends received deduction for dividends received from less than 20% owned taxable domestic corporations is not allowed and must be added back to compute ACE.

24. **(T)** Generally, any item that is not taken into account in computing pre-adjustment AMTI but would be taken into account in computing a corporation's earnings and profits must be included in determining ACE. Thus, tax-exempt municipal bond interest (less any related deductions) must be included in the computation of ACE.

Problem 9

For **items 1 through 6,** candidates were (a) required to determine the amount of Reliant's 2002 Schedule M-1 adjustment, and (b) to indicate whether the adjustment (I) increases, (D) decreases, or (N) has no effect, on Reliant's 2002 taxable income.

NOTE: Schedule M-1 is the schedule of the corporate income tax return that provides a reconciliation of net income (loss) per books with the corporation's taxable income before the net operating loss and dividends received deductions. If an item's treatment per books differs from its treatment for tax purposes, an M-1 adjustment will result.

1. **($15,000; I)** The $100,000 reimbursement for employee travel is deductible for both book and tax purposes and no adjustment is necessary. However, since only 50% of the $30,000 of reimbursed business meals that was deducted per books is deductible for tax purposes, an M-1 increase adjustment results in the amount of $15,000 ($30,000 x 50%).

2. **($7,000; I)** The $7,000 of term life insurance premiums on corporate officers that was deducted per books is not deductible for tax purposes because Reliant was the policy owner and beneficiary. As a result there is an M-1 increase adjustment of $7,000.

3. **($0; N)** The $18,000 of state franchise taxes and $15,000 of estimated state tax payments are fully deductible for both book and tax purposes and no M-1 adjustment is necessary.

4. **($6,000; D)** Since the computers are five-year recovery property and Reliant used MACRS and the half-year convention, depreciation would be computed using the 200% declining balance method (i.e., twice the straight-line rate) and the tax depreciation for 2001 would be ($50,000 x 40% x 1/2) = $10,000. The tax depreciation for 2002 would then be ($50,000 – $10,000) x 40% = $16,000. Since book depreciation was only $10,000, the book to tax difference in depreciation would result in an M-1 decrease adjustment of $6,000.

5. **($5,000; I)** Since only **long-term capital gain distributions** from a mutual fund pass through as capital gain, the $4,000 of **short-term capital gain distribution** from a mutual fund corporation must be reported by Reliant as ordinary dividend income, and cannot be netted against the $5,000 capital loss from the sale of the Retro stock held as an investment. As a result, Reliant's sale of the Retro stock results in a net capital loss of $5,000 for 2002. Since a corporation cannot deduct a net capital loss for tax purposes, the $5,000 of net capital loss deducted per books results in a book to tax difference and an M-1 increase adjustment of $5,000.

6. **($0; N)** Since Reliant had taxable income before the charitable contribution deduction of $500,000 for 2002, Reliant can deduct a maximum of ($500,000 x 10%) = $50,000 of charitable contributions for tax purposes. Reliant can deduct the $35,000 of contributions made during 2002, as well as the $15,000 paid on January 5, 2003, because Reliant is an accrual-basis taxpayer, the $15,000 contribution was authorized by Reliant's board of directors, and the $15,000 was paid within 2 1/2 months after the end of 2002. Since Reliant is deducting $50,000 of contributions for both book and tax purposes, there is no M-1 adjustment.

For **items 7 through 11,** candidates were required to indicate if the expenses are (F) fully deductible, (P) partially deductible, or (N) nondeductible for regular tax purposes on Reliant's 2002 federal income tax return.

7.   **(P)** The cost of the theater tickets qualifies as a business entertainment expense which is only 50% deductible for 2001.

8.   **(F)** Indirect costs that do not directly benefit a particular activity or are not incurred because of a particular activity may be currently deducted and are not required to be capitalized as part of the cost of inventory. Indirect costs that can be currently deducted include such costs as marketing, selling, advertising, distribution, and general and administrative expenses.

9.   **(N)** Since the proceeds of the loan were used to purchase municipal bonds which generate tax-exempt income, the interest expense on the loan is not deductible.

10.   **(N)** No deduction is allowed for the penalty that results from the underpayment of estimated income tax.

11.   **(F)** An accrual method taxpayer can deduct compensation for nonstockholder employees when there is an obligation to make payment, economic performance has occurred, the amount is reasonable, and payment is made not later than 2 1/2 months after the end of the tax year. Here, the amount of bonus was determined on December 9, 2002, and was paid February 3, 2003.

For **items 12 through 16,** candidates were required to indicate if the items are (F) fully taxable, (P) partially taxable, or (N) nontaxable for regular tax purposes on Reliant's 2002 federal income tax return.

12.   **(N)** Since the payment of federal income tax does not result in a deduction, a subsequent refund of federal income tax will be nontaxable.

13.   **(F)** Interest is generally fully included in gross income, including the interest on an overpayment of federal taxes.

14.   **(N)** A mutual fund that invests in tax-exempt municipal bonds is permitted to pass the tax exemption on the bond interest on to its shareholders when the tax-exempt interest is distributed in the form of dividends. To qualify, the mutual fund has to have at least 50% of the value of its total assets invested in tax-exempt municipal bonds at the close of each quarter of its taxable year.

15.   **(F)** Generally, a lessor will not recognize any income as a result of the capital improvements made by a lessee that revert to the lessor at the expiration of the lease. However, if the parties intend the improvements to be, in whole or in part, a substitute for rental payments, then the lessor must recognize the improvements as rental income equal in amount to the reduction in rental payments.

16.   **(P)** Since Reliant was a collateral assignee as a result of the insured's indebtedness, Reliant received the insurance proceeds as payment on the debt, rather than as life insurance proceeds paid "by reason of death of the insured." Consequently, the insurance proceeds are tax-free only to the extent of the amount of unpaid debt, and any proceeds in excess of the debt repayment must be included in Reliant's gross income.

For **items 17 through 21,** candidates were asked to indicate if the following (I) increase, (D) decrease, or (N) have no effect on Reliant's 2002 alternative minimum taxable income (AMTI) **prior to** the adjusted current earnings adjustment (ACE).

17.   **(N)** The dividends received deduction is not an adjustment in computing AMTI before the ACE adjustment. However, note that the 70% dividends received deduction is an increase adjustment in computing a corporation's ACE.

18.   **(N)** The tax-exempt interest on a state's **general obligation** bonds is not an adjustment is computing AMTI before the ACE adjustment. However, note that the interest from state and local **private activity** bonds would be an increase adjustment in computing AMTI prior to the ACE adjustment.

19.   **(I)** Generally for seven-year property, the 200% declining balance method would be used under MACRS for regular tax purposes, while the 150% declining balance method must be used for AMT purposes, resulting in an increase adjustment in computing AMTI prior to the ACE adjustment for the year placed in service.

20.   **(N)** For real property placed in service after December 31, 1998, the AMT adjustment has been eliminated because for AMT purposes, the recovery period is the same as that used for regular tax MACRS depreciation (e.g., thirty-nine years or 27 1/2 years). On the other hand, for real property that was placed in service before January 1, 1999, an AMT adjustment is necessary because for AMT purposes, real property must be depreciated using the straight-line method over a forty-year recovery period, rather than the thirty-nine-year or 27 1/2-year period used for regular tax purposes.

21.   **(N)** Allowable charitable contributions do not result in an adjustment in computing AMTI or ACE.

For **items 22 through 28,** candidates were asked to indicate if the statement is true (T) or false (F) regarding Reliant's compliance with tax procedures, tax credits and the alternative minimum tax.

22.   **(F)** Reliant's AMT exemption would be reduced by 25% of the excess of AMTI over $150,000.

23.   **(F)** If Reliant's return was fraudulent with the intent to evade tax, there would be no statute of limitations. This means that the IRS could assess the tax or begin a court proceeding to collect the tax and the interest thereon at any time.

24.   **(F)** The general statute of limitations on the assessment of tax is three years after the due date of the return, or three years after the return is filed, whichever is later. If gross income omissions exceed 25% of the gross income stated on the return, the assessment period is extended to six years.

25.   **(T)** The general business credit is composed of the (1) investment credit, (2) welfare-to-work credit, (3) alcohol fuels credit, (4) research credit, (5) low-income housing credit, (6) enhanced oil recovery credit, (7) disabled access credit,

(8) renewable resources electricity production credit, (9) empowerment zone employment credit, (10) Indian employment credit, (11) employer social security credit, (12) orphan drug credit, and (13) new markets credit.

26.   (T) A tax credit is available to an eligible small business for expenditures incurred to remove existing barriers in order to make the business accessible to disabled individuals.

27.   (T) A tax return preparer may take a corporation's tax return information into account, and may act on it without the consent of the corporation in the preparation of employees' tax returns if the information is relevant and its consideration is necessary for the proper preparation of the employees' returns.

28.   (F) An amended return claiming a refund must be filed within three years from the date the return was filed, or two years from payment of tax, whichever is later. For this purpose, a return filed early is treated as filed on its due date.

Problem 10

For **items 1 through 4,** candidates were asked to determine the amount for Lan Corp. (an accrual-basis calendar-year S corporation), using the fact pattern for each item.

1.   ($6,140) The requirement is to determine the amount of net business income that Lan should report on Schedule K of Form 1120S. The term "net business income" corresponds to an S corporation's "ordinary income (loss) from trade or business activities." The computation of this amount excludes any item that must be separately stated and passed through to shareholders in order to retain the item's special tax characteristics. Here, the interest income on investments is portfolio income and must be separately stated and passed through to shareholders as interest income. Similarly, the charitable contributions must be separately stated and passed through to shareholders in order to apply the appropriate percentage limitations at the shareholder level. As a result, Lan's net business income consists of its $7,200 of gross receipts reduced by the $1,120 of supplies expense, or $6,140.

2.   ($2,700) The requirement it to determine the amount of net business income to be reported on Pike's 2002 Schedule K-1 from Lan. If there is no election to terminate the tax year following the sale of stock, the income of an S corporation for the entire taxable year is allocated per share, per day to anyone who was a shareholder during the year. Lan was formed on January 6, 2002, and its tax year consists of 360 days. So its net business income per share, per day would be $14,400 ÷ 200 shares ÷ 360 days = $.20. Since Pike purchased his forty shares on January 31, he is considered to own his stock for a total of 334 days during the year (counting February 1 as the first day). Thus, the amount of net business income to be reported on Pike's Schedule K-1 is (40 shares x 334 days x $.20) = $2,672. Since the instructions indicated that the answer should be rounded to the nearest hundred, the correct answer is $2,700.

3.   ($3,150) The requirement is to determine Pike's basis for his Lan stock at December 31, 2002, assuming that he had purchased the stock for $4,000. An S corporation's items of income and deduction pass through to be reported on shareholder returns even though no distributions are made. As a result, a shareholder's S corporation stock basis is increased by the pass through of all income items (including tax-exempt income), and is decreased by all loss and deduction items (including nondeductible expenses). In this case, Pike's beginning basis of $4,000 would be increased by the $150 of municipal bond interest income, and decreased by the $1,000 of ordinary business loss.

4.   ($9,000) The requirement is to determine Taylor's basis in Lan shares for determining gain or loss from the sale of stock to Pike. Taylor's beginning stock basis of $10,000 must be increased by his $2,000 share of the ordinary income from Lan prior to the sale, and must be decreased by the $3,000 nontaxable cash distribution that Taylor received. Recall that distributions by S corporations without accumulated earnings and profits are treated as a return of stock basis and are excluded from gross income.

For **items 5 and 6,** candidates were asked to determine whether each statement regarding Lan's S corporation status is true (T) or false (F).

5.   (F) Eligibility requirements restrict an S corporation to one class of stock issued and outstanding. An S corporation will not be treated as having more than one class of stock solely because of differences in voting rights among the shares of common stock, but is not permitted to have issued and outstanding preferred stock.

6.   (F) An S corporation election will terminate as of the first day of the fourth year if it has passive investment income in excess of 25% of gross receipts for three consecutive taxable years and subchapter C accumulated earnings and profits at the end of each of those years. Subchapter C earnings and profits are earnings and profits accumulated during a year for which a subchapter S election was not in effect. Since Lan has been an S corporation since inception, it would have no subchapter C earnings and profits and there would be no restriction on the amount of its passive investment income.

Problem 11

For **items 1 through 4,** candidates were asked to determine the amount of Capital Corp.'s M-1 adjustment necessary to reconcile book income to taxable income, and to indicate whether the adjustment (I) increases, (D) decreases, or (N) has no effect, on Capital's 2002 taxable income.

1.   ($7,000; D) Capital's organizational costs of $40,000 that were incurred in 1999 can be amortized over sixty months (five years) for tax purposes. As a result, the tax amortization of organizational costs results in a tax deduction of $40,000 x 1/5 =

$8,000 for 2002. Since only $1,000 of organizational costs was deducted per books for 2002, a Schedule M-1 decrease adjustment is necessary for the $7,000 difference.

2. ($5,000; I) Only 50% of reimbursed employees' expenses for business meals and entertainment is deductible for tax purposes. As a result, an M-1 increase adjustment of $5,000 is necessary to reflect the fact that 50% of the $10,000 of reimbursed business meals and entertainment that was deducted for book purposes is not deductible for tax purposes.

3. ($0; N) The $15,000 of life insurance premiums treated as reasonable compensation is fully deductible for both book and tax purposes and no M-1 adjustment is necessary.

4. ($10,000; I) The reserve method of accounting for bad debts is not allowed for tax purposes. Instead, a bad debt deduction can be taken only when a specific debt is determined to be uncollectible. Since no bad debt was written off during 2002, an M-1 increase adjustment is necessary for the $10,000 addition to the allowance for uncollectible accounts for 2002.

For **items 5 and 6,** candidates were required to indicate if the items were (F) fully taxable, (P) partially taxable, or (N) nontaxable for regular tax purposes on Sunco Corp.'s 2002 federal income tax return.

5. (P) Dividends received from a 35%-owned domestic corporation would be eligible for an 80% dividends received deduction. As a result, only 20% of the gross dividends received would be included in taxable income.

6. (F) A lease cancellation payment is treated as rent and must be fully included in income when received.

For **items 7 and 8,** candidates were required to indicate whether the items are (F) fully deductible, (P) partially deductible, or (N) nondeductible for regular tax purposes on Quest's 2002 federal income tax return.

7. (P) Since Quest is an accrual method corporation, it can elect to deduct contributions authorized by its board of directors during 2002, so long as the contribution is actually paid no later than 2 1/2 months after the end of the tax year. Thus, to maximize its deduction for 2002, Quest can elect to treat the $38,000 contribution as a deduction for 2002 subject to the 10% of taxable income limitation that applies for 2002. Since Quest had 2002 taxable income of $200,000 before the charitable contributions and dividends received deductions, Quest's 2002 deduction for the $38,000 charitable contribution is limited to $200,000 x 10% = $20,000.

8. (N) A penalty that is paid for a failure to pay federal income taxes on time is not deductible.

For **items 9 through 11,** candidates were required to determine whether each item contributes to (O) overstating, (U) understating, or (C) correctly stating Gelco's 2002 alternative minimum taxable income (AMTI) prior to the adjusted current earnings adjustment (ACE).

9. (U) Generally for seven-year property, the 200% declining balance method would be used for MACRS, while the 150% declining balance method must be used for AMT purposes. Therefore, the use of MACRS would have the effect of understating AMTI before the ACE adjustment, and would necessitate an increase adjustment to convert 2002 regular taxable income to AMTI.

10. (U) MACRS depreciation for nonresidential real property placed in service during 1998 would be computed using the straight-line method and a thirty-nine-year recovery period. For AMT purposes depreciation would have to be computed using the straight-line method over a forty-year recovery period. Therefore, regular tax depreciation would have the effect of understating AMTI before the ACE adjustment, and would necessitate an increase adjustment to convert 2002 regular taxable income to AMTI. However, note that for real property placed in service after December 31, 1998, the AMT adjustment has been eliminated because for AMT purposes, the recovery period is the same as that used for regular tax MACRS depreciation (e.g., thirty-nine years or 27 1/2 years). Thus, if the building had instead been placed in service after **December 31, 1998,** no AMT adjustment would be necessary and the correct answer would be (C).

11. (C) Interest on a state's general obligation bonds is tax exempt for purposes of computing both regular taxable income, as well as for computing AMTI before the ACE adjustment, and would have the effect of correctly stating AMTI before the ACE adjustment. However, note that interest from a state's general obligation bonds is includible income for purposes of determining a corporation's ACE adjustment.

Keep practicing! Wiley's CPA Examination Review Software has over 2,800 questions.

Available at www.wiley.com/cpa

I. GIFT AND ESTATE TAXATION

The federal gift tax is an excise tax (imposed on donor) on the transfer of property by gift during a person's lifetime. The federal estate tax is an excise tax on the transfer of property upon death. The Tax Reform Act of 1976 combined these taxes into a **unified transfer tax** rate schedule that applies to both life and death transfers. To remove relatively small gifts and estates from the imposition of tax, a **unified transfer tax credit** of **$345,800** is allowed for 2002 against gift and estate taxes. This is equivalent to an **exemption** of the first **$1,000,000** of taxable gifts or taxable estate from the unified transfer tax.

A. The Gift Tax

1. Gift Tax Formula

Gross gifts (cash plus FMV of property at date of gift)		$xxx
Less:		
One-half of gifts treated as given by spouse	$ x	
Annual exclusion (up to $11,000 per donee)	x	
Unlimited exclusion for tuition or medical expenses paid on behalf of donee	x	
Unlimited exclusion for gifts to political organizations	x	
Charitable gifts (remainder of charitable gifts after annual exclusion)	x	
Marital deduction (remainder of gifts to spouse after annual exclusion)	x	xx
Taxable gifts for current year		$ xx
Add: Taxable gifts for prior years		x
Total taxable gifts		$ xx
Unified transfer tax on total taxable gifts		$ xx
Less: Unified transfer tax on taxable gifts made prior to current year		x
Unified transfer tax for current year		$ xx
Unified transfer tax credit	$ xx	
Less: Unified transfer tax credit used in prior years	x	x
Net gift tax liability		$ xx

2. A **gift** occurs when a transfer becomes complete and is measured by its fair market value on that date. A gift becomes **complete** when the donor has relinquished dominion and control and no longer has the power to change its disposition, whether for the donor's benefit or for the benefit of another.

   a. The creation of joint ownership in property is treated as a gift to the extent the donor's contribution exceeds the donor's retained interest.

   b. The creation of a joint bank account is not a gift; but a gift results when the noncontributing tenant withdraws funds.

3. Gross gifts less the following deductions equal taxable gifts:

   a. **Annual exclusion**—of up to $11,000 (for 2002) per donee is allowed for gifts of present interests (not future interests). A **present interest** is an unrestricted right to the immediate use, possession, or enjoyment of property or the income from property. A **future interest** includes reversions, remainders, and other interests that are limited to commence in use, possession, or enjoyment at some future date or time.

   (1) Trusts for minors (Sec. 2503(c) trusts) allow parents and other donors to obtain an annual exclusion for gifts to trusts for children under age twenty-one even though the trust does not distribute its income annually. To qualify, the trust must provide

   (a) Until the beneficiary reaches age twenty-one, the trustee **may** pay the income and/or the underlying assets to the beneficiary, and,

   (b) Any income and assets not distributed must pass to the beneficiary when the beneficiary reaches age twenty-one. If the beneficiary dies before age twenty-one, the income and underlying assets are either payable to the beneficiary's estate, or are payable to any person the minor may appoint if the minor possesses a general power of appointment over the trust property.

   (2) **Crummey** trusts allow a donor to obtain an annual exclusion upon funding a discretionary trust. This type of trust is more flexible than a Sec. 2503(c) trust because the beneficiary can be of any age and the trust can terminate at any age. To qualify, a beneficiary must have the power to demand a distribution equal to the lesser of the donor's annual exclusion ($11,000), or the beneficiary's pro rata share of the amount transferred to the trust each year.

b. **Gift-splitting**—a gift by either spouse to a third party may be treated as made one-half by each, if both spouses consent to election. Gift-splitting has the advantage of using the other spouse's annual exclusion and unified transfer tax credit.

> *EXAMPLE: H is married and has three sons. H could give $22,000 per year to each of his sons without making a taxable gift if H's spouse (W) consents to gift-splitting.*

	H	W
Gifts	$66,000	
Gift-splitting	(33,000)	$33,000
Annual exclusion (3 x $11,000)	(33,000)	(33,000)
Taxable gifts	$ 0	$ 0

c. **Educational and medical exclusion**—an unlimited exclusion is available for amounts **paid on behalf of a donee** (1) as tuition to an educational organization, or (2) to a health care provider for medical care of donee

d. **Political gifts**—an unlimited exclusion is available for the transfer of money or other property to a political organization.

e. **Charitable gifts**—(net of annual exclusion) are deductible without limitation

f. **Marital deduction**—is allowed without limitation for gifts to a donor's spouse

(1) The gift must not be a terminable interest (i.e., donee spouse's interest ends at death with no control over who receives remainder).

(2) If donor elects, a gift of **qualified terminable interest** property (i.e., property placed in trust with income to donee spouse for life and remainder to someone else at donee spouse's death) will qualify for the marital deduction if the income is paid at least annually to spouse and the property is not subject to transfer during the donee spouse's lifetime.

(3) The marital deduction for gifts to an alien spouse is limited to $110,000 per year.

4. The **tax computation** reflects the **cumulative nature** of the gift tax. A tax is first computed on lifetime taxable gifts, then is reduced by the tax on taxable gifts made in prior years in order to tax the current year's gifts at applicable marginal rates. Any available transfer tax credit is then subtracted to arrive at the gift tax liability.

5. A **gift tax return** must be filed on a calendar-year basis, with the return due and tax paid on or before April 15th of the following year.

a. A donor who makes a gift to charity is not required to file a gift tax return if the entire value of the donated property qualifies for a gift tax charitable deduction.

b. If the donor dies, the gift tax return for the year of death is due not later than the due date for filing the decedent's federal estate tax return (generally nine months after date of death).

6. The **basis of property acquired by gift**

a. Basis for gain—basis of donor plus gift tax attributable to appreciation

b. Basis for loss—lesser of gain basis or FMV at date of gift

c. The increase in basis for gift tax paid is limited to the amount (not to exceed the gift tax paid) that bears the same ratio to the amount of gift tax paid as the net appreciation in value of the gift bears to the amount of the gift.

(1) The amount of gift is reduced by any portion of the $11,000 annual exclusion allowable with respect to the gift.

(2) Where more than one gift of a present interest is made to the same donee during a calendar year, the $11,000 exclusion is applied to gifts in chronological order.

> *EXAMPLE: Joan received property with a FMV of $60,000 and an adjusted basis of $80,000 as a gift. The donor paid a gift tax of $12,000 on the transfer. Since the property was not appreciated in value, no gift tax can be added in the basis computation. Joan's basis for computing a gain is $80,000, while her basis for computing a loss is $60,000.*

B. The Estate Tax

1. **Estate Tax Formula**

Gross estate (cash plus FMV of property at date of death, or alternate valuation date)		$xxx
Less:		
Funeral expenses	$x	
Administrative expenses	x	
Debts and mortgages	x	
Casualty losses	x	
Charitable bequests (unlimited)	x	
Marital deduction (unlimited)	x	xx
Taxable estate		$xxx
Add: Post-76 adjusted taxable gifts		xx
Total taxable life and death transfers		$xxx
Unified transfer tax on total transfers		$ xx
Less:		
Unified transfer tax on post-76 taxable gifts	$x	
Unified transfer tax credit	x	
State death, foreign death, and prior transfer tax credits	x	x
Net estate tax liability		$ xx

2. **Gross estate** includes the FMV of all property in which the decedent had an interest at time of death.

    a. **Jointly held property**

        (1) If property was held by tenancy in common, only the FMV of the decedent's share is included.

        (2) Include one-half the FMV of community property, and one-half the FMV of property held **by spouses** in joint tenancy or tenancy by the entirety.

        (3) Include one-half of FMV if the property held by two persons in joint tenancy was acquired by gift, bequest, or inheritance (1/3 if held by three persons, etc.)

        (4) If property held in joint tenancy was acquired by purchase by **other than spouses,** include the FMV of the property multiplied by the percentage of total cost furnished by the decedent.

    b. The FMV of transfers with retained life estates and revocable transfers are included in the gross estate.

    c. Include the FMV of transfers intended to take effect at death (i.e., the donee can obtain enjoyment only by surviving the decedent, and the decedent prior to death had a reversionary interest of more than 5% of the value of the property).

    d. Include any property over which the decedent had a **general power of appointment** (i.e., decedent could appoint property in favor of decedent, decedent's estate, or creditors of decedent or decedent's estate).

    e. Include the value of life insurance proceeds from policies payable to the estate, and policies over which the decedent possessed an "incident of ownership" (e.g., right to change beneficiary).

    f. Income in respect of a decedent

3. Property is included at **FMV at date of decedent's death**; or executor may elect to use FMV at **alternate valuation date** (generally a date six months subsequent to death), if such election will reduce both the gross estate and the federal estate tax liability.

    a. If alternate valuation is elected, but property is disposed of within six months of death, then use FMV on date of disposition.

    b. Election is irrevocable and applies to all property in estate; cannot be made on an individual property basis.

4. **Estate tax deductions** include funeral expenses, administrative expenses, debts and mortgages, casualty losses during the estate administration, charitable bequests (no limit), and an unlimited marital deduction for the FMV of property passing to a surviving spouse.

    a. A terminable interest granted to surviving spouse will not generally qualify for marital deduction.

    b. If executor elects, the FMV of "qualified terminable interest property" is eligible for the marital deduction if the income from the property is paid at least annually to spouse and the property is not subject to transfer during the surviving spouse's lifetime.

    c. Property passing to a surviving spouse who is not a US citizen is not eligible for the estate tax marital deduction, except for property passing to an alien spouse through a qualified domestic trust (QDT).

    d. Property passing from a nonresident alien to a surviving spouse who is a US citizen is eligible for the estate tax marital deduction.

5. Post-76 taxable gifts are added back to the taxable estate at date of gift FMV. Any gift tax paid is *not* added back.

6. A unified transfer tax is computed on total life and death transfers, then is reduced by the tax already paid on post-76 gifts, the unified transfer tax credit, state death tax credit (limited to table amount), foreign death tax credit, and prior transfer tax credit (i.e., percentage of estate tax paid on the transfer to the present decedent from a transferor who died within past ten years).

7. An **estate tax return** must be filed if the decedent's **gross estate exceeds $1,000,000** in 2002. The return must be filed within **nine months** of decedent's death, unless an extension of time has been granted.

8. The **basis of property acquired from a decedent** is generally the FMV at date of decedent's death, or the alternate valuation date if elected for estate tax purposes.

    a. Use FMV on date of disposition if alternate valuation is elected and property is distributed, sold, or otherwise disposed of during the six-month period following death.

    b. FMV rule does not apply to appreciated property acquired by the decedent by gift within one year before death if such property then passes from the donee-decedent to the original donor or donor's spouse. The basis of such property to the original donor (or spouse) will be the adjusted basis of the property to the decedent immediately before death.

    EXAMPLE: Son gives property with FMV of $40,000 (basis of $5,000) to terminally ill father within one year before father's death. The property is included in father's estate at FMV of $40,000. If property passes to son or son's spouse, basis will remain at $5,000. If passed to someone else, the property's basis will be $40,000.

II. GENERATION-SKIPPING TAX

This tax is imposed in addition to the federal gift and estate taxes (i.e., unified transfer tax) and is designed to prevent individuals from escaping an entire generation of gift and estate taxes by transferring property to, or in trust for the benefit of, a person that is two or more generations younger than the donor or transferor.

A. The tax approximates the unified transfer tax that would be imposed if property were actually transferred to each successive generation, and is imposed on taxable distributions, taxable terminations, and direct skips to someone at least two generations below that of the donor or transferor.

1. A taxable distribution is a distribution out of a trust's income or corpus to a beneficiary at least two generations below that of the grantor (unless the grandchild's parent is deceased and was a lineal descendant of the grantor) while an older generation beneficiary has an interest in the trust.

2. A taxable termination means that by reason of death, expiration of time, or otherwise, the interest of a nonskip person terminates (i.e., someone less than two generations below the donor or transferor) and a skip person (i.e., someone at least two generations below the donor or transferor) becomes the recipient of the trust property or the only beneficiary.

3. A direct skip occurs when one or more generations are bypassed altogether and property is transferred directly to, or in trust for, a skip person.

B. The generation-skipping transfer tax is imposed at a flat rate that equals the maximum unified transfer tax rate of 50% for 2002 (49% for 2003).

C. Exemptions available

1. A $1,100,000 exemption per transferor for 2003.

2. An unlimited exemption is available for a direct skip to a grandchild if the grandchild's parent is deceased and was a lineal descendant of the transferor.

III. INCOME TAXATION OF ESTATES AND TRUSTS

Although estates and trusts are separate taxable entities, they will not pay an income tax if they distribute all of their income to beneficiaries. In this respect they act as a conduit, since the income taxed to beneficiaries will have the same character as it had for the estate or trust.

A. An estate or trust must **file** US Fiduciary Income Tax Return Form 1041 if it has **gross income of $600 or more**.

    1. Return is due by the 15th day of the fourth month following the close of the estate or trust's taxable year.

    2. A **trust must adopt a calendar year** as its taxable year. An estate may adopt a calendar year or any fiscal year.

    3. For 2002, estate and trusts are taxed as follows:

        a. First $1,850 of taxable income is taxed at 15%

        b. Over $1,850 but not over $4,400 is taxed at 27%

        c. Over $4,400 but not over $6,750 is taxed at 30%

        d. Over $6,750 but not over $9,200 is taxed at 35%

        e. Over $9,200 is taxed at 39.1%

    4. The alternative minimum tax applies to estates and trusts and is computed in the same manner as for individuals.

    5. Estates and trusts are generally required to make estimated tax payments using the rules applicable to individuals. However, estates do not have to make estimated payments for taxable years ending within two years of the decedent's death.

B.   Classification of Trusts

    1. **Simple trust** is one that (1) is required to distribute all of its income to beneficiaries each year, (2) cannot make charitable contributions, and (3) makes no distribution of trust corpus (i.e., principal) during the year.

    2. **Complex trust** is one in which (1) the trustee has discretion whether to distribute or accumulate its income, (2) may make charitable contributions, and (3) may distribute trust corpus.

C.   Computation of Estate or Trust Taxable Income

    1. **Gross income** for an estate or trust is generally the same as for individual taxpayers.

        a. Generally no gain or loss is recognized on the transfer of property to beneficiaries to satisfy specific bequests.

        b. Gain or loss is recognized on the transfer of property to beneficiaries in lieu of cash to satisfy specific cash bequests.

    2. **Allowable deductions** for an estate or trust are generally the same as for an individual taxpayer.

        a. A personal **exemption** is allowed.

            (1) $600 for estate

            (2) $300 for simple trust (i.e., a trust required to distribute all income currently)

            (3) $100 for a complex trust (i.e., a trust other than a simple trust)

        b. Charitable contributions can be deducted without limitation if paid out of income.

            (1) Contributions are not deductible to the extent paid out of tax-exempt income.

            (2) Only complex trusts can make charitable contributions.

        c. Expenses incurred in the production of tax exempt income are not deductible.

        d. Capital losses offset capital gains and a net capital loss of up to $3,000 can be deducted with the remainder carried forward.

        e. Medical and funeral expenses of a decedent are not allowed as deductions on estate's income tax return Form 1041. However, if medical expenses are paid within twelve months of the decedent's death, they are deductible on the decedent's final Form 1040, if the estate's executor waives the deduction on the decedent's estate tax return

        f. Any unused capital loss and NOL carryovers from the decedent's final Form 1040 are not allowed as deductions.

    3. An **income distribution deduction** is allowed for distributions of income to beneficiaries.

a. **Distributable net income (DNI)** is the maximum amount of deduction for distributions to beneficiaries in any taxable year and also determines the amounts and character of the income reported by the beneficiaries.

b. Generally, DNI is the same as the estate's or trust's taxable income computed before the income distribution deduction with the following modifications:

(1) Add

(a) Personal exemption
(b) Any net capital loss deduction (limited to $3,000)
(c) Tax exempt interest (reduced by related nondeductible expenses)

(2) Subtract

(a) Net capital gains allocable to corpus
(b) Extraordinary dividends and taxable stock dividends allocated to corpus of simple trust

c. Deduction will be the lesser of DNI or the amount distributed to beneficiaries (i.e., taxable income required to be distributed, plus other amount of taxable income distributed).

D. Treatment of Simple Trust and Beneficiaries

1. Income is taxed to beneficiaries, not to trust.
2. Beneficiaries are taxed on the income required to be distributed (up to DNI), even though not actually distributed during the year.
3. Income passes through to beneficiaries retaining its characteristics (e.g., tax-exempt income passes through retaining its exempt status).
4. If multiple beneficiaries, DNI is prorated in proportion to the amount of required distribution to each beneficiary.

E. Treatment of Complex Trust and Beneficiaries

1. A two-tier income distribution system is used.

a. First tier: Distributions of the first tier are income amounts that are required to be distributed and include distributions that can be paid out of income or corpus, to the extent paid out of income.
b. Second tier: Distributions of the second tier are all other amounts that are actually paid during the year or are required to be paid.

2. DNI is first allocated to distributions in the first tier. Any remaining DNI is prorated to distributions in the second tier.

EXAMPLE: A trust has DNI of $9,000. The trust instrument requires that $6,000 of income be distributed annually to Alan. Further, it permits distributions to Baker and Carr of income or corpus in the trustee's discretion. For the current year, the trustee distributes $6,000 to Alan, $4,000 to Baker, and $2,000 to Carr.

Since Alan's distribution is a first tier distribution, all $6,000 distributed is taxable to Alan. This leaves only $3,000 of DNI to be allocated to the second tier distributions to Baker and Carr. Since DNI would be allocated in proportion to the amounts distributed, $2,000 of Baker's distribution and $1,000 of Carr's distribution would be taxable.

F. Grantor Trusts are trusts over which the grantor (or grantor's spouse) retain substantial control. The income from a grantor trust is generally taxed to the grantor, not to the trust or beneficiaries. A grantor trust generally exists if any of the following conditions are present:

1. Trust income will, or in the grantor's or nonadverse party's discretion may be, distributed to the grantor or grantor's spouse (or used to pay life insurance premiums of either).
2. The grantor (or nonadverse party) has the power to revoke the trust.
3. The grantor (or grantor's spouse) holds a reversionary interest worth more than 5% of trust corpus.
4. The grantor (or nonadverse party) can deal with trust property in a nonfiduciary capacity (e.g., purchase trust assets for less than adequate consideration or borrow trust property at below market rate).
5. The grantor (or grantor's spouse) or nonadverse party controls the beneficial enjoyment of the trust (e.g., ability to change beneficiaries).

G. Termination of Estate or Trust

1. An estate or trust is not entitled to a personal exemption on its final return.

2. Any unused carryovers (e.g., NOL or capital loss) are passed through to beneficiaries for use on their individual tax returns.

3. Any excess deductions for its final year are passed through to beneficiaries and can be deducted as miscellaneous itemized deductions.

IV. EXEMPT ORGANIZATIONS

A. Types of Organizations

1. Tax-exempt organizations are listed by class of organization in the Internal Revenue Code. Generally, an exempt organization serves some common good, is operated as a not-for-profit entity, its net earnings do not inure for the benefit of specified individuals, and the organization does not exert undue political influence. To obtain exempt status, the organization must be one of those specifically identified in the Code, and generally must apply for and receive an exemption.

2. **Sec. 501(c)(3) organizations** (religious, educational, charitable, etc.) generally must apply for exemption by filing Form 1023 within fifteen months from the end of the month in which they were organized. To qualify, (1) the organization must meet an organizational and operational test, (2) no part of the organization's net earnings can inure to the benefit of private shareholders or individuals, and (3) the organization cannot, as a substantial part of its activities, attempt to influence legislation (unless it elects an exception permitting certain lobby expenditures) or directly participate to any extent in a political campaign for or against any candidate for public office.

    a. Some organizations do not have to file for exemption (e.g., churches or an organization [other than a private foundation] normally having annual gross receipts of not more than $5,000). They automatically are exempt if they meet the requirements of Sec. 501(c)(3).

    b. The **organizational test** requires the articles of organization limit the organization's purposes to one or more exempt purposes described in Sec. 501(c)(3), and must not expressly empower the organization to engage in activities that are not in furtherance of its one or more exempt purposes, except as an insubstantial part of its activities.

    c. The **operational test** requires that an exempt organization be operated exclusively for an exempt purpose. An organization will be considered to be operated exclusively for an exempt purpose only if it engages primarily in activities that accomplish its exempt purpose. An organization will not be so regarded if more than an insubstantial part of its activities is not in furtherance of an exempt purpose.

IRC 501	*Type of Organization*	*Description*
(c) (1)	Federal and Regulated Agencies	Federal Credit Unions, FDIC, Federal Land Bank
(c) (2)	Title Holding Corporation for Exempt Organization	Corporation holding title to fraternity or sorority house
(c) (3)	Religious, Educational, Charitable, Scientific, Literary, Testing for Public Safety, Foster National or International Amateur Sports Competition, Prevention of Cruelty to Children or Animals Organizations	Activities of a nature implied by description of class of organization (e.g., church, school, museum, zoo, planetarium, Red Cross, Boy Scouts of America)
(c) (4)	Civic Leagues, Social Welfare Organizations, and Local Associations of Employees	Promotion of community welfare (e.g., community association, volunteer fire companies, garden club, League of Women Voters)
(c) (5)	Labor, Agricultural, and Horticultural Organizations	Educational or instructive, to improve conditions of work, and to improve products and efficiency (e.g., teacher's association)
(c) (6)	Business Leagues, Chamber of Commerce, Real Estate Boards, etc.	Improvement of business conditions of one or more lines of business (e.g., trade of professional associations, Chambers of Commerce)
(c) (7)	Social and Recreation Clubs	Recreation and social activities (e.g., Country Club, Sailing Club, Tennis Club)
(c) (8)	Fraternal Beneficiary Societies and Associations	Lodge providing for payment of life, sickness, accident, or other benefits to members
(c) (9)	Voluntary Employees' Beneficiary Associations	Providing for payment of life, sickness, accident or other benefits to members

(c)(10)	Domestic Fraternal Societies and Associations	Lodge devoting its net earnings to charitable, fraternal, and other specified purposes, but no life, sickness, or accident benefits to members
(c)(11)	Teachers' Retirement Fund Associations	Payment of retirement benefits to teachers
(c)(12)	Benevolent Life Insurance Associations, Mutual or Cooperative Telephone Companies, etc.	Activities of a mutually beneficial nature
(c)(13)	Cemetery Companies	Operated for benefit of lot owners who purchase lots for burial
(c)(14)	State Chartered Credit Unions	Loans to members
(c)(15)	Mutual Insurance Companies or Associations	Providing insurance to members substantially at cost
(c)(16)	Farmers Cooperative Organizations to Finance Crop Operations	Financing of crop operations in conjunction with activities of marketing or purchasing association
(c)(17)	Supplemental Unemployment Benefit Trusts	Payment of supplemental unemployment compensation benefits
(c)(19)	Member of Armed Forces Post or Organization	Veterans of Foreign Wars (VFW)
(d)	Religious and Apostolic Associations	Communal religious community that conducts business activities. Members must include pro rata share of organization's income in their gross income
(e)	Cooperative Hospital Service Organizations	Performs cooperative service for hospitals (e.g., centralized purchasing organization)
(k)	Child Care Organizations	Provides care for children

    d. **Inurement** is private benefit provided to insiders who have the institutional opportunity to direct the organization's resources to themselves, to entities in which they have an interest, or to family members. Inurement issues may arise because of excessive compensation, payment of excessive rent, receipt of less than fair value from sales of property, and inadequately secured loans.

    e. An organization (other than churches and private foundations) can elect to replace the substantial part of activities test with a limit defined in terms of expenditures for influencing legislation. **Attempting to influence legislation** includes (1) any attempt to influence any legislation through an effort to affect the opinions of the general public (i.e., grassroots lobbying), and (2) any attempt to influence any legislation through communication with any member or employee of a legislative body, or with any government official or employee who may participate in the formulation of legislation (i.e., direct lobbying).

        (1) Attempting to influence legislation does **not** include appearing before or communicating with any legislative body with respect to a possible decision of that body that might affect the powers, duties, exempt status, or the deduction of contributions to the organization.

        (2) If the election to be subject to the lobbying expenditures limits (instead of the substantial part of activities test) is made, an organization will not lose its exempt status unless it normally makes lobbying expenditures in excess of 150% of lobbying nontaxable amount or normally makes grassroots expenditures in excess of 150% of grassroots nontaxable amount.

        (3) If the election is made, an organization will be subject to a 25% excise tax on the excess of its lobbying and grassroots expenditures over the lobbying and grassroots nontaxable amounts.

3. **Private foundations** are Sec. 501(c)(3) organizations other than churches, educational organizations, hospitals or medical research organizations operated in conjunction with hospitals, endowment funds operated for the benefit of certain state and municipal colleges and universities, governmental units, and publicly supported organizations.

    a. An organization is **publicly supported** if it normally receives at least one-third of its total support from governmental units and the general public (e.g., support received in the form of gifts, grants, contributions, membership fees, gross receipts from admissions, sales of merchandise, etc.)

    b. Private foundations may be subject to taxes based on investment income, self-dealing, failure to distribute income, excess business holdings, investments that jeopardize charitable purposes, and taxable expenditures. The initial taxes (with the exception of the tax on investment income) are imposed because the organization engages in prohibited transactions. Additional taxes are imposed if the prohibited transactions are not corrected with a specified period.

4. **Feeder organizations** do not qualify for tax-exempt status. A feeder organization carries on a trade or business for the benefit of an exempt organization and remits its profits to the exempt organization.

B. **Filing Requirements**

1. Most exempt organizations must file an **annual information return** Form 990 (Return of Organization Exempt from Income Tax). Organizations **not** required to file Form 990 include churches, federal agencies, organizations whose annual gross receipts do not exceed $25,000, and private foundations.
2. Exempt organizations with **unrelated business income** must file Form 990-T (Exempt Organization Business Income Tax Return) if the organization has gross income of at least $1,000 from an unrelated trade or business. Form 990-T may be required even though Form 990 is not required.
3. **Private foundations** must annually file Form 990-PF (Return of Private Foundation). If an organization is subject to any of the excise taxes imposed on private foundations, Form 4720 (Return of Certain Excise Taxes on Charities and Other Persons) must be filed with Form 990-PF.

C. **Unrelated Business Income (UBI)**

1. **UBI** is income from a business that is (1) **regularly carried on**, and (2) is **unrelated** to the organization's exempt purpose. A business is substantially related only if the activity (not its proceeds) contributes importantly to the accomplishment of the exempt purposes of the organization.
2. Income derived from debt-financed property unrelated to the exempt function of the organization is included in UBI. The amount of such income to be included in UBI is based on the proportion of average acquisition indebtedness to the property's average adjusted basis.
3. Income from commercial product advertising in journals and other publications is generally UBI.
4. Activities specifically treated as resulting in **related income** (not UBI) include

   a. An activity where substantially all work is performed without compensation (e.g., a church runs a second-hand clothing store with all work performed by volunteers).
   b. A trade or business carried on for the convenience of students or members of a charitable, religious, or scientific organization (e.g., university bookstore).
   c. The sale of merchandise received as gifts or contributions.
   d. Income from dividends, interest, annuities, and royalties. However, such income will be included in UBI if it results from debt-financed investments.
   e. Income derived from renting real property. However, income derived from renting personal property is considered UBI unless the personal property is leased with the real property and personal property rents do not exceed 10% of total rents.
   f. Conducting bingo games if the games are not in violation of any state or local law, and are conducted in a jurisdiction that ordinarily confines bingo games to exempt organizations.

5. UBI is **taxed to the extent in excess of $1,000.** UBI is taxed at regular corporate rates if the organization is a corporation, taxed at rates applicable to trusts if the organization is a trust.

V. INCOME TAX RETURN PREPARERS

A. **Preparer**—an individual who prepares for compensation, or who employs one or more persons to prepare for compensation, an income tax return, or a substantial portion of return.

1. Preparer need **not** be enrolled to practice before the Internal Revenue Service.
2. Compensation—must be received and can be implied or explicit (e.g., a person who does neighbor's return and receives a gift has not been compensated. Accountant who prepares individual return of the president of a company, for which he performs the audit, for no additional fee as part of a prior agreement **has** been compensated [implied])

B. **AICPA Statement on Standards for Tax Services**

1. **Tax Return Positions**

   a. With respect to tax return positions, a CPA

      (1) Should not recommend a position unless there is a **realistic possibility of it being sustained** administratively or judicially on its merits if challenged.

(2) Should not prepare or sign a tax return if the CPA knows the return takes a position that the CPA could not recommend under a. above.

(3) Notwithstanding a. and b., a CPA may recommend a position that is not frivolous so long as the position is adequately disclosed on the return or claim for refund. A frivolous position is one which is knowingly advanced in bad faith and is patently improper (e.g., a return position that is contrary to a clear, unambiguous statute).

(4) Should advise the client of the potential penalty consequences of any recommended tax position.

   b. A CPA should not recommend a tax position that exploits the IRS audit process, or serves as a mere arguing position advanced solely to obtain leverage in bargaining with the IRS.

   c. A CPA has both the right and the responsibility to be an advocate for the client.

2. **Realistic Possibility Standard**

   a. The CPA should consider the weight of each authority (e.g., Code, Regs., court decisions, well-reasoned treaties, article in professional tax publications, etc.) in determining whether this standard is met, and may rely on well-reasoned treatises and articles in recognized professional tax publications.

   b. Realistic possibility of success may require as much as a **one-third likelihood** of success.

   c. The realistic possibility standard is less stringent than the "more likely than not" and "substantial authority" standards, but is more strict than the "reasonable basis" standard.

3. **Answers to Questions on Returns**

   a. A CPA should make a reasonable effort to obtain from the client and provide appropriate answers to all questions on a tax return before signing as preparer.

   b. When reasonable grounds for omitting an answer exist, the CPA is not required to provide an explanation on the return of the reason for omission. Reasonable grounds for omitting an answer include

(1) Information is not readily available and the answer is not significant in terms of taxable income or tax liability.

(2) Uncertainty as to meaning of question.

(3) Answer is voluminous and return states that data will be supplied upon examination.

4. **Procedural Aspects of Preparing Returns**

   a. A CPA may in good faith rely without verification upon information furnished by the client or by third parties, and is not required to audit, examine, or review books, records, or documents in order to independently verify the taxpayer's information.

(1) However, the CPA should not ignore implications of information furnished and should make reasonable inquires if information appears incorrect, incomplete, or inconsistent.

(2) When feasible, the CPA should refer to the client's past returns.

   b. Where the IRS imposes a condition for deductibility or other treatment of an item (e.g., requires supporting documentation), the CPA should make appropriate inquiries to determine whether the condition for deductibility has been met.

   c. When preparing a tax return, a CPA should consider information known from the tax return of another client if that information is relevant to the return being prepared, and such consideration does not violate any rule regarding confidentiality.

5. **Use of Estimates**

   a. Where data is missing (e.g., result of a fire, computer failure), estimates of the missing data may be made by the client.

   b. A CPA may prepare a tax return using estimates if it is impracticable to obtain exact data, and the estimated amounts are reasonable.

   c. An estimate should not imply greater accuracy than actually exists (e.g., estimate $1,000 rather than $999.32).

6. **Departure from Position Previously Concluded in an IRS Proceeding or Court Decision**

   a.   Unless the taxpayer is bound to a specified treatment in the later year, such as by a formal closing agreement, the treatment of an item as part of concluding an IRS proceeding or as part of a court decision in a prior year, does not restrict the CPA from recommending a different tax treatment in a later year's return.

   b.   Court decisions, rulings, or other authorities more favorable to the taxpayer's current position may have developed since the prior proceeding was concluded or the prior court decision was rendered.

7. **Knowledge of Error: Return Preparation**

   a.   The term "error" as used here includes any position, omission, or method of accounting that, at the time the return is filed, fails to meet the standards as outlined in 1. and 2. above. An error does not include an item that has an insignificant effect on the client's tax liability.

   b.   A CPA should inform a client promptly upon becoming aware of a material error in a previously filed return or upon becoming aware of a client's failure to file a required return. A CPA

   (1)   Should recommend (either orally or in writing) measures to be taken.
   (2)   Is not obligated to inform the IRS of the error, and may not do so without the client's permission, except where required by law.

   c.   If the CPA is requested to prepare the client's current return, and the client has not taken appropriate action to correct an error in a prior year's return, the CPA should consider whether to continue a professional relationship with the client or withdraw.

8. **Knowledge of Error: Administrative Proceedings**

   a.   When a CPA is representing a client in an IRS proceeding (e.g., examination, appellate conference) with respect to a return that contains an error of which the CPA has become aware, the CPA should promptly inform the client and recommend measures to be taken.

   b.   The CPA should request the client's permission to disclose the error to the IRS, and lacking such permission, should consider whether to withdraw from representing the client.

9. **Form and Content of Advice to Clients**

   a.   No standard format is required in communicating written or oral advice to a client.
   b.   Written, rather than oral, communications are recommended for important, unusual, or complicated transactions.
   c.   A CPA may choose to communicate with a client when subsequent developments affect previous advice. Such communication is only required when the CPA undertakes this obligation by specific agreement with the client.

C. Preparer Penalties

1.   If (1) any part of an understatement of liability with respect to a return or refund claim is due to a position that has no **realistic possibility of success**, (2) the return preparer knew (or reasonably should have known) of that position, and (3) that position was not disclosed or was frivolous, then the preparer is subject to a $250 penalty unless there is reasonable cause for the understatement and the preparer acted in good faith.

   a.   Realistic possibility of success may require as much as a one-third likelihood of success.
   b.   A frivolous position is one that is knowingly advanced in bad faith and is patently improper.

2.   If any part of an understatement of liability with respect to a return or refund claim is due (1) to a willful attempt to understate tax liability by a return preparer with respect to the return or claim, or (2) to any reckless or intentional disregard of rules or regulations, the preparer is subject to a penalty of $1,000.

   a.   The $1,000 penalty is reduced by the penalty paid in 1. above.
   b.   Rules and regulations include the Internal Revenue Code, Treasury Regulations, and Revenue Rulings.

3. Additional penalties may be imposed on preparers if they fail to fulfill the following requirements (unless failure is due to reasonable cause):

    a. Preparer must sign returns done for compensation.

    b. Preparer must provide a copy of the return or refund claim to the taxpayer no later than when the preparer presents a copy of the return to the taxpayer for signing.

    c. Returns and claims for refund must contain the social security number of preparer and identification number of preparer's employer or partnership (if any).

    d. Preparer must either keep a list of those for whom returns were filed with specified information, or copies of the actual returns, for three years.

    e. Employers of return preparers must retain a listing of return preparers and place of employment for three years.

    f. Preparer must not endorse or negotiate a refund check issued to a taxpayer.

    g. Preparer must not disclose information furnished in connection with the preparation of a tax return, unless for quality or peer review, or under an administrative order by a regulatory agency.

MULTIPLE-CHOICE QUESTIONS (1-82)

1. Steve and Kay Briar, US citizens, were married for the entire 2002 calendar year. In 2002, Steve gave a $30,000 cash gift to his sister. The Briars made no other gifts in 2002. They each signed a timely election to treat the $30,000 gift as made one-half by each spouse. Disregarding the unified credit and estate tax consequences, what amount of the 2002 gift is taxable to the Briars?

 a. $20,000
 b. $10,000
 c. $8,000
 d. $0

2. In 2002, Sayers, who is single, gave an outright gift of $50,000 to a friend, Johnson, who needed the money to pay medical expenses. In filing the 2002 gift tax return, Sayers was entitled to a maximum exclusion of

 a. $0
 b. $10,000
 c. $11,000
 d. $50,000

3. During 2002, Blake transferred a corporate bond with a face amount and fair market value of $20,000 to a trust for the benefit of her sixteen-year old child. Annual interest on this bond is $2,000, which is to be accumulated in the trust and distributed to the child on reaching the age of twenty-one. The bond is then to be distributed to the donor or her successor-in-interest in liquidation of the trust. Present value of the total interest to be received by the child is $8,710. The amount of the gift that is excludable from taxable gifts is

 a. $20,000
 b. $11,000
 c. $8,710
 d. $0

4. Under the unified rate schedule for 2002,

 a. Lifetime taxable gifts are taxed on a noncumulative basis.
 b. Transfers at death are taxed on a noncumulative basis.
 c. Lifetime taxable gifts and transfers at death are taxed on a cumulative basis.
 d. The gift tax rates are 5% higher than the estate tax rates.

5. Which of the following requires filing a gift tax return, if the transfer exceeds the available annual gift tax exclusion?

 a. Medical expenses paid directly to a physician on behalf of an individual unrelated to the donor.
 b. Tuition paid directly to an accredited university on behalf of an individual unrelated to the donor.
 c. Payments for college books, supplies, and dormitory fees on behalf of an individual unrelated to the donor.
 d. Campaign expenses paid to a political organization.

6. On July 1, 2002, Vega made a transfer by gift in an amount sufficient to require the filing of a gift tax return. Vega was still alive in 2003. If Vega did **not** request an extension of time for filing the 2002 gift tax return, the due date for filing was

 a. March 15, 2003.
 b. April 15, 2003.
 c. June 15, 2003.
 d. June 30, 2003.

7. Jan, an unmarried individual, gave the following outright gifts in 2002:

Donee	Amount	Use by donee
Jones	$15,000	Down payment on house
Craig	12,000	College tuition
Kande	5,000	Vacation trip

Jan's 2002 exclusions for gift tax purposes should total

 a. $27,000
 b. $25,000
 c. $22,000
 d. $ 9,000

8. When Jim and Nina became engaged in April 2002, Jim gave Nina a ring that had a fair market value of $50,000. After their wedding in July 2002, Jim gave Nina $75,000 in cash so that Nina could have her own bank account. Both Jim and Nina are US citizens. What was the amount of Jim's 2002 marital deduction?

 a. $ 64,000
 b. $ 75,000
 c. $114,000
 d. $125,000

9. Raff created a joint bank account for himself and his friend's son, Dave. There is a gift to Dave when

 a. Raff creates the account.
 b. Raff dies.
 c. Dave draws on the account for his own benefit.
 d. Dave is notified by Raff that the account has been created.

10. Fred and Ethel (brother and sister), residents of a non-community property state, own unimproved land that they hold in joint tenancy with rights of survivorship. The land cost $100,000 of which Ethel paid $80,000 and Fred paid $20,000. Ethel died during 2002 when the land was worth $300,000, and $240,000 was included in Ethel's gross estate. What is Fred's basis for the property after Ethel's death?

 a. $140,000
 b. $240,000
 c. $260,000
 d. $300,000

11. Bell, a cash-basis calendar-year taxpayer, died on June 1, 2002. In 2002, prior to her death, Bell incurred $2,000 in medical expenses. The executor of the estate paid the medical expenses, which were a claim against the estate, on July 1, 2002. If the executor files the appropriate waiver, the medical expenses are deductible on

 a. The estate tax return.
 b. Bell's final income tax return.
 c. The estate income tax return.
 d. The executor's income tax return.

12. If the executor of a decedent's estate elects the alternate valuation date and none of the property included in the gross estate has been sold or distributed, the estate assets must be valued as of how many months after the decedent's death?

 a. 12
 b. 9

c. 6

d. 3

13. What amount of a decedent's taxable estate is effectively tax-free if the maximum unified estate and gift credit is taken during 2002?

a. $ 625,000

b. $ 650,000

c. $ 675,000

d. $1,000,000

14. Which of the following credits may be offset against the gross estate tax to determine the net estate tax of a US citizen dying during 2002?

	Unified credit	Credit for gift taxes paid on gifts made after 1976
a.	Yes	Yes
b.	No	No
c.	No	Yes
d.	Yes	No

15. Fred and Amy Kehl, both US citizens, are married. All of their real and personal property is owned by them as tenants by the entirety or as joint tenants with right of survivorship. The gross estate of the first spouse to die

a. Includes 50% of the value of all property owned by the couple, regardless of which spouse furnished the original consideration.

b. Includes only the property that had been acquired with the funds of the deceased spouse.

c. Is governed by the federal statutory provisions relating to jointly held property, rather than by the decedent's interest in community property vested by state law, if the Kehls reside in a community property state.

d. Includes one-third of the value of all real estate owned by the Kehls, as the dower right in the case of the wife or curtesy right in the case of the husband.

16. In connection with a "buy-sell" agreement funded by a cross-purchase insurance arrangement, business associate Adam bought a policy on Burr's life to finance the purchase of Burr's interest. Adam, the beneficiary, paid the premiums and retained all incidents of ownership. On the death of Burr, the insurance proceeds will be

a. Includible in Burr's gross estate, if Burr owns 50% or more of the stock of the corporation.

b. Includible in Burr's gross estate only if Burr had purchased a similar policy on Adam's life at the same time and for the same purpose.

c. Includible in Burr's gross estate, if Adam has the right to veto Burr's power to borrow on the policy that Burr owns on Adam's life.

d. Excludible from Burr's gross estate.

17. Following are the fair market values of Wald's assets at the date of death:

Personal effects and jewelry	$150,000
Land bought by Wald with Wald's funds five years prior to death and held with Wald's sister as joint tenants with right of survivorship	800,000

The executor of Wald's estate did not elect the alternate valuation date. The amount includible as Wald's gross estate in the federal estate tax return is

a. $150,000

b. $550,000

c. $800,000

d. $950,000

18. Which one of the following is a valid deduction from a decedent's gross estate?

a. State inheritance taxes.

b. Income tax paid on income earned and received after the decedent's death.

c. Federal estate taxes.

d. Unpaid income taxes on income received by the decedent before death.

19. Eng and Lew, both US citizens, died in 2002. Eng made taxable lifetime gifts of $100,000 that are **not** included in Eng's gross estate. Lew made no lifetime gifts. At the dates of death, Eng's gross estate was $850,000, and Lew's gross estate was $950,000. A federal estate tax return must be filed for

	Eng	Lew
a.	No	No
b.	No	Yes
c.	Yes	No
d.	Yes	Yes

20. With regard to the federal estate tax, the alternate valuation date

a. Is required to be used if the fair market value of the estate's assets has increased since the decedent's date of death.

b. If elected on the first return filed for the estate, may be revoked in an amended return provided that the first return was filed on time.

c. Must be used for valuation of the estate's liabilities if such date is used for valuation of the estate's assets.

d. Can be elected only if its use decreases both the value of the gross estate and the estate tax liability.

21. Proceeds of a life insurance policy payable to the estate's executor, as the estate's representative, are

a. Includible in the decedent's gross estate only if the premiums had been paid by the insured.

b. Includible in the decedent's gross estate only if the policy was taken out within three years of the insured's death under the "contemplation of death" rule.

c. Always includible in the decedent's gross estate.

d. Never includible in the decedent's gross estate.

22. Ross, a calendar-year, cash-basis taxpayer who died in June 2002, was entitled to receive a $10,000 accounting fee that had not been collected before the date of death. The executor of Ross' estate collected the full $10,000 in July 2002. This $10,000 should appear in

a. Only the decedent's final individual income tax return.

b. Only the estate's fiduciary income tax return.

c. Only the estate tax return.

d. Both the fiduciary income tax return and the estate tax return.

Items 23 and 24 are based on the following data:

Alan Curtis, a US citizen, died on March 1, 2002, leaving an adjusted gross estate with a fair market value of $1,400,000 at the date of death. Under the terms of Alan's will, $375,000 was bequeathed outright to his widow, free of all estate and inheritance taxes. The remainder of Alan's estate was left to his mother. Alan made no taxable gifts during his lifetime.

23. Disregarding extensions of time for filing, within how many months after the date of Alan's death is the federal estate tax return due?
   a.   2 1/2
   b.   3 1/2
   c.   9
   d.   12

24. In computing the taxable estate, the executor of Alan's estate should claim a marital deduction of
   a. $ 250,000
   b. $ 375,000
   c. $ 700,000
   d. $1,025,000

25. In 1997, Edwin Ryan bought 100 shares of a listed stock for $5,000. In June 2002, when the stock's fair market value was $7,000, Edwin gave this stock to his sister, Lynn. No gift tax was paid. Lynn died in October 2002, bequeathing this stock to Edwin, when the stock's fair market value was $9,000. Lynn's executor did not elect the alternate valuation. What is Edwin's basis for this stock after he inherits it from Lynn's estate?
   a. $0
   b. $5,000
   c. $7,000
   d. $9,000

26. The generation-skipping transfer tax is imposed
   a.   Instead of the gift tax.
   b.   Instead of the estate tax.
   c.   At the highest tax rate under the unified transfer tax rate schedule.
   d.   When an individual makes a gift to a grandparent.

27. Under the terms of the will of Melvin Crane, $10,000 a year is to be paid to his widow and $5,000 a year is to be paid to his daughter out of the estate's income during the period of estate administration. No charitable contributions are made by the estate. During 2002, the estate made the required distributions to Crane's widow and daughter and for the entire year the estate's distributable net income was $12,000. What amount of the $10,000 distribution received from the estate must Crane's widow include in her gross income for 2002?
   a. $0
   b. $ 4,000
   c. $ 8,000
   d. $10,000

Items 28 and 29 are based on the following:

Lyon, a cash-basis taxpayer, died on January 15, 2002. In 2002, the estate executor made the required periodic distribution of $9,000 from estate income to Lyon's sole heir. The following pertains to the estate's income and disbursements in 2002:

2002 Estate Income
  $20,000   Taxable interest
  10,000   Net long-term capital gains allocable to corpus

2002 Estate Disbursements
  $5,000   Administrative expenses attributable to taxable income

28. For the 2002 calendar year, what was the estate's distributable net income (DNI)?
   a. $15,000
   b. $20,000
   c. $25,000
   d. $30,000

29. Lyon's executor does not intend to file an extension request for the estate fiduciary income tax return. By what date must the executor file the Form 1041, US Fiduciary Income Tax Return, for the estate's 2002 calendar year?
   a.   March 15, 2003.
   b.   April 15, 2003.
   c.   June 15, 2003.
   d.   September 15, 2003.

30. A distribution from estate income, that was **currently** required, was made to the estate's sole beneficiary during its calendar year. The maximum amount of the distribution to be included in the beneficiary's gross income is limited to the estate's
   a.   Capital gain income.
   b.   Ordinary gross income.
   c.   Distributable net income.
   d.   Net investment income.

31. A distribution to an estate's sole beneficiary for the 2002 calendar year equaled $15,000, the amount currently required to be distributed by the will. The estate's 2002 records were as follows:

Estate income
$40,000   Taxable interest

Estate disbursements
$34,000   Expenses attributable to taxable interest

What amount of the distribution was taxable to the beneficiary?
   a. $40,000
   b. $15,000
   c. $ 6,000
   d. $0

32. With regard to estimated income tax, estates
   a.   Must make quarterly estimated tax payments starting no later than the second quarter following the one in which the estate was established.
   b.   Are exempt from paying estimated tax during the estate's first two taxable years.
   c.   Must make quarterly estimated tax payments only if the estate's income is required to be distributed currently.
   d.   Are not required to make payments of estimated tax.

33. A complex trust is a trust that
   a.   Must distribute income currently, but is prohibited from distributing principal during the taxable year.
   b.   Invests only in corporate securities and is prohibited from engaging in short-term transactions.
   c.   Permits accumulation of current income, provides for charitable contributions, or distributes principal during the taxable year.
   d.   Is exempt from payment of income tax since the tax is paid by the beneficiaries.

34. The 2002 standard deduction for a trust or an estate in the fiduciary income tax return is

a. $0
b. $650
c. $750
d. $800

35. Which of the following fiduciary entities are required to use the calendar year as their taxable period for income tax purposes?

	Estates	Trusts (except those that are tax exempt)
a.	Yes	Yes
b.	No	No
c.	Yes	No
d.	No	Yes

36. Ordinary and necessary administration expenses paid by the fiduciary of an estate are deductible
  a. Only on the fiduciary income tax return (Form 1041) and never on the federal estate tax return (Form 706).
  b. Only on the federal estate tax return and never on the fiduciary income tax return.
  c. On the fiduciary income tax return only if the estate tax deduction is waived for these expenses.
  d. On both the fiduciary income tax return and on the estate tax return by adding a tax computed on the proportionate rates attributable to both returns.

37. An executor of a decedent's estate that has only US citizens as beneficiaries is required to file a fiduciary income tax return, if the estate's gross income for the year is at least
  a. $ 400
  b. $ 500
  c. $ 600
  d. $1,000

38. The charitable contribution deduction on an estate's fiduciary income tax return is allowable
  a. If the decedent died intestate.
  b. To the extent of the same adjusted gross income limitation as that on an individual income tax return.
  c. Only if the decedent's will specifically provides for the contribution.
  d. Subject to the 2% threshold on miscellaneous itemized deductions.

39. On January 1, 2003, Carlt created a $300,000 trust that provided his mother with a lifetime income interest starting on January 1, 2003, with the remainder interest to go to his son. Carlt expressly retained the power to revoke both the income interest and the remainder interest at any time. Who will be taxed on the trust's 2003 income?
  a. Carlt's mother.
  b. Carlt's son.
  c. Carlt.
  d. The trust.

40. Astor, a cash-basis taxpayer, died on February 3. During the year, the estate's executor made a distribution of $12,000 from estate income to Astor's sole heir and adopted a calendar year to determine the estate's taxable income. The following additional information pertains to the estate's income and disbursements for the year:

Estate income

Taxable interest	$65,000
Net long-term capital gains allocable to corpus	5,000

Estate disbursements

Administrative expenses attributable to taxable income	14,000
Charitable contributions from gross income to a public charity, made under the terms of the will	9,000

For the calendar year, what was the estate's distributable net income (DNI)?
  a. $39,000
  b. $42,000
  c. $58,000
  d. $65,000

41. For income tax purposes, the estate's initial taxable period for a decedent who died on October 24
  a. May be either a calendar year, or a fiscal year beginning on the date of the decedent's death.
  b. Must be a fiscal year beginning on the date of the decedent's death.
  c. May be either a calendar year, or a fiscal year beginning on October 1 of the year of the decedent's death.
  d. Must be a calendar year beginning on January 1 of the year of the decedent's death.

42. The private foundation status of an exempt organization will terminate if it
  a. Becomes a public charity.
  b. Is a foreign corporation.
  c. Does **not** distribute all of its net assets to one or more public charities.
  d. Is governed by a charter that limits the organization's exempt purposes.

43. Which of the following exempt organizations must file annual information returns?
  a. Churches.
  b. Internally supported auxiliaries of churches.
  c. Private foundations.
  d. Those with gross receipts of less than $5,000 in each taxable year.

44. To qualify as an exempt organization other than a church or an employees' qualified pension or profit-sharing trust, the applicant
  a. Cannot operate under the "lodge system" under which payments are made to its members for sick benefits.
  b. Need **not** be specifically identified as one of the classes on which exemption is conferred by the Internal Revenue Code, provided that the organization's purposes and activities are of a nonprofit nature.
  c. Is barred from incorporating and issuing capital stock.
  d. Must file a written application with the Internal Revenue Service.

45. To qualify as an exempt organization, the applicant
  a. May be organized and operated for the primary purpose of carrying on a business for profit, provided that all of the organization's net earnings are turned over to one or more tax exempt organizations.

b. Need **not** be specifically identified as one of the classes upon which exemption is conferred by the Internal Revenue Code, provided that the organization's purposes and activities are of a nonprofit nature.

c. Must **not** be classified as a social club.

d. Must **not** be a private foundation organized and operated exclusively to influence legislation pertaining to protection of the environment.

46. Carita Fund, organized and operated exclusively for charitable purposes, provides insurance coverage, at amounts substantially below cost, to exempt organizations involved in the prevention of cruelty to children. Carita's insurance activities are

a. Exempt from tax.

b. Treated as unrelated business income.

c. Subject to the same tax provisions as those applicable to insurance companies.

d. Considered "commercial-type" as defined by the Internal Revenue Code.

47. The filing of a return covering unrelated business income

a. Is required of all exempt organizations having at least $1,000 of unrelated business taxable income for the year.

b. Relieves the organization of having to file a separate annual information return.

c. Is **not** necessary if all of the organization's income is used exclusively for charitable purposes.

d. Must be accompanied by a minimum payment of 50% of the tax due as shown on the return, with the balance of tax payable six months later.

48. A condominium management association wishing to be treated as a homeowners association and to qualify as an exempt organization for a particular year

a. Need **not** file a formal election.

b. Must file an election as of the date the association was organized.

c. Must file an election at the beginning of the association's first taxable year.

d. Must file a separate election for each taxable year no later than the due date of the return for which the election is to apply.

49. An organization wishing to qualify as an exempt organization

a. Is prohibited from issuing capital stock.

b. Is limited to three prohibited transactions a year.

c. Must **not** have non-US citizens on its governing board.

d. Must be of a type specifically identified as one of the classes on which exemption is conferred by the Code.

50. Which one of the following statements is correct with regard to exempt organizations?

a. An organization is automatically exempt from tax merely by meeting the statutory requirements for exemptions.

b. Exempt organizations that are required to file annual information returns must disclose the identity of all substantial contributors, in addition to the amount of contributions received.

c. An organization will automatically forfeit its exempt status if any executive or other employee of the organization is paid compensation in excess of $150,000 per year, even if such compensation is reasonable.

d. Exempt status of an organization may **not** be retroactively revoked.

51. To qualify as an exempt organization, the applicant

a. Must fall into one of the specific classes upon which exemption is conferred by the Internal Revenue Code.

b. **Cannot**, under any circumstances, be a foreign corporation.

c. **Cannot**, under any circumstances, engage in lobbying activities.

d. **Cannot** be exclusively a social club.

52. To qualify as an exempt organization,

a. A written application need **not** be filed if no applicable official form is provided.

b. No employee of the organization is permitted to receive compensation in excess of $100,000 per year.

c. The applicant must be of a type specifically identified as one of the classes upon which exemption is conferred by the Code.

d. The organization is prohibited from issuing capital stock.

53. Hope is a tax-exempt religious organization. Which of the following activities is(are) consistent with Hope's tax-exempt status?

I. Conducting weekend retreats for business organizations.

II. Providing traditional burial services that maintain the religious beliefs of its members.

a. I only.

b. II only.

c. Both I and II.

d. Neither I nor II.

54. The organizational test to qualify a public service charitable entity as tax-exempt requires the articles of organization to

I. Limit the purpose of the entity to the charitable purpose.

II. State that an information return should be filed annually with the Internal Revenue Service.

a. I only.

b. II only.

c. Both I and II.

d. Neither I nor II.

55. Which of the following activities regularly conducted by a tax-exempt organization will result in unrelated business income?

I. Selling articles made by handicapped persons as part of their rehabilitation, when the organization is involved exclusively in their rehabilitation.

II. Operating a grocery store almost fully staffed by emotionally handicapped persons as part of a therapeutic program.

a. I only.

b. II only.

c.   Both I and II.

d.   Neither I nor II.

56. An organization that operates for the prevention of cruelty to animals will fail to meet the operational test to qualify as an exempt organization if

	The organization engages in insubstantial nonexempt activities	*The organization directly participates in any political campaign*
a.	Yes	Yes
b.	Yes	No
c.	No	Yes
d.	No	No

57. Which one of the following statements is correct with regard to unrelated business income of an exempt organization?

a.   An exempt organization that earns any unrelated business income in excess of $100,000 during a particular year will lose its exempt status for that particular year.

b.   An exempt organization is not taxed on unrelated business income of less than $1,000.

c.   The tax on unrelated business income can be imposed even if the unrelated business activity is intermittent and is carried on once a year.

d.   An unrelated trade or business activity that results in a loss is excluded from the definition of unrelated business.

58. Which of the following activities regularly carried out by an exempt organization will **not** result in unrelated business income?

a.   The sale of laundry services by an exempt hospital to other hospitals.

b.   The sale of heavy-duty appliances to senior citizens by an exempt senior citizen's center.

c.   Accounting and tax services performed by a local chapter of a labor union for its members.

d.   The sale by a trade association of publications used as course materials for the association's seminars that are oriented towards its members.

59. If an exempt organization is a corporation, the tax on unrelated business taxable income is

a.   Computed at corporate income tax rates.

b.   Computed at rates applicable to trusts.

c.   Credited against the tax on recognized capital gains.

d.   Abated.

60. During 2002, Help, Inc., an exempt organization, derived income of $15,000 from conducting bingo games. Conducting bingo games is legal in Help's locality and is confined to exempt organizations in Help's state. Which of the following statements is true regarding this income?

a.   The entire $15,000 is subject to tax at a lower rate than the corporation income tax rate.

b.   The entire $15,000 is exempt from tax on unrelated business income.

c.   Only the first $5,000 is exempt from tax on unrelated business income.

d.   Since Help has unrelated business income, Help automatically forfeits its exempt status for 2002.

61. Which of the following statements is correct regarding the unrelated business income of exempt organizations?

a.   If an exempt organization has any unrelated business income, it may result in the loss of the organization's exempt status.

b.   Unrelated business income relates to the performance of services, but **not** to the sale of goods.

c.   An unrelated business does **not** include any activity where all the work is performed for the organization by unpaid volunteers.

d.   Unrelated business income tax will **not** be imposed if profits from the unrelated business are used to support the exempt organization's charitable activities.

62. An incorporated exempt organization subject to tax on its 2002 unrelated business income

a.   Must make estimated tax payments if its tax can reasonably be expected to be $100 or more.

b.   Must comply with the Code provisions regarding installment payments of estimated income tax by corporations.

c.   Must pay at least 70% of the tax due as shown on the return when filed, with the balance of tax payable in the following quarter.

d.   May defer payment of the tax for up to nine months following the due date of the return.

63. If an exempt organization is a charitable trust, then unrelated business income is

a.   Not subject to tax.

b.   Taxed at rates applicable to corporations.

c.   Subject to tax even if such income is less than $1,000.

d.   Subject to tax only for the amount of such income in excess of $1,000.

64. With regard to unrelated business income of an exempt organization, which one of the following statements is true?

a.   If an exempt organization has any unrelated business income, such organization automatically forfeits its exempt status for the particular year in which such income was earned.

b.   When an unrelated trade or business activity results in a loss, such activity is excluded from the definition of unrelated business.

c.   If an exempt organization derives income from conducting bingo games, in a locality where such activity is legal, and in a state that confines such activity to nonprofit organizations, then such income is exempt from the tax on unrelated business income.

d.   Dividends and interest earned by all exempt organizations always are excluded from the definition of unrelated business income.

65. Which of the following acts constitute(s) grounds for a tax preparer penalty?

I.   Without the taxpayer's consent, the tax preparer disclosed taxpayer income tax return information under an order from a state court.

II. At the taxpayer's suggestion, the tax preparer deducted the expenses of the taxpayers' personal domestic help as a business expense on the taxpayer's individual tax return.

a. I only.
b. II only.
c. Both I and II.
d. Neither I nor II.

66. Vee Corp. retained Water, CPA, to prepare its 2002 income tax return. During the engagement, Water discovered that Vee had failed to file its 1997 income tax return. What is Water's professional responsibility regarding Vee's unfiled 1997 income tax return?

a. Prepare Vee's 1997 income tax return and submit it to the IRS.
b. Advise Vee that the 1997 income tax return has not been filed and recommend that Vee ignore filing its 1997 return since the statute of limitations has passed.
c. Advise the IRS that Vee's 1997 income tax return has not been filed.
d. Consider withdrawing from preparation of Vee's 2002 income tax return until the error is corrected.

67. To avoid tax return preparer penalties for a return's understated tax liability due to an intentional disregard of the regulations, which of the following actions must a tax preparer take?

a. Audit the taxpayer's corresponding business operations.
b. Review the accuracy of the taxpayer's books and records.
c. Make reasonable inquiries if the taxpayer's information is incomplete.
d. Examine the taxpayer's supporting documents.

68. Kopel was engaged to prepare Raff's 2002 federal income tax return. During the tax preparation interview, Raff told Kopel that he paid $3,000 in property taxes in 2002. Actually, Raff's property taxes amounted to only $600. Based on Raff's word, Kopel deducted the $3,000 on Raff's return, resulting in an understatement of Raff's tax liability. Kopel had no reason to believe that the information was incorrect. Kopel did not request underlying documentation and was reasonably satisfied by Raff's representation that Raff had adequate records to support the deduction. Which of the following statements is correct?

a. To avoid the preparer penalty for willful understatement of tax liability, Kopel was obligated to examine the underlying documentation for the deduction.
b. To avoid the preparer penalty for willful understatement of tax liability, Kopel would be required to obtain Raff's representation in writing.
c. Kopel is **not** subject to the preparer penalty for willful understatement of tax liability because the deduction that was claimed was more than 25% of the actual amount that should have been deducted.
d. Kopel is **not** subject to the preparer penalty for willful understatement of tax liability because Kopel was justified in relying on Raff's representation.

69. A penalty for understated corporate tax liability can be imposed on a tax preparer who fails to

a. Audit the corporate records.
b. Examine business operations.
c. Copy all underlying documents.

d. Make reasonable inquiries when taxpayer information appears incorrect.

70. A tax return preparer is subject to a penalty for knowingly or recklessly disclosing corporate tax return information, if the disclosure is made

a. To enable a third party to solicit business from the taxpayer.
b. To enable the tax processor to electronically compute the taxpayer's liability.
c. For peer review.
d. Under an administrative order by a state agency that registers tax return preparers.

71. A tax return preparer may disclose or use tax return information without the taxpayer's consent to

a. Facilitate a supplier's or lender's credit evaluation of the taxpayer.
b. Accommodate the request of a financial institution that needs to determine the amount of taxpayer's debt to it, to be forgiven.
c. Be evaluated by a quality or peer review.
d. Solicit additional nontax business.

72. Which, if any, of the following could result in penalties against an income tax return preparer?

I. Knowing or reckless disclosure or use of tax information obtained in preparing a return.
II. A willful attempt to understate any client's tax liability on a return or claim for refund.

a. Neither I nor II.
b. I only.
c. II only.
d. Both I and II.

73. Clark, a professional tax return preparer, prepared and signed a client's 2002 federal income tax return that resulted in a $600 refund. Which one of the following statements is correct with regard to an Internal Revenue Code penalty Clark may be subject to for endorsing and cashing the client's refund check?

a. Clark will be subject to the penalty if Clark endorses and cashes the check.
b. Clark may endorse and cash the check, without penalty, if Clark is enrolled to practice before the Internal Revenue Service.
c. Clark may endorse and cash the check, without penalty, because the check is for less than $500.
d. Clark may endorse and cash the check, without penalty, if the amount does **not** exceed Clark's fee for preparation of the return.

74. A CPA who prepares clients' federal income tax returns for a fee must

a. File certain required notices and powers of attorney with the IRS before preparing any returns.
b. Keep a completed copy of each return for a specified period of time.
c. Receive client documentation supporting all travel and entertainment expenses deducted on the return.
d. Indicate the CPA's federal identification number on a tax return only if the return reflects tax due from the taxpayer.

75. A CPA owes a duty to

a. Provide for a successor CPA in the event death or disability prevents completion of an audit.

b. Advise a client of errors contained in a previously filed tax return.

c. Disclose client fraud to third parties.

d. Perform an audit according to GAAP so that fraud will be uncovered.

76. In general, if the IRS issues a thirty-day letter to an individual taxpayer who wishes to dispute the assessment, the taxpayer

a. May, without paying any tax, immediately file a petition that would properly commence an action in Tax Court.

b. May ignore the thirty-day letter and wait to receive a ninety-day letter.

c. Must file a written protest within ten days of receiving the letter.

d. Must pay the taxes and then commence an action in federal district court.

77. A CPA will be liable to a tax client for damages resulting from all of the following actions **except**

a. Failing to timely file a client's return.

b. Failing to advise a client of certain tax elections.

c. Refusing to sign a client's request for a filing extension.

d. Neglecting to evaluate the option of preparing joint or separate returns that would have resulted in a substantial tax savings for a married client.

78. According to the profession's standards, which of the following statements is correct regarding the standards a CPA should follow when recommending tax return positions and preparing tax returns?

a. A CPA may recommend a position that the CPA concludes is frivolous as long as the position is adequately disclosed on the return.

b. A CPA may recommend a position in which the CPA has a good faith belief that the position has a realistic possibility of being sustained if challenged.

c. A CPA will usually **not** advise the client of the potential penalty consequences of the recommended tax return position.

d. A CPA may sign a tax return as preparer knowing that the return takes a position that will **not** be sustained if challenged.

79. According to the standards of the profession, which of the following statements is(are) correct regarding the action to be taken by a CPA who discovers an error in a client's previously filed tax return?

I. Advise the client of the error and recommend the measures to be taken.

II. Withdraw from the professional relationship regardless of whether or not the client corrects the error.

a. I only.

b. II only.

c. Both I and II.

d. Neither I nor II.

80. According to the profession's ethical standards, a CPA preparing a client's tax return may rely on unsupported information furnished by the client, without examining underlying information, unless the information

a. Is derived from a pass-through entity.

b. Appears to be incomplete on its face.

c. Concerns dividends received.

d. Lists charitable contributions.

81. Which of the following acts by a CPA will **not** result in a CPA incurring an IRS penalty?

a. Failing, without reasonable cause, to provide the client with a copy of an income tax return.

b. Failing, without reasonable cause, to sign a client's tax return as preparer.

c. Understating a client's tax liability as a result of an error in calculation.

d. Negotiating a client's tax refund check when the CPA prepared the tax return.

82. According to the standards of the profession, which of the following sources of information should a CPA consider before signing a client's tax return?

I. Information actually known to the CPA from the tax return of another client.

II. Information provided by the client that appears to be correct based on the client's returns from prior years.

a. I only.

b. II only.

c. Both I and II.

d. Neither I nor II.

OTHER OBJECTIVE QUESTIONS

Problem 1 (10 to 20 minutes)

Indicate the amount of the donor's taxable gift for federal gift tax purposes resulting from each of the following independent transfers. Since a numeric answer is required, a list of amounts would be presented for the candidate to select from.

1. George gave $18,000 directly to Craig, his younger brother, which Craig used to pay for his college tuition at Southeastern University.

2. Brian purchased a diamond ring for $12,000 that he gave to Janie as an engagement ring during 2002. They are planning to get married in 2003.

3. During 2002, Lance deposited $50,000 in a joint bank account established in the names of Lance and Jackie, his sister. Jackie made no deposits, and during 2002 withdrew $25,000 to purchase an automobile for her personal use.

4. Ted gave $16,000 to Community Hospital during 2002 to pay for the medical expenses of his Aunt Amy's recent operation and hospitalization. The $16,000 represents the portion of the medical expenses that were not covered by Amy's insurance.

5. Wilma made a gift from her separate funds of $60,000 during 2002 to her favorite niece, Debra. Wilma's husband, Henry, consented to split the gift. Debra used the money as a down payment on a house.

6. Ernest transferred $11,000 during 2002 to a political organization that was formed to promote the campaign of his friend, Richard, for mayor. Richard lost the election.

7. During 2002, Gene purchased a mink coat for $30,000 that he gave to his wife, Charlene.

8. Uncle Harry sold his summer home at Lake Tomahawk for $60,000 to his nephew, Scott, during 2002. Uncle Harry had paid $60,000 for the home eight years ago, and the home was worth $110,000 at the date of sale.

9. Melissa purchased real estate for $150,000 during 2002 and immediately had the property titled in the names of Melissa and Gary (her brother) as joint tenants with right of survivorship.

10. During 2002, Jerome placed property in an irrevocable trust for the benefit of his ten-year-old niece, Linda. The property will be turned over to Linda when she reaches age twenty-one. The present value of Linda's future interest when she attains age twenty-one is $11,000.

11. Charles donated $14,000 to the Salvation Army during 2002 which was used to help flood victims.

12. John paid $15,000 to Ames University during 2002 for his cousin Gina's tuition. John also paid $7,000 to the University to cover Gina's room and board, books, and student fees.

13. Aunt Selma made a gift of real property worth $90,000 to her niece, Kim, under the condition that Kim would pay the resulting gift tax liability of $25,000. The property had cost Selma $40,000.

Problem 2 (10 to 20 minutes)

During 2002, various clients went to Rowe, CPA, for tax advice concerning possible gift tax liability on transfers they made throughout 2002.

Required:

a. For each client, indicate whether the transfer of cash, the income interest, or the remainder interest is a gift of a present interest (P), a gift of a future interest (F), or not a completed gift (N).

Assume the following facts:

Cobb created a $500,000 trust that provided his mother with an income interest for her life and the remainder interest to go to his sister at the death of his mother. Cobb expressly retained the power to revoke both the income interest and the remainder interest at any time.

Items to be answered

1. The income interest at the trust's creation.

2. The remainder interest at the trust's creation.

Kane created a $100,000 trust that provided her nephew with the income interest until he reached forty-five years of age. When the trust was created, Kane's nephew was twenty-five. The income distribution is to start when Kane's nephew is twenty-nine. After Kane's nephew reaches the age of forty-five, the remainder interest is to go to Kane's niece.

3. The income interest.

During 2002, Hall, an unmarried taxpayer, made a $10,000 cash gift to his son in May and a further $12,000 cash gift to him in August.

4. The cash transfers.

During 2002, Yeats transferred property worth $20,000 to a trust with the income to be paid to her twenty-two-year-old niece Jane. After Jane reaches the age of thirty, the remainder interest is to be distributed to Yeats' brother. The income interest is valued at $9,700 and the remainder interest at $10,300.

5. The income interest.

6. The remainder interest.

Tom and Ann Curry, US citizens, were married for the entire 2002 calendar year. Tom gave a $40,000 cash gift to his uncle, Grant. The Currys made no other gifts to Grant in 2002. Tom and Ann each signed a timely election stating that each made one-half of the $40,000 gift.

7. The cash transfer.

Murry created a $1,000,000 trust that provided his brother with an income interest for ten years, after which the remainder interest passes to Murry's sister. Murry retained the power to revoke the remainder interest at any time. The income interest was valued at $600,000.

8. The income interest.

9. The remainder interest.

b. For **item 10**, determine whether the transfer is subject to the generation skipping tax (A), the gift tax (B), or both taxes (C). Disregard the use of any exclusions and the unified credit.

10. Martin's daughter, Kim, has one child, Dale. During 2002, Martin made an outright $5,000,000 gift to Dale.

Problem 3   (5 to 10 minutes)

A CPA sole practitioner has tax preparers' responsibilities when preparing tax returns for clients.

Required:

Items 1 through 9 each represent an independent factual situation in which a CPA sole practitioner has prepared and signed the taxpayer's income tax return. For each item, select from the following list the correct response regarding the tax preparer's responsibilities. A response may be selected once, more than once, or not at all.

Answer List

    P. The tax preparer's action constitutes an act of tax preparer misconduct subject to the Internal Revenue Code penalty.

    E. The Internal Revenue Service will examine the facts and circumstances to determine whether the reasonable cause exception applies; the good-faith exception applies; or both exceptions apply.

    N. The tax preparer's action does **not** constitute an act of tax preparer misconduct.

1. The tax preparer disclosed taxpayer income tax return information under an order from a state court, without the taxpayer's consent.

2. The tax preparer relied on the advice of an advisory preparer to calculate the taxpayer's tax liability. The tax preparer believed that the advisory preparer was competent and that the advice was reasonable. Based on the advice, the taxpayer had understated income tax liability.

3. The tax preparer did **not** charge a separate fee for the tax return preparation and paid the taxpayer the refund shown on the tax return less a discount. The tax preparer negotiated the actual refund check for the tax preparer's own account after receiving power of attorney from the taxpayer.

4. The tax preparer relied on information provided by the taxpayer regarding deductible travel expenses. The tax preparer believed that the taxpayer's information was correct but inquired about the existence of the travel expense records. The tax preparer was satisfied by the taxpayer's representations that the taxpayer had adequate records for the deduction. Based on this information, the income tax liability was understated.

5. The taxpayer provided the tax preparer with a detailed check register to compute business expenses. The tax preparer knowingly overstated the expenses on the income tax return.

6. The tax preparer disclosed taxpayer income tax return information during a quality review conducted by CPAs. The tax preparer maintained a record of the review.

7. The tax preparer relied on incorrect instructions on an IRS tax form that were contrary to the regulations. The tax preparer was **not** aware of the regulations or the IRS announcement pointing out the error. The understatement was immaterial as a result of the isolated error.

8. The tax preparer used income tax return information without the taxpayer's consent to solicit additional business.

9. The tax preparer knowingly deducted the expenses of the taxpayer's personal domestic help as wages paid in the taxpayer's business on the taxpayer's income tax return.

Problem 4   (10 to 20 minutes)

Items 1 through 10 are based on the following fact pattern:

Before his death, Remsen, a US citizen, made cash gifts of $7,000 each to his four sisters. In 2002 Remsen also paid $2,000 in tuition directly to his grandchild's university on the grandchild's behalf. Remsen made no other lifetime transfers. Remsen died on January 9, 2002, and was survived by his wife and only child, both of whom were US citizens. The Remsens did not live in a community property state.

At his death Remsen owned

Cash	$650,000
Marketable securities (fair market value)	900,000
Life insurance policy with Remsen's wife named as the beneficiary	
(fair market value)	500,000

Under the provisions of Remsen's will, the net cash, after payment of executor's fees and medical and funeral expenses, was bequeathed to Remsen's son. The marketable securities were bequeathed to Remsen's spouse. During 2002 Remsen's estate paid

Executor fees to distribute the decedent's property (deducted on the	
fiduciary tax return)	$15,000
Decedent's funeral expenses	12,000

The estate's executor extended the time to file the estate tax return.

On January 3, 2003, the estate's executor paid the decedent's outstanding $10,000 medical expenses and filed the extended estate tax return.

Required:

a.   For **items 1 through 5,** identify the federal estate tax treatment for each item. A response may be selected once, more than once, or not at all.

Estate Tax Treatments

F. Fully includible in Remsen's gross estate.
P. Partially includible in Remsen's gross estate.
N. Not includible in Remsen's gross estate.

1.   What is the estate tax treatment of the $7,000 cash gift to each sister?

2.   What is the estate tax treatment of the life insurance proceeds?

3.   What is the estate treatment of the marketable securities?

4.   What is the estate tax treatment of the $2,000 tuition payment?

5.   What is the estate tax treatment of the $650,000 cash?

Required:

b.   For **items 6 through 10,** identify the federal estate tax treatment for each item. A response may be selected once, more than once, or not at all.

Estate Tax Treatments

G. Deductible from Remsen's gross estate to arrive at Remsen's taxable estate.
I.   Deductible on Remsen's 2002 individual income tax return.
E. Deductible on either Remsen's estate tax return or Remsen's 2002 individual income tax return.
N. Not deductible on either Remsen's estate tax return or Remsen's 2002 individual income tax return.

6.   What is the estate tax treatment of the executor's fees?

7.   What is the estate tax treatment of the cash bequest to Remsen's son?

8.   What is the estate tax treatment of the life insurance proceeds paid to Remsen's spouse?

9.   What is the estate tax treatment of the funeral expenses?

10.   What is the estate treatment of the $10,000 of medical expenses incurred before the decedent's death and paid by the executor on January 3, 2003?

Problem 5   (10 to 20 minutes)

Items 1 through 7 are based on the following fact pattern:

Scott Lane, an unmarried US citizen, made no lifetime transfers prior to 2002. During 2002, Lane made the following transfers:

• Gave an $11,000 cash gift to Kamp, a close friend.

- Made two separate $10,000 cash gifts to his only child.
- Created an **irrevocable** trust beginning in 2002 that provided his aunt with an income interest to be paid for the next five years. The remainder interest is to pass to Lane's sole cousin. The income interest is valued at $26,000 and the remainder interest is valued at $74,000.
- Paid $25,000 tuition directly to his grandchild's university on his grandchild's behalf.
- Created an **irrevocable** trust that provided his brother with a lifetime income interest beginning in 2004, after which a remainder interest passes to their sister.
- Created a **revocable** trust with his niece as the sole beneficiary. During 2002, the niece received $12,000 interest income from the trust.

Required:

For **items 1 through 7,** determine whether the tax transactions are fully taxable, partially taxable, or not taxable to Lane in 2002 for gift tax purposes after considering the gift tax annual exclusion. Ignore the unified credit when answering the items. An answer may be selected once, more than once, or not at all.

Gift Tax Treatments

F.   Fully taxable to Lane in 2002 for gift tax purposes.
P.   Partially taxable to Lane in 2002 for gift tax purposes.
N.   Not taxable to Lane in 2002 for gift tax purposes.

1. What is the gift tax treatment of Lane's gift to Kamp?

2. What is the gift tax treatment of Lane's cash gifts to his child?

3. What is the gift tax treatment of the trust's income interest to Lane's aunt?

4. What is the gift tax treatment of the trust's remainder interest to Lane's cousin?

5. What is the gift tax treatment of the tuition payment to Lane's grandchild's university?

6. What is the gift tax treatment of the trust's income interest to Lane's brother?

7. What is the gift tax treatment of the $11,000 interest income that Lane's niece received from the revocable trust?

1. c		18. d		35. d		52. c		69. d	
2. c		19. a		36. c		53. b		70. a	
3. d		20. d		37. c		54. a		71. c	
4. c		21. c		38. c		55. d		72. d	
5. c		22. d		39. c		56. c		73. a	
6. b		23. c		40. b		57. b		74. b	
7. a		24. b		41. a		58. d		75. b	
8. b		25. b		42. a		59. a		76. b	
9. c		26. c		43. c		60. b		77. c	
10. c		27. c		44. d		61. c		78. b	
11. b		28. a		45. d		62. b		79. a	
12. c		29. b		46. a		63. d		80. b	
13. d		30. c		47. a		64. c		81. c	
14. d		31. c		48. d		65. b		82. c	
15. a		32. b		49. d		66. d			
16. d		33. c		50. b		67. c		1st: __/82 = __%	
17. d		34. a		51. a		68. d		2nd: __/82 = __%	

MULTIPLE-CHOICE ANSWER EXPLANATIONS

I.A. Gift Tax

1. (c) The requirement is to determine the amount of the $30,000 gift that is taxable to the Briars. Steve and Kay (his spouse) elected to split the gift made to Steve's sister, so each is treated as making a gift of $15,000. Since both Steve and Kay would be eligible for an $11,000 exclusion, each will have made a taxable gift of $15,000 – $11,000 exclusion = $4,000.

2. (c) The requirement is to determine the maximum exclusion available on Sayers' 2002 gift tax return for the $50,000 gift to Johnson who needed the money to pay medical expenses. The first $11,000 of gifts made to a donee during calendar year 2002 (except gifts of future interests) is excluded in determining the amount of the donor's taxable gifts for the year. Note that Sayers does not qualify for the unlimited exclusion for medical expenses paid on behalf of a donee, because Sayers did not pay the $50,000 to a medical care provider on Johnson's behalf.

3. (d) The requirement is to determine the amount of gift that is excludable from taxable gifts. Since the interest income resulting from the bond transferred to the trust will be accumulated and distributed to the child in the future upon reaching the age of twenty-one, the gift (represented by the $8,710 present value of the interest to be received by the child at age twenty-one) is a gift of a future interest and is not eligible to be offset by an annual exclusion.

4. (c) The requirement is to determine the correct statement regarding the unified transfer tax rate schedule. The unified transfer tax rate schedule applies on a cumulative basis to both life and death transfers. During a person's lifetime, a tax is first computed on cumulative lifetime taxable gifts, then is reduced by the tax on taxable gifts made in prior years in order to tax the current year's gifts at applicable marginal rates. At death, a unified transfer tax is computed on total life and death transfers, then is reduced by the tax already paid on post-1976 gifts, the unified transfer tax credit, state death taxes, foreign death taxes, and prior transfer taxes.

5. (c) The requirement is to determine which gift requires the filing of a gift tax return when the amount transferred exceeds the available annual gift tax exclusion. A gift in the form of payments for college books, supplies, and dormitory fees on behalf of an individual unrelated to the donor requires the filing of a gift tax return if the amount of payments exceeds the $10,000 annual exclusion. In contrast, no gift tax return need be filed for medical expenses or college tuition paid on behalf of a donee, and campaign expenses paid to a political organization, because there are unlimited exclusions available for these types of gifts after the annual exclusion has been used.

6. (b) The requirement is to determine the due date for filing a 2002 gift tax return (Form 709). A gift tax return must be filed on a calendar-year basis, with the return due and tax paid on or before April 15th of the following year. If the donor subsequently dies, the gift tax return is due not later than the date for filing the federal estate tax return (generally nine months after date of death). Here, since Vega was still living in 2003, the due date for filing the 2002 gift tax return is April 15, 2003.

7. (a) The requirement is to determine Jan's total exclusions for gift tax purposes. In computing a donor's gift tax, the first $11,000 of gifts made to a donee during calendar year 2002 is excluded in determining the amount of the donor's taxable gifts. Thus, $11,000 of the $15,000 given to Jones, $11,000 of the $12,000 given to Craig, and all $5,000 given to Kande can be excluded, resulting in a total exclusion of $27,000. Note that Jan's gift to Craig does not qualify for the unlimited exclusion of educational gifts paid on behalf of a donee, because the amount was paid directly to Craig. All $12,000 could have been excluded if Jan had made the tuition payment directly to the college.

8. (b) The requirement is to determine the amount of Jim's gift tax marital deduction. An unlimited marital deduction is allowed for gift tax purposes for gifts to a donee, who at the time of the gift is the donor's spouse. Thus, Jim's gift of $75,000 to Nina made after their wedding is eligible for the marital deduction, whereas the gift of the $50,000 engagement ring does not qualify because Jim and

Nina were not married at date of gift. The gift tax annual exclusion of $11,000 applies to multiple gifts to the same donee in chronological order, reducing the taxable gift of the engagement ring to $50,000 – $11,000 = $39,000. Since there is no remaining annual exclusion to reduce the gift of the $75,000 bank account, it would be completely offset by a marital deduction of $75,000.

9. (c) The requirement is to determine when a gift occurs in conjunction with Raff's creation of a joint bank account for himself and his friend's son, Dave. A gift does not occur when Raff opens the joint account and deposits money into it. Instead, a gift results when the noncontributing tenant (Dave) withdraws money from the account for his own benefit.

I.B. Estate Tax

10. (c) The requirement is to determine Fred's basis for the property after the death of the joint tenant (Ethel). When property is held in joint tenancy by other than spouses, the property's fair market value is included in a decedent's estate to the extent of the percentage that the decedent contributed toward the purchase. Since Ethel furnished 80% of the land's purchase price, 80% of its $300,000 fair market value, or $240,000 is included in Ethel's estate. Thus, Fred's basis is $240,000 plus the $20,000 of purchase price that he furnished, a total of $260,000.

11. (b) The requirement is to determine the correct treatment of medical expenses paid by the executor of Bell's estate if the executor files the appropriate waiver. The executor may elect to treat medical expenses paid by the decedent's estate for the decedent's medical care as paid by the decedent at the time the medical services were provided. To qualify for this election, the medical expenses must be paid within the one-year period after the decedent's death, and the executor must attach a waiver to the decedent's Form 1040 indicating that the expenses will not be claimed as a deduction on the decedent's estate tax return. Here, since Bell died during 2002, and the medical services were provided and paid for by Bell's estate during 2002, the medical expenses are deductible on Bell's final income tax return for 2002 provided that the executor attaches the appropriate waiver.

12. (c) If the executor of a decedent's estate elects the alternate valuation date and none of the assets have been sold or distributed, the estate assets must be included in the decedent's gross estate at their FMV as of six months after the decedent's death.

13. (d) The requirement is to determine the amount of a decedent's taxable estate that is effectively tax-free if the maximum unified estate and gift credit is taken. The maximum unified estate and gift tax credit is $345,800 for 2002. Due to the graduated structure of the tax, this credit is the equivalent of an exemption of $1,000,000 and effectively permits $1,000,000 of taxable estate to be free of tax.

14. (d) The requirement is to determine which of the credits may be offset against the gross estate tax in determining the net estate tax of a US citizen for 2002. In computing the net estate tax of a US citizen, the gross estate tax may be offset by the unified transfer tax credit, and credits for state death taxes, foreign death taxes, and prior transfer taxes. For 2002, a unified transfer tax credit of $345,800 is allowed against gift and estate taxes and is equivalent to an exemption of the first $1,000,000 of taxable gifts or taxable estate from the unified transfer tax. Only taxable gifts made after 1976 are added back to a donor's taxable estate in arriving at the tax base for the application of the unified transfer tax at death. To the extent these taxable gifts exceeded the exemption equivalent of the unified credit and required the payment of a gift tax during the donor's lifetime, such tax is then subtracted from a donor's tentative estate tax at death in arriving at the gross estate tax. Thus, although post-1976 gift taxes reduce the net estate tax, they are not subtracted as a tax credit from the gross estate tax.

15. (a) The requirement is to determine the correct statement with regard to the gross estate of the first spouse to die when property is owned by them as tenants by the entirety or as joint tenants with right of survivorship. Under the general rule for joint tenancies, 100% of the value of jointly held property is included in a deceased tenant's gross estate except to the extent that the surviving tenants can prove that they contributed to the cost of the property. However, under a special rule applicable to spouses who own property as tenants by the entirety or as joint tenants with right of survivorship, the gross estate of the first spouse to die automatically includes 50% of the value of the jointly held property, regardless of which spouse furnished the original consideration for the purchase of the property.

16. (d) The requirement is to determine the amount of insurance proceeds included in Burr's gross estate with regard to a policy on Burr's life purchased by Adam in connection with a "buy-sell" agreement funded by a cross-purchase insurance arrangement. The gross estate of a decedent includes the proceeds of life insurance on the decedent's life if (1) the insurance proceeds are payable to the estate, (2) the proceeds are payable to another for the benefit of the estate, or (3) the decedent possessed an incident of ownership in the policy. An "incident of ownership" not only means ownership of the policy in a legal sense, but also includes the power to change beneficiaries, to revoke an assignment, to pledge the policy for a loan, or to surrender or cancel the policy. Here, since the policy owned by Adam on Burr's life was not payable to or for the benefit of Burr's estate, and Burr had no incident of ownership in the policy, the full amount of insurance proceeds would be excluded from Burr's gross estate.

17. (d) The requirement is to determine the amount includible as Wald's gross estate for federal estate tax purposes. If an executor does not elect the alternate valuation date, all property in which the decedent possessed an ownership interest at time of death is included in the decedent's gross estate at its fair market value at date of death. If property was held in joint tenancy and was acquired by purchase by other than spouses, the property's total fair market value will be included in the decedent's gross estate except to the extent that the surviving tenant can prove that he/she contributed toward the purchase. Since Wald purchased the land with his own funds, the land's total fair market value ($800,000) must be included in Wald's gross estate together with Wald's personal effects and jewelry ($150,000), resulting in a gross estate of $950,000.

18. (d) The requirement is to determine the item that is deductible from a decedent's gross estate. Unpaid income taxes on income received by the decedent before death would be a liability of the estate and would be deductible from the gross estate. State inheritance taxes, income tax paid on income earned and received after the decedent's death, and federal estate taxes are not deductible in computing a decedent's taxable estate. Note that although state inheritance taxes are not deductible in computing a decedent's taxable estate, a limited tax credit is allowed for state death taxes in computing the net estate tax payable.

19. (a) The requirement is to determine whether federal estate tax returns must be filed for the estates of Eng and Lew. For a decedent dying during 2002, a federal estate tax return (Form 706) must be filed if the decedent's gross estate exceeds $1,000,000. If a decedent made taxable lifetime gifts such that the decedent's unified transfer tax credit was used to offset the gift tax, the $1,000,000 exemption amount must be reduced by the amount of taxable lifetime gifts to determine whether a return is required to be filed.

Since Lew made no lifetime gifts and the value of Lew's gross estate was only $950,000, no federal estate tax return is required to be filed for Lew's estate. In Eng's case, the $1,000,000 exemption is reduced by Eng's $100,000 of taxable lifetime gifts to $900,000. However, since Eng's gross estate totaled only $850,000, no federal estate tax return is required to be filed for Eng's estate.

20. (d) The requirement is to determine the correct statement regarding the use of the alternate valuation date in computing the federal estate tax. An executor of an estate can elect to use the alternate valuation date (the date six months after the decedent's death) to value the assets included in a decedent's gross estate only if its use decreases both the value of the gross estate and the amount of estate tax liability. Answer (a) is incorrect because the alternate valuation date cannot be used if its use increases the value of the gross estate. Answer (b) is incorrect because the use of the alternate valuation date is an irrevocable election. Answer (c) is incorrect because the alternate valuation date is only used to value an estate's assets, not its liabilities.

21. (c) The requirement is to determine when the proceeds of life insurance payable to the estate's executor, as the estate's representative, are includible in the decedent's gross estate. The proceeds of life insurance on the decedent's life are always included in the decedent's gross estate if (1) they are receivable by the estate, (2) the decedent possessed any incident of ownership in the policy, or (3) they are receivable by another (e.g., the estate's executor) for the benefit of the estate.

22. (d) The requirement is to determine the proper income and estate tax treatment of an accounting fee earned by Ross before death, that was subsequently collected by the executor of Ross' estate. Since Ross was a calendar-year, cash-method taxpayer, the income would not be included on Ross' final individual income tax return because payment had not been received. Since the accounting fee would not be included in Ross' final income tax return because of Ross' cash method of accounting, the accounting fee would be "income in respect of a decedent." For estate tax purposes, income in respect of a decedent will be included in the decedent's gross estate at its fair market value on the appropriate valuation date. For income tax purposes, the income tax basis of the decedent (zero) transfers over to the estate or beneficiary who collects the fee. The recipient of the income must classify it in the same manner (i.e., ordi-

nary income) as would have the decedent. Thus, the accounting fee must be included in Ross' gross estate and must also be included in the estate's fiduciary income tax return (Form 1041) because the fee was collected by the executor of Ross' estate.

23. (c) The requirement is to determine within how many months after the date of Alan's death his federal estate tax return should be filed. The federal estate tax return (Form 706) must be filed and the tax paid within nine months of the decedent's death, unless an extension of time has been granted.

24. (b) The requirement is to determine the amount of marital deduction that can be claimed in computing Alan's taxable estate. In computing the taxable estate of a decedent, an unlimited marital deduction is allowed for the portion of the decedent's estate that passes to the decedent's surviving spouse. Since $375,000 was bequeathed outright to Alan's widow, Alan's estate will receive a marital deduction of $375,000.

25. (b) The requirement is to determine Edwin's basis for the stock inherited from Lynn's estate. A special rule applies if a decedent (Lynn) acquires appreciated property as a gift within one year of death, and this property passes to the donor (Edwin) or donor's spouse. Then the donor's (Edwin's) basis is the basis of the property in the hands of the decedent (Lynn) before death. Since Lynn had received the stock as a gift, Lynn's basis before death ($5,000) becomes the basis of the stock to Edwin.

II. Generation-Skipping Tax

26. (c) The requirement is to determine the correct statement regarding the generation-skipping transfer tax. The generation-skipping transfer tax is imposed as a separate tax in addition to the federal gift and estate taxes, and is designed to prevent an individual from escaping an entire generation of gift and estate taxes by transferring property to a person that is two or more generations *below* that of the transferor. The tax is imposed at the highest tax rate (50%) under the unified transfer tax rate schedule.

III. Income Taxation of Estates and Trusts

27. (c) The requirement is to determine the amount of the estate's $10,000 distribution that must be included in gross income by Crane's widow. The maximum amount that is taxable to beneficiaries is limited to the estate's distributable net income (DNI). Since distributions to multiple beneficiaries exceed DNI, the estate's $12,000 of DNI must be prorated to distributions to determine the portion of each distribution that must be included in gross income. Since distributions to the widow and daughter totaled $15,000, the portion of the $10,000 distribution that must be included in the widow's gross income equals ($10,000/$15,000) x $12,000 = $8,000.

28. (a) The requirement is to determine the estate's distributable net income (DNI). An estate's DNI generally is its taxable income before the income distribution deduction, increased by its personal exemption, any net capital loss deduction, and tax-exempt interest (reduced by related nondeductible expenses), and decreased by any net capital gains allocable to corpus. Here, the estate's DNI is the

$20,000 of taxable interest reduced by the $5,000 of administrative expenses attributable to taxable income, or $15,000.

29. (b) The requirement is to determine the due date for the Fiduciary Income Tax Return (Form 1041) for the estate's 2002 calendar year. Form 1041 is due on the 15th day of the fourth month following the end of the tax year. Thus, an estate's calendar-year return is generally due on April 15th of the following year.

30. (c) The requirement is to determine the maximum amount to be included in the beneficiary's gross income for a distribution from estate income that was currently required. Distributable net income (DNI) is the maximum amount of distributions that can be taxed to beneficiaries as well as the maximum amount of distributions deduction for an estate.

31. (c) The requirement is to determine the amount of the estate's $15,000 distribution that is taxable to the sole beneficiary. The maximum amount that is taxable to the beneficiary is limited to the estate's distributable net income (DNI). An estate's DNI is generally its taxable income before the income distribution deduction, increased by its exemption, a net capital loss deduction, and tax-exempt interest (reduced by related nondeductible expenses), and decreased by any net capital gains allocable to corpus. Here, the estate's DNI is its taxable interest of $40,000, reduced by the $34,000 of expenses attributable to taxable interest, or $6,000.

32. (b) The requirement is to determine the correct statement regarding an estate's estimated income taxes. Trusts and estates must make quarterly estimated tax payments, except that an estate is exempt from making estimated tax payments for taxable years ending within two years of the decedent's death.

33. (c) The requirement is to determine the correct statement regarding a complex trust. A simple trust is one that (1) is required to distribute all of its income to designated beneficiaries every year, (2) has no beneficiaries that are qualifying charitable organizations, and (3) makes no distributions of trust corpus (i.e., principal) during the year. A complex trust is any trust that is not a simple trust. Answer (a) is incorrect because a complex trust is not required to distribute income currently, nor is it prohibited from distributing trust principal. Answer (b) is incorrect because there are no investment restrictions imposed on a complex trust. Answer (d) is incorrect because an income tax is imposed on a trust's taxable income.

34. (a) The requirement is to determine the amount of **standard deduction** for a trust or an estate in the fiduciary income tax return (Form 1041). No standard deduction is available for a trust or an estate on the fiduciary income tax return. On the other hand, a personal exemption is allowed for an estate or trust on the fiduciary income tax return. The personal exemption is $600 for an estate, $300 for a simple trust (i.e., a trust required to distribute all income currently), and $100 for a complex trust (i.e., a trust other than a simple trust).

35. (d) The requirement is to indicate whether estate and trusts are required to use the calendar year as their taxable year. All trusts (except those that are tax exempt) are generally required to use the calendar year for tax purposes.

In contrast, an estate may adopt the calendar year, or any fiscal year as its taxable year.

36. (c) The requirement is to determine the proper treatment for ordinary and necessary administrative expenses paid by the fiduciary of an estate. Ordinary and necessary administrative expenses paid by the fiduciary of an estate can be deducted on either the estate's fiduciary income tax return, or on the estate's federal estate tax return. Although the expenses cannot be deducted twice, they can be allocated between the two returns in any manner that the fiduciary sees fit. If the administrative expenses are to be deducted on the fiduciary income tax return, the potential estate tax deduction must be waived for these expenses.

37. (c) The requirement is to determine when a fiduciary income tax return for a decedent's estate must be filed. The executor of a decedent's estate that has only US citizens as beneficiaries is required to file a fiduciary income tax return (Form 1041) if the estate's gross income is $600 or more. The return is due on or before the 15th day of the fourth month following the close of the estate's taxable year.

38. (c) The requirement is to determine the correct statement regarding the charitable contribution deduction on an estate's fiduciary income tax return (Form 1041). An estate is allowed a deduction for a contribution to a charitable organization if (1) the decedent's will specifically provides for the contribution, and (2) the recipient is a qualified charitable organization. The amount allowed as a charitable deduction is not subject to any percentage limitations, but must be paid from amounts included in the estate's gross income for the year of contribution.

39. (c) The requirement is to determine who will be taxed on the trust's 2003 income. During 2003, Carlt created a trust providing a lifetime income interest for his mother, with a remainder interest to go to his son, but he expressly retained the power to revoke both the income interest and remainder interest at any time. When the grantor of a trust retains substantial control over the trust, such as the power to revoke the income and remainder interests, the trust income will be taxed to the grantor and not to the trust or beneficiaries.

40. (b) The requirement is to determine the estate's distributable net income (DNI). An estate's DNI generally is its taxable income before the income distribution deduction, increased by its personal exemption, any net capital loss deduction, and tax-exempt income (reduced by related expenses), and decreased by any net capital gain allocable to corpus. Here, the estate's DNI is the $65,000 of taxable interest, reduced by the $14,000 of administrative expenses attributable to taxable income and the $9,000 of charitable contributions. Charitable contributions are allowed as a deduction if made under the terms of the decedent's will and are paid to qualified charitable organizations from amounts included in the estate's gross income.

41. (a) The requirement is to determine the correct statement for income tax purposes regarding the initial taxable period for the estate of a decedent who died on October 24. For income tax purposes, a decedent's estate is allowed to adopt a calendar year or any fiscal year beginning on the date of the decedent's death. Answer (b) is incorrect because an estate may adopt a calendar year and is not restricted to a fiscal year. Answer (c) is incorrect because the estate's first tax year would begin on October 24, not October 1. Answer (d) is incorrect because an estate is not restricted to a calendar year, and if it adopted a calendar year, its initial year would begin with the date of the decedent's death (October 24).

IV.A.1. Tax-Exempt Organizations

42. (a)   The requirement is to determine what will terminate the private foundation status of an exempt organization. The private foundation status of an exempt organization will terminate if it becomes a public charity. Answer (b) is incorrect because a private foundation can be organized as a foreign corporation. Answer (c) is incorrect because private foundations are not required to distribute their assets to public charities. Answer (d) is incorrect because a private foundation's exempt purposes are already severely restricted by the Code.

43. (c)   The requirement is to determine which exempt organizations must file annual information returns. Private foundations must file annual information returns specifically stating items of gross income, receipts, and disbursements, and such other information as may be required. In contrast, churches, religious groups, and exempt organizations other than private foundations are required to file an information return only if their gross receipts are more than $25,000.

44. (d)   Organizations that can qualify as exempt organizations are listed in Sec. 501 of the Internal Revenue Code, and can take the form of a trust or corporation. To receive exempt status, the organization must file a written application with the IRS. In no event will exempt status be conferred upon an organization unless the organization is one of those types of organizations specifically listed in the Code. A fraternal benefit society must operate under the lodge system. An organization operating under the lodge system carries on its activities under a form of organization that comprises local branches chartered by a parent organization and can be established to provide its members with sick benefits.

45. (d)   The requirement is to determine the correct statement regarding qualification as an exempt organization. To qualify as an exempt organization, the applicant must not be a private foundation organized and operated exclusively to influence legislation pertaining to protection of the environment. Exempt status is specifically denied to organizations if a substantial part of their activities consists of "carrying on propaganda, or otherwise attempting, to influence legislation," if expenditures exceed certain amounts. Answer (a) is incorrect because an exempt organization cannot be organized for the primary purpose of carrying on a business for profit. Answer (b) is incorrect because an organization must be one of those classes upon which exemption is specifically conferred by the Internal Revenue Code. Answer (c) is incorrect because a social club organized for recreation will qualify for exemption if substantially all of the activities of the club are for such purposes and none of the profits inure to the benefit of any shareholder.

46. (a)   The requirement is to determine the proper tax treatment of Carita Fund's insurance activities. An otherwise qualifying exempt organization will instead be subject to tax if a substantial part of its activities consists of providing commercial-type insurance. Sec. 501(m)(3) provides

that "commercial-type insurance" does not include insurance provided at substantially below cost to a class of charitable recipients. Since Carita Fund was organized and operated exclusively for charitable purposes, and provided below cost insurance coverage to exempt organizations involved in the prevention of cruelty to children, its insurance activities are exempt from tax. The insurance activities do not constitute unrelated business income because the insurance activities were substantially related to the performance of the fund's exempt purpose. Answer (c) is incorrect because Carita Fund qualifies as an exempt organization.

47. (a)   The filing of a return covering unrelated business income (Form 990-T) is required of all exempt organizations having at least $1,000 of unrelated business taxable income for the year. However, this does not relieve the organization of having to file a separate information return (Form 990) if it is otherwise required to file. Answer (c) is incorrect because in determining whether income is unrelated business income, the exempt organization's need for the income or the use it makes of the profits is irrelevant. Answer (d) is incorrect because the tax on unrelated business income of exempt organizations must be paid in full with the return.

48. (d)   A condominium management association wishing to be treated as a homeowners association and thereby qualify as an exempt organization for a particular year must file a separate election for each taxable year no later than the due date of the tax return for which the election is to apply.

49. (d)   An organization wishing to qualify as an exempt organization must be of a type specifically identified as one of the classes on which exemption is conferred by the Code. In no event will exempt status be conferred upon an organization unless the organization is one of those listed. Furthermore, in order to receive exempt status, the organization must file an application with the Internal Revenue Service. Answer (a) is incorrect since an exempt organization may be organized as a corporation. Answer (b) is incorrect because an exempt organization may lose its exempt status by engaging in any prohibited transaction. Answer (c) is incorrect because non-US citizens may be on an exempt organization's governing board.

50. (b)   The requirement is to determine the correct statement regarding exempt organizations. With the exception chiefly of churches, an exempt organization (other than a private foundation) must nevertheless file an annual information return specifically stating items of gross income, receipts, and disbursements unless its gross receipts are normally not more than $25,000. An exempt organization required to file a return must annually report the total amount of contributions received as well as the identity of substantial contributors.

Answer (a) is incorrect because an organization can only achieve exempt status by filing an application for exemption with the Internal Revenue Service. Answer (c) is incorrect because there is no limitation on the amount of compensation that can be paid to an employee if the compensation is reasonable. Answer (d) is incorrect because exempt status can be retroactively revoked if an organization's character, purposes, or methods of operation are other than as stated in the application for exemption.

51. **(a)** The requirement is to determine the correct statement regarding qualification as an exempt organization. To qualify as an exempt organization, the applicant for exemption must fall into one of the specified classes of organizations that are listed in Sec. 501 as being exempt from tax. Answer (d) is incorrect because a social club can be an exempt organization as long as substantially all its activities are for such purposes and no part of its net earnings inures to the benefit of any private shareholder. Answer (c) is incorrect because most exempt organizations are permitted specified levels of lobbying expenditures, and can even elect to be subject to a tax equal to 25% of their excess lobbying expenditures to prevent loss of exempt status. Answer (b) is incorrect because foreign corporations can qualify as exempt organizations.

52. **(c)** Organizations that can qualify as exempt organizations are listed in Sec. 501 of the Internal Revenue Code. An exempt organization can take the form of a trust or a corporation. In order to receive exempt status, the organization must file an application with the Internal Revenue Service. In no event will exempt status be conferred upon an organization unless the organization is one of those listed in the Code. Answer (b) is incorrect because there is no limitation on the amount of salary that can be paid an employee.

IV.A.2. Sec. 501(c)(3) Organizations

53. **(b)** The requirement is to determine which of the activities is(are) consistent with Hope's tax-exempt status as a religious organization. An exempt organization must be operated exclusively for its exempt purpose, and other activities not in furtherance of its exempt purpose must be only an insubstantial part of its activities. A religious organization's providing traditional burial services that maintain the religious beliefs of its members would be consistent with its tax-exempt status as a religious organization. However, conducting recreational functions such as weekend retreats conducted for business organizations ordinarily would not be consistent with the tax-exempt status of a religious organization unless there were tightly scheduled religious activities and only limited free time for incidental recreation activities.

54. **(a)** The requirement is to determine which statements are correct in regard to the organizational test to qualify a public service charitable entity as tax-exempt. The term "articles of organization" includes the trust instrument, corporate charter, articles of association, or any other written instruments by which an organization is created. To satisfy the organizational test, the articles of organization (1) must limit the organization's purposes to one or more exempt purposes described in Sec. 501(c)(3); and, (2) must not expressly empower the organization to engage in activities that are not in furtherance of one or more exempt purposes, except as an insubstantial part of its activities.

55. **(d)** The requirement is to determine which of two activities (if any) will result in unrelated business income. Unrelated business income (UBI) is income derived from a trade or business, the conduct of which is not substantially related to the exercise or performance of an organization's exempt purpose. For a trade or business to be related, the conduct of the business activity must have a causal relationship to the achievement of the organization's exempt purpose. Selling articles made by handicapped persons as part

of their rehabilitation would be substantially related to the exempt purpose of an organization exclusively involved in their rehabilitation. Similarly, operating a grocery store almost fully staffed by emotionally handicapped persons as part of a therapeutic program to allow the persons to become involved with society, assume responsibility, and to exercise business judgment, would be substantially related to the rehabilitation purposes of the exempt organization.

56. **(c)** The operational test requires that an exempt organization be operated exclusively for an exempt purpose. An organization will be considered to be operated exclusively for an exempt purpose only if it engages primarily in activities that accomplish its exempt purpose. An organization will not be so regarded if more than an insubstantial part of its activities is not in furtherance of an exempt purpose. Thus, an organization that engages in insubstantial nonexempt activities will not fail the operational test. In contrast, an organization that operates for the prevention of cruelty to animals will fail the operational test if it directly participates in any political campaign.

IV.C. Unrelated Business Income (UBI)

57. **(b)** The requirement is to determine the correct statement with regard to the unrelated business income of an exempt organization. An exempt organization is not taxed on unrelated business income of less than $1,000. Answer (a) is incorrect because the amount of unrelated business income will not cause the loss of exempt status. Answer (c) is incorrect because the tax will not apply to a business activity that is not regularly carried on. Answer (d) is incorrect because a loss from an unrelated trade or business activity is allowed in computing unrelated business taxable income.

58. **(d)** The requirement is to determine which one of the listed activities will not result in unrelated business income. Unrelated business income (UBI) is income derived from any trade or business, the conduct of which is not substantially related to the exercise or performance of an organization's exempt purpose. For a trade or business to be "related," the conduct of the business activity must have a causal relationship to the achievement of the exempt purpose. A business activity will be "substantially related" only if the causal relationship is a substantial one. Assuming that the development and improvement of its members is one of the purposes for which a trade association is granted an exemption, the sale of publications used as course materials for the association's seminars for its members would be substantially related.

Answer (a) is incorrect because even though a special rule permits an exempt hospital to perform services at cost for other hospitals with facilities to serve not more than 100 inpatients, the permitted services are limited to data processing, purchasing, warehousing, billing and collection, food, clinical, industrial engineering, laboratory, printing, communications, record center, and personnel services. Answer (b) is incorrect because even though an exempt senior citizen's center may operate a beauty parlor and barber shop for its members, selling major appliances to its members has been held to generate unrelated business income. Answer (c) is incorrect because the performance of accounting and tax services for its members would be unrelated to the exempt purpose of a labor union.

59. (a) The requirement is to determine the correct statement with regard to an exempt organization's unrelated business taxable income when the exempt organization is a corporation. An exempt organization's unrelated business income in excess of $1,000 is taxed at regular corporate income tax rates if the organization is a corporation. An exempt organization must be a trust in order for its unrelated business income to be taxed at the rates applicable to trusts.

60. (b) The requirement is to determine the correct statement regarding an exempt organization's income of $15,000 derived from conducting bingo games. If an exempt organization derives income from conducting bingo games, in a locality where such activity is legal, and in a state that confines such activity to nonprofit organizations, then such income is exempt from the tax on unrelated business income. Answer (d) is incorrect because unrelated business income will not cause the revocation or forfeiture of an organization's exempt status.

61. (c) The requirement is to determine the correct statement regarding the unrelated business income of exempt organizations. A tax-exempt organization may be subject to tax on its unrelated business income if the organization conducts a trade or business that is not substantially related to the exempt purpose of the organization, and the trade or business is regularly carried on by the organization. For an exempt organization, an unrelated business does not include any activity where all the work is performed for the organization by unpaid volunteers. Answer (a) is incorrect because although unrelated business income may result in a tax, it will not result in the loss of the organization's exempt status. Answer (b) is incorrect because the term "business" is broadly defined to include any activity conducted for the production of income through the sale of merchandise or the performance of services. Answer (d) is incorrect because using a trade or business to provide financial support for the organization's exempt purpose will not prevent an activity from being classified as an unrelated trade or business and being subject to the tax on unrelated business income.

62. (b) The requirement is to determine the correct statement regarding an exempt organization's payment of estimated taxes on its unrelated business income. An exempt organization subject to tax on its unrelated business income must comply with the Code provisions regarding installment payments of estimated income tax by corporations. This means that an exempt organization must make quarterly estimated tax payments if it expects its estimated tax on its unrelated business income to be $500 or more. Answers (c) and (d) are incorrect because any tax on unrelated business income must be paid in full by the due date of the exempt organization's return.

63. (d) The requirement is to determine the correct statement regarding the taxability of unrelated business income (UBI) to an exempt organization that is a charitable trust. Answer (c) is incorrect because an exempt organization that is a charitable trust is subject to tax on its UBI only to the extent that its UBI exceeds $1,000. Answers (a) and (b) are incorrect because an exempt organization with UBI in excess of $1,000 is subject to tax at rates applicable to trusts if it is organized as a charitable trust.

64. (c) Unrelated business income (UBI) is gross income derived from any trade or business the conduct of which is not substantially related to the exercise or performance of an organization's exempt purpose. Although dividends and interest are generally excluded from UBI, they will be included if they result from debt-financed investments. Answer (d) is incorrect because it states that dividends and interest are always **excluded** from UBI. Answer (a) is incorrect because the Code only imposes a tax on UBI, it does not revoke an organization's exempt status. Answer (b) is incorrect because a net operating loss is allowed in computing unrelated business taxable income. Answer (c) is correct because Code Sec. 513(f) specifically excludes from UBI an exempt organization's conducting bingo games where such activity is legal.

V. Income Tax Return Preparers

65. (b) The requirement is to determine which acts constitute(s) grounds for a tax preparer penalty. A return preparer will be subject to penalty if the preparer knowingly or recklessly discloses information furnished in connection with the preparation of a tax return, unless such information is furnished for quality or peer review, under an administrative order by a regulatory agency, or pursuant to an order of a court. Additionally, a return preparer will be subject to penalty if any part of an understatement of liability with respect to a return or refund claim is due to the preparer's willful attempt to understate tax liability, or to any reckless or intentional disregard of rules and regulations.

66. (d) The requirement is to determine Water's responsibility regarding Vee's unfiled 1997 income tax return. A CPA should promptly inform the client upon becoming aware of the client's failure to file a required return for a prior year. However, the CPA is not obligated to inform the IRS and the CPA may not do so without the client's permission, except where required by law. If the CPA is requested to prepare the current year's return (2002) and the client has not taken action to file the return for the earlier year (1997), the CPA should consider whether to withdraw from preparing the current year's return and whether to continue a professional relationship with the client. Also, note that the normal statue of limitations for the assessment of a tax deficiency is three years after the due date of the return or three years after the return is filed, whichever is later. Thus, the statute of limitations is still open with regard to 1997 since there is no time limit for the assessment of tax if no tax return was filed.

67. (c) The requirement is to determine which action a tax return preparer must take to avoid tax preparer penalties for a return's understated tax liability due to a taxpayer's intentional disregard of regulations. A return preparer may, in good faith, rely without verification upon information furnished by the client or by third parties, and is not required to audit, examine, or review books, records, or documents in order to independently verify the taxpayer's information. However, the preparer should not ignore the implications of information furnished and should make reasonable inquiries if the furnished information appears incorrect, incomplete, or inconsistent.

68. (d) According to the Statements on Standards for Tax Services, in preparing a tax return a CPA may in good faith rely upon information furnished by the client or third parties without further verification.

69.   **(d)**   The requirement is to determine the correct statement regarding the imposition of a preparer penalty for understated corporate tax liability. A return preparer may in good faith rely without verification upon information furnished, and is not required to audit, examine, or review books, records, or documents in order to independently verify a taxpayer's information. However, the preparer should not ignore the implications of information furnished and should make reasonable inquiries if information appears incorrect, incomplete, or inconsistent.

70.   **(a)**   A tax return preparer is subject to a penalty for knowingly or recklessly disclosing corporate tax return information, if the disclosure is made to enable a third party to solicit business from the taxpayer. Taxpayer return information can be disclosed by the preparer without penalty if the disclosure is made to enable the tax processor to electronically compute the taxpayer's liability, for purposes of the tax return preparer's peer review, or if the disclosure is made under an administrative order by a state agency that registers tax return preparers.

71.   **(c)**   The requirement is to determine the correct statement regarding a tax return preparer's disclosure or use of tax return information without the taxpayer's consent. Generally, a tax return preparer who knowingly or recklessly discloses **any** information furnished to him in connection with the preparation of a return, or uses any such information other than to prepare, or to assist in preparing a return, is guilty of a misdemeanor, and upon conviction may be subject to fine and/or imprisonment. A limited exception permits the disclosure or use of tax return information for purposes of being evaluated by quality or peer reviews.

72.   **(d)**   A penalty of up to $1,000 may be assessed against a tax return preparer who knowingly or recklessly discloses or uses any tax return information other than to prepare, or assist in preparing a return. Additionally, a penalty of $1,000 will be assessed against a return preparer who willfully attempts to understate any client's tax liability on a return or claim for refund.

73.   **(a)**   Under Internal Revenue Code Section 6695(f) any person who is an income tax return preparer who endorses or otherwise negotiates any check which is issued to a taxpayer shall pay a penalty of $500.

74.   **(b)**   A CPA who prepares a federal income tax return for a fee must keep a completed copy of the return for a minimum of three years. Answer (a) is incorrect because prior to preparing a tax return the CPA would not be required to file certain notices and powers of attorney with the IRS. Answer (c) is incorrect because a CPA would only be required to ask the client if documentation of these expenses exists. The CPA would not have to actually receive and examine this documentation. Answer (d) is incorrect because the CPA's federal identification number would be required on any federal income tax return prepared for a fee.

75.   **(b)**   A CPA generally does owe a duty to inform a client that there are errors in a previously filed tax return so that the client may file an amended tax return. Answer (a) is incorrect because the client chooses his/her own CPA. Answer (c) is incorrect because CPAs are not required to disclose fraud by the client but are usually engaged to give an opinion on the fairness of the financial statements. An-

swer (d) is incorrect because although the CPA has a duty to perform an audit in accordance with GAAS and consistent with GAAP, the CPA is not under a duty to discover fraud in the audit unless the fraud would have been uncovered in the process of an ordinary audit or unless the CPA agreed to greater responsibility to uncover fraud.

76.   **(b)**   If the IRS issues a thirty-day letter to an individual taxpayer who wishes to dispute the assessment, the taxpayer may ignore the thirty-day letter and wait to receive a ninety-day letter. Answer (a) is incorrect because a taxpayer must receive a ninety-day letter before a petition can be filed in Tax Court. Answer (c) is incorrect because a taxpayer has a thirty-day period during which to file a written protest. Answer (d) is incorrect because a taxpayer is not required to pay the taxes and commence an action in federal district court.

Generally, upon the receipt of a thirty-day letter, a taxpayer who wishes to dispute the findings has thirty days to (1) request a conference with an appeals officer or file a written protest letter, or (2) may elect to do nothing during the thirty-day period and await a ninety-day letter. The taxpayer would then have ninety days to file a petition with the Tax Court. Alternatively, a taxpayer may choose to pay the additional taxes and file a claim for refund. When the refund claim is disallowed, the taxpayer could then commence an action in federal district court.

77.   **(c)**   A CPA will be liable to a tax client for damages resulting from the following activities: (1) failure to file a client's return on a timely basis, (2) gross negligence or fraudulent conduct resulting in client losses, (3) erroneous advice or failure to advise client of certain tax elections, and (4) wrongful disclosure or use of confidential information. A CPA will not be liable to a tax client for refusing to sign a client's request for a filing extension, therefore answer (c) is correct.

78.   **(b)**   According to the Statements on Standards for Tax Services, a CPA should not recommend a position unless there is a realistic possibility of it being sustained if it is challenged. Furthermore, a CPA should not prepare or sign an income tax return if the CPA knows that the return takes a position that will not be sustained if challenged. Therefore, answer (d) is incorrect. Also, a CPA should advise the client of the potential penalty consequences of any recommended tax position. Therefore, answer (c) is incorrect. Answer (a) is incorrect as a CPA may not recommend a position that is frivolous even if the position is adequately disclosed on the return.

79.   **(a)**   While performing services for a client, a CPA may become aware of an error in a previously filed return. The CPA should advise the client of the error (as required by the Statements on Standards for Tax Services) and the measures to be taken. It is the client's responsibility to decide whether to correct the error. In the event that the client does not correct an error, or agree to take the necessary steps to change from an erroneous method of accounting, the CPA should consider whether to continue a professional relationship with the client.

80.   **(b)**   A CPA may in good faith rely without verification upon information furnished by the client when preparing the client's tax return. However, the CPA should not ignore implications of information furnished and should make reasonable inquiries if information appears incorrect, incomplete, or inconsistent.

81. (c) Answer (a) is incorrect because IRC §6695(a) imposes a $50 penalty upon income tax return preparers who fail to furnish a copy of the return to the taxpayer. Answer (b) is incorrect because IRC §6695(b) imposes a $50 penalty upon income tax return preparers who fail to sign a return, unless the failure is due to reasonable cause. Answer (d) is incorrect because IRC §6695(f) imposes a $500 penalty upon income tax return preparers who endorse or otherwise negotiate a client's tax refund checks. There is no code section imposing a penalty for the understating of a client's tax liability due to an error in calculation.

82. (c) A CPA should consider both: (1) information actually known to the CPA from the tax return of another client; and (2) information provided by the client that appears to be correct based on the client's returns from prior years. In preparing or signing a return, a CPA may in good faith rely without verification upon information furnished by the client or by third parties. However, the CPA should not ignore the implications of information furnished and should make reasonable inquires if the information furnished appears to be incorrect, incomplete, or inconsistent either on its face or on the basis of other facts known to the CPA.

OTHER OBJECTIVE ANSWERS AND ANSWER EXPLANATIONS

Problem 1

1. **($7,000)** Since it was a direct gift to Craig, only an $11,000 annual exclusion applies.

2. **($1,000)** Only an $11,000 exclusion applies.

3. **($14,000)** Since Jackie made no deposits, a gift was made when she withdrew $25,000. The $25,000 gift would be reduced by an $11,000 annual exclusion.

4. **($0)** Amounts paid to health care providers for medical services on behalf of a donee (Amy) qualify for an unlimited exclusion.

5. **($38,000)** Since Wilma receives a deduction for the half of the gift to be reported by Henry, Wilma's taxable gift is $60,000 − $30,000 − $11,000 = $19,000. Henry's taxable gift is $30,000 − $11,000 = $19,000.

6. **($0)** There is an unlimited exclusion for transfers to political organizations.

7. **($0)** There is unlimited marital deduction.

8. **($39,000)** A sale for less than FMV to a family member is treated as a gift. The amount of taxable gift is the FMV of $110,000 reduced by the $60,000 payment and an $11,000 exclusion = $39,000.

9. **($64,000)** The person furnishing the consideration to acquire the property is treated as having made a gift to the other joint tenant in an amount equal to the value of the other tenant's interest in the property. The amount of taxable gift would be computed as $150,000 x 50% = $75,000 reduced by an $11,000 exclusion.

10. **($11,000)** A gift of a future interest is not eligible for exclusion.

11. **($0)** There is an unlimited deduction for gifts to charity.

12. **($0)** There is an unlimited exclusion for the payment of educational tuition paid on behalf of a donee. The $7,000 payment for room and board, books, and student fees would be offset by the annual exclusion.

13. **($54,000)** The gift tax paid by Kim is treated as consideration paid in exchange for Selma's property. The taxable gift is $90,000 − $25,000 − $11,000 = $54,000.

Problem 2

A gift occurs when a transfer becomes complete and is measured by its fair market value on that date. A gift becomes **complete** when the donor has relinquished dominion and control and no longer has the power to change its disposition, whether for the donor's benefit or for the benefit of another. An annual exclusion of up to $11,000 is available for gifts of a present interest. A **present interest** is an unrestricted right to the immediate use, possession, or enjoyment of property or the income from property. A **future interest** includes reversions, remainders, and other interests that are limited to commence in use, possession, or enjoyment at some future date or time. Gifts of future interests do not qualify for the annual exclusion.

For items 1 through 9, candidates were asked to determine whether the transfer of cash, an income interest, or a remainder interest represents a gift of a present interest (P), a gift of a future interest (F), or not a completed gift (N).

1. **(N)** Since Cobb expressly retained the power to revoke the income interest transferred to his mother at any time, he has not relinquished dominion and control and the transfer of the income interest is not a completed gift.

2. **(N)** Since Cobb expressly retained the power to revoke the remainder interest transferred to his sister at any time, he has not relinquished dominion and control and the transfer of the remainder interest is not a completed gift.

3. **(F)** Kane's transfer of an income interest to a nephew and a remainder interest to a niece are completed gifts because Kane has relinquished dominion and control. Since Kane's nephew was twenty-five years of age when the trust was created, but income distributions will not begin until the nephew is age twenty-nine, the transfer of the income interest is a gift of future interest and does not qualify for the annual exclusion.

4. **(P)** Since Hall's gifts of cash to his son were outright gifts, they are gifts of a present interest and qualify for the annual exclusion.

5. **(P)** Yeats' gift of the income interest to her twenty-two-year-old niece is a gift of a present interest qualifying for the annual exclusion since Jane has the unrestricted right to immediate enjoyment of the income. The fact that the value of the income interest does not exceed $11,000 does not affect its nature (i.e., completed gift of a present interest).

6. **(F)** Yeats' gift of the remainder interest to her brother is a completed gift of a future interest since the brother cannot enjoy the property or any of the income until Jane reaches age thirty.

7. **(P)** Tom's gift of $40,000 cash to his uncle is an outright gift of a present interest and qualifies for the annual exclusion. Since gift-splitting was elected and Tom and Ann would each receive an $11,000 annual exclusion, Tom and Ann each made a taxable gift of $20,000 − $11,000 exclusion = $9,000.

8. **(P)** Murry's gift of the income interest to his brother is a completed gift because Murry has relinquished dominion and control. It is a gift of a present interest qualifying for the annual exclusion since his brother has the unrestricted right to immediate enjoyment of the income.

9. **(N)** Since Murry retained the right to revoke the remainder interest transferred to his sister at any time, the transfer of the remainder interest does not result in a completed gift.

For item 10, candidates were asked to determine whether the transfer is subject to the generation-skipping tax (A), the gift tax (B), or both taxes (C).

10. **(C)** Since Martin made an outright gift of $5,000,000 to Dale, the transfer is a gift of a present interest and is subject to the gift tax. Since Dale happens to be Martin's grandchild, the gift also is subject to the generation-skipping tax. The generation-skipping tax on the transfer of property is imposed in addition to federal gift and estates taxes and is designed to prevent individuals from escaping an entire generation of gift and estate taxes by transferring property to, or in trust for the benefit of, a person that is two or more generations younger than the donor or transferor. The tax approximates the unified transfer tax that would be imposed if the property were actually transferred to each successive generation.

Problem 3

For **items 1 through 9,** candidates were asked to determine for each item whether (P) the tax preparer's action constitutes an act of tax preparer misconduct subject to the Internal Revenue Code penalty; (E) the IRS will examine the facts and circumstances to determine whether the reasonable cause exception applies, the good faith exception applies, or both exceptions apply; or, (N) the tax preparer's action does not constitute an act of tax preparer misconduct.

1. **(N)** A return preparer will be subject to penalty if the preparer knowingly or recklessly discloses information furnished in connection with the preparation of a tax return, unless such information is furnished for quality or peer review, under an administrative order by a regulatory agency, or pursuant to an order of a court.

2. **(E)** The reasonable cause and good faith exception applies if the return preparer relied in good faith on the advice of an advisory preparer who the return preparer had reason to believe was competent to render such advice.

3. **(P)** A return preparer will be subject to penalty if the preparer endorses or otherwise negotiates (directly or through an agent) any refund check issued to a taxpayer (other than the preparer) if the preparer was the preparer of the return or claim for refund which gave rise to the refund check.

4. **(N)** A return preparer may in good faith rely without verification upon information furnished by the client or third parties, and is not required to audit, examine, or review books, records, or documents in order to independently verify the taxpayer's information. If the IRS requires supporting documentation as a condition for deductibility, the return preparer should make appropriate inquiries to determine whether the condition has been met.

5. **(P)** A return preparer will be subject to penalty if there is a willful attempt in any manner to understate the tax liability of any taxpayer. A preparer is considered to have willfully attempted to understate liability if the preparer disregards information furnished by the taxpayer to wrongfully reduce the tax liability of the taxpayer.

6. **(N)** A return preparer will be subject to penalty if the preparer knowingly or recklessly discloses information furnished in connection with the preparation of a tax return, unless such information is furnished for quality or peer review, under an administrative order by a regulatory agency, or pursuant to an order of a court.

7. **(E)** Under these facts, a position taken on a return which is consistent with incorrect instructions does not satisfy the realistic possibility standard. However, if the preparer relied on the incorrect instructions and was not aware of the announcement or regulations, the reasonable cause and good faith exception may apply depending upon the facts and circumstances.

8. **(P)** A return preparer will be subject to penalty if the preparer knowingly or recklessly discloses information furnished in connection with the preparation of a tax return, unless such information is furnished for quality or peer review, under an administrative order by a regulatory agency, or pursuant to an order of a court.

9. **(P)** A return preparer will be subject to penalty if there is a willful attempt in any manner to understate the tax liability of any taxpayer or there is a reckless or intentional disregard of rules or regulations. The penalty will apply if a preparer knowingly deducts the expenses of the taxpayer's domestic help as wages paid in the taxpayer's business.

Problem 4

For **items 1 through 5,** candidates were asked to identify the federal tax treatment for each item by indicating whether the item was fully includible in Remsen's gross estate (F), partially includible in Remsen's gross estate (P), or not includible in Remsen's gross estate (N).

1. **(N)** Generally, gifts made before death are not includible in the decedent's gross estate, even though the gifts were made within three years of death.

2.   (F) The gross estate includes the value of all property in which the decedent had a beneficial interest at time of death. Here, the life insurance proceeds must be included in Remsen's gross estate because the problem indicates that Remsen was the owner of the policy.

3.   (F) The fair market value of the marketable securities must be included in Remsen's gross estate because Remsen was the owner of the securities at time of death.

4.   (N) Generally, gifts made before death are not includible in the decedent's gross estate.

5.   (F) The $650,000 cash that Remsen owned must be included in Remsen's gross estate.

For **items 6 through 10,** candidates were asked to identify the federal tax treatment for each item by indicating whether the item was deductible from Remsen's gross estate to arrive at Remsen's taxable estate (G), deductible on Remsen's 2002 individual income tax return (I), deductible on either Remsen's estate tax return or Remsen's 2002 individual income tax return (E), or not deductible on either Remsen's estate tax return or Remsen's 2002 individual income tax return (N).

6.   (N) The $15,000 of executor's fees to distribute the decedent's property are deductible on **either** the federal estate tax return (Form 706) or the estate's fiduciary income tax return (Form 1041). Such expenses **cannot** be deducted twice. Since the problem indicates that these expenses were deducted on the fiduciary tax return (Form 1041), they cannot be deducted on the estate tax return.

7.   (N) A decedent's gross estate is reduced by funeral and administrative expenses, debts and mortgages, casualty and theft losses, charitable bequests, and a marital deduction for the value of property passing to the decedent's surviving spouse. There is no deduction for bequests to beneficiaries other than the decedent's surviving spouse.

8.   (G) Generally, property included in a decedent's gross estate will be eligible for an unlimited marital deduction if the property passes to the decedent's surviving spouse. Here, the life insurance proceeds paid to Remsen's spouse were included in Remsen's gross estate because Remsen owned the policy, and are deductible from Remsen's gross estate as part of the marital deduction in arriving at Remsen's taxable estate.

9.   (G) Funeral expenses are deductible only on the estate tax return and include a reasonable allowance for a tombstone, monument, mausoleum, or burial lot.

10.   (E) The executor of a decedent's estate may elect to treat medical expenses paid by the estate for the decedent's medical care as paid by the decedent at the time the medical services were provided. To qualify for this election, the medical expenses must be paid within the one-year period after the decedent's death, and the executor must attach a waiver to the decedent's Form 1040 indicating that the expenses will not be claimed as a deduction on the decedent's estate tax return. In this case, the medical expenses qualify for the election because Remsen died on January 9, 2002, and the expenses were paid on January 3, 2003.

Problem 5

For **items 1 through 7,** candidates were asked to identify the federal gift tax treatment for each item by indicating whether the item is fully taxable (F), partially taxable (P), or not taxable (N) to Lane in 2002 for gift tax purposes after considering the gift tax annual exclusion.

1.   (N) There is no taxable gift because the $11,000 cash gift is a gift of a present interest and is fully offset by an $11,000 annual exclusion.

2.   (P) The $20,000 of cash gifts given to his child would be partially offset by a $11,000 annual exclusion, resulting in a taxable gift of $9,000.

3.   (P) The gift of the income interest valued at $26,000 to his aunt is a gift of a present interest and would be partially offset by an $11,000 annual exclusion, resulting in a taxable gift of $15,000.

4.   (F) Since the remainder interest will pass to Lane's cousin after the expiration of five years, the gift of the remainder interest is a gift of a future interest and is not eligible for an annual exclusion. As a result, the $74,000 value of the remainder interest is fully taxable.

5.   (N) An unlimited exclusion is available for medical expenses and tuition paid on behalf of a donee. Since Lane paid the $25,000 of tuition directly to his grandchild's university on his grandchild's behalf, the gift is fully excluded and not subject to gift tax.

6.   (F) Since Lane created the irrevocable trust in 2002 but his brother will not begin receiving the income until 2004, the gift of the income interest to his brother is a gift of a future interest and cannot be offset by an annual exclusion. As a result, the gift is fully taxable for gift tax purposes.

7.   (P) The creation of a revocable trust is not a completed gift and trust income is taxable to the grantor (Lane). As a result, a gift occurs only as the trust income is actually paid to the beneficiary. Here, the $12,000 of interest income received by the niece during 2002 is a gift of a present interest and would be partially offset by an $11,000 annual exclusion.

EXAMINATION IN ACCOUNTING AND REPORTING
(Taxation; Managerial; and Governmental & Not-for-Profit Organizations)

NOTE TO CANDIDATES: *Information for Uniform CPA Examination Candidates*, published by the AICPA, states that candidates should allocate the total time for each examination section to the questions for that section in proportion to the point value given for the question. Thus, candidates should begin each examination session by calculating the estimated time to be spent on each question.

	Point Value
All questions are required:	
No. 1	60
No. 2	10
No. 3	20
No. 4	10
Total	100

Number 1

Select the **best** answer for each of the following items. **Mark only one answer for each item.**

Items 1 through 75 are in the areas of federal taxation. The answers should be based on the Internal Revenue Code and Tax Regulations in effect for the tax period specified in the item. If *no* tax period is specified, use the *current* Internal Revenue Code and Tax Regulations.

Items 1 through 4 are based on the following:

Laura Lewis has been legally separated from her husband, Herman, since 2001. Their three-year-old son, Ronald, lived with Laura for the entire year 2002. Under the written separation agreement between Laura and Herman, Herman was obligated to pay Laura $300 per month for alimony and $200 per month for child support, or a total of $6,000 annually. However, Laura received a total of only $300 from Herman during 2002. Laura's other income in 2002 was from the following sources:

Salary	$20,000
Interest on insurance dividends left on deposit with a life insurance company	100
Interest on federal income tax refund	60

In addition, Laura's father, Albert, gave Laura a gift of 500 shares of Liba Corporation common stock in 2002. Albert's basis for the Liba stock was $4,000. At the date of this gift, the fair market value of the Liba stock was $3,000.

1. What was Laura's filing status for 2002?
   a. Single.
   b. Married filing separate return.
   c. Unmarried head of household.
   d. Married head of household.

2. How much alimony was includable in Laura's 2002 taxable income?
   a. $0
   b. $ 300
   c. $3,600
   d. $6,000

3. How much interest was includable in Laura's 2002 taxable income?
   a. $0
   b. $ 60
   c. $100
   d. $160

4. How much was includable in Laura's 2002 taxable income as a result of the receipt of the 500 shares of Liba stock?
   a. $0
   b. $3,000
   c. $3,500
   d. $4,000

Items 5 through 8 are based on the following:

John Budd, who was 58 at the date of his death on July 1, 2002, received $1,000 interest from municipal bonds during 2002. John's wife, Emma, age 57, received a $300 television set in 2002 as a gift for opening a long-term savings account at a bank. Upon John's death, Emma received life insurance proceeds of $60,000 under a group policy paid for by John's employer. In addition, an employee death benefit of $7,500 was paid to Emma by John's employer. Emma did not remarry in 2002. Emma is executrix of John's estate.

5. With regard to John's and Emma's filing status for 2002, Emma should file
   a. As a single individual, and a separate return should be filed for John as unmarried head of household.
   b. As a qualifying widow, and a separate return should be filed for John as married head of household.
   c. As a qualifying widow, and a separate return should be filed for John as a single deceased individual.
   d. A joint return including John, as married taxpayers.

6. How much taxable interest was received by John and Emma in 2002?
   a. $0
   b. $ 300
   c. $1,000
   d. $1,300

7. How much of the group life insurance proceeds should be excluded from 2002 taxable income?
   a. $0
   b. $ 5,000
   c. $50,000
   d. $60,000

8. How much of the employee death benefit should be excluded from 2002 taxable income?
  a. $0
  b. $4,500
  c. $5,000
  d. $7,500

Items 9 through 13 are based on the following:

Eric Ross, who is single, and has no dependents, had an adjusted gross income of $60,000 in 2002, comprised of the following:

Salary	$54,000
Net investment income	6,000

During 2002, uninsured art objects owned by Eric, with a basis of $50,000 and a fair market value of $70,000, sustained casualty fire damage reducing the fair market value to $60,000. Also during 2002, Eric made the following payments:

Interest on margin account at stockbroker	$18,000
Real estate taxes on condominium owned by Eric's mother, in which Eric resides	3,000
State and city gasoline taxes	180
Medical insurance premiums	300
Unreimbursed dental expenses	4,500
Contribution to political committee of elected public official	500

Eric elected to itemize his deductions for 2002.

9. How much can Eric claim in his itemized deductions for interest on his 2002 return?
  a. $0
  b. $ 6,000
  c. $ 7,000
  d. $18,000

10. How much can Eric claim as taxes in itemized deductions on his 2002 return?
  a. $0
  b. $ 180
  c. $3,000
  d. $3,180

11. How much can Eric claim in his itemized deductions for medical and dental expenses on his 2002 return?
  a. $4,800
  b. $1,800
  c. $ 300
  d. $0

12. How much can Eric claim in his itemized deductions for the casualty loss on his 2002 return?
  a. $0
  b. $3,000
  c. $3,900
  d. $4,000

13. How much of a tax credit can Eric claim in his 2002 return for the $500 political contribution?
  a. $250
  b. $100
  c. $ 50
  d. $0

Items 14 through 16 are based on the following:

Carl Tice, an employee of Canova Corp., received a salary of $50,000 from Canova in 2002. Also in 2002, Carl bought 100 shares of Nolan Corp. common stock from

Canova for $30 a share, when the market value of the Nolan stock was $50 a share. Canova had paid $20 a share for the Nolan stock in 1999.

In addition, Carl owned a building that he leased to Boss Co. on January 1, 2002, for a five-year term at $500 a month. Boss paid Carl $8,000 in 2002 to cover the following:

Rent for January to December 2002	$6,000
Advance rent for January 2003	500
Security deposit, to be applied against the final three months' rent in the fifth year of the lease	1,500

Carl also received the following dividends in 2002 from:

Mutual Life Insurance Co., on Carl's life insurance policy (total dividends received have not yet exceeded accumulated premium paid)	$ 300
General Merchandise Corp., a Texas corporation, on preferred stock	400
Second National Bank, on bank's common stock	800

14. How much should Carl report in his 2002 income tax return as compensation income received from Canova?
  a. $50,000
  b. $51,000
  c. $52,000
  d. $53,000

15. How much rent income should Carl report in his 2002 income tax return for the amounts paid to him by Boss?
  a. $6,000
  b. $6,700
  c. $7,500
  d. $8,000

16. How much dividend income should Carl report in his 2002 income tax return?
  a. $ 400
  b. $1,100
  c. $1,200
  d. $1,500

17. Dr. Chester is a cash-basis taxpayer. His office visit charges are usually paid on the date of visit or within one month. However, services rendered outside the office are billed weekly, and are usually paid within two months as patients collect from insurance companies. Information relating to 2002 is as follows:

Cash received at the time of office visits	$ 35,000
Collections on accounts receivable	130,000
Accounts receivable, January 1	16,000
Accounts receivable, December 31	20,000

Dr. Chester's gross income from his medical practice for 2002 is
  a. $165,000
  b. $169,000
  c. $181,000
  d. $185,000

18. On January 1, 2002, Hubert Toast sold stock with a cost of $4,000 to his sister Melba for $3,500, its fair market value. On July 30, 2002, Melba sold the same stock for $4,100 to a friend, in a bona fide transaction. In 2002 as a result of these transactions
  a. Neither Hubert nor Melba has a recognized gain or loss.
  b. Hubert has a recognized loss of $500.
  c. Melba has a recognized gain of $100.
  d. Melba has a recognized gain of $600.

19. In Mona Lux's 2002 income tax return, Mona validly claimed the $3,000 personal exemption for her dependent seventeen-year-old son, Brett. Since Brett earned $5,000 in 2002 selling novelties at the college he attended full-time, Brett was also required to file a 2002 income tax return. How much should Brett claim as a personal exemption in his 2002 individual income tax return?

    a. $0
    b. $ 750
    c. $1,500
    d. $3,000

Items 20 through 35 are based on the following:

Bates Corporation, a manufacturer, is a solvent, domestic, calendar-year, accrual-basis taxpayer. All of the corporation's outstanding stock is owned equally by two brothers, John and Fred Bates. The controller has been unable to compute the corporation's 2002 taxable income or tax liability because he is unfamiliar with the tax treatment of several property dispositions. You have been requested to assist the controller in determining the appropriate tax treatment of the property dispositions in question.

The controller has prepared a schedule of these dispositions and a memorandum of significant information relevant to these properties. All depreciation has been correctly computed and recorded on the books by the controller, but no entries have been made to adjust the asset and related accounts for the property dispositions. The controller's schedule and memorandum appear below.

Schedule of Property Dispositions*

	Cost	Accumulated depreciation	Cash proceeds	Fair market value	Nature of disposition
Merchandise inventory	$4,800	$ --	$ --	$ 7,000	Distributions
Marketable securities	8,300	--	--	9,650	Consulting fee
Marketable securities	3,500	--	--	4,400	Settlement of debt
Land	22,000	--	20,000	20,000	Condemnation
Building	6,800	--	2,100	--	Demolition
Warehouse	60,000	21,000	58,000	58,000	Destruction by fire
Machine	4,000	1,700	600	3,300	Trade-in
Furniture	8,200	6,560	--	1,900	Contribution
Automobile	6,000	2,250	3,000	4,300	Sale
Investment—Subo Corp.	16,500	--	--	--	Worthless security
Patent	13,000	--	31,000	31,000	Sale

*All property disposed of has been held for more than twelve months.

Additional information regarding the property dispositions follows:

Merchandise inventory. On January 22, inventory, priced by the FIFO method, was distributed to a stockholder who assumed a $5,600 account payable in connection with the distribution.

Marketable securities. On May 8, certain securities were transferred to a nonstockholder as a fee for consulting services of $9,650 in connection with current operations. Other securities were transferred to him in settlement of a $4,400 liability appearing on the corporate books.

Land. On February 15, a condemnation award was received as consideration for unimproved land held primarily as an investment and on March 31, another parcel of unimproved land to be held as an investment was purchased at a cost of $21,500.

Building. On April 2, land and building were purchased at a total cost of $34,000 of which 20% was allocated to the building on the corporate books. The real estate was acquired with the intention of demolishing the building and this was accomplished during the month of November. Cash proceeds received in November represent the net proceeds from demolition of the building.

Warehouse. On June 30, the warehouse was destroyed by fire. The warehouse was purchased January 2, 1988, and MACRS straight-line depreciation was used. On December 27, part of the insurance proceeds was used to purchase a replacement warehouse at a cost of $53,000.

Machine. On December 26, the machine was exchanged for another machine having a fair market value of $2,700 and cash of $600 was received.

Furniture. On August 15, furniture was contributed to a qualified charitable organization. No other contributions were made or pledged during 2002.

Automobile. On November 3, the automobile was sold to Fred Bates, a stockholder.

Investment in Subo Corp. On December 31, the stock of Subo Corp. was declared worthless. The investment represents ownership of 100% of the stock of Subo, which has always derived all of its gross income from manufacturing operations. Subo has never filed a consolidated tax return with Bates.

Patent. On November 18, the patent was sold to an independent third party. The patent had been held as an investment.

Required:

In accordance with the current Internal Revenue Code and Tax Regulations, select the appropriate tax treatment for the property dispositions listed in questions 20 through 35.

20. How much income should be reported by Bates Corporation on the distribution of the inventory?
    a. $0
    b. $ 800
    c. $1,400
    d. $2,200

21. How much dividend income should be reported by the stockholder who receives the distribution of inventory and assumes the $5,600 account payable in connection with the distribution?
    a. $0
    b. $1,400
    c. $4,800
    d. $7,000

22. What will be the tax basis of the merchandise inventory to the stockholder who received the distribution of inventory?
   a. $1,400
   b. $2,200
   c. $4,800
   d. $7,000

23. How much and what type of income should be reported by Bates Corporation on the compensatory transfer of securities in satisfaction of the consulting fee?
   a. $0
   b. $1,350 ordinary income.
   c. $1,350 capital gain.
   d. $9,650 capital gain.

24. How much and what type of income should be reported by Bates Corporation on the transfer of securities in settlement of its indebtedness?
   a. $0
   b. $900 ordinary income.
   c. $900 capital gain
   d. $3,500 ordinary income.

25. What amount and type of loss would be recognized by Bates Corporation on the February 15 condemnation of the unimproved land?
   a. $0
   b. $2,000 ordinary loss.
   c. $2,000 Sec. 1231 loss.
   d. $2,000 capital loss.

26. What is Bates Corporation's tax basis for the parcel of unimproved land that was purchased as an investment on March 31?
   a. $19,500
   b. $21,500
   c. $22,000
   d. $23,500

27. What amount and type of loss should be reported by Bates Corporation on the demolition of the building in November?
   a. $0
   b. $4,700 ordinary loss.
   c. $4,700 capital loss.
   d. $6,800 ordinary loss.

28. What is the minimum amount of gain that must be included in gross income by Bates Corporation on the involuntary conversion and replacement of the warehouse?
   a. $0
   b. $ 5,000
   c. $ 7,000
   d. $19,000

29. What amount and type of gain would be recognized by Bates Corporation on the December 26 trade-in of the machine?
   a. $0
   b. $600 Sec. 1245 ordinary income.
   c. $600 Sec. 1231 gain.
   d. $1,000 Sec. 1245 ordinary income.

30. What is Bates Corporation's tax basis for the machine acquired in the December 26 like-kind exchange?
   a. $2,300
   b. $2,700

   c. $1,900
   d. $8,200

31. What amount of charitable contribution can Bates Corporation deduct as a result of its contribution of furniture to a qualified charitable organization?
   a. $ 260
   b. $1,640
   c. $1,900
   d. $4,000

32. What amount of gain or loss should be reported by Bates Corporation as a result of its sale of the automobile to Fred Bates on November 3?
   a. $0
   b. $550 gain.
   c. $750 loss.
   d. $1,300 gain.

33. What amount of constructive dividend should be reported by Fred Bates as a result of his November 3 purchase of the automobile from Bates Corporation?
   a. $0
   b. $ 550
   c. $ 750
   d. $1,300

34. What amount and type of loss should be reported by Bates Corporation on the worthlessness of its Subo stock?
   a. $0
   b. $ 8,250 capital loss.
   c. $16,500 ordinary loss.
   d. $16,500 capital loss.

35. What amount and type of gain should be reported by Bates Corporation on the sale of the patent?
   a. $18,000 ordinary income.
   b. $18,000 capital gain.
   c. $31,000 ordinary income.
   d. $31,000 capital gain.

36. In 2002, Dr. James Pyle, a cash-basis taxpayer, incorporated his dental practice. No liabilities were transferred. The following assets were transferred to the corporation:

Cash (checking account)	$ 1,000
Equipment	
Adjusted basis	60,000
Fair market value	68,000

Immediately after the transfer, Pyle owned 100% of the corporation's stock. The corporation's total basis for the transferred assets is
   a. $69,000
   b. $68,000
   c. $61,000
   d. $60,000

37. To qualify for tax-free incorporation, a sole proprietor must be in control of the transferee corporation immediately after the exchange of the proprietorship's assets for the corporation's stock. "Control" for this purpose means ownership of stock amounting to at least
   a.   80.00%
   b.   66.67%
   c.   51.00%
   d.   50.00%

38. Yuki Corp., which began business in 2002, incurred the following costs in 2002 in connection with organizing the corporation:

Printing of stock certificates	$ 5,000
Underwriters' commissions on sale of stock	100,000

What portion of these costs qualifies as amortizable organization expenses deductible ratably over a period of not less than sixty months?

    a. $105,000
    b. $100,000
    c. $ 5,000
    d. $0

39. If a corporation's tentative minimum tax exceeds the regular tax, the excess amount is

    a. Carried back to the preceding taxable year.
    b. Carried back to the third preceding taxable year.
    c. Payable in addition to the regular tax.
    d. Subtracted from the regular tax.

40. The partnership of Bull and Mash had the following items of income during the taxable year ended December 31, 2002:

Net income from sales	$35,000
Dividends from domestic corporations	3,000
Dividends from foreign corporations	2,000
Net long-term capital gain	4,000
Net short-term capital gain	1,000
Net rental income	7,000
	$52,000

What is the total ordinary income of the partnership for 2002?

    a. $35,000
    b. $43,000
    c. $44,000
    d. $52,000

41. Carter Partnership had 2002 net ordinary income of $45,000 and a net long-term capital gain of $5,000. Mr. Abbott, who has a 20% interest in the profits and losses of the partnership, had 2002 drawings of $12,500 from the partnership. The other partners withdrew $27,500 during 2002. The partnership agreement does not provide for partner salaries or bonuses. Mr. Abbott had no other capital gains or losses during 2002. By how much will Mr. Abbott's 2002 adjusted gross income increase because of his interest in Crater Partnership?

    a. $ 2,000
    b. $ 8,000
    c. $ 9,400
    d. $10,000

42. The partnership of Bond and Felton has a fiscal year ending September 30. John Bond files his tax return on a calendar-year basis. The partnership paid Bond a guaranteed salary of $1,000 per month during the calendar year 2001 and $1,500 a month during the calendar year 2002. After deducting this salary the partnership realized ordinary income of $90,000 for the year ended September 30, 2001, and $80,000 for the year ended September 30, 2002. Bond's share of the profits is the salary paid him plus 40% of the ordinary income after deducting this salary. For 2002, Bond should report taxable income from the partnership of

    a. $36,500
    b. $44,000

    c. $48,500
    d. $50,000

43. In January 2002, Martin and Louis formed a partnership with each contributing $75,000 cash. The partnership agreement provided that Martin would receive a guaranteed salary of $20,000 and that partnership profits and losses (computed after deducting Martin's salary) would be shared equally. For the year ended December 31, 2002, the partnership's operations resulted in a loss of $18,000 after payment of Martin's salary. The partnership had no outstanding liabilities as of December 31, 2002. What is the amount of Martin's partnership basis as of December 31, 2002?

    a. 46,000
    b. 66,000
    c. 76,000
    d. 86,000

44. On July 1, 2002, Bertram Bryant acquired a 30% interest in Windward Company, a partnership, by contributing property with an adjusted basis of $5,000 and a fair market value of $12,000. The property was subject to a mortgage of $8,000, which was assumed by Windward. What is Bryant's basis of his interest in Windward?

    a. $0
    b. $4,000
    c. $5,000
    d. $6,400

45. A partner's taxable income, arising from the partner's interest in a partnership, includes

    a. Only the partner's share of partnership income actually distributed to the partner during the year.
    b. The partner's share of partnership income, whether or not distributed to the partner during the year.
    c. Only the partner's salary actually paid to the partner during the year.
    d. Only the partner's salary and interest paid to the partner during the year, and deducted by the partnership during that year.

46. The basis of property (other than money) distributed by a partnership to a partner, in complete liquidation of the partner's interest, shall be an amount equal to the

    a. Fair market value of the property.
    b. Book value of the property.
    c. Adjusted basis of such partner's interest in the partnership, reduced by any money distributed in the same transaction.
    d. Adjusted basis of such partner's interest in the partnership, increased by any money distributed in the same transaction.

47. If an individual donor makes a gift of future interest whereby the donee is to receive possession of the gift at some time in the future, the 2002 annual exclusion for gift tax purposes is

    a. $0
    b. $ 3,000
    c. $10,000
    d. $11,000

48. For income tax purposes, all estates

    a. Must adopt a calendar year, except for estates in existence prior to 2002.

b.   May adopt a calendar year or any fiscal year.

c.   Must adopt a calendar year regardless of the year the estate was established.

d.   Must use the same taxable year as that of its principal beneficiary.

49. If the executor of Alan's estate elects the alternate valuation method, all remaining undistributed property included in the gross estate must be valued as of how many months after Alan's death?

    a.   12

    b.   9

    c.   6

    d.   3

50. For the year ended December 31, 2002, Kork Corp.'s book income, before federal income taxes, was $300,000. Included in this $300,000 were the following items:

Provision for state corporation income tax	$3,000
Interest income on United States obligations	8,000
Interest paid on loan to carry United States obligations	2,000

How much was Kork's 2002 taxable income?

    a. $292,000

    b. $294,000

    c. $300,000

    d. $303,000

51. Alston Corp. has three stockholders and derives all of its income from investments in stocks and securities. Alston regularly distributes 51% of its taxable income as dividends to its stockholders. Alston is a(n)

    a.   Corporation subject to the accumulated earnings tax.

    b.   Personal holding company.

    c.   Exempt organization.

    d.   Regulated investment company.

52. With regard to consolidated returns, which one of the following statements is correct?

    a.   The common parent must directly own 51% or more of the total voting power of all corporations included in the consolidated return.

    b.   Of all intercompany dividends paid by the subsidiaries to the parent, 70% are excludable from taxable income on the consolidated return.

    c.   Only corporations that issue their audited financial statements on a consolidated basis may file consolidated tax returns.

    d.   Operating losses of one group member may be used to offset operating profits of the other members included in the consolidated return.

53. The accumulated earnings tax can be imposed

    a.   On both partnerships and corporations.

    b.   On companies that make distributions in excess of accumulated earnings.

    c.   On personal holding companies.

    d.   Regardless of the number of stockholders of a corporation.

54. Bow, Inc., an S corporation, has three equal stockholders. For the year ended December 31, 2002, Bow has ordinary income of $300,000. Bow made cash distributions totaling $120,000 during 2002. For 2002, what amount from Bow should be included in each stockholder's gross income?

    a. $140,000

    b. $100,000

    c. $ 60,000

    d. $ 40,000

55. Grey, a calendar-year taxpayer, was employed and resided in New York. On February 2, 2002, Grey was permanently transferred to Florida by his employer. Grey worked full-time for the entire year. In 2002, Grey incurred and paid the following unreimbursed expenses in relocating.

Lodging and travel expenses while moving	$1,000
Premove househunting costs	1,200
Costs of moving household furnishings and personal effects	1,800

What amount was deductible as moving expense on Grey's 2002 tax return?

    a. $4,000

    b. $2,800

    c. $1,800

    d. $1,000

56. Matthews was a cash-basis taxpayer whose records showed the following:

2002 state and local income taxes withheld	$1,500
2002 state estimated income taxes paid December 30, 2002	400
2002 federal income taxes withheld	2,500
2002 state and local income taxes paid April 17, 2003	300

What amount was Matthews entitled to claim for taxes on her 2002 Schedule A of Form 1040?

    a. $4,700

    b. $2,200

    c. $1,900

    d. $1,500

57. Which item is subject to the phaseout of the amount of certain itemized deductions that may be claimed by high-income individuals?

    a.   Charitable contributions.

    b.   Medical costs.

    c.   Nonbusiness casualty losses.

    d.   Investment interest deductions.

58. Which of the following is(are) among the requirements to enable a taxpayer to be classified as a "qualifying widow(er)"?

  I.   A dependent has lived with the taxpayer for six months.

  II.   The taxpayer has maintained the cost of the principal residence for six months.

    a.   I only.

    b.   II only.

    c.   Both I and II.

    d.   Neither I nor II.

59. In 2002, Smith, a divorced person, provided over one-half the support for his widowed mother, Ruth, and his son, Clay, both of whom are US citizens. During 2002, Ruth did not live with Smith. She received $9,000 in social security benefits. Clay, a full-time graduate student, and his wife lived with Smith. Clay had no income but filed a joint return for 2002, owing an additional $500 in taxes on his wife's income. How many exemptions was Smith entitled to claim on his 2002 tax return?

    a.   4

b.   3

c.   2

d.   1

60. In 2002, Don Mills, a single taxpayer, had $70,000 in taxable income before personal exemptions. Mills had no tax preferences. His itemized deductions were as follows:

State and local income taxes	$5,000
Home mortgage interest on loan to acquire residence	6,000
Miscellaneous deductions that exceed 2% of adjusted gross income	2,000

What amount did Mills report as alternative minimum taxable income before the AMT exemption?

    a. $72,000

    b. $75,000

    c. $77,000

    d. $83,000

61. At partnership inception, Black acquires a 50% interest in Decorators Partnership by contributing property with an adjusted basis of $250,000. Black recognizes a gain if

I.   The fair market value of the contributed property exceeds its adjusted basis.

II.   The property is encumbered by a mortgage with a balance of $100,000.

    a.   I only.

    b.   II only.

    c.   Both I and II.

    d.   Neither I nor II.

62. On January 4, 2002, Smith and White contributed $4,000 and $6,000 in cash, respectively, and formed the Marco General Partnership. The partnership agreement allocated profits and losses 40% to Smith and 60% to White. In 2002, Marco purchased property from an unrelated seller for $10,000 cash and a $40,000 mortgage note that was the general liability of the partnership. Marco's liability

    a.   Increases Smith's partnership basis by $16,000.

    b.   Increases Smith's partnership basis by $20,000.

    c.   Increases Smith's partnership basis by $24,000.

    d.   Has **no** effect on Smith's partnership basis.

63. Hart's adjusted basis in Best Partnership was $9,000 at the time he received the following nonliquidating distribution of partnership property:

Cash		$ 5,000
Land		
Adjusted basis		7,000
Fair market value		10,000

What was the amount of Hart's basis in the land?

    a. $0

    b. $ 4,000

    c. $ 7,000

    d. $10,000

64. Stone's basis in Ace Partnership was $70,000 at the time he received a nonliquidating distribution of partnership capital assets. These capital assets had an adjusted basis of $65,000 to Ace, and a fair market value of $83,000. Ace had no unrealized receivables, appreciated inventory, or properties that had been contributed by its partners. What was Stone's recognized gain or loss on the distribution?

    a. $18,000 ordinary income.

b. $13,000 capital gain.

c. $ 5,000 capital loss

d. $0

65. On January 3, 2002, the partners' interests in the capital, profits, and losses of Able Partnership were

	% of capital, profits and losses
Dean	25%
Poe	30%
Ritt	45%

On February 4, 2002, Poe sold her entire interest to an unrelated party. Dean sold his 25% interest in Able to another unrelated party on December 20, 2002. No other transactions took place in 2002. For tax purposes, which of the following statements is correct with respect to Able?

    a.   Able terminated as of February 4, 2002.

    b.   Able terminated as of December 20, 2002.

    c.   Able terminated as of December 31, 2002.

    d.   Able did **not** terminate.

66. Curry's sale of her partnership interest causes a partnership termination. The partnership's business and financial operations are continued by other members. What is(are) the effect(s) of the termination?

I.   There is a deemed distribution of assets to the remaining partners and the purchaser.

II.   There is a hypothetical recontribution of assets to a new partnership.

    a.   I only.

    b.   II only.

    c.   Both I and II.

    d.   Neither I nor II.

67. The organizational test to qualify a public service charitable entity as tax-exempt requires the articles of organization to

I.   Limit the purpose of the entity to the charitable purpose.

II.   State that an information return should be filed annually with the Internal Revenue Service.

    a.   I only.

    b.   II only.

    c.   Both I and II.

    d.   Neither I nor II.

68. Which of the following activities regularly conducted by a tax-exempt organization will result in unrelated business income?

I.   Selling articles made by handicapped persons as part of their rehabilitation, when the organization is involved exclusively in their rehabilitation.

II.   Operating a grocery store almost fully staffed by emotionally handicapped persons as part of a therapeutic program.

    a.   I only.

    b.   II only.

    c.   Both I and II.

    d.   Neither I nor II.

69. A tax return preparer may disclose or use tax return information without the taxpayer's consent to

    a.   Facilitate a supplier's or lender's credit evaluation of the taxpayer.

b. Accommodate the request of a financial institution that needs to determine the amount of taxpayer's debt to it, to be forgiven.
c. Be evaluated by a quality or peer review.
d. Solicit additional nontax business.

70. A CPA who prepares clients' federal income tax returns for a fee must
a. File certain required notices and powers of attorney with the IRS before preparing any returns.
b. Keep a completed copy of each return for a specified period of time.
c. Receive client documentation supporting all travel and entertainment expenses deducted on the return.
d. Indicate the CPA's federal identification number on a tax return only if the return reflects tax due from the taxpayer.

71. A CPA will be liable to a tax client for damages resulting from all of the following actions **except**
a. Failing to timely file a client's return.
b. Failing to advise a client of certain tax elections.
c. Refusing to sign a client's request for a filing extension.
d. Neglecting to evaluate the option of preparing joint or separate returns that would have resulted in a substantial tax savings for a married client.

72. According to the profession's standards, which of the following actions should be taken by a CPA tax preparer who discovers an error in a client's previously filed tax return?
a. Advise the IRS.
b. Correct the error.
c. Advise the client.
d. End the relationship with the client.

73. Lyon, a cash-basis taxpayer, died on January 15, 2002. In 2002, the estate executor made the required periodic distribution of $9,000 from estate income to Lyon's sole heir. The following pertains to the estate's income and disbursements in 2002:

2002 Estate Income

$20,000	Taxable interest
10,000	Net long-term capital gains allocable to corpus

2002 Estate Disbursements

$5,000	Administrative expenses attributable to taxable income

For the 2002 calendar year, what was the estate's distributable net income (DNI)?
a. $15,000
b. $20,000
c. $25,000
d. $30,000

74. A distribution to an estate's sole beneficiary for the 2002 calendar year equaled $15,000, the amount currently required to be distributed by the will. The estate's 2002 records were as follows:

Estate income

$40,000	Taxable interest

Estate disbursements

$34,000	Expenses attributable to taxable interest

What amount of the distribution was taxable to the beneficiary?

a. $40,000
b. $15,000
c. $ 6,000
d. $0

75. Steve and Kay Briar, US citizens, were married for the entire 2002 calendar year. In 2002, Steve gave a $30,000 cash gift to his sister. The Briars made no other gifts in 2002. They each signed a timely election to treat the $30,000 gift as made one-half by each spouse. Disregarding the unified credit and estate tax consequences, what amount of the 2002 gift is taxable to the Briars?
a. $29,000
b. $10,000
c. $ 8,000
d. $0

Number 2

Mayne Manufacturing Co. has incurred substantial losses for several years, and has become insolvent. On March 31, 2000, Mayne petitioned the court for protection from creditors, and submitted the following statement of financial position:

Mayne Manufacturing Co.
STATEMENT OF FINANCIAL POSITION
March 31, 2000

	Book value	Liquidation value
Assets		
Accounts receivable	$100,000	$ 50,000
Inventories	90,000	40,000
Plant and equipment	150,000	160,000
	$340,000	$250,000
Liabilities and Stockholders' Equity		
Accounts payable—general creditors	$600,000	
Common stock outstanding	60,000	
Deficit	(320,000)	
Total	$340,000	

Mayne's management informed the court that the company has developed a new product, and that a prospective customer is willing to sign a contract for the purchase of 10,000 units of this product during the year ending March 31, 2001; 12,000 units of this product during the year ending March 31, 2002; and 15,000 units of this product during the year ending March 31, 2003, at a price of $90 per unit. This product can be manufactured using Mayne's present facilities. Monthly production with immediate delivery is expected to be uniform within each year. Receivables are expected to be collected during the calendar month following sales.

Unit production costs of the new product are expected to be as follows:

Direct materials	$20
Direct manufacturing labor	30
Variable overhead	10

Fixed costs (excluding depreciation) will amount to $130,000 per year.

Payments for direct materials will be paid during the calendar month following purchase. Fixed costs, direct manufacturing labor, and variable overhead will be paid as incurred. Inventory of direct materials will be equal to sixty days' usage. After the first month of operations, thirty days' usage of direct materials will be ordered each month.

The general creditors have agreed to reduce their total claims to 60% of their March 31, 2000 balances, under the following conditions:

• Existing accounts receivable and inventories are to be liquidated immediately, with the proceeds turned over to the general creditors.

• The balance of reduced accounts payable is to be paid as cash is generated from future operations, but in no event later than March 31, 2002. No interest will be paid on these obligations.

Under this proposed plan, the general creditors would receive $110,000 more than the current liquidation value of Mayne's assets. The court has engaged you to determine the feasibility of this plan.

Required:

Items 101 through 110 represent amounts that will be used in determining the feasibility of the liquidation plan.

101. Cash collections from customers for the year ending March 31, 2001.

102. Total cash disbursements for operations for the year ending March 31, 2001.

103. Cost of direct materials required for production for the year ending March 31, 2001.

104. Disbursements for direct materials for the year ending March 31, 2002.

105. Cash received from liquidation of accounts receivable and inventories.

106. Payments made to general creditors in the year ended March 31, 2002.

107. Direct materials inventory balance at March 31, 2002.

108. Accounts payable balance at March 31, 2002.

109. Disbursements for direct manufacturing labor for the year ended December 31, 2001.

110. Disbursements for variable overhead for the year ended December 31, 2002.

Number 3

The general fund trial balance of the city of Solna at December 31, 2002, was as follows:

	Dr.	Cr.
Cash	$ 62,000	
Taxes receivable—Delinquent	46,000	
Estimated uncollectible taxes—Delinquent		$ 8,000
Stores inventory—Program operations	18,000	
Vouchers payable		28,000
Fund balance reserved for stores inventory		18,000
Fund balance reserved for encumbrances		12,000
Unreserved undesignated fund balance		60,000
	$126,000	$126,000

Collectible delinquent taxes are expected to be collected within sixty days after the end of the year. Solna uses the "purchases" method to account for stores inventory. The following data pertain to 2003 general fund operations:

111. Prior year encumbrances are reestablished at the beginning of the fiscal year.

112. Budget adopted

Revenues and other financing sources	
Taxes	$220,000
Fines, forfeits, and penalties	80,000
Miscellaneous revenues	100,000
Share of bond issue proceeds	200,000
	$600,000
Expenditures and other financing uses	
Program operations	$300,000
General administration	120,000
Stores—Program operations	60,000
Capital outlay	80,000
Periodic transfer to capital projects fund	20,000
	$580,000

113. Taxes were assessed at an amount that would result in revenues of $220,800, after deduction of 4% of the tax levy as uncollectible.

114. Orders placed but not received

Program operations	$176,000
General administration	80,000
Capital outlay	60,000
	$316,000

115. The city council designated $20,000 of the unreserved fund balance for possible future appropriation for capital outlay.

116. Cash collections and transfer

Delinquent taxes	$ 38,000
Current taxes	226,000
Refund of overpayment of invoice for purchase of equipment	4,000
Fines, forfeits, and penalties	88,000
Miscellaneous revenues	90,000
Share of bond issue proceeds	200,000
Transfer of remaining fund balance of a discontinued fund	18,000
	$664,000

117. Canceled encumbrances

	Estimated	Actual
Program operations	$156,000	$166,000
General administration	84,000	80,000
Capital outlay	62,000	62,000
	$302,000	$308,000

118. Additional vouchers

Program operations	$188,000
General administration	38,000
Capital outlay	18,000
Transfer to capital projects fund	20,000
	$264,000

119. Albert, a taxpayer, overpaid his 2003 taxes by $2,000. He applied for a $2,000 credit against his 2002 taxes. The city council granted his request and updated the accounts to reflect actual property taxes collected.

120. Vouchers paid amounted to $580,000.

121. Stores inventory on December 31, 2003, amounted to $12,000.

122. The budgetary accounts are closed at year-end.

123. The actual accounts are closed at year-end.

124. An encumbrance reserve is established.

Required:

For each numbered item, determine which account(s) is(are) debited and which account(s) is(are) credited.

A. Appropriations control

B. Estimated revenues control

C. Estimated other financing sources control

D. Estimated other financing uses control

E. Budgetary fund balance

F. Budgetary fund balance reserved for encumbrances

G. Cash

H. Taxes receivable—Current

I. Taxes receivable—Delinquent

J. Estimated uncollectible taxes—Current

K. Stores inventory—Program operations

L. Accounts payable

M. Due to capital projects fund

N. Deferred revenue

O. Fund balance reserved for encumbrances

P. Fund balance reserved for stores inventory

Q. Fund balance designated for possible future appropriation for capital outlay

R. Unreserved undesignated fund balance

S. Encumbrances control

T. Expenditures control

U. Revenues control

V. Other financing sources control—Proceeds of bonds

W. Other financing sources control—Transfers in

X. Other financing uses control—Transfers out

Number 4

Items 125 through 130 represent various transactions pertaining to Crest Haven, a voluntary health and welfare organization, for the year ended December 31, 2002. To the right of these transactions is a listing of how transactions could affect the statement of activities (List A Effects) and the statement of cash flows (List B Effects). Assume Crest Haven uses the direct method of reporting cash flows from operations.

Transactions

125. Pledges of $500,000 were made by various donors for the acquisition of new equipment. The equipment will be acquired in 2003.

126. Dividends and interest of $40,000 were received from endowment investments. The donors have stipulated that the earnings from endowment investments be used for research in 2003.

127. Cash donations of $350,000 were received from donors who did **not** stipulate how the donations were to be used.

128. Investments of $250,000 were acquired from cash donated in 2001 by a donor who stipulated that the cash donation be invested permanently.

129. Depreciation expense of $75,000 was recorded for 2002.

130. $300,000 of the amount pledged in transaction (125) was received.

Required:

Indicate how each transaction should be reported by Crest Haven on (1) the statement of activities and (2) the statement of cash flows prepared for the year ended December 31, 2002. Crest Haven reports separate columns for changes in unrestricted, temporarily restricted, and permanently restricted net assets on its statement of activities. In addition, Crest Haven uses the direct method of reporting its cash flows from operation activities. A List A or List B effect may be used once, more than once, or not at all.

Statement of Activities *List A Effects*	*Statement of Cash Flows* *List B Effects*
A. Increases unrestricted net assets	H. Increases cash flows from operating activities
B. Increases temporarily restricted net assets	I. Decreases cash flows from operating activities
C. Increases permanently restricted net assets	J. Increases cash flows from investing activities
D. Decreases unrestricted net assets	K. Decreases cash flows from investing activities
E. Decreases temporarily restricted net assets	L. Increases cash flows from financing activities
F. Decreases permanently restricted net assets	M. Decreases cash flows from financing activities
G. Transactions not reported on the statement of activities	N. Transactions not reported on the statement of cash flows

ANSWERS TO SAMPLE EXAMINATION
ACCOUNTING AND REPORTING
(Taxation; Managerial; and Governmental & Not-for-Profit Organizations)

Answer 1

1.	c	14.	c	27.	a	40.	a	53.	d	66.	c
2.	a	15.	d	28.	b	41.	d	54.	b	67.	a
3.	d	16.	c	29.	b	42.	c	55.	b	68.	d
4.	a	17.	a	30.	a	43.	b	56.	c	69.	c
5.	d	18.	c	31.	b	44.	a	57.	a	70.	b
6.	b	19.	a	32.	b	45.	b	58.	d	71.	c
7.	d	20.	d	33.	d	46.	c	59.	c	72.	c
8.	a	21.	b	34.	c	47.	a	60.	c	73.	a
9.	b	22.	d	35.	b	48.	b	61.	d	74.	c
10.	a	23.	c	36.	c	49.	c	62.	a	75.	c
11.	c	24.	c	37.	a	50.	c	63.	b		
12.	c	25.	d	38.	d	51.	b	64.	d		
13.	d	26.	b	39.	c	52.	d	65.	b		

Hints for Multiple-Choice Questions

1. Individuals are considered unmarried if living apart under a separate maintenance decree at the end of the tax year.

2. Since Herman paid less than was required, amounts are first allocated to child support.

3. Interest income is taxable unless specifically excluded from gross income (e.g., interest on municipal bonds).

4. Property received as a gift is specifically excluded from gross income.

5. If your spouse dies during the year, you are considered married for the whole year for filing purposes.

6. A "gift" received as consideration for opening a bank account constitutes interest income on that account.

7. Life insurance proceeds paid by reason of death are always excluded from gross income.

8. $5,000 employee death benefit exclusion was repealed for decedents dying after August 20, 1996.

9. The deduction for investment interest expense is limited to net investment income.

10. Since Eric's mother was the owner of the condominium, the taxes were not imposed on Eric.

11. Qualifying medical expenses are deductible to the extent in excess of 7.5% of AGI.

12. The loss must be reduced by $100 and 10% of AGI.

13. No credit or deduction is available for political contributions.

14. A bargain purchase of stock at less than FMV may be treated as an additional form of compensation.

15. Security deposits that can be applied against rent are treated as advance rent.

16. Dividends on unmatured life insurance policies are treated as a reduction of cost so long as cumulative premiums have not been exceeded.

17. Under the cash method, income is reported when cash is collected.

18. A loss is disallowed on the sale of property to a related taxpayer.

19. No personal exemption is available on Brett's return because he qualifies as a dependency exemption on his mother's return.

20. The distribution is treated as if the inventory was sold for FMV to the stockholder.

21. The amount realized is the inventory's FMV reduced by the amount of liability assumed.

22. A shareholder's basis for distributed property is its FMV.

23. Marketable securities are capital assets and result in capital gain.

24. Gain must be recognized when appreciated property is used to satisfy a liability.

25. The property was primarily held as an investment.

26. Since the realized loss on the February 15 condemnation would be recognized, the basis of the replacement parcel would be its cost.

27. No loss can be recognized because the property was acquired with the intent to demolish the building.

28. Gain must be recognized to the extent that the insurance proceeds were not reinvested in the new warehouse.

29. In a like-kind exchange, gain is recognized to the extent of boot received.

30. The basis of the like-kind property received is the same as the basis of the machine exchanged.

31. Contributions of ordinary income property are deductible to the extent of the lesser of FMV, or adjusted basis.

32. The automobile is treated as if it had been sold for FMV.

33. A corporation's sale of property to a controlling shareholder for less than FMV results in a constructive dividend.

34. Generally an ordinary loss can be deducted on the worthlessness of securities in a subsidiary that is at least 80% owned.

35. The definition of capital assets includes property held as an investment.

36. Since no gain is recognized, basis is transferred to the corporation.

37. At least 80% of combined voting power and each class of nonvoting stock.

38. Costs of issuing stock are neither deductible nor amortizable.

39. The amount is subject to estimated payment requirements.

40. Net income from sales is the only item listed that does not have special tax characteristics.

41. Partners are taxed on their distributive shares of partnership income even though it is not distributed or withdrawn.

42. Distributive share of income and guaranteed payments are deemed to flow through to partners on the last day of the partnership tax year.

43. The basis for a partner's partnership interest is reduced by the partner's distributive share of partnership losses.

44. The basis of the partner's partnership interest is reduced (but not below zero) by a net reduction in the contributing partner's liabilities ($8,000 x 70% = $5,600).

45. Partners are taxed on their distributive share of partnership income.

46. In a complete liquidation, the basis of a partner's partnership interest must be reduced to zero.

47. An $11,000 exclusion is only allowed for gifts of a present interest.

48. Trusts must adopt a calendar year.

49. The alternate valuation date can be used if it reduces both the gross estate and the amount of federal estate tax.

50. No adjustments are necessary because the items included in book income can also be included in the computation of taxable income.

51. A PHC has more than 50% of the value of its stock owned by five or fewer individuals, and at least 60% of its gross income is investment income.

52. The common parent must own at least 80% of another includible corporation, and intercompany dividends are completely eliminated in the consolidation process.

53. The accumulated earnings tax cannot be imposed on personal holding companies.

54. Shareholders are taxed on their share of S corporation income even though it is not distributed.

55. Only direct moving expenses are deductible.

56. State and local taxes are deductible for the year in which withheld or paid.

57. Medical expenses, nonbusiness casualty losses, investment interest expenses, and gambling losses are not subject to reduction.

58. Surviving spouse's dependent child must live with taxpayer for entire year.

59. The $9,000 of social security benefits is excluded from gross income.

60. Personal taxes and miscellaneous itemized deductions in the 2% category are not deductible for AMT purposes.

61. Gain will be recognized if the amount of liability relief exceeds the adjusted basis of property transferred.

62. An increase in partnership liabilities has the same effect as a capital contribution.

63. The land's basis is limited to his remaining partnership basis.

64. Proportionate noncash property distributions do not cause the recognition of gain or loss.

65. A partnership must have associates.

66. A constructive liquidation and recontribution of assets occurs if the terminated partnership continues to operate.

67. The articles of organization must limit the scope of activities.

68. Unrelated business income is income from a business that is not substantially related to the organization's exempt purpose.

69. Tax return information generally must be used only to prepare or assist in preparing a return.

70. It is not necessary to review documentation supporting expenses.

71. A CPA is not required to sign an extension request.

72. A CPA is not obligated to inform the IRS of a client's error.

73. An estate's DNI is taxable income (not allocated to corpus) reduced by related expenses.

74. The amount taxable is limited to the estate's DNI.

75. Each spouse will receive an annual exclusion.

Explanation for items 20 through 35

Bates Corporation
SCHEDULE TO COMPUTE TAXABLE INCOME
For 2002

Net income before property distributions		$23,650
Add (deduct) ordinary income (loss):		
(21) Distribution of inventory	$2,200	
(26) Destruction of warehouse	5,000	
(24) Condemnation of land	(2,000)	
(27) Trade-in machinery	600	
(29) Sale of automobile	550	
(30) Worthless security	(16,500)	
		(10,150)
Add (deduct) capital gain (loss):		
(23) Settlement of debt with securities	$ 900	
(22) Compensatory transfer of securities	1,350	
(31) Sale of patent	18,000	
	20,250	
Compensatory transfer of securities	(9,650)	
Taxable income before contribution		$24,100
(28) Deduct contributions		(1,640)
(32) Taxable income		$22,460

Schedule 1

Computation of Gain on Warehouse

Insurance proceeds		$58,000
Less: Cost	$60,000	
Accumulated depreciation	(21,000)	
Adjusted basis		−39,000
Realized gain		$19,000
Insurance proceeds	$58,000	
Cost of replacement	−53,000	
Recognized gain		$5,000

Schedule 2

Computation of Gain on Machinery

Fair market value		$3,300
Less: Cost	$4,000	
Accumulated depreciation	(1,700)	
Adjusted basis		−2,300
Realized gain		$1,000
Recognized gain (to extent "boot" received)		$600

Schedule 3

Computation of Furniture Contribution

Ordinary income property: contribution equals lesser of (1) FMV = $1,900, or (2) adjusted basis = $8,200 − $6,560 = 1,640.

Schedule 4

Computation of Gain on Automobile

Fair market value		$4,300
Less: Cost	$6,000	
Accumulated depreciation	(2,250)	
Adjusted basis		−3,750
Recognized gain (Sec. 1245 ordinary income)		$550

Answer 2

101. $825,000	**103.** $200,000	**105.** $90,000	**107.** $50,000	**109.** $300,000
102. $750,000	**104.** $245,000	**106.** $270,000	**108.** $25,000	**110.** $120,000

Hints for Other Objective Answer Format Questions

101. Since AR are collected the month following sales, the AR will exist at 3/31/01.

102. Construct a direct materials (DM) budget and adjust for AP.

103. No tricks here.

104. Construct a DM budget and adjust for AP.

105. These amounts are given.

106. The proceeds from AR and inventories were paid to creditors in FY 2001.

107. On what production level should ending inventory be based?

108. How many units were purchased in the past month?

109. Use 2001 production levels.

110. Use 2002 production levels.

Answer 2: Complete Explanation

101. ($825,000)

Sales	$900,000	(10,000 units @ $90)
Beg. accounts receivable	0	
Total	900,000	
Less end accounts receivable	75,000	($900,000 x 1/12)
Collections from customers	825,000	

102. ($750,000)

Direct materials [1]	$220,000
Direct manuf. labor (10,000 units x $30)	300,000
VOH (10,000 units x $10)	100,000
Fixed costs	130,000
	$750,000

[1] Direct material required for production (10,000 units x $20)	$200,000
Required ending inventory (12,000 units x 2/12 x $20)	40,000
Total	240,000
Less beginning inventory	0
Purchases	240,000
Beginning AP	0
Total	240,000
Less ending AP (12,000 x 1/12 x $20)	20,000
Disbursements for direct materials	$220,000

103. ($200,000)

Units to be produced	10,000
Unit production cost for direct materials	$ 20
Cost of direct material required for production	$200,000

104. ($245,000)

Direct materials required for production (12,000 units x $20)	$240,000
Required ending inventory (15,000 units x 2/12 x $20)	50,000
Total	290,000
Less beginning inventory	40,000
Purchases	250,000
Beginning AP	20,000
Total	270,000
Less ending AP (15,000 x 1/12 x $20)	25,000
Disbursements for direct materials	$245,000

105. ($90,000)

Liquidation values at March 31, 2000

Accounts receivable	$50,000
Inventories	40,000
Total	$90,000

106. ($270,000) Total payments to general creditors should equal $360,000 ($600,000 x 60%) by March 31, 2002. Payments to creditors in the year ended March 31, 2001, totaled $90,000 ($50,000 from AR + $40,000 from inventory); thus, payments during the year ended March 31, 2002, should equal $270,000 ($360,000 – $90,000).

107. ($50,000) In 2002 Mayne has contracts to sell 15,000 units. Mayne must keep sixty days (two months) of inventory on hand. Accordingly, at March 31, 2002, Mayne needs 2,500 units (15,000 x 2/12) in inventory. Since these units cost $20 per unit, the inventory balance at March 31, 2002, is $50,000.

108. (25,000) Since purchases are paid in the month following purchase, the accounts payable balance at March 31, 2002, should equal one month's purchases. Purchases each month are equal to thirty days' usage; thus, AP at March 31, 2002, should equal $25,000 (15,000 units x 1/12 x $20).

109. ($300,000)

Production	10,000
Direct manufacturing labor cost	x $30
Disbursements for DML	$300,000

110. ($120,000)

Production	12,000
VOH cost	x $10
Disbursements for VOH	$120,000

*NOTE: The solutions approach to solving **items 101 through 110** involves preparing the cash budgets for 2001 and 2002. The portions of the cash budgets relating to specific items are indicated in parentheses.*

Mayne Manufacturing Co.
CASH BUDGET
For the Years Ending March 31

	2001	2002
Balance of cash at beginning	$0	$75,000
Cash generated from operations		
Collections from customers—Schedule A	$825,000 (111)	$1,065,000 [1]
Disbursements		
Direct materials—Schedule B	220,000	245,000
Direct labor	300,000	360,000
Variable overhead	100,000	120,000
Fixed costs	130,000	130,000
Total disbursements	750,000 (112)	855,000
Excess of cash collections over cash disbursements from operations	75,000	210,000
Cash available from operations	75,000	285,000
Cash received from liquidation of existing accounts receivable and inventories	90,000 (115)	0
Total cash available	165,000	285,000
Payment to general creditors	90,000	270,000 (116) [2]
Balance of cash at end	$ 75,000 [1]	$ 15,000

[1]   This amount could have been used to pay general
     creditors or carried forward to the beginning of the
     next year.

[2]   ($600,000 x 60%) – ($50,000 + $40,000)

Schedule A

Mayne Manufacturing Co.
COLLECTIONS FROM CUSTOMERS
For the Years Ending March 31

	2001	2002
Sales	$900,000	$1,080,000
Beginning accounts receivable	0	75,000
Total	900,000	1,155,000
Less ending accounts receivable	75,000	90,000
Collections from customers	$825,000	$1,065,000

Schedule B

Mayne Manufacturing Co.
DISBURSEMENT FOR DIRECT MATERIALS
For the Years Ending March 31

	2001	2002
Direct materials required for production	$200,000 (113) [3]	$240,000
Required ending inventory	40,000 [4]	50,000 (117) [5]
Total	240,000	290,000
Less beginning inventory	0	40,000
Purchases	240,000	250,000
Beginning accounts payable	0	20,000
Total	240,000	270,000
Less ending accounts payable	20,000	25,000
Disbursements for direct materials	$220,000	$245,000 (114)

[3]   10,000 units x $20 per unit = $200,000
[4]   12,000 units x 2/12 = 2,000; 2,000 x $20 per unit = $40,000
[5] ·15,000 units x 2/12 = 2,500; 2,500 x $20 per unit = $50,000

Answer 3

	Dr.	Cr.		Dr.	Cr.		Dr.	Cr.		Dr.	Cr.
111.	S O	R F	**115.**	R	Q	**119.**	H J	N U	**123.**	U V W	T S X R
112.	B C	A D E	**116.**	G	I H T U V W	**120.**	L	G	**124.**	F	O
113.	H U	J	**117.**	F T	S L	**121.**	P	K			
114.	S	F	**118.**	T X	L M	**122.**	A D E	B C			

Hints for Other Objective Answer Format Questions

111. An entry involving fund balance is also required.

112. Debt issue proceeds received are classified as "other financing sources."

113. An allowance must be recorded.

114. "Encumbrances" records an expected liability, while "Expenditures" records an actual liability.

115. This item gives away the account names.

116. The overpayment resulted in an overstatement of expenditures.

117. Reverse encumbrances entry at the estimated amount; charge expenditures at the invoice amount.

118. One account is not debited to expenditures.

119. Note the actual amount collected for current taxes in item **116.** above.

120. No tricks here.

121. Adjust the accounts to reflect the correct balance.

122. Estimated other financing uses is a budgetary account.

123. Other financing sources is an actual account.

124. Examine entry **111.** above.

City of Solna
GENERAL FUND JOURNAL ENTRIES
For the Year Ended December 31, 2003

		Dr.	Cr.
111.	Encumbrances control	$ 12,000	
	Unreserved undesignated fund balance		12,000
	Fund balance reserved for encumbrances	12,000	
	Budgetary fund balance reserved for encumbrances		12,000
112.	Estimated revenues control	400,000	
	Estimated other financing sources control	200,000	
	Appropriations control		560,000
	Estimated other financing uses control		20,000
	Budgetary fund balance		20,000
113.	Taxes receivable—Current	230,000	
	Estimated uncollectible taxes—Current		9,200
	Revenues control		220,800
114.	Encumbrances control	316,000	
	Budgetary fund balance reserved for encumbrances		316,000
115.	Unreserved undesignated fund balance	20,000	
	Fund balance designated for possible future appropriation for capital outlay		20,000

	Dr.	Cr.
116. Cash	664,000	
Taxes receivable—Delinquent		38,000
Taxes receivable—Current		226,000
Expenditures control		4,000
Revenues control		178,000
Other financing sources control—Proceeds of bonds		200,000
Other financing sources control—Transfers in		18,000
117. Budgetary fund balance reserved for encumbrances	302,000	
Encumbrances control		302,000
Expenditures control	308,000	
Accounts payable		308,000
118. Expenditures control	244,000	
Other financing uses control—Transfers out	20,000	
Accounts payable		244,000
Due to capital projects fund		20,000
119. Taxes receivable—Current	2,000	
Deferred revenue		2,000
Estimated uncollectible taxes—Current	3,200	
Revenues control		3,200

*A net of $224,000 has been collected for current year taxes, **whereas only** $220,800 was recognized as revenues in entry 113.*

	Dr.	Cr.
120. Accounts payable	580,000	
Cash		580,000
121. Fund balance reserved for stores inventory	6,000	
Stores inventory—Program operations		6,000

City of Solna
CLOSING ENTRIES
For the Year Ended December 31, 2003

	Dr.	Cr.
122. Appropriations control	560,000	
Estimated other financing uses control	20,000	
Budgetary fund balance	20,000	
Estimated revenues control		400,000
Estimated other financing sources control		200,000
123. Revenues control	402,000	
Other financing sources control—Proceeds of bonds	200,000	
Other financing sources control—Transfers in	18,000	
Expenditures control		548,000
Encumbrances control		26,000
Other financing uses control—Transfers out		20,000
Unreserved undesignated fund balance		26,000
124. Budgetary fund balance reserved for encumbrances	26,000	
Fund balance reserved for encumbrances		26,000

Answer 4

125.	B,N	**127.**	A,H	**129.**	D,N
126.	B,H	**128.**	G,K	**130.**	G,L

Hints for Other Objective Answer Format Questions

125. The pledges are recorded as support in 2002 even though no cash is received.

126. When the earnings are expended, the assets are reclassified as unrestricted. Interest and dividends would not be classified as an investing activity.

127. Assets can only be restricted by the donor's request. Donations are classified as financing activities only if they are permanently invested, or if contributed for plant.

128. The acquisition does not increase or decrease permanently restricted net assets, although it does affect cash flows.

129. Depreciation is deducted from unrestricted revenues. The **direct** method is used by Crest Haven.

130. The transaction would **decrease** pledge receivables by $300,000 and **increase** cash by $300,000. The cash received is classified as a financing activity.

APPENDIX B

AICPA Summary of Coverage (Last 6 Exams) from Accounting and Reporting (ARE) Section of Uniform CPA Examination[1]

Summary of Exam Coverage—May 1999 through November 2001 Uniform CPA Examinations

The following summary of coverage provides an analysis of the Content Specification Outline coverage for the May 1999 through November 2001 ARE Sections of the Uniform CPA Examinations. This summary is intended only as a study aid and should not be used to predict the content of future Examinations.

How to Interpret This Table

The percentages on the third line of the table indicate the percentage points allocated to each type of question on these Examinations. For example, on the May 1999 Accounting and Reporting Section (ARE), 60% of the examination points were allocated to multiple-choice questions, and 40% of the points were allocated to other objective answer format (OOAF).

The AICPA has also provided the **actual number** of multiple-choice questions asked for each area (identified with a roman numeral) and topic (identified with an uppercase letter) of the content specification outlines (e.g., for the May 1999 Examination, under area I., there were seven multiple-choice questions asked that were distributed among A. – H.). In addition, the AICPA has also indicated the **percentage** of OOAF questions asked for each area and topic in the outline.

---

[1] These Content Specification Outlines were published in **Selected Questions and Unofficial Answers Supplement Indexed to Content Specification Outlines** (2001 Edition); reprinted with permission of the AICPA

Accounting & Reporting— Taxation, Managerial, and Governmental and Not-for-Profit Organizations

	Multiple-Choice						OOAFs						Essays
	N01	M01	N00	M00	N99	M99	N01	M01	N00	M00	N99	M99	
	60 (60%)	60 (60%)	75 (60%)	75 (60%)	75 (60%)	75 (60%)	40 (40%)	40 (40%)	40%	40%	40%	40%	
I. Federal Taxation— Individuals	10	20	12	12	25	7	10%		10%	10%	0%	15%	
A. Inclusions in Gross Income					9	7						7%	
B. Exclusions and Adjustments to Arrive at Adjusted Gross Income					5	0							
C. Deductions from Adjusted Gross Income					4	0						3.5%	
D. Filing Status and Exemptions					1	0							
E. Tax Accounting Methods					1	0						1%	
F. Tax Computations, Credits, and Penalties					2	0							
G. Alternative Minimum Tax					2	0						3.5%	
H. Tax Procedures					1	0							
II. Federal Taxation— Corporations	20	10	25	13	19	13		10%	0%	10%	5%	10%	
A. Determination of Taxable Income or Loss					0	5							
B. Tax Accounting Methods					1	1							
C. S Corporations					6	1						10%	
D. Personal Holding Companies					0	1							
E. Consolidated Returns					2	1							
F. Tax Computations, Credits, and Penalties					2	1							
G. Alternative Minimum Tax					2	0							
H. Other					6	3							

Accounting & Reporting—Taxation, Managerial, and Governmental and Not-for-Profit Organizations

	Multiple-Choice						OOAFs						Essays
	N01	M01	N00	M00	N99	M99	N01	M01	N00	M00	N99	M99	
	(60%)	(60%)	75 (60%)	75 (60%)	75 (60%)	75 (60%)	40%	40%	40%	40%	40%	40%	
III. Federal Taxation—Partnerships	5	5	0	12	0	12	10%	5%	10%	0%	10%	0%	
A. Basis of Partner's Interest and Bases of Assets Contributed to the Partnership						2					5%		
B. Determination of Partner's Share of Income, Credits, and Deductions						2					2%		
C. Partnership and Partner Elections						1							
D. Partner Dealing with Own Partnership						1							
E. Treatment of Partnership Liabilities						1							
F. Distribution of Partnership Assets						3					3%		
G. Termination of Partnership						2							
IV. Federal Taxation—Estates and Trusts, Exempt Organizations, and Preparers' Responsibilities	5		7	7	0	12	5%	10%	5%	5%	10%	0%	
A. Estates and Trusts					0	6					5%		
B. Exempt Organizations					0	3							
C. Preparers' Responsibilities					0	3					5%		
V. Accounting for Governmental and Not-for-Profit Organizations	15	15	19	19	19	19	15%	15%	15%	15%	15%	15%	
A. Governmental Entities					11	8					10%		
B. Nongovernmental Not-for-Profit Organizations					8	11					5%		
VI. Managerial Accounting	10	10	12	12	12	12	0%		0%	0%	0%	0%	
A. Cost Estimation, Cost Determination, and Cost Drivers					1	1							

Accounting & Reporting—Taxation, Managerial, and Governmental and Not-for-Profit Organizations	Multiple-Choice						OOAFs						Essays
	N01	M01	N00	M00	N99	M99	N01	M01	N00	M00	N99	M99	
			75 (60%)	75 (60%)	75 (60%)	75 (60%)			40%	40%	40%	40%	
B. Job Costing, Process Costing, and Activity Based Costing					2	2							
C. Standard Costing and Flexible Budgeting					1	0							
D. Inventory Planning, Inventory Control, and Just-in-Time Purchasing					0	1							
E. Budgeting and Responsibility Accounting					1	2							
F. Variable and Absorption Costing					0	0							
G. Cost-Volume-Profit Analysis					1	1							
H. Cost Allocation and Transfer Pricing					2	1							
I. Joint and By-Product Costing					0	1							
J. Capital Budgeting					1	1							
K. Special Analyses for Decision Making					1	1							
L. Product and Service Pricing					2	1							